Microsoft® Office Word 2003 Inside Out

Mary Millhollon and Katherine Murray

PUBLISHED BY
Microsoft Press
A Division of Microsoft Corporation
One Microsoft Way
Redmond, Washington 98052-6399

Library of Congress Cataloging-in-Publication Data
Millhollon, Mary.
Microsoft Office Word 2003 Inside Out / Mary Millhollon, Katherine Murray.
p. cm.
Includes index.
ISBN 0-7356-1515-2
1. Microsoft Word. 2. Word processing. I. Murray, Katherine, 1961- II. Title.

Z52.5.M52M57 2003
005.52--dc22 2003061578

Printed and bound in the United States of America.

1 2 3 4 5 6 7 8 9 QWT 8 7 6 5 4 3

Distributed in Canada by H.B. Fenn and Company Ltd.

A CIP catalogue record for this book is available from the British Library.

Microsoft Press books are available through booksellers and distributors worldwide. For further information about international editions, contact your local Microsoft Corporation office or contact Microsoft Press International directly at fax (425) 936-7329. Visit our Web site at www.microsoft.com/mspress. Send comments to *mspinput@microsoft.com.*

Acquisitions Editor: Alex Blanton
Series Editor: Sandra Haynes
Project Editor: Laura Sackerman

Body Part No. X10-08605

"What lies before us and what lies behind us
is nothing compared to what lies within us."

—Ralph Waldo Emerson

Contents At A Glance

Table of Contents

Chapter 8
Aligning Information and Formatting Paragraphs and Lists 221

Part 3
Designing Pages for Maximum Visual Impact

Chapter 15
Mastering Page Setup and Pagination 463

Chapter 16
Formatting Documents Using Templates, Wizards, Add-Ins, and XML Schemas 485

Part 5
Collaborating Online and on Team Projects

Chapter 24
Working and Collaborating Online 635

Chapter 31
Working with Field Codes and Custom Forms 863

Acknowledgements

We want to send out a big "Thanks!" to all the people we worked with in the production of this book—it's been a team effort! Special thanks to our agents, Claudette Moore and Debbie McKenna of Moore Literary Agency; to Alex Blanton, acquisitions manager at Microsoft Press; to Laura Sackerman and Susan McClung; to Bob Hogan, the technical editor; and to the crew involved in the design, layout, and final production of the book. And last but never least, we'd like to thank our special guys—Cameron, Christopher, Robert, and Matthew—for the smiles and hugs and important reminders of what matters most at the end of every day.

We'd Like to Hear from You!

Our goal at Microsoft Press is to create books that help you find the information you need to get the most out of your software.

The INSIDE OUT series was created with you in mind. As part of our ongoing effort to ensure that we're creating the books that meet your learning needs, we'd like to hear from you. Let us know what you think. Tell us what you like about this book and what we can do to make it better. When you write, please include the title and author of this book in your e-mail, as well as your name and contact information. We look forward to hearing from you!

How to Reach Us

E-Mail: nsideout@microsoft.com
Mail: Inside Out Series Editor
Microsoft Press
One Microsoft Way
Redmond, WA 98052

Note: Unfortunately, we can't provide support for any software problems you might experience. Please go to http://support.microsoft.com *for help with any software issues.*

About the CD

The companion CD that ships with this book contains many tools and resources to help you get the most out of your Inside Out book.

What's on the CD

Your Inside Out CD includes the following:

- **Complete eBook** In this section you'll find an electronic version of *Microsoft Office Word 2003 Inside Out.* The eBook is in PDF format.
- **Insider extras** This section includes a reference to the built-in commands in Word, which you can run as macros and add to your toolbars and menus; an inside look at the new features in the Microsoft Office System; and tips for the best places on the Internet to learn Extensible Markup Language (XML).
- **Microsoft tools and information** In this section you'll find resources, demos, and tools for Microsoft Office Word 2003 and the Microsoft Office System.
- **Extending Word** In this section you'll find great information about third-party utilities and tools you can use to further enhance your experience with Word.
- **Microsoft Computer Dictionary, Fifth Edition, eBook** Here you'll find the full electronic version of the *Microsoft Computer Dictionary, Fifth Edition.*
- **Tablet PC Quick Reference** Here you'll find the full electronic version of the *Tablet PC Quick Reference.*

The companion CD provides detailed information about the files on this CD, and links to Microsoft and third-party sites on the Internet.

Note Please note that the links to third-party sites are not under the control of Microsoft Corporation and Microsoft is therefore not responsible for their content, nor should their inclusion on this CD be construed as an endorsement of the product or the site.

Software provided on this CD is in the English language only and may be incompatible with non-English language operating systems and software.

Using the CD

To use this companion CD, insert it into your CD-ROM drive. If AutoRun is not enabled on your computer, run StartCD.exe in the root of the CD. Accept the license agreement that is presented to access the starting menu.

System Requirements

The following are the minimum system requirements necessary to run the CD:

- Microsoft Windows XP or later or Windows 2000 Professional with Service Pack 3 or later
- 266-MHz or higher Pentium-compatible CPU
- 64 megabytes (MB) RAM
- 8X CD-ROM drive or faster
- Microsoft Windows–compatible sound card and speakers
- Microsoft Internet Explorer 5.01 or higher
- Microsoft Mouse or compatible pointing device

Note An Internet connection is necessary to access some of the hyperlinks. Connect time charges may apply.

Support Information

Every effort has been made to ensure the accuracy of the book and the contents of this companion CD. For feedback on the book content or this companion CD, please contact us by using any of the addresses listed in the "We'd Like to Hear from You" section.

Microsoft Press provides corrections for books through the World Wide Web at *http://www.microsoft.com/mspress/support*. To connect directly to the Microsoft Press Knowledge Base and enter a query regarding a question or issue that you may have, go to *http://www.microsoft.com/mspress/support/search.htm*.

For support information regarding Windows XP, you can connect to Microsoft Technical Support on the Web at *http://support.microsoft.com*.

Conventions and Features Used in this Book

This book uses special text and design conventions to make it easier for you to find the information you need.

Text Conventions

Convention	Meaning
Abbreviated menu commands	For your convenience, this book uses abbreviated menu commands. For example, "Click Tools, Track Changes, Highlight Changes" means that you should click the Tools menu, point to Track Changes, and click the Highlight Changes command.
Boldface type	**Boldface** type is used to indicate text that you enter or type.
Initial Capital Letters	The first letters of the names of menus, dialog boxes, dialog box elements, and commands are capitalized. Example: the Save As dialog box.
Italicized type	*Italicized* type is used to indicate new terms.
Plus sign (+) in text	Keyboard shortcuts are indicated by a plus sign (+) separating two key names. For example, Ctrl+Alt+Delete means that you press the Ctrl, Alt, and Delete keys at the same time.

Design Conventions

This icon identifies a new or significantly updated feature in this version of the software.

Inside Out

This statement illustrates an example of an "Inside Out" problem statement.

These are the book's signature tips. In these tips, you'll get the straight scoop on what's going on with the software—inside information about why a feature works the way it does. You'll also find handy workarounds to deal with software problems.

Tip Tips provide helpful hints, timesaving tricks, or alternative procedures related to the task being discussed.

Troubleshooting

This statement illustrates an example of a "Troubleshooting" problem statement.

Look for these sidebars to find solutions to common problems you might encounter. Troubleshooting sidebars appear next to related information in the chapters. You can also use the Troubleshooting Topics index at the back of the book to look up problems by topic.

Cross-references point you to other locations in the book that offer additional information about the topic being discussed.

This icon indicates information or text found on the companion CD.

Caution Cautions identify potential problems that you should look out for when you're completing a task or problems that you must address before you can complete a task.

Note Notes offer additional information related to the task being discussed.

Sidebars

The sidebars sprinkled throughout these chapters provide ancillary information on the topic being discussed. Go to sidebars to learn more about the technology or a feature.

Part 1

Professional Tools for Professional Documents

Chapter 1

Gearing Up with Word 2003

Microsoft Office Word 2003: It's the Word you've been waiting for. New, powerful features enable you to write something once and use it many times; new collaboration enhancements make it easy to share documents and work in teams; flexible document protection tools enable you to determine who can work with the documents you create and how much changing they are allowed to do. And all these high-end capabilities (and more) are easy to find and use within the familiar-but-improved Microsoft Office System interface.

This chapter gives you a bird's-eye view of the many capabilities of Word 2003. Along the way, you'll find out about the new features in this edition of the program and get a sense of how Word 2003 can help you create professional documents for all kinds of business functions and in all kinds of circumstances.

Keys to Improvements in Word 2003

With more than 450 million registered users of Office the world over, and more than 600,000 users involved in the beta testing done prior to release, Microsoft product developers have lots of opportunity for feedback. They hear what users struggle with and want; they know how our information needs are changing; and they can anticipate the tools, tricks, and program features that will enable us to take our computers with us and do our work in a faster, smarter, and more professional way.

In the years since the first version of Office was introduced, our worldwide workforce has become increasingly mobile and diverse. We may use Word on a traditional stand-alone desktop system, a laptop, or a Pocket PC. We may share documents with people who live and work in different countries, scattered all over the globe. We need to write, edit, print, fax, e-mail, and publish documents to the World Wide Web. We use the text we create in Word in myriad other documents—presentations, reports, e-mail, databases, and more. What do we need? The flexibility to work any way we need to; the extensibility to allow our data to be used many different ways, and the security to ensure that access to our critical documents is limited and controlled by the right people. Enter Word 2003, with new features that improve collaboration, extend data use beyond the barriers of different formats, enable us to connect and communicate seamlessly, and provide controls for protecting and restricting document access and editing.

What's New in Word 2003?

The biggest changes in Word can really be grouped into three different categories: the new look; new ways to find and enter information; and new ways to collaborate. This section gives you a quick overview on the new features, but you'll find much more detailed information in the specific chapters related to the changes.

A New Look

You can't have a new version of Word without having a new look. The new style of Word 2003 is rounded, slick, and modern. The boxy edges of menu bars and dialog boxes have been given a more sophisticated appearance. The toolbars are shaded so they appear almost three-dimensional—the menus, options, and colors all match up with what you're used to seeing in the Microsoft Windows XP operating system. Elements of the software's new look are as follows:

- **New task panes** Task panes were new in Word 2002 and they've been a hit with users worldwide. It's easy to understand why: the task pane pulls together commands, options, or settings you need to perform a specific task. You don't need to leave the current document or worry about what's behind the dialog box; the task pane displays everything off to the right so you can still see, scroll, and work in your document as needed. Word 2003 includes a number of new task panes, including Getting Started, Research, Shared Workspace, Document Updates, and XML Structure (available in Microsoft Office Professional Edition 2003 and the stand-alone edition of Microsoft Office Word 2003 only).
- **Changes in Help** There have been major changes—for the better—in Word's help system. Now if you're online your computer will automatically search Microsoft's online Help database to find you the most recent information about your issue or question. And at the end of every help entry, you are asked whether the information was what you were looking for—and if not, why not? This feedback goes directly to Microsoft to help product developers understand what's baffling users and what people are trying to find out. And that is bound to make the *next* incarnation of Word even better.
- **Reading Layout view** The Reading Layout view was designed for people who like to see the entire page on the screen at the same time and zoom in and out at will. The focus of Reading Layout is simply that: reading. When you open a document in Reading Layout view, Word displays the entire page, with thumbnails of other pages in the panel on the left side of the window. (If thumbnails do not appear automatically on your screen, click the Thumbnails button in the Reading Layout toolbar.) To move to another page, simply click the thumbnail you want to see. Reading Layout view makes it easy to scan a document quickly, tailor the display to your liking, and navigate through even a long document easily.
- **Compare Side-by-Side view** A new Compare Side-by-Side view (available from the Window menu) enables you to review two similar documents without having to merge the two documents into one. Scrolling in one scrolls them both; this makes it easy for you to see where the changes are in each document.

New Ways to Find and Enter Information

One of the biggest thorns in any writer's side is the *hurry-up-and-wait* syndrome. We try to *hurry up* gathering research, and then *wait* while we look for that one missing piece. Whether you are pulling together the narrative for the annual report, working on a Web page, or composing a draft letter to a prospective employer, you need to find and enter the information you need—preferably without interruptions—as you write your document. New features in Word make it easy for you to research and enter information on the fly, without ever leaving (or even minimizing) your Word document. Here is an overview of these new features:

- **Research task pane** The new Research task pane enables you to find more information about a word by holding down Alt and clicking it. If you are connected to the Internet, Word will automatically search the Web using any of the resources you've specified. In addition, you can access the Thesaurus and a Translation tool within the Research task pane.
- **Word on your Tablet PC** New Tablet PC support enables you to use ink technology to write on your documents, circling and underlining key phrases, drawing diagrams, handwriting e-mails, and more.
- **Improved Help system** Now when you look for help on a topic in Word, you're given access to all the resources you could possibly want—beyond the limits of your own stand-alone PC. If you're connected to the Internet, Word will automatically access the Microsoft Office System site to look for the latest information on the topic you entered. In addition, questions at the end of help entries enable you to tell Microsoft developers whether the help actually *did* help. If not, you can tell them why. If it did, you can say so. This improved feedback will be used in future versions of Word to make the help system even better.
- **Big changes on the Office Web site** Microsoft Office Online has been totally revamped to offer more information than ever. Now you'll find dozens of templates related to your specific task and new tricks, articles, clip art, and online courses to help you learn more about using Word effectively. A new Marketplace feature gives you access to Microsoft's partners for various business services.

New Ways to Collaborate

We've gone from working in single, isolated offices on stand-alone PCs to being part of a vast international network consisting of corporate networks as well as individual users. The Internet (or an internal corporate network) provides the connective tissue—the people and ideas give it the fuel. In this now-global workplace, the Microsoft Office System offers vastly improved collaboration features as well as the following new technologies that help you protect your critical business information:

- **Shared documents** Working collaboratively on documents is nothing new, but having an organized place to share them—and all the resources connected with them—*is* new. Word 2003 includes document workspaces, project-oriented Web sites created in a shared space on the Web that enable you to share and store documents, assign tasks, post events, and more. And sharing a document can be as simple as e-mailing it, if that's your style. Chapter 25, "Working with Shared Documents," will tell you about the interesting possibilities involved in sharing documents.

- **XML support** If you are using Microsoft Office Professional Edition 2003 or standalone Microsoft Office Word 2003, you can open, create, and save your documents in Extensible Markup Language (XML) format, which enables you to get more from your data and free up the information you have locked away in out-of-date legacy systems.

For more information on applying XML in your documents, see Chapter 29, "Working with XML."

- **Instant messaging** In this age of instant everything, is it any surprise that instant messaging would make its way into Word? Instant messaging is a great tool because it can give you answers *fast*. With instant messaging, you can jot a quick note to the department head to make sure you've used the most recent numbers in the sales projections; you can ask your assistant to confirm an appointment; you can trade a quick one-liner with a co-worker you just finished meeting with. The instant messaging feature in Word highlights the names of your online contacts wherever they appear in a document. To see whether the contact is currently online, you simply hover the mouse pointer over the name.
- **SharePoint Team Services** In Word 2003, SharePoint Team Services have been considerably improved and made more visible. The Shared Document Workspace relies on SharePoint Team Services, which create the space for the shared Web site and allow you to create and assign tasks, gather resources, create document libraries, and more—all while you're working in your Word document.
- **Improved security** The document protection features in Word 2003 let you control editing or formatting, or both. You can also restrict format changes to specific styles or restrict changes so that users can only read (but not edit) the file or make comments.

  With Information Rights Management (IRM), you can control the information you distribute to others. By setting different levels of permission, you can allow some users to read and change documents, while blocking others from printing, e-mailing, or changing the documents they read. This enables you to share sensitive information on a need-to-know basis, secure in knowing that once the information is received, it won't travel outside your organization.
- **Built-in fax support** Need to fax your current document over to the home office? Now you can do it from within Word. In the Microsoft Office System, the File menu includes the Send To option, which enables you to send a fax using either a fax modem or an Internet fax service.

What Is XML?

The acronym XML stands for *Extensible Markup Language*, but it's actually much more than a language—it's a data standard that allows you to create your own method for tagging data types and separating the data from the format. When you save a document as XML, you are able to reduce it to its data only, which enables you to then "pour" the data into other forms for other functions. This enables you to create something once and use it many times, which helps you do things faster and reduce the margin for error in your important data.

Investigating Word's Interface Tools

Start Word by clicking Start, All Programs, Microsoft Office, Microsoft Office Word 2003. The Word document window opens and a new blank document appears. Figure 1-1 shows the Word 2003 interface and the screen elements and tools you'll use as you create and work with documents.

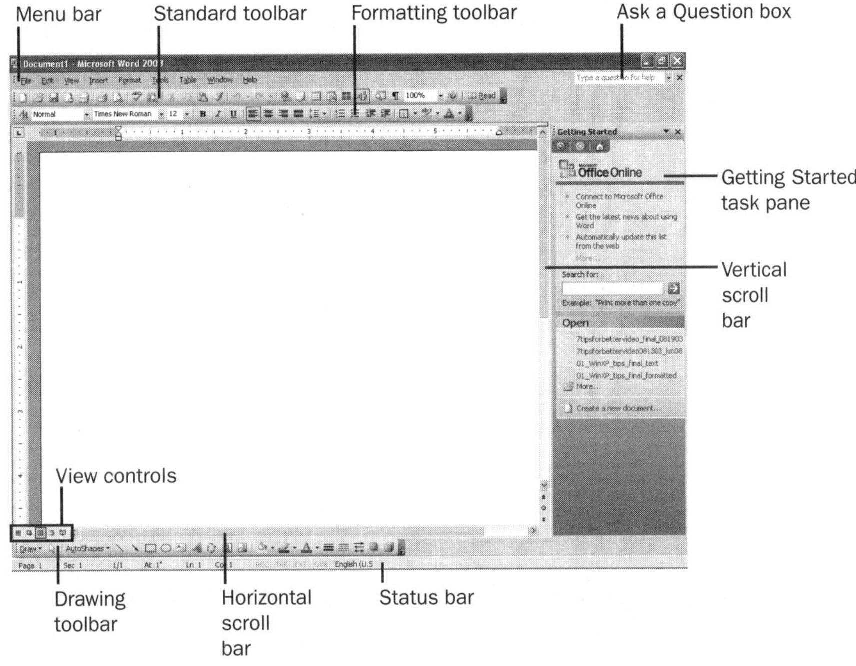

Figure 1-1. Word's new look is an inviting interface with a Getting Started task pane, ready to take you to the Web or open a new or existing document.

If you need help installing Word, see Appendix A, "Installing and Repairing Word 2003."

Working with Menus

You have several ways to work with Word. From personalized menu selections to shortcut menus to customizable toolbars, you have a range of flexible options for the way you make selections. What's more, Word attempts to learn the way you work, personalizing your menus and toolbars with the items you use most often and leaving off other items until you select them.

Personalized Menus

With a focus on keeping the screen uncluttered, the personalized menus in Word allow you to use the menu's "short form" unless you need a command that doesn't appear initially on the shortened menu. When you first display a menu, Word displays a short list of that menu's most commonly used commands. An Expand button at the bottom of the menu enables you to display the remaining commands if necessary, as shown in Figure 1-2.

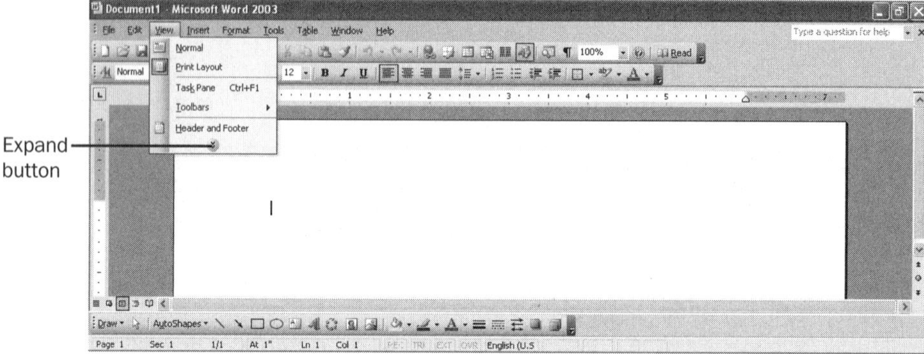

Figure 1-2. A personalized menu appears first in a short form; when you click the Expand button and select a command, it's automatically shown on the menu.

Shortcut Menus

Another type of menu that streamlines your use of Word is the shortcut menu. You display shortcut menus by right-clicking the mouse button in the editing window. The content of the menu varies, depending on what you're doing and what you clicked. For example, if you're editing a paragraph and you right-click, the menu shown in Figure 1-3 might appear.

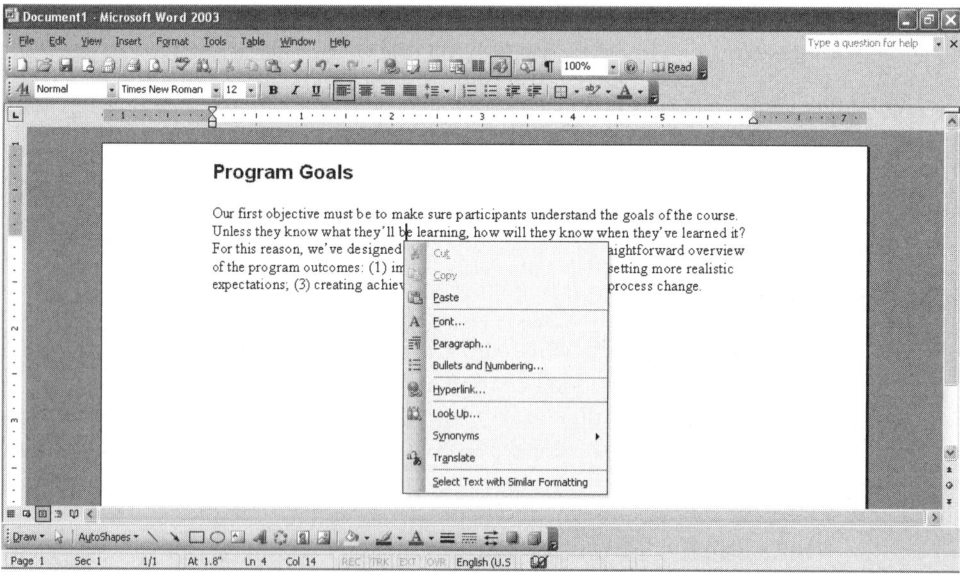

Figure 1-3. The shortcut menu displays commands that are related to the task you're carrying out and the type of data with which you're working.

By contrast, if you're adding a graphical object and right-click the object, the shortcut menu in Figure 1-4 appears.

Figure 1-4. The shortcut menu for a graphical object shows a different collection of commands.

> **Tip Get rid of the horizontal scroll bar**
> If you don't like using the horizontal scroll bar, you can wrap the text in your document to contain it completely within the window. Choose Tools, Options, and then click the View tab. In the Outlines And Normal Options section, select the Wrap To Window check box, and then click OK.

Putting Scroll Bars to Work

Scroll bars have been around for a long time—they are a staple in Microsoft Windows-based applications. Word scroll bars give you a quick way to move through the document. Simply drag the scroll box down the vertical scroll bar or to the right on the horizontal scroll bar. A ScreenTip appears, as shown below, revealing the heading nearest each scroll box position as you move the box on the scroll bar.

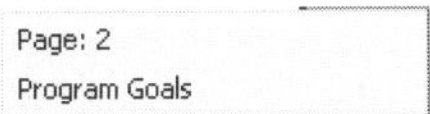

Troubleshooting

No ScreenTips?

You are scrolling through your document and ScreenTips don't appear.

If you can't see ScreenTips in your document, they may have been turned off on your system. Check it out by clicking Tools, and then Options. In the View tab, make sure ScreenTips is checked in the Show section. If it's not, select it, and then click OK to return to your document.

Using the Document Browser

Another way to move quickly through your document is to use the document browser. An effective little tool, the browser enables you to move through your document in a variety of ways. For example, you might browse by graphics, by headings, by sections, or by pages. To use the document browser, follow these steps:

1 Click the Select Browse Object button. The Select Browse Object menu appears, as shown below.

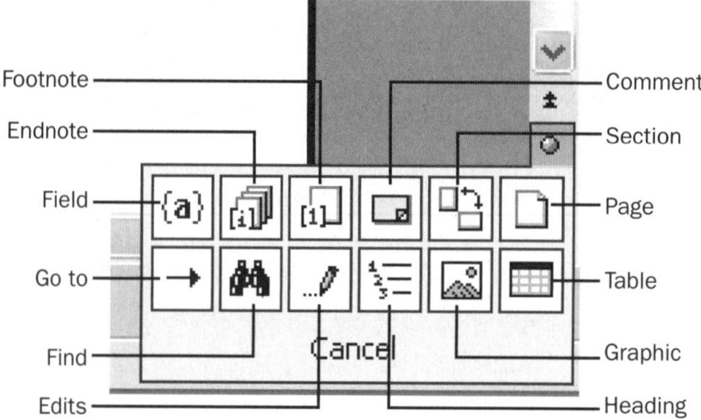

2 Choose from the Select Browse Object menu. Word moves the insertion point to the next occurrence of the item you selected.

3 To continue browsing forward in the document, click the double arrows below the Select Browse Object icon.

4 To browse backward, click the double up arrows above the Select Browse Object icon.

Tip **Identify elements in the document browser**
If you forget which element you've selected from the Select Browse Object menu, position the mouse pointer over the navigation arrows. If you've selected Browse By Comment, for example, Next Comment appears when you position the pointer over the double arrows.

Using Keyboard Shortcuts

If you're a consistent—if not fast—typist, you might be most comfortable moving through your document and selecting commands by using the keyboard. Word includes a library of keyboard shortcuts you can use to get your work done quickly.

Displaying Key Functions

Not sure what the function keys do? You can have Word display a toolbar of functions. Choose Tools, Customize, and then click the Toolbars tab. Locate the Function Key Display check box in the list, and then select it. The Function Key toolbar then appears at the bottom of the screen, as shown in Figure 1-5.

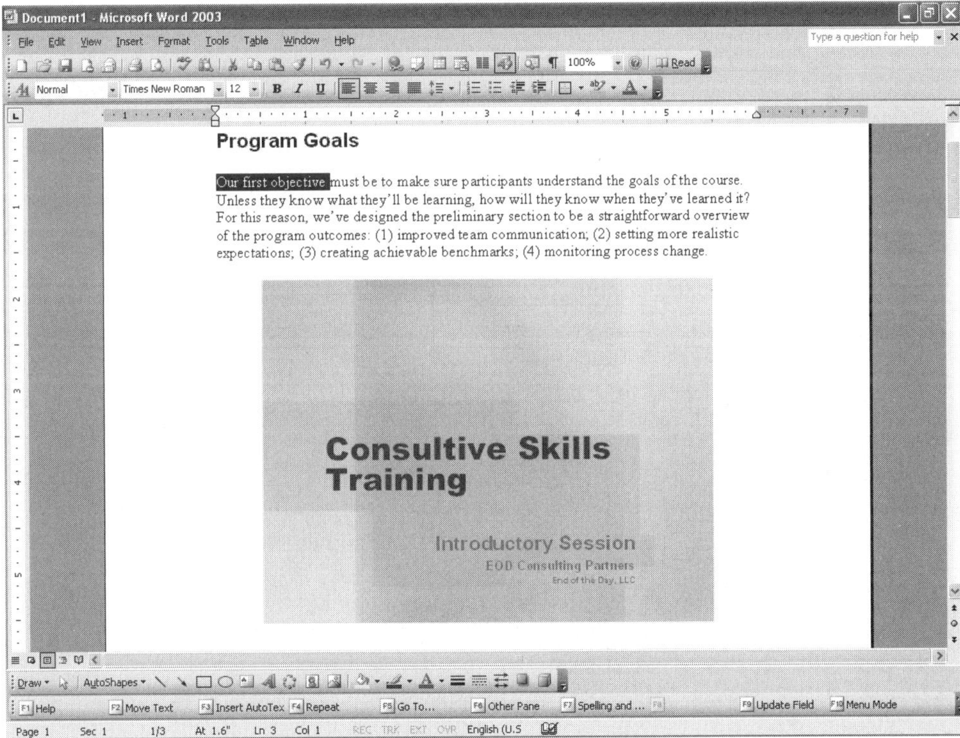

Figure 1-5. If you don't mind giving up the screen real estate, you can display the list of function keys at the bottom of the work area.

In addition, you can make many common menu selections by using keyboard shortcuts, as shown in Table 1-1.

Table 1-1. Bypassing Menu Selections Using Keyboard Shortcuts

Button	Menu and Command	Shortcut
	File, New	Ctrl+N
	File, Open	Ctrl+O
	File, Save	Ctrl+S
	File, Print	Ctrl+P
	Edit, Undo	Ctrl+Z
	Edit, Redo	Ctrl+Y
	Edit, Cut	Ctrl+X
	Edit, Copy	Ctrl+C
	Edit, Paste	Ctrl+V
NA	Edit, Select All	Ctrl+A
	Edit, Find	Ctrl+F
NA	Edit, Replace	Ctrl+H
NA	Edit, Go To	Ctrl+G
NA	View, Task Pane	Ctrl+F1
	Insert, Hyperlink	Ctrl+K
	Format, Reveal Formatting	Shift+F1
	Tools, Spelling And Grammar	F7
	Tools, Research	Alt+click
	Tools, Track Changes	Ctrl+Shift+E

Table 1-1. Bypassing Menu Selections Using Keyboard Shortcuts

Button	Menu and Command	Shortcut
	Tools, Macro, Macros	Alt+F8
	Tools, Macro, Visual Basic Editor	Alt+F11
	Tools, Macro, Microsoft Script Editor	Alt+Shift+F11
	Help, Microsoft Word Help	F1

Viewing Documents in Various Lights

Word provides many different ways for you to see what you're doing. Whether you choose outline form, full screen display, or something in between, you determine what you want on the screen as you work.

Document Views

Print Layout is one of the first views you'll see when you begin using Word. This view shows you how your document will look when printed. In this view, you'll see all the elements—text formats, graphics, rules, borders, and shading—that you add to the page.

Each view in Word gives you a different perspective on the developing document. Table 1-2 lists the views and gives suggestions for their use.

Table 1-2. Comparing Word Views

View	Description	Use	Access
Normal	Displays a single page with simple text formatting. No drawings, comments, or columns.	For entering text quickly and doing simple text editing	Click View, Normal or click the Normal View button to the left of the horizontal scroll bar.
Web Layout	Displays the page width, text position, and format as the document would appear on the Web. Drawings, graphics, and columns will appear.	For testing a page you're creating for the Web	Click View, Web Layout or click the Web Layout View button to the left of the horizontal scroll bar.
Print Layout	Displays the document as it will appear in print, with text formatting, graphics, headers and footers, columns, and all special elements.	For proofing the design, layout, and treatment of text and graphics before you print	Click View, Print Layout or click the Print Layout View button to the left of the horizontal scroll bar.

Table 1-2. Comparing Word Views

View	Description	Use	Access
Outline	Displays the headings and subheads in your document, providing the organizational structure.	For structuring the content of your document or organizing sections	Click View, Outline or click the Outline View button to the left of the horizontal scroll bar.
NEW FEATURE! Reading Layout	Shows the document in full-page view, enabling you to navigate through the document by clicking thumbnail images of individual pages or displaying multiple pages at once.	For reading, reviewing, or revising a document	Choose View, Reading Layout or click the Reading Layout button to the left of the horizontal scroll bar.
Document Map	Displays the document in two frames. On the left, the headings of the document enable you to navigate through the text on the right.	For moving through the document quickly, checking headings and corresponding sections	Click View, Document Map or click Document Map on the Standard toolbar.
Full Screen	Displays the editing window of your document in full-screen view, without rulers, toolbars, or the menu bar.	For viewing the maximum workspace available on the screen.	Click View, Full Screen; to return to the Preview view, click Close Full Screen on the Full Screen floating toolbar.

Normal

Displaying Your Document in Normal View Normal view is touted as the fastest and easiest view for entering and editing text quickly. If you need to just “get text in there,” without seeing special layouts such as columns and additional elements such as headers and footers, Normal view enables you to work with text efficiently and get the task done. In Normal view, you *won’t* see these elements:

- Multiple columns
- Drawings
- Headers and footers
- Footnotes and endnotes

In addition, the page and section breaks in Normal view are shown as dotted lines and it’s a bit more difficult to get a feel for how the text will actually look on the printed page. To know how the text will look in relation to the page, switch to Print Layout view.

Web Layout

Working in Web Layout View The Web Layout view shows the document the way it will appear in a Web browser—as one long page with no page breaks. Here the text will wrap to a wider margin and you’ll see how your headings, formatting, background color, and graphics will look. Working in this view is helpful when you’re creating a Web page in Word and when you’re creating a printed publication that you want to be able to export easily to a Web page.

Print Layout

Showing Print Layout View Print Layout view is the most complete view of all. With this view, you'll see the document as it will appear in print, with graphics, special formats, page breaks, and additional elements such as headers, footers, endnotes, and more. Special formats, such as multiple columns, will appear.

Outline

Working with Outline View Outline view enables you to see the organizational structure of your document. And not only can you *view* the levels, but you can also reorganize the outline, change heading subordination, and add and delete sections from within Outline view.

Reading Layout

Using Reading Layout View Reading Layout view gives you a quick way to review, edit, annotate, and check the layout of your documents by displaying pages in full-screen view, as shown in Figure 1-6. When you click Thumbnails from the toolbar, a panel of pages appears on the left side of the window; simply click the page you want to view to move to that page.

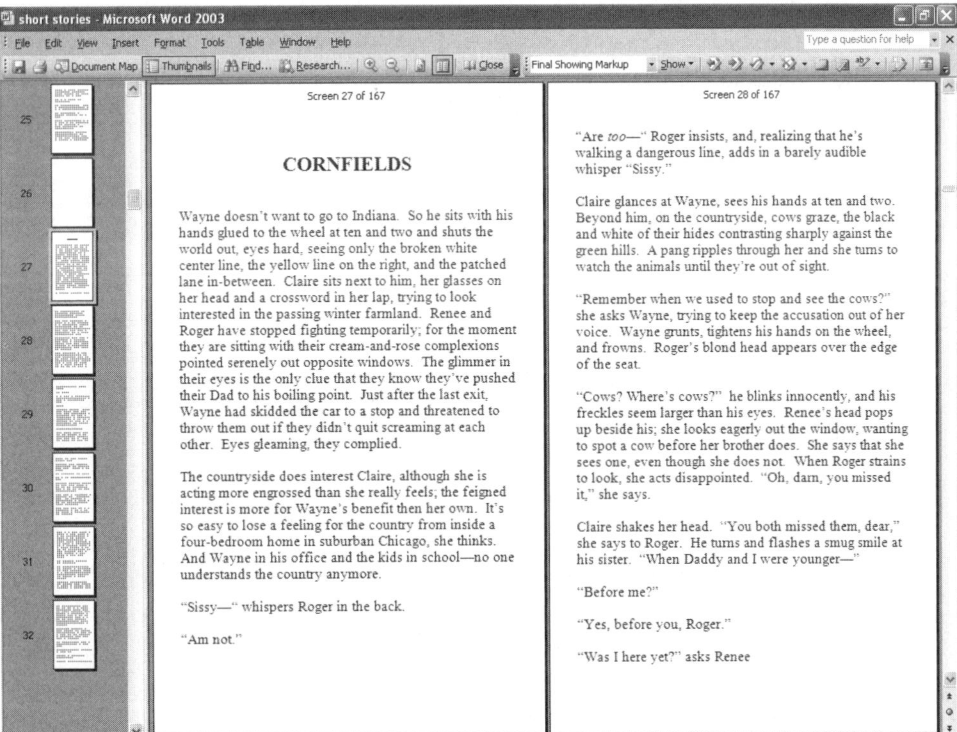

Figure 1-6. The new Reading Layout view in Word 2003 enables you to scan a document quickly without scrolling.

For more information on working with documents in Outline view, see Chapter 10, "Outlining Documents for Clarity and Structure."

Document Map

Displaying the Document Map Word's Document Map, shown in Figure 1-7, enables you to see both the structure and the content of your document at the same time. Display it by choosing View, Document Map or by clicking Document Map on the Standard toolbar. Although the left panel doesn't show the actual outline, it does enable you to navigate through your document by clicking the headings on the left to scroll the document to the desired section.

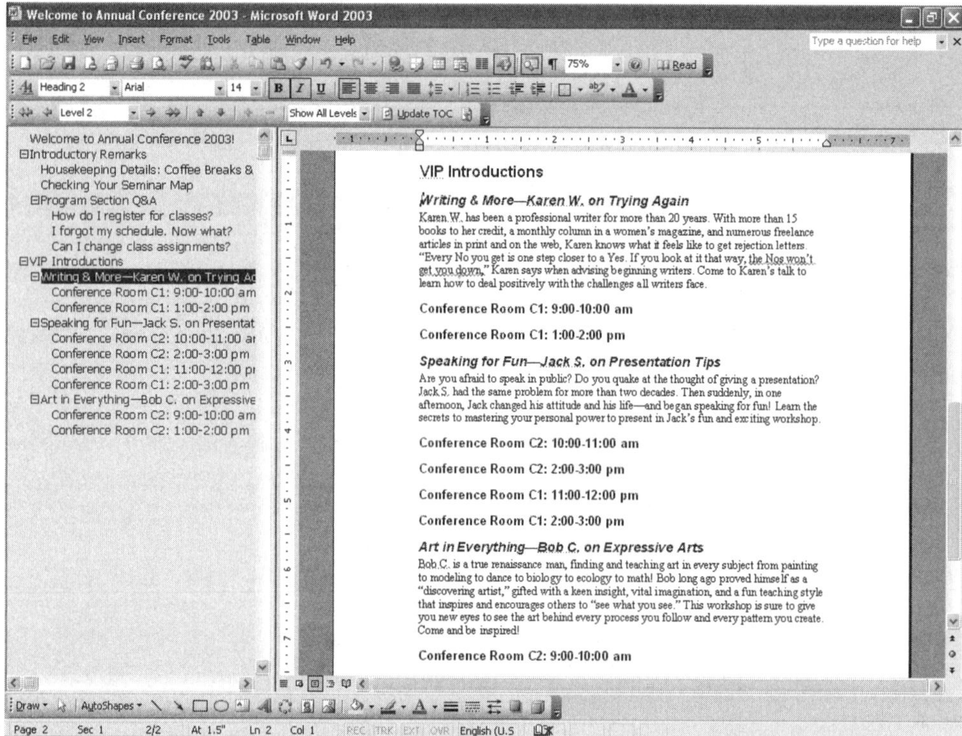

Figure 1-7. The Document Map lets you see both structure and content at the same time.

The Document Map might not leave when you're finished with it. If the Document Map stays on when you switch to a different view, click Document Map once more.

Working in Full Screen View Full Screen view, shown in Figure 1-8, isn't considered a document view, but it does change the way you see and work with your document. Full Screen view gets rid of everything except the text and a small toolbar, enabling you to write and edit flat out without menus, the Task pane, or—heaven forbid—the Office Assistant interrupting you. To select Full Screen view, click View, Full Screen. When you're ready to return to the previous view, click Close Full Screen on the floating Full Screen toolbar.

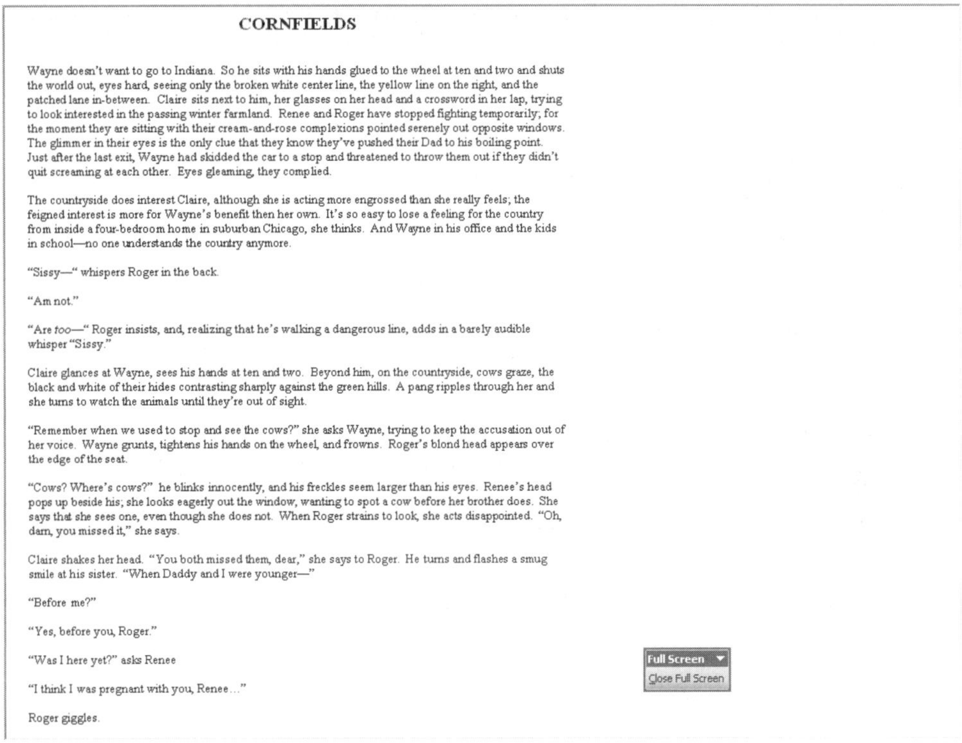

CORNFIELDS

Wayne doesn't want to go to Indiana. So he sits with his hands glued to the wheel at ten and two and shuts the world out, eyes hard, seeing only the broken white center line, the yellow line on the right, and the patched lane in-between. Claire sits next to him, her glasses on her head and a crossword in her lap, trying to look interested in the passing winter farmland. Renee and Roger have stopped fighting temporarily; for the moment they are sitting with their cream-and-rose complexions pointed serenely out opposite windows. The glimmer in their eyes is the only clue that they know they've pushed their Dad to his boiling point. Just after the last exit, Wayne had skidded the car to a stop and threatened to throw them out if they didn't quit screaming at each other. Eyes gleaming, they complied.

The countryside does interest Claire, although she is acting more engrossed than she really feels; the feigned interest is more for Wayne's benefit then her own. It's so easy to lose a feeling for the country from inside a four-bedroom home in suburban Chicago, she thinks. And Wayne in his office and the kids in school—no one understands the country anymore.

"Sissy—" whispers Roger in the back.

"Am not."

"Are *too*—" Roger insists, and, realizing that he's walking a dangerous line, adds in a barely audible whisper "Sissy."

Claire glances at Wayne, sees his hands at ten and two. Beyond him, on the countryside, cows graze, the black and white of their hides contrasting sharply against the green hills. A pang ripples through her and she turns to watch the animals until they're out of sight.

"Remember when we used to stop and see the cows?" she asks Wayne, trying to keep the accusation out of her voice. Wayne grunts, tightens his hands on the wheel, and frowns. Roger's blond head appears over the edge of the seat.

"Cows? Where's cows?" he blinks innocently, and his freckles seem larger than his eyes. Renee's head pops up beside his; she looks eagerly out the window, wanting to spot a cow before her brother does. She says that she sees one, even though she does not. When Roger strains to look, she acts disappointed. "Oh, darn, you missed it," she says.

Claire shakes her head. "You both missed them, dear," she says to Roger. He turns and flashes a smug smile at his sister. "When Daddy and I were younger—"

"Before me?"

"Yes, before you, Roger."

"Was I here yet?" asks Renee

"I think I was pregnant with you, Renee…"

Roger giggles.

Full Screen

Close Full Screen

Figure 1-8. Full Screen gives you the maximum amount of room on the screen for text entry and editing.

Other Ways to Control and Customize Your View

There are other ways you can change the view of your document while you're working. You might want to change the size of the text on the screen using Zoom, split the display, or customize the View options used as the defaults.

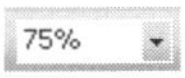

75%

Zoom

Zooming In on Your Document The Zoom control, shown in Figure 1-9, enables you to "get closer" or "move away from" the page while you work. The percentage you set controls the size of the display. A percentage of 100 displays the document at actual size. Percentages of less than 100 make the document appear smaller. Percentages greater than 100 enlarge the text and graphics, enabling you to work "up close" for line drawing or special positioning or spacing tasks.

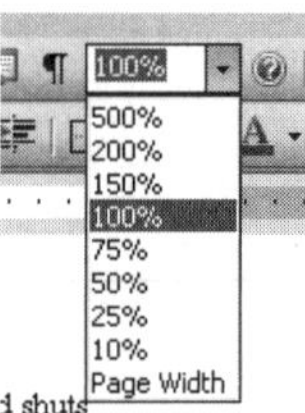

Figure 1-9. Click the Zoom arrow to display the list of choices. Click your choice to make the change.

> **Tip** **Choose Page Width or Text Width with Zoom**
> The Zoom list box offers Page Width, which enables you to display your text in a size that matches the width of the page. If you want to see the pages sized to match the width of the text, or displayed as whole pages or as multiple page configurations, switch to Reading Layout view.

Displaying Two Areas Simultaneously Your work in some documents might require you to split the screen so that you can see two sections of a document at the same time. Perhaps in an early part of your document you refer to a section covered later and you want to make sure that you've described the section accurately. You can have Word split the screen into two sections, as shown in Figure 1-10, which you can navigate independently by following these steps:

1. Position the pointer on the split box at the top of the vertical scroll bar. The pointer changes to a double-headed arrow.
2. Drag the box down to reveal the upper pane of the split window. When the pane is the size you want, release the mouse button.

> **Tip** **Perform multiple functions in multiple windows**
> You can perform other functions in the split document window: you can search, format, scroll, zoom in and out, and edit text as you would in a single window.

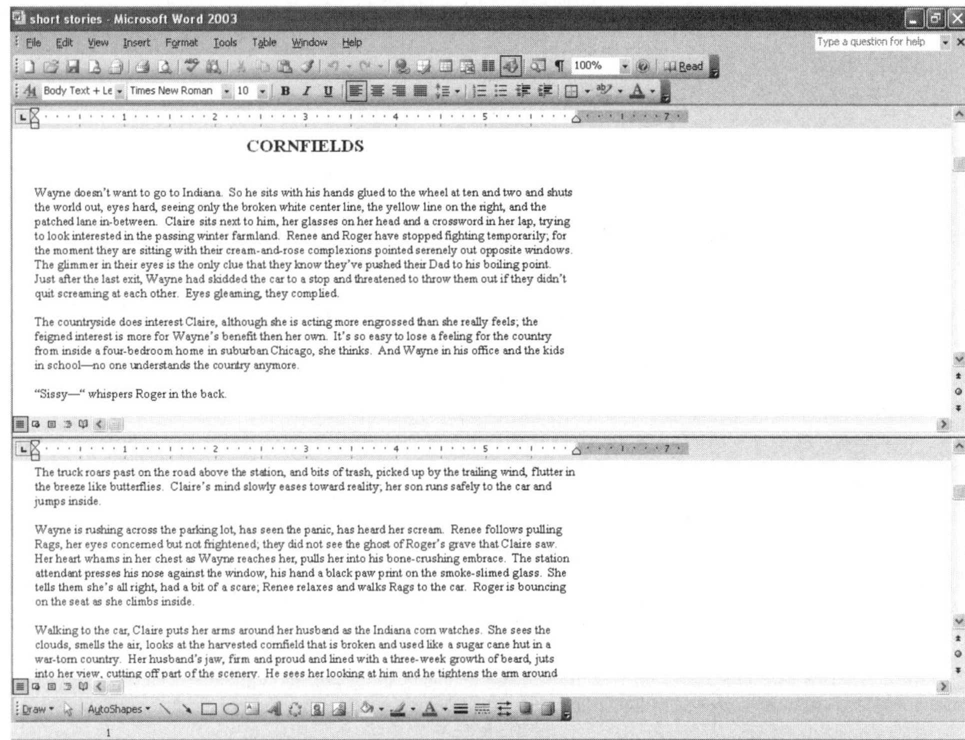

Figure 1-10. Clicking the split box and dragging it down opens a second display window at the pointer position. You can then scroll through the document to locate the text you need.

Compare Side by Side Now you can put revised documents side by side, as shown in Figure 1-11, and review changes by scrolling through and comparing the documents. This is a big improvement over using Merge Documents to add changes to a master document automatically. To compare two documents, open the ones you want to view, and then click Window, Compare Side By Side. If more than two documents are open, Word will display a message box prompting you to choose the document you want to compare to the current document. A small toolbar enables you to control whether the documents scroll together or independently.

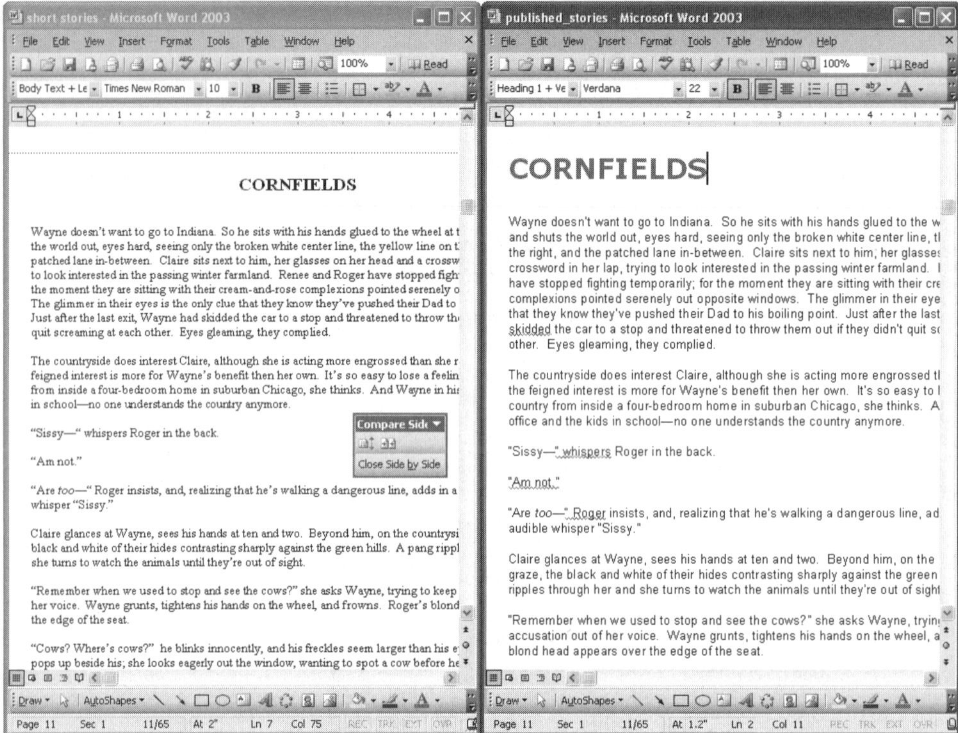

Figure 1-11. Compare Side by Side enables you to see what's changed in a document before you merge changes.

Customizing View Options You can make some major choices about the way your Word screen appears by changing the view options. Click Tools, Options, and then click the View tab, as shown in Figure 1-12.

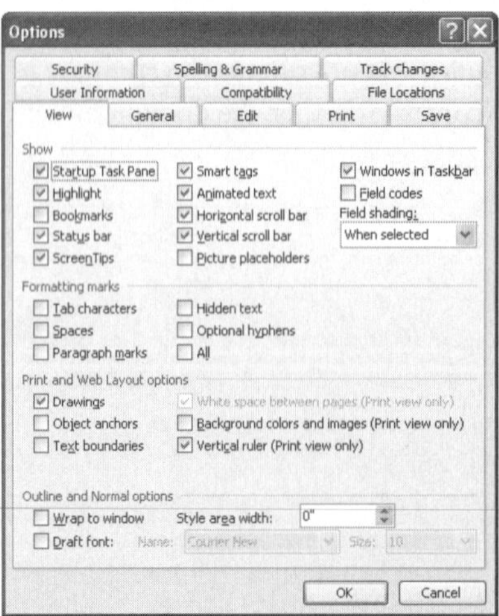

Figure 1-12. Setting View options enables you to control the elements that appear on the screen by default.

You'll find several options related to different aspects of the document display, as follows:

- **Show** The options in this section control whether additional elements appear in the Word window.
- **Formatting Marks** The options in this section determine whether formatting characters such as tabs, characters, hidden text, and paragraph marks appear.
- **Print And Web Layout Options** The options in this section control whether drawings, anchors, text boundaries, white space, and vertical rules appear.
- **Outline And Normal Options** The options in this section allow you to choose whether text wraps to the window, whether a draft font is used, and if a style area is specified, the width of the area assigned to the style column.

Creating Convenient Toolbar Displays

For several versions now, Word has given us customizable toolbars. The graphical nature of Word makes it easier to point and click than to open menus and search for commands. Tools are embedded in menus, reminding you what to look for when you don't feel like opening menus to find the same command. To display a toolbar, simply click View, Toolbars, and then select the toolbar you want to display.To remove a toolbar, just repeat the action.

Know Your Staples: the Standard and Formatting Toolbars

The two toolbars used most often and displayed by default are the Standard toolbar and the Formatting toolbar. The Standard toolbar, shown in Figure 1-13, includes the tools you use to manage files, create and edit documents, and add special but common elements to your document, such as tables, graphics, or charts.

Figure 1-13. Tools on the Standard toolbar take care of file management, document creation, and editing tasks.

> **Note** The selection of tools shown on your Standard and Formatting toolbars, and the order in which they appear, might differ from those shown here. As you work with Word and select previously hidden tools, the program adds them to the displayed toolbar, where they'll be within easy reach.

The Formatting toolbar, shown in Figure 1-14, includes the tools you use to control the font, size, style, alignment, format, and color of text. Also on the Formatting toolbar are tools for controlling indents and alignment.

Figure 1-14. Formatting tools enable you to change the look, alignment, and color of text.

> **Tip** **Add the Ink Comment toolbar**
>
> To go with ink support throughout the Office applications, Word 2003 includes an Ink Comment toolbar that enables you to draw or write on existing documents. You can use a Tablet PC and stylus or simply move your mouse pointer on the screen. Display the toolbar by clicking View, Toolbars, Ink Comment.

Relocating Toolbars

If you like to work with a number of toolbars but don't want your document overloaded at the top of the window, you can move toolbars to any of the four edges of the screen. In addition, you can create a *floating toolbar* by dragging the toolbar out into the work area.

To move a toolbar, follow these steps:

1. Display the toolbar you want to use.
2. Position the mouse pointer on the move handle, which resembles a dotted vertical line, at the far left edge of the toolbar. The pointer changes to a four-headed arrow.
3. Drag the toolbar to the new location.

Toolbars are "sticky," which means that you can drag one to a border of the work area and it will stay at that edge of the screen. For example, the Formatting toolbar shown in Figure 1-15 is positioned along the left edge of the work area.

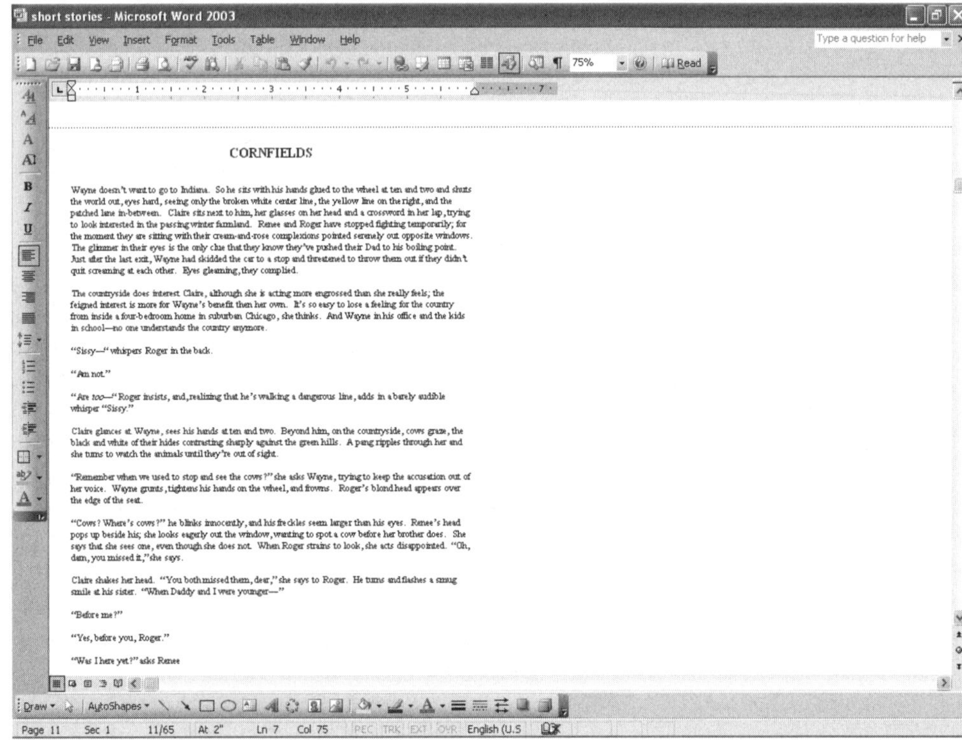

Figure 1-15. You can move a toolbar to another position on the screen by dragging it to the new location. If you want to create a floating toolbar, simply leave the toolbar in the document work area.

Adding and Removing Buttons Quickly

As mentioned earlier in this chapter, Word attempts to learn the way you use the program by adding the tools you select to the toolbars as you go along. This enables the menus to stay relatively small until you select the tools you need to add. But there's another way to add tools to the toolbars—you can click the Toolbar Options arrow (located at the far right end of each toolbar), and then select Add Or Remove Buttons.

When the tools appear, click the one you want to add. Alternatively, to remove a tool, click the tool, and then click to remove the check mark. The tool will be removed from the current display.

To find out how to create your own custom toolbars, see Chapter 5, "Customizing Word and Enhancing Accessibility."

Interpreting Status Bar Data

The status bar, located along the bottom edge of the Word window, helps you keep your bearings as you work on a document. The status bar gives you important information about where you are in the document and which features are currently enabled.

The left side of the status bar shows the location of the insertion point, specifying the page and section numbers, the current and total page count, and the line number and column location. On the right side of the status bar, you see information about the active settings and features affecting your document.

You may see the following indicators, depending on what you are doing and which features you've selected:

- REC When you are recording a macro
- TRK When Track Changes is enabled
- EXT When selected text is extended
- OVR When Overtype mode (as opposed to Insert mode) is in effect

Chapter 2

Mastering Document Fundamentals

If you've been using Word through its last few versions, you might have noticed that the program has been steadily growing beyond being a basic word-processing tool. If you haven't been using recent versions of Word, you might have heard through the grapevine (and be pleasantly surprised to find) that Word has evolved into a word-processing application that can be used to collaborate on documents with others on a network, create e-mail messages, create and manipulate Extensible Markup Language (XML) files, conduct mail merges, perform desktop publishing tasks, createWeb pages, and on and on. All these features add value to Word's complete package, but the root of Word's power remains in its fundamental capability—*document creation.*

Fortunately, Word's functionality has expanded without diminishing its word-processing features. In fact, in Word 2003 you'll find word-processing features are abundant and more powerful than ever. You'll be pleased to see that you can find many standard word-processing features and tools available in predictable and comfortable places. For example, the Exit command is still located at the bottom of the Find menu; the Minimize, Restore, and Close buttons are still in the window's upper-right corner; and you can still press Ctrl+S to save your current document. In addition, Word 2003 provides a number of new tools and innovative twists on familiar features that extend Word's capabilities and ease of use, which are introduced in Chapter 1, "Gearing Up with Word 2003." Because document creation is Word's primary functionality, this chapter is dedicated to the process—from start to finish—of working with documents. Along the way, you'll learn about Word's new and revised tools, features, and procedures as well as review standard formatting fundamentals. Whether you're a new user or an old hand, this chapter enables you to master Word's fundamental yet oh-so-important document formation and management tasks. And as you probably know, mastering the fundamentals clears the way for successful use of Word 2003's more advanced features.

Creating and Working with Content in Word

Frequently, the first task in Word is opening a blank document. This procedure sounds pretty straightforward, but just to warm up a little, let's look at the various ways you can create a blank document.

First, you can simply open Word. By default, a blank document and the Getting Started task pane open whenever you start Word. If you want to create a new blank document from within Word, you can use any of Word's traditional methods, including the following:

- Click the New Blank Document button on the Standard toolbar.
- Press Ctrl+N.
- Choose File, New to display the New Document task pane and then click Blank Document.
- Click Create A New Document under Open in the Getting Started task pane.

Tip Open Word automatically on system startup
To open Word automatically when you start the Microsoft Windows operating system, drag the Word 2003 icon from its Microsoft Office folder in the All Programs section on the open Start menu to the Startup folder on the Start menu.

At this point, you should take a moment to look over the new Getting Started task pane. This pane debuts in Word 2003 and serves as a home base, giving you a task pane view that can link you to a few helpful resources.

Working with the New Getting Started Task Pane

Home

When you open Word 2003, the Getting Started task pane (shown in Figure 2-1) appears docked along the right side of the window by default. You can display the Getting Started task pane from the other task pane views at any time by clicking the Home button on the task pane toolbar (directly below the task pane title bar) or by selecting Getting Started from the Other Task Panes list box that you access by clicking the task pane title bar. You can close the task pane by clicking the close button on the right edge of the task pane title bar, or you can move the task pane to various locations on your screen (even making the task pane a floating window) by dragging the line that appears along the left edge of the task pane's title bar.

Mastering Document Fundamentals

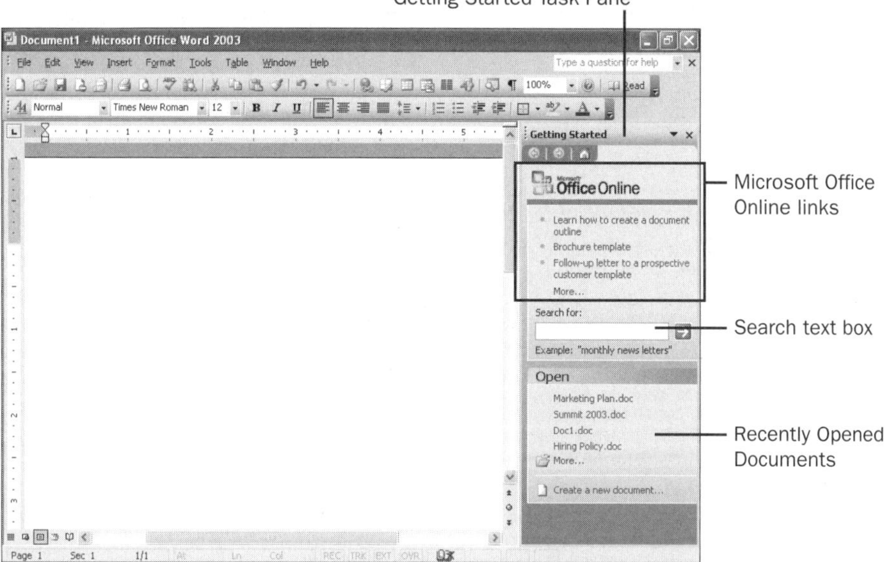

Figure 2-1. The Getting Started task pane provides hyperlinks to Microsoft Office Online resources, a search text box, and links that can expedite opening existing and new documents.

The Getting Started task pane is divided into three main sections:

- **Office Online** Enables you to configure Word to periodically download and list helpful hyperlinks from Microsoft.com. To have hyperlinks downloaded, click Automatically Update This List From The Web in the Getting Started task pane. After you activate this feature, the Office Online section lists helpful hyperlinks and a More hyperlink after Word is restarted. Click More to see additional hyperlinks in the Office Online Spotlight task pane, as shown in Figure 2-2. After you review hyperlinks in the Office Online Featured Links task pane, you can click the Home button in the task pane to return to the Getting Started task pane.

Figure 2-2. The Featured Links view in the task pane displays a changing set of additional hyperlinks from Microsoft Office Online and a Search text box.

- **Search** Enables you to enter keywords in the text box to search for information online. Search results appear in the Search Results task pane, which is discussed in detail in Chapter 4, "Honing Document Navigation Skills."
- **Open** Lists recently opened documents, a link to the Open dialog box, and a link to the New Document task pane. Note that in Microsoft Word Version 2002, recently opened documents appear in the New Document task pane; now, inWord 2003, recently used documents appear in the Getting Started pane. To display the Open dialog box, click the More hyperlink in the Open section, and to display the New Document task pane, click Create A New Document.

> **Tip** **Control whether Office Online featured links display**
> You can turn Office Online featured links on or off by configuring an option in the Help task pane. To do so, display the Help task pane, click Online Content Settings in the See Also section, and clear or select the Show Microsoft Office Online Featured Links check box.

You can control the content in the Getting Started task pane in several ways. Basically, you can turn the display of Microsoft Office Online hyperlinks on and off, hide the Search text box and display it again, and specify how many recently opened documents to display.

> **Tip** You can quickly display or hide the task pane by pressing Ctrl+F1.

Controlling the Display of Links and the Search Option in the Getting Started Task Pane

To specify whether Microsoft Office Online hyperlinks and the Search text box appear in the Getting Started task pane, follow these steps:

Service Options...

Service Options

1 Choose Tools, Options, click the General tab, and then click Service Options.

2 In the Category section of the Service Options dialog box, click Online Content, as shown in Figure 2-3. Then perform any of the following actions:

- To stop the display of Microsoft Office Online links, clear the Show Microsoft Office Online Featured Links check box, and then click OK twice.
- To show only the Open section in the Getting Started task pane (without the Office hyperlinks or the Search text box), clear the Show Content And Links From Microsoft Office Online check box. Note that clearing this check box also removes the hyperlink to online templates in the New Document task pane and to automatic help on templates. Click OK twice, and then restart Word.
- To turn options on after they've been turned off, select the Show Content And Links From Microsoft Office Online check box, select any additional check boxes (such as the Show Microsoft Office Online Featured Links check box), click OK twice, and then restart Word.

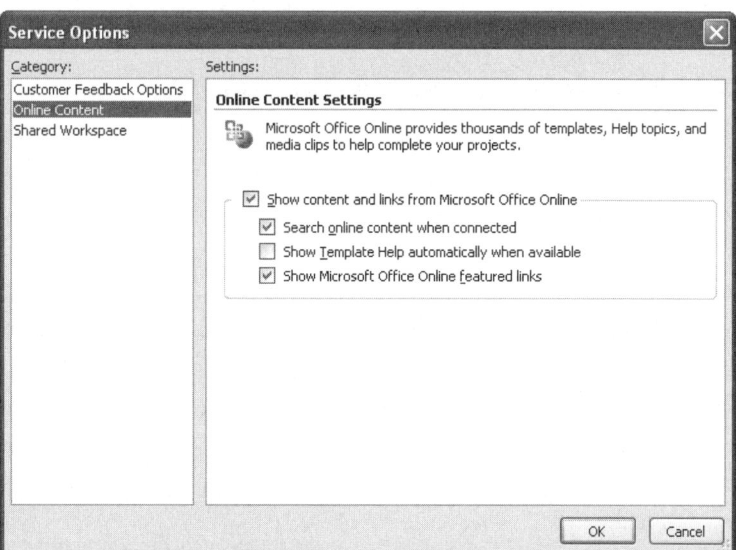

Figure 2-3. The Service Options dialog box enables you to control some ways that Word interacts with online resources.

After the Show Microsoft Office Online Featured Links option has been turned off and then back on, you'll have to click the Automatically Update This List From The Web hyperlink in the Getting Started task pane to enable Word to download hyperlinks from Microsoft Office Online.

Configuring the List of Recently Opened Documents

Another way you can customize the Getting Started task pane is to specify how many (if any) recently opened documents should be listed in the Open section. By default, the four most recently opened documents appear in the Getting Started task pane. To configure this setting, choose Tools, Options, click the General tab, and type a number from 0 through 9 in the Recently Used File List box to display up to nine recently opened documents in your task pane. If you choose not to display any previously opened documents, you can clear the check box or enter **0** in the Recently Used File List box.

Inside Out

Clearing your document history list

You might think that clearing your document history from the Windows Start menu (by right-clicking Start, choosing Properties, clicking the Start Menu tab, clicking Customize, clicking the Advanced tab, and then clicking Clear List) would automatically clear the Open list box in the Getting Started task pane—but it doesn't. Instead, this feature clears the history from the My Recent Documents feature found in the Windows operating system. To clear the task pane's document history list, you must choose Tools, Options, click the General tab, and then clear the Recently Used File List check box or type **0** in the Recently Used File List box.

Working with the New Document Task Pane

You can quickly create a variety of document types using the New Document task pane.To display the New Document task pane, perform any of the following actions:

- Choose File, New.
- Click Create A New Document in the Getting Started task pane.
- Choose View, Task Pane, or choose View, Toolbars, Task Pane to display the task pane if it's hidden (or press Ctrl+F1, which toggles the task pane's display), click the task pane title bar, and then click New Document in the title bar list box if necessary.

The New Document task pane, shown in Figure 2-4, provides the following options for creating documents:

- **Blank Document** Opens a new blank Word document based on the Normal.dot template.

For information about customizing the Normal.dot template, see Chapter 16, "Formatting Documents Using Templates, Wizards, Add-Ins, and XML Schemas."

- **XML Document** Opens a new document as an XML file. When you use this new document option, Word automatically specifies the document as an XML document when you save your work. You can save an XML document using Word's XML schema, or you can attach any XML schema to the document. When you save a document as an XML document, any software that can parse XML can read and process the data in your document. In other words, saving a document as an XML file makes the data available to any application that supports XML, not just to Microsoft Office programs. Further, you can use XML documents in various ways, such as using a document in Word as well as a Web page, without having to manipulate the content in any way.

For more information about working with XML documents in Word, see Chapter 29, "Working with XML."

- **Web Page** Opens a blank Web page and enables Web page components. By default, Word saves a Web Page created with this option as a Single File Web Page. You can also save a Web page using the Web Page and Web Page, Filtered designations in the Save As dialog box.

For more information about building Web pages using Word, see Chapter 26, "Creating Professional Web Sites."

- **E-mail Message** Displays an Untitled Message window that you can use to create and send an e-mail message. If Outlook hasn't been set up on the system yet, the Outlook Startup Wizard appears when you first select the E-mail Message hyperlink.

For more information about using Word to send e-mail messages, see Chapter 24, "Working and Collaborating Online."

- **From Existing Document** Displays the New From Existing Document dialog box, which is similar to the Open dialog box. You can then create a new document based on an existing document. You might feel as though you're working on an existing document, but your new document actually contains only a copy of the existing file's contents. The first time you save the new document, Word automatically displays the Save As dialog box so that you can save the file as a new file instead of replacing the existing document.

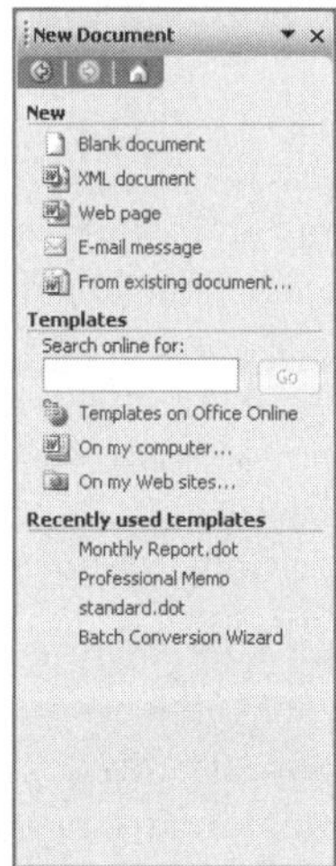

Figure 2-4. The New Document task pane provides a variety of methods you can use to create various types of new documents, including XML documents, Web pages, and e-mail messages.

In addition to creating new blank workspaces, the New Document task pane offers options to create new documents using templates stored on your computer and online, as described in the next section.

Working with Templates and Wizards

Word makes creating new documents based on *templates* a snap. Templates are predesigned documents that contain formatting and, in many cases, generic text. They are used as a foundation for creating new documents based on predetermined settings. For example, to create an office memo, you could use the Professional Memo document template, as shown in Figure 2-5. The Professional Memo template is a Word document template that you can access in the Memos tab in the Templates dialog box.

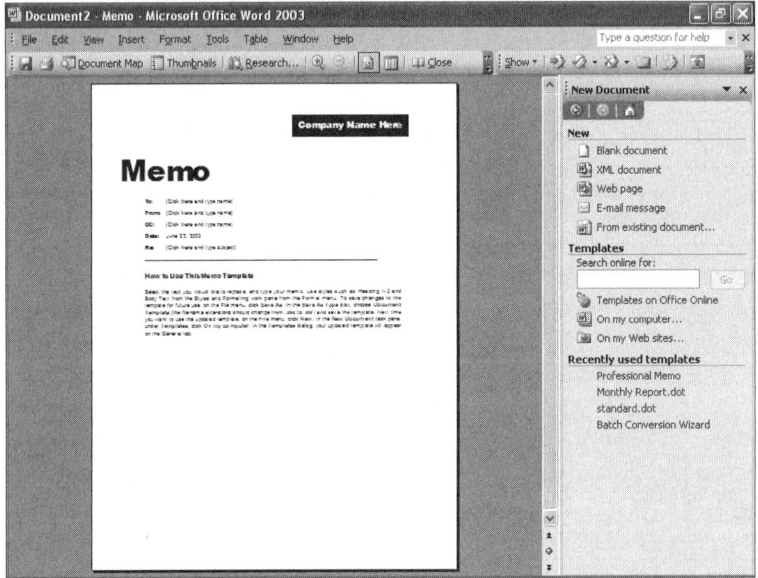

Figure 2-5. Templates can contain standard text elements and font styles as well as providing placeholder text and graphics—as seen here in the Professional Memo template.

By default, templates have the .dot extension, and blank Word documents are based on the standard global template, the Normal.dot template. The Normal template contains default styles but no generic text. You can access document templates by selecting from the Templates options in the New Document task pane.Template options include the following:

- **Search Online For** You can search online for templates by entering a keyword in the Search Online For text box, and then clicking Go. By default, when you download and use an online template, the Template Help task pane appears, offering assistance and the opportunity to rate the template. You can turn off the automatic display of Template

Help by displaying the Service Options dialog box, selecting Online Content, and then clearing the Show Template Help Automatically When Opening A Template check box, shown earlier in Figure 2-3.

- **Templates On Office Online** Clicking this link opens the Microsoft Office Online Templates home page in your Web browser, as shown in Figure 2-6. Microsoft's Templates home page provides a selection of templates ranging from staffing and management documents to stationery.

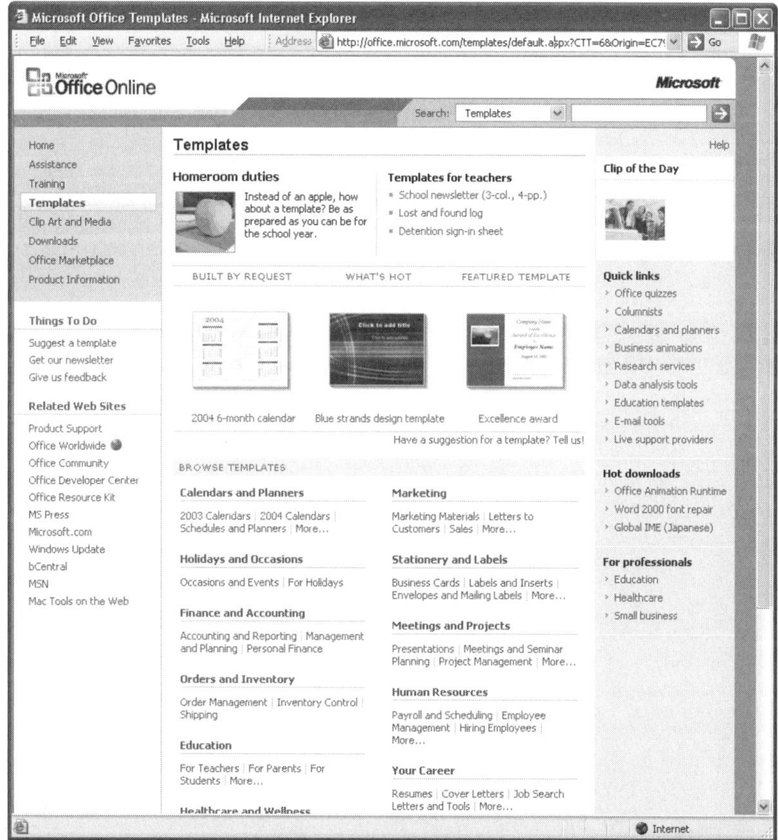

Figure 2-6. The Microsoft Office Online Templates home page provides free templates, arranged by category, that you can open in Office applications and modify to suit your purposes.

- **On My Computer** When you click the On My Computer hyperlink, the Templates dialog box appears, as shown in Figure 2-7. The Templates dialog box contains templates and wizards that can help you create basic documents. By default, the Templates dialog box organizes templates and wizards into the following categories: General (Blank Document, XML Document, Web Page, and E-mail Message), Legal Pleadings, Letters & Faxes, Mail Merge, Memos, Other Documents (including résumé templates), Publications, and Reports.

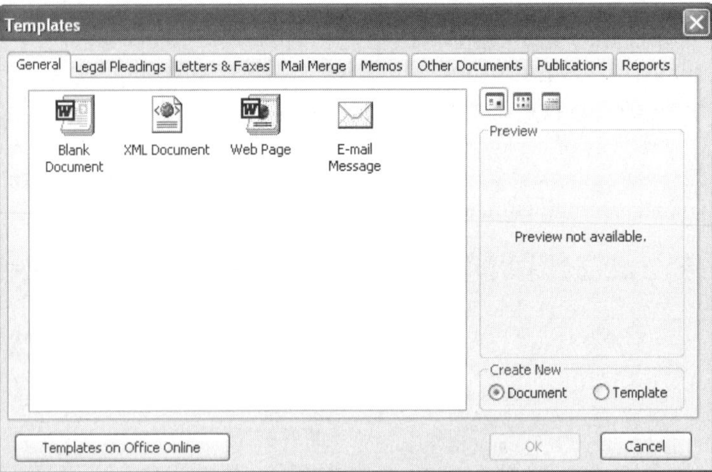

Figure 2-7. The Templates dialog box enables you to quickly access standard document templates and wizards installed with Office.

- **On My Web Sites** If you (or an associate) have a Web site on a network or on the Internet where templates are stored, you can click the On My Web Sites link to access your Network Places. Then, in the New From Templates On My Web Sites dialog box, navigate to the network place that stores the template you want.
- **Recently Used Templates** The task pane automatically displays links to recently used templates. This feature can dramatically speed the process of applying the same template to one document after another because you won't need to continually display the Templates dialog box to apply a previously accessed template.

Tip **Store templates online**

Occasionally, you might want to store templates online. If you don't have a Web site, you can work around this limitation without spending a dime, by using MSN's free Web space at *groups.msn.com*. You can use the free space to store templates (and other files), thereby making the files easily accessible on the Internet. You can also configure the Templates On My Web Sites link in the New Documents task pane to include a shortcut to your File Cabinet's contents. For more information about storing templates on a Web site and using MSN File Cabinets, see Chapter 24, "Working and Collaborating Online."

For in-depth information about templates, see Chapter 16, "Formatting Documents Using Templates, Wizards, Add-Ins, and XML Schemas."

Mastering Document Content Fundamentals

After you open a new document—whether it's blank or based on an existing document or template—the next order of business is to insert information into the document and format it.

Granted, that's a fairly obvious observation, but it's well worth discussing. Working with information is what this book's all about, so just to be sure we cover all our bases, we'll address content fundamentals here. First, we'll look at inputting information, and then we'll look at ways to navigate through documents and perform standard editing and formatting tasks. These topics might sound basic, but you should be able to pick up at least a few pointers here and there throughout the upcoming sections. If nothing else, scan the tables included on the next few pages to learn a new trick or two to help streamline your working style.

Inputting Information

You have a few options when it comes to inserting information into Word 2003 documents:

- **Click in the document and begin typing in the editing window.** Typed text appears to the left of the insertion point. You can reposition the insertion point by clicking elsewhere within the editing window.
- **Copy and paste information.** Using the Office Clipboard, you can easily copy information from within the current document, other Word documents, Web pages, other applications, and from almost any other application that allows you to copy selected data. After you copy data, you can paste the information directly into Word documents. For more information about using the Office Clipboard, see the section "Using the Office Clipboard" later in this chapter on page 46.
- **Insert the contents of another Word document or text file.** You can insert the contents of another document into the current document without copying and pasting by choosing Insert, File; navigating in the Insert File dialog box to the file that contains the information you want to insert into the current document; and then double-clicking the document. The document's contents are inserted into the currently displayed document (and the existing document remains unchanged).
- **Use speech recognition.** You can speak your piece by configuring and working with Word's speech features. Using speech recognition, you can dictate content and use voice commands by talking into a high-quality headset.
- **Handwrite content using the mouse or a stylus.** Word can recognize handwritten marks you make with your mouse or a *stylus*, which is a pencil-like tool used on electronic writing or drawing pads, tablet PCs, and so forth. When you use the handwriting recognition feature or Ink feature, you can retain your written marks, create drawings, or configure Word to interpret your handwriting and display the information as typed text.

Tip **Change from Insert mode to Overtype mode**

By default, new text you type in the middle of a line will be inserted between existing text. To change from Insert mode to Overtype mode, you can choose Tools, Options, and then clear the Overtype Mode check box in the Edit tab. For quicker results, double-click OVR on the status bar or press the Insert (sometime labeled Ins) button to toggle between Insert and Overtype modes.

Moving Within Documents Using Keyboard Shortcuts and Function Keys

After you enter information in documents, you'll frequently need to move around within your documents so that you can add, edit, and format your documents' contents. As you most likely know, you can move around within a document using the scroll bars located along the right and bottom edges of the editing window, and you can reposition the insertion point by clicking anywhere within your document. By learning a few keyboard shortcuts, you can speed up text navigation considerably. Table 2-1 lists common keyboard shortcuts and function key combinations that you might find handy as you work your way through Word documents. To print a list of keyboard shortcuts and function commands, follow these steps:

1. Click Tools, Macro, Macros, and then select Word Commands in the Macros In list box.
2. In the Macro Name list box, click ListCommands, and then click Run.
3. In the List Commands dialog box, select the Current Menu And Keyboard Settings option, and then click OK.
4. Click File, Print to print the shortcut list.

Tip **Use Shift to select text**

By pressing Shift in combination with a keyboard navigation shortcut, you can generally select all the text from the insertion point's current location to the location to which the shortcut takes you. For example, if you press End, the insertion point moves to the end of the line, but if you press Shift+End, you'll select all the text from the insertion point to the end of the line.

Table 2-1. Keyboard Shortcuts and Function Commands for Navigating Within Documents

Keyboard Shortcut	Action
Alt+Down Arrow	Moves to the next object
Alt+End	Moves to the end of the row
Alt+F1 (or F11)	Moves to the next field
Alt+F4	Closes the active document
Alt+F6	Moves to the next window
Alt+F7	Moves to the next misspelled word if the Check Spelling As You Type feature is turned on (the default)
Alt+Home	Moves to the start of a row
Alt+Left Arrow	Goes back to the previous page in Web view
Alt+Page Down	Moves to the end of the current column
Alt+Page Up	Moves to the top of the current column
Alt+Right Arrow	Goes forward to the next page in Web view
Alt+Shift+F1 (or Shift+F11)	Moves to the previous field

Table 2-1. Keyboard Shortcuts and Function Commands for Navigating Within Documents

Keyboard Shortcut	Action
ALT+Shift+F6	Displays the previous window
Alt+Up Arrow	Moves to the previous object
Arrow keys	Move the insertion point left, right, up, or down
Ctrl+Alt+Home	Opens the Select Browse Object menu
Ctrl+Alt+Page Down	Moves the insertion point to the bottom of the window
Ctrl+Alt+Page Up	Moves the cursor to the top of the window
Ctrl+Alt+S	Splits the window view
Ctrl+Alt+Y (or Shift+F4)	Finds the next instance of a search term
Ctrl+Alt+Z (or Shift+F5)	Moves to the previous location of the insertion point (even if the insertion point was in a different Word document)
Ctrl+Down Arrow	Moves to the next paragraph or next table cell
Ctrl+End	Moves to the end of the document
Ctrl+F	Displays the Find tab in the Find And Replace dialog box
Ctrl+F5	Restores a document's window from maximized to the previous window size
Ctrl+F6 (or Alt+F6)	Displays the next window
Ctrl+F7	Activates the window so you can move it using the arrow keys
Ctrl+F8	Activates the window so you can resize the window height and width using the arrow keys
Ctrl+F10	Maximizes the document window
Ctrl+G (or F5)	Displays the Go To tab in the Find And Replace dialog box
Ctrl+Home	Moves to the beginning of the document
Ctrl+Left Arrow	Moves one word to the left
Ctrl+O (or Ctrl+Alt+F2 or Ctrl+F12)	Displays the Open dialog box
Ctrl+Page Down	Browses to the next item (based on the current Browse Object setting)
Ctrl+Page Up	Browses to the previous item (based on the current Browse Object setting)
Ctrl+Right Arrow	Moves one word to the right
Ctrl+S (or Alt+Shift+F2 or Shift+F12)	Saves the current document
Ctrl+Shift+F6	Displays the previous window

Table 2-1. Keyboard Shortcuts and Function Commands for Navigating Within Documents

Keyboard Shortcut	Action
Ctrl+Up Arrow	Moves to the previous paragraph
Ctrl+W (or Ctrl+F4)	Closes the active document
End	Moves to the end of the current line
Esc	Closes an open menu or cancels the current action
F6	Moves to the next pane or frame
Home	Moves to the beginning of the current line
PageDown	Displays the next screen
PageUp	Displays the previous screen
Shift+F6	Moves to the previous pane or frame
Shift+Tab	Moves to the previous cell in a table
Tab	Moves to the next cell in a table

An easy way to view the commands associated with function keys is to display the Function Key Display toolbar on your desktop. To do so, choose Tools, Customize, select Function Key Display in the Toolbars tab, and then click Close.

By default, the Function Key Display toolbar shows the basic function key commands. You can press Shift, Ctrl, Alt, or any combination of those three keys to display other commands on the Function Key Display toolbar. To illustrate this little toolbar trick, Figure 2-8 shows the Function Key Display toolbar in normal, Shift, Ctrl, and Alt modes.

Figure 2-8. The Function Key Display toolbar adjusts to show various options when you press Shift, Ctrl, and Alt alone or in any combination.

> **Note** You can also browse through documents using the GoTo tab in the Find And Replace dialog box. To access the Go To tab, press F5, press Ctrl+G, or choose Edit, Go To. For more information about using the Find And Replace dialog box, see Chapter 4, "Honing Document Navigation Skills."

Using the Select Browse Object Feature

Another way to browse through documents is to use the Select Browse Object menu and its associated buttons. You can find the three browse buttons—Previous Find/Go To, Select Browse Object, and Next Find/Go To—in the lower-right corner of the editing window, as shown here. Table 2-2 describes the available options.

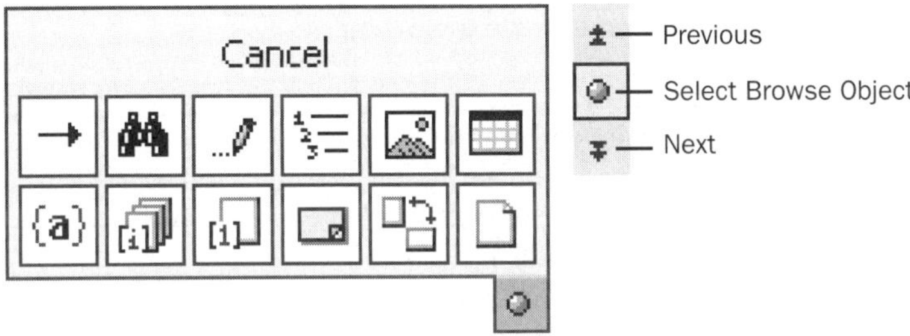

Figure 2-9. The Select Browse Object tool enables you to specify how you'd like to browse through a document based on the type of object.

To use the Select Browse Object feature, follow these steps:

1. Open the Select Browse Object menu by pressing Ctrl+Alt+Home or by clicking the Select Browse Object button on the vertical scroll bar.
2. Select the type of object you want to browse for (such as, browsing from heading to heading). See Table 2-2 for available options.
3. Click the Previous and Next buttons to navigate from one browse object to the next, or press Ctrl+Page Up to see the previous object and press Ctrl+Page Down to see the next browse object.

Table 2-2. Select Browse Object Menu Options

Button	Description
→	Browses by using the Go To tab in the Find And Replace dialog box
	Browses by using the Find tab in the Find And Replace dialog box
...	Browses by moving from edit to edit (if the Track Changes feature has been used)

Table 2-2. Select Browse Object Menu Options

Button	Description
	Browses by moving from heading to heading
	Browses by moving from graphic to graphic
	Browses by moving from table to table
{a}	Browses by moving from field to field
	Browses by moving from endnote to endnote
	Browses by moving from footnote to footnote
	Browses by moving from comment to comment
	Browses by moving from section to section
	Browses by moving from page to page

Performing Basic Editing Tasks

As you know, merely entering information into a Word document doesn't usually create a finished product. Instead, your documents are the result of entering information, and editing and formatting the entered text, images, and objects. Now that we've covered entering text and navigating within documents, it's time to work with text by performing basic editing tasks. This section provides information about selecting, copying, cutting, and pasting text; using the Clipboard; and undoing, redoing, and repeating changes—in other words, some of the common tasks you'll perform every time you work on documents in Word.

Selecting Text

Generally speaking, you can streamline many editing tasks by first selecting the text you want to edit. In fact, you can speed up most text modification tasks by mastering precise selection techniques. You can select text in a variety of ways. Usually (and not too surprisingly), you will select text using the mouse or keyboard commands. (You can also select text that contains similar formatting by using the Styles And Formatting task pane, but because that topic is slightly more advanced and is related to creating and using styles, that technique is addressed in Chapter 9, "Using Styles to Increase Your Formatting Power.") Regardless of how you select text, you can cancel a selection by clicking any area outside the selected text or by pressing an arrow key.

> **Note** You can access a couple of key text-selection options by choosing Tools, Options, and then clicking the Edit tab in the Options dialog box. In the Edit tab, you can specify whether to automatically select paragraph marks when you select paragraphs (the Use Smart Paragraph Selection check box) and whether to automatically select entire words when you're selecting text (the When Selecting, Automatically Select Entire Word check box). Both text selection settings are activated by default.

Selecting Information with Your Mouse Selecting information using the mouse is the most common way to select text and other elements (such as graphics, tables, objects, and so forth) in Word documents. To select information using the mouse, you can use any of the options described in Table 2-3.

Table 2-3. Methods of Selecting Text Using the Mouse

Selection	Method
Word or single element	Double-click the word or element.
Sentence	Press Ctrl and click in the sentence.
Paragraph	Triple-click within the paragraph, or double-click in the left margin next to the paragraph.
Entire line	Click in the left margin.
Multiple lines	Click and drag in the left margin.
Contiguous text or elements	Position the insertion point at the beginning of the text to be selected, click and drag to select the desired text, and then release the mouse button.
Multiple noncontiguous instances of text or elements	Select the first item (as described above), press Ctrl, and then select additional text or elements elsewhere within your document.
Entire section	Display your document in Outline view, and then triple-click a heading or click a heading.
Large block of text	Click at the start of the selection, scroll to the end of the selection, and then hold down Shift as you click.
Blocks of text using Extend mode	Click at the beginning of the text you want to select, double-click EXT on the status bar, and then click at the end of the text you want to select. To deactivate Extend mode, press Esc or double-click EXT again so that it appears dimmed on the status bar.
Vertical block of text	Press Alt, and then drag over the text.

Table 2-3. Methods of Selecting Text Using the Mouse

Selection	Method
Table Cell	Click the left edge of the cell.
Table Row	Click in the left margin next to the row.
Table Column	Click the column's top gridline or border.
Entire Table	Click in the table and press Alt+Num 5, with Num Lock turned on. Alternatively, click the table selection box that displays near the top-left corner of the table when you position the cursor over the table.
Text box or frame	Position the cursor over the edge of the text box until it changes to a four-headed arrow, and then click.
Graphic	Click the graphic.
Headers and Footers	In Print Layout View, double-click the dimmed header or footer text, and then click in the left margin.
Footnotes and Endnotes	In Print Layout View, click in the left margin.
Entire document	Triple-click in the left margin or press Ctrl+A.

Note When you want to select large areas of contiguous text, consider using Extend mode, which enables you to select contiguous blocks of text without holding down the mouse button.

Tip **Select all instances of an element**

You can select all instances of a word, a symbol, or a phrase. To do so, select the Find tab in the Find And Replace dialog box (press Ctrl+F), type the text you want to select in the Find What text box (or paste information, such as a symbol), select the Highlight All Items Found In check box, select Main Document in the list box if necessary, and then click the Find All button.

Chapter 9, "Using Styles to Increase Your Formatting Power," discusses how to select text based on formatting attributes.

Selecting Text Using Keyboard Commands As most people's Word proficiency increases, so does their desire to take advantage of Word's numerous keyboard commands. Keyboard commands increase productivity by limiting how frequently you move your hand from your keyboard to your mouse and back again. For the most part, selecting text using keyboard commands requires you to press Shift while you press the keyboard combination that moves the insertion point in the direction of the text you want to select. If you know the keyboard combinations used to move the insertion point (shown in Table 2-1), you can generally select text by using the same keyboard combinations while holding down Shift. For example,

Ctrl+Right Arrow moves the insertion point to the next word, and Shift+Ctrl+Right Arrow selects the text from the insertion point to the beginning of the next word. Table 2-4 lists the text selection keyboard commands that might be most useful for you.

> **Tip** Combine cursor-movement keyboard commands with text-selection commands to make selections precisely (for example, press Home to move to the beginning of a line before you select the line; see Table 2-1).

> **Tip** To select multiple noncontiguous areas, make your first selection, hold down Ctrl, and then select the other items.

Table 2-4. Keyboard Commands for Selecting Text

Keyboard Command	Selects
Alt+Shift+Page Down	From the insertion point to the end of a column
Alt+Shift+Page Up	From the insertion point to the beginning of a column
Ctrl+A	Entire document
Ctrl+Alt+Shift+Page Down	From the insertion point to the bottom of the window
Ctrl+Alt+Shift+Page Up	From the insertion point to the top of the window
Ctrl+Shift+Down Arrow	From the insertion point to the end of the current paragraph
Ctrl+Shift+End	From the insertion point to the end of the current document
Ctrl+Shift+F8 + arrow keys or mouse button	Vertical or horizontal blocks of text beginning at the insertion point (press Esc to cancel selection mode)
Ctrl+Shift+Home	From the insertion point to the beginning of the current document
Ctrl+Shift+Left Arrow	From the insertion point to the beginning of a word; to select preceding words, press Left Arrow repeatedly while holding down Ctrl+Shift
Ctrl+Shift+Right Arrow	From the insertion point to the end of a word; to select subsequent words, press Right Arrow repeatedly while holding down Ctrl+Shift
Ctrl+Shift+Up Arrow	From the insertion point to the beginning of the current paragraph
Esc (or double-click EXT on the status bar)	To turn off Extend mode
F8	To turn Extend mode on and increase the size of a selection (press twice to select a word, three times to select a sentence, and so forth)

Table 2-4. Keyboard Commands for Selecting Text

Keyboard Command	Selects
F8+F8	Current word
F8+F8+F8	Current sentence
F8 + arrow key	From the insertion point to a specific location in a document (press Esc to cancel selection mode)
F8+Left Arrow or F8+Right Arrow	The character nearest to the insertion point to the left or right
Shift+Down Arrow or Shift+Up Arrow	Entire line above or below the insertion point, beginning from the insertion point
Shift+End	From the insertion point to the end of the current line
Shift+F8	To reduce the size of a selection
Shift+Home	From the insertion point to the beginning of the current line
Shift+Left Arrow	One character to the left of the insertion point
Shift+Page Down	One screen down, beginning from the insertion point
Shift+Page Up	One screen up, beginning from the insertion point
Shift+Right Arrow	One character to the right of the insertion point
Shift+Tab	Preceding cell's contents in a table
Tab	Next cell's contents in a table

Tip **Use F8 to select text**

You can use the F8 key to turn on Extend mode and then to progressively select the current word, sentence, paragraph, and so forth. For example, to turn on Extend mode and select the current word, press F8 twice. To select the current sentence, press F8 three times. To select the current paragraph, press F8 four times or press and hold F8 down.To turn off Extend Mode, press Esc. or double-click EXT in the Word status bar. To control the status bar display, choose Tools, Options, and then select or clear the Status Bar check box on the View tab.

Copying, Cutting, and Pasting

Copying, cutting, and pasting are probably among the top word-processing features responsible for saving countless trees. Thousands of sheets of paper have been conserved as people copy, cut, and paste text instantaneously instead of painstakingly retyping documents on fresh paper each time a sentence or paragraph needs to be moved or revised. Using Word, you can easily copy, cut, and paste selected text without retyping or wasting a single sheet of paper.

Word provides a number of ways to go about your copying, cutting, and pasting business, as shown in Table 2-5. To use the Copy and Cut features, select the text you want to manipulate, and then choose one of the listed commands. To paste information, position the insertion point where you want to insert the information, and then choose one of the Paste commands. Alternatively, you can right-click selected text and choose Cut, Copy, or Paste from the shortcut menu. In addition to cutting and pasting, you can reposition text by using Word's drag-and-drop feature, which essentially enables you to use the mouse to cut and paste text without using the Cut and Paste commands.

Table 2-5. Copy, Cut, and Paste Features

Action	Menu Command	Keyboard Shortcut	Toolbar Button
Copy	Edit, Copy	Ctrl+C or Ctrl+Insert	
Copy Format	None	Ctrl+Shift+C	
Cut	Edit, Cut	Ctrl+X or Shift+Del	
Paste	Edit, Paste	Ctrl+V or Shift+Insert	
Paste Format	None	Ctrl+Shift+V	NA

> **Tip** You can configure your Insert key to serve as a Paste key. To do so, choose Tools, Options, click the Edit tab, and then select the Use The INS Key For Paste check box.

When you paste an item, Word displays the Paste Options smart tag, as shown in Figure 2-10. This smart tag provides paste-specific formatting options. To apply a paste option, position the pointer over the Paste Options smart tag, click the arrow to display the menu, and then choose a command. To ignore a smart tag after pasting, simply continue to work within your document or press Esc—the smart tag will quietly disappear until the next time you paste an object.

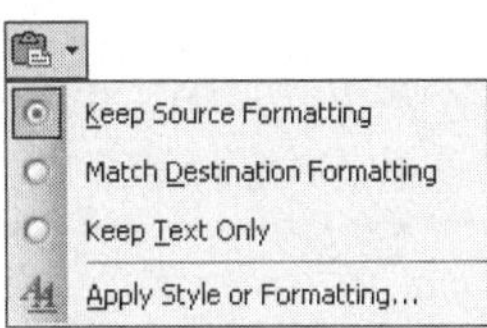

Figure 2-10. By default, the Paste Options smart tag appears whenever you paste an element into your Word document.

If you prefer not to use the Paste Options smart tag, you can configure Word to not display the Paste Options smart tag when you paste. To do this, choose Tools, Options, display the

Edit tab, clear the Show Paste Options Buttons check box, and then click OK.

For more information about the ins and outs of smart tags, see Chapter 7, "Putting Text Tools to Work."

Using the Office Clipboard

You can copy, cut, and paste within the same document, between multiple documents, and even between different applications, thanks to the Office Clipboard. The Office Clipboard allows you to store up to 24 items, including text, objects, and graphics, which means you can copy or cut 24 elements from various applications without losing data in the digital abyss. (Of course, as soon as you copy item 25, the first item you copied to your Clipboard is removed.) Further, the Clipboard provides an easy way to see which Clipboard item contains the information you want to access. As shown in Figure 2-11, the Clipboard contents are displayed in the task pane. In this example, 4 items are stored on the Clipboard (notice the *4 of 24* in the task pane's title bar), including Excel data, a Jasc Paint Shop Pro image, some text copied from a Word document and a clip art image. Each Clipboard item's parent application is identified by an accompanying icon.

Figure 2-11. The Clipboard holds up to 24 items and displays some of the copied and cut items' contents to help you identify the item you want to paste into a document.

Opening the Clipboard To open the Clipboard manually, perform any of the following actions:

- Choose Edit, Office Clipboard.
- Select Clipboard in the task pane's menu.
- Press Ctrl+C+C.
- Select text or other items and double-click the Copy button on the Standard toolbar.

You can also open the Clipboard using the Clipboard icon, shown in Figure 2-12, which appears on the taskbar by default whenever the Clipboard appears in any Office program.

You double-click the icon to display the Clipboard in the current window. For example, if the Clipboard is open in Word, you can start Excel, and then double-click the Clipboard icon on the taskbar to display the Clipboard in Excel.

Figure 2-12. Whenever the Clipboard is open in an Office application, the Clipboard icon appears in the status area of the Windows taskbar by default.

> **Tip** To prevent the Office Clipboard icon from appearing on the taskbar, click the Options button in the Clipboard task pane, and then clear the Show Office Clipboard Icon On Taskbar check box.

Pasting Clipboard Information After information is stored on the Clipboard, you can paste the information into a document by positioning the insertion point where you want to insert the information, displaying the Clipboard, and then clicking the item you want to paste. If you want to paste everything stored on the Clipboard into your document, click the Paste All button in the task pane.

Deleting Clipboard Information To delete items from the Clipboard, you can either click the down arrow that appears when you position your pointer over a Clipboard item, or right-click an item to display the menu, as shown in Figure 2-13, and then choose Delete. If you want to clear the entire Clipboard, click the Clear All button in the task pane.

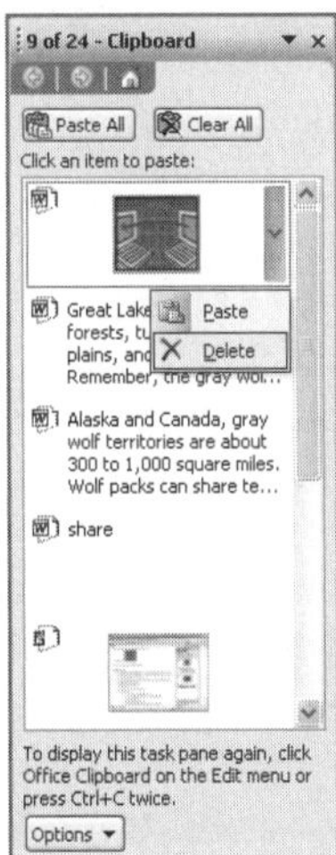

Figure 2-13. You can delete Clipboard items one at a time, or you can clear the entire Clipboard by clicking the Clear All button.

Inside Out

The Office Clipboard and the system Clipboard

You might be wondering how the Office Clipboard relates to the system Clipboard. Here's a quick rundown of how the two Clipboards relate to one another:

- The last item you copy to the Office Clipboard is stored on the system Clipboard.
- Clearing the Office Clipboard also clears the system Clipboard.
- When you click the Paste toolbar button, choose Edit, Paste, or press Ctrl+V to paste information, you paste the contents of the system Clipboard (which by default is the last item you added to the Office Clipboard).

Undoing, Redoing, and Repeating

Fortunately, changes you make to documents are not immediately set in stone. You have ample opportunity to change your mind when it comes to editing text—not only can you undo edits you've recently made but you can also redo undone edits and even repeat an action if you need to. Most likely, you'll use the Undo command more frequently than the Redo and Repeat commands, so let's look at that feature first.

Using the Undo Feature The Undo feature enables you to undo one or many changes made to a document during the current session. In fact, the Undo feature can store over 100 actions, so you have plenty of time during the current session to discard your edits. Keep in mind that some actions are too large to store, such as reformatting large tables. When Word encounters a change that the Undo command can't handle, you'll receive a warning message indicating that you won't be able to undo a particular action. In addition to not being able to undo the current action, you'll also lose the ability to undo prior actions. If you're sure that's OK, you simply proceed, and Word will begin a new Undo list box.

Note If you receive a message that you won't be able to undo a current action and you're a little leery about moving ahead without the Undo safety net, you can take precautionary action. One easy approach is to simply perform the "risky" action last so that you won't lose your current Undo list box until you're sure you'll no longer need it. Another workaround is to copy the element you want to perform the action on, paste the information into a blank document, perform the desired action on the copied version of your information, and then copy and paste the modified information into the original document. Using this method, you can ensure that if the action doesn't go as planned, your original document remains intact.

To Undo one or more actions, use any of the following procedures:

- Choose Edit, Undo to undo the last action.
- On the Standard toolbar, click the Undo button to undo the last change (or click it multiple times to undo a series of changes).
- On the Standard toolbar, click the Undo arrow and click the action you want to undo. (If you don't see the action you're looking for, scroll through the list.) When you undo an action in the list, you also undo all the actions that appear above it in the list.

- Press Ctrl+Z to undo the last action.
- Press Alt+Backspace to undo the last action.

Tip To undo all the changes to a picture, select the picture you want to restore, and then click Reset Picture on the Picture toolbar.

Using the Redo Feature As soon as you undo an action, you automatically activate the Redo command. The main role of the Redo command is to enable you to redo an undone action before you make any further changes. If you want to redo an undone action, use any of the following techniques:

- Choose Edit, Redo immediately after you've undone an action—before you've made any other changes.
- On the Standard toolbar, click the Redo button to redo the last undone change (or click the Redo button multiple times to undo a series of changes).
- On the Standard toolbar, click the Redo arrow, and then click the action you want to redo. (If you don't see the action you're looking for, scroll through the list.) When you redo an action in the list, you also redo all the actions that appear above it in the list.
- Press Ctrl+Y to redo the last undone change.
- Press Alt+Shift+Backspace to redo the last undone change.
- Press F4 to redo the last undone change.
- Press Alt+Enter to redo the last undone change.

Caution If you type or perform any other action after you undo a change, you lose the ability to redo the undone action.

Using the Repeat Command The Repeat command is related to the Undo and Redo commands. When the Redo feature isn't activated (Redo is activated only after you undo an edit), the Edit menu displays a Repeat command. The Repeat feature is fairly self-explanatory—choosing this command repeats the last action you performed. For example, if you typed your name in a form, you could use the Repeat command to insert your name elsewhere in the form. To do so, simply click or press Tab to reposition the insertion point, and then choose the Repeat command. To use the Repeat command after you have added content to your document, you can perform any of the following actions:

- Choose Edit, Repeat. (If you clicked the Undo command immediately before displaying the Edit menu, the Redo command appears in place of the Repeat command.)
- Press Ctrl+Y.
- Press F4.
- Press Alt+Enter.

The Repeat command comes in handy when you use it as a cut-and-paste shortcut.

Note If you can't repeat the last action, the Repeat command on the Edit menu changes to Can't Repeat.

Positioning Content Effectively

Whenever you create documents (reports, brochures Web pages, and so forth)—regardless of their purpose—you'll need to position (and reposition) text, graphics, and other elements within the documents. You can easily align and move contents within a Word document by using the Formatting toolbar buttons as well as the Click And Type and drag-and-drop features.

For a full discussion on aligning information in Word documents, see Chapter 8, "Aligning Information and Formatting Paragraphs and Lists."

Aligning Text Using the Toolbar

Word offers four quick and easy paragraph and element alignment options:

- **Left** Aligns text and other elements (such as graphics, tables, and so on) along the left margin, leaving a ragged right edge. Left alignment is the default setting in most versions of Word.
- **Center** Aligns the midpoint of the selected element with the center point between the page's margins.
- **Right** Aligns text and other elements along the document's right margin, leaving the left margin ragged.
- **Justified** Creates straight (or flush) left and right edges by adding white space between text to force the text to align with the left and right margins.

To apply an alignment setting, click anywhere within the paragraph or element you want to align, highlight the text or element you want to align, or select multiple elements within the document, and then use one of the options shown in Table 2-6.

Table 2-6. Text Alignment Options

Setting	Toolbar Button	Keyboard Shortcut
Left		Ctrl+L
Center		Ctrl+E
Right		Ctrl+R
Justified		Ctrl+J

Tip Activate the automatic hyphenation feature
To steer clear of having too much white space inserted within justified text, you might want to activate the automatic hyphenation feature. To do so, chooseTools, Language, Hyphenation to display the Hyphenation dialog box. Select the Automatically Hyphenate Document check box, and then click OK. To learn more about hyphenation, see Chapter 8, "Aligning Information and Formatting Paragraphs and Lists."

Using the Click And Type Feature

The Click And Type feature, which was introduced in Word 2000, continues to be available in Word 2003. This feature enables you to click anywhere in a page to position the insertion point and add text, graphics, tables, or other items in a blank area of a document. Before Click And Type came along, you had to insert carriage returns, tabs, and spaces before you could properly position your insertion point away from existing page elements.

By default, the Click And Type feature is enabled in Word 2003. You can verify whether the feature is currently activated by choosing Tools, Options; displaying the Edit tab; and making sure that the Enable Click And Type check box is selected.

To use Click And Type, you must be working in Print Layout or Web Layout view (choose View, Print Layout, or View, Web Layout). From Layout view, double-click in the page to position the insertion point. Watch the insertion point; it will indicate the default alignment of the text you enter.

Keep in mind that you can't use the Click And Type feature to position text in the following situations:

- With multiple columns
- With bulleted and numbered lists
- Next to floating objects
- To the left or right of pictures that have top and bottom text wrapping
- To the left or right of indents
- To insert a table next to an existing table
- While recording macros

Tip You can turn the Click And Type feature off and on by configuring the feature's options. To do so, choose Tools, Options; click the Edit tab; select the Enable Click And Type check box to turn on the feature, or clear the check box to turn off the feature; and then click OK.

Using the Drag-and-Drop Feature

The drag-and-drop feature is a favorite with most people because it seems to come naturally. It reflects how we arrange our lives—we pick up items and put them down elsewhere, without issuing a complex series of cut and paste commands.

To use the drag-and-drop feature, select the text (or other element, such as a graphic or table) that you want to move, click and hold down the mouse button within the selected area, and then drag the selected element to another area in the current document or in another document. When you release the mouse button, the element will be repositioned in the document, and the Paste Options smart tag will appear (because when you use the drag-and-drop feature, you are essentially cutting and pasting). If you right-click when you click and drag, a shortcut menu opens when you release the mouse button, which provides Move Here, Copy Here, Link Here, and Cancel commands.

By default, the drag-and-drop feature is activated. You can control whether this feature is enabled by choosing Tools, Options; displaying the Edit tab; and then selecting the Drag-and-drop Text Editing check box to turn on the feature, or clearing the check box to turn off the feature.

Formatting Text Efficiently

As with most Word tasks, you can format text using menu options, keyboard shortcuts, or toolbar buttons. In addition, you can set formatting options before you enter text, or you can apply formatting to existing text. One of the most common methods of formatting text is to use the buttons readily available on the Formatting toolbar, shown in Figure 2-14.

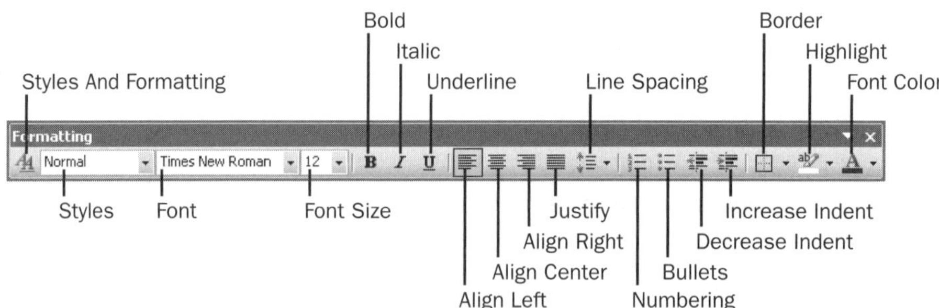

Figure 2-14. The Formatting toolbar appears by default; it provides quick access to the most frequently used formatting commands.

> **Tip** **Add and remove toolbar buttons**
>
> You can easily add buttons to and remove buttons from the Formatting toolbar by clicking the arrow at the right end of the Formatting toolbar, pointing to Add Or Remove Buttons, selecting Formatting, and then selecting the buttons you want to show or hide. The following Formatting toolbar buttons can be added: Grow Font, Shrink Font, Superscript, Subscript, and Language.

For more information about customizing toolbars, see Chapter 5, "Customizing Word and Enhancing Accessibility."

Using the Formatting toolbar is often the quickest way to get formatting results, but once you memorize key combinations, keyboard shortcuts also enable you to format text quickly and efficiently. Finally, while choosing menu options to format text is generally the slowest method, menus can provide more control and flexibility when you are formatting text as well as allow you to apply multiple formatting settings at one time.

Regardless of whether you use toolbar buttons, keyboard shortcuts, or menu options, the procedure is basically the same: You select the text you want to format (or position the insertion point where you want formatting to begin when you start typing), and then click the appropriate toolbar button, press the keyboard shortcut, or choose a menu option. In this section, you'll learn how to manipulate text using all three techniques.

Note Most toolbar buttons and keyboard shortcuts are *toggle commands*, which means that you perform the same action both to apply and to remove a formatting attribute. For example, selecting unformatted text and pressing Ctrl+B (or clicking the Bold button on the Formatting toolbar) applies boldface formatting to the selected text, and pressing Ctrl+B (or clicking Bold) again removes the boldface formatting from the selected text.

Specifying Fonts and Sizes

As you know, the world of documents embraces numerous fonts. Thus, it should come as no surprise that Word can handle thousands of fonts that are compatible with the Windows operating systems, including Adobe PostScript fonts (if the Adobe Type Manager is installed) and TrueType fonts. The quickest way to specify a font is to select the text you want to format, and then select a font in the Font list box on the Formatting toolbar, as shown in Figure 2-15. The Font list box contains all the currently available fonts.

Note The default fonts installed with the Microsoft Office System are all TrueType fonts. With TrueType fonts, the text that appears on your screen is the same as the text in your printed document.

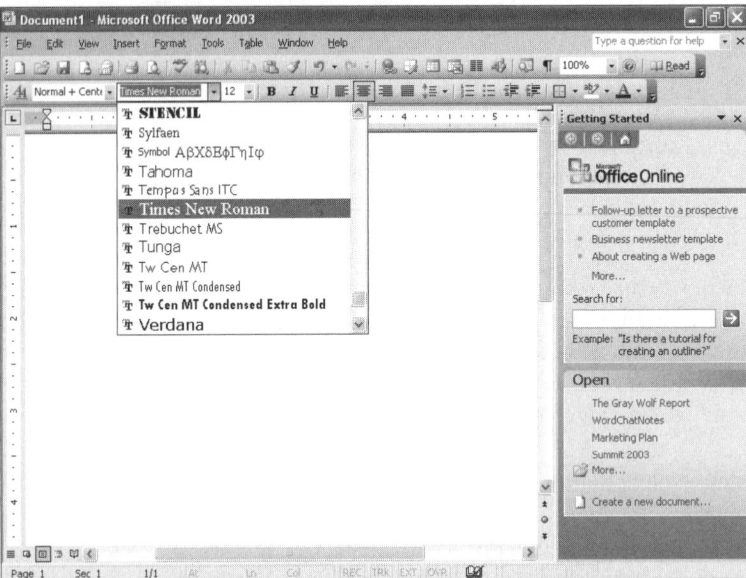

Figure 2-15. By default, the Font list box displays font names in their respective fonts.

You can specify whether the font names in the Font list box appear in their respective fonts or in plain text. To configure this setting, follow these steps:

1. Choose Tools, Customize, and then click the Options tab in the Customize dialog box.
2. Select or clear the List Font Names In Their Font check box.

Serif vs. Sans Serif Fonts

All fonts can be classified as *serif* or *sans serif*. You can easily differentiate between the two font types. Serif fonts add "hooks" to their letters, similar to the font used in the following paragraph's text. Examples of serif fonts are Times and Times New Roman. In contrast, sans serif fonts have plain-edged letters, like the font used in the headings throughout this book. Examples of sans serif fonts are Arial and Helvetica. Using sans serif fonts for headings and serif fonts for body text is common practice in the print community because most readers find it easiest to read in hard copy. For online documents, the print setup is often switched for easier onscreen reading; frequently in online documents, serif fonts are used for headings and sans serif fonts are used for body text.

After you select a font for your text, you'll most likely want to specify a size. The quickest way to size text is by using the Size list box, located to the right of the Font list box on the Formatting toolbar (shown previously in Figure 2-14). As you probably know, font sizes are measured in points, and 72 points equals an inch. By default, the Size list box provides a variety of common point sizes. To apply a font size using the Size list box, you simply select the text you want to resize or position your cursor at the point where you want the size specification to apply to newly entered text, click the Size arrow, and select a size from the list.

If you want to use a font size not listed in the Size list box, you need to do the following:

1. Select the text you want to resize or position your cursor at the point where you want the size specification to apply to newly entered text.
2. Click the Size box to select the currently displayed font size (or press Ctrl+Shift+P), and then enter a new value.

You can enter half-point sizes in the Size box using decimal notation (for example, 10.5), and you can specify sizes as tiny as 1 point and as large as 1,638 points (which is approximately two feet high).

Tip When you type large numbers in the Size box, don't include a comma separator—it will only confuse Word and slow you down.

As a Word veteran, you won't be surprised to hear that you can also resize text using keyboard shortcuts. Table 2-7 lists the keyboard shortcuts you can use to change the font size.

Table 2-7. Keyboard Shortcuts for Sizing Text

Keyboard Shortcut	Sizing Effect
Ctrl+Shift+P, and then enter a font size or press the Up Arrow and Down Arrow keys to choose a font size from the Size list box	Changes font to a specified size
Ctrl+]	Enlarges font by 1 point
Ctrl+[	Reduces font by 1 point
Ctrl+Shift+>	Increases font to the next larger size in the Size list box
Ctrl+Shift+<	Decreases font to the next smaller size in the Size list box

Specifying Default Fonts for Templates, Web Pages, and E-Mail Messages

Instead of applying font sizes and styles to each document, you can speed up document formatting by specifying default fonts for templates, Web pages, and e-mail messages. You might find changing the default font settings especially useful if you frequently use formatting other than Word's default styles. When you change default settings, you essentially use Word's dialog boxes to modify the template used by a particular document type.

Specifying Default Fonts for Templates To specify a template's default font, first open a document and attach the template (choose Tools, Templates and Add-Ins, and then attach the template you want to modify). If you set a default font for a document that doesn't have an attached document template, you will modify Word's Normal template, which is a global template and affects all documents created in Word. To modify a template's default font, follow these steps:

1. Choose Format, Font.
2. In the Font tab, select the settings you want to configure for the template's default font, and then click Default.
3. In the message box (shown in Figure 2-16), click Yes to change the template's default font.

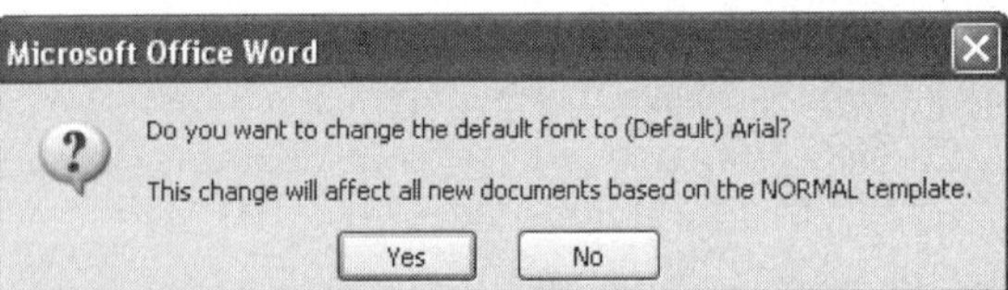

Figure 2-16. When you specify a change to a template's default font, Word shows you which template you are modifying before you complete your changes.

After you set a default font, all new documents created using the template will be based on the new default font settings.

For more information about creating, modifying, and attaching templates, see Chapter 16, "Formatting Documents Using Templates, Wizards, Add-Ins, and Schemas."

Specifying Default Fonts for Web Pages To specify a default font for Web pages, follow these steps:

1. Choose Tools, Options, and then display the General tab.
2. Click Web Options, and then display the Fonts tab.
3. Specify proportional and fixed-width font settings, and then click OK twice.

For more information about creating and formatting Web pages, see Chapter 26, "Creating Professional Web Sites."

Specifying Default Fonts for E-Mail Messages You can also specify a default font for e-mail messages that you create using Word. To do this, follow these steps:

1. Choose Tools, Options, and then display the General tab.
2. Click E-mail Options, and then display the Personal Stationery tab in the E-mail Options dialog box, as shown in Figure 2-17. As you can see in the E-mail Options dialog box, you can configure settings for new messages, for replies and forwarded messages, and for plain text messages.

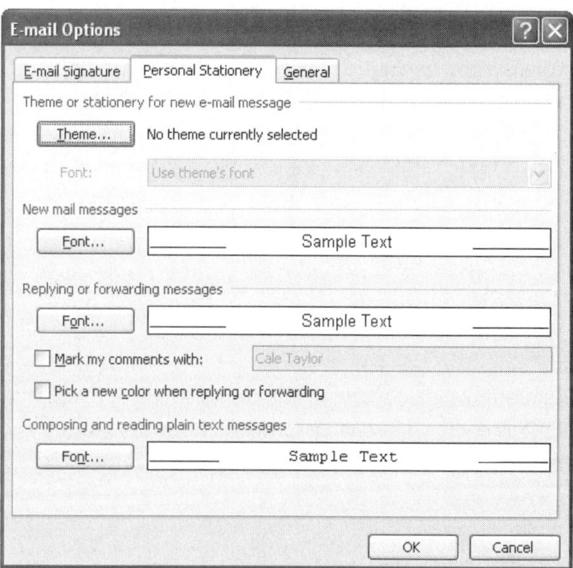

Figure 2-17. E-mail messages open using the formatting specified in the Personal Stationery tab in the E-mail Options dialog box.

3 Click the Theme button (which displays the Theme Or Stationery dialog box) or any Font button (which displays the Font dialog box, shown in Figure 2-18) to specify default settings for the particular types of e-mail.

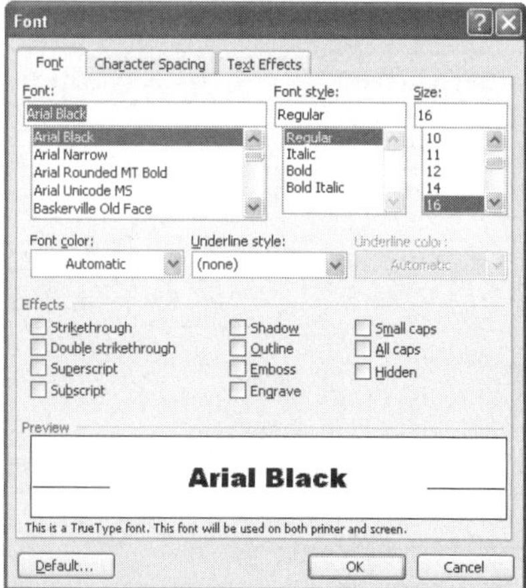

Figure 2-18. The Font dialog box enables you to select additional formatting effects as well as format multiple font attributes at one time, including font, size, color, and effects.

For more information about using Word to create e-mail messages, see Chapter 24, "Working and Collaborating Online."

Applying Multiple Font Attributes at One Time

Formatting toolbar buttons and keyboard shortcuts are great for simple formatting needs. But, in other instances, you might want to take advantage of a not-so-readily-accessible formatting effect (such as Emboss or Superscript) or apply a number of formatting attributes at one time. In those cases, a better approach would be to use the Font dialog box. To format text using the Font dialog box, follow these steps:

1. Select the text you want to format, click within the word you want to format, or position the insertion point where you want formatting to start when you begin typing.
2. Choose Format, Font (or right-click the text and choose Font on the shortcut menu, or press Ctrl+D).

In the Font dialog box, you can specify the font name, font style (including italic, bold, and bold italic), size, underline style, character spacing, text effects, and more. The Font dialog box also contains a preview window, so you can see how your font selections will appear in your document.

Applying Bold, Italic, and Underline Attributes

In addition to selecting fonts and resizing text, you can apply formatting attributes. The Formatting toolbar includes buttons for the three most commonly used formatting attributes—Bold, Italic, and Underline. To apply boldface, italic, or underlining to your text, simply click the appropriate toolbar button or press the keyboard shortcut, as listed in Table 2-8.

Table 2-8. Toolbar Buttons and Keyboard Shortcuts for Applying Boldface, Italic, and Underlining

Format	Toolbar Button	Keyboard Shortcut
Bold	**B**	Ctrl+B
Italic	*I*	Ctrl+I
Underline	U	Ctrl+U
Underline Words Only	None	Ctrl+Shift+W
Double Underline	None	Ctrl+Shift+D

The Underline button and keyboard shortcuts allow you to quickly apply standard underlining, but you can access a greater variety of underline styles using the Font dialog box. To choose an underline style in the Font dialog box, display the Font dialog box (press Ctrl+D), click the Underline Style arrow (shown previously in Figure 2-18), and select an underline style in the list. Figure 2-19 shows some of the Underline Style options in action.

Tip **Remove or change a custom underline**
To quickly remove a custom underline or to change the underline to a standard underline, select the underlined text (or click within the word you want to remove the underline from), and press Ctrl+U or click the Underline button on the Formatting toolbar once to remove the custom underline and twice to remove the underline altogether. The first time you execute the Underline toggle command, the custom underline changes to a standard (single-line) underline, and the second time you execute the command, the standard underline is removed.

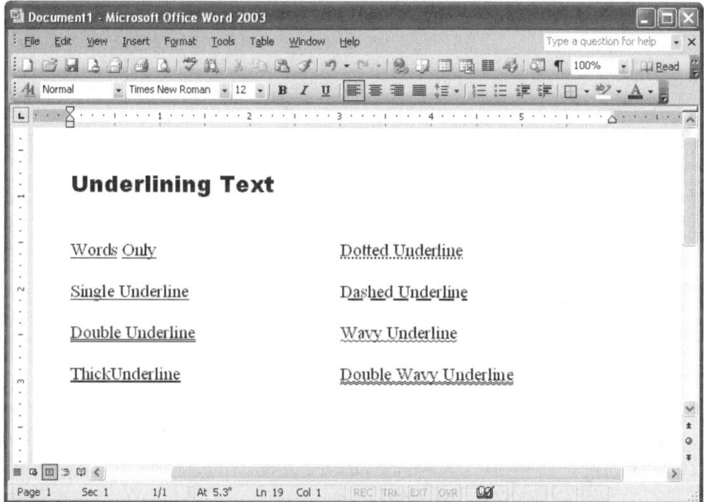

Figure 2-19. Word provides a variety of underline styles, including the styles shown here, which you can apply to text by using the Font dialog box.

Note You can quickly underline a blank line using Word's Click And Type feature. To do this, ensure that you're working in Page Layout View or Web Layout View, position your cursor where you want the line to start, click the Underline button on the Formatting toolbar, double-click where you want the line to end, and then click the Underline button to turn off the underline option. If you need a more accurately placed line, you can manually set a tab instead of using Click and Type.

Changing Text Color

Applying color to text and underlines provides another avenue for customizing text attributes. By default, Word displays and prints black text on a white background. (You can configure your view in Word to display white text on a blue background by choosing Tools, Options, clicking the General tab, and selecting the Blue Background, White Text check box, but keep in mind that this setting changes your *view*, not the printed text color.) In many cases, you might want to change the color of text to add pizzazz to your documents. For example, you might add color to text when you're creating a brochure, a Web page, an e-mail message, or any other document in which the text will appear on a colored background.

The most straightforward way to apply color to text is to follow these steps:

1. Select the text you want to color.
2. Click the Font Color arrow on the Formatting toolbar.
3. Select a color from the color palette shown in Figure 2-20.

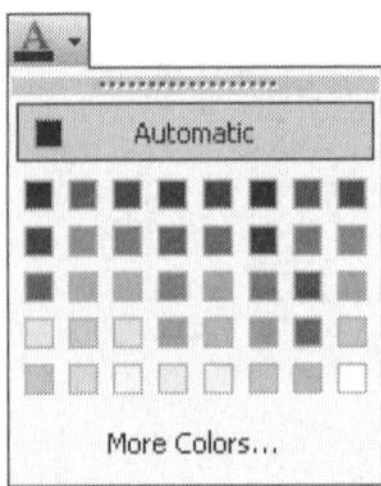

Figure 2-20. You use the color palette to specify the color you want to apply to selected text.

After you've applied color to some text, the Font Color button retains that color setting for the rest of your current session (or until you select another color in the color palette). The thick underline under the *A* on the Font Color button reflects the most recently selected color. You can select other text and simply click the Font Color button to apply the same color to the text; you don't have to repeatedly select the same color in the color palette each time you want to apply the color. By default, the Font Color button is set to Automatic (which generally equates to black).

If you're going to color text frequently within a document, you can drag the top bar of the color palette to display it as a floating toolbar that remains available as you work, as shown in Figure 2-21. To close the Font Color toolbar after you've detached it from the Formatting toolbar, simply click the Close button—the color palette will be available from the Font Color arrow on the Formatting toolbar whenever you need it.

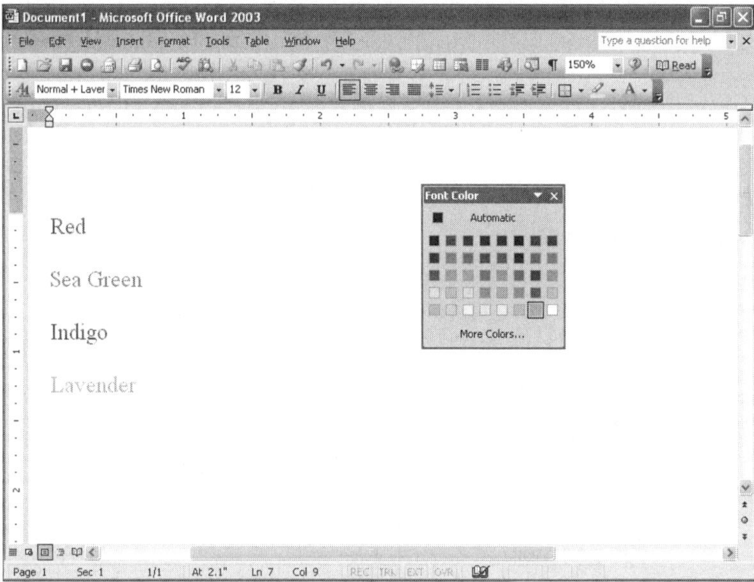

Figure 2-21. You can drag the color palette by its top bar to display it as a floating toolbar.

In addition to these methods of changing font color, you can also color text using the Font dialog box, shown earlier in Figure 2-18. Notice that you can specify a font color as well as an underline color. Clicking either color arrow in the Font dialog box displays the color palette, which you can use to apply an appropriate color to your text.

For more information about creating custom colors, see Chapter 12, "Enlivening Documents with Drawings and AutoShapes."

Copying Styles Using the Format Painter

Format Painter

After you've formatted your text, you might want to apply similar attributes to other text. For example, suppose you've used the following settings to style a book title that's embedded in body text: bold italic, 12 points, Arial, red. When you type the next book title in your document, you could either apply all the formatting settings manually, create a style, or use the Format Painter tool to copy and paste the settings from the last book title to the current book title. Usually, the quick-and-convenient route of copying formatting settings will be preferable to manually applying a set of attributes over and over.

Using the Format Painter tool is a breeze. By default, the Format Painter tool is available on the Standard toolbar. To use the Format Painter, follow these steps:

1. Click in or select the text that has the formatting you want to apply to other text.
2. Click the Format Painter button.
3. Click or select the text you want to format.

To format multiple instances of text using the Format Painter, select the text with the desired format, and then double-click the Format Painter; this keeps the Format Painter turned on until you turn it off. All text you select or words you click while the Format Painter is activated will be reformatted. To turn off the Format Painter, click the Format Painter button on the Standard toolbar or press Esc.

You can also use keyboard commands to copy formatting. To do so, follow these steps:

1. Click in or select the text with the desired format, and press Ctrl+Shift+C.
2. Click in a word or select the text you want to format, and press Ctrl+Shift+V to apply the formatting attributes.

The advantage of using keyboard shortcuts in this case is that you can repeat the Ctrl+Shift+V command as many times as necessary on various instances of selected text—the formatting settings are retained during the current session until you execute another Ctrl+Shift+C command. Sometimes, having a group of formatting commands available with a single keyboard shortcut can prove to be a real time-saver.

Adding Text Effects and Animation

In addition to basic formatting, Word provides a number of other text effects that you can access from the Font dialog box (shown previously in Figure 2-18). Figure 2-22 illustrates these text effects.

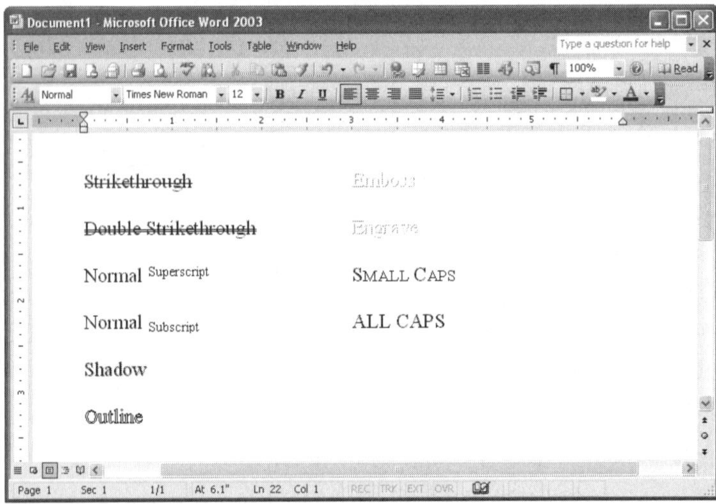

Figure 2-22. Word offers a number of font effects that you can apply to existing text.

The following options are available in the Effects section in the Font tab:

- Strikethrough
- Double Strikethrough

- Superscript (Ctrl+Shift+=)
- Subscript (Ctrl+=)
- Shadow
- Outline
- Emboss
- Engrave
- Small Caps (Ctrl+Shift+K)
- All Caps (Ctrl+Shift+A)
- Hidden (Ctrl+Shift+H)

Adding an effect to text using the Font dialog box is accomplished in a predictable manner, as follows:

1. Click within a word, select the text you want to format, or position the insertion point where you want an effect to begin when you start typing.
2. Choose Format, Font, select the appropriate check box in the Font tab, and then click OK.

You can also add animation effects by clicking the Text Effects tab in the Font dialog box. The following animations are available in Word:

- **(None)** Applies no animation effects (the default selection).
- **Blinking Background** Creates a blinking effect by alternating reversed text within a black rectangle with regular text.
- **Las Vegas Lights** Surrounds selected text with a looping series of blinking colored shapes.
- **Marching Black Ants** Borders selected text with a black dashed line that moves clockwise.
- **Marching Red Ants** Borders selected text with a red dashed line that moves clockwise.
- **Shimmer** Repeatedly blurs and unblurs selected text.
- **Sparkle Text** Displays moving colored "sparkles" on top of the selected text.

To see each effect in action, press Ctrl+D to display the Font dialog box, click the Text Effects tab, and then click each option in the Animations list box. The Preview section at the bottom of the Text Effects tab shows a small animated display as you select each option.

Show/ Hide

Working with Hidden Text

You can't see it in Figure 2-22, but the word *Hidden* is inserted below *ALL CAPS* and formatted using the Hidden effect. You can create hidden text by selecting text, and then selecting the Hidden check box in the Font tab in the Font dialog box or by pressing Ctrl+Shift+H. Hidden text is useful for making notes to yourself. Word uses hidden text for certain components, including index fields, bookmarks, and table of contents fields.

To display hidden text on screen, click the Show/Hide button on the Standard toolbar or press Ctrl+Shift+8 to toggle your display. Hidden text is identified with a dotted underline, as shown in the following graphic:

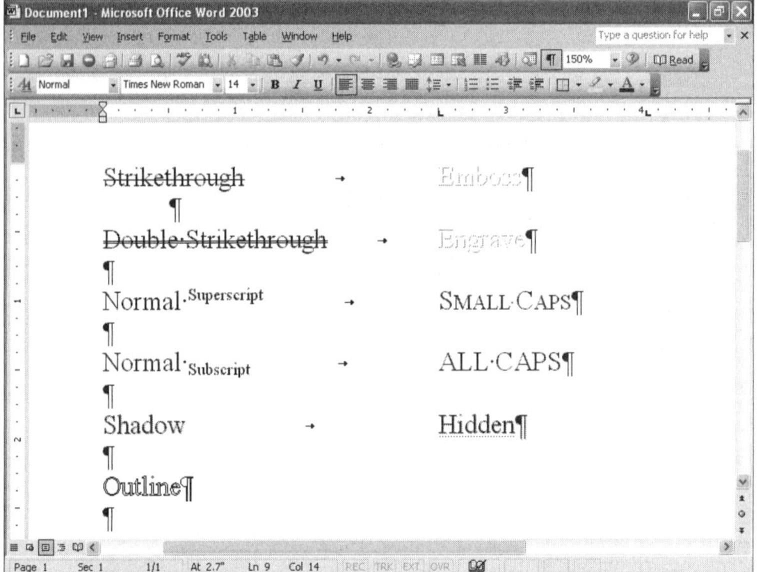

Keep in mind that if you print your document while hidden text is displayed on your screen, the text will be printed by default. Likewise, if you click the Show/Hide button to hide all hidden text, the hidden text will not be printed by default when you print your document. However, if you want, you can print hidden text that's in a document even if the hidden text doesn't appear on screen. To do so, verify that the hidden text does not appear on screen; choose Tools, Options; click the Print tab; select the Hidden Text check box in the Print tab; click OK; and then print the document.

Tip **Animate with care**

Animated text should be used sparingly. Animation can serve a purpose in a few select cases, but the effects are frequently distracting and can be downright annoying when overused. In addition, you need to consider software limitations when you use animated text. For example, earlier versions of Word, such as Microsoft Word 95 and Microsoft Word 6, don't recognize animations, and of course animated text can't be printed (which could be a concern).

Troubleshooting

I can't use animations in Word documents saved as Web pages

Although using the text animation feature seems like a natural fit for creating Web pages, the feature doesn't work in Word documents saved as Web pages. When you save a document containing animated text, Word displays a message box stating that the animated text will appear as italicized text. If you truly need to show animated text in an online document, the only workaround at this time is to create a link on your Web page that points to the Word document containing the animation or to insert an animated Graphics Interchange Format (GIF) file. For more information about creating Web pages, see Chapter 26, "Creating Professional Web Sites."

Changing Case

Occasionally, you might want to change lowercase text to all caps, all caps to lowercase, or mixed-case text to all caps or all lowercase. Fortunately, you can perform these potentially tedious maneuvers without displaying the Font dialog box or retyping text. In fact, all you need to do is select the text you want to change and press Ctrl+Shift+A to alternate between all lowercase and all uppercase or press Shift+F3 to cycle through all lowercase, initial capped, and all uppercase.

In addition, Word offers more advanced capitalization schemes in the Change Case dialog box. To display the Change Case dialog box, shown in Figure 2-23, choose Format, Change Case (or press Alt+O+E). Notice that you can format selected text using the following options: Sentence Case, Lowercase, Uppercase, Title Case, or Toggle Case.

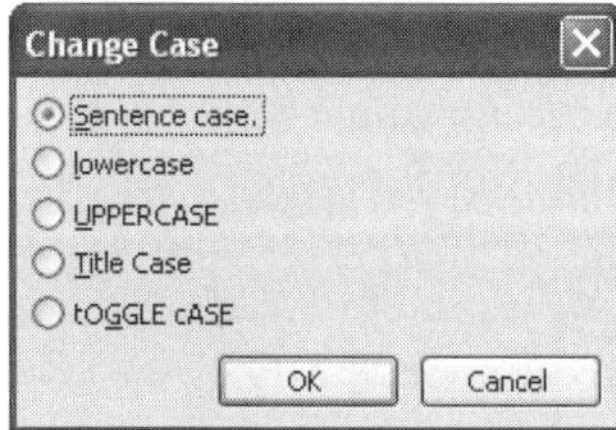

Figure 2-23. The Change Case dialog box enables you to quickly revise uppercase and lowercase letters.

Controlling Character Spacing

Another key font formatting issue is character spacing. Word provides space-tweaking features that were once available only to professional typesetters. You can (and should) use character spacing features to improve the look and readability of your documents. To view the primary character spacing options, choose Format, Font (or press Ctrl+D), and click the Character Spacing tab, as shown in Figure 2-24.

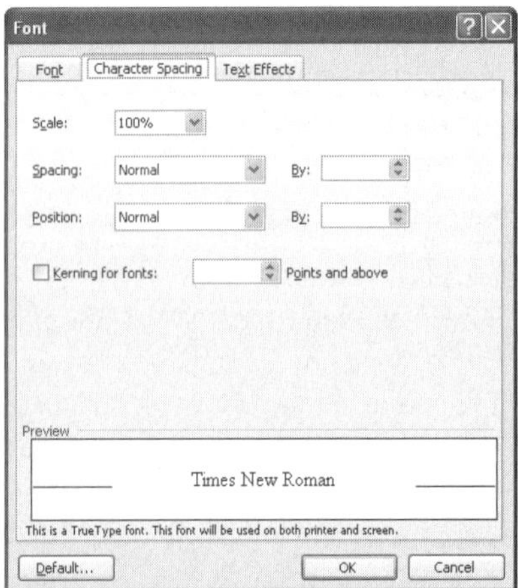

Figure 2-24. The Character Spacing tab in the Font dialog box enables you to rescale selected text, adjust spacing between characters, and reposition text.

You can control the following spacing parameters:

- **Scale** Lets you stretch or compress selected text characters horizontally as a percentage of the text's current size. You can choose a scaling option from the list box, or you can manually enter a scaling value from 1% to 600%. The Scale option is set to 100% for normal text.
- **Spacing** Enables you to expand or condense the spacing between text characters by the amount you enter in the By box. If you decide you don't like the expanded or condensed spacing settings, you can choose Normal in the Spacing list box to revert to standard letter spacing.
- **Position** Allows you to raise or lower selected text relative to the text's baseline by the amount you enter in the By box. To reset the text on the baseline, choose Normal in the list box.
- **Kerning For Fonts** Enables Word to automatically adjust the amount of space between specific character combinations so that words and letters look evenly spaced. You can specify the minimum font size that should be automatically kerned in the Points And Above box. Generally, kerning is used for headings and larger fonts sizes (12 to 14 points and larger). In Word, kerning works only with TrueType or Adobe Type Manager fonts. Be aware that turning on the Kerning For Fonts feature can slow processing. If you want to manually kern characters, select the characters and use the Spacing option to tighten or loosen the characters' positions.

Note To reiterate, the Scale option narrows and widens the actual characters, whereas the Spacing option adjusts the space between characters.

The Character Spacing tab also includes a Default button. This Default button enables you to store all the current settings in the Font, Character Spacing, and Text Effects tabs in the Font dialog box as the default settings for the active document as well as for all new documents based on the current template. If your current document uses the Normal template, clicking the Default button will change the defaults for all new blank documents you create, so be careful.

Clearing Formatting Attributes

Up to now, we've been looking at adding font formatting attributes, but at times you might want to remove all formatting attributes from within a paragraph. Word provides a quick way to clear all formatting attributes from text at one time. To clear all formatting from a single word or selected text, follow these steps:

1. Select the word or text you want to convert to plain text.
2. Press Ctrl+Spacebar.

Tip You can remove formatting from an entire document by pressing Ctrl+A to select the entire document, and then pressing Ctrl+Spacebar.

Similarly, you can remove formatting by using the Styles And Formatting task pane. To do so, follow these steps:

1. Select the word or text you want to clear.
2. Click the Styles And Formatting button on the Formatting toolbar (or select Styles And Formatting in the Task Pane list box if the task pane is already open).
3. In the Formatting Of Selected Text section, click Select All.
4. In the Pick Formatting To Apply section, choose Clear Formatting in the list box, or in the Formatting Of Selected Text section, position the pointer over the style box, click the arrow, and then choose Clear Formatting.

Styles And Formatting

Inserting Symbols and Special Characters

Sometimes your text will require symbols and special characters that aren't readily available on your keyboard. For example, you might want to show a copyright symbol, insert words containing accent marks, include small "dingbat" graphics, insert a nonbreaking space, and so forth. Quite a few symbols and special characters are available in Word if you know where to look. Nicely enough, when you find what you're looking for, Word makes it easy to insert and reuse symbols and special characters in the future.

Adding Symbols

Word provides the Symbol dialog box to take care of your symbol and special character needs. (To access the Symbol dialog box, choose Insert, Symbol.) Figure 2-25 shows the Symbols tab in the Symbol dialog box.

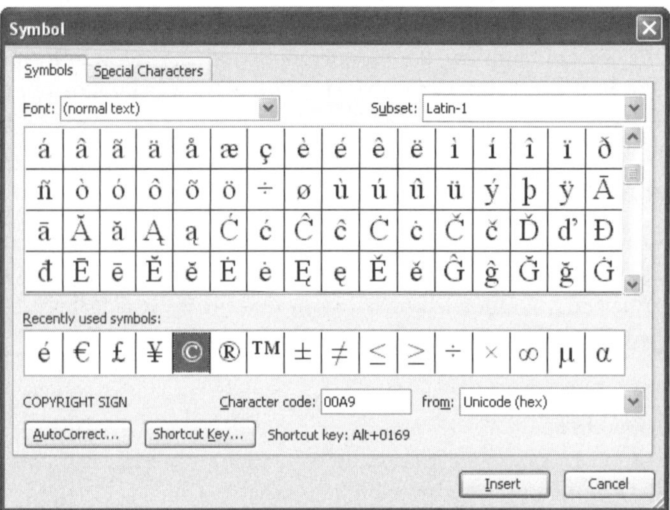

Figure 2-25. The Symbols tab in the Symbol dialog box enables you to browse and insert symbols.

You can insert symbols in three main ways:

- Click a symbol in the symbol table, and then click the Insert button.
- Double-click a symbol in the symbol table.
- Press the symbol's shortcut key.

Tip Pressing a keyboard shortcut command to insert a symbol inserts the symbol without displaying the Symbol dialog box. If you don't know the keyboard shortcut for a symbol, you can click the symbol in the Symbol dialog box and view the associated keyboard command in the lower portion of the dialog box or by clicking the Shortcut button.

When you're inserting symbols from within the Symbol dialog box, keep in mind that you can insert multiple symbols during a single visit. In fact, inserting all the symbols you'll need for a while can prove to be fairly efficient. (After all, cutting and pasting or dragging and dropping inserted symbols is quicker and easier than repeatedly accessing the Symbol dialog box.) When you've inserted the symbols you need, click Close to close the Symbol dialog box.

Troubleshooting

I want to insert symbols without repeatedly displaying the Symbol dialog box

In some instances, you can quickly display the Symbol dialog box by double-clicking a symbol that's been inserted into your document. Unfortunately, you can't always count on this being the case. For example, you can double-click smiley faces and arrows to display the Symbol dialog box, but you can't display the Symbol dialog box by double-clicking copyright and registered trademark symbols.

If you're going to need more than a few symbols, you can either paste in a number of symbols you think you'll need or leave the Symbol dialog box open while you work. Fortunately, you can enter text in your document while the Symbol dialog box is open. The main drawback to this approach is that the Symbol dialog box stays on top, so you'll probably have to drag the dialog box out of your way a few times as you work. In addition, although you can resize the Symbol dialog box by making it larger, you can't make it smaller. The capability to reduce the Symbol dialog box can't be too far in the future, however, now that resizable dialog boxes are becoming more widely available in Office applications.

Adding Special Characters

Inserting special characters is similar to inserting symbols. Logically enough, special characters can be found in the Special Characters tab in the Symbol dialog box, as shown in Figure 2-26. Most of the special characters are typesetting characters that you use when refining document text. You will find that a number of the special characters can also be inserted by using the Symbols tab or by using the AutoCorrect feature.

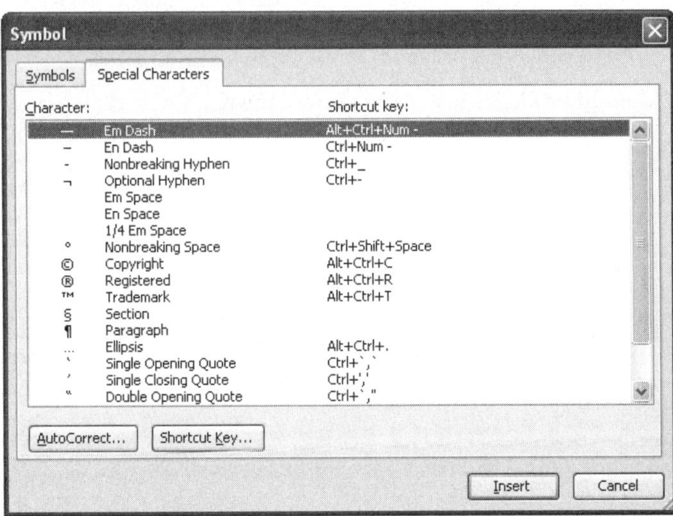

Figure 2-26. The Special Characters tab in the Symbol dialog box provides quick access to special characters.

You can insert special characters using any of these techniques:

- Double-click an entry in the Special Characters tab.
- Select an entry in the Special Characters tab, and then click Insert.
- Press the character's keyboard shortcut.

Using Shortcut Keys to Insert Symbols and Special Characters

If you frequently need to insert a symbol or special character that requires displaying the Symbol dialog box, you can simplify your life by memorizing preassigned keyboard shortcuts or by creating custom keyboard shortcuts. In Figures 2-25 and 2-26, you can see that both tabs in the Symbol dialog box contain a Shortcut Key button. In addition, both tabs display currently assigned keyboard shortcuts for quick reference. In the Symbols tab, available keyboard shortcuts appear next to the Shortcut Key button when a symbol is selected; in the Special Characters tab, keyboard shortcuts are listed in the Shortcut Key column.

If you find that you use a symbol or special character that isn't already assigned a keyboard shortcut (or if you want to associate your own command with a symbol or special character even though it already has a shortcut), you can create a custom shortcut for future use. To do so, follow these steps (from either the Symbols or the Special Characters tab):

1. Display the Symbols dialog box (choose Insert, Symbol), and select a symbol or special character.
2. Click the Shortcut Key button. The Customize Keyboard dialog box appears.
3. By default, the cursor is positioned in the Press New Shortcut Key box; therefore, you can just type the keyboard shortcut you'd like to assign to the symbol. If the combination is already associated with another operation, the dialog box indicates which operation uses the keyboard shortcut. If the keyboard shortcut is not already associated with another operation, the dialog box indicates that the combination is currently unassigned, as shown in Figure 2-27.
4. Click Assign, and then click Close twice to close the remaining dialog boxes.
5. Test your newly created keyboard shortcut within your document to verify that it is working properly.

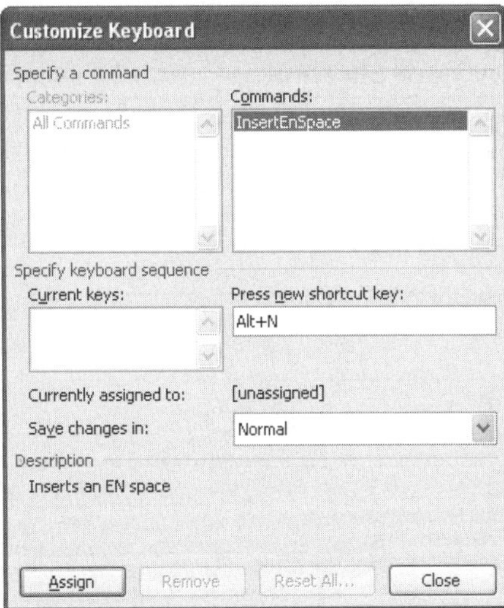

Figure 2-27. The Customize Keyboard dialog box enables you to assign a custom keyboard shortcut to a symbol or special character.

As you might imagine, you can remove keyboard shortcut commands assigned to symbols and special characters. To do so, display the Customize Keyboard dialog box (as described in preceding steps 1 and 2), select the key combination you want to delete in the Current Keys list box, click Remove, and then click Close twice to close the open dialog boxes.

Inserting Symbols Automatically

In addition to inserting symbols manually and using keyboard shortcuts, Word enables you to automatically create symbols as you're typing, without displaying the Symbol dialog box. The magic behind this trick is the AutoCorrect feature. When the AutoCorrect feature is turned on, you can automatically insert symbols that are included in the built-in list of AutoCorrect entries. Table 2-9 lists the symbols you can create using the AutoCorrect feature.

When symbols are inserted automatically, Word 2003 accompanies the symbol with a smart tag. (If the smart tag doesn't appear immediately, position the pointer over the symbol until it appears.) Figure 2-28 shows the AutoCorrect smart tag associated with the automatically generated right arrow symbol.

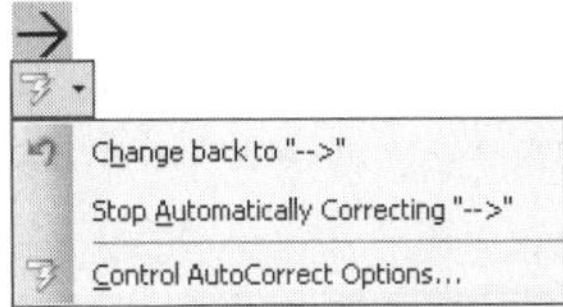

Figure 2-28. The AutoCorrect smart tag enables you to control whether automatically generated symbols should replace typed text.

Table 2-9. Symbols That Can Be Inserted Using AutoCorrect

Symbol	Keyboard Shortcut
©	(c)
®	(r)
™	(tm)
…	...
☺	:) or :-)
😐	:| or :-|
☹	:(or :-(
→	->
←	<-
➔	==>
🡐	<==
⇔	<=>

If an AutoCorrect symbol is inserted but you would prefer to display the typed text, simply press the Backspace key once after you type the text. For example, if you want to display (c) instead of ©, type an opening parenthesis, c, and then a closing parenthesis (at which point, the text changes to the copyright symbol automatically), and then press the Backspace key (which removes the copyright symbol and redisplays the (c) text).

In some cases, you might find yourself removing a symbol repeatedly. Instead of driving yourself crazy, hold the pointer over the symbol's smart tag before you remove it, click the arrow, and then choose the Stop Automatically Correcting command from the smart tag's menu. This action forces Word to stop converting the typed combination to a symbol throughout the remainder of the document. If you want to stop the action in all Word documents, choose Control AutoCorrect Options from the smart tag menu, and then delete the action from the AutoCorrect tab.To delete an AutoCorrect option, select the option in the table in the AutoCorrect tab, and click Delete.

For more information about AutoCorrect, see Chapter 7, "Putting Text Tools to Work."

Inserting Date and Time Elements—The Quick Way

Word offers a variety of elements that you can use to insert dates and times into documents. Basically, date and time elements are fields (which are discussed in greater depth in Chapter 31, "Working with Field Codes and Custom Forms"), but Word provides a quick and easy method of inserting date and time components without your having to delve into the nitty-gritty of fields. If you want to simply enter the current date and time without manually configuring fields, you can do so as follows:

1. Choose Insert, Date And Time. The Date And Time dialog box appears, as shown in Figure 2-29.

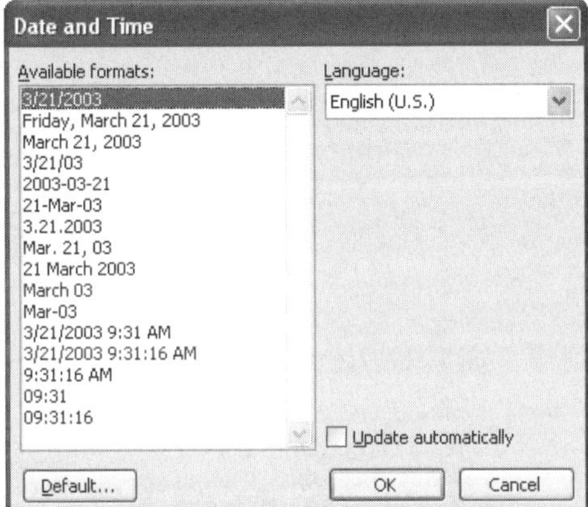

Figure 2-29. The Date And Time dialog box enables you to insert date and time elements that will either show the date and time when the element was inserted or will update automatically each time the document is opened or printed.

2. Select a date and time format in the Available Formats list box, and, if necessary, choose a language in the Language list box.
3. If you'd like the date and time to be updated automatically, select the Update Automatically check box; if you prefer to keep the date and time unchanged, leave the check box empty.
4. Click OK. The date and time information is inserted into your document and is accompanied by a smart tag that enables you to schedule a meeting or display your calendar. You can format the date and time elements just as you format other text within your document.

You can also insert a current time or date that is updated when you update the document's fields by pressing Alt+Shift+T to insert a time field or Alt+Shift+D to insert a date field. By default, fields are updated each time you open a Word document, as specified in the General tab in the Options dialog box (using the Update Automatic Links At Open check box). In addition, you can choose to update fields when you print by selecting the Update Fields check box in the Print tab in the Options dialog box, or you can select fields (or press Alt+A to select the entire document, if desired) and press Alt+Shift+U or F9 to update the fields in the active document.

Saving Documents

Whenever you create and edit documents, you need to save your work—an obvious statement, but one well worth emphasizing. You should save your work as frequently as possible, not just when you're closing a document. In this section, we'll take a quick look at techniques that make saving documents as seamless as possible.

Saving Changes to Existing Documents

Saving your document in the same location with the same name is easy. Simply follow any of these procedures:

- Choose File, Save.
- Click the Save button on the Standard toolbar.
- Press Ctrl+S.
- Press Shift+F12.
- Press Alt+Shift+F2.

Tip **Save, save, save**

Take advantage of the simplicity of the save procedure. Whenever you're about to take a break, press Ctrl+S as you start to roll your chair away from your desk. When your phone rings, click the Save button as you reach for the receiver. Saving your work periodically helps you avoid major data loss headaches when you least expect them (because, as everyone knows, system crashes or disasters usually strike at the most inopportune times).

Troubleshooting

Word states that my document is too large to save

Documents that are too large to save can be divided into smaller parts. You can cut and paste parts of the document into new documents, and then save each part individually. To print all the files in sequence, you can use INCLUDETEXT fields to associate and connect the files (see Chapter 3, "Printing with Precision"). Another option would be to divide your document into a master document with subdocuments, as described in Chapter 20, "Creating and Controlling Master Documents."

Saving All Open Documents Simultaneously

When you want to shut down in a hurry but multiple documents are open, you can save all open documents at the same time. To do so, press Shift, and then choose File, Save All. Word saves all the open documents and templates at the same time. If you have open documents that have never been saved, the Save As dialog box appears so that you can name any newly created files.

Tip You can close all documents without saving them by pressing Shift and choosing File, Close All.

Saving Files by Using the Save As Dialog Box

The Save As dialog box appears every time you save a new document or opt to save an existing document as a new file or in a new location by choosing File, Save As (or by pressing F12). Figure 2-30 shows the latest incarnation of the Save As dialog box, which is similar to the Save As dialog box in Word 2002, except for a slight modification to the buttons on the default My Places Bar in the leftmost area of the dialog box.

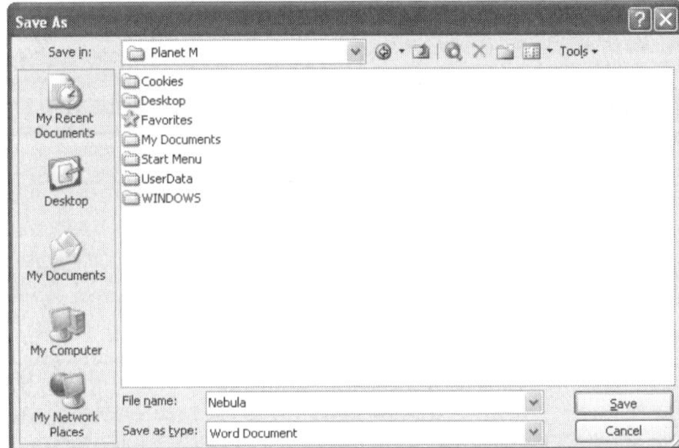

Figure 2-30. The Save As dialog box provides all the options you need to specify how and where to save new and existing documents.

To save a new document using the Save As dialog box or to save an existing document with new parameters (including a new location, a new file type, or a new file name), follow these steps:

1. Choose File, Save As, or press F12. (Or, if you're saving a newly created document for the first time, click the Save button on the Standard toolbar.)
2. Navigate to the folder in which you want to save the current document (the save location appears in the Save In text box), type a file name in the File Name box, and then select the file type in the Save As Type list box. The Word Document file type appears by default, and Word saves documents with the .doc extension. You can, however, save Word documents using a variety of file types, which can come in especially handy if you're saving a file for someone who is using an application other than Word or if you're creating Hypertext Markup Language (HTML) or XML documents. (Table 2-10 lists the file formats available in the Save As dialog box.)
3. Click Save.

Note Keep in mind that the Save feature replaces an existing file with an updated version of the file and the Save As feature creates a new file. When you use the Save As feature while working on an existing file, you create a new version of the file, and the original copy of the file remains intact in its original location.

Tip At times, you'll want to create a folder to contain a newly created file. You can easily create a new folder during the save procedure by clicking the Create New Folder button on the Save As dialog box's toolbar.

Reviewing the Available File Formats in the Save As Type List Box

Table 2-10 describes the file format types available in the Save As dialog box.

Table 2-10. File Formats Available in the Save As Type List Box

Format Type	Description
Word Document (.doc)	Saves the file as a Word 2003 document.
NEW FEATURE! XML Document (.xml)	Saves the document in standard XML format using either the Word XML schema or any custom XML schema. Further, you can apply Extensible Stylesheet Language Transformations (XSLT) files to XML documents to render XML data in a desired format.
NEW FEATURE! Single File Web Page (.mht, mhtlm)	Saves all the elements of a Web site, including text and graphics, as a single file. In Word 2002, this feature was called *Web Archive*.
Web Page (.htm, .html)	Saves the file as a Web page with full Word editing capabilities.
Web Page, Filtered (.htm, .html)	Saves a document as a Web page without including extraneous source code that enables many Word editing features. Using this option creates smaller HTML files than files saved with the Web Page option.
Document Template (.dot)	Saves the file as a template that you can use to build similar documents.
Rich Text Format (.rtf)	Saves the file using a standard text format that's widely recognized among word-processing applications and used to exchange word-processing information.

Table 2-10. File Formats Available in the Save As Type List Box

Format Type	Description
Plain Text (.txt)	Eliminates all formatting; converts lines, section breaks, and page breaks to paragraph marks; and uses the American National Standards Institute (ANSI) character set. A useful option for cross-platform availability when formatting isn't a major consideration.
Word 97-2002 & 6.0/95 – RTF (.doc)	Saves the file in Rich Text Format with the .doc extension, which can be recognized by Word 6, Word 95, Word 97, Word 2000, and Word 2002.

Obtaining Additional File Format Converters

At some point, you might face the task of converting a document for which Word has not supplied a converter, and no converter for the file type is available on the Office CD-ROM. When this situation arises, you'll have to install another converter. In some cases, you can easily obtain a converter from the Office Web site or in the Office Resource Kit. If you have an Internet connection, you can access the Office Web site by choosing Help, Office On Microsoft.com. If neither the Web site nor the Office Resource Kit provides what you're looking for, your next step should be to dig up a third-party solution. One well-known, third party, file-conversion solution is Dataviz's Conversions Plus software. In addition, you can search shareware sites (such as *http://www.tucows.com*) for file conversion programs.

Specifying a Default Save Format

The default setting when you save Word documents saves documents using the Word Document (*.doc) format. You have the opportunity to save files as other file types when you save a file using the Save As dialog box (to do so, select another file type in the Save As Type list box). If you frequently save your documents in a format other than the default .doc format, you can change the default setting to another file format by configuring Word's Save options. When you change the default file format setting, all documents you save in the future will be saved with the specified format unless you change the setting during the save process. To change the default file format setting, follow these steps:

1. Choose Tools, Options, and click the Save tab, as shown in Figure 2-31. Alternatively, click Tools, Save Options in the Save As dialog box.

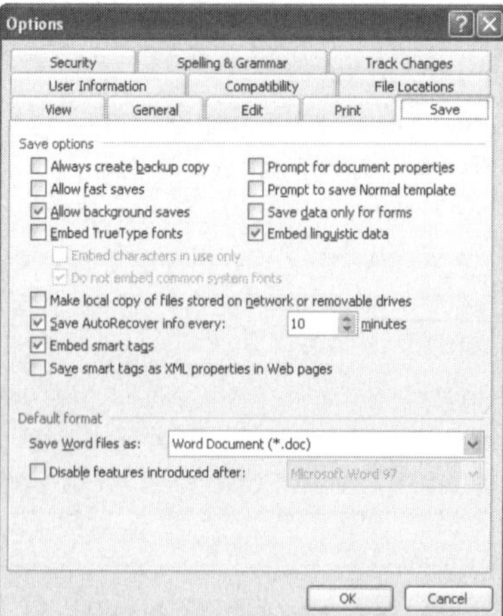

Figure 2-31. The Save options in Word enable you to configure default Save settings.

2 In the Default Format section, select a new default format setting in the Save Word Files As list box, and click OK.

Saving as an XML Document

Expanded support for XML is one of the biggest and most exciting changes incorporated into the Microsoft Office System. In Word 2003, XML support has been greatly expanded. In the past, XML support in Word came in the form of Web page source code and smart tag development. Now, you can create and customize XML documents in Word. This capability gives your data added flexibility and enables you to use your data across platforms and other data barriers. In other words, the ability to save a Word document as an XML document helps you separate the document's content from the confines of the document.

In a nutshell, XML is the standard language used to describe and deliver data. Using XML, developers can use customized XML tags to organize and present information. While XML is often associated with HTML and can work closely with HTML, HTML's strength and main purpose is to display information rather than to describe and deliver data, which are XML's strengths.

Tip **Understand key XML terms**

Grasping the meaning of the following few key terms can help you use XML technology more effectively:

- *XML data* refers to the raw XML data stored independently of the form in which the data is presented.
- An *XML schema* is a document that defines the structure of an XML document, including the element names, entities, attributes, and content that's allowed in the XML document.
- *XSLT* files transform the structure of an XML document to create various views.

By combining XML data, schemas, and XSLT files, you can create, store, transmit, and deliver data in a wide variety of ways.

In Word 2003, you can create documents using Word's standard XML schema (a schema is a set of rules that determine the language elements used in the document) or you can attach a custom XML schema. By default, when you save a file as an XML document, Word applies the default Word XML schema (WordML), which applies XML tags that store information. When you attach a custom schema, Word attaches both the WordML schema and the custom schema to your document by default.

One of the notable benefits of increased XML support in Word is that you can work on XML documents using Word's familiar interface options. You can open, create, and save XML documents in Word without even knowing that you're working with XML (although you can also work directly with the XML markup if you desire). You can save any file as an XML document. Further, when you save XML documents, you can specify whether to save the data only or apply an Extensible Stylesheet Language Transformation (XSLT), which enables you to display the saved XML document in a specific view.

To save a file as an XML document, you use the Save As dialog box, as described here:

1. Choose File, Save As, or press F12. (Or, if you're saving a newly created document for the first time, click the Save button on the Standard toolbar.)
2. Navigate to the folder in which you want to save the current document (the save location appears in the Save In text box), type a file name in the File Name box, and select XML Document in the Save As Type list box. The Save As dialog box displays the Apply Transform and Save Data Only check boxes. When you select Apply Transform, the Transform button becomes available as shown in Figure 3-32.
3. To apply an XSLT to format the document, click Transform, select an XSLT file, and then click Open. The name of the XSLT file appears to the right of the Transform label in the Save As dialog box.

Caution If you apply an XSLT when you save a file, Word discards any data that the XSLT does not use.

4. Click Save. A warning box displays that asks if you'd like to keep WordML. You can choose Continue, Keep WordML (which preserves your entire document, including the data that the XSLT would exclude), or Cancel.

Tip To apply the same XSLT every time you save a document, you can attach an XSLT file in the same way you attach templates and add-ins. To learn how to attach XSLT files in this way, see Chapter 16, "Formatting Documents Using Templates, Wizards, Add-Ins, and XML Schemas."

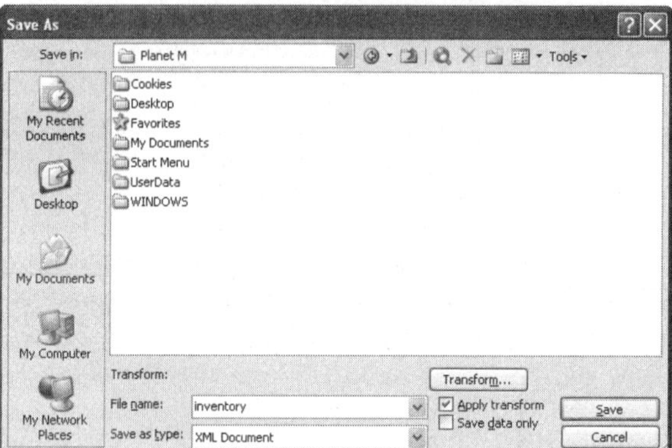

Figure 2-32. You can apply an XSLT file or save data only when you save a file as an XML document.

For more information about creating and working with XML documents in Word, see Chapter 29, "Working with XML."

Saving a File as a Web Page

You can save any document in Word as a Web page by using the Save As Type list box in the Save As dialog box. In Word 2003, three Web-related file types are available in the Save As Type list box:

1. Single File Web Page (formerly *Web Archive*) (.mht, .mhtml)
2. Web Page (.htm, .html)
3. Web Page, Filtered (.htm, .html)

When you're creating Web pages in Word, you'll probably want to begin by saving the document in the Web Page file type format. This format creates an HTML document and enables you to continue using all the Word editing features while you work. Later, when you're ready to upload your Web page to a network or the Internet, you might want to then save the document using the Web Page, Filtered option to streamline your document's source code and create a smaller HTML file than is created by the Web Page option. (The Web Page, Filtered option removes some of the source code that's inserted into Word-generated Web pages for the sole purpose of providing Word editing capabilities.) Finally, when you're ready to archive a Web site or you want to send an entire Web site as a single file to someone, you'd probably use the Web Archive file type, which saves all the elements of your Web site—graphics and text—as a single .mht or .mhtml file.

When you elect to save a Web page in Word using the Save As dialog box, the dialog box is slightly modified to include a Change Title button. You can click the Change Title button to display the Set Page Title dialog box, and then specify a page title for your Web page. The text you enter in the Set Page Title dialog box will appear in the title bar when the page is viewed in a browser.

For more information about creating Web pages in Word, see Chapter 26, "Creating Professional Web Sites."

Saving a File to an FTP Site

If you or your company has access to a site that uses File Transfer Protocol (FTP), you can save documents directly to a folder on the site. To do so, follow these steps:

1. Choose File, Save As.
2. In the Save In list box, choose FTP Locations.
3. Double-click a listed FTP site or create a connection to an FTP site by clicking Add/Modify FTP Locations (and then double-click the newly created link).
4. Enter a name in the File Name text box, and click Save.

Saving a File as Encoded Text

Generally, you can freely share text files without worrying about how the text is stored. However, in some cases, you might need to share text files with people working in other languages or using other computer systems. In those instances, you might need to save a Word document using an encoding standard. Using an encoding standard helps other programs to determine how to represent stored text so that it's readable. To save a Word document as encoded text, follow these steps:

1. Click File, Save As.
2. Specify a location and file name for the file.
3. In the Save As Type list box, select Plain Text.
4. Click Save. The File Conversion dialog box appears.
5. Under Text encoding, select Windows (Default), MS-DOS, or Other Encoding, and then select an encoding standard in the list box.
6. Select any other desired options, and click OK.

Saving a Document as a TIFF File

Office includes Microsoft Office Document Imaging (MODI), which enables you to work with scanned documents. With this feature, you can use the Microsoft Office Document Image Writer print driver to save any Office document as a Tagged Image File Format (TIFF) image file. To do so, follow these steps:

1. Open the document, and then choose File, Print or press Ctrl+P.
2. In the Name list box, select Microsoft Office Document Image Writer, and then click Properties.
3. In the Microsoft Office Document Image Writer Properties dialog box, click the Advanced tab.

4. In the Advanced tab, select TIFF – Monochrome Fax, and then click OK.
5. In the Print dialog box, click OK.
6. In the Save As dialog box, ensure that the View Document Image check box is selected, configure any other desired options, and then click OK.

After you save a document as a TIFF file, you can edit the file and work with the content using Microsoft Office Document Imaging.

Saving a File on a Network

My Network Places

Saving a file in a network location is similar to saving a file in a folder on your local computer. The main difference is that in the Save As dialog box you navigate to a network location instead of to a local folder. Word 2003 makes saving a file in a network location easy by providing the My Network Places button on the My Places Bar. (The My Places Bar is discussed in the section "Taking a Closer Look at the My Places Bar," on page XX.)

Creating Automatic Backups

By default, Word's AutoRecover feature stores unsaved changes to a file every 10 minutes. For added assurance, you can configure Word to create a backup file every time you save a file. To set this option, choose Tools, Options; click the Save tab; and select the Always Create Backup Copy check box. When this feature is activated, you'll notice that your folders contain two versions of each document you've saved: One file displays the standard file name, and the other file is named "Backup of *file name*.wbk." To open a backup file, simply double-click the file in the same manner you double-click other files to open them.

Note You can't use the fast save feature and the automatic backup feature at the same time. The automatic backup feature creates a backup file each time you save your document. When the Allow Fast Saves check box is selected in the Save tab in the Options dialog box, Word saves only the changes you make to a document (instead of saving the entire document). When the list of changes grows fairly large, Word performs a normal save and integrates all the changes. By default, neither the fast save nor the automatic backup feature is activated.

Retrieving Local and Shared Documents

The poet William Wordsworth once claimed that he wrote his best works in a single sitting. But most of us don't work that way—instead, we return to documents time and again for one reason or another as well as often collaborate and review information with others while we work. Therefore, Word provides a few techniques you can use to retrieve and share existing documents. This section lays out the various document retrieval options—you can sift through and determine which method best suits your working style.

Displaying Existing Documents

As with other files in Windows, you can retrieve documents in a variety of ways using the Windows interface. For example, you can open a document by choosing the Documents option from the Start menu, opening My Computer, navigating to a document within your browser, and so forth. In Word, the best sources for retrieving Word documents are the Open dialog box and the Getting Started task pane.

> **Note** If you are using Office on an Apple computer, you can open any Office file that has been created or stored on a computer running Microsoft Windows. Simply access the file from a floppy disk or CD drive, or over your network or the Internet (for instance, by opening an e-mail attachment or logging on to an FTP site).

Surveying the Open Dialog Box

The Open dialog box, shown in Figure 2-33, is your key to finding and retrieving Word documents. To display the Open dialog box, perform any of the following actions within Word:

- Choose File, Open.
- Click the Open button on the Standard toolbar.
- Click a document's link in the Getting Started task pane.
- Press Ctrl+O.
- Press Ctrl+F12.
- Press Ctrl+Alt+F2.

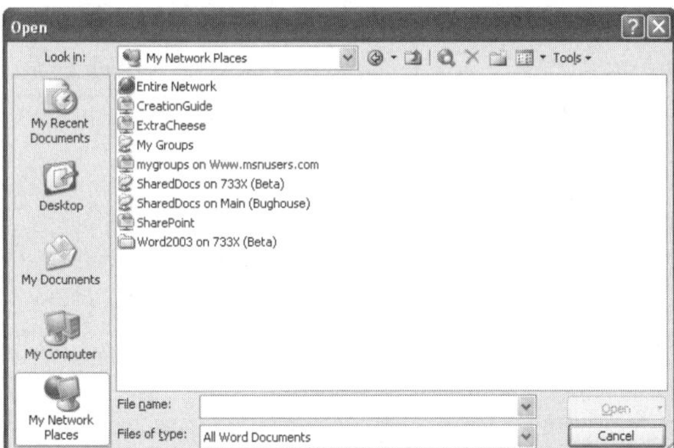

Figure 2-33. The Open dialog box serves as a gateway to existing files on your system, your network, and the Internet.

Taking a closer look at the My Places Bar The My Places Bar enables you to move quickly around your system and network as you retrieve documents. The default My Places Bar buttons are described in Table 2-11. You can rearrange the My Places buttons by right-clicking an icon and choosing Move Up or Move Down from the shortcut menu. In addition, you can right-click the My Places Bar and specify whether to view large or small icons. Finally, you can add and remove custom icons on the My Places Bar by completing the following steps:

1. Click File, Open.
2. In the Open dialog box, display and select the folder you want to create a shortcut to in the My Places Bar.
3. Click Tools, and then click Add To "My Places".

To remove a custom link from the My Places Bar, right-click the icon and choose Remove.

Table 2-11. Default My Places Bar Buttons

Button	Name	Function
My Recent Documents	My Recent Documents	Displays Windows shortcuts to files you've opened recently, listed in date and time order, starting with the most recently opened document. If you've worked on a document a number of times, clicking the shortcut in the History folder takes you to the most recent version.
Desktop	Desktop	Displays the contents of your desktop. You should probably avoid saving Word documents to your desktop so that you don't clutter up your desktop. Although if you are saving documents only temporarily, you might want to save them to your desktop so you can delete them easily later.
My Documents	My Documents	Opens the default document folder named My Documents.
My Computer	My Computer	Displays the contents of the My Computer folder, which generally includes disk drives, CD-ROM drives, network locations, shared documents, and so forth.
My Network Places	My Network Places	Displays your network locations (shown in Figure 2-33).

Selecting views in the Open dialog boxes As with most Windows-based applications, Word lets you specify how you'd like to display the documents and folders listed in the Open dialog box. To do so, you click the arrow on the Views toolbar button and select a view in the list box. You can display files and folders in the Open and Save As dialog boxes using the following views:

- Thumbnails
- Tiles
- Icons
- List
- Details
- Properties
- Preview
- WebView

In addition, you can change the sort order of documents and folders in a dialog box by clicking the column heading buttons, such as Name, Size, Type, and Modified.

Perfecting the Art of Opening Existing Documents

After you become familiar with the ins and outs of the Open dialog box, opening documents is fairly straightforward. The basic premise behind using the Open dialog box to open files is to select a file name and then click the Open button, or to simply double-click a file name.

> **Tip** To open multiple files from within the Open dialog box, select files while pressing Shift or Ctrl, and then click the Open button.

As you might have noticed, the Open button in the Open dialog box sports a menu that provides a few extra commands, as shown in Figure 2-34. This menu enables you to open a file as read-only, open a copy of a file, open a file in a browser (if the document's an HTML file), open an XML document with a transform, or open and repair a faulty file.

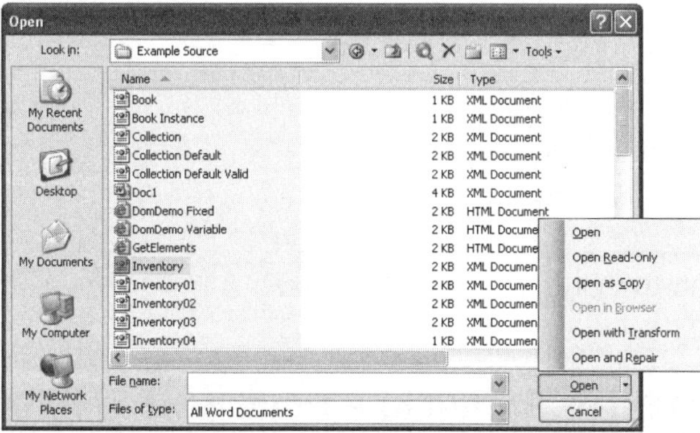

Figure 2-34. The Open button menu provides options that let you control how you open a document.

Tip Remember, when you open a read-only file, you must use the Save As feature to save any changes you make to the document (in which case, you create a new document based on the read-only document without affecting the original file).

To bypass the Open dialog box altogether when opening documents, you can use one of these methods:

- Double-click a Word document's icon in a folder.
- Drag a Word document's icon from its folder into the Word application.
- In the Getting Started task pane, click a document link listed under the Open heading.

Note Take special note of the Open And Repair command. You can use Open And Repair to attempt to open a file that's been damaged or corrupted.

Opening an XML Document

You open XML documents in Word in the same way you open other documents. After you open an XML document, you can control whether the XML tags appear. To do so, open the XML document; the XML task pane appears by default. Click the XML Document task pane title bar, and select XML Structure in the list box. In the XML Structure task pane, you can select or clear the Show XML Tags In The Document check box to control the display of XML tags. Figure 2-35 shows two views of the same XML document—one with the tags visible and one with the tags hidden.

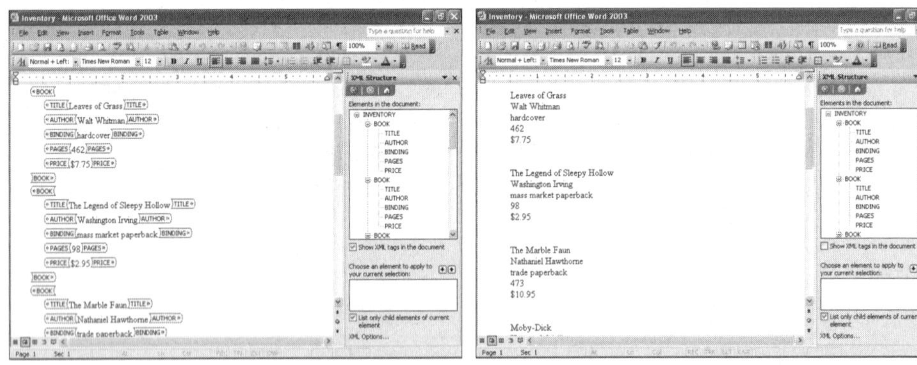

Figure 2-35. You can display and hide XML tags while you work with XML documents in Word 2003.

Opening a Document Stored in a Document Workspace

When you open a shared document that's stored in a document workspace, such as a SharePoint Team Services Web site, you're basically opening a document stored in a network location. Therefore, to open a shared document, you access your network places. To open a shared document, click File, Open, click My Network Places in the My Places Bar, double-click the network location, and then open the document. When you work with a shared document, the Shared Workspace task pane appears in Word by default, as shown in Figure 2-36.

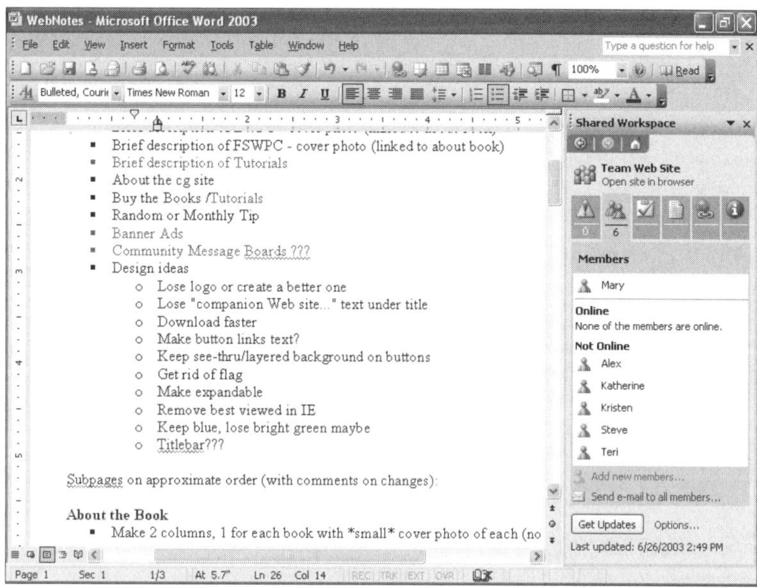

Figure 2-36. Word's Shared Workspace task pane streamlines online document collaboration and helps team members access the most up-to-date information.

For more information about working with shared documents and SharePoint Team Services, see Chapter 25, "Working in the Shared Document Workspace."

Taking Advantage of AutoRecover and Background Saves

As all computer users intuitively know, there's always a risk of losing data when you least expect it. To help reduce the risk of losing data, Word is installed with the AutoRecover and Background Saves features activated. These two features work together to help save your information without interrupting your workflow too much. These features can be summarized as follows:

- **AutoRecover** Automatically stores information about an active document that might be useful if your system crashes or if there's a power failure. By default, Word gathers AutoRecover information every 10 minutes.
- **Background Saves** Enables you to continue working in Word while you save a document. A pulsing disk icon appears on the status bar when a background save is taking place.

To verify that your system has these two features activated, choose Tools, Options; click the Save tab; and then make sure that the Save AutoRecover Info Every and Allow Background Saves check boxes are selected.

Tip **Working around the "same name" error when saving long documents**
If you attempt to save a long document while Word is performing an automatic background save, you might get a "same name" error, because Word uses the same name to complete both save operations. If this occurs, simply wait a moment while the background save completes, and then save the document normally. You can tell when a document is being saved (automatically or otherwise) by looking for the pulsing disk icon on the status bar.

Keep in mind that the AutoRecover feature isn't a replacement for saving your file. Instead, it's a tool you can use to recover a file after a system crash. You need to continue to save your documents regularly. If your system seems a bit shaky, you can also configure AutoRecover to gather information more frequently by clicking the Save tab in the Options dialog box and changing the interval time in the Save AutoRecover Info Every text box.

Note By default, AutoRecover files are stored in \%*UserProfile*%\Application Data\Microsoft\Word. You can change the default location using the File Locations tab in the Options dialog box. (See Chapter 5, "Customizing Word and Enhancing Accessibility" for instructions about changing default file locations.)

If you experience a system crash while working in Word, Word displays a Document Recovery task pane along the left side of the Word window after you restart your system and reopen Word. You can select which files you want to recover from among the recovered versions of documents that appear in the Document Recovery task pane. The documents are referred to as recovery files, and they have the .asd extension.

To open a recovered document, double-click the entry in the Document Recovery task pane or choose Open in the item's menu. In addition, you can save or delete a recovered file or view repairs made to a recovered file by clicking the item's arrow, and then selecting the desired command.

Tip **Recover the most recent versions of files**
Frequently you'll see a few versions of the same file listed in the Document Recovery task pane's Available Files list box. When this occurs, keep in mind that a recovered file with *"[Recovered]"* in its title is usually in better shape than a file with *"[Original]"* in its title. Be sure to check the Last Saved time listed with each recovered document to verify that you're recovering the most recent version.

After you've made your recovery decisions, click Close in the lower-right corner of the Document Recovery task pane to close the pane. If you have not taken specified recovery action (such as deleting, saving, or opening and closing without saving) for each file in the Document Recovery task pane, a message box will appear asking whether you want to view the recovered files later or remove the files because you've saved the file you need. Select the action you want Word to take, and then click OK to complete the recovery process.

Caution When you close a recovery file without saving it, the recovery file is deleted—you can't recover a deleted recovery file.

Troubleshooting

Recovery files aren't displayed in Word after a crash

In some instances, your recovery files might not appear when you reopen Word. Don't worry (yet)—all is not lost at this point. You can try to locate and open a recovery file manually when necessary. To do so, follow these steps:

1. Click the Open button on the Standard toolbar, and navigate to the folder that contains the recovery files (usually *%UserProfile%*\Application Data\Microsoft\Word).
2. In the Files Of Type box, select All Files. You'll be looking for .asd files, but Word doesn't include a list item for that file type. (If you want to get really fancy, you can simply search for recovered files using the parameter AutoRecovery*.* in the Windows Search Results dialog box. To display the Windows Search Results dialog box, choose Start, Search, and then click Documents.)
3. Find the recovery file named "AutoRecovery save of *file name*.asd", and then open the document.
4. Click Save on the Standard toolbar, type or select the file name of the existing document, and then choose Yes when you're asked whether you want to replace the existing file.

Caution In a couple of situations, AutoRecover doesn't work. Most notably, AutoRecover doesn't recover master document files, although it does recover individual subdocuments. In addition, AutoRecover doesn't save changes you make in the Microsoft Visual Basic Editor while you have a document open in Word. The only time edited macros are included in an AutoRecover file is when macro changes are made in the Word document itself instead of in the Visual Basic Editor.

Chapter 3

Printing with Precision

The phenomenal surge of personal computing that began in the 1980s introduced the concept of a "paperless" society, but 20 years later, the world has yet to realize that ideal (as plenty of buried desks and bulging file cabinets can attest). For the most part, people continue to rely heavily on printed matter. When you work in Word, you'll probably need to print information frequently. In most cases, printing a document requires you simply to click the Print button on the Standard toolbar—not a complex task. However, as a more experienced Word user, you might want a higher level of control over your print jobs—especially if you want to do more than simply print single copies of entire documents. For example, you might want to print selected sections of a document, print more than one copy of a document, print several document pages per printed page, print a series of related documents, or print a summary of the formatting styles or markup used in a document. Fortunately, the printing options included in Word give you this additional control over printing—and that's what this chapter is all about.

Previewing Before Printing

Even before you familiarize yourself with the nuances of printing, you should make a habit of using the Print Preview feature. Like a painter stepping back from her canvas, you can use Print Preview to take a big-picture look at a page or series of pages before you commit the information to hard copy. In Print Preview mode, you can examine entire pages at once, checking for obvious page setup errors and oddities and even applying minor fixes to correct some of the errors you discover. For example, using Print Preview, you can quickly see when an image box overlays text (or vice versa), when a single line runs onto the next page, or when indented text is misaligned.

Getting Comfortable in Print Preview Mode

Print Preview

Print Preview gives you a chance to view your document from a variety of perspectives before you print. By default, when you activate Print Preview, the current page is shown. To activate Print Preview mode, open your document in Word, and then use one of the following techniques:

- Choose File, Print Preview.
- Click the Print Preview button on the Standard toolbar.
- Press Ctrl+Alt+I or Ctrl+F2.

Figure 3-1 shows a document in Print Preview mode. The Print Preview toolbar buttons are described in Table 3-1.

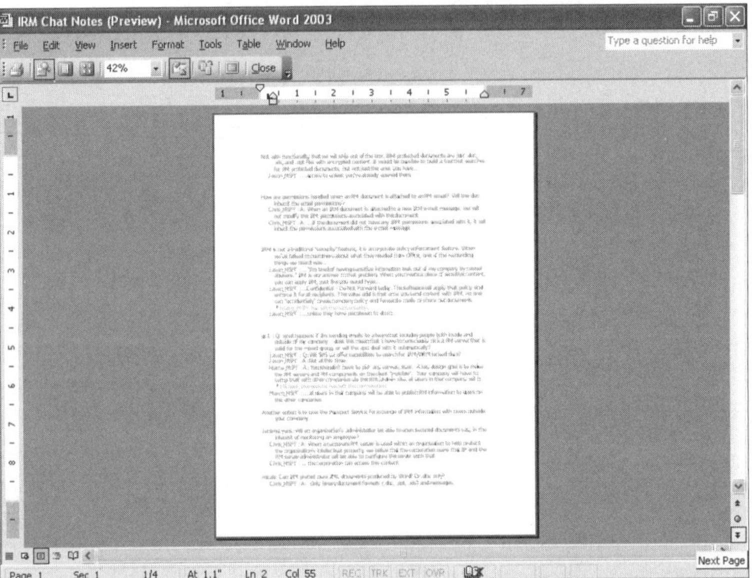

Figure 3-1. Previewing documents can help you troubleshoot page layout issues before you print.

Table 3-1. Print Preview Toolbar Buttons

Name	Button	Description
Print		Prints a single copy of the previewed document without displaying the Print dialog box.
Magnifier		Enlarges and reduces the view and enables you to edit content.
One Page		Displays a single page in Print Preview.
Multiple Pages		Enables you to arrange, display, and print multiple pages at one time.
Zoom list	42%	Enables you to enlarge or reduce the current view.
View Ruler		Toggles rulers on and off. Rulers enable you to modify margins and indents and set tabs from within Print Preview mode.
Shrink To Fit		Reduces the number of pages in the current document by one. This feature helps you avoid having a small amount of text spilling onto an extra page.

Table 3-1. Print Preview Toolbar Buttons

Name	Button	Description
Full Screen		Maximizes the viewing area by hiding standard components of the Word window, such as the title bar, menu bar, status bar, and scroll bars.
Close Print Preview	Close	Exits Print Preview mode and returns to the same page and view that appeared before you activated Print Preview.

To exit Print Preview mode, you can use any of the following methods:

- Press Esc.
- Press Ctrl+F2.
- Choose View, Normal.
- Click Close on the Print Preview toolbar.
- Click a view button (located to the left of the horizontal scroll bar).

When you exit Print Preview, Word returns the insertion point to the position in which it was located before you selected Print Preview.

Controlling How Print Preview Displays Documents

In Print Preview mode, you can examine your document by zooming in to see details. You can also maximize your viewing area by shifting to Full Screen mode, pull back to display the flow of content on multiple pages, or select a specific page to focus on. Let's look at each viewing option, listed below:

- **Zooming in on information** You can increase the viewing size of your document by using the Magnifier button (which displays the document at actual size) or by indicating a size in the Zoom box (either by selecting a size in the Zoom list or by typing a percentage value). To zoom in on a selected area, click the Magnifier button, and then click in the area of the document that you want to examine more closely. You can use the Zoom box to further modify your view, if necessary. To return your document to its original size, make sure that the Magnifier button is selected (it remains selected until you click another toolbar button), and then click in the document. In other words, you click once to enlarge your view to 100 percent, and click a second time to reduce the view. As you'll see in "Editing in Print Preview Mode," later in this chapter, you can also use the Magnifier button to activate Print Preview mode's editing options.
- **Working in Full Screen mode** To maximize the Word window's viewable area, click the Full Screen button. Figure 3-2, on the next page, shows two pages of a document in Full Screen mode. Notice that all standard window elements are hidden except the Print Preview toolbar and a small floating toolbar containing the Close Full Screen button. To display menu options when in Full Screen mode, position the pointer at the top of the window. To revert to standard Print Preview mode, click the Close Full Screen button on the Full Screen toolbar, click the Full Screen button, or press Esc.

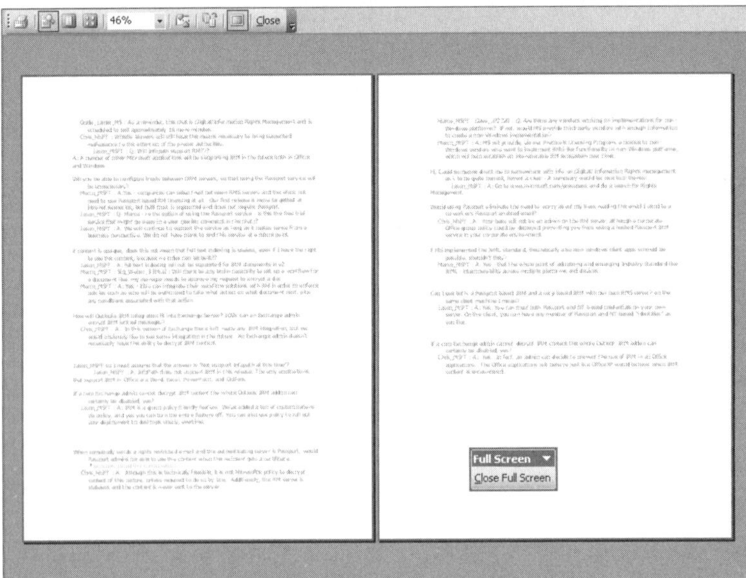

Figure 3-2. Full Screen mode maximizes your Print Preview viewing area.

- **Displaying multiple pages** One of the greatest benefits of Print Preview is the ability to view multiple pages at once. This feature enables you to see how your document will flow from page to page before you create a hard copy. You can view up to 24 pages (three rows by eight columns). To show multiple pages, click the Multiple Pages button, and then drag your mouse across the menu's page icons to select the number of rows and columns you want to display. Figure 3-3 shows 24 pages (the maximum number) in the Print Preview window.

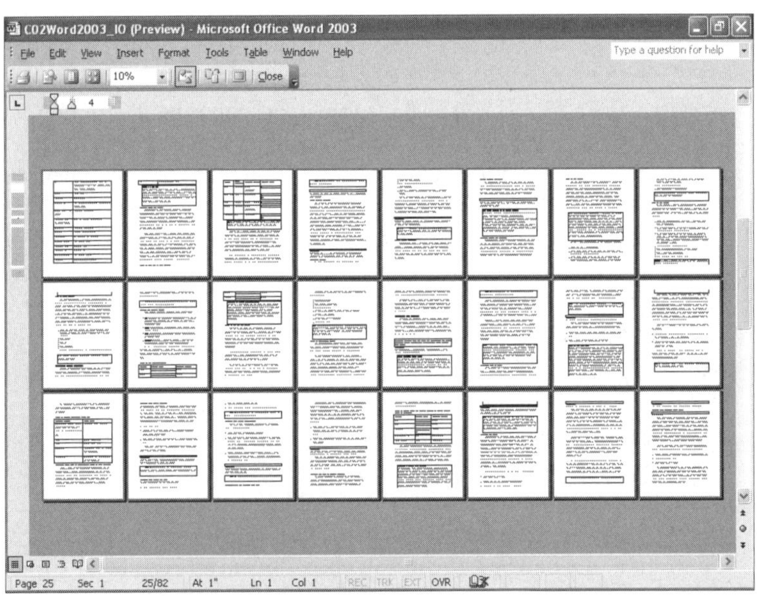

Figure 3-3. Using the Multiple Pages feature, you can display up to 24 thumbnail pages at a time.

- **Viewing a selected page** Obviously, you can click the One Page button on the Print Preview toolbar to display a single page. Conveniently enough, you can also select which page you want to view if you have displayed multiple pages. To do so, click the page you want to view, and then click the One Page button.

Differentiating Between Print Layout View and Print Preview

Keep in mind that *Print Layout view* and *Print Preview* are two different views. (Print Layout view and Print Preview are discussed in detail in "Viewing Documents in Various Lights," on page 13.) To summarize:

- **Print Layout view** Displays a document as it will print, showing the standard Word interface. Print Layout view enables you to work with standard Word editing controls while viewing how page elements will print. To switch to Print Layout view, choose View, Print Layout or click the Print Layout view button in the lower-left corner of the Word window.
- **Print Preview** Displays your document in a custom interface that contains the Print Preview toolbar. In Print Preview mode, you can view multiple pages at one time as well as making editing and formatting changes before you print.

In general, Print Layout view should be used as a working environment, and Print Preview mode should be used to verify your document's layout when you're almost ready to print and when you want to make minor fixes.

Actual Page

Note Pages in Reading Layout view do not represent how pages will appear when the document is printed. Instead, Reading Layout view optimizes the view of a document for online reading. To display how pages will print while using Reading Layout view, click the Actual Page button on the Reading Layout toolbar. For more information about the Reading Layout view, see Chapter 1, "Gearing Up with Word 2003."

Editing in Print Preview Mode

As you zoom in, out, and around in Print Preview, you'll occasionally see details you want to adjust. If you exit Print Preview mode to fix the problems, you'll be returned to your original location, which means that you might have to search all over again for the areas you identified in Print Preview mode. Fortunately, you don't have to leave Print Preview mode to make minor editing adjustments. If you need to edit some text, condense a document slightly, or adjust alignment, you can do so in Print Preview mode using the techniques described here:

Inside Out

Displaying a Print Preview page in another view

When you exit Print Preview, your insertion point returns to the position in which it was located before you selected Print Preview. In some instances, you might prefer to go directly to the page you were viewing in Print Preview mode. Unfortunately, Word doesn't provide an option to display the current page in Print Preview mode in other views—you're forced to return from whence you came. A quick workaround to this little impediment is to take note of the relevant page number while you're in Print Preview mode (click in the page, and then check out the page number on the status bar), close Print Preview, and then use Go To (press Ctrl+G or display the Select Browse Object menu) to move to the desired page.

- **Editing text in Print Preview mode** You can modify text in Print Preview mode by deleting, adding, cutting, copying, pasting, moving, and formatting text and other document components—in much the same way you edit documents in other views. To activate text editing mode in Print Preview mode, click Magnifier, which changes the insertion point to a magnifying glass. To edit at actual size (100 percent), position the magnifying glass on the page in the area you want to edit, click to zoom in to 100 percent, and then click Magnifier again to change the magnifying glass to an insertion point. Keep in mind that you don't have to edit in 100 percent view; you can edit in any view size. At 100 percent, you can edit text in detail; at smaller sizes with several pages on the screen, you can easily drag elements from page to page.
- **Condensing text to shorten a document by one page** You can use the Shrink To Fit feature to tighten up a document that's just a tad too long. To do so, click the Shrink To Fit button on the Print Preview toolbar. If desired, you can click Shrink To Fit multiple times. Each time you click the Shrink To Fit button, you shrink your document by at least one page. Be forewarned that you might not like the changes Word makes (for instance, fonts can be reduced up to four point sizes). In some cases, Word will simply give up and present a message box stating that it was unable to shrink the document by one page. For instance, in shrinking an 82-page document, Word gave up at 33 pages. To undo shrinking, use Word's Undo feature.

Caution If you want to print but not store the Shrink To Fit results, click Shrink To Fit to shrink your document, click Print on the Print Preview toolbar, and then undo the Shrink To Fit action before you save the document. Once you save a document that's been shrunk, you can't undo the Shrink To Fit changes.

- **Adjusting margins, indents, and tabs** You can click the Rulers button on the Print Preview toolbar to toggle rulers on and off in Print Preview mode. When the rulers appear, you can drag the margin, indent, or tab icons to adjust margins, indents, or tabs. If you're displaying multiple pages, the rulers move to the top and left of the page that's currently selected. In Figure 3-3, the rulers correspond to the first page in the first row (which is actually page 25 in the document, as you can see in the status bar).

For more information about using rulers to adjust margins, indents, and tabs, see Chapter 8, "Aligning Information and Formatting Paragraphs and Lists."

Tip **Access Page Setup options quickly**

When rulers are visible, you can quickly display the Page Setup dialog box, which enables you to reset a document's margins, page orientation, and other page setup options. To display the Page Setup dialog box, double-click anywhere within the ruler areas except the white portion of the top ruler. If you click within the white portion of the top ruler, you might accidentally set unwanted tabs.

Tip **Print booklets using landscape orientation**

Word is designed to have landscape orientation for booklets; therefore, you can't print a booklet using portrait orientation. If you're working in portrait orientation and select Book Fold from the Multiple Pages list in the Pages section of the Margins tab in the Page Setup dialog box, Word will automatically switch the page orientation to landscape.

Inside Out

Undoing changes in Print Preview mode

Notice that the Print Preview toolbar doesn't contain an Undo button. Luckily, this doesn't mean that you can't undo changes in Print Preview mode. To undo changes, choose Edit, Undo, or press Ctrl+Z. If you find that you frequently need to undo changes in Print Preview mode, display the Formatting toolbar (choose View, Toolbars, Formatting) in Print Preview mode, or customize the Print Preview toolbar by adding the Undo button, as described in Chapter 5, "Customizing Word and Enhancing Accessibility."

Printing Quickly and Efficiently

Print

After you've approved your document's appearance using Print Preview mode, you're ready to print. By far the easiest and most common printing task is printing an entire document.You've probably done this a million times, but to make sure we don't overlook any obvious procedures, here's a quick rundown of the ways you can print a single copy of the current document:

- Choose File, Print, and then click OK.
- Click Print on the Standard toolbar.
- Press Ctrl+P or Ctrl+Shift+F12, and then click OK.

You can also print a Word document without opening it by right-clicking the file's icon and choosing Print from the shortcut menu. From within Word, you can print multiple documents in the same folder at one time by following these steps:

1. Choose File, Open.
2. In the Open dialog box, open the folder that contains the documents you want to print, and then select the documents.
3. Right-click the selected documents and then choose Print, or select Print from the Tools menu.

Troubleshooting

An extra blank page prints when I print

If an extra blank page prints at the end of your print job, there might be an extra paragraph return or two inserted at the end of your document. To delete the empty paragraphs, display hidden characters in your document (by clicking the Show/Hide button on the Standard toolbar), and then delete the extra paragraph markers. After you delete the extra paragraph marker or markers, you can verify that the extra blank page has been removed by viewing your document in Print Preview mode.

Troubleshooting

The wrong font appears in my document onscreen or when printed

In some cases, a font that you're using might not show up in your document. Instead, Word substitutes another font for the unavailable font. You can control which font is used as the substitute font by performing the following steps:

1. Click Tools, Options, and then click the Compatibility tab.
2. Click the Font Substitution button.
3. Under Font Substitutions, click the missing font name under Missing Document Font, and then click a substitute font in the Substituted Font box.

Similarly, some fonts might show up onscreen, but print differently from the way they appear onscreen. In these cases, Word might be printing a draft copy (check the Draft Output option on the Print tab in the Options dialog box), or the font you're using might not be available in your printer. To fix a missing printer font, you should change the offending font to a TrueType font or another font that's supported by your printer.

Note To print from Word, you must have a printer and printer driver installed. If you're in charge of configuring your own printer, check your printer manufacturer's Web page for updated drivers to download if you run into Word 2003 compatibility issues. For additional assistance, visit the Microsoft Knowledge Base at *http://support.microsoft.com*.

For information about printing envelopes and labels, see Chapter 30, "Performing Mail Merges."

Canceling a Print Job

Sometimes, you might decide at the last moment that you want to cancel a print job. The way you cancel a print job depends on whether background printing is turned on. By default, Word activates background printing, which means that you can continue working while you print a document. To change this setting, choose Tools, Options, click the Print tab, and then clear the Background Printing check box. To halt printing from within Word while your computer is sending a document to the printer, follow one of these two procedures:

- If background printing is disabled, click Cancel or press Esc.
- If background printing is enabled, double-click the animated printer icon on the status bar while the document is being sent to the printer. If you're printing a short document, the animated printer icon might not be visible long enough for you to cancel the printing task.

Managing Print Jobs Using the Print Queue Window

You can also manage your print jobs after you have sent them to the printer by using the print queue window. To display the print queue window, double-click the Printer icon on the taskbar in the Microsoft Windows user interface after you've sent a document to the printer. You can perform the following key tasks from the print queue window:

- **Delete a single print job** Select the print job you want to cancel, and then choose Document, Cancel Printing to remove it from the print queue.
- **Reprioritize print jobs** Drag print icons up or down in the print queue list to change the order in which documents are printed.
- **Cancel all print jobs** Choose Printer, Cancel All Documents to delete all documents from the print queue.

Controlling Print Jobs

As an experienced user, you probably need to perform printing tasks that are more complex than merely printing single copies of entire documents. Thus, instead of clicking the Print button on the Standard toolbar, you'll probably benefit more by pressing Ctrl+P or choosing File, Print so that you can take advantage of the options available in the Print dialog box, shown in Figure 3-4, on the next page. In this part of the chapter, you'll learn how to customize and control many of Word's printing settings.

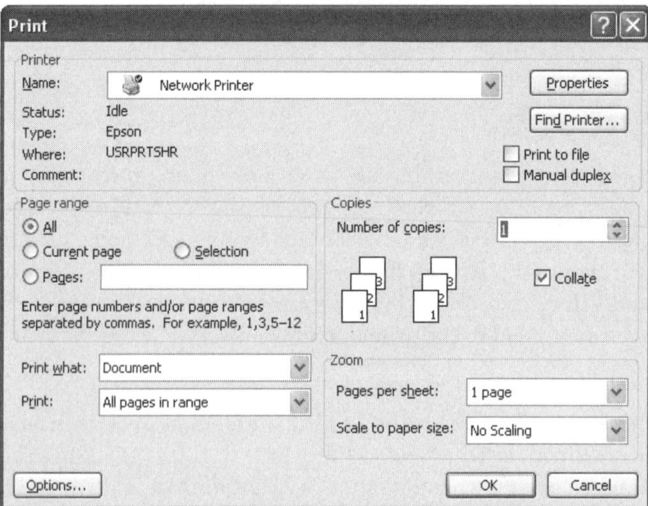

Figure 3-4. The Print dialog box provides many of the options that you can use to control your print jobs.

Printing More Than One Copy of a Single Document

To print multiple copies of a document, display the Print dialog box, and then select or type a value in the Number Of Copies box. By default, Word collates multiple copies of a print job. (Notice that the Collate check box is selected in the Copies section in the Print dialog box.) When collating is enabled, Word sends one copy of your print job to the printer, waits a moment, sends the next copy to the printer, and so on. The result is that the entire selection or document is printed, then the next copy is printed, and so forth. In the long run, this method is probably easier for an end user, but it takes longer to process and can cause bottlenecks in a print queue if the document contains many large graphics or extensive formatting. If you prefer, you can clear the Collate check box. Word will then send the printer all copies of the first page, all copies of the second page, and so forth, leaving you to collate the copies manually. On some laser printers, printing without collating might speed the process and avoid bottlenecks in the print queue because the printer won't have to reprocess information for each copy of a page.

Printing Ranges

In many cases, you'll want to print a selection of pages instead of an entire document. For example, you might want to select and print a few paragraphs of text instead of an entire Web page; you might want to print two or three noncontiguous sections within a long report; or you might want to print the cover letter attached to your updated résumé. To print specific pages and sections within a document, use the following options in the Page Range section of the Print dialog box:

- **All** Prints the entire document; the default selection. To print an entire document, display the Print dialog box, and then click OK.

- **Current Page** Prints the page in which your insertion point is currently located. To use this option, click in the page you want to print, display the Print dialog box, click Current Page, and then click OK.
- **Selection** Prints selected text. To use this option, select the content you want to print, display the Print dialog box, click Selection, and then click OK.

To review text selection methods, see Chapter 2, "Mastering Document Fundamentals."

- **Pages** Prints only the pages, page ranges, and sections you specify. You can use commas and hyphens with the letters *s* (for *section*) and *p* (for *page*) to specify which pages, sections, and page ranges you want to print. For example, enter **1-5,9,15-18** to print pages 1 through 5, page 9, and pages 15 through 18; enter **s2,s4** to print sections 2 and 4; and enter **p3s4-p6s5** to print from page 3, section 4, to page 6, section 5.

For more information about defining and using sections, see Chapter 15, "Mastering Page Setup and Pagination," and Chapter 19, "Formatting Columns and Sections for Advanced Text Control."

Printing Odd and Even Pages to Simulate Duplex Printing

If you want to print using both sides of each sheet of paper but you don't have a *duplex printer* (a printer that can automatically print on both sides of a sheet), you can use the Odd Pages and Even Pages print options in Word to work around the limitation. To accomplish this, you can print all the odd pages first, turn the printed pages over, reinsert the paper into your printer's paper tray, and then print the even pages. You'll probably have to experiment with your printer tray to ensure that you insert the paper properly. (Usually, the odd pages would go in face down with the top of the page positioned to feed into the printer first.) Bear in mind that printing this way too often can cause printers to jam eventually as a result of the ink from the already printed pages building up as they pass through your printer. If you do a lot of two-sided printing, you should probably invest in a printer that is designed to handle it.

To configure a print job to print only odd or even pages, display the Print dialog box and select either Odd Pages or Even Pages in the Print drop-down list. By default, the All Pages In Range option is selected.

You can use the Odd Pages and Even Pages options in combination with specified page ranges. For example, you can print only the odd pages in the range from page 110 through page 213 by specifying **110-213** in the Pages box and selecting Odd Pages in the Print list.

Printing Document Elements

As you know, documents consist of much more than just the content that appears on a page. Documents can include property settings, editing marks, comments, keyboard shortcut assignments, formatting styles, and so forth. In some cases, you might want to print a document's informational elements instead of the actual document. The Print dialog box enables you to print some common document elements by selecting them in the Print What list. Using this technique, you can print the following elements:

- **Document** Prints the entire document; the default setting.
- **Document Properties** Prints basic information about a file, such as the file name, directory, template, title, author, creation date, last saved date, number of words, and so forth. This information is similar to the information stored in the file's Properties dialog box. You can view a file's properties without printing the information by opening a document and choosing File, Properties.
- **Document Showing Markup** Prints the document and all the tracked changes made in the text. In addition, each comment inserted into the document is printed in the margin of the corresponding page in a box called a *bubble box*, with dashed lines indicating the insertion point of each comment. You can see how a marked-up document will be printed by previewing the document in Print Preview mode, as shown in Figure 3-5. Keep in mind that if you have turned on tracking so that all revisions appear in your document when you send that document to print, the Document Showing Markup print option is selected in the Print dialog box by default.

For information about using markup features, see Chapter 27, "Revising Documents Using Markup Tools."

- **List Of Markup** Prints each tracked change made in a document on a separate line below a color-coded heading. The color-coding is based on who made each change, and each heading's text indicates page number, action (deleted, inserted, or comment), name of the user who made the change, and the date and time of the modification. This printout provides a very detailed list of changes. If the document contains more than a few changes or comments, this print job could take a few minutes to queue and even longer to print. Keep in mind that this option can create fairly large print files, so use this option with discretion.

Tip **Print additional document information**

You can print other document components in addition to those in the Print What list, as we describe throughout this book. For example, to print hidden text and field codes, display them in your document before you print (as described in "Setting Printing Options," later in this chapter); to print an outline of your document, display the document in Outline view before you print; and to print a Web page's HTML source code, choose View, HTML Source before printing.

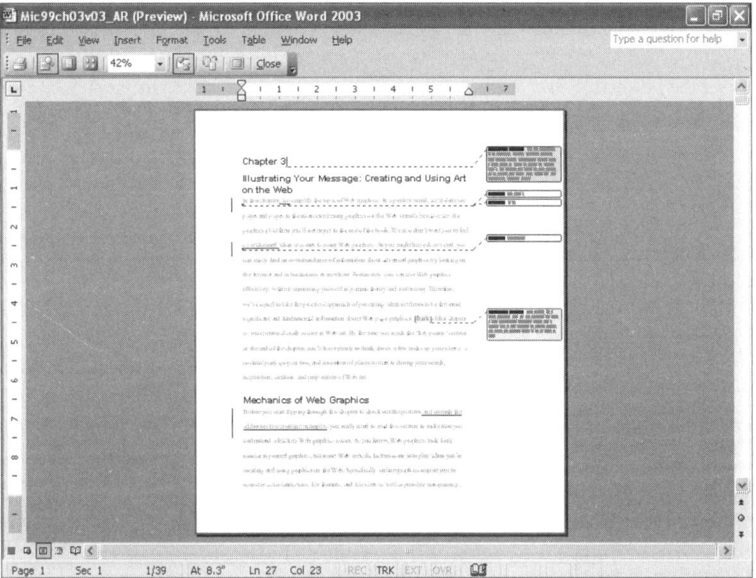

Figure 3-5. A document printed with markup shows all tracked changes and comments along with the document's contents, similar to how a marked-up document appears in Print Preview mode.

- **Styles** Creates an alphabetical list of styles used in the current document. Each list entry includes the style's parameters, in *reveal formatting* style. For example, an excerpt from a Styles printout might look like this:

> **Bull List**
> Normal + Indent: Left: 0", Hanging: 0.25", Line spacing: 1.5 lines, Space Before: 3 pt, After: 6 pt, Tabs: 0.5", Left, Bulleted
>
> **Caption**
> Style for Next Paragraph: Normal
> Normal + Font: Italic, Indent: First line: 0", Line spacing: 1.5 lines, Space Before: 0 pt, After: 6 pt
>
> **Comment Reference**
> Default Paragraph Font + Font: 8 pt

For more information about creating and using styles, see Chapter 9, "Using Styles to Increase Your Formatting Power."

- **AutoText Entries** Prints a complete alphabetical list of the AutoText entries associated with the template attached to the current document. By default, the Normal.dot template is attached to documents if no other template has been specified.

For more information about AutoText, see Chapter 7, "Putting Text Tools to Work."

- Key Assignments Prints an alphabetical list of custom shortcut keys created for standard Word commands or macros.

For more information about working with macros, see Chapter 32, "Creating and Working with VBA Macros."

Troubleshooting

Printing a markup list for a page range doesn't work

Unfortunately, you can't print a markup list for a range of pages—you have to print either a complete list of all the changes made to an entire document or none at all. Luckily, if you're flexible, you can work around this limitation. The easiest approach is to forget about the list and instead print a range of pages using the Document Showing Markup option. You'll be able to see the tracked changes and comments in this view—it just won't be printed in list format (and in many cases, the changes make more sense when you see them in a document instead of listed one after another). Of course, in some instances, you might really need to print a list of markups for a range of pages. Don't worry—there's still hope. One way you can accomplish this is to follow these easy steps:

1. Make sure the marked-up document is open in Word with the changes visible.
2. Select the range you want to use to generate a markup list, and copy it to the Clipboard (press Ctrl+C or click Copy on the Standard toolbar).
3. Click the New Blank Document button.
4. Paste the copied selection into the new blank document.
5. Display the Print dialog box (press Ctrl+P or choose File, Print), select List Of Markup in the Print What drop-down list, and then click OK.
6. After the list is printed, close the new blank document without saving it.

Printing Draft Copies

In some instances, you might want to quickly print a document's text without "extras" like formatting and graphics. In these cases, you can print a draft copy, if your printer supports this option. You can activate the draft printing feature using one of these techniques:

- Choose Tools, Options, click the Print tab (shown in Figure 3-6), select the Draft Output check box in the Printing Options section, and then click OK.

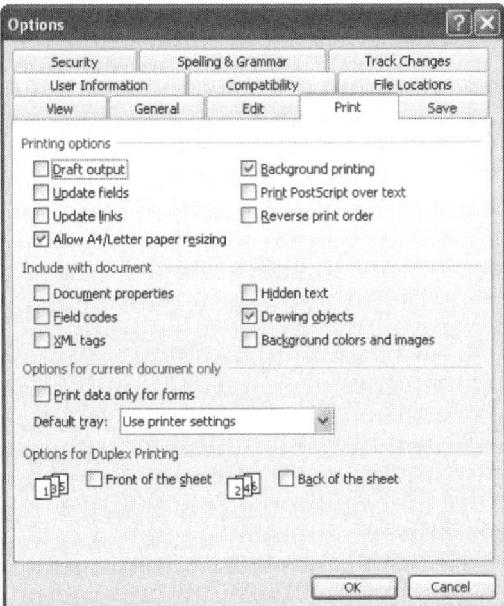

Figure 3-6. Print options are available in the Print tab in the Options dialog box, as shown here, or by clicking the Options button in the Print dialog box.

- Display the Print dialog box, click the Options button, select the Draft Output check box, and then click OK.

When you print a document using Draft mode, your printed document will contain minimal formatting and no graphics.

Printing Several Pages Per Sheet

In Word, you can print more than one document page on a single sheet of paper. This feature, introduced in Word 2000, helps you to better see a document's layout and can be used to present information in a visually concise manner. You'll find that printing several pages per sheet is similar to previewing multiple pages in Print Preview mode. (The difference is that the printed pages generally provide a clearer view of the pages' contents.) When you print multiple pages on a single sheet of paper, Word shrinks the pages to the appropriate size for printing purposes. To set up this arrangement, follow these steps:

1. Press Ctrl+P or choose File, Print.
2. In the Zoom section of the Print dialog box, select the number of pages per sheet you want to print in the Pages Per Sheet drop-down list. You can print up to 16 pages per sheet.

> **Note** The Pages Per Sheet feature has a few limitations. First, you must use the values in the Pages Per Sheet drop-down list to specify the number of pages to be printed—you can't type a value. In addition, the feature is available only when the Document or Document Showing Markup option is selected in the Print What list.

Scaling Printed Documents

Just as you can reduce and enlarge copies when you use a photocopier, you can reduce and enlarge your print output in Word by using the Scale To Paper Size feature. Scaling documents can come in handy when you are printing on nonstandard paper sizes or when you want to shrink your output slightly to ensure that information isn't cut off by margin settings.

The key to scaling documents is to use the Scale To Paper Size list, which is located in the Zoom section in the Print dialog box. The Scale To Paper Size list includes a variety of sizing options, including Letter, Legal, A4, various envelope sizes, and so forth. To view the list of options, click the Scale To Paper Size list. By default, the No Scaling option is selected.

> **Note** Scaling a document using the Print dialog box scales your document for the current printing session only; it doesn't resize or alter the document's contents, unlike the Shrink To Fit feature in Print Preview mode, which modifies the formatting in your document.

Printing XML Tags

When you work with an XML document, you can configure Word to include the XML tags in the printed document whether or not you're working with the XML tags visible onscreen. Printing an XML document—XML tags and all—is a simple matter of selecting the XML Tags check box before you print, in either of the following ways:

- Choose Tools, Options, click the Print tab (shown previously in Figure 3-6), select the XML Tags check box, and then click OK.
- Display the Print dialog box, click Options, select the XML Tags check box, and then click OK.

After you select the XMLTags check box, the tags will appear, embedded in the document, when you print. To hide the XML tags in a printed document, ensure that the XML Tags check box in the print options is cleared.

Printing Background Colors and Images

If your document uses background colors or images (such as a watermark), you can specify whether to print the colors or images when you print the document. To control background color and image printing, perform either of the following actions:

- Choose Tools, Options, click the Print tab (shown previously in Figure 3-6), select the Background Colors And Images check box, and then click OK.
- Display the Print dialog box, click Options, select the Background Colors And Images check box, and then click OK.

To revert to the default setting of not printing background colors and images, make sure the Background Colors And Images check box in the print options is cleared.

Using INCLUDETEXT to Print Information from Multiple Documents

You can use the INCLUDETEXT field to insert (and subsequently print) text and graphics from named documents into the current document. To accomplish this, simply insert the INCLUDETEXT field where you want to insert the contents of another document (for example, at the end of the active document), and then print.

To include the contents of an entire document within the current document when you print, follow these steps:

1. Position the insertion point where you want the included text to display and print.
2. Click Insert, Field.
3. In the Field dialog box, select IncludeText in the Field Names list, and specify the included document's path in the File Name Or URL text box, as shown in Figure 3-7.

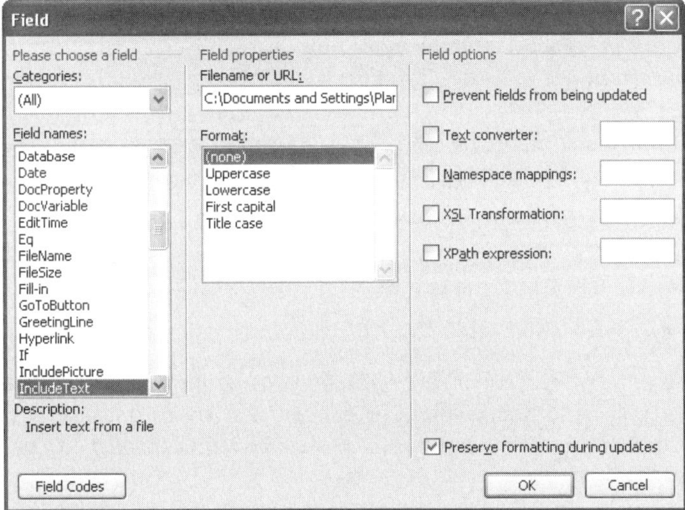

Figure 3-7. You can use the INCLUDETEXT field to help manage and print long documents and multipart publications.

4. Click OK.

You can control how field codes appear in your document by selecting the Field Codes check box and setting the Field Shading list in the View tab in the Options dialog box (by choosing Tools, Options, and then display the View tab). After you add the INCLUDETEXT field, the content of the included documents will print when you print the active document.

For more information about using fields, see Chapter 31, "Working with Field Codes and Custom Forms."

Printing Data from a Form

In Word, you can print only the data entered in a form by selecting the settings in the Print tab, as described here:

1. Open the document containing the data you want to print.
2. Choose Tools, Options, and then click the Print tab.
3. In the Options For Current Document Only section, select the Print Data Only For Forms check box, and then click OK.
4. Click the Print button on the Standard toolbar.

Creating a Print File

At times, you might want to create a print file instead of sending your document to your local printer. Usually, print files are created when a file needs to be printed on another printer (generally one of higher quality). For example, if you create a work document in your home office, you might want to create a print file so that you can print the document on your company's high-quality color printer. Alternatively, perhaps you have developed a magazine or newsletter on your computer at work, but you want to submit a print file to a print shop so that they can create the final version.

Essentially, when you create a print file, you save your document in a format that another printer can recognize. When you print to a file, Word preserves the document's layout information, such as font spacing, line breaks, and page breaks.

To create a print file, follow these steps:

1. Determine which printer (for example, a PostScript printer) will be used, and install a printer driver for that printer, if necessary. (Ask your print shop or network administrator for a copy of the appropriate printer driver if you need one, or download it from the Web.)
2. Display the Print dialog box (by choosing File, Print, or pressing Ctrl+P).
3. In the Name list, select the printer that will print the file.
4. Select the Print To File check box, and then click OK to display the Print To File dialog box, which looks similar to the Save As dialog box.
5. Navigate to the location in which you want to save the print file, type a name for the print file in the File Name box, and then click OK. Word saves the file with a .prn extension.

Setting Printing Options

In addition to the options available in the Print dialog box, Word offers a number of other printing options, some of which are discussed in more detail earlier in this chapter. You can find these print options by choosing Tools, Options, and then clicking the Print tab, or by clicking Options in the Print dialog box. Table 3-2 summarizes the options available in the Printing Options section (the top portion) of the Print tab and Print dialog box.

Table 3-2. Printing Options

Option	Description
Draft Output	Prints a document without formatting and graphics (as described in the section "Printing Draft Copies," on page 104).
Update Fields	Updates fields before printing. For example, when this option is selected, date and time fields will be updated when you print.
Update Links	Updates links to other documents before printing. For example, if a linked document has changed, the linked content will be updated before printing.
Allow A4/Letter Paper Resizing	Enables automatic switching between standard 8 ½-by-11 paper and the narrower, slightly longer A4 paper size used in most countries. This option is selected by default.
Background Printing	Enables you to continue working while print tasks are being processed (although you might notice a slight slowing in response times as you work). This option is selected by default.
Print PostScript Over Text	Prints PostScript code (such as watermarks or overprinted text) inserted in a document on top of the text, not underneath it.
Reverse Print Order	Prints a document in reverse order, beginning with the document's last page.

In addition to the options listed in Table 3-2, the Print tab offers options that enable you to perform the following tasks (some of which are discussed in more detail earlier in this chapter):

- Print various elements of a document in addition to your print tasks, such as printing a summary of the document properties, field codes (instead of field contents), XML tags, hidden text, drawing objects, and background colors and images.
- Print only the data inserted in a form.
- Specify a default paper source.
- Configure duplex page order printing options for printers that can print on both sides of a sheet of paper.

For more information about selecting paper sources, see Chapter 15, "Mastering Page Setup and Pagination."

Troubleshooting

A printing error message appears after I send a document to be printed

First and foremost, if your printer generally works without a hitch but is not responding at the moment, check your hardware. Perform the following simple (yet important and sometimes overlooked) checks:

- Make sure that the toner or ink cartridge isn't empty.
- Verify that the paper tray contains paper.
- Clear any paper jams, and reset the printer if necessary.
- Check that the printer connections (wires, plugs, and contacts) are secure and firmly in place.
- Make sure that the online light is lit, if the printer is an older model.
- Verify that you can manually print a test page. (Refer to your printer's manual for instructions on manually printing a test page.)

If all the hardware components seem to be in working order, your next step is to look at the software side of the problem. The main software tasks you might have to perform if Word can't find a printer when you send your document to be printed are listed here.

- **Installing or reinstalling a default printer driver** You might have to install a printer driver from the printer's installation CD-ROM or the Windows CD-ROM, or download a driver from the manufacturer's Web site.
- **Fixing a damaged Windows registry entry** You can try to fix a damaged Windows registry entry for your default printer by setting another printer as the default printer, and then resetting your original printer as the default to overwrite the damaged Windows registry entry.
- **Correcting a device conflict on the printer port** If you can't print on your local printer, you might have a printer port conflict. To correct this conflict, try using the Windows Device Manager to remove and reinstall the printer port.

For detailed instructions regarding these procedures, visit the Microsoft Knowledge Base online, at *http://support.microsoft.com*. You might want to start by reviewing article number 291336.

Chapter 4

Honing Document Navigation Skills

As an experienced Word user, you've undoubtedly grown accustomed to using a few standard techniques for finding files and winding your way through documents. For instance, most people locate and open documents using common navigation tools such as Windows Explorer and the Open dialog box. They can then navigate through open Word documents using scroll bars, keyboard keys (such as Page Up and Page Down), and keyboard shortcuts. In addition to these standard means of document navigation, you can use several other Word tools to find and navigate through documents, including the Basic File Search and Advanced File Search task panes; the Document Map; the Find, Replace, and Go To features; and the File Search dialog box. This chapter takes a look at Word's document navigation tools—the ones that go above and beyond basic document navigation.

The Many Faces of Document Navigation

Word provides numerous document navigation tools, some of which don't even seem like document navigation tools on the surface. This chapter presents the main navigation tools beyond basic browsing, but other means of moving through documents are discussed elsewhere in this book. For example, you can move through documents using the following techniques:

- Jump to marked locations within your document by using bookmarks. (Bookmarks are introduced in "Creating Bookmarks for Document Navigation," on page 133, and are described in more detail in Chapter 23, "Configuring Footnotes, Endnotes, and Cross-References.")
- Browse from component to component using the Select Browse Object options. (Browsing is introduced in Chapter 2, "Mastering Document Fundamentals," and is discussed further in this chapter in "Jumping to Document Areas Using the Go To and Select Browse Object Options," on page 132.)

- Move quickly from section to section using outline levels. (See Chapter 10, "Outlining Documents for Clarity and Structure.")
- Work with multiple-file documents using Master Documents. (See Chapter 20, "Creating and Controlling Master Documents.")

Keep in mind that the ultimate goal is to become comfortable with the various document navigation tools so that you can access the information you need efficiently and almost automatically.

Conducting Basic and Advanced Searches

Before you learn how to search within documents, you should take a look at how to search among documents. As mentioned, you can find documents using the Basic File Search and Advanced File Search task pane as well as the File Search dialog box. Using these tools, you can conduct basic and advanced searches. You use the Basic File Search task pane when you want to find files, Outlook items, or Web pages containing various forms of text, and you use the Advanced File Search task pane when you want to find files based on file properties, such as author name, file name, date last modified, and so forth. To access the Basic File Search task pane, choose File, File Search (or press Alt+F+H). To access the Advanced File Search task pane, click the Advanced File Search link in the Basic File Search task pane.

By default, the search task pane appears in the last search view you used to conduct a search—either Basic File Search or Advanced File Search. If the Advanced File Search view is visible, you can access the Basic File Search options by clicking the Basic File Search link in the See Also section of the task pane. Likewise, if the Basic File Search view is visible, you can access the Advanced File Search view by clicking the Advanced File Search link in the See Also section in the task pane. Figures 4-1 and 4-2 show the Basic File Search and Advanced File Search task pane views.

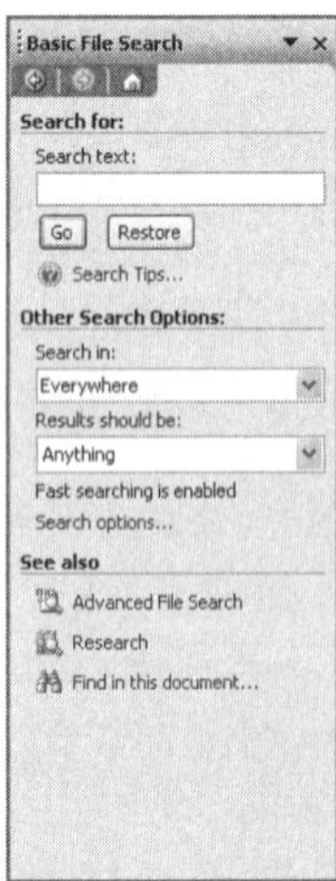

Figure 4-1. The Basic File Search task pane view enables you to search documents using text strings, file location information, and file types.

Figure 4-2. The Advanced File Search task pane view enables you to search for documents based on properties and conditions in addition to file location information and file types.

The File Search dialog box offers search capabilities similar to those of the File Search task panes. You display the File Search dialog box from within the Open dialog box. This approach to searching for documents is handy if you're already in the Open dialog box and you're not sure where a particular document is stored.To view the File Search dialog box, perform the following steps:

1. Choose File, Open, press Ctrl+O, or click the Open button on the Standard toolbar to display the Open dialog box.
2. In the Open dialog box, choose Tools, Search.

The File Search dialog box contains Basic and Advanced tabs, shown in Figures 4-3 and 4-4, which provide options similar to those available in the Basic File Search and Advanced File Search task panes (compare Figures 4-1 and 4-2).

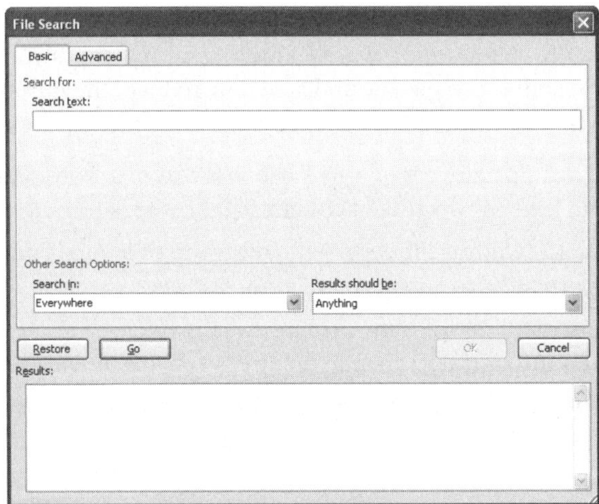

Figure 4-3. The options in the Basic tab in the File Search dialog box correspond to the Basic File Search task pane options.

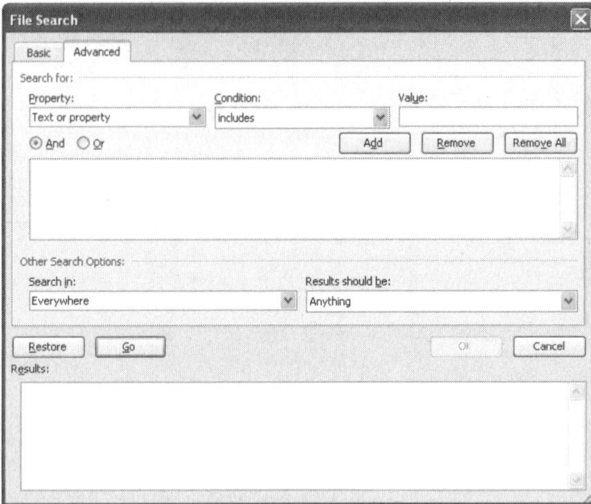

Figure 4-4. The options in the Advanced tab in the File Search dialog box correspond to the Advanced File Search task pane options.

To use the File Search dialog box and the File Search task pane options, you perform similar procedures. In this chapter, we look primarily at how to use the File Search task pane options, but you can use the same techniques in the File Search dialog box.

Using Basic File Search to Find Documents

One of the most common ways to search for documents is to look for a particular character, word, or phrase in your documents' file names and contents. In Word, you can search among documents located on your computer and in network locations by entering text strings in the Basic File Search task pane view.

Using Basic File Search is similar to using online search engines, such as Google and MSN Search. Word (and other programs in the Microsoft Office System, for that matter) lets you base your search on one or more characters or words. Entering more than one word in the Search Text box makes your search more specific and generally reduces the number of documents returned in your Search Results. In addition, keep in mind the following search tips:

- By default, a basic search finds files containing various forms of a word. For example, searching for **run** would find any document containing the words *run*, *running*, or *ran*.
- You can use the asterisk (*) wildcard to represent any group of letters. For example, entering **l*st** would return any documents containing *last*, *least*, *lowest*, and so forth.
- You can use the question mark (?) wildcard to represent any single character. For example, entering **l?st** would return any documents containing *last*, *lest*, *list*, *lost*, or *lust*.
- If you're searching among Outlook items only (including e-mail messages, calendar items, contacts, tasks, journal entries, and notes) and you're using an English-language version of Word 2003, you can use *natural language searching*. With natural language

searching, you can enter phrases, such as **Find all tasks completed yesterday**, to find information. (Note that natural language searches have some limitations—for example, you can't use a natural language search to look through Outlook public folders.)

> **Tip** For additional search tips, click the Search Tips link in the Basic Search task pane view.

After you define your search text, you can choose to search any of the following document storage areas, found in the Search In list box:

- **Everywhere** Searches all folders and embedded folders included in My Computer, My Network Places, and Outlook.
- **My Computer** Includes all the drives and folders on your computer, including mapped drives.You can select My Computer to search through everything on your computer, or you can pick and choose which folders and files you want to include in your search.
- **My Network Places** Includes all folders stored on network file servers,Web servers, or Microsoft Exchange servers that are configured as Network Places. Keep in mind that some networked locations don't support searching.
- **Outlook** Searches all the messages, appointments, contacts, tasks, and other information stored in your Outlook folders.

> **Tip** If you know exactly where the folder you want to search is located, you can type the folder's path directly in the Search In box.

The steps for conducting a basic file search are as follows:

1. Choose File, File Search.
2. In the Search For section of the Basic File Search task pane view, type your search text in the Search Text box.
3. In the Other Search Options section, click the Search In arrow. Select check boxes for the drives, folders, files, or whatever you want to search for in the intended document, as shown in Figure 4-5, and then click outside the list to close it. If you select folder check boxes other than Everywhere, My Computer, My Network Places, or Outlook, you can use multiple clicks to achieve the following results:
   - One click selects the folder.
   - Two clicks selects the folder and the folders within it.
   - Three clicks selects only the folders within the top-level folder.
   - Four clicks deselects all folders within the folder.

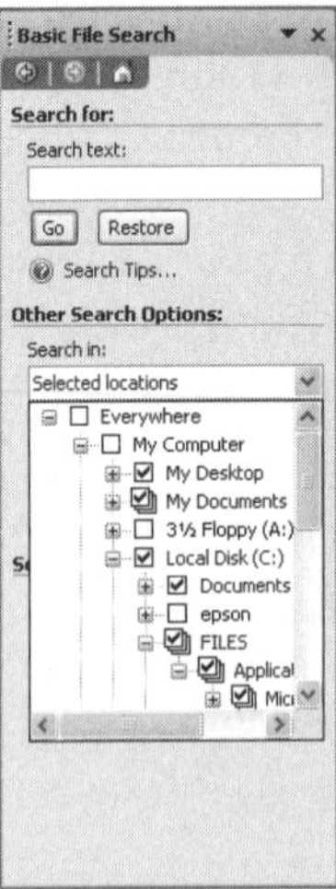

Figure 4-5. Click plus sign icons to expand your view, and select check boxes to indicate that you want Word to search within a selected drive, folder, or file. Notice the "stacked" check boxes, which indicate that subfolders will be included in the current search.

4 Click the Results Should Be list box, select which types of files you want to include in your search, and click outside the list box to close it. For example, if you want to search only Word files, make sure that only the Word check box is selected under Office Files, as shown in Figure 4-6.

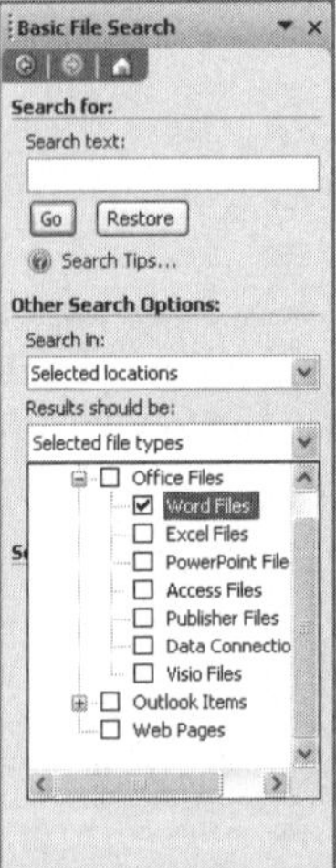

Figure 4-6. You can pick and choose which types of files you want to include in your document search.

The Results Should Be options include the following:

- **Anything** Specifies the broadest set of file types, including file types not typically associated with Office.
- **Office Files** Specifies Office documents, including Word, Excel, PowerPoint, Access, Publisher, Data Connection, and Visio files. You can limit which Office documents to search among by selecting the check boxes next to specific Office applications.
- **Outlook Items** Specifies e-mail messages, appointments, contacts, tasks, and notes.
- **Web Pages** Specifies Web pages (.htm or .html), Web archives (.mht or .mhtml), and other Web-related formats (such as .asp).

5 After you've configured your basic search parameters, click Go.

When you click Go, the Basic File Search task pane view changes to the Search Results task pane view. The search results are divided into My Computer, My Network Places, and Outlook categories which correspond to the options you selected in the Basic File Search task pane (for example, if you didn't check My Computer, the My Computer search results heading won't appear in the Search Results task pane). While the search is being processed, you'll see *(Searching)* next to category headings. If no results are found in a particular category, you'll see *(No Results Found)* next to the category heading. If the search seems to be taking too long, you can click the Stop button to end the procedure. (After the search is completed, the Stop button changes to the Modify button.) Figure 4-7 shows the results of a completed search. Notice that each search result item is accompanied by an icon that identifies the item's file type.

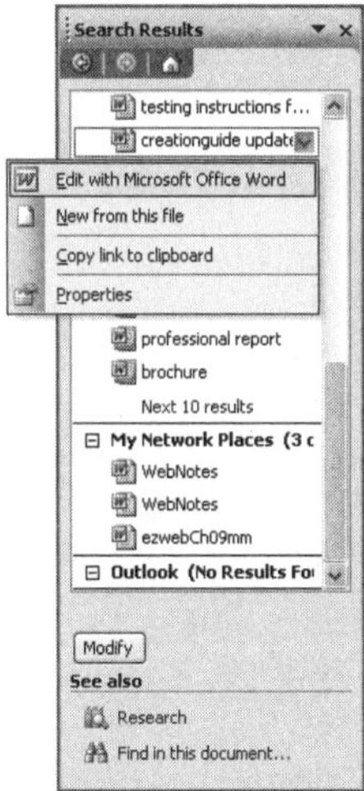

Figure 4-7. You can perform a variety of actions on your search results using the menu commands associated with each item.

After the search is completed, you can perform any of the following actions on the items in the Search Results task pane view:

- **View document properties.** Hover the pointer over an item in the search results list, or hover over the item, and then click the item's arrow and choose Properties from the menu to view a more comprehensive summary of the document's properties.

- **Open an item in its default application.** Click a search result item.
- **Edit an item using a corresponding Office application.** Click the item's arrow (as shown in Figure 4-7), and choose to edit the document.
- **Create a new document based on the existing document.** Click the item's arrow, and choose New From This File.
- **Store a hyperlink to an item on the Office Clipboard.** Click the item's arrow, and choose Copy Link To Clipboard.
- **View additional search result items.** Click the Next *x* Results link at the bottom of the list of search results.
- **Conduct a new search or modify the search text.** Click the Modify button, and change your search parameters.

Note Unfortunately, when you open a document from the search results list, the search term isn't selected within the document. To further compound the problem, you can't reliably use the Find utility (as described in the section "Finding Text and Elements Within the Current Document," on page 123) to highlight your search term(s) within documents because all forms of the search term are included in the results (such as eat, eating, and ate for the search term eat). To help eliminate extraneous documents in your search results list, consider using at least two-word target phrases when searching and enclose exact phrases in quotation marks whenever possible. By enclosing multiple words or phrases in quotation marks, you indicate that the search terms should be combined to make a single search string.

Conducting Advanced File Searches Based on Document Properties

As mentioned, in addition to searching for text strings in documents, you can conduct advanced searches based on document properties. Advanced file searches enable you to enter more detailed search criteria by specifying document properties, conditions, and values. To conduct an advanced file search, follow these steps:

1. Choose File, File Search, and then click the Advanced File Search link in the See Also section of the Basic File Search task pane to display the Advanced File Search task pane view.
2. In the Advanced File Search task pane view, click the Property arrow, and select the document property you want to use to conduct your search.
3. Click the Condition arrow, and select a condition. Only certain conditions are available for each property.
4. In the Value box, type a value associated with the specified property and condition.
5. Click Add. The search parameter (consisting of the property, condition, and value you specified) will appear in the list, which is located below the Add button.

Note If you type a value that's invalid for a property or condition, the Add button will remain unavailable.

6 You can narrow your search by adding more search parameters if desired. To do so, select another property and condition, type a value, and then click And or Or. If you click And, each search result document must match both search parameters before it can be included in your search results. If you click Or, any document containing either search parameter is included in your search result.

7 Click Add.

Tip If you add a search parameter to an advanced search that you later decide you don't want to include, select the search parameter, and click Remove in the Advanced File Search task pane. Or if you want to clear your search parameters entirely, click Remove All.

8 After you've specified your search parameters, select an item in the Search In and Results Should Be list boxes in the Other Search Options section. (The settings in these list boxes are described in "Using Basic File Search to Find Documents," on page 114.) Then click Go.

Figure 4-8 shows an example of an advanced search, with two search parameters set and a third search parameter about to be added to the list.

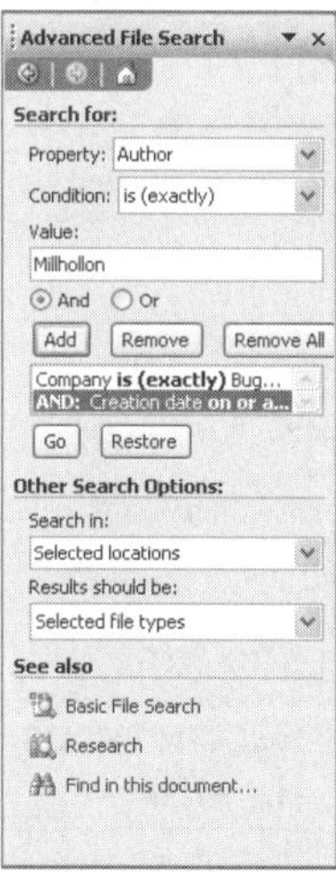

Figure 4-8. Using the And option narrows an advanced search, whereas using the Or option expands your search.

You can perform the same actions on advanced search results as on basic search results, as described earlier in the chapter. For example, you can hover the pointer over a search result item to view document properties, or you can click a search result item to open the item in its default application.

Speeding Search Tasks Using the Indexing Service

You can speed up your searches by enabling Fast Searching and keeping your index up to date. Fast Searching speeds up your searches by taking advantage of the Windows Indexing Service. The Indexing Service extracts information from a set of documents and organizes the information in a way that makes searching quick and easy. This information includes text (content) as well as characteristics (properties) of documents.

Fast Searching is enabled by default in Microsoft Windows 98, Windows Millennium Edition (Windows Me), and Windows NT 4. To enable Fast Searching in Windows 2000 and Windows XP or to verify your Fast Searching status if you're using another version of Windows, perform these steps:

1. Choose File, File Search to display the Basic File Search task pane view. Directly above the Search Options link in the Other Search Options section, you should see a statement indicating whether Fast Searching is enabled or disabled.
2. Click the Search Options link.
3. In the Indexing Service Settings dialog box, choose Yes, Enable Indexing Service And Run When My Computer Is Idle, as shown in Figure 4-9, and then click OK. The File Search task panes will now show that fast searching is enabled.

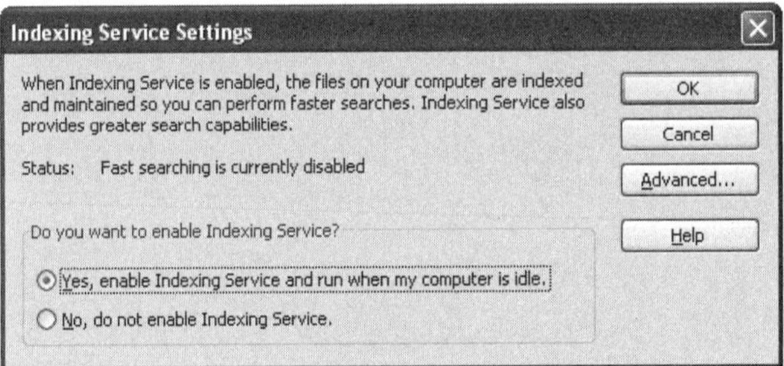

Figure 4-9. You can enable the Indexing Service from within Word.

To help guide your decision regarding whether you should enable the Indexing Service, Microsoft provides the "best practices" guidelines shown in Table 4-1.

Table 4-1. Recommended Computer Configuration for the Indexing Service

Number of Documents to Be Indexed	Minimum Memory (in MB)	Recommended Memory (in MB)
Fewer than 100,000	64	64
From 100,000 through 250,000	64	From 64 through 128
From 250,000 through 500,000	64	From 128 through 256
500,000 or more	128	256 or more

Troubleshooting

No search results appear for a search term after the indexing service is enabled

When the Indexing Service indexes documents, it ignores the words, letters, and numbers found in the Noise-Word List. If you try to search for a term that appears in the Noise-Word List, you won't get any search results.

Noise-Word List files are named Noise.*xxx*, where the three-letter extension indicates the language of the list. For example, Noise.enu refers to an English Noise-Word List. You can view the words your index disregards by choosing Start, Search, For Files Or Folders and searching for a file named Noise.*. You can edit the Noise.* document in any text editing program (such as WordPad). If you see a word in the list that you want indexed, simply delete the word from the Noise-Word List, and save the file.

Adhering to Search Query Rules After the Indexing Service Is Enabled

After you start the Indexing Service, keep the following rules in mind when you search for documents:

- Queries are not case-sensitive.
- You can't search for words appearing in the Noise-Word List.
- If you use a special character in your query (such as &, |, ^, #, @, or $), you must enclose the query in quotation marks to identify the enclosed information as a single search string unit.
- Date and time values should be in the form *yyyy/mm/dd hh:mm:ss* or *yyyy-mm-dd hh:mm:ss*. The first two characters of the year and the entire time can be omitted. If you omit the first two characters of the year, the date is assumed to be between 1930 and 2029. Further, you can add a 3-digit millisecond value after the seconds value. All dates are in Coordinated Universal Time, for example, 2002/11/20 13:42:03:123.
- Dates and times can be expressed relative to the current date and time by using a minus sign (-) followed by integer and time unit pairs. The acceptable time units are *y* (year), *q* (quarter, which is three months), *m* (months), *w* (week), *d* (day), *h* (hour), *n* (minutes), and *s* (seconds).
- Numeric values can be decimal or hexadecimal. Hexadecimal values should be preceded by *0x*.
- You can use the following Boolean operators or symbols: AND (&), OR (|), and NOT (&!). You can also use NEAR (~) in content queries (but not in property queries).

Accessing Document Areas Using the Document Map

Document Map

You can navigate through open documents in a number of ways. One way to navigate through a document is to use the Document Map feature. The Document Map appears as a separate pane along the left side of your window and contains a list of the headings in the document. The Document Map enables you to quickly jump to specific sections in your document in any view; it also serves as a quick reminder of your current location within the open document. Figure 4-10 shows a document with the Document Map open.

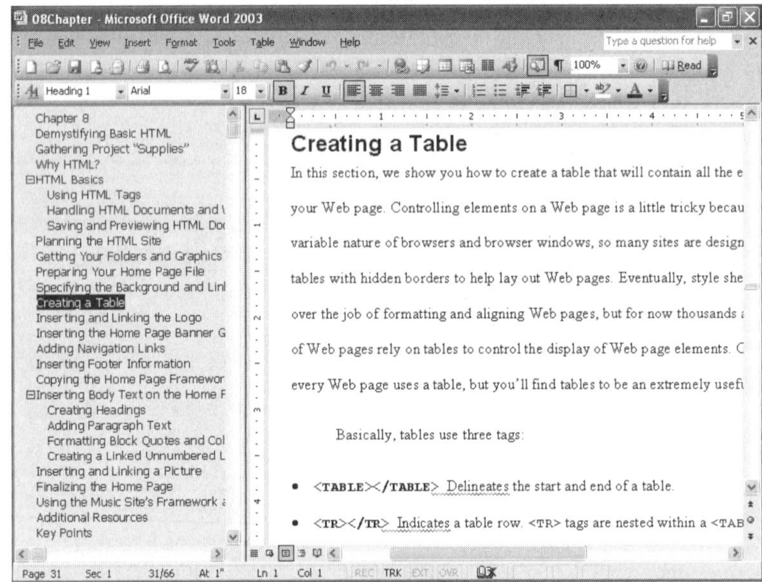

Figure 4-10. The Document Map enables you to click a section heading to display the section.

To use the Document Map effectively, your document must be formatted with built-in heading styles or outline-level paragraph formats. If your document doesn't use either of these built-in formatting settings, Word attempts to identify paragraphs that seem to be headings and displays them in the Document Map, but this approach is only nominally effective. To navigate through a document using the Document Map, follow these steps:

1. Click the Document Map button on the Standard toolbar, or choose View, Document Map. By default, all levels of headings are visible. To change the default setting, right-click the Document Map, and choose a heading level. You can also click the plus (+) and minus (-) signs next to headings with subheadings to expand and collapse sections.
2. Click a heading to jump to the corresponding section in the document window. The current section's heading is highlighted, so you can quickly see the current position of the insertion point within the document.
3. Close the Document Map by clicking the Document Map button, double-clicking the Document Map's resize bar (the bar adjacent to the vertical scroll bar), or choosing View, Document Map.

Troubleshooting

The text in the Document Map is too large

You can format the text in the Document Map to make it easier to work with. For example, changing the font and font size can make the Document Map text easier to read and headings easier to find. (When you reformat the Document Map text, you do not alter the actual heading styles in the document.) To modify the Document Map text, follow these steps:

1. Display the Document Map pane by clicking the Document Map button on the Standard toolbar or choosing View, Document Map.
2. Click the Styles And Formatting button on the Formatting toolbar, or choose Format, Styles And Formatting.
3. In the Styles And Formatting task pane, click the Show arrow, and select Custom.
4. In the Format Settings dialog box, select the Document Map check box in the Styles To Be Visible list box, and then click OK to return to the Styles And Formatting task pane.
5. Right-click Document Map in the Pick Formatting To Apply list box, choose Modify, configure the font style and size, and then click OK.

You can resize the Document Map by dragging the right edge of the Document Map pane. However, the custom settings are only retained for the current session. After you close and reopen the document, Word automatically sets the Document Map to one-fourth of the window's width.

Finding Text and Elements Within the Current Document

In addition to searching for documents and navigating through documents using the Document Map, you can search for text, graphics, and other document elements within the current document by using the Find, Replace, and Go To features. Find, Replace, and Go To are extremely popular tools among seasoned Word users because they are quick, accurate, and easy to use.

To access the Find tab in the Find And Replace dialog box, shown in Figure 4-11, choose Edit, Find, or press Ctrl+F. Alternatively, you can click the Find button on the Select Browse Object menu. (To display the Select Browse Object menu, click the Select Browse Object button located near the bottom of the vertical scroll bar, or press Ctrl+Alt+Home.)

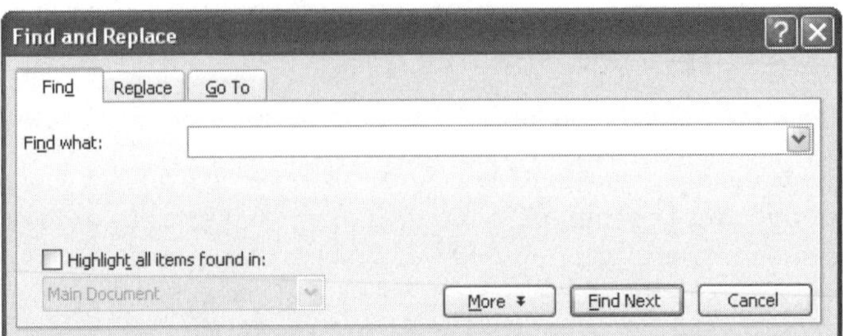

Figure 4-11. You can use the Find tab to locate instances of words, phrases, special characters, styles, and more.

In this section, you'll learn how to use the Find tab's various options; many of these options also appear in the Replace tab.

Tip **Add the Find button to the Standard toolbar**
To add the Find button to the Standard toolbar, click the arrow on the right end of the Standard toolbar, choose Add Or Remove Buttons, point to Standard, and then select the Find option.

Finding and Selecting Items

As an experienced Word user, you know that you can find characters, words, phrases, and text elements by typing a search string in the Find dialog box, and then clicking Find Next to move from one instance of the search string to the next. In addition to the standard instance-by-instance Find capabilities, you can select every instance of a character, word, phrase, or text element at one time with a single click. To select every instance of a search text string, follow these basic steps:

1. In the Find tab in the Find And Replace dialog box, type your search text in the Find What box.
2. Select the Highlight All Items Found In check box, ensure that Main Document is selected in the list, and then click Find All. (The Find Next button changes to the Find All button after you select the Highlight All Items Found In check box.)
3. Click Close to close the dialog box.

When all instances of a search string are selected, you can globally format the selected text by clicking toolbar buttons or applying Format menu options. You can also delete all the selected text by pressing Delete or Backspace. To deselect the selected text, simply click any area in your document that isn't highlighted.

Configuring Options in the Find Tab

In many cases, conducting a simple text search using the Find tab adequately serves your needs. But you'll also encounter situations when you want to further refine your search parameters. To define more specific searches or to search for document elements, you'll need to use the Find And Replace dialog box's additional options. To view the additional options in the Find tab, click the More button. The fully expanded Find tab is shown in Figure 4-12.

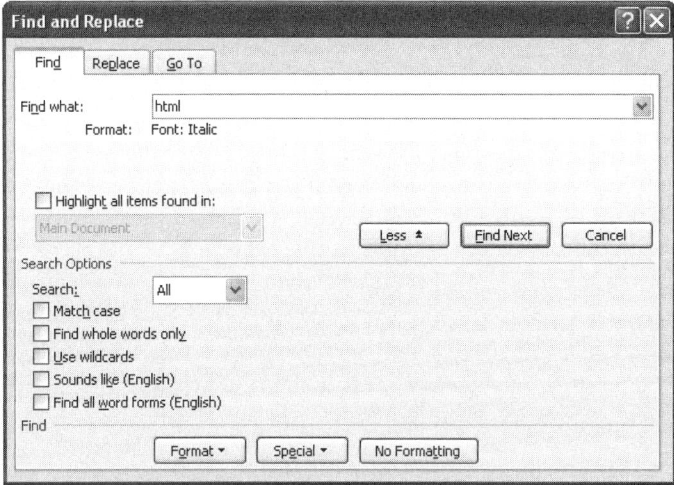

Figure 4-12. The expanded version of the Find dialog box provides access to search options as well as the Format, Special, and No Formatting buttons. Notice that the More button has changed to a Less button; you can click the Less button to shrink the dialog box to its original view.

The Find options in Word 2003 are fundamentally the same as the Find options in Word 2002 with a few added Special character options, so the advanced Find capabilities in this version of Word will be very familiar to Word 2002 users. But let's take a moment to review the expanded Find tab's options. (Keep in mind that most of these options are also available in the Replace tab.)

The following Search options are available in the expanded Find tab:

- **Search** Enables you to specify whether to search Down, Up, or All. When you choose All, Word searches the entire document by starting at the insertion point, searching to the end of the document, moving to the beginning of the document, and then searching until reaching the insertion point again. When you choose Down or Up, Word starts from the insertion point and searches only in the specified direction; with the Up and Down options, Word does not search headers, footers, footnotes, or comments.
- **Match Case** Specifies a search that distinguishes between uppercase and lowercase letters based on the text entered in the Find What box. This option is unavailable when you select the Use Wildcards, Sounds Like, or Find All Word Forms check box.
- **Find Whole Words Only** Searches only for whole words, not parts of longer words. For example, if you type **the** in the Find What box and select Find Whole Word Only, Word will ignore words that contain *the*, such as *them, there, other,* and so forth. This option is unavailable when you select the Use Wildcards, Sounds Like, or Find All Word Forms check box.

- **Use Wildcards** Enables you to use wildcard characters in place of text to expand and refine your searches. If you enter wildcard characters in the Find What box without selecting the Use Wildcards option, Word will treat the wildcards as plain text. Table 4-2 lists the wildcards you can use in the Find And Replace dialog box. When the Use Wildcards check box is selected and you want to search for a character that is also a wildcard, precede the character with a backslash (\). For example, to search for an asterisk, you must enter *.
- **Sounds Like (English)** Searches for terms that sound like the word or words entered in the Find What box. For example, if you enter **eight** in the Find What box, and then select the Sounds Like check box, Word will find all instances of *eight* as well as *ate*. This feature works only with legitimate words—entering the number **8** and selecting the Sounds Like check box won't return *eight*, *ate*, or *8*, and entering **u r** won't return *you are*.
- **Find All Word Forms (English)** Searches for all forms of the word entered in the Find What box. For example, if you enter **speak** in the Find What box, Word will find *speak*, *speaking*, *spoke*, *spoken*, *speaks*, and so forth.

Table 4-2. Using Wildcards in the Find And Replace Dialog Box

Wildcard	Specifies	Example
?	Any single character	**p?t** finds *pet*, *pat*, *pit*, and so forth.
*	Any string of characters	**p*t** finds *pest*, *parrot*, *pit*, and so forth.
<	Finds the text at the beginning of a word	**<(mark)** finds *market* but not *demark*.
>	Finds the text at the end of a word	**(ter)>** finds *winter* but not *terrain*.
[ ]	Finds one of the enclosed characters	**t[oa]n** finds *ton* and *tan*.
[-]	Finds any character within the specified range	**[r-t]ight** finds *right*, *sight*, and *tight*.
[!x-z]	Finds any single character except characters in the range inside the brackets	**cl[!a-m]ck** finds *clock* and *cluck* but not *clack* or *click*.
{*n*}	Finds exactly *n* occurrences of the preceding character or expression	**ble{2}d** finds *bleed* but not *bled*.
{*n*,}	Finds at least *n* occurrences of the preceding character or expression	**fe{1,}d** finds *fed* and *feed*.
{*n*,*m*}	Finds from *n* to *m* occurrences of the preceding character or expression	**10{1,3}** finds *10*, *100*, and *1000*.
@	Finds one or more occurrences of the preceding character or expression	**mo@d** finds *mod* and *mood*.

Finding Instances of Formatting

In addition to finding text strings, you can find (and replace) various formatting settings. To view the available formatting parameters in the expanded Find tab, click Format, as shown in Figure 4-13.

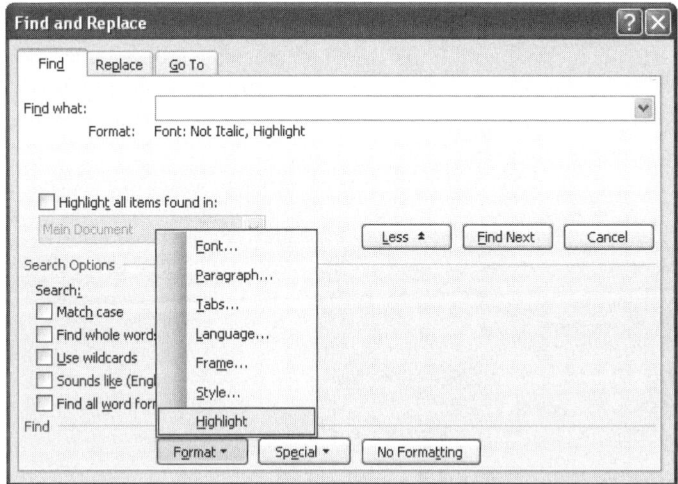

Figure 4-13. You can find instances of formatting by choosing options from the Format menu.

Choosing Font, Paragraph, Tabs, Language, Frame, or Style from the Format menu displays the corresponding formatting dialog box. For example, choosing Font displays a dialog box named Find Font, which looks very similar to the Font dialog box. Choosing the Highlight option lets you specify highlighted or unhighlighted text in the Find What box. For example, choose Highlight once to find highlighted text, choose Highlight again to indicate that you want to find text that is not highlighted, and choose Highlight a third time to find all instances of the search text regardless of highlighting. When formatting is applied to text in the Find What box, the formatting information appears below the Find What box, as you can see in Figure 4-13.

Tip **Control formatting using keyboard shortcuts**

You can control basic character formatting by using keyboard shortcuts. To do so, click in the Find What box and press keyboard shortcuts such as Ctrl+B (bold), Ctrl+I (italic), and Ctrl+U (underline) to toggle among applied, not applied, and neither (which equates to no formatting) settings.

You can find instances of formatting without entering text in the Find What box. For example, the configuration shown in Figure 4-13 will find only instances of highlighted text that isn't italic in the current document. You can, of course, specify text in combination with formatting settings if that's what you need to find.

To clear all formatting commands in the Find What box, click the No Formatting button. You'll want to clear formatting when you complete one Find operation and are ready to conduct another.

Finding Special Characters Using Codes

Word further expands your search capabilities by providing special codes you can use to find document elements, such as paragraph marks, tab characters, endnote marks, and so forth. To view the available special characters, click Special in the Find And Replace dialog box, as shown in Figure 4-14. Notice that this list has grown from past versions of Word to include the Section Character and Paragraph Character options.

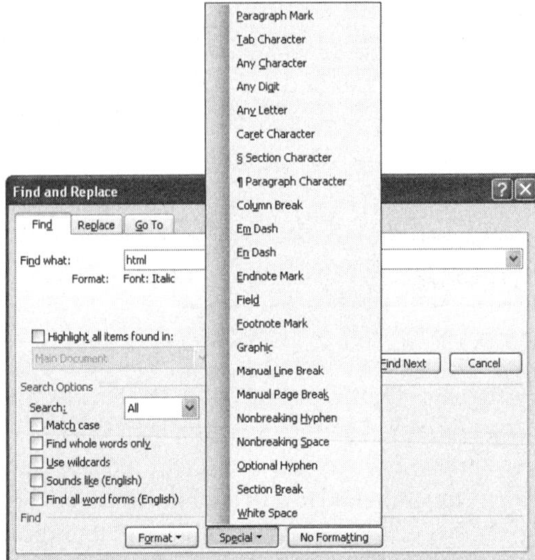

Figure 4-14. You can search for special character and document elements by choosing options from the Special menu or by inserting character codes directly in the Find What box (or the Replace With box in the Replace tab).

When you choose an option from the Special menu, a code is inserted in the Find What box. If you'd prefer, you can enter a code directly in the Find What box. Table 4-3 lists some commonly used special character codes. (Notice that some codes can be used only in the Find What or Replace With box, and that the Use Wildcards option must be turned on or off in certain instances.)

> **Note** Word can't find floating objects, WordArt, text effects (such as Marching Black Ants), watermarks, or drawing objects. However, if you change a floating object into an inline object, Word can find the object.

Table 4-3. Using Special Character Codes in the Find And Replace Dialog Box

Special Character	Code	Find And Replace Box
ANSI or ASCII characters	^0*nnn* (where *nnn* is the character code)	Find What; Replace With
Any Character	^?	Find What (with the Use Wildcards check box cleared)
Any Digit	^#	Find What (with the Use Wildcards check box cleared)
Any Letter	^$	Find What (with the Use Wildcards check box cleared)
Caret Character	^^	Find What; Replace With
Clipboard Contents	^c	Replace With
Column Break	^n	Find What; Replace With
Em Dash	^+	Find What; Replace With
En Dash	^=	Find What; Replace With
Endnote Mark	^e	Find What (with the Use Wildcards check box cleared)
Field	^d	Find What (with the Use Wildcards check box cleared)
Find What Text	^&	Replace With
Footnote Mark	^f	Find What (with the Use Wildcards check box cleared)
Graphic	^g	Find What (with the Use Wildcards check box selected)
Manual Line Break	^l	Find What; Replace With
Manual Page Break	^m	Replace With
Nonbreaking hyphen	^~	Find What; Replace With
Nonbreaking space	^s	Find What; Replace With
Optional Hyphen	^-	Find What; Replace With
NEW FEATURE! Paragraph Character	^v	Find What, Replace With
Paragraph Mark	^p	Find What (with the Use Wildcards check box cleared); Replace With
Section Break	^b	Find What (with the Use Wildcards check box cleared)
NEW FEATURE! Section Character	^%	Find What, Replace With
Tab Character	^t	Find What; Replace With
White Space	^w	Find What (with the Use Wildcards check box cleared)

Replacing Text

Often, you'll want to find text to replace it with something else. In Word, you use the Replace tab in the Find And Replace dialog box. The Replace tab contains the options available in the Find tab, but it also includes a Replace With box, as shown in Figure 4-15. You can enter text, wildcards, formatting, and special characters codes in the Replace With box in the same way you enter information in the Find What box.

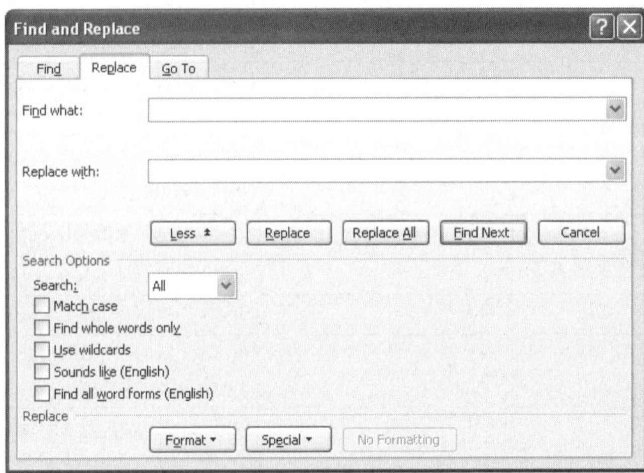

Figure 4-15. The expanded view of the Replace tab offers the same options found in the expanded Find tab in the Find And Replace dialog box.

To display the Replace tab in the Find And Replace dialog box, choose Edit, Replace, or press Ctrl+H. Type the text you want to find in the Find What box, and type the replacement information in the Replace With box. Then click one of the following buttons:

- **Replace** Replaces the currently selected instance of the Find What information with the Replace With information, and selects the next instance.
- **Replace All** Replaces all instances of the Find What information with the Replace With information. (Be careful when using Replace All—unless you have a very specific search element, it's usually safer to replace text and components on a case-by-case basis.)
- **Find Next** Skips the currently selected instance of the Find What information without replacing it, and selects the next instance.

Tip **Transpose words using the Replace feature**

Just as you did in the Find tab, you can use wildcards in the Replace tab. Here's a wildcard trick that uses parentheses and backslash wildcards to transpose words. It's especially useful when you'd like to switch a name from last name first to first name first. For example, type (Dunn), (Matthew) in the Find What box and type \2 \1 in the Replace With box. Select the Use Wildcards check box, click Find Next, and then click Replace. Word finds *Dunn, Matthew* and replaces it with *Matthew Dunn*. Placing the comma outside the parentheses ensures that it's eliminated when the replacement text is inserted.

Troubleshooting

I can't replace text with a graphic or an object

Although the Find And Replace dialog box doesn't directly support replacing text with graphics or objects, you can easily perform this action using the Clipboard and the ^c wildcard. You might want to use this feature to insert elements such as margin icons or recurring field combinations. To perform this procedure, follow these steps:

1. If placeholder text (such as **@@@**) is not already present, enter it where you want to insert the graphic or other element.
2. Copy the graphic or component you want to insert to the Clipboard.
3. Press Ctrl+H to display the Replace tab in the Find And Replace dialog box.
4. In the Find What box, type the placeholder text.
5. In the Replace With text box, enter **^c** to indicate the last item copied to the Clipboard.
6. Click Find Next and then click Replace, or click Replace All.

Finding or Replacing Special Characters—Keyboard Commands to the Rescue!

At times, you might want to find or replace special characters or symbols that aren't included on the Special menu in the Find And Replace dialog box. Don't worry—just because the character isn't included on the menu doesn't mean you can't find and replace it. You might have considered copying and pasting symbols into the Find And Replace dialog box, but when you open the Find And Replace dialog box, the Copy and Paste commands are unavailable on the Standard toolbar and the Edit menu. The trick is to use keyboard commands to copy (Ctrl+C) and paste (Ctrl+V) the characters into the Find And Replace dialog box.

For example, let's say you want to replace all ™ symbols (which are created by typing **(tm)** in your document) with ® symbols (which are created by typing **(r)** in your document). To replace ™ with ® throughout a document, follow these steps:

1. Press Ctrl+H to display the Replace tab in the Find And Replace dialog box.
2. Select an instance of ™ in your document (you might have to scroll through your document or drag the dialog box out of your way to do this), press Ctrl+C to copy the symbol, click in the Find What text box in the Find And Replace dialog box, and then press Ctrl+V to paste the symbol.
3. Next, select an instance of ® in the document (if it's not already in your document, you might have to create it so you can copy it), press Ctrl+C to copy the symbol, click in the Replace With text box in the Find And Replace dialog box, and then press Ctrl+V to paste the symbol.
4. Click Replace All.

Jumping to Document Areas Using the Go To and Select Browse Object Options

The third tab in the Find And Replace dialog box is the Go To tab, shown in Figure 4-16, which enables you to move quickly through a document, and go just about anywhere you'd like. For example, you can go directly to a page, section, line, bookmark, comment, footnote, endnote, field, table, graphic, equation, object, or heading.

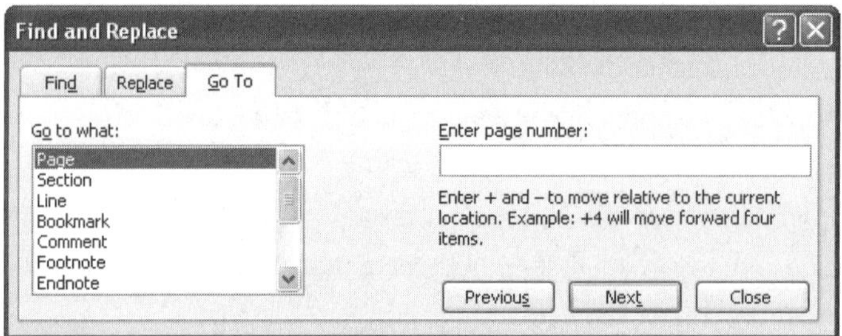

Figure 4-16. You can jump from area to area within a document using the Go To feature.

To display the Go To tab in the Find And Replace dialog box, perform any of the following actions:

- Choose Edit, Go To.
- Press F5 or Ctrl+G.
- Click the Go To button in the Select Browse Object menu. (To display the Select Browse Object menu, click the Select Browse Object button toward the bottom of the vertical scroll bar.)

To use the Go To tab, select a component in the Go To What list box, enter the appropriate value or parameter in the box to the right if necessary, and then click Go To (or click Previous or Next if no value or parameter is specified). Here are two possible uses for the Go To feature:

- To display a particular page in the document, select Page in the Go To What list box, type the page number in the Enter Page Number box, and then click Go To.
- To display the next heading in the document, select Heading in the Go To What list box, and then click Next without entering text in the text box.

You can also use the Select Browse Object menu to move from document element to document element. To display the Select Browse Object menu, click the Select Browse Object button on the vertical scroll bar. The Select Browse Object menu, shown in Figure 4-17, contains buttons that enable you to perform the following tasks:

- Display the Go To tab in the Find And Replace dialog box
- Display the Find tab in the Find And Replace dialog box
- Browse by edits (see Chapter 27, "Revising Documents Using Markup Tools")
- Browse by heading

- Browse by graphic
- Browse by table (see Chapter 13, "Organizing Concepts in Tables")
- Browse by field (see Chapter 31, "Working with Field Codes and Custom Forms")
- Browse by endnote (see Chapter 23, "Configuring Footnotes, Endnotes, and Cross-References")
- Browse by footnote (see Chapter 23, "Configuring Footnotes, Endnotes, and Cross-References")
- Browse by comment (see Chapter 27, "Revising Documents Using Markup Tools")
- Browse by section (see Chapter 19, "Formatting Columns and Sections for Advanced Text Control")
- Browse by page

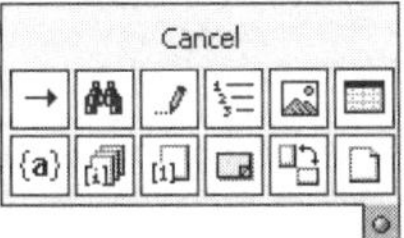

Figure 4-17. The Select Browse Object menu enables you to jump from component to component within a document.

After you choose an option from the Select Browse Object menu, you can click the Previous and Next arrow buttons (located above and below the Select Browse Object button on the vertical scroll bar) to move to the next and previous instances of the selected object.

For more information about the Select Browse Object tool, see Chapter 2, "Mastering Document Fundamentals."

Creating Bookmarks for Document Navigation

In addition to using the Go To tab in the Find And Replace dialog box and the Select Browse Object menu, you can navigate documents by creating bookmarks. If you frequently need to access a particular area within a document, you can insert a bookmark to make returning to the area a snap. To insert and name a bookmark, follow these steps:

1. Position the insertion point where you want to insert a bookmark, and then, from the Insert menu, click Bookmark.
2. In the Bookmark dialog box, type a name for the bookmark, and then click Add.

After you insert a bookmark, you can use the Go To tab to find the bookmarked area, or you can choose Insert, Bookmark to display the Bookmark dialog box, select the bookmark's name, and then click Go To.

Chapter 5

Customizing Word and Enhancing Accessibility

As your experience with Word grows, you'll look for ways to speed up routine tasks and streamline cumbersome procedures. You'll also discover things you like—and don't like—about the way Word operates and learn what you like in menus, toolbars, and keyboard shortcuts.

This chapter shows you how to tailor Word 2003 to your liking and make the program more accessible for other users. Specific tasks include customizing toolbars, menus, and keyboard shortcuts. In addition, you'll get ideas on how you can make your documents easier to read and work with so that they are more accessible to a wide variety of users.

Saving Time by Starting Word Automatically

This first idea is a timesaving tip. If you start Word every time you start Microsoft Windows, why not have Windows start Word automatically? Follow these steps to add Word to your Startup folder so that it launches automatically when you start your system:

1. Click the Windows Start menu, and then point to All Programs.
2. From the Microsoft Office folder, select and drag the Microsoft Office Word 2003 icon to the Startup folder.
3. Hold the icon over the Startup folder until the folder's contents appear, and then place the icon in the list in the order you want it to be started, as shown below.

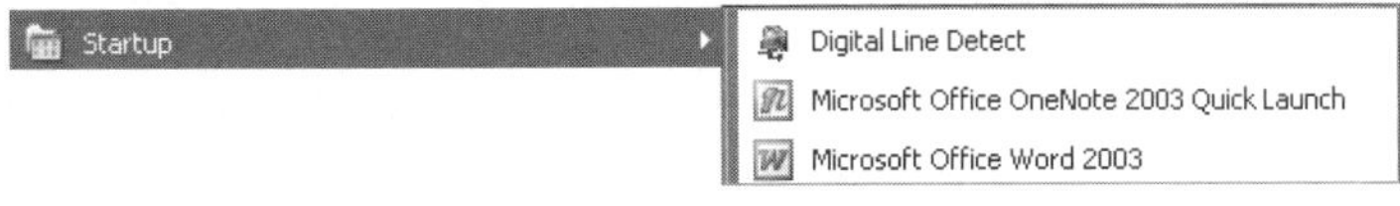

Word adds the shortcut icon to the Startup folder, and the next time you start Windows, Word will start automatically.

Inside Out

Enable drag-and-drop

If you drag the Word icon to the Startup menu and nothing appears to happen, check that the drag-and-drop feature is enabled on your system. Right-click Start, choose Properties, click the Start Menu tab, and then click Customize. Finally, in the Customize Start Menu dialog box, click the Advanced tab and make sure that Enable Dragging And Dropping is checked in the Start Menu Items list. (If it's not, click it to enable the feature.) Click OK twice to return to Word.

Customizing Startup by Adding Switches

If you regularly open Word documents and then attach the same template time after time, you may want to streamline things by adding a switch to the startup command. This causes Word to open a new document automatically with the template you want already attached.

To use a switch at startup, click Start, and then choose Run. In the Run dialog box, enter the path to Word (for example, C:\Program Files\Microsoft Office\Office\Winword.exe) or click Browse to navigate to the folder and have Windows enter the path for you, and then press the Spacebar and type the letter t, followed by the template file name. For example, if the template is named Mspressnew.dot, to have Word automatically open a new document with this template attached, your command line would look like this:

C:\Program Files\Microsoft Office\Office\Winword.exe t Mspressnew.dot

Click OK to enter the command and start Word.

If you really like this technique, you can create a desktop shortcut that enables you to bypass using the Run command. Right-click the Windows desktop, select New, and then choose Shortcut. Enter the path to the template file (shown above) in the Type The Location Of The Item box, and then click Next. Type a name for the shortcut, and then click Finish. Now you'll be able to start Word the way you want it, right from your desktop.

Specifying the Default Document's Location

If you often retrieve files from and save files to the same folder, you can automate that process to make the open and save procedures faster. You enter your settings for default file locations in the Options dialog box. To tell Word where to save your files by default, follow these steps:

1. Choose Tools, Options. The Options dialog box appears.
2. Click the File Locations tab, as shown in Figure 5-1. You see a listing of the file location assignments that are currently active.

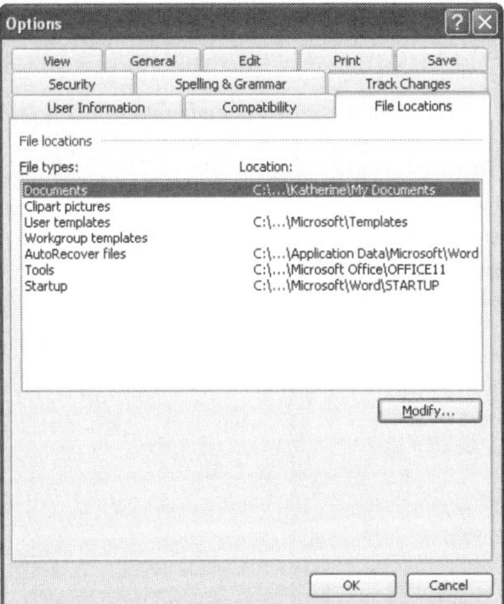

Figure 5-1. You can change the default folder in which Word stores and retrieves documents.

3 To change where Word stores the documents you create, click Documents, and then click Modify.

4 Navigate to the folder you want Word to use as the default documents location. Click the folder, and then click OK. When you return to the dialog box, click OK again to return to the document. Word records the change and now, by default, both saves files to and retrieves files from the specified folder.

> **Tip** You also can specify the location Word uses to store AutoRecover files, the files created if Word encounters a problem. Word saves any open files automatically (which is a good thing), but you might want to know where they are so you can get to them later if you need to. To specify where Word puts your AutoRecover files, choose Tools, Options, and then click the File Locations tab. In the File Types list, click AutoRecover Files, and then click Modify to choose a different default location. Navigate to the folder you want, and then click OK to save your changes.

Customizing Word Toolbars

Word comes equipped with a great many toolbars—some old, some new. The toolbars customize themselves to suit you—the buttons you use most often are the ones that appear on the Standard and Formatting toolbars. You can further customize the toolbars by adding or removing selected buttons or by creating new buttons and toolbars as you need them.

Showing ScreenTips and Shortcut Keys on Toolbars

By default, Word displays ScreenTips when you position the mouse pointer over buttons on your toolbars. You can disable ScreenTip display, if you choose, and you can add shortcut keys to your ScreenTips. Here are the steps:

1. Choose Tools, Customize. The Customize dialog box appears.
2. Click the Options tab, as shown in Figure 5-2. Then select your options as follows:
   - To disable ScreenTips, clear the Show ScreenTips On Toolbars check box.
   - To add shortcut keys to the ScreenTips, select both the Show ScreenTips On Toolbars and the Show Shortcut Keys In ScreenTips check boxes.

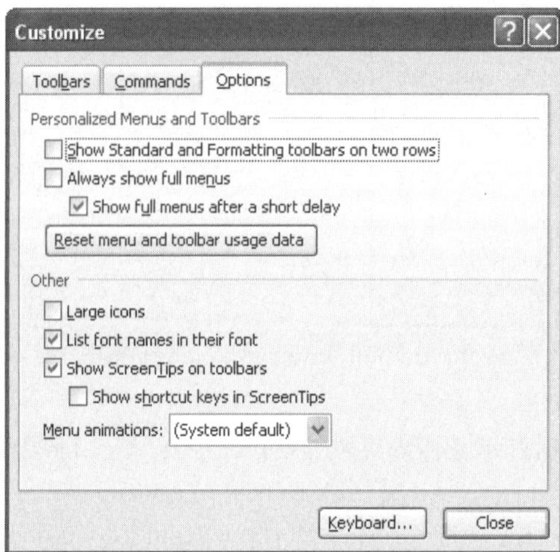

Figure 5-2. You can configure how ScreenTips and shortcut keys in ScreenTips are displayed.

3. Click Close. If you've enabled both options, the ScreenTips now appear when you position the pointer over buttons on toolbars, and shortcut keys will be included in the ScreenTip.

Displaying Large Toolbar Buttons

If you want to increase the size of the buttons on your toolbars, you use a Word customization setting. To increase the size of your toolbar buttons, follow these steps:

1. Chose Tools, Customize. The Customize dialog box appears.
2. Click the Options tab.
3. Select the Large Icons check box, but be forewarned: the icons in your workspace will be HUGE! If you want to reverse the effect, clear the Large Icons check box. Click Close to make the change.

Modifying Existing Toolbars

You can also change existing toolbars by adding or removing toolbar buttons, adding new buttons, moving buttons among menus, or reordering the buttons that appear on individual toolbars.

Adding a Button to an Existing Toolbar

Every toolbar in Word has its own Toolbar Options button. Position the pointer over the arrow at the far right end of a toolbar, and theToolbar Options ScreenTip will appear, as shown below. Click the arrow and a menu of toolbar choices appears. Depending on how you have your toolbars configured, the options you see may include tools that aren't visible on the current toolbar.

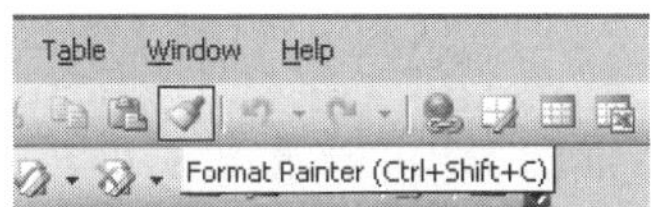

To add a button to a toolbar, follow these steps:

1. Click the Toolbar Options arrow. A menu appears.
2. Choose Add Or Remove Buttons, and then choose the toolbar's name from the menu. (For example, for the Standard toolbar you would choose Add Or Remove Buttons, Standard.) A submenu appears, displaying all buttons available for the selected menu, as shown in Figure 5-3. Buttons that currently appear on the toolbar are marked with a check mark; buttons not used show only the button image and name.

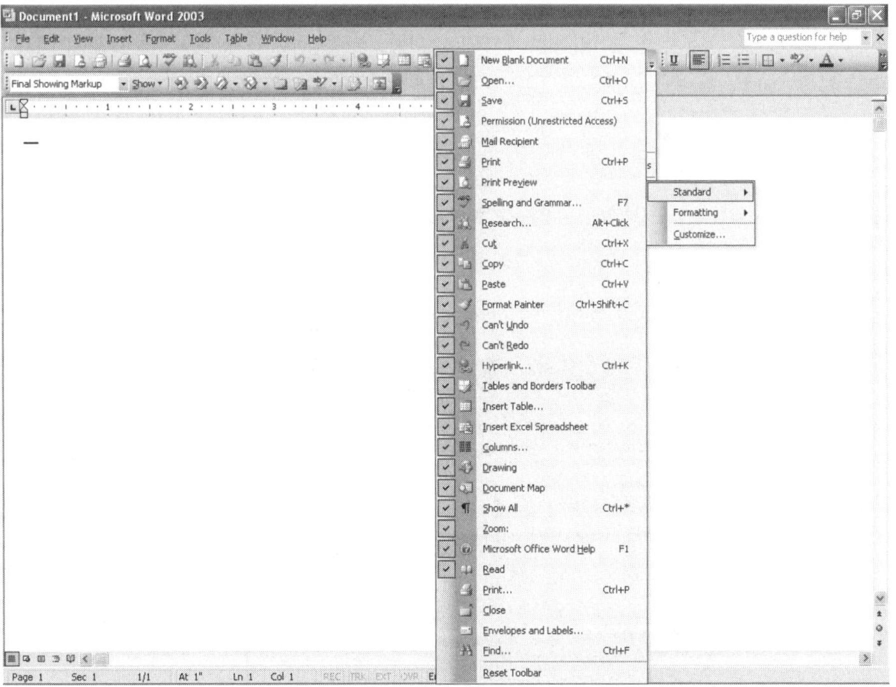

Figure 5-3. The Standard submenu shows all the buttons available for the Standard toolbar, with a check mark next to each one currently shown on the toolbar.

3. Click the button or buttons you want to add. The button is instantly added to the toolbar you're working with.
4. Click outside the menu to close it.

Tip **Reset toolbars**

If you make changes to a toolbar and then decide to change what you've done, you can restore the toolbar's previous setup. To revert to the original toolbar, choose Tools, Customize to display the Customize dialog box. Click the Toolbars tab. Click the name of the toolbar you want to reset, and then click Reset. The Reset Toolbar dialog box appears, asking you to indicate the name of the template that stores the toolbar you want to restore. Click the arrow and choose the template, and then click OK to restore the original toolbar settings.

Creating Custom Toolbars

If you have special applications or a set of tools that you use frequently, you can create your own custom toolbar to make those tools available the way you want them.You can create a custom toolbar using the Customize dialog box by following these steps:

1. Choose Tools, Customize. The Customize dialog box appears.
2. Click the Toolbars tab, and then click New. The New Toolbar dialog box appears.
3. Type a name for the new toolbar in the Toolbar Name box.
4. Click the Make Toolbar Available To arrow, and then choose the name of the template in which you want to make the toolbar available. Click OK, then Close. A new toolbar is placed in your work area.

Adding Buttons to a New Toolbar

Next, you need to add tools to the toolbar you've just created. Follow these steps:

1. In the Customize dialog box, click the Commands tab, as shown in Figure 5-4.

Figure 5-4. Create your own toolbar by copying and combining existing buttons.

2 In the Categories list, click the name of the menu that contains the command you want to add to your new toolbar.

3 In the Commands list, scroll to the command button you want to use. Drag the button to your new toolbar. A copy of the button is placed on the new toolbar.

4 Repeat steps 2 and 3, selecting first the menu and then the command, until you've added all desired buttons to your toolbar.

5 Click Close to close the Customize dialog box and begin working with your toolbar.

> **Tip** **Copy buttons between toolbars**
>
> The process of creating a new toolbar requires that you copy buttons from one toolbar to another. How do you do this? Just drag and drop. Whether you're creating a new toolbar or simply copying buttons from one toolbar to another, dragging works the same way: select the button in the Commands list in the Commands tab in the Customize dialog box (choose Tools, Customize to open), and then drag the button to the new location on the toolbar you're modifying.

Changing the Look of Toolbar Buttons

When you're working with the buttons on your toolbars, you might want to change the look of a button you're adding or copying. To change a toolbar button, follow these steps:

1 Choose Tools, Customize to display the Customize dialog box.

2 Click the button on the toolbar you want to modify, and then click Modify Selection in the Commands tab in the Customize dialog box.

3 Choose Change Button Image. A palette appears, giving you a number of images you can use in place of the current image on the selected button (as shown in Figure 5-5).

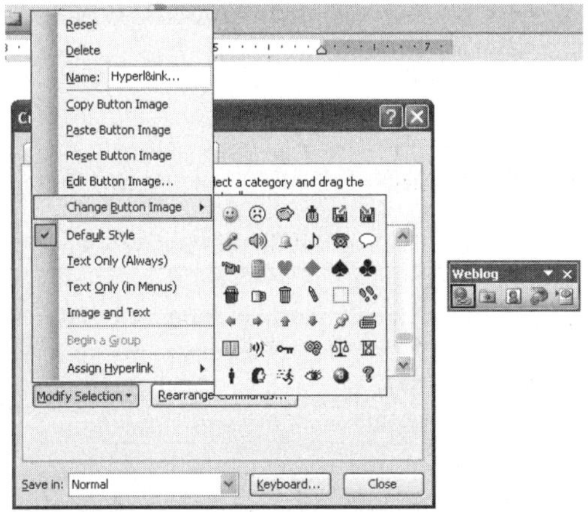

Figure 5-5. You can modify the toolbar button to display a different image.

4 Click the image you want to use. The button image is updated on the toolbar. Click Close.

Editing Button Images

If you really enjoy customizing your buttons, you might want to edit button images to create your own look. To edit a button image, follow these steps:

1. Display the Customize dialog box by clicking Tools, Customize.
2. Click the button on the toolbar you want to change.
3. Click Modify Selection in the Commands tab in the dialog box.
4. Choose Edit Button Image from the menu. The Button Editor dialog box appears, as shown in Figure 5-6.

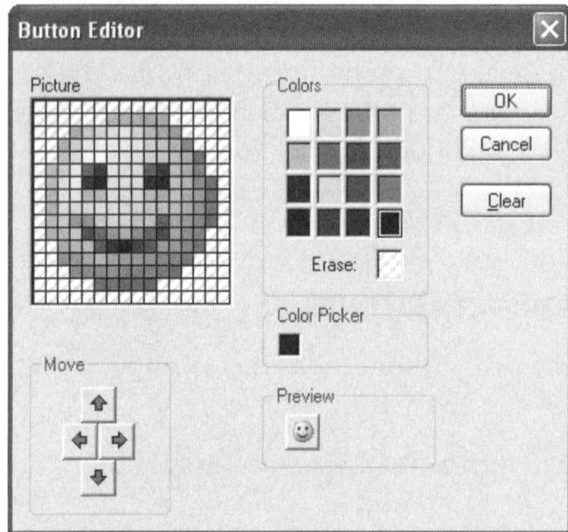

Figure 5-6. The Button Editor dialog box enables you to edit button images.

To edit the button image, click the color you want to use and click individual pixels to change the color of the image or to turn the color on or off. Use the directional buttons in the lower-left corner of the dialog box to move the image on the surface of the button. When you've made all the modifications you want, click OK to close the dialog box and record the changes.

Adding Divider Lines to Toolbars

Divider lines on toolbars help you visually group buttons with similar functions. If you've added a number of buttons to your custom toolbar, you might need to add divider lines to help you locate the tools you need more easily. To add a divider line, follow these steps:

1. Display the toolbar you want to change.
2. Choose Tools, Customize to display the Customize dialog box.
3. Click the Commands tab.
4. Click the button to the left of which you'd like to add the divider line.
5. Click Modify Selection, and then choose Begin A Group from the menu that appears. A divider line is added to the left of the button you selected.
6. Click Close to close the dialog box.

Tip **Rename a custom toolbar**
You can easily rename a toolbar you've created by choosing Tools, Customize and then clicking the Toolbars tab. Next, select the toolbar you want to rename in the Toolbars list, and then click Rename. When the Rename Toolbar dialog box appears, type the new name, and then click OK.

Customizing Menus for Added Functionality

In addition to all these toolbar changes, you can make modifications to the Word menus, as well. Not only can you change existing menus built into Word, you can add new menus to the Word menu bar and add submenus to menus already in use.

Creating Your Own Menu

Creating custom menus in Word is a fun feature you can use to create a list of the options you use most often, and then plug them into a menu you name and use yourself. To create a new menu for your Word menu bar, follow these steps:

1. Choose Tools, Customize. The Customize dialog box appears.
2. Click the Commands tab. In the Categories list, scroll down to New Menu, and then click it.
3. In the Commands list, click New Menu, and then drag it to the Word menu bar. The insertion point appears, showing you where the menu name will be placed. When the menu is situated where you want it, release the mouse button.
4. With New Menu selected on the menu bar, click Modify Selection in the Commands tab in the Customize dialog box. Choose Name from the menu that appears, and then type a name for the menu in the box.
5. Click Close to close the Customize dialog box. The new menu appears in the Word menu bar at the top of your screen.

Tip **Remove a menu**
If you want to remove a menu, press and hold Alt while dragging the menu name into the Word work area. The menu name is deleted from the menu bar.

Adding Menu Options to a New Menu

After you create a new menu, how do you add commands to it? The process is similar to adding a menu: you display the Commands tab in the Customize dialog box and drag the commands you want to the newly created menu. The insertion point shows you where the command will be added; release the mouse button when you've positioned the command where you want it.

Rearranging Menu Commands

You can easily rearrange the commands in a menu by simply dragging them to the positions you want. Here's how:

1. Choose Tools, Customize. The Customize dialog box appears.
2. On Word's menu bar, click the menu you wish to rearrange. The menu opens.
3. In the open menu, click the menu command you want to move and drag it to a new location.
4. Repeat as needed to move other commands in the menu.
5. Click Close to close the Customize dialog box and return to your document. The menu is updated so the new commands appear the next time you open the menu.

Removing Commands from Menus

If you want to remove a command from a menu, begin by displaying the Customize dialog box. On Word's menu bar, click the menu that contains the command. Drag the command off the menu and into the document window to remove it. Release the mouse button. The command is removed from the menu.

> **Tip** Restore default menus
> If you decide that you've changed too much on an existing menu, you can return the menu to the configuration it had before the last change you made. To restore a menu to its previous setting, display the Customize dialog box, click the Commands tab, click the menu on the menu bar, click the Modify Selection button, and then click Reset to return the selected menu to its former setting.

Creating Keyboard Shortcuts

If you like working quickly with the keyboard instead of using the mouse to open menus and choose commands, you might be interested in working with keyboard shortcuts and adding more of them to your Word document templates. You can add shortcuts to existing buttons and include symbols and special characters while you're at it. This part of the chapter gives you the steps for customizing your Word settings by adding keyboard shortcuts.

> **Note** All shortcut keys begin with Alt, Ctrl, or a function key.

Assigning Keyboard Shortcuts to Existing Buttons and Commands

In the Customize dialog box, you'll find options that enable you to add keyboard shortcuts to commands you use frequently. When the Customize dialog box appears (choose Tools, Customize), click Keyboard to see the Customize Keyboard dialog box shown in Figure 5-7.

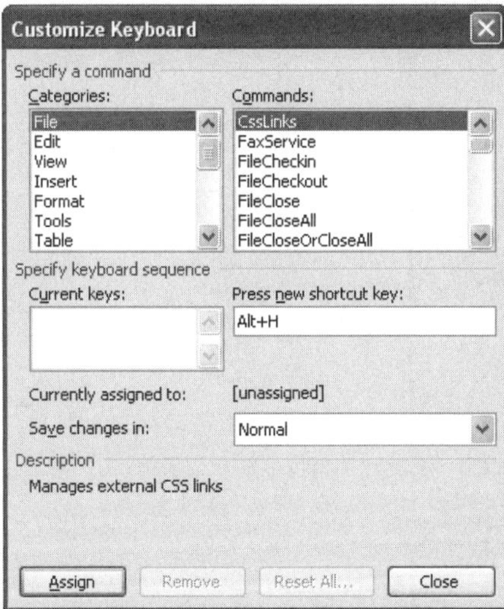

Figure 5-7. In the Customize Keyboard dialog box, you can choose a shortcut key for a command you use frequently.

To add a keyboard shortcut, select the menu and the command you want to use. In the Press New Shortcut Key box, press the key combination you want to use. Click Assign to apply the change to the document, and then click Close to close the dialog box.

> **Note** Any keyboard shortcuts you create will be saved only with the current document. Be sure to save your changes to a template if you want to use the same settings with other documents.

Using Keyboard Shortcuts for Symbols or Special Characters

You can assign a symbol or a special character to a keyboard shortcut if you want to create a quick key combination for a symbol or special character you use often. For example, if you frequently need to insert a copyright symbol into documents you write, you can create a keyboard shortcut to add the symbol for you. To create a keyboard shortcut for a symbol, follow these steps:

1. Choose Insert, Symbol. The Symbol dialog box appears. Click the Special Characters tab if you want to insert a special character; otherwise, leave the Symbols tab selected.
2. Click the Shortcut Key button. The Customize Keyboard dialog box appears, as shown in Figure 5-8.

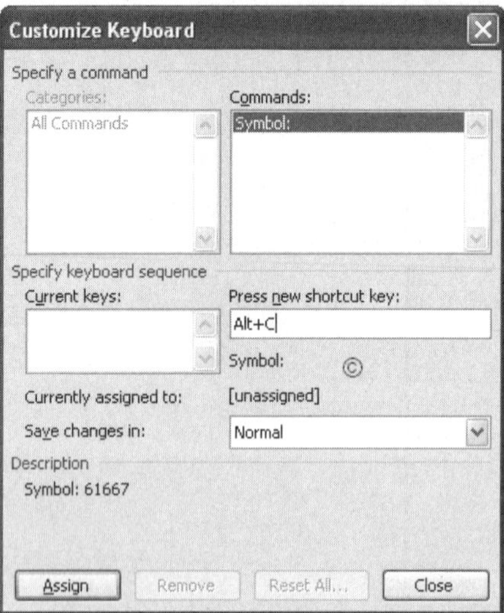

Figure 5-8. Assign a keyboard shortcut to a symbol or special character.

3. Click in the Press New Shortcut Key box, and press the new key combination you want to assign to the symbol or special character.
4. Click Assign. Word applies the shortcut keys to your selection.
5. Click Close twice to close both dialog boxes.

> **Tip** **Reset keyboard shortcuts**
> You have the option of resetting all your keyboard shortcuts if you want to wipe the slate clean. To do this, display the Customize Keyboard dialog box by choosing Tools, Customize. Click the Keyboard button, and then click Reset All. Word alerts you that continuing with this operation will remove all macros you've previously assigned to the template you're currently using. Click Yes to continue; otherwise, click No to cancel the procedure. Click Close twice to close both dialog boxes.

Incorporating Additional Accessibility Features

The accessibility features in Word were created and developed over time to help make the program usable for a wide variety of users—including those with visual impairments, limited dexterity, and other physical challenges that make using a word processing program difficult. A number of the features in this chapter—such as the ability to enlarge command buttons, and the addition of keyboard shortcuts—can make the program easier to use. This section rounds out our customizing discussion by providing suggestions for ways you can make your documents more accessible to a wide variety of users.

Changing Text Color for Easier Reading

The color of your text and the color of the background on which it's displayed both play a large role in the readability of your document. You can change the color of your text easily by following these steps:

1. Select your text, and then click the arrow to the right of the Font Color button, on the Formatting toolbar.
2. On the color palette, click a different color.
3. Repeat as needed for other text sections.

> **Tip** **Choose a good contrast**
> Experts tell us that the amount of contrast between background and text colors contributes as much to the readability of the text as the color of the text itself. When you're creating your document, be sure that there is a significant contrast between the text color and the color of the background of your document. If the two shades are too close, readers will find your document hard—even impossible—to read.

Customizing Sound

Some people have difficulty hearing sounds that are easy for others to pick up; others are highly sensitive to certain kinds of sounds and might prefer that you not use sound at all in your documents. You can tailor the sounds on your system to create the effect you want. You can customize the sound on your system with these simple procedures:

- To disable sound, choose Tools, Options, and then click the General tab. Clear the Provide Feedback With Sound check box. Note, however, that selecting this option will affect all the programs in the Microsoft Office System, so disable the option only if you don't want to play sound with any of your programs.
- You can change the sounds that are used by making changes in the Control Panel. Double-click Sounds And Audio Devices in the Control Panel. In the Sounds tab in the Sounds And Audio Devices dialog box, click the event in the Program Events list to which you want to apply the sound. Click the Sounds arrow, and then choose the sound you want to use. Click Apply, and then click OK to close the dialog box. Windows makes the necessary changes in your sound settings, and you'll hear the new sounds you selected the next time the event is triggered.

> **Tip** **Add voice commands**
> The sound events you hear while you're working on your document may be limited—you might hear a beep when you click a wrong command or a chime when a new e-mail message is delivered—but you can take sound a step further if need be. Word allows you to add audio clips and comments, adding real voice-over capability to your documents. This means that you can add notes, suggestions, and instructions to documents, forms, or brochures, as well as using Word's dictation features to display menus, choose commands, and enter text with voice commands.

Chapter 6

Making the Most of Research Services and Reference Tools

Word adds resources to your reference library without taking up an inch of shelf space. By default, when you install Word, you also install several standard reference tools, including research resources, a dictionary, a grammar guide, a thesaurus, a translation tool, and a document statistics tool.

The greatest advantage that reference tools in Word have over traditional reference books is that you can access and customize the Word tools while you work—without stopping midsentence, digging out your trusty encyclopedia, dictionary, or grammar guide, flipping through pages, and then modifying your text after you find the answer to your question. In fact, you don't even have to close or minimize your Word window. Furthermore, Word reference tools enable you to apply information you find—such as spelling and grammatical changes—automatically, thereby speeding up your word-processing tasks even more. Once you learn how to use Word reference tools properly, you'll find that they can be extremely handy. In this chapter, we focus on getting the most out of the electronic research and reference tools that are readily available every time you work in Word.

Researching Information Using the Research Task Pane

Research

The newest reference tool on the Office block is the Research task pane. This new task pane provides access to a number of free and fee-based reference tools, including reference books, research sites, business and financial sites, and other services. A taste of the offerings available in the Research task pane includes the following:

- **Thesaurus** Provides word choices in selected languages.
- **eLibrary** Serves as an online library, offering information from newspapers, newswires, magazines, reference books, and a variety of transcripts.
- **Encarta Dictionary** Provides definitions of words or phrases. You can choose from a variety of Encarta dictionaries.

- **Factiva News Search** Provides news about companies, industries, and business topics.
- **Gale Company Profiles** Pulls together information about a variety of businesses to enable you to efficiently research enterprises for career and investment purposes.
- **Encarta World Dictionary** Provides definitions and spelling assistance.
- **Encarta Encyclopedia** Links you to articles found in the online Encarta encyclopedia.
- **MSN Search** Serves as a typical search engine and presents links to World Wide Web sites related to specified research keywords.
- **MSN Money Stock Quotes** Provides stock information from the MSN Money Web site.
- **Translation** Translates words or sentences from one selected language into another and offers links to online translation services that can translate entire documents.

Figure 6-1 shows the Research task pane. You can display the Research task pane in any of the following ways:

- Click the Research button on the Standard toolbar.
- Press Ctrl+Shift+O.
- Press Alt, and then click a word or selected text that you want to research.
- Choose Tools, Research.
- Display the task pane (choose View, Task Pane or press Ctrl+F1), and then select Research in the task pane's title bar list.

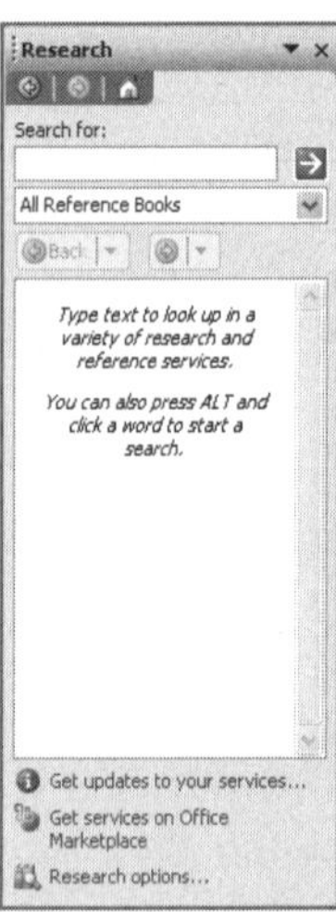

Figure 6-1. The Research task pane enables you to look up facts, figures, and words without minimizing or closing the Word window.

Generally, you'll quickly refer to the Research task pane while you work and then move on. In addition to using research services, you can also customize the task pane by adding and removing services as well as applying filters by turning on the parental control feature. The next few sections describe the ins and outs of using the Research task pane.

Using Research Services

When you use research services in the Microsoft Office System, you can access information that's stored online and on your computer without leaving your Office application. The fundamental process is to specify your research keyword or keywords, and then select the type of resource you want to access. To specify keywords, you can perform any of the following actions:

- Press Alt, and then click a word or selected text. The Research task pane appears, the text that was clicked appears in the Search For box, and a search is performed.
- Right-click a word or selected text, choose Look Up, the Research task pane appears, the text that was clicked appears in the Search For box, and a search is performed.
- Display the Research task pane (choose Tools, Research; click Research on the Standard toolbar; or press Ctrl+Shift+O), and type text in the Search For box.

After you've entered text in the Search For box, you're ready to select the type of research resource you want to use. To select a resource, display the list in the Research task pane (as shown in Figure 6-2), and then select either a group of resources (such as All Reference Books, All Research Sites, or All Business And Financial Sites), or choose a particular service to streamline your research results. After you select a service, the research process begins. By default, the Research task pane is configured to look in All Reference Books. If the research service you want to use is already selected in the list, you can simply click the green Start Searching arrow button next to the Search For box after you enter research keywords.

Figure 6-2. The Research task pane enables you to select the type of resource you want to use for your research.

Depending on your research selection, your results might look similar to any of the examples shown in Figure 6-3. After research results appear, click any item to expand the listing or click associated links to view additional information.

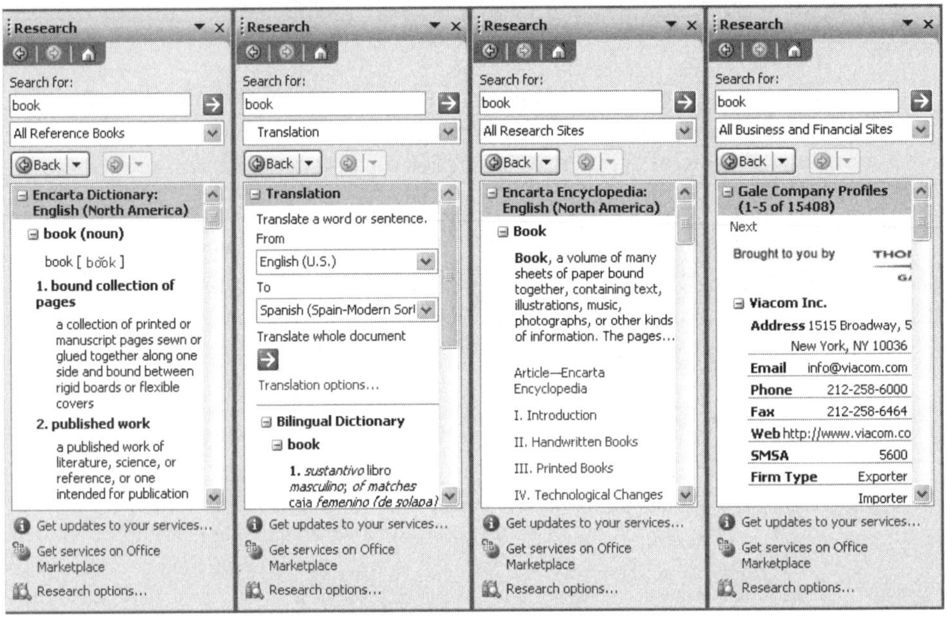

Figure 6-3. The Research task pane presents information in a variety of ways depending on the research service you choose.

If you don't find what you're looking for when you conduct your research, expand the Can't Find It? section in the Research task pane (which appears at the bottom of your research results list), and click a link to another research service, such as All Reference Books or All Research Sites.

Looking Up Words, Dictionary Style

Another added benefit of the new Research task pane is that you can quickly look up definitions and spelling while working in Word. To research a word's definition or origin, right-click the word, and choose Look Up from the shortcut menu. The Research task pane appears and displays potentially relevant information.You can conduct further research on the term by choosing another research service in the list below the Search For box. To track down a word's spelling, you can type your best guess in the Search For box (just as you might open a dictionary to a page near your best guess), and then click Start Searching. If you guessed correctly, the Research task pane displays definitions and other relative links. If you guessed incorrectly, the Research task pane lists some possible spelling alternatives, with links to definitions of the suggested words.

Controlling Research Services

Although some research services are free, a number of research services available in the Research task pane are fee-based. Therefore, you can pick and choose which services (if any) you'd like to use and configure your task pane accordingly by activating, deactivating, adding, updating, and removing research service options available in the task pane.

Notice that you can activate and deactivate services as well as add and remove services. When you activate or deactivate a service, you control whether an installed service is used for searching. In contrast, adding or removing a service controls the list of services that you can activate or deactivate. Let's look at activating and deactivating services first.

Activating and Deactivating Research Services

The key to controlling installed research services lies in the Research Options dialog box. To display the Research Options dialog box, click Research Options in the Research task pane. Activated services appear selected in the Research Options dialog box, as shown in Figure 6-4. You can activate and deactivate installed research services by selecting and clearing the check boxes.

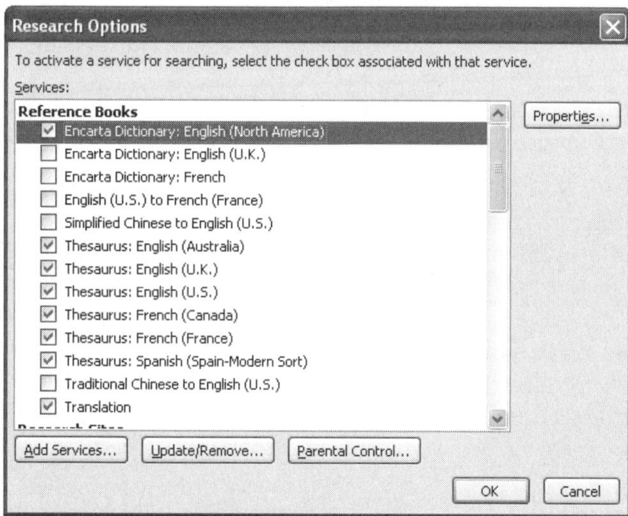

Figure 6-4. The Research Options dialog box enables you to set up the research options that will be available when you conduct searches that involve research.

Adding Research Services

You can install additional research services on your system if they are available. To do so, follow these steps:

1. Display the Research task pane, and then click the Research Options link.
2. In the Research Options dialog box, click Add Services to display the Add Services dialog box, which is shown in Figure 6-5.

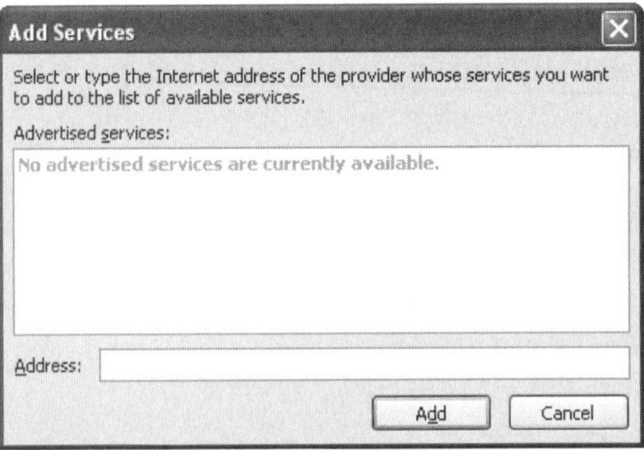

Figure 6-5. Adding research services enables you to expand the available research services on your computer.

3. Select an advertised service in the Advertised Services list (if any are available) or type the address of the service you want to add in the Address box, and then click Add.

After you add a service, it is automatically enabled for searching. Further, it will appear in the Search For list in the Research task pane the next time you display the list. You can control whether the service is included in your searches by activating or deactivating the service in the Research Options dialog box.

Tip **Add a SharePoint Portal Server 2003 site as a research service**
To add a SharePoint Portal Server 2003 site, enter *http://your root directory/_vti_bin/search.asmx* in the Address box in the Add Services dialog box. For more information about SharePoint Services and Team Web sites, see Chapter 25, "Working with Shared Documents."

Updating and Removing Research Services

When you use research services and subscribe to research service providers, you might find that you want to update or remove existing services. In both cases, you'll use the Update Or Remove Services dialog box, as shown in Figure 6-6.

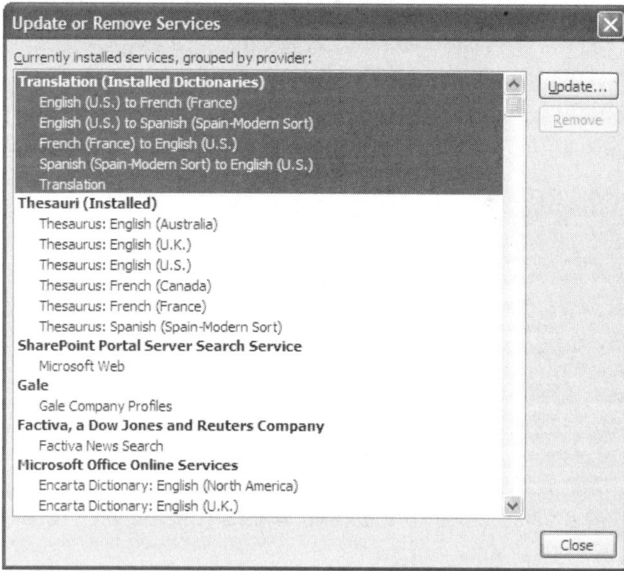

Figure 6-6. To update or remove a research service, select the service in the Update Or Remove Services dialog box, and then click Update or Remove.

To update a research service, display the Research task pane and then perform either of the following procedures:

- If updates are available, the Service Updates Are Available link appears at the bottom of the Research task pane. Click this link, select the service you want to update (if necessary), and click Update.
- Click Research Options, click Update/Remove, select the service you want to update, and click Update.

To remove a research service provider from your system, follow these steps:

1. Display the Research task pane, and click Research Options.
2. Click Update/Remove, select the research service provider you want to remove, click Remove, and click Close.

Remember, you can deactivate a research service instead of removing a research provider. You might opt to deactivate a service instead of removing it if you think you might want to use the service in the future.

Using Parental Control to Block Offensive Content

To some extent, you can control the type of content that can be included in research results that appear in the Research task pane by applying a filter that blocks questionable content. The parental control feature for the Research task pane is similar to parental controls available in some Web browsers.To block content, you turn on the parental control feature and provide a password, as follows:

1 Display the Research task pane, and click Research Options.

2 Click Parental Control, select Turn On Content Filtering To Make Services Block Offensive Results; if desired, select Allow Users To Search Only The Services That Can Block Offensive Results; enter a password; and click OK. Figure 6-7 shows the Parental Control dialog box with both filtering options selected and a password entered.

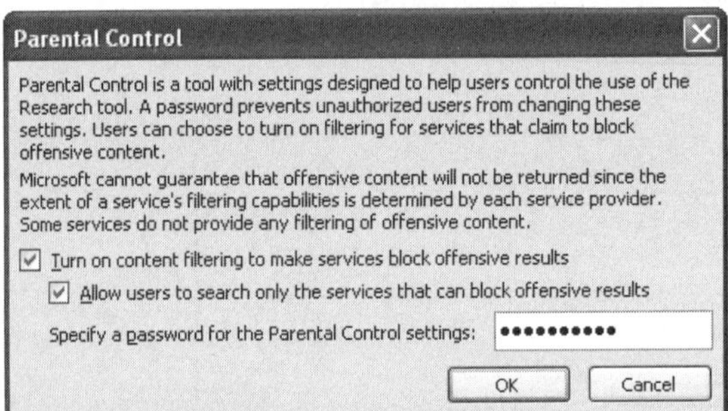

Figure 6-7. You can filter research results as well as limit research activities to services that can block offensive content.

3 In the Confirm Password dialog box, reenter your password, and click OK.

4 After you turn on the Parental Control feature, the Research Options dialog box displays a statement that the feature is turned on and that some services might be unavailable or produce limited results. Figure 6-8 shows the modified Research Options dialog box with the Parental Control message. Click OK to close the Research Options dialog box.

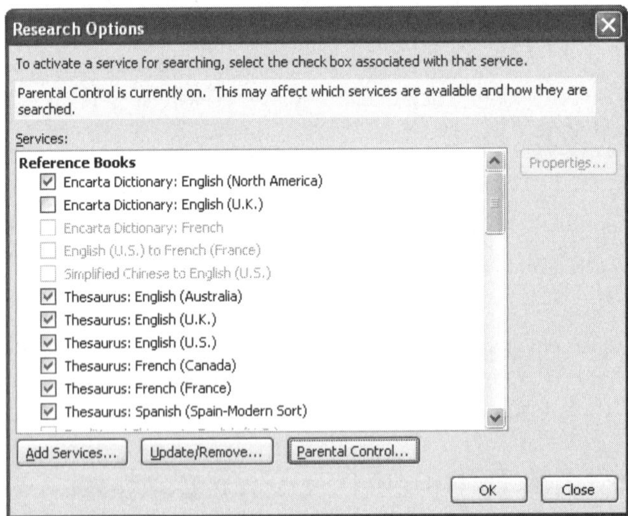

Figure 6-8. The Research Options dialog box alerts users when the Parental Control feature is turned on.

Building a Document's Credibility Using Spelling and Grammar Tools

Two frequently used reference tools in Word are the spelling and grammar tools. The popularity of these tools is understandable—most people know that nothing detracts from a document's credibility more than spelling and grammatical errors. To help you avoid the pitfalls of these kinds of errors, let's look at the ins and outs of the spelling and grammar tools in Word.

Caution Using the spelling and grammar tools to check your documents shouldn't replace proofreading. These features are helpful, but they can't definitively correct your text in all instances. Instead of thinking of the spelling and grammar checking tools as a teacher correcting your work, visualize an assistant who taps you on the shoulder whenever your text seems to go astray, and then offers advice on how to fix the problem. Ultimately, you'll need to read through your document carefully to ensure its accuracy.

Benefiting from Automated Spelling and Grammar Checking

By default, Word checks spelling and grammar whenever you open a document or type information in a document. With automatic spelling and grammar checking, Word flags potential spelling errors with a wavy red underline and potential grammatical errors with a wavy green underline, as shown in Figure 6-9 (although you won't be able to differentiate between green and red here).

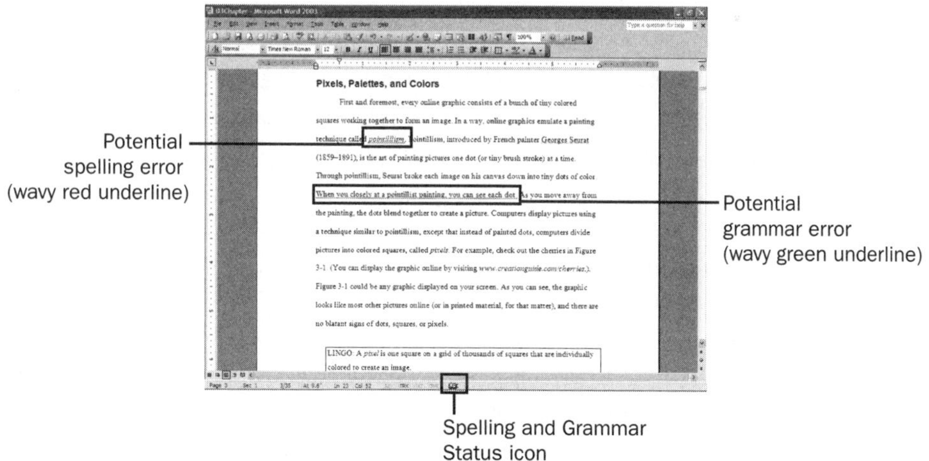

Figure 6-9. By default, Word automatically checks your document for spelling and grammar errors and flags the errors with wavy underlines.

Note The red and green wavy underlines used to flag spelling and grammar errors are not printed when you print your document—they appear only on-screen.

Word also displays the Spelling And Grammar Status icon on the status bar. This icon indicates whether your document contains any potential errors. If errors are detected, the icon contains an X mark; if no errors are found, the icon contains a check mark. (In the example in Figure 6-9, the Spelling And Grammar Status icon contains an X, indicating that the document contains potential spelling or grammar errors.)

Tip **Flag formatting inconsistencies**

In addition to displaying red and green wavy underlines to denote spelling and grammatical issues, you can configure Word to flag formatting inconsistencies with a blue wavy underline. Word marks text when it appears similar to but not exactly the same as other formatting in your document. For example, Word can recognize when a list is formatted slightly differently than other lists in your document (maybe one list is indented more than other lists, for instance) or when normal text appears in boldface in paragraph text. To use the formatting checker, choose Tools, Options, click the Edit tab, and then select the Mark Formatting Inconsistencies check box. In addition, the Keep Track Of Formatting check box must be selected in the Edit tab (the default setting).

Understanding the Underlines in Your Document

You might have noticed that Word frequently uses combination of colors and underlines to draw attention to text in your document. By default, Word uses a number of colors and underlines as visual cues to flag potential errors. By understanding Word's color-coded underlining scheme, you can review and correct documents more efficiently. The main visual cues you'll find in Word include the following:

- **Red wavy underline** Indicates a possible spelling error.
- **Green wavy underline** Indicates a possible grammar error.
- **Blue wavy underline** Indicates a possible instance of a formatting inconsistency.
- **Purple wavy underline** Indicates that an XML structure doesn't adhere to the attached XML schema in an XML document,.
- **Blue (default) underline** Indicates that the text is a hyperlink. Hyperlinks appear as blue underlined text by default but the settings can be customized.
- **Purple (default) underline** Indicates a visited (or followed) hyperlink. Visited hyperlinks appear as purple underlined text by default but the settings can be customized.
- **Red single or double underlines** Indicate newly inserted text when the Track Changes feature is turned on. Other colors can also indicate inserted text, and a different color can correspond to each author who makes changes to the document.
- **Purple dotted underlines** Accompany smart tags and appear under the text relevant to the smart tag.

Fixing Marked Text Quickly Case by Case

After Word marks potential spelling and grammar errors, you can resolve each issue on a case-by-case basis. To access options for fixing a potential error, you can right-click text that has a wavy underline or double-click the Spelling And Grammar Status icon to select the next instance of a potential error. Both techniques display a shortcut menu containing error-fixing options. Different options are available depending on whether the potential error is a spelling issue or a grammar issue. The shortcut menu for a spelling issue is shown in Figure 6-10.

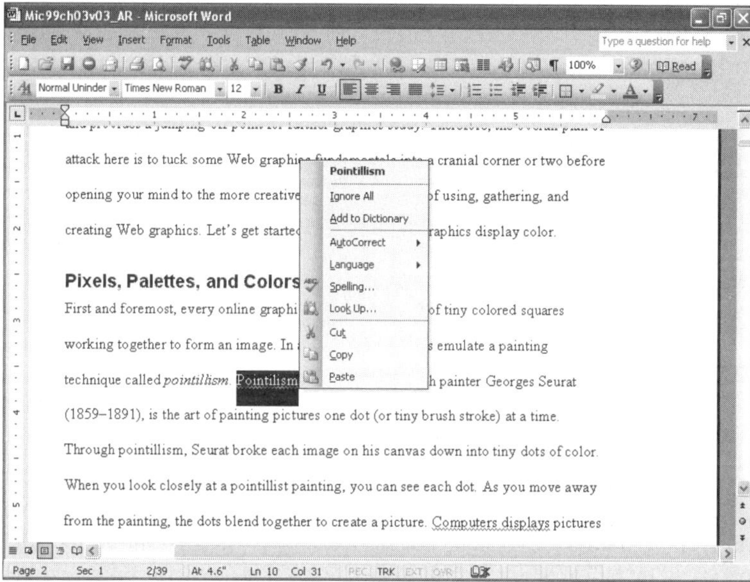

Figure 6-10. Word provides a selection of relevant error correction options when you right-click text flagged as a potential error.

The possible remedies are as follows:

- **List of possible replacement words** Provides one or more words that might represent the correctly spelled version of the word in your text. To replace a misspelled word with a correctly spelled word, simply click the word in the shortcut menu.
- **Ignore All** Instructs Word to ignore all instances of the flagged spelling within the current document. When you ignore all instances of a particular flagged word, the red wavy underline is removed from the specified text throughout the document.
- **Add To Dictionary** Adds the word as it's spelled in your document to your custom dictionary, which ensures that the term won't be flagged as a potential error in the future. (Custom dictionaries are discussed in detail in "Managing Custom Dictionaries," on page 167.)

- **AutoCorrect** Enables you to configure an AutoCorrect setting for the misspelled word. You can have the misspelled word automatically replaced with the correctly spelled word by clicking the correctly spelled word in the AutoCorrect submenu, as shown in Figure 6-11. Alternatively, you can manually configure an AutoCorrect entry in the AutoCorrect dialog box by clicking AutoCorrect Options in the Auto-Correct submenu.

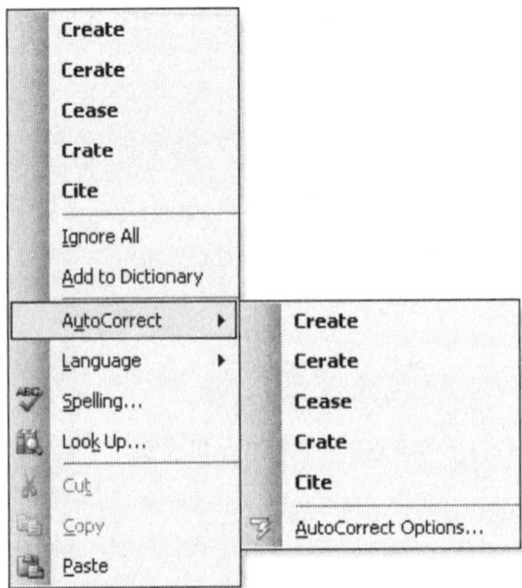

Figure 6-11. You can select a correctly spelled word in the AutoCorrect submenu so that future instances of the mistyped text you've selected are automatically replaced with the correctly spelled word.

- **Language** Enables you to specify that a particular word or phrase is written in another language. If proofreading tools are installed for that language, Word uses the appropriate language dictionary to check the text. If a corresponding language dictionary is not installed, Word will skip the specified words without marking them as potential errors.
- **Spelling** Displays the Spelling dialog box, which provides additional spelling checking options. The Spelling dialog box is similar to the Spelling And Grammar dialog box, which you can access by choosing Tools, Spelling And Grammar or by pressing F7.
- **Look Up** Displays the Research task pane and presents typical dictionary type information, including definitions and spelling alternatives. Furthermore, if your computer is online, you can find additional information about the term by using other research services and resources such as encyclopedias and Web sites.
- **Cut** Deletes the selected text and puts it on the Clipboard. (If you right-click text without selecting it, the Cut command is dimmed and unavailable.)
- **Copy** Copies the selected text to the Clipboard. (If you right-click text without selecting it, the Copy command is dimmed and unavailable.)

- **Paste** Pastes the last item copied to the Clipboard. To replace a misspelled word using Paste, be sure that the entire misspelled word is selected.

Grammar correction options are accessed in much the same way as spelling correction options. In this case, you right-click text flagged with a green wavy underline or double-click the Spelling And Grammar Status icon. Both techniques display a shortcut menu containing the following options:

- **Short error explanation or replacement text** Provides a brief description of the problem or possible replacement text. For example, the error explanation might state *Fragment (Consider Revising)*, or it might show the flagged phrase followed by the plural form of the verb instead of the singular form.
- **Ignore Once** Disregards the current instance of the grammatical error but doesn't disregard other text that breaks the same grammar rule.You might want to ignore an error once if a particular construct is acceptable in a specific area of your document but you don't want to ignore the construct in other areas. For example, you might want to allow a sentence fragment in a figure caption but still want Word to continue to scan for sentence fragments in the rest of your document.
- **Grammar** Displays the Grammar dialog box, which provides additional grammar checking options. The Grammar dialog box is similar to the Spelling And Grammar dialog box; you can access it by choosing Tools, Spelling And Grammar or by pressing F7.
- **About This Sentence** Provides additional information about the potential error flagged by Word.
- **Look Up** Displays the Research task pane and presents information from reference sources about the flagged text. If your computer is online, you can find additional information about the term by using other research services and resources such as encyclopedias and Web sites. Note that this option provides information about the flagged text but doesn't necessarily present a grammatical fix.
- **Cut** Deletes the selected text and puts it on the Clipboard. (If you right-click a word or text without selecting it, the Cut command is dimmed and unavailable.)
- **Copy** Copies the selected text to the Clipboard. (If you right-click text without selecting it, the Copy command is dimmed and unavailable.)
- **Paste** Pastes the last item copied to the Clipboard. To replace a word using Paste, be sure that the entire word is selected.

You can also resolve spelling and grammar issues by correcting your text without accessing the shortcut menus. When you manually correct a misspelling or a grammatical error, Word automatically removes the wavy underline.

Tip To jump to the next spelling or grammatical error without displaying the Spelling And Grammar dialog box, double-click the Spelling And Grammar Status icon or press Alt+F7.

Disabling Automatic Spelling and Grammar Checking

By default, Word checks for spelling and grammar errors automatically, but you can turn off one or both of these features at any time. For instance, many users appreciate the spelling checker but some find that the grammar checker doesn't serve their needs particularly well. To control automatic spelling and grammar checking, perform one of the following actions:

- Right-click the Spelling And Grammar Status icon, and choose Hide Spelling Errors or Hide Grammatical Errors from the shortcut menu.
- Choose Tools, Options, and click the Spelling & Grammar tab (or right-click the Spelling And Grammar Status icon, and choose Options). In the Spelling & Grammar tab, shown in Figure 6-12, clear the Check Spelling As You Type check box to turn off the spelling checker, or clear the Check Grammar As You Type check box to turn off the grammar checker.

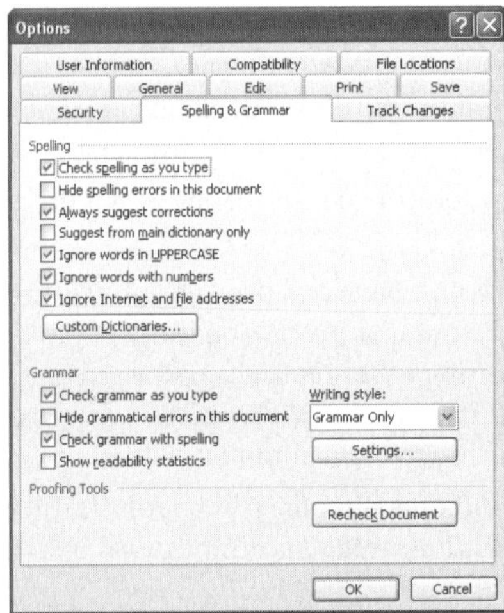

Figure 6-12. The Spelling & Grammar tab enables you to customize how Word performs spelling and grammar checking tasks.

Tip **Turn off the wavy lines**

If you want to use the Spelling Checking and Grammar Checking features but you don't want to see red and green wavy underlines throughout your document, you can turn off the underlines. To do so, choose Tools, Options, click the Spelling & Grammar tab, and then select the Hide Spelling Errors In This Document check box to hide red (spelling) underlines and select the Hide Grammatical Errors In This Document check box to hide green (grammar) wavy underlines. Or you can right-click the Spelling And Grammar Status icon on Word's status bar, and choose Hide Spelling Errors or Hide Grammatical Errors from the shortcut menu.

Tip **Turn off spelling and grammar completely**

You might notice that when you disable the spelling and grammar checking tools the Spelling And Grammar Status icon continues to appear on the status bar. To remove the status bar icon, you must also turn off smart tags, because the grammar checker is used to recognize smart tags. To turn off smart tags, choose Tools, AutoCorrect Options, and then click the Smart Tags tab. Clear the Label Text With Smart Tags check box, and click OK. The next time you start Word the Spelling And Grammar Status icon will not appear.

Scrutinizing Your Spelling in an Entire Document

Spelling And Grammar

At times, you might prefer to check your spelling and grammar in one fell swoop instead of right-clicking every instance of a potential error. In those cases, your best bet is to work through your document or block of selected text using the Spelling And Grammar dialog box. To access the Spelling And Grammar dialog box, perform any of the following actions:

- Choose Tools, Spelling And Grammar.
- Click the Spelling And Grammar button on the Standard toolbar.
- Press F7.

When the Spelling And Grammar dialog box appears, it displays the first potential error it encounters after the insertion point in the current document. For each potential problem, the word or phrase in question appears in color: red for a spelling issue, and green for a grammar issue. Figure 6-13 shows the Spelling And Grammar dialog box when a potential spelling error is being addressed, and Figure 6-14 shows the Spelling And Grammar dialog box when a potential grammar error is being reviewed. Take a moment to compare the options in the two versions of the dialog box—you'll notice many similarities and a few differences. In this part of the chapter, you'll learn how to handle potential spelling errors. The grammar options are discussed in "Brushing Up Your Grammar," on page 173.

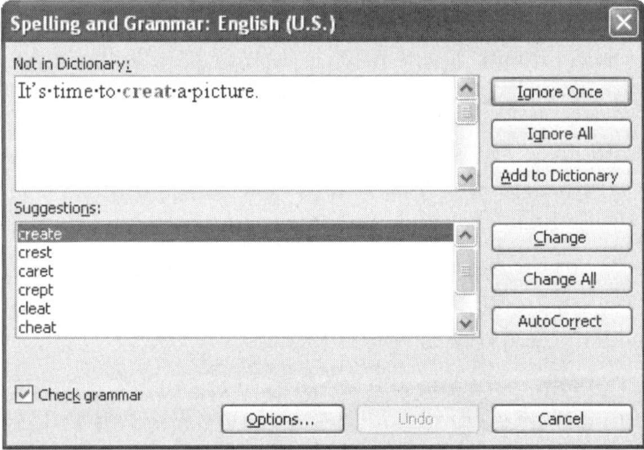

Figure 6-13. When you use the Spelling And Grammar dialog box to correct errors, you have a greater selection of suggestions and options to pick from than when you right-click potential errors. This version of the dialog box shows the options available for a potentially misspelled word.

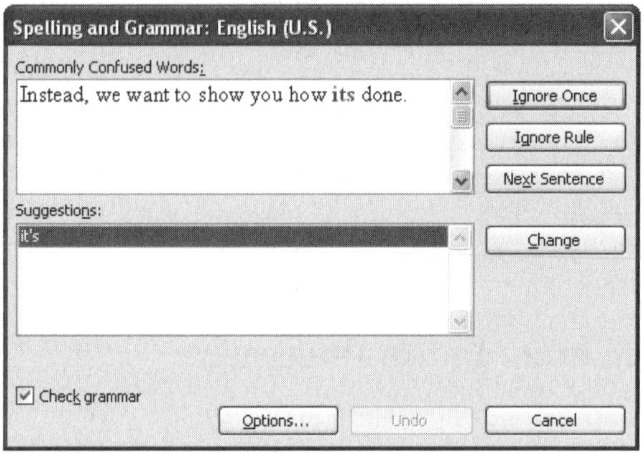

Figure 6-14. The grammar checker provides error-checking options similar to the options available in the spelling checker. This version of the dialog box draws attention to the word "its" as a commonly confused word.

Inside Out

Activating the grammar checker

You can control whether the grammar checker is activated by selecting or clearing the Check Grammar check box in the Spelling And Grammar dialog box, but you can access this particular check box only when you choose Tools, Spelling And Grammar or press F7. If you display the Spelling dialog box or the Grammar dialog box by right-clicking an underlined potential error, this check box will not be available.

Specifying How to Handle Spelling Errors

When a potential spelling problem appears in the Spelling And Grammar dialog box, you can modify the highlighted text by typing in the top box, or you can handle the flagged text using one of the following techniques:

- **Ignore the current instance.** You can disregard the current instance of a particular spelling of a word by clicking Ignore Once. If the same misspelling occurs elsewhere in your document, the spelling checker will continue to flag subsequent instances.
- **Ignore all instances.** You can disregard all instances of a particular spelling of a word throughout the current document by clicking Ignore All. After you click Ignore All, Word won't flag or query you about any other instances of the misspelled word.
- **Add a word to the dictionary.** You can add the current instance of a particular spelling of a word to your dictionary by clicking Add To Dictionary. The word will be added to your custom dictionary without further configuration on your part. For more information about controlling your custom dictionary, see "Managing Custom Dictionaries," on page 167.

- **Change the current instance.** You can replace the selected text with a suggested word by double-clicking the correct word in the Suggestions list or by selecting a word in the Suggestions list, and then clicking Change.
- **Change all instances.** You can replace the selected text and all other instances of the same text with a particular word by selecting a word in the Suggestions list, and then clicking Change All.
- **Add terms to the AutoCorrect list.** You can add a correction to the AutoCorrect list by selecting a word in the Suggestions list, and then clicking AutoCorrect. The misspelled and correctly spelled versions of the word are automatically added to your AutoCorrect list without further configuration on your part.

Caution If you click Change All but close the dialog box before checking the entire document, the spelling checker will not make the specified change in the unchecked portion of the document. To change all instances of a correction, ensure that you check the entire document.

For more information about the AutoCorrect list, see Chapter 7, "Putting Text Tools to Work"

After you resolve the current spelling issue, Word automatically jumps to the next potential spelling error. If you change your mind about a spelling modification, you can undo the last spelling change by clicking Undo in the Spelling And Grammar dialog box, by clicking in the document and pressing Ctrl+Z, or by clicking the Undo button on the Standard toolbar.

Tip **Edit text while checking spelling and grammar**
You can click in your document and make changes directly to your text while the Spelling And Grammar dialog box is open. After you finish making changes to your document, you can continue your spelling check by clicking Resume in the Spelling And Grammar dialog box.

When every spelling issue has been addressed, Word displays a message box informing you that the spelling check is complete. If you want to stop the spelling checker before you've checked the entire document, simply click Close in the Spelling And Grammar dialog box.

Selecting the Text You Want to Check

By default, when you use the Spelling And Grammar dialog box, you check the entire document, starting at the current location of the insertion point. But if you prefer, you can check only selected text. To check only selected text, select the text, and then click the Spelling And Grammar button on the Standard toolbar. (Of course, if you select a single word, you can right-click to access the word replacement options in the shortcut menu.) The spelling checker works through the selected text. When the end of the selected text is reached, Word displays a dialog box stating that Word has finished checking the selected text and asking whether you'd like to continue checking the remainder of the document.

> **Tip** **Omit selected text from spelling and grammar checking**
> In addition to selecting specific text you want to check, you can also indicate that portions of text should never be checked for spelling or grammar errors. (When you use this feature, you have to eliminate both spelling and grammar checking—you can't turn off only one feature for selected text.) To turn off spelling and grammar checking procedures for specific text, select the text you want to omit, choose Tools, Language, Set Language, and then select the Do Not Check Spelling Or Grammar check box and click OK. Keep in mind that any text you omit from spelling and grammar checks is also excluded from AutoSummarize processes, which means that the text won't be included in any automatically generated summaries.

Configuring Spelling Options

As mentioned, you can control a few spelling checker options by configuring settings in the Spelling & Grammar tab in the Options dialog box (accessed by choosing Tools, Options, and clicking the Spelling & Grammar tab). The first two options in the Spelling section in the Spelling & Grammar tab—Check Spelling As You Type and Hide Spelling Errors In This Document—are discussed in "Disabling Automatic Spelling and Grammar Checking" on page 162. The other options you can configure are as follows:

- **Always Suggest Corrections** By default, Word provides a list of suggested corrections for each misspelled word. If you find that Word doesn't provide the correct spelling in the majority of instances (for example, you might be working on a document that contains highly specific jargon, such as a medical document), you can clear this check box to save time.
- **Suggest From Main Dictionary Only** Word checks all open dictionaries during spelling checks, including the main dictionary and your custom dictionaries. If you prefer to use only the main dictionary, select the Suggest From Main Dictionary Only check box.
- **Ignore Words In UPPERCASE** This check box excludes words in all uppercase from spelling checks. The spelling checker would be hard pressed to understand all acronyms, so this check box is selected by default. If you use a number of acronyms and you'd like to check them, you can add the acronyms to your custom dictionary and clear the Ignore Words In UPPERCASE check box.
- **Ignore Words With Numbers** By default, any words that contain numbers are ignored by the spelling checker. You'll especially appreciate this option if you're proofreading documents such as catalogs or price lists in which product codes are combinations of numbers and letters.
- **Ignore Internet And File Addresses** By default, the spelling checker ignores Internet addresses, file path names, and e-mail addresses. For example, text such as *C:\clients\microsoft* and *www.microsoft.com* is automatically ignored by the spelling checker. If you prefer to check these types of elements, clear the Ignore Internet And File Addresses check box.

By configuring these spelling checker options, you can customize spelling tasks to be as streamlined as possible for particular document types.

Making the Most of Research Services and Reference Tools

Rechecking Your Document

Once you've checked a document using the appropriate spelling checker options, Word doesn't recheck any of the spelling or grammar issues that you've addressed or dismissed. If you want to check your document a second (or third) time, you'll have to tell Word to catch previously caught spelling and grammar issues again. To do so, follow these simple steps:

1. Click the Options button in the Spelling And Grammar dialog box, or choose Tools, Options, and click the Grammar & Spelling tab in the Options dialog box.
2. Click Recheck Document. A message box appears, stating that the operation will reset the spelling and grammar checkers so that Word can recheck your document for potential errors, even if you've previously dismissed the error marks.
3. Click Yes to close the message box, and then click OK to close the Options dialog box.
4. After Word has finished resetting the spelling checker and grammar checker, click the Spelling And Grammar button on the Standard toolbar or press F7 to display the Spelling And Grammar dialog box, and then check your document.

You can recheck a document as many times as necessary. This feature is especially handy if you've ignored particular corrections and later want to change the ignored text.

Managing Custom Dictionaries

When you install Word, you also install a main dictionary. The spelling checker uses the main dictionary whenever it checks your document for spelling errors. You can also add words to your custom dictionary or add existing dictionaries to the list of dictionaries Word uses to check documents.

When you click Add To Dictionary in the Spelling And Grammar dialog box, Word adds the selected term to your custom dictionary. After you add terms to your custom dictionary, Word checks both the main dictionary and your custom dictionary (named CUSTOM.DIC by default) whenever you run the spelling checker. You can also edit and delete terms in your custom dictionary as well as create additional custom dictionaries that you can use whenever necessary.

Modifying Custom Dictionaries

As mentioned, you can add terms to your default custom dictionary by clicking Add To Dictionary in the Spelling And Grammar dialog box. You can also add terms to your custom dictionary by right-clicking words that are flagged by a red wavy underline and choosing Add To Dictionary from the shortcut menu. Because adding terms to the custom dictionary is so easy, many users mistakenly add words that shouldn't be included, such as words or abbreviations that should be ignored in one document but might be incorrect in other documents. For example, you might want to allow the word *lite* in a marketing piece but have Word catch the misspelling in other documents. If you regularly add terms to your custom dictionary or if you suspect that you've added incorrect terms, you should review and manually correct your dictionary to ensure accuracy.

To access and modify your custom dictionary, follow these steps:

1 Display the Spelling & Grammar tab (by choosing Tools, Options, and clicking the Spelling & Grammar tab; by pressing F7, and clicking Options; or by right-clicking the Spelling And Grammar Status icon, and choosing Options).

2 Click Custom Dictionaries. The Custom Dictionaries dialog box appears, as shown in Figure 6-15. Notice that the CUSTOM.DIC dictionary is selected by default.

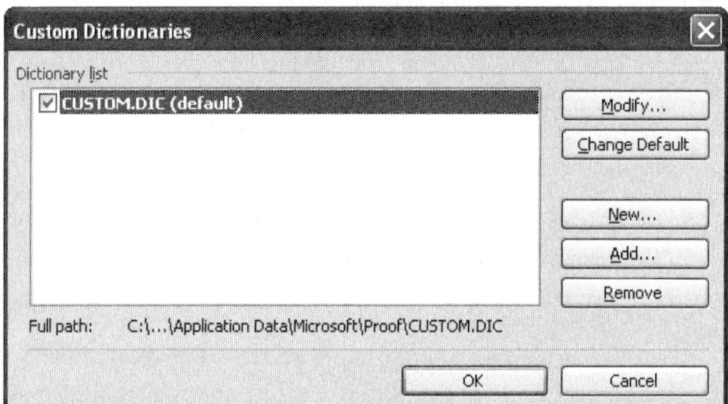

Figure 6-15. The Custom Dictionaries dialog box provides options for creating and modifying custom dictionaries that Word uses in conjunction with the main dictionary.

3 Select a dictionary in the Dictionary List, and then click Modify to display a dictionary editing dialog box, as shown in Figure 6-16.

Figure 6-16. The dictionary editing dialog box provides an easy way to create and modify custom dictionaries. In early versions of Word, editing dictionaries entailed modifying a plain text file.

Within this dialog box, you can perform the following actions:

- *Manually add a term to a custom dictionary.* Enter a term in the Word box, and click Add or press Enter. The dictionary automatically arranges terms alphabetically.
- *Delete a term included in a custom dictionary.* Choose a word in the Dictionary list, and click Delete.
- *Specify a language for a custom dictionary.* Click the Language box, and choose a language in the list. By default, the CUSTOM.DIC dictionary is set to All Languages.

4 Click OK twice when you have finished modifying your custom dictionary.

Tip Remember the limitations of custom dictionaries

When you add terms to a custom dictionary, you should keep a few minor limitations in mind, namely the following:

- Ensure that the words are 64 characters or fewer and do not contain spaces.
- Ensure that the custom dictionary doesn't include over 5,000 words or is larger than 64KB.
- Keep in mind that dictionaries are American National Standards Institute (ANSI) text files, which can only contain characters that conform to the ANSI encoding standard.

With careful maintenance of your custom dictionary, including adding frequently used terms, you can keep your spelling checker working at peak performance and increase your efficiency. With a well-maintained custom dictionary, you'll avoid having to continually dismiss terms that appear regularly in your documents but aren't included in the main dictionary.

Creating New Custom Dictionaries

At times, you might work on jargon-laden documents that use very specific terminology. For example, if you occasionally work on medical documents that contain terms such as *brachytherapy, echography,* and *osteotomy,* you could create a custom dictionary named Medical that you could activate whenever you're using medical terminology. To create a custom dictionary that you can use in addition to CUSTOM.DIC, follow these steps:

1 Display the Spelling & Grammar tab in the Options dialog box (by choosing Tools, Options, and clicking the Spelling & Grammar tab; by pressing F7, and clicking Options; or by right-clicking the Spelling And Grammar Status icon, and choosing Options), and click Custom Dictionaries.

2 In the Custom Dictionaries dialog box, click New. The Create Custom Dictionary dialog box appears. This dialog box displays a list of the custom dictionaries currently available to Word in the Proof folder. Figure 6-17 shows the Create Custom Dictionary dialog box, which contains the CUSTOM.DIC file and three additional custom dictionaries.

Figure 6-17. The Create Custom Dictionary dialog box enables you to create new dictionaries that you can use on an "as-needed" basis whenever you check documents.

3 Type a name for the new custom dictionary in the File Name box, and click Save. When you create a custom dictionary, the file is saved with the .dic extension in the Proof folder, along with the CUSTOM.DIC file and any other custom dictionaries you've created.

After you create a new dictionary, it is added to the Dictionary List in the Custom Dictionaries dialog box and its check box is selected. When the spelling checker runs, it refers to the main dictionary and all custom dictionaries that are selected in the Dictionary List.

Tip **Avoid suggestions from the main dictionary only**

When you use custom dictionaries, make sure that the Suggest From Main Dictionary Only check box is cleared (the default setting) in the Spelling & Grammar tab in the Options dialog box. If this check box is selected, Word won't refer to your custom dictionaries when the spelling checker is started.

To add terms to a new custom dictionary, select the dictionary in the Custom Dictionaries dialog box, click Modify, and then manually enter terms. You can also add terms to the dictionary as you work, as described in "Choosing a Default Dictionary," on page 171.

Tip **Create a Names dictionary**

You might want to create a Names dictionary that contains the names of people you interact with on a regular basis. Not only will this streamline spell checks by eliminating the repeated flagging of correctly spelled names, but you'll also avoid misspelling people's names in your documents because your custom dictionary will be keeping an eye on your spelling.

Adding Custom Dictionaries

Most of the time, you'll either use the CUSTOM.DIC dictionary or create a new custom dictionary. However, you can also add existing dictionaries to the Dictionary List in the Custom Dictionaries dialog box. For example, if you have *Stedman's Medical Dictionary* on your computer, you can add it to Word's list of custom dictionaries. Adding an existing dictionary is similar to creating a new custom dictionary. To do so, follow these steps:

1. In the Spelling & Grammar tab in the Options dialog box, click Custom Dictionaries.
2. In the Custom Dictionaries dialog box, click Add to display the Add Custom Dictionary dialog box, which looks almost identical to the Create Custom Dictionaries dialog box.
3. Navigate to the desired dictionary file, and double-click the dictionary's file name. The dictionary will appear in the Dictionary List and its check box will be selected.

By default, custom dictionaries are stored in the \\%UserProfile%\Application Data\Microsoft \Proof folder. If you have a custom dictionary file (with a .dic extension), you can store the file in the Proof folder; it will then be easily accessible from the Custom Dictionaries dialog box.

Converting an Existing List of Terms to a Custom Dictionary

If you have an existing list of terms or a style sheet containing terms you frequently use, you can create a custom dictionary without having to retype or copy all the terms in the dictionary editing dialog box. To convert a list to a custom dictionary, follow these steps:

1. Verify that each term appears on a separate line with no blank lines inserted between terms. Then save your document as a plain text (.txt) file, and close the file.
2. Right-click the file name in Windows Explorer, and rename the file using the .dic extension. (You might have to clear the Hide File Extensions For Known File Types check box in the View tab in the Folder Options dialog box in Windows Explorer in order to view file name extensions.)
3. After you rename the file, store it in *%UserProfile%*\Application Data \Microsoft\Proof.

The next time you display the Add Custom Dictionary dialog box, you'll see your newly created dictionary listed among the available custom dictionaries. Double-click the newly added dictionary to add it to the Dictionary List in the Custom Dictionaries dialog box.

Choosing a Default Dictionary

By default, all terms you add to a dictionary while running a spelling check are added to the CUSTOM.DIC dictionary. You can change the custom dictionary in which added words are stored by changing the default custom dictionary. By reconfiguring your default dictionary, you can quickly build very specific custom dictionaries without having to enter terms manually.

Let's return to the Medical dictionary example. While you're working on a medical document, you could specify the Medical dictionary as your default custom dictionary. Then whenever you click Add To Dictionary, the specified term would be added to the Medical dictionary instead of CUSTOM.DIC. Configuring Word in this way would serve two purposes: it would avoid adding unnecessary terms to the CUSTOM.DIC dictionary, and it would save you from manually typing terms in the Medical dictionary.

To specify which custom dictionary serves as the default file, perform the following simple actions:

1. Choose Tools, Options, click the Spelling & Grammar tab, and then click Custom Dictionaries to display the Custom Dictionaries dialog box.
2. Select the custom dictionary you want to be the default in the Dictionary List.
3. Click Change Default.

The default custom dictionary will appear at the top of the list with *(default)* after its name, as shown in Figure 6-18. Now when you add a word to your custom dictionary (by clicking Add To Dictionary in the Spelling And Grammar dialog box or right-clicking a word with a red wavy underline and then clicking Add To Dictionary in the shortcut menu), the term will be added to the new default custom dictionary.

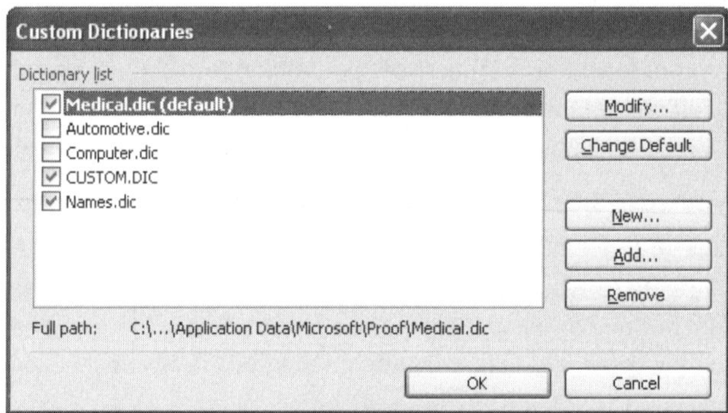

Figure 6-18. The default custom dictionary appears at the top of the Dictionary List, above the alphabetical list of custom dictionaries.

Disabling, Removing, and Deleting Dictionaries

Most of the time, you won't need to have Word check all your custom dictionaries every time you're working on a document. Therefore, you might want to disable some custom dictionaries until you need them. Other times, you might want to remove a custom dictionary from your Dictionary List altogether. Word allows you to do this without deleting the dictionary file. In some cases, you might want to delete a dictionary file because you no longer use it. You can perform all these tasks easily, from within the Custom Dictionaries dialog box, as follows:

- **Disable a dictionary** Clear the dictionary's check box in the Dictionary List. When a dictionary's check box is cleared, Word doesn't refer to the dictionary when it checks spelling.

- **Remove a dictionary** Select the name of the dictionary you want to remove in the Dictionary List, and click Remove. This action does not delete the file; it simply removes it from the Dictionary List.
- **Delete a dictionary** Click New or Add, select the dictionary file name in the Create Custom Dictionary or Add Custom Dictionary dialog box, and press Delete (or right-click the dictionary file name, and choose Delete from the shortcut menu). Click Yes in the Confirm File Delete message box, and click Cancel to close the dialog box. This operation sends the dictionary file to your Recycle Bin. Finally, you'll want to remove the reference to the dictionary in the Custom Dictionaries list, as described in the preceding bulleted item.

Brushing Up Your Grammar

In addition to checking spelling, Word can check documents for grammatical correctness. In a nutshell, Word's grammar checker works by reviewing standard grammar-related issues in your documents and flagging potential errors with a wavy green underline. By design, the grammar checker focuses only on the most typical and frequent types of grammar problems, meaning that most but not all grammar issues will be flagged by the grammar checker.

As you become familiar with the grammar checker and its capabilities, you'll find that its usefulness varies quite markedly from one document to the next. In some documents, the grammar checker might catch all sorts of useful errors, but in other documents, the grammar checker might flag numerous potential errors that are in fact grammatically correct. Therefore, you'll probably want to turn the Grammar Checking feature on and off depending on the document you're working on.

Tip **Control the grammar checker**

You can turn the grammar checker on and off by selecting or clearing the Check Grammar check box in the Spelling And Grammar dialog box. Similarly, you can hide the green wavy underlines without disabling grammar checking by right-clicking the Spelling And Grammar Status icon, and choosing Hide Grammatical Errors from the shortcut menu.

Using the grammar checker in Word is similar to using the spelling checker, so you might want to refer to the descriptions of the spelling checker in this chapter to answer some of your questions about the grammar checker. However, the grammar checker has a few grammar-specific features of its own, which are discussed next.

Checking Your Grammar

To run the grammar checker, right-click a potential grammar error, and choose Grammar from the shortcut menu, or choose Tools, Spelling And Grammar, as described in "Benefiting from Automated Spelling and Grammar Checking," on page 157. To resolve a grammar issue in the Spelling And Grammar dialog box (or in the Grammar dialog box), you can modify the marked text (which appears green) by typing in the top box, or you can choose from among the following options:

- **Ignore Once** Leaves the text as it is, without making any changes. Word removes the green wavy underline and displays the next grammar issue. If you click in the body of your document while the dialog box is open, the Ignore Once button changes to Resume, which you can click to continue checking grammar whenever you're ready to move on.
- **Ignore Rule** Ignores the text and all other grammar issues that are classified as the same type of error. Word removes the green wavy underline from all instances and displays the next grammar issue.
- **Next Sentence** Retains the current text without making changes and jumps to the next grammatical error.
- **Change** Replaces existing text with the text selected in the Suggestions list.
- **Explain** Displays the Office Assistant, which briefly describes the currently selected grammatical error.

In addition to these options, you can undo the last implemented correction (by clicking Undo), or display the grammar options (by clicking Options), as described next.

Configuring Grammar Options

Like the spelling checker, the grammar checker has options that you can configure in the Spelling & Grammar tab in the Options dialog box. As described earlier in this chapter, the first two check boxes in the Grammar section—Check Grammar As You Type and Hide Grammatical Errors In This Document—control whether the grammar checker is turned on or off and whether green wavy underlines appear in the document.

The third option—the Check Grammar With Spelling check box—performs essentially the same function as the Check Grammar check box in the Spelling And Grammar dialog box: It enables you to turn off the grammar checker while you're using the spelling checker. When you clear this check box, you can check spelling without addressing grammar issues. (The green wavy underlines used to flag potential grammar problems will continue to appear in your document if the Check Grammar As You Type check box is selected.) Selecting this option usually speeds up document checking because Word skips the grammar issues and presents only the potential spelling errors.

The remaining options in the Spelling & Grammar tab—the Writing Style and Settings options—enable you to define grammar rules that Word should follow, as discussed next.

For more information about the Show Readability Statistics check box (found in the Grammar section of the Spelling & Grammar tab), see "Judging a Document's Readability Level," on page 183.

Specifying Grammar Rules

The grammar checker in Word can check up to 35 types of fundamental grammar rules and writing style options, ranging from finding double negatives and clichés to identifying incorrect verb tenses and passive sentence structures. To specify grammar rule settings, follow these steps:

1. Choose Tools, Options, click the Spelling & Grammar tab, and then specify whether you want the grammar checker to check grammar only or grammar and style by selecting the appropriate option in the Writing Style list.
2. Click Settings. The Grammar Settings dialog box appears, as shown in Figure 6-19.

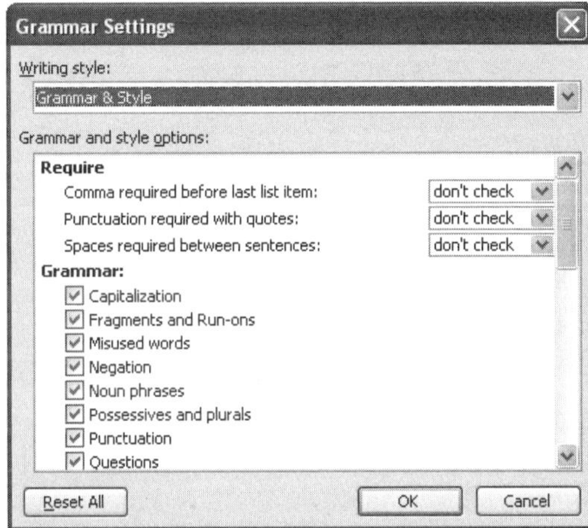

Figure 6-19. You can pick and choose which grammar and style rules you want Word to use when it searches for potential grammatical errors.

3. Select and clear the check boxes to configure which grammar rules you want Word to use when it searches for potential grammatical problems.

> **Tip** **View details of grammar and style options**
> To view brief descriptions of the grammar and writing style settings you can configure in the Grammar Settings dialog box, type *grammar and writing style options* in the Search For box in the Help task pane, and then click the green Start Searching button. In the results list, click the Grammar And Writing Style Options entry. To view details about each option, click the Show All link in the Microsoft Word Help window. The Help window presents a brief summary and examples of each grammar and style rule.

Enlivening Your Vocabulary Using the Thesaurus

As you write, you might encounter instances when you just can't think of the right word or you find yourself using the same word repeatedly. At those times, you should consider turning to a thesaurus. Instead of lugging out a heavy book every time you want to find a synonym, you can turn to a much lighter resource—the Word Thesaurus. Just as the Word spelling and grammar checkers suggest replacements for potential spelling and grammar errors, Word provides a thesaurus that lists a variety of terms you can use in your document.

Replacing Existing Text with a Synonym or Antonym

You can use the Word Thesaurus to look up synonyms and antonyms for selected words. To use the Thesaurus, right-click the word you want to replace, and then choose Synonyms from the shortcut menu to display a list of potential synonyms and antonyms, as shown in Figure 6-20.

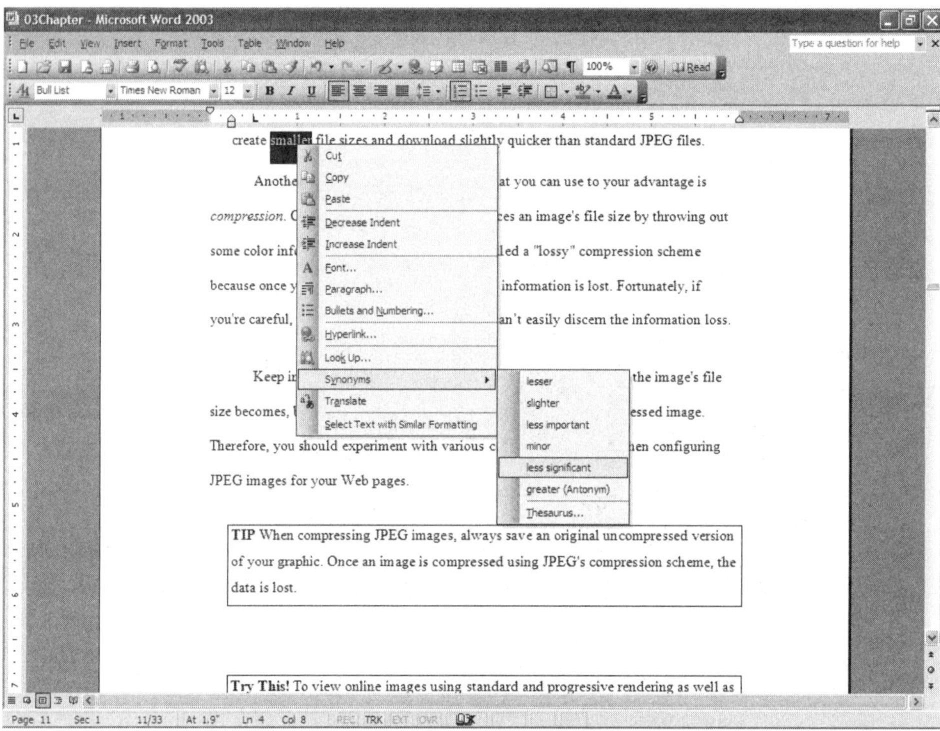

Figure 6-20. Notice that this synonym list for the word "smaller" includes an antonym, which is identified by the word (Antonym) after the suggested term.

> **Note** **Use the Thesaurus on flagged terms**
>
> You can't right-click to access the Thesaurus for a word that's flagged as a potential spelling or grammar error (a word marked with a red or green wavy underline). When you want to replace a flagged word with a synonym, you need to right-click and address the spelling or grammar error first, even if you merely want to choose Ignore Once to overlook the issue. Then you can right-click the word again to access the Thesaurus.

To replace existing text with a suggested term, click the appropriate suggestion; the original text is automatically replaced with the alternative.

Thumbing Through the Virtual Pages of the Online Thesaurus

If you right-click a word to access a list of synonyms (or antonyms) and none of the alternatives suits your purposes, you can click Thesaurus to open the Thesaurus in the Research task pane, as shown in Figure 6-21.You can use the Research task pane to search for additional terms.

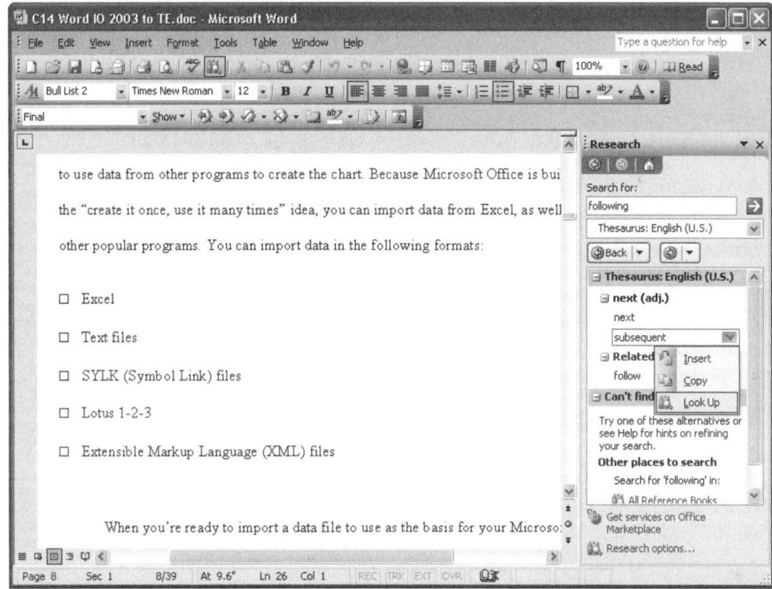

Figure 6-21. The Research task pane displays the Thesaurus entries and enables you to jump from term to term in the same fashion you might flip through a hard-copy thesaurus.

The Thesaurus enables you to look for synonyms and antonyms by searching through a wider range of suggestions than those presented by the right-click method. To open the Thesaurus in the Research task pane, position the insertion point in or near the word you want to look up, and then use one of the following procedures:

- Choose Tools, Language, Thesaurus.
- Press Shift+F7.
- Right-click the word you want to replace, choose Synonyms, and choose Thesaurus from the shortcut menu.
- Display the Research task pane, enter a word in the Search For box, and choose Thesaurus in the list.

The word you looked up appears in the results list in the Research task pane, as shown previously in Figure 6-21. To look up additional related terms, click a word in the results list, or hover the pointer over the word, click the arrow that appears, and then click Look Up. The results list will change to show words related to the clicked word. Further, you can also look up a word by typing the word in the Search For box and pressing Enter. If you find a word that suits your needs, you can insert the word into your document by hovering the pointer over the word, clicking the arrow, and then clicking Insert.

> **Tip** If you don't find an acceptable replacement word in the Replace With Synonym list after clicking Look Up, you can click Back in the Research task pane to return to the previous selected meaning and associated synonyms.

Translating Text into Other Languages

Using Word, you can perform basic translation tasks, such as translating words or phrases and inserting translated text into your documents. Word uses bilingual dictionaries installed on your computer as well as online (if you're connected to the Internet) to translate single words or short phrases. If you want to translate longer phrases, paragraphs, or documents, you can access online machine translation services as well as professional human translation services from within Word's Research task pane. The main interface for using Word's translation feature is the Translation reference resource in the Research task pane, which is shown in Figure 6-22.

Figure 6-22. The Translation reference resource in the Research task pane helps you translate words and phrases.

To open the Translation reference resource, use one of the following methods:

- Choose Tools, Language, Translate.
- Press Alt+Shift+F7.

- Display the Research task pane (choose Tools, Research, or click Research in the Standard toolbar), and select Translation in the Search For list.
- Right-click a word in your document that you want to translate, and choose Translate from the shortcut menu.

Note The first time you use translation services in an Office 2003 application, you will need to install the client dictionaries. After you install them, the dictionaries are available automatically when you connect to the Internet.

You can control which installed language pairs are available by clicking the Translation Options link in the Research task pane, and configuring the options in the Translation Options dialog box. If the Translation Options dialog box doesn't show a bilingual dictionary that you need, you might need to install Microsoft Office Proofing Tools, which is an add-in package that Microsoft offers for more than 45 languages (for more information, visit *http://shop.microsoft.com*).

To use the Translation tool, follow these steps:

1. Specify the text you want to translate by clicking a word or selecting text before you display the Research task pane (as described earlier). If you want to translate an entire document, you don't need to specify the text you want to translate—just open the document, and then display the Research task pane. If the Research task pane is already open, you can type the text you want to translate directly into the Search For box.
2. Ensure that Translation is selected in the Search For list.
3. Select From and To translation dictionaries in the lists. For example, you can select from English (U.S.) to Italian (Italy).
4. To translate the word or phrase that appears in the Search For text box, click the Start Searching button next to the Search For box. Your translation results appear in the results list in the Research task pane. To translate the entire document, click Translate Whole Document. Entire document translations appear in your Web browser, with a link to human translation services if you'd like a more accurate translation than the machine translation results.

Tip **Translate documents using online machine or human translation services**
When you click Translate Whole Document in the Research task pane, your document is translated using a machine translation service. Machine translation services can help you determine the main ideas in documents, but they shouldn't be used for important or sensitive documents because computers cannot preserve your text's full meaning, detail, or tone. To translate critical documents, you should use a professional human translator.

If you are having trouble finding appropriate translations, try looking up the singular forms of nouns (for example, *child* instead of *children*) and search using the infinitive forms of verbs (for example, *swim* instead of *swam*). Searching for root words generally results in greater success during translation. Also, keep in mind that theWord translation tool serves approximately the same function as a language dictionary—it's not a full-service translation utility, but it's a nice way to interpret a few words or phrases.

Scrutinizing Document Statistics

In addition to the standard reference book features included in Word, you have several other electronic reference tools that you can use to analyze your documents. Namely, you can instruct Word to quickly summarize the content in a document by using the AutoSummarize feature, you can analyze a document's readability level using Flesch Reading Ease and Flesch-Kincaid Grade Level scores, and you can display word count statistics to track the length of your text while you work.

Getting to the Point with AutoSummarize

Word can automatically summarize key points in documents, enabling you to create brief versions of documents that readers can quickly scan. You'll find that AutoSummarize works best on structured documents such as reports, white papers, technical documents, articles, and so forth. AutoSummarize doesn't work especially well for fiction, correspondence, and other more loosely structured documents.

The AutoSummarize feature determines key points in your document by analyzing and scoring sentences. Sentences are given higher scores if they contain words that are frequently used in the document.

You can choose one of the following four options for displaying the summary information:

- **Highlight Key Points** Summarizes the current document by highlighting summary information (in yellow, by default). The remainder of the document text appears in gray. The AutoSummarize toolbar appears by default; it includes a Highlight/Show Only Summary button, a Percent Of Original slider that enables you to adjust the percentage of the document included in the summary, and a Close button that returns you to your original document. Figure 6-23 shows a sample document with key points highlighted; notice the AutoSummarize toolbar in the upper-right corner.

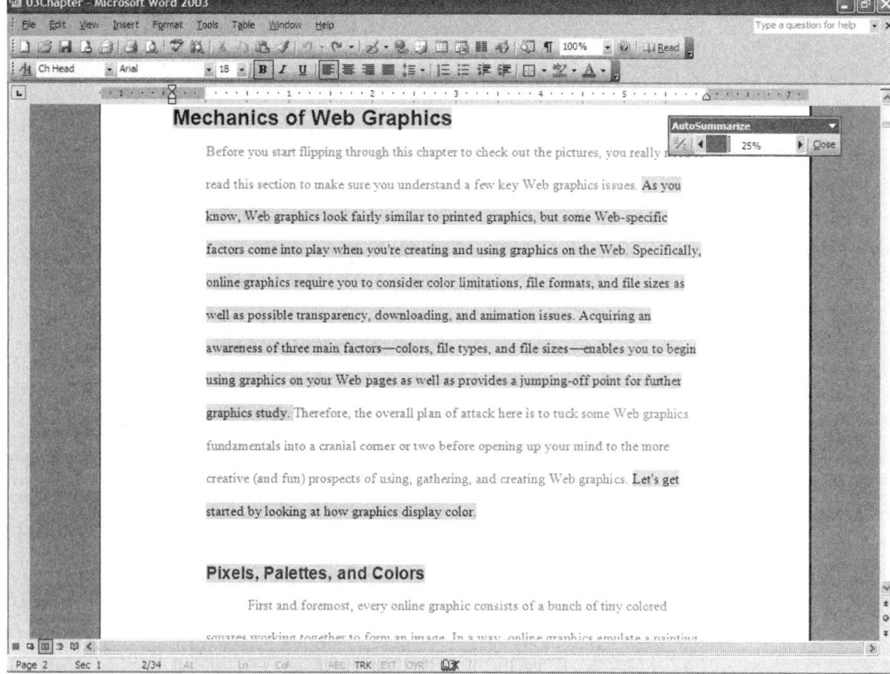

Figure 6-23. You can temporarily highlight a document's key points using the AutoSummarize feature, which automatically displays the AutoSummarize toolbar.

- **Create A New Document And Put The Summary There** Displays the summarized information in a new document. This option creates a separate document with no link to the original text. The only way you can adjust the percentage of information in this type of summary is to re-create the summary. This type of summary is helpful if you want to create an abstract or executive summary of a document.
- **Insert An Executive Summary Or Abstract At The Top Of The Document** Inserts the summary at the beginning of the document under the heading *Summary*. Using this option, the summary becomes part of your document. To remove the summary, click Undo (or press Ctrl+Z), or delete the added text manually.
- **Hide Everything But The Summary Without Leaving The Original Document** Hides all document text except the text included in the summary. This option doesn't change your text; it merely temporarily hides the text not included in the summary. If you print your document, only the summary will be printed. To return to the display of the complete document, click the Close button on the AutoSummarize toolbar.

> **AutoSummarize can't summarize text in textboxes, frames, or tables. For more information about text boxes and frames, see Chapter 17, "Formatting Layouts Using Text Boxes, Frames, Backgrounds, and Themes," and for more information about tables, see Chapter 13, "Organizing Concepts in Tables."**

To summarize a document using the AutoSummarize tool, follow these steps:

1. Open the document you want to summarize, and then choose Tools, AutoSummarize to display the AutoSummarize dialog box, shown in Figure 6-24.

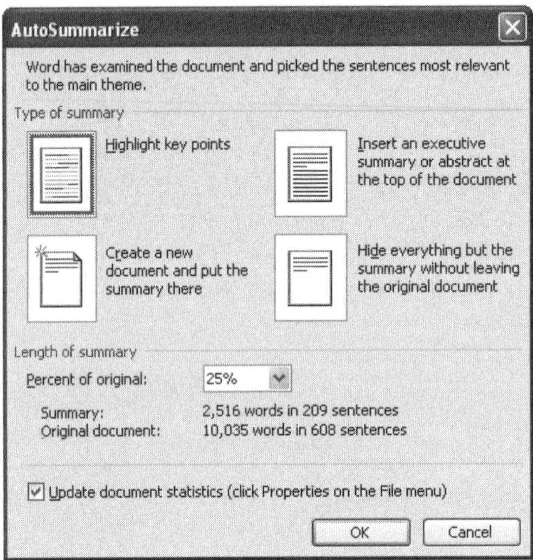

Figure 6-24. AutoSummarize provides various options for displaying a summary of the current document.

> **Tip** The AutoSummarize processing can take a few moments to complete. If you find the processing is taking too long, you can stop it by pressing Esc.

2. In the AutoSummarize dialog box, choose the type of summary you want to create.
3. In the Percent Of Original box, specify the level of detail that you want to include in your summary. You can choose among the following options: 10 Sentences, 20 Sentences, 100 Words Or Less, 500 Words Or Less, 10%, 25%, 50%, or 75%. A higher percentage includes more details in your summary, whereas a lower percentage includes less detail.
4. Specify whether you want AutoSummarize to replace existing keywords and comments in the Summary tab in the document's Properties dialog box (the document's Properties can be viewed by choosing File, Properties, and clicking the Statistics tab). If you don't want AutoSummarize to replace this information, clear the Update Document Statistics check box.
5. Click OK to create the summary.

After you create a summary using the AutoSummarize feature, you should proofread and edit the summary to smooth any rough edges, especially if you chose to create a new document or inserted the summary at the beginning of your document. Sometimes, you might find that it's better to include more in your summary at first and then pare down the information as needed—generally, it's easier to cut text than to put text back in.

Note AutoSummarize creates summaries based on the language in use when Office was installed on the computer. If you use AutoSummarize on a document written in another language, the summary is created in the document's language. Further, if multiple languages are used in a document that's being summarized, AutoSummarize generates the summary in the language that's used most frequently in the document.

Tip **Include text formatted with the No Proofing option in a summary**
AutoSummarize can't summarize text that's marked not to be checked for spelling or grammar. To ensure that text isn't formatted with the No Proofing option, choose Tools, Language, Set Language, and ensure that the Do Not Check Spelling Or Grammar check box is not selected.

Judging a Document's Readability Level

You can configure Word to display a readability level for a document after you finish checking spelling and grammar. Word determines readability levels by assigning Flesch Reading Ease scores and Flesch-Kincaid Grade Level scores to documents. These scores are obtained by rating the average number of syllables per word and average number of words per sentence. The Flesch Reading Ease score is based on a 100-point scale, in which a higher score means that a document is easier to read. You should aim for scores ranging from 60 to 70 in most cases. The Flesch-Kincaid Grade Level score rates text based on U.S. school grade level. For example, a score of 8.0 means that an eighth grader should be able to understand the text. Most documents intended for the general public should score near the 7.0 or 8.0 level.

To display reading statistics, you must select the Show Readability Statistics option and completely check your document's spelling and grammar as follows:

1. Choose Tools, Options, and click the Spelling & Grammar tab. Select the Check Grammar With Spelling check box (if necessary), select the Show Readability Statistics check box, and click OK.
2. Run a complete spelling and grammar check by choosing Tools, Spelling And Grammar. When the check is complete, Word automatically displays information about the reading level of the document, as shown in Figure 6-25.

Readability Statistics

Counts	
Words	2234
Characters	11653
Paragraphs	376
Sentences	92
Averages	
Sentences per Paragraph	1.8
Words per Sentence	13.0
Characters per Word	4.6
Readability	
Passive Sentences	8%
Flesch Reading Ease	61.0
Flesch-Kincaid Grade Level	7.8

OK

Figure 6-25. The Readability Statistics dialog box shows readability levels in addition to other details, such as word count, average words per sentence, and so forth.

Displaying Word Count Statistics

At times, you might want to show word count statistics without obtaining readability or AutoSummarize information. For example, you might have been given a limit on how many words a document can be for a particular assignment—magazines and newspapers commonly set this type of limit. You can easily count the words in your document in Word. To do so, choose Tools, Word Count. The Word Count dialog box appears, displaying page, word, character, paragraph, and line count information, as shown in Figure 6-26.

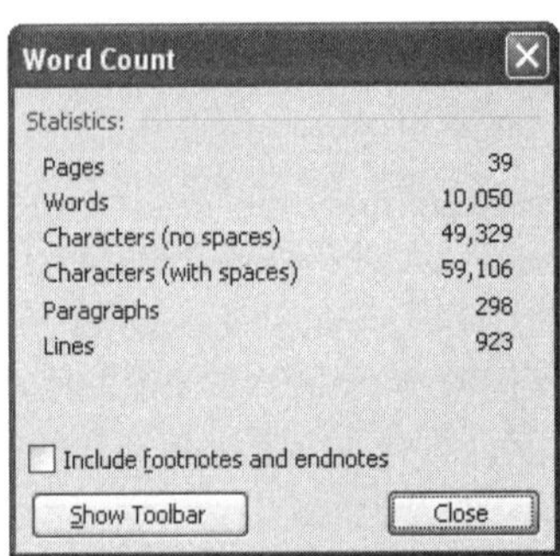

Figure 6-26. The Word Count dialog box gives you a quick summary of your document's statistics.

You can also use the following keyboard shortcuts to conduct word counts:

- Ctrl+Shift+G displays the Word Count dialog box.
- Ctrl+Shift+R conducts a recount to update the word count statistics.

The Word Count dialog box includes the Include Footnotes And Endnotes check box so you can choose whether to include those elements in your word count. Further, the Word Count dialog box contains a Show Toolbar button. Click this button to display the Word Count toolbar, shown in Figure 6-27, and then close the Word Count dialog box. The Word Count toolbar remains on your desktop while you work; you can click Recount at any time to quickly check your word count statistics, and click the arrow to view additional count statistics, including page, word, character (with and without spaces), paragraph, and line counts. Note that if your document has the revisions feature turned on, the Word Count feature will include the revisions in the count totals.

Figure 6-27. You can display various word count statistics on the Word Count toolbar by selecting the type of statistic from the list.

Finally, you can also perform a word count on selected text, including noncontiguous selections. To do so, select the text you want to count, and then choose Tools, Word Count or click Recount on the Word Count toolbar bar (if it's open).

Chapter 7

Putting Text Tools to Work

Part of the challenge of working with a word processing program that's as full-featured and powerful as Word is getting to the tools you need quickly. Some tasks are very simple—entering text, running the spelling checker, printing a simple page. Others are more complicated and require an investment of time and effort. Applying a format to a heading, for example, requires you to think about the overall design of your document (or the standards for publication in your department) and to choose the text font, size, style, and spacing settings you want in order to create just the right effect. But to cut down on the time you spend making those choices, Word includes an automated tool called AutoFormat that enables you to apply and change formats quickly in your documents. And if you want to reuse formats from other documents or sections of your work, you can use another feature—Reveal Formatting—to view the formats applied to selected text sections.

You also spend time going back and tracking down the bugs that sneak into your documents. Word includes tools to help you cut down on error-correction time. AutoText is a feature that inserts words or phrases you use often in your work (you can train AutoText to use terms native to your business or industry). AutoCorrect corrects typos as you go, giving you a cleaner document right from the start. This chapter explores all these tools as well as the Office Clipboard, which holds up to 24 different items and offers a "smart" paste feature that helps you easily repeat routine tasks.

Applying Quick Format Changes

Word 2003 includes a number of automatic features that help you control the formatting in your document. AutoFormatting, which enables you to add predesigned formats to paragraphs, headings, and tables, is covered in detail in the next part of the chapter. Here we'll look at the Format Painter, which gives you the means to copy formats from place to place, and a new offering that enables you to copy formats without creating new styles to do it.

Automatic? Your Call

If you granted three wishes to experienced Word users, at the top of the list would be improved control over automatic features. Until you understand what's going on behind the scenes with the various tools—including spelling, font choice, spacing, and more—you don't often know where to go when Word begins indenting lists you don't want indented, adding numbers you don't want added, or swapping words against your will. Such is the downside of automated functionality.

But the good news is that you have control over those automatic features. You can turn each feature on and off and control the items you want Word to change on the fly. This chapter looks at each of these features individually and shows you how you can set them up to work most efficiently for you.

Copying Formats Without Styles

One of the simplest formatting changes you're likely to make involves applying a format you like to another place in your document. Suppose, for example, that you like the indents and spacing you used in a citation in your report, and now you want to use that same format later in the document. You can use the Styles and Formatting task pane to apply that format with a single click of the mouse. Here are the steps to follow:

1. Open a document.
2. Create (or select) the text with the format you want to copy.
3. Choose Format, Styles And Formatting. The Styles And Formatting task pane appears, as shown in Figure 7-1.
4. Select the text to which you want to apply the format.
5. Click the format you want to use in the Styles And Formatting task pane. The format is then applied to the selected text.

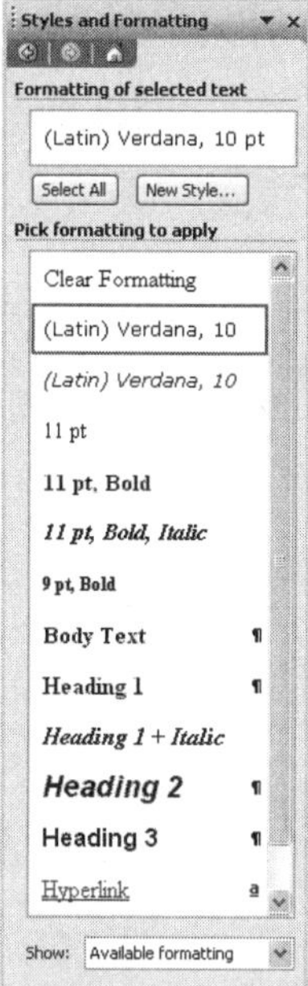

Figure 7-1. The Styles And Formatting task pane lists all the formats used in the current document, whether they've been saved as styles or not.

Note Styles sometimes get a bad reputation for being difficult to create and use. But styles can save you valuable time and effort, especially when you have specific formats and text treatments you use often. A style can include your choices for the font, size, color, style, spacing, and alignment of text. If you need to use a consistent standard for headings, body text, captions, or list items in your document, styles can save you time in applying the same format throughout your work.

Choosing Formats to View

You can change the formats that are available in the Styles And Formatting task pane by clicking the Show arrow in the Styles And Formatting task pane and choosing one of the following options:

- **Available Formatting** Displays all the formats that are currently available to the open document.

- **Formatting In Use** Shows only the styles that are currently being used in the open document.
- **Available Styles** Shows only the created and named styles available to the open document. This option does not display the unnamed styles you might have added to the text.
- **All Styles** Displays all styles available in the style sheets available to Word and the open document.
- **Custom** Opens a dialog box that enables you to choose the elements for which styles are displayed in the Styles And Formatting task pane (as shown in Figure 7-2).

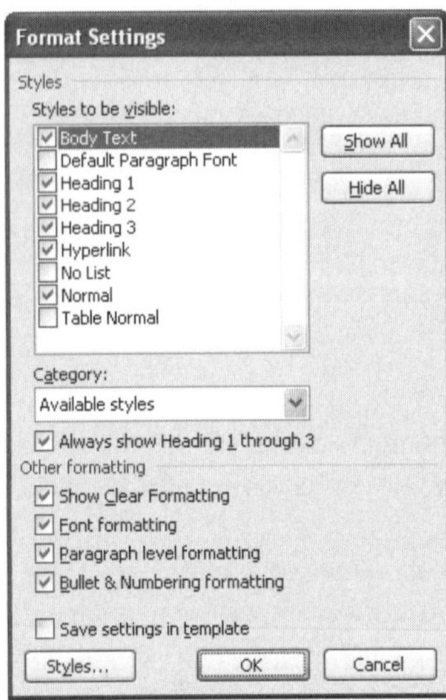

Figure 7-2. You can control where Word looks for styles by changing the selection in the Category list box.

For more information about creating, applying, and organizing styles, see Chapter 9, "Using Styles to Increase Your Formatting Power."

Employing the Format Painter

Format Painter

The Format Painter is a tool that enables you to copy and apply a format quickly. To apply the Format Painter, select the text you want to use, and then click the Format Painter tool on the Standard toolbar. Finally, click in the text or phrase to apply the format.

Inside Out

Format Painter tricks

- If you want to apply the format multiple times in your document, double-click the Format Painter to activate it, apply the format as needed, and then click Format Painter again or press Esc to deactivate it.
- If you want to apply the format to a single word, click once anywhere in the word to be formatted.
- To apply the format to an entire paragraph, click to the left of the paragraph.
- To apply the format to a phrase, select the entire phrase you want to format.
- To cancel a Format Painter operation, press Esc.
- To copy and paste the format quickly, use Ctrl+Shift+C to copy and Ctrl+Shift+V to paste.

Painless AutoFormatting

A good format is worth its weight in gold. A format that is inviting, professional, and easy to read can make the difference between your document's getting a second look or a toss in the trash. Because of a clean format, your grant proposal might get closer scrutiny; your book might catch an editor's attention; and your report could get passed up the line of command to the CEO's desk.

Word makes formatting easier by anticipating what you need and automating format changes with AutoFormat. You can work with AutoFormat as you type or you can apply AutoFormat to an existing document. AutoFormat is activated by default, so as soon as you begin using Word 2003, AutoFormat will kick in and help you.

Inside Out

What can you do with AutoFormat?

AutoFormat can jump in and quickly format items you use often in your documents. You might use AutoFormat to do the following:

- Format numbered lists.
- Assign a particular bullet style to a bulleted list.
- Take care of typographical issues, such as inserting open and close quotation marks.
- Format fractions.
- Make font style changes as needed.

Applying AutoFormatting

When you open an existing document in Word, you can have AutoFormat go through and correct any inconsistencies or errors in the format. You can choose both the form of the document you want Word to check (select General Document, Letter, or Email) and the way that Word alerts you about the changes that need to be made.

Start the process by choosing Format, AutoFormat. The AutoFormat dialog box appears, as shown in Figure 7-3.

Figure 7-3. You can choose the document type and set AutoFormat options in the AutoFormat dialog box.

Your first major decision is whether you want to review each AutoFormat suggestion as it arises or give AutoFormat carte blanche to make changes. If you want to apply AutoFormat to the entire document right now, click AutoFormat Now. Word goes through the document and makes changes according to the AutoFormat options selected by default.

If you want to see the changes AutoFormat wants to make before they're made, click the AutoFormat And Review Each Change option. After you click OK, Word begins to AutoFormat the document and displays the AutoFormat dialog box so that you can accept or reject the changes it proposes, as shown in Figure 7-4.

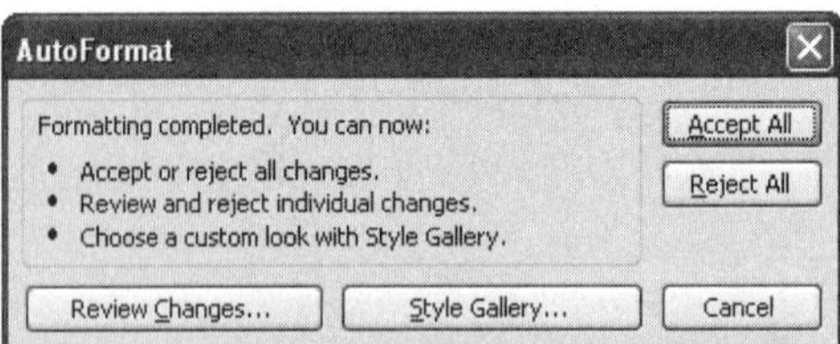

Figure 7-4. When you elect to have accept-and-reject privileges with AutoFormat, you're asked to make decisions about each change as it's proposed.

Tip If you want to apply AutoFormat to a selected portion of your document, select it before you display the AutoFormat dialog box.

Setting AutoFormat Options

You control the types of items you want AutoFormat to format for you. Display the choices by clicking the Options button in the AutoFormat dialog box. The AutoFormat tab in the AutoCorrect dialog box appears, as shown in Figure 7-5, and you can review all the AutoFormat options set by default for your document. Table 7-1 provides a quick description of the various AutoFormat options and gives examples of when they might affect your work.

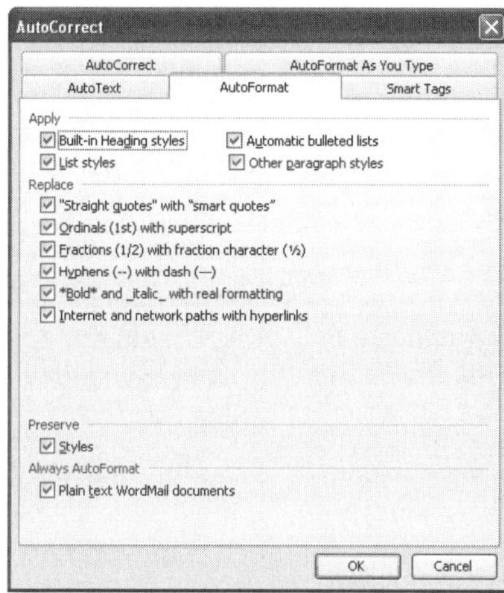

Figure 7-5. The check boxes in the AutoFormat tab control the items Word looks for when it AutoFormats your document.

Table 7-1. AutoFormat Options Selected by Default

AutoFormat Check Box	Description	Use
Built-in Heading Styles	Formats the headings in your document	You have a particular style sheet you want to apply to a long document.
List Styles	Uses the default list style to automatically indent and number your lists.	You have a multistep process that you want to format in a consistent way.
Automatic Bulleted Lists	Takes its cue from the first bullet you enter and formats subsequent lines accordingly	You want to use standardized bulleted lists throughout your document.
Other Paragraph Styles	Anticipates the styles of your paragraphs, adding spacing and indent levels according to paragraph styles in your document, letter, or e-mail message	You want to use spacing consistent with that already used in your document and existing styles.

Table 7-1. AutoFormat Options Selected by Default

AutoFormat Check Box	Description	Use
"Straight Quotes" With "Smart Quotes"	Replaces straight quotation marks with open and close quotation marks	You want to create a document that is typographically accurate with correct punctuation.
Ordinals (1st) With Superscript	Inserts ordinals (such as 1st, 2nd, 3rd) when you type full-sized ordinals	You want to increase the professional look of your document and make ordinals easier to read.
Fractions (1/2) With Fraction Character (½)	Replaces full-sized fractions (1/2) with reduced fractions (½)	Again, you want to increase the professional look of your publication and make the fraction easier to read.
Hyphens (-) With Dash (—)	Replaces two hyphens (-) with a dash character (—)	You want to add to the professional look of your document.
Bold And _Italic_ With Real Formatting	Applies text styles Bold and Italic to words as you type	You want to type quickly without interrupting your process to choose bold and italic styles.
Internet And Network Paths With Hyperlinks	Adds hyperlinks automatically to text strings that Word recognizes as URLs and network paths	You want to create hyperlinks to other documents online.
Preserve Styles	Keeps any styles you create in the existing document and does not replace them with named styles	You want to keep custom styles in the current document and don't want other formatting applied automatically.
Always AutoFormat Plain Text WordMail Documents	Enables you to use automatic formatting in e-mail messages	You want to include formatting in your e-mail messages and you've selected Word as your e-mail editor.

Note If you try to use dashes in your current document and AutoFormat doesn't automatically change them for you, make sure that you don't include spaces before and after the hyphens. Word will format the hyphens as dashes only if you type the hyphens between two text characters.

Disabling AutoFormat Features You Don't Use

No big surprise here—if you want to disable AutoFormat features, clear the check box to the right of the option you want to leave out. Which options might you want to disable in AutoFormat? Here are a few possibilities:

- **List Styles** If you have customized lists or need to enter project-specific codes as you type, clear the List Styles check box so Word doesn't apply its own format.
- **Automatic Bulleted Lists** If you have a specific style you want to apply to your document, or you want to use the dashes or asterisks commonly used to denote bullets, clear the Automatic Bulleted Lists check box.
- **Preserve Styles** If you want Word to automatically update styles in a document to fit the styles in the applied style sheet, clear the Styles check box. Word will then automatically format modified paragraphs to fit accepted styles.

AutoFormatting as You Type

Word also gives you the option of automatically formatting your text as you type, allowing you to improve the consistency of your document as you create it. Because AutoFormat is enabled by default, the feature will already be turned on when you begin to type. If you want to change the formatting options, however, you can change the settings in the AutoFormat As You Type tab in the AutoCorrect dialog box. To set AutoFormat As You Type options, choose Format, AutoFormat. Click the Options button in the AutoCorrect dialog box, and then click the AutoFormat As You Type tab. The options are similar to the options you've just set in the AutoFormat tab, but there are a few differences, as you can see in Figure 7-6.

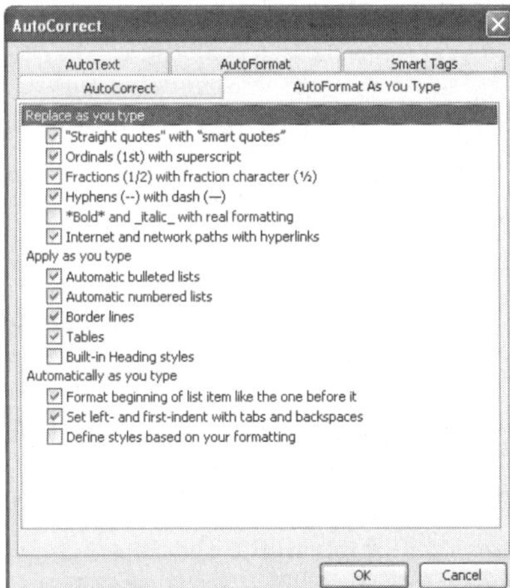

Figure 7-6. Catching formatting problems while you type is the function of the AutoFormat As You Type options.

The only options that are not enabled by default are the ones that replace words enclosed in asterisks and underscores with bold and italic, respectively, and the Built-in Heading Styles option. The Set Left- And First-Indent With Tabs And Backspaces item, available in the Automatically As You Type section, picks up the indents you set as you type, repeating them in subsequent similar paragraphs.

After you've finished setting the options for AutoFormat As You Type, click OK to close the AutoCorrect dialog box.

Seeing What's Going On Using Reveal Formatting

You can find out how text at the cursor position is formatted by choosing Format, Reveal Formatting to display the Reveal Formatting task pane, shown in Figure 7-7.

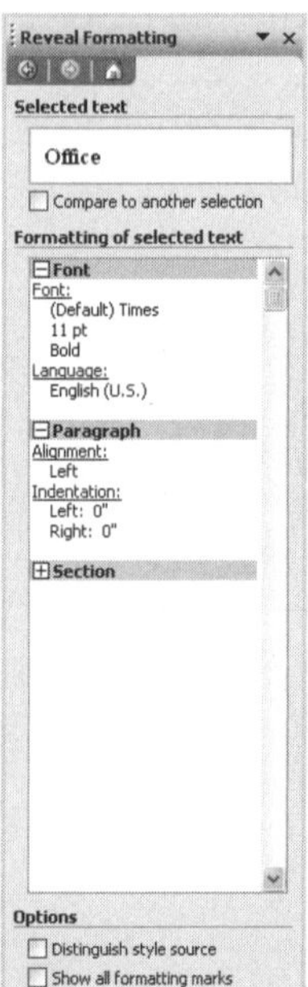

Figure 7-7. The Reveal Formatting task pane lists the format settings for the text at the insertion point.

The Reveal Formatting task pane lists all the format specifications for the selected text. The format items are divided into three groups:

- **Font** This group includes format settings that apply to the characters used in the document, including the font type and size, as well as the language selected for the document.
- **Paragraph** This group contains format settings for aspects of the paragraph such as the selected paragraph style, text alignment, indentation settings, and paragraph spacing (before and after spacing, as well as line spacing).
- **Section** This group includes the format settings you use to control larger portions of the document, including overall margin settings, page layout choices, and paper selections.

Making Changes from the Reveal Formatting Task Pane

You can make formatting changes to the text at the insertion point right from the Reveal Formatting task pane. By simply clicking the format setting you want to change (the links are shown in blue, underlined text), you can move directly to the relevant dialog box. To make formatting changes directly from the task pane, follow these steps:

1. Select the text for which you want to change the format.
2. Choose Format, Reveal Formatting. The Reveal Formatting task pane appears.
3. Click the format setting you want to change. For example, click the Indentation link in the task pane. The Paragraph dialog box appears with the Indents And Spacing tab displayed, as shown in Figure 7-8.

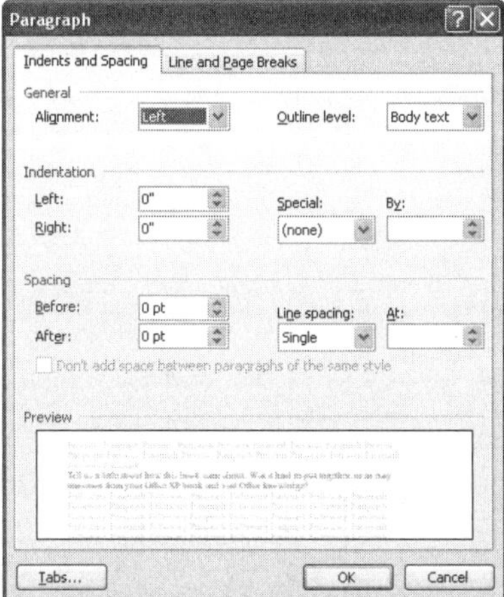

Figure 7-8. You can save time and effort by moving directly to the changes you want to make from the Reveal Formatting task pane.

4. Make your changes and close the dialog box. You are returned to the current document.

Displaying Formatting Marks from Reveal Formatting

For times when you need to grab the last paragraph mark, move blocks of text from one section to another, or make sure you have only one space between words, you can display and work with formatting marks in your document.

You can display formatting marks easily from the Reveal Formatting task pane by selecting the Show All Formatting Marks check box at the bottom of the task pane. The marks then appear in your document, as shown in Figure 7-9.

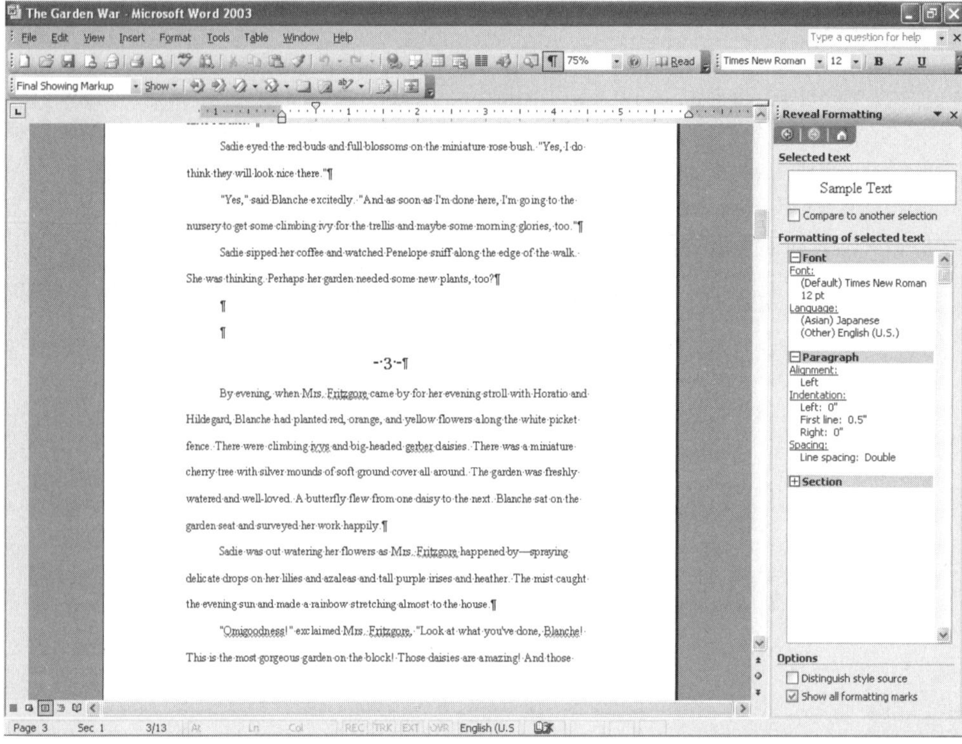

Figure 7-9. Display formatting marks by selecting the check box at the bottom of the Reveal Formatting task pane.

Changing the Formatting Marks That Appear

By default, all available formatting marks—tabs, spaces, paragraph marks, hidden text, and hyphens—are shown when you select Show All Formatting Marks in the Reveal Formatting task pane. You can change which marks are displayed by following these steps:

1. Choose Tools, Options. The Options dialog box appears, as shown in Figure 7-10.
2. Click the View tab, if necessary. In the Formatting Marks section, select check boxes for the marks you want to appear in the document.

Figure 7-10. Switch to the View tab in the Options dialog box to change which formatting marks are displayed.

> **Tip** **Avoid screen clutter**
> Some people are able to work with formatting marks on and barely notice them; others are distracted by the dots and symbols stuffed between words and paragraphs in their text. You can hide formatting marks quickly by clicking the Show/Hide button on the Standard toolbar.

Comparing Other Text Formats

Another option available to you in the Reveal Formatting task pane is the ability to compare and contrast similar text styles with subtle differences. Have you ever studied a heading, wondering why it doesn't look quite right compared to another heading in your document? Now Reveal Formatting enables you to click on one text item, and then compare it to another, showing the differences in font styles and sizes, spacing, and so forth.

To compare the formats of two text segments in your document, follow these steps:

1. Select the text you want to start with. You can either select a block of text or simply place the insertion point in the text you want to use.
2. Display the Reveal Formatting task pane, if needed, by choosing Format, Reveal Formatting.
3. Select the Compare To Another Selection check box, just beneath the Selected Text box in the Reveal Formatting task pane. Another text selection box opens in the task pane, showing a duplicate of the text you selected.

4 Now select the text to which you want to compare the original text. The task pane shows the formatting differences between the two selections, as shown in Figure 7-11.

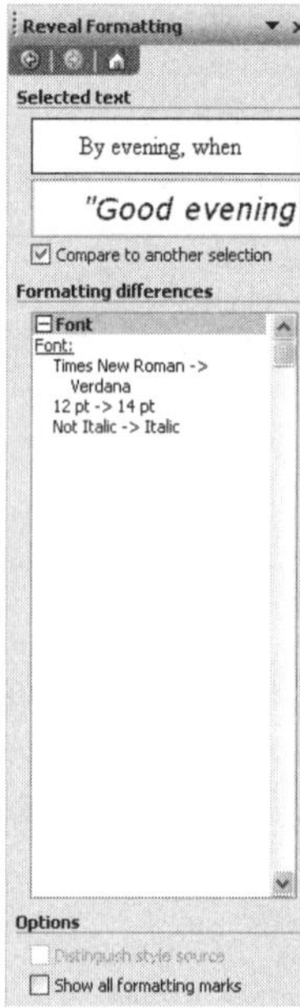

Figure 7-11. The Reveal Formatting task pane displays the formatting differences between two text selections.

> **Tip** The Reveal Formatting task pane is perfect for comparing the format of one piece of text with another. But when you want to see and compare the contents of documents (and not just the format), choose Compare Side By Side from the Window menu to view two open documents together on the screen.

Making Changes in Text Under Comparison

Suppose that comparing two different types of heading reveals the need to reformat one type of heading throughout your entire document. Word gives you a way to do this easily. Right there in the Reveal Formatting task pane, you can choose an option that will modify every heading formatted with particular settings in the rest of your document. To make this kind of change, follow these steps:

1 Click the arrow to the right of the compared text. A menu appears, as shown in Figure 7-12.

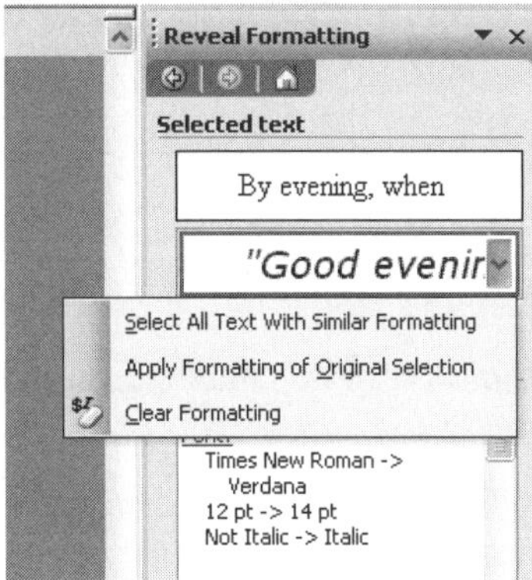

Figure 7-12. Select the action in the Reveal Formatting task pane.

You can choose Select All Text With Similar Formatting, which highlights all text in the document with the same specifications; Apply Formatting Of Original Selection, which applies the format of the first item to the second item; or Clear Formatting, which clears the formatting of the second Selected Text item.

Tip **Find similar formats**
When the Reveal Formatting task pane is not visible, you can easily find and highlight all text with the same format as the text at the insertion point. Just right-click the text and choose Select Text With Similar Formatting from the shortcut menu. All similar text items throughout your document will be selected, and you can make your changes as needed.

2 Choose the option you want, and then Word reformats the text accordingly. If you don't like the change, choose Edit, Undo to reverse your changes.

Where Did That Style Come From?

One final offering in the Reveal Formatting task pane that's worth a mention: you can find out the source of a particular style by selecting the Distinguish Style Source check box at the bottom of the Reveal Formatting task pane.

Selecting this check box causes Word to display the style from which the new style was created; for example, if a Note style applied to a segment of text in your document was created based on your Body Text style, the task pane will show you that information. That's helpful to know if you're planning to change the Body Text style at some point—you'll be able to see at a glance which other items in your document will be affected by the change.

Using AutoCorrect to Fix Typos Effortlessly

AutoCorrect is a terrific Word feature that anticipates your possible errors and corrects them—almost before you know you've made them. AutoCorrect comes with a library of more than a thousand different items, and it learns from you as you work. Are you forever typing **yuor** when you mean to type **your**? AutoCorrect will automatically reverse the characters in words it recognizes without any further action from you.

AutoCorrect locates several types of problems in your document. You can relax and let the thoughts flow, knowing that Word will catch and correct the following types of errors:

- **Problems with capitalization** If you accidentally type too many capital letters in a row, forget to capitalize the beginning of a sentence or a table heading, or enter the name of a day of the week in lowercase (**tuesday**), Word will fix it for you.
- **Problems with garbled typing** If your fingers get tied in a knot when you try to type the word **can** and type **acn** instead, Word will untangle the characters for you.
- **Problems with spacing** If your words run together, as in **nextime** instead of **next time**, Word will add the missing letter and character space.
- **Inserting special symbols** Instead of going through the menu selections needed to insert a special symbol like a Wingding, you can rely on AutoCorrect to substitute the symbol for the text you type (for example, replacing (r) with ®).

Controlling AutoCorrect

AutoCorrect is a great feature that can cut down the time and effort you spend ensuring the accuracy and professionalism of your documents. It can also get in your way sometimes, when you *mean* to enter a word in all caps, or you want to spell something incorrectly, or you decide to lowercase the labels in a table. You have the option of changing AutoCorrect options one at a time, while you're working in your document, and all at once, by changing the selections in the AutoCorrect dialog box.

Working with AutoCorrect in Your Document

AutoCorrect Options

The first time you notice AutoCorrect might be when it has just changed something you've typed. Suppose, for example, that you began typing a sentence and neglected the first capital letter. AutoCorrect makes the change. You then have the option of continuing and accepting the change or stopping and undoing it (assuming, of course, that you *meant* to leave the character lowercase). To see your AutoCorrect choices after a change is made, follow these steps:

1. Position the pointer over the word that was changed. A blue underline appears at the beginning of the word.
2. Hover the mouse pointer over the line for a second, and the line changes to the AutoCorrect Options button. To the right of the button is an arrow.

3 Click the arrow to see a menu. The choices reflect the type of change that's been made and give you the option of undoing the change or changing other AutoCorrect options, as shown in Figure 7-13.

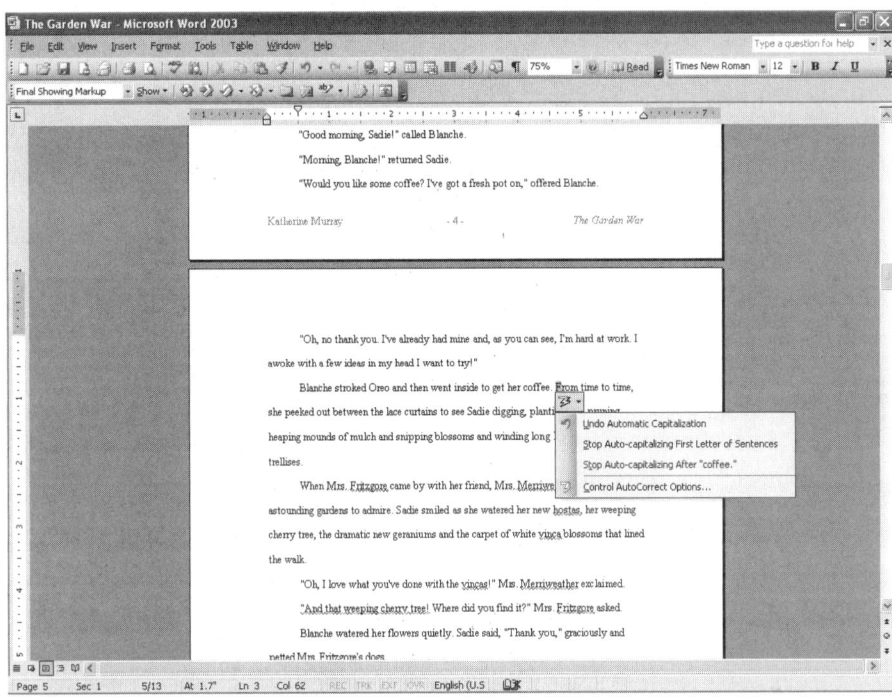

Figure 7-13. You can make changes to the kinds of corrections AutoCorrect makes while continuing to work in your document.

4 Click the command you want in the menu and Word makes the change. You can then continue with your text entry and editing.

Setting AutoCorrect Options

It's good to know how to set the AutoCorrect options just the way you want them. You can control the items that AutoCorrect fixes; you can also create your own words and phrases for AutoCorrect to insert (you can even add images in place of text). You can have AutoCorrect apply correct spellings from the spelling checker as you type.

To display the AutoCorrect dialog box, shown in Figure 7-14, choose Tools, AutoCorrect Options. The AutoCorrect dialog box allows you to control the changes AutoCorrect makes for you. Table 7-2 describes the choices in the AutoCorrect dialog box.

Figure 7-14. Use the AutoCorrect Options dialog box to specify which items you want AutoCorrect to catch.

Table 7-2. Setting Autocorrect Options

AutoCorrect Option	Description	Use
Show AutoCorrect Options Button	Displays the AutoCorrect Options button when a change is automatically made in your document.	You want to be able to go back and undo AutoCorrect changes.
Correct TWo INitial CApitals	Finds and changes any capitalization inconsistencies at the beginning of a word.	You are not entering data with acronyms or unusual capitalization.
Capitalize First Letter Of Sentences	Capitalizes the first word in a new sentence.	You are typing sentences.
Capitalize First Letter Of Table Cells	Capitalizes the data entered in the cells of a table.	You want to capitalize table data.
Capitalize Names Of Days	Capitalizes the full names of days of the week.	You want the days of the week to be shown traditionally; if you want days to appear in lowercase as part of a design element, clear this check box.
Correct Accidental Usage Of cAPS LOCK Key	Catches the accidental pressing of the Caps Lock key, releases it, and changes the erroneous capitalization of characters.	You want AutoCorrect to watch for and catch unusual capitalization.

Table 7-2. Setting Autocorrect Options

AutoCorrect Option	Description	Use
Replace Text As You Type	Enables AutoCorrect to make changes as you type. If you disable this option, AutoCorrect will not make changes on the fly.	You want AutoCorrect to make changes as you work.
Replace: With:	Enables you to add your own AutoCorrect entries to the AutoCorrect library.	There are words, phrases, text blocks, or graphics that you want to insert automatically in your document.
Automatically Use Suggestions From The Spelling Checker	Looks for suggestions for misspelled words by consulting the spelling checker's dictionary.	You want to include words and phrases the spelling checker recognizes as part of the AutoCorrect library.
Exceptions	Enables you to "teach" AutoCorrect which items *not* to correct automatically.	You have particular words, phrases, acronyms, or items that you don't want AutoCorrect to change.

Adding AutoCorrect Entries

One of the great features of AutoCorrect, besides its ability to catch your errors and make you look good, is that you can reduce data entry time by having Word automatically insert words, phrases, or even logos or graphics when it finds an AutoCorrect item you've entered.

For example, suppose that it's part of your company's policy to use the real company logo whenever the name of the company is shown in text.You can create an AutoCorrect entry that does that for you, automatically. Here's how:

1. Start by creating the item you want to place in the document, complete with the formatting, coloring, and spacing you want.
2. Select the item.
3. Choose Tools, AutoCorrect Options. The AutoCorrect dialog box appears.
4. Click Formatted Text in the Replace Text As You Type section if you've added formatting features to the word or phrase.
5. In the Replace box, type the characters you want to use to trigger the replacement, as shown in Figure 7-15.

Figure 7-15. You can create AutoCorrect entries that replace text you type with words, phrases, logos, graphics, and even blocks of text.

6 Click Add. Word then adds the new AutoCorrect entry to the list.

7 Test the new item. Click in your document and type the characters you entered in the Replace box. AutoCorrect will place the new addition at the insertion point.

> **Tip** Save keystrokes
>
> You can use AutoCorrect to enter blocks of text you type often, saving you the trouble of typing the same text over and over again. For example, if you include your organization's mission statement on everything you print, you can create an AutoCorrect entry that inserts the entire mission statement when you type the letters **ms**.

Replacing and Deleting AutoCorrect Entries

You can edit the AutoCorrect entries you create by simply creating them again, and then replacing them. For example, if you want to modify the logo you entered as an AutoCorrect item, you can simply make the change to the logo in the document, select it, and then enter the same trigger word in the Replace box in the AutoCorrect tab in the AutoCorrect dialog box. The button beneath the list changes from Add to Replace. Click Replace to insert the new AutoCorrect entry in place of the original. Word will display a message box asking you to confirm the action. Click Yes and the AutoCorrect entry is replaced.

You can delete entries in a similar way. Display the AutoCorrect dialog box and type the characters for the trigger in the Replace box in the AutoCorrect tab. When AutoCorrect displays the item you want to delete, click it to select it, and then click Delete.

Tip **Catch accidental deletions**

A warning about deleting AutoCorrect entries: Word doesn't prompt you to confirm that you do, in fact, mean to delete the item. The item is simply removed from the list. If you clicked Delete accidentally and want to save the AutoCorrect entry you've just deleted, you have one last chance—until you click OK or select another entry, AutoCorrect displays the item just deleted in the Replace and With boxes. You can click Add to add the item back to the list, if you catch the error in time.

Entering Exceptions

As helpful as AutoCorrect is, there will be times you don't want it interfering with what you're trying to do. You might be typing a document full of chemical compounds, for example, or creating a list of access codes for the new mainframe. You don't want AutoCorrect to get in there and change the capitalization and perhaps your character order while you type. In this case, you have two options: you can disable AutoCorrect while you're working on this document, or you can create an exception to teach AutoCorrect what you don't want it to change.

Tip **Add exceptions automatically**

If you've selected Automatically Add Words To List in the AutoCorrect Exceptions dialog box, Word automatically updates your list of selections if you press Backspace after Word uses AutoCorrect to change a word, and then type the word the way you want it to appear. If you use Undo, Word will not update your list with the change.

To enter AutoCorrect exceptions, you click Exceptions in the AutoCorrect tab in the AutoCorrect dialog box. The AutoCorrect Exceptions dialog box shown in Figure 7-16 appears.

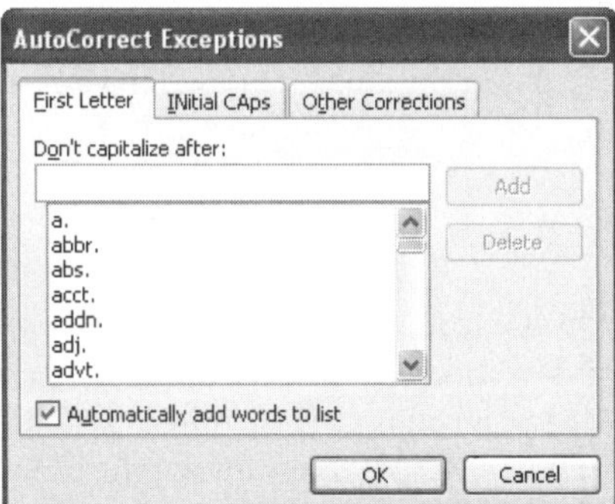

Figure 7-16. You can teach AutoCorrect not to correct certain items that are particular to the documents you create.

AutoCorrect lets you create three different kinds of exceptions:

- **First Letter** This form of capitalization controls the words immediately following abbreviations. (For example, you might have a phrase such as "after the merging of Lake Ltd. and Smith Co.," in which the word "and" should not be capitalized.)
- **INitial CAps** Allows you to enter words and phrases with unusual capitalization that you don't want changed. This might include company names or abbreviations or terms peculiar to your business or industry.
- **Other Corrections** Enables you to add additional items you don't want AutoCorrect to change. This might include names, locations, unusual spellings, and phrases that reflect terminology particular to your work.

To add an exception to one of the Exception lists, follow these steps:

1. Display the AutoCorrect Exceptions dialog box, if necessary, by clicking Exceptions in the AutoCorrect dialog box.
2. Click the tab for the exception type you want to enter.
3. Click in the box, and then type the item you want to add.
4. Click Add to add the exception to the AutoCorrect Exceptions list box.
5. Click OK twice to close the dialog boxes and return to your document.

Making AutoText Work for You

Although AutoCorrect and AutoText can be used in similar ways—cutting down the time and effort you spend entering text—AutoText really has a different function. Instead of catching errors in spelling, capitalization, and spacing, the focus of AutoText is simply to help you enter text as quickly as possible. AutoText works with the AutoComplete feature to anticipate the words you are preparing to enter and to insert them for you. By spending the time to educate Word about the terms, phrases, and descriptions often used in your documents, you can both save text entry time and reduce your margin for error.

Inserting AutoText Entries

AutoText gives you a long list of entries to choose from, including standard elements of documents such as the attention line, mailing instructions, company name, salutations, e-mail options (which include a complete list of the e-mail addresses Word recognizes from your Outlook Contacts list), and a Person selection, which lists the names of the individuals in your Address Book.

You begin the process of using AutoText by choosing Insert, AutoText. A menu of AutoText choices appears, and you can point to a selection to display specific AutoText choices, as shown in Figure 7-17.

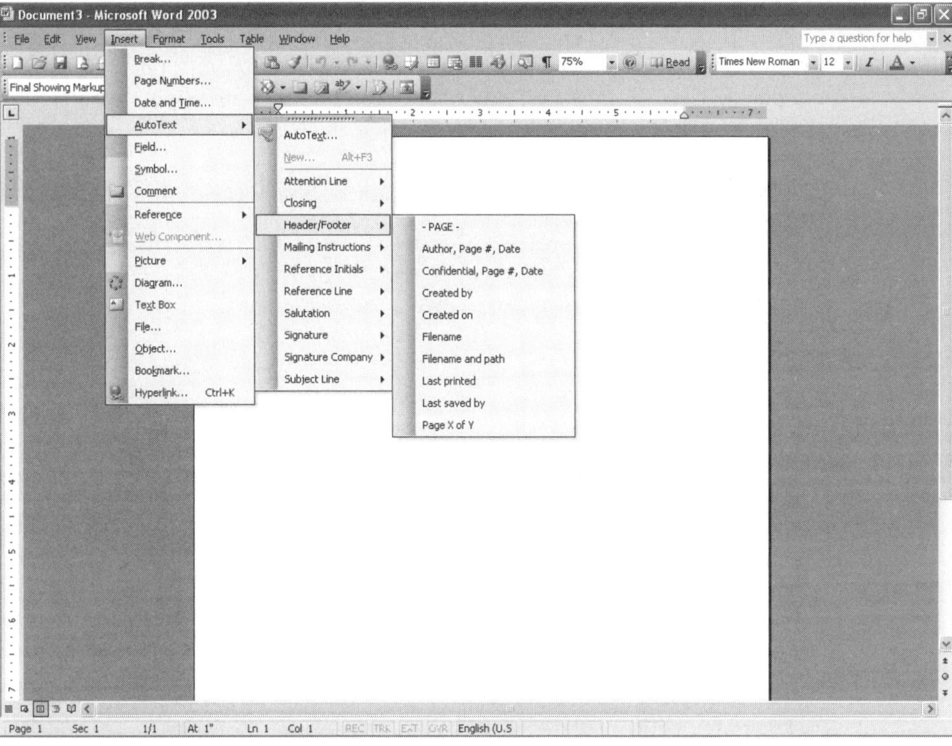

Figure 7-17. AutoText uses the text you often add and the text you've already entered to create the fastest means of text entry for your documents.

AutoText in Headers and Footers

When you want to add AutoText to a header or footer in your document, start by displaying the Header And Footer toolbar by choosing View, Header And Footer. Then click in the header (or footer) and follow these steps:

1. Choose Insert, AutoText. A list of Header and Footer AutoText items appears.
2. Choose the item you want to add as AutoText. The text is added at the insertion point.

You'll notice that although the AutoText menu choice appears as, for example, Author, Page #, Date once the AutoText is inserted in the document, the actual data appears—your name, the current page number, today's date. The Header and Footer AutoText entries are actually field codes, meaning that they are replaced with data when they are used in the document. Every time you open a document, these fields will be updated as needed.

Inserting AutoText in Your Document

AutoText is enabled by default. When you begin typing a word or phrase AutoText recognizes, it displays the rest of the phrase in a ScreenTip above the word you are typing, with the instruction "(Press ENTER to Insert)," as shown in Figure 7-18.

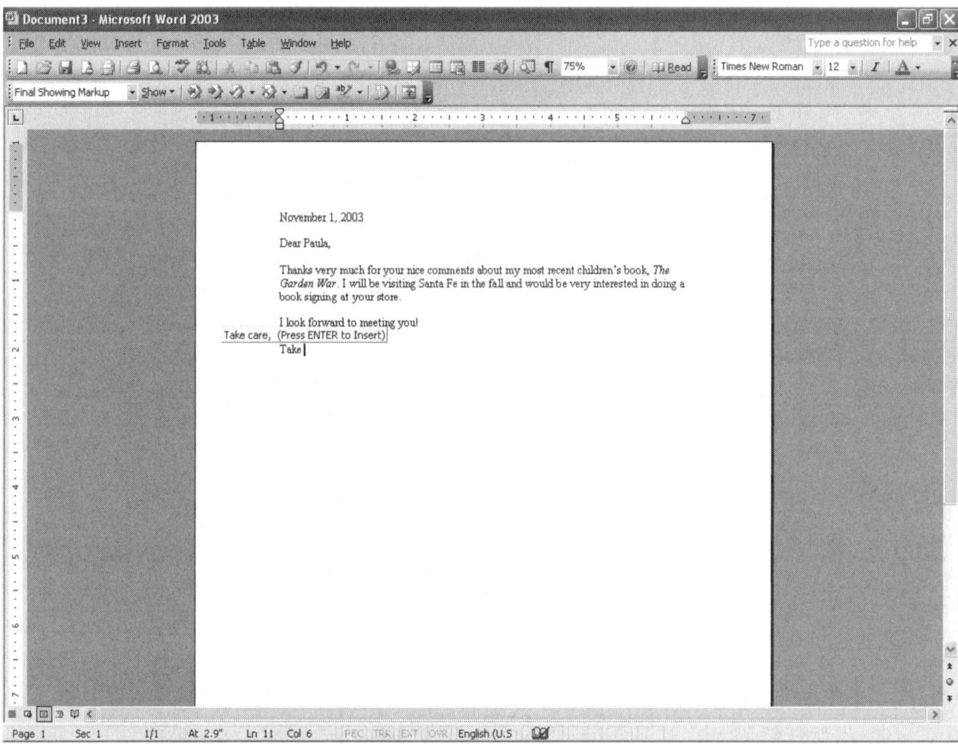

Figure 7-18. AutoComplete offers to complete a word or phrase for you. Press Enter to add the text as prompted.

> **Tip** If AutoText doesn't come to your rescue when you begin typing a phrase it should recognize, make sure AutoComplete is enabled by choosing Tools, AutoCorrect Options, and then clicking the AutoText tab. The first check box, Show AutoComplete Suggestions, should be selected. If it isn't, check the box, and then click OK to save your changes. Now AutoText should work as expected.

Although entering AutoText on the fly, as you're prompted, offers the fastest way of inserting AutoText entries, you can add entries from the AutoText tab in the AutoCorrect dialog box if you choose. Simply scroll through the AutoText entry list box until you find the item you want, click it, and then click Insert. Word adds the text you selected at the insertion point in your document.

Inside Out

Comparing AutoText and AutoComplete

Confused about the difference between AutoComplete and AutoText? The two terms are actually two parts of the same process. AutoText entries are the words and phrases you enter by choosing the AutoText selection from the Insert menu. AutoComplete is the process of finishing a partially typed word or phrase for you. But when you want to enter new phrases for AutoComplete, where do you go? To the AutoText tab in the AutoCorrect dialog box.

Adding Your Own AutoText Entries

What other entries will AutoText insert for you? Months, days of the week, and names it recognizes. The best way to get the full effect of AutoText, however, is to teach it to enter the words and phrases you use most often. This is really a simple thing to do.

The quickest way to add AutoText entries is just to type your document. When you get to a word or phrase that you'd like to enter as AutoText, select it, and then press Alt+F3. The Create AutoText dialog box appears, as shown in Figure 7-19, and all you need to do is click OK. The phrase is added to your list and will be suggested for insertion the next time Word recognizes that you're beginning to type it.

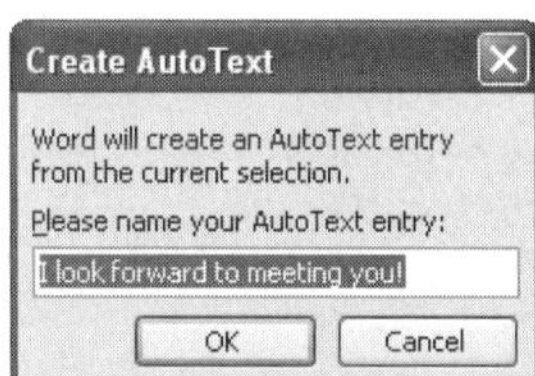

Figure 7-19. Fast and simple—add an AutoText entry by selecting the phrase and pressing Alt+F3.

Note You can also add AutoText entries in the AutoText tab in the AutoCorrect dialog box. Simply type the entry in the Enter AutoText Entries Here box, and then click Add. Using this method is best when you have several entries to create. When you're finished adding entries, click OK to return to your document.

Managing AutoText Entries

You've already spent some time in the AutoCorrect dialog box, which includes a tab for AutoText. Here you have another way to add your own AutoText entries. You can also manage the entries you have by inserting and deleting them. Figure 7-20 shows the AutoText tab in the AutoCorrect dialog box.

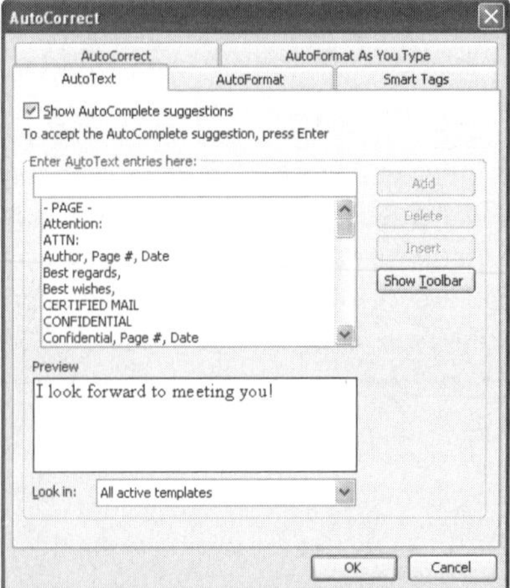

Figure 7-20. You can manage the AutoText entries you add and insert in the AutoText tab in the AutoCorrect dialog box.

Disabling AutoText

If AutoText just gets under your skin and you want to disable the feature (but *why?*), you can do so easily by displaying the AutoCorrect dialog box (choose Tools, AutoCorrect Options), clicking the AutoText tab, and then clearing the Show AutoComplete Suggestions check box. That suppresses the display of the AutoText ScreenTips that come to your rescue as you type. When and if you want to use AutoText again, simply repeat the steps and select Show AutoComplete Suggestions check box.

Tip **Improve speed by disabling AutoText**

Some users feel that ScreenTips slow Word down, especially in large documents and documents that are heavily loaded with graphics. If you find this to be true on your system, try disabling AutoText to see whether the change makes a difference in performance.

Choosing Templates for AutoText

By default, AutoText looks in all active templates to find the AutoCorrect entries used in your document. The items you add are saved in Normal.dot, the global template Word traditionally uses for newly created files (unless you specify otherwise). To choose a different template, click the Look In arrow in the AutoText tab in the AutoCorrect dialog box, and then click the template you want to use.

Saving AutoText Entries to Other Templates

If you've added other templates to Word, you can save AutoText entries in them by following these steps:

1. Choose Tools, Templates And Add-Ins to display the Templates And Add-Ins dialog box.

2 Click Organizer, and then click the AutoText tab. The listing on the left shows the AutoText entries in Normal.dot, the global template. The listing on the right shows the AutoText entries in the current document. If you want to change the template from which you are copying the AutoText entries, click Close File on the left to close the selected file, and then click Open File and choose the file you want to use.

3 Select the AutoText entries in the left listing that you want to copy to the file on the right side of the Organizer dialog box, as shown in Figure 7-21. Click Copy. The Auto-Text entries are added to the template on the right.

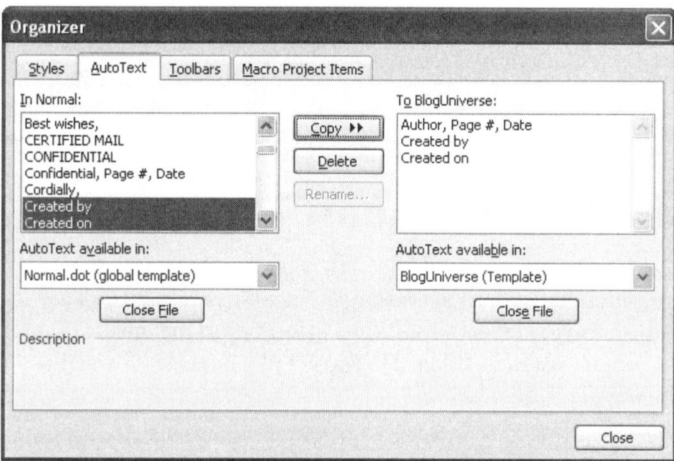

Figure 7-21. Copying AutoText entries to another document template is a simple matter when you use the Organizer available through Tools, Templates, And Add-Ins.

4 Click Close to exit the Organizer dialog box and return to your document.

> **Tip** **Why copy AutoText entries?**
> If AutoText is capable of looking in all available templates for possible entries, why is it necessary to copy entries from one template to another? If you're creating a standard template for your department or group, or you simply want a backup copy for yourself, having all the same AutoText entries saved in the template you use helps ensure consistency in the documents you create. It also can save your co-workers time, depending on how complete your AutoText entries are.

Using the AutoText Toolbar

Word includes an AutoText toolbar you can use to insert entries, add new words and phrases, and display the AutoText options.You can display the toolbar in one of two ways:

- Choose View, Toolbars, and then click AutoText.
- Click Show Toolbar in the AutoText tab in the AutoCorrect dialog box.

The AutoText toolbar is shown in Figure 7-22. You can use this toolbar to insert, create, and manage your AutoText entries.

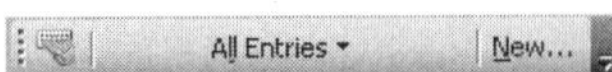

Figure 7-22. The AutoText toolbar gives you tools for displaying the dialog box, inserting, and adding entries.

> **Tip** List AutoText entries
> Want to see a complete list of all your AutoText entries? You can print a list from the Print dialog box. Press Ctrl+P to display the Print dialog box, choose your printing options, and, in the Print What list box, select AutoText Entries, and then click OK. A full listing of your AutoText entries will be printed.

Getting the Scoop on Smart Tags

One of the exciting features Word 2003 offers is smart tags, which have been significantly improved in this release of the Microsoft Office System. Smart tags deliver what their name suggests—they provide links to additional information that gives you more data on a recognized item, person, place, or thing. They make you "smarter" by giving you wider access to the data in your applications.

Smart tag functionality is included with Word, Excel, Outlook, and PowerPoint, and smart tags can be displayed in Microsoft Internet Explorer. A smart tag is meant to be an intuitive link, an easy connection to more information about the tagged item. For example, suppose that you're writing a report that summarizes new research your department has recently completed. When you type the list of contributing writers, you see the name of a person you recognize, but you can't recall her department. In theory, if the information about the employee has been entered, you should be able to position the pointer over the employee's name and see a ScreenTip containing information about her, complete with her name, e-mail address, and other contact information. The fact that this data is retained in Excel and potentially in Web documents makes this transfer of data smarter and more consistent.

> **Note** In earlier versions of Word, this kind of "smart" technology helped users locate URLs and e-mail addresses. In the Microsoft Office System, "smart tags" have been expanded to offer more meaningful information, including full contact information and customized data. In addition, tools for developers make it easy for organizations to create their own customized smart tags that deliver information relevant to the tasks and procedures information workers most need to accomplish.

Changes to Smart Tags in Word 2003

Smart tags in Word 2003 now do more, reach farther, and are more flexible than ever before. Developers will find they have more control over the smart tags they create and will be able to develop and deploy smart tags easily. Support for Extensible Markup Language (XML) throughout Microsoft Office Professional Edition 2003 adds an extra boost by enabling developers to use XML to extend Microsoft Office Smart Tag List Tool (MOSTL), the smart tag recognizer and action handler, without going back into the code.

How will your organization use smart tags? In terms of corporate possibilities, companies that want their employees to be able to link to critical resources inside the company will use smart tags. Smart tags will be ideal for documents that have to be processed such as invoices or expense reports. For example, suppose that a user enters a tracking number. A smart tag recognizes the item and when the user clicks the smart tag, the menu offers the user the ability to view—right from the current document—that particular order in the inventory system. Another option in the smart tag menu might fill in the details from that invoice automatically, saving the user keystrokes, time, and error checking.

Smart Tags: Quick Facts for Developers

Here are some quick facts about the changes in smart tags in the Microsoft Office System:

- Smart tags recognize regular expressions and context-free grammatical rules.
- New properties enable developers to create customizable smart tags that perform specialized functions.
- Smart tag actions can run as soon as a recognizer identifies a string as a smart tag.
- Cascading menus give developers the option of providing users with additional choices.
- Developers can control tag properties and customize the look of smart tags that appear in user documents.
- Developers can create temporary smart tags with limited functionality.
- Smart tags can be assigned a time limit so they expire automatically.
- Developers can use XML to create and modify smart tags.
- Developers have more control over hiding, displaying, or changing the look of customized smart tags.

Inside Out

Learn more about smart tags

If you're interested in finding out more about developing custom smart tags, visit *www.microsoft.com*, enter "Smart Tags" in the Search box, and click Go. To learn more about planning, implementing, and deploying enterprise smart tags, you can download and read the Smart Tag Enterprise Resource Kit from the same site.

Following a Smart Tag

A smart tag in your document appears the way a ScreenTip appears in other uses. The first item you see is a small circular tag and a purple dotted underline. When you click the circular tag, a menu appears, as shown in Figure 7-23. Table 7-3 describes the different functions of the smart tag choices.

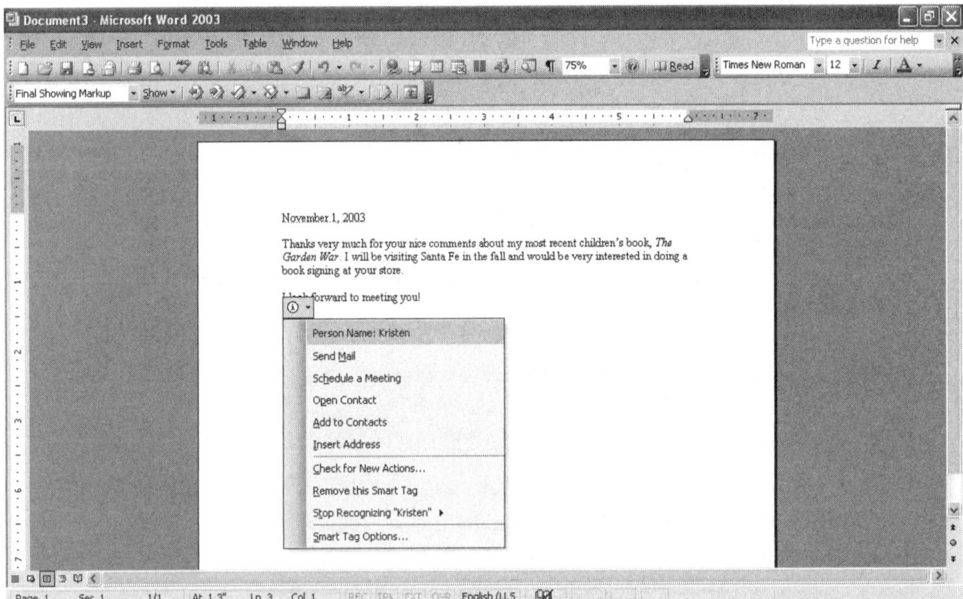

Figure 7-23. Smart tags expand the ways you can use data among applications, enabling you to create mail, schedule meetings, add contacts, and insert addresses as you work.

Table 7-3. Smart Tag Choices

Smart Tag Option	Description
Send Mail	Opens an e-mail message with Word as the editor
Schedule A Meeting	Opens Outlook so that you can schedule a meeting and invite the selected person
Open Contact	Displays the Outlook Contact List so that you can look up, add to, or edit the person's information
Add To Contacts	Adds the selected person to Outlook's Contact List
Insert Address	Inserts the address of the person at the current insertion point
Remove This Smart Tag	Deletes the smart tag at this occurrence in the document
Smart Tag Options	Displays the Smart Tags tab, enabling you to choose additional options

Turning Off Smart Tags

If you decide that you don't want to use smart tags in your document, simply display the Smart Tags tab in the AutoCorrect dialog box (as shown in Figure 7-24), clear the Label Text With Smart Tags check box, and then click OK. Smart tags will be disabled for the current document.

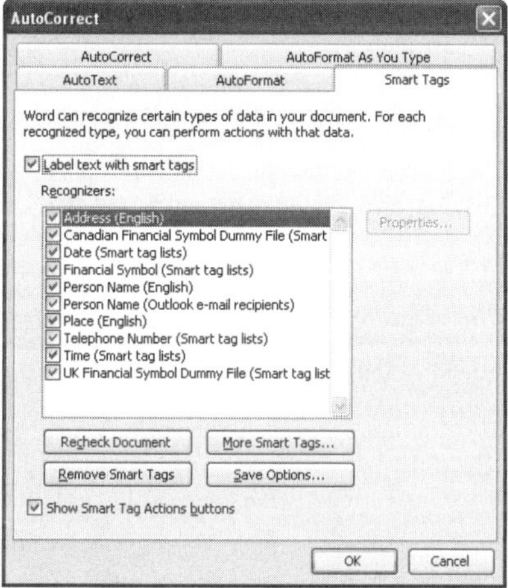

Figure 7-24. You turn smart tags on and off and select the options you want in the Smart Tags tab in the AutoCorrect dialog box.

Understanding Recognizers

A *recognizer* is an item that the smart tag recognizes: a person, place, date, time, or thing that has been added to your application data. By default, all types of recognizers are selected. To disable any type of recognizer, simply clear the check box to the left of the item. Word will then use only the selected item to display information in smart tag form.

Rechecking Your Document

After you make a change to smart tags, you should recheck your document by clicking Recheck Document in the Smart Tags tab in the AutoCorrect dialog box. Word warns you that changes made by the grammar checker might be reversed as you recheck smart tags. If you want to continue, click Yes; otherwise, click No.

Getting Additional Smart Tags

You can get additional smart tags from the MicrosoftWeb site. Start by establishing your Internet connection, and then display the Smart Tags tab in the AutoCorrect dialog box. Click More Smart Tags, and Word will start Internet Explorer and take you to a page where you can find out more. Follow the prompts on the screen to navigate to and download the smart tags you'll use to extend the functionality of Word 2003.

Removing Smart Tags

You might want to remove selected smart tags in your document, depending on how many you have and how often you need them. Word gives you the option of removing selected tags or getting rid of all of them at once.

Removing an Individual Smart Tag

To remove a specific smart tag, follow these steps:

1. In your document, click the smart tag to display the menu for the tag you want to remove.
2. Choose Remove This Smart Tag from the menu. The underline and the identifier are removed for that smart tag.

Note If you've cleared the Label Text With SmartTags check box and then copied text with a smart tag into your document, the smart tag will appear even though you've turned smart tags off.

Removing All Smart Tags

If you want to do something really drastic and get rid of all the smart tags in your document, display the Smart Tags tab in the AutoCorrect dialog box, and then click Remove Smart Tags. Word will display a warning that the action will remove all smart tags permanently—both in the existing document and in any copies of this document that are on someone else's computer. If you want to remove the smart tags, click Yes; otherwise, preserve them by clicking No.

Exploring the Improved Clipboard

Using the Clipboard isn't rocket science—we've all been working with the Windows Clipboard since the earliest incarnations ofWord. The Office Clipboard inWord 2003 enables you to store up to 24 different items (text, graphics, sound objects, and more). When you choose Edit, Office Clipboard, its contents appear in the Clipboard task pane so that you can work with the items easily, as shown in Figure 7-25.

Note In addition to the old standby Clipboard keystrokes—Ctrl+C to copy and Ctrl+V to paste—you can paste all Clipboard items at once by clicking a single button in the Clipboard task pane.

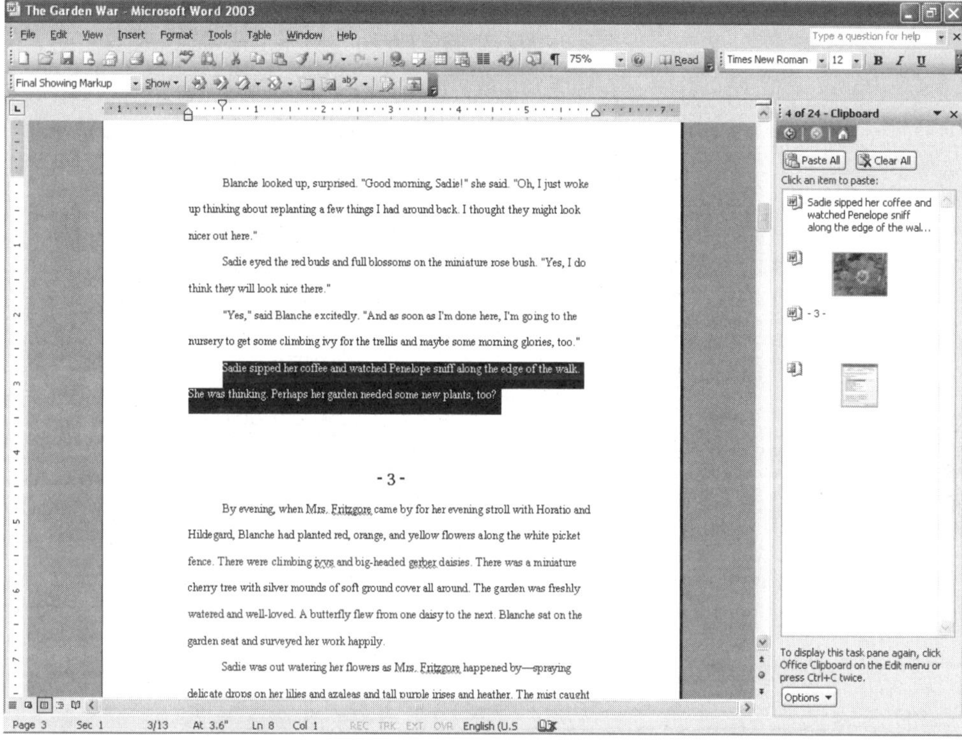

Figure 7-25. The Clipboard is available in a task pane so that you can easily see and manipulate the images and text stored there.

Pasting from the Office Clipboard

The fastest way to paste something from the Office Clipboard is to press Ctrl+V. The most recent item you copied to the Clipboard is pasted at the insertion point in your document. If you want to paste an item other than the most recent one, however, you'll need to use the Clipboard task pane. To do this, choose Edit, Office Clipboard, and then position the pointer over the item you want to paste. An arrow appears. Click the arrow to display a short menu that offers the Paste and Delete commands. This is also a handy feature when you want to remove items from the Clipboard in order to free up memory.

Setting Clipboard Options

The Office Clipboard includes a number of options you can control from the Clipboard task pane. When you click Options in the lower-left corner of the task pane, you're given four commands in the menu. Table 7-4 gives you an overview of each.

Table 7-4. Office Clipboard Options

Office Clipboard Option	Description	Use
Show Office Clipboard Automatically	Automatically displays the Clipboard task pane whenever the Clipboard is used.	You want to see what is stored on the Clipboard.
Show Office Clipboard When Ctrl+C Pressed Twice	Opens the Clipboard task pane when you press Ctrl+C two times consecutively.	You want to view the Clipboard quickly while you work.
Collect Without Showing Office Clipboard	Hides the display of the Clipboard but collects up to 24 items.	You want maximum available space on the screen.
Show Office Clipboard Icon On Taskbar	Displays a small Clipboard icon in the lower-right corner of the Windows taskbar.	You want to be reminded when something is stored on the Clipboard without having an application maximized.
Show Status Near Taskbar When Copying	Displays a ScreenTip showing how many items of the possible 24 are currently stored on the Clipboard.	You want to keep an eye on the resources you're using for the Clipboard, particularly if you're switching among Office applications.

Chapter 8

Aligning Information and Formatting Paragraphs and Lists

Professional-looking documents rely on accurate content alignment and styling—no matter how avant-garde a document's layout happens to be. Typesetters and layout artists have long recognized that effectively aligning page elements plays a large role in increasing a document's readability and "keeping the reader's eye on the page." Even people untrained in design can quickly see that "something's wrong" when they view a page that's been slapped together without regard to formatting and alignment. Therefore, when you work in Word, you should give serious thought to formatting and aligning document elements. If you learn to use Word formatting and alignment tools effectively—maybe even automatically—you'll be able to seamlessly integrate design tasks throughout the document creation process.

In this chapter, we look at formatting and alignment commands associated with a single type of element: *paragraphs*. And because a list is basically a series of paragraphs, we cover lists here as well. Now, paragraph formatting and alignment isn't as narrow a topic as it might sound at first. As a Word veteran, you probably know (or can intuit) that Word addresses document formatting and layout issues on three levels: character, paragraph, and section (or page). Character formatting issues include applying font styles and attributes (as discussed in Chapter 2, "Mastering Document Fundamentals," and Chapter 9, "Using Styles to Increase Your Formatting Power"). At the other end of the formatting spectrum, section formatting options control margins, headers, footers, gutters, and other page setup configurations (as covered in Chapter 15, "Mastering Page Setup and Pagination"). Paragraph formatting represents the middle ground of document formatting and alignment. Clearly, paragraph issues aren't as narrowly focused as character formatting tasks, and they aren't as encompassing as section setup commands. But don't let paragraph formatting's midlevel classification fool you—working with paragraphs is one of the most fundamental and essential skills you need to master to use Word effectively.

Understanding the Significance of Paragraphs in Word Documents

¶ Show/Hide

Surprisingly, even experienced Word users aren't fully aware of how extensively Word formatting relies on paragraphs. Part of this emphasis on paragraphs stems from the fact that, in Word, the term *paragraph* refers to far more than a group of sentences related to a theme. Instead, a paragraph in Word includes a paragraph mark (¶) along with all content preceding the paragraph mark, up to (but not including) the preceding paragraph mark. Each time you press Enter after a letter, heading, graphic, table, chart, list item, or any other element, you insert a paragraph mark and create what Word considers a paragraph. Figure 8-1 illustrates the concept of various paragraph elements in Word; notice the paragraph mark after each bulleted list item, each paragraph of text, each heading, and the graphic. You can display paragraph marks (along with other hidden text) in your documents by clicking the Show/Hide button on the Standard toolbar or by selecting Show All Formatting Marks in the Reveal Formatting task pane.

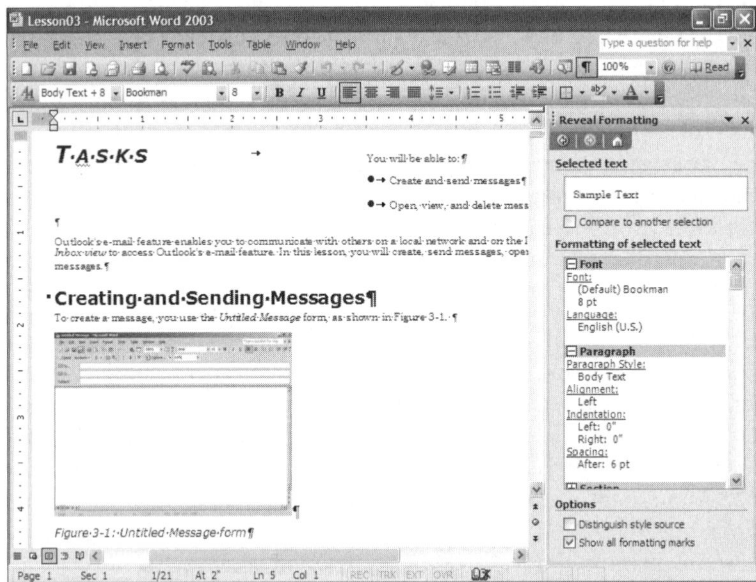

Figure 8-1. In Word, any content followed by a paragraph mark is considered a paragraph.

Inside Out

Showing selected hidden characters

The Show/Hide button on the Standard toolbar provides a quick way to display paragraph marks along with other typically hidden characters (like spaces and tab marks). In some cases, you might find that having hidden characters appear all over your document is a bit distracting. Fortunately, showing hidden characters isn't an all-or-nothing proposition. You can easily circumvent the Show/Hide button and configure your view to show selected hidden characters as follows:

1. Choose Tools, Options, and click the View tab.
2. In the Formatting Marks section in the View tab, clear the All check box (if it's selected), and select the hidden characters you want to display. For example, select only the Paragraph Marks check box to show only paragraph marks.
3. After you specify which formatting marks you want to display, those marks will appear in your document, regardless of whether you click the Show/Hide button. (Note that the Show/Hide button continues to show all hidden characters when you toggle the button on, regardless of your View tab settings.) To hide formatting marks activated using the View tab, you'll need to revisit the View tab to reconfigure the formatting marks settings.

In addition to imposing a broader definition of paragraphs, Word enables you to associate specific formatting information with your paragraphs. When you format a paragraph, the formatting information is stored in that paragraph's paragraph mark. Word can then use the information stored in paragraph marks to apply paragraph properties to text inserted within formatted paragraphs. This setup also enables Word to apply a current paragraph's formatting to the next paragraph when you press Enter at the end of the paragraph. This process is fairly logical. When you click at the end of a paragraph, the insertion point's position precedes the existing paragraph mark. (You can easily demonstrate this behavior by displaying paragraph marks, and then clicking at the end of any paragraph—you'll be able to click to the left but not to the right of a paragraph mark.) Pressing Enter at the end of a paragraph essentially simulates the act of inserting information within the existing paragraph, thereby retaining the paragraph formatting for any subsequently added information.

In Word, you can format paragraphs by setting the following paragraph formatting parameters:

- Paragraph alignment
- Indentation
- Spacing between lines
- Spacing before and after paragraphs
- Tabs
- Line and page breaks
- Hyphenation

In the following sections of the chapter, you'll learn how to manage these paragraph features. The final topic before we tackle the particulars of list-making describes how to create drop caps, because drop caps are most commonly used when formatting paragraphs.

Note Technically speaking, some tasks performed while you are in Outline view relate to paragraph formatting, but those topics aren't addressed in this chapter. Word offers a comprehensive collection of outlining tools and features; for an in-depth look at outlining, see Chapter 10, "Outlining Documents for Clarity and Structure."

Formatting Paragraphs by Aligning and Indenting Text

One of the most common paragraph formatting tasks is aligning paragraphs within a document. As you know, you can set margins to specify overall page and document alignment. But alignment matters don't stop there. You can also control alignment at the paragraph level by specifying text alignment and indentation. You can configure paragraph alignment settings using these familiar methods:

- Click buttons on the Formatting toolbar or press keyboard shortcuts to quickly format paragraphs.
- Use the horizontal ruler to align paragraphs visually.
- Configure settings in the Paragraph dialog box.

This portion of the chapter examines the intricacies of each of these techniques.

For more information about setting margins and configuring overall page setup parameters, see Chapter 15, "Mastering Page Setup and Pagination."

Aligning Paragraphs Using Toolbar Buttons and Keyboard Shortcuts

The quickest way to apply paragraph formatting is to click within a paragraph or select a few paragraphs, and then click a button on the Formatting toolbar or press a keyboard shortcut. Of course, these processes are limited by their default settings, but in many cases, the easiest route proves to be the best when it comes to paragraph formatting. To review which Formatting buttons and keyboard shortcuts can help you format paragraphs, see Table 8-1.

Table 8-1. Toolbar Buttons and Keyboard Shortcuts for Aligning and Formatting Paragraphs

Format	Toolbar Button	Keyboard Shortcut	Description
Align Left		Ctrl+L	Aligns information along the left margin of the page or specified area, with a ragged right edge.
Align Center		Ctrl+E	Aligns the midpoint of each line with the horizontal center of the page or area.
Align Right		Ctrl+R	Aligns information along the right margin of the page or specified area, with a ragged left edge.
Justify		Ctrl+J	Aligns text flush with both the left and right margins of the page or specified area.
Line Spacing		Ctrl+1 (single-space), Ctrl+2 (double-space), or Ctrl+5 (1.5-space)	Controls the vertical spacing between lines of text. Clicking the Line Spacing arrow displays a list of line spacing options.
Decrease Indent		Ctrl+Shift+M	Decreases a paragraph's indent by one tab stop. By default, tab stops are set every 0.5 inch.
Increase Indent		Ctrl+M	Increases a paragraph's indent by one tab stop. By default, tab stops are set every 0.5 inch.
Border		None	Applies a border to specified text. Clicking the Borders arrow displays a menu of common border options.

Aligning Paragraphs Using the Ruler

Formatting toolbar buttons and keyboard shortcuts give you quick access to paragraph formatting options, but the Word ruler offers visually oriented people an intuitive and more precise method for controlling paragraph alignment as well as providing a greater variety of alignment settings. The trick to using the ruler effectively is to become comfortable with the ruler's markers. To get up to speed, look at Figure 8-2, which shows the Word 2003 ruler (which looks extremely similar to the ruler in earlier versions of Word). The next few sections describe how to use the ruler markers to format paragraphs.

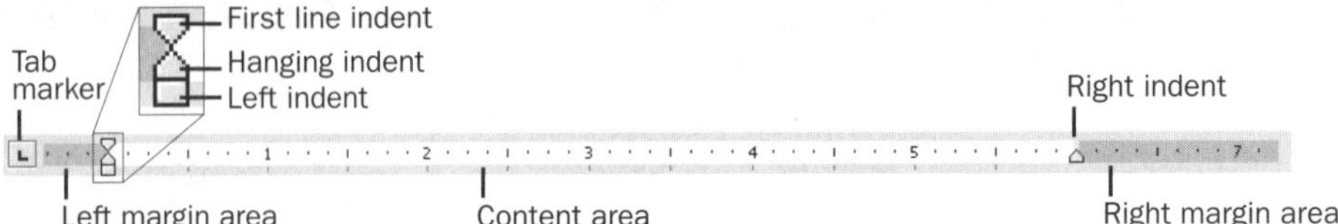

Figure 8-2. You can use the Word ruler to quickly and accurately align document content.

Displaying and Configuring the Ruler

By default, Word displays the ruler in Normal, Web Layout, and Print Layout views and does not display the ruler in Outline and Reading Layout views. If you don't see the ruler in Normal, Web Layout, or Print Layout view, you can display it by choosing View, Ruler.

> **Tip** To control whether the *vertical ruler* appears in Print Layout view, you must configure the View tab in the Options dialog box. To do so, choose Tools, Options, click the View tab, and then select or clear the Vertical Ruler (Print View Only) check box, in the Print And Web Layout Options section. Note that the vertical ruler isn't available in other Word views.

As you can see in Figure 8-2, the *0* (zero) spot on the ruler corresponds to the left margin setting. By default, the left and right margins are set to 1.25 inches on 8.5-by-11-inch paper. Thus, the default setup provides 6 inches between the margins for content.

You've probably noticed that the ruler measurements are shown in inches. If you prefer to use other units of measurement, you can change the default measurement unit setting as follows:

1. Choose Tools, Options, and click the General tab.
2. In the General tab, click the Measurement Units arrow, select a measurement unit in the list, and click OK. Available options are Inches, Centimeters, Millimeters, Points, and Picas.

Adjusting Left and Right Indents

To adjust left and right indents using the ruler, click within the paragraph (even if it's an empty paragraph) or select the paragraphs you want to adjust, or select the entire document (press Ctrl+A). Then click and drag the Left Indent or Right Indent marker on the ruler.

> **Tip** To move the First Line Indent marker along with the Hanging Indent marker, drag the small rectangle below the Hanging Indent marker (the Left Indent marker) on the ruler. Dragging the Left Indent marker retains the relative settings of the first line and left margin.

When you're working with tables, the ruler offers additional alignment markers, as shown in Figure 8-3. Namely, you can drag column markers to alter margin widths and row height markers to adjust row height; the margin markers move to correspond to the currently selected row and column. You can also indent table cell contents or entire columns.

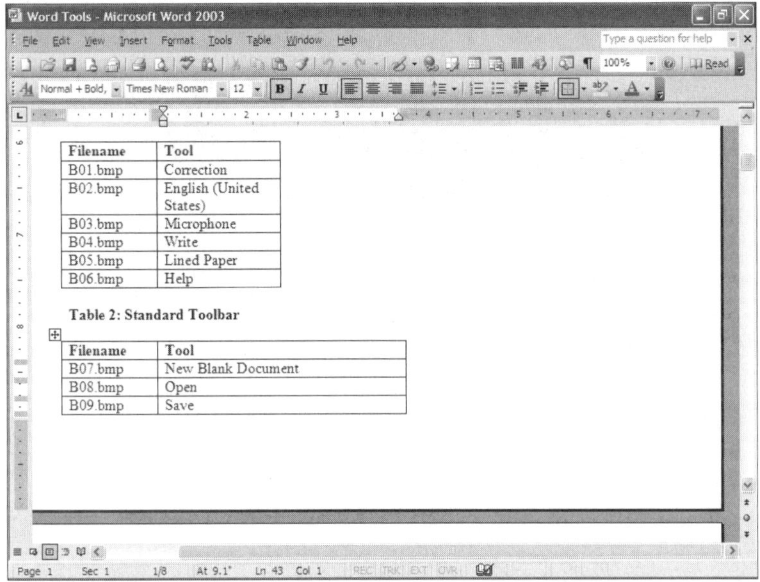

Filename	Tool
B01.bmp	Correction
B02.bmp	English (United States)
B03.bmp	Microphone
B04.bmp	Write
B05.bmp	Lined Paper
B06.bmp	Help

Table 2: Standard Toolbar

Filename	Tool
B07.bmp	New Blank Document
B08.bmp	Open
B09.bmp	Save

Figure 8-3. When you're working with tables in Print Layout view, you can use the vertical and horizontal rulers to adjust row heights and column widths.

For more information about resizing and aligning tables and table contents, see Chapter 13, "Organizing Concepts in Tables."

Creating First Line and Hanging Indents

You can use the ruler to create a hanging indent or a first-line indent, as illustrated in Figure 8-4. To do so, click in the paragraph you want to format or select multiple paragraphs, and then drag the First Line Indent marker left or right to the desired location.

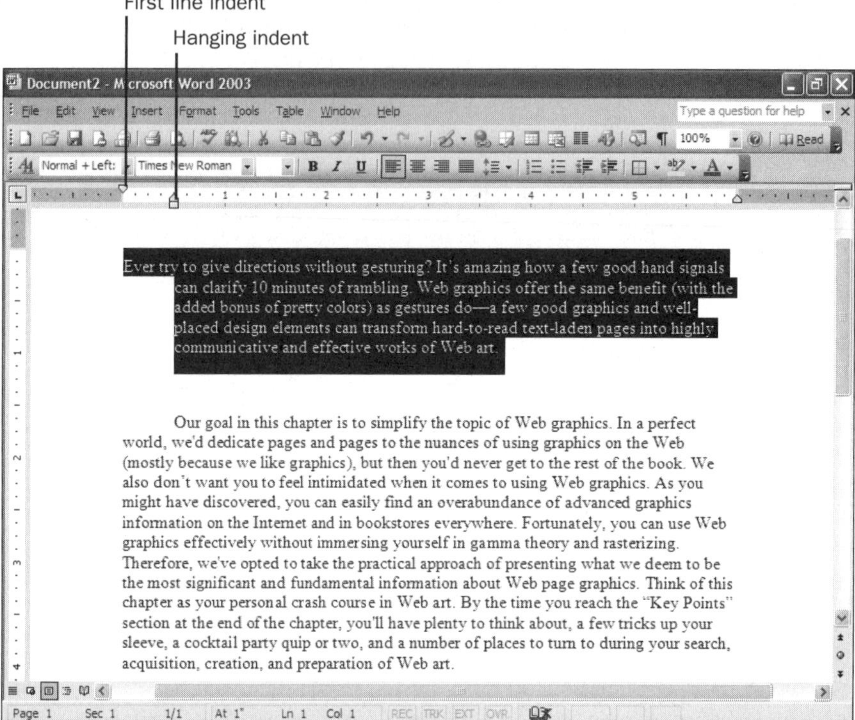

Figure 8-4. You can drag the First Line Indent marker to create a hanging indent or a first-line indent.

> **Tip** You can press Ctrl+T to create a hanging indent that aligns body text with the first tab marker. (By default, tabs are set every 0.5 inch.) You can press Ctrl+Shift+T to "unhang" an indent, regardless of how the hanging indent was created.

Aligning Paragraphs Using the Paragraph Dialog Box

Using toolbar buttons, keyboard shortcuts, and ruler markers to align paragraphs can be quick, but aligning paragraphs by using the Paragraph dialog box offers its own advantages. By configuring settings in the Paragraph dialog box, you can align paragraphs precisely as well as apply a number of paragraph formatting settings at one time.

To display the Paragraph dialog box, shown in Figure 8-5, choose Format, Paragraph, or right-click a paragraph (or selected paragraphs), and choose Paragraph from the shortcut menu.

> **Tip** You can also display the Paragraph dialog box by clicking the Alignment, Indentation, or Spacing link in the Reveal Formatting task pane, as described in "Modifying Paragraph Attributes Using Reveal Formatting," on page 237.

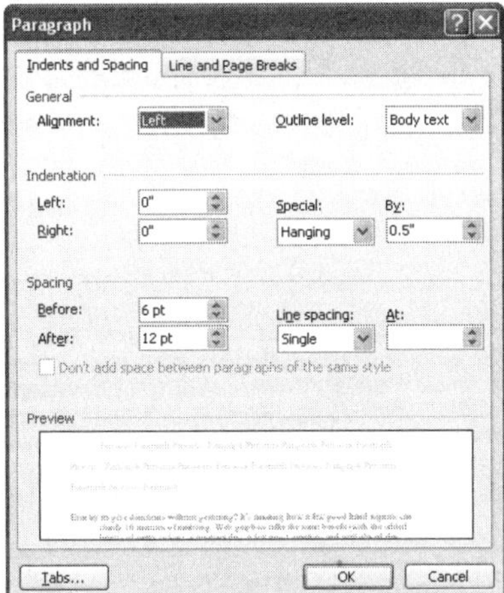

Figure 8-5. The Paragraph dialog box provides precise and complete control of paragraph formatting.

The Indents And Spacing tab offers the following paragraph alignment options:

- **Alignment** Sets the position of paragraph contents relative to the margins. Available alignment options are Left, Centered, Right, and Justified. The options in this list correspond to the alignment buttons on the Formatting toolbar.
- **Left Indentation** Indents the paragraph from the left margin by the amount you specify. To display text or graphics within the left margin, enter a negative number in the Left box.
- **Right Indentation** Indents the paragraph from the right margin by the amount you specify. To display text or graphics within the right margin, enter a negative number in the Right box.
- **Special and By** Controls the paragraph's first-line indentation. The Special list box has three options: (None), First Line, and Hanging. The (None) option is selected by default. To specify the first-line indent, enter a value in the By box; the Special list box changes to display First Line automatically.

You can configure other paragraph settings in the Paragraph dialog box, including paragraph spacing parameters, as you'll see next.

Language-Specific Paragraph Options

If you have additional languages enabled for Office (which is achieved by selecting Start, All Programs, Microsoft Office, Microsoft Office Tools, Microsoft Office 2003 Language Settings), you might see an additional tab in the Paragraph dialog box that contains paragraph options relevant to the particular language. For example, the following graphic shows the Asian Typography tab, which appears when Japanese is enabled in an English (US) version of Office:

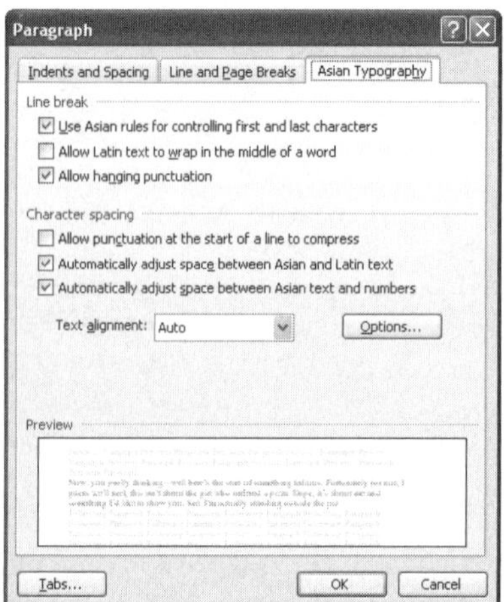

For more information about working with language features in Word, see Appendix B, "Implementing Multilanguage Features."

Addressing Spacing Issues

You can adjust line spacing in your documents to help create an aesthetic impression or improve readability. In particular, you can control line spacing within paragraphs as well as specify the amount of space above and below paragraphs.

Specifying Line Spacing

Long gone are the days when you had to press Return twice at the end of each line of text to double-space your paragraphs. Now creating line spacing is a simple matter of configuring paragraph settings before, during, or after you enter text. In Word, you can adjust line spacing in several ways, including using the Formatting toolbar, keyboard shortcuts, and the Paragraph dialog box.

Line Spacing

One fast way to configure a paragraph's line spacing is to click in the paragraph you want to configure or select multiple paragraphs, and then click the Line Spacing button on the Formatting toolbar. The Line Spacing menu offers the following options: 1.0, 1.5, 2.0, 2.5, 3.0, or More. Selecting a number option instantly adjusts the selected paragraphs' line spacing. If you select More, the Paragraph dialog box appears.

Tip **Apply line spacing to subsequent paragraphs**
After you select a line spacing option from the Line Spacing menu, you can click the Line Spacing button to apply the specified line spacing to subsequently selected paragraphs. To view the current line spacing setting, simply hover the pointer over the Line Spacing button. The ToolTip will display the current setting in parentheses—for example, *Line Spacing (2)*.

Using the Paragraph dialog box, you can adjust paragraph line spacing to a precise 1/10 of a point by using the Line Spacing option in conjunction with the At box in the Indents And Spacing tab (shown previously in Figure 8-5). By default, Word formats paragraphs using single-line spacing that is adjusted automatically based on the size of the font in the paragraph. The Line Spacing list box provides the following options:

- **Single** Accommodates the largest font per line plus a small amount of extra space to create the appearance of a single-spaced paragraph. This is the default setting.
- **1.5 Lines** Inserts one-and-one-half times the space allotted for a single line space to selected paragraph(s).
- **Double** Inserts twice the space allotted for a single line space to the selected paragraph(s).
- **At Least** Sets a minimum amount of space for each line as specified in the At box. When Word encounters a larger font size or a graphic that won't fit in the minimum space, Word increases that line's spacing to accommodate the text or graphic.
- **Exactly** Forces Word to apply an exact line spacing, as specified in the At box, regardless of what size text or graphics Word encounters. (Otherwise, Word accommodates the largest text or graphic in a line by default.) If Word encounters text or graphics too large to fit in the allotted line space, the text or graphics will appear "cut off" in your document.
- **Multiple** Allows you to use the At box to specify a line spacing setting from 0.06 through 132 lines, in increments of 1/100 of a line. This option provides extra-fine control over line spacing.

To apply a line spacing setting using the Paragraph dialog box, click in the paragraph you want to format or select multiple paragraphs, and then do either of the following:

- Choose Format, Paragraph, and click the Indents And Spacing tab.
- Right-click in the text, choose Paragraph from the shortcut menu, and click the Indents And Spacing tab.

After you display the Indents And Spacing tab, specify your line spacing settings, and click OK.

Last but not least, you can quickly adjust a paragraph's line spacing by clicking in a paragraph or selecting multiple paragraphs, and then pressing any of the following keyboard shortcuts:

- Ctrl+1 applies single-line spacing to selected paragraphs.
- Ctrl+2 applies double-line spacing to selected paragraphs.
- Ctrl+5 applies 1.5-line spacing to selected paragraphs.

Adjusting Spacing Above and Below Paragraphs

In addition to adjusting spacing between lines within paragraphs, you can configure the space displayed above and below paragraphs. Adding space around paragraphs is an old typesetters' trick used to create a particular look and feel for a document and to improve readability. In Word, adding space above and below paragraphs produces the desired typesetting results and provides added control during document adjustment tasks. For example, you're not limited to separating paragraphs by one or two lines—you can separate paragraphs by 0.5 inch, 3 points, and so forth. In addition, if you use spacing consistently within your document and you find that your document (or a section within your document) runs a little long or comes up a tad short, you can select the entire document, a section, or a few paragraphs, and adjust the paragraph spacing options using the Paragraph dialog box to tighten up or lengthen your document in just a few steps.

To add spacing above and below selected paragraphs, follow these steps:

1. Click in the paragraph you want to configure, or select multiple paragraphs.
2. Choose Format, Paragraph, and click the Indents And Spacing tab.
3. Enter values in the Before and After boxes in the Spacing section, and click OK. The Before and After spacing options require you to specify in points how much space to insert before and after paragraphs. Keep in mind that 72 points equals approximately 1 inch.

If you create styles for your documents, you'll want to consider configuring the Before and After settings when you create paragraph styles. Adding before and after spacing to paragraph styles helps to ensure that spacing will be applied consistently and automatically throughout your document.

For more information about creating styles, see Chapter 9, "Using Styles to Increase Your Formatting Power."

Tip **Add line spaces before paragraphs**

You can instantly add a full line space before a paragraph by selecting the paragraph(s) you want to format and pressing Ctrl+0 (zero). If you select multiple paragraphs, pressing Ctrl+0 adds a blank line space before each paragraph in the selection.

Controlling Alignment Using Tabs

Back in the typewriter's heyday, tab stops were the end-all when it came to formatting tables, charts, and columns. Now Word offers a variety of text alignment tools, including specific features you can use to create columns, tables, and charts. But even with the advanced Word formatting features, tab stops continue to play a key role in aligning text and performing other tab-related activities. For example, tabs frequently come into play when you want to create simple lists, tables of contents (including dotted leader lines between titles and page numbers), center-aligned or decimal-aligned text, and so forth. Figure 8-6 shows a variety of tab styles in action.

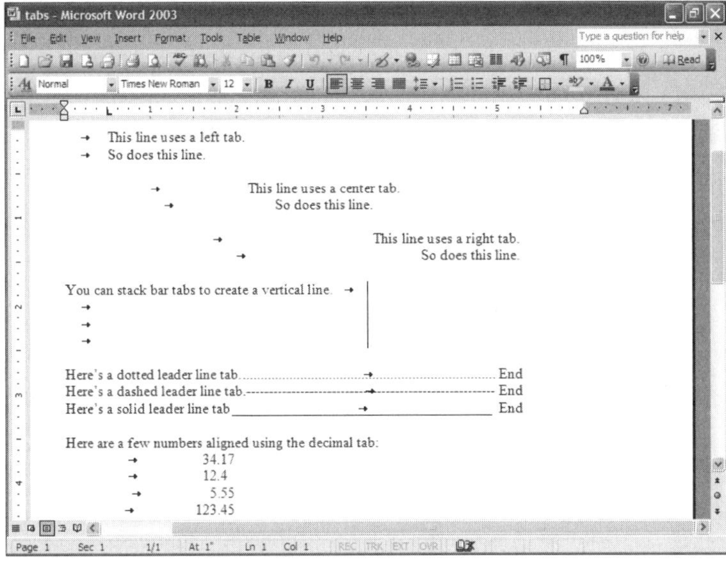

Figure 8-6. Word enables you to select from a variety of tab styles when you're adding tab stops.

New documents based on the default Normal.dot template include left-aligned tab stops every 0.5 inch, although the tab settings don't appear in the ruler. You can adjust the default tab stop setting, add custom tabs, clear all tabs, and create tabs with leader lines. To adjust tabs, use the ruler or Tabs dialog box, as discussed in the following sections.

> **Tip** **Display hidden characters**
> You can see where tabs are inserted in your document by displaying characters that are typically hidden. To do so, click the Show/Hide button on the Standard toolbar, or choose Tools, Options, click the View tab, select Tab Characters in the Formatting Marks section, and then click OK. Tabs appear as arrows, as shown in Figure 8-6.

Putting the Ruler to Work to Set Tabs

You can set tabs using the horizontal ruler inWord. Using the ruler has a couple of advantages: you get visual feedback as soon as you set the tabs, and you can drag the ruler tabs to the left or right until you're satisfied with their positions. (You can even drag tabs off the ruler to delete them.) As soon as you set a tab on the ruler, your selected text moves to reflect the setting. To set tabs using the ruler, you need to complete the following steps:

1. Click in a paragraph or select multiple paragraphs in which you want to set tabs, or position the insertion point at the location where you want to create a new paragraph containing the tab settings.
2. Set the desired tab style by clicking the button at the left end of the horizontal ruler. To cycle through the available tab styles, click the button repeatedly. Table 8-2 lists the tab styles along with other available ruler markers, and Figure 8-6 shows the various tab styles in action.

3 After you select a tab style, click the ruler to insert a tab. If you position a tab incorrectly, you can drag it off the ruler to delete it or drag it left or right to reposition it.

Table 8-2. Ruler Markers

Button	Name	Description
	Left Tab	Text begins at the tab stop and continues right. This is the most commonly used tab style.
	Center Tab	Text is centered on the tab stop as you type.
	Right Tab	Text begins at the tab stop and moves left as new text is typed.
	Decimal Tab	Rows of numbers are aligned on the decimal point, regardless of the number of decimal places in each number.
	Bar Tab	Creates a vertical line. This setting enables you to draw vertical lines that span any number of horizontal lines of text.
	First Line Indent	Activates the First Line Indent feature. Click the ruler to set a first-line indent. (Using this method, you can create a first-line indent with a single click instead of dragging the ruler marker.)
	Hanging Indent	Activates the Hanging Indent feature. Click the ruler to position a hanging indent.

Carrying Tabs from One Paragraph to the Next

If you set tabs in a paragraph, the tab settings will automatically be included in the next paragraph if you press Enter at the end of the paragraph and continue typing to create a new paragraph. On the other hand, if you format tabs in a paragraph that's already embedded among other paragraphs, the tab settings will not automatically extend to the existing paragraphs that follow.

If you want to extend tab formatting to existing paragraphs, you need to select all the paragraphs you want to format before you set the tabs, or you can format a single paragraph, and then use the Format Painter to copy the paragraph attributes to other paragraphs. Be sure to use the Format Painter option cautiously—Format Painter copies all paragraph formatting attributes, not just the tab settings. (For more information about the Format Painter, see Chapter 2, "Mastering Document Fundamentals.")

Finally, if you want to set tabs throughout an entire document, press Ctrl+A to select the document, and then set your tabs on the ruler. Be aware that setting tabs for an entire document might affect existing tabs, so be sure to review your document after you make wide-ranging changes. In addition, you might want to clear any existing tabs before inserting your new "global" tags. The process of deleting tabs is described in "Clearing Custom Tabs," on page 236.

Creating Tabs Using the Tabs Dialog Box

In addition to clicking the ruler to create tabs, you can add tabs using the Tabs dialog box. When you use the Tabs dialog box, you can set tabs using precise measurements. You can also create tabs that use leader lines. (*Leaders* insert formatting, such as dots or dashes, in the space leading to the tab stop, as shown in Figure 8-6.) Neither of these tasks can be accomplished using the ruler. The main drawback of creating tabs using the Tabs dialog box is that you won't be able to see how your tabs affect your text until after you close the dialog box and view your document. To display the Tabs dialog box, perform any of the following actions:

- Choose Format, Tabs.
- Click Tabs in the Paragraph dialog box.
- Double-click an existing tab in the horizontal ruler.

Figure 8-7 shows the Tabs dialog box. If the currently selected paragraph contains tabs when you display the Tabs dialog box, the tab positions will be listed in the Tab Stop Position list box. Notice that the DefaultTab Stops option is set to *0.5* by default.

Figure 8-7. The Tabs dialog box enables you to modify the default tab stop settings, insert tabs at precise positions, create leader lines, and clear existing tabs.

To set tabs using the Tabs dialog box, follow these steps:

1. Click in the paragraph or select multiple paragraphs in which you want to set tabs, or position your insertion point at the location where you want to create a new paragraph containing the tab settings.
2. Display the Tabs dialog box (by choosing Format, Tabs or double-clicking an existing tab marker in the ruler).
3. Type a tab location, such as *1.75*, in the Tab Stop Position box.
4. In the Alignment section, specify whether you want a left, center, right, decimal, or bar tab.

5. Select a leader line style, if desired, and then click Set. The tab will be listed in the Tab Stop Position list box.
6. Add more tabs, if necessary, by repeating steps 3 through 5, and then click OK to close the Tabs dialog box when you've finished setting tabs.

Tip **Adjust the default tab and indent setting**

To change the default tab and indent setting, you can type a new setting in the Default Tab Stops box in the Tabs dialog box. For example, you could change the default 0.5-inch setting to 0.75 inch. The default setting is used if custom tabs aren't set when you press Tab or click the Increase Indent and Decrease Indent buttons on the Formatting toolbar.

Clearing Custom Tabs

Just as you can add custom tabs using the horizontal ruler and the Tabs dialog box, you can also clear tabs using these same tools. You can even clear all tabs at one time if you're really in "spring cleaning" mode. To remove tabs, select the paragraph(s) you want to modify, and then perform one of the following procedures:

- Drag the tab markers off the ruler. (Simply click a tab marker and drag it down into the document area.)
- Display the Tabs dialog box (by choosing Format, Tabs or double-clicking an existing tab marker in the Ruler), select the tab you want to delete, and click Clear.
- Display the Tabs dialog box, and click Clear All.
- Click the Tabs link in the Reveal Formatting task pane (as described in the next section of the chapter).

Troubleshooting

Ruler options are unavailable when multiple paragraphs are selected

In some instances, you might want to modify several paragraphs that have different tab settings so that they all have consistent tab settings. You can do so using both the horizontal ruler and the Tab dialog box. The easiest way to accomplish this task is by performing the following steps:

1. Select the paragraph(s) you want to format. If the tab markers in the horizontal ruler appear shaded or dimmed, the tab settings aren't currently applied to the entire selection. (You probably already know this, so the dimmed tab markers shouldn't faze you.)
2. Double-click a dimmed tab marker (or choose Format, Tabs) to display the Tabs dialog box.
3. Click Clear All, click OK, and then click the horizontal ruler to define tab settings that will apply to the entire selection.

Modifying Paragraph Attributes Using Reveal Formatting

After you apply paragraph alignment settings (as well as font and section formatting settings), you can view your settings in the Reveal Formatting task pane. To display the Reveal Formatting task pane, choose Format, Reveal Formatting, or select Reveal Formatting from the task pane's menu. Figure 8-8 shows the Reveal Formatting task pane in action.

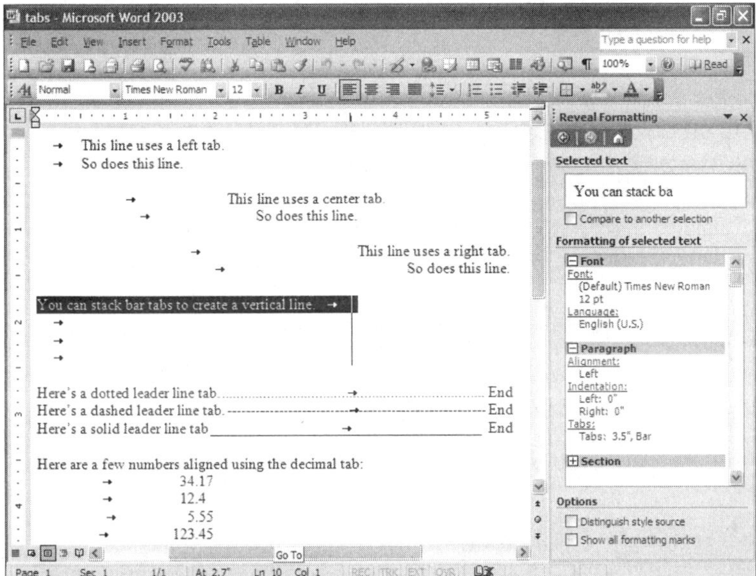

Figure 8-8. The Reveal Formatting task pane provides quick access to font, paragraph, and section formatting settings. Click a link to display the appropriate formatting dialog box.

As you can see, the Reveal Formatting task pane is a wellspring of formatting information, but its usefulness doesn't stop there. The Reveal Formatting task pane also provides links to the appropriate dialog boxes if you need to modify any format settings. Notice that the task pane is divided into Font, Paragraph, and Section sections (representing the three levels of formatting used in Word documents). Within each section, you can see links to formatting attributes set within the current selection or active area. You can click any link to display the dialog box associated with the selected settings. For example, if you click the Tabs link, the Tabs dialog box appears so that you can easily configure tab settings for the current paragraph. Table 8-3 lists more examples of which dialog box appears when you click a formatting link.

Table 8-3. Reveal Formatting Links and Dialog Box Associations

Link	Associated Dialog Box and Tab
Font	Font dialog box, Font tab
Language	Language dialog box

Table 8-3. Reveal Formatting Links and Dialog Box Associations

Link	Associated Dialog Box and Tab
Alignment	Paragraph dialog box, Indents And Spacing tab
Indentation	Paragraph dialog box, Indents And Spacing tab
Tabs	Tabs dialog box
Margins	Page Setup dialog box, Margins tab
Layout	Page Setup dialog box, Layout tab
Paper	Page Setup dialog box, Paper tab

After you click a link in the task pane and modify settings in a particular dialog box, click OK to return to the task pane and document window. You'll be able to see your new format settings implemented in the document.

For more information about Reveal Formatting, see Chapter 7, "Putting Text Tools to Work."

Controlling Line and Page Breaks

In addition to aligning paragraphs, adjusting line spacing, and setting tabs, you can fine-tune the flow of your paragraphs by controlling line and page breaks. The main area to turn to when you want to control line and page breaks is the Line And Page Breaks tab in the Paragraph dialog box, shown in Figure 8-9.

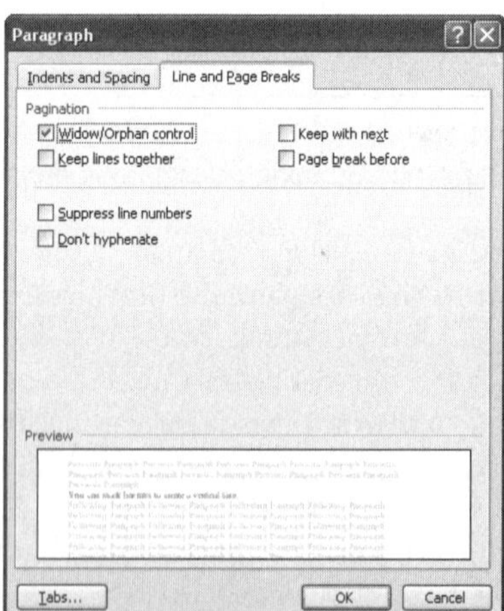

Figure 8-9. You can control line and page breaks to some extent in Word by selecting check boxes in the Line And Page Breaks tab.

To apply the line and page break settings, select the text you want to format, display the Line And Page Breaks tab, and select the appropriate check boxes. The following line and page break options are available:

- **Widow/Orphan Control** Ensures that the last line of a paragraph doesn't appear by itself at the top of a new page (a widow) or that the first line of a paragraph doesn't appear by itself at the bottom of a page (an orphan). Typesetters have been struggling to avoid widows and orphans for centuries. The Widow/Orphan Control check box is selected by default.
- **Keep Lines Together** Prevents page breaks from occurring within selected paragraphs. When a page break is needed, Word moves the entire paragraph to the next page.
- **Keep With Next** Prevents a page break from occurring between the selected paragraph and the following paragraph. This feature can come in handy when you're using paragraphs that work together to create a single element, such as a table and a table caption.
- **Page Break Before** Inserts a manual page break before the selected paragraph. You might want to configure this option if you think the selection might cause pagination problems or if you want to ensure that content, such as a section title, appears at the top of a new page.

> **Tip** To apply the pagination controls in the Line And Page Breaks tab in the Paragraph dialog box to an entire document, press Ctrl+A to select the entire document before configuring the pagination check boxes.

The Line And Page Breaks tab also contains a Suppress Line Numbers option, which prevents line numbers from appearing if you're using the line numbering feature. For more information about line numbering, see Chapter 15, "Mastering Page Setup and Pagination." In addition, the Line And Page Breaks tab contains a Don't Hyphenate check box. Hyphenation is covered next.

Taking Charge of Hyphenation

When you work with paragraphs, you need to decide whether you're going to hyphenate words at the ends of lines to create more evenly aligned edges within ragged-edge paragraphs or control "rivers" of white space within justified paragraphs. By default, hyphenation is turned off in Word. This means that if a word is too long to fit on a line, the entire word is moved to the beginning of the next line. If you prefer, you can activate Word's built-in Hyphenation feature to eliminate white space and gaps along the edges of your text. When you use the Hyphenation feature, you can opt to apply hyphenation manually or automatically, as follows:

- **Automatic hyphenation** Word automatically hyphenates an entire document. If you later change the document's contents, Word re-hyphenates the document as needed, while you work.
- **Manual hyphenation** Word searches for instances in which hyphenation is needed, and then you manually confirm whether to add a hyphen at each instance. If you later modify the document, Word displays and prints only the hyphens that fall at the ends of lines. To re-hyphenate the document, you would have to repeat the manual hyphenation process.

Note If you want to apply hyphenation to text that's written in a language other than the default language for the Microsoft Office System, you need to ensure that the language is enabled for editing (through the Microsoft Office 2003 Language Settings), and you need to install Microsoft Office 2003 Publishing tools for the language.

Either way, the process of adding hyphenation begins in the Hyphenation dialog box, shown in Figure 8-10. To display the Hyphenation dialog box, choose Tools, Language, Hyphenation. The following sections briefly describe how to control hyphenation.

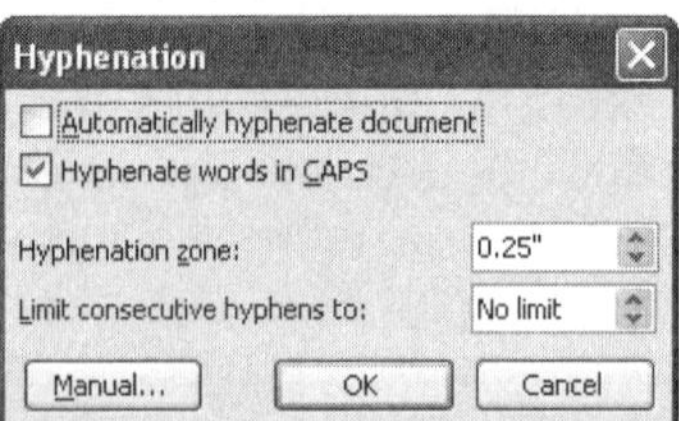

Figure 8-10. The Hyphenation dialog box enables you to automatically or manually hyphenate your documents.

Tip **Insert nonbreaking hyphens**
You can format nonbreaking hyphens to prevent a hyphenated word, number, or phrase from breaking if it falls at the end of a line. For example, you might not want to break a phone number at the end of the line. To insert a nonbreaking hyphen, press Ctrl+Shift+hyphen.

Hyphenating an Entire Document Automatically

To hyphenate an entire document automatically, follow these steps:

1. Choose Tools, Language, Hyphenation to display the Hyphenation dialog box.
2. Select the Automatically Hyphenate Document check box.
3. In the Hyphenation Zone box, enter the amount of acceptable white space to leave between the end of the last word in a line and the right margin. If you want fewer hyphens, make the Hyphenation Zone value larger; if you want to reduce ragged edges, make the Hyphenation Zone value smaller.
4. In the Limit Consecutive Hyphens To box, type the maximum number of consecutive lines that can end with a hyphen, and then click OK.

Tip If you want to turn off the automatic hyphenation feature as well as remove automatically inserted hyphens, simply display the Hyphenation dialog box, clear the Automatically Hyphenate Document check box, and click OK.

Hyphenating Part of a Document Automatically

To hyphenate part of a document automatically, follow these steps:

1. Select the text you don't want to hyphenate.
2. Choose Format, Paragraph, and click the Line And Page Breaks tab. Select the Don't Hyphenate check box, and click OK.
3. Choose Tools, Language, Hyphenation to display the Hyphenation dialog box.
4. Select the Automatically Hyphenate Document check box.
5. Configure the Hyphenation Zone and Limit Consecutive Hyphens To settings (as described earlier), and then click OK.

This procedure will hyphenate your document in all areas except the section(s) you've excluded.

Hyphenating All or Part of a Document Manually

When you hyphenate a document manually, you can hyphenate the entire document or you can select part of the document before you display the Hyphenation dialog box. To hyphenate text manually, either select the text you want to hyphenate or make sure that no text is selected if you want to hyphenate the entire document, and then follow these steps:

1. Choose Tools, Language, Hyphenation to display the Hyphenation dialog box.
2. Click Manual to have Word scan the document. When Word identifies a word or phrase that should be hyphenated, the Manual Hyphenation dialog box appears, as shown in Figure 8-11. You can click Yes to insert the specified hyphen; use the arrow keys or mouse to reposition the hyphen location, and then click Yes; click No to ignore the suggestion, and then move to the next word; or click Cancel to end the hyphenating process.

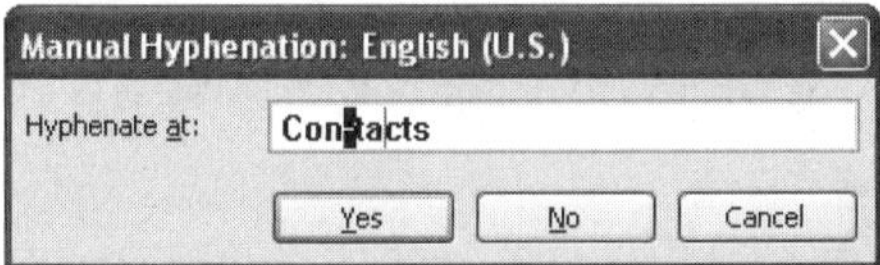

Figure 8-11. When you manually hyphenate a document, the Manual Hyphenation dialog box appears each time a word needs to be hyphenated and Word suggests locations where you can hyphenate that word.

Creating Drop Caps in Existing Paragraphs

A popular format frequently associated with paragraphs is the drop caps. *Drop caps* refer to the large letters that appear at the very beginning of chapters or sections, as shown in Figure 8-12.

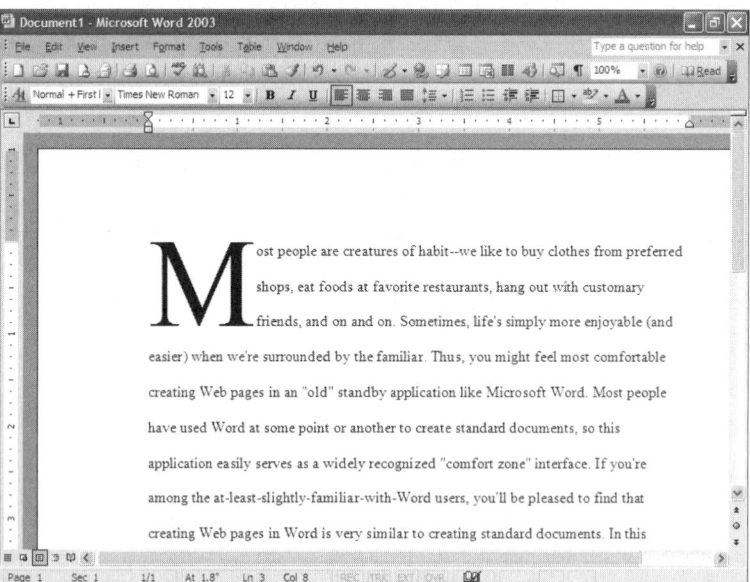

Figure 8-12. Drop caps are large, stylized letters that are frequently used to identify the beginning of a prominent section in a document, such as a chapter.

Word provides an easy way for you to add drop caps to paragraphs. When you use the Drop Cap feature, Word basically converts the first letter of a paragraph to a graphic. After the graphic is automatically created and situated, you can further modify the drop cap just as you modify any graphic element. To create a drop cap, follow these steps:

1. Click in the paragraph that you want to customize with a drop cap, or, if you want to enlarge more than just the first letter in the paragraph, select the letters or word(s) you want to format as drop caps.
2. Choose Format, Drop Cap. The Drop Cap dialog box appears, as shown in Figure 8-13.

Figure 8-13. The Drop Cap dialog box enables you to set parameters before the graphic for the first letter is created and inserted in your document.

For more information about working with graphics, see "Part 2: Reinforcing Your Message with Tables, Charts, Diagrams, and Pictures."

3 Click the Position option—None, Dropped, or In Margin—and then configure any formatting parameters you want to customize, including Font, Lines To Drop, and Distance From Text. Click OK.

If you decide not to display a drop cap in your paragraph, you can easily remove the formatting. To do so, click in the paragraph containing the drop cap, display the Drop Cap dialog box, click None, and then click OK.

Finally, note that drop caps appear above your paragraph in Normal View and Outline View. To view drop caps properly on screen, view documents that contain drop caps in Web Page Layout view, Print Layout view, or Reading Layout view.

Perking Up Paragraphs with Borders and Shading

Another common method of customizing paragraphs is to add borders around and/or shading behind selected paragraphs. To accomplish this simple feat, follow these steps:

1 Select the paragraph you want to format.

2 Choose Format, Borders And Shading.

3 Select the border or shading options you want to apply to the selected paragraph, and then click OK.

For more information about the ins and outs of creating borders and shading, see Chapter 18, "Drawing Attention to Documents by Using Borders and Shading."

Creating Effective Lists

Another way to align text is to create bulleted and numbered lists. Adding bulleted and numbered lists to your document can go a long way toward making your document more readable, which is an achievement your readers will be grateful for. Lists can also help you make your point clearly and succinctly, enabling the ideas to stand out instead of being lost inside a large paragraph. The remainder of this chapter shows you how to create lists—both bulleted and numbered—in Word documents. You'll learn the ins and outs of list-making and discover how lists can make your work easier and more effective, whether you create short articles, long dissertations, or something in between.

Like its predecessors, Word 2003 includes automated features that make creating lists a fairly simple process. Within that process, however, you have a number of choices to make—and some quirks to navigate around.

Throughout this chapter, both bulleted and numbered lists are referred to simply as lists, because they behave the same way. When you choose a bullet, of course, you're using a special symbol, character, or graphic to start a text line. When you use a number, you're selecting the font, size, and color of the numeral you want to use. In addition, you can use roman numerals, letters, and other line identifiers in numbered lists (a technique covered later in this chapter in "Improving Numbered Lists" on page 256).

When Bullets Work

Word gives you the capacity to create bulleted lists with a number of looks. For instance, you can select bullet characters, colors, and indents. Further, you can place bulleted lists side by side in a multicolumn format. Here are some guidelines to remember when you create bulleted lists:

- **Be concise.** Fewer words make a larger impact. Unless you *must* include paragraphs of text for each bullet item, pare your prose down to fewer than three sentences if you can.
- **Stick to the point.** A general rule is "one point, one bullet." Don't try to cram more than one idea into each bullet item.
- **Be clear.** Flowery language isn't necessary—clear and simple is best.
- **Don't overdo it.** Bullets can be so much fun (and easier to write than big blocks of text) that you might be tempted to use them liberally throughout your document. Resist the temptation to overuse bullets in your work and use them only when they bring clarity to your content.
- **Choose a bullet that makes sense.** If your report is about a new drive train your company is manufacturing, would baby-bottle bullet characters really make sense? Probably not. Be sure to fit the bullet characters you choose to the style and expectation of your audience.
- **Don't use too many at once.** Don't make your lists burdensome for your readers. If possible, say what you need to say in five to seven bullet points and move back to paragraph style.

Tip **Use bullets for unordered lists**
Bullets are ideal for those times when you want to convey short, to-the-point pieces of information. The fact that you use bullets instead of numbers implies to your reader that the points can be read and applied in any order; there's no necessary sequence in a bulleted list.

When Numbers Matter

The type of information you create determines whether you need numbered lists in your documents. If you're writing a how-to manual about fly-fishing, you might have quite a few numbered steps, explaining important steps for preparing equipment, finding the right spot, and setting up for your first cast. If you're creating a marketing plan with a timeline and an action sequence, your steps will define a process that builds a bigger promotions system. Whatever the purpose of your numbered list, you can make sure it's most effective in these ways:

- **Use numbers that fit your style.** In an upbeat publication, you might want to use specialty numbers or a casual font with oversized numbers. In a more serious piece, you'll want the numbers you select to carry a more professional tone.

- **Keep steps clear.** Most often, numbered steps are used to describe a process. Conveniently enough, steps can add clarity to a complex procedure. Therefore, don't muddy the waters by overburdening a numbered step with too much information. Include one or two instructions per step and then move on to the next numbered step.
- **Remember the white space.** Whether you're working with bulleted or numbered lists, the white space in your document is as important as the text on the page—it might be a humbling statement, but it's true. White space gives your readers' eyes a rest, so space list items and avoid crowding steps too closely.
- **Align by design.** As with spacing for bulleted and numbered lists, the alignment of lists matters. Make sure the indents in the second line of the list item align with the first character of text, and make sure that lists present a consistent alignment pattern throughout your document.

Tip Use numbered lists when order matters

A numbered list communicates a sequence: First, we have the team meeting; next, we implement the plan; then we write the report; and finally, we present our results. These items, in a list, would be numbered because they show a definite order and a logical process.

Preparing to Create Lists

You need to make sure that you have AutoFormat configured for lists and bullets if you want to create bulleted and numbered lists automatically as you type. To do so, follow these steps:

1. Choose Tools, AutoCorrect Options. The AutoCorrect dialog box appears.
2. Click the AutoFormat As You Type tab and make sure the Format Beginning Of List Item Like The One Before It check box is selected in the Automatically As You Type section. (Note that this option is selected by default.)
3. Next, click the AutoFormat tab and make sure that List Styles and Automatic Bulleted Lists are both selected in the Apply section at the top of the tab.
4. Click OK to return to your document.

For more about working with automatic text tools like AutoFormat, AutoCorrect, and AutoText, see Chapter 7, "Putting Text Tools to Work."

Creating a Quick List

Numbering

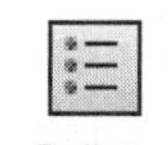

Bullets

Word enables you to create both numbered and bulleted lists from existing text as well as on the fly. To create a list from existing text, select the text, and then click either the Numbering or Bullets button on the Formatting toolbar. Each selected paragraph will be formatted as a single numbered or bulleted list item. As mentioned, you can also create lists while you type. To create a quick list while you type by using the Formatting toolbar buttons, follow these steps:

1. Place the insertion point where you want to add the list.

2 Click the Numbering button on the Formatting toolbar if you want to create a numbered list, or click the Bullets button on the Formatting toolbar if you want to create a bulleted list.

3 Type your first item, and press Enter. The list item is added and the next bullet or number is added (as shown in Figure 8-14).

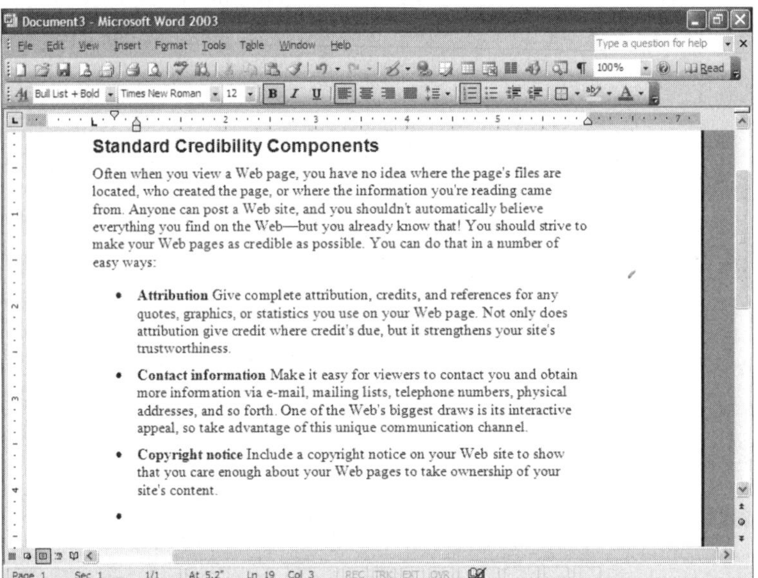

Figure 8-14. Adding a quick list uses Word's default bullet style.

4 Continue entering your list items, pressing Enter after each item.

> **Tip** You can easily rearrange list items by selecting the item you want to move, and then dragging it to another location in the list.

Creating Lists While You Type

You can also create lists while you type by taking advantage of AutoCorrect features that are turned on in Word by default. You can create both bulleted and numbered lists while you type.

To create a bulleted list in Word without clicking a toolbar button, type an asterisk (*), press Tab, type a list entry, and then press Enter. By default, Word will change the asterisk to a bullet and a smart tag will appear that enables you to control the AutoCorrect automatic bulleted list feature. If you want to create the bulleted list, simply continue to type, and the smart tag will disappear.

Similarly, to create a numbered list while you type, enter a number (you can enter any number, but generally, you'd probably want to start with the number 1), press Tab, enter text, and press Enter. Word will format the entry as a numbered list item and display a smart tag that enables you to control the creation of a numbered list. Again, to continue creating the numbered list, simply continue to type the next numbered list entry and the smart tag will close by itself.

Lists created using the techniques described in this section use the default bullet or number style—you didn't have any say in the font, color, design, or spacing of the list. But those items are all easily changed and controlled, as described in the remainder of this chapter.

> **Tip** **Add paragraphs to list items without inserting the next list number or bullet**
> If you want to start a new paragraph within a bulleted or numbered list, but you're not yet ready for the next bullet or number, press Shift+Enter instead of Enter. Pressing Shift+Enter ensures that the added information appears as a paragraph within the current bulleted or numbered item. When you press Enter later, a bullet or number will appear, to continue your list.

Ending a List—the Way You Want

One of the challenges users often face with bulleted and numbered lists is that the lists seem to want to go on forever. After you press Enter on your last list entry, yet another bullet (or number) shows up. Get rid of the extra bullet or number by doing one of three things:

- Click the Bullets or Numbering toolbar button to turn off the feature.
- Press Backspace to delete the number or bullet.
- Press Enter twice after the last item instead of once.

> **Note** If spacing is important in your document, avoid pressing Enter twice to end a list because it adds an unnecessary line space.

Enhancing Bulleted Lists

The default Word settings for bulleted and numbered lists are fine when you're creating a quick, simple document that will be passed around the office and eventually end up in the dumpster. But what about those special reports you create or the procedure manuals that others rely on? Those need to have a more professional look and feel, and the treatment of the lists in your document suddenly become more important.

You can improve a basic bulleted list in several ways. You might want to customize your list by choosing your bullet style from the bullet library, selecting a picture bullet, creating your own bullets, or changing indents and spacing for your bullet items.

Choosing a New Bullet from the Bullet Gallery

Word gives you a gallery of seven preset bullet styles to choose from and a virtually unlimited supply of bullet options you can pull from symbol typefaces, graphics libraries, and more. To choose a new bullet character for a list, follow these steps:

1. Select the list items with the bullets you want to change, or position your cursor where you want to add a list.

2 Choose Format, Bullets And Numbering. The Bullets And Numbering dialog box appears, as shown in Figure 8-15.

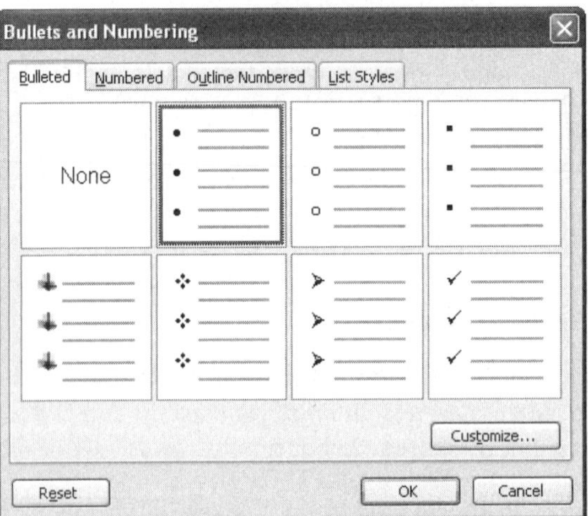

Figure 8-15. Changing the default bullet to another Word bullet style is a simple matter of point-and-click.

3 Select the new bullet you want to use by clicking the preview box of your choice.

4 Click OK to return to your document. The bullet character is added and your list is updated with the new style.

> **Tip** **Right-click to format bullets or numbering**
> A quick way to access the Bullets And Numbering dialog box is to select your list, right-click, and then choose Bullets And Numbering from the shortcut menu.

Selecting a Bullet Character Outside the Default Preset Gallery

If the preset gallery bullets don't work for you, you can select one of the preset options that you won't need, and click Customize in the Bullets And Numbering dialog box to start the process of changing your bullet character choices. When you click Customize, the Customize Bulleted List dialog box appears. In this dialog box, bullet character choices appear across the top of the dialog box, and below the bullet characters, three buttons enable you to access three types of bullet modifications: Font, Character, and Picture. Figure 8-16 shows the Customize Bulleted List dialog box.

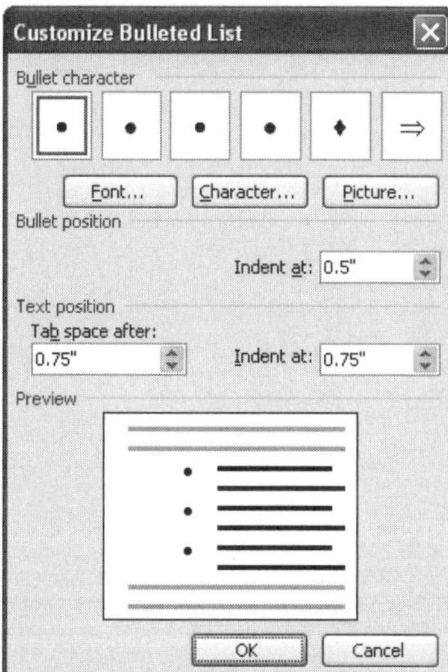

Figure 8-16. The Customize Bulleted List dialog box gives you the means to change the font and character you use for bullets. You can also change bullet spacing and text position here.

Resetting a Default Preset Bullet Gallery

Keep in mind that when you specify a custom bullet, the new bullet will appear in the Bulleted tab in the Bullets And Numbering dialog box in place of the bullet you selected before you clicked Customize. If you'd like to revert to the default bullet, you can do so, as follows:

1. Choose Format, Bullets And Numbering, and click the Bulleted tab if necessary.
2. Select the preview box that you'd like to return to the default setting.
3. Click Reset. A message box appears, asking if you'd like to reset the gallery position to the default setting.
4. Click Yes, and the default bullet for the selected gallery position appears in the Bulleted tab.

To reset the entire bullet gallery to the default settings, you'll have to select and reset each gallery position in the Bulleted tab in the Bullets And Numbering dialog box.

Changing the Bullet Font

When you click Font in the Customize Bulleted List dialog box, the Font dialog box appears, as shown in Figure 8-17. Here you can select a typeface and change font settings for bullet characters.

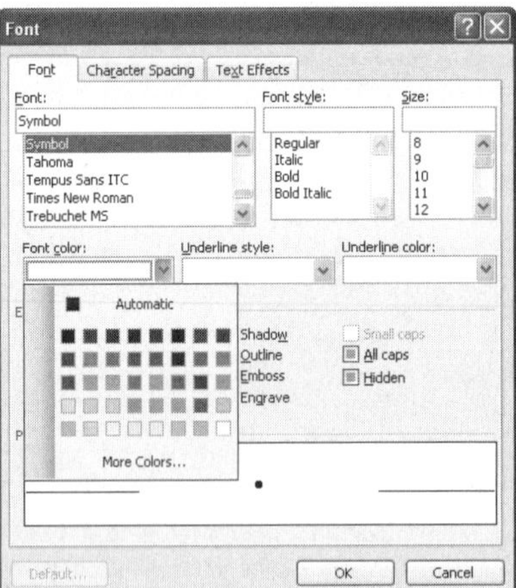

Figure 8-17. The Font dialog box enables you to change a bullet character's typeface, style, color, and text effects.

From within Word, you can access a few typefaces that include symbols that can be used as bullet characters. Some typefaces you might find useful for custom bullets include MS Outlook, Symbol, Webdings, and Wingdings. Of course, you can use *any* character, alphabetic or otherwise, as a bullet character. But unless you're creating an outline, letters as bullets can be less clear for readers than graphical symbols.

Changing a Bullet Character

When you customize bullets, you can click Character in the Customized Bulleted List dialog box to display the Symbol dialog box, as shown in Figure 8-18. The Symbol dialog box displays available characters for selected fonts. You can change font selections in the Symbol dialog box by choosing a font in the Font list box. After you find a character you want to use, simply click the character, and then click OK.

For more information about working with the Symbol dialog box, see Chapter 2, "Mastering Document Fundamentals."

Notice that you can see the numeric character code in either decimal or hexadecimal format for each character you select in the Symbol dialog box. This enables you to be sure you've used the same bullet throughout this document and in other documents that need a consistent style.

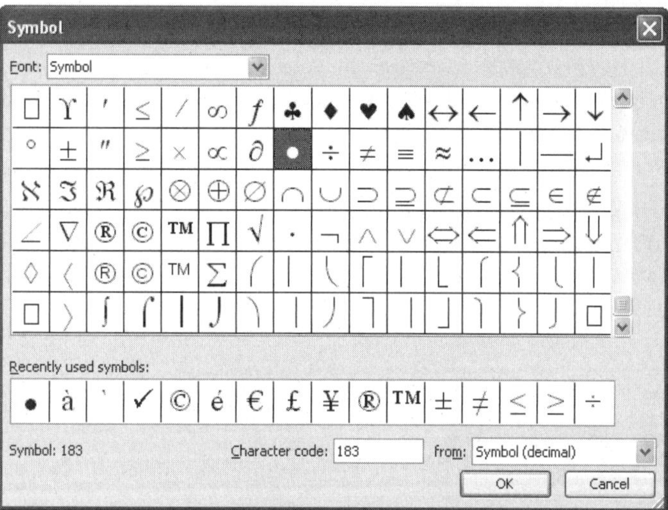

Figure 8-18. Click the symbol you want to select as a new bullet character. Make note of the character code of the item you select if you need to be consistent with lists in other documents.

Tip You can resize the Symbol dialog box to view additional rows and columns of symbols at a time.

Troubleshooting

My default bullet characters show up as clock faces

If your default bullets appear as clock faces, the most likely cause is that the Symbol font on your system is damaged. By default, Microsoft Word uses the bullet character from the Symbol font. If the Symbol font (Symbole.fon) is damaged or unavailable, Word replaces the bullet with a character from the Wingdings font. In the Wingdings font, the corresponding ASCII character is a clock face. To resolve this issue, delete the Symbole.fon file in the \%*Windir*%\Font folder, and then reinstall the Symbol font from your Microsoft Windows CD or from another computer that's running the same version of Microsoft Windows. Alternatively, if you don't want to reinstall the Symbols font, you can simply select another character from the Wingdings font in the Symbol dialog box, as described in this chapter.

Using a Picture Bullet

We live in an age of pictures—television and the Web have raised the bar on what we expect in terms of aesthetic presentation of information. One way you can subtly add imagery to your documents is to use picture bullets. Used judiciously, picture bullets in your documents can effectively liven up a document by adding color and interest to text.

What is a picture bullet? Simply, it's a graphic image that's small enough to use as a bullet character. Word offers a range of bullet styles and shapes, included animated bullets that you can use online. To display the Picture Bullet dialog box and see the available offerings, ensure that a bullet gallery position is selected in the Bullets tab in the Bullets And Numbering dialog box, click Customize, and then click Picture in the Customize Bulleted List dialog box. The Picture Bullet dialog box appears, as shown in Figure 8-19.

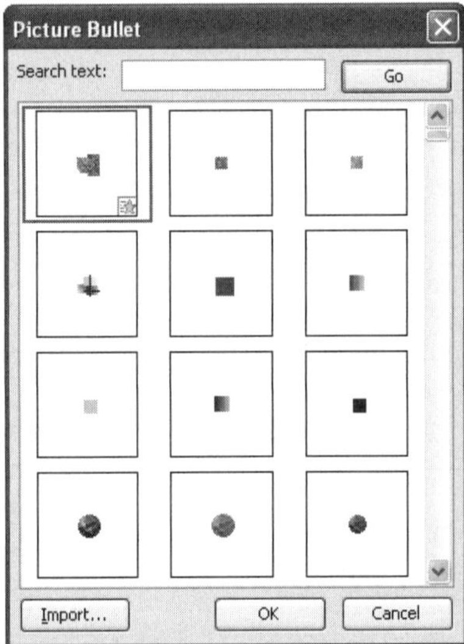

Figure 8-19. Picture bullet options appear in a dialog box that includes a Search Text option.

To select a picture bullet, you simply click the one you want, and click OK. Word adds the picture bullet to the Bullet Character choices section in the Customize Bulleted List dialog box. Ensure that the newly added bullet is selected in the Bullet Character section, and then click OK. You'll then be able to select the picture bullet as the bullet of choice in the Bullets And Numbering dialog box.

If you don't see a picture bullet that you want to use in the Picture Bullet dialog box, enter text in the Search Text box, and click Go. Word will search clip art and online files. Online bullet options appear with an image of the world in the lower-left corner of the preview picture. Further, animated bullets (bullets that will appear with small movements, size changes, or color changes when the bullet is viewed online in a Web page) appear with a star in the lower-right corner of a preview picture, as you can see in the first button preview shown in Figure 8-19.

Creating a Multilevel List with Picture Bullets

At times, you might want to create complex bulleted lists that consist of multiple sublevels. In many cases, you'll probably display a complex list as a numbered or lettered outline, but in some instances, you might want to create a list with picture bullets using a different picture for each level. If you're using a built-in theme in your document, many Office themes already supply pictures or symbols for each level in a multilevel bulleted list. But if you'd like to create a custom bulleted list, you can do so by following these steps:

1. Select the list items with the bullets you want to change, or position your cursor where you want to add a list.
2. Choose Format, Bullets And Numbering, and then click the Outline Numbered tab. The Outline Numbered tab (shown in Figure 8-20) enables you to format the styles of bullets or numbers that will appear for each level in a complex list.

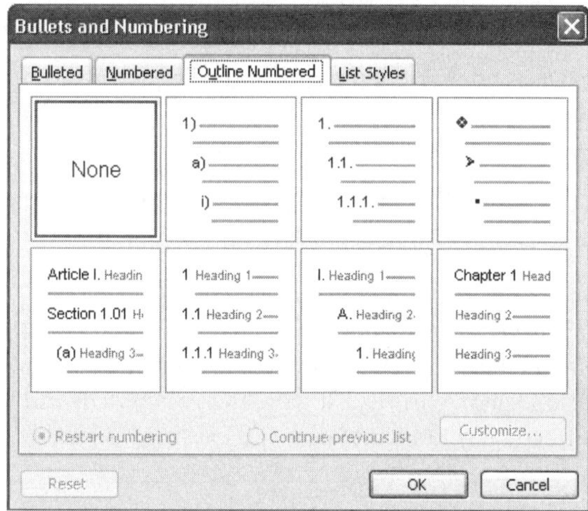

Figure 8-20. The default Outline Numbered gallery includes a preset option for multilevel lists that uses character bullets.

3. Select a gallery option that you'd like to replace with your custom settings (for simplicity's sake, you might want to choose a list style from the top row), and click Customize. The Customize Outline Numbered List dialog box appears, as shown in Figure 8-21.

Chapter 8

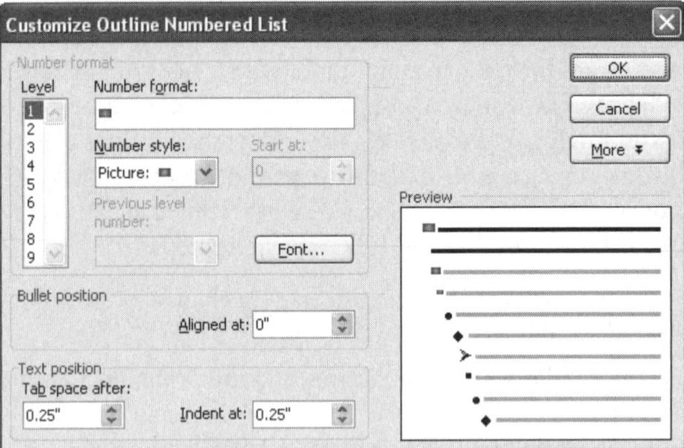

Figure 8-21. To create complex lists with custom bullets, you specify a bullet style for each list level by configuring the Customize Outline Numbered List dialog box.

4. In the Level box, click 1, or click the top row in the Preview window.
5. In the Number Style box, select New Picture. The Picture Bullet dialog box appears, as shown earlier in Figure 8-19.
6. Select a picture bullet, click OK, and then repeat steps 4 and 5 to format the sublevels in your list (remember to select a level number or click the level in the Preview window).
7. When you finish adding pictures to all the levels in your list, click OK.

After you configure a multilevel picture bullet list, you can insert the custom bullets while you type. To insert a sublevel item with its accompanying bullet, press Enter, and press Tab for each level. You can also format a list by using the Increase Indent and Decrease Indent buttons on the Formatting toolbar to format new and existing bulleted text.

Tip To reset an Outline Numbered list to the default setting, click the gallery position in the Outline Numbered tab in the Bullets And Numbering dialog box, and then click Reset.

For more information about creating outlines and numbered outline lists, see Chapter 10, "Outlining Documents for Clarity and Structure."

Importing Custom Bullets

If you create other bullets you want to use in your Word documents, you can add them in the Picture Bullet dialog box. To do so, follow these steps:

1. Choose Format, Bullets And Numbering, and click the Bulleted tab.
2. Select a gallery position in the Bulleted tab, and click Customize.
3. Click a Bullet Character position that contains a picture you'd like to replace, and click Picture.

4. In the Picture Bullet dialog box, click Import. The Add Clips To Organizer dialog box appears, as shown in Figure 8-22.

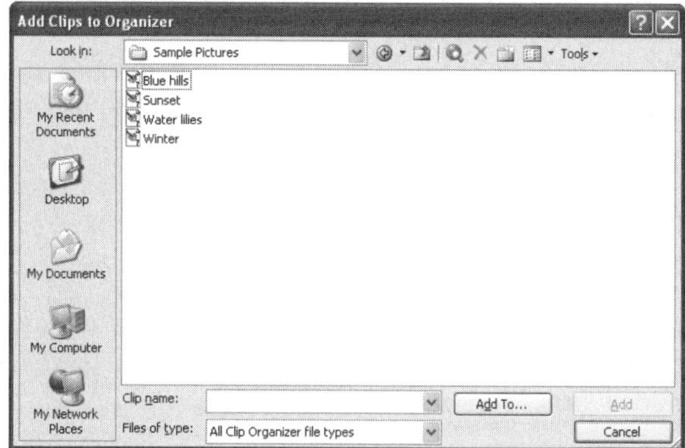

Figure 8-22. Add your own picture bullets by clicking the Import button in the Picture Bullet dialog box, browse to and select the file you want, and then click Add To. Word provides some sample pictures you can use to test this feature.

> **Note** To use your images as Word picture bullets, save the files in Graphics Interchange Format (GIF), bitmap (BMP), or Joint Photographic Experts Group (JPEG) format.

5. Browse to the folder containing the picture you want to add, click the picture, click Add To, and then click OK. The picture appears in the Bullet Character section in the Customize Bulleted List dialog box.
6. Ensure that the newly added picture is selected, and click OK.

Word adds the picture to the Bulleted tab in the Bullets And Numbering dialog box, thereby making it easily accessible in the future.

Changing the Bullet Indent

When you first create a bullet the Word-default way, the program indents the bullet by ¼ of an inch, or 0.25 on your ruler. Text begins at the 0.5 marker. Although this is the default setting, you might want to change the indent level to either move the bullet farther out toward the text margin, or inward, to put more space between the edge of the page and the bullet character and text. To make your changes, select a bullet style in the bullet gallery in the Bulleted tab in the Bullets And Numbering dialog box, click Customize, and then make changes in the Customize Bulleted List dialog box in either of the following ways:

- **Increase indent** To increase the space between the left edge of the page and the bullet character, click the Indent At up arrow in the Bullet Position section of the Customize Bulleted List dialog box, or enter a value in the box.

- **Decrease indent** To decrease the indent, click the down arrow, or click in the Indent At box and type the value you want.

> **Tip** **Use the ruler to adjust list formatting**
> You can also reformat a list by using the ruler (to display the ruler, choose View, Ruler). To format a list using the ruler, simply select your list, and then change alignment and indent settings by moving the indent and tab markers on the ruler.

Modifying Text Position in Lists

Depending on the bullet character you choose, you might want to add more space between the character and the beginning of the text. By default, Word separates the bullet and the text beginning by ¼ of an inch, or 0.25 on your ruler. The text itself begins at the 0.5 marker.

You can change both these settings by changing the Text Position settings in the Customize Bulleted List dialog box. Here's how:

1. Make sure the bullet items are selected in your document or that your cursor is positioned in an empty paragraph where you want to start a bulleted list.
2. Choose Format, Bullets And Numbering.
3. In the Bullets And Numbering dialog box, select the bullet style you want to customize, and click Customize. The Customize Bulleted List dialog box appears.
4. In the Text Position section of the dialog box, click the up or down arrow in the Tab Space After box to change the amount of space between the bullet character and the beginning of the text.
5. In the Indent At box, click the up or down arrow to increase or decrease the position at which you want the text to begin. In both this step and the previous one, you can click in the box and type the value if you prefer.
6. Click OK to accept the new bullet settings and return to your document.

> **Note** As always, if you don't like the changes, you can press Ctrl+Z to undo your last operation or you can reset the gallery position. Also, remember that you can modify list alignment settings by dragging indent and tab markers on the ruler.

Improving Numbered Lists

Like bulleted lists, numbered lists allow you to make your own choices about the look and format of the numerals used. Many procedures you use to customize bulleted lists can also be used to fine-tune numbered lists. Most notably, in numbered lists, you can make modifications by specifying a font, selecting the number style you want, and choosing the number and text position of the items in your list.

Note Because the process of changing the font, number position, and text position in the Customize Numbered List dialog box is the same as for changing the bullet and text font and position (covered earlier in this chapter in the sections "Changing the Bullet Font," "Changing the Bullet Indent," and "Modifying Text Position in Lists"), those steps are not repeated here for numbered lists. Refer to the procedures for bulleted lists for information.

Choosing a Numbering Scheme

Numbers can add character to numbered lists. You might use simple traditional characters or larger, colorful characters, depending on the nature of your publication. Begin by selecting the numbered list you want to change, or position your cursor in an empty paragraph in which you want to start your list, and then follow these steps:

1. Choose Format, Bullets And Numbering, and then click the Numbered tab. Figure 8-23 shows the Numbered tab with the first gallery position selected.

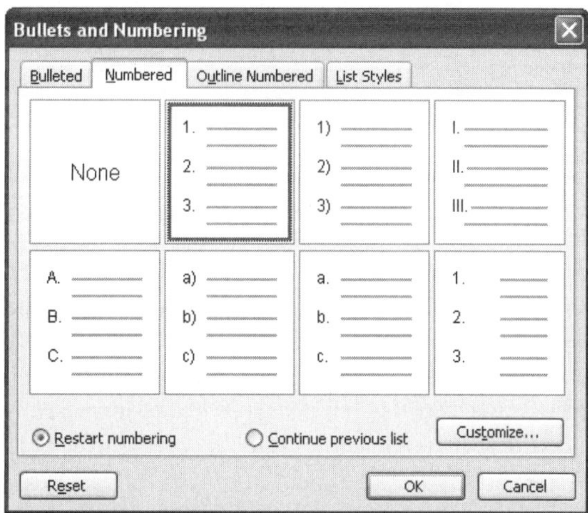

Figure 8-23. The Numbered tab in the Bullets And Numbering dialog box displays preset numbering styles that you can use when you create numbered lists.

2. Click one of the numbering styles shown in the gallery.
3. Click OK. Word updates the numbering style in your list if you selected an existing list or it implements the numbering style when you begin typing.

Modifying the Numbering Style

If you aren't particularly happy with the default numbering styles in the Numbered tab's gallery, you can customize the numbering style you use in much the same way you can customize bulleted list options. Basically, you display the Numbered tab in the Bullets And

Numbering dialog box, select a number style in the gallery that you'd like to replace with a custom style, and then click Customize. The Customize Numbered List dialog box appears, which provides formatting options for numbered lists (as shown in Figure 8-24).

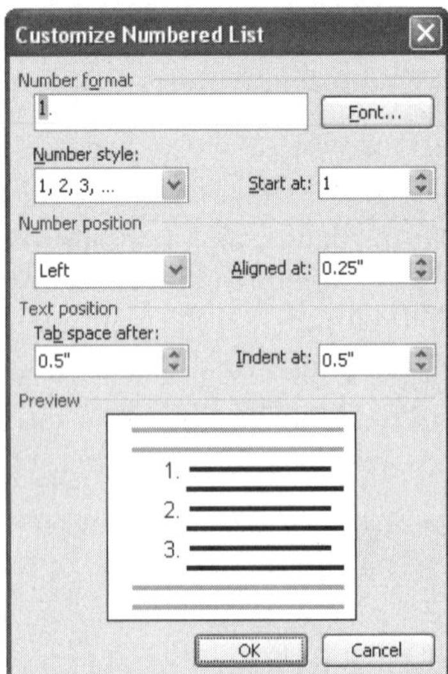

Figure 8-24. The Customize Numbered List dialog box gives you the means to change the number style you use in your list. You can also change number spacing and text position here.

Choose the Font you want to use by clicking Font, and then using the Font dialog box. To choose a number style, from the Customize Numbered List dialog box, click the Number Style arrow to see the available style choices. You can determine at which number you want the list to start by clicking in the Start At box, and then typing the number for the starting point. If you prefer, you can use the up or down arrows on the Start At box to increase or decrease the number by one. Further, you can customize the text position by configuring the Number Position and Text Position options (for additional alignment information, see the sections "Changing the Bullet Indent," on page 255, and "Modifying Text Position in Lists," on page 256).

> **Note** To configure multilevel lists, see the section "Creating a Multilevel List with Picture Bullets" on page 253. Also, see Chapter 10, "Outlining Documents for Clarity and Structure," for more information about working with complex lists and outlines.

Continuing Numbering

Some of your numbered list items might be separated by elements such as charts, explanatory paragraphs, or sidebars. But instead of starting over again with number 1, as Word does by default when you click the Numbering button on the Formatting toolbar, you might want to pick back up with the next numbered step in your process. You can continue numbers in an existing numbered list in a couple of ways:

- Right-click the first incorrect number in a numbered list, and choose Continue Numbering.
- Click the numbered item that you want to renumber; choose Format, Bullets And Numbering; and click Continue Previous List. The numbering scheme in use is selected in the gallery and changes to show the continuation numbers (as shown in Figure 8-25). Click OK.
- Click a numbered item in the accurately numbered part of your list, click Format Painter in the Standard toolbar, and then click the incorrectly numbered item.

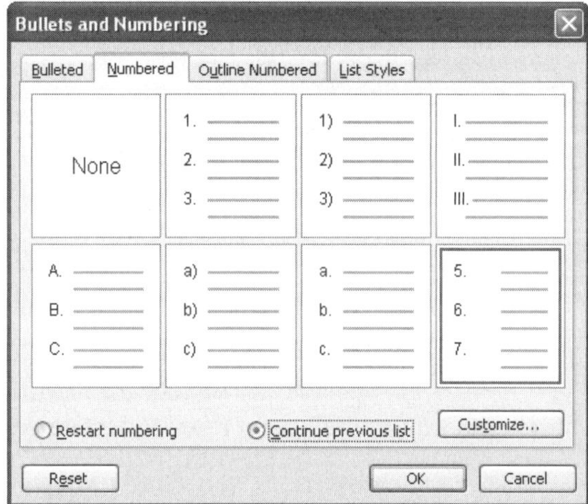

Figure 8-25. When you click Continue Previous List, the styles update to show the extended numbering sequence.

To continue a numbered list while you type, use any of the following procedures:

- Type the next number in the series, press Tab, and then type your text. The AutoFormat feature will kick in and automatically continue your previous numbered list.
- Click the smart tag when you start the continued numbered series, and then choose Continue Numbering in the smart tag list.
- Click a numbered item in the accurately numbered part of your list, click Format Painter in the Standard toolbar, and then click in the paragraph where you want to add the next numbered step.

A word of caution: you should carefully evaluate the length of your numbered lists. In some cases, your information might be clearer if you create a series of shorter numbered lists (separated by headings, if possible), instead of creating a long numbered list.

Restarting Numbering

Restarting numbered lists is similar to continuing numbered lists, as described in "Continuing Numbering" on page 258. The main difference is that you'll want to choose the Restart Numbering option instead of the Continue Previous List option. To restart a numbered list with the number 1, take any of the following actions:

- In a numbered list, right-click the number that you want to change to the number 1, and choose Restart Numbering.
- If you're currently creating the list, type 1, press Tab, and then type text to begin the new numbered list.
- Click the numbered item that you want to renumber; choose Format, Bullets And Numbering; click Restart Numbering, and then click OK.

Tip **Restart a list with a number other than 1**
If you want to restart a list with a number other than 1 (but you don't want to continue the preceding list), select Restart Numbering in the Bullets And Numbering dialog box, click Customize, enter a number in the Start At box, and then click OK.

Insert a Numbered Step into an Existing List

If you find that you've forgotten a step, you can easily insert the step into an existing list. To do so, place your cursor at the end of the step that will precede the newly inserted step, and press Enter. Word will automatically insert the next number and renumber the following existing steps.

Tip You can combine lists by cutting and pasting existing lists together. Further, you can easily rearrange list items by selecting an item you want to move, and dragging it to another location in the list.

Converting a Bulleted List to a Numbered List (or Vice Versa)

You can easily convert bulleted lists to numbered lists and vice versa. To do so, simply select the list, and then click either the Bullets button or the Numbering button on the Formatting toolbar. After you convert a list, you can tweak the list's appearance and settings while the list is selected by choosing Formatting, Bullets And Numbering (or right-clicking the selected list and choosing Bullets And Numbering), and then configuring the settings in the Bullets And Numbering dialog box.

Resolving List Challenges

Word's bulleted and numbered list feature is basically simple to use once you understand the ins and outs of lists, but a few headaches occur now and then. The biggest workaround that you might find useful when you're facing list challenges is to turn off the AutoFormat feature.

Sometimes the automatic features can conflict with the way you've chosen to format lists. If you want to make your own changes to Word's bullet and numbering schemes, disable Auto-Format before you begin list-making. To do that, follow these steps:

1. Choose Tools, AutoCorrect Options, and then click the AutoFormat tab.
2. Clear the List Styles and Automatic Bulleted Lists check boxes.
3. In the AutoFormat As You Type tab, clear the Automatic Bulleted Lists and Automatic Numbered Lists check boxes.

For more information about AutoFormatting, see Chapter 7, "Putting Text Tools to Work."

Tip Go with custom styles rather than the default

One way to ensure that you've saved a list's bullet or numbering formatting is to create your own styles. When you create a list style, opt to create a custom style; don't base the new style on any of Word's list styles. When you use the default list styles, Word returns to its default settings at shutdown, which means that when you open your document the next time, your changes will be gone. For more information about creating styles, see Chapter 9, "Using Styles to Increase Your Formatting Power."

Chapter 9

Using Styles to Increase Your Formatting Power

Formatting takes on new meaning when you create complex or long documents that contain recurring elements, such as headings, formatted paragraphs, figure captions, table headings, and so forth. Spending time formatting components one by one in a document that contains a variety of elements can easily lead to hours of tedium and increased chances of formatting errors. Conveniently, you can eliminate repetitive formatting tasks in Word by using *styles*.

A *style* is a named set of formatting characteristics that you can apply to characters, paragraphs, tables, and lists. When you use styles, you can quickly apply multiple formatting settings to specified text. In addition, styles enable you to modify the look of a document easily by changing a style (or styles) instead of manually reformatting components throughout your document. Styles also enable you to take advantage of the following powerful automation and organization features available in Word:

- **AutoFormat** See Chapter 7, "Putting Text Tools to Work."
- **AutoSummarize** See Chapter 6, "Making the Most of Research Services and Reference Tools."
- **Master Documents** See Chapter 20, "Creating and Controlling Master Documents."
- **Outlining** See Chapter 10, "Outlining Documents for Clarity and Structure."
- **Tables of contents, tables of figures, and similar elements** See Chapter 21, "Generating First-Class Tables of Contents and Related Elements."
- **Themes, templates, and add-ins** See Chapter 16, "Formatting Documents Using Templates, Wizards, Add-Ins, and XML Schemas."
- **Web page wizards and templates** See Chapter 26, "Creating Professional Web Sites."

The bottom line is that instead of formatting each character, paragraph, table, and list in a document individually by using toolbar buttons, keyboard shortcuts, menu commands, and dialog box options, you can make better use of your time and resources by creating and using styles.

Unfortunately, the concept of styles tends to make most Word users feel a bit uncomfortable; even some experienced Word users rarely bother with styles (or they use styles only sporadically). Fortunately, if you're comfortable using Word but are new to styles, you needn't worry—creating, using, and modifying styles are skills that are well within your grasp. Most cases of the style heebie-jeebies are quickly eliminated with a little information and some hands-on experience. If you take a little time to understand and experiment with the concepts presented in this chapter, you'll be able to use styles whenever you need them during document creation and modification. More importantly, you'll discover that using styles can dramatically improve productivity.

Understanding Styles

In Word, the term *style* refers to a collection of formatting commands that are grouped together and given a name. To apply a style, you can simply select the text you want to format (or position the insertion point in a new paragraph where you want the formatting to begin when you enter text), and then select a style in the Style list box on the Formatting toolbar—with a single click, you can apply a complete set of format settings to text. When you apply a style, all the formatting settings in the style are applied at once. As mentioned, styles in Word come in four types:

- **Character** Formats selected text within a paragraph, including properties such as font, size, boldface, italic, and underlining.
- **Paragraph** Affects all the properties associated with a paragraph's appearance, such as text alignment, tab stops, line spacing, borders, and shading. Paragraph styles can include character formatting.
- **Table** Gives a uniform appearance to table borders, colors, shading, alignment, and fonts.
- **List** Affects alignment, numbering or bullet components, and fonts used within lists.

Note Prior to Word 2002, you could create and use only two types of styles—paragraph and character. The table and list styles became available in Word 2002, and continue to be available in Word 2003.

You create, use, and modify the four types of styles in the same basic manner, and you can access all style types in the Styles And Formatting task pane, the Style list box on the Formatting toolbar, and the Style dialog box. But before you start customizing your documents using homegrown styles, you should take a look at the sizable collection of built-in styles provided with Word, described next.

Working with the Default Styles in Word

As you probably know, Word uses the Normal.dot template to create new documents, and you use the Normal default style when you start entering text in a new, blank document. (By default, the Normal style settings are Times New Roman, 12 point, left-aligned, single-spaced.) The Normal.dot template includes over 150 built-in styles, including paragraph, character, list, and table styles. Five of the most widely used built-in styles also have keyboard shortcuts. Two additional keyboard shortcuts let you promote and demote headings by one level. Table 9-1 summarizes these built-in style keyboard shortcuts.

Note Remember, a *template*, such as Normal.dot, is a document that contains the formatting settings and other layout components used in a document, including styles, standard (or boilerplate) text, graphics, page components, and so forth. For more information about templates, see Chapter 16, "Formatting Documents Using Templates, Wizards, Add-Ins, and XML Schemas."

Table 9-1. Keyboard Shortcuts For Build-in Styles

Style	Keyboard Shortcut
Normal	Ctrl+Shift+N
List Bullet	Ctrl+Shift+L
Heading 1	Ctrl+Alt+1
Heading 2	Ctrl+Altl+2
Heading 3	Ctrl+Alt+3
Demote Heading Level	Alt+Shift+Right Arrow
Promote Heading Level	Alt+Shift+Left Arrow

For more information about creating a keyboard shortcut for any style, see "Assigning Keyboard Shortcuts to Styles," on page 280.

In a Word document, default styles are available for you to use and customize. You can opt to use only the default styles (which are effective, albeit a bit conservative); customize existing styles on a document-by-document basis; create custom styles from scratch, and then save them in the document or in a custom template; or customize the Normal.dot template if you want the changes to appear in all new documents.We'll look at each of these alternatives in the following sections.

Note Keep in mind that although you can customize the styles in the Normal template, you can't delete them.

Mastering the Styles And Formatting Task Pane

Styles And Formatting

In Word, you can view available styles in three places: the Style list box on the Formatting toolbar, the Style dialog box (accessed by double-clicking a style name in the Style Area, as described in the section "Configuring the Width of the Style Area" on page 269, or by clicking Styles in the Format Settings dialog box), and the Style And Formatting task pane. The Style list box and the Style dialog box are familiar tools that have been around for a few versions of Word. Their functionality remains fairly consistent with earlier versions of Word. Figure 9-1 shows the Style dialog box, and Figure 9-2 shows the Style list box.

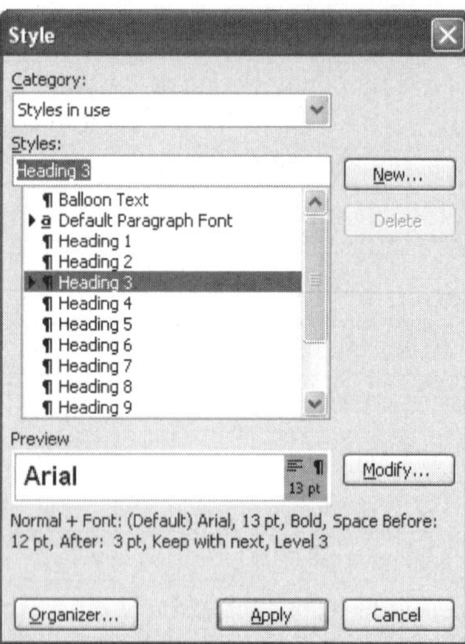

Figure 9-1. The Style dialog box includes a Preview area so you can see how text will look when it's formatted with a selected style.

On the other hand, the Styles And Formatting task pane, shown in Figure 9-2, is a more recent feature, which debuted in Word 2002. The Styles And Formatting task pane is designed to make using, creating, modifying, and deleting or hiding styles easier than traditional dialog box methods.

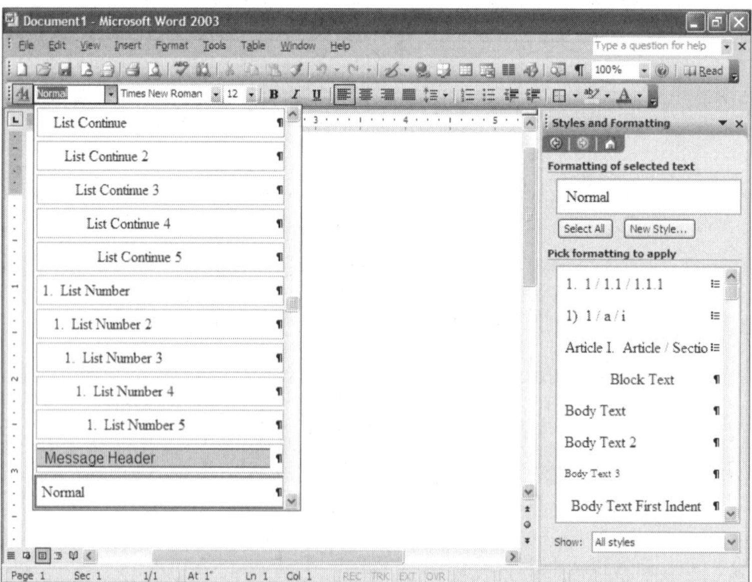

Figure 9-2. The Style list box provides quick access to available styles, and the Styles And Formatting task pane displays style names with their associated formatting.

To open the Styles And Formatting task pane, click the Styles And Formatting button on the Formatting toolbar (to the left of the Style list box), or if your task pane is open, click the arrow in the task pane's title bar and choose Styles And Formatting. The Styles And Formatting task pane contains the following elements:

- **Formatting Of Selected Text** Displays the style of the current paragraph or selected text. If you hover the pointer over the text box, a summary of the style's settings appears in a ToolTip window and an arrow appears. You can click the arrow to access a shortcut menu that enables you to select all instances of the style, clear formatting, create a new style, modify the style, or reveal formatting.
- **Select All** Selects all instances of the current style, as indicated in the Formatting Of Selected Text list box as well as in the Style list box on the Formatting toolbar.
- **New Style** Displays the New Style dialog box, where you can create and modify styles and templates. (The New Style dialog box is discussed in detail in "Creating New Styles," on page 273.)
- **Pick Formatting To Apply** Displays a list of styles, as specified in the Show list box. As with the Formatting Of Selected Text list box, hovering the pointer over the text box displays a ToolTip summary of the style's attributes and displays the arrow. Further, in the Pick Formatting To Apply list box, most style names are followed by a symbol that identifies the style type—character, paragraph, list, or table. If no symbol appears next to a list item, the item represents a formatting combination, used in the document, that hasn't been named and saved as a style.
- **Show** Enables you to specify which styles appear in the Pick Formatting To Apply list box and in the Style list box on the Formatting toolbar. You can choose Available Formatting, Formatting In Use, Available Styles, All Styles, or Custom.

> **Tip** **Display all built-in Word styles**
> When you first open a blank document in Word 2003, the Styles And Formatting task pane and Style list box show only four built-in styles: Heading 1, Heading 2, Heading 3, and Normal. To show all the built-in Word styles in the Styles And Formatting task pane and in the Styles list box, open the Styles And Formatting task pane, click the Show list box, and select All Styles.

Customizing the Style List Box in the Styles And Formatting Task Pane

You can temporarily customize the Styles And Formatting task pane by selecting Custom in the Show list box. When you select Custom, the Format Settings dialog box appears, as shown in Figure 9-3.

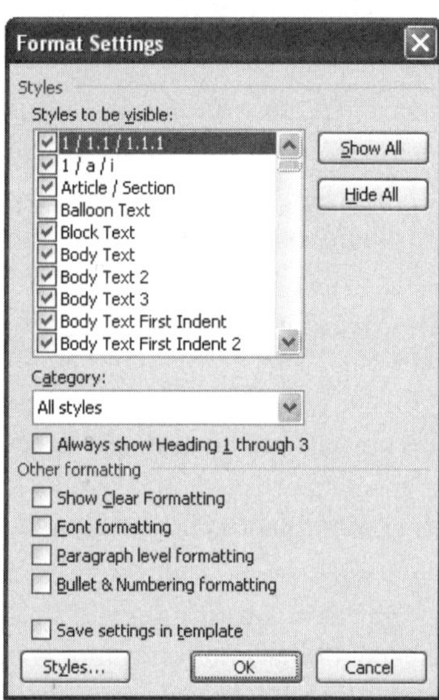

Figure 9-3. The Format Settings dialog box enables you to control which styles appear in the Styles And Formatting task pane.

In the Format Settings dialog box, you can specify which styles will appear by selecting a style category, and then selecting check boxes in the Styles To Be Visible list box. You can configure additional settings in the Other Formatting section, including the Show Clear Formatting option, which adds the Clear Formatting option to the Style list box. The Clear Formatting option is discussed in "Clearing Formatting in Selected Text," on page 272.

Finally, you can customize the Style And Formatting task pane view for all documents that use the template that's attached to the current document. To do so, select the styles you want to make visible, choose the Save Settings In Template check box, and click OK. Word will automatically display the selected styles in the Style And Formatting task pane for the current document as well as for future documents created using the same template. Nicely enough, you can change which styles appear at any time by revisiting the Format Settings dialog box.

Configuring the Width of the Style Area

Often you'll find it convenient to view styles while you work. For example, you might want to verify that you're properly applying a defined set of styles, or you might need to differentiate between styles with similar appearances. When you view styles as you work, you can easily distinguish which styles are applied to which paragraphs because Word displays each paragraph's style name in the Style Area when you're working in Normal view.

To display style name in the Style Area while you work, first make sure that you're working in Normal or Outline view, and then configure the Style Area Width display setting. By default, Style Area Width is set to 0 inches, so it is hidden from view. To increase the width of the Style Area, follow these steps:

1 Choose Tools, Options, and click the View tab if necessary.

2 In the Styles Area Width box near the bottom of the View tab, type an appropriate value. Figure 9-4 shows the result of specifying a Style Area Width of 1 inch.

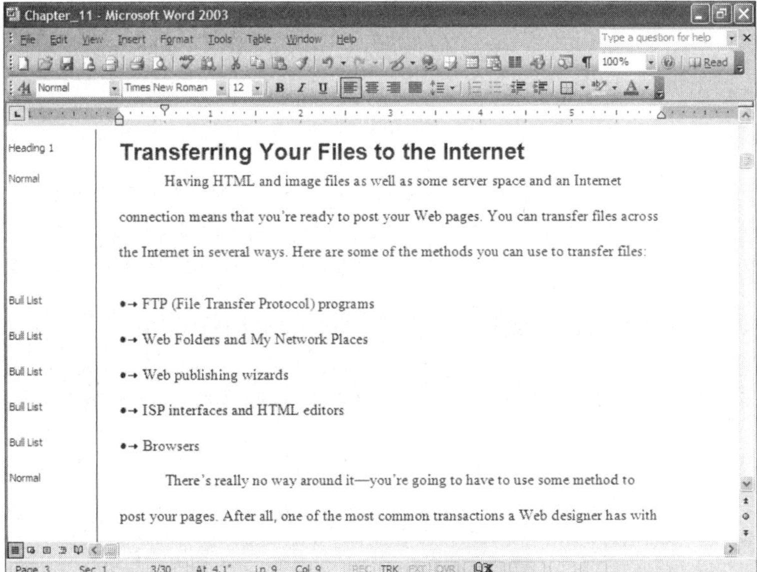

Figure 9-4. The Style Area identifies each paragraph's style in an adjustable-width column located to the left of a document's content.

After you display the Style Area, you can change its width by dragging the border left or right. You can select a paragraph (or paragraphs) in your document by clicking the paragraph's style name in the Style Area, and you can access the Style dialog box by double-clicking a style name. To hide the Style Area, either drag the border all the way to the left or change the Style Width Area setting on the View tab to 0.

Making Styles Work for You

Before you create and customize styles to suit your purposes, you should be comfortable using and applying existing styles. Word provides plenty of styles that you can use to format your documents while you hone your style skills. Incidentally, the quickest way to apply styles to documents is to use the styles that already exist. Don't be intimidated when it comes to using styles. In Word, you can easily change all occurrences of a style. In fact, after you've applied styles, you'll be able to select and modify all instances of a style as well as clear formatting if you determine you'd rather not use a specified style. The next few sections examine how to apply, select, change, and clear existing styles.

Applying Styles to Text

Logically enough, applying a style entails first specifying the element you want to format. You can specify text to be styled by clicking within a paragraph, selecting text within a paragraph or multiple paragraphs, or positioning the insertion point at the beginning of an empty paragraph in which you want the selected style to be applied when you type. After you've specified what you want to format, you can perform any of the following procedures to apply an existing style to the text:

- Choose a style in the Style list box on the Formatting toolbar. You can click the Style arrow or press Ctrl+Shift+S to select the list and then use the Up Arrow and Down Arrow keys to navigate through the style options.

Tip To avoid having to scroll through the Style list box, click the Style down arrow, and then type the first letter of the style name. Styles are listed alphabetically, so the list will jump to the style names starting with the letter you typed.

- Select a style in the Pick Formatting To Apply list box in the Styles And Formatting task pane.
- Double-click the paragraph's existing style name in the Style Area, and choose a style in the Style dialog box.
- Press a preassigned keyboard shortcut (see Table 9-1) or a custom keyboard shortcut.

When you apply a style, the selected text is immediately reformatted in that style. If you find that the newly applied style isn't what you were looking for, you can replace it by applying another style, or you can undo the formatting by clicking Undo on the Standard toolbar, pressing Ctrl+Z, or choosing Edit, Undo.

Selecting and Changing All Instances of a Style

After you apply styles to your text, you can easily select all instances of a style whenever the need arises. In Word 2000 and earlier, you had to use the Find And Replace dialog box to find instances of a formatting style, and you were limited to finding instances one at a time—in other words, you couldn't select all instances of similarly styled text at once. In Word 2002 and Word 2003, you can use the Style And Formatting task pane to select all instances of a specified style quickly. This capability can considerably speed up a number of tasks related to global styles. For example, you might want to select all instances of styled text because you want to replace one style with another, or you might want to delete all text that appears in a particular style, or you might want to copy all similarly styled elements to a new document. Regardless of your reasons, you can select all instances of a style by following these steps:

1. Click a paragraph or word that uses the style you want to select. (You can display the Style Area to simplify the process of selecting a paragraph that has been formatted with the sought-after style.)
2. Click the Styles And Formatting button on the Formatting toolbar to open the Styles And Formatting task pane if it isn't already visible.
3. Click Select All, or hover the pointer over the text in the Formatting Of Selected Text section, click the style's down arrow, and choose Select All *x* Instance(s), as shown in Figure 9-5.

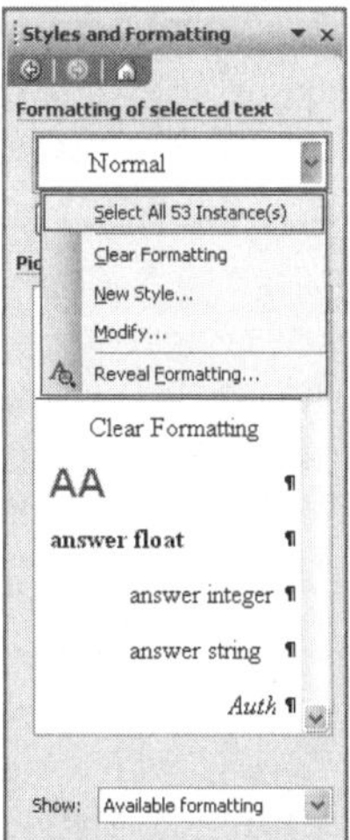

Figure 9-5. Using the Formatting Of Selected Text list box, you can see exactly how many times a style is applied in the current document.

After you select all instances of text with a particular style, you can reformat the selected text by selecting another style in the Style list box on the Formatting toolbar or by selecting a style in the Pick Formatting To Apply list box in the Styles And Formatting task pane. You can delete all selected text with the specified style by pressing Backspace or Delete.

For information about modifying a style's settings, see "Modifying Existing Styles," on page 280.

Clearing Formatting in Selected Text

In addition to simplifying the process of selecting all instances of styled text, the Styles And Formatting task pane enables you to clear formatting quickly. In Word, both the Pick Formatting To Apply list box in the Styles And Formatting task pane and the Style list box on the Formatting toolbar include a Clear Formatting option. You can use this option to remove all formatting settings from selected text, paragraphs, or entire documents. To do so, follow these steps:

1. Select the text or click within the paragraph you want to clear.
2. Perform any of the following actions:
   - Select Clear Formatting in the Style list box on the Formatting toolbar.
   - Display the Styles And Formatting task pane, and select the Clear Formatting option in the Pick Formatting To Apply list box.
   - Choose Edit, Clear, Formats.
   - Display the Styles And Formatting task pane, hover the pointer over the text in the Formatting Of Selected Text list box, click the arrow, and select Clear Formatting.

After you clear the formatting, the text reverts to Normal style (which is Times New Roman, 12 point, left-aligned, single-spaced by default). If you realize immediately that you don't want to clear the formatting, click Undo on the Standard toolbar, press Ctrl+Z, or choose Edit, Undo. Further, you can later reapply the style or apply a new style to the text the same way you apply styles to other text.

Tip **Clear formatting**

To clear all text formatted with a particular style, select all instances of the style (as described in "Selecting and Changing All Instances of a Style," on page 270), and then, in the Styles And Formatting task pane, select Clear Formatting in the Formatting Of Selected Text list box.

Troubleshooting

The Clear Formatting option isn't shown in the Pick Formatting To Apply list box

If you select text, and then find that the Clear Formatting option isn't listed in the Styles And Formatting task pane, it might be because the All Styles option is selected in the Show list box. By default, the All Styles view doesn't include the Clear Formatting option. To eliminate this little annoyance, click the Show arrow, and then choose Available Formatting, Formatting In Use, or Available Styles, all of which are configured to show the Clear Formatting option by default. The Clear Formatting option will appear at or near the top of the list after you change the Show setting.

Creating New Styles

Up to this point in the chapter, we've been looking at existing styles. Most likely, you could create the majority of your documents using the built-in styles found in the Normal.dot template. Doing so would ensure that your documents look consistent, your formatting time is reduced, and your documents are able to interact with the Word tools that rely on styles. But keep in mind that millions of other people use Word as well, and your documents might look rather familiar (and possibly mundane) to them (and to you). And even though Word includes numerous styles in the Normal.dot template, you might find that you need a style that's not provided, such as a boxed tip element or a shaded sidebar. When you want to add some formatting spice or find you need an additional style, you can create your own styles, as described in this section.

Your primary tool when you create new styles is the New Style dialog box. The New Style dialog box offers options specific to the type of style you're creating (character, paragraph, table, or list), as shown in Figure 9-6. To access the New Style dialog box, click the New Style button in the Styles And Formatting task pane.

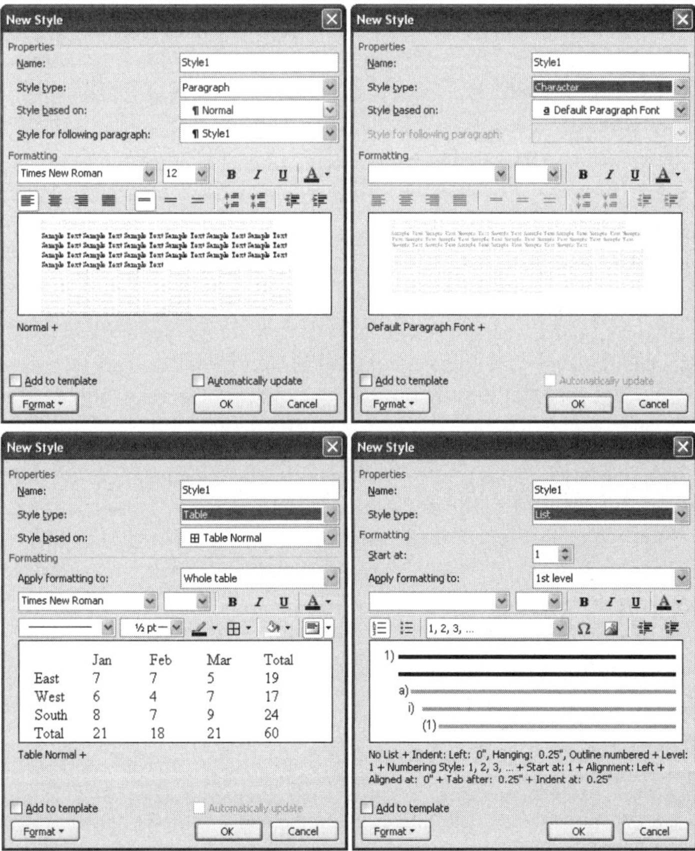

Figure 9-6. The New Style dialog box enables you to configure a variety of properties when you create a new style; the dialog box's options change slightly based on whether you're creating a character, paragraph, table, or list style.

Tip Learn more information about formatting

Formatting characters, paragraphs, lists, and tables from within the New Style dialog box is similar to formatting the same elements from within the main Word window. If you're unsure of a formatting feature in the New Style dialog box that's not addressed in this chapter, check the table of contents for a related chapter that clarifies the effects of a formatting feature. For example, table formatting options are discussed in Chapter 13, "Organizing Concepts in Tables."

Creating New Styles Based on Preformatted Text

One of the easiest ways to create a style is to format existing text, and then define a style based on the formatted text. To successfully create a style using this technique, select and format text within your document (remember to consider font characteristics as well as paragraph settings), and then perform any of the following actions:

- Click the Style box on the Formatting toolbar or press Ctrl+Shift+S, type a name for the new style, and press Enter. To create a paragraph style, your cursor simply needs to be positioned in the formatted paragraph; to create a character style, ensure that the cursor is positioned in a formatted word or select an instance of the formatted text before you name the new style.
- Display the Styles And Formatting task pane, and click New Style. In the New Style dialog box, type a style name in the Name box, configure any other settings, and then click OK. Notice the Style Type list box, where you can specify whether you want to create a paragraph, character, table, or list style, as described in the section "Creating New Styles," on page 273.
- Double-click a style name in the Style Area to display the Style dialog box, and click New to display the New Style dialog box. In the New Style dialog box, type a style name in the Name box, specify the style type, select any other formatting options, and then click OK.

When you create a new style using the New Style dialog box, you can define the style for the current document only (which is the default action), or you can apply the style to the current template. To add a style to the current template (which is Normal.dot by default, if no other template has been attached to the document), select the Add To Template check box. This option saves the style information as part of the current template and makes the style available to other documents using the same template. If you want to save custom styles to a template without adding the styles to the Normal.dot template, you can save your styles to a custom document template, and then attach the template to other documents that use the formatting.

For an in-depth discussion about the New Style dialog box, see "Creating New Styles Using the New Style Dialog Box," on page 275, and for more information about the Add To Template option, see "Adding Styles to Documents and Templates," on page 279.

Using the AutoFormat Feature to Create Styles as You Type

In Word, you can also create styles automatically while you work. By using the AutoFormat feature, you can configure Word to automatically create styles for the current document based on your formatting commands. After you turn on the AutoFormat feature, you'll notice that the formatting and styles you use are automatically added to the Styles And Formatting task pane. To best see the feature in action while you work, display the Styles And Formatting task pane, and select Formatting In Use in the Show list box. To automatically create styles while you format text, follow these steps:

1. Choose Tools, AutoCorrect Options to display the AutoCorrect dialog box.
2. Click the AutoFormat As You Type tab.
3. In the Apply As You Type section, select the Built-In Heading Styles check box. (The other check boxes should already be selected by default.)
4. In the Automatically As You Type section, select the Define Styles Based On Your Formatting check box.
5. Click OK to close the AutoCorrect dialog box.

After you activate the AutoFormat As You Type feature, Word will automatically apply heading and text styles (such as Heading 1, Body Text, List, and so forth) to text as you type. If you don't agree with the AutoFormat feature's treatment, you can apply a different style to a text component. If AutoFormat seems to regularly misinterpret your formatting needs, you might consider turning the feature off. To do so, you simply undo the settings you used to turn the feature on, as follows:

1. Choose Tools, AutoCorrect Options, and click the AutoFormat As You Type tab.
2. Clear the Built-In Heading Styles check box, and clear the Define Styles Based On Your Formatting check box.

For more information about using the AutoFormat feature, see Chapter 7, "Putting Text Tools to Work."

Creating New Styles Using the New Style Dialog Box

As you've seen, you can create styles by formatting text and basing a style on the formatted text. But if you want a somewhat higher degree of control over your style creation endeavors, you should consider creating styles by using the New Style dialog box (shown previously in Figure 9-6). When you use the New Style dialog box, you can easily incorporate alignment, line spacing, indents, paragraph spacing, font colors, and more into your style. To create a new style using the New Style dialog box, follow these steps:

1. Click the Styles And Formatting button on the Formatting toolbar to display the Styles And Formatting task pane, and then click the New Style button. The New Style dialog box appears.

2 In the New Style dialog box, type a name for your new style in the Name box. Think carefully when you consider names to associate with styles—the more descriptive your style names are, the easier it will be for you (and others) to identify each style's purpose and apply the proper style within documents.

3 In the Style Type list box, specify whether your style will be a paragraph, character, table, or list. Most styles are paragraph styles.

4 In the Formatting section, configure your style's properties using the Font and Size list boxes as well as the formatting, color selection, alignment, line spacing, above and below spacing, and indent buttons.

5 If necessary, click Format to access additional formatting options, as shown in Figure 9-7.

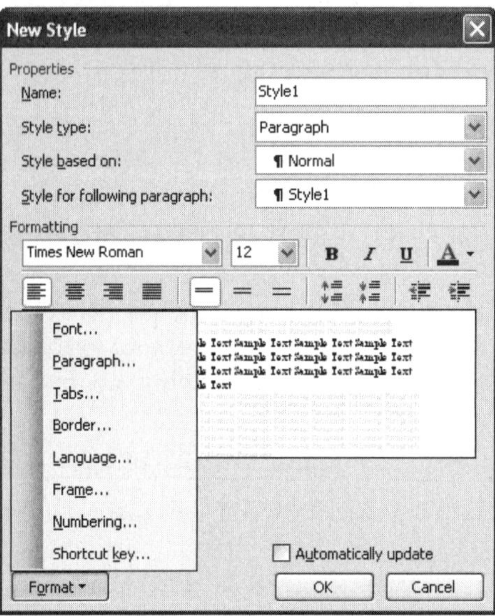

Figure 9-7. The Format button enables you to access dialog boxes that provide more detailed formatting options.

6 When you've finished configuring formatting options, click OK.

The newly created style will appear in the Styles And Formatting task pane as well as in the Style list box. You can use and modify your new styles just as if they were built-in styles. Further, unlike built-in styles, custom styles are easy to delete when you no longer need them. The next few sections address some of the additional configuration options found in the New Style dialog box.

Basing New Styles on Existing Styles

By default, the styles you create in the New Style dialog box (or by typing a name in the Style box on the Formatting toolbar) are based on the Normal style. This means that your styles contain all the settings for the Normal style plus whatever modifications you make to the style.

Word makes it easy for you to create a new style based on an existing style of your choice. When you base a new style on an existing style, some of the new style's properties are already configured, which can simplify the style creation process. In addition, whenever you alter a base style, all styles created using the base style are automatically altered as well—this provides an added level of consistency. (But it can also create a mess if you're not careful.)

To illustrate the trickle-down theory of base styles, let's look at an example. Suppose you want to create a style named Heading 1 Centered that's based on the existing Heading 1 style. By default, the Heading 1 style is Arial, 18 point, and left-aligned. You can create Heading 1 Centered by basing the new style on the existing Heading 1 style, and then changing the Alignment setting to Centered. Let's say that a few days later, you learn that the headings in your document should be formatted using the Verdana font, not Arial. You can alter the Heading 1 style to use Verdana, and, because you based the Heading 1 Centered style on the Heading 1 style, the text formatted with the Heading 1 Centered style will automatically be reformatted to use Verdana as well.

By default, many built-in Word styles are based on the Normal style. The styles you create will also be based on the Normal style unless you specify otherwise. To review, the Normal style includes the default settings listed in Table 9-2, which are the settings that will serve as a basis for any style you create based on the Normal style.

Table 9-2. Default Normal Style Settings

Element	Settings
Formatting	Times New Roman, 12 point, and English (U.S.)
Paragraph	Left aligned, 0" left indentation, 0" right indentation, single-spaced, and 0" spacing above and below paragraphs

> **Tip** **View a style's formatting in the Reveal Formatting task pane**
> You can view a style's formatting settings by clicking a paragraph formatted with the style you want to investigate, and then displaying the Reveal Formatting task pane. The Reveal Formatting task pane shows all the details about the style's font, paragraph, and section properties.

To base a style on an existing style other than Normal or to specify that you don't want to base your style on any existing style, you can use the Style Based On list box in the New Style dialog box, shown in Figure 9-8. This list contains a (No Style) option that enables you to avoid basing your new style on any existing style.

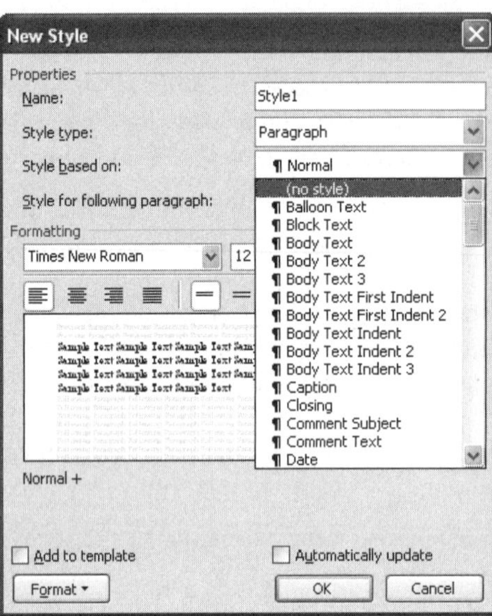

Figure 9-8. You can select any existing style to serve as a base style when you're creating new styles.

> **Tip** **Disassociate a style from a base style**
>
> If you don't want a custom paragraph style to change when you change the base style, you should ensure that your style is not based on another style. To do this, display the New Style dialog box or the Modify Style dialog box, select Paragraph in the Style Type list box, choose the (No Style) option in the Style Based On list box, and then click OK.

Specifying Styles for Following Paragraphs

Some styles are predictable—you can predict which style elements are likely to precede or follow them 99 percent of the time. For example, most of the headings in your documents are probably followed by Normal text, or maybe your documents use a figure number element that's almost always followed or preceded by a figure caption. You can take advantage of style predictability and save yourself unnecessary formatting steps by configuring settings for paragraphs that follow specific elements.

When you specify a style for a paragraph that will automatically follow text that has a particular style, you specify that you want to apply that style after you press Enter at the end of the current style. You can easily specify a style for a subsequent paragraph as you're creating a new style. To do so, choose a style in the Style For Following Paragraph list box in the New Style dialog box.

> **Note** If you don't specify a subsequent paragraph style, Word continues to use the current style for subsequent paragraphs until you choose another style.

After you configure the Style For Following Paragraph option and click OK, Word takes care of the rest. The next time you press Enter after a paragraph with a style that includes a setting for a subsequent paragraph style, the style for the subsequent paragraph will automatically be applied. If you display your Style Area in Normal view while you work, you can easily verify that you've configured your subsequent paragraph styles correctly.

You can modify the following paragraph setting for existing styles as well, as described in "Revising Style Properties," on page 282.

Adding Styles to Documents and Templates

By default, Word adds a new style only to the active document. If you modify a built-in style, that modification applies only to the existing document. But when you create a style, you have the opportunity to add the style to the template attached to the active document. You can easily add a new style to a template by selecting the Add To Template check box in the New Style dialog box before you click OK.

Keep in mind that when you add a style to a template, you add the style to the template that's attached to the current document. As you might imagine, because the Normal.dot template is the default template in Word, the Normal.dot template is associated with a great number of documents. Therefore, when you add a style to a template, you're very likely adding the style to the Normal.dot template. When you modify the Normal.dot template, you effectively modify the template associated with all those other documents. Adding a style to a template gives users access to the style in the list of available styles in all documents that are based on that template. But usually you won't want to change an existing style because it might negatively affect another document's appearance. Instead, consider creating a custom template, as described in Chapter 16, "Formatting Documents Using Templates, Wizards, Add-Ins, and XML Schemas."

Tip **Identifying an attached template**

To identify the active document's attached template, choose Tools, Templates And Add-Ins. In the Templates And Add-Ins dialog box, the name of the currently attached template appears in the Document Template box. In many instances, you'll see that the Normal template serves as the active document's attached template.

For more information about the interrelationship of templates and styles, see Chapter 16, "Formatting Documents Using Templates, Wizards, Add-Ins, and XML Schemas."

Controlling Automatic Style Updates

When you create a paragraph style, you can configure Word to update the style whenever you apply manual formatting to text formatted in the selected style. To illustrate, let's say a style applies boldface formatting to text. While working in a document, you decide that you don't want the paragraph style to include boldface text, so you select a paragraph that uses the style you want to modify (making sure to include the paragraph mark), and then press Ctrl+B to turn off the Bold attribute. When you alter text that's configured with an automatically updating style, you adjust all text that's formatted with the same style. In addition, the style definition is revised to match your manual change.

To activate automatic updating, select the Automatically Update check box in the New Style dialog box, if you're creating a new style, or the Modify Style dialog box, if you're changing an existing style. (The Modify Style dialog box is discussed in more detail later in this chapter.) Keep in mind that an automatic update made to a style is reflected only in the active document, even if the style is saved in the attached template.

Note When a paragraph style is configured to update automatically, you can still perform character formatting tasks within the paragraph without affecting the style or other paragraphs formatted with the style. Automatic updates come into play only when you select the entire paragraph (paragraph mark and all) and apply a formatting change.

Modifying Existing Styles

After you learn how to create styles, modifying existing styles is a snap. The main difference between creating and modifying styles is that you use the Modify Style dialog box instead of the New Style dialog box. To access the Modify Style dialog box, perform any of the following actions:

- In the Style Area, double-click the style name you want to modify to display the Style dialog box, and then click Modify.
- In the Styles And Formatting task pane, hover the pointer over a style in the Formatting Of Selected Text list box or the Pick Formatting To Apply list box, click the arrow, and choose Modify.
- In the Styles And Formatting task pane, right-click a style in the Formatting Of Selected Text box or the Pick Formatting To Apply list box, and choose Modify.

The Modify Style dialog boxes for paragraph, character, table, and list styles look very similar to their counterpart New Style dialog boxes. These dialog boxes allow you to configure most of the same settings that are available when you create a new style.

Assigning Keyboard Shortcuts to Styles

One style modification trick that will come in handy when you're working with styles is to assign keyboard shortcuts to commonly used styles. If you use the same few styles throughout a document, you might find it tiresome to repeatedly click a style in the Styles And Formatting task pane or select a style in the Style list box. In those cases, it's quicker to create a keyboard shortcut that you can press whenever you need a particular style. Creating a shortcut is quick and easy. To do so, follow these steps:

1. In the Styles And Formatting task pane, right-click the style you want to associate with a keyboard shortcut, and then choose Modify. The Modify Style dialog box appears.

2 In the Modify Style dialog box, click Format, and then click the Shortcut Key option. The Customize Keyboard dialog box appears, as shown in Figure 9-9.

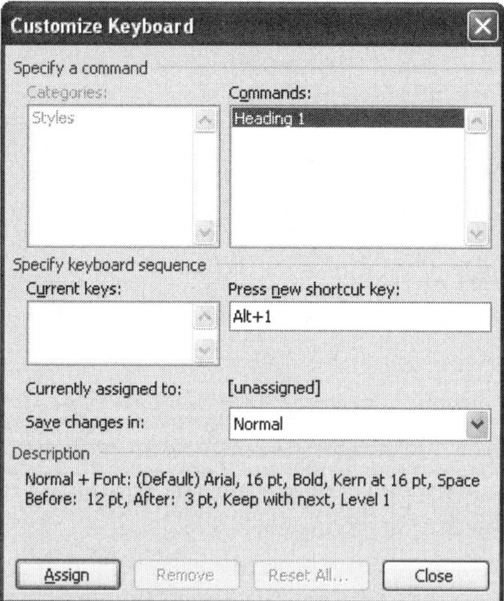

Figure 9-9. You can use the Customize Keyboard dialog box to create keyboard shortcuts for styles.

3 Press the keyboard shortcut you want to use. If the combination is already in use, the dialog box will indicate which feature uses the keyboard shortcut; if the combination is available, the Currently Assigned To label will indicate that the keyboard command is unassigned.

4 In the Save Changes In list box, specify whether you want to save the keyboard shortcut in the global Normal template, in another template, or in the active document.

5 Click Assign.

After you create a keyboard shortcut, you can type text, click within the paragraph or select the text you want to format, and then press the keyboard shortcut.

Renaming a Style

Sometimes you might want to rename a style—maybe the style's purpose has changed since the style was created, or maybe you want to make the style's name more descriptive. Regardless of your reasons, you can change a style name easily by following these steps:

1 Right-click a style name in the Styles And Formatting task pane, and choose Modify.

2 In the Modify Styles dialog box, click in the Name box, edit the style's name, and then click OK.

Keep in mind that the name change is effective only in the active document. If you want to apply the name change globally, you need to save the style in the active template by selecting the Add To Template check box before you click OK.

You can also rename styles stored in documents and templates using the Organizer, as discussed in "Copying Styles from One Document to Another," on page 284.

Revising Style Properties

As described in this chapter, you can select all instances of a given style of text, and then apply formatting to those instances. But an easier and more efficient method (especially if the document is still in the creation stage) is to modify the style's properties. When you modify an existing style's properties, all text currently formatted with that style is updated to match the new settings. This reaction to modifications enables you to change the look of your document quickly and efficiently, without having to revisit every instance of a style and manually apply formatting changes. This feature can potentially save you from making hundreds of changes by hand.

To modify a style's properties, open the Modify Style dialog box, and then remove and apply the appropriate formatting settings. You can use the controls in the Formatting section as well as the Format button's menu. After you've made your changes, click OK. Your document will be reformatted with the modified style settings.

Tip **Modify the default style settings**
Because many styles are based on the Normal style, you can easily change the entire look of your document by modifying the Normal style's default font—for example, you might want to use Bookman Old Style in place of Times New Roman to create a more "open" look. (The Bookman Old Style font is wider than Times New Roman, which is considered fairly narrow.) The modifications you make to a style will apply only to the active document if the Add To Template check box is cleared when you implement style modifications.

Note Changing a built-in style and saving it in a template—especially the Normal template—can wreak havoc on documents that are based on the template. Therefore, make changes judiciously.

Updating an Existing Style to Match Selected Text

In addition to modifying style properties and using the Automatically Update feature, Word 2003 provides another shortcut to reformatting the styles in an active document. Namely, you can change an existing style by having Word modify the style to conform to selected text. To take advantage of this back-door approach to formatting, follow these steps:

1. In your document, format and select the text you want to use to modify a style.
2. In the Styles And Formatting task pane, right-click the style you want to change, and then choose Update To Match Selection.

After you choose Update To Match Selection, the style is modified to match the selected text's formatting, and all text formatted with the style takes on the new formatting settings. The changes you make using this option apply to the active document only.

Deleting Styles

Naturally, when you create and modify styles, you'll probably want to delete a few as well. You can delete styles from the active document's task pane or completely obliterate a style from a template. This section describes how to delete styles from the active document.

To learn more about editing templates (including deleting styles from templates), see Chapter 16, "Formatting Documents Using Templates, Wizards, Add-Ins, and XML Schemas."

When you delete a style from an active document, you are either deleting a custom style you created for the active document or instructing Word to not use a particular style found in the document's template. If you delete a paragraph style, Word applies the Normal style to all text that was formatted with the deleted style and removes the style definition from the task pane. You can delete styles in two main ways:

- Right-click a style in the Styles And Formatting task pane, and choose Delete.
- Double-click a style name in the Style Area, select the style (if necessary) in the Style dialog box, and click Delete.

Further, you can delete multiple styles at once by using the Organizer window. To do so, follow these steps:

1. Choose Tools, Templates And Add-Ins, and then click Organizer.
2. In the Styles tab, select the styles you want to delete from your document or template (you can press Ctrl or Shift to select multiple styles).
3. Click Delete, click Yes, and then click Close.

Note You can't delete the built-in Word styles from the All Styles view in the Styles And Formatting task pane. You can delete built-in styles from other views in the Show list box in the Styles And Formatting task pane, because in those cases you're merely configuring the active document's task pane view, not modifying the template.

Restoring Styles in the Normal Template

If you find that you've modified the styles in your Normal template but you'd like to revert to Word's default settings, you can do so easily. To restore Word's default Normal.dot template, close Word and rename the Normal file (usually located in \%*UserProfile*%\Application Data\Microsoft\Templates). You should rename the file with a recognizable name, such as Normal2 or OLD_Normal; do not delete the Normal.dot file. After you rename the Normal file, Word will create a new Normal.dot file the next time you open Word. The new Normal file will contain the default Normal template settings.

> **Tip** **Locate the Normal.dot template**
>
> To find the Normal template, you can look in the File Locations tab in the Options dialog box. The File Locations tab shows abbreviated versions of the locations of user template files. To see the complete path to the Templates folder, choose Tools, Options, click the File Locations tab, select User Templates, and then click Modify. In the Modify Location dialog box, click the Look In list box to view the path to your templates.

Copying Styles from One Document to Another

After you've created a document using just the right styles, you might want to share those styles with another document. You can easily copy styles from one document to another without having to create or modify templates. In a nutshell, the procedure entails opening the Organizer window (by choosing Tools, Templates And Add-Ins, Organizer), displaying the style lists in the Styles tab for the two documents involved in the copying endeavor, and then copying styles from one document to another. Here's the procedure:

1. Choose Tools, Templates And Add-Ins, and then click Organizer. The Organizer dialog box appears, as shown in Figure 9-10.

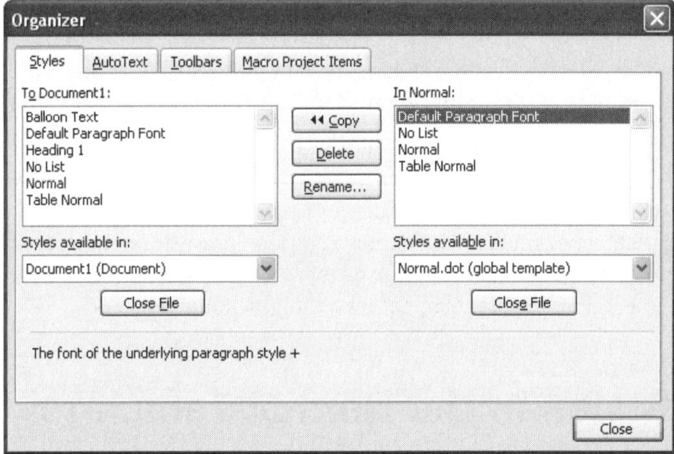

Figure 9-10. The Organizer assists you when you want to copy styles, templates, and other features from one document to another. You can also delete and rename styles within the Organizer.

2. At this point, in the Styles tab, you want to navigate to the two documents you want to work with. Therefore, if necessary, click Close File below the left style list. The style list is cleared, and the button changes to an Open File button.
3. Click Open File. The Open dialog box appears.
4. In the Open dialog box, click the Files Of Type list box, choose All Files (*.*), and then double-click the name of the file you want to copy styles to.

5. Now you need to display the document styles you want to copy into a document. To do so, click Close File below the right style list. The style list is cleared, and the button changes to Open File.
6. Click Open File. The Open dialog box appears.
7. In the Open dialog box, double-click the name of the file that contains the styles you want to copy.
8. To select all the styles in the right style list, you can click the first style, press and hold Shift, and then click the last style. Or, if you prefer, you can pick and choose which styles you want to copy by clicking one style and then pressing Ctrl and clicking additional styles.
9. After you select the styles you want to copy, click Copy, and then click Yes To All (or click Yes each time Word asks whether you want to overwrite an existing style with the same name).
10. Click Close, and click Yes to save the modified document.

In addition to copying styles from one document to another in the Organizer, you can also delete and rename styles as well as copy, delete, and rename AutoText entries, custom toolbars, and macro project items. These topics are covered in chapters devoted to each subject.

Tip **Understand the Organizer's limitations**

In some cases, you might not be able to use the Organizer to copy styles, macros, or AutoText entries from one document to another. This restriction might occur for several reasons. For example, the document you are copying to may be protected except for comments or tracked changes; the document might require a password before you can make changes to it; the document could be a read-only file; or the document might be stored on a network on which you don't have the user privileges necessary to change the document.

Chapter 10

Outlining Documents for Clarity and Structure

With all the "wizard" technology around, wouldn't you think somebody would come up with a wizard that could write your document for you? Word 2003 doesn't go quite that far, but by using its outlining capabilities, you can make planning, creating a structure, drafting, and reorganizing your document a clean and simple process. Many professional writers (present company included) use outlining to provide a "road map" for the documents they'll create. Outlines enable you to think about the logical foundation of your document first, so that when it's time to write, you can let your creative energies flow from your fingertips.

In this chapter, you'll learn all about the outlining capabilities of Word. Whether you love outlining and want to make the best use of all available tools or you're only creating the blasted thing because your supervisor asked for it, you'll find the tools easy to understand and use. And with practice and a few tips and techniques, you might find yourself actually enjoying it.

10 Reasons to Outline Your Next Long Document

Remember those awful research projects you had to do in junior high school, when you had to turn in first your outline, then your note cards, then your draft, and then your final? Composing in Word isn't like that, thank goodness. Once you create an outline in Word, you've got something to start with. Not something you'll type once and then type again later—but something you can use to build your document, edit it, and organize (or reorganize) it. And with that outline, you can even move seamlessly to and from a table of contents that's linked to the work in progress.

So if you have a resistance to outlining (and you're not alone), consider these reasons for outlining long documents in Word:

1. **You're more likely to meet your goals.** If your job involves writing grant proposals, producing product evaluations, writing annual reports, or composing print publications, you know that your document must reach a particular goal. You need to know where you're going, why you're going there, and the people you're trying to take with you. When you first type the document headings in Word, you're defining the steps

that will take you to the goal of your publication. Your headings reflect the major categories of information your audience will want to know. As you create the outline, you can make sure you're covering all the topics that you need to reach your result.

2 **You can create an organized, thoughtful document.** Your outline will list not only the large categories but also smaller subtopics within each category. The multi-level capabilities Word outlines offer (up to nine levels) enable you to organize your thoughts down to the smallest detail.

3 **The headings remind you where you're going.** Once you have an outline that you're happy with, you're free to write the document as the muse strikes. If you're a stream-of-consciousness writer, you can simply go with the flow and let the words fly—in the appropriate sections, of course. (Actually, you can always move the sections later if you choose.) If you're more of a left-brain, analytical writer, you can craft your sentences within the structured topics, making sure you've got the requisite topic sentence, supporting sentences, and closing or transition sentence.

4 **You can easily reorganize your document later.** Word gives you the means to move parts of your document easily, even after your long document is filled with text: you can collapse topics to their headings and move them around as you like. And of course, Undo always reverses your action if you later decide it was a bad move.

5 **You can expand and collapse topics.** The expand and collapse features of Word's outline enable you to change what you're viewing in the document. A fully expanded outline will show everything entered thus far—so all the text you've written, subheadings you've added, and notes you've inserted will be visible in a fully expanded outline view. If you want to limit the display to only headings and subheadings, you can collapse the outline to show only those items. This enables you to check to make sure that your organization is logical, that you've covered everything you want to cover, and that you have your topics in the right order.

6 **You can divide long documents and make assignments to get documents done faster.** Word's Master Document feature enables you to divide long documents into smaller chunks that you can then assign to other writers. When you pull the document back together, all the pieces can be merged into one coherent whole. Using the outlining feature enables you to see at a glance the most logical places for divisions.

7 **You can see what doesn't fit.** Outlining also gives you a way to see what *doesn't* work in your document. If there's a topic that really needs to be a separate document, or a heading that is begging for a rewrite, it will stand out. Of course, you can edit, move, and enter text in Outline view, so making those changes is a simple matter.

8 **You can easily change heading levels.** Word's outlining feature comes with its own toolbar, giving you the means to promote or demote headings and text. If you want to change a level 1 heading to a level 2 heading, for example, you can do that with the click of a button. This also works for text you want to raise to a heading or headings you want to drop to body text.

9 **You can work seamlessly with the table of contents** (TOC). If you've created a TOC for your document, you can update it on the fly and move directly to it to make changes, if needed. This saves you the hassle—and potential error—of creating a document with a separate TOC that might not be updated when the document is.

Outlining Documents for Clarity and Structure

10 **You can print your outline for handouts, reviews, or talking points.** Word gives you the option of printing only the outline of your document, which is a nice feature when you want to show others key points in a document or presentation but don't want them reading along word for word. Whether you do this in the review stage, as part of a collaborative effort, or to condense your finished document to a printable outline, you can display and print only the headings you want your readers to see.

For more about creating and working with Master Documents, see Chapter 20, "Creating and Controlling Master Documents."

Using the Document Map vs. Using the Outline

Document Map

You might have already discovered a Word feature that gives you a quick-look outline in a side panel along the left edge of your work area. Word's Document Map, shown in Figure 10-1, creates a listing of headings in your document that are linked to the document so that you can use the Document Map to move easily from one part of the document to another. To display the Document Map, click the Document Map button on the Standard toolbar or choose View, Document Map.

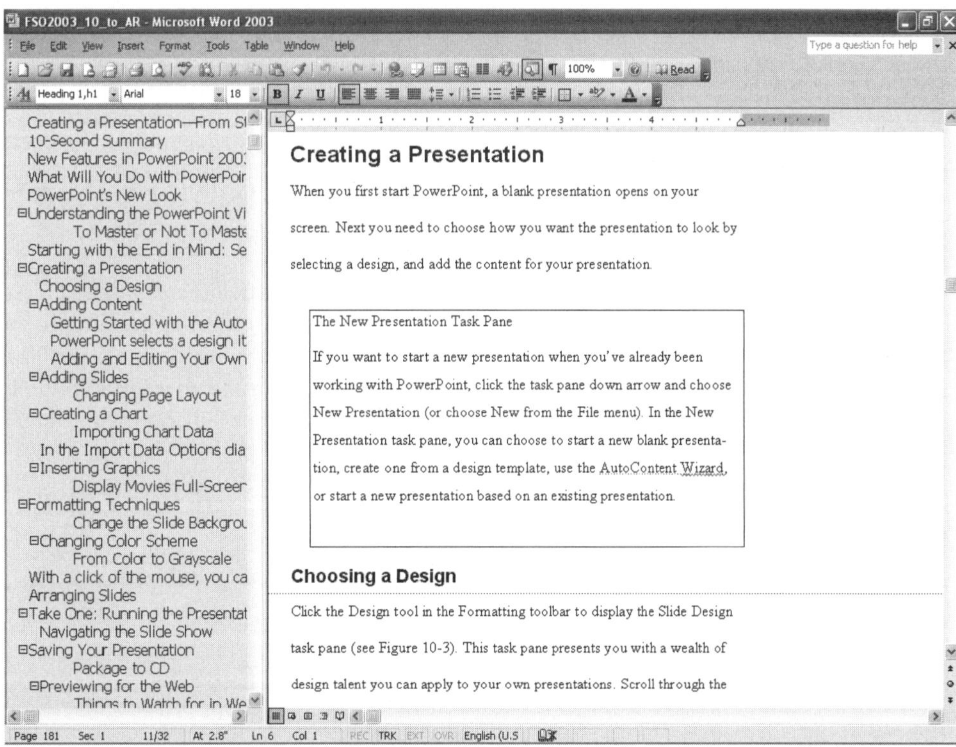

Figure 10-1. Document Map view gives you a quick look at the way an outline develops naturally from a document. The headings are those to which you've applied heading styles.

Tip **Think Document Map perks**
Two great things about the Document Map: you can view your document two ways at once—in outline form and in either Print Layout or Web Layout form—and you can easily move to the topic you want to see by clicking the heading in the left panel of the work area.

Why have a Document Map *and* an outlining feature? First, the Document Map is a handy tool when you want to do things like check the wording of a topic, make sure the text you've added fits the heading, and see at a glance that you've covered all the topics you intended to cover.

What you *can't* do in Document Map view is what makes Word's outline capabilities necessary: you can't change the heading levels of text, reorganize parts, or affect the table of contents in any way. For major structuring changes, text reorganizations, heading modifications, and more, you'll want to work in Outline view. For simple, lay-of-the-land operations, the Document Map will give you a clear picture of your document in a form that you can access and navigate quickly.

Viewing a Document in Outline View

Whether you're starting a document from scratch or you're working with an existing one, with text and headings already entered and formatted, you can use outlines to your benefit. To display Outline view, click the Outline View button to the left of the horizontal scroll bar, at the bottom of the page.

Note You can also change to Outline view by pressing Ctrl+Alt+O or by choosing View, Outline.

If you've entered headings in your document and formatted them with one of Word's heading styles (Heading 1, Heading 2, or Heading 3), they'll appear as headings in Outline view, as shown in Figure 10-2. The basic text styles applied to your document will be reflected in the outline, but all paragraph formatting (indents, before and after spacing, and line spacing) is suppressed. When you return to Print Layout or Web Layout view, the paragraph formatting will be intact.

Outlining Documents for Clarity and Structure

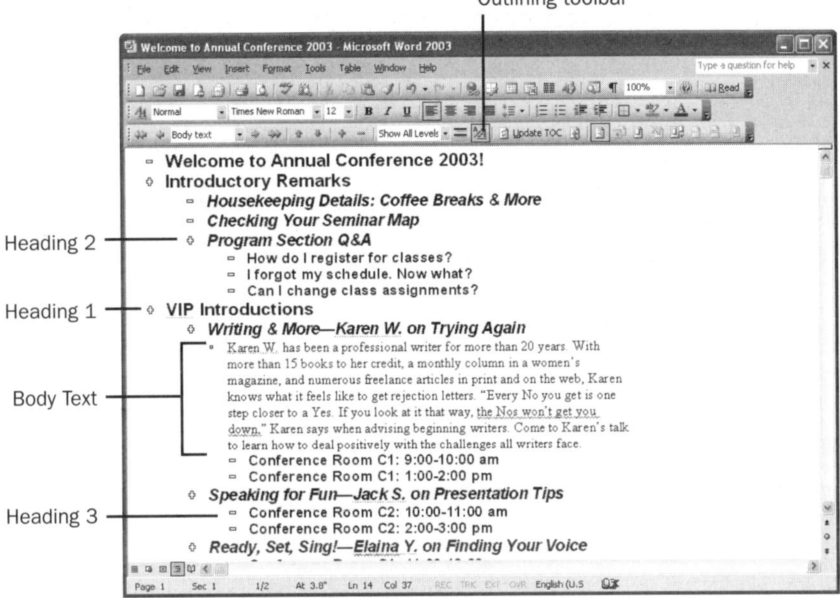

Figure 10-2. Outline view makes use of the headings you've formatted in your document. Paragraph text also appears by default when you first display the outline.

Troubleshooting

Headings don't show up in Outline view

When you switch to Outline view, why don't any of your headings appear? If you didn't use the built-in heading styles Word offers—Heading 1, Heading 2, or Heading 3—Word won't automatically recognize the headings as outline levels. To correct the problem, click the headings one by one, click the Outline Level arrow on the Outlining toolbar, and choose the heading level you want in the list. If you want to change all the headings at once, select all your headings, choose Outline Level, Level 1, and then use Demote as needed to move headings down to Level 2 and Level 3.

Several different types of symbols appear in Outline view, as shown in Table 10-1. They provide clues as to what action to take while working in an outline.

Table 10-1. Outline Symbols

Symbol	Name	Description
	Expand button	If double-clicked, alternately displays and hides subordinate headings and text paragraphs
	Collapse button	Indicates that there are no subordinate headings or text paragraphs

Table 10-1. Outline Symbols

Symbol	Name	Description
& More	Underlined heading	Shows that the topic includes body text
▭	Topic marker	Applied to lowest-level outline entry, indicating that it's formatted as body text

Exploring the Outlining Toolbar

When you display your document in Outline view, the Outlining toolbar appears automatically. Like other Word toolbars, the Outlining toolbar is *dockable*, which means that you can move it to any place on the screen you find convenient. Figure 10-3 shows the workspace with the Outlining toolbar in the document area as a floating toolbar. Table 10-2 lists and describes the tools on the Outlining toolbar.

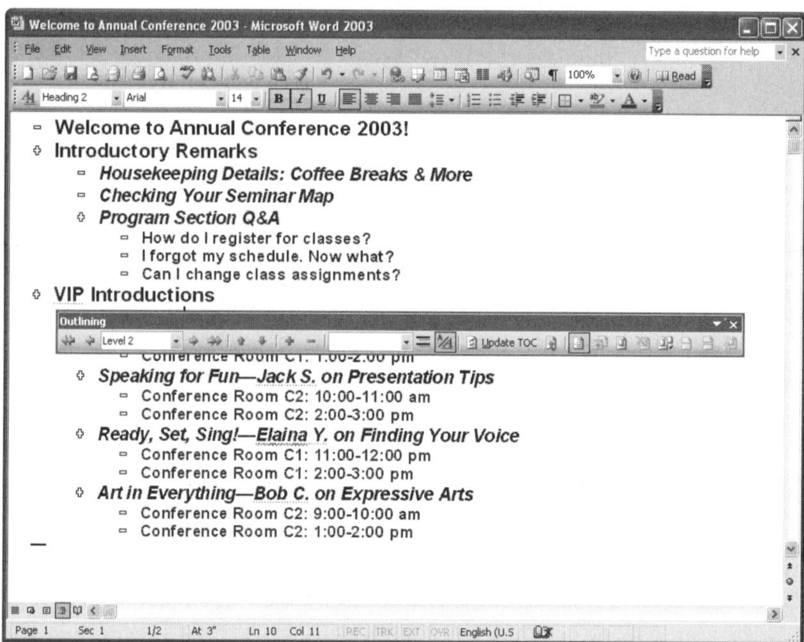

Figure 10-3. The Outlining toolbar can be docked along any edge of your document window or pulled anywhere on the screen as a floating toolbar.

> **Note** When you display the Outlining toolbar by choosing View, Toolbars, and then selecting Outlining, only the tools shown in Table 10-2 appear. When you change to Outline view, the Outlining toolbar and the Master Document tools appear in the same button row. You can choose the outline level right from the Outlining toolbar by clicking the Outline Level arrow and choosing the level you want in the list. You can also update the TOC from Outline view and go directly to the TOC while you work.

Outlining Documents for Clarity and Structure

Table 10-2. Outlining Tools

Tool	Name	Description
	Promote To Heading 1	Raises the outline level of the selection to the highest outline level, Heading 1
	Promote	Raises the outline level of the selection by one level
Level 2	Outline Level	Enables you to view and change the outline level of the selection
	Demote	Lowers the outline level of the selection by one level
	Demote To Body Text	Lowers the outline level of the selection to the lowest outline level, body text
	Move Up	Moves the selection up one level in the outline
	Move Down	Moves the selection down one level in the outline
	Expand	Expands the outline heading to show subheadings and text
	Collapse	Reduces selection to top-level headings, hiding subordinate headings and text
Level 2	Show Level	Displays a list of heading levels; select the level to which you want the outline displayed
	Show First Line Only	Reduces text entries to show a single line; good for reviewing paragraph topics
	Show Formatting	Alternately hides and displays the character formatting shown in Outline view
Update TOC	Update TOC	Automatically updates a table of contents you've generated for the current document
	Go To TOC	Moves the display to the table of contents (usually positioned at the end of the document)

Creating a New Outline

Creating a new outline in Word is simple. If you're just starting a document, simply click the Outline View button to the left of the horizontal scroll bar. Follow these steps to start the new outline:

1. Type the text for your heading. The heading is automatically formatted in the Heading 1 style.
2. Press Enter. The insertion point moves to the next line in the outline.

Chapter 10

Demote

3 To create a sublevel, click Demote on the Outlining toolbar. Word indents the insertion point and changes the first outline symbol (-) to a plus (+) symbol, indicating that the heading now has a subordinate entry. Type the text for that entry.

4 Press Enter to move to the next line in your outline. By default, Word creates the next heading at the same level as the heading you last entered. If you want to create another sublevel, click Demote.

Promote

5 To raise an entry one heading level, click the Promote button. If you want to move all the way out to the left margin and create a Heading 1 outline level, click the Promote To Heading 1 button.

6 Continue typing entries until your outline is completed. Figure 10-4 shows a sample outline with multiple outline levels.

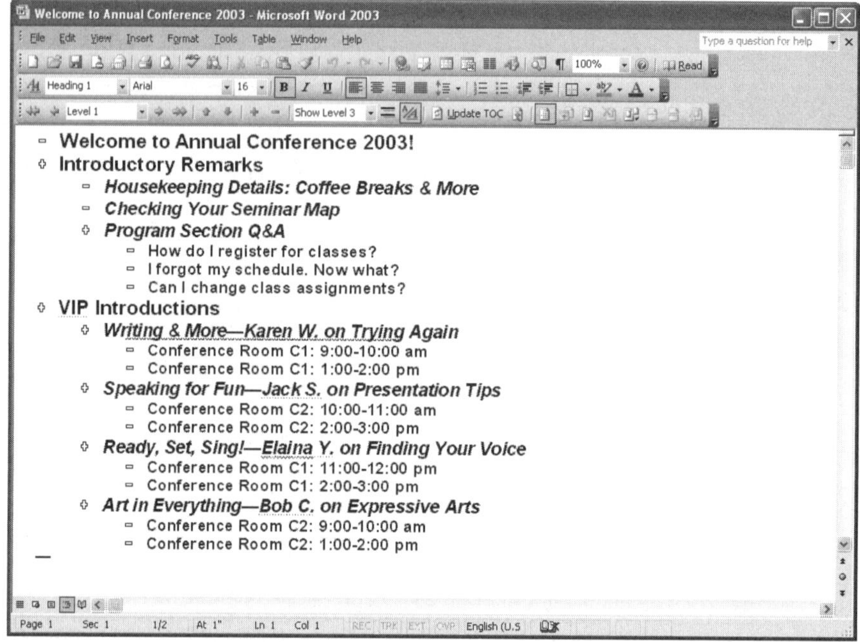

Figure 10-4. Outlining is a simple matter of identifying key topics in your document, naming them, and ordering them the way you want.

> **Tip** **Change the look of Heading 1**
>
> It's true that you must have your headings formatted in the styles Word will recognize—Heading 1, Heading 2, or Heading 3—in order for them to act and display properly in the Outline window, but you can create styles you like for those headings. You can use the Reveal Formatting task pane to change the formatting choices for those styles and save the changes in the current document. You can also have Word automatically make the changes to all similar heading styles in your document. For more information on using the Reveal Formatting task pane to format headings easily, see Chapter 7, "Putting Text Tools to Work."

> **Note** In some instances, you might want to use the Tab key not to indent a heading level in your outline but to actually insert a Tab character between words. When you want to insert an actual tab in your outline, press Ctrl+Tab instead of simply pressing the Tab key.

Choosing the Way You Want Your Outline Displayed

Working in Word's Outline view enables you to customize the display so you see only the heading levels you want to work with. For example, you might want to see only the first-level heads in your outline so that you can check that all your most important topics are covered. Or perhaps you want to see every level, to check the completeness of the subtopics. You can easily move back and forth between various outline displays by using the buttons on the Outlining toolbar.

Displaying Different Levels of Text

Level 2

Show Level

You can easily control how much of the outline you want to see. If you want to limit the display of your outline to only Heading 2 levels, for example, you click the Outline Level arrow to display the list of levels. Click Show Level 2 to display every level down to and including level 2, as shown in Figure 10-5.

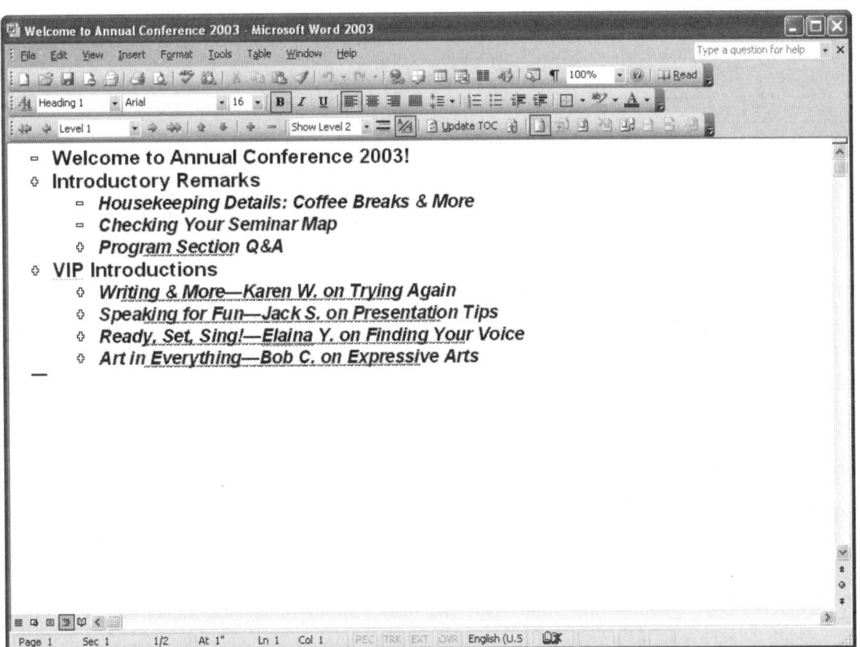

Figure 10-5. Control the levels displayed in Outline view by choosing what you want to see in the Show Level list box.

Inside Out

Copy document headings without all the text

Being able to collapse the outline display to headings only gives you a quick look at the overall organization of your document. If only you could copy and paste only the headings of your outline as well. Unfortunately, when you highlight the entire outline, copy it, and paste it into another document, the whole thing—headings and subordinate text—goes along for the ride. The workaround is to create a table of contents (Chapter 21, "Generating First-Class Tables of Contents and Related Elements," tells you how) and then convert the TOC to regular text by pressing Ctrl+Shift+F9. Then you can copy the headings and paste them into a document.

Tip **Dictate your outline**

If you prefer dictation to typing, you can "speak" your outline into being. If you've enabled the Speech Recognition feature, created a profile, and taught Word how to recognize your speech patterns by using the Speech Recognition Training Wizard, you can dictate your outline as you would any other document. To dictate your outline, follow these steps:

1. Open a new document and click Outline view or choose View, Outline.
2. Place the insertion point where you want to begin.
3. Display the Language bar, if necessary (double-click the EN symbol to the left of the clock on the Windows taskbar).
4. Make sure your microphone is connected and turned on, and then click Microphone on the Language bar.
5. Click Dictation. Word begins "listening" to your speech.
6. Slowly and clearly speak your first heading. After a brief delay, Word enters the words at the insertion point.

The first few times you use Word's Dictation feature, don't expect miracles. It's a long process of training the program to recognize the way you say the words you use. Using the training wizard and creating your own profile help, but it's a continual process. It's fun, and hopefully worth the effort, but a process nonetheless.

One word of caution, however: If you forget to turn your microphone off and you mutter to yourself as you work, you can have odd words appear in your paragraphs. A laugh apparently sounds like "Lincoln" to Word, and the phrase "You talkin' to me?" was interpreted as "Utah in the." So be forewarned: remember to turn your microphone off when you're no longer using dictation. Something's listening to every word you say.

Note There are other methods of changing which heading levels appear: you can click the Expand or Collapse button on the Outlining toolbar, or you can double-click the Expand button to the right of a heading to display subordinate items.

Showing the First Line of Text

When you get to the point in the work on your outline that you're ready to look at the paragraph text you've entered, you can have Word display only the first line of text so that you can see what the content of the paragraph is without displaying the entire paragraph. Why might you want to display only the first line of text?

- You might want to check the order in which you discuss topics.
- You're considering whether to move text to a different part of the document.
- You're reviewing the primary points you've covered under subheadings.

Show First Line Only

To display only the first line of text for the paragraphs in your document, click the Show First Line Only button on the Outlining toolbar. The display changes to show the first text lines, as Figure 10-6 shows. To display full paragraphs again, click the button a second time.

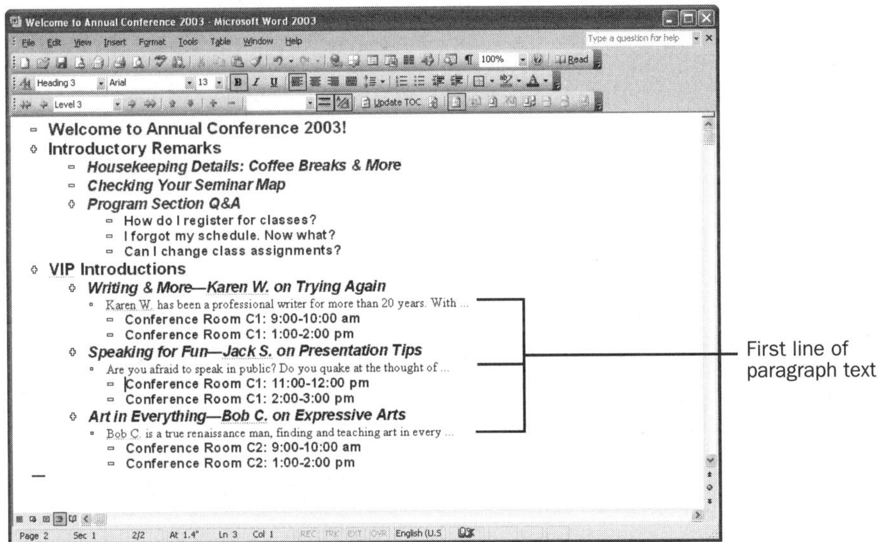

Figure 10-6. Displaying only the first line of a paragraph lets you see the general subject of your text so that you can make informed choices about reordering topics.

Removing and Showing Formatting

Another quick change you might want to make is to suppress the display of formatting in your outline. As you know, when you change to Outline view, the headings are shown with whatever character formatting they're assigned in the other Word views. Heading 1, by default, is in the Arial 16 point font, for example. When you're working in the outline, however, you might find formatting differences distracting while you consider the content and organization of your topics.

Show Formatting

To hide the formatting assigned to heading levels in your outline, click the Show Formatting button on the Outlining toolbar. This button actually functions as a toggle, meaning that the first click hides the formatting and the second displays it again. Figure 10-7 shows you what a simple outline looks like when all formatting has been suppressed.

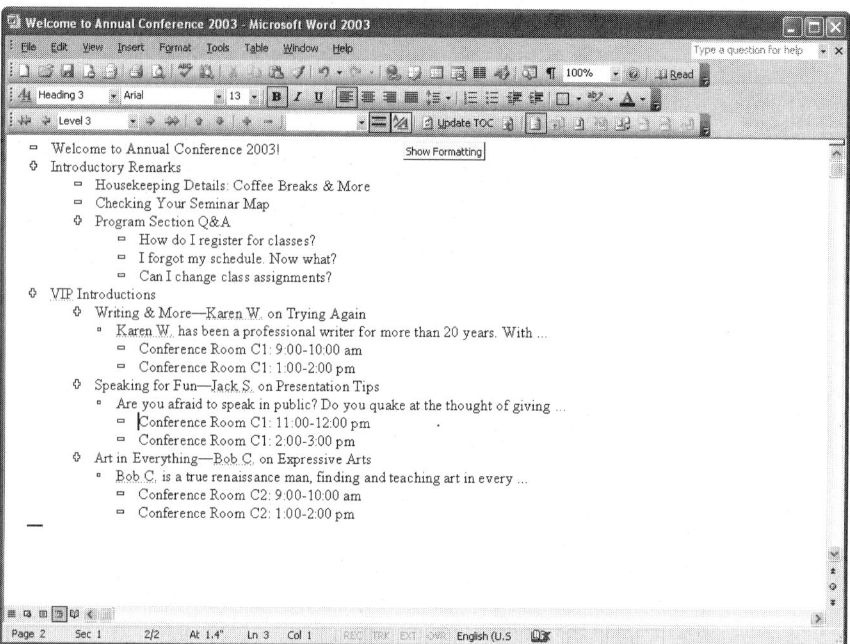

Figure 10-7. When you want to focus on the thoughts in your outline, you might want to hide the formatting applied to heading levels.

Working with Headings in Outline View

Whether you create an outline from scratch or use the outline created as part of your existing document, you'll invariably want to change some headings and insert and delete others. Headings are easy to work with in Outline view—with a simple click of a tool, you can change heading levels, move headings in the outline, and even demote the heading to body text, if you like.

Adding a Heading

When you want to insert a heading in an existing outline, in Outline view, find the heading you want the new heading to follow and simply place the insertion point after that heading, and then press Enter. If you want the heading to be at the same level as the heading preceding it, simply type your new heading. If you want to promote or demote the heading level, click the appropriate button before typing your text.

Applying Outline Levels

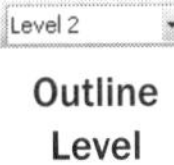

Outline Level

You can choose the outline level for your heading by using the Outline Level list box on the Outlining toolbar. Simply click in the heading to which you want to apply the outline level, and then click the Outline Level arrow to display the list, as shown in Figure 10-8. Click your choice, and the format is applied to the heading.

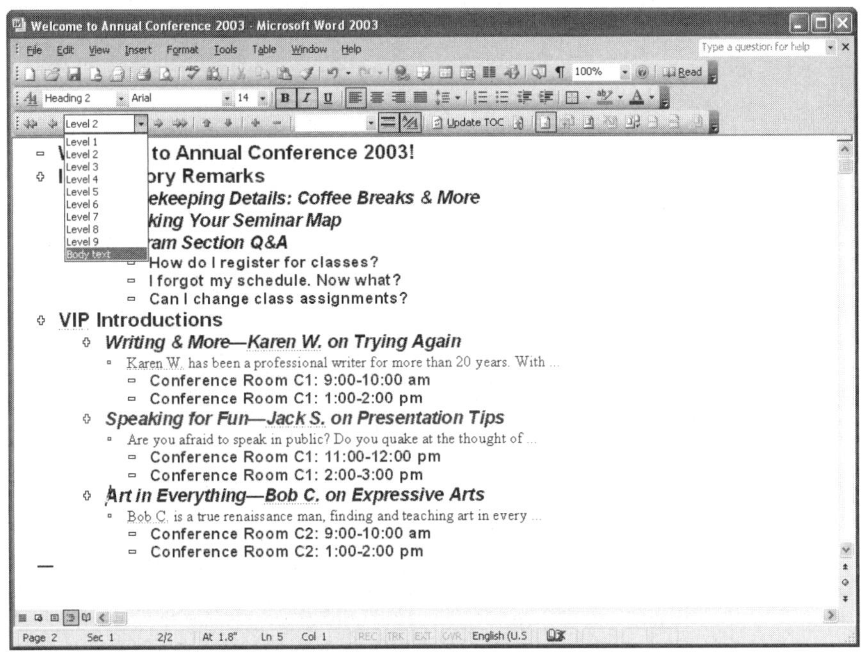

Figure 10-8. If you know which outline level you want to assign to the new heading, choose it directly from the Outline Level list box.

> **Tip Get different perspectives on a document**
> You can easily view your document in both Outline view and Print Layout view at the same time. Just drag the screen divider (located at the top of the vertical scroll bar) down the scroll bar; another pane opens above the current one. To change that area to another view, click in it to give it focus, and then select the view you want. You can then see how your document looks while you're working in Outline view.

Promoting and Demoting Headings

Promote

Once you have text in your outline, you can easily change outline levels, moving a heading from level 1 to level 2, for example, or from body text up to level 3. Put simply, promoting a heading takes it one level higher in the outline, and demoting a heading moves it one level down in the outline. Figure 10-9 shows the various levels available as you promote and demote headings.

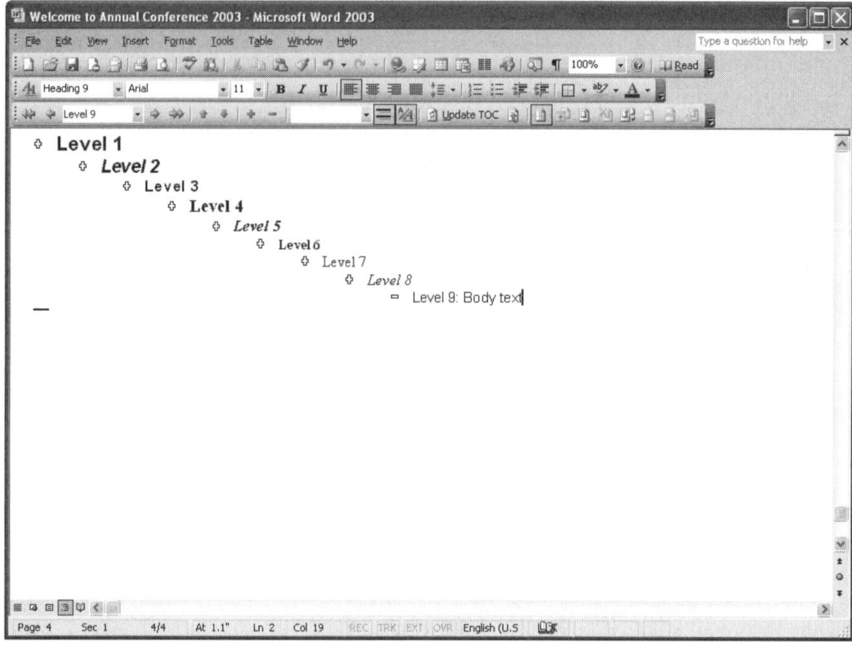

Figure 10-9. Promote and Demote give you a simple way to change the outline level of selected headings.

Demote

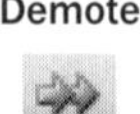

Demote To Body Text

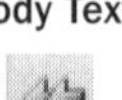

Promote to Heading 1

Each time you click the Demote button, Word moves the heading one level down the Outline Level scheme. Outline view shows the change by indenting the heading another 0.5 inch and changing the formatting. Conversely, the Promote button raises the heading level of the selected text until you reach Heading 1, which is the highest outline level available.

When you want to demote and promote in larger increments, moving a heading all the way to the topmost level, for example, or changing a heading to body text, use the Promote To Heading 1 or Demote To Body Text button.

When might you want to promote or demote text? You could be working on a report, for example, and realize that a topic you've placed at a Heading 2 level is really part of another topic. You can first change the heading level to reflect the level the heading should be to fit in the outline where you want it to go, and then you can move the selection to that point.

Changing Your Outline

Once you have all the heading levels the way you want them, you might decide that you want to move some of your outline topics around. That's one of the biggest benefits of using Outline view—you can easily see which topics fit and which don't, or which topics would work better somewhere else.

Expanding and Collapsing the Outline

As you learned earlier in this chapter, symbols in the Outline window give you clues about what, if anything, is subordinate to the level displayed in the outline. The visual clues are as follows:

- A minus sign (-) means a heading has no subordinate headings or text.
- A plus sign (+) means subheadings appear beneath the heading level.
- An underlined heading indicates that body text is present.
- A small square shows you that the item is body text, the lowest outline item available.

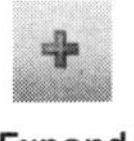

Expand

You'll find two easy methods for expanding and collapsing the topics in your outline. You can double-click the plus sign to the left of the heading you want to expand. Or, if you prefer, you can simply make sure the heading is selected, and then click Expand. Figure 10-10 shows an expanded outline.

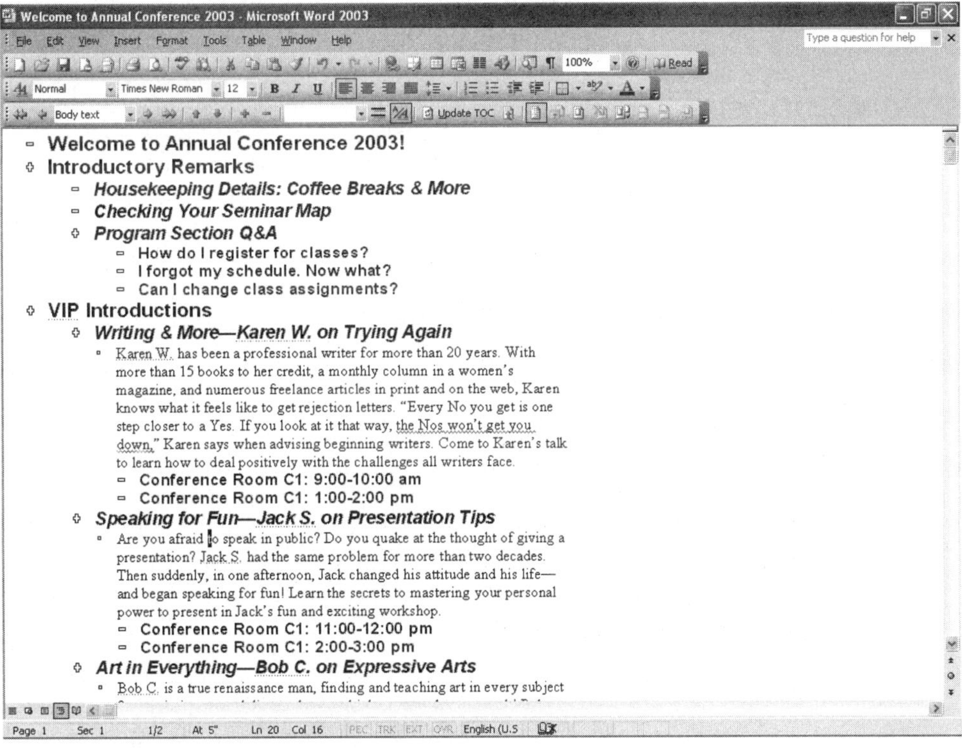

Figure 10-10. When you click Expand, Word expands the selection to the level previously displayed. If you've selected Show First Lines Only, Word will stop at first-line display.

Collapse

Collapse works the same way; simply click in the heading of the topic you want to hide; then double-click the plus sign or click Collapse on the Outlining toolbar.

Moving Outline Topics

Another benefit to Outline view is that you can move entire topics easily. Whether you choose to use Word's Outlining tools, cut and paste text using the Office Clipboard, or drag what you've selected from place to place, you can easily move portions of your document as needed.

Moving Topics Up and Down

Move Up

When you want to move part of an outline to an earlier point in your document or closer to the end, you can use two of Word's Outlining tools—Move Up and Move Down—to do the trick. Start by selecting the entire part you want to move, and then click Move Up to move the selection up one heading. If you want to move it more than one level up, click Move Up as many times as needed to position the selection in the right place.

Move Down

You use Move Down the same way: select the part of your outline you want to move, and then click Move Down on the Outlining toolbar. If you want to move the selection more than one level farther down, keep clicking Move Down. Remember to press Ctrl+S occasionally to save your file.

Tip **Move only a heading**

If you want to move only a heading—not an entire topic—simply click in the heading before choosing Move Up or Move Down. Word moves only the selected heading and leaves any subordinate headings and text in place.

Cutting and Pasting Parts of the Outline

You can also cut and paste parts of your documents in Outline view. This is helpful when you know you want to move a topic, but you're not exactly sure where you want to put it. You can cut and paste part of an outline by following these steps:

1. Select the entire portion you want to move.

Cut

2. Click Cut on the Standard toolbar. The selected portion is removed from the outline to the Office Clipboard.
3. Scroll through the outline until you find the place where you'd like to paste your selection and click to place the insertion point there.

Paste

4. Click Paste on the Standard toolbar. The selection is pasted at the new location.

Tip **Forget what's on the clipboard?**
You can easily take a look at what's on the Office Clipboard if you forget what you've placed there. Choose Edit, Office Clipboard to view the Clipboard task pane along the right side of your document window.

Dragging to a New Location

If the part of your outline you want to move is within dragging distance of the new location, you can simply highlight it and drag it to the new position. As you drag, the pointer changes, showing a small box beneath the arrow. A text insertion bar moves from line to line, tracking the point at which the selection will be inserted when you release the mouse button.

Tip **Keep it at a high level**
For best results, show only high-level headings before you move part of your outline. This enables you to display more of your outline on the screen and you'll have a shorter distance to drag what you're moving. Even if text is not displayed, subordinate headings and text will be moved with the heading.

Numbering Your Outline

For some documents, you might need to use Word's outline numbering feature. This enables you to choose one of Word's preset numbering schemes (seven are displayed by default) or create one of your own. When might you need to use outline numbering?

- You're creating a long paper that will be reviewed by other people. (Having the numbers is helpful for times when, for example, Arnie in sales says, "Hey, I'm not sure I get what you're saying in paragraph 34.")
- You're drawing up a contract for a new associate to sign.
- You're drafting an outline for a book and want the chapters to be numbered automatically.
- You've finally decided to go back to finishing that dissertation.

Adding a Numbering Scheme

You can add numbers to an existing outline or you can create a numbered outline as you go. To add numbers to an outline you've already created, follow these steps:

1. Display the outline to which you want to add numbers.
2. Choose Format, Bullets And Numbering. The Bullets And Numbering dialog box appears.

3 Click the Outline Numbered tab, as shown in Figure 10-11.

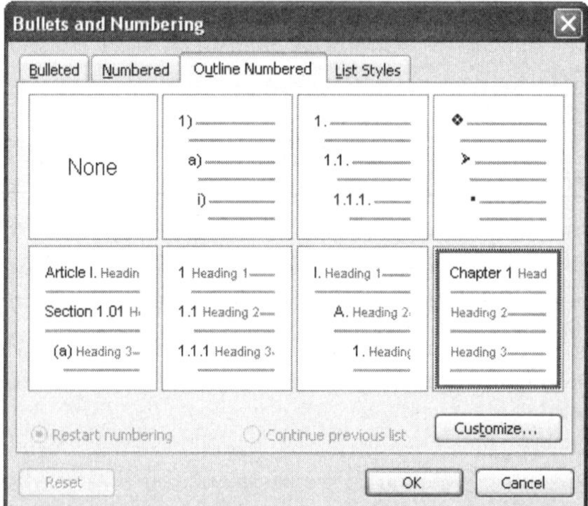

Figure 10-11. Word offers a number of preset outline numbering styles you can use as they are or customize to meet your needs.

4 Review the preset selections, click your choice, and then click OK. The style you selected is applied to your outline.

You'll notice that each preset numbering scheme includes different character styles (some use numbers; some use symbols; some use a mix of numbers and letters, and so on.). The preset numbering schemes also act differently depending on which elements in your outline you want to number. Table 10-3 gives you a quick look at the preset numbering schemes in Word's outline numbering feature.

Tip **Display and hide outline numbers**

You might want to use numbering in your outline only while the document is in its draft stages. While you're working on it and others are reviewing it, you might find it helpful to have numbers in the outline so that others can refer to sections without a lot of searching. When you're finished with the document and you're ready to finalize it, you can simply remove the numbering by selecting the entire document, right-clicking, and choosing Bullets And Numbering from the shortcut menu. In the Outline Numbered tab, select None, and then click OK.

Table 10-3. Preset Outline Numbering Schemes

Scheme	Characters Used	Use
1) a) i)	Numbers, letters, and Roman numerals	You're following a traditional outlining format.

Outlining Documents for Clarity and Structure

Table 10-3. Preset Outline Numbering Schemes

Scheme	Characters Used	Use
1. / 1.1. / 1.1.1.	Numbers	You have a multilevel document with multiple subtopics.
❖ / ➢ / ▪	Symbol characters	You want to call attention to the major points in your document and don't need a more traditional numbering sequence.
Article I. Headin / Section 1.01 H / (a) Heading 3	Article and Section numbering plus letters	You're creating a paper that is a compilation of multilevel documents or a reference work consisting of several fully developed pieces.
1 Heading 1 / 1.1 Heading 2 / 1.1.1 Heading 3	Numbers	You want to number main points and provide a numeric reference among subpoints.
I. Heading 1 / A. Heading 2 / 1. Headinç	Roman numerals, letters, and numbers	You want to use a traditional literary outline style.
Chapter 1 Heac / Heading 2 / Heading 3	Chapter numbering plus numbers	You're creating an outline for a book project and want only major headings labeled in the outline.

Customizing the Numbering Scheme

If you're working on a unique project and you want to create your own numbering scheme, you can customize one of the outline numbering sequences. To start the customizing process, follow these steps:

1. Display the outline you want to number.
2. Right-click in the work area. The shortcut menu appears.
3. Click Bullets And Numbering. The Bullets And Numbering dialog box appears.
4. Click the Outline Numbered tab.
5. Select the numbering scheme that's closest to the one you want, and then click Customize. The Customize Outline Numbered List dialog box appears, as shown in Figure 10-12.

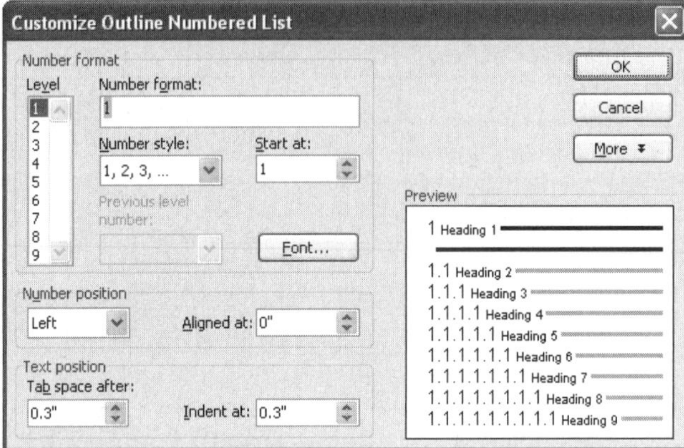

Figure 10-12. You can create your own outline numbering scheme based on one of Word's preset styles.

Tip **Renumber safely**

If you try one outline numbering sequence, and then want to change to another, first remove the previous outline numbering sequence by displaying the Bullets And Numbering dialog box, clicking the Outline Numbered tab, clicking None, and then clicking OK. That removes the numbering style from your outline. Now go back and repeat the steps to choose the numbering scheme you want. If you go directly from one numbering style to another, you might get unexpected results; occasionally Word changes outline levels and could introduce errors into your document.

Troubleshooting

The numbers in the numbered outline disappear

You're creating a numbered outline and you selected the style you want in the Outline Numbered tab of the Bullets And Numbering dialog box. But when you return to the outline, not all the headings are numbered as you selected. What's going on?

Word only recognizes and formats headings that are assigned to the built-in heading styles. If only some of your headings are formatted with the built-in styles, Word numbers only those headings. If you've created custom styles for your outline, you can still use those styles (and number them the way you want). In order to do this, you need to create a link that ties the custom style to one of Word's outline levels. Create this link by right-clicking in the work area and choosing Bullets And Numbering. Click the Outline Numbered tab, and then click Customize. In the Customize Outline Numbered List dialog box, select the outline level you want, click More (if necessary) to display the advanced options, and then click the Link Level To Style arrow. Choose the name of the style you used for the heading, and then click OK. Word links the style you selected to the outline level in the numbering scheme.

Selecting the Level

Word provides the option of customizing different outline levels separately. Click the level you want to work with by selecting it in the Level list box, on the left side of the Customize Outline Numbered List dialog box. In the Preview section, you see the outline level you've selected.

Tip **Change a portion of your outline**

By default, Word applies to the entire document the changes you make in the Customize Outline Numbered List dialog box. If you want to apply a change only to a portion of your outline, however, you can display the dialog box, click More (if necessary) to display the advanced options, and then click the Apply Changes To arrow. Choose Current Paragraph to apply the changes to the paragraph at the insertion point, This Point Forward to apply the changes throughout the remainder of the document, or Selected Text to apply the changes only to the text that's selected.

Choosing Your Style

The number style you select determines whether the numbering scheme uses numbers, letters, words, or characters. You can choose from 17 different styles, which include several bullet styles and a picture bullet style. To choose the number style you want to use for your customized outline, click the Number Style arrow in the Customize Outline Numbered List dialog box, and then click your choice.

Tip **Create legal briefs**

If your work involves preparing legal briefs, you'll be pleased to know that Word has an option that numbers using legal style. To activate this option, perform the following steps:

1. Right-click in the Outline window, and then choose Bullets And Numbering from the shortcut menu.
2. Click the Outline Numbered tab, and then click Customize.
3. Click More in the Customize Outline Numbered List dialog box and then select the Legal Style Numbering check box.
4. Finally, click OK, and Word renumbers your outline.

Controlling the Format of Outline Numbers

All the selections you make in the Customize Outline Numbered List dialog box, with the exception of the indent for a particular item, are shown in the Number Format box at the top of the dialog box. The number format controls the way your numbering style is displayed. If you want to use additional characters or words in your numbering style, enter them here. For example, you might want to use some of the following: (1) 1: 1 –New Item! ** 1 ** <1> ~ 1 ~.

As you make each change, the Preview window shows you how your new outline format will look. You can continue revising the format as many times as you want; Word doesn't record the change until you click OK.

Customizing Your Start Point

You also have the option of starting the numbering of your outline with a number other than 1. To choose a new number, click the Start At up and down arrows or click in the box, and then type the number you want to use.

Tip **Link outline levels to styles**
Don't want all these changes to go to waste? You can link the changes you make in your outline levels to corresponding styles in the style sheet of the current document. To do so, display the Customize Outline Numbered List dialog box, choose the Level style you want to use, and then click More. Click the Link Level To Style arrow and choose the style to which you want to link the outline level, and then click OK.

Customizing the Font Selection

You aren't stuck with the fonts Word assigns by default—or even the fonts you've already used in your document heading styles—when it comes to customizing your outline. To select a different font, click Font in the Customize Outline Numbered List dialog box. When the Font dialog box appears, make your choices, and then click OK. The Number Format box and the Preview section in the Customize Outline Numbered List dialog box will reflect the changes you made.

Choosing Fonts for Outlines

Which fonts work best for intricate outlining? By default, Word uses Arial 16 for Heading 1, Arial 14 Bold Italic for Heading 2, and Arial 13 Bold for Heading 3. Pretty unexciting stuff. The point, however, when you're in Outline view, is to create something that's easy to read. Arial, while it's not going to make anybody's pulse race, is a straightforward, readable font.

The most readable fonts for text, according to typographically savvy designers, are serif fonts like Times Roman, New Century Schoolbook, and Garamond. The most interesting fonts for headings are often those that give a contrast to the rest of your document—so if you have page upon page of Times New Roman text, looking at an Arial heading isn't such a bad idea. Unusual fonts that have personality, like Comic Sans, are great as occasional attention-getters but won't go far toward readability in an outline.

The best advice for choosing fonts for your particular outline is to try a few in your document to see which font best complements the text.

Changing Number and Text Position

If you're creating a custom outline and want to change the alignment and spacing of the numbers in your outlining scheme, you can make those changes in the Number Position section of the Customize Outline Numbered List dialog box. To change alignment, click the alignment arrow in the Number Position section and make your choice. You can select Left, Centered, or Right.

To indent the text so that it's aligned where you want it, click the up or down arrow in the Aligned At box. You might want to increase the alignment value, for example, if you want the outline to be indented within another section of text or printed within a customized layout scheme.

You can also control where you set a tab for text following an outline number. You can enter the spacing for the tab, which helps with text alignment throughout your outline. The default setting is 0.5 inch; to increase the setting, in the Text Position section, click the Tab Space After up arrow or type the new value. To decrease the amount of space, click the down arrow or enter the setting you want.

Finally, you can change the amount of space by which you indent the text following the number or letter in your numbering scheme. If you're using a phrase instead of a single character, you might want to increase the indent to give readers more white space as they read. Changing the text position simply requires entering another value in the Indent At box in the Text Position section. Again, the Preview section shows the change.

Printing Your Outline

At various stages throughout the process of viewing, editing, arranging, reorganizing, and formatting the headings in your outline, you might want to print a copy to see how things are shaping up. Printing is the same basic process, whether you're printing a long document or a simple outline. Here are the steps:

1. Switch to Outline view, and then display your outline.
2. Display only those headings you want to print by using the Collapse and Expand buttons and selecting the outline levels you want to see.

Print

3. Click Print on the Standard toolbar. The outline will be printed as displayed on the screen.

Troubleshooting

Too many page breaks in printed outlines

You've finished working on the outline for the new product report, and the development team is waiting to see what you've come up with. You've gone back over it several times to make sure you've got all the sections organized properly and the outline levels set correctly. Everything looks good.

But when you print the outline, there are big blank spots in the center of the pages. In the file, the text looks fine—what's the problem? Chances are the blank spots are due to Word's treatment of manual page breaks. If you've inserted manual page breaks in your document, you'll need to remove them before printing the outline; otherwise, the blank spots will prevail.

To remove the manual page breaks, click Show/Hide to display all the formatting marks in your outline, then move to each page break symbol, and then press Delete. Save your document and print again. The unwanted breaks should be gone.

Part 2

Reinforcing Your Message with Tables, Charts, Diagrams, and Pictures

Chapter 11

Adding Visual Impact with Pictures and Objects

You've probably heard that "a picture is worth a thousand words," and that's not just rhetoric. Think about what we see around us on the World Wide Web, in our mailboxes, in the newspaper, on TV. The words alone don't carry the message: the color, presentation, pictures, and style of the document capture our attention and ignite our imaginations. Consider this book, for example. It contains information that you want and need, but it wouldn't be as effective without the careful design of the pages and the screenshots, captured to show you what to look for as you try the procedures for yourself.

A picture can show at a glance what it takes words time to paint inside our heads. In a report, you'll need an entire paragraph (or a page!) to explain how a new product goes through a development cycle, but showing a diagram of the cycle will let your readers know instantly what the whole process looks like. This chapter explores ways you can use Word 2003 to bring images into your documents that add spark and interest, and just may get your point across more clearly, effectively, and persuasively.

What a Difference an Image Makes!

Need reasons to put images in your documents? There are many different reasons to use clip art, pictures, photos, drawings, and special graphic designs in the publications you produce. The goals of your publication will determine whether artwork is appropriate. Here are a few ways in which images help you reach your audience in an effective way:

- **They capture—and hold—the reader's interest.** In this time of colorful, slick marketing pieces and sophisticated Web pages, we need something that will make us take notice. A well-planned picture, whether it's a photo, a logo, or a drawing, can catch the reader's eye and get your document a closer look.
- **They give the reader's eyes a break.** It's a well-established fact that readers won't struggle through page after page of single-spaced text. They want healthy margins on the page, and they want both visual interest and rest—something that images on the page can give them. A well-placed image in a brochure can help lead the reader's eye from place to place. A diagram in a long report can provide a much-needed reading break.

- **They support an idea in your story or report.** An image in your document or on your Web page can help reinforce the theme or concept of your writing. If you're the publications director for a women's health center, for example, and you're creating your organization's annual report, photos of healthy, happy women help communicate your message and your mission. Likewise, in other documents, photos of products help build brand identity in your readers' minds, and organizational charts help befuddled staff understand who they report to in the aftermath of a corporate merger.

Finding Art You Can Use

What kind of art do you want to use? You can import all kinds of art into Word—drawings, paintings, images you create in high-end graphics programs, and art you download off the Web. You can also create your own diagrams and drawings inside the document you're working on. There's room for everything, and unless you've got an art file created in an ancient (or virtually unheard-of) format, you'll be able to get a filter that enables Word to import it.

Inside Out

Unusual graphics format?

If you have a logo or an image saved in a file format Word doesn't recognize, try opening the file in an image editing program (Microsoft Digital Image Pro 9 is a good example of a program that works with a variety of files). If you can open the file in the image editor, you can then save the file in a more common file format, such as .bmp, .tif, or .jpg.

Distinctions Between Paint and Draw Graphics

When you work with graphics, you create one of two types of images: bitmapped or vector graphics. You might see bitmapped graphics referred to as *paint graphics* or *raster images.* This type of image is created based on a pattern of pixels (or a map of bits). When you enlarge a bitmapped graphic, the dots are stretched, resulting in a loss of clarity because the larger the dots, the greater the space between the dots.

This chapter deals specifically with placing, importing, and working with images and objects. But Word also includes specialized drawing tools, for times when you want to hand-draw items on your Word page, and AutoShapes, which enable you to create and customize common shapes. For more about using Word's drawing tools to create images in your documents, see Chapter 12, "Enlivening Documents with Drawings and AutoShapes."

Vector images (also called *draw graphics* and *object-oriented graphics*) are drawings made of shapes, lines, and curves. Because these items are based on mathematical calculations, the images can be grouped into a single object and later divided again into individual objects. This means they can be resized, moved, and enlarged with no loss of quality. Table 11-1 lists some popular images you'll use, identifies their type, lists common file formats, and suggests possible sources or programs.

Table 11-1. Paint and Draw File Types

Item	Image type	File formats	Source
Clip art	Depends on the image—bitmapped or vector graphics	.bmp, .dib, .gif, .jpg, .pcx, .png, .tif, .wmf	Microsoft Clip Organizer, purchased clip art collections, Web clip art sources
AutoShapes	Vector graphics	.wmf	Microsoft Windows-based programs
Scanned images	Bitmapped graphics	.bmp, .gif, .png, .jpg	Microsoft Paint, Adobe Photoshop, Paint Shop Pro
Web graphics	Usually bitmapped graphics	.gif, .png	Available online and in some Web-generation programs
Page backgrounds	Bitmapped graphics	.bmp, .dib, .gif, .pcx, .png, .jpg, .tif, .htm	Paint images, HTML files
Picture bullets	Bitmapped graphics	.gif	Images created in programs such as Paint

Enhancing Your Documents with Clip Art

Word includes a collection of clip art you can use in your own documents. Both bitmapped and vector images are included in the collection—and you'll find all sorts of different topics represented, from animals to transportation to people and holidays. When you want to insert a piece of clip art in a document, you'll use the Clip Art task pane to do so. It's an easy and intuitive process.

Clip Art vs. the Clip Organizer

The Clip Organizer is a full-fledged art collection utility, tracking not only images but sound and motion files as well. You'll use the Clip Organizer to organize, add, review, and sometimes delete media clips of all types. You'll also use this utility to access additional clips and services on the Web, a feature that's built right into the interface. For more about the Clip Organizer, see "Using the Clip Organizer" on page 318.

Inserting Art from the Task Pane

The easiest way to get clip art into your document is to use the Clip Art task pane. Start by clicking in your document where you want the art to appear. Then choose Insert, Picture, Clip Art. The Clip Art task pane appears, as shown in Figure 11-1.

Figure 11-1. The Clip Art task pane gives you a fast and easy way to place images in your document.

Note The first time you click Organize Clips, at the bottom of the Clip Art task pane, the Add Clips To Gallery dialog box appears so that you can add your own clip art to the Clip Organizer. To have Word automatically scan your hard disk for media clips, which can include video segments, sound, or pictures, click OK. Otherwise, click Cancel.

Enter a word or phrase in the Search For box that describes the type of art you're looking for. You don't need to know the name of a specific category—simply enter a word that describes the topic you want, such as "border." Click Go. A list of clips that meet your criteria appears in the task pane, as shown in Figure 11-2. Click the one you want, and then Word adds it to your document.

Figure 11-2. Choose from the list of clips that meet your criteria.

Searching for Art in the Task Pane

When you search for a specific piece of clip art, by default Word searches all available categories: My Collections, Office Collections, and Web Collections. View the available collections by clicking the Search In arrow, as shown in Figure 11-3.

Figure 11-3. You can change Word's default search options by selecting only the collections you want.

You'll find three collections:

- **My Collections** Includes the art you add to the Clip Organizer.
- **Office Collections** Includes 40 major categories, some with subcategories, in which you're sure to find something that fits your topic.
- **Web Collections** Includes all the Web-friendly graphics included in the Clip Organizer. When you click Clips Online for the first time, a folder is created for storing clips downloaded from the Web.

At the bottom of the Clip Art task pane, you see further choices that take you to the Microsoft Clip Organizer, to the Web to gather more clips, and to tips that can help you locate the right art for your documents.

Searching for Clips Online

Microsoft Office Online now offers more clips—art, music, and video—than ever before. If you haven't visited the site yet, check it out. It's a great resource.

To find additional clips online, click Clip Art On Office Online at the bottom of the Clip Art task pane or, if the Clip Organizer is displayed, click Clips Online. If you are connected to the Internet, Word takes you right to the Microsoft Office Clip Art and Media Web page, where you can search for, select, and download clips to use in your documents.

Using the Clip Organizer

The Microsoft Clip Organizer helps you keep all your image, sound, and motion files in one place, arranged according to topic. To start the Microsoft Clip Organizer, click the Organize Clips link at the bottom of the Clip Art task pane. The first time you do this, you are asked whether you want the Clip Organizer to scan your hard disk for media files. On subsequent uses, the Clip Organizer appears as shown in Figure 11-4.

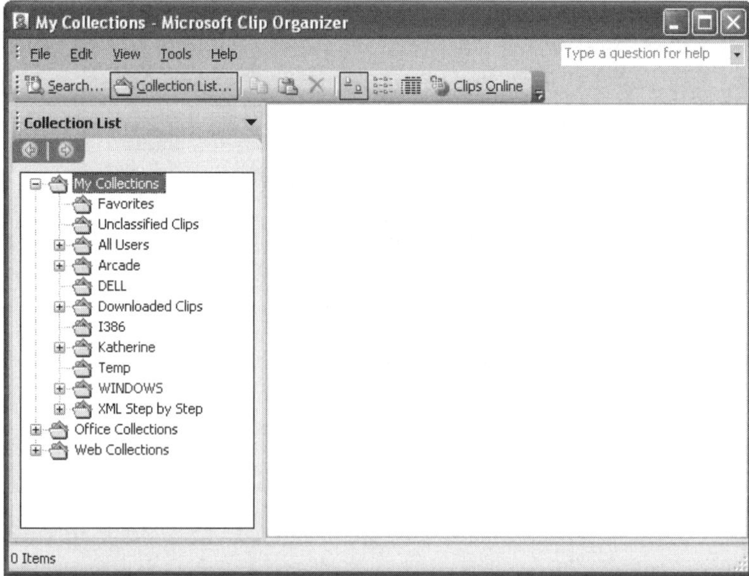

Figure 11-4. Click the folder of the collection you want to view.

The layout of the Microsoft Clip Organizer is similar to that of Microsoft Windows Explorer; you can easily see the number of collections available for your selection. You'll use the following items to help you locate and work with the clips you need:

- **Menu bar** Contains the commands you need to create new categories, organize your clips, copy and paste clips between collections, view individual images, search for more help on the Web, and get help using the Clip Organizer.
- **Toolbar** Provides tools for searching, choosing collections, copying, pasting, and deleting images, controlling the display in the Microsoft Clip Organizer window, and accessing the Web to search for more clips.
- **Collection List** Shows all available folders in which you can search for images.
- **View window** Shows selected clips. By positioning the pointer on a specific clip, you can display information about the file. In Figure 11-5, the file description shows the name of the file, the width and height in pixels, the file size, and the file format.

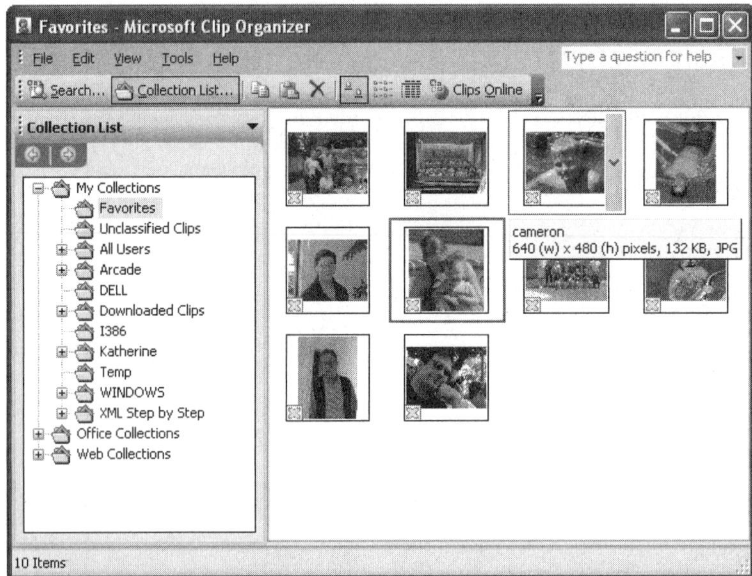

Figure 11-5. The Clip Organizer brings all your media clips together in one place.

Working with an Image in the Clip Organizer

To choose a clip from the Microsoft Clip Organizer, simply navigate to the clip you want and select it in the view window. The image is selected and an arrow appears along the right edge of the image. Click the arrow to display the menu; a range of choices appears, as shown in Figure 11-6.

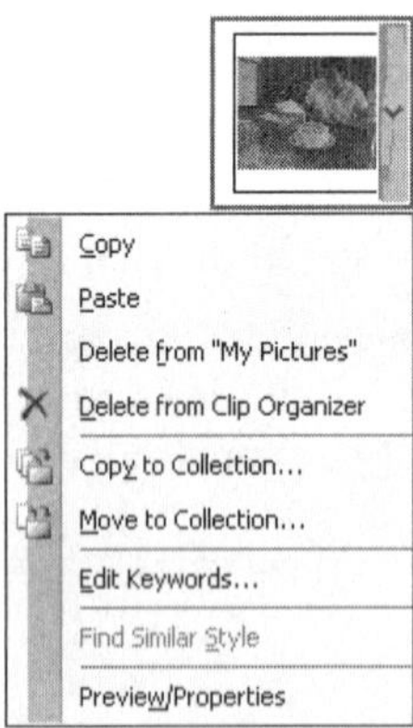

Figure 11-6. Right-click an image and choose an option to work with your images.

How will you use the Clip Organizer to work with your images? Most of the things you'll do in the Clip Organizer have to do with organizing and accessing your images. For example, you can use the Clip Organizer to do the following:

- Scan your hard drive for clip art images to add to the Clip Organizer
- Copy and paste images into other folders, files, and applications
- Reorganize art collections
- Locate images with a similar style
- Add and edit keywords that describe individual images
- Access Web tools for working with Clip Organizer images
- Display the properties of an individual image

Saving Favorite Clips

Over time, you might find that you have a group of images that qualify as "favorites." You can save those clips to your Clip Organizer Favorites collection so that you can access them easily. Here's how:

1. In the Clip Organizer, expand the My Collections section so that the Favorites folder is visible.
2. Navigate to the collection and folder storing the clip art you want to copy.
3. Drag the clip art image from the view window to the Favorites folder, as shown in Figure 11-7. The Clip Organizer makes a copy of the file and leaves the original in the Collection folder.

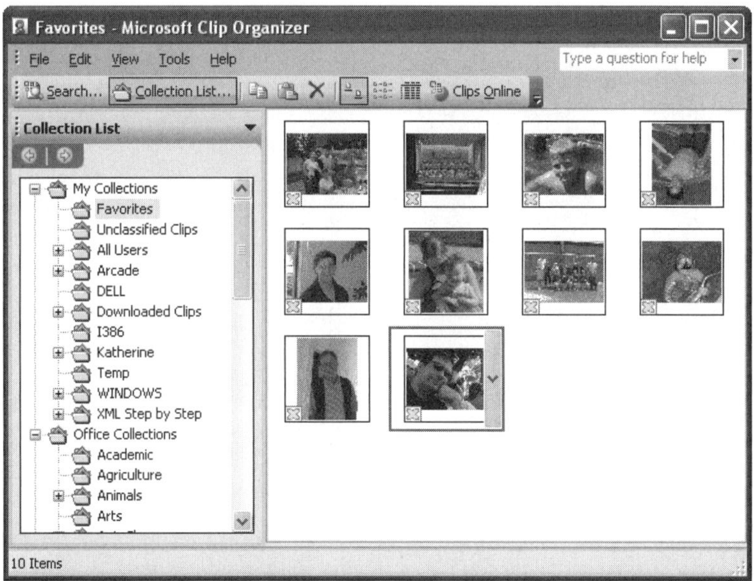

Figure 11-7. You can drag a copy of an image to your Favorites folder to keep a collection of files you use often.

Chapter 11

Tip **Copy images from the Clip Art task pane**

You can copy an image from the Clip Art task pane to your Favorites folder in the Clip Organizer by clicking the image's arrow and choosing Make Available Offline. When the Copy To Collection dialog box appears, you can choose your Favorites collection (or another collection as applicable), and then click OK. The image is then copied to the specified collection.

Adding Your Own Images—Automatically

If you're using your own clip art collections or you want to use clip art from a previous version of Office, you can have the Clip Organizer search and add clips automatically. To add the clips to the Clip Organizer, follow these steps:

1. Display the Microsoft Clip Organizer by choosing Insert, Picture, Clip Art, and then click Organize Clips in the bottom section of the task pane.
2. In Microsoft Clip Organizer, choose File, Add Clips To Organizer, and then click Automatically to have Word search and add the clips it finds automatically. The Add Clips To Organizer dialog box appears, alerting you that Word will catalog all media files (including picture, sound, and motion files) if you click OK.
3. Click Options in the Add Clips To Organizer dialog box to specify which folders the Clip Organizer will search for the files you want to add. The Auto Import Settings dialog box appears, listing all the folders found on your system, as shown in Figure 11-8. If you want the Clip Organizer to skip any of the selected folders, simply clear the folder check boxes.

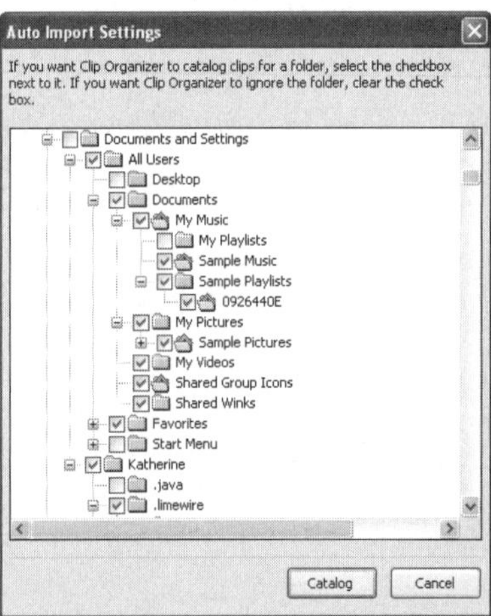

Figure 11-8. The Clip Organizer will search all available folders on your computer unless you specify otherwise.

4. Click Catalog in the Auto Import Settings dialog box to begin the process. The Clip Organizer displays a status dialog box showing you the progress of searching for clips and adding keywords to link the clips to the Clip Organizer. You can click Stop any time you want to cancel the process.

Adding Images on Your Own

The Clip Organizer also gives you the option of selecting the images you want to add and specifying where they go. You can also add keywords that you'll use to refer to the images later. To add images on your own, follow these steps:

1. Display the Microsoft Clip Organizer.
2. Choose File, Add Clips To Organizer, and then select On My Own. The Add Clips To Organizer dialog box appears, as shown in Figure 11-9.

Figure 11-9. You can add your clips to the Clip Organizer manually by navigating to the folder you want and choosing a destination collection.

3. Click the file you want to add, and then click Add To. The Import To Collection dialog box appears so you can choose the collection folder for the clip you are importing.
4. Choose a collection, click OK, and then click Add. You're returned to the Clip Organizer and the clip is added to your collection as specified.

Creating a New Collection

You can create a new collection in two ways: by clicking New in the Import To Collection dialog box or by choosing File, New Collection in the Clip Organizer. The New Collection dialog box (shown in Figure 11-10) appears, where you can choose a parent folder, if necessary, and enter a name for the collection.

Figure 11-10. You can create new collections in the Clip Organizer to store clips specific to your interests or industry.

> **Tip** **Review clip properties**
> For some documents, you'll need to look carefully for just the right images to fit the design and layout of your project. In these cases, you might want to see the file type, the size, the orientation, and any keywords associated with the image. To view the properties of an image, select the image and choose Preview/Properties from the menu. The Preview/Properties dialog box displays file specifications and lists the full path to the file, along with any caption and keywords.

Adding and Editing Keywords

Keywords are important in helping you find the images you want. Each file in the Clip Organizer is assigned a certain number of keywords—these words help characterize the image so that the Clip Organizer knows what to display when you enter a word in the Search For box. Keywords are what make it possible for you to enter *baby* in either the Microsoft Clip Organizer or the Clip Art task pane and display the images of children in the collections.

To display the keywords for a specific image, follow these steps:

1. Select the image in either the Microsoft Clip Organizer or the Clip Art task pane, and click its arrow.
2. Choose Edit Keywords. The Keywords dialog box appears, as shown in Figure 11-11.

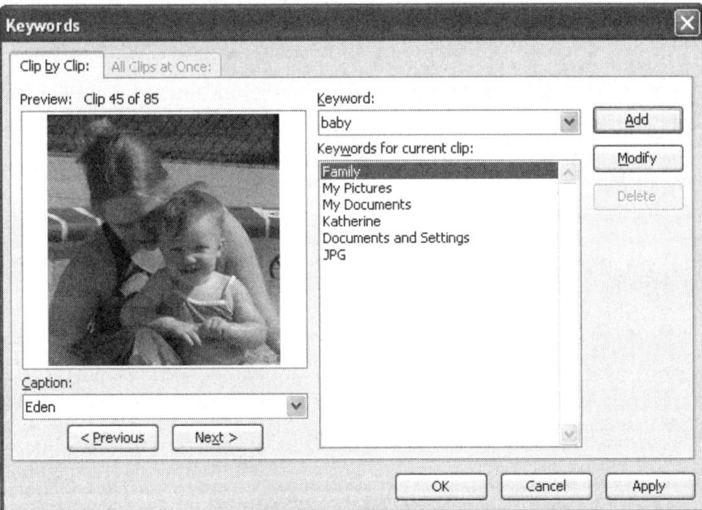

Figure 11-11. You can review, add, edit, or delete keywords in the Keywords dialog box.

3 By default, the name of the image appears in the Caption list. You can select the caption name from the list, and then enter the caption (or name) you want to appear.

4 Click in the Keyword list, and then choose a word from the list or type a word you want to use to refer to the image. Click Add to add the keyword.

Note If you want to delete any keyword in the list for the selected clip, simply select it, and then click Delete.

Deleting Unwanted Images

If the Clip Organizer acquires files you don't want included, you can select and delete them using the image menu. Click the file you want to delete, and you'll see two delete options in the menu: you can delete the clip from the selected folder, or you can delete the file from the Clip Organizer completely. If you choose the first option, the image is deleted without any further action from you. If you choose the second option, the Clip Organizer alerts you that the action will cause the image to be deleted from all collections on your system. Click OK to proceed, or click Cancel.

Inserting Pictures

Although letting the Clip Organizer scan your computer and add files for you is a convenient, timesaving feature, there will be times that you want to import directly into your document specific files you've created in another program or brought in on disk. You can import images from other programs, and you can bring in images you created with your scanner or digital camera.

Tip **Use pictures as backgrounds**

You can turn a picture you like into a background for your Word document. Choose Format, Background, click Fill Effects, and then click the Picture tab. Click Select Picture to display the Select Picture dialog box in which you can choose the picture for your background. Click the image, click Insert, and then click OK. The image is copied, tile-fashion, the width and length of your document.

Importing Images into Word

The process of importing an image simply involves choosing Insert, Picture, From File. Word automatically goes to the My Pictures folder and displays all files that can be imported, as shown in Figure 11-12. Navigate to and click the file you want, and then click Insert. Word adds the file to the document at the insertion point.

Figure 11-12. Word displays all the file types it recognizes.

Tip **Limit file display**

If you want to see only files of a certain type, click the Files Of Type arrow and choose the file format you want to see in the list that appears. Only files with the extension you selected will appear in the Insert Picture dialog box.

Using Scanned and Digital Images in Word

Many of the best images you use in your documents might be real, live photos of real, live people. Your annual report could show the smiling faces of real people helped by your organization; your business plan could include scanned images of the site where your new building will be erected; your classroom project could include pictures of the 22 students who helped prepare it.

To scan an image or use a digital photograph in Word, follow these steps:

1. Open the document to which you want to add the image.
2. Choose Insert, Picture, From Scanner Or Camera. The Insert Picture From Scanner Or Camera dialog box appears, as shown in Figure 11-13.

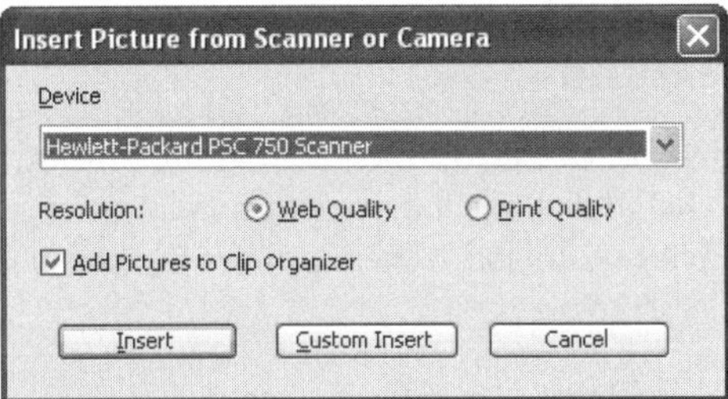

Figure 11-13. The Insert Picture From Scanner Or Camera dialog box gives you the means to scan your photos or pictures directly into your Word document.

3. If you have more than one scanner or camera installed on your system, click the Device arrow and choose the one you want to use.
4. Choose the resolution you want to use. Web Quality is of lower quality (fewer pixels and colors are used to create the image) than Print Quality, but the files are smaller and they're suitable for screen display.
5. If you want the image to be added to the Clip Organizer by default, leave the Add Pictures To Clip Organizer check box selected.
6. Finally, if you want to add a picture from your scanner, click Insert; if you want to add a picture from a digital camera, click Custom Insert.

Tip **Find lost images**

If you elected to have the scanned image or captured photo saved to the Clip Organizer, look for it in your Unclassified Clips collection. You can then drag it to your Favorites folder or another collection of your choosing.

Working with Pictures

The pictures we've been talking about thus far have been pictures you choose from the Clip Art task pane, pictures you import from another program, or images you scan or capture with a digital camera. These different ways of bringing images into Word produce different types of files:

- Clip art can be either bitmapped or vector images.
- Imported files can also be either bitmapped or vector images.
- Scanned images and captured photos are always bitmapped images.

Although bitmapped images and vector images each require different editing techniques, you'll use basically the same procedures with them in Word. The primary difference between the two types of image files is what happens to them when you resize them. A bitmapped image will become stretched and blurrier as the graphic is enlarged; a vector image can be resized with no loss of quality or clarity.

Checking Out the Picture Toolbar

When you click one of the images you've added to your document, the Picture toolbar appears by default. This toolbar includes all the tools you need to make simple changes to the images you bring into Word. Table 11-2 introduces each of the Picture toolbar buttons and gives you an idea of when to use each one.

Table 11-2. Picture Tools for Editing Images

Button	Name	Description	Use
	Insert Picture	Displays the Insert Picture dialog box so you can import a new file	You want to add another picture as you work in your document.
	Color	Gives you a set of four options that range from full color to black and white	You want to use a special treatment on an image—removing color, turning it to black and white.
	More Contrast	Makes the darks darker and the lights lighter	You want to make an image appear more abstract by creating sharp contrasts, with less subtle shading.
	Less Contrast	Lessens the division between dark and light, blurring the image	You want to create a subtle effect with no sharp contrasts.
	More Brightness	Increases the lightness of the overall image	You want to lighten a too-dark photo or image.
	Less Brightness	Tones down the brightness, taking the edge off light colors and reflections	You want to darken a too-light photo or image.
	Crop	Appears to cut off the edges of an image (in reality preserves the entire image)	You want to select a portion of a photo or image to be used in a document.
	Rotate Left	Rotates image to the left 90 degrees each time you click on its side	You want to turn the image, angle text, or skew a line or border.

Table 11-2. Picture Tools for Editing Images

Button	Name	Description	Use
	Line Style	Sets the width of the line style used to border the image	You want to create a boundary or frame for the image.
	Compress Pictures	Reduces the space required to save picture files (Web or Print resolution)	You're concerned about file size and want to optimize your document for the Web.
	Text Wrapping	Controls the way text wraps around the selected object	You're creating a document that incorporates text and images together in a continuing layout.
	Format Picture	Displays the Format Picture dialog box so that you can make choices in one place about cropping, brightness, compression, and more	You want to choose a number of settings for your picture at once.
	Set Transparent Color	Creates a "see-through" effect in an image when you click the areas you want changed	You're creating an image with a special effect—for example, a stylized photo or drawing.
	Reset Picture	Returns the picture to its size, shape, and brightness and contrast levels before you made any changes to it	You've modified an image and want to discard the changes you've made.

Inserting Pictures

Insert Picture

You're already familiar with the function of the Insert Picture tool on the Picture toolbar. When you want to add an image to your document, click this button. The Insert Picture dialog box appears, enabling you to navigate to the folder storing the image you want to import. Select the picture, and then click Insert to add it to your document.

> **Tip Add multiple images**
> You can add more than one picture at once using the Insert Picture tool. When the Insert Picture dialog box appears, click the first image you want to import, and then press and hold Ctrl while you click additional images. When everything you want is selected, click Insert, and then Word imports all selected images at once into the current document.

From Color to Black & White and Back

Color

The next button on the Picture Toolbar offers you the choice of turning your color photograph or picture into a grayscale or black and white image. By default, the image is assigned Automatic coloring. If you're preparing a document that will be printed in black and white only, you can change the image to grayscale (which turns each color into a shade of gray) or to black and white, which does away with subtleties and gives you a sharply defined black and white image. Figure 11-14 shows the four different effects of the Color tool settings.

Automatic

Grayscale

Black & White

Wash Out

Figure 11-14. The Color tool enables you to create different looks for the images in your documents.

Changing Picture Contrast and Brightness

More Contrast

Less Contrast

In Word, the contrast and brightness controls for your images influence the overall effect of the image in a significant way. The Contrast setting controls the amount of differentiation between light and dark. When you increase the contrast by clicking More Contrast, the darks get darker and the lights get lighter. When you decrease the contrast by clicking Less Contrast, the darks lighten and the lights darken.

The brightness of your image controls the light-to-dark ratio your graphic displays. Click More Brightness to increase the brightness, and the entire image lightens. When you click Less Brightness, the entire image darkens. The buttons are incremental, meaning that each time you click them, Word changes the amount of brightness just a bit.

Tip **Test brightness and contrast levels**

There's no hard and fast rule for brightness and contrast settings for your images. Test out different settings and see what looks best. If you're creating a print document, remember to print a copy as a test, because what you see on the screen won't match the quality of what you see in print.

Cropping Pictures

Crop

Cropping images is a simple process. With the image displayed on your screen, click the Crop button on the Picture toolbar. The pointer changes to a cropping tool. You can then place the tool on the edge or corner of the image where you want to begin cropping and drag the side or corner of the image inward until the amount you want to remove has been cropped out.

Tip Reverse a bad crop
If you decide after you've cropped an image that you liked it better the way it was before you changed it, you can undo the operation by clicking Undo on the Standard toolbar. If you want to reverse not only the cropping but other changes as well, you can return the picture to its original state by clicking Reset Picture on the Picture toolbar.

Resizing Pictures

An operation that goes hand-in-hand with cropping is resizing the images you import. This is one technique you'll use all the time—pictures rarely come into your documents at just the right size.

To resize a picture in Word, click the image. Handles appear around the edges of the object. If you want to enlarge the image, click in one corner of the picture and drag the handle outward. A dotted outline follows the pointer, showing the new size of the image, as shown in Figure 11-15. When the image is the size you want, release the mouse button.

Figure 11-15. Resizing follows the same rule of thumb in Word as it does in other applications—click and drag to resize quickly.

Tip Resize accurately
If you need to resize your picture to fit a space exactly, click Format Picture on the Picture Toolbar to display the Format Picture dialog box, click the Size tab, and then enter the exact measurements for your picture.

If you're working with bitmapped graphics, like the one in Figure 11-15, you'll notice a loss of clarity when you enlarge the image. To maintain the best clarity possible for scanned and digitized images, keep their sizes as small as your design allows. Several small focused images are better than one large fuzzy one.

One of the headaches with image size and placement is how well—or how poorly—the text wraps (or doesn't wrap) around the picture. For more about text wrapping, see "Controlling Text Wrapping" on page 334.

Rotating Pictures

Rotating is fun. If you're creating a special border effect, a text-and-graphics look in which your logo pitches sideways, a rolling star, or some other creative addition to your documents, the Rotate Left tool will come in handy. To rotate an image in Word, follow these steps:

1. Display your document in Print Layout view.
2. Select the image you want to rotate. The PictureToolbar appears.
3. Click Rotate Left. Word rotates an image to the left 90 degrees each time you click. A small green handle appears at the top edge of the rotated image; this is the handle that enables you to freely rotate the image.

Rotate Left

4. Position the pointer over the handle. The pointer changes shape to a curved arrow.
5. Drag the handle in the direction you want to free rotate the image. You can control the rotation in either direction, right or left, and modify the rotation as many times as you like. Figure 11-16 shows an image being rotated.

Figure 11-16. You can use both block rotate and free rotate functions right from the Picture Toolbar.

> **Note** A *block rotate* is the process of turning the picture by a certain number of degrees, in this case, 90 degrees. A *free rotate* is the process of grabbing an image by a handle and moving it to the desired rotation position.

Controlling Line Style

Line Style

Not all images need a frame—you'll discover how best to use the line style control settings on a case-by-case basis. With the Line Style options you can select a variety of line styles and widths, and you can further control them in the Format Picture dialog box, which appears when you choose More Lines at the bottom of the Line Style menu, shown below. To choose the line style you want, simply click the picture, click Line Style, and then make your choice.

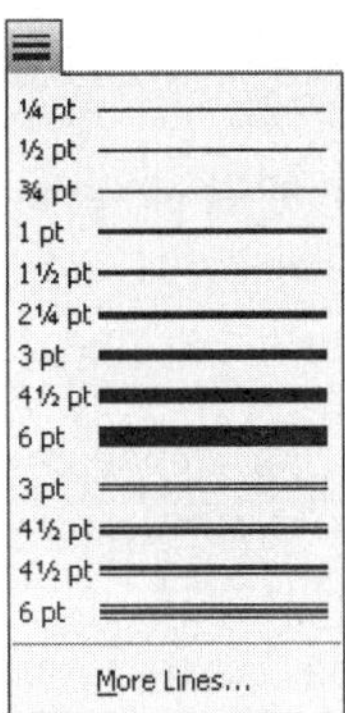

Compressing Pictures

Compress Pictures

Pictures can take up a hefty amount of disk space as well as use your computer resources in printing. Because of the amount of data stored in an image—especially a color image—the files tend to be huge. Word offers the Compress Pictures tool as a way to reduce the amount of space taken up by your picture files. To compress the pictures in the current document, follow these steps:

1. Select one of the pictures in the document. The Picture Toolbar appears.
2. Click the Compress Pictures button. The Compress Pictures dialog box appears, as shown in Figure 11-17.

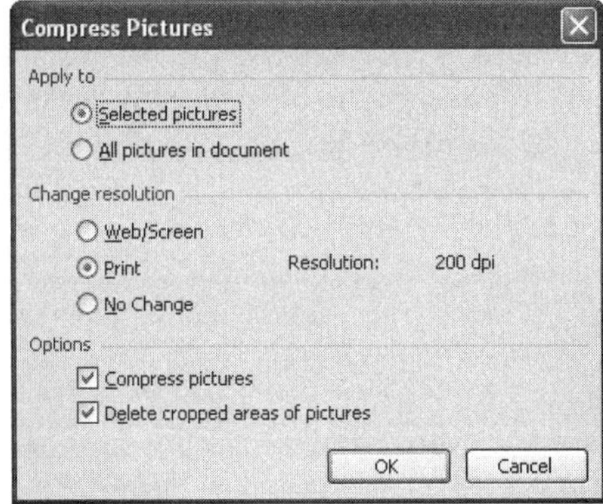

Figure 11-17. You can reduce the amount of space a graphics-heavy file requires by compressing images.

3. If you want only the selected picture compressed, leave the default selection of Selected Pictures. If you want to compress all pictures in the document, click the All Pictures In Document option.

   In choosing resolution, you can tell Word to lower the resolution for the screen (which also affects Web viewing) or for printing only.

Note If you have Word change the resolution to Web/Screen, the image will be displayed at 96 dots per inch (dpi) on your monitor. If you choose Print, Word reduces resolution to 200 dpi. For best results, test both resolution changes and see whether either works for you. If not, choose No Change, and then Word will compress the file as much as possible without affecting the display or print resolution.

4. For optimum compression, leave the last two check boxes, Compress Pictures and Delete Cropped Areas Of Pictures, selected. They ensure that the pictures are compressed as fully as possible.
5. Click OK to compress the images. Word displays a warning that compression might reduce the quality of the picture and asks you whether you want to apply picture optimization. If you want Word to step in and attempt to optimize your picture in light of the lost resolution, click Apply. If you click Cancel, the compression process is stopped.

Cutting Your Files Down to Size

If you're working on high-quality documents and file size is a concern but not a priority, you might want to think of ways to creatively reduce the size of your file without resorting to compression. In our experience, compressing images can cause a dramatic loss of quality, and if your objective in using pictures is to make your documents look their best, including a fuzzy or ill-defined image might not be quite good enough.

There are ways, however, that you can control file size as you work:

- **Limit your use of photos.** Because of the information stored in a digitized image file, it can be very large. Consider how many photos you want to use in your document and use them effectively.
- **Watch your file types.** Some files are larger than others. A small JPG or GIF file takes up less space than the average BMP or TIF file.

Controlling Text Wrapping

The whole point of adding pictures is to illustrate your text, right? So you need a way to help your text and graphics flow together naturally. You coordinate this text-and-art relationship by using the Text Wrapping tool, which is available on the Picture Toolbar.

Tip **Make a Text Wrapping toolbar**
You can grab the top of the Text Wrapping list and drag it off in a toolbar by itself. This is convenient if you're working with text wrapping and want to save yourself a few toolbar clicks.

To set up text wrapping in your document, follow these steps:

Text Wrapping

1. Select the picture you want to wrap text around. The PictureToolbar appears.
2. Click Text Wrapping. A list of Text Wrap choices appears.
3. Select the Text Wrapping style you want to apply to your picture. Experiment if you like; you can always Undo your choice if you don't like the effect. The Text Wrapping options are the following:
   - *In Line With Text*—Selected by default; positions the picture in line with text as it appears at the current position.
   - *Square*—Causes the text to wrap left and right of the bounding box enclosing the picture.
   - *Tight*—Secures the text to the picture itself, not the bounding box (which might appear to be the same border, depending on the picture you are working with).
   - *Behind Text*—Causes the text to flow over the top of the picture.
   - *In Front Of Text*—Causes the text to flow behind the picture.
   - *Top And Bottom*—Wraps the text above and below the image in the document, if there's room. White space is left bordering the picture on the sides.
   - *Through*—Wraps text against the border of your picture, which is a nice effect if you have an uneven boundary that text could fill.
   - *Edit Wrap Points*—Enables you to fine-tune the way the text wraps around the picture. By controlling individual points, you can set a boundary for the text that follows the line of the picture.

Adding and Editing Wrap Points

Word gives you the means to create your own kind of text wrapping by creating boundaries for text to flow along. You do this by using Edit Wrap Points selection from the Text Wrapping tool on the Picture toolbar. For example, consider the example shown in Figure 11-18. In this example, the top and bottom edges of the wrap area were extended to make room for handwritten comments.

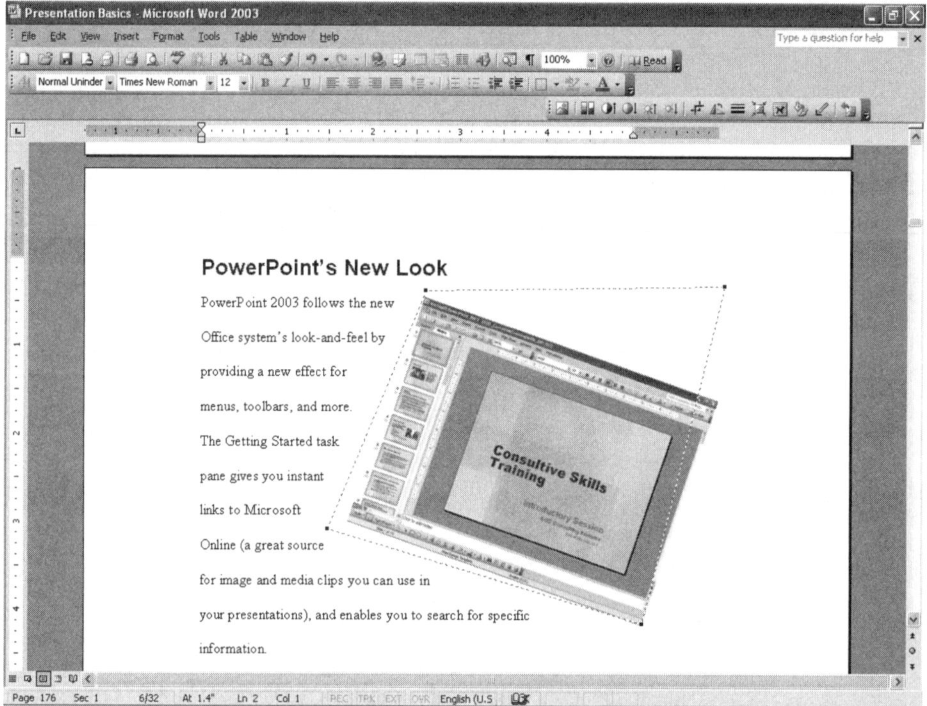

Figure 11-18. You can create your own text wrapping boundaries with Edit Wrap Points.

Here's the process for creating and working with edit wrap points:

1. Select the picture you want to work with. The PictureToolbar appears.
2. Click Text Wrapping, and then choose Edit Wrap Points from the menu. A red dashed boundary with several black handles appears around your picture.
3. Grab one of the handles with the mouse pointer and drag it outward, to the edge of the boundary you want to create. The line stays where you put it.
4. To create another handle (you aren't limited to following the shape of the image—you can stretch and add edit points any place you choose), simply click in the boundary line and drag it out to the point at which you want it. This creates another handle at that point and establishes the boundary where you put it.
5. After you finish creating your text boundary, click Text Wrapping again, and then click Through. The text wraps up to, but not into, the new text boundary you created.

Formatting Pictures

When you're comfortable working with pictures and you're used to getting the color, shading, brightness, and text wrap choices just the way you want them, you might want to handle all these choices in one place rather than selecting them individually. That's what the Format

Picture dialog box is for. Also available from the Picture Toolbar, the Format Picture dialog box, shown in Figure 11-19, enables you to make choices for colors and lines, picture size, text wrapping, alignment, brightness and contrast, cropping settings, and Web text settings.

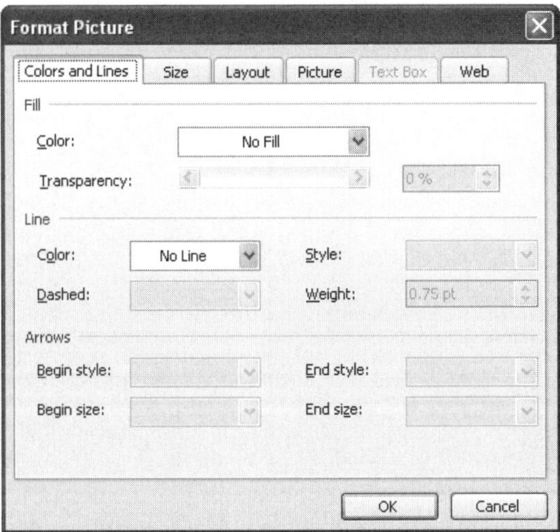

Figure 11-19. The Format Picture dialog box combines many of the options you've worked with individually on the Picture toolbar.

Because most of this is covered elsewhere in this chapter, and because finding your way around a dialog box is doubtless a technique you mastered long ago, it's necessary to describe only one item in the Format Picture dialog box: setting alternative text for Web display.

Creating Web Alternative Text

If you're using Word to create a Web page, when you put graphics on a page, it's possible that the visitors to your site won't ever view them. That's not because of bandwidth issues; that's because some users prefer to browse with their graphics capabilities disabled. It enables them to move more quickly through Web pages and get on with the business of surfing. But if your visitors don't have their graphics enabled and you've got all these great pictures on your site, what are they going to see?

That's where alternative text comes in. You can add a text message that explains what the image *would* look like if the user chose to view it. Also, alternative text can provide a message while a large file loads or alert a user if a file is missing.

To add alternative text to your document, follow these steps:

Format Picture

1. Click the picture to which you want to add alternative text and make sure the Picture Toolbar appears. (If it doesn't appear automatically, right-click the image, and then choose Show Picture Toolbar from the menu.)
2. Click Format Picture. The Format Picture dialog box appears.

3 Click the Web tab. This tab gives you a note box where you can type the message you want to appear in place of the picture, as shown in Figure 11-20.

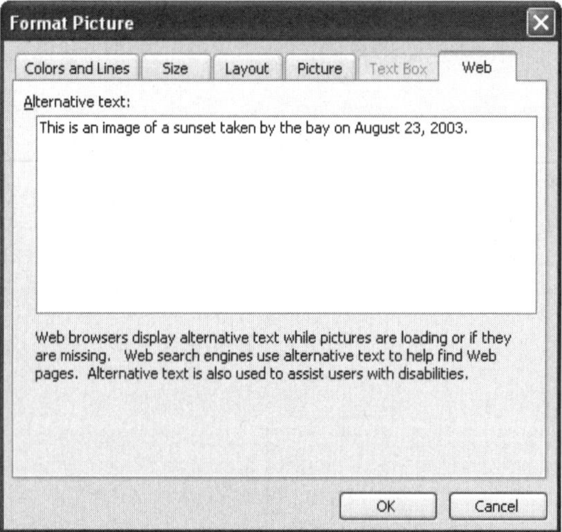

Figure 11-20. Alternative text gives Web visitors something to view if they don't have graphics enabled in their browsers.

Troubleshooting

Graphics are missing from my document

If you don't see graphics in your document, make sure that you haven't enabled the Picture Placeholders option in the Options dialog box. This feature helps speed up screen display by showing only the outlines of graphics. Choose Tools, Options, and then click the View tab. Make sure the Picture Placeholders check box, located in the Show section, is not selected.

Inserting Multimedia Objects

Up to this point in the chapter, you've learned about adding images to Word documents. But did you know that you can use Word to communicate using more than words and pictures? Your Word documents can literally sing, if you choose to add audio clips or voiceovers. They can show something in action, if you choose to add a video segment. Your Web pages can teach, if you want to add a PowerPoint presentation to the page you create in Word.

Word makes it easy to both link and embed files (which are called *objects* for this operation). That means you can work with files you create in other programs, whether they're programs in the Microsoft Office System or not. This next part of the chapter shows you how to incorporate objects in your documents, whether you want to add multimedia effects or something more sedate, like an Excel spreadsheet or a bit of Access data.

What kinds of things might you want to link? You've got all sorts of choices: a sound file, a table, a video clip, an equation, data tables, images, a presentation file, or another Word document.

Create It Once, Use It Again

One of the great things about using a multi-application system like Office is the way you can reuse what you create. You can open your Excel spreadsheet in your sales report. You can attach an organization chart to the announcement of the new spring promotions. You can add a voiceover segment to a section of a speech you're testing with your coworkers. You can use these different items in your Word document by importing them as objects.

Although you can copy and paste these items into a document, keeping the data current can be a problem if your information changes often. If you paste a segment of your Excel worksheet in your document, and then the original worksheet changes, your document will be out of date. To create multidimensional documents and keep them current, you can link the objects to their original files using object linking and embedding (OLE) and Dynamic Data Exchange (DDE).

Note You can import objects from programs outside the Microsoft Office System. As long as a program supports OLE and DDE, you can link and edit that program's objects.

Linking vs. Embedding: A Comparison

Linking a file and *embedding* a file might seem like the same process. In fact, they are two very different processes, each providing a different function, as follows:

- **Linking** Establishes a link between the original (source) file and the file to which you copied the data (destination). Whenever you change the information in the source file, the destination file is updated.
- **Embedding** Places an intact copy of the source file in the destination file. Although changing the source file doesn't affect the destination file, you can *edit* the object in the destination file by double-clicking it. You can then edit the object without quitting Word.

Tip **Cut to the chase**
The biggest difference between linking and embedding is which file (source or destination) contains the data and how this file is updated (at the source, or originating program, or in the destination document).

Chapter 11

Good Candidates for Linking and Embedding

Linking an object is a good choice when you need to keep data in your documents up to date. Here are a few examples:

- You're creating a draft of a report that includes slides from a PowerPoint presentation that's not yet finished. If the document is linked to the presentation file, when you finish the presentation, the document will reflect the changes.

- You have a new logo design for your business, and you're trying it out on letterhead. If you maintain the link to the draw file in which the logo is stored, when you change the logo, the letterhead will reflect the changes.
- You have a sales report due this afternoon, but not all the numbers are in from your regional sales staff. If you import the part of the Excel spreadsheet that's ready and establish a link when you update the information later, the file will reflect the changes.

Embedding objects is a good idea when you don't need to maintain a link but want to edit the object in your document. Here are some examples of embedding:

- You want to send a snapshot of current Excel data to a coworker, but the information is likely to change.
- You want to add a finished spreadsheet object. You don't need to maintain the link, but you might want to change the format or values later.
- You've added an organization chart, but when you send the document to different audiences, you need to change the roles that are displayed.

Note Linking an object to a file establishes a one-way link to the source document. When you change the information in the source—for example, when you change the name of a product in the PowerPoint presentation you've imported—the same change is reflected in the document to which you've linked the information.

Tip **Use linking to minimize file size**
When you want to keep your files small, linking is your best bet. Because a linked file stores only a pointer to the source file, the destination file size increases only a little. Although these types of links introduce other potential problems (such as broken links to deleted or moved source files), they give you the flexibility you might need when size is a consideration.

Linking Objects

Word provides two different ways for you to bring linked objects into your documents. You can use the Insert Object dialog box to place an existing object in your document, and you can use the Paste Special command to use the basic copy-and-paste procedure to establish and maintain a link with the source file.

Inserting a Linked Object

Suppose you have a great new banner ad design that you want to incorporate in the document you're preparing for a client. Although the banner ad isn't quite finished, you want to show the client how the ideas are developing in the presentation. You decide to add the entire presentation to your document as a link in the report.

To insert the object and create a link to the source file, follow these steps:

1. Place the insertion point where you want to include the object.
2. Choose Insert, Object. The Object dialog box appears.
3. Click the Create From File tab, as shown in Figure 11-21. Here you can enter the name for the file you want to insert and choose whether to link or embed the file.

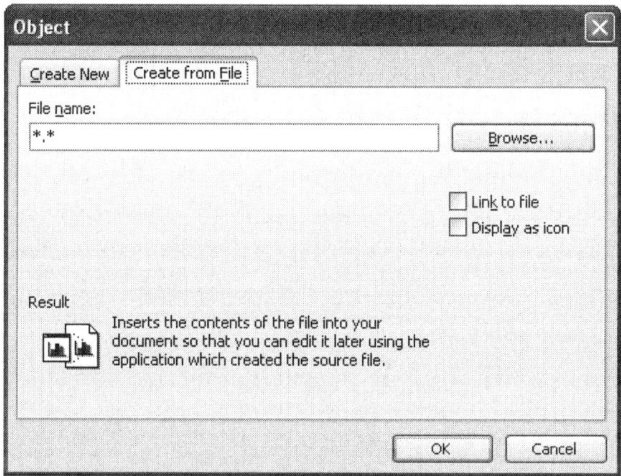

Figure 11-21. The Object dialog box gives you the means to link or embed objects.

4. Click Browse. The Browse dialog box appears. Navigate to the folder in which the file you want to link is stored, select the file, and then click Insert.You are returned to the Object dialog box.
5. Select the Link To File check box. This tells Word to establish the link to the source.
6. Click OK. The object is inserted at the insertion point.

Tip **Run a presentation**

If your linked object is a PowerPoint presentation, run the presentation by double-clicking it. You won't be able to edit the presentation, however, without opening the source file.

Troubleshooting

The linked object is missing

So after you go through the steps to insert a linked object, it starts to appear in your file and then—nothing. Just an outline, no object. What's going on?

If you have enabled Picture Placeholders in the Options dialog box, Word is saving memory and screen update time by showing only the outline of the object. You can fix this by choosing Tools, Options, and then clearing the Picture Placeholders check box in the Show section of the View tab.

Tip **Create objects with Create New**
The process of embedding uses the Create New tab in the Object dialog box. Embedding an object enables you to include in your document objects you have created in other programs, and it also lets you actually create the objects from scratch while you are working with Word. When you select the options in the Create New tab to create an embedded object, Word launches the program you used to create the object; after you save and close the other program, you are returned to Word, and the object is embedded in your current document.

Adding Linked Objects with Paste Special

Another way to add a linked object to your document is to use Paste Special. This command (available from the Edit menu) copies and pastes not only the data but also a link to the source file. Start in the Word document to which you want to add the linked object, and then follow these steps:

1. Position the insertion point where you want to add the object.
2. Start the program in which you have created the object. Select the section or object, and then copy the item to the Clipboard.
3. Return to Word, and then choose Edit, Paste Special. The Paste Special dialog box appears, as shown in Figure 11-22.

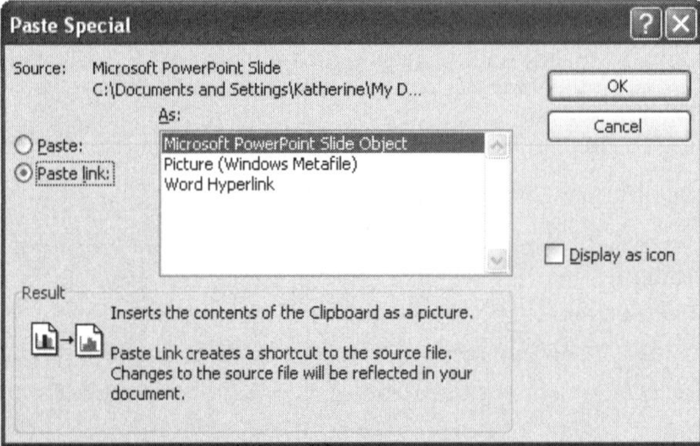

Figure 11-22. The Paste Special dialog box enables you to both link and embed data.

4. Click the Paste Link option, select the object type in the As list box, and then click OK. Word adds the data and the link to your document.

Note The Paste Link option is available only for objects you've created in programs that support linking.

Note When you want to review the links in your current document, choose Edit, Links to display the Links dialog box.

Changing Linked Objects

Any editing you do on a linked object actually takes place in the source file. You can edit a linked object in several different ways:

- You can double-click the object to launch the source program.
- You can click the object, choose Edit, Linked Object, and then click Edit Link.
- You can right-click the object to display the shortcut menu. You can then click Linked Object and select Edit Link. This takes you to the source file so that you can make changes, as shown below.

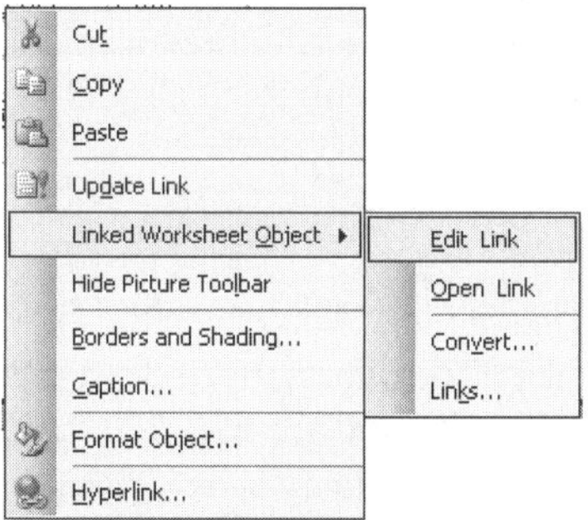

To modify the source object directly, make your changes in the originating program. Save and close the object as you would normally.

When you return to the linked document, select the linked object and choose Edit, Update Link (or press F9). Depending on how you've set up your options for updates, the destination file might be updated as soon as you return to it or it might be delayed until you manually choose an update.

Working with Links

The only tricky part to working with linked objects in your documents is that managing a variety of links can be confusing and a drain on your system's resources. For this reason, Word pulls link management together in one place—the Links dialog box, shown in Figure 11-23. To display this box, choose Edit, Links.

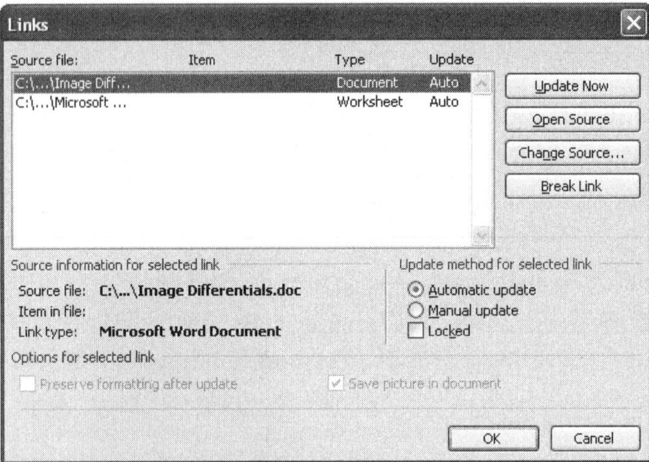

Figure 11-23. The Links dialog box gives you the means to review, change, update, and remove links to objects you've inserted in your document.

The following list provides you with a quick overview of the techniques you'll use to keep your links in order.

- **Reviewing links** In the Source File list of the Links dialog box, you see a list of the currently active links in your document. The information tells you the type of link, the update method (Auto is selected by default), and any options that have been selected.
- **Updating links** By default, Word updates any links in your document. Each time you open the file, Word checks whether any links have changed—a process that can take a few minutes if you've added many links to your current document. Similarly, when you make a change to the source file and the destination file happens to be open, Word updates the destination file if you've set the updating options to update automatically.
- **Manually updating links** If you want to update links manually, display the Links dialog box, select the link you want to change, click the Manual Update check box (under Update Methods), and then click OK. When you want to update the link, press F9.
- **Locking a link** To lock a link, display the Links dialog box, select the linked object in the Source File list, and then select the Locked check box in the Update Method For Selected Link section. You can unlock a link later if you choose by repeating the first two steps, and then clearing the Locked check box.
- **Going to the source** When you want to look at the source file for your document, you can use the Open Source button in the Links dialog box to get to it. Simply select the link in the Source File list, and then click Open Source. The source program runs, and the file appears.
- **Changing the source** When you move a source file, the linked document needs to know about the move. To update the linked document about the source's new location, choose Edit, Links, and then, with the link selected, click Change Source in the Links dialog box. The Change Source dialog box appears. Navigate to the folder where the

source file is now located, click the file, and then click Open. Click OK to close the Links dialog box.

- **Breaking links** When you have a file in its finished state, you might want to break a link to protect the object from future modifications.To break the link of a selected object, click the link in the Source File list in the Links dialog box. Click Break Link, and then click Yes to confirm.

Tip **Update now**

It's possible for some links in the Source File list in the Links dialog box to show Auto updates and others to show Manual updates. You can force the update of a Manual link by selecting it in the Source File list, and then clicking Update Now.

Troubleshooting

My changes are lost

If Word crashes and then AutoRecover restores your document, you might find that your linked object has lost its most recent changes and is appearing as an outline instead of a fully displayed object. To fix these problems, save the document, click the object, and then choose Tools, Options. Clear the Picture Placeholders check box in the Show section of the View tab, and then click OK to close the dialog box. Then, with the object still selected, press F9 to force a manual update. Word compares the object to the source file and updates any missing changes.

Note If you want to reestablish the link you just broke, pressing Ctrl+Z does the trick.

Embedding Objects

Embedding objects, in contrast to linking objects, is a pretty straightforward process. There are no links to worry about or maintain. You simply place an object in the document and there it stays. Pretty clean and simple.

The downside of embedded objects is the size of the file they create. When you add a PowerPoint presentation to your destination document, for example, your Word file takes on the weight of the additional file. With a linked file, only the link to the source file is actually stored in the document.

Pasting Data as an Embedded Object

When you want to embed a portion of a file, you can use Paste Special to import the information, keeping the formatting intact. Select the data you want to embed, and then copy it to the Clipboard. Open your destination document, and place the insertion point where you want to add the data. Choose Edit, Paste Special to display the Paste Special dialog box shown previously in Figure 11-22. Choose the format in the displayed list, and then click OK to embed the data.

Creating a New Embedded Object

To create a new embedded object, start in the document to which you want to add the embedded object. Place the insertion point where you want to add the object, and then choose Insert, Object. The Insert Object dialog box appears, with the Create New tab selected, as shown in Figure 11-24.

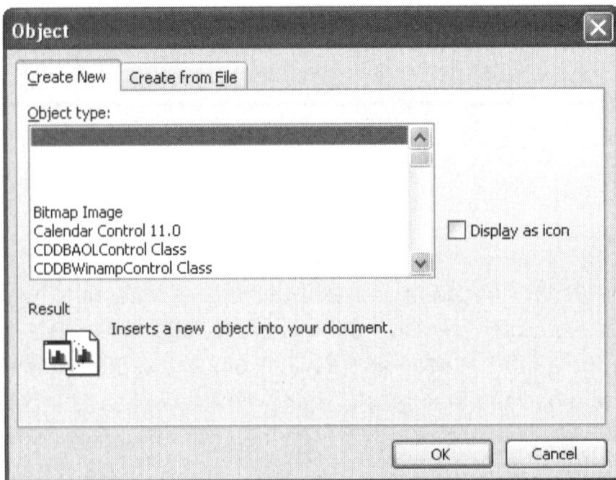

Figure 11-24. You can create an embedded object from within your Word document.

Scroll through the Object Type list, and select the one you want. If you want to have the embedded object displayed as an icon instead of a file, select the Display As Icon check box; and then click OK. The program that creates the object you selected launches so that you can create the item for your Word document. When you're finished creating the document, choose the File menu, and then choose the command that enables you to return to Word.

Note Depending on the program you're using to create the embedded object, the menus you see might differ from the ones you see here. Different programs offer different levels of support for object linking and embedding. If you need help with the program you're using to create the embedded object, consult that program's help system or your program documentation.

Adding an Existing Object

Adding a file or data section to your document as an embedded object allows you to keep all the data in one place, which makes your file portable. The benefit of embedding a file as opposed to copying it into your document is that you can edit an embedded object—in its originating program—from within your Word document. To add a file as an embedded object, click the spot where you want to add the object, and then choose Insert, Object. Click the Create From File tab, choose Browse, select the file you want to embed, and click Insert. Click OK to add the object.

Editing an Embedded Object

You edit an embedded object by double-clicking it—whether the object is a section of a file or an entire embedded file. Double-clicking starts the program in which the file was created. You can make your changes as needed, and then choose File, Close And Return To Microsoft Word to accept the changes in your document.

Troubleshooting

I can't edit an embedded object

You double-click an object to edit it, and nothing happens. What's going on? These are the possibilities:

- Make sure the source program is still installed. If it's not, install it or convert the embedded object to a file format you can use.
- Make sure that you're not running low on system memory. If that appears to be the problem, close all other programs to free up resources.
- If you're working with a linked object on a network, make sure that no one else has the source file open at the same time, or that the network location still exists.
- Make sure that the source file hasn't been moved or renamed. Check this by clicking the object and choosing Edit, Links.

Chapter 12

Enlivening Documents with Drawings and AutoShapes

You can liven up your Word documents with two basic types of graphics—pictures and drawing objects. A *picture* in Word is a graphic created from another file, such as a bitmap, a scanned image, a photograph, or most types of clip art. *Drawn graphics* (also called *vector drawings*) are created from lines, curves, rectangles, and other objects that can be changed, formatted, moved, and enhanced. In Word, you can create drawings by combining objects such as AutoShapes, freeform shapes, diagrams, curves, lines, arrows, WordArt, and similar constructs. In this chapter, we focus on creating and inserting drawing objects in Word.

For more information about working with pictures in Word, including clip art, see Chapter 11, "Adding Visual Impact with Pictures and Objects."

Getting Acquainted with Word's Drawing Features

Semantically, it might sound odd that you can *draw* in *Word*, but drawing capabilities have been steadily evolving in Word throughout the last few versions. As an experienced Word user, you're probably familiar with the basic drawing tasks you can perform in Word, such as creating lines and inserting shapes. In Word 2003, the drawing capabilities continue to be an integral part of the application. But, as you know, Word is designed to be a document creation program, not a painting program. Therefore, you should expect some drawing limitations in Word, and you should use a true painting program to create detailed graphics. On the other hand, the Word drawing tools are advanced enough to be extremely handy when you want to create particular types of drawings, including the following:

- Arrows or connection lines
- Simple iconlike illustrations

- Schematic office or room layout illustrations
- Diagrams, flowcharts, and organizational charts (see Chapter 14, "Showcasing Data with Charts, Graphs, and Diagrams")
- Images created by combining regular shapes, such as squares, ovals, and lines
- Splash starbursts and shapes containing text blocks
- Stylized WordArt text

You can find the tools for creating drawing objects by using the Drawing toolbar, the AutoShapes menu (which is on the Drawing toolbar), or the WordArt Gallery. In addition, you can control your drawings by mastering the relationship between drawing objects and the drawing canvas, which appears by default whenever you create a drawing (except WordArt) in Word. In the next few sections, we look at using the Drawing toolbar and AutoShapes; WordArt is discussed in more detail later in the chapter, in "Working with WordArt" on page 388.

Sketching Your Ideas in Word 2003

In Word 2003, you can sketch and draw in documents using other tools in addition to the program's basic drawing tools. Namely, you can use the following tools:

- **Ink** If you're using a Tablet PC, you can use your tablet pen to insert comments, create drawings and handwritten content, and add ink annotations.
- **Handwriting Tools** Using the Language bar, you can use the Drawing Pad and Handwriting feature to add drawings and handwritten content to documents. The handwriting tools are available in the Simplified Chinese, Traditional Chinese, English, Japanese, and Korean language versions of Office.

To learn more about using ink with Tablet PCs, see Chapter 27, "Revising Documents Using Markup Tools" in this book, as well as "A Tablet PC Quick Reference," on this book's companion CD.

Familiarizing Yourself with the Drawing Toolbar and the AutoShapes Menu

Drawing

When you create drawings in Word, you work with the Drawing toolbar, a central location for drawing tools. To display the Drawing toolbar, click Drawing on the Standard toolbar; choose View, Toolbars, Drawing; or choose Insert, Picture, New Drawing. Table 12-1 describes the buttons available on the Drawing toolbar.

Table 12-1. **Drawing Toolbar Buttons**

Button	Name	Function
Draw	Draw	Provides a menu with drawing and editing commands, such as Order, Group, and Text Wrapping
	Select Objects	Enables you to select one or more drawing objects
AutoShapes	AutoShapes	Provides ready-made shapes, including lines, basic shapes, arrows, stars, banners, callouts, and others
	Line	Enables you to click and drag to draw a line
	Arrow	Enables you to click and drag to draw an arrow
	Rectangle	Enables you to click and drag to create a square or a rectangle
	Oval	Enables you to click and drag to draw a circle or an oval
	Text Box	Enables you to create a text box so that you can add text to drawing objects
	Insert WordArt	Displays the WordArt Gallery dialog box
	Insert Diagram or Organizational Chart	Displays the Diagram Gallery dialog box
	Insert Clip Art	Displays the Clip Art task pane in the current view
	Insert Picture	Displays the Insert Picture dialog box
	Fill Color	Enables you to control the color, texture, pattern, or picture used to fill drawing objects, including the Drawing Canvas
	Line Color	Enables you to control the color, texture, pattern, and effect of line objects and borders
	Font Color	Enables you to color text
	Line Style	Provides a variety of line styles and settings you can apply to lines and borders

Table 12-1. Drawing Toolbar Buttons

Button	Name	Function
	Dash Style	Provides a variety of dashed line styles and settings you can apply to lines and borders
	Arrow Style	Provides a variety of arrow styles and settings you can apply to lines
	Shadow Style	Enables you to add and control shadow effects for drawing objects
	3-D Style	Enables you to add and control 3-D settings for drawing objects
	Select Multiple Objects	Opens the Select Multiple Objects dialog box (by default, this button does not appear, but it can be displayed using the Add Or Remove Buttons arrow at the right end of the Drawing toolbar)

In addition to using Drawing toolbar buttons to draw shapes, you can insert standard shapes into your documents by using the AutoShapes menu, which you can display by clicking AutoShapes on the Drawing toolbar, as shown in Figure 12-1. The AutoShapes menu provides a library of shapes that you can use to create custom drawings. After you insert an AutoShape, you can color, resize, reshape, and otherwise customize the object, as you'll see throughout this chapter. You can also combine AutoShapes and other drawing components to create more complex graphics.

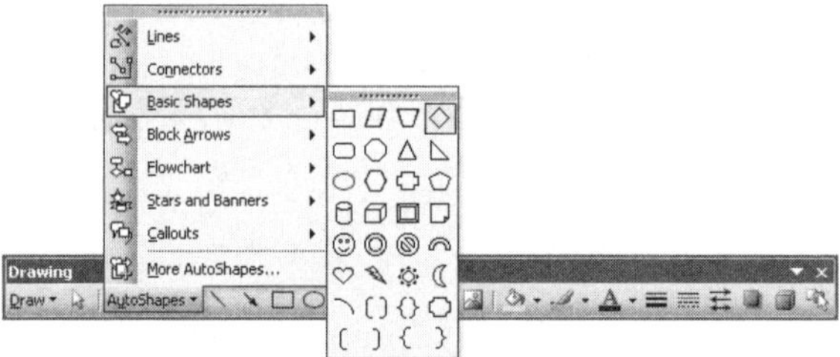

Figure 12-1. The AutoShapes menu provides a collection of shapes you can insert and combine to create custom graphics.

Understanding the Role of the Drawing Canvas

Before you create a drawing using the Word drawing tools, you should understand how drawings work in Word. By default, when you create a drawing in Word, the drawing is placed on a fully customizable drawing canvas. The *drawing canvas* is a frame-like object (like a text box) that enables you to draw multiple shapes in one area as a group to create a complete drawing. When a drawing's shapes are contained in a drawing canvas, you can move and resize the drawing as a unit as well as position the drawing relative to surrounding text and graphics. Of course, you don't have to use the drawing canvas when you create drawings, but you will probably find it useful.

Tip Keep in mind that if you create a drawing on the drawing canvas, you can later drag it off the drawing canvas.

To display a drawing canvas, perform one of the following actions:

- Choose Insert, Picture, New Drawing.
- On the Drawing toolbar, choose an AutoShape in the AutoShapes menu.
- On the Drawing toolbar, click the Line, Arrow, Rectangle, Oval, or Text Box button.

Figure 12-2 shows a couple of objects placed on an active drawing canvas.

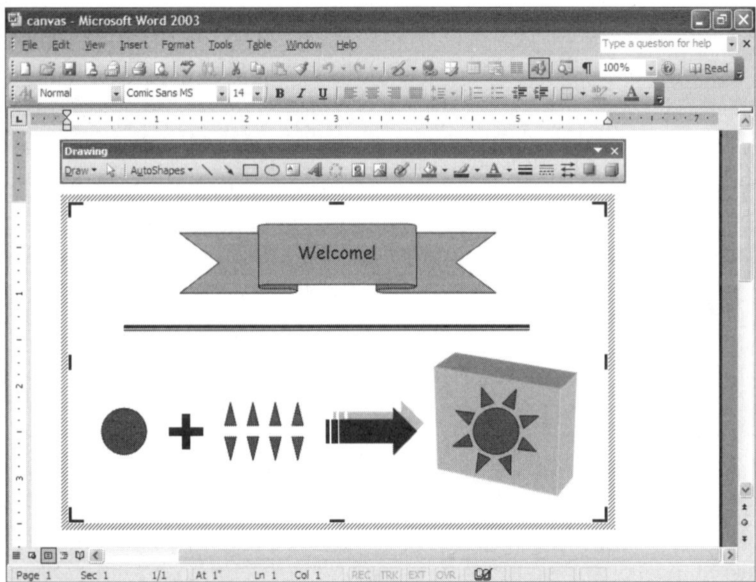

Figure 12-2. The drawing canvas helps you control drawing objects relative to other drawing objects in a drawing as well as control the overall relationship between the complete drawing and the document's contents.

Notice that the drawing canvas displays a frame-like boundary while you work. The frame outlines the drawing canvas's current working area, and it includes solid black lines and corners that you can drag to resize the canvas. By default, the drawing canvas doesn't have borders or background formatting, but you can customize the drawing canvas just as you can customize any other drawing object. For example, you can add color, apply shading, resize the frame, add 3-D effects, and so forth. To access formatting options for the drawing canvas, you can do any of the following:

- Right-click anywhere in the drawing canvas or in its border, and choose Format Drawing Canvas from the shortcut menu
- Double-click a blank area in the drawing canvas

Both of these techniques display the Format Drawing Canvas dialog box, which is discussed in more detail in "Integrating the Drawing Canvas with Document Text" on page 386.

If you prefer that the drawing canvas not appear every time you insert a drawing object, you can change this setting. To do so, follow these steps:

1. Choose Tools, Options, and click the General tab.
2. Clear the Automatically Create Drawing Canvas When Inserting AutoShapes check box, and click OK.

Keep in mind that the drawing canvas is highly customizable and helps you to easily move combined drawing objects as a unit. For the most part, you'll probably want to use the drawing canvas when you create drawings unless you're inserting a single object, such as a line or an arrow.

Tip **Delete a drawing canvas without deleting a drawing**
If you create a drawing on a drawing canvas and later decide that you don't want to use the drawing canvas, you can drag your drawing off the drawing canvas, select the drawing canvas, and then press Delete (or right-click the drawing canvas and choose Cut from the shortcut menu). This action enables you to keep your drawing while deleting the drawing canvas.

Drawing Basic Lines and Shapes

Although drawing capabilities continue to expand in Word, the old standby tools remain intact and readily available. As with earlier versions of Word, Word 2003 enables you to draw basic lines and shapes in your documents by clicking Drawing toolbar buttons. Basic lines and shapes frequently serve as the foundation for more complex drawings that you create by combining and formatting objects.

Note When you draw in Word, you must work in Print Layout, Web Layout, or Reading view. If you're in Normal or Outline view when you click a line or shape button on the Drawing toolbar, Word automatically changes your view to Print Layout.

Working with Straight Lines and Arrows

In Word, you can use the Drawing toolbar to create straight lines and arrows. To do so, follow these steps:

1. Click Line or Arrow on the Drawing toolbar. The pointer changes to a crosshair pointer whenever a drawing tool is selected.
2. Click in the drawing canvas where you want to start the line or arrow.
3. Drag to draw the line or arrow.

After you draw a line or an arrow, you can manipulate and control it in the following ways:

- **Change the appearance of a line or an arrow.** Click the line or arrow to select it; click the Line Style, Dash Style, or Arrow Style button on the Drawing toolbar; and choose a new style for the line or arrow from the menu. You can apply multiple settings to a single object. For example, you can apply a dash style and an arrow style to the same object. Figure 12-3 shows the Arrow Style menu.

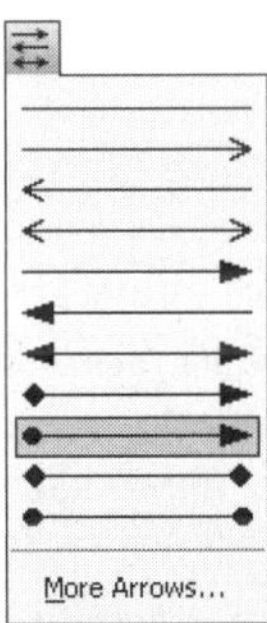

Figure 12-3. You can change the appearance of arrows and lines by choosing options from the Line Style, Dashed Style, and Arrow Style menus.

- **Constrain a line or an arrow to move in 15-degree-angle increments from the starting point.** Press Shift as you draw the line or arrow. As you move the mouse pointer, the angle of the object will change in 15-degree increments.
- **Lengthen a line or an arrow in opposite directions.** Press Ctrl as you draw the line or arrow.
- **Reposition a line or an arrow.** Click the line or arrow to select it, click the selected object (but do not click a selection handle), and then drag the object to a new location.
- **Resize a line or an arrow.** Select the line or arrow, and then drag a selection handle to lengthen, shorten, or change the angle of the object.

You can also double-click an existing line or arrow to display the Format AutoShape dialog box, shown in Figure 12-4. The Format AutoShape dialog box enables you to configure a number of shape formatting settings . The techniques for formatting objects are discussed throughout this chapter.

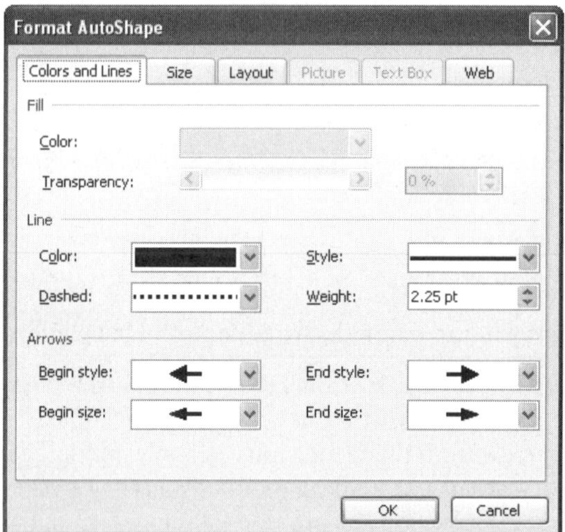

Figure 12-4. You can double-click an object in the drawing canvas to display the object's formatting dialog box.

> **Tip** **Add a vertical line between columns**
> When you want to add a line between columns, you can do so without creating a drawing canvas or using Drawing toolbar buttons. To add a vertical line between columns, click in a column, and then choose Format, Columns. In the Columns dialog box, select the Line Between check box. For more information about working with columns, see Chapter 19, "Formatting Columns and Sections for Advanced Text Control."

Creating Ovals and Rectangles

Creating ovals, circles, rectangles, and squares is similar to creating lines and arrows. To create an oval or a rectangle, click the Oval or Rectangle button on the Drawing toolbar, click in the drawing canvas, and then drag to create the object. To create a circle or square, click the Oval or Rectangle button, and then press Shift as you drag to create your shape. You can move and resize an oval or a rectangle by selecting and dragging the object to move it or by dragging the object's selection handles to resize it.

> **Tip** **Create a box around paragraph text**
> If you want to draw a box around text, use the the Border button's menu on the Formatting toolbar. For more information about adding borders, see Chapter 18, "Drawing Attention to Documents by using Borders and Shading."

Working with AutoShapes

As mentioned, AutoShapes are ready-made shapes that you insert into your documents by choosing a shape from the AutoShapes menu. AutoShapes come in a variety of forms, including basic shapes, lines, connectors, flowchart symbols, stars, banners, callouts, and other common shapes (as shown previously in Figure 12-1). After you insert an AutoShape, you can format, move, resize, and otherwise manipulate the shape in the same way you manipulate other drawing objects, as described in "Customizing Lines and Shapes," on page 365, and in "Controlling Objects in Drawings," on page 379.

Tip **Display a menu as a floating toolbar**
If you find that you use a particular AutoShape menu repeatedly, you can drag the menu by its top bar to create a floating toolbar. When you've finished with the floating toolbar, simply close it; you'll be able to display the menu from its normal position in the AutoShapes toolbar.

Format a Series of Objects Automatically

At times, you might want to create a series of AutoShapes that use the same formatting. For example, maybe you're creating coupons and you want to draw four yellow rectangles with two 1/4-inch-thick dashed line borders. Instead of formatting each rectangle separately, you can format the first rectangle, and then copy the settings before you create the next three rectangles.

You can easily create a default drawing style that will be implemented automatically when you create new shapes. To do this, right-click the AutoShape that contains the formatting you want to use to create new objects, and then choose Set AutoShape Defaults from the shortcut menu. The next objects you draw (regardless of their shapes) will automatically be formatted with the settings you applied to the object you used to set the defaults.

Drawing Nonstandard Lines and Freeform Shapes

The first menu in the AutoShapes menu is Lines. The Lines menu enables you to draw lines that are more complex than the straight lines and arrows you can create using the Line and Arrow buttons on the Drawing toolbar. To use one of these more complex lines, choose an AutoShape from the Lines menu, and then click and drag on the drawing canvas to create your line, shape, or arrow. The Lines menu provides the following tools:

- **Line** Draws a straight line, similar to using the Line button on the Drawing toolbar.
- **Arrow** Draws a standard arrow, similar to using the Arrow button on the Drawing toolbar.
- **Double Arrow** Draws an arrow with arrowheads at both ends of the line.
- **Curve** Draws a smooth-turning line or shape that curves at each point you click in the drawing canvas. To turn off the Curve tool, double-click or press Esc.

- **Freeform** Draws objects by using straight lines and hand-drawn lines. To create straight lines, click two points; to create curvy lines, hold down the mouse button as you draw. To delete the most recent freeform element you've drawn while you're creating your object, press Backspace or Delete; to turn off the Freeform tool, double-click or press Esc; or to delete the entire freeform object after you create it, press Ctrl+Z or choose Edit, Undo Insert Freeform. To change the shape of a freeform object, click Draw on the Drawing toolbar, choose Edit Points, and then drag the edit handles to modify the object; to change the dimensions of the freeform object, click the object and then drag the selection handles.
- **Scribble** Draws a line wherever you click and drag. To turn off the Scribble tool, release the mouse button, and the tool is automatically deactivated.

> **Tip** Freeform drawings, curved lines, and scribble lines can be formatted with fill effects, color, and line style options the same way other drawing objects are formatted, as described throughout this chapter.

Adding Basic Shapes and Block Arrows

As mentioned, the AutoShapes menu provides a number of basic shapes and arrows that you can insert into your document. Figure 12-5 shows the Block Arrows and Basic Shapes menus as floating toolbars. After you insert a shape or an arrow, you can drag the object to reposition it, drag selection handles to resize or reshape it, and format the object's line and fill settings, as described in "Customizing Lines and Shapes," on page 365, and "Controlling Objects in Drawings," on page 379.

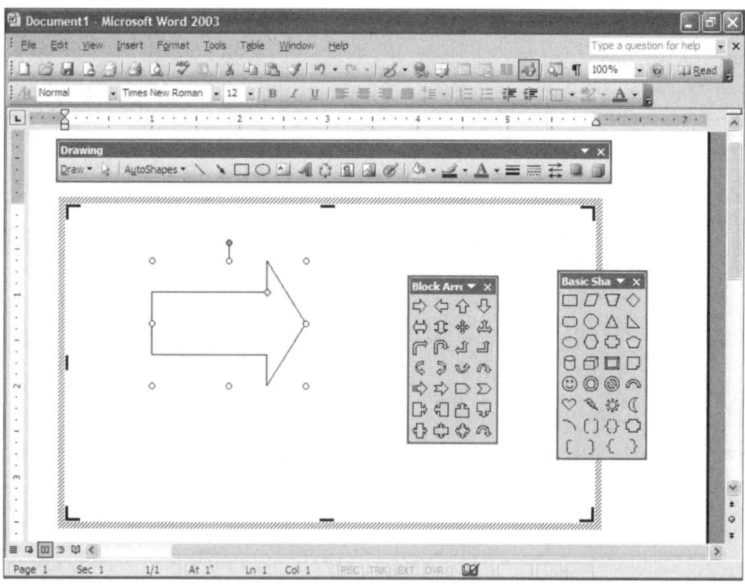

Figure 12-5. The Block Arrows and Basic Shapes menus—shown here as floating toolbars—provide a variety of shapes that you can insert into your documents and customize.

Changing a Shape without Losing Formatting

You can always replace an existing AutoShape or standard shape (such as a rectangle or an oval) with a different shape without losing your format settings. To do so, follow these steps:

1. Select the AutoShape, click Draw on the Drawing toolbar, and choose Change AutoShape. The Change AutoShape menu appears, which in turn includes menus for Basic Shapes, Block Arrows, Flowchart, Stars And Banners, and Callouts.
2. Choose a shape from any of the Change AutoShape menus to replace the existing shape.

Keep in mind that you can replace only standard shapes. For example, you can replace a rectangle or an AutoShape with another AutoShape, but you can't replace a line or a freeform shape with an AutoShape.

Using Connectors

Connectors enable you to use a line or an arrow to connect shapes and keep them connected. A connector joins two shapes at specified points (called *connection sites*) on the shapes. If you move or resize shapes joined by a connector, the connector adjusts and continues to connect the two objects at the connection sites using the predetermined line shape. Connectors can be lines or arrows, as shown in Figure 12-6.

Figure 12-6. A connector creates a line or an arrow between shapes and remains connected even when the shapes are moved, reshaped, or resized.

To join objects using a connector, follow these steps:

1. On the Drawing toolbar, click AutoShapes, choose Connectors from the menu, and then click the type of connector you want to create.
2. Hover the pointer over the first shape you want to attach to the connector. When you choose a connector and position the pointer over a shape, connection sites appear as blue circles on the shape.
3. Click near a blue connection site on the first object, and hover the pointer over the object you want to connect to. (Blue connection sites will appear on the second shape when you position the pointer over the shape.) Then click on or near a connection site on the second object.

Figure 12-7 illustrates the process of creating a connector and shows how the objects remain connected even after they have been moved and resized.

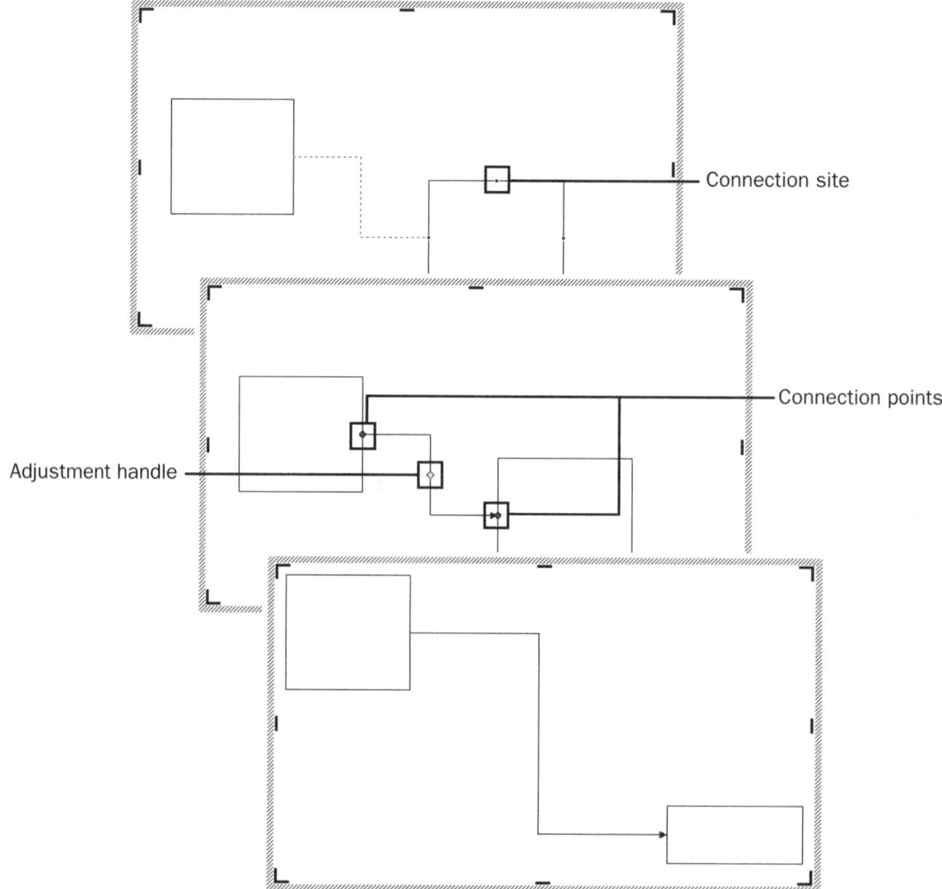

Figure 12-7. A connector is a line between objects that remains connected even if the connected objects are moved or resized.

After you connect two objects, you can move, reshape, and resize the objects without losing the connection. To modify a connector, you can drag an endpoint (indicated by red circles) to a new connection site, or you can right-click the connector to display a shortcut menu. The shortcut menu enables you to sever the connection (by choosing Cut), change the connector's style (by choosing the straight, elbow, or curved option), or reroute the connector (by choosing Reroute Connectors). You can also automatically reroute connectors by clicking Draw on the Drawing toolbar, and choosing Reroute Connectors.

Note Some connectors have a yellow diamond-shaped adjustment handle. You can drag this handle to change the shape of the connector line without detaching the line from the connection sites.

Creating Flowcharts

Another group of AutoShapes available in Word consists of flowchart shapes. You can draw a flowchart fairly easily in Word by using the flowchart AutoShapes and connector lines. To use the flowchart objects, click AutoShapes on the Drawing toolbar, and choose Flowchart to open the Flowchart menu and view the flowchart AutoShapes. The Flowchart floating toolbar, shown in Figure 12-8, contains 28 flowchart AutoShapes that you can use to create standard flowcharts.

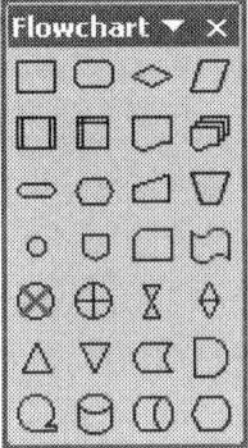

Figure 12-8. Word includes flowchart AutoShapes that you can combine with connectors to create flowcharts.

Flowcharts are frequently used to illustrate processes and relationships in an abbreviated form. For example, you might use a flowchart to illustrate a decision-making process (in which, if you choose Yes, you follow one path, and if you choose No, you follow another), or you might use a flowchart to illustrate relationships among pages on a small Web site. To create a flowchart, you combine a number of drawing tasks, as summarized here:

1. Using the flowchart AutoShapes, draw the shapes you need for your flowchart .
2. Arrange the shapes by dragging them on the drawing canvas, and then connect the shapes using connectors. Connectors work better than standard lines and arrows when you're creating flowcharts because you might have to move or resize the flowchart shapes.
3. Right-click each flowchart shape, choose Add Text from the shortcut menu, and then type the appropriate text.

After you create a flowchart, you can color and format lines and shapes in the flowchart, as described in "Customizing Lines and Shapes," on page 365.

Creating and Customizing Stars and Banners

When you want to create a visual splash on a flyer, an advertisement or marketing piece, a newsletter, or another eye-catching publication, you can use objects from the Stars And Banners AutoShapes menu. Inserting a star or banner is similar to inserting other AutoShapes, as described in the following steps:

1. Click AutoShapes on the Drawing toolbar, and choose Stars And Banners from the menu.
2. Choose a star or banner, and then click and drag in the drawing canvas to create the object.

An example of an inserted star and banner is shown in Figure 12-9.

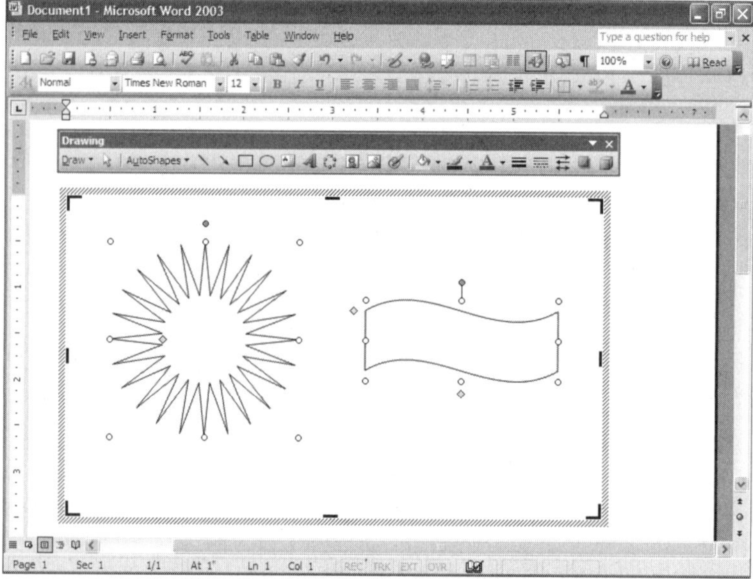

Figure 12-9. You can modify the appearance of stars and banners by using the rotation, adjustment, and sizing handles.

As with most AutoShapes, stars and banners are customizable, as described in "Customizing Lines and Shapes" on page 365, and "Controlling Objects in Drawings," on page 379. For example, you can customize stars and banners by performing any of the following actions:

- Adding text
- Applying color or a fill effect
- Modifying the outline style
- Rotating the object
- Adjusting the shape of the star or banner
- Resizing the star or banner

Keep in mind that the purpose of using star and banner objects in documents is to draw attention to particular bits of information or sections of your documents. If you overuse these types of objects, you'll tend to drive readers away instead of attract them.

Drawing Callouts

Sometimes you might want to associate certain pieces of information with a particular spot on a graphic, or you might want to annotate areas of a document. You can easily do so by using *callouts*. A callout object combines a text box with an arrow, a line, or a pointer. Word provides 20 types of callout AutoShapes, which you can find on the Callouts floating toolbar, shown in Figure 12-10.

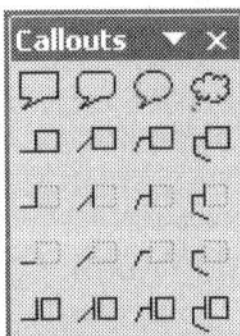

Figure 12-10. Word provides a variety of callout objects that you can use to annotate documents, identify areas in graphics, or present other types of information.

To use a callout, follow these steps:

1. Click AutoShapes, choose Callouts, and then choose a callout style from the Callouts menu.
2. Click the location in the drawing canvas where you want to insert the callout, and drag to create the object.
3. After you insert a callout, you can click the callout's leader line and drag the yellow diamond-shaped adjustment handle to reposition the leader; drag the green rotation handle to rotate the callout; or drag selection handles to resize the callout.
4. Click in the callout's text area, and type the relevant information.

As with other AutoShapes, you can format callouts using standard formatting techniques, such as applying colors, formatting text, adding fill effects, resizing, and moving.

Accessing More AutoShapes in the Clip Art Task Pane

If you find that you need an object that is not available in the AutoShapes menus, you can access additional shapes by choosing More AutoShapes, located at the bottom of the AutoShapes menu. When you click this option, Word opens the Clip Art task pane, shown in Figure 12-11. If you don't see the additional shapes, you might first need to click Organize Clips.

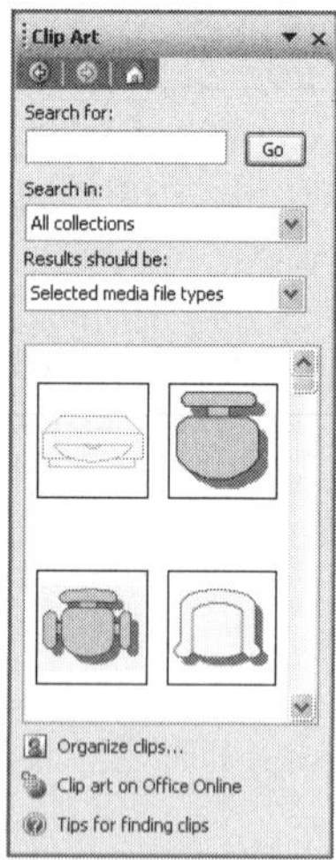

Figure 12-11. When you choose the More AutoShapes option, you gain quick access to additional drawing objects that are easy to customize.

The additional AutoShapes include the following:

- Room layout objects, such as outlines of desks, chairs, wastebaskets, and door swing marks
- Computers and computer-related objects, such as mainframes, modems, firewalls, and folders
- Commonly used objects, such as musical notes, light bulbs, and padlocks
- Web site-related objects, such as objects that represent a home page, a film clip, a feedback form, and an e-mail icon

You insert items associated with the More AutoShapes category in the same way you insert other clip art items—simply by clicking the object you want to insert. The main difference between the More AutoShapes objects and standard clip art is that you can more easily customize and format the AutoShapes as drawing objects than you can most clip art.

Tip **Integrating clip art into drawings**

In addition to the clip art items associated with the More AutoShapes option, you can add any other clip art item to a drawing. You can also right-click a clip art item and choose Edit Picture from the shortcut menu to customize the clip art as a drawing object. If you've inserted a clip art item that's a picture and not a drawing object, Word displays a message box when you click Edit Picture that asks whether you want to convert the picture to a drawing object. Click Yes to make the conversion.

Customizing Lines and Shapes

Most likely, you'll want your drawings to be displayed in color rather than in black, white, and shades of gray. In Word, you can colorize your lines and fill objects using standard and custom colors, including a full range of gray shades. You can also customize your shapes by using fill effects to insert multicolor gradient blends, textures, and pictures.

> **Note** When you use colors, keep in mind how your document will be displayed and printed. If your document will always be displayed in electronic form or printed on high-quality paper with four colors, you won't have to worry too much about color reproduction. On the other hand, if your document will be printed on a black-and-white printer (even if it's also viewed online) or on colored paper, you'll want to make sure that the colors you use in your drawings create adequate contrast; otherwise, your drawings might print as indiscernible blobs.

Specifying Lines and Fill Colors

As a rule, drawing objects created in Word can contain color in two main areas: borders (called *lines*) and interior spaces (called *fills*). The easiest way to color lines and fills is to use the Drawing toolbar, as follows:

- **Color a line** Select an object, click the Line Color arrow on the Drawing toolbar, and then choose a color in the color palette, shown in Figure 12-12.

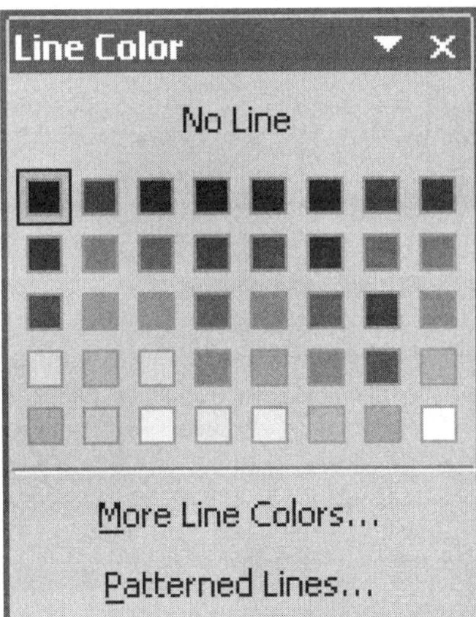

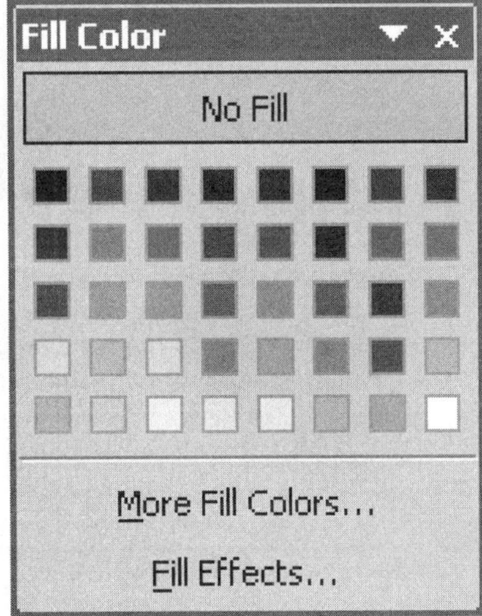

Figure 12-12. To color a line or fill, simply click a color in the Line Color or Fill Color menu or floating toolbar. The row of colors below the default color palette contains the last eight custom colors you've used for either lines or fills.

- **Color a fill** Select an object, click the Fill Color arrow, and then choose a color in the color palette. The Fill Color menu is similar to the Line Color menu.

The Line Color and Fill Color menus also contain No Line or No Fill options. You can use these options to display an object without any lines (not even black) or with no fill color (which means that the background color will show through the object's outlined form).

Using Custom Colors and Transparent Colors

You can apply custom colors and transparent colors to objects by choosing More Fill Colors from the Fill Color menu or More Line Colors from the Line Color menu. Either option displays the Colors dialog box, shown in Figure 12-13.

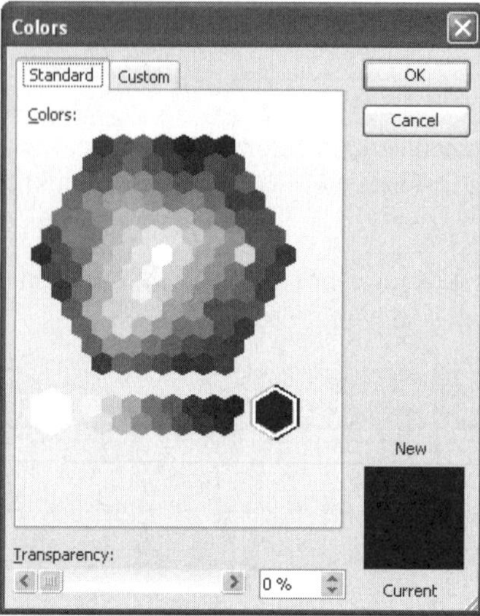

Figure 12-13. Choose more colors in the Colors dialog box.

Click a color in the Standard tab to use it and add the color to your custom color area in the color palette. If you want to choose from 16 million predefined colors, click the Custom tab, shown in Figure 12-14.

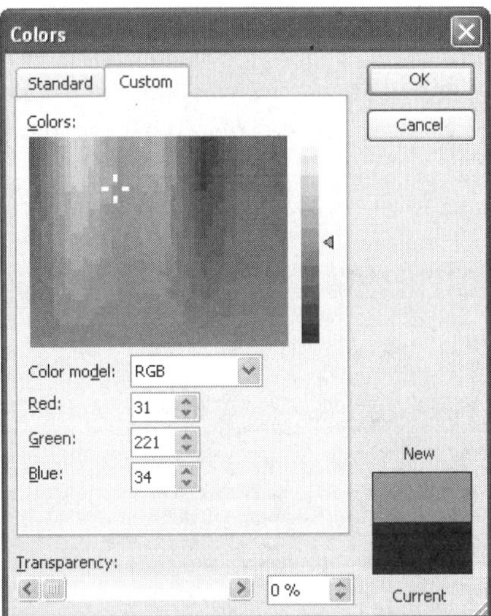

Figure 12-14. You can choose from 16 million predefined colors in the Custom tab.

Choose a color using the crosshair and slider bar. The Custom tab also includes Red, Green, and Blue value boxes that reflect the color values indicated by the crosshair and slider bar. The Red, Green, and Blue value boxes specify exact RGB color values for graphics. If you know a color's RGB values, you can enter them in the appropriate boxes, or you can click the up and down arrows to scroll through values. In addition to using the RGB Color Model option, you can click the Color Model arrow to access HSL (hue, saturation, luminance), CMYK (cyan, magenta, yellow, black), and PANTONE color models. HSL is generally used to control colors for devices that transmit light, such as video monitors, and CMYK and PANTONE color models are used for printed publications.

Both the Standard and Custom tabs include a Transparency option. This option helps you designate a particular color to serve as a transparent or semitransparent color. A transparent color lets a page's background color or texture show through. When you make a color transparent or semitransparent and you place your picture on a page that has a background color or texture, the background color or texture shows through the picture wherever the transparent color is applied. For example, you have a drawing of a mouse and you want to show the mouse on your Web page without the rectangular picture background. You could color all areas in the picture—except the mouse—pink. Then you could choose pink in the Standard or Custom tab and set the Transparency option to 100%. After you specify that pink is transparent, all pink areas within your picture will allow the page's background color or texture to show through in certain applications (such as Web browsers and HTML editors).

Transparency is frequently used in Web graphics to create images that seem to be cut out (instead of rectangular). For example, in the Web page graphic shown in Figure 12-15, the picture of the News Guy on the left doesn't use transparency, whereas the picture on the right has Orange set to 100% transparency. (Notice that the colored background shows through in the image on the right but that the background is solid orange in the image on the left. To see this example online and in color, visit *www.creationguide.com/newsguy*.)

Figure 12-15. The picture on the left does not use transparency.

Adding Fill Effects and Patterns

In addition to coloring lines and fills, you can apply fill effects and patterns to further customize drawing objects. To add a fill effect to an object, select the object, click the Fill Color arrow on the Drawing toolbar, and then choose Fill Effects from the Fill Color menu to display the Fill Effects dialog box. To add a pattern to a line, select the line, click the Line Color arrow on the Drawing toolbar, and then choose Patterned Lines from the Line Color menu to display the Patterned Lines dialog box. The available effects are discussed next.

Tip **Copying an object's formatting**

After you format an object—including adding color and fill effects—you can copy the object's formatting to other objects. To do so, select the formatted object, click Format Painter on the Standard toolbar, and then click the object that you want to have the same formatting.

If you want to apply the formatting to multiple objects, select the formatted object, double-click Format Painter on the Standard toolbar, and then click the objects you want to format. You then press Esc or click Format Painter to turn off the feature.

Adding Color Gradients to Shapes

The Gradient tab in the Fill Effects dialog box is shown in Figure 12-16. This tab enables you to custom-blend color gradients for selected objects. You can create a gradient from one or two colors, or you can choose from among a number of preset gradients, such as Daybreak, Horizon, and Chrome. In addition, you can specify the direction of your gradient in the Shading Styles section in the Gradient tab.

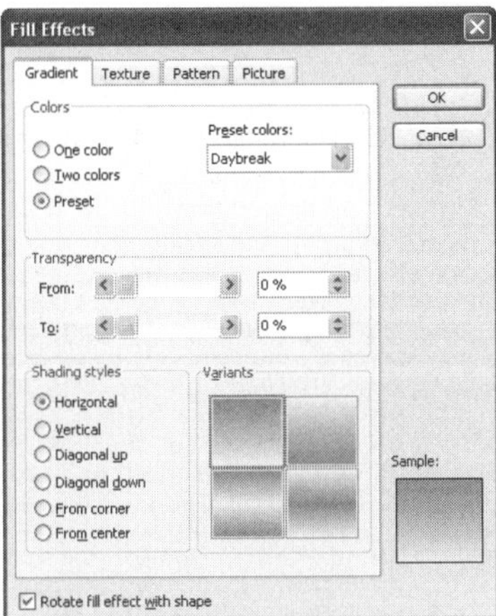

Figure 12-16. The Gradient tab, shown here with the Preset option selected, enables you to blend colors to create shading effects in your objects.

To create a gradient, follow these steps:

1. Double-click the object you want to format with a color gradient. The Format AutoShape dialog box appears.
2. Click the Colors And Lines tab, and, in the Fill section, click the Color arrow and choose Fill Effects. The Fill Effects dialog box appears.

> **Tip** You can also display the Gradient tab in the Fill Effects dialog box by selecting the object you want to format, clicking the Fill button's arrow on the Drawing toolbar, and then clicking Fill Effects.

3. In the Colors section in the Gradient tab, click the Two Colors option and choose colors in the Color 1 and Color 2 lists to create a custom gradient, or click Preset to select from a group of built-in gradient schemes in the Preset Colors list.
4. Choose a Shading Styles option, and click a Variants option. Notice that the Sample window displays a preview of your gradient options; you can experiment with a few shading styles and variants until you find the effect you're after.
5. When you're satisfied with your color gradient settings, click OK to close the Fill Effects dialog box, and then click OK to apply the gradient to the selected object. If you don't like the results, simply change your settings in the Gradient tab in the Fill Effects dialog box.

Note The Fill Effects dialog box contains two options that appear in each of the tabs in the Fill Effects dialog box: the Sample window, which lets you preview each fill effect as you select or create it, and the Rotate Fill Effect With Shape check box, which enables you to control whether the fill effect should be repositioned whenever you rotate or flip an object. (This option is unavailable when you're working with the Patterns tab.)

Applying Textures to Shapes

The Texture tab in the Fill Effects dialog box, shown in Figure 12-17, lets you add textures to drawing objects. By default, Word includes 24 textures that you can use to customize objects. You can import your own textures.

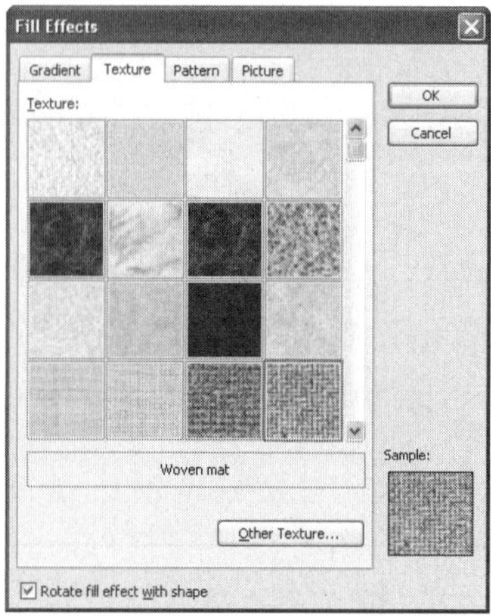

Figure 12-17. The Texture tab provides textures that you can apply to selected objects.

To apply a texture to a shape, follow these simple steps:

1. Select the drawing object you want to fill with a texture.
2. Click the Fill Color arrow on the Drawing toolbar, choose Fill Effects from the menu, and then click the Texture tab in the Fill Effects dialog box.
3. In the Texture tab, click the texture you want to use, or click Other Texture to display the Select Texture dialog box, navigate to your custom texture file and select it, and then click Insert.
4. Click OK in the Fill Effects dialog box to complete the procedure.

If you find that you don't like a texture's appearance, simply click Undo on the Formatting toolbar (or press Ctrl+Z), or apply a new texture to the object using the same procedure.

Inside Out

Coloring textures

Because textures are images that you insert into an object's background, you can't apply a color and a texture to an object at the same time. If you apply a texture to an object that contains a color fill, the texture replaces the color. Likewise, if you apply color to an object that contains a texture, the color replaces the texture. A workaround might be to colorize a texture image in a painting program or to use a pattern, as described in the next section.

Creating Patterns for Shapes and Lines

Patterns can be used to create fill and line effects that are not as complex as textures and yet not as flat as solid color fills. Word offers 48 patterns that you can apply to objects and lines. In addition to adding a pattern to an object, you can also specify foreground and background colors to be used by the pattern. The processes of adding patterns to fills and lines are similar, as you can see here:

- **Add a pattern to a fill** Select an object, click the Fill Color arrow on the Drawing toolbar, choose Fill Effects from the menu, click the Pattern tab, select a pattern, specify foreground and background colors, and then click OK.
- **Add a pattern to a line** Select an object, click the Line Color arrow on the Drawing toolbar, choose Patterned Lines from the menu, select a pattern, specify foreground and background colors, and then click OK.

Figure 12-18 shows the Pattern tab, which is available for both lines and fills.

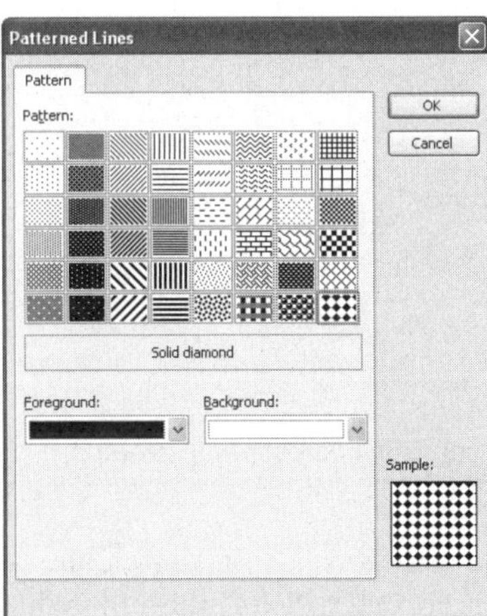

Figure 12-18. The Pattern tab enables you to apply patterns with custom colors to selected objects.

You can use custom colors to create patterns, and you can preview your patterns in the Sample window before you apply the patterns to your objects.

Tip Change pattern colors

If you add a pattern to a shape that already has a fill color, Word uses the existing color for the foreground (the pattern) by default. Further, if you change an object's color after applying a pattern by using standard fill color tools (the Fill button on the Formatting toolbar or the Color list in the Colors And Lines tab in the Format AutoShape dialog box), Word will fill the object with a solid color and drop the pattern settings. To avoid losing pattern settings, you should change the colors of an object that contains a pattern by using the Pattern tab in the Fill Effects dialog box and configuring the Foreground and Background lists.

Inserting Pictures into Shapes

Like adding a background graphic to your objects, inserting a picture can serve as a fill effect. To use a picture as a fill, follow these steps:

1. Select the object, click the Fill Color arrow on the Drawing toolbar, and choose Fill Effects from the menu.
2. In the Fill Effects dialog box, click the Picture tab, shown in Figure 12-19, and then click the Select Picture button to display the Select Picture dialog box.

Figure 12-19. The Picture tab enables you to fill objects with picture backgrounds.

3. In the Select Picture dialog box, navigate to the location of your picture, and then double-click the picture. The picture appears in the Picture tab and in the Picture and Sample areas.
4. Click OK to display the picture as the selected object's fill.

Figure 12-20 shows an object formatted with a picture fill.

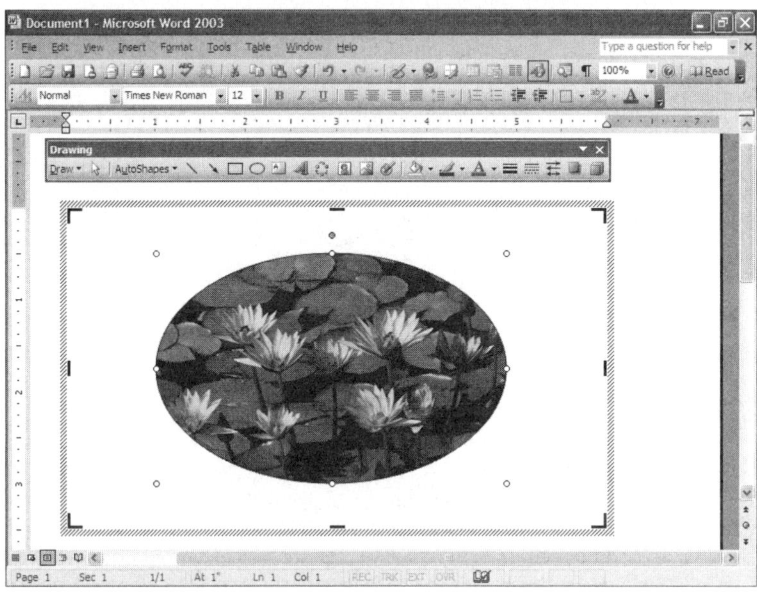

Figure 12-20. You can use graphics images to create a custom fill.

Formatting Shadows and 3-D Effects

In addition to adding textures and colors, you can apply shadow and three-dimensional (3-D) effects to lines, arrows, shapes, AutoShapes, backgrounds, and freeform shapes. Generally, you'll want to use shadow and 3-D effects when you want to create a sense of depth in your drawing. Both the shadow and the 3-D effects are accessible from the Drawing toolbar.

Note You can apply either a shadow or a 3-D effect to an object—but you can't apply both. This means that if you apply a 3-D effect to a drawing object that has a shadow, the shadow will disappear. Likewise, if you add a shadow effect to a 3-D object, the 3-D formatting will be removed.

Adding and Controlling Shadows

You can instantly add depth to drawing objects in Word by adding a shadow to the edge of an object. The Shadow Style effects in Word enable you to add various shadow styles to objects, adjust shadow position, and change shadow color. Figure 12-21 shows a few flowchart objects formatted using the Shadow Style effects.

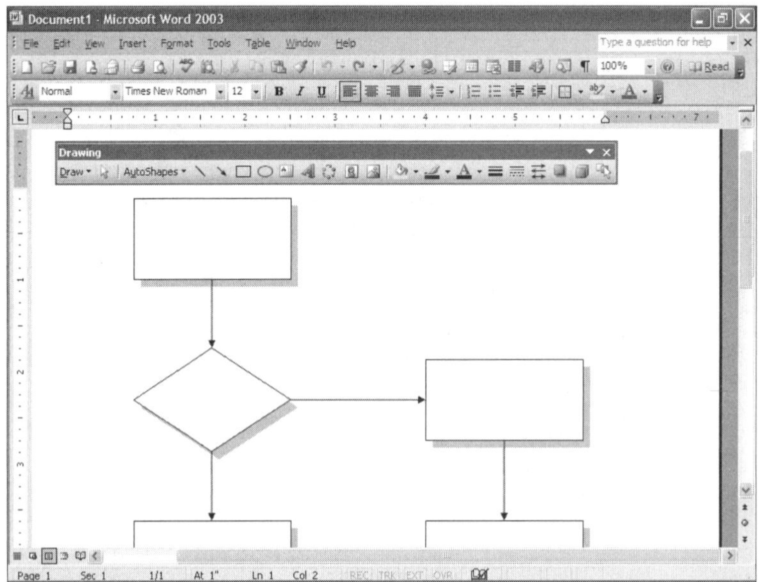

Figure 12-21. You can add shadows to basic objects, as shown in this flowchart structure.

Creating Shadows

You can add a 50 percent gray shadow to any selected object by using a preset shadow style in Word. To do so, you use the Shadow Style menu on the Drawing toolbar, shown in Figure 12-22.

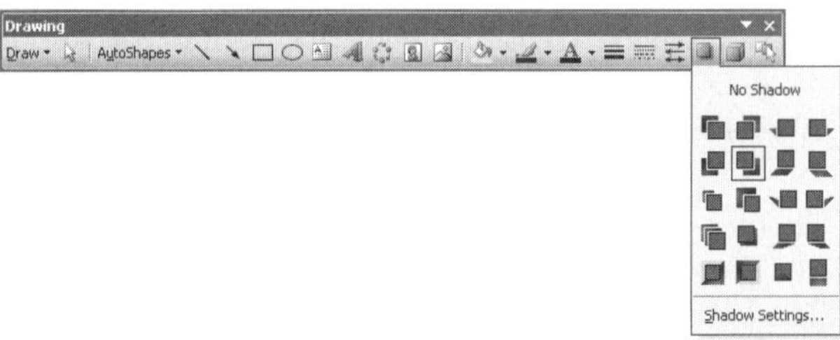

Figure 12-22. Word provides 20 preset styles in the Shadow Style menu.

To add a preset shadow style to an object, select the object you want to add a shadow to, click Shadow Style on the Drawing toolbar, and choose a shadow style from the Shadow Style menu. To remove a shadow, select the object, and click No Shadow in the Shadow Style menu.

Changing the Position of Shadows

After you apply a shadow, you can manually adjust the shadow's position relative to the object. To do so, follow these steps:

1. Select the object that has the shadow you want to adjust.

2 Click the Shadow Style button on the Drawing toolbar, and choose Shadow Settings from the menu. The Shadow Settings toolbar appears.

 The buttons on the Shadow Settings toolbar are described in Table 12-2.

3 Click the appropriate buttons to reposition the shadow. Each time you click a nudge button, the shadow moves 1 point in the specified direction.

Table 12-2. Shadow Settings Toolbar Buttons

Button	Name	Description
	Shadow On/Off	Adds or removes an object's shadow
	Nudge Shadow Up	Moves an object's shadow up by 1 point
	Nudge Shadow Down	Moves an object's shadow down by 1 point
	Nudge Shadow Left	Moves an object's shadow left by 1 point
	Nudge Shadow Right	Moves an object's shadow right by 1 point
	Shadow Color	Displays a color palette that you can use to color a shadow (the default color is 50 percent gray)

Tip To nudge a shadow 6 points instead of 1 point, press Shift while you click the appropriate nudge button on the Shadow Settings toolbar.

Coloring Shadows

In addition to adjusting a shadow's position, you can also color a shadow. To do so, follow these steps:

1 Select the drawing object that contains the shadow you want to change.

2 Click the Shadow button on the Drawing toolbar, and choose Shadow Settings from the menu. The Shadow Settings toolbar appears.

3 On the Shadow Settings toolbar, click the Shadow Color arrow, and choose the color you want to apply to the shadow from the menu.

If you don't see the color you want in the Shadow Color menu, click More Shadow Colors to access the Standard and Custom tabs in the Colors dialog box (as discussed in "Specifying Line and Fill Colors," on page 365). The Shadow Color menu also includes a Semitransparent Shadow option. This option is selected by default; it creates a lighter shadow that you can see text through. Clear the Semitransparent Shadow selection if you want to make your shadow darker and to ensure that text is not visible through the shadow.

Inside Out

Redrawing borders previously removed by embossed or engraved shadows

If you apply an embossed or engraved shadow to an object (Shadow Style 17 or Shadow Style 18 in the Shadow Style menu), Word hides the object's borders by default. If you later apply a different shadow effect to the object, you might have to redraw the object's borders (especially if the object is the same color as the background). To do so, select the object, and choose a line color from the Line Color menu on the Drawing toolbar.

Applying and Customizing 3-D Effects

By using 3-D effects, you can format and customize simple 3-D objects. To add a 3-D effect to an object, Word adjusts the two-dimensional object by expanding (or extruding) the object's edges and rotating the object to appear at an angle. In Word, you can control the depth of a 3-D object's extrusion as well as the object's angle. In addition, you can specify how light and shadow reflect off the shape, and you can specify how the object's surface should be formatted by choosing the Wire Frame, Matte, Plastic, or Metal option.

Adding 3-D Effects

To create a 3-D effect, you use the 3-D Style menu, shown in Figure 12-23.

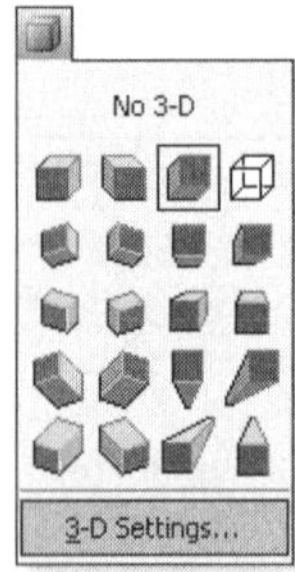

Figure 12-23. Word provides 20 preset styles in the 3-D Style menu.

To format a 3-D object, follow these steps:

1. Select the object you want to modify.
2. On the Drawing toolbar, click the 3-D Style button, and then click a 3-D setting in the 3-D Style menu.

After you create a 3-D object, you can remove a 3-D effect by choosing No 3-D from the 3-D Style menu. You can also change which 3-D setting is applied by selecting the 3-D object and choosing a different setting from the 3-D Style menu.

Tip To add the same 3-D effect to several objects at one time (including applying the same lighting effects and other settings), select or group the objects before you apply the 3-D settings.

Controlling Light, Color, Angle, and Other Settings

After you apply a 3-D style to an object, you can change the 3-D style's appearance, including its color, rotation, depth, lighting, and surface texture. To modify an object's 3-D effects, you select the object, click 3-D on the Drawing toolbar, and then click 3-D Settings in the 3-D Style menu to display the 3-D Settings toolbar. Table 12-3 describes the buttons available on the 3-D Settings toolbar.

Table 12-3. 3-D Settings Toolbar Buttons

Button	Name	Description
	3-D On/Off	Adds or removes a 3-D effect.
	Tilt Down	Tilts the object down by 5 degrees. Press Shift while clicking to move the object in 45-degree increments. Press Ctrl while clicking to move the object in 1-degree increments.
	Tilt Up	Tilts the object up by 5 degrees. Press Shift while clicking to move the object in 45-degree increments. Press Ctrl while clicking to move the object in 1-degree increments.
	Tilt Left	Tilts the object 5 degrees to the left. Press Shift while clicking to move the object in 45-degree increments. Press Ctrl while clicking to move the object in 1-degree increments.
	Tilt Right	Tilts the object 5 degrees to the right. Press Shift while clicking to move the object in 45-degree increments. Press Ctrl while clicking to move the object in 1-degree increments.
	Depth	Displays a menu that enables you to change the size of the object's extrusion.
	Direction	Displays a menu that enables you to control the direction of the object's extrusion. You can choose from nine preset values as well as specify a diminishing perspective (Perspective) or a flat-plane perspective (Parallel).
	Lighting	Displays a menu that enables you to choose a light direction. You can choose from nine preset values as well as Bright, Normal, or Dim.
	Surface	Displays a menu containing four surface options you can assign to the selected object: Wire Frame, Matte, Plastic, and Metal.
	3-D Color	Displays a color palette that you can use to control the color of the 3-D object's extrusion.

To use any of the 3-D Settings toolbar buttons, select the 3-D object and then click the appropriate toolbar button. Like the procedure for applying color settings to other objects, the 3-D Color menu enables you to create custom colors (in this case, for a 3-D object's extrusion) by choosing More 3-D Colors to display the Colors dialog box. (The Colors dialog box was shown previously in Figures 12-13 and 12-14.)

Adding Text to Drawings

A picture may be worth a thousand words, but you'll often find that you want to add text to your drawings. You can add text as a separate element by drawing a text box, or you can enter text directly into an existing object. For example, you might want to insert text into a star shape or a banner. To add text to drawings, use one of the following methods:

- **Add text box properties to an existing shape.** To enter text directly in an object, right-click the object, and choose Add Text from the shortcut menu. The shape will become a text box, with an insertion point inside. You simply type and format the text you want to appear in the shape.
- **Create a text box.** To create a freestanding text box, click Text Box on the Drawing toolbar and draw a text box in the drawing canvas. After you draw a text box, you simply type text in the box. Text boxes can be treated as shapes, which means that they can be resized and formatted in many of the same ways shapes are formatted, including modifying fills, borders, shadow, and 3-D effects.

In addition to entering text in text boxes and objects, you can add WordArt to your drawings as described in "Working with WordArt" on page 388.

Inside Out

Adding text to freehand drawings

When you create a freehand drawing, you can't right-click the drawing and choose Add Text. To work around this limitation, you can click Text Box on the Drawing toolbar, and draw a text box on top of your freehand drawing. Then type and format text in the text box. If you want to ensure that the text and drawing aren't separated or layered incorrectly in the future, choose the shape and the text box (by pressing Shift as you click the objects), and then click Draw on the Drawing toolbar and choose Group from the menu to group the two objects together.

> **Tip** **Create Web page buttons**
> By combining basic objects and text boxes, you can create custom buttons for Web pages. To make these custom buttons active hyperlinks, you simply add hyperlink properties to your drawing objects, as described in Chapter 26, "Creating Professional Web Sites."

Controlling Objects in Drawings

When you create a drawing using objects, you'll find that you frequently need to adjust existing objects in a number of ways. Because drawn pictures are made of lines and shapes, you can reshape, group and ungroup, reorder, and change the color of one or all parts of a picture. This part of the chapter describes the numerous ways you can work with existing objects when you create drawings in Word.

Modifying Objects

Rarely will you instantly create a shape in the exact position and size required by your drawing. Therefore, you need to become proficient at resizing, reshaping, rotating, and flipping objects before you can successfully create drawings in Word.

Resizing Objects

To resize an object, select the object, and then drag the object's selection handles. You can resize a single shape, a group of selected shapes, or the entire drawing canvas. When you resize drawing objects, Word redraws the lines and shapes to meet the newly designated dimensions.

Reshaping Objects

Many AutoShapes display a yellow diamond-shaped adjustment handle when you select them. This adjustment handle enables you to change the most prominent feature of a shape. For example, you can change the length and width of a star's points by dragging the star's adjustment handle. Figure 12-24 shows a star shape that has been modified using this technique.

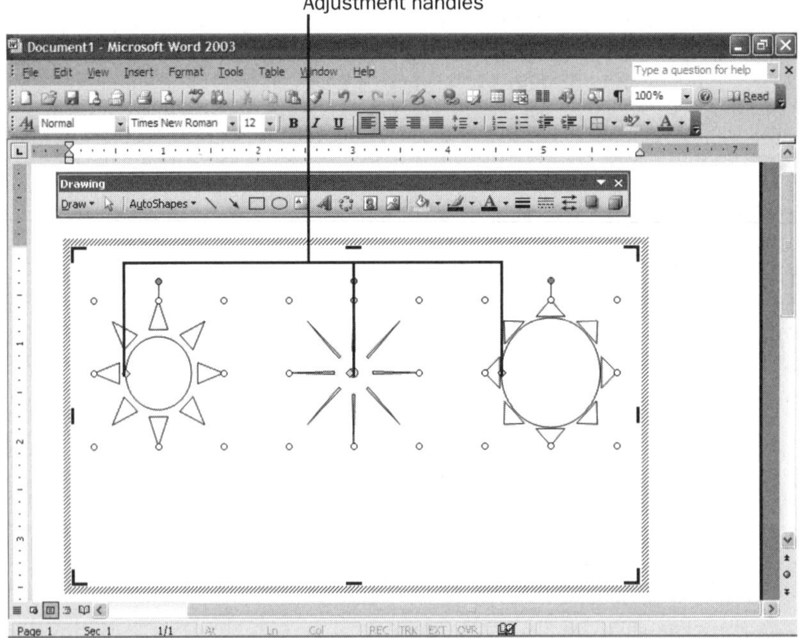

Figure 12-24. These shapes were created from the same AutoShape (Sun in the Basic Shapes menu); each has been modified by dragging its yellow diamond-shaped adjustment handle.

Rotating Objects

In addition to resizing and reshaping objects, you can rotate them. To do so, use either of the following methods:

- Drag the green round rotation handle located near the top of the object, and then click outside the object to set the rotation position.
- On the Drawing toolbar, click Draw, choose Rotate Or Flip from the menu, and then choose Free Rotate, Rotate Left, or Rotate Right. When you choose Rotate Left or Rotate Right, you rotate the object by 90 degrees. When you choose Free Rotate, you can rotate the object to any angle by using the rotation handle that appears.

Remember, if your object contains a fill effect and you want the fill to rotate with the object, you must make sure that the Rotate Fill Effect With Shape check box is selected in the Fill Effects dialog box.

Tip To restrict the rotation of objects to 15-degree angles, press Shift while you drag the rotation handle.

Flipping Objects

Flipping an object literally means to flip an object over. (It might help to visualize flipping pancakes when using this feature.) You can flip an object horizontally or vertically. To flip an object, select the object, click Draw on the Drawing toolbar, choose Rotate Or Flip from the menu, and then choose Flip Horizontal or Flip Vertical. Figure 12-25 shows the results of flipping an object horizontally and vertically.

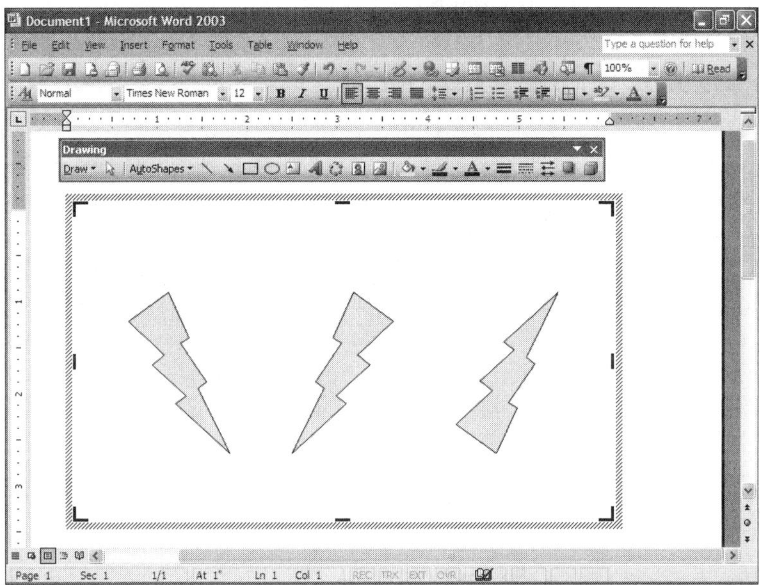

Figure 12-25. To create this figure, three identical lightning bolts were drawn and then the lightning bolt in the center was flipped horizontally while the lightning bolt on the right was flipped vertically.

> **Tip** You can flip AutoShapes, pictures, clip art, and WordArt objects.

Selecting Multiple Drawing Elements at One Time

Sometimes you might want to select multiple objects at one time because you want to perform one of the following tasks:

- Apply formatting to all selected objects
- Move all the selected objects without losing the spacing between the objects
- Delete all the selected objects
- Prepare to group the objects (as described next)

To select multiple objects, press Shift or Ctrl, and then click each object you want to include. Alternatively, you can click in the drawing canvas, click the Select Multiple Objects button on the Drawing toolbar in the Select Multiple Objects dialog box, click the check boxes that appear next to the names of the objects that you want to select, and then click OK. You can tell which objects have been selected because they now have selection handles. After a group of objects is selected, you can right-click to apply shortcut menu options, click Drawing toolbar buttons to apply formatting, press Delete or Backspace to delete the objects, or drag the selected items to move them as a group.

Repositioning and Aligning Drawing Objects with Precision

As an experienced Word user, you know that you can reposition drawing objects by clicking and dragging them. Moving objects this way to create drawings is especially effective when you use Word's drawing canvas. Sometimes, however, you might want to position objects with more precision. You can control how objects are positioned by using a drawing grid, nudging objects into place, and using the aligning and distributing options provided on the Drawing toolbar, as described here:

- **Using the drawing grid** You can use the drawing grid with or without the drawing canvas to help you position graphics. To turn on the drawing grid, click in your document or in the drawing canvas, click Draw on the Drawing toolbar, and choose Grid from the menu. In the Drawing Grid dialog box, select the Display Gridlines On Screen check box, as shown in Figure 12-26, and then click OK. The drawing grid appears. To turn off the grid, in the Drawing Grid dialog box, clear the Display Gridlines On Screen check box.

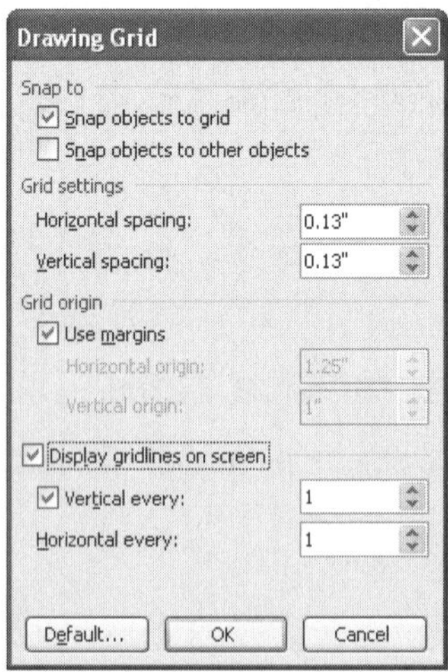

Figure 12-26. The Drawing Grid dialog box provides options you can use to control how the drawing grid looks and behaves.

- **Nudging objects into place** You can move (nudge) an object up, down, left, or right by 1 pixel by selecting the object, and then pressing the arrow keys, or by selecting the object, and then clicking Draw on the Drawing toolbar, choosing Nudge on the menu, and then choosing Up, Down, Left, or Right. If you have the Snap Objects To Grid option turned on while you are using the drawing grid, as shown in Figure 12-27, choosing the Nudge option moves your object one grid measurement. You can also nudge objects in smaller increments while using the grid by pressing Ctrl while you press the arrow keys.

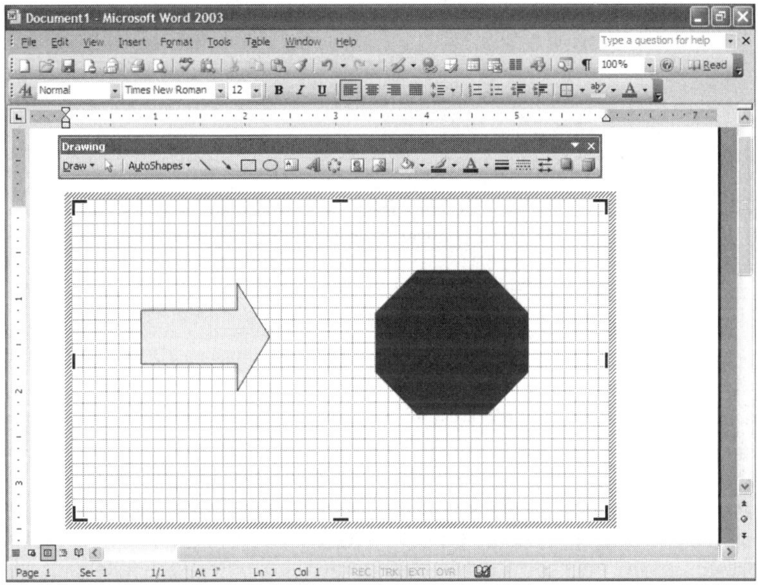

Figure 12-27. You can use the drawing grid to help size, position, and align objects accurately.

- **Aligning and distributing objects** To help you align and arrange objects evenly relative to each other, you can use the alignment and distribution options in the Draw menu. To do so, select the objects you want to position, click Draw on the Drawing toolbar, and choose Align Or Distribute from the menu. As shown in Figure 12-28, you can align objects vertically (Left, Center, or Right), horizontally (Top, Middle, or Bottom), and distribute selected objects evenly horizontally or vertically.

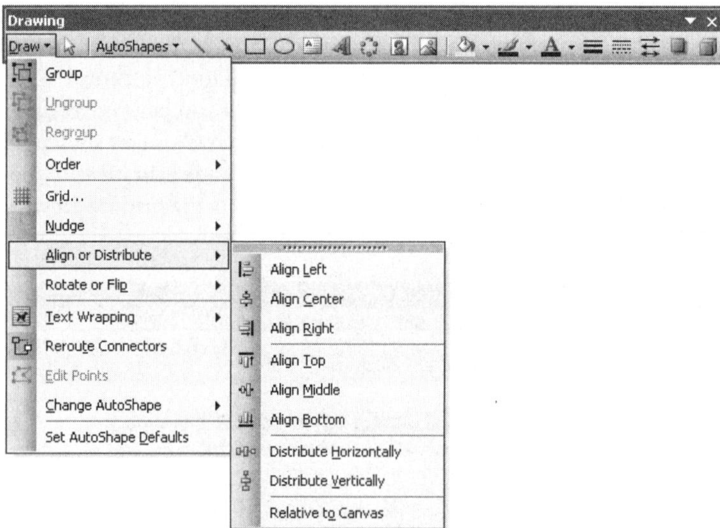

Figure 12-28. After you learn how to align and distribute objects, you'll find that you use these alignment options frequently to create professional-looking drawings.

Note If you have the Snap Objects To Grid feature turned on while you work on the drawing grid, you can override the feature by pressing Alt while you drag an object.

Tip By default, objects are distributed relative to each other when you choose an Align Or Distribute setting. To distribute objects relative to the drawing canvas instead, choose Relative To Canvas from the Align Or Distribute menu, before you select an alignment option. To distribute objects that are not on a drawing canvas, you can choose Relative To Page on the Align Or Distribute menu from the Draw menu.

Note The Distribute Horizontally and Distribute Vertically options are available only when three or more objects are selected.

Tip **Move drawing objects**

You can freely move drawing objects only if they are floating objects. If an object is formatted as an inline object, you can only position the object within text lines.

When you move a floating object, you can press Shift while you move it to restrict the object so that it can move only along the horizontal and vertical planes.

Grouping and Ungrouping Objects

You can group objects to ensure that certain objects stay positioned together no matter what. Grouping comes in handy when you want to copy or move drawings as well as ensure that layered objects don't inadvertently become incorrectly layered (for more about layering, see "Controlling Object Layering," next). For example, if you've overlaid a text box on an AutoShape, you might want to group the two objects so that you won't have to reposition the text box within the shape every time you move the shape. In addition, you won't have to worry about the text box being accidentally layered beneath the object, which would hide the text. You can ungroup grouped items at any time, which enables you to edit any part of a grouped object whenever necessary.

To group objects, position your objects, select the objects you want to group (by pressing Shift and clicking each object you want to include or by dragging your cursor to select the objects), click Draw on the Drawing toolbar, and then choose Group from the menu. Alternatively, select the objects you want to group, right-click, choose Grouping from the shortcut menu, and then choose Group.

To ungroup objects, click the group to select it, click Draw on the Drawing toolbar, and then choose Ungroup. Alternatively, right-click the group, choose Grouping from the shortcut menu, and then choose Ungroup.

Tip **Regrouping your objects**
If you ungroup a group to make a minor change—maybe you want to resize an object in the group, for example—you can easily regroup the objects after you make your changes. To do so, select any object that was part of the group, click Draw on the Drawing toolbar, and choose Regroup from the menu, or right-click the object, choose Grouping from the shortcut menu, and then choose Regroup.

Controlling Object Layering

When you create a drawing that contains many objects, you'll need to control which objects are layered in front of and behind other objects. Paying attention to how objects are layered can save you from inadvertently obscuring parts of your drawings that should be visible. The order in which objects are stacked is sometimes referred to as the *z-order*, based on standard coordinate references, in which *x* refers to horizontal positioning, *y* refers to vertical positioning, and *z* refers to depth positioning. To control the z-order of objects in your drawing, select an object, click Draw on the Drawing toolbar, and choose Order from the menu (or right-click an object and choose Order from the shortcut menu) to access the layering options, as shown in Figure 12-29. You can position an object in front of all layers, in back of all layers, in front of the next layer, or in back of the preceding layer. In addition, you can specify drawing canvases to be placed in front of or behind text if your drawing is a floating object or is a drawing that's not bounded by the drawing canvas.

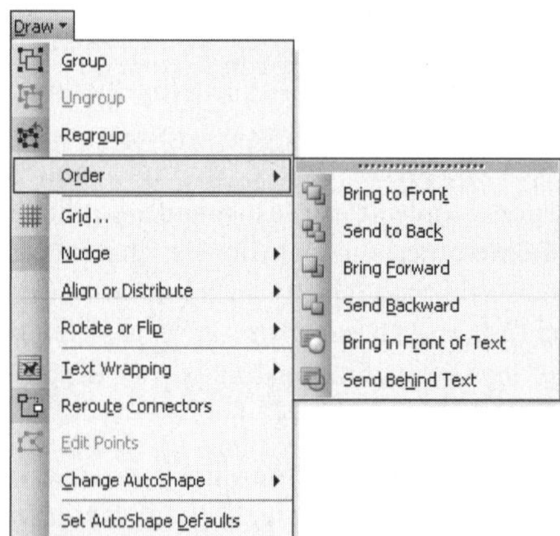

Figure 12-29. Layering objects helps you control which objects appear in the foreground of your drawing and which appear in the background.

Tip If you're having trouble selecting an object (perhaps it's buried under other objects), you can press Tab repeatedly to move your selection focus from one object to the next.

Integrating the Drawing Canvas with Document Text

Most of this chapter describes how to work with drawing objects, both inside and outside the drawing canvas. You can control drawings formatted as floating objects the same way you control other floating objects. Similarly, when you create drawings within the drawing canvas, you can control how the drawing canvas wraps around the drawing as well as how the drawing canvas is positioned relative to a document's text. To configure the drawing canvas settings, you use the Drawing Canvas toolbar, shown in Figure 12-30.

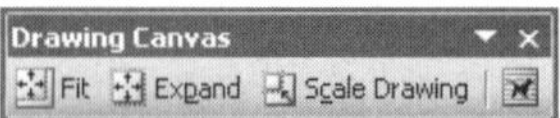

Figure 12-30. You can resize the drawing canvas as well as specify how text should wrap around the canvas by using the Drawing Canvas toolbar buttons.

To display the Drawing Canvas toolbar, right-click a blank area in the drawing canvas, and choose Show Drawing Canvas Toolbar from the shortcut menu. The Drawing Canvas toolbar buttons are described in Table 12-4.

Table 12-4. Drawing Canvas Toolbar Buttons

Button	Name	Description
Fit	Fit Drawing To Contents	Reduces the drawing canvas frame to the size of the drawing when your drawing contains two or more objects.
Expand	Expand Drawing	Expands the drawing canvas. You can click this button multiple times to expand the canvas incrementally.
Scale Drawing	Scale Drawing	Displays selection handles on the drawing canvas that enable you to resize the drawing canvas and the drawing at the same time.
	Text Wrapping	Displays the Text Wrapping menu, which enables you to specify how text should wrap around the drawing canvas. The text wrapping options are the same options you use when formatting pictures. (See Chapter 11, "Adding Visual Impact with Pictures and Objects," for more information about text wrapping options.)

You can also access drawing canvas options by displaying the Format Drawing Canvas dialog box using one of the following methods:

- Double-click in a blank area of the drawing canvas or the drawing canvas frame.
- Right-click in a blank area in the drawing canvas or on its frame, and choose Format Drawing Canvas from the shortcut menu.

The Format Drawing Canvas dialog box is shown in Figure 12-31. This dialog box is similar to the formatting dialog box that appears when you double-click a drawing object.

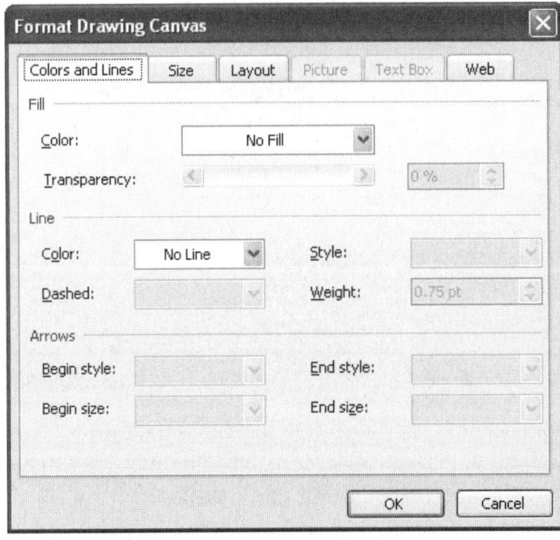

Figure 12-31. The Format Drawing Canvas dialog box enables you to precisely control the settings for your drawing canvas.

Using the Format Drawing Canvas dialog box, you can customize the color, line, size, and layout options. You can also enter alternative text (called ALT text) if you'll be using the drawing on a Web page. ALT text appears in Web pages in place of graphics when graphics are turned off in a browser or a user is using a text-only browser. (See Chapter 26, "Creating Professional Web Sites," for more information about ALT text.)

You can also control the drawing canvas directly in a few ways. For example, you can reposition a drawing canvas in a document by dragging the drawing canvas frame. In addition, you can drag drawings off the drawing canvas, and then delete the drawing canvas by right-clicking it and choosing Cut from the shortcut menu. Last, you can delete an entire drawing—canvas and all—by right-clicking the drawing canvas and choosing Cut from the shortcut menu or pressing Delete.

Working with WordArt

If your Word documents leave you with that nagging "it's just missing something" feeling, you might want to add some graphical text. Graphical text works especially well in intentionally eye-catching types of documents, such as brochures, flyers, newsletters, Web pages, and advertisements. If you decide to add graphical text, you're in luck—the WordArt feature helps you create and customize graphical text quickly and easily.

Used creatively (and sparingly), WordArt can add a splash of color, a bit of dimension, a touch of originality, and a professional polish to your documents. The sample document in Figure 12-32 illustrates how a couple of default WordArt styles can be combined to create a Web page logo. These default WordArt styles and colors are certainly adequate, but if creating a unique look is a concern, you should seriously consider customizing WordArt objects whenever you use them—otherwise, people might recognize that you're using a standard WordArt style. If you master the WordArt features described in this chapter, you'll be able to create highly customized graphical text for your documents.

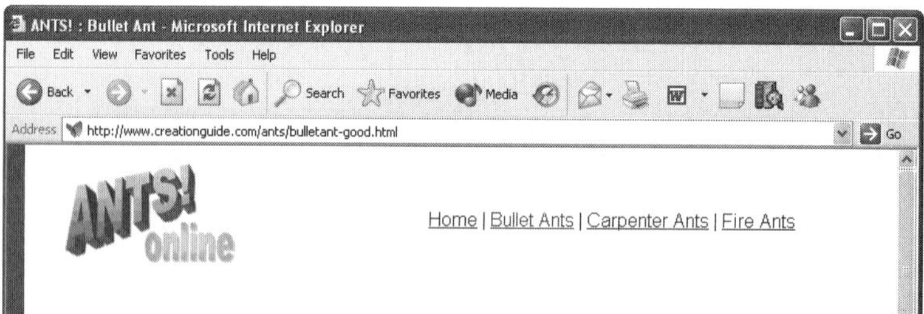

Figure 12-32. Two WordArt styles combined to create a simple fictitious Web page logo.

> **Note** After you create WordArt objects, you can manipulate them much as you customize other drawing objects in Word, as described throughout this chapter.

At the most basic level, including a WordArt object in your document entails selecting a WordArt style and entering the WordArt object's display text. To accomplish these two tasks, you'll use the WordArt Gallery, shown in Figure 12-33, and the Edit WordArt Text dialog box, shown in Figure 12-34.

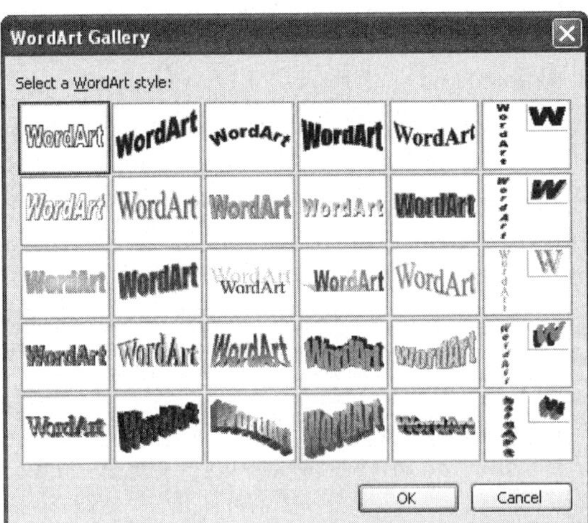

Figure 12-33. The WordArt Gallery offers 30 base styles that you can use as a foundation when you create a WordArt object.

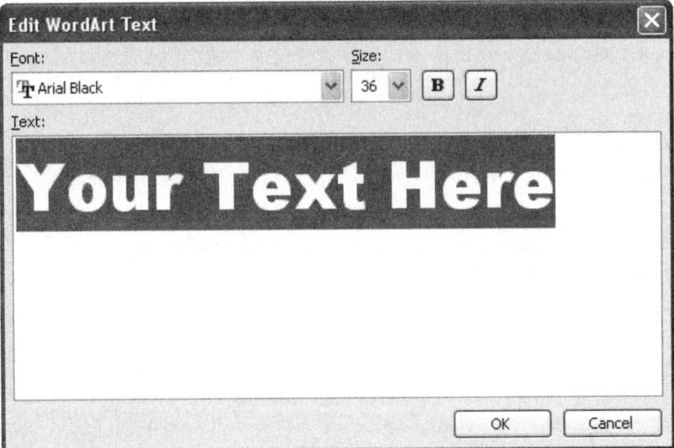

Figure 12-34. You can enter custom text for a WordArt object in the Edit WordArt Text dialog box, as well as configure font, size, boldface, and italic formatting settings.

Adding WordArt Using the WordArt Gallery

To create a WordArt object, follow these steps:

1. Click in your document where you want to insert theWordArt object.
2. Ensure that you're working in either Print Layout, Web Layout, or Reading view, and then choose Insert, Picture, WordArt, or display the Drawing toolbar (by clicking Drawing on the Standard toolbar) and click Insert WordArt.

Insert WordArt

3. In the WordArt Gallery, select a WordArt style, and click OK (or simply double-click the WordArt style of your choice). The Edit WordArt Text dialog box appears.
4. Type the WordArt object's display text in the Text box, and configure the Font, Size, Bold, and Italic text attributes. (You can easily reconfigure these settings later, so don't worry about getting them right the first time.)
5. After you configure the WordArt object's text, click OK. The WordArt object appears in your document.

Tip If you want to convert existing text into a WordArt object, select the text before you choose Insert, Picture, WordArt. The selected text will appear automatically in the Text box in the Edit WordArt Text dialog box.

After you insert a WordArt object, you'll most likely want to customize the object to suit your purposes. You can customize WordArt objects in a number of ways. For example, you can adjust a WordArt object's content and style, change the object's shape, combine WordArt objects, control text alignment, and so forth. To help you make changes to your WordArt objects, Word provides the WordArt toolbar, shown in Figure 12-35.

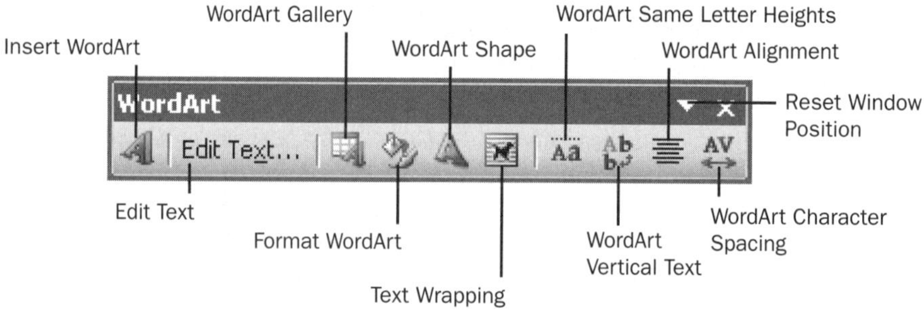

Figure 12-35. The WordArt toolbar contains most of the tools you need to fully customize WordArt objects.

The next few sections of this chapter describe the ways you can alter WordArt characteristics to morph standard WordArt objects into custom graphical text elements. As you'll discover, customizing WordArt is a breeze.

Modifying WordArt Properties

After you create a standard WordArt object, you might decide that you want to change your basic font selection, apply a different WordArt base style, or edit the text.To do this, you'll have to return to the WordArt Gallery or the Edit WordArt Text dialog box. Backtracking is easy, and can be done as follows:

WordArt Gallery

- To apply a different WordArt base style to an existing WordArt object, click the WordArt object you want to modify, click WordArt Gallery on the WordArt toolbar, and double-click a style in the WordArt Gallery.

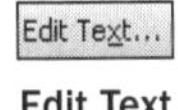

Edit Text

- To edit text in an existing WordArt object, double-click the WordArt object, or click the WordArt object (which selects the WordArt object and opens the WordArt toolbar by default) and click the Edit Text button on the WordArt toolbar. In the Edit WordArt Text dialog box, make changes, including adjusting text and formatting, and click OK.

When you apply a different style using the WordArt Gallery or edit WordArt text in the Edit WordArt Text dialog box and click OK, the changes are instantly reflected in your document.

Troubleshooting

Formatting applies to the entire WordArt object, but I want to format only part of the object

Conveniently enough, Word provides numerous formatting options when it comes to customizing WordArt objects, but one drawback sticks out like a sore thumb—WordArt formatting options almost always apply to the entire WordArt object. If you want to format various parts of a WordArt object differently, you have to get a little creative. Specifically, you have to create separate pieces of WordArt, format the pieces as individual objects, and then group the objects together. You can accomplish this in two ways: by using the grouping option, or by using the drawing canvas.

Positioning WordArt Objects in Documents

After you create a WordArt object, you'll want to specify how and where the object will appear in your document. By default, a WordArt object is inserted as an *inline object.* This means that the object is inserted at the insertion point and embedded within a regular line of text, as shown in Figure 12-36. You can drag inline WordArt objects from line to line and from paragraph to paragraph. You can also resize inline WordArt objects just as you resize other objects (by dragging the object's sizing handles or configuring the object's Size properties). But if you want to wrap text around a WordArt object, rotate the object, angle the object's text, position the object behind or in front of document text, or drag the object around a page that doesn't contain text, you'll need to change the format settings for the WordArt object.

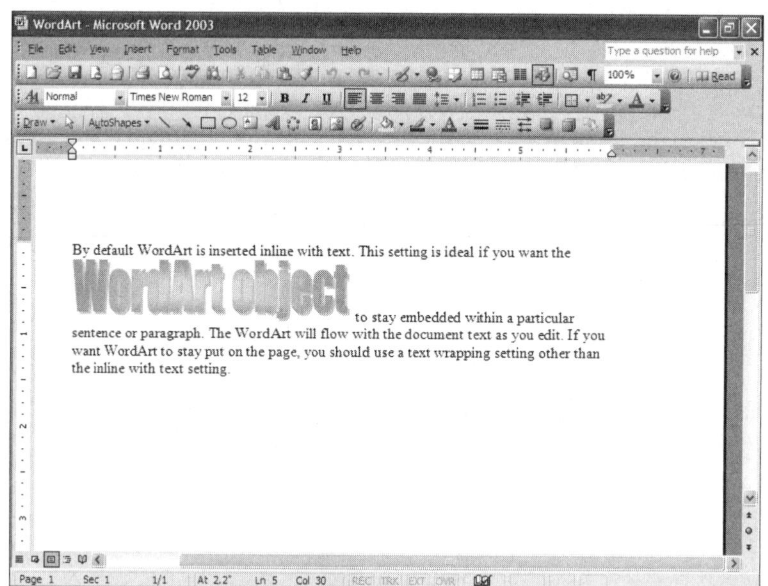

Figure 12-36. By default, a WordArt object is formatted as an inline object. You can change an object to a floating object by changing the object's text wrapping setting.

To change a WordArt object's text wrapping setting, follow these steps:

Text Wrapping

1. Click the WordArt object, and click Text Wrapping on the WordArt toolbar.
2. From the Text Wrapping menu, choose a text wrapping setting.

The Text Wrapping menu, shown in Figure 12-37, provides the following standard text wrapping styles: In Line With Text (the default setting), Square, Tight, Behind Text, In Front Of Text, Top And Bottom, Through, and Edit Wrap Points.

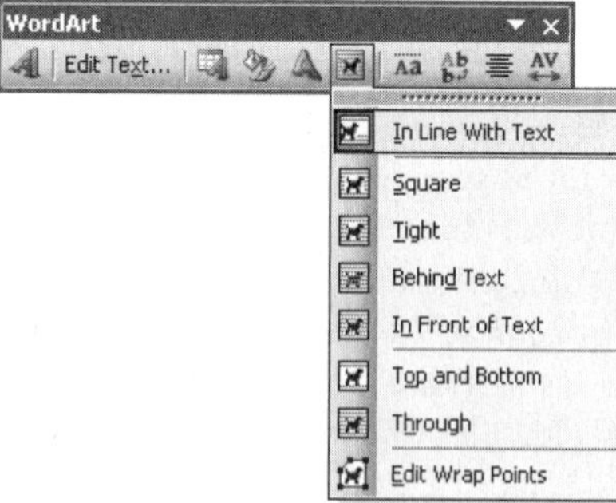

Figure 12-37. You can control how WordArt appears relative to document text by configuring the text wrapping setting.

After you specify how you'd like a WordArt object to be positioned within text, you can move the object by dragging it around your page in Web Layout, Print Layout, or Reading view. In addition, you can specify exact object placement settings by configuring the Layout tab in the Format WordArt dialog box.

> **Tip** **Move WordArt objects incrementally**
> You can move floating (not inline) WordArt objects in small increments using the arrow keys. To nudge a WordArt object, click the object to select it, and then press the Up Arrow, Down Arrow, Left Arrow, and Right Arrow keys to move it in the desired direction.

To access advanced layout properties for a selected WordArt object, you need to display the Advanced Layout dialog box. To do so, follow these steps:

Format WordArt

1. Click the WordArt object, and click Format WordArt on the WordArt toolbar (or right-click the WordArt object, and choose Format WordArt from the shortcut menu) to display the Format WordArt dialog box.
2. In the Format WordArt dialog box, click the Layout tab. The Layout tab provides basic text wrapping and text alignment settings.
3. In the Layout tab, click the Advanced button. The Advanced Layout dialog box appears, as shown in Figure 12-38. Notice that the Advanced Layout dialog box contains two tabs: Picture Position and Text Wrapping.

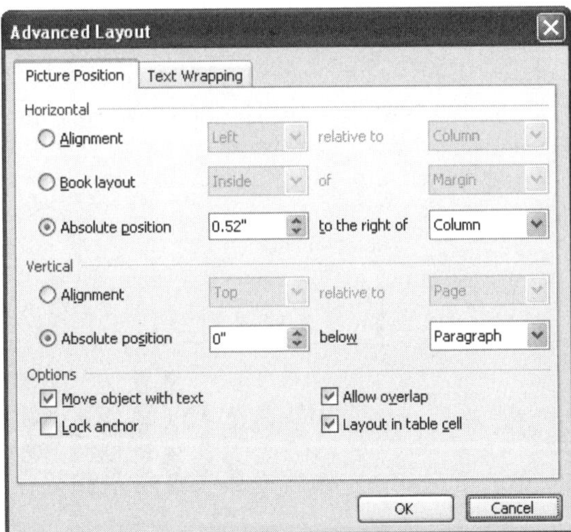

Figure 12-38. The Advanced Layout dialog box enables you to precisely configure a WordArt object's position, alignment, and text wrapping settings.

4. Configure your settings in the Picture Position and Text Wrapping tabs, click OK to close the Advanced Layout dialog box, and then click OK in the Format WordArt dialog box to apply the settings.

For more information about setting Advanced Layout options, see Chapter 11, "Adding Visual Impact with Pictures and Objects."

If you're attempting to apply advanced layout settings to a WordArt object but find that the Picture Position options are unavailable, change the Wrapping Style setting in the Text Wrapping tab to something other than In Line With Text. The Picture Position tab also contains a Move Object With Text check box. If you want to position a WordArt object on a particular page regardless of text flow, be sure to clear this check box.

Changing the Shape of WordArt

After you insert and position a WordArt object, you'll probably want to resize and reshape the object to suit your purposes. You can resize and reshape WordArt using three key tools: handles, WordArt shapes, and the Format WordArt dialog box.

Putting Handles to Work

As with other objects and graphics, you can display handles on WordArt objects and use the handles to modify the size and appearance of the objects. Both inline and floating WordArt objects provide sizing handles, which you can drag to resize the object.

To display a WordArt object's handles, simply click the object. Inline WordArt objects display standard black square sizing handles that you can drag to resize the object horizontally, vertically, and diagonally (which resizes the height and width proportionally). WordArt objects that aren't formatted as inline objects display a more colorful set of handles. Namely, a non-inline object provides clear circle-shaped handles for resizing, a green circle-shaped handle for rotating, and a yellow diamond-shaped handle for angling text. Figure 12-39 shows a WordArt object and its handles. To use a handle, simply drag the handle to the desired position.

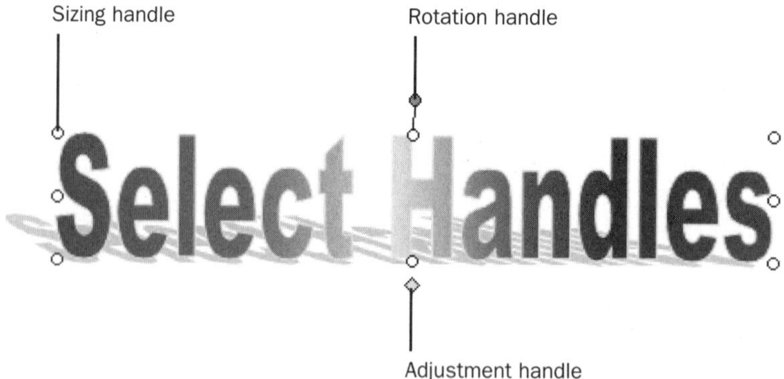

Figure 12-39. Handles enable you to resize, rotate, and angle WordArt text. The handles shown in this image appear when an image is a floating object. Inline objects only provide sizing handles.

Note Remember, when you are working with an inline WordArt object, you can only drag the sizing handles to resize the WordArt object—you can't rotate or angle the text.

Tip Keep an eye on the dashed lines when you move, rotate, angle, and resize WordArt text. Dashed lines appear as you drag handles so that you can get an idea of how you are reshaping a WordArt object.

Applying WordArt Shapes

In addition to resizing, rotating, and angling WordArt text, you can distort a WordArt object's shape. To do so, select theWordArt object, click theWordArt Shape button on the WordArt toolbar, and choose one of the 40 shapes available in the WordArt Shape menu, shown in Figure 12-40.

Figure 12-40. To get a feel for WordArt shapes, experiment with the WordArt Shape menu by applying various shapes to selected WordArt objects.

Sizing, Rotating, and Scaling WordArt with Precision

As you've seen, you can use handles to resize, rotate, and adjust WordArt objects until they look just right, but you can also perform these actions by specifying precise measurements. Using precise measurements to define your WordArt objects is an effective method when you want to create a uniform appearance across documents or among similar components within the same document. To control WordArt size and rotation settings precisely, you configure the settings in the Size tab in the Format WordArt dialog box, shown in Figure 12-41. To access the Size tab, right-click a WordArt object, choose Format WordArt from the shortcut menu (or double-click the WordArt object), and click the Size tab. You can set sizing options for WordArt objects just as you set sizing options for other graphics or objects. After you configure Size And Rotate and Scale options, click OK to apply the settings.

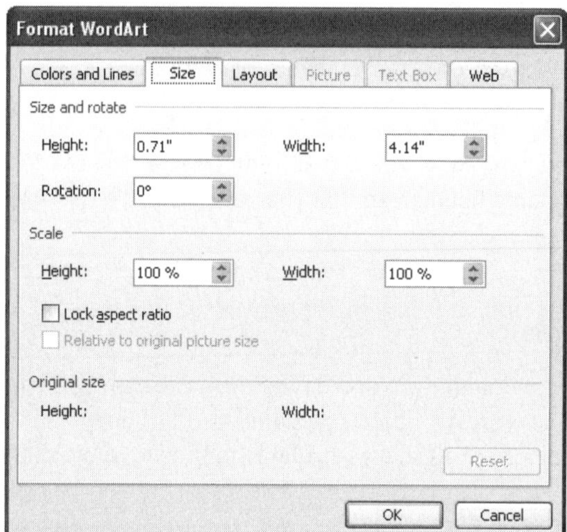

Figure 12-41. The Size tab enables you to precisely configure the size, rotation, and scale settings for WordArt objects. Notice that the Size tab includes a Lock Aspect Ratio check box, which allows you to resize the height and width of a WordArt object proportionally based on a percentage of its current size.

Modifying WordArt Colors and Line Properties

Whenever you use WordArt, you should modify the default style to present custom graphical text. Because so many people use Word, applying a default WordArt style without adding your own flair can result in others recognizing your use of WordArt. This recognition isn't necessarily a negative factor, but you'd probably prefer people to admire your graphical text, read the content, and move on, without pondering the sources of your design. Originality has its benefits. You can easily customize a WordArt object by changing the object's colors, texture, and line properties.

Changing a WordArt object's color scheme is as simple as selecting the WordArt object, clicking Format WordArt on the WordArt toolbar, and configuring the Colors And Lines tab in the Format WordArt dialog box. Figure 12-42 shows the Colors And Lines tab with the Color menu open. The Color setting in the Line section comes into play when you use a WordArt style that incorporates an outline around the graphical text.

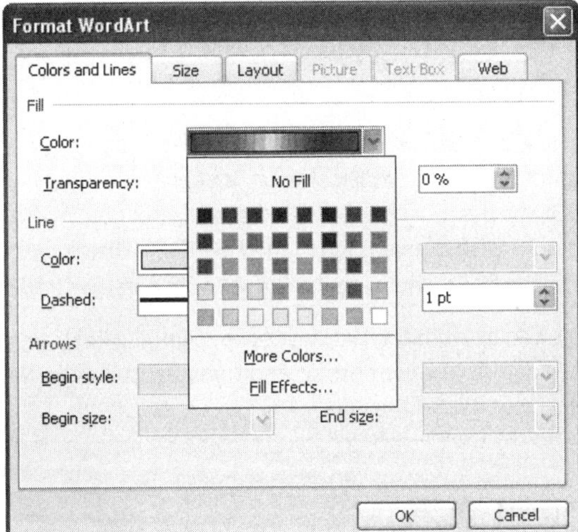

Figure 12-42. You can modify WordArt colors and line settings by configuring the Colors And Lines tab in the Format WordArt dialog box.

The Color menu includes the standard color palette as well as options that allow you to access additional colors and fill effects. If you select the Fill Effects option, the Fill Effects dialog box appears, as shown in Figure 12-43.You can use this dialog box to configure shading colors and gradients, textures, patterns, and pictures used to fill the WordArt object.

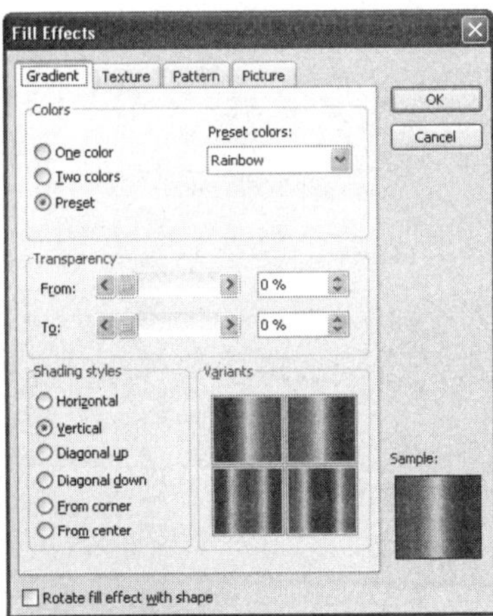

Figure 12-43. If a default WordArt style uses gradients, multiple colors, textures, or patterns, you can change the default settings using the Fill Effects dialog box.

Changing the Shading or Texture of a WordArt Object

Some WordArt objects use a two-color (or more) gradient and shading scheme. If you apply a single color to this kind of WordArt object, the objects will look a bit flat because of the change to a one-dimensional coloring scheme. If you want to change the color of a two-tone WordArt object, you have to modify the object's colors in the Gradient tab in the Fill Effects dialog box. You can also select a preset gradient color scheme by choosing the Preset option in the Gradient tab.

If you want to change the texture used in a default WordArt style, click the Texture tab in the Fill Effects dialog box. You can choose from a number of additional textures as well as navigate to any textures or graphics stored on your system.

Formatting WordArt as Vertical Text

WordArt Vertical Text

At times, you might want to display WordArt vertically instead of horizontally. You can create a vertical WordArt object by choosing one of the five vertical WordArt styles in the WordArt Gallery, or you can select an existing WordArt object and click WordArt Vertical Text on the WordArt toolbar.

You can also create columns of WordArt text by pressing Enter after each word you type in the Edit WordArt Text dialog box. Then, after the WordArt appears in your document, click WordArt Vertical Text. Your WordArt text will look something like the example in Figure 12-44.

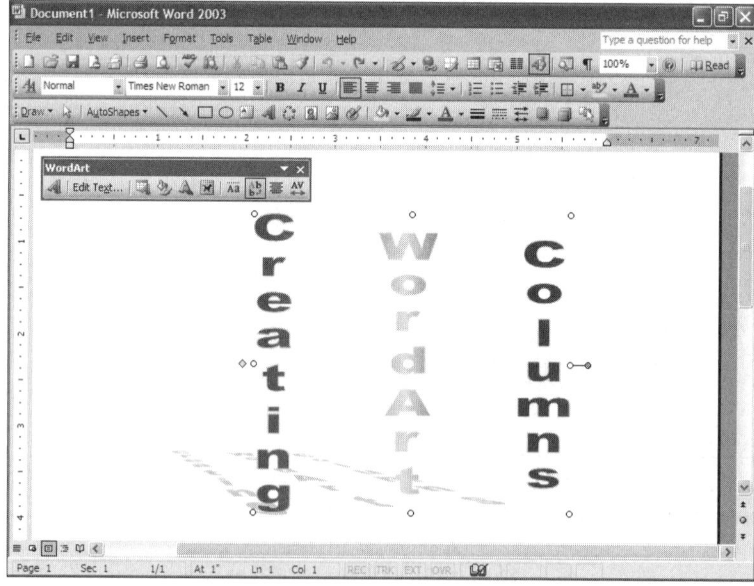

Figure 12-44. You can convert horizontal WordArt to vertical text by using the WordArt Vertical Text button on the WordArt toolbar.

Aligning and Justifying WordArt Text

WordArt Alignment

If your WordArt object includes multiple words on more than one line, you can control how the WordArt text is aligned. Aligning WordArt text is similar to aligning standard paragraph text. To view the available WordArt alignment options, select theWordArt object, and click WordArt Alignment on the WordArt toolbar, as shown in Figure 12-45.

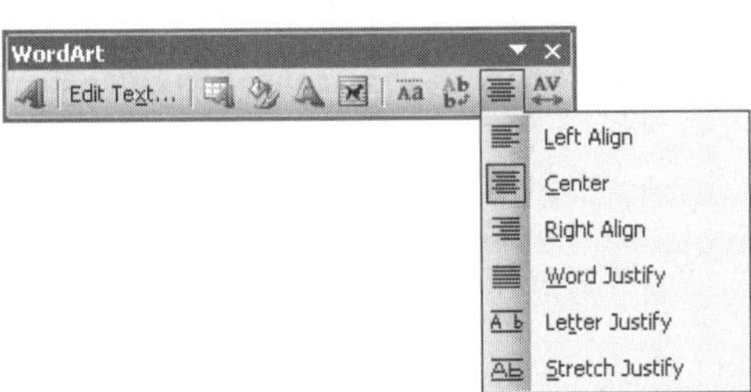

Figure 12-45. You can align WordArt text within the object's frame by choosing alignment options from the WordArt Alignment menu.

The WordArt Alignment menu provides the following alignment commands:

- **Left Align** Aligns the text along the left edge of the WordArt frame.
- **Center** Centers the text within the frame.
- **Right Align** Aligns the text along the right edge of the frame.
- **Word Justify** Justifies the text within the frame by adding space between words.
- **Letter Justify** Justifies the text within the frame by adding space between letters and increasing existing spaces between words. Single-word lines are treated the same as they would be using the Word Justify option.
- **Stretch Justify** Justifies the text within the frame by stretching the letters and the spaces between words.

Tip **Align vertical columns**

You can use the alignment options to align vertical columns of WordArt text as well. To top-align vertical columns of text, choose the Left Align option on the WordArt Alignment menu; to bottom-align vertical columns of text, choose the Right-Align option.

Using the WordArt Same Letter Heights Option

WordArt Same Letter Heights

Another effect you can apply to WordArt is to display lowercase letters the same height as uppercase letters. You might want to use this option to create a somewhat avant-garde artistic effect in a flyer or newsletter. To apply this formatting option, select the WordArt object, and click the WordArt Same Letter Heights button on the WordArt toolbar. Like other WordArt formatting options, you can't selectively apply this format setting within a WordArt object—it's an all-or-nothing proposition unless you use a workaround, such as grouping WordArt objects or arranging objects on the drawing canvas.

Adjusting WordArt Character Spacing and Kerning

Before word-processing applications came along, most people left concepts like *character spacing* and *kerning* to professional typesetters. But now everyone who uses a word-processing application is a bit of a typesetter. Thus, character spacing and kerning issues have made it to the fringe of mainstream document creation. If you've been ignoring character spacing and kerning options, here are a couple of quick definitions to get you going:

- **Character spacing** Refers to the space between characters. You can expand or condense space evenly between all WordArt characters.
- **Kerning** Refers to adjusting spacing between pairs of characters to create the appearance of even spacing. For example, you might want to tighten the space between letter pairs such as *YO* and *WA*.

To adjust character spacing and kerning in WordArt objects, you can click WordArt Character Spacing on the WordArt toolbar, as shown in Figure 12-46. TheWordArt Character Spacing menu lets you specify whether you want to set character spacing as Very Tight, Tight, Normal, Loose, Very Loose, or Custom. In addition, you can turn the Kern Character Pairs option on or off.

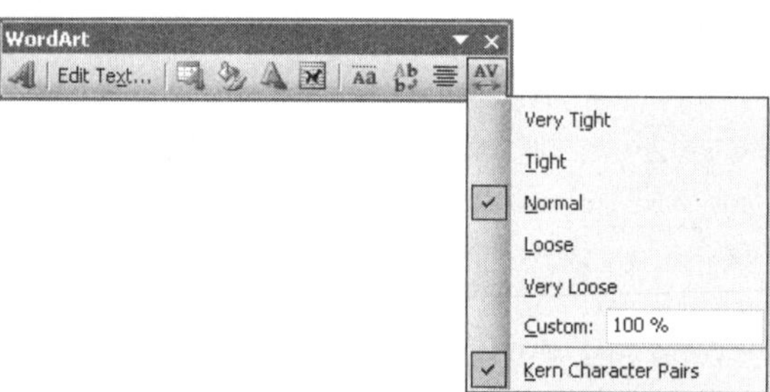

Figure 12-46. The WordArt Character Spacing menu provides options for expanding or condensing WordArt text.

Using WordArt in Online Documents

Web page creation has introduced an entire new genre of word processing, and Word offers a number of features for Web design. Among the plethora of Word features, WordArt is a natural for creating Web page components. In fact, WordArt can be customized using a couple of options specific to the Web. In particular, you can add *alternative text* (usually referred to as *ALT text* by Web designers) to WordArt, and you can format WordArt objects as hyperlinks. The next two sections describe these two basic Web formatting options.

For more information about creating Web pages in Word, see Chapter 26, "Creating Professional Web Sites."

Adding ALT Text to WordArt

ALT text is text that appears on Web pages in place of graphics if a user has graphics capabilities turned off or if the user is using a text-only browser. ALT text also appears while graphics are loading (to give users a hint about the graphic before it loads) and when users hover the pointer over a graphic. Basically, ALT text helps users identify the purpose of a Web page graphic. To add ALT text to a WordArt object, follow these steps:

1. Select the WordArt object, and click Format WordArt on the WordArt toolbar, or right-click the WordArt object, and choose Format WordArt from the shortcut menu.
2. In the Format WordArt dialog box, click the Web tab. By default, the WordArt text appears as the ALT text, as shown in Figure 12-47.

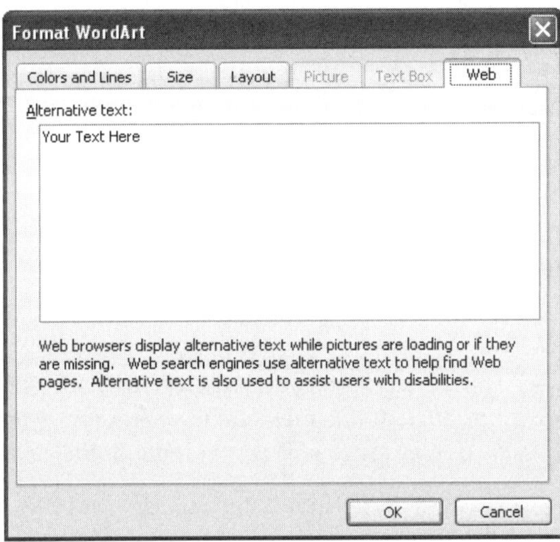

Figure 12-47. The Web tab in the Format WordArt dialog box is used to set the ALT text that appears for a WordArt object.

3. To change the ALT text (by default, the ALT text is the same as the WordArt text), select the existing ALT text, type the text you want to associate with your WordArt object, and then click OK.

When your WordArt appears as part of a Web page, the ALT text will appear in place of your graphic as the graphic downloads and whenever users opt to hide graphics or use a text-only browser.

Creating WordArt Hyperlinks

Another way you can configure a WordArt object for the Web is to format the object as a hyperlink. Often, graphics (and remember, graphical text is fundamentally the same as a graphic) also serve as Web page hyperlinks. When you use WordArt on a Web page, you're basically inserting a graphic in your page. You might want to convert your WordArt object to a hyperlink for a number of reasons. For example, you might want to use a WordArt object as a button that links to a subordinate page, or you might want to use WordArt to create a linked logo image that users can click to return to your home page.

To configure WordArt as a hyperlink, you use the same procedure you use to add a hyperlink to other graphics or objects. To link a WordArt object, follow these steps:

1 Select the WordArt object, and click Insert Hyperlink on the Standard toolbar, or right-click a WordArt object, and choose Hyperlink from the shortcut menu. The Insert Hyperlink dialog box appears, as shown in Figure 12-48.

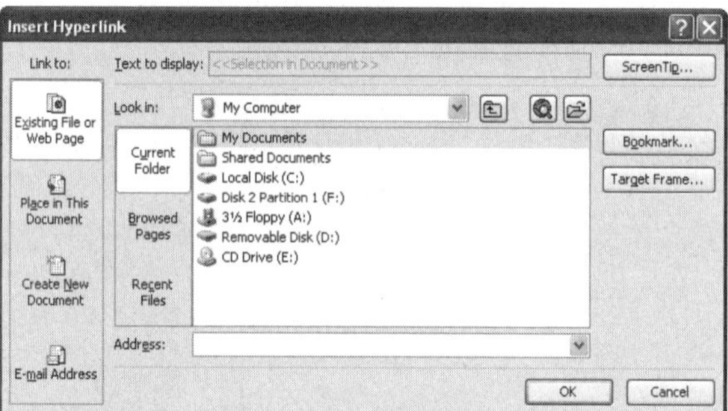

Figure 12-48. The Insert Hyperlink dialog box enables you to format a WordArt object as a hyperlink.

2 In the Link To list, specify the type of link you want to create. You can link to an existing file, another place in the current document, a new file, or an e-mail address. Then insert the link's address by navigating to a file or typing it in the Address box.

Using linked WordArt, you can easily add clickable banners, logos, buttons, and icons to your online documents.

Chapter 13

Organizing Concepts in Tables

Word 2003 might surprise you with the flexibility it offers when it comes to creating tables. You can use the left-brained approach—planning your table, choosing the right number of columns and rows, and designing it to an exact specification—or you can use the right-brained approach—just click Draw Table on the Tables And Borders toolbar and draw what you want on the page.

Whichever table generation method suits your style best, Word complements the table creation basics with a wealth of special table features. You'll soon be able to apply styles to give your tables a professional look; search for and sort table information according to your specifications; easily add, delete, and reorder rows and columns; drag table data; create your own custom styles; and much more. This chapter sprints with you through the basics and spends some time on features you can use to really make your Word documents stand out.

Creating Effective Tables

Half the battle in creating a logical, usable table is in the planning. What do you want to show in table form? What will your readers be looking for, and how can you best organize that data to help them find what they need? Here are some additional questions to ask as you're thinking about the table you're going to create:

- Do you need to create the table in a limited space in your document?
- How many rows and columns will you need?
- Will the table content include text, numbers, or both?
- Will you use functions for totaling and averaging columns?
- Will you have other, similar tables in your document?
- Will you use a predesigned table style or create your own?

Knowing ahead of time what you want to create helps you get a "big picture" of the resulting table. Throughout this chapter, you'll find the necessary procedures for creating tables with each of the above characteristics.

Creating a Simple Table

Word gives you several different ways to create a table, and a full set of tools to use after the table has been created. The easiest way to create a simple table is to use Insert Table on the Standard toolbar. Follow these steps:

1. Place the insertion point where you want to create the table in your document.
2. Click Insert Table on the Standard toolbar. A menu will display a grid of rows and columns.
3. Drag the mouse pointer down and to the right until you've highlighted the number of rows and columns you want to create, as shown in Figure 13-1.

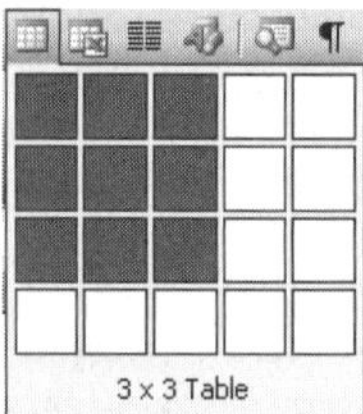

Figure 13-1. Select the desired number of rows and columns by highlighting them in the Insert Table menu.

4. When you have highlighted the number of cells you want to create, release the mouse button. The resulting table will be placed at the insertion point, as shown in Figure 13-2.

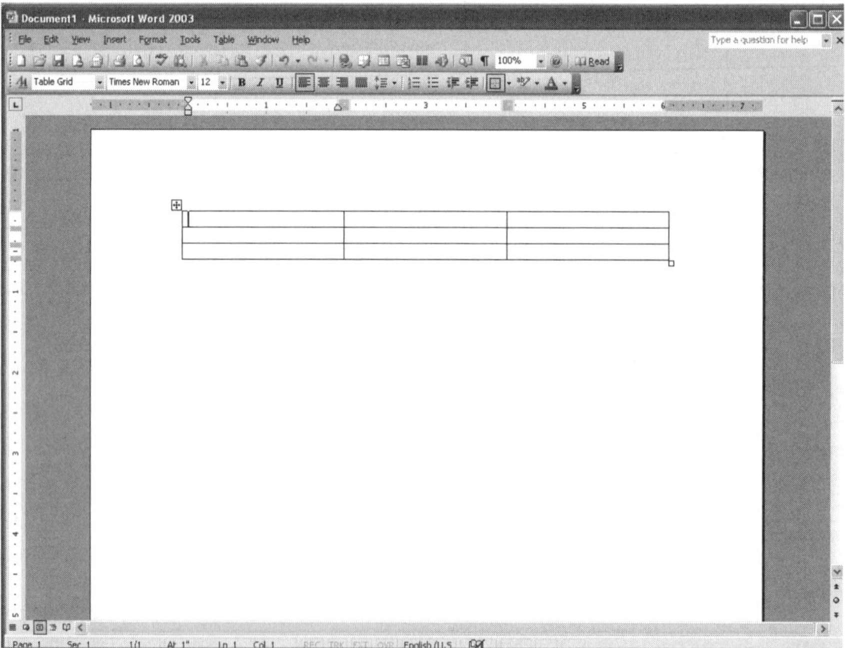

Figure 13-2. The table created with Insert Table on the Standard toolbar is uniform in size and shape.

Drawing a Table Freehand

Tables And Borders

If you prefer to draw tables as you go rather than rely on menus and tools, you can choose Table, Draw Table or click Table and Borders on the Standard toolbar. The Draw Table feature on the Table and Borders toolbar enables you to take an electronic "pencil" and draw a table the way you want it. You can also add lines for rows and columns and make editing changes while you work.

Create Special Table Effects Easily

Using Word's Draw Table feature, you can create uneven rows and columns, remove line segments in areas of your table that you want to open up, and control borders and shading, all with the click of the mouse.

To draw a table in your Word document, follow these steps:

1. Place the insertion point where you want to create the table.
2. Click the Tables And Borders button on the Standard toolbar, and then click Draw Table. The pointer will change to a pencil tool. Table 13-1 describes the various tools on this toolbar.
3. Drag the pointer down and to the right to draw the table. You can create the table to the exact size and specification you want, using the horizontal and vertical rulers as a guide, or you can resize the table later by dragging a corner. Release the mouse button when you're finished.
4. Use the mouse pointer to draw rows and columns. Word adds the straight line as you draw. Figure 13-3 shows a table created with the Draw Table tool. Both rows and columns have been added.

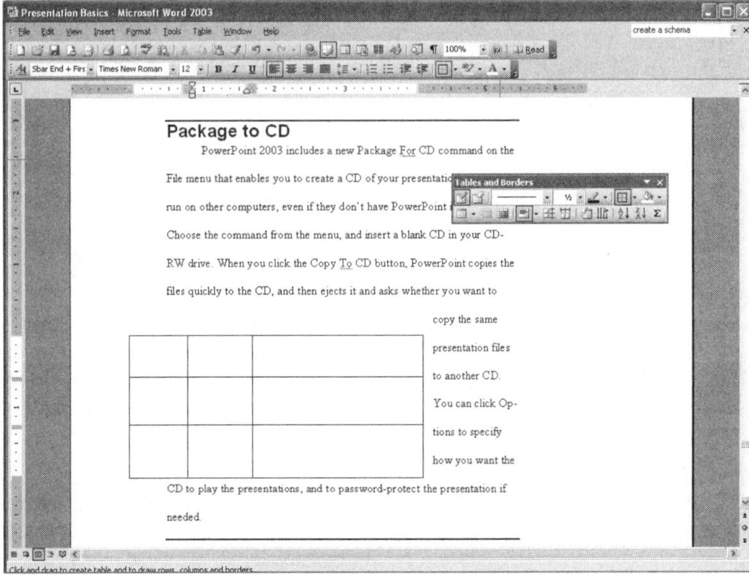

Figure 13-3. You can draw a table at any point in your document using the Draw Table tool.

> **Tip** **Wrap text automatically**
> If you want to create a table in the middle of a text section and have the text automatically wrap around it, press Ctrl while you draw the table.

Eraser

> **Tip** **Use the eraser**
> If you don't want a segment of a line to extend all the way across the table (you might want to underline only the Totals column in a table, for example), you can erase the pieces of the line you don't want. Simply click the Eraser button and click the line segment you want to erase.

Table 13-1. Buttons on the Tables And Borders Toolbar

Button	Name	Description
	Draw Table	Enables you to draw a table freehand
	Eraser	Erases line segments you don't want
	Line Style	Displays choices for the style of the table border line
½	Line Weight	Sets the width of the border line
	Border Color	Displays choices for the color of the border line
	Outside Border	Enables you to choose whether (and how) you want to border the table
	Shading Color	Displays shade color choices for selected cells
	Insert Table	Displays the Insert Table dialog box
	Merge Cells	Merges cells in a specified segment of the table
	Split Cells	Splits selected cell into individual cells
	Cell Alignment	Lets you choose the alignment for data in cell entries
	Distribute Rows Evenly	Arranges data evenly within a row

Table 13-1. **Buttons on the Tables And Borders Toolbar**

Button	Name	Description
	Distribute Columns Evenly	Arranges data evenly within a column
	Table AutoFormat	Displays the Table AutoFormat dialog box so that you can choose a predesigned table format or create your own
	Change Text Direction	Rotates text in the selected cell
	Sort Ascending	Sorts selected cells in ascending (A to Z) order
	Sort Descending	Sorts selected cells in descending (Z to A) order
	AutoSum	Totals the values in the cells in the corresponding row or column and places the result in the current cell

Tip **Move or delete a line**
If you don't like where you just drew a line in your table, you have one of two options. You can press Ctrl+Z to delete the line. Or you can close the Tables And Borders toolbar and position the text cursor over the line; the pointer will change to a double-headed arrow. You can now click the line and drag it to where you wanted it in the first place.

Setting Rows and Columns

If drawing a table freehand is too freewheeling an approach for you, you can use the Insert Table dialog box to set up the table the way you want it. Use this method when you want to create a table to precise specifications, with a set number of rows and columns. Follow these steps:

1. Place the insertion point where you want to begin the table.
2. Choose Table, Insert, Table. The Insert Table dialog box appears, as shown in Figure 13-4.

Figure 13-4. The Insert Table dialog box enables you to plan a table before creating it by choosing the number of columns and rows, the fit behavior, and the predesigned format used, if any.

3. Enter the number of columns and rows you want to create in the table.
4. Choose the AutoFit Behavior option that best suits your needs.

Note **Apply a predesigned style**
You can apply a predesigned style to your table by usingTable AutoFormat. For more information, see "Producing a Finished Table with AutoFormat" on page 418.

Tip **Apply table dimensions across the board**
If you want Word to apply the table selections you make in the Insert Table dialog box to other new tables you create in the current document, select the Remember Dimensions For New Tables check box.

Entering Table Data

Getting the data into the table is the easy part. You might enter data by hand, copy it from an Excel spreadsheet, drag it from another table, download it from a SharePoint data list box, or import it from a text-delimited file. To add data by hand, simply click in the cell in which you want to add data and type. Move to the next cell by pressing the Right Arrow key, if there's no data in the cell, or by pressing Tab. To move back to a previous cell, press the Left Arrow key or Shift+Tab.

SharePoint Team Services is a collection of Web-based services that enable you to create team Web sites, organize meetings, and do much more. For more information, see Chapter 25, "Working with Shared Documents."

Perhaps the easiest way to get data into your table, if it already exists in another table, is to use the drag-and-drop technique. If you want to copy an entire table, simply click the table move handle in the upper left corner of the selected table, press Ctrl, and drag to the new location. (If you don't press Ctrl while you drag, the entire table will move but not copy.)

Troubleshooting

Drag-and-drop technique doesn't work

If you've been trying to drag and drop text from one place to another in your document and find that it doesn't work, check to make sure you've got the feature enabled. To check this, follow these steps:

1. Choose Tools, Options.
2. Click the Edit tab, and select the Drag-And-Drop Text Editing check box, in the Editing Options section.
3. This activates the feature, and you should be able to drag and drop items as needed.

Editing Tables

Getting the data into table form is only half the battle. Once your data is entered, you'll no doubt want to reorganize it, edit it, add to it, and delete some of it. That means adding rows and columns—perhaps moving the rows you already have—and deleting others. You might decide to rearrange the order of columns, which means moving data from one side of the table to the other. That's where Word's formatting features come in.

Displaying Table Formatting Marks

Show/Hide

One of the secrets in moving and editing table data successfully lies in seeing the unseen. Each table cell, row, and column is given a marker that delineates the end of the items in the table format. When you move, copy, or paste information, these unseen markers might go along, giving you unexpected results at best, or overwriting your existing data at worst.To display the hidden marks in your current Word table, select the table by clicking the table move handle and then click Show/Hide on the Standard toolbar. The various table formatting marks will appear, as shown in Figure 13-5.

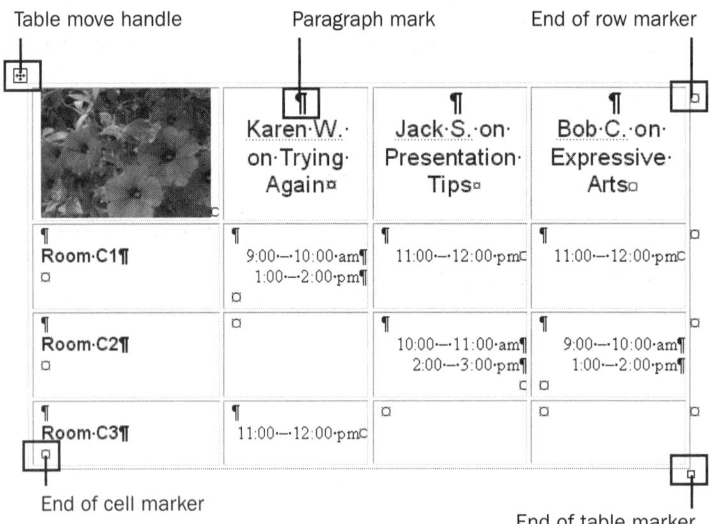

Figure 13-5. Table Formatting Marks identify the end of individual cells, rows, columns, and the table itself.

> **Tip** **Control the way formatting marks are displayed in your document**
> If you don't see all the formatting marks you expect, someone may have set the View options to limit the ones that are displayed by default. You can turn all the formatting marks back on by choosing Tools, Options, and clicking the View tab. In the Formatting Marks section, click All; then click OK. Now all of your formatting marks will appear automatically whenever you click Show/Hide.

Selecting Table Cells

To move and copy rows, columns, and cells, start simply by selecting them to let Word know which data you want to work with. As you get comfortable working with tables, you'll discover the tricks to selecting just the data you want for various operations. Table 13-2 lists selection methods you'll use in working with tables.

> **Tip** **Use multiple table selections**
> You can select noncontiguous sections of a table by pressing and holding Ctrl while you click additional selections. In a product listing, for example, this capability enables you to choose only the products that will be included in the 2003 catalog and copy them to a new table, leaving behind all the 2002 offerings.

Table 13-2. Selecting Table Segments

Selection	Method	Use
Entire table	Click the table and then click the table move handle that appears in the upper left corner of the table.	You want to move, copy, format, or delete an entire table.
Single row	Click outside the table to the left of the row.	You want to reorder, format, copy, move, insert, or delete a row.
Single column	Click outside the table just above the column.	You want to move, format, copy, insert, or delete a column.
Single cell	Click to the left of any data entered in the cell.	You want to move, copy, delete, or clear that cell.
Multiple cells, rows, or columns	Drag across the elements you want to select.	You want to move, format, copy, or delete sections of a table.

Copying Table Data

Although copying is basically a simple operation, copying table data can be a pain. The data can sometimes go where you don't expect it; for example, if you want to copy all the information into one cell in the new table, the data might instead be spread over the entire row, replacing existing data. If you want to copy multiple cells to multiple cells in the new table, the incoming cells might all be lumped into the cell at the insertion point. How do you avoid these kinds of copy surprises?

First, know what you're copying. The trick is to select cell data if you want to copy cell data; likewise, select the cells themselves (or rows or columns) if that's what you want to copy. By capturing the table formatting marks when you highlight the section you want to copy, you can be sure you get the results you expect.

Next, know where you're copying to. If you are copying a row or a column, make sure you've allowed enough room for the incoming data so that important entries won't be overwritten and lost. Once you've selected what you want to copy and you've planned the copy destination, press Ctrl+C to copy and Ctrl+V to paste, as usual.

Inserting Columns

You can expand and add to your table easily. One way to do this is by adding new columns. There are two different ways to add columns to the right or left of an existing column. One method causes Word to reconfigure the width of the existing columns, so that the width of the overall table is no wider than it was before you inserted a column. The other method maintains the widths of existing columns and widens the table by the width of the new column.

To add a new column to your table, select the column beside which you want to create the new column. To select the entire column, click on the top border of the column. When the column is selected, the Insert Table button on the Standard toolbar will change to Insert Columns. Click Insert Columns to add the new column. If your table is already the width of the text column, the new column is added without any widening of the table. If your table is narrower than the text margins allow, the new column is inserted and the columns to the right of the column move to make room.

Tip **Choose right or left, above or below**
The buttons on the Standard toolbar don't give you quite as much flexibility as menu commands do. Here's an example: by default, Word inserts columns to the left of the selected column and rows above the selected row. If you use the Insert Column button to add a column to your table, you must accept this default. However, if you choose Table, Insert and then select Columns To The Right or Rows Below, you can tell Word exactly where to insert a column or row.

Inserting Rows

Inserting rows is similar to inserting columns. Begin by selecting the row below which you want to insert a new row. Select the entire row by clicking to the left of the first cell of the row. The entire row is highlighted.

Click Insert Rows on the Standard toolbar (this button replaces the Insert Table button when a row is selected). Word inserts the new row just above the currently selected row.

Tip **Insert multiple rows and columns**
If you want to insert more than one row or column, select the number of rows or columns you want to add. (It doesn't matter whether the rows and columns have data in them or not.) For example, if you want to insert three rows, select three rows in the current table before choosing the commands necessary to add the rows.

Inserting Cells

In some circumstances, you might want to insert cells in a table without adding an entire row or column. You might need to do this, for example, when you have overlooked a product name and number in your listing and need to add it without changing the entire table. To insert cells in a table, simply select the cell (or cells) below which you want to insert new cells. Choose Table, Insert, Cells. The Insert Cells dialog box appears, as shown below. Click Shift Cells Down to place the new cells above the selected cells. Click Shift Cells Right if you want to move the existing cells to the right to make room for the new cells. Click OK to insert the cells. The cells are added and the existing cells are moved as specified.

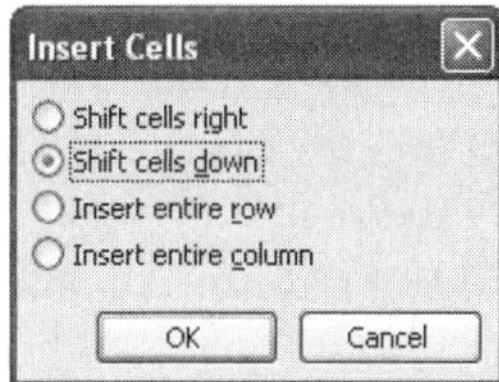

Deleting Columns, Rows, and Cells

If you decide that you don't need certain rows or columns after all, or if you have empty rows you didn't use, you can easily delete them. Simply highlight the rows or columns, choose Table, Delete, and choose what you want to delete from the Delete submenu.

When you choose to delete cells in a table, Word displays the Delete Cells dialog box so that you can identify where you want remaining cells to be shifted. Click your selection, and click OK to return to the document.

Moving Rows and Columns

In some instances, you might want to select parts of your table and move them to other parts of your document, perhaps creating a new table, moving rows to another position in the table, or turning the table information into text. When you want to move rows or columns, simply select the rows or columns you want to move and drag the selected block to the new location. The table rows or columns are relocated as you specified.

Merging Cells

Sometimes tables seem to grow out of proportion. If this has happened to your table and you're looking for a way to consolidate data, you can use Word's Merge Cells command to take data from separate cells and combine it in one cell. To merge cells in your table, select the rows or columns you want to merge and choose Table, Merge Cells. The data is combined into a single cell.

> **Note** You'll probably need to do some editing to get your data looking the way you want after a merge. Data takes on the format of the receiving cell, and you might wind up with extra lines and odd capitalization as a result.

Splitting Cells

As you might imagine, splitting cells is the opposite of merging them. When you've got a collection of data that you want to divide into separate cells, rows, or columns, you can use Split Cells on the Tables And Borders toolbar (or the Split Cells command on the Table menu). To split cells, begin by selecting the cell, row, or column you want to split. Click Split Cells on the Tables And Borders toolbar. In the Split Cells dialog box, enter the number of columns and rows over which you want to divide the data. If you have previously merged the data you are now splitting, Word "remembers" the number of columns and rows and suggests those values for the division. To retain the basic format and apply existing row and column formatting to the new columns and rows, leave the Merge Cells Before Split check box selected. Click OK to split the cells.

Tip **Adjust column sizes**

After you split cells in your table, you'll probably need to redistribute the space in the columns. To resize a column quickly, point to the column border in the top row of the column you want to change. When the pointer changes to a double-headed arrow, drag the column border in the direction you want to resize the column. When the column is the size you want it, release the mouse button.

Resizing Tables

You won't always know how large a table is going to be when you first begin creating it. Word provides options for helping you control the size of your table and offers flexibility for resizing your table exactly the way you want. This section explains how you can work with Word to best handle table-sizing issues.

Understanding AutoFit

When you first create a table using the Insert Table dialog box, you're given the option of choosing AutoFit for your table. AutoFit enables you to automatically resize your window as needed, and it is actually already working, by default, to create fixed column widths in your table. AutoFit offers three options:

- **Fixed Column Width** Enables you to choose a specific width for the columns you create.
- **AutoFit To Contents** Adjusts the width of columns to accommodate the data you enter.
- **AutoFit To Window** Sizes a table so that it fits within a Web browser window. This size changes depending on the size of the window, which means that the table will be automatically redrawn as many times as the user resizes his or her browser window.

Tip **Test AutoFit To Window**
If you want to see how resizing your table will affect the rest of the text displayed in your document, you can easily test AutoFit To Window by creating your table, choosing AutoFit To Window (you can do this before you create the table or afterward), and then displaying the table in Web Layout view. When the table is displayed, resize your document window. The table is automatically reformatted so that it always fits within the borders of the window.

Resizing an Entire Table

Although AutoFit does a fine job of keeping on top of the way your table needs to grow (or shrink), there will be times when you want to make those changes yourself. Resizing a table is a simple matter of click-and-drag editing. Start by selecting the table (click the table move handle). Then follow these steps:

1. Scroll to the end of the table. In the lower right corner, you see a table resize handle.
2. Position the pointer over the table resize handle. The pointer changes to a double-headed arrow.
3. Drag the corner of the table in the direction you want the table to be resized. The cells of the table are redrawn to reflect the new size.

Note You can resize tables only in Print Layout and Web Layout views. Although you can see a table in Normal view, the table resize handle is not available.

Setting Preset and Percent Table Sizes

The Table Properties dialog box gives you two very different sizing options. To open this dialog box, click in your table and choose Table, Table Properties. To create a table based on a fixed measurement, click the Table tab and in the Size section, select the Preferred Width check box and enter the width for the table you're going to create. Click the Measured In arrow and select Inches; then click OK.

The best use of this feature, however, is in creating a table that reformats automatically based on the size of the browser window. In other words, if you're viewing your table as part of a Web page, and you reduce the size of your browser window, the table will reformat so that it will stay visible, even in the smaller window. This is a great feature if you're often switching back and forth between applications and want to keep your information open on the screen. To create a table whose dimensions are based on a percentage of screen display, click the Measure In arrow, select Percent, and then click OK. The table will be reformatted as needed to stay within the size of the Web browser window.

Changing Column Width

The fastest way to change the width of a column is also the easiest. You simply position the pointer over the dividing line of the column you want to change and, when the pointer changes to a double-headed arrow, drag the border in the desired direction. Be sure that you've "grabbed" the border for the entire column, however; it's possible to move the border for a single cell, which won't help if you want to make an entire column wider or narrower. (You'll be able to tell that you've grabbed the entire column when you see the dotted column guide along the length of the table.)

Changing Row Height

Changing row height is similar to changing column width. Position the pointer on the row border you want to change. When the pointer changes to a double-headed arrow, drag the border in the desired direction.

Tip **Add space to table rows**

We don't need statistics to tell us that nobody wants to read a cramped table. You can help the readers of your document get your point more easily by providing enough space in your table rows. By default, Word is a bit skimpy on row height (less than a quarter of an inch); you might want to increase your rows to at least 0.25 inch if the space in your document allows.

Distributing Data Evenly in Rows and Columns

Distributing your data refers to the process of spacing and aligning data within cells. By default, when you create a basic table and enter text, the text aligns along the left border of the cell, placed in the first line of the cell. To distribute your data evenly in the rows in your table (spacing it evenly between the top and bottom margins of the row), click Distribute Rows Evenly on the Tables And Borders toolbar.

To distribute the data evenly among the columns in your table, as shown in Figure 13-6, click Distribute Columns Evenly.

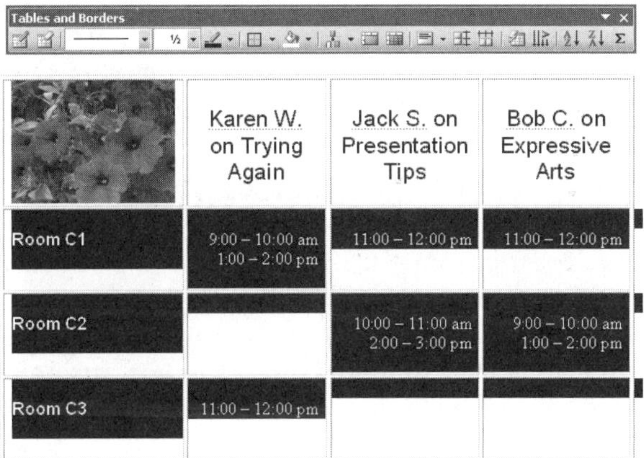

	Karen W. on Trying Again	Jack S. on Presentation Tips	Bob C. on Expressive Arts
Room C1	9:00 – 10:00 am 1:00 – 2:00 pm	11:00 – 12:00 pm	11:00 – 12:00 pm
Room C2		10:00 – 11:00 am 2:00 – 3:00 pm	9:00 – 10:00 am 1:00 – 2:00 pm
Room C3	11:00 – 12:00 pm		

Figure 13-6. Data is distributed evenly among columns and rows in the selected table.

Changing Text Direction

While we're talking about distributing data, how about rotating the text in your table cells? Word provides a capability that enables you to turn your horizontal text to the vertical axis, which gives you the means to create interesting column headings for your tables.

You can change the direction of your text whether you've already entered data or you're just beginning to add data to your table. If you're changing the direction of existing text, select the text, and then click Change Text Direction on the Tables And Borders toolbar. Clicking this button rotates the text 90 degrees to the left. The vertical column headings in the table in Figure 13-7 were created using this button.

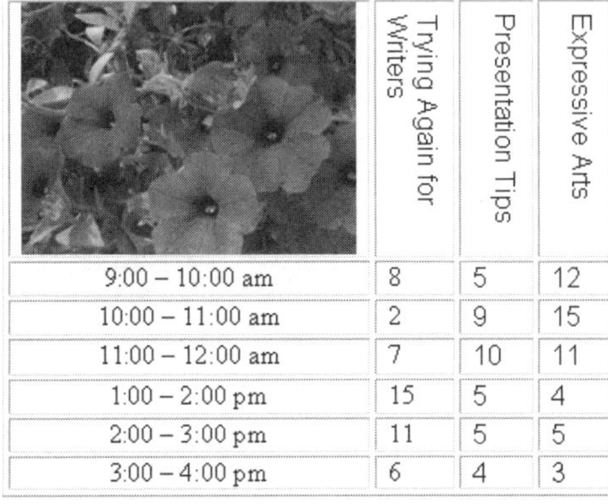

Registration

	Trying Again for Writers	Presentation Tips	Expressive Arts
9:00 – 10:00 am	8	5	12
10:00 – 11:00 am	2	9	15
11:00 – 12:00 am	7	10	11
1:00 – 2:00 pm	15	5	4
2:00 – 3:00 pm	11	5	5
3:00 – 4:00 pm	6	4	3

Figure 13-7. The column headings in this table have been rotated 90 degrees.

If you want to change the direction yet again, click Change Text Direction a second time. Now the text rotates a further 180 degrees, so that it faces the other edge of the table. Click the button again, and the text returns to normal. If you're setting the direction for text that you are about to enter, simply click the button and then type your text.

Enhancing Your Tables with Formatting

Tables come in all shapes and sizes, from simple to sophisticated. Word includes a number of formatting features you can apply to your tables to give them the look you want. Word now supports custom table styles, which means you can create your own Table AutoFormats from scratch or modify existing formats to meet your needs. In this section, you'll also find out about creating borders, adding shading, and using table colors.

Producing a Finished Table with AutoFormat

Word's Table AutoFormat feature gives you a library of different formats you can apply to your tables. When you want to create a table in a hurry, you can rely on Word's Table AutoFormat to give you the look you want, and then you can just plug in the data. Or, if you've already created a basic table, as discussed in the first half of this chapter, you can apply an AutoFormat to your table. To apply an AutoFormat to an existing table,, simply click in the table you want to reformat, open the Table menu, and choose Table AutoFormat. In the Table AutoFormat dialog box (shown in Figure 13-8), scroll through the list to find the format you want to try, then click the desired format and click Apply.

Figure 13-8. Table AutoFormat enables you to apply predesigned table styles to your tables.

In the Table AutoFormat dialog box, you have the option of disabling any of the special features Table AutoFormat applies that you *don't* want to use. You can select the Heading Rows, First Column, Last Row, and Last Column check boxes if you want the entire table to be formatted in a uniform fashion.

Tip **Select a default table style**

If you want to choose a particular Table AutoFormat as the default table style for your document, select it in the Table Styles list box and click Default. Word will display the Default Table Style dialog box, asking whether you want to make this style the default style for this document only or for all documents based on the Normal template. Click your choice, and click OK.

Tip **Create a new table with AutoFormatting**

If you want to start using AutoFormat immediately to set up a new table, you can do so by clicking Insert Table on the Tables And Borders toolbar. The Insert Table dialog box appears. Enter the number of columns and rows you want to create; then click AutoFormat. This action takes you to the Table AutoFormat dialog box, where you can choose the style you like.

Modifying an Existing Table AutoFormat

Once you get used to working with Table AutoFormat, you might discover that you like some styles more than others. Perhaps you like light shading behind columns but find it distracting in heading rows. You might prefer one color to another, or perhaps a certain font matches the standard design of your business documents.

You can modify an existing AutoFormat to create a new style that accommodates the settings you like best. Follow these steps:

1. Click in the table that has been formatted with the Table AutoFormat style you want to enhance.
2. Choose Table, Table AutoFormat. The Table AutoFormat dialog box appears, with the current AutoFormat style selected in the Table Styles list box.
3. Click Modify. The Modify Style dialog box appears, as shown in Figure 13-9.

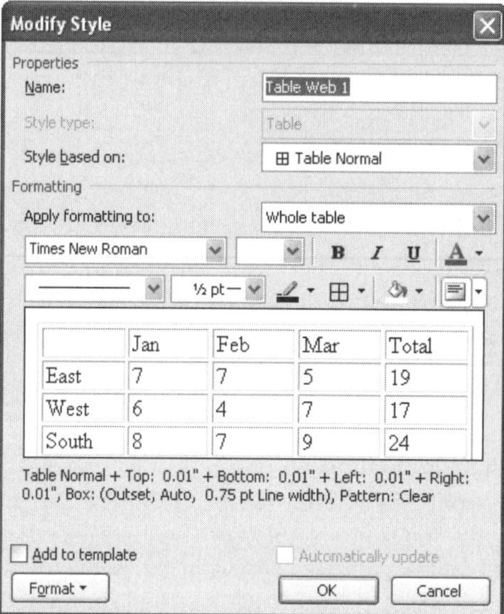

Figure 13-9. You can modify an existingTable AutoFormat style to create a unique table style.

4 Enter a name for the new table style.

> **Tip** **Name table styles memorably**
> Name any new styles you create in such a way that you'll be able to identify the style later. For example, you might choose to name a new shaded table BlueShade1 if that will help you remember what is unique about that style.

5 By default, the table style already applied to the table (if applicable) is shown in the Style Based On list box. Click the arrow and choose a different style if you want to change the format the new style is based on.

6 In the Formatting section, choose the item you want to modify.

> **Note** For those times when you want to modify only a single element of the table format (for example, removing the bold from the last row in the table), choose just the item you want to change, select the new format settings, and click OK.

7 Make your formatting changes in the Modify Style dialog box. When you're finished, click OK to return to the Table AutoFormat dialog box and then click Close to return to the document. Your changes will be reflected in the table.

Note If you want to add the new Table AutoFormat style you create to the template for this document, select the Add To Template check box in the Modify Style dialog box.

Tip **Create your own table style**
The process of modifying an existing Table AutoFormat isn't too different from creating your own from scratch. To create your own AutoFormat table style, click Table AutoFormat on the Tables And Borders toolbar to display the dialog box; then click New. The New Style dialog box appears, containing all the same choices you worked with in the Modify Style dialog box.

Adding Borders and Shading

Borders and shading are two of those fun Word features in which the caveat "a little goes a long way" is particularly meaningful. Think carefully about how and why you'll use borders, shading, and colors, and then create the table effect to match your thoughtful vision.

Using Borders: Do's and Don'ts

Applying borders to your documents isn't rocket science, of course. But by following these simple guidelines, you can make sure your use of borders is a help to your readers, rather than a hindrance.

Do

- Use a border to set a table off from surrounding text.
- Create a type of border that gives the reader's eye a rest.
- Use gridlines when your table includes columns of numbers.

Don't

- Create a heavy, overwhelming border that crowds the text.
- Mix heavy line weights, dark colors, and multi-line styles for traditional documents.
- Use designer lines as a grid in the center of your table.

Choosing Borders

Word provides a number of border styles for your table. When you want to add a border to your table, follow these steps:

Border Color

1. Click anywhere in the table.
2. Click Border Color on the Tables And Borders toolbar. The Borders And Shading dialog box appears, as shown in Figure 13-10.

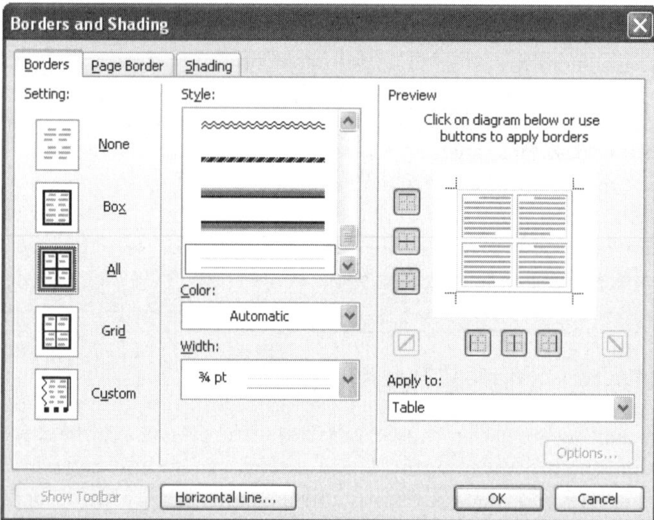

Figure 13-10. Choose from a number of preset border styles in the Borders and Shading dialog box.

3 Select the Setting type you want to use. Word offers five different choices:

- *None*—Doesn't apply a border to the table.
- *Box*—Draws a boundary around the table.
- *All*—Includes an outer border and an internal grid between table cells and applies a shadow format and current style and width settings to the table.
- *Grid*—Creates a three-dimensional effect with an internal grid.
- *Custom*—Enables you to create a custom border, using the settings you select in the Preview section. You might, for example, elect to have only top and bottom borders for your table and forgo any side boundaries or gridlines.

4 Choose the style for the line used in the border. You can scroll through the Style list box to find and select the line style you want.

5 Click the Color arrow to locate and select the color you want to use for the border.

6 Click the Width arrow, and select your choice of width.

7 If you want to customize the display of the selected border by adding or removing border edges, click your selections in the Preview section.

> **Note** If you want to apply a border to a single cell, display the Borders And Shading dialog box and make your selections. Then click the Apply To arrow and select Cell.

Selecting Shading

Right behind the Borders and Page Borders tabs in the Borders And Shading dialog box, you'll find the Shading tab. Shading is often used effectively in tables to perform different functions. For example, shading can be used for these purposes:

- Help the reader see a distinction between data types (for example, the column showing last year's revenue might be light gray, while the column for this year's is white).
- Call attention to important data items.
- Enhance design. Table headings and column labels are often placed in shaded bars.

When you want to add shading to your table, you can use either the Borders And Shading dialog box or Shading Color on the Tables And Borders toolbar. Just click in the table you want to shade and click Border Color. In the Fill area of the Shading tab, click the Fill color you want to apply to the table. The Preview window shows the change. Click the Style arrow and choose the percentage of shade you want to apply; these settings control how dark the shade will be on your table. Click OK and the shade is added to the table.

Note If you want to apply shading to a selected portion of a table, select those cells (or rows or columns) before opening the Borders And Shading dialog box.

If you want to see additional color choices, or enter your own custom color (with RGB percentages), click More Colors. This option comes in handy when you need to match a specific hue for professional documents.

You can later change the table color quickly by clicking Shading Color on the Tables And Borders toolbar. This displays the Borders And Shading dialog box, and you can make your changes as needed.

Working with Table Properties

Now that you've been through many of these table features on your own—from creating tables to editing, resizing, and formatting them—you can work on some of the finer points of table management. The Table Properties dialog box enables you to make choices about how you want your table to behave, both with text in a document and in a Web browser window. To display the Table Properties dialog box, shown in Figure 13-11, click in the table and then choose Table, Table Properties.

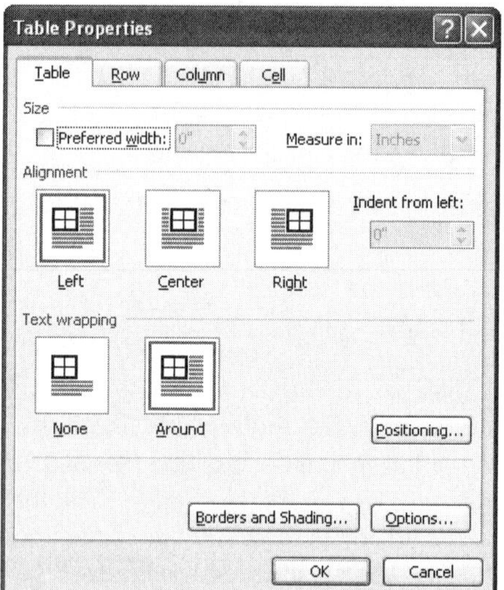

Figure 13-11. The Table Properties dialog box enables you to make sizing and behavior choices for your tables.

Controlling Table Size

In the Table Properties dialog box, the Size options in each of the tabs—Table, Row, Column, and Cell—include the choices you need to set the preferred width or height measurements for each item.

- **Preferred Width** Refers to the size at which the item is displayed by default, if space allows.
- **Measure In** Determines whether the size is kept to a precise measurement or is figured as a percentage of available display space.

> **Tip** **Use the Percent option**
> The Percent option in the Measure In box enables you to create a table that's reformatted to fit a Web page each time a user resizes his or her browser window. Having this kind of flexibility makes your tables that much more effective. Table, Column, and Cell tabs all have the capacity to accept a Percent setting. The Row tab doesn't need the Percent option because rows are controlled by the Column settings for the table.

Aligning Tables with Text

The way in which your text aligns with the table you create is controlled on the Table tab in the Table Properties dialog box. You can choose Left, Center, and Right alignment, which act as follows:

- **Left** Positions the table along the left text margin.
- **Center** Centers the table between the left and right text margins.
- **Right** Aligns the table along the right text margin.

Another option in the Alignment section of the Table tab in the Table Properties dialog box enables you to indent the table from the left margin by a specific increment. The default is set to 0, and you can increase that setting as needed.

Aligning Cells

The Cell tab in the Table Properties dialog box includes an alignment setting that controls the vertical alignment of data in table cells. This setting enables you to choose the alignment of text within a cell, and is related to the choices you can make on the Tables And Borders toolbar when you click Align.

Controlling Text Wrap

Text wrap becomes a very important consideration when you're working with multiple tables in a long document. On the Table tab in the Table Properties dialog box, you have the option of choosing None—which means text will not wrap around the table at all but appear above and below it—or Around, which flows text up to and around the table.

When you click Around, the Positioning button becomes available. Click Positioning to display the Table Positioning dialog box (shown in Figure 13-12), which allows you to make choices that control where the table is positioned in your document by default.

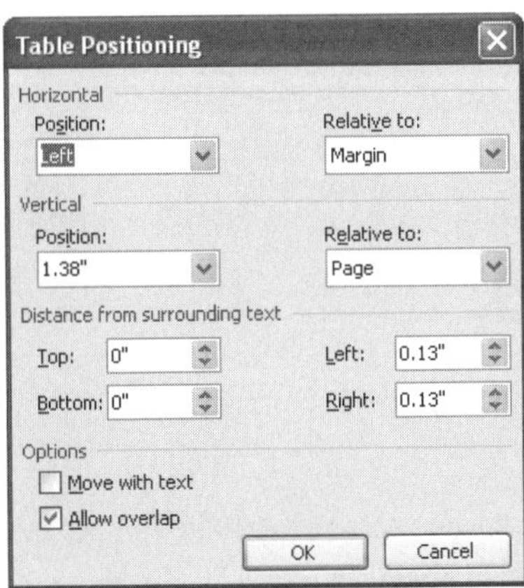

Figure 13-12. The Table Positioning dialog box enables you to control the default table position for your document.

These choices include the following:

- The horizontal and vertical positioning of the table (choose Left, Right, Center, Inside, or Outside)
- The element to which the table position is relative (choose Margin, Page, Column for the horizontal position and Margin, Page, Paragraph for the vertical position)

- The space you want to leave between the table and surrounding text
- Whether you want to allow the text to overlap the table boundary and whether you want the table to stay fixed in place or move with text if it is reformatted

Note Different tables require different settings. Take the time to experiment with the best effects for your particular table.

Controlling Table Breaks

Two options on the Row tab of the Table Properties dialog box, shown in Figure 13-13, control the way in which the table is divided in the event of a section or page break. If you want to allow Word to break the table at a specified point in the table, click Next Row or Previous Row to select the row after which you would allow a break. Then select the Allow Row To Break Across Pages check box.

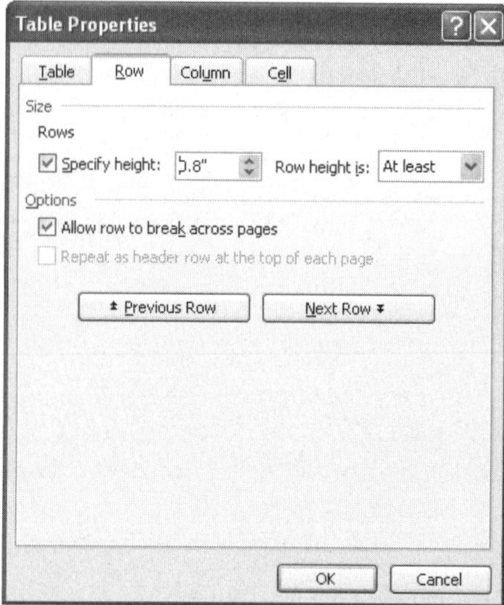

Figure 13-13. Choose whether you want to allow a table to be divided by a page or section break on the Row tab in the Table Properties dialog box.

If you want to repeat the column headings in the second section of the divided table, select the Repeat As Header Row At The Top Of Each Page check box. This will ensure that your table heads are replicated at the beginning of the next table segment.

Sorting Your Table Data

One of the great things about Word tables is that they provide more than a clear way of organizing data—they also give you a means of *reorganizing* data. Word includes a Sort function, so you can easily reorder the information in your table by searching and sorting on certain key words or phrases. You might, for example, want to organize a conference registration list by sorting first according to state and then alphabetically by last name.

The easiest way to sort data in a Word table is to simply click in the table and click Sort Ascending or Sort Descending on the Tables And Borders toolbar. If you want to use Word to perform a more specialized sort, you can display the Sort dialog box (shown in Figure 13-14) by clicking in the table and then choosing Table, Sort. The Sort dialog box provides you with the means to sort by three different fields, data types, and document elements.

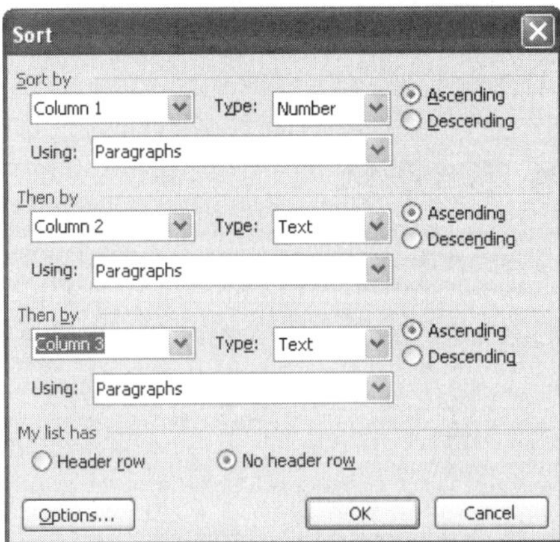

Figure 13-14. The Sort dialog box gives you the means to search on three fields.

To enter sort specifications in the Sort dialog box, follow these steps:

1. In the Sort By section, click the arrow of the first item and choose the name of the column by which you want to sort.
2. Click the Type arrow and select the data type (Text, Number, or Date).
3. Leave Ascending selected if that's the sort order you choose; otherwise, click Descending.
4. If you have a secondary sort, select that column in the Then By section. (For example, you might want to arrange the products first by Type, then by Shelf, and finally by Product number.)
5. Select the data type for the secondary sort and select the sort order.
6. Define a third sort in the second Then By section if needed.
7. If you want Word to leave the header row out of the sort, click the Header Row option.
8. Click OK to perform the sort.

Tip **Sort non-tabular data**

Word includes options that enable you to search information that isn't in table form. To sort non-tabular data, highlight it and choose Table, Sort. Click Options in the Sort dialog box to open the Sort Options dialog box and specify the character you've used to separate data entries. If you want Word to distinguish between uppercase and lowercase letters (which it ignores by default), select the Case Sensitive check box. Click OK to return to the Sort dialog box.

Troubleshooting

A two-name search produces unexpected results

If your two-name search doesn't give you the results you expect, make sure that you've used the right character to separate the words. If you're searching for <FirstName> <LastName>, you need to insert a space to separate the words. If you're searching <LastName>, <FirstName>, you need to include a comma and space between the words. To enter the separator character, choose Table, Sort, and click Options. Select the separator you want in the Separate Fields At section.

Working with Functions in Tables

Although Word is happy to leave the truly complicated calculations to its sister, Excel, the program includes support for working with a number of functions in your tables. Some of the Word tables you create will no doubt include numbers—and some of those columns will require totals, averages, and more.

Adding with AutoSum

The function you'll use most often will probably be AutoSum, included as a button on the Tables And Borders toolbar. AutoSum will total the cell values in contiguous cells in a column or row. To use AutoSum, follow these steps:

1. Click in the cell at the end of a column of numbers (or the right end of a row).
2. Click the AutoSum button on the Tables And Borders toolbar. Word automatically totals the column or row of numbers and inserts the total at the insertion point.

Note Whenever you change a value in the column used to create the AutoSum total, the change will be reflected in the sum. To force an update of calculations in your table, highlight the previous total, and then press F9.

Using Other Functions

AutoSum isn't the only function you can include in your Word tables. You can create a number of calculations, depending on what you want the data in your tables to do. You can create your own formulas and work with other Word functions by using the Formula dialog box shown in Figure 13-15.

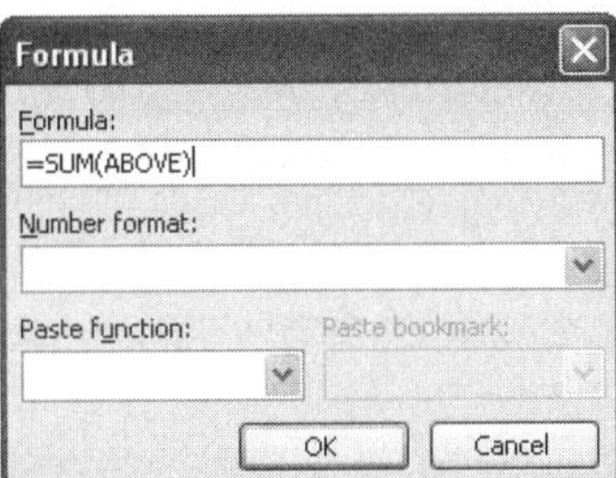

Figure 13-15. You can create your own formulas in the Formula dialog box.

You can display the different functions Word allows by clicking the Paste function arrow. These functions are available for your selection:

ABS	IF	OR
AND	INT	PRODUCT
AVERAGE	MAX	ROUND
COUNT	MIN	SIGN
DEFINED	MOD	SUM
FALSE	NOT	TRUE

To insert your own formula in a table, follow these steps:

1. Click in a cell at the end of a column of numbers where you want to add the formula.
2. Choose Table, Formula. The Formula dialog box is displayed.
3. Type = in the Formula box to tell Word you're entering a formula.
4. Click the Paste function arrow and choose the function you want from the displayed list box. The function is added to the Formula box, and parentheses are supplied.
5. Click OK to close the Formula dialog box. Word will then calculate the answer and display it in the table cell.

> **Tip** **Choose a number format**
> You can have Word display a numeric result in the format you want. Simply click the Number format arrow and choose from the displayed options.

Converting Tables to Text

What happens when you don't want a table to be a table anymore? Suppose that you've created a great table for the annual report, but now someone in marketing wants it in text form—no tables allowed. How do you preserve the data and lose the grid? You can make the change easily. Click in the table and choose Table, Convert, Table To Text. In the Convert

Table To Text dialog box, select the character you want Word to use to delineate individual text entries. You might have Word separate your table entries by inserting commas, paragraph marks, or another character between them. Click OK to convert the table.

Changing Text to a Table

The process for changing text to a table is equally simple. When you select text in Word to be formatted as a table and you choose Table, Convert, Text To Table, the Convert Text To Table dialog box asks for input similar to what you entered in the Insert Table dialog box. The program will want to know how many columns and rows you want to use, how you want to use AutoFit, which Table AutoFormat you want to use (if any), and finally, which characters have been used to delineate the individual text entries. Click your choices and click OK. Word converts the text to a new table.

Chapter 14

Showcasing Data with Charts, Graphs, and Diagrams

A chart can give you an image and an understanding of your data in a way that words alone can't. With a single picture, you can show how sales in all four regions compare—you know at a glance who comes out the winner. You can capture and portray important buying trends among your customers; you can give upper management a picture of staff productivity; you can give an instant picture of the healthy progress your business is making in new venues. If your business is considering reorganization, a diagram can help the group understand the new chain of command and settle into their new roles more easily. In all cases, seeing a chart or diagram helps communicate relationships quickly—much faster than reading about upcoming changes and forming the new image in your mind.

Note What's the difference between a chart and a graph? Nothing, really. The terms are used interchangeably to describe the graphical depiction of data—early on, the term *charting* referred to a type of mapmaking. *Graphing*, on the other hand, involved plotting data points and discerning trends and relationships. Today, the terms mean essentially the same thing; for example, you use Microsoft Graph to create *charts* in your Word documents. *Diagramming* refers to the process of generating a flowchart or diagram using a specific model. The second half of this chapter deals with planning, creating, and enhancing diagrams in your documents.

The Smart Use of Charts and Graphs

Charts are used to illustrate relationships—how one item relates to another, how an item this year relates to the same item last year. There are several different types of charts available to you as you create your Word documents. Some of the most commonly used charts include the following:

- **Column charts** A column chart is used to show data comparisons. You might show, for example, how two data series "stack up" against each other for the first quarter.
- **Bar charts** Word shows a bar chart as horizontal bars, graphing data items over time (or other categories). You might use a bar chart to compare the stages of different products in a production cycle.
- **Line charts** A line chart plots data points over time or by category. You might use a line chart to show a trend in product returns over a six-month period.
- **Pie charts** A pie chart shows the relationship of different data items to the whole. Each pie comprises 100 percent of the series being graphed, and each slice is shown as a percentage of the pie. You might use a pie chart to show the relative size of individual departments in the northeastern sales division of your company.
- **XY (Scatter) charts** An XY chart enables you to plot pairs of data points over time. You might use an XY chart to contrast the test scores from a battery of exams given at two different universities.
- **Area charts** An area chart gives you the means to compare data two different ways: You can show the accumulated result of the data items, and you can show how the data (and their relationship to one another) change over time. For example, you might use an area chart to show how many students took each module of the exam at two different universities.
- **Doughnut charts** A doughnut chart is similar to a pie chart in that it shows the relationship between data items. Doughnut charts enable you to compare two sets of data and the way in which they relate to the whole and to each other. You might use a doughnut chart to portray two different sales campaigns. The sections of the doughnut could represent the different sales channels, and you could compare and contrast the different effects of each channel.
- **Radar charts** A radar chart plots multiple data points and shows their relation to a center point. You might use a radar chart to show how each regional sales division fared in the recent sales competition.
- **Bubble charts** A bubble chart enables you to plot three different data series. Each item is plotted at a particular point in time and shows the data value as a bubble. This would enable you to see, for example, which accounts had the highest charges during the second quarter.

Introducing Microsoft Graph

Word relies on Graph to help you create the charts you want in your documents. Graph is a full-featured graphing utility that enables you to use any of the 14 standard charts or the 20 built-in custom charts. You can also create your own custom chart types when you need to show unique data relationships for your documents. Table 14-1 lists the chart types you can create in Graph.

Table 14-1. Chart Types in Graph

Standard	Column, Bar, Line, Pie, XY (Scatter), Area, Doughnut, Radar, Surface, Bubble, Stock, Cylinder, Cone, Pyramid
Custom	Area Blocks, B&W Area, B&W Column, B&W Line-Timescale, B&W Pie, Blue Pie, Colored Lines, Column-Area, Columns with Depth, Cones, Floating Bars, Line-Column, Line-Column on 2 Axes, Lines on 2 Axes, Logarithmic, Outdoor Bars, Pie Explosion, Smooth Lines, Stack of Colors, Tubes

Note Graph is built into Word and all other Microsoft Office System applications as well. You begin a chart by choosing Insert, Picture, Chart. When you want to edit a chart, simply double-click the chart and Graph launches automatically.

Creating a Basic Chart

When you're ready to create a simple chart with Graph, start by selecting the data you want to use. You can do this by entering the data in the datasheet Graph gives you, by copying the data from another program, or by selecting data in your current Word document.

Starting with Word and Selecting Chart Data

The easiest way to create a chart is to begin with a table of data you've created in your Word document. Create your information as you want it, and then follow these steps to use it to create a chart:

1. Click in the table, and then choose Table, Select, Table (or click the table move handle to select the entire table).
2. Choose Insert, Picture, Chart. Graph starts, and then creates a chart based on the information in the table you selected. (See Figure 14-1.)

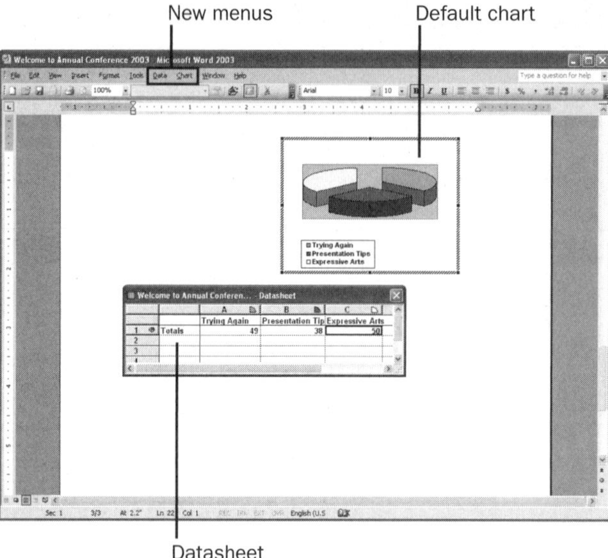

Figure 14-1. You can easily create a chart based on data you've already entered in your Word document.

> **Tip** **Select table sections only**
> If you want only a portion of the table to be used for your chart, select only the segment you want to use, and then choose Insert, Picture, Chart.

Checking Out the Graph Window

When Graph starts in Word, it brings with it several key components. Graph inserts additional menus in the Word menu bar and adds graph-related buttons to the Standard toolbar. The default chart that Graph draws based on the data you selected is a column chart.

- **Default chart** Graph chooses a column chart as the default chart type for the data you select. You can easily change the chart type to better represent the data you're working with.
- **Datasheet** The information you selected in your Word document is shown in the datasheet. Here you can modify information as needed to customize the values and labels shown in the chart.
- **Additional menus** Graph brings two additional menus—Data and Chart—that enable you to work with the data and charts you create. The commands in the other menus are also changed to reflect chart-related commands.

Note **Get Graph Help**
Graph comes with a fully developed Help system of its own, which means that you can get help on any chart operations you're attempting. Simply press F1 to start Help.

Importing Data from Other Programs

Although you're creating a chart for use in your Word document, you might want to use data from other programs to create the chart. Because the Microsoft Office System is built on the "create it once, use it many times" idea, you can import data from Excel, as well as other popular programs. You can import data in the following formats:

- Excel
- Text files
- SYLK (Symbol Link) files
- Lotus 1-2-3
- Extensible Markup Language (XML) files

When you're ready to import a data file to use as the basis for your Graph chart, follow these steps:

1. Double-click the chart with the datasheet you want to modify.

View Datasheet

2. Make sure the datasheet appears. If it isn't in view, click the View Datasheet button on the Standard toolbar.

Import File

3. Choose Edit, Import File or click Import File on the Standard toolbar. The Import File dialog box appears.
4. Click the arrow in the Files Of Type box and select the format of the file you're importing. (This example assumes you've selected an Excel file, but the process for the other file types is similar.)
5. Navigate to the folder you want, select the file, and then click Open. The Import Data Options dialog box appears, as shown in Figure 14-2.

Figure 14-2. You can use data from other programs in the charts you create in Graph.

6. Choose the worksheet from which you want to import the chart data.
7. Enter the data range of cells you want to import if you're importing only selected data; otherwise, leave the Entire Sheet option selected.
8. If you want to be prompted before Graph overwrites the existing data in your datasheet, clear the Overwrite Existing Cells check box. (By default, Graph selects this check box, which causes your data to be overwritten without any action by you.)
9. Click OK. The data is brought into the datasheet and the chart is changed accordingly.

Tip **Link or embed chart data**

You can choose to link or embed chart data in a Word document. If you link a chart, the chart in your Word document will be updated whenever the source document changes. If you embed a chart in your document, you'll be able to edit the chart as you would normally, by double-clicking it in the hosting document.

Creating the Right Chart for the Job

Making sure you've got the right chart for the data you're displaying is key to communicating your point most effectively. Some charts, such as bar and column charts, are best for comparing data items—for example, tracking the sales of apples compared to oranges. Other charts, such as pie charts, are better for showing the relation of individual items to a whole—such as the sales of apples and oranges as they compare to total produce sold in May 2004.

Tip **Create your own custom chart types**

You can also create your own custom chart types with Graph. When there's a specific type of chart you want, or a mix of chart types, you can create your own specifications and save them with the current document. To find out more about creating a custom chart type, see "Creating Your Own Chart Types," on page 439.

Checking Out the Chart Types

Graph makes it simple for you to select and change chart types. Start by creating a new chart or by displaying the chart you've already created. Double-click the chart, if necessary, so that the Graph additions to the Standard toolbar are displayed. Then choose Chart, Chart Type. The Chart Type dialog box appears, as shown in Figure 14-3, containing all the different charts—both Standard and Custom—that are available to you.

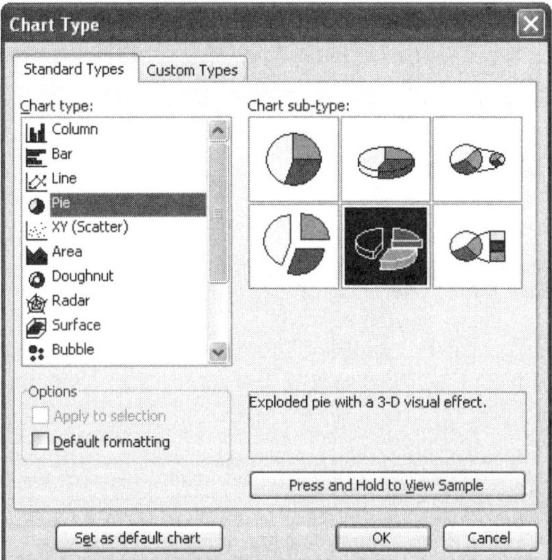

Figure 14-3. The Chart Type dialog box includes more than 30 different chart types you can use to illustrate your data.

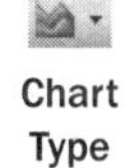
Chart Type

Tip **Change chart types—the fast way**

If you've used the Chart Type dialog box before, Graph will have placed the Chart Type button on the Standard toolbar. To change a chart type quickly, simply click the Chart Type button's arrow, and then select the chart you want from the menu. The selected chart is automatically replaced with the new chart type.

Selecting a Standard Chart Type

The Standard Types tab in the Chart Type dialog box is the first to appear. The type of chart selected in the Chart Type list (and in the Chart Sub-Type section) depends on the type of chart selected in your document.

To choose another chart type, simply scroll through the Chart Type list, and then select the one you want. The examples in the Chart Sub-Type section change to reflect your new choice. Select the sub-type you want by clicking it as well. When you click OK, you are returned to Graph and your chart is updated to show the new chart type.

Tip **Test your choice**

If you're not sure how your choice will look and want to test it before you make the change, select the type and the sub-type, and then click Press And Hold To View Sample in the Standard Types tab in the Chart Type dialog box. Graph gives you a preview of your chart, redrawn in the format of the new type. If you like what you see, click OK, and the chart is replaced in your document.

Choosing a Custom Chart Type

If you don't see what you want in the Standard Types tab in the Chart Type dialog box, you can try the Custom Types tab, shown in Figure 14-4. Click that tab and scroll through the Chart Type list box. You'll see many different styles of all kinds and colors. When you find the one you want, select it, and then click OK. You are returned to your document and the chart change is made.

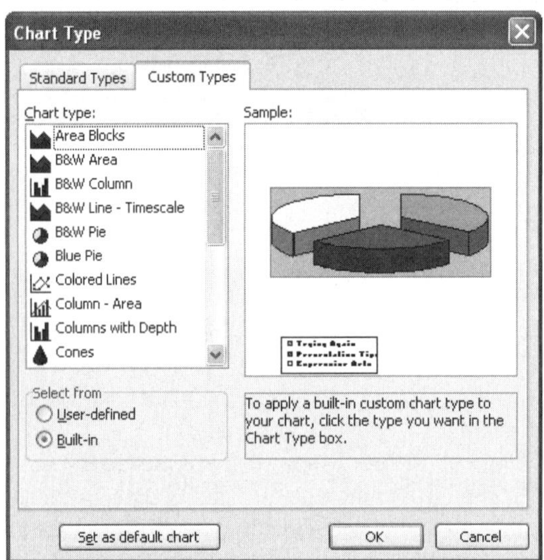

Figure 14-4. The Chart Type Custom Types tab gives you additional choices for more specialized graphs.

> **Tip** Notice that if you select a chart you created before you click Chart Type, Graph will display your chart in the preview window so that you can see how it will look when you change it to a different type.

Setting a New Default Chart Type

If you really like the chart type you've selected, you can make it the default chart that Graph automatically uses whenever you create a new chart. Double-click the chart in your document, and then choose Chart, Chart Type. Click Set As Default Chart to store this chart type as the type Graph uses when you create a new chart.

Creating Your Own Chart Types

If you just can't find the exact chart you want, or if your data needs are specialized for a particular document type, you can create a custom chart type to handle your unique situation. Like creating a style, creating a custom chart style is based on an existing style. You can tailor the existing style by changing colors, bar type, three-dimensional (3-D) or two-dimensional (2-D) effects, background, titles and labels, and more.

To create your own custom chart type, follow these steps:

1. Place the insertion point where you want to create the chart.
2. Choose Insert, Picture, Chart. The default chart and datasheet appear.
3. Change the data as needed and close the datasheet, and then select other chart options such as chart type, color, and style in the way you want them to appear.
4. Click Chart, Chart Type.
5. In the Chart Type dialog box, click the Custom Types tab.
6. In the Select From section, click the User-Defined option. The Custom Types tab changes to show the Default chart type. An Add button appears so that you can add the new chart type to the Chart Type list.
7. Click Add. The Add Custom Chart Type dialog box appears, as shown in Figure 14-5.

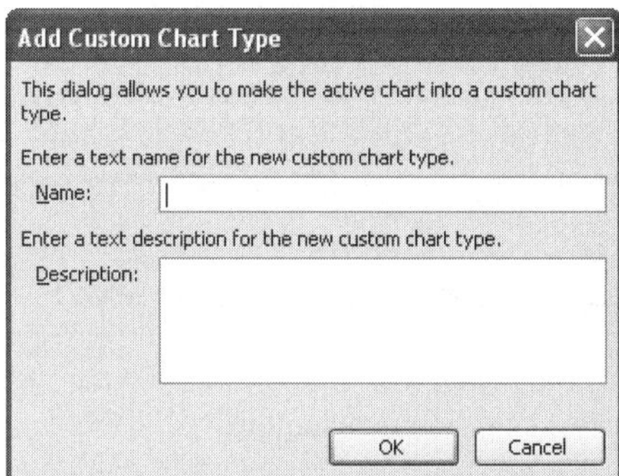

Figure 14-5. When you create a custom chart type, you name the type and add a description in the Add Custom Chart Type dialog box.

8. In the Name box, type a name for the chart type.
9. If you want to add a description of the chart or the way it is to be used, click in the Description box, and then type the explanation of the chart type.
10. Click OK to add the custom chart type, and then click OK in the Chart Type dialog box to finish creating the custom chart type.

Tip **Use your own chart types**

When you want to use one of your own custom-designed chart types in a document, choose Insert, Picture, Chart, click the Custom Types tab in the Chart Type dialog box, and then click the User-Defined option. Select the chart you want to use from the Chart Types list, and then click OK. Graph inserts the custom chart in your document.

Working with the Datasheet

When you first create a chart, whether you're basing the information on data in your current Word document or entering it as you go, Graph displays a datasheet along with the newly created chart. The datasheet shows you the data, including categories, data series, and values, that's used to make your chart. (See Figure 14-6.)

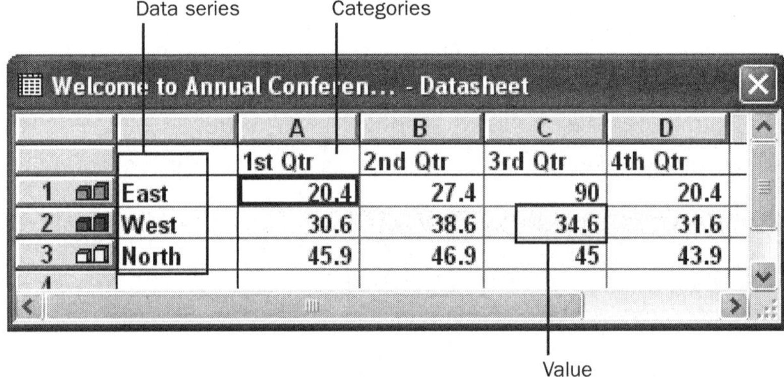

		A	B	C	D
		1st Qtr	2nd Qtr	3rd Qtr	4th Qtr
1	East	20.4	27.4	90	20.4
2	West	30.6	38.6	34.6	31.6
3	North	45.9	46.9	45	43.9
4					

Figure 14-6. The datasheet displays the data values and labels used to create your chart.

You can easily modify this data and change the way the chart is drawn by editing the values in the datasheet. The datasheet includes the following elements:

- **Categories** The items in the columns are the categories placed along the horizontal axis of the chart. Categories might include months, quarters, stages of a project, or some other unit by which value can be measured.
- **Data Series** The data series show the items that are being graphed, according to the categories selected.
- **Values** The data entered in the cells of the datasheet is compared to the value axis, which is the vertical axis in the created chart.

Datasheet Tips

Here are some quick tips for working with your chart's datasheet:

- To select everything in the datasheet quickly, click the Select All button (the gray rectangle in the upper-left corner of the datasheet).
- To hide a data series, double-click the row label of the series you want to hide.
- To add a data series, simply click in the next available row, type a label, and then enter your data. To insert or delete a row or column in the datasheet, right-click inside the datasheet, and then click Insert or Delete. Select the way you want to shift cells (down or to the right), select whether you want to insert or delete a row or column, and then click OK.
- To control the way the datasheet treats empty cells, choose Tools, Options, and then click the Chart tab in the Graph Options dialog box. Click the empty cell option you want, and then click OK.
- To copy datasheet values for use in a Word table, select the information you want, and then press Ctrl+C. This places a copy on the Clipboard, and you can paste the data as needed by pressing Ctrl+V.

Chapter 14

Note If you close the datasheet, you can display it again while you edit the chart by clicking the View Datasheet button on the Standard toolbar.

Changing the Data Arrangement

By default, Graph displays the categories along the horizontal axis and the values along the vertical axis, but if you choose, you can flip that arrangement to display your data differently. Consider, for example, the chart shown in Figure 14-7. Although the default configuration for the chart compares the quarterly sales results of each region, the flipped version compares the regions with each other, spotlighting how well each did during the different quarters of the year.

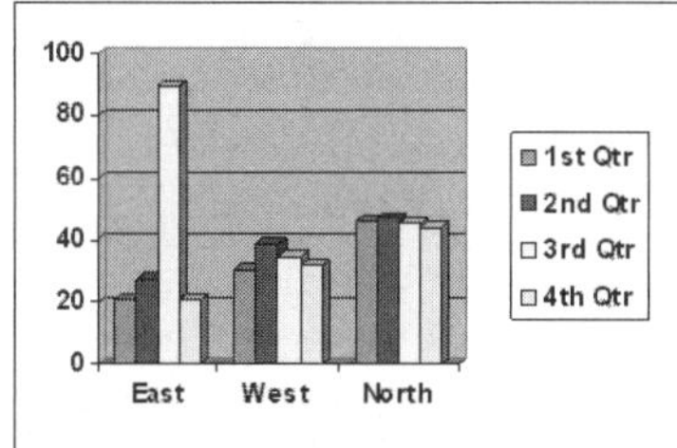

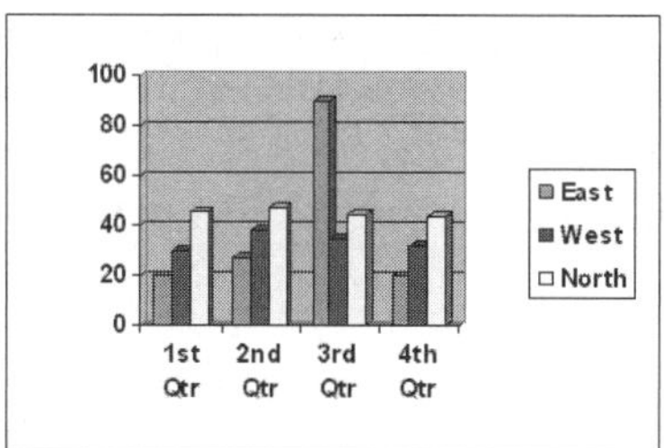

Figure 14-7. Flipping the data arrangement in your chart enables you to see in a new way the data you've used to build your chart.

By Column

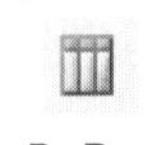

By Row

You can change the data arrangement of your chart in two ways:

- Choose Data, Series In Columns or Series In Rows (the default).
- Click the By Column button or the By Row button on the Standard toolbar while editing the chart to change the data arrangement. By Row is the default setting.

Editing and Enhancing Chart Information

Creating your chart is only half the fun. Once you decide on the basic style you want, you can add to, edit, and enhance your chart by using chart options to add titles and labels, and you can make other modifications as well. You use the Chart Options dialog box, shown in Figure 14-8, to add titles, axis controls, gridlines, legends, labels, and more.

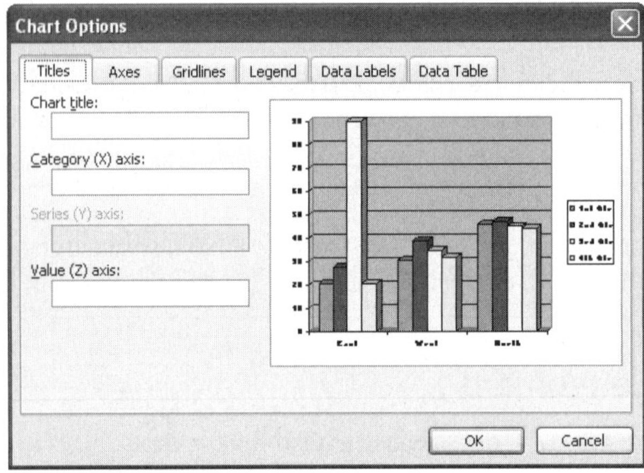

Figure 14-8. You add titles, labels, and other chart elements in the Chart Options dialog box.

> **Note** Although most of the elements you'll find in the Chart Options dialog box apply to all the different chart types, some controls are disabled for certain charts. For example, the Series (Y) Axis check box is disabled in a default column chart. And the only tabs available for a pie chart are Titles, Legend, and Data Labels.

To display the Chart Options dialog box, double-click the chart in your document, and then choose Chart, Chart Options. Then use the following items as a guide to help you set the options for your chart:

- **Title the chart.** The Titles tab appears by default. Click in the Chart Title box, type your title, and then click Tab. The preview window is automatically updated to reflect your change.

Tip **Choose chart titles that work**

Chances are that you won't have a lot of room in your document for lengthy chart titles. Try to choose a title that pulls out key words reflecting what the chart's portraying. If you're comparing product sales, "Product Sales Comparison" works. If you're comparing your private school's test results with the local public school system, "Test Score Comparison" would be accurate. Not exciting, but accurate. If you can think of something exciting too, all the better.

- **Name the axes.** The process of naming the axes is similar to naming the chart: simply click in the appropriate box, and then type your title. The Category (X) Axis is the horizontal axis; the Value (Z) Axis is the vertical axis. Remember that each title you enter takes up space around your chart and that you run the risk of giving the readers too much to read—so make sure your axes' titles, if you use them, truly add to the information you're trying to convey.
- **Hide axis tick marks.** To suppress the display of the tick marks used along the axes, click the Axes tab, as shown in Figure 14-9. The Axes tab gives you the choice to display or hide the marks and labels along the Category (X) axis and the Value (Z) axis. If your chart has a Series (Y) axis, this option will be enabled as well. By default, all labels and marks are displayed. To suppress the display, clear the check box beside each axis item you want to hide.

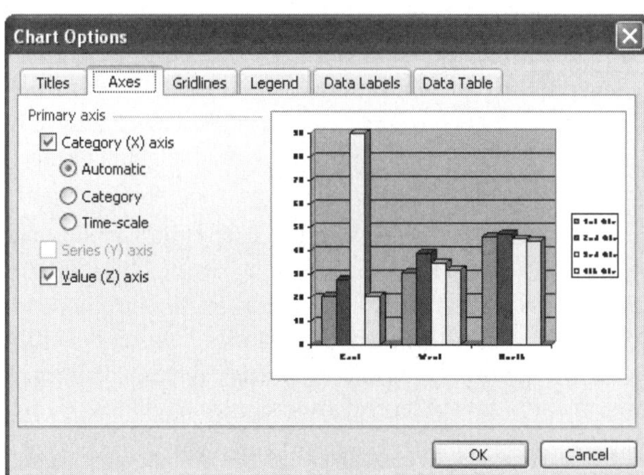

Figure 14-9. If you're pressed for space in your document, you can suppress the display of axis labels and tick marks.

- **Add gridlines.** If you're working with complicated charts that have multiple data series, gridlines can help clarify the comparisons and conclusions you want readers to draw from your chart. Select the Gridlines tab in the Chart Options dialog box, and then click either Category Axis Gridlines or Value Axis Gridlines. Alternatively, you can click in the chart and click either the Category Axis Gridlines button or Value Axis Gridlines button on the Standard toolbar.

> **Tip** By default, Graph adds gridlines at each major category or value mark in your chart. But you can add additional gridlines in smaller increments, if you find that your data warrants it. With the chart selected, choose Chart, Chart Options to display the Chart Options dialog box, and then click the Gridlines tab. You'll find a series of options that enable you to select both Major and Minor gridlines for your chart.

Be forewarned, however: with gridlines, a little goes a long way. Be sure to add only what your reader needs in order to understand your data—too many lines will clutter up your chart and make it more difficult for readers to decipher.

> **Tip** **Get the particulars right**
> If you want more control over where gridlines are placed and how tick marks appear, select the axis you want to change, and then right-click and choose Format Axis from the shortcut menu. In the Format Axis dialog box, click the Scale tab, and then enter the settings you want for the display and number of tick marks used.

Legend

- **Work with a legend.** Graph assumes that you want a legend for your chart when you first create it. You can have Graph remove the legend by clicking Legend on the Standard toolbar. This hides the legend and causes your chart to be enlarged to fill the space the legend previously occupied.
- **Control legend placement.** You can control where the legend is placed in the chart by selecting the chart in Graph, and then choosing Chart, Chart Options to display the Chart Options dialog box. Click the Legend tab and you'll see a number of options that enable you to hide the legend (simply clear the Show Legend check box) or, in the Placement section, position the legend by clicking Bottom, Corner, Top, Right, or Left. Graph repositions or hides the legend after you click OK.
- **Enter data labels.** Data labels are helpful when you need to give the reader further clues about which data items go with which series or category. Graph gives you the ability to add several different kinds of data labels to your charts. You might want to add percentages to pie slices, for example, or category labels to stacked bars. Click the Data Labels tab, and then choose the type of labels you want to use, as shown in Figure 14-10.

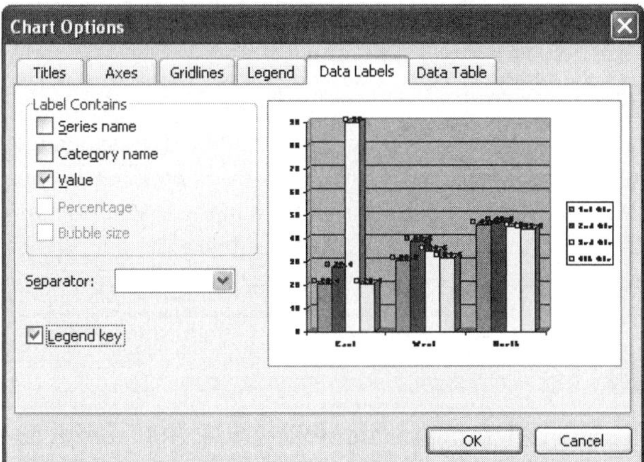

Figure 14-10. Data labels can add a bit of extra description to the data series in your chart.

> **Tip** **Choose multiple labels**
> You can choose to display more than one type of label if you choose. For example, you might want to display both percentages and category names on a pie chart. If you select more than one label type, use a separator to separate the labels. Click the Separator arrow to display a list of choices, and then click the separator you want to use.

One more way to make sure that readers get the connection between your data trends and the categories being plotted: you can use the Legend Key feature to add small legend tags to the left of each data label. Readers will be able to see at a glance which items relate to the categories in your chart legend.

> **Tip** **Change labels in the datasheet**
> The data labels Graph uses are taken right from your datasheet. If you want to change a data label on the chart, it's best to go back to the datasheet and make the change. Otherwise, the label change might not "stick" and you might see the same old label displayed the next time you display your chart.

Data Table

- **Create a data table.** A data table can give readers another way to understand the data being graphed. Click the Data Table tab, and then click the Show Data Table check box. When you click OK, the data table is added to your document. Alternatively, you can click in the chart and then click the Data Table button on the Standard toolbar.

Troubleshooting

I can't see axis titles in my chart

If you're having trouble seeing the axis titles along the Category and Values axes on your chart, the chart area might be too small to display all the chart information successfully. Try resizing the chart by clicking it, and then dragging one of the resize handles outward, enlarging the chart. If that doesn't do the trick, click the axis title while editing the chart, and then choose a smaller Font Size on the Formatting toolbar.

Formatting Charts

Graph gives you the ability to format all the different elements your chart includes. You might want to change the font of a title, resize the labels, change the background color, change the line thickness, apply a pattern, or do any number of other things.

To choose the chart object you want to work with, double-click the chart, and then click the Chart Objects arrow on the Standard toolbar. A list of possible objects appears, as shown in Figure 14-11. Click your choice, and then Graph selects that item in the chart. You can then right-click the item to display a format choice—for example, right-clicking a legend displays a shortcut menu with Format Legend. When you select that command, a formatting dialog box appears in which you can select the Patterns, Font, and Placement for the legend.

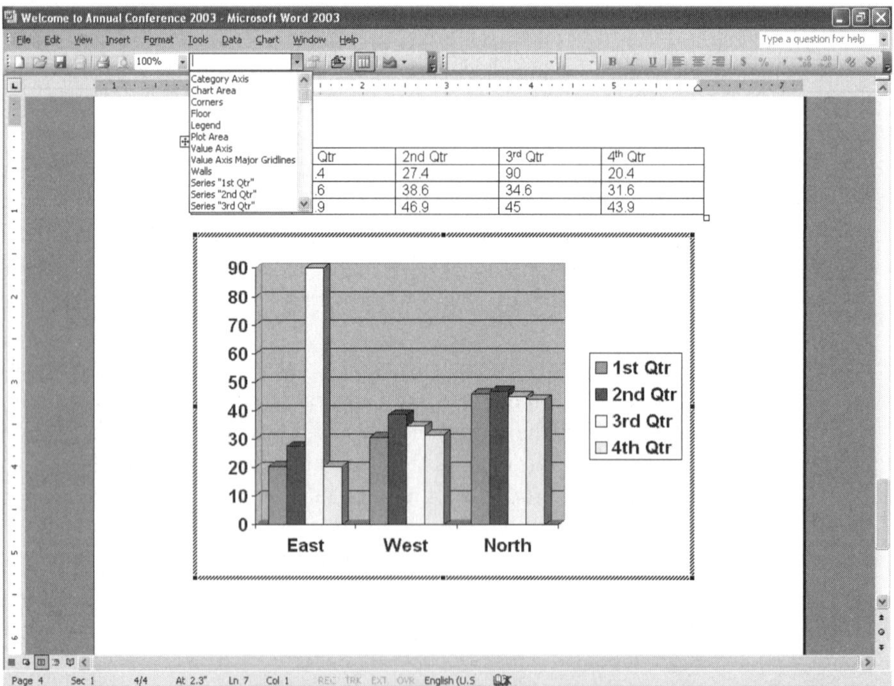

Figure 14-11. Use the Chart Objects list to select the chart element you want to work with.

Note The formatting commands available—and the tabs in the different Formatting dialog boxes—vary widely depending on the type of chart you're creating and the chart element you've selected. Right-clicking a chart axis, for example, displays a very different set of choices than right-clicking the legend does.

Working with Patterns

You work with patterns in Graph to format a number of different items:

- Do you want a border around your chart? If so, what kind? You make those choices in the Patterns tab in the Format dialog box.
- Do you want to choose a different color for the lines in your chart?
- Would you like to add a drop shadow to the chart?
- Do you plan to recolor any or all of the data series lines or bars in your chart?

You can change each of these items by displaying the Format dialog box and clicking the Patterns tab, as shown in Figure 14-12. By default, Graph includes a single-line border, but you can customize and modify the lines used to enclose your chart. Additionally, you can experiment with fill colors for the chart area. The Sample preview box in the lower-left corner shows you the effect of your changes.

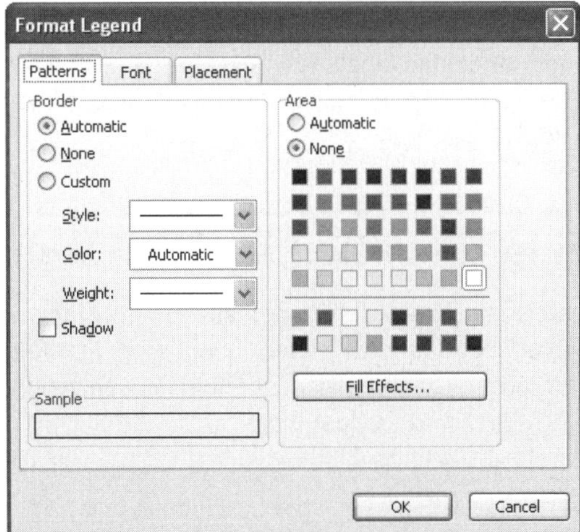

Figure 14-12. You can modify settings in the Patterns tab in the Format Legend dialog box to change the chart's border and color scheme.

Changing Fonts

There's no big secret about changing fonts in a chart—simply select the text you want to change and change it as you would text in your document. You can use the buttons on the Formatting toolbar (which is available even when Graph is active), or you can choose Format, Font. The

Format dialog box appears with the Font tab selected, as shown in Figure 14-13, and you can modify the font, style, size, underline, color, background, and effects.

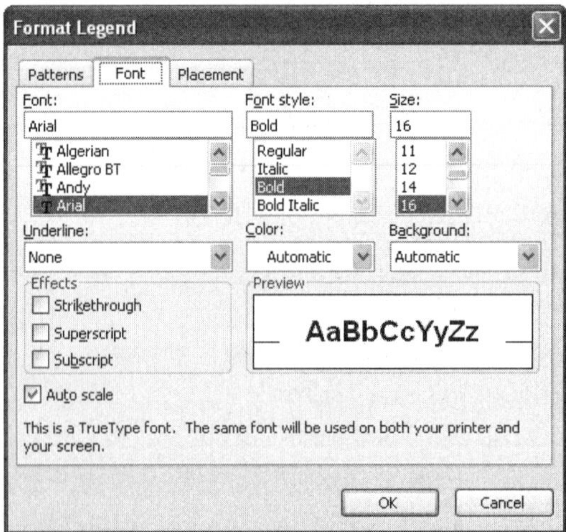

Figure 14-13. You can easily change the fonts used for titles and labels in your chart by using the Font tab in the Format Legend dialog box.

Tip **Control the size of titles and labels**

The Auto Scale check box in the Font tab in the Format dialog box is selected by default—this means that Graph will resize your titles and labels to fit the chart if you resize it. If you want the titles and labels to stay the same size no matter how much the chart is enlarged or reduced, clear the Auto Scale check box.

3-D Charts: Changing Elevation and Rotation

You might notice that your 3-D chart angles to the left by default. You might find, however, that the other design elements on your page have a different orientation. In this case, you need to be able to change the chart layout. Graph provides the following elevation and rotation options for 3-D charts, which enable you to do just that:

- **Elevation** The vertical distance from which the reader's perspective of the chart is measured. For example, with an elevation of 30, the elevation is twice as "high" as the same chart viewed with an elevation of 15.
- **Rotation** The degree to which the chart is rotated away from the head-on view. Raising Microsoft's default value of 20 to 40 turns the chart further to the left.
- **Perspective** Another option available for some charts. This option enables you to change the depth of the chart by increasing or decreasing the value.

To change the elevation, rotation, and perspective for your 3-D chart, double-click the chart, and then choose Chart, 3-D View. Experiment with the Elevation and Rotation until you get the effect you want. Click Apply and then OK to return to your document.

Adding Error Bars and Trendlines

Two additional visual cues, error bars and trendlines, can help your readers understand your data more quickly. Error bars show the error margin built into each data marker, and trendlines use an analysis of existing data to predict future behavior.

Inserting Error Bars

You can create error bars for the data series in your 2-D area, bar, column, and line charts, as well as bubble and XY (scatter) charts. To add error bars to your chart, follow these steps:

1. Double-click your chart to select it.
2. Use the Chart Objects list to select the data series to which you want to add error bars.
3. Right-click the selected series, and then choose Format Data Series from the shortcut menu.
4. Click the Y Error Bars tab, and then select the Display option you want.You can choose one of the following, as Figure 14-14 shows:
   - *Both*—Displays an error amount above and below the displayed value
   - *Plus*—Displays an error amount above the displayed value
   - *Minus*—Shows an error amount below the displayed value
   - *None*—No error bars are displayed

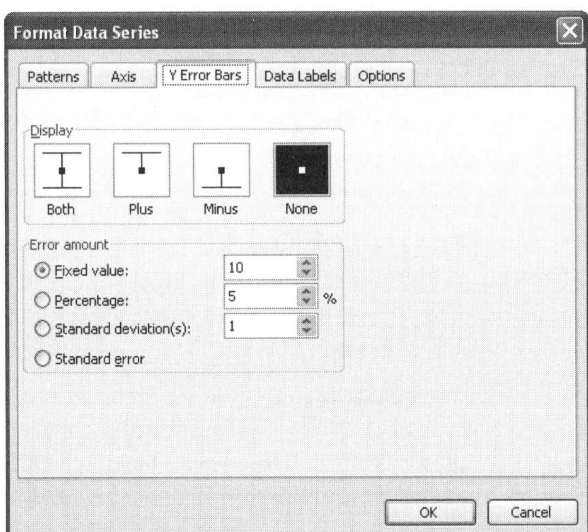

Figure 14-14. Use the Format Data Series dialog box to add error bars that show a margin for error in which the result could be a bit higher or lower than what's shown in your chart.

5. In the Error Amount section, choose the amount of the difference between actual and plus or minus that you want to show.
6. Click OK to add the error bars and return to the chart.

Plotting Trendlines

Trendlines are helpful when you want to use your chart as a basis for either looking ahead to future possibilities or seeing trends in the past. You can add trendlines to area, bar, bubble, column, line, stock, or XY (scatter) charts. When you've created one of these chart types, adding a trendline is simple. Here are the steps:

1. Double-click the chart to select it.
2. Choose Chart, Add Trendline. The Add Trendline dialog box appears, as shown in Figure 14-15.

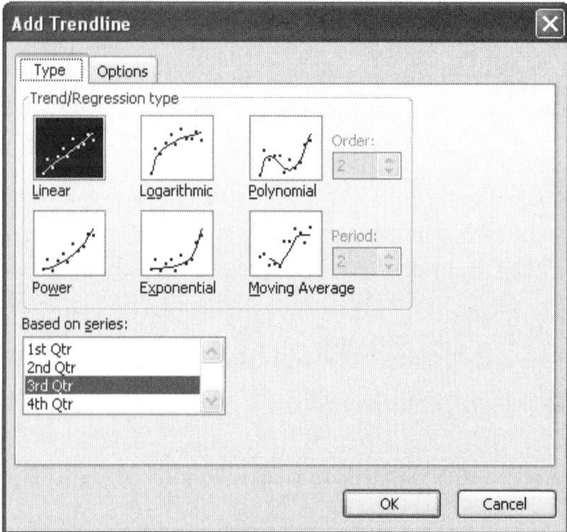

Figure 14-15. In the Add Trendline dialog box, select the formula you want Graph to use to plot your projections.

3. In the Trend/Regression Type section, choose the type of trendline you want to create. Each of these types is based on a formula that calculates and projects data patterns based on the information in your datasheet.
4. In the Based On Series section, select the data series you want to use to create the trendline.
5. Click the Options tab. Here you'll enter a name for the trendline (if necessary), choose the length of the periods forward and backward you want to project, and choose whether you display equations or values on the chart. Make your choices, and then click OK. You're returned to Graph, and the trendline has been added, as shown in Figure 14-16.

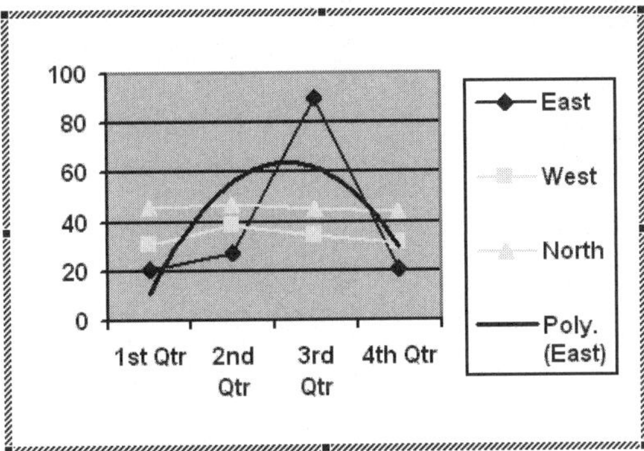

Figure 14-16. A trendline in your chart can show a general direction for your data and help readers understand at a glance what the significant changes in your data might be.

Creating an Organization Chart

When you create an organization chart in Word, you can create a new chart on the fly and enter text as you go, or you can build your chart from existing text in Word, PowerPoint, or Excel. Either way, creating the organization chart is a simple process that gives you the flexibility you need to fit the chart in your document and format it the way you want. Here are the steps:

1. Place the insertion point where you want to create the chart.
2. Choose Insert, Picture, Organization Chart. Word creates your basic chart—now you can enter text and add shapes as needed, as shown in Figure 14-17.

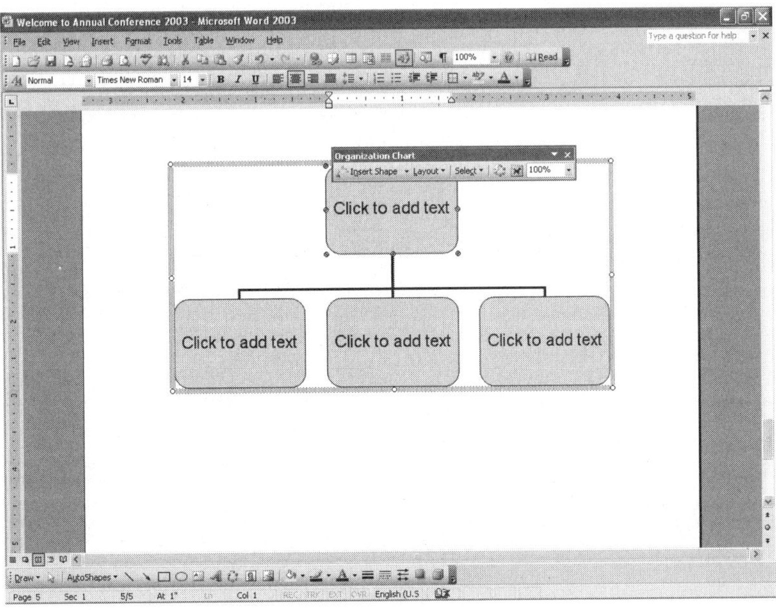

Figure 14-17. Word draws a simple organization chart and gives you the tools to add shapes as needed.

Organization Chart Elements

There aren't many parts to deal with in an organization chart. You'll use basic shapes to create relationships—subordinates, peers, and assistants—and you'll design, move, and change branches that show the relationships among people or processes. Here are the items you'll be working with in your organization charts:

- **Shapes** Boxes used to name a person, identify a role, or describe a step or department.
- **Connector lines** Lines that connect each shape in your chart.
- **Chart frame** Border surrounding the organization chart. This is a nonprinting border, although you can add a border to the chart if you choose.
- **Organization Chart toolbar** Provides the menus and tools you need to add, move, and wrap text around the chart in your document. Table 14-2 introduces the tools and gives examples of when each could be used.

Table 14-2. Organization Chart Tools

Button	Name	Description	Use
Insert Shape	Insert Shape	Adds subordinate, co-worker, or assistant shapes	You want to add a new position, person, or project to your chart.
Layout	Layout	Changes the layout of the organization chart	You want to display the chart information in a different form.
Select	Select	Displays choices for selecting chart elements	You want to select a particular level, type of shape, or branch.
	AutoFormat	Provides a gallery from which you can choose predesigned chart styles	You want a professional look with coordinated colors and lines.
	Text Wrapping	Displays text wrap options for the placement of text around the chart	You want to arrange text around, next to, or even across your chart.
100%	Zoom	Changes the size in which the organization is displayed	You want to increase the size of the chart so that you can work with it more easily.

Entering Text

Once you create the basic chart, you're ready to add text in the individual shapes. Simply click in the shape at the top of the chart, and then type the name of the person, position, or process. The text appears center-aligned in the shape by default, as shown in Figure 14-18.

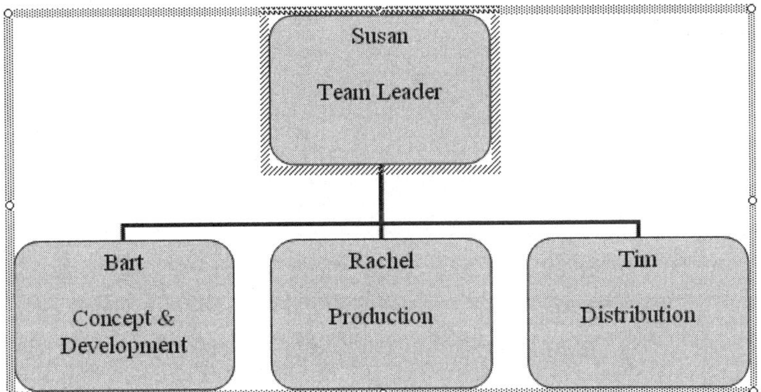

Figure 14-18. Word adds text in the default font for the current template; you can change the font, style, color, and alignment as needed.

> **Note** The typical text navigation keys—Enter, Tab, and the arrow keys—don't work in the organization chart. Just move the mouse pointer, and then click to move from shape to shape.

Inserting Shapes

When you first create an organization chart, Word gives you one superior, or lead, shape and three subordinates. For most charts, you'll want to add and reorder shapes as you build your chart. To insert shapes in your organization chart, click the shape to which you want to add a relationship. The frame for the shape changes, showing that it's selected. Next, click the Insert Shape arrow on the Organization Chart toolbar or simply click Insert Shape to add a subordinate. If you displayed the shortcut menu, choose the relationship you want to add from the menu:

- **Subordinate** Adds a shape beneath the selected shape.
- **Coworker** Adds a shape on the same level.
- **Assistant** Adds a shape below and to one side, off the main branch.

Changing the Layout

The basic tree structure is the default arrangement for new organization charts, but you have other layouts to choose from. To see the different layouts, click Layout on the Organization Chart toolbar, as shown in Figure 14-19.

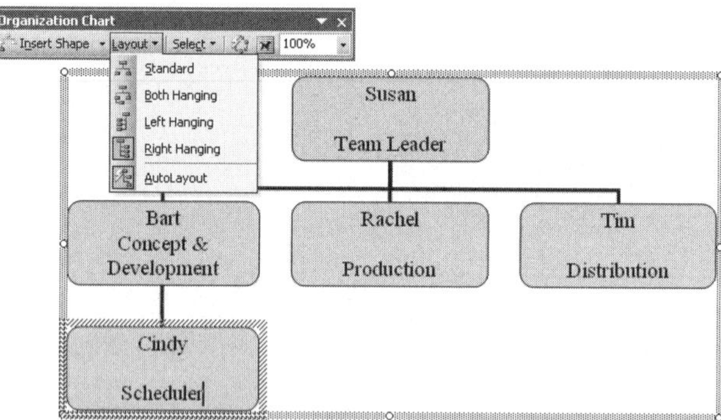

Figure 14-19. You can select a different layout for the organization chart.

Different types of organizations will lend themselves to different chart layouts, so try experimenting with the different choices to see what works best for your data. Also consider where the chart appears on the page, how it fits with your overall design, and which alignment might lead the reader's eyes in the most effective way.

Selecting Branches

As you work with your organization chart, you might find that you want to work with several items at once. You might, for example, want to change the line color for all connector lines to blue. Or you might want to add a drop-shadow to all management level shapes. Or you might want to change the fill color of individual shapes. Whatever change you want to make, you need to select the shapes before you can modify them.

You tell Word which items you want to select by using the Select menu. Then make your selection from the following choices:

- **Level** All shapes on the current level
- **Branch** All shapes in the current branch
- **All Assistants** All assistant shapes in the chart
- **All Connecting Lines** All lines in the chart so that you can change color, thickness, and so on

Note Can you raise a shape from one level to another? No—but you can simply delete the existing shape and create a new one, showing the correct relationship.

Moving Shapes and Sections

Once you select the shape or branch you want to work with, you can reorder the selections the way you want. Click the shape you want to move. If the frame appears around the shape, click the item again to display the shape handles. Next, position the pointer over one of the handles. The pointer changes to a four-sided arrow. Drag the shape to the new location in a position that is at the same level. (The shape will not move if you try to move it to a superior position.) An outline moves with the shape, and when you release the mouse button, the shape is moved to the new location.

To move an entire branch, simply click the shape at the top level of the branch you want to move so the handles appear. Then click Select on the Organization Chart toolbar, and then choose Branch from the menu. All shapes in that branch are selected. Drag the branch to the new location.

Using AutoFormat to Modify the Look

You can apply predesigned formatting to your organization chart by using AutoFormat. Click in the chart, and then click AutoFormat on the Organization Chart toolbar, and the Organization Chart Style Gallery dialog box appears, as shown in Figure 14-20. Click through the various Gallery styles to find the one you want. When you find a style that fits your document, click Apply.

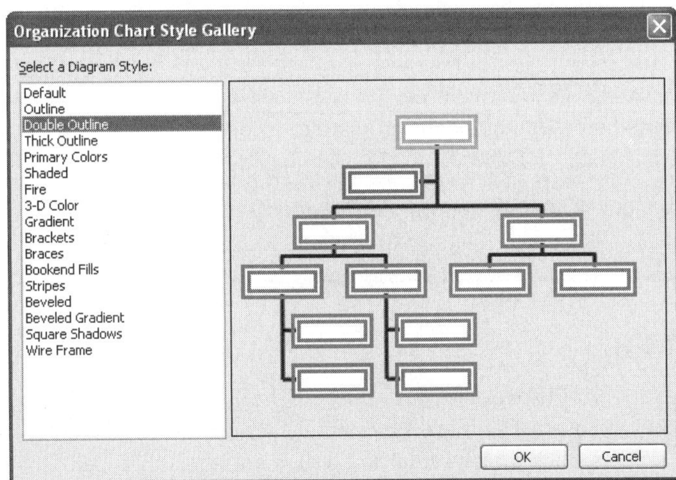

Figure 14-20. Select a style from the Organization Chart Style Gallery dialog box.

Controlling Text Wrap Around Charts and Diagrams

The text wrap feature works the same way for organization charts that it does for pictures and other objects in your Word documents. Simply click the Text Wrapping tool, and then choose the wrapping style that fits what you're trying to do. Here's a quick review of the choices:

- **In Line With Text** Places the chart on the same line as the current text
- **Square** Runs text up to the edge of a squared area around the chart

- **Tight** Wraps the text tightly against the outline of the organization chart
- **Behind Text** Runs text over the top of the chart
- **In Front Of Text** Places text behind the chart
- **Top And Bottom** Wraps text above and below the chart
- **Through** Runs text through the white space in the organization chart
- **Edit Wrap Points** Allows you to add custom points so that you can create your own text wrap boundary around the chart

Designing Conceptual Diagrams

Going beyond organization charts, diagrams enable you to show more complicated relationships, dependencies, processes, and more. Word gives you five different diagram types to choose from—a full complement of tools for illustrating concepts.

Inside Out

Selecting the right diagram for the job

In addition to the Organization Chart type, Word includes the following diagram types that you can use and customize for your documents:

- **Cycle** Shows a cyclical process
- **Radial** Shows how different elements relate to a core element
- **Pyramid** Shows how elements build on a foundation
- **Venn** Shows how elements overlap other elements
- **Target** Shows individual relationships to a core element or goal

Creating the Diagram

Adding a diagram is a simple two-click process. Just click where you want to add the diagram, and then choose Insert, Diagram. When the Diagram Gallery dialog box (shown in Figure 14-21) appears, click the one you want to use, and then click OK. The diagram is added to your document, and the Diagram toolbar appears. Click a shape's default text, and then type the text you want to add. Table 14-3 describes each button on the Diagram toolbar.

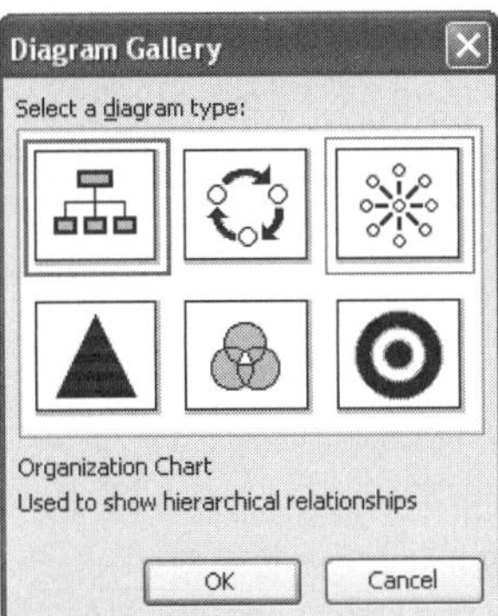

Figure 14-21. Choose the diagram type you want to create in the Diagram Gallery dialog box.

Table 14-3. Diagram Tools

Button	Name	Description	Use
Insert Shape	Insert Shape (Note: This tool changes based on the type of diagram you select.)	Enables you to add a shape in the form suitable to the diagram type	You want to add another element to your diagram.
	Move Shape Backward	Moves the currently selected shape one item down or back	You want to change the order of the elements in your diagram.
	Move Shape Forward	Moves the currently selected shape one item forward or up	You're changing the order of the elements in the diagram.
	Reverse Diagram	Reorders the selected diagram element	You want to move the top element to the bottom of the diagram.
Layout ▾	Layout	Provides options for resizing the diagram	You're reducing the size of the chart to make room for text to wrap around it.
	AutoFormat	Displays a Gallery of preset diagram formats	You want to create a professional-looking diagram.
Change to ▾	Change To	Displays options for other diagrams	You want to change your current diagram into another diagram type.
	Text Wrapping	Shows the options for wrapping text around diagrams	You want to flow text around the select diagram.

Adding to the Diagram

The default diagram appears with several preset shapes—but you'll probably want to add more on your own. Simply select the shape next to or above which you want to add a shape. Click Insert Shape on the Diagram toolbar. A new shape is added to the diagram. The type of shape depends on which diagram you're creating, as follows:

- A stripe for a Pyramid
- An overlapping circle for a Venn chart
- A circle and connector line for a Radial chart
- A segment for a Cycle chart
- A ring for a Target diagram

Moving Diagram Elements

Moving shapes in a diagram is slightly different from moving shapes in an organization chart. Instead of selecting and moving an entire branch, you work with single elements. Select the shape you want to move, and then choose Move Shape Backward, Move Shape Forward, or Reverse Diagram to move the shape in the direction you want.

Changing the Diagram Layout

Resizing your diagram involves using Layout on the Diagram toolbar. When you click Layout, you're given three choices in addition to the AutoLayout option:

- **Fit Diagram To Contents** Tightens up the white space surrounding the diagram.
- **Expand Diagram** Widens the diagram box.
- **Resize Diagram** Resizes the actual diagram. Resize handles appear at the outer edges of the diagram box. Click a handle and drag the diagram box inward or outward.

Using AutoFormat for Diagrams

The AutoFormat button displays the Diagram Style Gallery dialog box, shown in Figure 14-22. Similar to the Organization Chart Style Gallery dialog box, this AutoFormat collection displays different styles you can apply to your diagram. You'll find different color schemes and shapes for each diagram type. Experiment with the different formats until you find a style that suits your document. Click Apply to apply the style to your diagram.

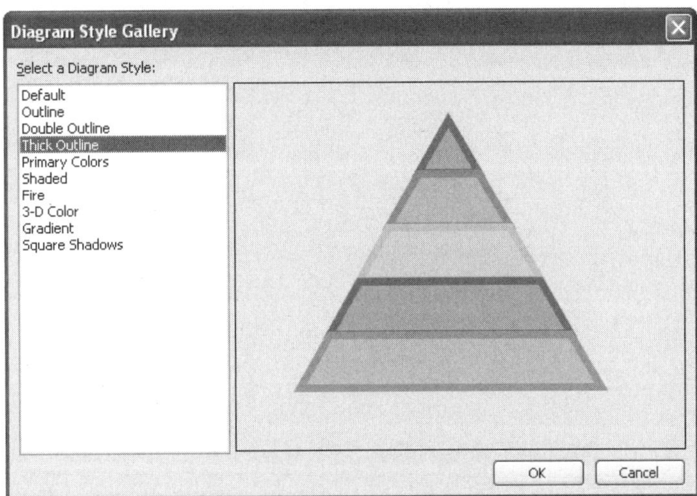

Figure 14-22. Choose a style from the Diagram Style Gallery dialog box.

Changing to Another Diagram Type

One great feature about Word's diagramming capability is the ease with which you can change from type to type. For example, if you use a cycle diagram to show the process of bringing a new product to market and it just doesn't seem quite right, you can change the diagram—with data intact—to a radial diagram type. To change to another diagram type, click in the diagram, click Change To on the Diagram toolbar, and then click the type of diagram you want. The diagram is redrawn as the type of diagram you selected.

Part 3

Designing Pages for Maximum Visual Impact

Chapter 15

Mastering Page Setup and Pagination

Have you ever started creating a document with one vision of its final form and then found that the document's design was traveling down an entirely different path, seemingly on its own? Maybe a single-column publication suddenly became a multiple-column document, or a piece that wasn't supposed to be a booklet turned out to work perfectly in a booklet format. In those types of cases, everything changes—margins, orientation, column specifications, and headers and footers. These aren't the kinds of changes you want to be making when you have a tight deadline, but fortunately, with Word, you can control these types of changes efficiently with a little know-how.

Whether you plan your publication in advance or change strategies midstream, Word's page setup features help you control page layout basics. Specifically, when you plan your pages, you can make choices about the following page setup specifications and options:

- Sections, headers, footers, and page number settings
- Top, bottom, left, and right margin sizes
- Document orientation
- Paper size and tray or cartridge to use when printing
- Whether to print one or two pages per sheet
- Spaces between columns
- Page, column, and text breaks
- Header and footer content and positioning
- Text flow and spacing for languages that use vertical orientation

This chapter covers the preceding topics as well as related page setup features provided in Word.

Planning Page Setup

Although you can select your page settings at any point during the creation or editing of your document, taking time up front to plan basic document settings can save you time, trouble, and corrections later. In addition, if you're creating a standard document for others in your department to use, getting the basics set early can ensure that you don't have to open multiple documents to readjust margin settings, page size, and more. You can even create a template with your settings to further simplify applying current settings and future changes.

When you make drastic changes in your document setup—such as changing the page from portrait to landscape orientation—the content of your page will be dramatically affected. For instance, if you switch to landscape orientation after you've entered text and graphics, set headers and footers, and created section divisions in portrait orientation, you'll most likely have quite a bit of changing to do to display your information properly on the shorter, wider page.

Preparing Your Document

In most cases, you'll use the Page Setup dialog box to enter page settings. To display the Page Setup dialog box use any of the following techniques:

- Choose File, Page Setup.
- In Print Layout view, double-click anywhere in the vertical or horizontal ruler or in the upper-left corner of the page (or, if you have a language setting such as Japanese enabled, in any corner of the page).
- Press Alt+F+U.
- Click Page Setup on the Header And Footer toolbar.
- Double-click a Section Break marker.

The Page Setup dialog box inWord 2003 (shown in Figure 15-1) looks similar to the Page Setup dialog box inWord 2002. If you have support for Simplified Chinese,Traditional Chinese, Japanese, or Korean enabled through Microsoft Office 2003 Language Settings (to set this up, choose Start, All Programs, Microsoft Office, Microsoft Office Tools, and finally Microsoft Office 2003 Language Settings), you'll also see the Document Grid tab in your Page Setup dialog box. To summarize, the Page Setup tabs enable you to enter basic page settings as follows:

- **Margins** Allows you to specify settings for the top, bottom, left, right, and gutter margins; choose page orientation; and select the format for multiple pages.
- **Paper** Includes options regarding the paper size and the source for the paper and envelopes on which you'll print your information. In addition, you can access the Print dialog box from this tab by clicking Print Options.

- **Layout** Enables you to set options for sections, headers and footers, and overall content alignment. In addition, you can access the Line Numbers dialog box by clicking Line Numbers and the Borders And Shading dialog box by clicking Borders.
- **Document Grid** Enables you to control the horizontal and vertical text flow as well as line and character spacing in documents that use East Asian languages. Using this tab, you can also specify Drawing Grid settings (click Drawing Grid), which give you control over the grid display and other grid settings.

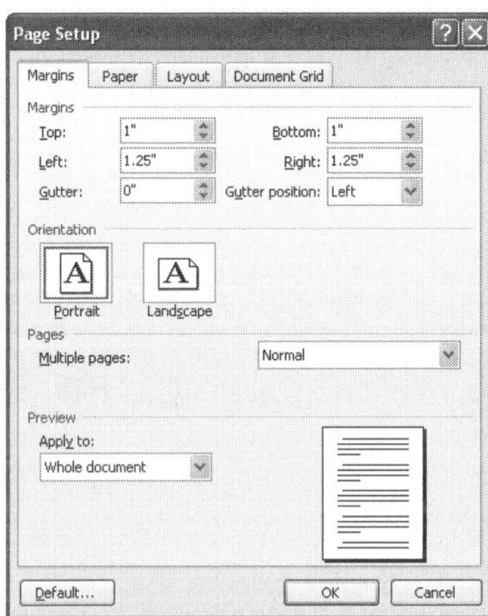

Figure 15-1. The Page Setup dialog box enables you to choose the settings that affect the margins, paper type, layout, and spacing of your document.

Setting Up a Document as a Whole

One of the first choices you'll make controls how far-reaching you want a particular set of page setup settings to be. You can apply page settings to an entire document, to the current section, from the insertion point forward, or to selected text. To make your choice, follow these steps:

1. Open the document you want to format and, if desired, position the insertion point where you want the page setup settings to apply, or select the text and objects that you want to be formatted by the new page setup settings.
2. Choose File, Page Setup to display the Page Setup dialog box.
3. In the Margins tab, click the Apply To arrow. Then choose one of the following:
   - To apply settings to the entire document, select Whole Document.
   - To apply settings to the current section if you're working in a document with multiple sections, choose This Section.
   - To apply settings to text starting at the insertion point's current position, choose This Point Forward.
   - To apply settings to selected text, choose Selected Text.
   - To apply settings to selected sections, choose Selected Sections.

Note The This Point Forward and Selected Text/Selected Sections options are mutually exclusive, so either one or the other will be available, depending on whether content is selected or not.

Any changes you make in the Page Setup dialog box will be applied to your document according to your selection in the Apply To list.

Tip **Combine global settings with selected text settings**
You can apply page setup settings for an entire document along with additional settings for selected text or sections. For example, you can set a specific left margin for an entire document as well as add line numbers or additional indentation for selected sections or blocks of text.

Working in Sections

If you want to enter page setup settings for a section only, place the insertion point where you want to make the change or select the content (such as text, graphics, sections, objects, or other components) that you want to modify. Then choose File, Page Setup to display the Page Setup dialog box. Click the Apply To arrow, select the appropriate Apply To option, and then make your page setup changes. When you choose the This Point Forward option, the settings you enter are applied throughout the rest of the document. When you specify more than one group of page setup options in a document, Word automatically inserts a *Section Break (Next Page)* marker at the point at which page setup settings change. You can see Section Break markers in Normal view by default; in Web Layout, Print Layout, Outline, and Reading Layout views, you must click the Show/Hide button on the Standard toolbar to display hidden characters.

Tip To view the page setup options that are configured for a section, double-click the Section Break marker to display the Page Setup dialog box.

If you want to end the page setup settings in a section at a certain point (for example, you increased the right indent for a particular section but want to return to the normal margin after that section), place the insertion point where you want to make the change. Then choose File, Page Setup to display the Page Setup dialog box a second time, click the Apply To arrow, choose From This Point Forward, and return the settings to normal.

Tip You can quickly format certain sections differently from the overall document by entering the content and then formatting the sections. To do this, simply enter and select the content that should receive custom page setup settings, and then apply the page setup settings to the selected text. Taking this approach is often quicker than revisiting the Page Setup dialog box each time you want to start or stop applying a particular page setup configuration.

Saving Page Setup Defaults to the Current Template

After you get the page settings set up the way you want them in your document, you can save the specifications as your page setup default settings in the document's template. When you save page setup settings as default settings, Word saves the settings to the current template. If your document isn't based on a custom template, the changes will be applied to the Normal template (by default, all new Word documents use the Normal template if they aren't based on another template). When you create default page setup settings, your page setup settings will be applied to all new documents that are created based on the template. To save your page setup settings as the default settings, follow these steps:

1. Place the insertion point where you want page settings to take effect or where you've configured the settings you want to use as the default page setup settings.
2. Choose File, Page Setup to display the Page Setup dialog box.
3. Enter the page setup choices you want to apply to the document's template.
4. In the lower-left corner of the Page Setup dialog box, click Default. A message box, shown in Figure 15-2, asks whether you'd like to change the default settings in the current template. To do so, click Yes; if you decide you would rather not alter the template settings, click No.

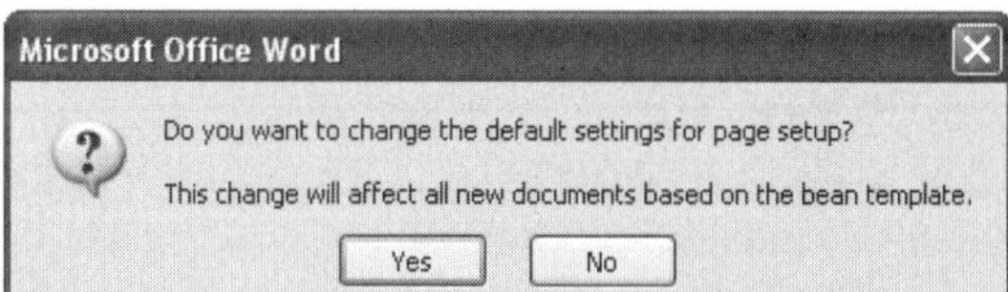

Figure 15-2. Making the current page setup settings the new default alters the existing template. In this figure, the template being altered is named bean. If the current document isn't based on a custom template, the message box shows that changes you're applying will be made to the NORMAL template.

> **Tip** **Make a backup copy or reset the Normal template**
> For best results, always keep a clean backup copy of your standard template in a directory other than the Template directory on your hard disk or server. That way, if you need to return to earlier default specifications, you can do so without having to reenter the original Word settings. If you want to reset your Normal template, simply exit Word, rename the Normal.dot file (choose an easy-to-recognize name, such as Normal_old.dot), and then restart Word. Word will automatically create a new Normal.dot template based on Word's default settings.

Changing Margins and Orientation

The page setup items you'll adjust most often are likely to be the margins and page orientation settings. The margins of your document control the amount of white space at the top, bottom, right, and left edges of the document. You can also control the amount of space used for the gutter, which is the space reserved on the interior edges of pages to save room for binding. In Word, you can customize the gutter setting along the left or top margin of the page.

Tip **Plan your margins for double-sided printing**
If you'll be binding the document you create, be sure to specify a gutter margin large enough to accommodate the binding. If your document is printed single-sided, every gutter margin will show the spacing you enter along the left margin. If your document is to be printed double-sided, display the Page Setup dialog box, click the Multiple Pages arrow, and then choose Mirror Margins to make sure that the margin settings are applied to the left and right interior margins. For more information about printing, see Chapter 3, "Printing with Precision."

Entering Margin Settings

When you begin working with a new Word document, the left and right margins are set to 1.25 inches, and the top and bottom margins are set to 1 inch.You can change margin settings in Word in two basic ways:

- Drag the Left Indent and Right Indent markers in the horizontal ruler or the edge of the shaded area in the vertical ruler (in Normal, Web Layout, and Print Layout views) to the margin setting you want.

Tip To show and hide the horizontal and vertical rulers, choose View, Ruler.

- Display the Page Setup dialog box (choose File, Page Setup), type values in the appropriate Margins options boxes, and then click OK.

Note By default, the Gutter Position option in the Margins tab in the Page Setup dialog box enables you to choose whether to create a left or top gutter. If you choose any option other than Normal in the Multiple Pages list in the Pages section of the Page Setup dialog box, Word disables the Gutter Position option and adds the gutter setting to the left margin (or alternating right and left margins, if Mirror Margins is selected in the Multiple Pages list).

Choosing Orientation

A document's orientation affects the way the content is printed on a page. By default, portrait orientation prints documents in traditional, 8.5-by-11-inch format; landscape orientation prints documents in a horizontal, 11-by-8.5-inch format. When should you use each orientation? Here are a few ideas.

- **Portrait orientation** Traditional documents, letters, reports, newsletters, Web pages, and invoices.
- **Landscape orientation** Slides, signs, title pages, charts, calendars, tri-fold brochures, and tables.

To change the orientation of a document, open the document, choose File, Page Setup to display the Page Setup dialog box, and then click the Margins tab. Click Landscape to change the orientation so that the document is printed with the long edge of the paper serving as the top of the page, or click Portrait to print the document with the short edge of the paper serving as the top of the page.

Note You can change the orientation from landscape to portrait and back again in a single document, if you choose. Simply place the insertion point where you want to change the orientation, display the Page Setup dialog box, click the Margins tab, and then choose the appropriate setting in the Apply To list. Then click the orientation you want. After you click OK, Word inserts a Section Break (Next Page) marker, and begins a new page using the new page setup settings. To view the page setup changes, click Print Preview on the Standard toolbar.

Working with Varying Page Settings

Depending on a document's complexity, you might want to vary the margins. For instance, a standard report might have equal margins on the right and left, a format that makes setting margins a snap. In contrast, a document you want to bind or fold, or a publication that's designed so that the left and right pages complement each other, might require more finely tuned adjustments to page settings.

When you want to set up a multiple-page document that requires varying page settings, you can simplify your task by using the Multiple Pages setting in the Page Setup dialog box. The Multiple Pages setting enables you to specify whether your document should include mirror margins, two pages per sheet, book fold, or reverse book fold, as described in Table 15-1. To change the page settings for a multiple-page document, follow these steps:

1. Open your document, and then choose File, Page Setup to display the Page Setup dialog box.
2. Enter the Margins, Paper, and Layout settings in their respective tabs.
3. In the Pages section in the Margins tab, click the Multiple Pages arrow. Table 15-1 shows the effects of the Multiple Pages choices.
4. Click your choice, and then click OK. Word applies the changes to the current document.

Table 15-1. Choosing Page Settings for Multiple Pages

Setting	Preview	Description
Normal		Creates single pages, with the same margin, header, and footer selections for every page.
Mirror Margins		Creates a document in which the margins on the left and right pages mirror each other.

Table 15-1. Choosing Page Settings for Multiple Pages

Setting	Preview	Description
2 Pages Per Sheet		Divides the current page into two pages.
Book Fold		Treats each left and right page as a spread, using a gutter and mirroring margins as applicable.
Reverse Book Fold		Enables you to create a booklet written in a right-to-left text orientation, such as one written in Arabic or Hebrew, or in an East Asian language that has vertical text. (This option is available only when a relevant language is enabled in Microsoft Office 2003 Language Settings.)

Selecting Paper Size and Source

Another page setup task involves preparing your document for final printing. Specifically, you need to specify a paper size and paper source. Word offers a range of paper sizes. The standard basics are there—from letter (traditional 8.5-by-11-inch) to legal (8.5-by-14-inch) to traditional business envelopes. In addition to the usual paper sizes, Word also supports statement, executive, and index card sizes. You'll also find numerous envelope options.

Choosing a Paper Size

To select a paper size, choose File, Page Setup to display the Page Setup dialog box, and then click the Paper tab. The options on the Paper tab all have to do with the paper size and source you'll use, as shown in Figure 15-3. Click the Paper Size arrow, and then choose the size you want from the list that appears.

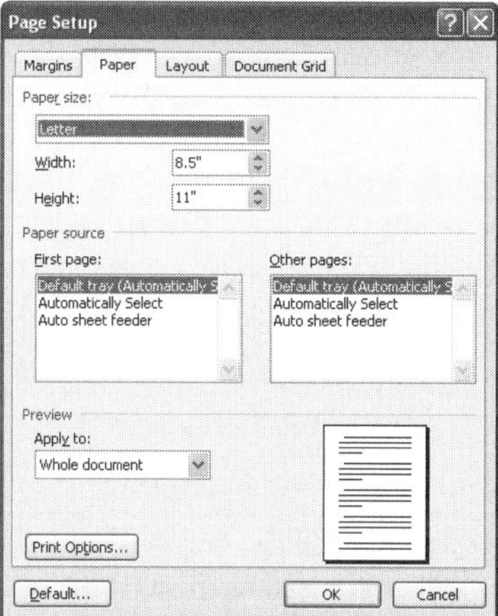

Figure 15-3. Choose the size and source for paper in the Paper tab in the Page Setup dialog box.

Selecting the Paper Source

The paper source is where Word gets the paper, envelopes, or other medium you'll use when you print a document. If you're working with a printer that has several trays, you can customize the documents you print, for example, printing one page on letterhead in one tray and printing subsequent pages on blank stock.

To select a paper source, choose File, Page Setup, and then click the Paper tab. Then, click the paper tray you want to use as the source in the First Page and Other Pages lists.

Tip **Check print options in the Paper tab**
Because so many Page Setup options overlap the Print Options settings, Word makes it easy to access the print options in the Paper tab in the Page Setup dialog box. When you're working with page setup settings, take a moment to check your print options by clicking the Print Options button in the lower-left corner of the Paper tab. Coordinating print and page setup options might come in handy, for instance, if you want to use A4 or legal paper sizes or you plan to use duplex printing. In those cases, you can set your print and page setup options at the same time, thereby avoiding having to remember to set appropriate print options when you print the document.

For more information about printing in Word 2003, see Chapter 3, "Printing with Precision."

Making Layout Choices

Depending on a document's specific characteristics, you might need to make layout choices that affect the number of columns you use, the settings you choose for headers and footers, text alignment, line numbering, and more. The Layout tab in the Page Setup dialog box presents all these options together so that you can make your choices in one place.

Selecting and Formatting Sections

Word gives you the option of choosing where you want your new sections to begin. Whenever you choose the This Point Forward option in the Apply To list while you're creating a document, Word begins a new section and applies the page settings you've selected. To change the settings for an existing section, click in the section. After you've positioned the insertion point, display your section choices by clicking the Section Start arrow in the Layout tab in the Page Setup dialog box (as shown in Figure 15-4). Then select your choice from the list that appears:

- **Continuous** Begins the new section at the insertion point.
- **New Column** Starts a new column when you begin a new section.
- **New Page** Jumps to a new page to begin a new section.
- **Even Page** Moves to the next even page to begin a new section.
- **Odd Page** Moves to the next odd page to begin a new section.

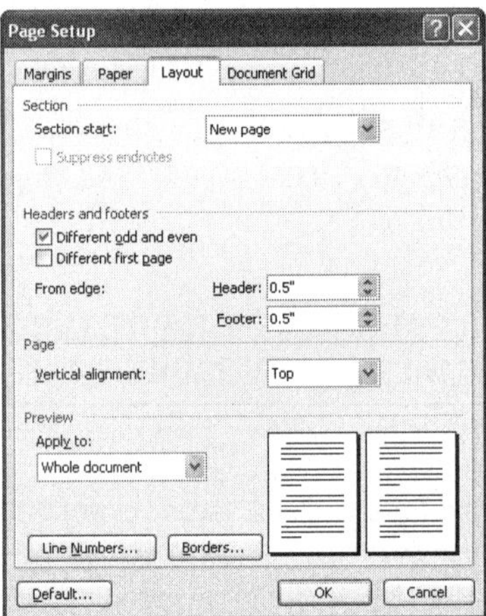

Figure 15-4. The Layout tab provides options that enable you to control section starting positions, header and footer displays, vertical content alignment, line numbers, and page borders.

For more information about working with sections, see Chapter 19, "Formatting Columns and Sections for Advanced Text Control."

Accessing Page Setup Options for Headers and Footers

Headers and footers are an important part of long documents. Headers appear at the tops of pages, while footers provide information at the bottoms of pages. For example, in a book, the chapter name and book title often appear in the header, while the page number appears in the footer. You'll often use headers and footers to provide readers with important information about the publication, which could include the title, the author, the page number, creation date, last modified date, confidentiality statements, and other items. Using the Page Setup dialog box, you can control whether headers and footers are different for odd and even pages, whether the first page should have a different header or footer, and where headers and footer are placed relative to the edge of a printed page. To access these options, follow these steps:

1. Choose File, Page Setup to display the Page Setup dialog box, and click the Layout tab.
2. Make your selections in the Headers And Footers section. You can configure the following settings:
   - *Different Odd and Even*—Enables you to create headers and footers that are different for right and left pages. This allows you, for example, to place the page numbers in the outside bottom corner of every page, whether you're printing an odd or even page.
   - *Different First Page*—Enables you to disable the display of headers or footers on the first page. Or, if you prefer, you can enter header or footer information that prints only on the first page.
   - *From Edge*—Controls the amount of spacing between the edge of the page and the headers and footers. To enter this setting, type in the value box or use the up or down arrow to adjust the measurement.

Note For more information about using headers and footers, see "Including Headers and Footers" on page 477.

Aligning Sections Vertically

Word gives you the option of indicating how you want the content between the top and bottom margins of your page to be aligned. To control vertical alignment, display the Page Setup dialog box (choose File, Page Setup), click the Layout tab, click the Vertical Alignment arrow, and then select an alignment option. You can choose among Top, Center, Justified, or Bottom. Word aligns the page content based on your selection. For example, if you click Center, Word will center the page contents between the top and bottom margins. If you choose Bottom, Word will align the page contents with the bottom margin and place whatever extra space remains at the top of the page.

Adding Line Numbers

If you're working on a document that requires line numbering, you can use Page Setup settings to add the numbers automatically. You can choose whether you want to number the entire document, selected content, or a particular section. To turn on line numbering, follow these steps:

1. Position your cursor where you want to start numbering or in a section you want to number, or select existing text that you want to display with line numbers.
2. Choose File, Page Setup, and then click the Layout tab.

3 In the Apply To list, select where you want to apply numbering. Some options you might see include This Section, This Point Forward, Selected Sections, Selected Text, and Whole Document.

Tip By default, Word creates a new section on a new page when you add numbers to selected text. If you want to add numbers to selected text without placing the numbered text on a separate page, remember to select Continuous in the Section Start list in the Layout tab. When you select Continuous, Word creates a section without adding a page break.

4 In the Layout tab, click Line Numbers. The Line Numbers dialog box appears, as shown in Figure 15-5.

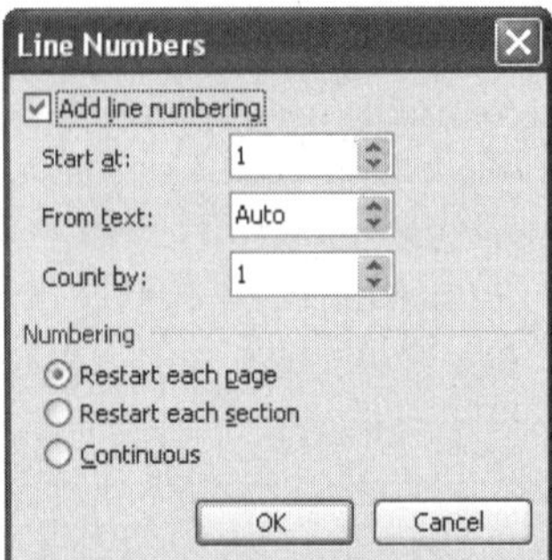

Figure 15-5. In the Line Numbers dialog box, you can choose to add line numbering for a section, selected text, or the entire document.

5 Select the Add Line Numbering check box. In the Start At box, type the number with which you want numbering to begin.

6 In the From Text box, specify number placement by using the up or down arrows or typing a number (by default, the From Text spacing is measured in inches), or accept Auto (the default setting).

7 In the Count By box, enter a value to specify which lines should be accompanied by numbers. For instance, if you want to show a number next to every other line, you would enter *2* in the Count By box. To display a number next to each line, retain the default Count By setting of *1*.

8 In the Numbering section, click Restart Each Page if you want each page to be individually numbered, click Restart Each Section if you want the numbering to begin again with each subsequent section, or click Continuous if you want numbers to increase throughout the document.

9 Click OK to close the Line Numbers dialog box and return to the Page Setup dialog box. Click OK to close the Page Setup dialog box.

Inside Out

Making room for line numbers

If you've created heading styles that extend all the way to the left margin of your page, you might find them truncated when you add line numbering. You can fix this by displaying the Line Numbers dialog box and changing the From Text setting. By default, From Text is set to Auto, but by decreasing the amount of space between numbering and text, you can usually make room for both line numbering and headings.

Creating a Page or Section Border

If you want to set up page and section borders for your document while you're taking care of the rest of your page settings, you can do so in the Page Setup dialog box. To access border settings, display the Page Setup dialog box (choose File, Page Setup), click the Layout tab, and then click Borders. The Borders And Shading dialog box appears. Using this dialog box, you can add borders to selected text and paragraphs, sections, and pages, as well as to the entire document.

For full coverage of adding page borders, see Chapter 18, "Drawing Attention to Documents by Using Borders and Shading."

Controlling Page Breaks

As you know, if you've created documents of any length, Word automatically adds page breaks at the appropriate points to indicate page divisions and show you how printed pages will look. In Print Layout and Reading views, an automatic page break looks truly like a break between pages—you can see where one page ends and another begins. In Normal view, page breaks appear as dotted lines. Often, instances arise when you might want to add page breaks manually. In Word, you can easily add manual breaks to control pages, sections, and columns.

Adding Manual Page Breaks

In some cases, you might want to enter your own page break to control where data is positioned on the page. For example, you might want to insert a manual page break in the following instances:

- To create a page containing minimal information, such as a cover page or acknowledgements page
- To prevent a paragraph from being divided across two pages
- To ensure that a figure or table and its caption appear on the same page
- To begin a new section with a heading at the top of a page
- To end a section when you don't want anything else printed on the current page

To create a manual page break, place the insertion point where you want to insert the break, and then press Ctrl+Enter. Or, if you prefer, you can choose Insert, Break. When you choose Insert, Break, the Break dialog box appears, as shown in Figure 15-6. The Break dialog box gives you greater control over a break's settings than the Ctrl+Enter keyboard shortcut, including enabling you to create column and text wrapping breaks.

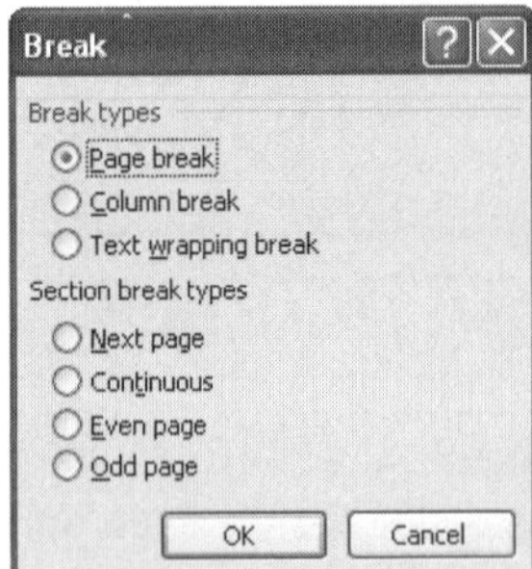

Figure 15-6. You can insert a page, column, or text wrapping break using the Break dialog box.

Inserting Column and Text Breaks

In addition to creating page breaks, you can control content layout by manually inserting column breaks and text wrapping breaks. When you add a column break by choosing Insert, Break, and then selecting Column Break in the dialog box, Word inserts a column break at the insertion point and wraps any remaining text to the next available column.

Similarly, you can use the Text Wrapping Break option in the Break dialog box when you want to force a text break for layout reasons, but you don't want to start a new paragraph. For instance, you might want to break text at a particular position to appear before and after an inline graphic or object, or you might want to present lines of poetry without applying the document's paragraph style (including paragraph spacing) to each line of text. The Text Wrapping Break option is similar to inserting soft returns in your document, which you can add by pressing Shift+Enter. Frequently, text wrapping breaks are used to separate text from Web page objects or other text and are the equivalent of inserting a <BR> tag in HTML code.

Troubleshooting

My printed document includes unwanted breaks

You finish your document and print a draft. What's this? The document is breaking at odd places? You seem to have mysterious phantom page breaks somewhere in your document. To resolve this problem, click Show/Hide on the Standard toolbar. This displays all formatting characters, and you'll be able to look for and delete unwanted page break characters before you print.

For more information about working with sections, see Chapter 19, "Formatting Columns and Sections for Advanced Text Control."

Including Headers and Footers

Adding text to the Header (top) and Footer (bottom) areas in a Word document serves a number of purposes. In addition to making documents look professional, headers and footers can also provide helpful information, including titles, publication dates, author information, copyright or confidentiality notices, page numbers, and so forth. In Word, you can easily insert text, AutoText, and graphics in document headers and footers.

Tip You can see a document's headers and footers only in printed documents, Print Layout view, Reading Layout view, and Print Preview mode. Headers and footers are hidden in the Normal, Web Page, and Outline views.

Adding Page Numbers

Word enables you to add page numbers in two main ways. You can add basic page numbers by choosing Insert, Page Numbers, and then configuring the Page Numbers dialog box, as shown below. When you choose Insert, Page Numbers, Word automatically configures the Header or Footer area in your document to contain page numbers.

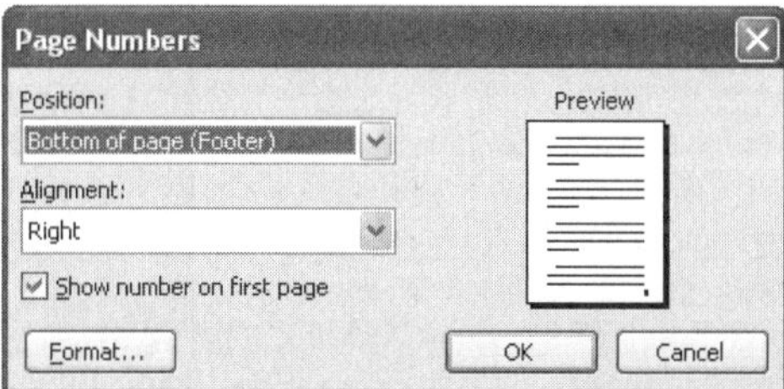

If you want to add more complex page numbering and additional information, you can create custom headers and footers, as described next.

Finally, if you want to include a page number outside the header or footer area, you can drag the page number's text box out of the header or footer area. To do so, follow these steps:

1. Insert a page number, either by creating a header or footer, or by choosing Insert, Page Number.
2. Double-click the header or footer area, or choose View, Header And Footer.
3. Click the page number to display the number's text box.
4. Position your pointer over the page number text box until it appears in the form of crossed arrows, and then drag the text box out of the header or footer area into your document.

The page numbers will then be enclosed in floating text boxes within your document. However, they will still be anchored in the header or footer, which means that you'll have to open the header or footer before you can change the floating page number's location or properties.

Creating Headers and Footers

To add content to a document's Header and Footer areas, choose View, Headers And Footers. When you choose this command, the Header and Footer areas become accessible and the Header And Footer toolbar appears, as shown in Figure 15-7. The Header And Footer toolbar buttons are described in Table 15-2. After you access the Header and Footer areas, you can add text, AutoText, field codes, graphics, and objects to customize your document's headers and footers. Keep in mind that you can only view headers and footers in Print Layout and Reading Layout views and in printed documents. The next section of the chapter describes how you can edit and customize headers and footers in Word documents.

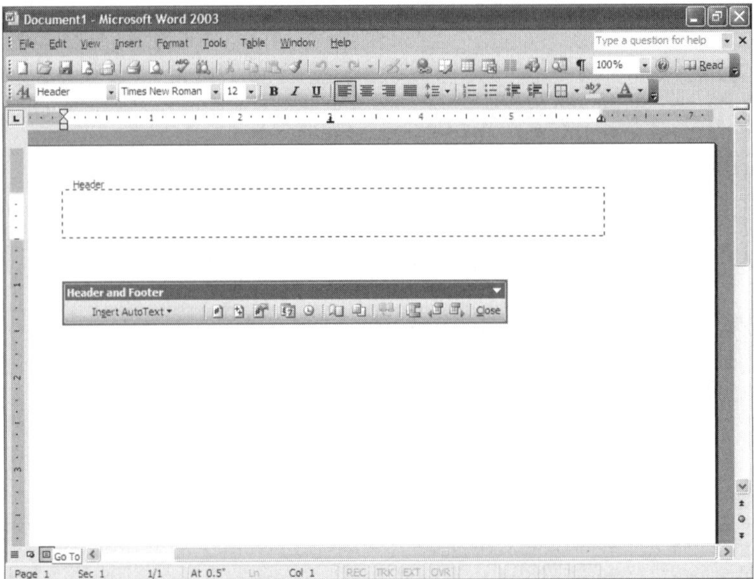

Figure 15-7. To create headers and footers in documents, you enter and format text and graphics in the header and footer areas.

Table 15-2. Header And Footer Toolbar Buttons

Button	Name	Function
Insert AutoText ▾	Insert AutoText	Enables you to insert AutoText entries in headers and footers. Options include Created By, Created On, Last Saved By, Page X of Y, and so forth.
	Insert Page Number	Inserts a page number field, { PAGE }, and displays the current page number.
	Insert Number of Pages	Inserts the page number field, { NUMPAGES }, and displays the total number of pages in the document.

Mastering Page Setup and Pagination

Table 15-2. Header And Footer Toolbar Buttons

Button	Name	Function
	Format Page Number	Displays the Page Number Format dialog box, which enables you to apply number formatting, include chapter numbers, continue numbering from prior pages, or start numbering at a specified page number.
	Insert Date	Inserts the date field using the default display setting, { DATE \@ "M/d/yyyy" }.
	Insert Time	Inserts the time field using the default display setting, { TIME \@ "h:mm"ss am/pm" }.
	Page Setup	Displays the Page Setup dialog box. You can use options in the Layout tab to specify different odd and even pages for headers and footers as well as to create a different first page.
	Show/Hide Document Text	Toggles the display of the document's contents. You can hide document text to simplify your view as you create and edit headers and footers.
	Link to Previous	Links the headers and footers in the current section to the preceding section. This enables you to create a continuous flow from section to section.
	Switch Between Header and Footer	Switches the view from header to footer and vice versa, thereby enabling you to jump quickly from the Header area to the Footer area and back again.
	Show Previous	Displays the previous header or footer that is different from the current header or footer.
	Show Next	Displays the next header or footer that is different from the current header or footer.
Close	Close Header and Footer	Closes the Header and Footer areas as well as closing the Header And Footer toolbar.

Working with Field Codes in Headers and Footers

When you use the Header And Footer toolbar to add elements such as page numbers, dates, times, and so forth to headers and footers, Word often inserts field codes. You can control field codes in a number of ways, including the following:

- You can edit a field code by right-clicking the field code in the Header or Footer area, and then choosing Edit Field. The Field dialog box appears, which enables you to select from various formats that you can use to display the field's data.
- You can toggle the display between field data and field codes by right-clicking a field and choosing Toggle Field Codes.
- To update a field, select the field and press F9.
- To control whether fields appear with or without gray backgrounds online, choose Tools, Options, click the View tab, and then select an option in the Field Shading list. Available field shading options are Never, Always, and When Selected.

For more information about working with field codes, see Chapter 31, "Working with Field Codes and Custom Forms."

Positioning and Editing Headers and Footers

After you add information to headers and footers, you can position and edit the headers and footers. You can modify the contents as well as the position and size of the Header and Footer areas. To reopen headers and footers for modification, choose View, Header And Footer, or double-click in the Header or Footer area while working in Print Layout or Reading Layout view.

By default, header and footer content is left-aligned and the Header and Footer areas are 0.5 inches deep. You can adjust alignment and positioning for headers and footers as follows:

- **Horizontal alignment of header and footer information** To change horizontal alignment within headers and footers, you click the alignment buttons on the Formatting toolbar, which include Align Left, Center, Align Right, and Justify. You can also align data by positioning your cursor or selecting information, and then pressing Tab once to center information or pressing Tab twice to right-align information.
- **Vertical alignment of header and footer information** To adjust the distance of headers and footers from the top or bottom edge of a page, you apply settings in the Layout tab in the Page Setup dialog box. You can easily access the Page Setup dialog box by clicking Page Setup on the Header And Footer toolbar or by choosing File, Page Setup. Then click the Layout tab, and configure the From Edge settings in the Header and Footer boxes.
- **Distance between headers or footers and document content** To adjust the space between headers or footers and document content, make sure that you're working in Print Layout view and that the rulers are visible (to display rulers, choose View, Ruler). Then, open the header or footer, position the insertion point on the top or bottom margin boundary in the vertical ruler until the pointer appears as a double-headed arrow, and then drag the top or bottom margin up or down.

Keep in mind that when you change alignment and position in headers or footers, the changes affect all headers or footers in the current section by default. If the document is not divided into sections, the changes are reflected throughout the document.

Tip Control headers and footers from section to section

To create a different header for part of a document, you must divide the document into sections and then create headers and footers for each section. If you are working in a document divided into sections but you want to continue using the same headers and footers from section to section, click in a section, and then, in the Header And Footer toolbar, click Link To Previous. For more information about working with sections, see "Working in Sections" on page 466, as well as Chapter 19, "Formatting Columns and Sections for Advanced Text Control."

Deleting Headers and Footers

To delete a header or footer, simply open the Header and Footer areas (by choosing View, Header And Footer), select the contents of the header or footer you want to delete, and then press Delete or Ctrl+X. When you delete the contents of a header or footer, you delete the contents for all instances of the same header or footer throughout the document. If you want to delete the headers and footers in only part of a document, you must first divide the document into sections by inserting section breaks. After you divide your document, you can create and clear headers and footers for each section.

Working with the Document Grid

If support for Simplified Chinese, Traditional Chinese, Japanese, or Korean is enabled through Microsoft Office 2003 Language Settings, you can use Word's Document Grid to help you control line and character placement in your documents.To choose grid settings, you use the Document Grid tab in the Page Setup dialog box, as shown in Figure 15-8.

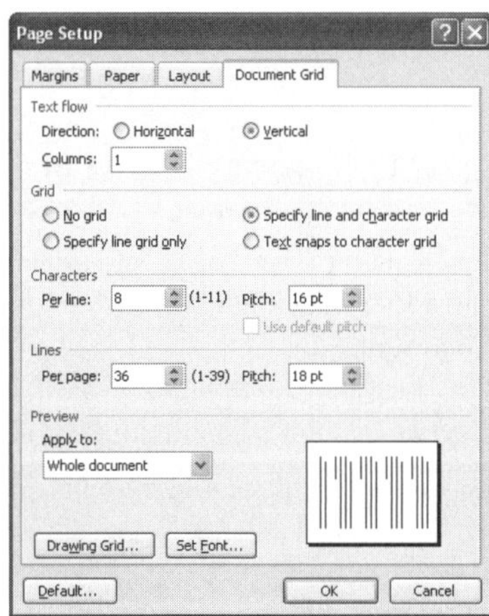

Figure 15-8. The Document Grid enables you to precisely control the line and character spacing in documents that contain East Asian text.

Specifying Document Grid Settings

Using the Document Grid tab, you can control the number of characters per line, number of lines per page, character *pitch* (spacing between characters), and line spacing. To use the Document Grid features, follow these steps:

1. Choose File, Page Setup, and then click the Document Grid tab.
2. If you want to text to be shown vertically, appearing top to bottom as you type, click Vertical in the Text Flow section. Otherwise, for traditional right-to-left text display, leave Horizontal selected. If desired, specify a number of columns in the Columns box. Notice that the Preview image adjusts to display your page setup settings while you work.
3. To turn on the grid feature, select one of the following options:
   - *Specify Line Grid Only*—Makes only the settings in the Lines section in the Document Grid tab available, so that you can choose the amount of space between lines (by selecting the number of lines you want to appear on the page) and the pitch, or spacing between lines.
   - *Specify Line And Character Grid*—Makes all settings in both Character and Lines sections available. This setting enables you to choose both the number of characters per line and the number of lines per page. You can also choose the pitch of both characters and lines.
   - *Text Snaps To Character Grid*—Disables the Pitch settings and gives you the means to choose number of Characters Per Line and Lines Per Page.
4. Click the Apply To arrow, choose the option that specifies the portion of the document to which you want to apply the grid, and then click OK.

If you changed the text direction in the Document Grid tab, Word starts a new page with the grid choices in effect. If you retained the original text direction, Word applies the grid effects as soon as you begin typing in the current section. As you type, you'll be able to see the effects of the new spacing selections you've chosen.

Displaying the Document Grid

If you want to see the Document Grid while you work, choose File, Page Setup to display the Page Setup dialog box, and then click the Document Grid tab. In the lower-left portion of the dialog box, click the Drawing Grid button. In the Drawing Grid dialog box, select the Display Gridlines On Screen dialog box, as shown in Figure 15-9. Click OK twice to return to the document. The gridlines appear throughout the document.

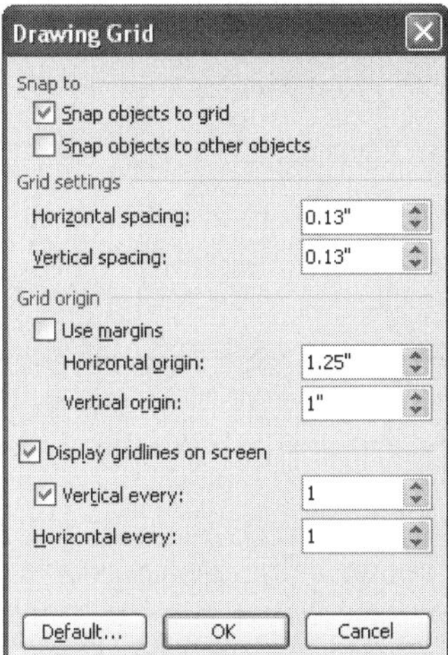

Figure 15-9. You can customize the Document Grid's display by modifying the Drawing Grid dialog box settings.

Note You can see the Document Grid while you work only when you're working in Print Layout view.

Chapter 16

Formatting Documents Using Templates, Wizards, Add-Ins, and XML Schemas

Computers are powerful, but they still need to be told what to do—no matter how automated a task might seem. It should come as no surprise, therefore, that whenever you create a new document in Word, your document is based on a *template* that provides default document creation settings. Templates are available locally on your computer as well as online, and they serve as patterns for documents: they define styles, AutoText entries, toolbars, standard (or *boilerplate*) text, placeholder text, and so forth. You can control how documents and templates interact in a number of ways. For example, you can base documents on existing templates, create custom templates for new and existing documents, attach templates to documents, load global templates, and edit templates.

In addition to controlling documents using templates, you can use interactive *wizards* to create documents styled in particular ways. Word provides a set of wizards and you can access additional wizards at Microsoft Office Online. Each wizard presents a series of dialog boxes that walk you through the construction of a particular type of document. For instance, you can use wizards to create memos, calendars, Web pages, résumés, letters, and other common documents.

You can also control your Word environment by adding custom commands and features with *add-ins*. Add-ins are supplemental programs that add specific capabilities to Word. For example, some add-ins install Microsoft Office updates, proofreading tools, helper applications (such as Stamps.com, ScanSoft PDF converter, MSN Stock Quotes, and ActiveDocs), troubleshooting tools, sound files, graphics filters, and additional templates and wizards.

Finally, using the stand-alone edition of Word 2003 or the version of Word 2003 in Microsoft Office Professional Edition, you can create XML documents and attach XML schemas. By default, Word uses an XML schema named WordML when you save a Word document as an

XML document. If you have another XML schema that you'd like to attach to a document, you can do so in much the same way that you attach a template to a document.

In this chapter, you'll learn how to add, use, and control templates, wizards, add-ins, and XML schemas to enhance and automate document creation, editing, and formatting.

Understanding How Templates Work

As mentioned, every Word document is based on a template. A template is a .dot file (or group of related files) that contains the structure and tools for shaping the style and page layout of finished files. Templates can contain settings for fonts, styles, page layout parameters, toolbars, macros, AutoText entries, key assignments, menus, headers, footers, and special formatting. By default, Word bases new blank documents on the Normal template (discussed in more detail in "Getting the Scoop on Word's Normal Template," on page 487).

The main purpose of templates is to make formatting and inserting information into documents as efficient, error-free, and automatic as possible. The fewer formatting and typing tasks you have to perform, the better. In addition to speeding document creation, templates enable you to provide custom editing environments for particular projects and clients because templates can include interface tools (such as toolbars, macros, and menus) as well as formatting and layout settings. To clarify, templates can assist in document creation tasks in the following ways:

- **Provide all relevant styles for a particular document** As described in Chapter 9, "Using Styles to Increase Your Formatting Power," you can create and use a series of styles to generate a particular look for a document. By creating a template that contains a set of styles, you can easily access and consistently apply the styles throughout similar and related documents.
- **Include boilerplate text, AutoText entries, headers, footers, and placeholder text** Templates can save you from repeatedly typing information that recurs in related documents by enabling you to create new documents that automatically contain default text, include relevant custom AutoText entries (such as company names and contract text), and display placeholder text. For more information about AutoText entries, see Chapter 7, "Putting Text Tools to Work," and for more information about adding headers and footers, see Chapter 15, "Mastering Page Setup and Pagination."
- **Display necessary and customized toolbars and menus** If a particular type of document always uses specificWord tools, you can create a template that displays a Word interface that caters to the tasks associated with the document type. To learn about customizing toolbars and menus, see Chapter 5, "Customizing Word and Enhancing Accessibility."
- **Include specialized macros for a particular document type** To help streamline tasks in certain types of documents, you can include macros in a template. Macros are routines that are created to perform a task or set of tasks, and are assigned to a toolbar button or keyboard shortcut. For more information about macros, see Chapter 32, "Creating and Working with VBA Macros."

Regardless of the information included in templates, you can use two main types of templates when you work in Word: *global templates* and *document templates*. Global templates (most notably the Normal template) contain settings that are available to all documents. In contrast, document templates, such as memo and Web page templates, contain settings that are available only to documents based on that template. When a document is based on a template, the template is attached to the document. (For more information about attaching templates, see "Attaching Templates to Documents," on page 499.) If this difference between global and document templates seems a little cloudy at the moment, don't despair. After you review the information in this chapter and experiment with templates for a while, you'll see the value of knowing how to use and customize global and document templates as you work.

Getting the Scoop on Word's Normal Template

No matter what template you use to format a specific document, the Normal global template is always open. Normal.dot is stored in the \%*UserProfile*%\Application Data\Microsoft \Templates folder by default. Whenever you start Word, it automatically looks for the Normal template in the location specified in the File Locations tab in the Options dialog box. (You display this dialog box by choosing Tools, Options.)

For more information about changing the default location of template files, see Chapter 5, "Customizing Word and Enhancing Accessibility."

The Normal template contains default styles and built-in AutoText entries (but no boilerplate text) that are automatically available whenever you create new, blank documents. As you work in a document, any styles, AutoText entries, macros, toolbars, or other customizations you save are stored in the Normal template unless you specify otherwise. In addition, you can modify the Normal template to change the default document formatting in Word. As you can imagine, the longer you work with Word, the more customized your Normal.dot file can become.

If the Normal template is damaged, moved, missing, or renamed, Word creates a new Normal template the next time you start Word, which is based on the default settings. This automatically generated Normal template won't include any customizations you've made to a previous version of Normal.dot. Of course, you can intentionally rename your Normal template to force Word to create a new Normal template. If you do this, Word will create a fresh Normal template, and then you can copy selected components from the renamed template into the newly generated Normal template by using the Organizer, as described in "Renaming, Deleting, and Copying Styles Using the Organizer," on page 504. To rename the Normal template after you've altered the default template by adding customizations, close Word, then display the Normal.dot template in the the \%*UserProfile*%\Application Data\Microsoft\Templates folder, right-click the Normal template, choose Rename, and enter a new name for the template. The next time you open a new blank document in Word, the document will be based on the standard Normal.dot template without any custom settings.

Troubleshooting

I can't find the Normal template in the templates folder

After you rename or delete the Normal template from the Templates folder, you won't see the Normal.dot file in the Templates folder at first. Word will continue to open using the default Normal.dot template, but the file won't appear in the Templates folder until you customize the Normal template by adding a style, toolbar, macro, or other customization, or close Word.

Caution Because the Normal template is so necessary and so widely used, it's often the first target of macro virus authors. Therefore, if you work with a highly customized Normal template, you might want to back up your system's Normal.dot file every few weeks. If you don't need to change your Normal.dot file on a regular basis, you can provide added security by making the Normal template read-only. Making your Normal template read-only protects it from virus attacks that attempt to overwrite or add information to Normal.dot files.

Troubleshooting

Word crashes during startup—could the Normal template be corrupted?

If Word crashes during startup, you can use a switch to quickly determine whether the problem is due to a damaged Registry entry or a corrupt Normal.dot file. To get to the root of the problem, try opening Winword.exe using the **/a** switch (see Table 16-1 for all Word startup switches). When you use the **/a** switch, Word opens but prevents add-ins and global templates (including Normal.dot) from loading automatically. To start the Winword program without loading add-ins and global templates, follow these steps:

1. Click Start, and then choose Run.
2. In the Run dialog box, type "**c:\program files\microsoft office\office11\winword.exe" /a** (or replace the text in quotation marks with a different path if you installed Word elsewhere) in the Open box, and then click OK.

If Word opens properly using this method, you can deduce that you have a damaged Registry or a corrupt Normal.dot file. To test whether the Normal.dot file is the culprit, use Microsoft Windows Explorer to find and rename the Normal.dot file, and then attempt to start Word normally. If Word starts, a new Normal.dot file will be created, and you can use the Organizer to copy any components you need from the renamed file into the newly created Normal.dot file.

If Word still doesn't start properly after you rename your existing Normal.dot file, you probably have a damaged Registry. You can try to correct this problem by opening Word using the Run dialog box (as described previously) and choosing Help, Detect And Repair from the Word Help menu. Alternatively, you can run the Microsoft Windows Installer. To do so, choose Start, Settings, Control Panel. In Control Panel, double-click Add Or Remove Programs, select Microsoft Office or Microsoft Word in the Currently Installed Programs list of the Add Or Remove Programs dialog box, and then click Change. In the setup dialog box, choose the Reinstall Or Repair option to restore your original Word files and Registry settings.

Table 16-1. Word Startup Switches

Switch	Result
/a	Word starts but prevents add-ins and global templates (including the Normal.dot template) from loading automatically.
/l*addinpath*	Word starts and then loads the specified add-in.
/m	Word starts without running any AutoExec macros. You can also suppress macros during startup without using a switch by pressing Shift while you start Word.
/m*macroname*	Word starts, and then runs the specified macro.
/n	A new instance of Word starts without an open document. Documents opened in each instance of Word will not be listed in the Window menu in other instances.
/p*xslt*	Word starts and opens a new XML document based on the specified Extensible Stylesheet Language Transformation (XSLT).
/safe	Word starts in Office Safe Mode.
/t*templatename*	Word starts and opens a new document based on a template other than the Normal template.
/w	A new instance of Word starts with a new blank document. Documents opened in each instance of Word will not be listed in the Window menu in other instances.

Creating New Documents Based on Existing Templates

When you install Word, the setup program provides numerous wizards and templates. You can find additional wizards and templates on the Web, most notably by accessing the Templates page on the Microsoft Office Online Web site. With all these prebuilt templates at your disposal, you can easily create new documents based on templates without having to create a custom template. In this part of the chapter, you'll learn how to create new documents based on templates that you have on hand or can access easily. Building templates from scratch is discussed later in this chapter.

Troubleshooting

Some built-in Word templates aren't available

When Word is installed as part of a typical Office installation, some built-in wizards and templates are installed directly onto your computer, but other wizards and templates are loaded by the Windows Installer the first time you try to access them. If you click Customize instead of Install Now when you first run the setup program, you can install additional templates and wizards at that time.

To make additional built-in templates available after Word is installed, follow these steps:

1. Run the setup program (either from disk or from the Add Or Remove Programs in the Control Panel, in which case you'd click Microsoft Office 2003, and then click Change), choose Add Or Remove Features in the setup dialog box, and then click Next.
2. Click the Choose Advanced Customization Of Applications check box, and then click Next.
3. Expand the Microsoft Office Word node by clicking the plus sign, and then expand Wizards And Templates to view the list of built-in wizards and templates.
4. Click the Wizards And Templates arrow, and choose Run All From My Computer from the menu that appears. To install only a few additional templates and wizards, click the arrow next to each wizard or template you want to add, and then choose Run From My Computer.
5. Click Update to install the wizards and templates.

By indicating that you want templates and wizards to run on your computer, you'll be able to access the templates and wizards without having to run the Windows Installer program.

Using the Templates Dialog Box to Create New Documents

As mentioned, Word provides a number of built-in templates that you can use to create new documents. For easy access, Word displays links to templates in the New Document task pane. To access the Word templates, choose File, New to display the New Document task pane, and then click the On My Computer link in the Templates section. The Templates dialog box will appear, as shown in Figure 16-1.

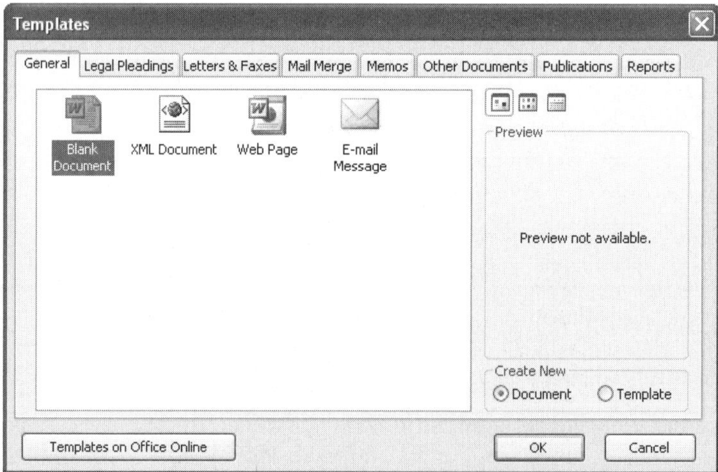

Figure 16-1. The Templates dialog box provides easy access to built-in Word templates as well as custom templates.

The Templates dialog box lets you access all default Word templates (to find the location of the default templates, choose Tools, Options, and then click the File Locations tab; default templates are in the Workgroup Templates, File Types list) as well as any templates you create and save in the \%*UserProfile*%\Application Data\Microsoft\Templates folder. Each tab in the Templates dialog box indicates a subfolder. When you create or copy custom templates (as described in "Creating Custom Templates" on page 494), you can include your custom templates in the Templates dialog box by storing the files in the Templates folder.

To create a new document using a template available in the Templates dialog box, follow these steps:

1. Choose File, New to display the New Document task pane, and then click On My Computer in the Templates section.
2. In the Templates dialog box, click the tab for the subfolder that contains the template you want to use for the new document.
3. In the Create New section, make sure that Document is selected, and then double-click the template (or select the template, and then click OK).

If you're opening a template or wizard that's installed on your computer, Word immediately creates a new document. If the template isn't installed on your computer, Windows Installer installs it and then Word creates the document.

Adding and Removing Word Templates and Tabs in the Templates Dialog Box

To some extent, you can control which templates and tabs appear in the Templates dialog box. To do so, you display the setup dialog box and select which templates and wizards you want to be available, as described in the following steps:

1. Close all Office programs, and then click Start, Control Panel.
2. Double-click Add Or Remove Programs, select Microsoft Office 2003 or Microsoft Word 2003 from the list (depending on your system's setup), and then click Change.
3. In the setup dialog box, select Add Or Remove Features, and then click Next.
4. In the Custom Setup screen, select the Choose Advanced Customization Of Applications check box, and then click Next.
5. Click the plus sign to expand the Microsoft Office Word node, and then expand the Wizards And Templates node.
6. To remove a tab, click the arrow next to the template or wizard component (such as Memos), and then choose the Not Available option in the list.
7. After you configure the settings for the Wizards And Templates node, click Update.

The next time you open the Templates dialog box, the tabs and available templates will reflect the changes you've indicated. If you want to restore the tabs and templates, simply reconfigure the Wizards And Templates group in the setup dialog box.

To add custom tabs that store custom templates to the Templates dialog box, simply create a folder in %*UserProfile*%\Application Data\Microsoft\Templates and store your templates in that folder. The folder's name will display as a tab in the Templates dialog box.

Obtaining Templates from Office Online

If you find that the Templates dialog box doesn't contain the template you need or you want to expand your template options, you can download additional templates from the Microsoft Office Online Templates page. Figure 16-2 shows some of the template categories available on the Office Online Web site.

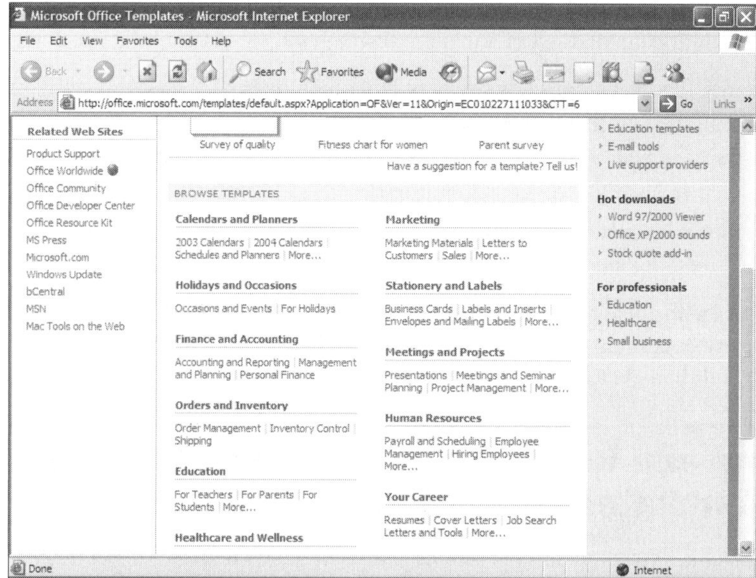

Figure 16-2. In addition to clicking category headings to find templates, you can type a search string in the Office Online Search box located at the top of the Office Online Web page to search for templates online.

To access templates on the Office Online site, verify that you're connected to the Internet, and then follow these steps:

1. Choose File, New, and then click the Templates On Office Online link in the New Document task pane.
2. On the Office Templates Web page, click a main category or a subcategory listing, and then scan the available templates. To preview a template, click the template's name or associated icon (an icon appears next to each template name to indicate the template's Office file type, such as Word or Excel).
3. When you find a template that suits your needs, click it, click Download Now, and then, if necessary, click Accept if you accept the Terms Of Use agreement.

> **Tip** You can also access templates on Office Online by clicking the Templates On Office Online button in the Templates dialog box.

The template will be downloaded to your system and displayed in Word. At that point, you can edit the template and save it as a local document or template. You should spend some time checking out the extensive selection of templates on the Office Template Web site—ranging from marketing and business forms to stationery and résumés.

Using Templates Stored on Your Web Sites and in Network Locations

In addition to retrieving templates from the Templates dialog box and the Office Online Web site, you can access templates stored on a network or Web site. Frequently, workgroups need to share templates, so storing templates online provides an ideal way to share templates and ensure that the most up-to-date templates are readily available to team members. In Word, you can easily create new documents based on templates that are stored on Web sites and on networks. To do so, make sure you're connected to your network or the Internet, and then follow these steps:

1. Choose File, New, and then click the On My Web Sites link in the Templates section of the New Document task pane. The New From Templates On My Web Sites dialog box appears, as shown in Figure 16-3.
2. Double-click the shortcut to the folder on the Web server that contains the template you want to use. By default, templates saved on Web sites are stored in the sharedtemplates folder, as shown in Figure 16-3. Templates can be stored in any folder, though, depending on your network setup or personal preferences.

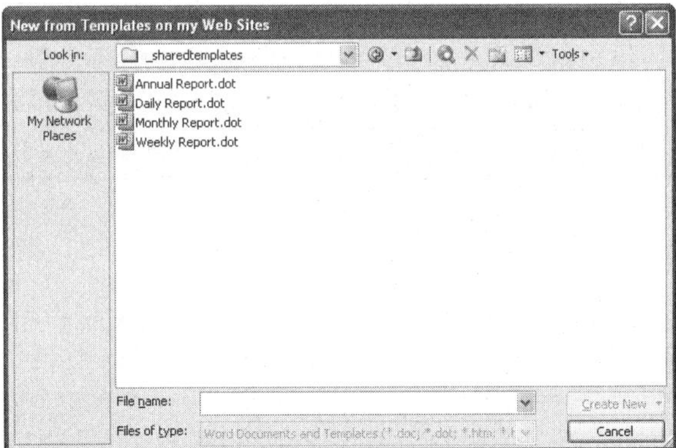

Figure 16-3. The New From Templates On My Web Sites dialog box serves as a gateway to the contents of the My Network Places folder, which can include links to templates stored on your network or Web sites.

3. If necessary, double-click the folder that contains the template you want to use, and then double-click the template file.

After you open an online template file, a new document is created on your desktop that's based on the template settings. You can then type the contents of the new document and save the document locally or store it on the server, just as with any other document.

Troubleshooting

Links to templates do not appear when I click the Templates On My Web Sites link

Before you can create a new document based on a template that's stored online, the template must be stored in an online folder, and you need to create a shortcut to the network or Web server that contains the template you want to use. If these conditions aren't met, you won't have any Web site shortcuts in the New From Templates On My Web Sites dialog box.

If you don't have a Web site or network server space, you can obtain file storage space online from free Web space servers. For instance, you can visit *groups.msn.com* and create an MSN Group site to use for storing and sharing documents.

After you have created an online folder in which you can store files and templates, the next order of business is to create a shortcut to the online location. To do so in Microsoft Windows XP, follow these steps:

1 Open the My Network Places folder (choose Start, My Network Places), and then double-click the Add Network Place in the Network Tasks task pane.

2 In the Add Network Place Wizard, click Next, click Choose Another Network Location, and then click Next.

3 Type the address of the network location or Web server (or click Browse to locate the network location or Web server), click Next, type a name for the shortcut, click Next, and then click Finish.

After you create shortcuts to network and Web site locations, you can click the links to the sites in the New From Templates On My Web Sites dialog box to access the online folder and any files or templates stored within the folder.

Creating Custom Templates

After you're familiar with how templates work and how to use existing templates, you're ready to start creating your own templates. In Word, you can create templates in three ways. You can base a template on an existing document, base a new template on an existing template, or create a template from scratch. The method you use should depend on the resources you have on hand, as follows:

- **Create a template based on a document** You have a document that contains most or all of the settings you want to use in your template.
- **Create a template based on an existing template** You have a template that contains many of the settings you want to use in your new template but you want to add or change a few settings without affecting the existing template.
- **Create a template from scratch** You have no model to use as a starting point for your template.

When you create custom templates, you should save your templates in the *%UserProfile%*\Application Data\Microsoft\Templates folder so that they'll be easily accessible in the Templates dialog box. Templates you save in the Templates folder appear in the General tab in the Templates dialog box (which means, logically enough, that templates stored elsewhere won't appear in the Templates dialog box). If you want to store your templates in a custom tab in the Templates dialog box, create a new subfolder (or a few subfolders, if necessary) in the Templates folder, and save your templates in the subfolder. Each custom tab in the Templates dialog box has the same name as a subfolder you create in the Templates folder, so name your subfolders carefully. Note that you must save at least one template or Word document in a subfolder; otherwise, the subfolder won't appear as a tab in the Templates dialog box.

Now that we have a few details out of the way, let's look more closely at the three ways you can create templates.

Note You should save your template with the .dot extension, but any document file that you save in the Templates folder will also act as a template by default. To ensure that your files are saved as template files, you might want to display file extensions in Windows Explorer. In Windows XP, known file extensions are hidden by default. To show extensions, choose Start, Control Panel, and then double-click the Folder Options item. In the Folder Options dialog box, click the View tab, clear the Hide Extensions For Known File Types check box, and then click OK.

Document templates can be stored on your hard disk, included in a document library, or used as a workgroup template. For more information about sharing documents and using workgroup templates, see Chapter 24, "Working and Collaborating Online." For more information about using shared document workspaces and document libraries, see Chapter 25, "Working with Shared Documents."

Basing a Template on an Existing Document

When you base a template on an existing document, you create a template that contains all the styles, macros, toolbars, menus, layout, and other settings in the document. Most likely, you'll want to modify the document's settings slightly to fine-tune your template. You can do so, but be careful. You don't want to modify the document—you want to modify the template. So create your template first, close the existing document (if necessary), and then make all your modifications within the template document, as follows:

1. Choose File, Open.
2. In the Open dialog box, open the document that contains the formatting and/or text you want to include in your template.
3. Choose File, Save As.
4. In the Save As dialog box, select Document Template in the Save As Type list, as shown in Figure 16-4.

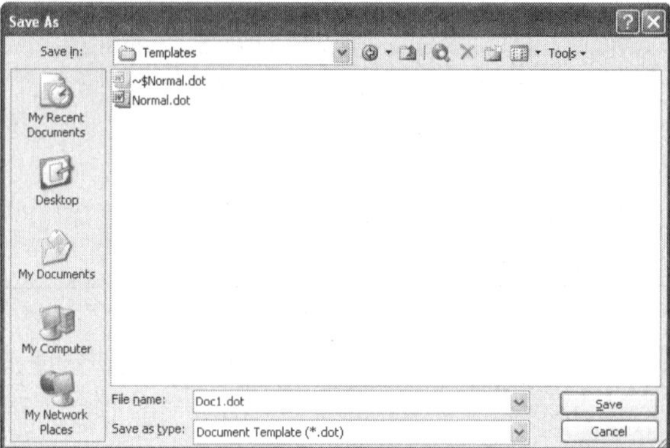

Figure 16-4. When you select Document Template in the Save As Type drop-down list, Word displays the Templates folder by default.

5 By default, the document will be saved in the Templates folder, and the template will appear in the General tab in the Templates dialog box. To display the template in a custom tab, create a new subfolder. The subfolder's name will also appear as the name of the tab.

6 In the File Name box, type a name for the new template, and then click Save.

7 In the new template, add any text or graphics you want to appear in new documents that you base on the template, and delete any information you don't want to appear in documents using the template.

8 Make setup changes in the new template, if desired. For example, you can change the margin settings, page size and orientation, styles, paragraph formatting, header or footer information, add placeholder text, and so forth.

9 Save and close the new template.

After you create a new template, you should test the template to verify that it works as intended by creating a document using the template. To do so, click the On My Computer link in the New Document task pane, click the tab in which the template is located (if necessary), make sure that the Document option is selected in the Create New section in the Templates dialog box, and then double-click the new template.

Providing Single-Click Access to Templates

If you create a custom document template that you'll access frequently to create new documents, you might consider adding a custom button to one of your toolbars or creating a desktop shortcut that enables you to quickly open a new blank document based on a particular template. For example, on the Standard toolbar, you could add a button next to the New Blank Document button. With one click, the new button would open a new document based on a specific template. To learn how to display and link custom toolbar buttons, see Chapter 5, "Customizing Word and Enhancing Accessibility."

To create a desktop shortcut, right-click on your desktop, choose New, select Shortcut, enter the path to the template or use the Browse button to locate the template, click Next, enter a shortcut name (or use the default name, which is the same as the file name), and then click Finish.

Creating a New Template Based on an Existing Template

If you have a template that you want to use as a starting point for a new template, you can do so in much the same way that you create a template based on an existing document. The main procedural difference is that you open a template (.dot) file instead of a document (.doc) file.

To create a template based on an existing template, follow these steps:

1. Choose File, New.
2. In the New Document task pane, click the On My Computer link in the Templates section. The Templates dialog box appears.
3. Select a template similar to the one you want to create, click the Template option in the Create New section, and then click OK.
4. After the template opens, choose File, Save As, and then save the template as a new template with a new name.
5. In the new template, add and modify settings as necessary, and then save the template.

Customizing existing templates comes in especially handy when you download templates using the Templates On Office Online link in the New Document task pane. The Web site provides a wide variety of generic templates; you can customize the generic templates by modifying them to suit your needs, and then save the modified templates as your own templates for future use.

For more information about templates available on the Microsoft Office Online Web site, see "Obtaining Templates from Office Online" on page 492.

Building a Template from Scratch

In addition to basing templates on existing documents and templates, you can build templates from scratch. Building a template from scratch is similar to creating a document from scratch. To create a new, blank template, follow these steps:

1. Choose File, New, and then click On My Computer in the New Document task pane.
2. In the Templates dialog box, choose Template in the Create New section, and then double-click Blank Document in the General tab.

Tip Another way to create a blank template is to open a new, blank document, open the Save As dialog box, and then save the document as a template.

After you create a blank template file, you can add styles, boilerplate text, custom toolbars, macros, and any other elements you want to include in your template. For information about creating specific elements in your template, see the corresponding chapters in this book.

Tip Use themes to create template settings
When you create templates, you might want to incorporate built-in themes to streamline the process. A *theme* is a set of colors, fonts, and graphics elements (such as ruled lines and bullets) that work together to provide a unified look for your document. Even if you don't see a built-in theme that exactly meets your needs, you can use a theme as a starting point to identify the elements you might want to include in your template. After you apply a theme to your template, you can reformat the theme components to suit your style. For more information about themes, see Chapter 17, "Formatting Layouts Using Text Boxes, Frames, Backgrounds, and Themes."

Previewing Templates Using the Style Gallery

One convenient aspect of using templates with defined styles is that you aren't forever committed to using particular formatting. You can change a document's formatting at any time by adjusting the properties of the styles defined in the template. If you're considering modifying a document's styles, you should visit Word's Style Gallery. The Style Gallery enables you to preview how an entire document will look if styles are applied from another template. If you like what you see, you can copy the styles from within the Style Gallery directly into your document.

To preview a document with other template styles and to apply new styles to a document, follow these steps:

1. Open the document you want to format, and then choose Format, Theme.
2. In the Theme dialog box, click Style Gallery. The Style Gallery appears, as shown in Figure 16-5.
3. Select a template in the Template list, and choose an option in the Preview section, as follows:
   - *Document*—Displays how your document will appear if it's formatted with the selected template.
   - *Example*—Displays an example of a sample file formatted with the template, if an example is available.
   - *Style Samples*—Displays the format for each style in the template in list format.

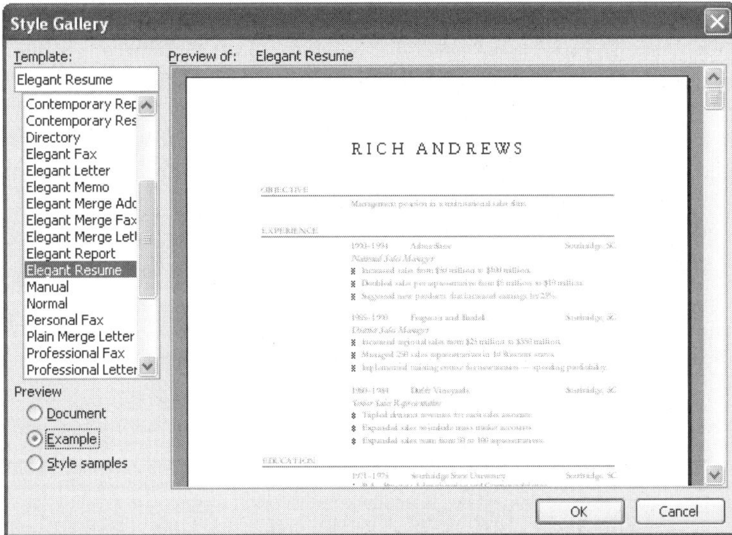

Figure 16-5. The Style Gallery enables you to preview and apply text formatting styles from other templates to the current document.

4 To apply the selected styles to the current document, click OK.

Keep in mind that when you apply styles using the Style Gallery, you aren't changing the template that's attached to the current document. Instead, the Style Gallery lets you view and apply styles from other templates to the contents of the current document. To attach a different template to a document, follow the instructions in the next part of the chapter. To modify a template, refer to "Creating a New Template Based on an Existing Template" on page 497.

Attaching Templates to Documents

Every document has a template associated with it, or "attached" to it, that controls the basic layout and settings used in the document by default. If you create a new, blank document, the Normal.dot template, which is a global template, is attached to the document. When you create a document from an existing template, that document template is automatically attached to the document as well. You can specify which document template you want to attach to a document, regardless of which template is currently attached. And when you replace the existing document template with a new one, you can specify to automatically update the document's text with the new styles, which makes changing templates and formatting later a snap.

To attach a document template to a document and update the document's styles based on the newly attached template, follow these steps:

1 Open your document, and then choose Tools, Templates And Add-Ins. The Templates And Add-Ins dialog box appears, as shown in Figure 16-6.

Figure 16-6. The Templates And Add-Ins dialog box helps you attach a different template to a document, automatically update styles, and control global templates and add-ins.

2. Click Attach to display the Attach Template dialog box, which looks very similar to the Open dialog box. The contents of the Templates folder are displayed by default.
3. Select the template you want to attach to the current document, and then click Open (or simply double-click the desired template). If you want to attach a template that's not stored in the Templates folder, you'll need to navigate to the template's location in the Attach Template dialog box.
4. To automatically apply the newly attached template's styles to the current document, select the Automatically Update Document Styles check box in the Templates And Add-Ins dialog box.
5. Click OK to attach the selected template to the current document.

If you direct Word to automatically update styles, keep in mind that the document text must be formatted with styles that have the same style names as the style names included in the newly attached template. If the style names are the same, Word will update the text formatting to match the newly attached template's style formats. If the document's style names are different from the attached template's style names, you'll have to select and replace instances of each style. If you find that you're faced with changing styles manually, consider using the Select All feature in the Styles And Formatting task pane to choose all instances of an "old" style, and then click the new style name in the Styles And Formatting task pane to replace the styles.

For more information about changing all instances of a style, see Chapter 9, "Using Styles to Increase Your Formatting Power."

Modify Attached Templates

Instead of replacing an attached template with a different one, you might occasionally want to modify an attached template. You might want to modify a template when you're satisfied with the current template for the most part but you want to do some minor tweaking or add a new component. Modifying an attached template has the following effects:

- Macros, AutoText entries, custom toolbars, and custom command settings in the modified template are available for use in any document based on the template, including existing documents.
- Modified styles are not immediately updated in existing files to match the template's new styles.
- Added or modified boilerplate text, graphics, and format settings (such as page margins, column settings, and so forth) are applied to new documents subsequently based on the modified template. Existing documents aren't affected.

If you want to update an existing file that was created using a template before it was modified, open the document, display the Templates And Add-Ins dialog box (by choosing Tools, Templates And Add-Ins), and then select the Automatically Update Document Styles check box. After you click OK, the document will be reformatted using the template's new settings.

For more information about how to modify existing templates, see "Modifying Existing Templates," on page 503.

Working with Global Templates

As mentioned, Word uses two types of templates—global and document. All documents have access to the Normal global template, and many documents have document templates attached that provide formatting instructions. In addition, you can load other templates as needed to serve as global templates. Keeping all these template possibilities in mind, you can see that the interface features and formatting styles available in a current document can be based on the following templates:

- The *Normal template*, which is a global template
- A *document template*, which applies custom formatting and style settings
- Any additional *global templates* that are installed, which contain features such as macros and toolbars that can benefit any open Word document

If several templates that define the same style name are open, the attached document template's settings override all global template settings. The reason document templates take precedence when it comes to styles is that the purpose of document templates is to apply formatting while global templates are generally used to store macros, AutoText entries, and custom toolbar, menu, and keyboard shortcut settings that you can use while you work with any document, not just documents based on a particular document template. By design, templates should be used as global templates when they contain features that benefit any open document.

Typically, when you work on a document, you use only the settings stored in the attached document template or in the Normal template. But when you need to use items that are stored in another template, you can load the other template as a global template. This enables you to use the template's features without having to modify the Normal.dot file or replace the attached document template. After you load a global template, items stored in the template are available to any document during the remainder of the Word session.

Loading Global Templates

When you load global templates, you can specify whether they are to be available for the current session only or available whenever you start Word. To load a global template for the current session, follow these steps:

1. Choose Tools, Templates And Add-Ins to display the Templates And Add-Ins dialog box.
2. In the Global Templates And Add-Ins section on the Templates tab, click Add to display the Add Template dialog box (which displays the contents of the Templates folder by default), and then double-click the name of a template that you want to include in the global template list.
3. Select the check boxes next to any templates you want to load during the current session, as shown in Figure 16-7.

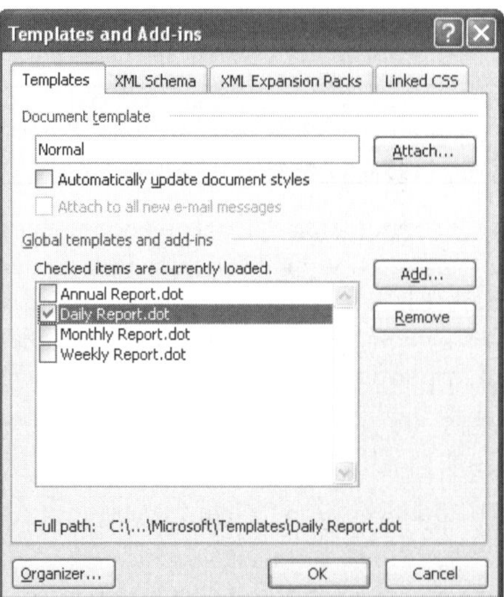

Figure 16-7. You can choose which templates you want to load as global templates during the current session.

4. Click OK to complete the setup.

If you often load the same global template, you can configure Word to load the global template automatically whenever you start Word. The easiest way to accomplish this is to copy the template into the Word Startup folder, which is located at *%UserProfile%*\Application Data\Microsoft\Word\Startup by default.

Caution Be careful when choosing to load global templates automatically. Configuring your system to load global templates each time Word starts uses up system memory and slows Word startup.

Unloading Global Templates

By default, global templates are unloaded (but not removed) when you exit Word, unless you've placed the global template in your Word Startup folder. But if you prefer, you can unload global templates before then. When you've finished with a global template, you can unload it or remove it from the global template list. Note that neither action deletes the template file; unloading and removing a global template from the global template list merely stops the template from serving as a global template. To unload a global template, open the Templates And Add-Ins dialog box (choose Tools, Templates And Add-Ins), and perform either of the following actions:

- Clear the check box next to the template's name in the Global Templates And Add-Ins list to stop using the global template.
- Select the global template in the Checked Items Are Curently Loaded list, and then click Remove to stop using the global template and to remove the template from the list.

Inside Out

Removing global templates from the startup folder

The Remove button in the Templates And Add-Ins dialog box is unavailable when the global template you select to remove is stored in your Startup folder. To work around this, cut and paste the template in the Startup folder to a new location, or, if you have another copy of the template, simply delete the template from the Startup folder.

Modifying Existing Templates

You can modify existing templates by opening and manually changing the template file; modifying a document that has the template attached and saving changes to the template; or by copying, deleting, and renaming template components using the Organizer. Regardless of how you make changes to a template, when you modify a template, the modifications affect new documents based on the template, but the contents of existing documents are not affected by template modifications unless you specifically instruct Word to apply the new template settings to the document, by configuring options in the Templates And Add-Ins dialog box.

Modifying an Existing Document Template File

To modify an existing document by working directly in the template, you must first open the file as a template from the Open dialog box, as follows:

1. Choose File, Open, select Document Templates in the Files Of Type list, and then locate and open the template you want to modify. By default, templates are stored in the \%*UserProfile*%\Application Data\Microsoft\Templates folder.
2. Change any of the template's text and graphics, styles, formatting, macros, AutoText entries, AutoCorrect settings, toolbars, menu settings, and keyboard shortcuts, and then click Save on the Standard toolbar.

Remember, whenever you make changes to a document template, you should test the changes by creating a sample new document based on the template. Also, to apply the changes to any existing document to which the template is attached, ensure that the Automatically Update Document Styles check box in the Templates And Add-Ins dialog box is selected after you open the document. (If the option has been previously selected from within a document, the template will update automatically when that document is opened.)

Modifying an Existing Document Template While Working in a Document

You can modify a template while you work in a Word document. For instance, you can add a style to the attached document template by creating a style (as described in Chapter 9, "Using Styles to Increase Your Formatting Power"). In the New Style dialog box (or in the Modify Style dialog box), select the Add To Template check box to add the new style to the currently attached template. When you save the document, Word displays a message box that asks if you want to update the attached document template, as shown in Figure 16-8.

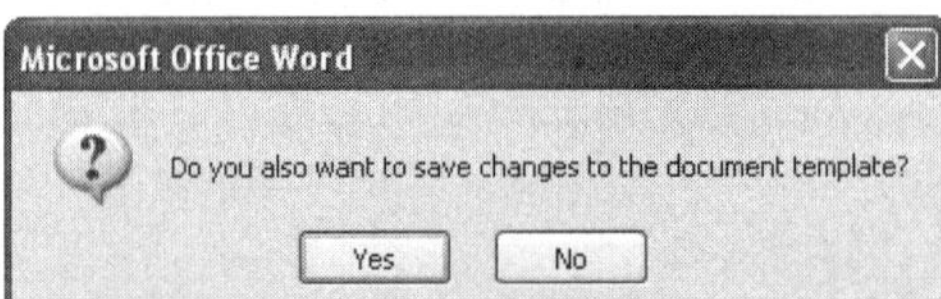

Figure 16-8. You can modify and save changes to an attached document template while you work in a document.

Renaming, Deleting, and Copying Styles Using the Organizer

In addition to modifying templates by making changes in template and document files, you can use the Organizer to manage template components. The Organizer dialog box contains tabs for Styles, AutoText, Toolbars, and Macro Project Items, as shown in Figure 16-9.

Formatting Documents Using Templates, Wizards, Add-Ins, and XML Schemas

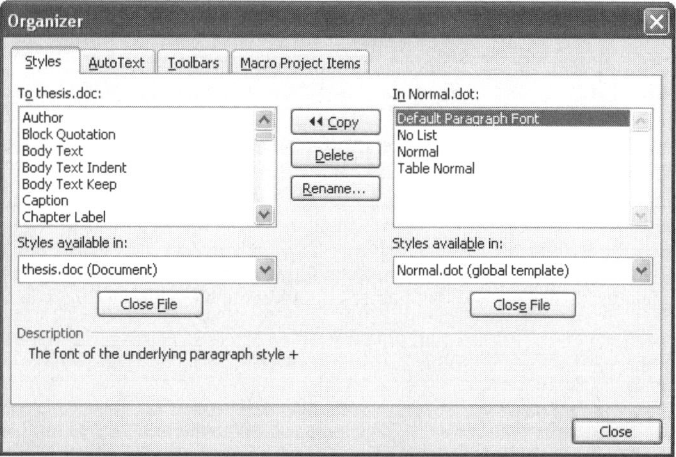

Figure 16-9. You can copy, delete, and rename styles, AutoText, toolbars, and macros stored in specific documents and templates by using the Organizer.

To use the Organizer to copy and manage any of these types of elements in documents and templates, follow these steps:

1. Choose Tools, Templates And Add-Ins, and then click Organizer.
2. In the Organizer dialog box, click the tab for the items you want to copy, delete, or rename.
3. To copy items to or from templates or files, click Close File to close the active document and its attached template or to close the Normal template. Then click Open File, and select the template or file you want to open by double-clicking it in the Open dialog box. Select the items you want to copy, delete, or rename, and then click Copy, Delete, or Rename as appropriate.
4. Click Close when you've finished with the Organizer.

Troubleshooting

I can't copy items to a particular template

If you try to copy styles, macros, toolbars, or other items to a template that's protected in some way, you might not be able to open the template, accept or reject tracked changes in the template, or save changes to the template. This problem might be due to any of the following reasons:

- The template is protected for tracked changes, comments, or forms.
- The template is encrypted and requires you to enter a password.
- The template is protected by a password (in other words, a password was added to the Security tab in the Options dialog box). If you don't know the password, you can open the template only as a read-only file.
- The file attributes are set to read-only.

- You don't have access to the server on which the template is stored.
- The template might be open on another computer on your network.

To save changes to a template, the protection settings must be removed from the template, you must gain the proper access permissions, or you must wait until the template is no longer open on another computer on the network.

In some instances, you might want to protect templates. To learn more about protecting documents, see "Protecting Templates," below, as well as Chapter 28, "Addressing Document Protection and Security Issues."

Protecting Templates

Protecting your templates can ensure that templates remain intact, without unintentional alterations. Protecting your templates can be especially important if you're sharing them with other people on a network or online. You can protect templates the same way you protect standard Word documents. In particular, you can protect your templates in the following ways:

- **Suggest that they be opened as read-only** Choose Tools, Options, click the Security tab, select the Read-Only Recommended check box, and then click OK.
- **Encrypt the template** Choose Tools, Options, click the Security tab, enter a password in the Password To Open box, click OK, re-enter your password, and then click OK again.
- **Create a file-sharing password** Choose Tools, Options, click the Security tab, enter a password in the Password To Modify box, click OK, re-enter your password, and then click OK again.

- **Protect formatting and editing changes** Choose Tools, Protect Document. The Protect Document task pane appears, which enables you to apply detailed formatting and editing restrictions.

- **Prevent the template from being forwarded, edited, or copied by unauthorized people** Apply Information Rights Management (IRM) by clicking Permission on the Standard toolbar.

For more information about tracking changes and adding comments, see Chapter 27, "Revising Documents Using Markup Tools," and for more information about creating and protecting forms, see Chapter 31, "Working with Field Codes and Custom Forms." For more information about IRM and security in Word, see Chapter 28, "Addressing Document Protection and Security Issues."

Constructing Documents and Other Publications Using Word's Wizards

By now, most experienced Word users are familiar with Word's wizards. These wizards provide a series of dialog boxes that walk you through the process of constructing a document. In other words, the wizard asks questions, you provide responses, and then a feature is activated or an item is created—such as a form, a network place, or a Web page—in accordance with your answers. The aim of a wizard is to create a foundation for a document. After the document is created, you fill in the gaps with more detailed information.

By default, wizards are accessible through the Templates dialog box with document templates. You can easily identify wizards in the Templates dialog box because wizard icons include a magic wand. To open a wizard, you simply double-click the wizard of your choice. To work through a wizard, you follow the instructions on the screen. For example, the Welcome screen for the Memo Wizard (available in the Memos tab in the Templates dialog box) is shown in Figure 16-10. The wizard steps are listed on the left side of the screen; the current step is shown in bold green text. By referring to this area while you work, you can follow your progress throughout the process. Note that not all wizards provide this step-by-step display.

Figure 16-10. Wizards apply information you supply to create a document or set of documents.

Customizing Word with Add-Ins

Another way you can modify your Word environment is to use *add-ins*. An add-in is a supplemental program that adds custom commands or custom features to Word. Like global templates, some add-ins can be loaded for the current session only or whenever you start Word. For loading instructions, see "Loading Global Templates," on page 502. In addition to Microsoft Office add-ins (which are available when you install Word or from the Office Online Web site), your system can be configured to use Component Object Model (COM) add-ins, which are usually designed by developers and solutions providers. You view and control COM add-ins a little differently than Microsoft add-ins and global templates, as described later in this part of the chapter.

Examples of typical add-ins offered by Microsoft and third-party developers and vendors include the following:

- **Microsoft Office Proofing Tools** Contains proofreading tools that Microsoft makes for over 30 languages, including fonts, spelling and grammar checkers, AutoCorrect lists, AutoSummarize rules, translation dictionaries, and for Asian languages, Input Method Editors (IMEs).

- **MSN Money Stock Quotes** Provides summary information about recent stock activity.
- **Office Troubleshooters** Includes troubleshooting tools that can help you diagnose and correct common Office problems.
- **Stamps.com** Enables you to print your own postage.
- **Supplement Templates And Wizards** Provides additional wizards for home and work use.

To find add-ins, visit the Microsoft Office OnlineWeb site by choosing Help, Microsoft Office Online on the Word Help menu.

> **Note** Keep in mind that when you download an add-in, you might have to follow specific installation procedures to ensure that the add-in runs properly. Generally, the download site provides the information you need for correct installation. Before you download an add-in, you should print the installation instructions so that you'll have them on hand for easy reference.

View Word COM Add-Ins

To see which COM Add-Ins are available in Word, display the COM Add-Ins For Word 2003 node in the System Information window by following these steps:

1. In Word, choose Help, About Microsoft Word, and then click System Info.
2. In the System Information window, expand the Office 2003 Applications group, expand the Microsoft Office Word 2003 group, and then click the COM Add-Ins entry.

The COM add-ins are listed in the right pane of the System Information window, with the total number of add-ins at the top of the list, as shown in Figure 16-11. Note that if you click the Summary item in the Microsoft Office Word 2003 group, Word doesn't list COM add-ins; you must click the COM Add-Ins item to view the installed add-ins.

Chapter 16

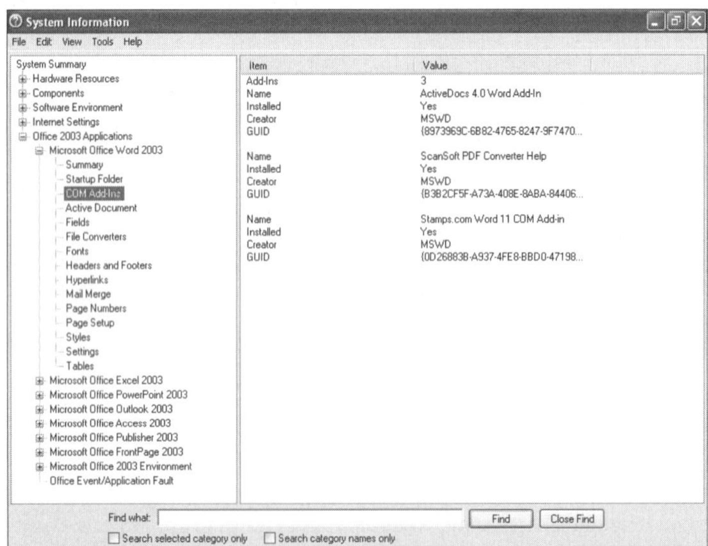

Figure 16-11. The System Information dialog box can show you which COM add-ins are installed for each Office application that is currently running.

Load and Unload Word COM Add-Ins

Loading and unloading Word COM add-ins is generally a software developer's task, but on occasion, you might want to load and unload COM add-ins instead of merely adding and removing them. To load and unload COM add-ins, you must first customize the Tools menu in Word to make the COM Add-Ins dialog box accessible. To do this, follow these steps:

1. Choose Tools, Customize, and then click the Commands tab.
2. Select Tools in the Categories list, drag the COM Add-Ins item to a position in the Tools menu, and then click Close.
3. Choose the COM Add-Ins item from the Tools menu. The COM Add-Ins dialog box appears, as shown in Figure 16-12.

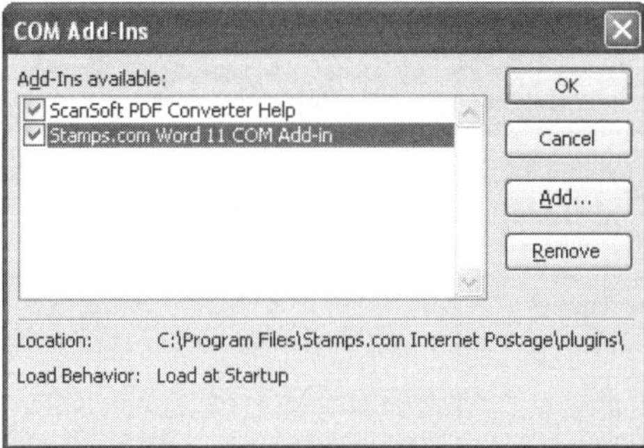

Figure 16-12. The COM Add-Ins dialog box enables you to load and unload COM add-ins as well as control the list of available COM add-ins.

Note Most Word users will either install or remove add-ins (which usually have the .exe or .dll extension) on and from the system instead of loading or unloading them. Generally, add-ins can be removed by using the Windows Add Or Remove Programs dialog box in Control Panel. To access this dialog box, choose Start, Settings, Control Panel, and then, double-click Add Or Remove Programs.

Using the COM Add-Ins dialog box, you can add COM add-ins (click Add, and then navigate to the desired add-in); remove add-ins from the list of available add-ins; and load and unload add-ins by clearing or selecting the add-in check boxes. Keep in mind that you can neither add nor remove a COM add-in from the system by using the COM Add-Ins dialog box; the COM Add-Ins dialog box merely provides access to add-ins, permitting you to control whether add-ins are active, inactive, available, or hidden.

Attaching XML Schemas

If you save a Word document as an XML document, Word uses an XML schema named WordML. The schema applies XML tags that define the document's file properties and structure (such as paragraphs, headings, and tables) as well as formatting and layout information. In addition, you can attach any custom XML schema to an XML document while working in Word. When you save the document, both the Word schema and the custom attached XML schema are attached to the document by default.To attach an XML schema to a document, choose Tools, Templates And Add-Ins, and then click the XML Schema tab. Figure 16-13 shows the XML Schema tab with two available XML schemas. You can add schemas to the list of available schemas (click Add Schema) as well as select which schemas you want to attach to the current XML file (select and clear the check boxes next to the names of available schemas). For a complete discussion about using Word's XML features, see Chapter 29, "Working with XML."

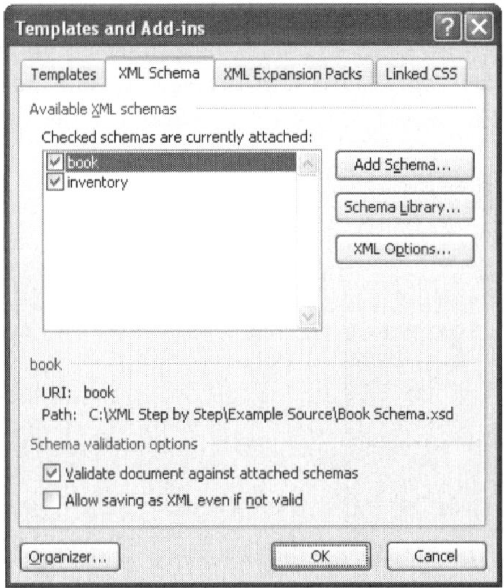

Figure 16-13. The Templates And Add-Ins dialog box now enables you to attach templates, XML schemas, XML expansion packs, and cascading style sheets.

Note Except for the ability to save documents as XML files using the Word XML schema, XML features are available only in Microsoft Office Professional Edition 2003 and the stand-alone edition of Word 2003.

Chapter 17

Formatting Layouts Using Text Boxes, Frames, Backgrounds, and Themes

When you work in Word, you probably take for granted how Word seamlessly flows text from margin to margin and page to page. On occasion, however, you might want to venture beyond basic word processing and into the realm of desktop publishing. For example, instead of filling a page with text, you might want to position and format blocks of text precisely within your document, or you might want to customize the overall "look" of your document by applying a uniform color scheme. Although Word doesn't offer all the bells and whistles incorporated in high-end desktop publishing applications such as Microsoft Publisher, it does include a nice collection of desktop publishing tools that can serve most of your workaday desktop publishing needs.

Specifically, the desktop publishing capabilities in Word let you control text layout by using text boxes, AutoShapes formatted to serve as text containers, and frames. Further, you can add pizzazz to your page layouts by including backgrounds, watermarks, or themes in onscreen and printed documents. In this chapter, you'll learn how to use these common desktop publishing tools to create professional and imaginative document layouts.

Controlling Text Placement and Formatting with Text Boxes and AutoShapes

When you use Word, you might occasionally find that you need control over your text layout beyond setting margins, formatting paragraphs, and creating columns. At those times, you might benefit from entering your information into shapes that can contain text, such as AutoShapes that can serve as *text containers* or *text boxes*. Text boxes are free-floating objects, independent of the regular document, that you can use to enclose information. You can then format these objects in the same ways you format drawings, by using the Drawing toolbar.

For more information about working with AutoShapes and the Drawing toolbar, see Chapter 12, "Enlivening Documents with Drawings and AutoShapes."

In Word, you can use two main types of text containers: standard text boxes and AutoShapes formatted to serve as text containers. Generally, you'll want to use text boxes and AutoShapes when you want to position several blocks of text on a page or flow a continuing story from one area in your document to another. For example, you might be creating a newsletter in which a story starts on the cover page but concludes on another page, later in the newsletter.

> **Note** In Word, text and graphics contained in a single text box or a chain of linked text boxes are referred to as a *story*.

In addition to creating interesting page layouts and continuing a story from one text block to another (also referred to as flowing text in linked text boxes), you might also want to use text boxes to accomplish the following tasks:

- Format text blocks using Drawing toolbar buttons
- Rotate or flip text
- Change text orientation
- Group text blocks and change their alignment or distribution as a group

This part of the chapter describes how you can manipulate and control text using text boxes—both standard rectangular text boxes and AutoShapes formatted as text containers. Keep in mind that when you're working with text boxes and AutoShapes, you must work in Print Layout view. In Print Layout view, the text boxes and AutoShapes appear on the screen as you work. Figure 17-1 shows a Print Layout view of a text box and an AutoShape formatted to contain text.

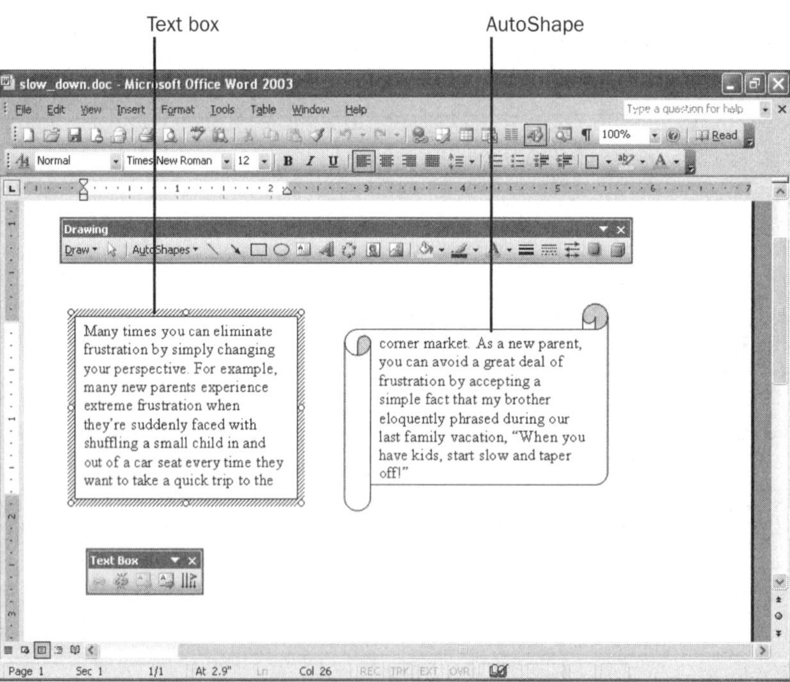

Figure 17-1. You can control text placement and generate unique page designs using text boxes and AutoShapes.

Formatting Layouts Using Text Boxes, Frames, Backgrounds, and Themes

As you can see, the active text box is shown surrounded by a frame-like border. This border appears whenever you click a text box, and it serves a number of purposes, including enabling you to move and resize the text box as well as access text box properties.

Creating Text Boxes

Creating a text box is as easy as drawing a box or shape in the drawing canvas. You can create a text box by performing any of the following actions:

Vertical Text Box

Text Box

- Choose Insert, Text Box, Horizontal, or Insert, Text Box, Vertical, and then drag the pointer in your document to draw a text box.
- Click the Text Box or Vertical Text Box button on the Drawing toolbar, and then drag the pointer in your document to draw a text box.
- Create an AutoShape, right-click the AutoShape, and then choose Add Text from the shortcut menu.

For more information about creating AutoShapes, see Chapter 12, "Enlivening Documents with Drawings and AutoShapes."

By default, when you draw a text box or an AutoShape, a drawing canvas appears. You can work with a text box in the drawing canvas, or you can drag the text box off the drawing canvas and then delete the canvas. (To delete the drawing canvas, select it and press Delete, or right-click and choose Cut.) If you prefer to avoid placing text boxes and AutoShapes in the drawing canvas in the first place, you can turn off the drawing canvas's default action by configuring the Options dialog box, as follows:

1. Choose Tools, Options, and then click the General tab.
2. Clear the Automatically Create Drawing Canvas When Inserting AutoShapes check box.
3. Click OK.

After you close the Options dialog box, the drawing canvas will no longer appear when you create text boxes and drawings.

Regardless of whether you work on or off the drawing canvas, you'll notice that the Text Box toolbar opens automatically after you create a text box, as shown previously in Figure 17-1. This toolbar appears whenever a text box is selected. When no text boxes are selected, the Text Box toolbar is hidden. To display the toolbar again, simply click a text box in your document.

Tip **Display the Text Box toolbar again**

By default, the Text Box toolbar appears when you select (or click in) a text box and disappears when the text box is no longer selected. If you manually close the Text Box toolbar while you're working by clicking the Close button, the toolbar won't appear automatically when you click text boxes. To display the Text Box toolbar after you close it, you need to click a text box and then choose View, Toolbars, Text Box. The Text Box option appears on the Toolbars menu only when you've selected a text box in your document.

As you create text boxes in your document, you can move and resize the text boxes in the same manner you move and resize drawing objects—by dragging them by their borders. To move a text box, click anywhere on its border other than on a sizing handle, and then drag the text box. To resize a text box, you can drag the sizing handles (which appear as circles in text box frames) to change the text box's width and height. Figure 17-1 shows a selected text box with its border and sizing handles.

Inserting Text into Text Boxes and AutoShapes

After you create text boxes or format AutoShapes to hold text, you are ready to add text and formatting. You can insert text into containers in a few predictable ways, including the following:

- Type text directly into a text box.
- Paste copied information into a text box.
- Drag information into a text box.
- Click a text box, and then choose Insert, File to insert a file's contents into the text box.

If you're planning to insert a longer story into a text box or a series of linked text boxes, you should consider typing and editing the story in a plain Word document before importing the information into the text box or text boxes. That way, you can conduct most of your editing, formatting, and fine-tuning tasks in a standard document, which generally provides a larger viewing area.

> **Tip** **Format text in text boxes**
> You can format text in text boxes in the same way you format document text. First click in the text box, and then format the text using keyboard shortcuts, Formatting toolbar buttons, Font and Paragraph dialog boxes, and the Styles And Formatting task pane.

In addition to inserting text, you can insert graphics, tables, and some fields into text boxes. Among the items that you cannot include in text boxes are the following:

- Columns
- Comments
- Drop caps
- AutoFormatting
- Endnotes
- Footnotes
- Indexes
- Page and column breaks
- Tables of contents

To be able to include these elements in a text container, you'll have to convert your text box into a floating frame, as described next, or you'll need to use a framed document, as discussed in "Adding Frames When Designing Online Documents," on page 522.

Note A nice feature of text containers is that when you run the spelling checker and grammar checker, Word also checks the information in text boxes and AutoShapes.

Using Floating Frames for Comments, Footnotes, Tables, and Fields

Generally, your best bet when placing text into text containers is to use text boxes and AutoShapes formatted to contain text, because they are highly customizable. But if you need to insert text that includes comments, footnotes, endnotes, tables, or certain fields (such as tables of contents and index fields) in a container, you'll have to use a *floating frame* instead of a text box, because text boxes can't properly support these types of elements. Although a floating frame looks like a text box, you can't format it as extensively as a text box, and it supports Word fields.

You can easily convert an existing text box into a floating frame whenever necessary by following these steps:

1. If the text box you want to convert is in the drawing canvas, drag the text box off the canvas.
2. Click the text box you want to convert, and then right-click the text box's frame.
3. Choose Format Text Box from the shortcut menu, and then click the Text Box tab in the Format Text Box dialog box.
4. Click Convert To Frame. A message box appears, warning that you are about to change the text box to a frame and that some drawing formatting might be lost. Click OK.

After you convert a text box into a frame, the Text Box toolbar and some Drawing toolbar buttons, such as the Fill Color and Line Color buttons, will be unavailable.

Note You can't convert a frame element into a text box in the same way you can covert a text box into a frame. Therefore, if you want to move frame contents into a text box, you must draw a text box, cut and paste the frame's contents into the text box, and then delete the frame.

Formatting Text Boxes and AutoShapes

By default, when you create a text box, it appears as a white (not transparent) box surrounded by thin (0.75 point) black lines. Fortunately, text boxes don't have to be limited to plain white rectangles strategically placed around your document. You can format text boxes and AutoShapes formatted to be text containers in the same manner you format other drawing objects. For example, you can apply fill and line colors by using the Fill Color and Line

Color buttons on the Drawing toolbar, or you can add a shadow to a text box by using the Shadow Style button. To format text boxes and AutoShapes using the Drawing toolbar, select the text box or AutoShape, and then click the appropriate Drawing toolbar button.

In addition to the standard formatting buttons available on the Drawing toolbar, you can format text boxes using the Format Text Box dialog box. Namely, you can control the position of text inside text boxes and AutoShapes, you can change a text box's shape, and you can have Word automatically resize a text box or an AutoShape to accommodate the complete text of a story.

For more information about using the Drawing toolbar to format drawing objects, see Chapter 12, "Enlivening Documents with Drawings and AutoShapes."

Controlling Text in Text Boxes and AutoShapes

You can change a text box's internal margin settings to control the distance between text and a text box's or an AutoShape's edges. You can do this as described in the following steps:

1 Click a text box or an AutoShape, hover the pointer over the container's frame until it appears as crossed arrows, double-click the container's frame (or right-click the frame, and then choose Format Text Box or Format AutoShape from the shortcut menu; or click a text container, and then choose Format, AutoShape, or Format, Text Box). The Format Text Box or Format AutoShape dialog box appears, depending on the type of text container you're formatting.

2 Click the Text Box tab, shown in Figure 17-2. The Text Box tab is the same in both the Format Text Box and Format AutoShape dialog boxes.

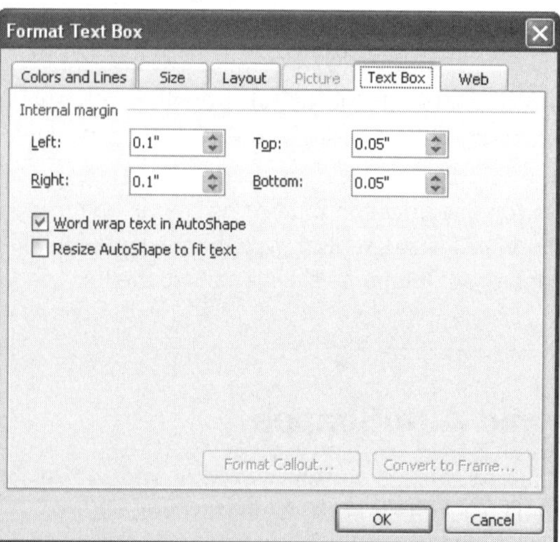

Figure 17-2. You can control the spacing around text in text boxes and AutoShapes by configuring the internal margin settings in the Text Box tab.

3 In the Internal Margin section, increase or decrease the left, right, top, and bottom margin measurements to control the distance between the text and the selected object's edges. Click OK to apply the settings.

Change Text Direction

In addition to controlling internal margins, you can change the direction of text inside text boxes. To do so, click in a text box, and then click Change Text Direction on the Text Box toolbar. You can continue to click the button to cycle through the available text direction options: down, up, and standard.

> **Note** When you change the text direction in a linked text box, you change the text direction in all linked text boxes in the story. In other words, you can't change the text direction in a single text box if it's part of a linked series of text boxes. For more information about linked text boxes, see "Linking Text Boxes to Flow Text from One Text Box to Another," on page 518.

Changing Text Box Shapes

The beauty of using AutoShapes is that you can change your mind regarding which AutoShape you want to use at any time, even if the AutoShape is formatted as a text box. Changing the shape of a text box or an AutoShape is similar to changing shapes that don't contain text. To do so, ensure that you're working in Print Layout view, and then follow these basic steps:

1 Click the text box whose shape you want to modify. To select multiple text boxes, press and hold Shift while clicking each text box.

2 On the Drawing toolbar, click Draw, and then choose Change AutoShape from the menu.

3 In the Change AutoShape menu, choose a category, and then click the shape you want to apply to the selected text boxes.

All the selected shapes take on the new shape but retain all other format settings, such as color, internal margins, and so forth.

Resizing Text Boxes or AutoShapes Automatically to Show All Content

You can automatically resize a text box or an AutoShape that contains text, graphics, and objects so that it is as long or as short as necessary to display all the content inserted in it. You can use this option only with nonlinked (stand-alone) text containers because linked text containers are designed to flow text to the next linked container if content is longer than the current container's boundaries. To automatically size a nonlinked text container to accommodate inserted text, graphics, and objects, follow these steps:

1 Double-click a text container's frame, and then click the Text Box tab in the Format Text Box or Format AutoShape dialog box.

2 Select the Resize AutoShapeTo FitText check box, and then click OK.

The text container will automatically stretch or shrink to accommodate the text.

Linking Text Boxes to Flow Text from One Text Box to Another

If you've ever created a newsletter or a brochure, you know how tricky it can be to fill text areas and manage jumps from one page to another properly. In Word, you can simplify these kinds of tasks by linking text boxes. When you link text boxes, you indicate that any text you insert into one text box will automatically flow into the next text box when the first text box cannot accommodate all of the inserted text. After you insert text into linked text boxes, you can edit the text to make your story longer or shorter, and Word will automatically reflow the text throughout the series of linked text boxes.

Note The maximum number of links you can have in one document is 31, which means that you can have up to 32 linked text containers in one document.

When you want to link text boxes or AutoShapes, you need to keep the following limitations in mind:

- Linked text boxes and AutoShapes must be contained in a single document (note that they cannot be in different subdocuments of a master document).
- No text box or AutoShape may already be linked to another series or story.

Before you flow text into a series of linked text boxes, you should be sure that you've made most of your changes to your text. Then draw the text boxes you want to link and into which you'll import your story. When your text is ready and your text boxes are drawn, follow these steps to link the text boxes and insert the text:

Create Text Box Link

1. In Print Layout view, click the first text box you want to insert text into, and then click Create Text Box Link on the Text Box toolbar (or right-click the text box border, and then choose Create Text Box Link). The pointer changes to an upright pitcher, as shown below.

2. Move the pointer to the text box you want to link to the first text box. When you move the upright pitcher pointer over a text box that can receive the link, the pitcher tilts and turns into a pouring pitcher, as shown below. Click the second text box to link it to the first text box.

3. To link a third text box, click the text box you just linked to the first text box, click Create Text Box Link, and then click the third text box. You can create a chain of linked text boxes using this method.

Tip **Cancel the linking process**
If you click Create Text Box Link and then decide that you don't want to link to another box, press Esc to cancel the linking process.

4 After you link your text boxes, click in the first text box, and then insert text by typing, pasting, or choosing Insert, File. Generally, the latter approach is recommended because it enables you to insert prepared and edited text into your linked text boxes.

Tip **Insert a story while linking text boxes**
If you have a complete story that's ready to flow into text boxes, you can insert the story into the text boxes while you link them. To do this, insert your story into the first text box, and then link to the next text box as described in steps 1 and 2. When you use this approach, the text flows into the text boxes while you link them.

Inside Out

Obtaining word count statistics for text box content

Word excludes all text in text boxes from both word and line count statistics when you use the Word Count command on the Tools menu to perform counts on your entire document. If you need to obtain word count statistics for text in text boxes, you can work around this limitation with a little effort. Basically, you can get the count for the text in each text box or series of linked text boxes, and then add the numbers together to get a total count for the story. To do this, click a text box, press Ctrl+A to select all the text in the story, and then choose Tools, Word Count. If your story is inserted into a series of linked text boxes, you'll obtain the word count statistics for the entire story. If your text boxes aren't linked, you'll need to repeat the process in every text box, and then add the numbers to produce a grand total.

Moving Among Linked Text Boxes

Next Text Box

Previous Text Box

After you link text boxes, you can easily jump from one text box to another by using the Text Box toolbar. To do so, select a text box that's part of a linked series of text boxes. Then, on the Text Box toolbar, click Next Text Box to move to the next linked text box, or click Previous Text Box to move to the previous text box. You can also move to the next text box by positioning your insertion point at the end of text in a filled text box and then pressing the right arrow key, or you can jump to the preceding text box by positioning your insertion point at the beginning of the text in a text box and then pressing the left arrow key.

Copying or Moving Linked Text Boxes

You can copy or move a story (including text boxes and their contents) to another document or another location in the same document. If your story consists of multiple linked text boxes that aren't contained in a single drawing canvas, you will have to select all the linked text boxes in the story before you can copy the story and text boxes. If the story's linked text boxes are in a single drawing canvas, you can select and copy any text box in the series of linked text boxes to copy the entire story and the selected text box to another location. Or, you can select all the text boxes in the drawing canvas to copy the story and all the associated text boxes.

When you copy a text box (or a few linked text boxes but not an entire story) that's not in a drawing canvas, you copy only the selected text box or boxes, without the content. When you copy a single text box that is part of an entire story that appears in text boxes in a single drawing canvas, you copy the entire story along with the selected text box. This means that when you paste the text box, you will probably need to resize the text box to see the entire story or you will need to add text boxes and link them to the newly inserted text box.

If you want to copy an entire story along with all the text boxes containing the story, you can do so by selecting the text boxes before copying them, as described here:

1 In Print Layout view, select a text box in the story by clicking the text box's frame.

Tip **Copy text boxes**

You must select a text box by its frame if you want to copy the text box. If you click inside the text box and then press Ctrl+C or choose Edit, Copy, Word won't copy anything.

If you want to copy multiple text boxes, you can click anywhere in each frame, including the first frame, while you press Shift to select the text boxes.

2 Press Shift and then click the text boxes you want to copy or move—if all the text boxes appear either on or off a single drawing canvas, you'll copy the text boxes' contents as well as the text box containers.

3 Click Copy or Cut on the Standard toolbar (or press Ctrl+C or Ctrl+X, or right-click a selected text box border, and then choose Copy or Cut from the pop-up menu).

4 Click where you want to reposition the text boxes, and then click Paste on the Standard toolbar (or press Ctrl+V, or right-click and then click Paste).

To copy or move content that appears within a text box without copying or moving the text box, select just the text or content in the same way that you select standard text and content, and then copy or move it in the same way you normally copy or move content in Word documents. To select and copy all the text in a linked story, click in the story, press Ctrl+A, and either copy and paste or drag the text to the desired location.You can select all the text in a story using Ctrl+A regardless of whether the story's text boxes are in a drawing canvas.

Breaking Text Box Links

You can break links between text boxes just as easily as you create them. When you break a link, you remove only the link between the selected text box and the text box that follows it in the series—you don't remove all the links in a linked series. Essentially, when you break a link, you divide a story into two series of linked text boxes or segments. By default, the first series of linked text boxes contains the story, and linked text boxes in the second series are empty.

To break a link between text boxes, follow these steps:

1. In Print Layout view, click the border of the text box from which you want the text to stop flowing. The selected text box will become the last text box in the first linked series of text boxes.
2. On the Text Box toolbar, click Break Forward Link (or right-click the text box border and then choose Break Forward Link).

Break Forward Link

At this point, text will stop flowing in the last text box before the broken link, and the second series of linked text boxes will be empty. If the text doesn't fit in the first series of linked text boxes after you break a link, you can create and link additional text boxes or enlarge existing text boxes to provide enough room to display the text.

> **Tip** **Eliminate a text box in the middle of a story**
> You can cut a text box in the middle of a linked series of text boxes without deleting any parts of your story. To do so, simply right-click a text box's border, and then choose Cut from the shortcut menu. When you cut a linked text box, the story readjusts and flows the text into the next text box.

Deleting Linked Text Boxes Without Losing Text

To delete a text box, you simply select a text box and press Delete, or right-click the text box border and choose Cut. Performing this action on a nonlinked text box deletes both the text box and its contents. In contrast, when you delete a text box that's part of a linked series of text boxes, the text from the deleted text box automatically flows into the remaining linked text boxes. If the remaining text boxes aren't large enough to properly display the story in its entirety, you'll have to resize the remaining text boxes, create additional text boxes, or edit your story to fit in the existing text boxes. Keep in mind that Word doesn't notify you when text overflows the final text box's boundaries, so you should always be extra diligent about checking the flow of stories and making sure that no text is hidden.

> **Note** **Delete a text box while keeping the story**
> To avoid deleting an entire story when you delete a stand-alone, nonlinked text box, click in the text box, press Ctrl+A to select the story, and then either drag or copy the selected story into your document before you delete the text box.

Adding Frames when Designing Online Documents

If you're creating documents that will be viewed online, you can take advantage of *frames* to organize your documents. Frames enable you to create areas for the text on your screen that allow you to divide a window into multiple areas so that you can show several documents at one time. Frames are frequently used in Web page design and for long documents on enterprise networks. For example, frames might be used to create an interface for a human resource manual.

Web designers commonly use frames to create several window regions, each of which shows specific types of information. For example, frames are sometimes used to create a menu bar that contains links to pages on a Web site. Users click links on the menu bar in one frame to display selected information in another *target* frame that serves as the main content area. Figure 17-3 shows a Web page that uses three frames—one title area frame, a navigation bar frame, and a body frame.

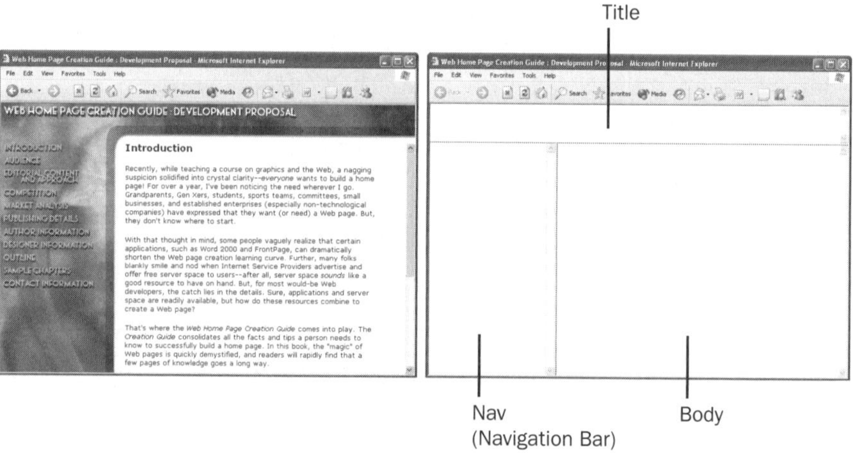

Figure 17-3. The Web page design on the left is based on a framework of three frame areas, as shown on the right.

The basic idea behind a *frames page* is that you create a page that defines how the window will be divided (which acts somewhat like your page's skeleton), and then you specify which document should appear in each frame. When you upload a page that uses frames to a server, you must copy the frames page as well as the files that contain the frames' contents. When you save a document that uses frames in Word—whether you save the document as a Word document or a Web page—Word creates a separate file for the content in each area as well as a frames page that defines the view. Thus, the Web page shown in Figure 17-3 would consist of at least four files—the title bar file, the navigation bar file, the main body text file, and the frames page file (which defines how the content files are shown in the window). To reopen a document that uses frames in Word, you simply open the frames page document.

Note that creating frames pages in Word differs from converting a text box into a frame or using a floating frame to contain information (such as field codes) on a page. When you use a frame container in a Word document and then save the document as a Web page, Word converts the floating frame into a table (using the <TABLE></TABLE> Hypertext Markup Language (HTML) tag set). In this case, browsers will show floating frames as standard content held in position by tables, and Word won't save the frame content in a separate file.

Note Using frames to create Web pages can take some finagling. If you're new to frames and you're creating a Web page, you should do some research about frames online or consult some of the many Web page design books.

Adding Frames to Documents

You can add frames to a document using any of the following techniques:

- Choose Format, Frames, New Frames Page to open a new document and display the Frames toolbar, which you can use to add frames to the new document.
- Choose View, Toolbars, Frames to display the Frames toolbar, which you can use to create frames in the current document.
- Choose Format, Frames, Table Of Contents In Frame to create a left frame that contains links to the headings in the current document. (The document must be formatted with built-in Word headings for this option to work properly.)

For more information about creating Web pages, see Chapter 26, "Creating Professional Web Sites."

The tools you need to create and manage frames can be found on the Frames toolbar, shown in Figure 17-4. (You can also access frames options when you're working in a frames page by choosing Format, Frames.)

Figure 17-4. You can click buttons on the Frames toolbar to add and delete frames in a frames page.

Using the Frames toolbar, you can add a frame to the current document by clicking one of the position buttons: New Frame Left, New Frame Right, New Frame Above, or New Frame Below. After you add a frame, you can resize it by dragging the frame's border.

Tip **Insert top and bottom frames**

If you're going to include top or bottom frames in your document along with a left or right frame, you should create the top or bottom frames first. That way, the top or bottom frame will span the entire width of the page.

Tables Of Contents In Frame

In addition to creating standard frames, you can have Word automatically generate a frame that contains links to the headings in your document. If your document uses built-in Word heading styles, you can click the Table Of Contents In Frame button (or choose Format, Frames, Table Of Contents In Frame) to create a linked table of contents in a left frame, as shown in Figure 17-5. You can format an automatically generated table of contents frame in the same way you format other frames and documents.

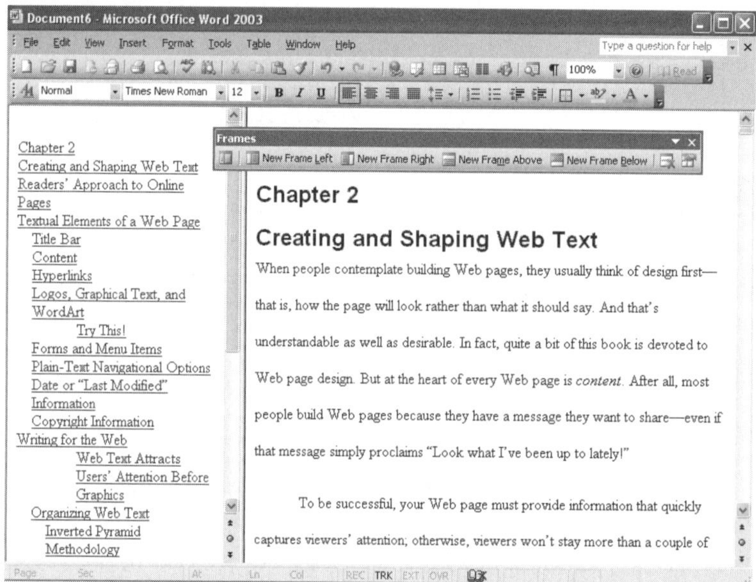

Figure 17-5. The Tables Of Contents In Frame option enables you to quickly create a left frame that contains links to each heading in your document.

When you use this option and then save the document as a Web page (.htm or .html), Word automatically creates three documents—one document that defines the structure of the page (the frameset page), a document that contains the main content, and a document that contains the table of contents frame information. To reopen the frame page, open the frameset document, which is often the smallest document (such as 1 KB) and has the name you assigned to the document when you saved it as a Web page. Word names the table of contents page by using the first item in the list of contents.

Tip **Specify how to follow hyperlinks while working in Word**

To use the links in a table of contents frame in Word, press Ctrl as you click the link. If you want to be able to click links without having to press Ctrl, choose Tools, Options, click the Edit tab, and then clear the Use Ctrl+Click To Follow Hyperlink check box.

Controlling Frame Properties

Frame Properties

As with most constructs created in Word, a frame's properties can be controlled by configuring settings in a properties dialog box, in this case the Frame Properties dialog box. The two main areas of concern when you're working with frames are the content and frame's appearance. To open the Frame Properties dialog box, click the frame you want to format, and then click Frame Properties on the Frames toolbar or choose Format, Frames, Frame Properties. The Frame Properties dialog box is described in more detail in the next section of the chapter.

Assigning Documents and Names to Frames

When you create a frames page, Word displays a different document in each frame. You might have to tell Word which document to display in which frame. (If you create a frames page from scratch, Word will automatically generate file names and documents for you.) You can specify documents to associate with a frame by configuring settings in the Frame tab in the Frame Properties dialog box, shown in Figure 17-6.

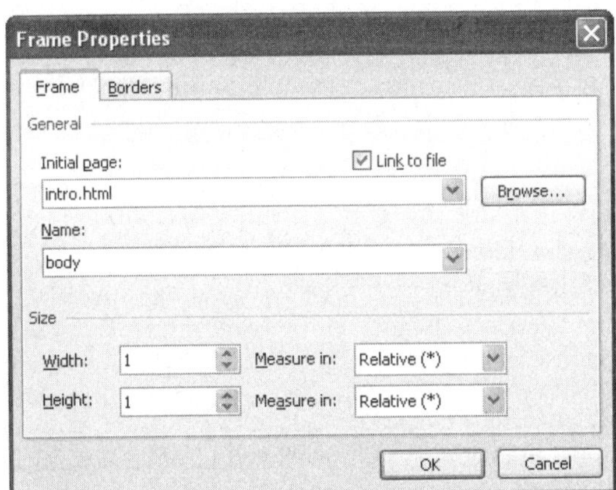

Figure 17-6. Using the Frame tab, you can perform a number of frame configuration tasks, including naming a frame and assigning a document to appear in the frame when the frames page opens.

In the Frame tab, you can indicate which page to display in a frame by inserting the file's path and name in the Initial Page box. The file specified in the Initial Page box is the file that appears each time the frames page is opened. You can also select the Link To File check box to ensure that the document used in your frames page is updated each time the Initial Page file is changed.

In addition to specifying which file is initially displayed in a frame, you can assign a name to each frame. When you use frames, the frames must be named so that you can refer to specific frames when you create hyperlinks. For example, the Frame tab shown in Figure 17-6 specifies that the intro.html file appear in a frame named *body*. The Introduction hyperlink in the navigation frame shown previously in Figure 17-3 is configured to open the intro.html file in the frame named *body* when the hyperlink is clicked. The frames page shown in Figure 17-3 contains frames named *title*, *body*, and *nav* (short for navigation bar).

To learn more about creating hyperlinks and specifying frame targets, see Chapter 26, "Creating Professional Web Sites."

Note Frame names are case-sensitive and can include numbers and letters. Also, because each frame must have a name, Word automatically provides default names for frames that aren't named manually.

The remaining frame parameters that you can configure in the Frame tab are the frame's height and width. You can assign height and width measurements in the Height and Width boxes and use the Measure In lists to specify whether the measurements are a percentage of the screen size, a fixed size in inches, or relative to the other frames, as follows:

- **Percent** Specifies that a frame's height or width should be sized as a percentage of the window. For example, if a frame's width is set to 50 percent, the frame will consume half the width of a user's window, regardless of the size of the window.
- **Inches** Specifies a fixed width or height in inches. The frame will always be displayed at the specified height, regardless of the size of the window.
- **Relative** (*) Indicates that the frame's height or width should fill the remaining area of the window after the other frame settings are applied. For example, if a top frame is set to 1 inch and a bottom frame is set to 1 inch, the body frame could be set to Relative so that the frame fills the area between the top and bottom frames, regardless of the size of the window.

Frequently you'll find that your document uses a combination of Percent, Inches, and Relative settings. If you prefer, you can adjust the sizes of the frames in your document by dragging frame borders, and Word will automatically configure your frame size settings for you.

Troubleshooting

Some of my frame pages are missing

If you find that a frame doesn't display an initial page when you open your frames page, you need to check the Initial Page setting in the frame's Frame Properties dialog box.

To display the Frame Properties dialog box, click in the frame; choose Format, Frames, Frame Properties; and then click the Frame tab. After you display the Frame tab, make sure that the path and file name in the Initial Page box are accurate and point to a valid file. Keep in mind that whenever you rename a file that's referred to in a frames page, you must modify the frames page's Frame Properties settings as well.

Formatting Layouts Using Text Boxes, Frames, Backgrounds, and Themes

Controlling Frame Borders, Resizing Capabilities, and Scroll Bars

In addition to controlling which documents are displayed in frames and assigning sizes and names to frames, you can control frame borders and scrollbars. To access frame border and scrollbar properties, follow these steps:

1. Click the frame you want to format.
2. Click Frame Properties on the Frames toolbar, or choose Format, Frames, Frame Properties.
3. Click the Borders tab, shown in Figure 17-7.

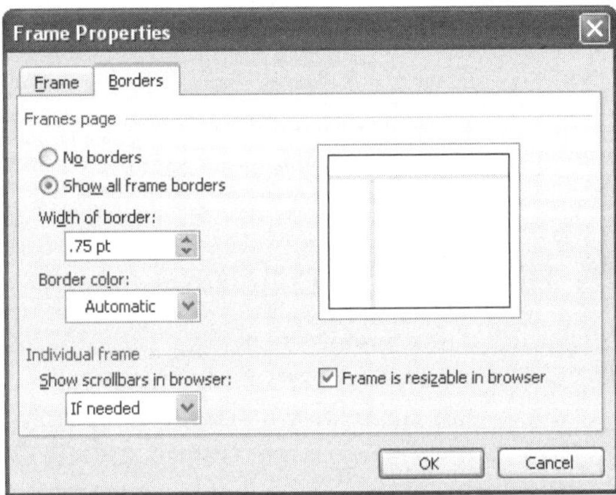

Figure 17-7. The Borders tab in the Frame Properties dialog box provides settings you can use to specify how frame borders and scrollbars appear in the current document.

The settings available on the Borders tab are as follows:

- **No Borders** Choose this option if you want your frames to be displayed seamlessly, without borders.
- **Show All Frame Borders** Choose this option if you want borders to be displayed.
- **Width Of Border** If you choose to show frame borders, you can type a value in this box or click the up or down arrow to specify the size of the border that appears between frames.
- **Border Color** Click the Border Color arrow to access the color palette, which enables you to specify the color of frame borders displayed in your document.
- **Show Scrollbars In Browser** Click the arrow and choose an option from the list to specify whether you want scroll bars to be displayed for the selected frame always, never, or only if needed.
- **Frame Is Resizable In Browser** Select this check box if you want users to be able to resize the selected frame. If you want the frame to always appear according to your frame size settings, clear the check box. Keep in mind that if you want the current frame to be resizable, adjacent frames must also be formatted as resizable.

As you configure border settings, notice that the preview box shows how your borders will appear. When you finish configuring border settings, click OK to apply the settings to the current document.

Deleting Frames

If you decide to modify a frames page, you can easily delete a frame. Remember, when you delete a frame, you delete only the frame in the frames page—you don't delete the file that contains the content that appears in the frame. To delete a frame, click the frame, and then click Delete Frame on the Frames toolbar or choose Format, Frames, Delete Frame.

Note When you delete a frame, you can't click Undo to revert to the previous frame setup. If you want to restore a deleted frame, you'll have to re-create the frame by using the Frames toolbar. Then you'll need to configure the frame's Initial Page setting so that the frame can display the document that appeared in the frame before you deleted it.

Using Backgrounds and Watermarks

To add information or visual interest to your documents, you can add *backgrounds* and *watermarks* to online and printed documents. Backgrounds are generally used to create backdrops for Web pages, online documents, and e-mail messages and usually aren't optimal for printing. You can view backgrounds in all views except Normal view and Outline view. If you want to create a more print-friendly background, you should consider creating a watermark. A watermark is faded text or a pale picture that appears behind document text. Watermarks are often used to add visual appeal to a document or to identify a document's status, such as "Draft" or "Confidential." You can see watermarks in Print Layout view, Print Preview, or in printed documents. In this section of the chapter, you'll learn how to create, control, and delete backgrounds and watermarks in your Web pages and printed documents.

Creating Backgrounds and Watermarks

You can create custom backgrounds and watermarks for online pages (including Web pages and e-mail messages) as well as printed documents. When you create a background for a document, you can use color gradients, patterns, pictures, solid colors, or textures that repeat, or *tile*, to fill the page. When you create a watermark, you can use a light-colored picture (usually gray) or light-colored text to appear behind your document's contents. If you use text, you can choose from built-in phrases or enter your own.

Adding Backgrounds to Online Pages

To add a background to a page (such as a Web page, an online document, or an e-mail message), choose Format, Background, and then perform any of the following actions:

- Click a color on the color palette to add a background color.

- Choose More Colors to access additional colors that you can apply to your background.
- Choose Fill Effects to access the Gradient, Texture, Pattern, and Picture tabs in the Fill Effects dialog box, which enable you to create custom backgrounds.

For more information about using fill effects, see Chapter 12, "Enlivening Documents with Drawings and AutoShapes."

After you choose a color or create a fill effect, Word automatically applies the background to the current document. You can see the background in all views except the Normal and Outline views. If you print the document, the background won't be printed by default. To print a document with its background configuration, you must configure the Options dialog box before you print, as follows:

1. Choose Tools, Options, and then click the Print tab.
2. Select the Background Colors And Images check box in the Include With Document section, and then click OK.

Note When you save a Web page with a background, Word saves background textures and gradients as JPEG files and patterns as GIF files.

Adding Watermarks to Printed Documents

To add a watermark to a printed document, display your document in Print Layout view (if you're working in Normal view, Word will switch to Print Layout view automatically after you add a watermark), and then choose Format, Background, Printed Watermark. The Printed Watermark dialog box appears, as shown in Figure 17-8.

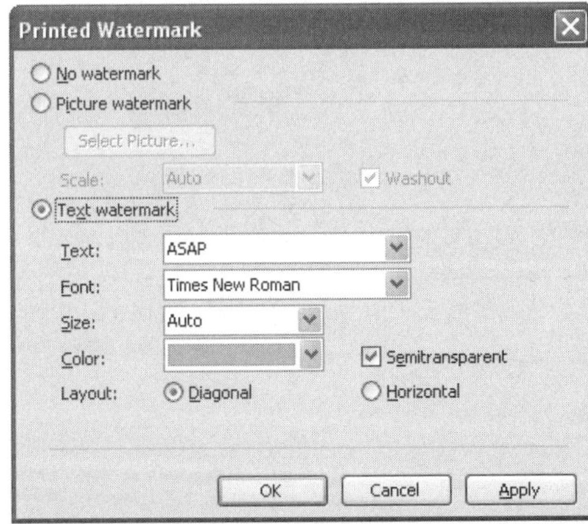

Figure 17-8. You can use the Printed Watermark dialog box to add picture and text watermarks to your documents.

You can insert a picture or text watermark by configuring the settings in the Printed Watermark dialog box, as described here:

- **Picture Watermark** To insert a picture watermark, click the Picture Watermark option, and then click the Select Picture button to choose a picture for the watermark. You can use color or grayscale pictures for watermarks. The Scale option lets you specify a size for the watermark picture. In most cases, you should select the Washout check box so that the watermark doesn't interfere with your document's readability.
- **Text Watermark** To insert a text watermark, click the Text Watermark option, and then type custom text in the Text box or choose from text in the Text list. Then configure the Text, Font, Size, Color, and Layout settings. You can display the watermark text diagonally or horizontally. In most cases, you should select the Semitransparent check box so that the watermark doesn't interfere with your document's readability.

After you configure your picture or text watermark settings, click OK to apply the watermark to the current document. Figure 17-9 shows a document that has a *Confidential* watermark in Print Preview mode.

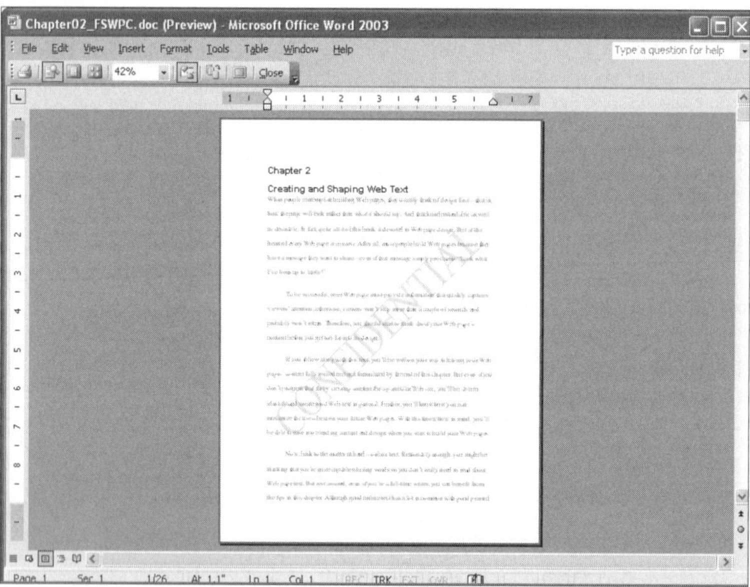

Figure 17-9. You can add standard or custom watermarks to documents that will be printed.

Including Watermarks in Document Headers

Before Word 2002, many people created watermarks by adding objects (such as AutoShapes) and images to document headers. You can continue to create watermarks in this manner. To do so, you manually paste or insert the watermark object or image into the document header. If you create watermarks this way, you can't use the Printed Watermark dialog box to configure the watermark's settings. For simplicity's sake, you should use the Printed Watermark dialog box to create watermarks whenever possible.

Changing and Removing Backgrounds and Watermarks

After you add backgrounds and watermarks to online pages and printed documents, you're free to change your mind at any time. You can easily change or remove backgrounds and watermarks that have been added to documents.

To change backgrounds or watermarks, use one of the following methods:

- **Change a background.** Choose Format, Background, and then choose new background settings.
- **Change a watermark.** Choose Format, Background, Printed Watermark, and then specify new settings in the Printed Watermark dialog box.

To remove backgrounds and watermarks, use one of these methods:

- **Remove a background.** Choose Format, Background, No Fill.
- **Remove a watermark.** Choose Format, Background, Printed Watermark. In the Printed Watermark dialog box, click the No Watermark option, and then click OK.

When you remove a background from a Web page, the page will be displayed using the default background colors specified by the user's Web browser. Generally, the default background color is white or gray.

Note If you created a watermark by inserting a watermark in a document's header, you must open the header and manually delete or change the watermark. You can't use the Printed Watermark dialog box to modify and remove watermarks inserted into headers.

Stylizing Documents with Themes

If you want to go one step beyond adding backgrounds when you format documents, you can apply *themes* to all types of documents, including Web page documents, online documents, e-mail messages, documents that you know will be viewed in Word only, and printed documents. Note that if you use themes in printed documents, you might want to remove any background colors or graphics applied by a theme. A theme is a set of unified design elements and color schemes. When you apply a theme to a document, Word customizes the background colors, bullets, heading styles, body text, lists, horizontal lines, hyperlinks, colors, tables, and so forth. For information about adding a theme to e-mail messages, see Chapter 24, "Working and Collaborating Online."

Note You can also use themes when you create Web sites and templates. For more information about creating Web sites in Word, see Chapter 26, "Creating Professional Web Sites," and for more information about creating templates, see Chapter 16, "Formatting Documents Using Templates, Wizards, Add-Ins, and XML Schemas."

Previewing and Implementing Themes

Your gateway to using themes is the Theme dialog box. You can use the Theme dialog box to preview and apply themes. In addition, you can use the Theme dialog box to configure the following settings for a selected theme:

- **Vivid Colors** Changes the colors used for styles and table borders to brighter settings. You can instantly see the difference the Vivid Colors setting makes to a selected theme by keeping an eye on the preview box as you select and clear the Vivid Colors check box.
- **Active Graphics** Includes animated graphics, such as spinning bullets, when the page is displayed in a Web browser. For the most part, you'll probably want to avoid active graphics because they generally require users' browsers to perform extra processing for little visual gain.
- **Background Image** Applies the background image shown in the preview box to the current document. If you prefer to use a solid color background or plan to print the document without the background image, clear the Background Image check box.
- **Set Default** Sets the selected theme as the default theme. When you click this button, the theme will be applied automatically whenever you create a new, blank document or a new, blank Web page (depending on the type of document that's currently open when you click the Set Default button).
- **Style Gallery** Displays the Style Gallery dialog box, which enables you to access a variety of templates.

For more information about the Style Gallery, see Chapter 16, "Formatting Documents Using Templates, Wizards, Add-Ins, and XML Schemas."

To apply a theme to a document, follow these steps:

1. Open a document that you want to format, or open a blank document or blankWeb page.
2. Choose Format, Theme.

3 In the Theme dialog box, click theme names in the Choose A Theme list to preview available themes. (If a theme isn't installed on your system, Word provides an Install button, which enables you to install the theme from the installation CD, as described in the next section of the chapter, "Installing Additional Themes.") Figure 17-10 shows the Theme dialog box, with the Global Marketing theme selected.

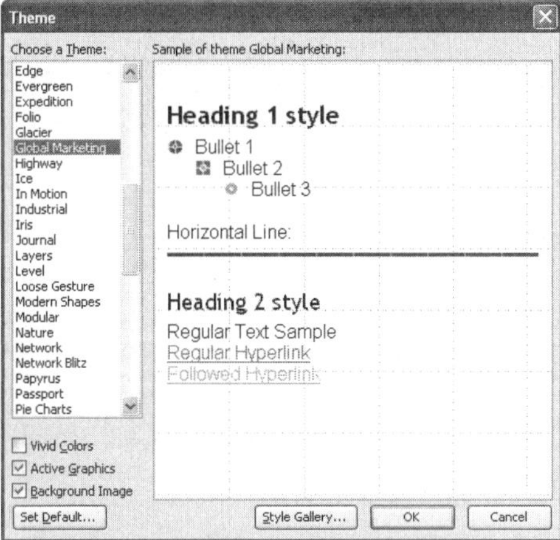

Figure 17-10. Word provides a selection of themes that you can use to format Web pages and online documents.

4 Select a theme, and then configure the Vivid Colors, Active Graphics, and Background Image check boxes as desired.

5 Click OK to apply the theme to the current document.

If you clicked Set Default in the Theme dialog box, you can create new documents based on the theme by clicking New Blank Document on the Standard toolbar or by choosing File, New to display the New Document task pane and then clickingWeb Page or Blank Document. To reset the default theme, choose (No Theme) in the Choose A Theme list in the Theme dialog box.

Installing Additional Themes

If you select a theme in the Theme dialog box that isn't installed on your system, the Theme dialog box presents an Install button in place of the preview box. To install the additional themes, insert the installation CD, and then click Install. You'll see a progress dialog box as the theme is installed on your system, as shown in Figure 17-11. When the installation is complete, the theme will be displayed in the preview box in the Theme dialog box.

Figure 17-11. By default, Word doesn't install all themes when you perform a typical installation; in some cases, you might need to install additional themes from the installation CD or installation network location.

> **Tip** **Download additional themes**
> You can download additional themes from the Microsoft Office Online site. To access the site, make sure you're connected to the Internet, and then choose Help, Microsoft Office Online. After you reach the site, use the search feature to find additional themes.

Changing and Removing Themes

You can easily change or remove the current document's theme or the default theme at any time. To change and remove themes, perform any of the following procedures:

- **Change the current document theme.** Choose Format, Theme to display the Theme dialog box, select a new theme, and then click OK.
- **Change the default theme.** Display a document or Web page to specify the type of default page you want to format, and then choose Format, Theme. In the Theme dialog box, select a new theme, click Set Default, click Yes to confirm and then click OK.
- **Remove a theme from the current document.** Choose Format, Theme to display the Theme dialog box, select (No Theme) in the Choose A Theme list, and then click OK.
- **Reset the default to create new Web pages or blank documents without a theme.** Choose Format, Theme to display the Theme dialog box, select (No Theme) in the Choose A Theme list, click the Set Default button, and then click OK.

> **Note** As mentioned, you can also use themes to format e-mail messages. For more information about using Word to create and format e-mail messages, see Chapter 24, "Working and Collaborating Online."

Chapter 18

Drawing Attention to Documents by Using Borders and Shading

Sometimes producing a simple document on a clean white page is the best approach for communicating a message as clearly as possible. But other times, you might want to impress your audience with a little pizzazz by enhancing a document's look, sparking up the design, and showing readers you really know what you're doing. One approach you can use to present more than simple text-on-paper is to use borders and shading to create effective, eye-catching document designs.

A few ways you can use borders and shading include:

- Creating a border around a table
- Setting a heading as white text in a dark box
- Showcasing a special section of text that accompanies an article
- Setting off a table of contents so readers can read it easily
- Offsetting areas of Web pages with shading

Of course, you'll probably come up with numerous other ways to use borders and shading after you master the basics of Word 2003.

> **Tip** **Make custom border choices**
> Keep in mind that the borders you create don't have to go all the way around an item or page. You can apply borders to only the top or bottom, or sides, of an object as described in "Creating Partial Borders" on page 543.

Adding a Simple Border

Border

The easiest way to add a nothing-fancy border to an item in your document is to select the item, and then click the Border button on the Formatting toolbar. If you click the Border button, the selected border option (the border option shown on the face of the button) is applied; if you click the Border button's arrow, you can select from a number of border options, as described in Table 18-1. Keep in mind that the Border button is a toggle button; this means that with a click of the button, you can add borders if they aren't present or remove borders if they are present.

Tables And Borders

You can also create borders by using the Tables And Borders toolbar. To display the Tables And Borders toolbar, click the Tables And Borders button on the Standard toolbar or choose View, Toolbars, Tables And Borders. The Tables And Borders toolbar, shown in Figure 18-1, contains a Border button in the same way the Standard toolbar contains a Border button.

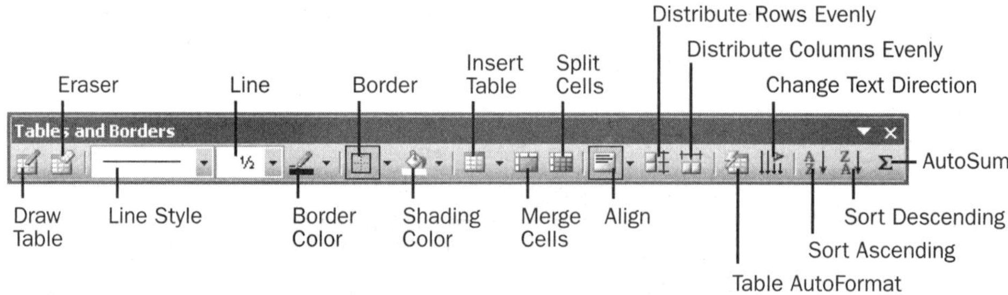

Figure 18-1. You can use the Tables And Borders toolbar to draw tables and add borders of various weights and colors.

Note If you've previously used the Border button on the Tables And Borders toolbar or the Standard toolbar, the border choice you last used will appear on the Border button during the current session. For example, if you chose Outside Border from the menu the last time you used the Border button on the Standard toolbar, the Outside Border option will appear on the Border button as the default border style on the Standard toolbar. But don't expect your border style choices to carry over from the Standard toolbar Border button to the Border button on the Tables And Borders toolbar—they won't. Adjusting one toolbar's Border button doesn't affect the border choice on the other toolbar. When you restart Word, the Border button resets to the default border style, which is Outside Border, on both toolbars.

Tip To create a simple border that outlines a selection, click Outside Border in the Border button's list.

Note The various buttons on the Tables And Borders toolbar are described in Table 13-2 in Chapter 13, "Organizing Concepts in Tables."

Table 18-1. Border Choices

Button	Name	Description
	Outside Border	Adds or removes the outline around the selected or current table or cells, paragraph, element, or image
	All Borders	Adds or removes the border around the selected or current element (if the selected element is text, horizontal and vertical lines are added to outline each paragraph; if the selected element is a table, cells are outlined)
	Top Border	Adds or removes the border at the top of the selected or current table or cells, paragraph, element, or graphic
	Left Border	Adds or removes the border along the left edge of the selected or current element
	Inside Horizontal Border	Adds or removes the horizontal line or lines between the selected paragraphs, table cells, or other elements
	Descending Diagonal	Draws or removes a descending (top right to bottom left) diagonal line through a cell or selected cells in a table
	Horizontal Line	Adds a graphical horizontal line at the cursor position (to insert a line above the current line of text, position the cursor at the beginning of the text; to insert a line below the current line of text, position the cursor at the end of the text or press Enter and insert it on a separate line); you can add horizontal lines in text as well as in table cells and adjust which graphic to use for the horizontal lines (see "Inserting Graphical Horizontal Lines" on page 550.)
	Inside Border	Adds or removes the border between rows and columns in a table but excludes the outside border; in text, horizontal lines are placed between each paragraph
	No Border	Applies no borders and clears all existing borders
	Bottom Border	Adds or removes the border along the bottom edge of the selected table or cells, paragraph, or element
	Right Border	Adds or removes the border along the right edge of the selected table or cells, paragraph, or element
	Inside Vertical Border	Adds or removes a vertical line in a table or through selected cells
	Ascending Diagonal	Draws an ascending (bottom right to top left) diagonal line through a cell or selected cells in a table

Tip Clear all borders before applying new border settings
Although you can use the toggle effect of the Border button to remove border lines, frequently you'll want to clear all existing borders before you apply new settings. To clear existing borders, select the section you want to modify, click No Border in the Border button's list, and then, while the section is still selected, click the border style you want to use.

Creating Enhanced Borders

When you want to create a border that has a more dramatic look than a simple line, you can take matters into your own hands using the Borders And Shading dialog box. By setting the options in this dialog box, you can choose a variety of looks for your border (including 3-D and shadow effects) and change the style, color, and width of the lines you use.You can also create partial borders by selecting only the line segments you want to display.

To create a customized border, begin by placing the insertion point where you want the border to begin or by selecting the data around which you want to create the border. Then choose Format, Borders And Shading. The Borders And Shading dialog box appears as shown in Figure 18-2.

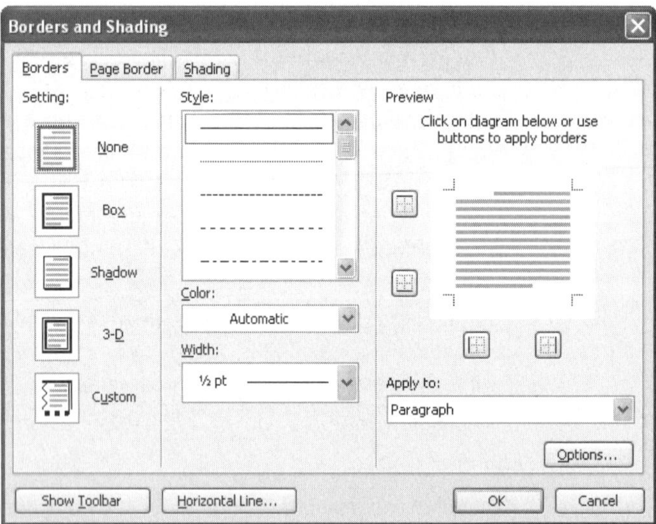

Figure 18-2. The Borders And Shading dialog box enables you to specify border types and border placement as well as line styles, colors, and widths.

Word offers some basic border settings that you can use, although you can create an almost unlimited number of combinations by adjusting the style, color, width, line, and shading settings. The borders Setting option is the first major choice you'll probably make when you use the Borders And Shading dialog box. This option controls the overall look of the border itself.

Drawing Attention to Documents by Using Borders and Shading

The Setting options vary depending on whether you're working in a table or with standard text. If you're working with standard text, you can choose from the following Setting options:

- **None** Shows no border around selected text and objects. This is the default.
- **Box** Encloses the selection in a simple line box.
- **Shadow** Outlines the selection with a box and adds a drop shadow below and to the right of the selection.
- **3-D** Creates a three-dimensional effect for the selected border, making it appear to "stand out" from the page.
- **Custom** Enables you to configure the Preview area so you can choose and customize the line segments you want to include in your border.

If you're working with a table or cells, you can choose among the following Setting options:

- **None** Shows no border around the table or selected cells.
- **Box** Encloses the table or selected cells in a simple line box without internal lines.
- **All** Outlines the entire table or selected cells, including borders between cells. This is the default.
- **Grid** Outlines a table or selected cells with a heavier exterior border and lighter interior borders.
- **Custom** Enables you to configure the Preview area so that you can choose and customize the line segments you want to include in your border.

Tip **Mix and match borders**
You can mix and match border types to achieve the effect you want. For example, you can add borders to part of a table and hide borders in other parts to create the appearance of advanced layouts. You can further combine border options, such as color and line widths, to make borders visually appealing.

To apply one of the Setting options shown in the Borders And Shading dialog box, click in the paragraph, table, image, or other element that you want to format or select text or cells. Next, display the Borders And Shading dialog box, and then click the Setting selection in the Borders tab. If you don't want to make any additional customizations, you can simply click OK to return to your document. The border will be added to the current text, table, or selected object. If the cursor was positioned in a new blank paragraph before the Borders And Shading dialog box was displayed, the border will appear around the insertion point and will expand as you type, including added paragraphs, images, tables, and other elements.To end the expansion of the border, either click outside the formatted area or press Enter at the end of the formatted area, and then format the new blank paragraph marker using the No Border setting on the Border button.

Tip **Undo or remove a border**
If you add a border and decide you really don't like it, you can do away with it immediately by choosing Edit, Undo or pressing Ctrl+Z. You can also choose Format, Borders And Shading, and then select a different border type, or select the No Border option or the existing border format on the Border button to clear or toggle the border lines off.

Troubleshooting

The changes I made to the borders in my table disappeared

If you change the border or shading of a table and discover that when you close the Borders And Shading dialog box the changes you specified weren't made, it could be because the table's formatting marks weren't selected properly before you applied formatting options. To avoid this problem, click Show/Hide on the Standard toolbar to display all the formatting characters in your document before you apply formatting. Then select the table, making sure to include the end-of-cell marks at the ends of the rows. Next, choose Format, Borders And Shading to display the Borders And Shading dialog box, and then enter your settings. Because the table formatting marks are included, the changes should stick after you close the Borders And Shading dialog box.

Selecting Line Styles for Borders

Word provides 24 line styles you can use to create border effects. From simple, straight lines to dotted, double, and triple lines, a variety of looks can be created by changing line styles. Figure 18-3 shows a few examples of borders created with different line styles.

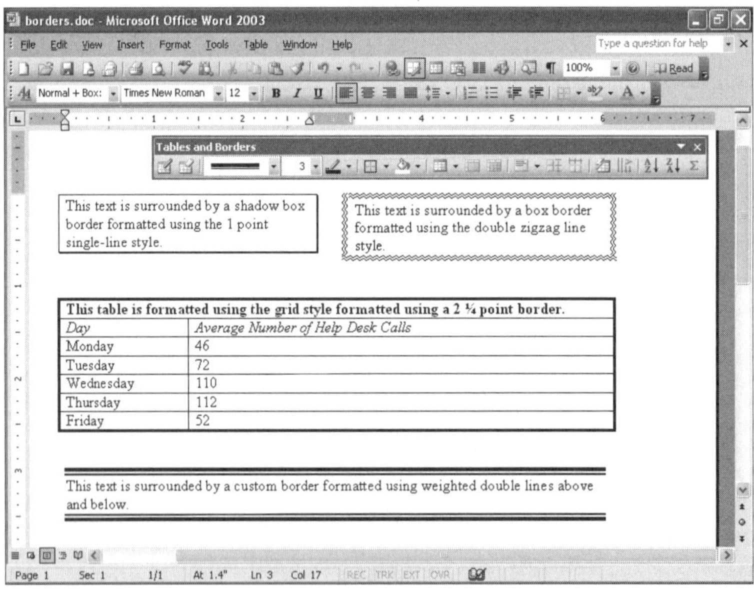

Figure 18-3. The line style you choose has a dramatic effect on the overall look of a border.

To choose a line style for a border, display the Borders And Shading dialog box and select a line style in the Style list in the Borders tab. The Preview section shows the effect of your choices. Set any other border choices you want, and then click OK. The document is updated with your changes.

Troubleshooting

There's not enough contrast in my double line

If you create a double line and can't see enough contrast between lines of different weights, you can play around with the line widths to get a better contrast. Start by clicking in or selecting the area with the border and choosing Format, Borders And Shading to display the Borders And Shading dialog box. In the Width list, choose a new line width setting, and then click the line you want to change in the Preview section in the dialog box.

Choosing Color

When you first start adding lines and borders to your publication, Word selects black by default. But you have all the colors of Word at your disposal, so you can get as colorful as your needs and presentation medium allow. To specify border colors, follow these steps:

1. Click in or select the elements you want to format with border colors. If the content already has a border and you only want to color the existing lines, you can retain the current border and simply apply a color setting to the existing border settings.
2. Choose Format, Borders And Shading.
3. In the Borders tab, select a Setting option and line style if you're creating a new border. If you're working with an existing border, you can make changes if desired.
4. Click the Color arrow. The color palette appears, as shown in Figure 18-4.

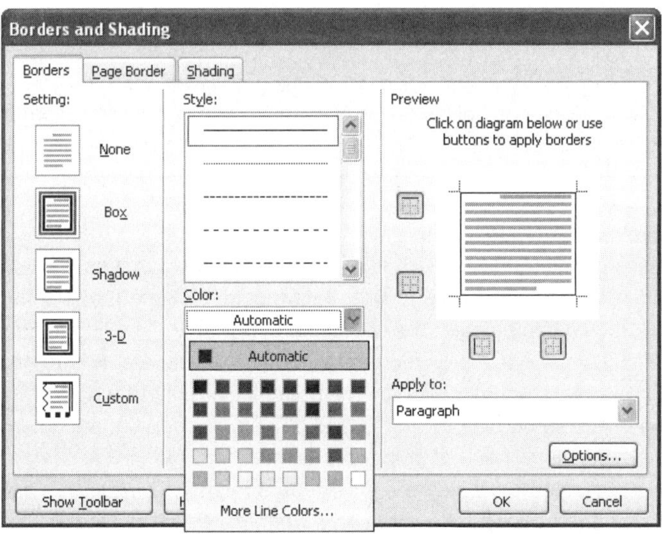

Figure 18-4. You can use the color palette to select a color for lines and shading.

5. Click the color you want to use from the color palette, or, if you don't see the color you were hoping for, click More Line Colors. The Colors dialog box appears so that you can find the color you're looking for. Click the color you want. If you're creating a new border, the color setting will be reflected in the Preview area immediately. If you're adjusting the color setting for an existing border, you will need to click each line in the Preview area to apply the color setting. In this way, you can control the line color for each border line.
6. Click OK. The color settings are applied in your document, and the Line Style list box on the Tables And Borders Toolbar displays the selected line style and color.

When You Need to Match Colors Exactly

Suppose that you're using Word to create a Web page or document that has to conform to last year's departmental annual report, right down to the color scheme. When you need to match colors, choosing accurate border colors can become an important issue. For times like these, you can use the Custom tab in the Colors dialog box to enter the exact RGB (Red, Green, and Blue) or HSL (Hue, Saturation, and Luminance) color percentages for custom colors. To configure the Custom tab in the Colors dialog box for borders, perform the following steps:

1. Choose Format, Borders And Shading.
2. Display the Color menu, and then click More Line Colors on the color palette.
3. Click the Custom tab, choose RGB, HSL, or another available color scheme in the Color Model list.
4. Enter values in the Red, Green, and Blue text boxes, or enter values in the Hue, Sat, and Lum text boxes.
5. Click OK to close the Colors dialog box, finish configuring your border settings, and then click OK in the Borders And Shading dialog box to apply the custom color.

Tip **Pick the best colors for borders**

The trick to selecting effective colors for a document's text, images, table borders, lines, shading, and other components is to work with a color scheme that consists of three or four main colors that complement the document's design and provide appropriate contrast. After you identify a color scheme, you can play with the colors a little to add interest. For instance, if headings are dark blue, you might consider using the same blue or a slightly lighter shade of the same blue for borders and lines. In addition, document design often benefits from a consistent use of color across the board for similar design elements. For instance, in a magazine or newsletter, all sidebars might be placed in a green box while quotations appear in yellow boxes. That way, when readers see "green" they know they're about to read a sidebar and when they see "yellow," they recognize that they're reading a quotation. Color used wisely can greatly increase the readability and eye appeal of a publication.

Controlling Border Width

When you create a simple border, the default line width is ½ point, which is a simple, thin line. If you want to create a more dramatic effect—whether you leave the line black or add color—you can change the width of the line. To change the line width, display the Borders And Shading dialog box, click the Width arrow, and then click the width you want. Available point sizes include ¼, ½, ¾, 1, 1 ½, 2 ¼, 3, 4 ½, and 6.

Tip **Create a special effect with separator lines**
You can use line widths to create a special effect for partial borders. For example, to add a wide line above and below content, select the area you want to enclose between the lines, choose Format, Borders And Shading, and then click the Custom Setting option. Select a line style, click the Width arrow, and then choose a larger point size, such as 3 pt. In the Preview section, click the top horizontal edge of the preview page. A line is added to the top border. Next, click the bottom horizontal edge of the preview page, and then click OK. Word adds the thick line border above and below the selected area.

Creating Partial Borders

Not every paragraph, table, or object you enclose in a border will need four lines all the way around. You might want to add two lines, along the top and right side of a paragraph, for example, to help set it apart from an article that appears beside it. You might use only a top and bottom rule to contain your table of contents. Or you might use a single line to set off a quotation from the main text in a report.

Creating a partial border is a simple matter. You use the Custom Setting option and the Preview area to accomplish this. Here are the steps:

1. Click in a table or paragraph or select the information around which you want to create the border.
2. Choose Format, Borders And Shading.
3. In the Borders tab, click the Custom Setting option. Specify the border's line style, color, and width.
4. In the Preview area, click each edge of the preview paragraph to indicate where border lines should appear, or click the buttons that correspond to the edge or edges that should have a border line. Table 18-2 describes the available Preview buttons.

Table 18-2. Preview Buttons

Button	Description
	Adds a line along the top border
	Adds a line along the bottom border
	Adds a line along the left border
	Adds a line along the right border

> **Tip** You can toggle border lines on and off by clicking the borders in the Preview area's sample page or by clicking the Preview buttons surrounding the sample page.

Applying a Page Border

Many of the techniques you use to add a border to a section, table, or object in a document can be used to add borders to entire pages as well. Figure 18-5 shows a document with a page border. You can create standard page borders or use Art Border, as described in this part of the chapter.

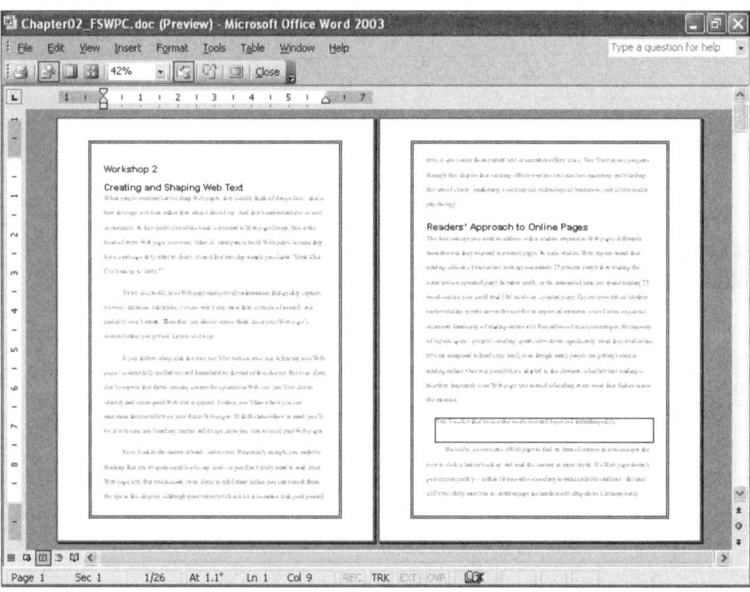

Figure 18-5. By default, page border settings are applied to all pages in the current document.

Creating a Page Border

When you add a page border, you start the process by choosing Format, Borders And Shading. When the Borders And Shading dialog box appears, click the Page Border tab. The main visual difference between the Borders tab and the Page Border tab is the addition of the Art list (which is covered in the next section of this chapter). In the Page Border tab, after you make all your border choices, the border will be applied to an entire page, section, or document. Here's the process:

1. Click in a page or a section that will have a border.
2. Choose Format, Borders And Shading, and then click the Page Border tab.
3. Click a page border setting (Box, Shadow, 3-D, or Custom).
4. Select a line style from the Style list.
5. Select a color in the Color list, if desired.
6. Click the Width arrow, and then choose the line width you want. The Style, Color, and Width settings are reflected in the Preview area.
7. If desired, use the Preview image to select which edges of the page will have a page border.
8. In the Apply To list, specify where the border should apply. Available options are Whole Document, This Section, This Section–First Page Only, and This Section–All Except First Page. By default, Whole Document is selected in the Apply To list, and the border is added to all the pages in the current document.

> **Tip** To apply a page border to a single page (other than the first page) or to a few pages in a long document, you first have to set off the page or pages by creating a section. To learn more about creating and working with sections, see Chapter 19, "Formatting Columns and Sections for Advanced Text Control."

9. Click OK to close the dialog box and apply the page border settings to the current document.

> **Tip** **Skip the first page border or apply a page border to the first page only**
> When you add a page border, Word applies the border to all the pages in your document. What if you want to skip the border on the first page or apply the border only to the first page? You can easily employ these options by using the Apply To setting in the Page Border tab in the Borders And Shading dialog box. To suppress the display of the border for first pages, choose Format, Borders And Shading, click the Page Border tab, click the Apply To arrow, and then select This Section – All Except First Page. To apply the border to the first page only, choose This Section – First Page Only in the Apply To list in the Page Border tab.

Adding an Artistic Border

The Art Page Border feature, known in earlier versions of Office as BorderArt, enables you to add an artistic touch to entire pages in your document. Special graphics are placed in patterns—either in black and white or in color—and used as borders for a page, group of pages, or selected sides of pages. To apply an artistic page border, follow these steps:

1. Click in the document to which you want to add the border.
2. Choose Format, Borders And Shading, and then click the Page Border tab.
3. Click the Art arrow, and then scroll through the art borders. Select an Art option. The Preview section shows your change, as shown in Figure 18-6. To control which borders will contain graphics, you can click the borders in the Preview Page area to add and remove the images.

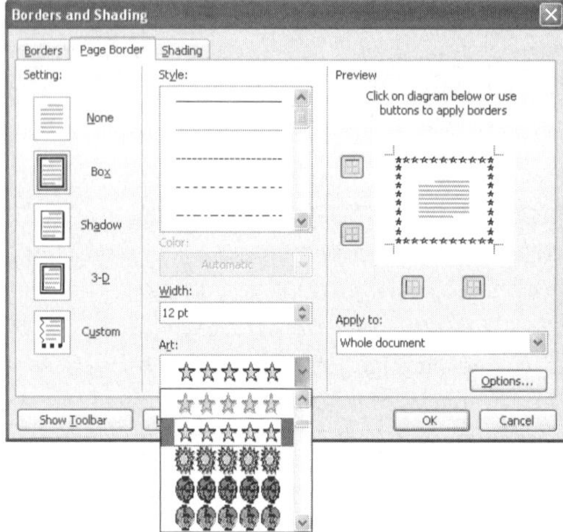

Figure 18-6. You can select from a number of art borders provided in Word. The first time you use the Art page border feature, you might need to install the feature (which entails following instructions on the screen and possibly inserting your Office CD).

4. In the Apply To list, choose which pages should include the border. You can include the border on the Whole Document, This Section, This Section – First Page Only, or This Section – All Except First Page.
5. Click OK. The border is added to the document according to the settings you configured in the Borders And Shading dialog box.

Caution Artistic borders can be colorful and vibrant—but they can also be a bit much for some professional documents. For that reason, you should use art borders sparingly and use discretion on a case-by-case basis.

Adding Borders to Sections and Paragraphs

Whether you're interested in applying borders to a single word, paragraph, image, section, or page, you can do it easily by using the Apply To list in the Borders And Shading dialog box. The tab you choose—Borders or Page Border—depends on the element you want to enclose in a border:

- If you want to create a border around a section in your document, click the Page Border tab. In the Apply To list, you'll find what you need to specify section bordering options.
- If you want to add a border around a paragraph, text, tables, images, selected table cells, or other elements in your document, click the Borders tab. The Apply To options in that tab will give you choices specific to the item you chose.

Bordering Sections

You might want to create a border around a section when you have specific information you want to highlight or when you want to set a section apart from the flow of the text. To create a section border, start by placing the insertion point in the section you want to surround with a border. Choose Format, Borders And Shading to display the dialog box, and then click the Page Border tab. Next, configure the border effects—including the borders Setting option and line style, color, and width—and then click the Apply To arrow and select your choice. Depending on the border you're creating (these options are not available for every type of border), you might see the following options:

- **Whole document** Adds a border to every page in your document.
- **This Section** Adds a border only to the pages between the previous section break and the next section break. If the document doesn't contain any section breaks, the border is applied to every page in the document.
- **This Section—First Page Only** Finds the first page of the current section and adds a border only to that page. If you're working in a document without sections, the first page of your document will contain the border.
- **This Section—All Except First Page** Adds a border to all pages in the current section except the first page of the section. If you're working in a document without section breaks, all pages in the document will have a border except the first page.

To apply a border to a section, simply click the appropriate Apply To selection in the Page Border tab, and then click OK to close the dialog box. The border is added to the section as specified. If you want to see how the border looks for the entire section, choose File, Print Preview (or click Print Preview on the Standard toolbar), click Multiple Pages on the Print Preview toolbar, and then select the number of pages to display. By using Print Preview's multipage display feature, you can see the effect of your border selection in your document. Click Close on the Print Preview toolbar to return to the document window.

For more information about using Print Preview, see Chapter 3, "Printing with Precision."

Tip **Add write-in spaces using the Inside Horizontal Border option**
Here's a great way to add horizontal lines for write-in spaces in your documents. Press Enter to insert a number of blank lines in your document in the area where you want to create horizontal lines. Then select the blank lines, click the Border button's arrow, and then click the Inside Horizontal Border option. Evenly spaced lines are added automatically, extending from the left to the right margin.

Adding Borders to Text, Pictures, Tables, and Cells

If you want to create a border around a smaller portion of text, such as a paragraph, selected text, image, or selected table cells, you use a different set of choices. Start by selecting the item you want to create the border around, and then choose Format, Borders And Shading. When the dialog box appears, leave the Borders tab selected, make your border choices as usual, and then click the Apply To arrow. Depending on the text you've selected, you might see the following choices:

- **Paragraph** Creates a border around the currently selected paragraph
- **Text** Adds a border to the highlighted text
- **Picture** Adds a border around the selected picture
- **Cell** Draws a border around the cells you've selected
- **Table** Creates a border around the entire table at the insertion point

Click the appropriate Apply To setting, and then click OK to close the Borders And Shading dialog box. The border is added to the selection as you specified.

Choosing Border Options

Word makes a few assumptions about the way borders appear in documents. By default, Word applies a small margin to borders applied to a paragraph and a larger margin to borders for sections and pages. When you add a border to a paragraph, Word adds a 1-point margin to the top and bottom and a 4-point margin along the left and right edges of the border. When you add a page or section border, Word adds 24-point margins measured from the edge of the page all the way around.

To access border options that enable you to adjust spacing between borders and content, choose Format, Borders And Shading. Display the Borders tab if you're changing the options for a paragraph border, or click the Page Border tab if you're working with a document or section border. Then click Options in the lower-right corner of the dialog box. The Border And Shading Options dialog box appears, as shown in Figure 18-7.

Drawing Attention to Documents by Using Borders and Shading

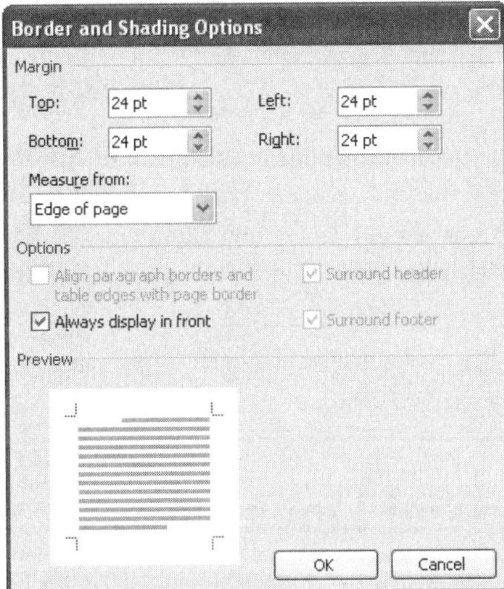

Figure 18-7. You control border margins and make choices about border alignment in the Border And Shading Options dialog box.

To make changes to the border margins, click in the box you want to change and type a new value, or use the up and down arrows to increase or decrease the value shown.

For page borders, Word automatically measures the margin from the edge of the page, but you can change the setting so that the measurement reflects spacing between text and the surrounding border. To make this change, click the Measure From arrow and choose Text. When working with the Borders tab, the Border And Shading Options dialog box only allows you to configure the space between the border and text.

The other options in the Border And Shading Options dialog box are available only if you're working with a page or section border. By default, Word includes any headers and footers inside the bordered area and, also by default, enables the Always Display In Front check box, which causes the border to be in front of any text or graphic objects that might overlap it. If you have other borders or tables within the bordered section, the Align Paragraph Borders And Table Edges With Page Border check box will also be available to you. If you want Word to align all these borders, select this check box.

After you've finished choosing border options, click OK to close the dialog box, and then click OK a second time to return to your document.

Note If you select a table before you display the Borders And Shading dialog box, your options in the Apply To list will show Paragraph, Table, and Cell. Similarly, if you select an image, the Apply To list will show Picture as an available border option.

Troubleshooting

My border isn't printing correctly

If your page border doesn't print along one edge of the page or is positioned too close to an edge, check the border's margin options. To do this, choose Format, Borders And Shading, click the Page Border tab, and then click Options. In the Margin section, increase the margin values to make sure the border is not placed outside your printer's printing range.

If you've set up your border to be measured from Text, the space between the text and the border might be pushing the border into the nonprintable area. (Most printers will not print in the 0.5-inch area around the perimeter of the page.)

Inserting Graphical Horizontal Lines

In some situations, you'll want only a divider line, not a complete border, to set off sections or special elements in a document. For example, if you're creating a Web page, you might want to add a line to mark the end of one section and the beginning of the next. In those cases, you can use the Inside Horizontal Border option, insert only a top or bottom partial border, or you can insert a graphical horizontal line. Applying the Inside Horizontal Border setting and creating partial borders are discussed earlier in this chapter. The particulars of working with graphical horizontal lines—lines that are images—are covered in the next couple of sections.

Adding a Graphical Horizontal Line

Word provides a collection of graphical horizontal lines that you can insert in documents. To add a graphical horizontal line to a document, follow these steps:

1. Place the insertion point where you want to add the line.
2. Choose Format, Borders And Shading, and then click the Border or Page Border tab on the Borders And Shading dialog box.
3. Click Horizontal Line to display the Horizontal Line dialog box, as shown in Figure 18-8.

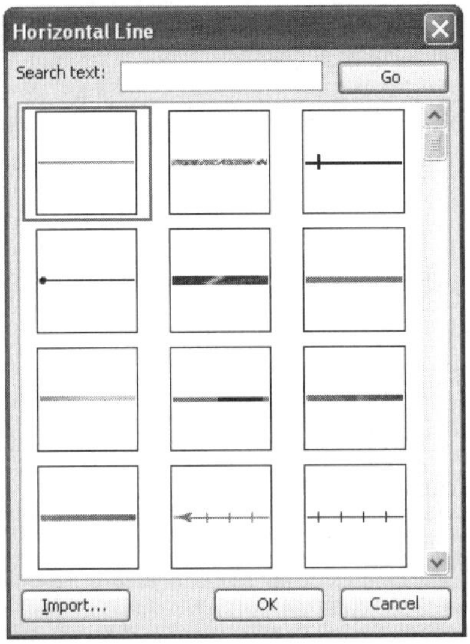

Figure 18-8. The Horizontal Line dialog box displays predesigned graphical lines that you can insert in your document.

4 Scroll through the selections and click a line style to add the line.

After you place a horizontal line in a document, you can select, copy, paste, resize, move, and color it as you would other graphical items. Furthermore, you can insert additional instances of the line by choosing the Horizontal Line option from the Border button menu. The next section of the chapter describes some ways you can format a graphical horizontal line in Word.

Formatting a Graphical Horizontal Line

When you insert a graphical horizontal line using the Horizontal Line dialog box, you're not committed to using the image as is. You can adjust several of the line's properties, including its width, height, and color. Specifically, you can perform either of the following actions:

- **Resize and position a line manually** To resize and position a graphical line manually, click the line, and then drag the line's selection handles to resize it or drag the selected line to move the image. Figure 18-9 shows some examples of graphical lines that have been resized by dragging the selection handles.

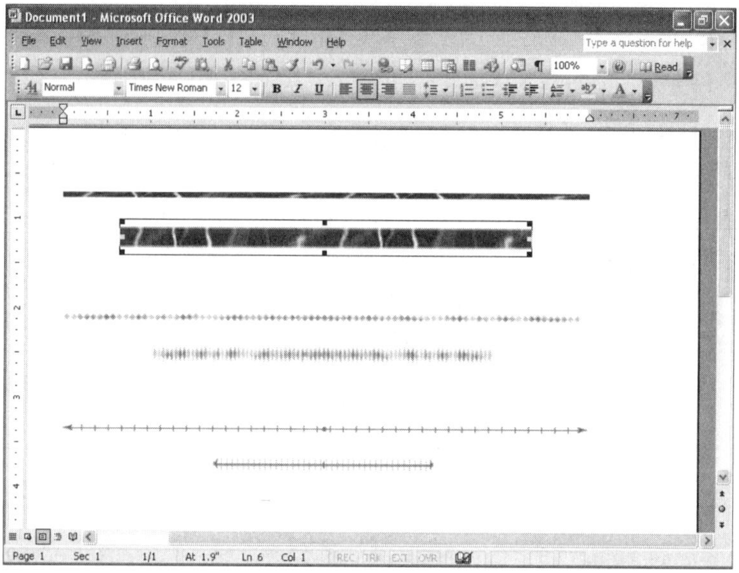

Figure 18-9. You can customize a graphical line by dragging the line's selection handles to resize the line's length and height.

- **Adjust a graphical line's properties** You can make changes to a graphical line's width, height, color, alignment, brightness, and contrast and crop some graphical lines by using the Format Horizontal Line dialog box (shown in Figure 18-10). To access the Format Horizontal Line dialog box, right-click a graphical line, and then choose Format Horizontal Line (or select the line, and then press Alt+O+L or choose Format, Horizontal Line).

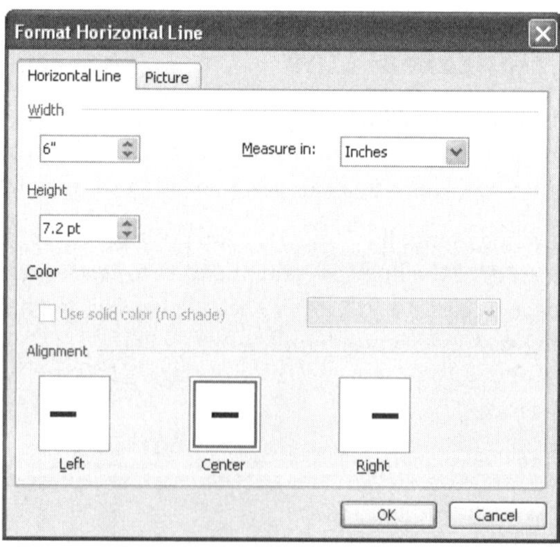

Figure 18-10. The Format Horizontal Line dialog box enables you to customize a graphical line's appearance and placement by configuring the line's properties. For instance, the Color option in the Picture tab enables you to recolor a graphical line as grayscale, black and white, or washed out.

Importing a Custom Line

If you create your own graphical lines in Word or another program (such as Microsoft Paint or PowerPoint), you can add the customized line files to your Horizontal Line gallery. Word can import files in the following formats:

- BMP, RLE, DIB (Microsoft Windows Bitmap)
- EMF (Enhanced Metafile)
- EPS (Encapsulated Postscript)
- GIF (Graphics Interchange Format)
- JPEG (Joint Photographic Experts Group)
- PNG (Portable Network Graphics)
- TIFF (Tagged Image File Format)
- WMF (Windows Metafile Graphics)

For more information about importing images into Word documents, see Chapter 11, "Adding Visual Impact with Pictures and Objects."

To add a custom line to your Horizontal Line gallery so that it's available in the Horizontal Line dialog box, follow these steps:

1. In the graphics program you're using, save the file in one of the supported file formats.
2. In Word, choose Format, Borders And Shading to display the Borders And Shading dialog box.
3. Click Horizontal Line. The Horizontal Line dialog box appears.
4. Click Import. The Add Clips To Organizer dialog box appears.
5. Navigate to the file you want to use, click it, and then click Add. The line is added to the gallery and remains selected.
6. Click OK to add the clip to your document. The Horizontal Line dialog box closes and the line is placed at the insertion point in your document.

After you add a graphical horizontal line, you can insert future instances of the line image in your document by using the Formatting and Tables And Borders toolbars. Simply choose the Horizontal Line option from the Border button's menu.

Tip To remove an imported image from the Horizontal Line dialog box, you can use the Clip Art task pane to find and delete the image.

Applying Shading Behind Content

Sometimes you need more than a border—you need something to help the text, heading, or image really stand out as different from the rest of the publication. For those times, you might consider adding a background shade to provide color, contrast, and visual appeal for your document.

Applying Shades to Tables and Paragraphs

Word includes a number of predesigned table formats that include many shading possibilities. You can use one of the preset shading schemes by selecting the table, and then choosing Table, Table AutoFormat. You can then click each format choice to see the shading that's been used in the AutoFormats.

Shading Color

When you want to apply custom shading to text, paragraphs, table cells, tables, or headings, you can use the Shading Color button on the Tables And Borders toolbar or the Shading tab in the Borders And Shading dialog box. To apply shading effects using the Shading tab in the Borders And Shading dialog box, follow these steps:

1. Select the item you want to shade.
2. Choose Format, Borders And Shading.
3. Click the Shading tab. The Shading tab contains various options you can use to add and modify shades, as shown in Figure 18-11.

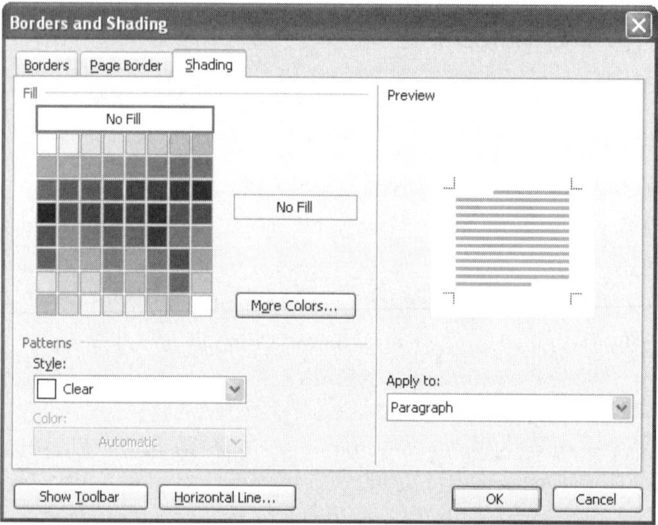

Figure 18-11. Adding shading can be as simple as selecting the information you want to appear on a shaded background, and then choosing a shade color in the Shading tab or from the Shading Color button's menu.

> **Note** The borders and shading features of Word work independently, which means that if you add shading without adding a border, the item will appear with only the shade behind it—no outer border will be added automatically. To add a border to a shaded item, select it, and then choose Format, Borders And Shading; configure border settings in the Borders tab; and then click OK to apply the border to the shaded selection.

4. In the Fill section, click the color you want to apply. If you don't see the color you want, you can click More Colors to open the Colors dialog box and choose from another selection. Alternatively, you can click the Custom tab in the Colors dialog box to enter the RGB or HSL values for a custom color.
5. In the Patterns section, click the Style arrow to display your choices for the density or pattern of the color you select. Choose a lower percentage for a lighter shade. The Preview area shows the effect of each selection.
6. Click OK to apply the shading settings.

To remove shading, select the shaded content, and then perform either of the following actions:

- On the Tables And Borders toolbar, click the arrow on Shading Color, and then choose No Fill.
- Choose Format, Borders And Shading, click the Shading tab, choose No Fill, and then click OK.

Note Shading applied to fields and forms is different from the shading you create by using the Shading tab in the Borders And Shading dialog box. To control whether fields and forms appear with shading, you need to configure the Options dialog box. To do so, choose Tools, Options. In the View tab, configure the Field Shading option, in the Show section, by making a selection in the list. For more information about fields and forms, see Chapter 31, "Working with Field Codes and Custom Forms."

Shading Considerations

As with the caveat given earlier about art borders, remember that a little shading goes a long way. Done thoughtfully and with readers' needs in mind, shading can be very effective in calling attention to certain elements and helping special design objects stand out on the page (especially in Web page design). But overusing shading or using the wrong mix of colors and patterns can make your document or Web page harder for people to read, which means they'll turn the page or click away from your site—and you'll lose your audience.

To use shading effectively, adhere to the following guidelines:

- **Use shading on a need-to-use basis.** Don't sprinkle shades all the way through your document at random. Give a shade a reason, such as, "Every time we mention a new board member we'll provide a brief biography in a shaded sidebar."
- **Choose intensities carefully.** A shade that looks light on the screen might be much darker in print. Always look at information online and in print form whenever possible, even for online content. You never know when a reader will decide to print an online page for later reference.

- **Test your contrasts.** When you add a colored shade behind text, be sure to increase the contrast between the color of the shade and the color of the text. If you choose a dark blue background, black text won't show up clearly. If you choose a dark background, select a light (white or yellow) text.
- **Do test prints on a printer that produces comparable output.** If you're printing colored shades, be sure to print a test page on a color printer.
- **If you're creating a Web page, use Web-safe colors for your shades.** Most Web browsers today can support the standard colors used in the Windows palette. If you choose customized colors, however, some browsers might not display the color accurately. Test the display of the page with different browsers to check the colors you've selected. To see a listing of Web-safe colors and their RGB values, visit *http://www.creationguide.com/colorchart.html.*

Part 4

Publishing Long or Complex Documents

Chapter 19

Formatting Columns and Sections for Advanced Text Control

Depending on the types of documents you create, you may rely heavily on Word's ability to create columns and sections. When you combine these two elements, you can control how the text flows in various parts of the same document. You can create single or multiple columns, even or uneven columns, columns with line dividers or with blank spaces, or gutters, in between. This chapter explores the use of both columns and sections in Word and helps you create interesting formats for your newsletters, reports, and more.

Planning Your Document

If the design of your document is up to you, it's a good idea to start out not at the computer keyboard but at the drawing board, literally sketching out how you want your pages to look. Will you use two columns or three? Do you want the columns to have equal widths or will one be narrow and the other two wide? Thinking carefully about your document's final appearance will go a long way toward helping you create it the way you want.

Word gives you the capability of creating up to 13 columns, but in all but the rarest circumstances (such as a simple word or number list) you won't use 13 columns—the width of each column would be a scant 0.5 inch! Most traditional documents use one, two, or three columns. In some instances, you might use four, but even those columns will provide little room for more than a few small words on a line.

As you prepare your document plan, consider these questions:

- How many columns do you want? Table 19-1 lists the column widths Word uses by default for a table with one to six columns on an 8.5-by-11-inch portrait page with the Equal Column Width option selected.
- Will you include graphics around which your columns need to flow?
- How much space do you want to leave between columns?
- Do you want your columns to be of equal width or varied widths?

- Will you include a table of contents column that might require more space than a traditional text column?
- Do you want the column settings to extend the full length of the page, or do you want to include a section at the top of the page that is only a single column?

Table 19-1. Word's Default Column Widths

Number of Columns	Width of Each Column
1	6 inches
2	2.75 inches with 0.5 inch spacing
3	1.67 inches with 0.5 inch spacing
4	1.13 inches with 0.5 inch spacing
5	.8 inches with 0.5 inch spacing
6	0.58 inches with 0.5 inch spacing

Choosing Predesigned Columns

Word includes a number of professionally designed templates that can help you get a jump start on using columns in your documents. The Brochure and Directory templates are two of these. You can get a closer look at the templates by following these steps:

1. Choose File, New. The New Document task pane appears on the right side of your work area.
2. Click On My Computer in the Templates area. The Templates dialog box appears. Click the Publications tab, as shown in Figure 19-1.

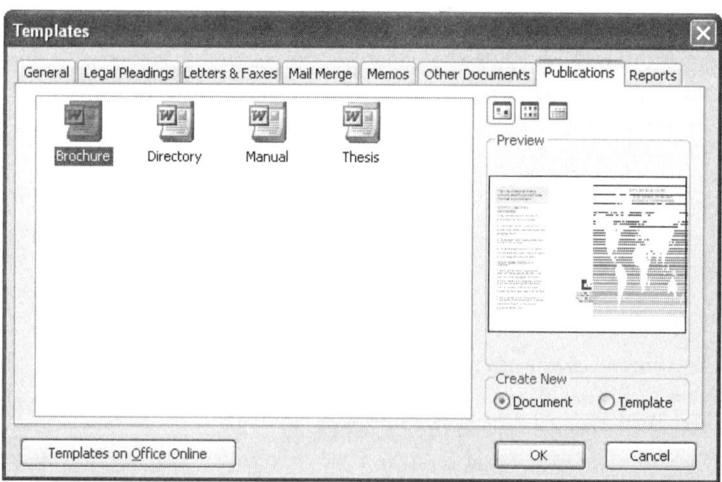

Figure 19-1. You can begin working with columns by using Word's predesigned templates.

3 To see a preview of the different document templates, click each one that you want to see. You may be prompted to install templates that are not installed by default. The Brochure and Directory types, shown in Figure 19-2 and Figure 19-3, include the use of columns.

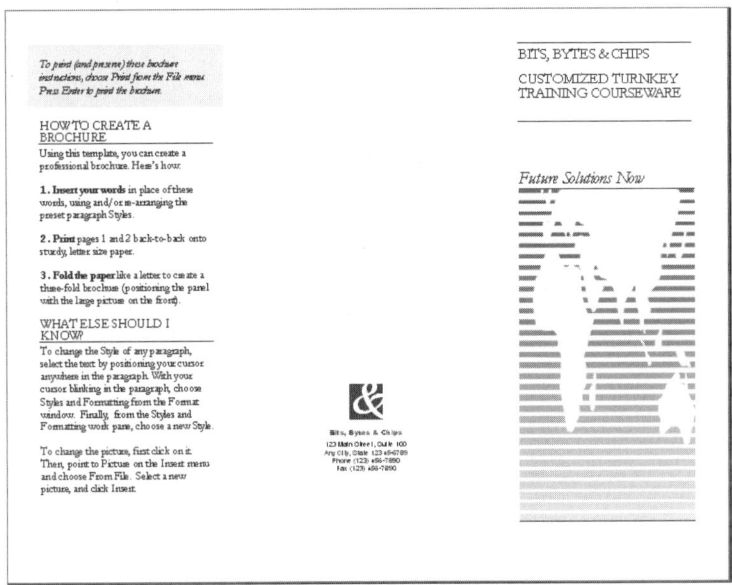

To print (and preserve) these brochure instructions, choose Print from the File menu. Press Enter to print the brochure.

HOW TO CREATE A BROCHURE

Using this template, you can create a professional brochure. Here's how:

1. Insert your words in place of these words, using and/or re-arranging the preset paragraph Styles.

2. Print pages 1 and 2 back-to-back onto sturdy, letter size paper.

3. Fold the paper like a letter to create a three-fold brochure (positioning the panel with the large picture on the front).

WHAT ELSE SHOULD I KNOW?

To change the Style of any paragraph, select the text by positioning your cursor anywhere in the paragraph. With your cursor blinking in the paragraph, choose Styles and Formatting from the Format window. Finally, from the Styles and Formatting work pane, choose a new Style.

To change the picture, first click on it. Then, point to Picture on the Insert menu and choose From File. Select a new picture, and click Insert.

Bits, Bytes & Chips
123 Main Street, Suite 100
Any City, State 12345-6789
Phone (123) 456-7890
Fax (123) 456-7890

BITS, BYTES & CHIPS

CUSTOMIZED TURNKEY TRAINING COURSEWARE

Future Solutions Now

Figure 19-2. Brochure uses a three-column layout in landscape mode to create a tri-fold brochure.

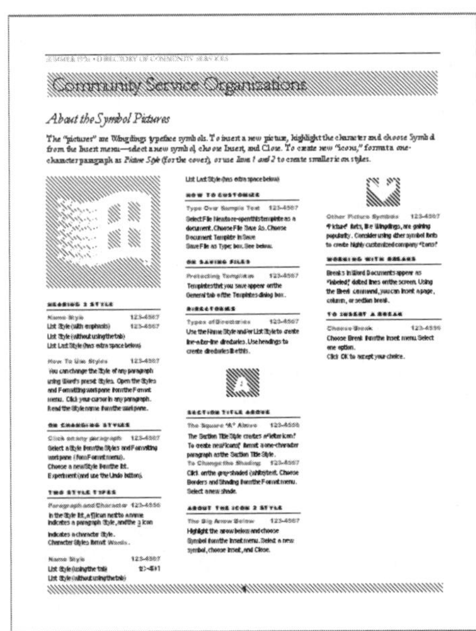

Community Service Organizations

About the Symbol Pictures

Figure 19-3. Directory uses a three-column layout in portrait mode to provide the template for a directory-type document.

4 To open one of the templates, simply click your choice and click OK.

Note The terms *landscape* and *portrait* are layout terms used to describe the way in which a page is positioned for printing. In landscape mode, the document is printed so that the long edge of the paper is the top of the document, in 11-by-8.5-inch layout. In portrait mode, the document is printed in the traditional 8.5-by-11-inch layout.

For more about working with Word's templates, see "Working with Templates and Wizards" on page 32.

Creating a Multi-Column Document

There are several ways to format your document in multiple columns. If you want to create columns on the fly, click the Columns button on the Standard toolbar. If you have certain specifications—for example, exact column measurements, a spacing requirement of a certain size, or more than four columns—use the Columns dialog box to choose those settings.

Tip **Switch to Print Layout view**
Be sure to display your document in Print Layout view before you begin working with columns. Normal view, Web Layout view, and Outline view won't enable you to see columns as they will appear in print. To display Print Layout view, Choose View, Print Layout or click Print Layout View to the left of the horizontal scroll bar.

Using the Columns Button

Columns

The easiest way to create a multi-column document is to click Columns on the Standard toolbar. When you click the button, a menu presents the choice of one to four columns, as shown in Figure 19-4. Click the column setting you want, and Word will automatically update the layout in your document.

Tip **Define columns the quick way**
If you want to create columns for only a portion of a document, select the area to which you want to apply the column format before you click the Columns button.

Note The only way you can see that Word has, in fact, created columns in your document is that the margins on the ruler will show the new boundaries. If the ruler isn't currently displayed in your document, choose View, Ruler to display it.

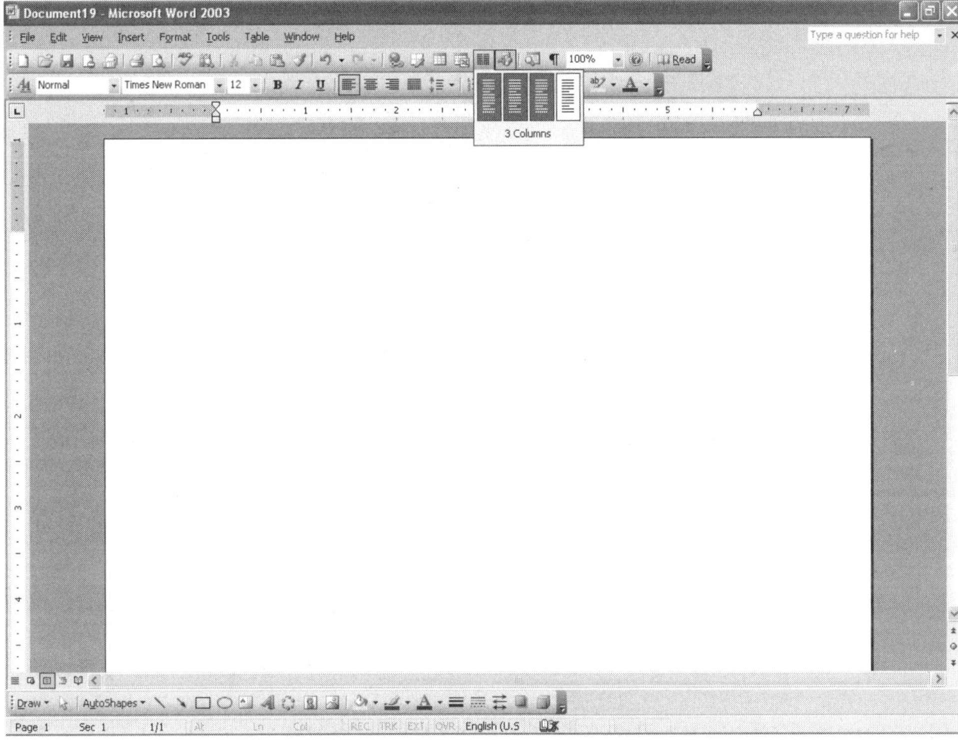

Figure 19-4. The Columns button allows you to select up to four columns from the Standard toolbar.

Choosing Column Specs in the Columns Dialog Box

If you have certain column specifications that you need to enter—for example, you're creating a follow-up report based on a format your department has adopted as its report format of choice—you can create and work with columns by using the Columns dialog box. Follow these steps:

1. Choose Format, Columns. The Columns dialog box is displayed.
2. Click the preset column format you want, if you see one that meets your needs. The Preview section will show you the format you've selected, as shown in Figure 19-5.

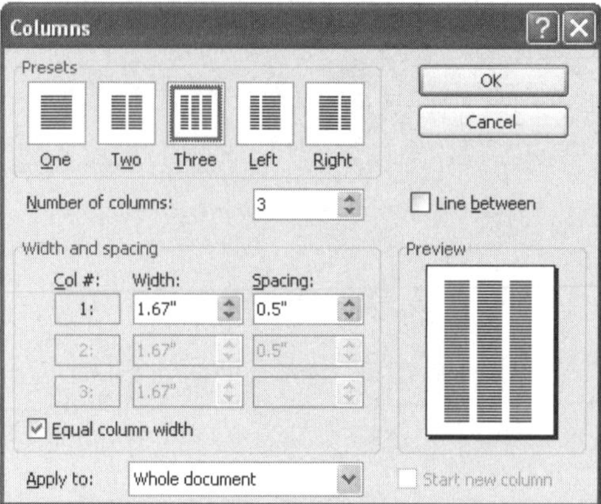

Figure 19-5. You can enter more specific column settings in the Columns dialog box.

3 Click OK to apply your formatting.

By default, Word assumes that you want your columns to be created equally (unless you choose either the Left or Right preset selection) and that you don't want a line to be placed between the columns you create. If you want to add a line between columns, select the Line Between check box, and Word will add the necessary rule.

Creating Columns for Part of a Document

Another assumption Word makes is that you want to apply the column format to the entire document. If you want to apply the format only from this point forward, click the arrow in the Apply To box and select This Point Forward. You might want, for example, to open your document with a paragraph or two in single-column format and then break up the rest of the document into three columns, as shown in Figure 19-6.

> **Note** Once you add section breaks to your document, you'll discover that This Section becomes one of your choices in the Apply To box.

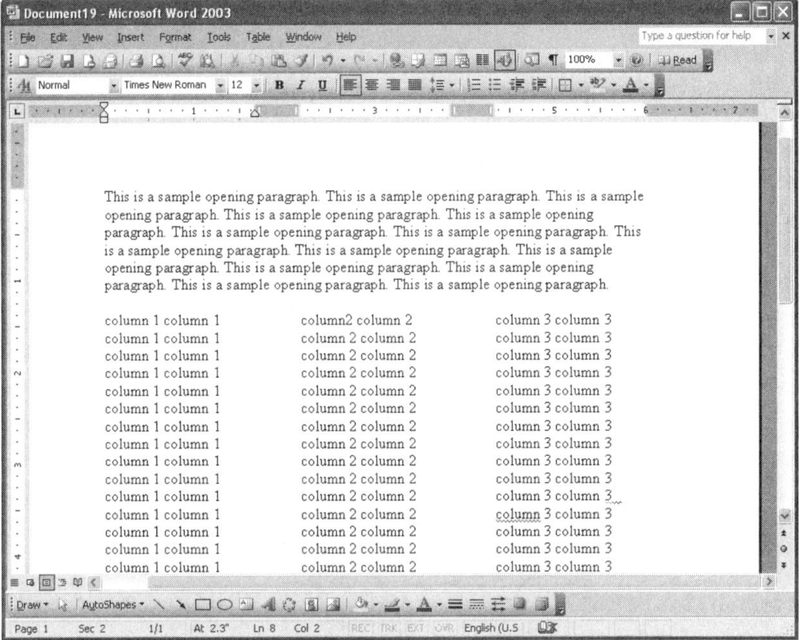

Figure 19-6. You can mix single-column and multi-column formats in the same document.

To create a mixed format, follow these steps:

1. Type the opening paragraph, leaving the document set to single-column format.
2. At the point where you want to create columns, Choose Format, Columns. The Columns dialog box is displayed.
3. Choose the number of columns you want; enter any spacing specifications as needed.
4. Select the Line Between check box if you want a line to be displayed between columns.
5. Click the Apply To arrow and choose This Point Forward. Click OK. The Columns dialog box closes and you're returned to the document.

Creating Unequal Column Widths

Although Word sets a number of options for you in the Columns dialog box, you can change those options to create columns that suit your document specifications. By choosing the Left or Right preset format, you can tell Word to create unequal formats, meaning the columns should not be of equal width. When you choose the Left preset format, the column to the left will be proportionately smaller than the one to the right. When you choose the Right preset, the right column will be the smaller one.

To customize column widths using the Columns dialog box, follow these steps:

1 Choose Format, Columns to display the Columns dialog box.
2 Click in the Number Of Columns box and type the number of columns you want to create.
3 Clear the check box to the left of Equal Column Width. The Width settings will become available for columns 1 through *n*, so that you can customize the settings, as shown in Figure 19-7.

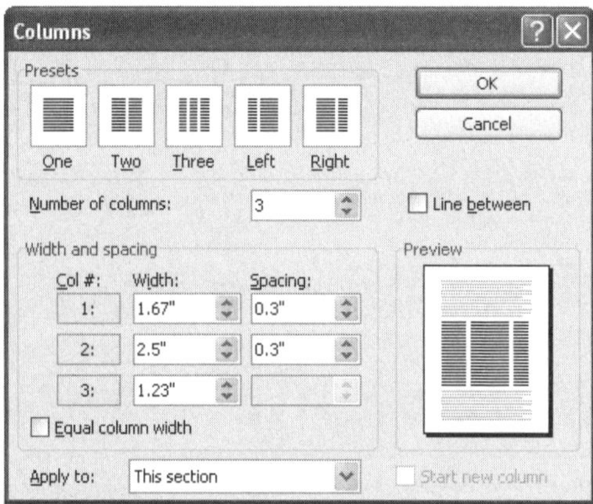

Figure 19-7. Use the Columns dialog box to specify the width and spacing for unequal columns.

4 Modify the Width and Spacing settings for your columns to get the effect you want. The Preview section shows the result of your choices.
5 Click OK to save your choices and return to the document.

Changing Column Width on the Ruler

You can also change the width of columns by dragging the column margins in the ruler at the top of your work area. If you want to keep the spacing the same between columns, position the pointer on the center of the spacing bar. When the pointer changes to a double-headed arrow, move the spacing bar in the direction you want to change the column. For example, to make the left column narrower, drag the spacing bar to the left.To make the left column wider, drag the spacing bar to the right. (See Figure 19-8.)

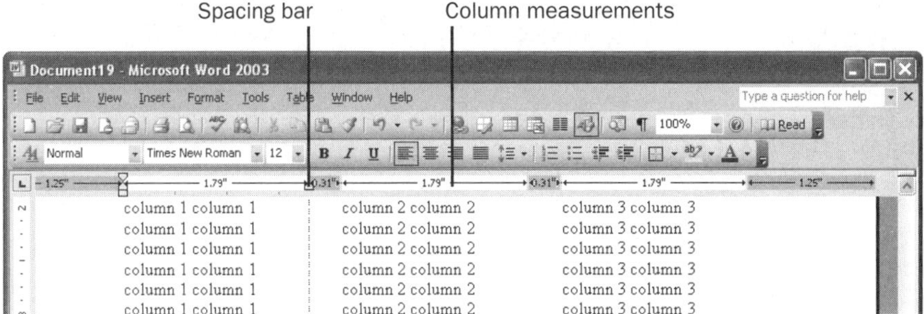

Figure 19-8. You can easily change the width of a column by dragging the spacing bar in the ruler.

You can also increase or decrease the amount of spacing between columns by dragging the edge of the spacing bar to the right or left. For example, to extend the spacing into the right column, drag the right edge of the spacing bar to the right. The size of the right column is reduced by the same amount of space you added to the spacing bar.

> **Tip** **Use the ruler to make precise column measurements**
> You can also display and control the accurate size of your columns when you're resizing them by using the ruler. Press and hold Alt while you drag the edge of the spacing bar in the ruler. The measurements of the column appear in the ruler, helping you know when the column you're working with is just the size you want it.

Getting Text into a Column Layout

Everything in Word should be as simple as getting text into a column layout. When you're turning a single-column document into a multiple-column document, Word does all the work for you. You simply display the Columns dialog box, choose the number of columns you want, specify any width and spacing settings, choose whether you want a line divider, and click OK. Word then puts the text in the format you selected, whether you already have a document full of text or an empty page.

If you're entering text into columns as you go, no text will appear in the second column until the previous column has been filled; that is, if you intend to have only headings in the left column and flow your text into the right column of a two-column format, you'll need to fill the left column with line spaces between headings until you get to the end of the column and Word wraps back up to the top of the right column. In the example shown in Figure 19-9, you can see the paragraph marks showing the line spacing inserted to cause the text to wrap to the next column.

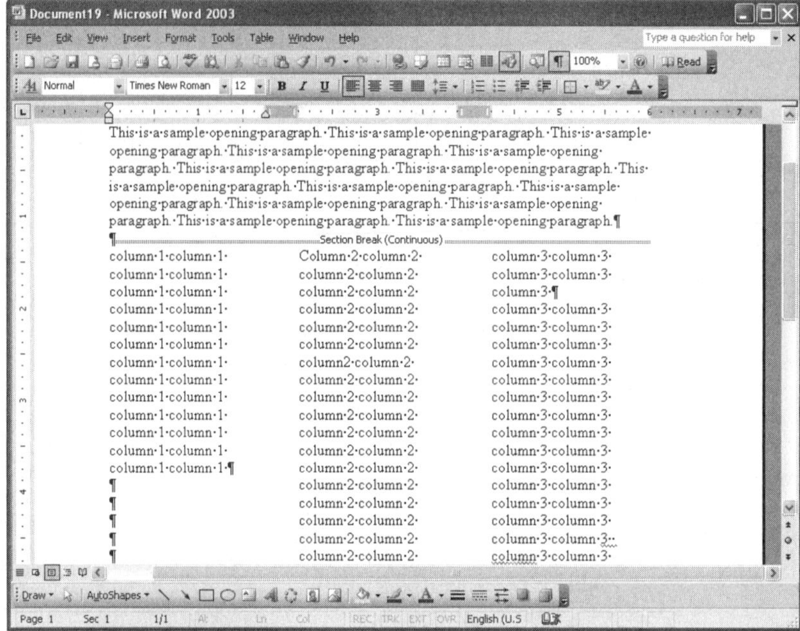

Figure 19-9. Before text will wrap to the second column, the first column must be filled.

> **Note** There *is* a quicker way to do this, if your left column is going to be blank except for perhaps a heading at the top. When you know you've entered all you want in a column, you can add a column break. You'll learn how to do this in the section "Inserting Column Breaks," on page 570.

Choosing Text Alignment

The way your text looks—and how readable your readers think it is—has a lot to do with the alignment you choose for the text. Traditional document alignment is often left justified, in which the text is aligned along the left margin of the page only. Other alignments include centered, which is often used for headings, and right justified, which aligns text along the right margin and rarely is used for traditional documents. Another alignment, full-justified text, aligns text along both the left and right margins, adding spaces in between words to spread out the text enough to make the both-edge alignment possible. Table 19-2 gives you a look at alignment differences.

Table 19-2. Text Alignment Differences

Example		Alignment Type	Use
This·is·a·sample·opening· paragraph.·This·is·a· sample·opening· paragraph.·This·is·a·	column·1·column·1·column·1·column·1·Column·1· column·1·column·1·column·1·column·1·Column·1· column·1·column·1·column·1·column·1·Column·1· column·1·column·1·column·1·column·1·Column·1·	Left	For traditional body text, headlines, captions, and more
This·is·a·sample·opening· paragraph.·This·is·a· sample·opening· paragraph.·This·is·a·	column·1·column·1·column·1·column·1·Column·1· column·1·column·1·column·1·column·1·Column·1· column·1·column·1·column·1·column·1·Column·1· column·1·column·1·column·1·column·1·Column·1·	Centered	For headlines, special text effects, captions or callouts
This·is·a·sample·opening· paragraph.·This·is·a· sample·opening· paragraph.·This·is·a·	column·1·column·1·column·1·column·1·Column·1· column·1·column·1·column·1·column·1·Column·1· column·1·column·1·column·1·column·1·Column·1· column·1·column·1·column·1·column·1·Column·1·	Right	For specialty text designs, table text, captions
This·is·a·sample·opening· paragraph.· This· is· a· sample· opening· paragraph.· This· is· a·	column·1·column·1·column·1·column·1·Column·1· column·1·column·1·column·1·column·1·Column·1· column·1·column·1·column·1·column·1·Column·1· column·1·column·1·column·1·column·1·Column·1·	Full	For text in columns, some special text elements, quotes

Users often prefer left-justified text for just about everything; however, some people like using full-justified text for documents with multiple columns. In some cases, formats work well with the left column right justified, lining up along the leftmost edge of the right column, which is full justified. (See Figure 19-10 for examples of the various types of alignment.)

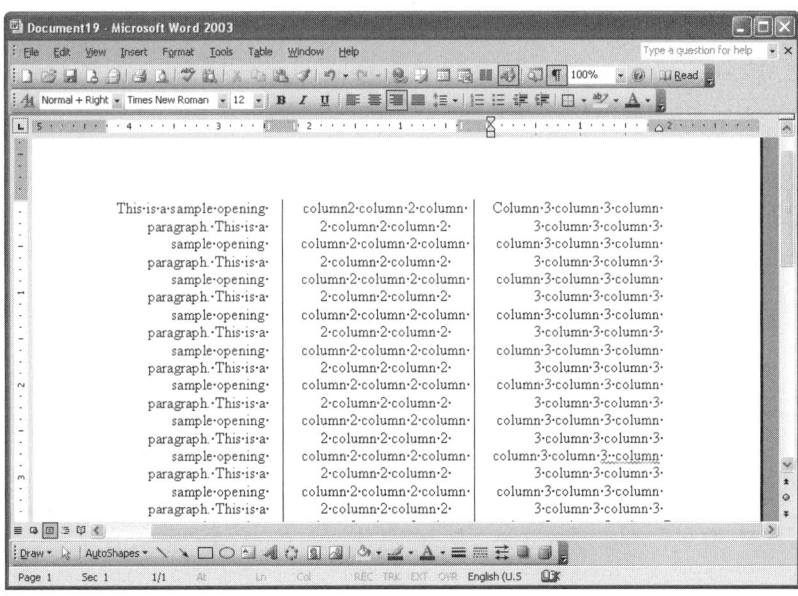

Figure 19-10. Mix and match alignment to see what looks best in your particular publication.

Beginning a New Column Layout

Longer documents often require a number of different general layouts—the introduction and summary of your report might read story-like, in a single-column format. When you begin to talk about the specification of your new product line, however, you might go to a multi-column format that presents information in the clearest way possible. You might also want to incorporate graphs and tables in the body of those columns.

How can you easily switch between column layouts without disturbing the way text flows in your document? The easiest way to change to a multi-column format is to place the insertion point where you want to start the new column layout and then follow these steps:

1. Choose Format, Columns. Select the number of columns you want to include in the Columns dialog box; add width and spacing settings, if necessary.
2. Select the Line Between check box if you want a line separating the columns.
3. In the Apply To box, click the arrow and choose This Point Forward.
4. Select the Start New Column check box.
5. Click OK to return to the document. Word moves to the top of the next column, and your column settings are in effect.

Inserting Column Breaks

When you've entered everything you want in a specific column and you're ready to wrap text to the next column, you can add a column break to force the wrap. To add a column break, follow these steps:

1. Place the insertion point where you want to insert the column break.
2. Choose Insert, Break. The Break dialog box appears, as shown in Figure 19-11.

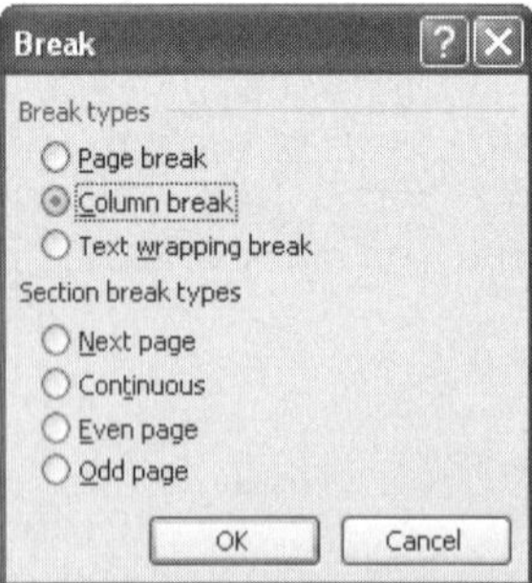

Figure 19-11. You can force a column break to cause text remaining in that column to wrap to the top of the next column.

3. In the Break Types section, click Column Break.

4. Click OK. You will be returned to the document, and Word will add a Column Break at the insertion point. The text in the column past that point will be wrapped to the top of the next column.

Removing Column Breaks

In Word, you can delete columns as easily as you add them. They can be removed simply by removing a character—just position the insertion point immediately following a break and press Backspace (or select the break itself and press Delete). The column break is removed and the text is flowed back into the previous column.

Balancing Your Columns

Lining up text isn't always easy, and Word includes a feature that can help you automatically balance the text in your columns. When you create a column break, as described in the preceding section, you can have Word create a continuous break, which ensures that the columns will be balanced. The "continuous" part of the break gives Word permission to end the column wherever necessary to even out the text placement.

To create a continuous break, follow these steps:

1. Place the insertion point where you want the break to be added.
2. Display the Break dialog box by choosing Insert, Break.
3. Select Column Break as usual and, in the Section Break Types section, click Continuous. Word then adds the continuous break, which will break the text at the appropriate point to balance the text columns most effectively.

Working in Sections

Since Word includes features that stretch to give you a variety of formats and controls for long documents, you need a way to limit the changes made to individual portions of your document. That's what sections are all about. By using sections, you can control a change from a single-column format to multiple columns and back again. You can create layouts that look different on odd and even pages. You can modify the margins of a section and then revert to the regular document formatting when the section is completed.

Creating a Section

Starting a section is almost as easy as starting a column. You can begin a new section anywhere—in the middle of a page or at the beginning of a new one. To start a new section, follow these steps:

1. Place the insertion point where you want to start the new section.
2. Choose Insert, Break. The Break dialog box (shown previously in Figure 19-9) appears.

3. Click one of the section break types (further described in Table 19-3) and click OK. The section is created, and the text flows accordingly.

> **Tip** **Create sections in Page Setup**
> If you have a larger vision of your document when you first use Page Setup, you can elect to create sections there as well. Choose File, Page Setup to display the Page Setup dialog box, and then click the Layout tab. The first group of settings on the Layout tab in the Page Setup dialog box deals with sections. You can choose Continuous, New Column, New Page, Even Page, or Odd Page in the Section Start list, just as you can in the Break dialog box. As always, you can change any of your selections at any time, and making changes in the Break dialog box later will carry through to the settings you entered in the Page Setup dialog box.

Table 19-3. A Quick Look at Section Types

Section Type	Description	Use
Next Page	Creates a new section at the top of the next page.	You want to start a new section with different formatting specifications on the next page in the document.
Continuous	Creates a new section beginning at the document insertion point.	You want to begin a new section in the middle of the current page.
Even Page	Creates a new section beginning on an even page. If the current page is an even page, an odd page is inserted and left blank.	You want to create a new section with a format used uniquely for even pages.
Odd Page	Creates a new section beginning on an odd page. If the current page is an odd page, an even page is inserted and left blank.	You want to create a section for odd pages only.

Selecting Multiple Sections

Word gives you the means of selecting different portions of your document at the same time. Whether you want to copy large and nonsequential sections, run the spelling checker on selected text, or reformat or delete selected blocks, you can use the multiple-select feature to select noncontiguous blocks and sections. To select multiple sections, follow these steps:

1. Select the first section you want to work with.
2. Press and hold the Ctrl key, and scroll to the next section and select it.
3. Continue adding sections as necessary and then perform the operation you have in mind. No longer is Word limited to an all-or-nothing selection method, which means you can work with just the text you want, when and how you want to.

Removing Section Breaks

You can remove the section breaks in your Word document in the same way you delete column breaks—simply select them and press Delete. Once you delete a section break, the document settings that were in effect before the break are applied to that section.

Saving Formats as Your Own Templates

A reminder: any time you go to any significant trouble to create your own format, especially if there's a chance you'll use the format again, consider saving the format you've created as a template you can use again as the basis for other documents.

To create a template from a document you've made, follow these steps:

1. Choose File, Save As. The Save As dialog box will appear.
2. Type a name for the template in the File Name box.
3. Click the Save As Type arrow and choose Document Template (*.dot).
4. Click Save to save the template file.

Chapter 20

Creating and Controlling Master Documents

When you work on longer documents, consistency and continuity become important. You need to make sure that all the parts of your document use the same styles, treat tables and figures the same way, and have consistent headers and footers. You need to be able to check the overall organization of your document, making sure that the topics flow logically and that you've arranged them in the best possible order.

This is easy to do when you're working with 10, 20, or even 30 pages. But what about those book-length projects for which various team members are taking a chapter or two, somebody else is plugging in the charts, and yet another person is checking the citations and references? It's in this type of situation that Word's master and subdocument features really shine. By using those features, you can divide a large document into pieces—for example, giving a chapter to each team member—and then integrate them back into one piece; you can have both the benefit of working with a team to get a major project done and the confidence that the consistency and continuity of your document are intact.

Using Master Documents

At its most basic level, a master document holds several separate files together. You might create a master document to handle the following projects:

- A book-length manuscript in which each team member writes and edits one chapter.
- A grant proposal in which different committee members are responsible for different pieces (for example, your executive director writing the Executive Summary, your financial officer providing the budget, and your development committee chairperson writing the objective and evaluation sections).

- An annual report that's a compilation of a number of different sections, including the introduction, the program descriptions, the donor thank-you section, and letters from clients served. Each person on your publications team could research and write a different piece of the report.
- A technical manual that's a collaborative effort between your IT department and a technical illustrator. After each chapter is written, you can send it as a subdocument to the illustrator, who can create and place the illustrations, and then return the subdocument to be integrated into the master.

Master documents and subdocuments create a great opportunity for you to use Word's team review and collaboration features. For more about tracking, comparing, and integrating changes in a collaborative document, see Chapter 24, "Working and Collaborating Online."

No matter what type of project you're working on—whether you're working with a team or doing it all yourself—you can use master documents to do the following things:

- Keep track of disparate sections and open and print them all rather than working with individual files
- Display and collapse subdocuments to switch between views easily
- Coordinate pieces of a project that are distributed to other team members
- Review and easily reorganize a long document
- Control styles, margins, and other formats throughout a long document
- Work with a long document as a whole for operations such as printing, checking spelling, and using the Find and Find And Replace features

What's in a Master Document?

In Chapter 10, "Outlining Documents for Clarity and Structure," you worked in Outline view to create, check, and change the basic organization of your document. The idea behind master documents builds on this basic philosophy and takes it to a higher level. By working with the "big picture" of your document, you can easily see how your sections or chapters compare, what needs to be moved, and which pieces you want to assign to other team members. The best place for this big picture approach is Outline view. That's where you'll do all your work with master and subdocuments.

When you first change to Outline view, either by choosing View, Outline or by clicking Outline View to the left of the horizontal scroll bar, the Outlining toolbar appears. On the toolbar, you'll see the master document buttons. Table 20-1 introduces these tools.

Note For a review of the other buttons on the Outlining toolbar, see Chapter 10, "Outlining Documents for Clarity and Structure."

Table 20-1. Master Document Buttons

Button	Button Name	Description
	Master Document View	Switches the display to master document view so that you can see subdocument icons
	Collapse Subdocuments	Limits the display of subdocument sections to their heading levels
	Create Subdocument	Creates a subdocument of the current selection
	Remove Subdocument	Removes the subdocument designation and returns the selection to being a normal part of the master document
	Insert Subdocument	Inserts an existing document as a subdocument
	Merge Subdocument	Puts two or more selected subdocuments together
	Split Subdocument	Divides a subdocument into two subdocuments
	Lock Document	Secures the subdocument so that no further changes can be made

Master documents can include text, graphics, charts—anything you put in your documents. One of the best things about working with master and subdocuments is the ability to build documents from segments and vice versa. Once you set up your master document to include subdocuments, you'll see a number of items in Outline view, as shown in Figure 20-1:

- **Subdocument icons** Once you create a subdocument from a selection in a document, Word displays the subdocument with an icon in outline form.
- **Document text** When the master document is fully expanded, you can see everything in your document, all the way to text level.
- **Subordinate headings** The subdocument headings enable you to see at a glance how your document is organized. You can also easily determine how to assign the various portions to other team members.
- **Master and subdocument buttons on the Outlining toolbar** Any time you work in Outline view, the master and subdocument buttons are available at the right end of the Outlining toolbar.

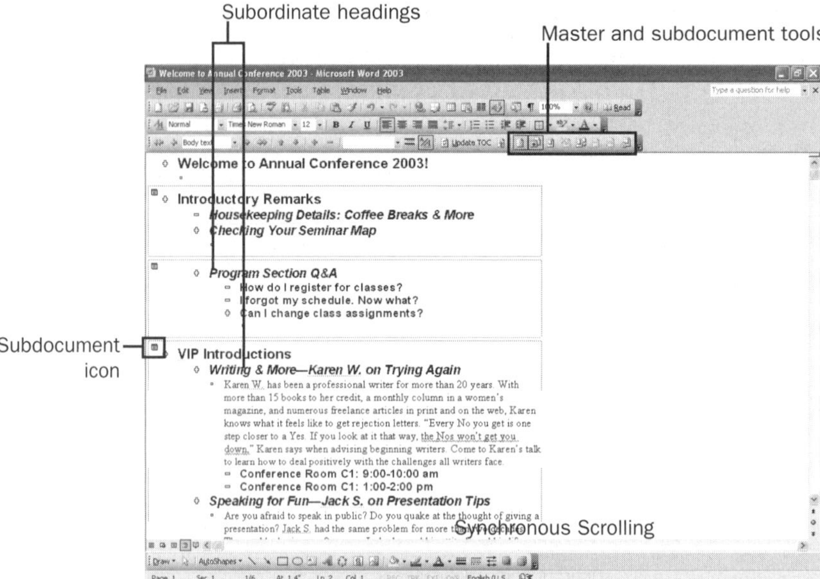

Figure 20-1. Working with master documents in Outline view, you can easily see and work with the subdocuments you create.

Preparing Master Documents and Subdocuments

You can see the benefits of working with master and subdocuments—especially if you're managing a large project. Like anything else that requires the cooperation of a number of people, it's best to start with a plan. Take some time to consider all the different aspects of your document and plan the types of assignments you want to make before you get started. Be sure to create a table or listing of various assignments that will enable you to track the different parts of your document.

Tip **Create an assignment list**

You might want to use Word's Table of Contents (TOC) feature to automatically generate a table of contents that you can use as an assignment list. If you have a large project with many different pieces (and as many team members), you'll need to track the list so that you know who has which piece. For more about using Word's TOC feature, see Chapter 21, "Generating First-Class Tables of Contents and Related Elements."

File Organization for Master and Subdocuments

In addition to the organization of the various pieces and people, you'll need to think about a physical location for the files as they come and go. All files for master and subdocuments must be stored in the same folder—otherwise, Word won't know where to look to integrate the various pieces.

Choose a folder in which you'll store both the master and subdocument files. If you're working on a network, make sure that this is a place on a shared drive to which all team members have access. If you'll be using existing documents to build the master document, be sure to move those documents to the newly created directory before you begin creating the master document.

Creating a Master Document

You have two different options for creating a master document—and both procedures are simple ones:

- You can start with an existing document and turn it into a master document by creating subdocuments within it.
- You can create a master document from scratch, creating the outline headings and subdocuments as you go.

Starting with an Existing Document

If you have a document you want to use as a master document, start by opening the file you want to use by choosing File, Open, navigating to and selecting the file you want, and then clicking Open. Change to Outline view by choosing View, Outline. The document appears in Outline view, with the heading styles you've selected, as shown in Figure 20-2.

The heading styles you've assigned to the text in your document specify which headings to use for the master document outline. You divide the master by selecting the portion you want to mark as a subdocument; Word inserts a link in place of the actual text in the master, and then saves the text as a subdocument. In "Creating Subdocuments," you'll learn how to select sections and create the subdocuments you need.

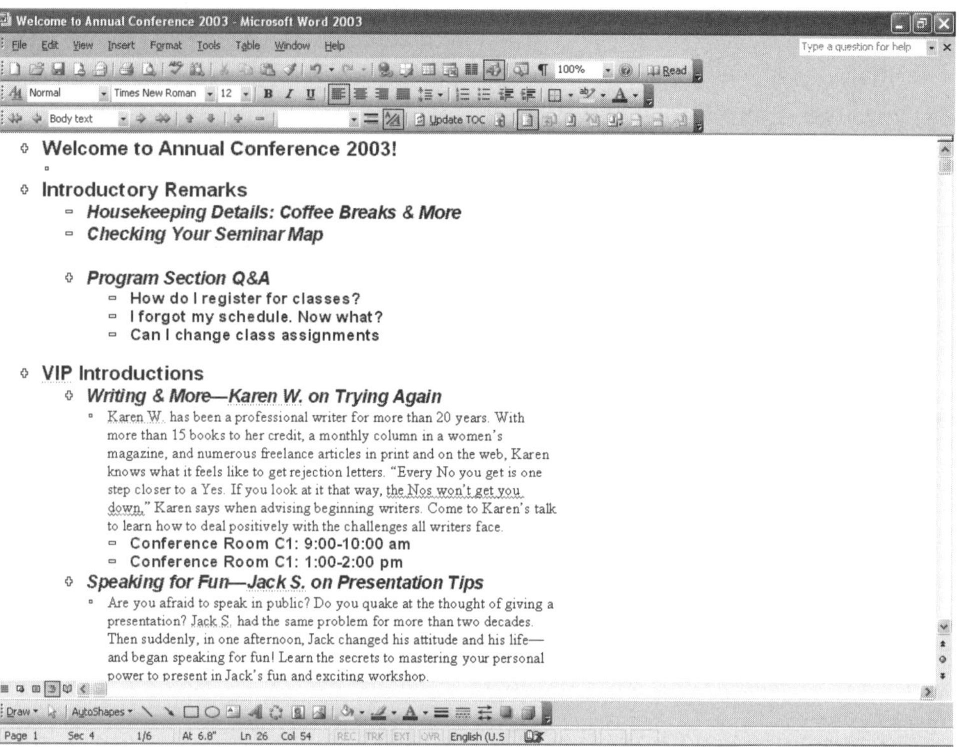

Figure 20-2. When you start with an existing document for your master, Word displays the existing heading levels in Outline view.

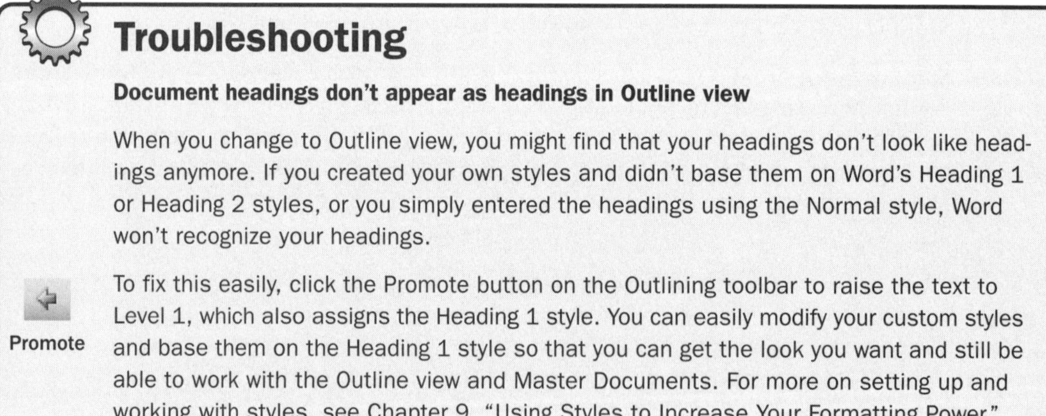

Troubleshooting

Document headings don't appear as headings in Outline view

When you change to Outline view, you might find that your headings don't look like headings anymore. If you created your own styles and didn't base them on Word's Heading 1 or Heading 2 styles, or you simply entered the headings using the Normal style, Word won't recognize your headings.

Promote

To fix this easily, click the Promote button on the Outlining toolbar to raise the text to Level 1, which also assigns the Heading 1 style. You can easily modify your custom styles and base them on the Heading 1 style so that you can get the look you want and still be able to work with the Outline view and Master Documents. For more on setting up and working with styles, see Chapter 9, "Using Styles to Increase Your Formatting Power."

Starting from Scratch

You can create a master document right from the beginning of your project. Once you have a concept and thoughts for a beginning outline, you can create the outline in Outline view, and then make the assignments for your subdocuments as needed. Here are the steps for starting a new master document from scratch:

1. Start a new document, and then change to Outline view by choosing View, Outline.
2. Enter the headings for the document title and subdocument titles. Word automatically creates the headings with the default style Heading 1. Make sure each heading you intend to turn into a subdocument is assigned the Heading 1 style. This is the style Word will use in dividing into subdocuments.

> **Tip** **Create a backup copy**
> If you think you might like to keep a copy of your outline before it's been divided into subdocuments, click File, Save As to save a backup copy of the outline file. Although you can easily remove subdocument divisions and integrate subdocuments into the master later, that's a big hassle if you simply want an original version of the outline to play around with.

Demote

Save

3. Create subheadings (sections within the subdocument) by clicking Demote to assign Heading 2 to subhead text.
4. When you have your outline the way you want it, save the file by clicking Save on the Standard toolbar, typing a name for the file, and then clicking Save.

Creating Subdocuments

Once you have the basic outline in place, you can determine how you want to divide the master document. Create a subdocument by following these steps:

1. Make sure that all headings and subheadings you want to include in the subdocument are displayed by clicking the Show Level arrow on the Outlining toolbar and selecting Show All Levels.
2. Click the symbol to the left of the heading for the text you want to use for the subdocument. For example, if you want to create a subdocument of the "Introductory Remarks" in Figure 20-3, click the plus (+) symbol, and the entire topic is selected.

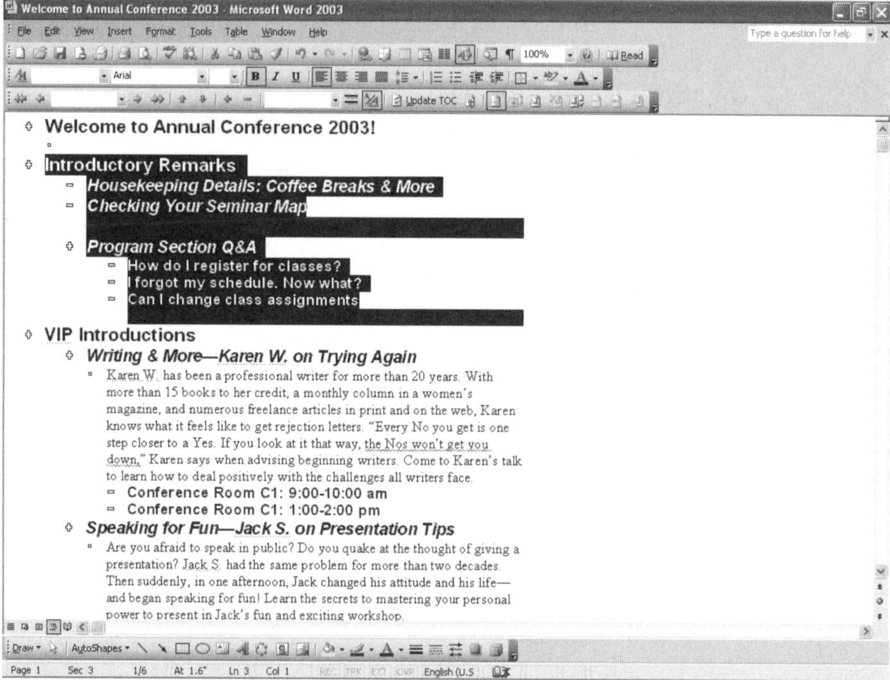

Figure 20-3. Be sure to display and select all text you want to include in your subdocument before clicking the Create Subdocument button.

3. Click Create Subdocument on the Outlining toolbar. The topic is marked as a subdocument, as Figure 20-4 shows.
4. Save the document. Word saves the subdocument as a separate file in the same folder. The Heading 1 text at the beginning of the file is used as the file name.

> **Note** This is one reason to create a different folder for each master document you work with—if there's any chance you'll have subdocuments with the same name in two different master documents, one subdocument might overwrite the other if you have too many files together. Better to be safe than sorry—create a new folder for each master document project.

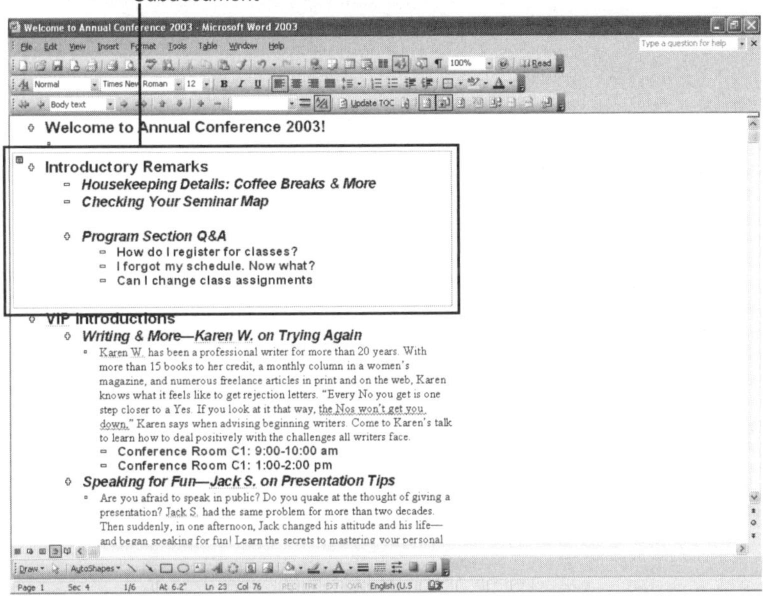

Figure 20-4. Word creates the subdocument and names it using the text in the first line of the selection.

Importing Data for Subdocuments

You can also create subdocuments by inserting other files into your master document. In this case, you might have a partial outline you're working with, or you might start a new file for your master and then open existing files into it. However you get the document pieces together, begin with your master document open on the screen. Place the insertion point where you want to add the subdocument, and then click Insert Subdocument on the Outlining toolbar. This opens the Insert Subdocument dialog box, shown in Figure 20-5.

Navigate to the file you want to import, select it, and then click Open. The subdocument is added to the master document at the insertion point. Add or create other subdocuments as needed. When you're finished creating subdocuments, save the file. Word saves the master and the subdocuments in the folder you specify.

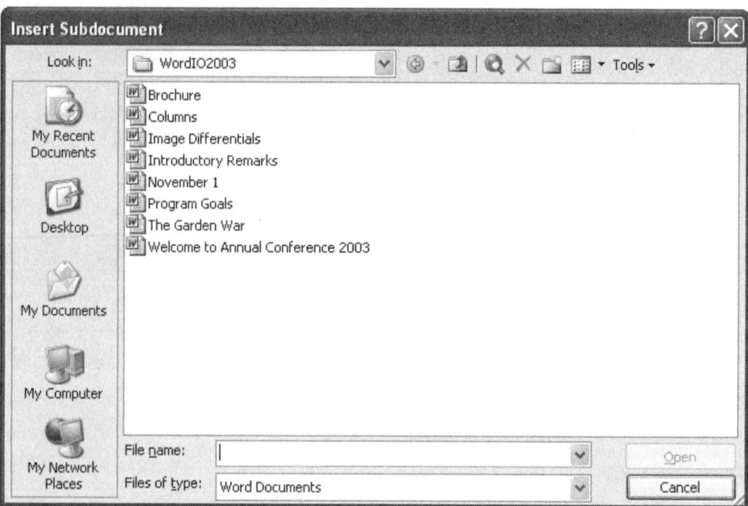

Figure 20-5. Importing an existing file into a master to use as a subdocument saves you data entry and organizing time.

Navigating to and from the Master Document

The basic idea behind master documents is that you can have one large file in which all pieces are represented, but for convenience and expediency's sake, you can have each of these different pieces in a different place, theoretically being worked on by different people. As you begin to work with and edit the text of your long document, you'll need to know how to navigate among the files in order to make the changes you want to make.

Working with the Master Document

After you create a master document and create subdocuments within it, Word changes the way it saves the file information. No longer is everything stored within the single document. Now the master document contains links to the subdocuments, and when you expand and work with the subdocuments within the master, you are really, through links, working in the individual subdocument files themselves.

After you save and close your master document, reopen it and notice the change. As Figure 20-6 shows, the master document for the Annual Conference publication now stores links to the subdocuments.

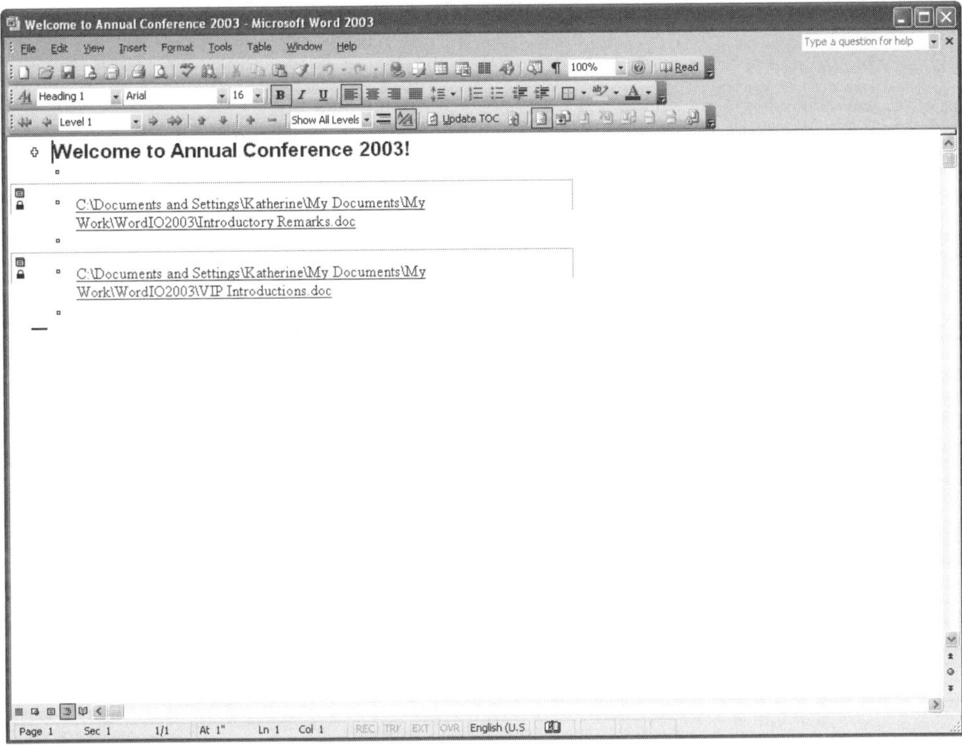

Figure 20-6. After you save, close, and then reopen the master document, Word shows the links to the subdocuments in place of the text.

Following Links to Subdocuments

To move to the subdocument, simply click the link. The subdocument file opens in a new Word window on your screen. You can now expand and edit the file as needed.

> **Note** If you later reorganize your files and move subdocuments from one place to another—even if you are moving them within the same directory to new subfolders—Word will display the message "Cannot open the specified file." To re-establish links between your master and subdocuments, first delete the broken subdocument link and then use Insert Subdocument on the Outlining toolbar to relink the document.

Expanding and Collapsing Subdocuments

You can collapse an outline to move and reorganize the document easily. As you learned when working in Outline view, however, you can collapse and expand only text that's been formatted with Word's built-in heading styles or preset outline levels. To expand and display the subdocuments in the master document, begin by clicking at the beginning of the document. (Change to Outline view, if necessary.) Click Expand Subdocuments on the Outlining toolbar. All subdocuments in your master are displayed, as shown in Figure 20-7. The subdocument icon and any subordinate text and graphics also appear.

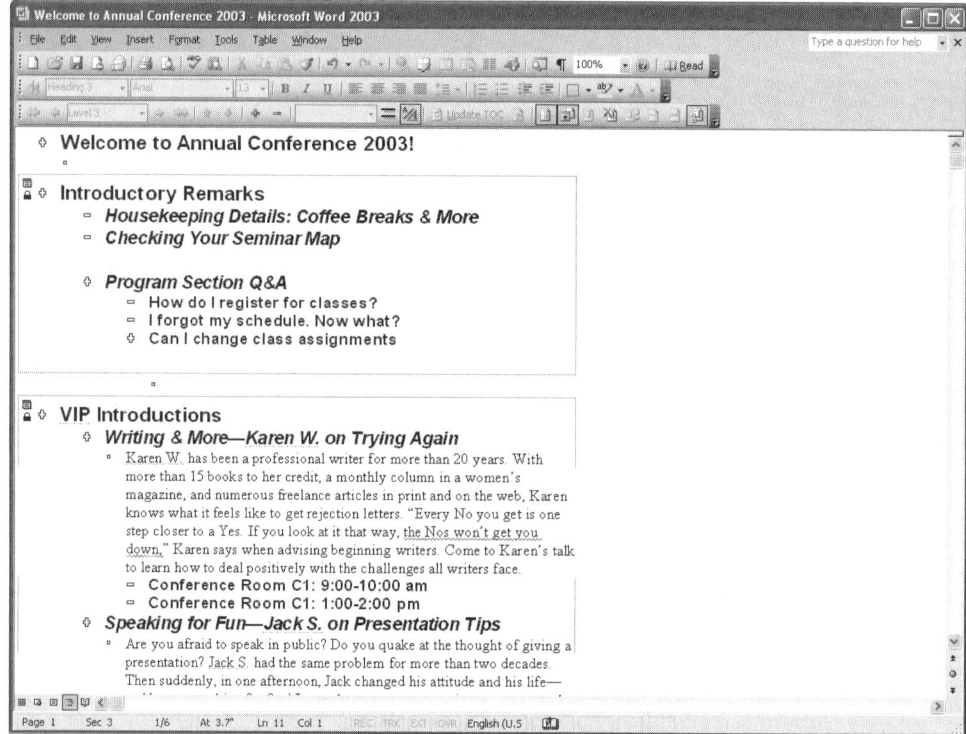

Figure 20-7. Expanding subdocuments shows all text in the master document, keeping the subdocument breaks and icons intact.

> **Tip** Check things out in Print Layout view
>
> When you expand subdocuments in the master document, you can change to Print Layout view to see how the sections will look in print form. You can make formatting changes, check spelling, and use Find and Replace to your heart's content while you're in Print Layout view so that you can see how the format is affected. Then return to Outline view to finish working with the master document and to move sections, if needed.

Once you've expanded the subdocuments in the master, the Expand Subdocuments button changes to Collapse Subdocuments so that you can again suppress the display of the subdocuments. You'll want to do this before you reorder subdocuments in your master document. To collapse the master display, click anywhere in the document and select Collapse Subdocuments. The master goes back to its links-only display.

Note If you want to collapse only the heading levels within a subdocument, use the traditional Collapse button on the Outlining toolbar to control that display.

Editing Master and Subdocuments

Because master documents and subdocuments are two different kinds of files, each storing different things, you'll make different editing changes in each of them. Table 20-2 lists the editing tasks you'll want to perform and shows where you'll make those changes in master and subdocuments.

Table 20-2. Editing Master and Subdocuments

Editing Task	Master Document	Subdocument
Text editing and correction	✓	✓
Applying heading levels	✓	
Changing topic order	✓	
Checking spelling	✓	
Global formatting	✓	
Local formatting of individual elements	✓	✓
Changing margins and page setup	✓	
Adding headers and footers	✓	
Adding borders and shading to specific objects		✓

Making Master Changes

The types of changes you'll make to your master document include those that will affect the entire publication. For example, you'll add styles to a template in the master document so that all the styles can be consistent among the various pieces of the publication. You'll also change margins, specify column settings, and do things like run the spelling checker and print while you have everything together in your master document.

You'll also add headers and footers to your master document so that you can ensure consistent treatment throughout all your subdocuments.

Entering Subdocument Changes

The most basic changes will have to happen in the subdocuments, especially if you are assigning subdocuments to different team members to write, edit, proofread, and ultimately return to the master. The line-by-line editing, word choice, and object work (such as the addition of tables, graphics, and text boxes) all need to happen in the subdocument file.

Each person working on a subdocument can make changes as needed, and then save the file in the designated folder. When the master document is opened and the document is expanded, all changes made in the various subdocuments will be reflected in the master. The person working with the master can then change global formatting options, check spelling, add headers and footers, and print the document as needed.

Troubleshooting

Different styles appear in the master document and subdocuments

If you notice that the headings in your master document and subdocuments look different, check the template you've applied by choosing Tools, Templates And Add-Ins. In the Document Template section, check each file to make sure that both the master and the subdocument have the same template selected and that the Automatically Update Document Styles check box is selected. If necessary, attach a different template by clicking Attach and, in the Attach Template dialog box, navigating to the template file you want. Make your selection and click Open, and then click OK to close the Templates And Add-Ins dialog box and return to the document.

Locking Subdocuments

Word provides a subdocument locking feature that enables you to protect documents so that no further changes can be made to them. This is particularly helpful if you're working as part of a team and want to make sure another team member doesn't modify a file after it's been finalized.

Lock Document

To lock a subdocument, simply click the subdocument icon and click Lock Document on the Outlining toolbar. A small lock symbol appears beneath the subdocument icon to the left of the subdocument text, as shown in Figure 20-8.

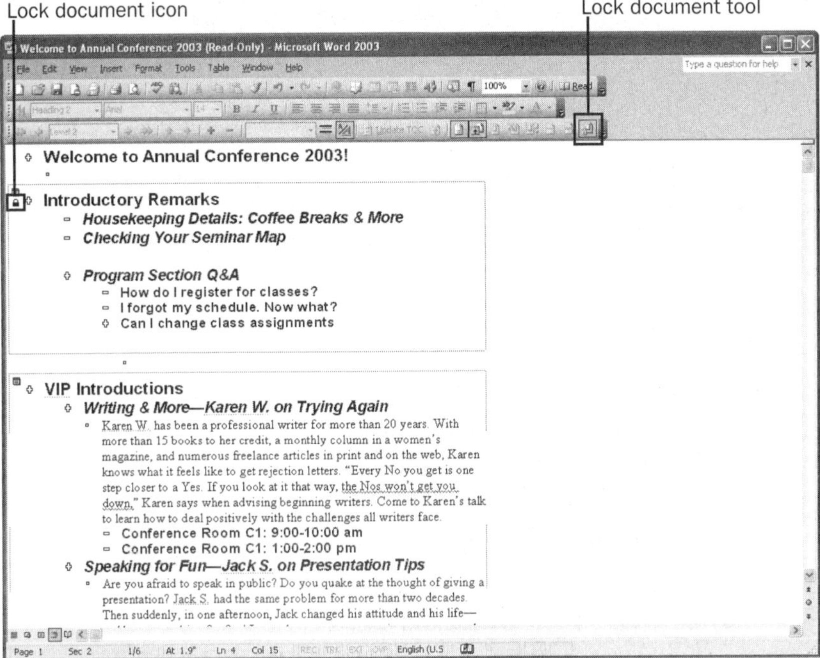

Figure 20-8. Once you finish editing a subdocument, you can lock it against further changes by clicking Lock Document on the Outlining toolbar.

Rearranging a Master Document

One of the greatest perks of working in a master document is the ease with which you can rearrange subdocuments. Start by opening your master document and reviewing the order of the subdocuments you've got listed. Click Expand Subdocuments to show all the headings and text of the subdocuments within the master. Drag the subdocument icon of the item you want to move to the new location. A heavy indicator line moves with the pointer, showing you the placement of the subdocument, as shown in Figure 20-9.

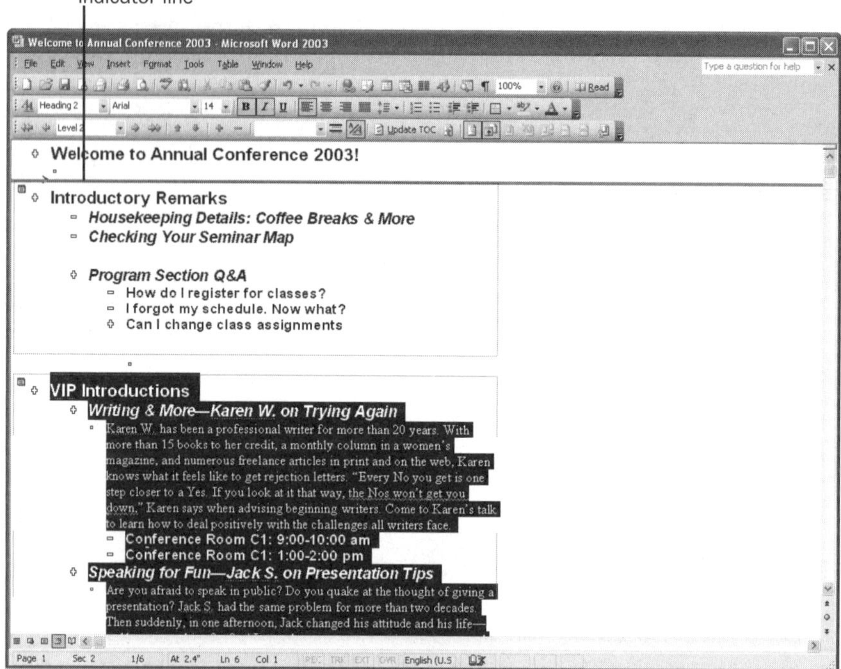

Figure 20-9. When you rearrange subdocuments, the indicator line shows you where the subdocument will be placed when you release the mouse button.

When the indicator line is positioned where you want to insert the subdocument, release the mouse button. The subdocument is then moved to that position.

> **Tip** **Don't accidentally bury your subdocument**
> Be sure to place the indicator line outside another subdocument boundary before you release the mouse button. Otherwise, Word will create a "nested" subdocument, placing the subdocument you just moved inside another subdocument. If this was not your intention, drag the subdocument icon to a new location outside an existing subdocument area or press Ctrl+Z to undo your action and start again.

> **Tip** **Work with multiple subdocuments**
> You can select multiple subdocuments by pressing and holding Shift while clicking the subdocument icons. If you want to select noncontiguous subdocuments, press and hold Ctrl while selecting the subdocuments you want to move.

Merging Subdocuments

Although splitting documents into subdocuments for organizing, editing, and enhancement purposes is a useful function, there will be times when you want to combine subdocuments after you've worked with them independently. To merge two subdocuments, follow these steps:

1. Open the master document with links to the subdocument files.
2. Click Expand Subdocuments to display the contents of the subdocument files.
3. Make sure that the subdocuments you want to combine are next to one another. For more on moving subdocuments, see "Rearranging a Master Document," on page 589.
4. Select both subdocuments by clicking their subdocument icons. (Press and hold Shift while you select the second subdocument.)
5. Click Merge Subdocument on the Outlining toolbar. The second subdocument is combined with the first.

> **Note** When Word combines subdocuments, the first file "takes on" the addition of the new data and everything is saved into that file.

Separating Subdocuments

If you create a new topic or want to divide a subdocument into two, simply create a new heading at the point where you want to make the break (or raise an existing heading to a Heading 1 level), and then click Split Subdocument on the Outlining toolbar. The subdocument is divided at the insertion point.

Converting Subdocuments

Depending on the nature of the document you're creating, you might want to convert all the subdocuments back to a single document. This is an easy process. Start with the master document open and display the document in Outline view. Select the first subdocument you want to convert, and then press and hold Shift while clicking subsequent subdocuments.

When you've selected all the subdocuments you want to convert, click Remove Subdocument on the Outlining toolbar. The subdocument icons and boundaries are removed, and the subdocuments become part of the master document—once again, you have a whole document. Save your file by choosing File, Save, or by pressing Ctrl+S.

Printing a Master Document

When you're ready to print your master document, begin by opening the master document and expanding the document display to the level you want to print. First click Expand Subdocuments on the Outlining toolbar to show the headings of all subdocuments, and then use the Expand buttons to expand the text level as desired. Finally, change to Print Layout view by choosing View, Print Layout, or clicking Print Layout View to the left of the horizontal scroll bar.

Choose File, Print, select any necessary print options, and then click Print. The entire master document, including the subdocument text, is printed.

Tip **Get a bird's-eye view**
Take a look at the document as it will appear in print by choosing File, Print Preview. You can select a multi-page view to see the overall look applied to the combined subdocuments in the master document. Click Close to return to the Print Layout view and make any necessary changes before printing.

Troubleshooting

The master document is incomplete when printed

If you find that some sections are missing when you print your master document, return to Outline view and scroll through the document to make sure all sections have been expanded. Anything left collapsed will not be printed, so make sure that you expand the entire document, if that's your intention, before selecting Print.

Managing Master Documents

As you can see, working with master and subdocuments is a great way to manage and manipulate large files. The only downside to master documents is the sometimes complicated task of keeping your files straight. Some procedures you take for granted with ordinary files—such as saving, opening, renaming, and moving—take a little more thought when it comes to working with master documents. Here are some reminders for times when you need to manage your master document files.

Saving Subdocument Files

Word saves the master document and all subdocuments when you choose File, Save or press Ctrl+S. The master document is saved under the name you entered the first time you saved the file, and Word names all the subdocuments automatically, using the first words of each heading as the file name. If you have several headings with the same title, Word adds numbers to the file names, such as "Lesson Plan1," "Lesson Plan2," and so on.

If you want to save a master document to a new location, choose File, Save As. Remember to create a new folder for the new master document and files. Then you'll need to select each subdocument and use Save As to save it to the new folder. Otherwise, the next time you open your master document, you'll see an error message telling you that the subdocument cannot be found. Click Close to save the file and return to the document.

Renaming Subdocuments

If you want to rename a subdocument, start in the master document and select the subdocument you want to rename. Then choose File, Save As. When the Save As dialog box appears, enter the new name for the file, and then click Save. Because you renamed the file from within the master document, the link will be updated and preserved within the master document.

Selecting Subdocuments

One of the tricks to dividing a document into subdocuments accurately is displaying and selecting the text you want to include. Make sure that you expand the selection fully before clicking Create Subdocument; otherwise, Word might not include all the text you want in the new subdocument.

> **Note** If you don't get the whole subdocument the first time, click Remove Subdocument to merge the text back into the master document, and then select all the text for the subdocument again and click Create Subdocument.

Chapter 21

Generating First-Class Tables of Contents and Related Elements

No matter where you're going, you need a good road map to get there. Even if you're the type of person who refuses to stop for directions, having a good table of contents (TOC) handy when you need to find something quickly in a long document can be a lifesaver. It's three minutes until the board meeting and you can't remember the name for the new program you're championing (oops). Where's that section on fall programs? If only you'd added that TOC…

A TOC lists the important headings in your document, giving you a quick glance at the topics, along with page numbers, so that you can easily move to the parts of the document you want. Whether you're creating a print document or a Web page, you can generate the tables you need for reference using Word's TOC feature.

This chapter introduces you not only to the TOC feature in Word, but also to other quick-look reference tables, including the table of authorities and the table of figures. You'll learn to create, edit, customize, and update your table of contents and add entries for special reference tables that make it easy to locate figures, citations, and more in your long documents.

Tips for Creating an Effective TOC

Headings are the real secret to creating a helpful table of contents. If you've written clear, understandable headings, your readers will know where to turn for the information they want. The next consideration is the way in which you format those headings—if you don't use styles Word recognizes, the program won't collect the headings the way you want.To create the TOC you want, keep these guidelines in mind:

- **Use Word's built-in heading styles—or create your custom styles based on them.** When you're working in Outline view or working with master documents, it's important that you use Word's built-in heading styles—Heading 1, Heading 2, and Heading 3. Additionally, you can use the various outline levels—1 through 9—but any other style won't be included in the table of contents Word generates for you.

- **Make your headings clear and concise.** The best headings are short—between four and ten words—and communicate the subject clearly. The headings for your document will vary, of course, depending on content, but if your objective is to help readers find what they want quickly, you'll be closer to meeting your goal if you keep your headings short, sweet, and smart.
- **Avoid confusing headings.** If the tone of your document is conversationally hip, you might be tempted to throw in little humorous sayings or quips as headings throughout your text. As a wise editor once asked, "Would readers understand what this heading means if they opened the book at this page?" If helping readers is your main goal, avoid phrases that might confuse them.

You can include literally any text in your document as part of the TOC by selecting entries manually. For more information on manual table of contents entries, see "Adding TOC Entries Manually," on page 597.

Creating a TOC

Once you've checked your headings to make sure they're clear and concise and that you've assigned a heading style Word will recognize, you can generate the table of contents. Here are the steps to follow:

1. Place the insertion point where you want to add the table of contents.
2. Choose Insert, Reference, Index And Tables. The Index And Tables dialog box appears.
3. Click the Table Of Contents tab. Here you choose options for the table of contents you generate, as shown in Figure 21-1.

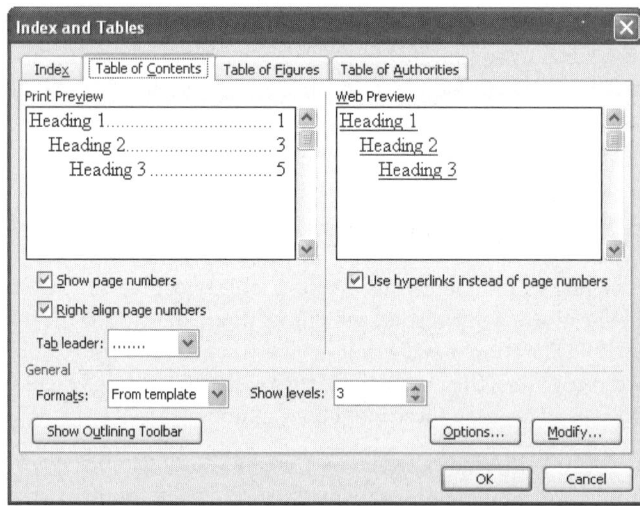

Figure 21-1. You generate a table of contents using the Index And Tables dialog box.

4 By default, Word right-aligns the page numbers in your table of contents. If you want no page number displayed, clear the Show Page Numbers check box; if you want to left-align the page numbers, clear the Right Align Page Numbers check box.

5 Click the Tab Leader arrow. Click the leader character you want to use, if any. You can choose from None, periods, en dashes (–), or em dashes (—).

6 Click OK to generate the TOC. Word places the table at the insertion point, as shown in Figure 21-2.

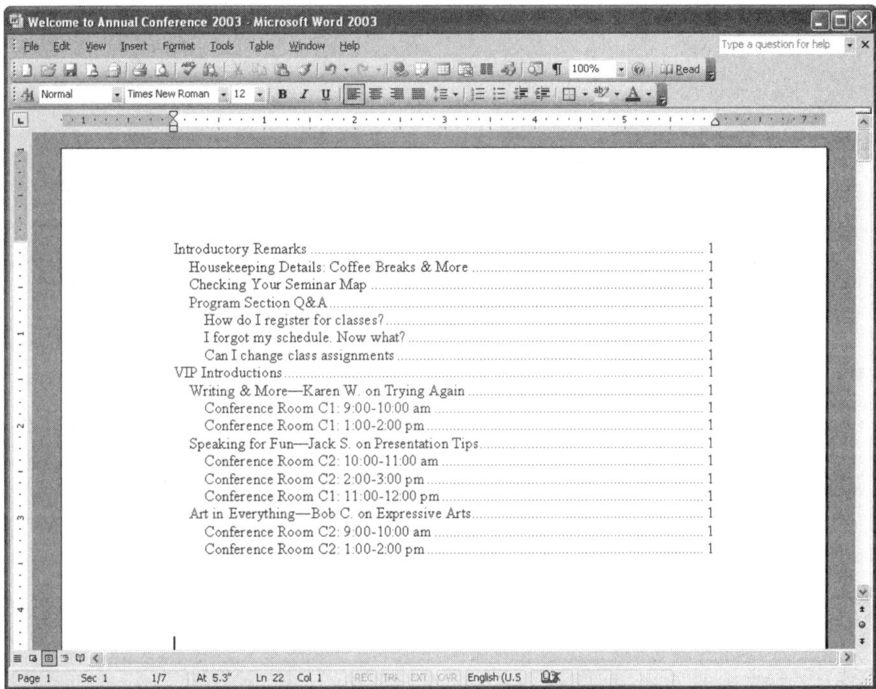

Figure 21-2. The table of contents Word generates by default right-aligns page numbers and includes dot leaders.

> **Tip** **Take a look at your TOC**
>
> You can view the table of contents you create in two different ways: when you change to Print Layout view, you see the TOC complete with page numbers and leaders; if you display the TOC in Web Layout view, you'll see hyperlinks in the document.

Adding TOC Entries Manually

You aren't limited to using headings in your table of contents. You can select any word or phrase in your document for inclusion in the TOC by following these steps:

1 Select the text you want to use in the TOC.

2. Press Alt+Shift+O. The Mark Table Of Contents Entry dialog box appears, as shown in Figure 21-3. The entry you selected appears in the Entry box.

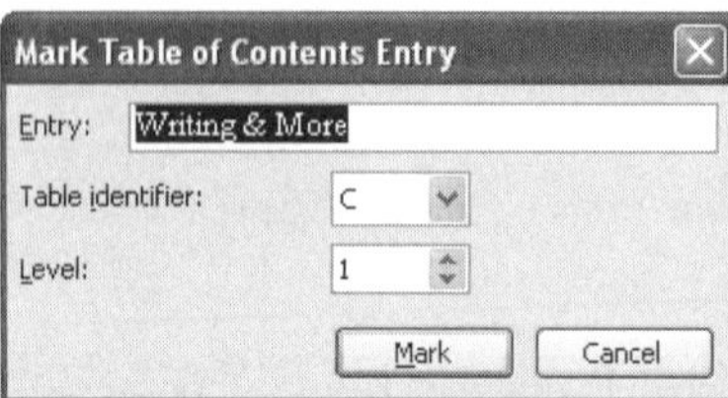

Figure 21-3. Enter TOC entries manually in the Mark Table Of Contents Entry dialog box.

3. If you use more than one TOC listing in a document, click the Table Identifier arrow to assign this entry to a TOC. (This step is unnecessary if you're creating only one TOC at a time.)
4. Enter the level at which you want the entry to be listed in the Level box. The first-level entry is the default.
5. Click Mark to add the entry. Word adds the table of contents field code to the entry.
6. For subsequent entries, select the text you want to use in your document, click in the Entry box (which causes the word to be added to the box), and then click Mark.
7. When you're finished adding entries, click Close.

Tip **Display only the entries you want to see**
If you want your table of contents to include only the entries you've added manually, clear the Styles and Outline Levels check boxes in the Table Of Contents Options dialog box. If you want all the elements included, leave those items selected and select the Table Entry Fields check box as well.

Next, to generate the table of contents to include the manual TOC entries, follow these steps:

1. Place the insertion point where you want to insert the TOC.
2. Choose Insert, Reference, Index And Tables.
3. Click Options in the Table Of Contents tab.
4. In the Table Of Contents Options dialog box, select the Table Entry Fields check box. This adds the TOC entries to the table of contents. (To find out more about the Table Of Contents Options dialog box, see "Customizing a TOC" on page 602.)
5. Click OK twice to close the dialog boxes; if you are replacing an existing TOC, click OK once more to confirm the operation. Word adds the new TOC at the insertion point.

Choosing a Format

The simple table of contents format gives you a standard TOC with right-aligned page numbers, dot leaders, and left-aligned headings. You can choose from a number of specially designed TOC formats so that your table of contents fits the style of your publication.

You can choose a format for your table of contents when you first generate it. When you choose Insert, Reference, Index And Tables and the Index And Tables dialog box appears, click the Formats arrow in the Table Of Contents tab. The formats shown there—From Template, Classic, Distinctive, Fancy, Modern, Formal, and Simple—offer different combinations of text styles for your TOC. Click the one you want; the style is shown in the Print Preview and Web Preview windows. When you find the one you want, click OK. The table of contents is created and formats are assigned as you selected.

Tip **Update the TOC format after the fact**

If you want to change the format for a table of contents you've already created, select the table, and then choose Insert, Reference, Index And Tables. Click the Table Of Contents tab, select the Formats arrow, and then choose the style you want. Finally, click OK. Word displays a message box asking whether you want to replace the selected TOC. Click Yes to replace the selected TOC, and then Word updates the TOC with the new format.

Troubleshooting

Headings are missing in my TOC

After you generate a table of contents for your Word document, review the document and check your headings carefully. If any headings are missing in the TOC, determine whether you've added text boxes or callouts in the drawing layer.

Word creates your table of contents by gathering all the headings and table of contents entry fields; if you've added text to the drawing layer, the entries won't be found automatically. To add these items to the TOC, just select the items, copy them, and paste them on the text layer. Finally, press F9 to update the TOC.

Editing and Updating a TOC

As you work with your document, you might move sections around and add and edit headings and text. That means that as soon as you make a heading change, your TOC is out of date because it won't reflect your most recent changes. You can update the table of contents in two different ways:

Update TOC

- Press F9 to update the table of contents.
- Click Update TOC on the Outlining toolbar to update the TOC.

Word searches the document and updates the TOC to reflect any changes you've made to headings.

Go To TOC

You can also move to the table of contents in case you want to do additional formatting or editing there. Just click Go To TOC on the Outlining toolbar. The display moves to the TOC so that you can make your changes.

Preparing a TOC for the Web

When you generate a table of contents for your document, a preview for the TOC in the Web page appears next to the TOC print preview in the Table Of Contents tab in the Index And Tables dialog box. Try out a Web TOC in your document by placing the insertion point where you want to add the TOC, clicking Insert, Reference, Index And Tables, and then clicking the Table Of Contents tab. Make sure the Use Hyperlinks Instead Of Page Numbers check box is selected, and then click OK. The TOC is added at the insertion point. To see the TOC in Web format, choose View, Web Layout. The TOC appears as a table of active hyperlinks, as shown in Figure 21-4, each of which takes you to the corresponding document section.

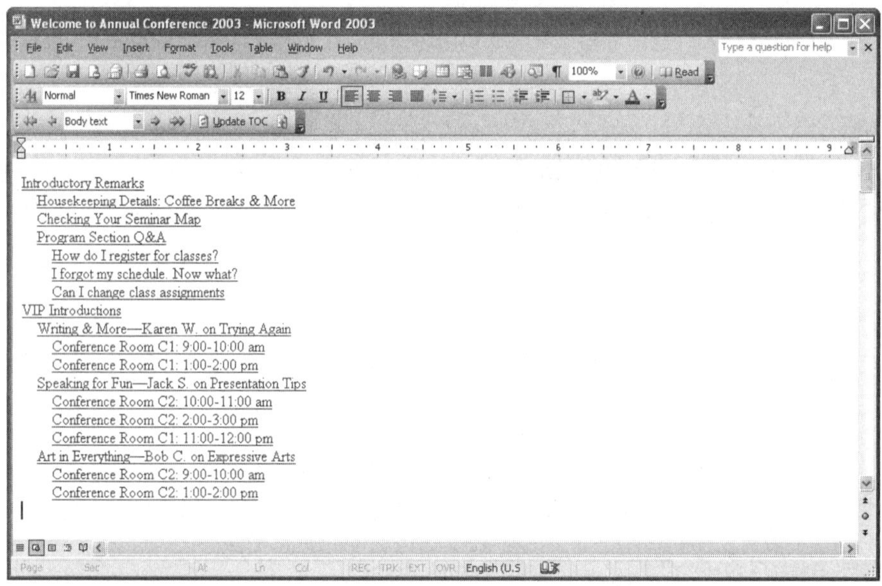

Figure 21-4. When you display Web Layout view, you'll see hyperlinks in your Web TOC.

Creating a Web TOC in a Frame

If you use frames in your Web page, you have the ability to show more than one item, file, or image on the screen at any one time. Using a TOC frame in your document allows your users to access the various sections of a document easily. By simply clicking a topic heading in the TOC frame, users can display the content of a topic in another frame.

Just as with traditional TOCs for your document, you must use Word's built-in heading styles in order for Word to recognize the headings for the table of contents. If the headings are based on the built-in styles, you can automatically create a TOC that appears in the left frame of a framed Web page. You can click the link in the left frame, and the frame on the right shows the page you've selected.

To create the table of contents in your Web page, follow these steps:

1. Select Format, Frames, Table Of Contents In Frame.
2. If prompted, click Yes, and then save the document. Word displays the Web page, with the new TOC in the left frame, as shown in Figure 21-5.

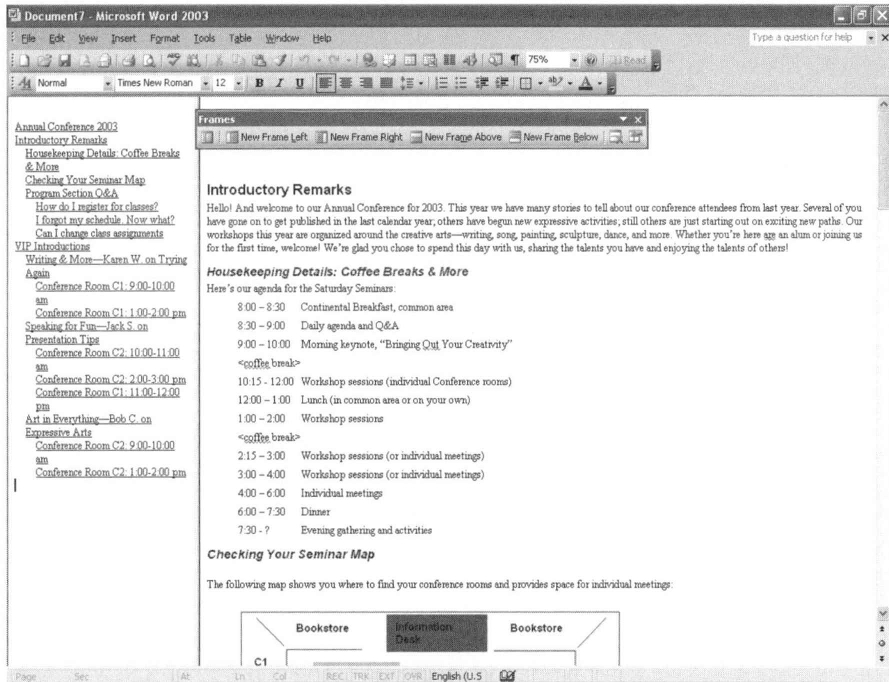

Figure 21-5. You can create a table of contents in the left frame of your Web page.

To learn more about working with frames in your Web pages, see Chapter 26, "Creating Professional Web Sites."

Note If you've created a table of contents for your Web page and the TOC appears in a Web frame, click inside the TOC frame before you press F9 to update; otherwise, the table will not be updated correctly.

Customizing a TOC

You can make additional changes to your table of contents by customizing both the elements you include in the TOC and the styles you use to include them. Figure 21-6 shows the Table Of Contents Options dialog box and the features available to you. To display these options, choose Insert, Reference, Index And Tables, and then select theTable Of Contents tab. Finally, click Options.

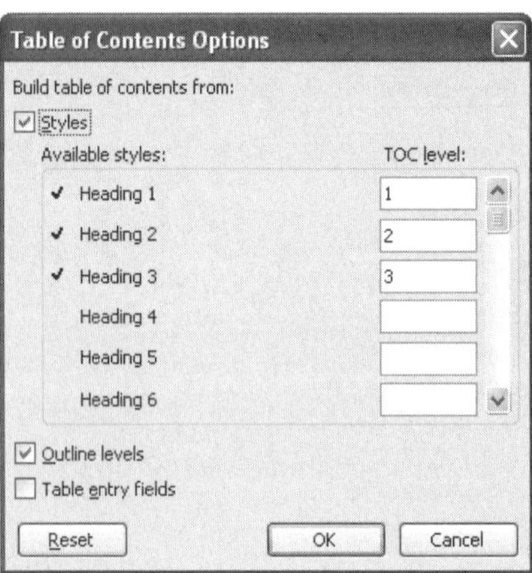

Figure 21-6. You can choose the elements you want to use in the Table Of Contents Options dialog box.

In the Table Of Contents Options dialog box, you can also select the styles you apply to the different elements in your table of contents. For example, in Figure 21-6, Headings 1, 2, and 3 are assigned to TOC levels 1, 2, and 3. If you choose, however, you can scroll down through the list to find other styles in your document—either styles you've created or existing styles—and then enter a TOC level in the text boxes on the right. The styles and levels you select are included in the TOC when it's generated. Click OK to update the table of contents.

Note If you want to undo your selections and reset the options to their default settings, click Reset in the Table Of Contents Options dialog box.

Tip **Modify styles in your document template**

If you've selected From Template in the Formats list in the Table Of Contents tab, the Modify button is enabled. When you click Modify, the Style dialog box appears, and you're given the choice of adding, deleting, or changing the styles used in the table of contents. When you click Modify in the Style dialog box, the Modify Style dialog box appears, so that you can make font and formatting changes to the selected style.

Incorporating Other Reference Tables

TOCs aren't the only reference tables you'll use as you work with long documents. If you use illustrations, tables, diagrams, or equations, you'll like having the choice of numbering and labeling those elements automatically. If you work with legal briefings and citations, the ability to create a table of authorities will save you considerable time and trouble.

Building a Table of Figures

When you have Word generate a table of figures to use as a reference tool in your document, Word searches for and collects the figure captions in your document. This means that you need to set up your captions before you generate the table.

Adding Captions

First things first. Start by adding labels to the items you want to include in your table of figures. You can add captions while you work by using Word's AutoCaption feature. Here are the steps to follow:

1. Choose Insert, Reference, Caption. The Caption dialog box appears.
2. Click AutoCaption. The AutoCaption dialog box, shown in Figure 21-7, appears.

Figure 21-7. AutoCaption enables you to add labels and numbers to your figures automatically.

3. In the Add Caption When Inserting box, select the check boxes next to the elements for which you want to add captions.
4. In the Options section, choose the label you want to use, click the Position arrow, and then select Above Item or Below Item.
5. Click OK to have Word search for and update the elements in your document.

Chapter 21

Note To view and work with the various options available for your table of figures, choose Insert, Reference, Index And Tables, and then click the Table Of Figures tab.

Controlling Figure Numbering

If you want to add figure numbering to your captions, choose Insert, Reference, Caption to display the Caption dialog box. Select the element to which you want to add the numbering (or update your other caption choices), and then click Numbering. The Caption Numbering dialog box appears, as shown in Figure 21-8.

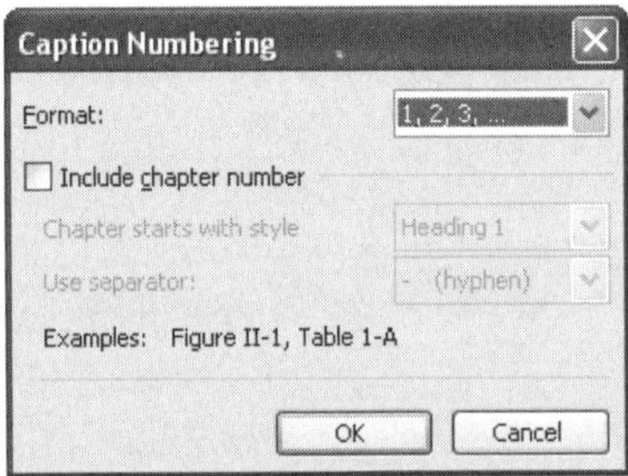

Figure 21-8. The Caption Numbering dialog box enables you to choose the format and style of the numbering sequence.

Begin by choosing the format you want to use for the numbering sequence. You can choose the traditional 1, 2, 3 or A, B, C, or you can choose roman numerals for figure numbering in the Format list box. If you want to include chapter numbers (which Word picks up from the text), select the Include Chapter Number check box. Next, specify the first heading style in the chapter (this showsWord where to begin looking), and then select a separator character from the Use Separator list box (Word will place this between the chapter number and the figure number in the caption). Click OK to save the settings. When you add your next figure, the caption will be applied automatically.

Generating a Table of Figures

After you've added captions to your illustrations by choosing Insert, Reference, Caption, you can use those captions to create a table of the figures in your document. Follow these steps to generate a table of figures:

1. Place the insertion point where you want to create the table of figures.
2. Click Insert, Reference, Index And Tables. The Index And Tables dialog box appears.
3. Click the Table Of Figures tab. The default selections for the table are displayed in the preview boxes, as shown in Figure 21-9.

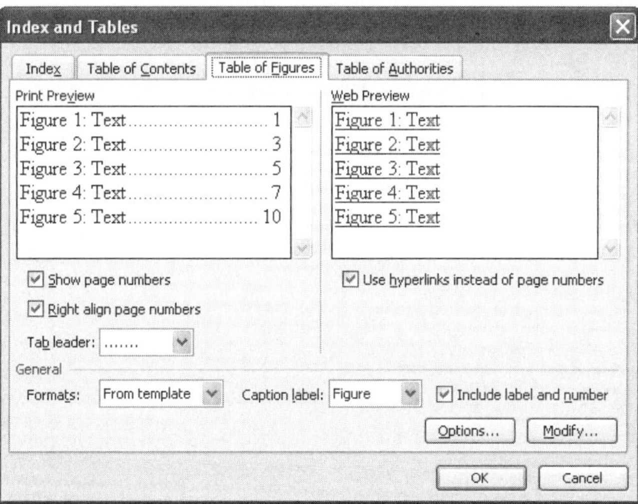

Figure 21-9. The preview boxes in the Index and Tables dialog box show the default selections.

4 Change the settings as needed, and then click OK to create the table. The table of figures is placed in the document at the insertion point.

Building a Table of Authorities

A table of authorities is a more specialized table reference that helps you track, compile, and display citations in your document.You'll use this feature most often for legal documents that reference cases, rules, treaties, and other documents. Before you can create a table of citations, obviously, you need to have placed those citations within the body of the document.

Adding Citations Manually

You can easily track citations for inclusion in the table of authorities as you work in your document. To begin the process of adding a citation, follow these steps:

1 Select the citation in the document.

2 Press Alt+Shift+I. The Mark Citation dialog box appears with the selected citation displayed in the Selected Text box, as shown in Figure 21-10.

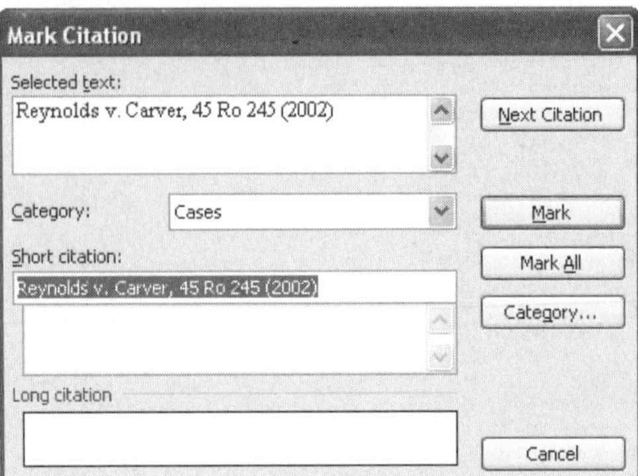

Figure 21-10. Use the Mark Citation dialog box to include citations in your table of authorities.

3. Click the Category arrow, and then choose the type of citation you're creating.
4. Edit the citation, if needed, in the Short Citation box.
5. Click Mark. Word adds the necessary codes to your document to identify the citation for inclusion in the table of authorities.
6. In your document, select another citation, and then click in the Selected Text box. This adds the citation to the box. Again, click Mark to add the citation.
7. Click Close to close the dialog box when you're finished adding citations.

Tip **Add citations directly**

You can also add citations from the Table Of Authorities tab in the Index And Tables dialog box. To display the tab, choose Insert, Reference, Index And Tables, and then click the Table Of Authorities tab. Click Mark Citation to display the Mark Citation dialog box. Enter your citation as needed, and then click Mark to complete the entry.

Generating the Table of Authorities

After you've entered the citations you want to reference, you can start the process of creating a table of authorities by following these steps:

1. Click Insert, References, Index And Tables.
2. Click the Table Of Authorities tab to choose the settings for the table of authorities you create, as shown in Figure 21-11.

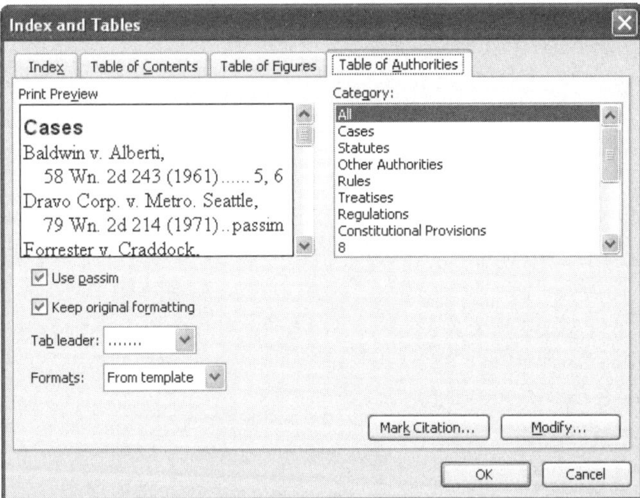

Figure 21-11. The Table Of Authorities tab includes everything you need for entering and formatting the table.

3. Choose your category from the list on the right.
4. Choose the formatting and styles you want, and then click OK to create the table of authorities.

> **Note** If you've created multiple tables in your document, be sure to update each table independently. To update, click in the table, and then press F9.

Chapter 22

Creating Effective Indexes

If you're creating a long document that covers a lot of ground—a textbook on the principles of modern economics, a procedural manual for a new computer program, or a parts catalog for an auto supply store—it's important for readers to find the subjects they're looking for. Creating a good index is part of making your document accessible for readers, by providing a listing of topics and subtopics and the pages on which they can be found. It's been said that your table of contents might be what helps readers decide whether to read your document in the first place, but the index determines whether or not they'll come back to it. If your index helps readers find what they're looking for quickly, they'll turn to it again and again.

In this chapter, you'll learn how to create indexes for your Word documents. Whether you create entries one by one or use a table to automate index entries, you'll find the process fairly intuitive and fast.

Constructing a Good Index

There are a number of things you can do to ensure that you create an index that readers will use. Think of the various indexes you've used in the past—no doubt some were better than others. Some seemed to lack all the main topics you were looking for, or they seemed disorganized. Here are some characteristics you should be sure to check in the indexes you create:

- **Usability** An index is first and foremost a reader service. Make sure that you've included all major topics and that you've thought through the alternative ways readers might be looking for those topics. Include topics, subtopics, and references to other topics for related information (for example, "*See* Parenting teens").
- **Readability** Using terms your readers will recognize—whether or not they're familiar with the content of your document—is important. If you're unsure about the various ways a reader might reference a certain topic, ask around. Talk to others on your team or in your department to make sure you've used words and phrases that will be easily understood.

- **Cross-references** Cross-references in an index refer readers to other topics where they'll find more information. For example, a listing with a subentry that sends others to the section on *Needs assessment* might look like this:

  Feasibility studies, 3-10
  Creating audience surveys, 3-4. *See* Needs assessment
  Hosting focus groups, 4-6
  Tabulating results, 6-8

- **Logical structure** One mistake new indexers often make is to include every important-sounding word—plus the kitchen sink. You'll help your readers find what they are looking for if you think carefully through your index. Which topics are most important? How many different ways might a reader refer to them? What are the words that will be searched for most often?

Note **Ask for feedback on your topic list**
After you identify key words and phrases for your index, create a list and send it to others in your department, asking for input, additions, and suggestions. Testing the topics in your index before you create it can save you editing time later.

Note **Find the index topics you need**
One place you can get clues for important index terms is your table of contents. Which words and phrases are used in your headings? Definitely include those topics in your index and look for plenty of opportunities to create subentries from the topics within those sections.

Indexing with Word

Creating indexes in Word is an interactive process that is part hands-on and part automatic. You create a Word index in three basic stages:

1. Mark index entries in your document (or create a concordance file, which allows you to mark index entries automatically).
2. Choose Insert, Reference, Index And Tables, and then click the Index tab to set indexing options, which control the way the index is placed and formatted in your document.
3. Word then sorts all the index entries in alphabetical order, adds the page numbers, and deletes any repeated entries. Figure 22-1 shows an example of a completed index.

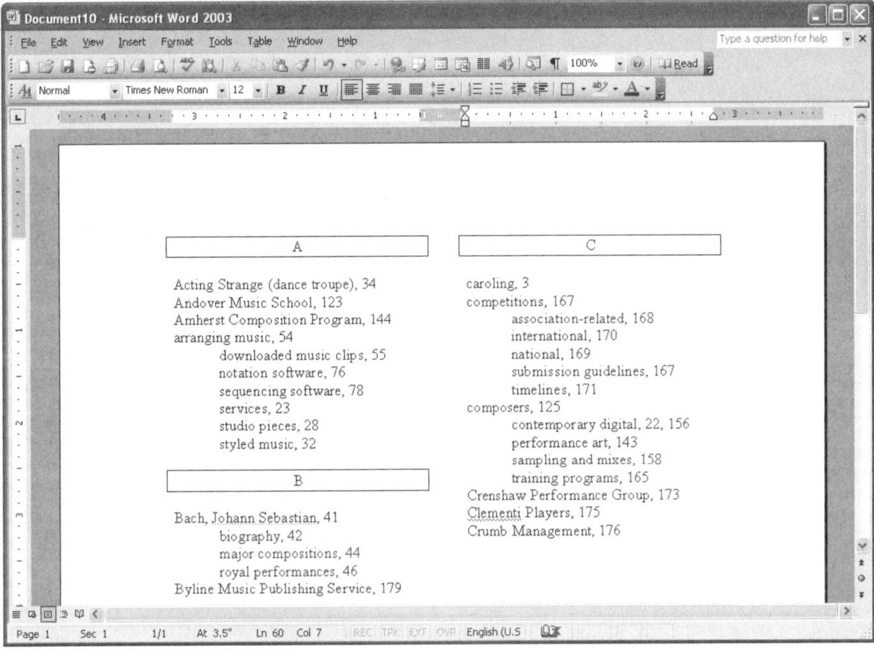

Figure 22-1. Word alphabetizes your entries, subordinates subentries, and adds alphabetic headings.

¶ Show/Hide

When Word compiles your index, the program inserts codes that mark the beginning and end of a topic and lists the page numbers on which the topics appear. Word marks each entry with the code XE, but the codes are hidden.You can display the hidden codes by clicking Show/Hide on the Standard toolbar.

Tip **Use a concordance file to add entries automatically**

If there are terms you're sure to include in your index, you can create them in a concordance file. Word will use the file to quickly mark the index entries you want. For more about creating a concordance file, see "AutoMarking Entries with a Concordance File," on page 619.

Creating Index Entries

Word makes it easy for you to enter index entries as you go—and once you display the Mark Index Entry dialog box, you can mark additional entries, add subentries, and add cross-references and page ranges.

Marking Index Entries

You can create an index entry in two different ways:

- If you want to begin with text that is already in the document, select and use existing text.
- If you want to add an entry that is not based on an existing word or phrase in your document, click to place the insertion point in the paragraph where you want to add the index entry.

To add index entries, follow these steps:

1. Select the text or place the insertion point, and then press Alt+Shift+X. The Mark Index Entry dialog box appears, as shown in Figure 22-2.

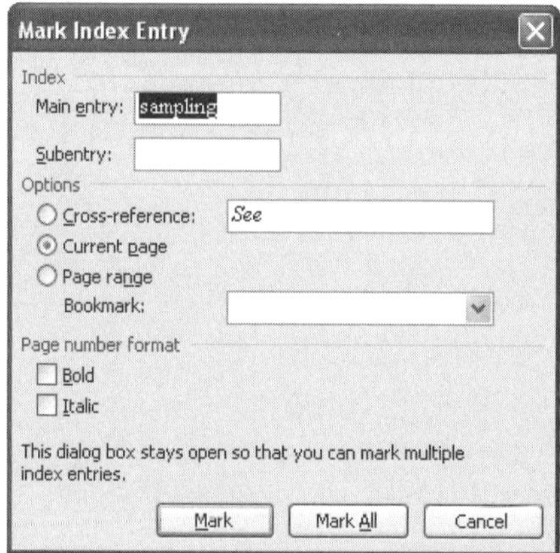

Figure 22-2. You use the Mark Index Entry dialog box to enter index entries and subentries.

2. If you selected text before opening the Mark Index Entry dialog box, the text appears in the Main Entry box. If necessary, edit the text that appears. If you placed the insertion point rather than selecting text, type the entry you want in the Main Entry box.
3. Click Mark to mark the entry, and then click Close to close the dialog box.

> **Tip** **Create clear index entries**
> Edit the entry in the Mark Index Entry dialog box to make it as clear as possible. For example, instead of a phrase that appears in your document, such as "served in the state legislature," you might enter "legislature," or "government service."

Creating Subentries

A subentry is a secondary topic you use to narrow the search on a specific topic. For example, if your report is about a new HR training program your company offers, one main index entry and the related subentries might look like this:

Life Essentials / Work Skills program, 5
    Overview, 6
    Program timeline, 7
    Reporting procedures, 7
    Retreat sessions, 8
    Training opportunities, 8

A subentry provides readers with additional references they can look up. It also adds depth and functionality to your index as a whole, and it makes reading the index easier on the eye.

Here's a quick way to enter subentries if you want to avoid repeated clicks in the dialog box: Just type the main entry and the subentry in the Mark Index Entry dialog box, separating the entries with a colon. You can use this technique to create up to seven levels of subentries, although an index that complex would no doubt baffle your readers! For best results, stick to one or perhaps two subentry levels. Examples of subentries entered in this way include the following:

Life Essentials / Work Skills program: Overview
    Life Essentials / Work Skills program: Program timeline
    Life Essentials / Work Skills program: Reporting procedures
    Life Essentials / Work Skills program: Retreat sessions
    Life Essentials / Work Skills program: Training opportunities

> **Tip** **Divide long subentry lists**
> If you find yourself entering too many subentries for a particular topic, you might want to create another main entry to divide the list. If your index lists a whole column of subentries, your readers might get lost in the list and not remember the main entry heading above.

Selecting Repeated Entries

When you're putting together a quick index and want to reference all occurrences of a particular word or phrase, you can do that easily using the Mark Index Entry dialog box. Start by selecting the text you want to index, and then pressing Alt+Shift+X to display the Mark Index Entry dialog box. Change the Main Entry text to show the entry you want, and then enter a subentry, if you want to include one. Finally, click Mark All. Word searches for the word or phrase and applies an index entry to every occurrence.

Note One of the limitations of Mark All is that the program marks every occurrence as it appears. This means that not only will you have the same index entry for each item (which doesn't give you the flexibility of creating multiple references to the same topic), but also Word will find only the words or phrases that exactly match the text you've entered. For example, if you enter **composer**, words like *composers* will be found, but not *composing* or *composition*.

Formatting Entries

As you add index entries, you can specify formatting for the characters and page numbers, thus cutting down the editing and formatting time you'll spend after you create the index. Here are the steps to apply formatting to your index entries:

1. Select the text for the index entry.
2. Press Alt+Shift+X to display the Mark Index Entry dialog box.
3. Edit the text in the Main Entry box as needed.
4. Select the text in the Main Entry box you want to format.
5. Press Ctrl+B to apply bold, Ctrl+I for italic, or Ctrl+U for underline styles.
6. Complete the entry as desired, and then click Mark to create the entry.

Note Word won't allow you to add any specialized formatting to entries at this stage. If you add color, change the font, or make any changes beyond a change to bold, italic or underline style, the change will be applied to the selected text in the document and not to the index entry.

You can also control the format of the page numbers Word adds to the index by selecting or clearing the check boxes in the Page Number Format section of the Mark Index Entry dialog box . You might want to use bold or italic to highlight certain entries. For example, a bold page number might indicate the most in-depth coverage of an item, and an italic page number might include biographical information or reference another work.

Adding Cross-References

Not all your entries will provide page number references. Some might point readers to other topics in your index instead. A cross-reference gives readers a pointer to an entry (or group of entries) for related information. To create a cross-reference in your index, follow these steps:

1. Select the text for the index entry or position the insertion point in the document.
2. Press Alt+Shift+X to display the Mark Index Entry dialog box.
3. Enter the Main Entry text, if needed.
4. Click the Cross-Reference option.

5. After the word *See*, type the index entry you want to refer readers to. For example, you might create cross-references that look like this:

   Training sessions. *See* Retreat sessions.

Specifying Page Ranges

By default, Word assigns the index entry the number of the current page. If you select and create an entry on page 3, for example, Word shows that page number with the index entry. If you want to indicate a span of pages so that you can give your readers the full range of pages on which a specific topic is covered, you can do so by using bookmarks you've already created.

> **If you haven't created bookmarks to mark places in your document and want to find out how, see Chapter 4, "Honing Document Navigation Skills."**

To use a bookmark to indicate a page range in your index, follow these steps:

1. Press Alt+Shift+X to display the Mark Index Entry dialog box.
2. Enter the text you want in the Main Entry and Subentry boxes, if needed.
3. Click the Page Range option.
4. Click the Bookmark arrow to display the list of bookmarks in the current document, and then click the bookmark you want to use.
5. Click Mark to add the entry.

When you create the index later, Word will insert an en dash (a long dash) between the page numbers in the range. A page range entry looks like this:

Physical response to stress, 1–2

Generating the Index

Once you've marked all the entries you want to include in your index, you're ready for Word to compile the index and place it in your document. When Word compiles the index, it gathers all the entries you've marked, assigns page numbers as you've specified, and alphabetizes the entries. Finally, after you click OK, Word places the index at the insertion point.

> **Tip** **Review your document**
>
> Although you can update an index easily by pressing F9 (which means you can go back and edit your index entries if you choose), you'll lose any additional formatting choices you make after the index is compiled. So it's worth your time, *before* Word compiles the index, to go back through the document and review your index entries to make sure you haven't missed anything important. To display the index entry codes, click the Show/Hide button on the Standard toolbar. Then page through the document to review important headings, sections, and captions for inclusion in your index.

Start the process of creating the index by placing the insertion point where you want to create the index, and then clicking Insert, Reference, Index And Tables. The Index And Tables dialog box appears, with the Index tab selected, as shown in Figure 22-3. In this dialog box you'll choose the format for both text entries and page numbers.

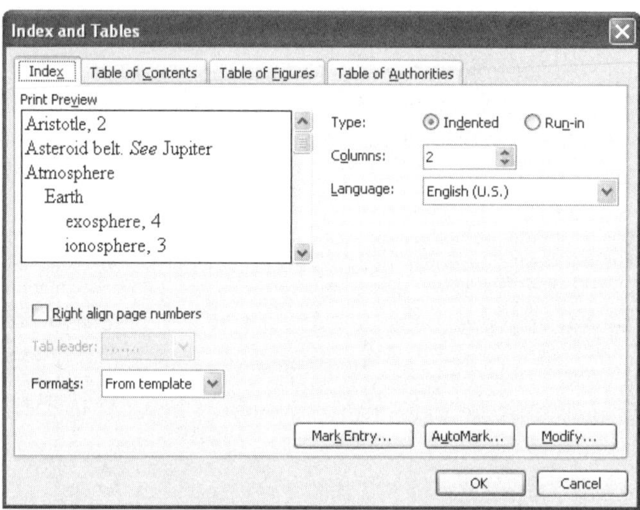

Figure 22-3. The Index tab includes the options and commands you need to create the index.

Note Notice the Mark Entry button in the Index tab in the Index And Tables dialog box. If you begin making your formatting choices for the index and suddenly remember a topic you want to include in the index, you can click Mark Entry to open the Mark Index Entry dialog box.

Choosing the Index Format

One of the most important choices you'll make in the Index tab in the Index And Tables dialog box involves the format you select for the compiled index. How do you want the index to look? When you click the Formats arrow, Word gives you the following choices:

- **From Template** The default; leaves out headings
- **Classic** Centers the alphabetic headings over the index column
- **Fancy** Encloses the heading in a shadowed box
- **Modern** Italicizes the heading and places a rule above it
- **Bulleted** Formats the heading as a block letter and centers it over the index column

- **Formal** Right-aligns page numbers, adds dot leaders, italicizes the heading, and indents the heading from the left margin
- **Simple** Removes all alphabetic headings and special formats

Choosing each of these options produces a different index format, which is displayed in the Print Preview window. To make your choice, click the Formats arrow, and then click the selection you want.

If you later decide to change the default alignment of the numbering or choose a different leader character, those changes will override the settings belonging to the different formats.

> **Tip** **Choose your format**
> Experiment with the different formats before selecting the one you want by clicking your different choices in the Formats list in the Index tab in the Index And Tables dialog box. When you choose a format style, the Print Preview window shows your selection so you can see the formatting effect of each style.

Choosing Alignment

After you create your index, you might want to make changes to the alignment and leaders the format applied. You can change these settings so that page numbers are aligned along the right edge of the index column and dot leaders are added to help lead the reader to the related page number. To change the alignment of page numbers in your index, follow these steps:

1. Display the Index And Tables dialog box by choosing Insert, References, Index And Tables.
2. In the Index tab, click the Indented option if necessary, and then select the Right Align Page Numbers check box.
3. Click the Tab Leader arrow, and select the type of leader you want.
4. Click OK to create the index and the page numbers are formatted as you selected.

Changing the Way Entries Are Displayed

Another choice in the Index And Tables dialog box allows you to choose whether you want index subentries to be run in with the index main entries or indented below them. Simply click your choice and Word will format the index accordingly.

When you choose Indented, your index subentries are indented beneath the main entries, like this:

When you choose Run-In, the subentries are placed on the same line with the main entries, like this:

Stress: controlling, 3; managing, 5; reducing, 7

Tip **Save space in cramped documents**
If you're getting to the end of your document and you're running out of space, you can use the Run-In setting to pick up extra space your index might otherwise use. To do this, choose Insert, Reference, Index And Tables, click the Index tab, select the Run-In option, and then click OK.

Troubleshooting

Error messages appear in my index

You've marked your index entries and created the index by choosing Insert, Reference, Index And Tables and clicking the Index tab. But after Word places the index in your document, you notice that error messages appear instead of the page numbers. The most likely cause is that you created the index in a subdocument rather than in the master document of your publication.

To resolve the problem, close the current document by choosing File, Close, and then open the master document. (For more information on working with master documents, see Chapter 20, "Creating and Controlling Master Documents.") Expand all subdocuments by clicking the Expand Subdocuments button on the Outlining toolbar in the Master Document, and then press F9 to update your index. The page numbers should be displayed correctly.

Changing Index Columns

Depending on the length of your document and the index you're creating, you might want to format your index in multiple columns. By default, Word compiles your index in two columns, but you might want to change this setting if you have a short index that will occupy only a partial column, or you want to run text in the column beside the index you create.

You can create up to four columns for the index. To make a change, display the Index And Tables dialog box, and on the Index tab, click the Columns up or down arrow to increase or decrease the number of columns you want.

Troubleshooting

My index columns don't line up

You've finally finished marking all the entries in your long document. You choose Insert, Reference, Index And Tables, click the Index tab, and then select the format you want. You elect to create an indented index that's displayed in three columns. With a second look over your choices, you click OK to have Word compile the index. But when you see the index on the screen, you notice that the middle column seems out of alignment with the other two. What's going on?

Although Word automatically creates a section break both before and after your index, it's possible that an extra line space is preceding the first line in the second column. Click the Show/Hide button on the Standard toolbar to display hidden paragraph marks in your document and review the top and bottom entries in each column. If you see an unwanted paragraph mark, select it and press Delete to remove it. Then press F9 to have Word update your index and balance the columns.

Updating an Index

You can update an index at any time by clicking it and pressing F9. This means that after you look at the compiled index, you can go back into the document and add entries you missed. The index is updated, and the choices you made in the Index And Tables dialog box are preserved.

Note If you've made any formatting changes, such as selecting a different format style or changing from Indented to Run-In style, Word asks whether you want to replace the existing index with the new one. If you haven't made any editing changes in the current index—or you're willing to re-enter the changes you've made—select Yes. Word replaces the existing index with the new, updated one, and you'll need to re-enter those edits. If you select Cancel, the operation is canceled and your changes are not made.

AutoMarking Entries with a Concordance File

A concordance file is really a simple table you create to track and enter index entries easily. The table you create is a two-column table: in the first column you enter the text you want Word to mark as the entry and in the second column you enter the index entry you want to use. Here are the steps to create a concordance:

Insert Table

1. Create a table in a new document by clicking the Insert Table button on the Standard toolbar, and then creating a two-column table.
2. In the first column, enter the words or phrases you want Word to mark for the entry.

3. In the second column, type the index entry for the text in the first column. Be sure to type each entry in a separate cell.
4. Save and close the concordance file.
5. Choose File, Open, select the name of the file you want to index in the Open dialog box, and then click Open.
6. Choose Index, Reference, Index And Tables. In the Index And Tables dialog box, click the Index tab.
7. Click the AutoMark button to display the Open Index AutoMark File dialog box.
8. Navigate to and select the concordance file, and then click Open. Word automatically searches your document and locates each entry with the words you specified in the concordance file. (Word marks only the first occurrence of an entry in any one paragraph.)

Inside Out

Creating a lean and effective concordance file

You think you're saving lots of time and trouble by creating a concordance file that lists topics you want to be sure to include in your index. After you finish creating and saving the list, you create the index, but you wind up with all kinds of unnecessary entries. For example, in your publication on contemporary music, you wanted to index references to *jazz*, but found instead that the word *jazz* appeared in many different places and contexts. As a result, there are many more references than you need.

A workaround for compiling huge indexes full of unnecessary AutoMarked entries is to create the majority of the index entries manually, using the Mark Index Entry dialog box (which you display by pressing Alt+Shift+X). Then use the concordance file and AutoMark in the Index tab in the Index And Tables dialog box to add to your basic index entries, including only key words or phrases that are used in the sections to which you want to refer your readers.

Chapter 23

Configuring Footnotes, Endnotes, and Cross-References

Most of us dread the kind of documents that demand the careful and painstaking attention that footnotes, endnotes, and cross-references require. Who has time to do all that notating? Luckily, Word 2003 makes it easy to insert, edit, and work with footnotes, endnotes, and cross-references in your documents. You make a few choices and enter your text, and Word takes care of the numbering, even if you move the notes from one place to another in your document. This chapter shows you how to quickly add and work with these kinds of notes—so they give you the added accuracy you need without the extra hassle.

Adding Footnotes and Endnotes

If you're working on a document that's based on research, that points to other documents, or that references a URL, you can easily add the source information at either the bottom of the page or the end of the document.

Footnotes appear in an area at the bottom of your page, with a separator line and a note reference mark to identify the note. (See Figure 23-1 for an example.) A matching note reference mark appears in the text at the place you create the footnote.

Endnotes look similar to footnotes, except that they're placed at the end of a document. Only one separator line separates the text and the endnotes, and the note reference marks are placed to the left of the noted items.

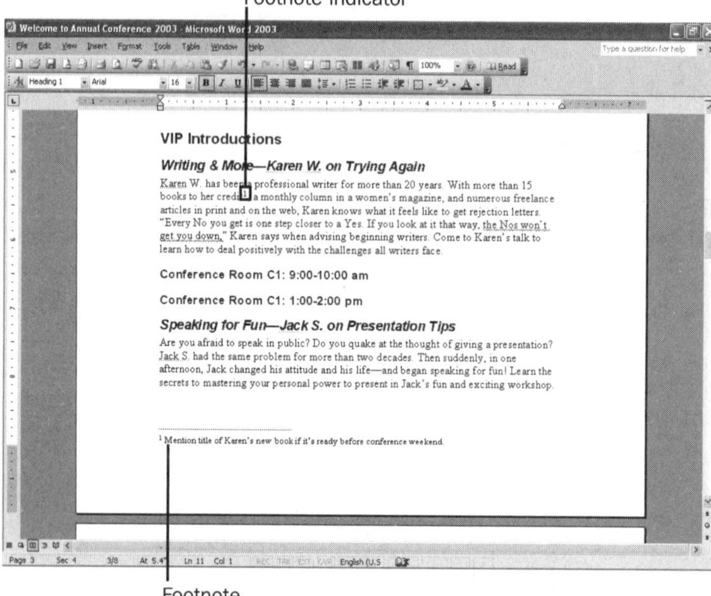

Figure 23-1. Footnotes appear at the bottom of the page and include a separator line and a note reference mark.

You can enter footnotes and endnotes of any length, but because the notes are created in a typeface that's smaller than regular text and because they take up room in your document otherwise reserved for text, your reader will be happier if you keep your footnotes and endnotes as short as possible.

Inserting Footnotes and Endnotes

When you're ready to insert a footnote or endnote in your document, follow these steps:

1. Place the insertion point where you want to add the footnote or endnote.
2. Choose Insert, Reference, Footnote. The Footnote And Endnote dialog box appears, as shown in Figure 23-2.

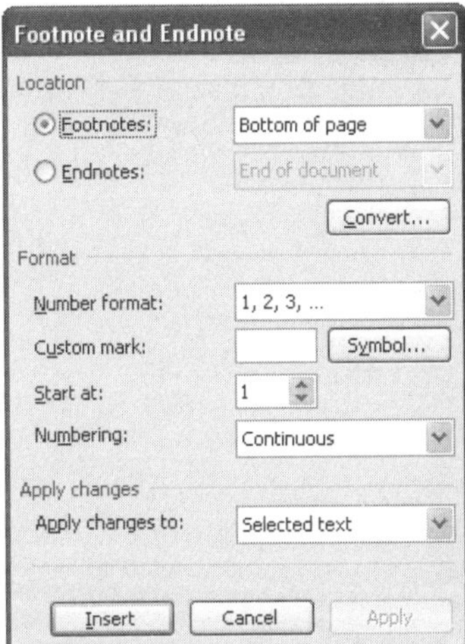

Figure 23-2. Enter footnote and endnote format choices in the Footnote And Endnote dialog box.

3 In the Location section of the Footnote And Endnote dialog box, click either the Footnotes or Endnotes option.

4 In the Format section, click the Number Format arrow, and then choose the numbering scheme you want to use for the note reference marks that identify your footnotes and endnotes. You'll find all the traditional choices—numeric, alphabetic, and roman numerals—plus something different: a collection of special symbols.

5 If you want to start the footnote or endnote with a number other than 1, click in the Start At box, and then type the number you want.

6 Click Insert to add the note. Word adds the note reference mark and, if you're viewing the document in Normal view, opens either the Footnotes pane (shown in Figure 23-3) or the Endnotes pane at the bottom of the Word window so that you can enter and later edit the note. If you're working in Print Layout view, Word places the insertion point following the footnote or endnote identifier at the bottom or end of the document.

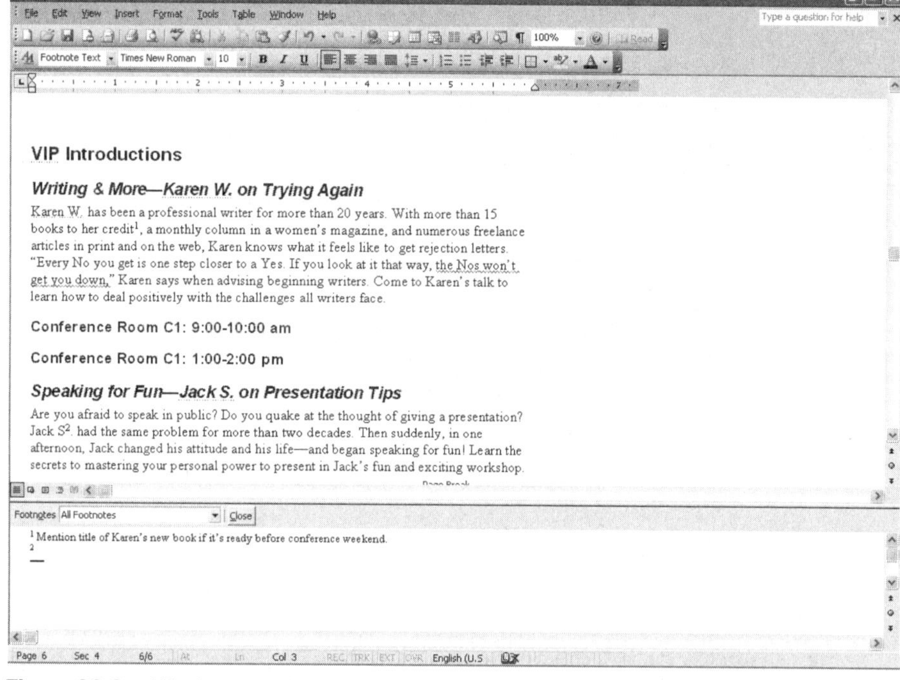

Figure 23-3. Word opens the Footnotes pane so that you can enter footnotes.

> **Tip** **Add notes in sections**
>
> If you want to apply the changes you make in the Footnote And Endnote dialog box to only a section in your document, begin by clicking in the section and displaying the dialog box by choosing Insert, Reference, Footnote. Make your changes in the dialog box, and then click the Apply Changes To arrow. Choose This Section to apply the changes only to the current section, and then click Apply.

Viewing Footnotes

As you work with the text in your document, the only clues you'll get about the placement of your footnotes and endnotes are the note reference marks inserted in the text. If you want to view the footnotes or endnotes you've entered, you can do so by displaying them as ScreenTips, by double-clicking the note reference mark, or by opening the Footnotes or Endnotes pane.

To display a footnote as a ScreenTip, position the pointer over the note reference mark in the document. The footnote appears as a tip above the pointer, as shown in Figure 23-4.

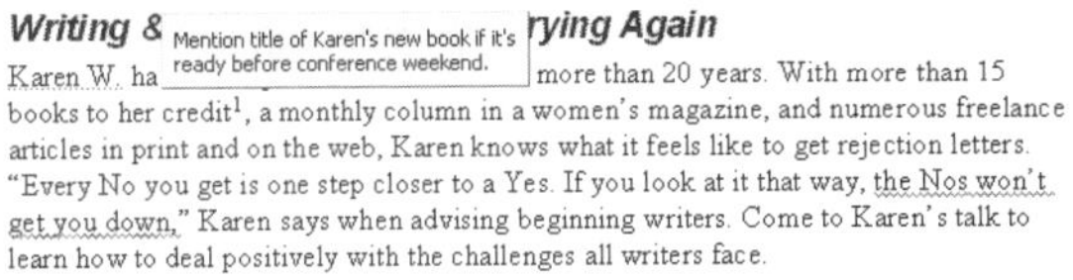

Writing & Mention title of Karen's new book if it's ready before conference weekend. **rying Again**

Karen W. ha more than 20 years. With more than 15 books to her credit[1], a monthly column in a women's magazine, and numerous freelance articles in print and on the web, Karen knows what it feels like to get rejection letters. "Every No you get is one step closer to a Yes. If you look at it that way, the Nos won't get you down," Karen says when advising beginning writers. Come to Karen's talk to learn how to deal positively with the challenges all writers face.

Figure 23-4. Displaying a footnote as a ScreenTip is a quick way to review a footnote you've entered.

> **Note** You can display a footnote or endnote in the Footnotes or Endnotes pane quickly by double-clicking the note reference mark.

To have Word display your footnotes in the Footnotes pane at the bottom of your screen, follow these steps:

1. Choose View, Normal or click the Normal View button to the left of the horizontal scroll bar.
2. Choose View, Footnotes. If you have both footnotes and endnotes, the View Footnotes dialog box appears. Click either View Footnote Area or View Endnote Area, and then click OK.

> **Note** The Footnotes option on the View menu is available only after you've chosen Insert, Reference, Footnote to add a footnote to your document.

Editing Footnotes and Endnotes

When you want to edit a footnote or endnote, you need to display the Footnotes or Endnotes pane for the item you want to edit. You can then edit and enhance the text as needed. Follow these steps:

1. Double-click the note reference mark of the footnote or endnote you want to edit. The Footnotes or Endnotes pane appears at the bottom of theWord window.
2. Edit the note as needed.
3. Click Close to close the pane.

Moving Footnotes and Endnotes

If you want to move a footnote or endnote from one position to another, select and drag the mark to the new location. If you want to move the mark to a location that's too far away to drag, you can cut and paste the mark by using Ctrl+X to cut and Ctrl+V to paste.

> **Note** If the position to which you move the footnote precedes another footnote, Word changes the numbering automatically.

Copying Footnotes and Endnotes

If you have a footnote or endnote you plan to use more than once, you can copy a note reference mark instead of typing a duplicate entry. Simply select the note reference mark, and then press and hold Ctrl while dragging the mark to the new place in the document.

Deleting Footnotes and Endnotes

When you want to remove a footnote or endnote from your document, go to the place in the document where the note reference mark appears and delete it. Simply removing the text in the Footnotes or Endnotes pane doesn't remove the note itself—Word will still keep the note reference mark in place and reserve the space at the bottom or end of your document for the note.

Troubleshooting

Deleted footnotes won't go away

If you've deleted a footnote or endnote that keeps reappearing, chances are that a portion of the note has been left behind. To find the culprit character, click the Show/Hide button on the Standard toolbar. All the paragraph marks will appear, and you can move to the footnote area and delete the stray paragraph mark. The reference in the text will then be deleted.

Adding Symbols to Footnotes

If you want to use a symbol instead of a numeric or alphabetic character as the identifier in your note reference marks, display the Footnote And Endnote dialog box by choosing Insert, Reference, Footnote. Then click Symbol. The Symbol dialog box appears, as shown in Figure 23-5. Choose the font and character you want to use, and then click OK. Word adds the symbol to the Custom Mark box in the Footnote And Endnote dialog box and, when you click Insert, the symbol is added as the note reference character in the text and in the Footnotes or Endnotes pane.

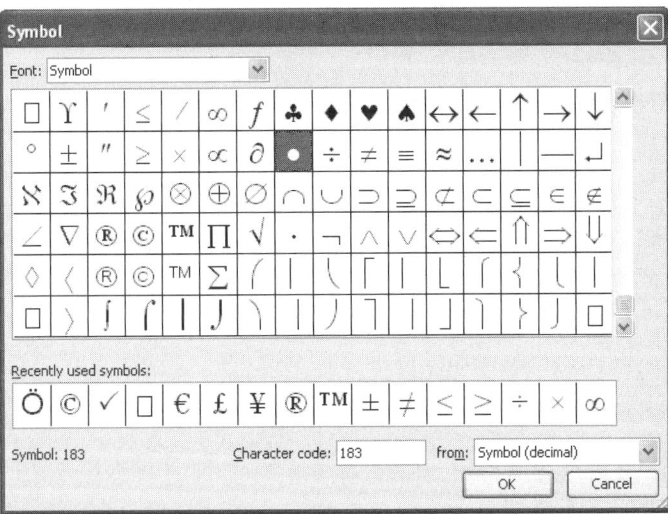

Figure 23-5. You can use symbols instead of numbers as note reference marks.

Troubleshooting

My footnotes disappear on my Web page

If you created a document, complete with footnotes and endnotes, and then saved it as a Web page, your footnotes haven't disappeared completely—they've simply been moved to the end of the Web document. The footnotes are turned into hyperlinks, so you can access them easily from within the page.

Click the note reference mark to activate the link; the footnote is then displayed in your browser. To return to the Web page, click your browser's Back button to return to the previous page.

Creating a New Separator Line

The separator line Word uses to show where the document text ends and the footnote text begins is a fairly nondescript line that extends a short distance across the page. If you want to change the separator line—perhaps to add color or choose a different line style or thickness—use the Borders And Shading dialog box to make the change. To do this, follow these steps:

1. In Normal view, choose View, Footnotes to display the Footnotes pane.
2. Click the Footnotes arrow, and then select Footnote Separator in the Footnotes list.
3. Delete the existing separator line by clicking it, and then pressing Delete.

4 Choose Format, Borders And Shading. The Borders And Shading dialog box appears.
5 Click the Borders tab.
6 In the Style list, select the border style you want.
7 Click the bottom and side segments in the Preview section to remove them, leaving only the top line.
8 Click OK to add the new separator line to the document.

Troubleshooting

My footnote is split across two pages

Sometimes getting footnotes to print just where you'd intended can be a bit tricky. You might wind up with too many additional blank lines on the page after the footnote, or you could find that your footnote has been divided, with one line appearing on the first page and a second line printing on the next page.

If you find that part of your footnote has moved to the next page, look at the margin settings for the page. The text on the page, the margins, and the footnote length all play a part in the amount of space reserved for your footnote area. Click File, Page Setup to display the Page Setup dialog box, and note the space you have entered for the margins. Try reducing the bottom margin setting to allow more room for the footnote, and then click OK to return to the document.

For best results, try to keep your footnotes short—one or two lines if possible. If you need to insert a long footnote, consider converting it to an endnote so that it can be placed at the end of the document.

Using Cross-References

When you're working on a long document in which you want to refer to other parts of that document, you can use cross-references to help readers find the information they seek. Word lets you refer to a number of different elements in your document—including captions, headings, footnotes and endnotes, and bookmarks you've created.

Tip **Expand subdocuments before referencing**

You can create cross-references only within the current document. You might create a reference at the beginning of a long report, for example, that points readers to a table in a later section that lists statistics related to a new study. You can't create a cross-reference to refer to a table in another document, however.

If you're working with master and subdocuments, be sure to expand the master document by clicking the Expand Subdocuments button on the Outlining toolbar. This makes all text accessible before you enter cross-references.

Creating a Cross-Reference

When you're ready to create a cross-reference, start by placing the insertion point where you want the cross-reference to appear in your document. Then follow these steps:

1. Add the text that refers to the cross-reference (for example, a phrase such as "To review the results of our survey, see").
2. Choose Insert, Reference, Cross-Reference. The Cross-Reference dialog box appears, as shown in Figure 23-6.

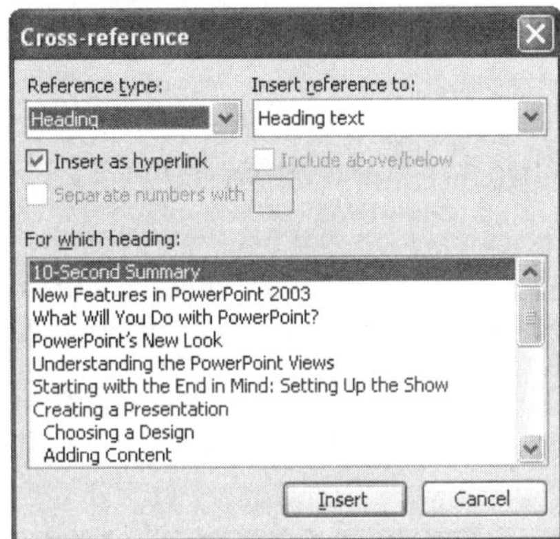

Figure 23-6. Cross-references enable you to point readers to different elements in your document.

3. Click the Reference Type arrow, and then make your selection. You can choose from the following document elements:
   - *Numbered Item*—Lists all the text entries beginning with a number throughout the document.
   - *Heading*—Shows all headings based on Word's Heading 1, 2, 3 styles or outline levels
   - *Bookmark*—Displays all the bookmarks currently listed in the document
   - *Footnote*—Shows all footnotes inserted in the document
   - *Endnote*—Lists the endnotes you have created
   - *Equation*—Shows any equations you've inserted in the document
   - *Figure*—Lists all figure references
   - *Table*—Shows all available tables in the document
4. Click the Insert Reference To arrow, and then choose the element you want Word to insert in the document. This item will be inserted at the insertion point.
5. Select the item to which you want to refer by clicking it in the For Which Numbered Item list box.

6. Click Insert, and Word adds the cross-reference to your document as you directed.
7. Click Close to return to your document.

Tip **Create links for a Web page**
If you plan to save your document as a Web page or make it available as an electronic file, you can have Word turn your cross-references into hyperlinks, so that readers can easily move from one page to another. To create links for cross-references, select the cross-reference you've created, and then display the Cross-Reference dialog box by choosing Insert, Reference, Cross-Reference. Select the Insert As Hyperlink check box, and then click Insert. The inserted cross-reference is created as a link to the other location in the document.

Modifying, Moving, and Updating Cross-References

You can edit and delete the text that introduces a cross-reference the same way you would modify any other text in your document. If you want to modify the item to which a reference refers, you need to make a different kind of change. Here are the steps:

1. Select the item inserted as the cross-reference (for example, you might select *Table 1-1*).
2. Display the Cross-Reference dialog box by choosing Insert, Reference, Cross-Reference.
3. In the For Which Numbered Item list in the Cross-Reference dialog box, click the new item to which you want the cross-reference to refer.
4. Click Insert, and then click Close to close the Cross-Reference dialog box.

Tip **Make a reference relative**
You can have Word create a relative reference to a cross-reference you enter by selecting the Include Above/Below check box in the Cross-Reference dialog box. Create your cross-reference as usual, and then after selecting the item you want inserted in the Insert Reference To list box, select the Include Above/Below check box. If the insertion point is on the same page as the section or item referenced, Word will insert "above" or "below," based on the position of the reference.

If you want to move a cross-reference, simply select the reference in your document, and then cut and paste it as you would normally. Once you have the reference in the location you want, press F9. Word updates the reference and makes the connection to the new location. If you want to update all references in a document, select the entire document before pressing F9.

Note When you want to delete a cross-reference, simply select the reference, and then delete it as you would any other text.

Troubleshooting

Cross-referencing in my document produces an error message

If you go through the steps to create a cross-reference and instead of the reference you expect, you get an error message saying, "Error! Reference source not found," check to make sure that the information you're referring to hasn't been removed from your document. If the item is still in your document but the reference still displays an error message, try fixing the problem by selecting the cross-reference and pressing F9 to update the reference. If the problem is caused by a broken link or a moved reference, the item should now be displayed properly.

Part 5

Collaborating Online and on Team Projects

Chapter 24

Working and Collaborating Online

In this era of telecommuting, long-distance associations, and on-the-move lifestyles, online communication plays a much larger role in collaboration than it has in the past. Online communication gives people a convenient way to work together by sharing documents and ideas in near real time across networks, regardless of where participants are located. To help make online communication possible, the Microsoft Office System offers a number of online collaboration features.

The online collaboration features in Word work in conjunction with other Office applications to expand the Internet and network options available to you from within Word. For example, Word works with Outlook to enable you to create and send e-mail messages; Word works with Microsoft Windows Messenger to enable you to send and receive instant messages; Word works with Microsoft Office Document Imaging (MODI) to create Tagged Image File Format (TIFF) files and fax documents; and Word works in conjunction with Microsoft Internet Explorer to provide Microsoft NetMeeting conferencing capabilities. In this chapter, you'll learn about a few of the most common online collaboration tools accessible from within Word. In particular, you'll learn how to useWord to send instant messages and e-mail messages, send faxes, conduct online conferences and meetings, and participate in Web discussions. Let's start by looking at one of the newest forms of integrated online communication—sending instant messages.

Using Instant Messaging While Working in Word

Working in conjunction with Microsoft Windows Messenger, Microsoft Network (MSN) Messenger, the Microsoft Exchange Instant Messaging (IM) Service, and Microsoft NetMeeting, Word lets you initiate and participate in instant messaging exchanges with other people who have access to instant messaging while you work in Word. When you send and receive instant messages, you can communicate back and forth in near real time. Figure 24-1 shows a sample Windows Messenger contacts window and a sample conversation window that you can use for IM communication.

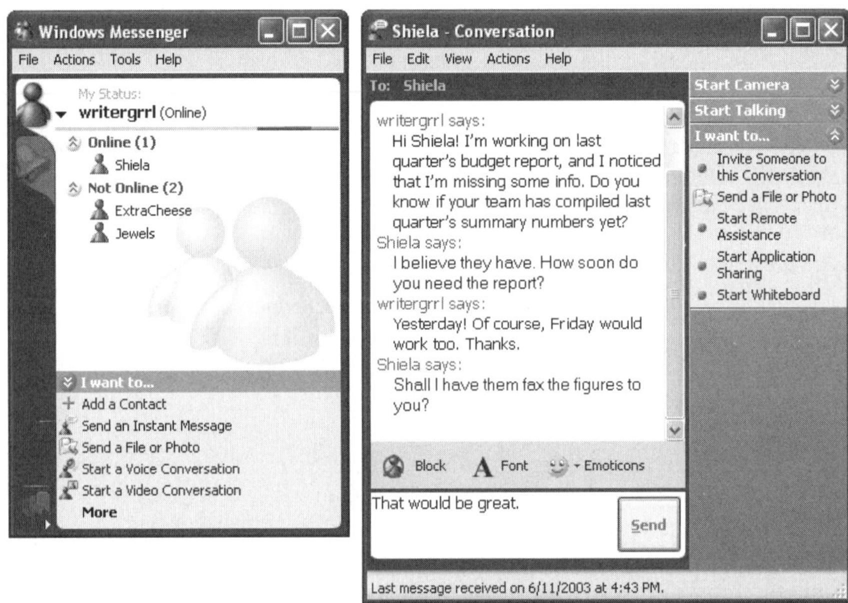

Figure 24-1. You can add contacts and initiate IM communication using Windows Messenger. The Windows Messenger window shows which contacts are online, and the conversation window displays the current conversation.

You can send instant messages to contacts who are online while you work in Word 2003. You can also send instant messages when you make changes to shared documents or workspaces. One of the easiest ways to take advantage of instant messaging is to enable Person Name smart tags. When Person Name smart tags are enabled, you can click the smart tag next to a contact's name in your document, and then open a message window or a contact's folder item for the contact if the person has a Contact folder entry in your Outlook application. To enable Person Name smart tags, follow these steps:

1. Choose Tools, AutoCorrect Options, and then click the Smart Tags tab.
2. Select the LabelText With SmartTags check box, which activates the Recognizers options.
3. In the Recognizers list, select the Person Name (Outlook E-Mail Recipients) check box, and then select the Person Name (English) check box if you're using the English-language version of Word, as shown in Figure 24-2.
4. Click OK to save the smart tag settings.

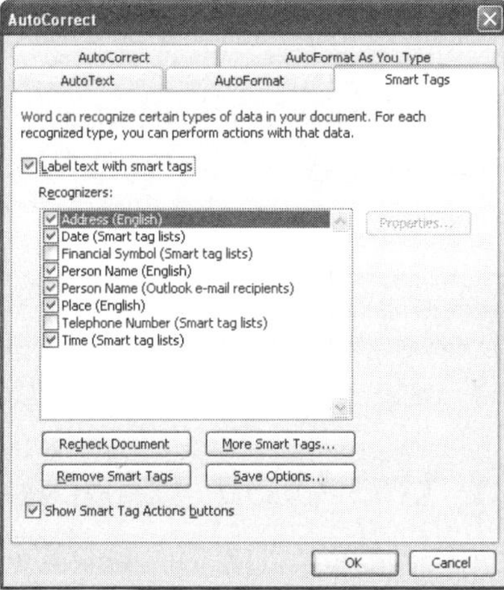

Figure 24-2. After you enable smart tags for names of individuals, these names will be accompanied by smart tags that you can click to initiate online communication right from Word documents.

Person Name Smart Tag

If smart tags are enabled to recognize names of individuals, you'll see a smart tag in your documents in association with text that is recognized as a person's name. When you see a smart tag or the telltale purple dotted lines beneath text (which you can hover the pointer over to display the smart tag), you can click the smart tag to access various communications options, such as sending an e-mail message, scheduling a meeting, inserting the contact's address, and so forth. To send a message to a contact, click the Person Name Smart Tag button and choose a message option from the menu. Then type your message and click Send.

Note Person Name smart tags become available after you complete a sentence by inserting closing punctuation (such as a period) or after you press Enter, whichever action comes first.

One caveat to using Person Name smart tags is that a contact's name and e-mail address information must be entered in your Outlook address book or your instant messaging application (such as Windows Messenger or MSN Instant Messenger), or the contact must be someone to whom you've previously sent an e-mail or instant message from Outlook or an instant messaging application. Although smart tags will appear for any text that appears to be a name, Word can insert proper addressing information into messaging applications only if a contact's addressing information is properly configured on your system or network.

> **Tip** If MSN Messenger is installed on your system, you can open it from within Word by choosing Tools, Online Collaboration, Meet Now, and then clicking the Open Messenger link. Keep in mind that before you can use this option, you must first set up NetMeeting in Internet Explorer. To do so, open Internet Explorer, choose New, Internet Call, and then work through the NetMeeting Wizard.

For more information about the ins and outs of using instant messaging as well as using instant messaging with shared documents and workspaces, see Chapter 25, "Working with Shared Documents."

Accessing the Web Using the Web Toolbar

One of the most obvious means by which Word integrates with the Web is the Web toolbar, shown in Figure 24-3. As an experienced Word user, you're probably familiar with the Web toolbar. It has been around since Word 97, and its appearance and functionality haven't changed since its introduction. Primarily, this toolbar is provided as a convenience so that you can access Web pages and browse hyperlinks included in documents displayed in Word. By default, when you open a Web page using the Web toolbar, the Web page opens in your browser.

Figure 24-3. The Web toolbar enables you to access Web pages and network locations from within Word.

To open the Web toolbar, choose View, Toolbars, Web. The Web toolbar provides buttons that are frequently found in Web browsers, as follows:

- **Back** Takes you to the previously displayed document. You can display Word documents or Web pages using the Back button.
- **Forward** Takes you to the next document if you've clicked the Back button.

> **Tip** **Move backward and forward between Web pages**
> You can use keyboard shortcuts to move backward and forward between pages while surfing the Internet. To move back, press Alt+Left Arrow, and to move forward, press Alt+Right Arrow.

- **Stop** Stops the current page loading process.
- **Refresh** Reloads the currently displayed page in Word.
- **Start Page** Opens your browser and displays the first page that appears when you open your default Web browser. A start page can be a Web site or a local file on your hard disk or network.
- **Search The Web** Opens your browser and loads the default search page.

- **Favorites** Opens your Favorites list, which can contain local files and folders as well as locations on networks and the Internet. This list is the same Favorites list available to you from within Internet Explorer.
- **Go** Provides a menu with options that enable you to open a hyperlink, move backward or forward, display the start or search page, and set the default start or search page to the currently displayed page.
- **Show Only Web Toolbar** Maximizes your viewing area by hiding all toolbars except the Web toolbar and the menu bar. When you'd like to display the hidden toolbars again, click the Show Only Web Toolbar button again.
- **Address** Lets you enter a local or an online path name to access information. You can click the Address arrow to display the same history list of links that are available from the Internet Explorer Address box.

> **Tip** **Specify a Start Page**
> You can control which Web page opens when you click the Start Page button by configuring your browser's Start Page settings. For example, in Internet Explorer, you control your start page by choosing Tools, Internet Options, and then configuring the Home Page section in the General tab in the Internet Options dialog box.

Using the Task Pane to Initiate Online-Related Tasks

The task pane introduced in Office XP continues to play a major role in Office 2003. Among the task pane's many features, you'll find a number of Web and network related options that enable you to use the task pane to integrate online capabilities as you work. In particular, you can open the task pane by choosing View, Task Pane (or pressing Ctrl+F1) and then use the Getting Started task pane along with other task pane views (accessible by clicking the task pane title bar) to perform the following Internet-related tasks:

- **Create a new blank Web page or e-mail message.** In the New Document task pane, click the Web Page or E-Mail Message link.
- **Access templates stored on your Web sites and in the online Microsoft Office Template Gallery.** In the Templates section in the New Document task pane, click the On My Web Sites or Templates On Office Online link.
- **Access Microsoft Office Online and the Office Update Web sites.** In the Word Help task pane, you can access online help as well as assistance and training from the Microsoft Online Web site. Furthermore, you can access newsgroups by clicking the Communities link, and you can visit the Office Update site by clicking the Downloads link. Finally, in the See Also section, you can link to additional help information, including Microsoft contact information.
- **Search online.** In the Search Results task pane, you can search Microsoft Office Online as well as Office Marketplace.
- **Search for additional clip art items online.** In the Clip Art task pane, click the Clip Art On Office Online link.

- **Research facts and update research tools.** In the Research task pane, you can update your research services as well as obtain new services from Office Marketplace. In addition, many research services require you to be online to benefit from their services.
- **Translate documents via the Web.** In the Research task pane, you can select Translation as your research tool, and then click the Translate Whole Document arrow to access an online translation service.
- **Share documents, schedules, lists, and other information in shared workspaces.** The Shared Workspace task pane enables you to access and work with shared documents and workgroup members.

For more information about obtaining online technical assistance from Microsoft (including information about Office On The Web features), see Chapter 1, "Gearing Up with Word 2003." For more information about using the Research task pane, see Chapter 6, "Making the Most of Research Services and Reference Tools." For more information about downloading clip art from the Web, see Chapter 11, "Adding Visual Impact with Pictures and Objects." For more information about using templates and wizards from the Microsoft Office Template Gallery, see Chapter 16, "Formatting Documents Using Templates, Wizards, Add-Ins, and XML Schemas." And for more information about working with the Document Workspace, see Chapter 25, "Working with Shared Documents."

Looking at Your Documents from the Web's Perspective

As you might know, many features in Word make the application a viable interface for creating and editing Web pages. Many Web page developers found the Web page capabilities in Word 2000 intriguing but not particularly practical, because Word automatically generated Hypertext Markup Language (HTML) source code that was bloated with lots of extra Word-specific commands. Beginning with Word 2002, the application enabled developers to strip out the extra code before sending their pages online. This makes Word much more appealing as a Web page development tool.

When you create and edit Web pages in Word, you can use the following Web-specific views:

- **Web Page Preview** Displays the current document in your Web browser so that you can see how it will look as a Web page. To preview a document as a Web page, choose File, Web Page Preview. If your Web browser is not running when you choose Web Page Preview, Word starts it automatically. You can return to your document in Word at any time.
- **Web Layout view** Enables you to work on a document while displaying it in Word in a way that simulates how the document will appear in a Web browser. For example, in Web Layout view, a document appears as one long page (without page breaks), text and tables wrap to fit the window, and backgrounds are displayed. You should work in Web Layout view when you are creating Web pages or documents that will be viewed on the screen. To change to Web Layout view, choose View, Web Layout.
- **Microsoft Script Editor** Enables you to edit Web scripts and HTML source code by editing a document's script and markup directly. You can open the Microsoft Script Editor by choosing View, HTML Source or by choosing Tools, Macro, Microsoft Script Editor. The first time you open the Script Editor, you will have to open it using the

Tools menu so that you can install the editor. After you install the editor, you can access it by using the Tools menu, and then selecting HTML Source command from the View menu, or by pressing Alt+Shift+F11.

When you're working in Web Layout view, keep in mind that Word offers a few additional configuration options for this view. Namely, you can control whether *object anchors* and *text boundaries* appear while you work. Object anchors indicate where objects are attached to paragraphs or positioned within tables, and text boundaries are dotted lines that show spacing and cell padding settings within page margins, columns, tables, and objects. To access the Object Anchors and Text Boundaries options, choose Tools, Options, and then click the View tab; the options appear in the Print And Web Layout Options section. Figure 24-4 shows a sample Web page with the Text Boundaries check box selected.

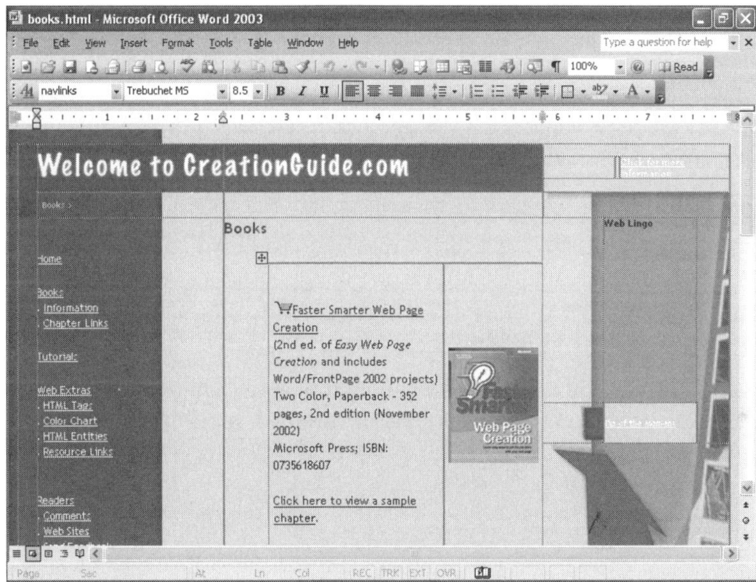

Figure 24-4. When you configure the Web Layout view to show margin spacing, Word uses dotted lines to indicate margin and spacing settings within pages, tables, and columns.

For more information about creating Web pages in Word, see Chapter 26, "Creating Professional Web Sites."

Working with My Network Places

In the true spirit of Web and desktop integration, you can use Word to create, copy, save, and manage folders and files that reside on a network, the Web, FTP servers, or in a shared workspace. After you create shortcuts to online folders (and if you have the proper permissions), you can work with online files and folders as though they were on your local computer. Of course, taking advantage of working with networks and the Web implies that you are connected to a network or have a connection to the Internet. The first order of business when you're working with online documents involves configuring your system so that you can access network places and File Transfer Protocol (FTP) sites.

Creating a Network Place

Although you can access documents and folders in existing Network Places from within Word, you need to set up links to new network places by using the Add Network Place Wizard.

To create a network place in Windows 2000 or later, follow these steps:

1. Click Start, My Network Places.
2. In the My Network Places task pane, click Add A Network Place.
3. Work through the Add Network Place Wizard pages to create a link to the network place.

After you add a network place, you can access documents and folders on the network place from within Word.

Linking to FTP Sites

In the same way that you access other network places, you can add FTP sites to your list of Internet sites if you have access to a network or the Internet. You can also add FTP sites to your list of network places while you're working in Word. To create shortcuts to FTP sites, follow these steps:

1. Click Open on the Standard toolbar to display the Open dialog box.
2. Click the Look In arrow, and then choose Add/Modify FTP Locations. The Add/Modify FTP Locations dialog box appears.
3. In the Name Of FTP Site box, enter the name or IP address of the FTP site (for example, **ftp.microsoft.com**, or **207.46.133.140**).
4. Specify whether you need to log on anonymously or will need to provide a user name by clicking either Anonymous or User. If you must supply a user name, type the user name in the User box, and type a password (if necessary) in the Password box. A sample completed Add/Modify FTP Locations dialog box is shown in Figure 24-5.

Figure 24-5. Adding FTP locations to your list of available network locations can streamline FTP procedures, such as transferring large files and uploading Web pages to servers.

5. When you finish configuring the Add/Modify FTP Locations dialog box, click Add to add the new FTP location, and then click OK to close the dialog box.

After you create an FTP link, you can double-click the link in the Open dialog box to access the contents of the FTP site. To modify or delete the link to an FTP site, right-click the link, and then choose Remove or Modify from the shortcut menu.

Accessing Resources Stored in Network Locations

You access network locations in the same way you access local files and folders—you simply navigate to the online file and folder locations in the Open dialog box, and then create a local shortcut to the document, if desired. To open an online folder or file using the Open dialog box, follow these steps:

1. Choose File, Open (or click Open on the Standard toolbar or press Ctrl+O).
2. Click the Look In arrow, choose My Network Places or FTP Locations (or click My Network Places on the Places bar), and then double-click the location you want to access.

When you access network locations, Word identifies each type of network connection with an icon. Table 24-1 summarizes the common icons you'll see associated with network locations.

Table 24-1. Network Location Icons

Icon	Description
	FTP server
	Shared folder on a network
	Folder on a Web site

Saving Documents to a Network Location

In addition to opening files from network locations, you'll probably want to save files to online locations. The process of saving files to online locations is similar to saving files locally. To save a newly created file to an online location, follow these steps:

1. Choose File, Save As.
2. In the Save As dialog box, click My Network Places.
3. Double-click the shortcut to the network location where you want to save the document, and then double-click any subfolders you want to access as well.
4. In the File Name box, type a name for the file (or retain the current name), and then click Save.

Note If you open a document from a network location, you can save your changes to the online document by clicking Save on the Standard toolbar or by pressing Ctrl+S. To save the document locally, you must first use the Save As command to save the document to a location on your computer.

Whenever you work with online files, you need to consider how other people will be (or are) interacting with files. For example, if you're updating Web pages, make sure that no other people are working on the pages when you replace existing files. Otherwise, you might overwrite each other's changes, which can be an extremely annoying experience. The next section of the chapter provides more information about sharing files and folders on networks.

Sharing Files and Folders

Part of the beauty of working on a network is that you can easily share files, folders, networked locations, and hardware resources (such as Zip drives, printers, scanners, and so forth) with anyone linked to your network. In addition, you can access networks from various locations. This capability can come in quite handy and can save you time because you won't have to continually copy information to a disk to use the information on another computer, and you won't be stranded in one location while your files sit in another. Because Word is a document creation program and sharing files and folders represents one of the most significant reasons for networking, we'll look at sharing those resources in more depth here.

Sharing Word Information Online

You can share information with other Word users in a number of ways. To share your information effectively, you should design your resource-sharing setup based on who will be accessing the information and how the information should appear. You can share files or folders using any of the following techniques:

- **Post the information to a public folder on Microsoft Exchange Server.** For example, you can open a file and choose File, Send To, Exchange Folder if your network has the Exchange Server extensions installed.
- **Save the information in a shared workspace.** A shared workspace is a Microsoft Windows SharePoint Team Services Web site. Shared workspaces are discussed in more detail in Chapter 25, "Working with Shared Documents."
- **Save the information in a shared network or Internet folder.** To learn more about Internet folders and network locations, refer to the discussion earlier in this chapter.
- **Send a copy of a file to others using an instant messaging (IM) application.** Many instant messaging services enable you to send documents to contacts. Windows Messenger and MSN Messenger provide this capability, and you can access IM from within Word as described earlier in this chapter.
- **Send a copy of a file to others or collaborate online using Word e-mail, fax, or NetMeeting features.** Word's e-mail, fax, and meeting capabilities are discussed later in this chapter.

- **Store comments about a document on a discussion server.** You can discuss online documents by participating in Web Discussions hosted by discussion servers or SharePoint Team Services, as described later in this chapter.

Choosing how you want to share resources can be fairly straightforward. For example, if you're sharing a few computers on a peer-to-peer network made up of trusted resources, you'll probably feel comfortable simply specifying files and folders as shared resources through Windows itself. On the other hand, if you know you have resources that people will need to access from many parts of the world, you'll be better served by sharing documents in a Web folder. To take advantage of other sharing options, such as public folders and SharePoint Web sites, you'll need to determine whether your server has Exchange Server extensions, Office Server extensions, or SharePoint Team Services installed.

Using Microsoft Windows 2000 and Windows XP to Share Folders on Your Intranet

Windows 2000 and Windows XP make it easy to share folders on intranets. The minor catch is that before you can share a folder with others on your intranet, you must be logged on as a member of the Administrators group or as another type of user with sufficient privileges. After you've verified your logon status, follow these steps to share a resource:

1. In Windows Explorer, right-click the folder you want to share, and then choose either Sharing And Security (Windows XP) or Sharing (Windows 2000) from the shortcut menu.
2. In the Sharing tab in the folder's Properties dialog box, click Share This Folder On The Network (Windows XP) or Share This Folder (Windows 2000).
3. Click OK to close the Properties dialog box.

After you share a folder, the folder icon changes to a hand holding a folder. This lets you quickly determine which folders on your computer are shared. Others on your network can now navigate to your computer and view the contents of the folders you've shared.

You can also share documents on your computer with other users by placing the documents in your computer's Shared Documents folder. You can access your Shared Documents by choosing Start, My Computer. In the My Computer window, you'll see the Shared Documents folder.

Sharing Documents with People Using Other Versions of Word

As you know, the software world changes much more frequently than many offices and people tend to update their systems. In addition, people use a variety of hardware platforms and operating systems. Therefore, you'll find that you occasionally want to share Word documents with people who are using earlier versions of Word or using Apple Macintosh versions of Word. Conveniently, Word includes several features that assist you when you want to share documents with people using other versions of Word (or people who aren't using Word at all).

> **Note** You can use Word 2003 to open documents created in Word 2003, Word 2002, Word 2000, Word 97, Word 95, or Word 6. All data and formatting in documents using those versions of Word are fully supported in Word 2003.

Sharing Documents with Users of Word 97 and Later

If you share documents with people who use Word 97 or later versions, you can save your documents in the standard Word document format. If desired, you can quickly create new documents or modify existing documents specifically for use in these versions of Word by turning off features not supported in that version. To do this, follow these steps:

1. Ensure that the document you want to save is open inWord.
2. Choose Tools, Options, and then click the Save tab. The Save tab in the Options dialog box is shown in Figure 24-6.

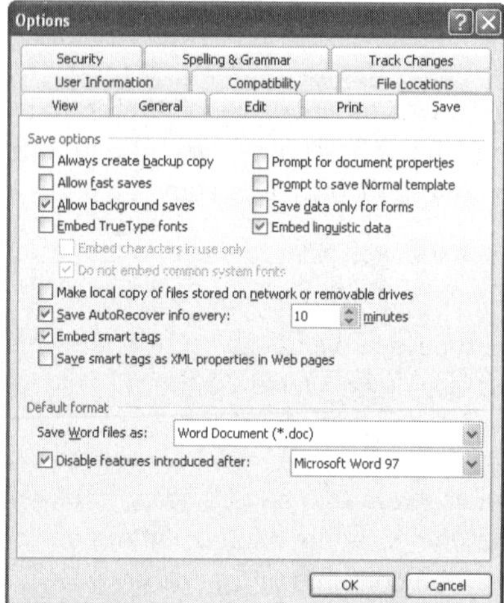

Figure 24-6. You can configure the settings in the Save tab to establish a default file format for new documents as well as to disable features that aren't supported in earlier versions of Word.

3. Select the Disable Features Introduced After check box, select the version of Word you want in the list, and then click OK. If appropriate, Word will display a summary of features in the document that aren't supported in the selected version of Word, as shown in Figure 24-7. Click Continue to proceed.

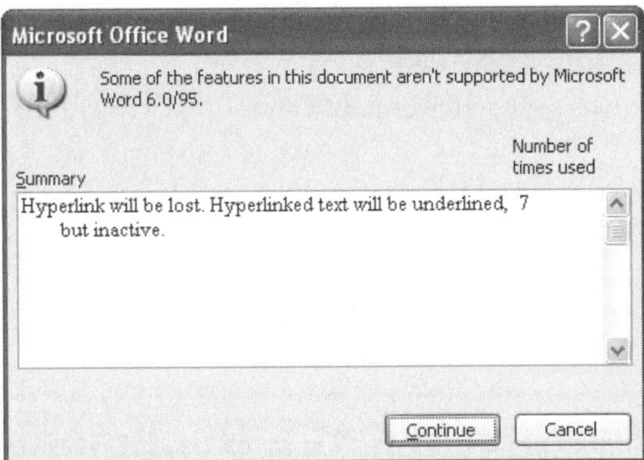

Figure 24-7. Word displays a summary of features found in the current document that aren't supported in the newly selected document format.

After you turn off features not supported by earlier versions of Word and save the document, the document can be used in the specified version of Word. If you work with the document in later versions of Word, you'll notice that some of the features are not available on menus. If you choose an unavailable option (such as choosing Insert, Hyperlink when you're working on a document for Word 6), a dialog box will appear, stating that the feature is currently disabled. The dialog box includes a Tell Me More button that you can click for further information about the disabled feature.

Note You can't use the Disable Features Introduced After option when you're saving Web pages—Word 97 and earlier versions don't support HTML documents.

Sharing Documents with Word for Windows 95 Users

In addition to saving documents for people who use Word 97 and more recent versions, you can prepare your documents so that they're accessible in Word 6 or Word 95 for Microsoft Windows 95. You can achieve this compatibility using one of the following techniques:

- **Save existing documents in Rich Text Format (RTF) for most versions of Word, including Word 6 or Word 95.** To save your document as an RTF file, choose File, Save As, and then select Word 97-2003 & 6.0/95 – RTF (*.doc) in the Save As Type list. When you save a document with this format, many word processing programs can read and display the document. The drawback to using this format to save a Word document is that some types of data or formatting might be lost. Furthermore, documents saved with this file format or the standard RTF format will often be larger than documents saved in more recent versions of Word because Word 97 and later versions of Word handle image compression better than earlier versions of Word and RTF.
- **Turn off unsupported features while you work.** To turn off unsupported features while you work, choose Tools, Options, click the Save tab, and then configure the Disable Features Introduced After setting. (For more detailed information, see the "Sharing Documents with Users of Word 97 and Later" on page 646.) When you turn off

unsupported features, you can create new documents or modify existing documents specifically for use in Word 6 or Word 95.

- **Send users a Word converter or viewer application.** Microsoft includes converters and viewers with Word, and they are also available for download from the Microsoft Office Resource Kit Web site and the Microsoft Office Online Web site. You can send a converter or a viewer application to users of Word 6, Word 95, or Microsoft Works, for Microsoft Windows, Microsoft Windows NT, or Apple Macintosh operating systems. After users install a converter or viewer, they can directly open Word documents.

Receiving Notification When a Document Is Converted

If you want to know which converter (if any) is being used when you open a document, you can display the Convert File dialog box, shown here:

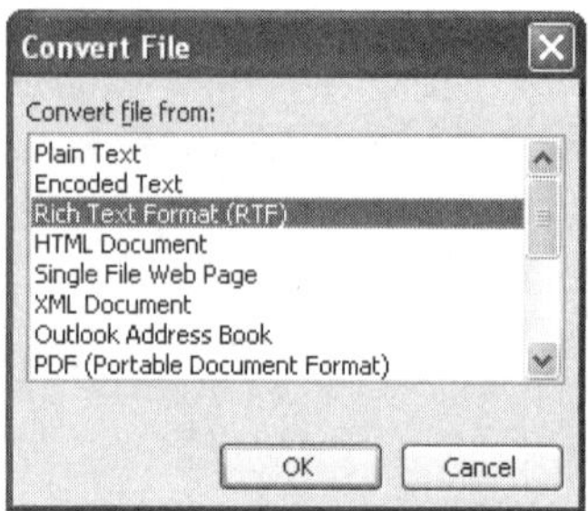

To configure Word to notify you when files are converted, follow these steps:

1. Choose Tools, Options, and then click the General tab.
2. Select the Confirm Conversion At Open check box, and then click OK.

After you set this option, the Convert File dialog box will appear when you open a file that must be converted. When you see the Convert File dialog box, simply click OK to open the document normally. (The file's default file format will be selected unless you specify another format.) If you click Cancel, the process will be aborted, and the document won't be opened. If you select another file format in the Convert File dialog box, the document will be opened in the selected format. For example, if you select Plain Text in the Convert File dialog box when you're opening a Web page document, you'll see a text document that shows the HTML source code for the Web page instead of the standard WYSIWYG view Word normally displays when you open HTML documents.

Converting a Batch of Files to or from Word Format

Although you can easily convert a document into another format by using the Save As feature, in some cases you might want to convert a number of Word files to another format. For example, you might want to convert a collection of files from a client who uses WordPerfect. You can easily convert a batch of files by using the Conversion Wizard included with Word. To do so, follow these steps:

1. Put the documents that you want to convert in a single folder.
2. Choose File, New to open the New Document task pane.
3. In the Templates section, click On My Computer.
4. In the Templates dialog box, click the Other Documents tab.
5. Double-click the Batch Conversion Wizard icon. The Start page is shown in Figure 24-8.

> **Note** The first time you use the Batch Conversion Wizard, you might have to wait a moment or two while the wizard is installed.

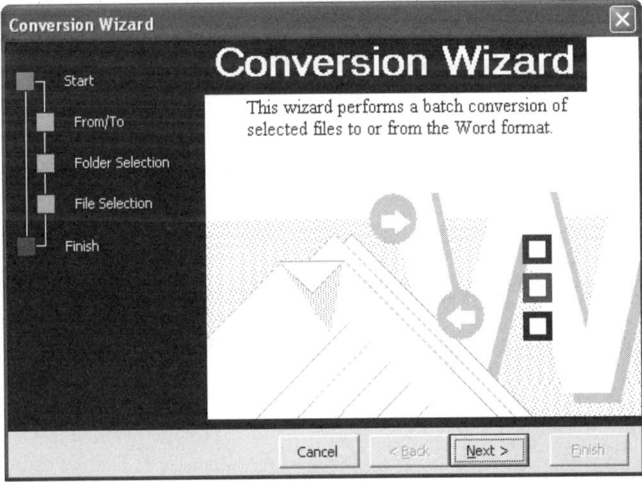

Figure 24-8. The Conversion Wizard walks you through the process of converting a number of files at one time.

6. Click Next, and then specify whether you want to convert documents to Word format or convert Word documents to another format by selecting the appropriate option and choosing the file type in the list.
7. Click Next, and on the Folder Selection page, click the Source Folder Browse button. The Browse For Folder dialog box appears, as shown in Figure 24-9. Select the appropriate folder, and then click OK.

Figure 24-9. You can use the Browse For Folder dialog box to specify the folder that contains the files you want to convert and the location where you want to store the converted files.

8 Click the Destination Folder Browse button, select the folder in which you want to store the converted files, and then click OK.

9 Click Next to display the File Selection page, shown in Figure 24-10, where you can specify the files you want to convert. To select a file, double-click the file name in the Available list; the file name will appear in the To Convert list. Continue to double-click file names in the Available list until all the files you want to convert appear in the To Convert list. If you want to convert all the files, click Select All. You can filter the Available list view by choosing a file type in the Type list.

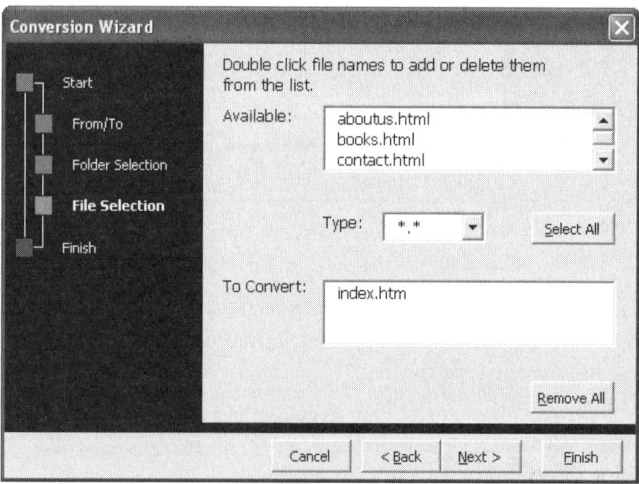

Figure 24-10. The File Selection page enables you to pick and choose the files you want to convert.

10 After you've added files to the To Convert list, you can remove a single file by double-clicking it or click Remove All if you decide not to convert any of the specified files. When you've completed the File Selection page, click Next, and then click Finish to complete the conversion. You'll see the Batch Conversion Progress dialog box, and then a final message box will appear, asking whether you want to perform another conversion. Click Yes to perform another conversion, or click No to close the dialog box.

Keep in mind that when you perform a batch conversion, you don't delete or change the original files. Instead, you create copies of existing files that are stored in another file format.

Setting a Default File Format

If you frequently save documents in a format other than the standard Word document format (for example, perhaps you need to share most of the documents you create with a client who uses Microsoft Works 6 or Works 7), you can change the default file format Word uses to save new documents. To do so, follow these steps:

1. Choose Tools, Options, and then click the Save tab.
2. In the Default Format section, click the Save Word Files As arrow, and choose the file format you want to use as your default file format in the list.
3. Click OK.

Remember that when you configure the default file format, the setting affects only new documents you create. Word saves existing documents in the same format in which they were opened.

Using Workgroup Templates

A convenient way to keep a group supplied with the most up-to-date templates is to store common templates centrally on a network server. (These shared templates are generally referred to as *workgroup templates*.) By doing this, you can ensure that everyone working on similar projects can access the same versions of templates at any time. A central repository for workgroup templates also saves everyone the headache of distributing and obtaining individual copies of the latest templates and can greatly help to standardize documents across the board.

You create workgroup templates in the same way you create other templates. You then designate a folder as the workgroup template container and make sure that everyone's computer is configured to point to that file. Generally speaking, you'll want to make workgroup templates read-only files so that no one accidentally changes the template information. If you want to ensure that only certain people can access the files, you might want to assign passwords to the templates or make the network share read-only.

For more information about creating templates, see Chapter 16, "Formatting Documents Using Templates, Wizards, Add-Ins, and XML Schemas." For information about making documents read-only and password-protected, see Chapter 28, "Addressing Document Protection and Security Issues."

To specify the location of workgroup templates on an individual's computer, follow these steps:

1 Choose Tools, Options, and then click the File Locations tab.

2 In the File Types list, select Workgroup Templates, as shown in Figure 24-11.

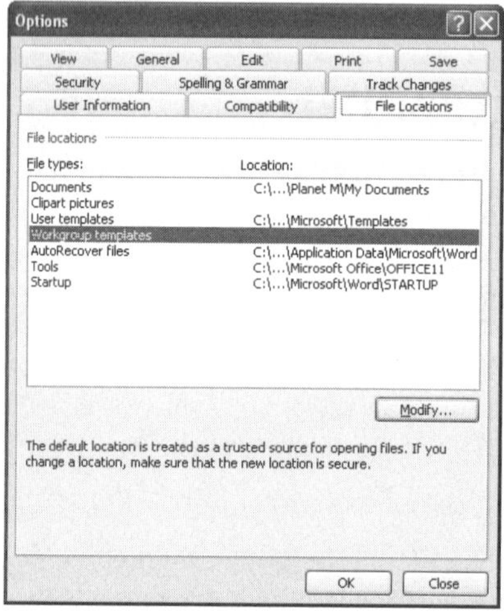

Figure 24-11. You can use the File Locations tab to specify locations for a number of file types, including workgroup templates.

3 Click Modify to open the Modify Location dialog box, which looks similar to the Open dialog box.

4 Create a new folder or navigate to and select the folder that contains the workgroup templates, click OK to close the Modify Location dialog box, and then click OK to close the Options dialog box.

To access templates stored in the workgroup templates folder, users can click the On My Computer link in the New Document task pane, and then click the General tab in the Templates dialog box. If workgroup templates are stored in a subfolder in the workgroup templates folder, the Templates dialog box will include a tab with the same name as the subfolder, and the templates stored within the subfolder will appear in that tab.

Tip **Store workgroup templates in a Web folder**

You can't indicate an Internet location for your workgroup templates in the File Locations tab in the Options dialog box—the workgroup templates folder must be stored in a location on your computer or network. If you want to store templates in a Web folder, you should create a My Network Places link to the Web folder. You can then access the folder by clicking the On My Web Sites link in the New Document task pane.

Using Word as an E-Mail Editor

Almost everyone has had at least a brush with e-mail in one form or another. As an experienced Word user, you've probably sent more e-mail messages than you care to think about. What you need to know about sending e-mail messages in Word is rooted in the Word-specific "how-to's." In this part of the chapter, you'll see how you can get the most out of the e-mail features in Word.

As you might imagine, you can use Word to send messages formatted as plain text, rich text, or HTML. Most new and updated versions of e-mail applications (including Outlook 2003) offer a choice of plain text or HTML; earlier or scaled-down e-mail applications generally support plain-text messages only. When you use Word, you can use any of the three formats described in the following list. The pros and cons given below should help you decide which format best suits your needs:

- **Plain text e-mail messages** The most common e-mail message format is still plain text, although HTML messages are beginning to make their presence known. Although plain text messages seem to be losing favor, they provide a few benefits over HTML or RTF messages. Namely, plain text e-mail messages are small, which makes sending and receiving messages quick. In addition, plain text e-mail messages are easily interpreted by all e-mail applications. The main drawback of plain text e-mail messages is that they are just that—plain text. You can't specify fonts, create layouts, include color, or apply any other text or document formatting (such as adding boldface or italics). Using plain text, you can send only a typed message (with an occasional emoticon to spice up your note). To work around this limitation, most people send a plain text e-mail message and attach document files that contain desired formatting. For more information about attaching files to e-mail messages, see "Sending an Attachment," on page 660.
- **HTML e-mail messages** HTML messages represent a newer wave of e-mail messaging. Using HTML messages, you can send highly formatted messages that incorporate font formatting, color, backgrounds, themes, and so forth. You can also use existing documents as e-mail messages without losing the document formatting. The drawbacks of HTML e-mail messages are significant. First, not all e-mail applications support HTML messages. When an HTML message is sent to a person who's using a text-only e-mail application, the recipient will receive a plain text version of your message, which means that they might have to wade through some HTML code before getting to the body of your message. A second drawback of HTML messages is that they are larger, which means that the messages can take longer to send and receive if they contain a lot of formatting and graphics. (This might be a particular concern if you know the recipient will be using a dial-up connection to receive your message.) Before you send HTML messages, make sure that the recipient can view HTML messages and has a relatively speedy Internet or network connection.
- **Rich-text e-mail messages** You can also format e-mail messages in Word as rich text, which sends a plain text e-mail message along with a .dat file (usually named Winmail.dat) containing information about message formatting as well as other data, such as voting button information. If recipients are using Outlook or the Exchange Client, a

rich-text message will appear fully formatted. If recipients aren't using Outlook or the Exchange Client, they will receive a plain text message with the Winmail.dat file attached (and the file's contents will seem meaningless). Unless you're working on an intranet and you need to use some of Outlook's special features, you'll usually want to format your e-mail messages using either the Plain Text or HTML setting.

By default, Word formats new, blank e-mail messages using the HTML format. You can change this setting by configuring the Mail Format tab in the Options dialog box in Outlook. To access this setting, follow these steps:

1. In Outlook, choose Tools, Options, and then click the Mail Format tab in the Options dialog box.
2. Click the Compose In This Message Format arrow, and then choose HTML, Rich Text, or Plain Text in the list. (HTML is selected by default.)
3. Click OK.

Keep in mind that if you format a document before you convert the document into an e-mail message, Word will automatically retain your formatting and send the message as an HTML e-mail message—even if you've specified plain text as your default e-mail message format. The default setting comes into play only when you create new, blank e-mail messages by clicking the E-Mail Message link in the New Document task pane.

Many e-mail options provided by Word are available only if you're using Outlook in conjunction with Word. For more information about using Outlook, see *Microsoft Office Outlook 2003 Inside Out* (Microsoft Press, 2004).

Turning Word On or Off as Your E-Mail Editor or Viewer

By default, Outlook is configured to use Word as your e-mail editor. This means that when you click New Mail Message on the Standard toolbar in Outlook, the blank e-mail document that opens includes many of Word's features. Although Word offers numerous formatting advantages over the standard Outlook message window, you can specify not to use Word as your e-mail editor if you prefer to use a scaled-down version of the Outlook message window. To control this setting, follow these steps:

1. In Outlook, choose Tools, Options, and then click the Mail Format tab in the Options dialog box.
2. Select or clear the Use Microsoft Office Word 2003 To Edit E-Mail Messages check box, and then click OK.

You can change this setting at any time if you find you prefer one message window to the other.

Sending a Document, E-Mail-Style

E-Mail

If you want to use Word to send an e-mail message, you can open the e-mail pane, which appears across the top of your Word window, or use the Untitled Message window. When you display the e-mail pane in Word, you'll see several buttons and text boxes that you can use to format and send your e-mail messages. When you access an Untitled Message window, you can work in a window similar to an Outlook e-mail message window.

You can create new, blank e-mail messages in Word or you can create e-mail messages from existing Word documents, as follows:

- **To create a new, blank e-mail message** Choose File, New to open the New Document task pane, and then click the E-Mail Message link. An Untitled Message window opens, as shown in Figure 24-12.

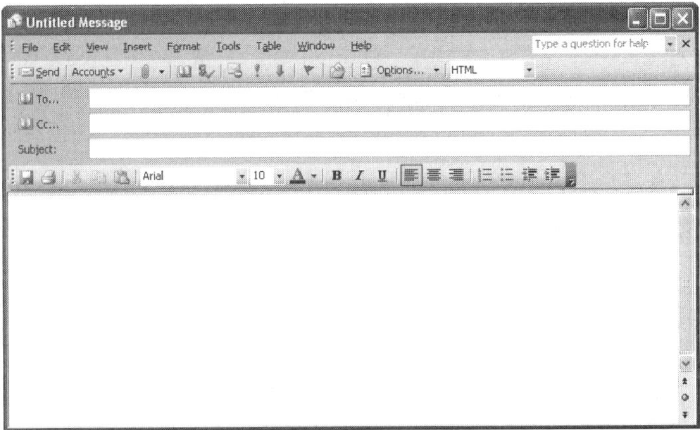

Figure 24-12. You can create a new, blank e-mail message by clicking the E-Mail Message link in the New Document task pane.

- **To create an e-mail message using an existing document** Open an existing document or enter information into a new, blank document, and then click E-Mail on the Standard toolbar. The e-mail pane opens above the document's contents, as shown in Figure 24-13. Notice that the Subject box contains the document's file name. (If the document has been saved, the file name appears in the Subject box automatically.)

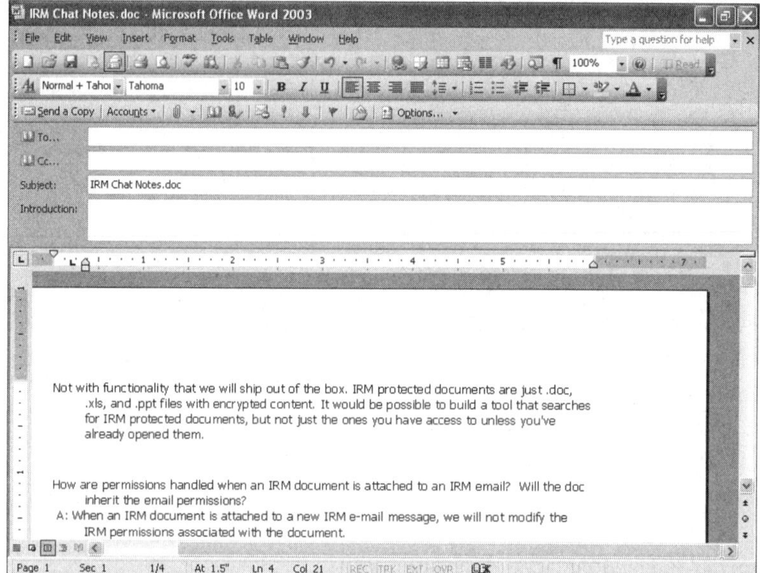

Figure 24-13. You can display the e-mail pane in an existing document, which enables you to send the entire document in an e-mail message.

As you can see in Figures 24-12 and 24-13, the e-mail window varies slightly depending on how you create your e-mail message. When you click E-Mail on the Standard toolbar to add the e-mail pane to an existing document, the e-mail pane includes an Introduction box (discussed in more detail in "Including an Introduction in an E-Mail Message" on the next page). When you click the E-Mail Message link in the New Document task pane, the e-mail pane includes a list that allows you to specify whether you want to format the message as HTML, rich text, or plain text.

After you display the e-mail pane in a document—regardless of whether it's a new document or an existing document—you are ready to configure the e-mail settings. Completing the e-mail pane is similar to addressing standard e-mail messages, as described here:

1. In the e-mail pane, enter recipient names in the To box and the Cc box, if necessary. (For more information about adding recipients, see "Specifying Sender and Recipient Identities" on the next page.)
2. Enter a subject in the Subject box, enter the document contents if necessary, and then click Send or Send A Copy (depending on how you created the e-mail message).

In addition to this basic procedure, you can use a number of other addressing and formatting features provided in Word. For example, you can include introductory text, specify a sender other than yourself, set e-mail priority levels, include an attachment, create a custom signature, and control a number of other e-mail features, as described in the next part of the chapter.

Including an Introduction in an E-Mail Message

If you click E-Mail on the Standard toolbar from an open document, Word includes an Introduction box in the e-mail pane. This box allows you to add text without inserting it into the existing document. You might want to do this if you're sending a document for review or sending a copy of a Web page. When you add an introduction, the recipient sees the introduction text separated from the main text by a horizontal rule, as shown in Figure 24-14.

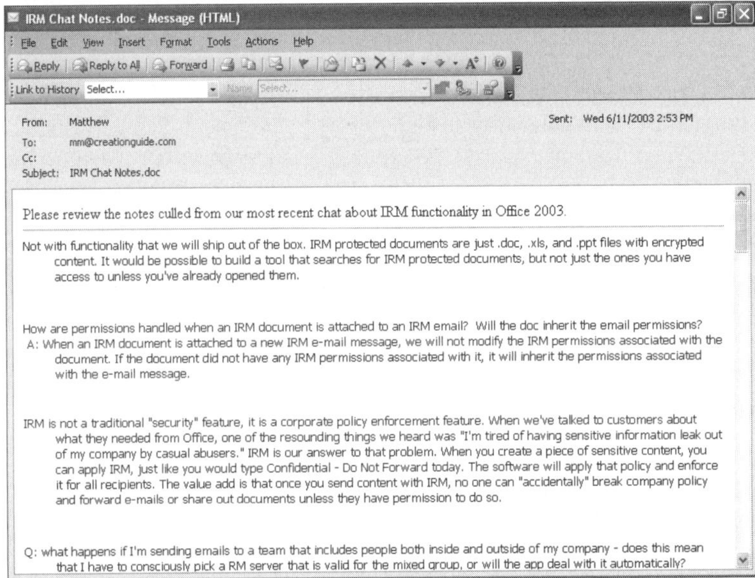

Figure 24-14. The Introduction box enables you to include ancillary text above your e-mail message's main contents.

Specifying Sender and Recipient Identities

When you send e-mail from within Word, you can specify the following participating parties:

- **Accounts** If you have multiple e-mail accounts set up on your computer, you can specify from which account you'd like to send the current e-mail message. To do so, click Accounts in the e-mail pane, and then select the account you want to use to send the message. Figure 24-15 shows an Accounts list on a computer configured with three e-mail accounts.

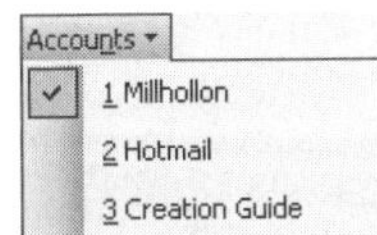

Figure 24-15. The Accounts list enables you to choose which account you want to use to send a message.

- **From** You can send an e-mail message on behalf of someone else by specifying a name in the From box. (If the From box doesn't appear in the e-mail pane, click the Options arrow, and then choose From in the menu.) When you send a message with a From name to a recipient using Outlook, the message header will show the From name in the Inbox, and the message itself will read ***Your Name** on behalf of **Sender's Name*** when the message is open. To specify a From name, type a name or an e-mail address in the From box, or click From in the e-mail pane to open the Choose Sender dialog box. In the Choose Sender dialog box, choose a name, and then click OK.

Caution Be careful when using the From box because this option can produce misleading results. If the recipient is using Outlook, the on behalf of statement appears in the message header and the communication is clear. But if the recipient is using another e-mail application, such as Outlook Express, the message header might simply show the name you inserted in the From box—the recipient won't know that the message was created and sent by someone other than the listed name.

- **To** Obviously, you need to specify a recipient (or recipients) for your message. You can do so by entering e-mail addresses in the To box. If you manually enter multiple recipients, separate each e-mail address with a semicolon.You can also enter e-mail addresses by clicking To, selecting Contacts in the Show Names From The list, and then double-clicking names in the Name list, as shown in Figure 24-16. After you've added all the names you want to include, click OK.

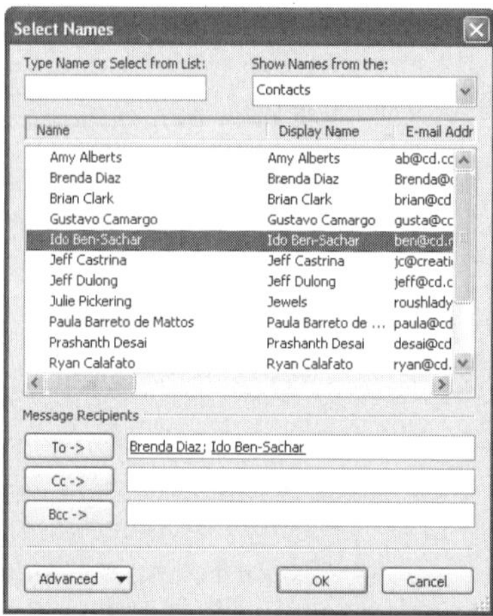

Figure 24-16. The Select Names dialog box enables you to specify e-mail addresses for the To, Cc, and Bcc boxes all at once.

- **Cc** You can send copies of e-mail messages to other people by entering their e-mail addresses in the Cc (short for *carbon copy*) box, either by typing the addresses or by clicking Cc, selecting a name in the Select Names dialog box, clicking Cc, and then clicking OK. When you enter names in the Cc box, all recipients can see the names of all the people who've been sent a copy of the message.

- **Bcc** You can use the Bcc (short for *blind carbon copy*) option to send a copy of an e-mail message to the person indicated in the Bcc box without revealing to the recipients specified in the To and Cc boxes that the additional copy was sent. To send blind copies of any e-mail message, enter e-mail addresses in the Bcc box, either by typing the address or by clicking Bcc, selecting a name in the Select Names dialog box, clicking Bcc, and then clicking OK. If you don't see the Bcc box in the e-mail pane, click the Options arrow, and then choose Bcc in the list.

> **Tip** **Verify the address resource**
> If you don't see the name you're looking for in the Choose Sender dialog box (which appears when you click From in the e-mail pane) or in the Select Names dialog box (which appears when you click To, Cc, or Bcc), verify that the proper address resource appears in the Show Names From The list. You can choose to display the names stored in your Outlook Contacts folder, as shown in Figure 24-16.

Setting E-Mail Priority

At times, you might want to mark e-mail messages as urgent or not-at-all urgent (also known as *high-priority* and *low-priority messages*). Marking your messages indicates instantly to recipients who are using Outlook or Outlook Express whether they should give special attention to a message. To set e-mail priority for a message, use the following techniques:

Importance: High

- **To send a high-priority message** Click the Importance: High button in the e-mail pane. The button appears as selected in your e-mail pane. If the recipient is using Outlook or Outlook Express, a red exclamation point will appear next to the message in the Importance column in the recipient's Inbox. (The treatment may vary in other e-mail applications.)

Importance: Low

- **To send a low-priority message** Click the Importance: Low button in the e-mail pane. The button appears as selected in your e-mail pane. In Outlook or Outlook Express, a blue down arrow will appear next to the message in the Importance column in the recipient's Inbox.

By default, e-mail messages are classified as normal priority; normal-priority messages aren't accompanied by any priority marker. You can also configure message priority levels by clicking the Options button in the e-mail pane to open the Message Options dialog box, clicking the Importance arrow, and then choosing Low, Normal, or High in the list.

Adding a Message Flag

You can add flags to e-mail messages to indicate that you or the recipient need to perform some type of follow-up action relevant to the message. The flag will appear only in Outlook (not Word), in the Sort By: Flag Status column. To flag a message, follow these steps:

Message Flag

1. In the e-mail pane, click the Message Flag button. The Flag For Follow Up dialog box appears.
2. Click the Flag To arrow, and then choose a flag type, such as Call, Follow Up, Do Not Forward, and so forth.

3. Click the Due By arrow, and then choose a due date on the pop-up calendar. You can also click the arrow for the adjacent list and specify a due-by time.
4. Click OK to close the Flag For Follow Up dialog box.

When you send the message, it will be accompanied by a flag in your Sent Items folder in Outlook and in the recipient's Inbox if the recipient is using Outlook or Outlook Express. You can also add flags to and remove flags from existing messages in your Inbox.

Sending an Attachment

One of the most frequent tasks associated with e-mail messages is transferring files and objects as attachments. You might want to send attachments if a recipient doesn't use an HTML e-mail application or if you're sending a large document, graphic, movie file, spreadsheet, or other file type. You attach files in Word in the same manner you attach files in other e-mail applications. To do so, use one of the following techniques:

- Open the document you want to send as an attachment, and then choose File, Send To, Mail Recipient (As Attachment).
- In the e-mail pane, click Insert File to open the Insert File dialog box (or click the Insert File arrow, and then choose File from the menu). Select the file you want to attach to the current e-mail message, and then click Insert. Notice that the file name appears in the Attach box in the e-mail pane, as shown in Figure 24-17.

Insert File

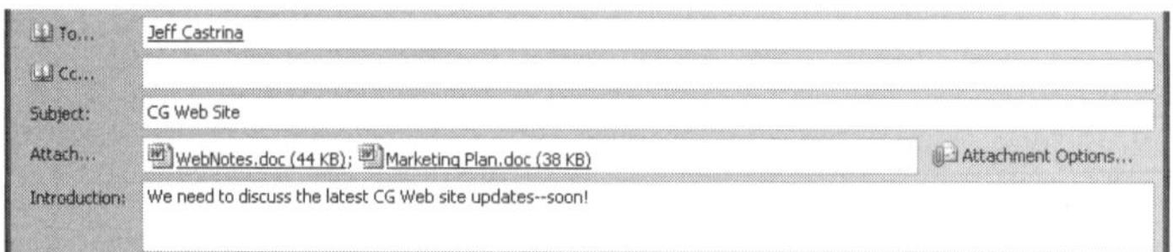

Figure 24-17. The e-mail pane displays the file names of any files attached to the current e-mail message.

- In Windows Explorer, right-click any document, and then choose Send To, Mail Recipient.

> **Tip** After you attach one document or item, you can access the Insert File dialog box by clicking the Attach button in the e-mail pane.

When you send an attached file, recipients can save a copy of the file on their computers, and then view it locally.

Adding an E-Mail Signature

As you've probably seen during your e-mail encounters, many people include a small blurb of information at the end of their e-mail messages. These blurbs are referred to as *signatures*. Signatures often supply extra contact information, links to Web pages, and sometimes witty or clever comments. Conveniently, you can edit or delete signatures just as you manipulate other text after it's inserted. To create a custom signature that you can use as you need, follow these steps:

1 Choose Tools, Options, click the General tab, and then click E-Mail Options. If necessary, click the E-Mail Signature tab. The E-Mail Options dialog box appears, as shown in Figure 24-18.

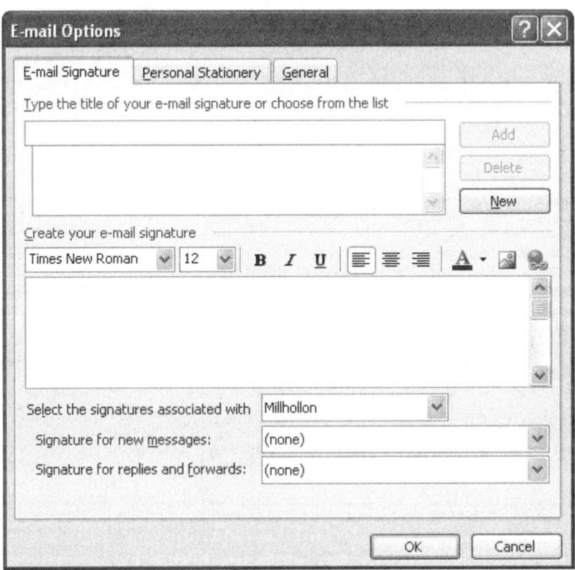

Figure 24-18. You can use the E-Mail Options dialog box to create a collection of signatures that you can choose from when you create e-mail messages in Word.

2 If more than one e-mail account is configured on your computer, display the e-mail account in the Select The Signatures Associated With list.

3 In the top box, enter a title for the signature you're creating so you can quickly identify the signature when you want to add its content to your e-mail messages.

4 Press Tab, enter the signature's content (including text, graphics, and hyperlinks) in the box in the Create Your E-Mail Signature section, and then click Add. By default, the newly created signature is assigned to be the default e-mail signature.

> **Tip Choose a default signature**
> You can set any signature to be your default signature by configuring the E-Mail Signature tab in the E-Mail Options dialog box. To do so, select the signature's name in the Signature For New Messages and Signature For Replies And Forwards lists, and then click OK.

5 To add another signature, click New, name the signature, enter the signature information, specify the e-mail account association, and then click Add.

6 When you have finished creating signatures, click OK to close the E-Mail Options dialog box, and then click OK to close the Options dialog box.

After you create and set a default signature, Word inserts the default signature in new, blank e-mail documents you create by clicking the E-Mail Message link in the New Document task pane. In addition, your default signature will be added to messages that you create by replying to or forwarding messages sent to you. If you create a number of signatures in Word, you can easily change which signature is inserted in an e-mail message by right-clicking the existing signature and choosing another signature from the shortcut menu. When you do this, the existing signature is removed and the selected signature is inserted in your document. You can also use this shortcut menu to access the E-Mail Options dialog box (in which you can create a new signature, modify existing signatures, and change your default signature setting). Figure 24-19 shows a blank e-mail document containing a signature accompanied by the shortcut menu showing other available signatures.

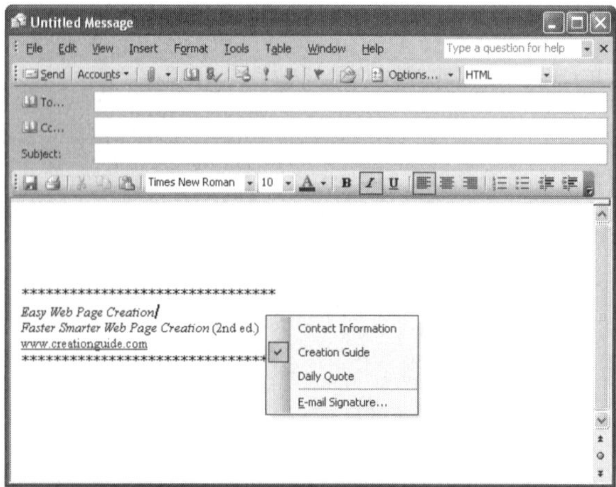

Figure 24-19. You can replace an existing signature by right-clicking it, and then choosing another signature name from the shortcut menu.

Routing Documents via E-Mail

You're probably familiar with the *routing slips* used in office settings. In plain language, a routing slip is a list of names of people who need to review an item. When a person on the list reviews the item, she checks off her name and then passes the item to the next person on the list. Routed items can be anything from policy updates to "secret" birthday cards for a co-worker. In Word, you can attach the online equivalent of a routing slip to a document, and you can route the document to each person on the list in sequence or all at once. You might want to use this feature if you want a number of people to review and return a particular document.

To create a routing slip, you must ensure that you have an e-mail program installed on your system. Then follow these steps:

1 Open the document you want to route, and then choose File, Send To, Routing Recipient. If a security warning appears, asking whether it's OK to check your Outlook Address Book, click Yes. The Routing Slip dialog box appears, as shown in Figure 24-20.

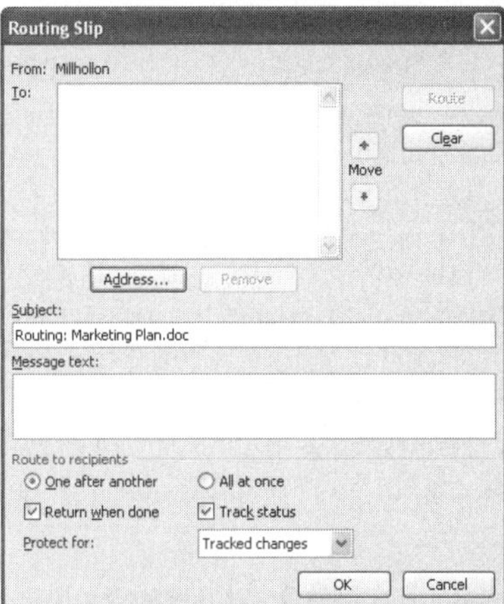

Figure 24-20. You can use the Routing Slip dialog box to create an online routing slip for a Word document.

2 In the Routing Slip dialog box, click Address. The Address Book dialog box appears.

3 In the Address Book dialog box, select the Show Names From The list, and then choose an address book, such as Contacts.

4 In the name list, double-click names or select the names you want to include on your routing slip (to select multiple names, press Ctrl while you select names), and then click To. Click OK to close the Address Book dialog box. The selected names will appear in the To list in the Routing Slip dialog box, as shown in Figure 24-21.

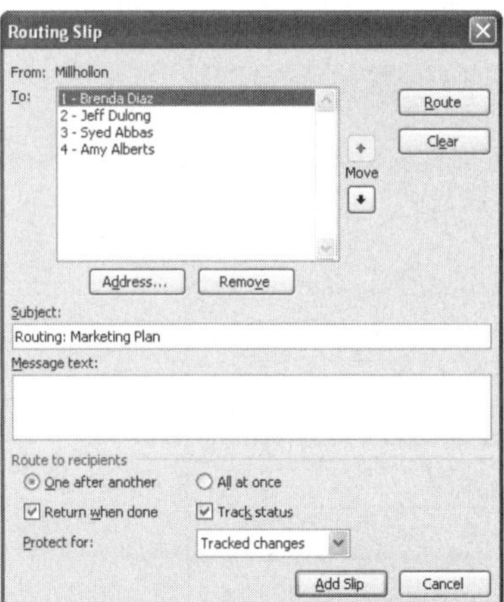

Figure 24-21. The To list in the Routing Slip dialog box specifies the users who will be included in the routing process. You can move names up and down the list to set the routing order.

5 Adjust the order of recipients in the To list to suit your needs by selecting names and clicking the up or down arrow buttons to the right of the To list to move the selected name up or down the list.

6 Enter text in the Message Text box, and in the Route To Recipients section, specify whether you want to route the document to each routing slip recipient in sequence or all at once.

7 Click Route to begin routing your document. If you receive a security warning, click Yes to continue.

Recipients of a document with a routing slip will receive an e-mail message stating that the attached document is being routed. After the recipient opens and reviews the document in Word, he should choose File, Send To, Next Routing Recipient to forward the document to the next person on the routing slip. If the recipient wants to route the document to another name in the list, he can choose File, Send To, Other Routing Recipient. As the document is routed, the originator of the routed document receives update e-mail messages indicating the latest action (such as "Bill routed the document *name of document* to Julie").

Formatting Messages with Stationery and Themes

If you choose to send HTML-formatted e-mail messages, you can send highly customized messages. You can use the themes provided in Word to format your e-mail messages as described in Chapter 17, "Formatting Layouts Using Text Boxes, Frames, Backgrounds, and Themes." You can also add *stationery* to e-mail messages. Fundamentally, stationery is a scaled-down version of a theme, and the process of applying stationery is similar to applying themes, as described here:

1 Choose Tools, Options, click the General tab, and then click E-Mail Options. The E-Mail Options dialog box appears.

2 In the E-Mail Options dialog box, choose the Personal Stationery tab, shown in Figure 24-22.

Figure 24-22. The Personal Stationery tab provides a number of format settings for e-mail messages, including the Theme button, which you can use to access the Theme Or Stationery dialog box.

3 Click the Theme button. The Theme Or Stationery dialog box appears, as shown in Figure 24-23.

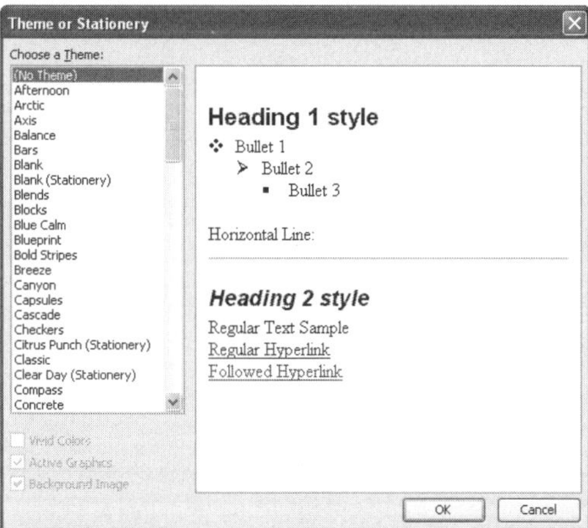

Figure 24-23. You can use the Theme Or Stationery dialog box to select and preview e-mail stationery and themes before applying them.

4 Choose a name in the Choose A Theme list. Notice that a number of themes include the word Stationery after the theme name; themes labeled as stationery are scaled-down themes that specify an e-mail message's background and standard text settings (such as color and font).

5 View themes in the preview box until you find one you want to use. Select the theme, click OK to close the Theme Or Stationery dialog box, click OK to close the E-Mail Options dialog box, and then click OK to close the Options dialog box.

When you set a default theme, Word applies the theme to all future e-mail messages you create until you reconfigure the default theme setting. The theme won't be applied to e-mail messages or documents you've already created.

Tip **Apply a theme to only the current e-mail message**
You can apply a new theme to an existing e-mail message before you send it, regardless of whether the e-mail message has a theme already applied. To do so, choose Format, Theme to access the Theme dialog box. Select a theme, preview the theme, and then click OK. When you use this option, you won't see themes specially formatted as stationery, so you won't find themes listed with the *(Stationery)* identifier after the theme names.

Setting E-Mail Message Options

You can set a number of e-mail message options within Word by configuring settings in the Message Options dialog box, shown in Figure 24-24. To display the Message Options dialog box, click the Options button in the e-mail pane.

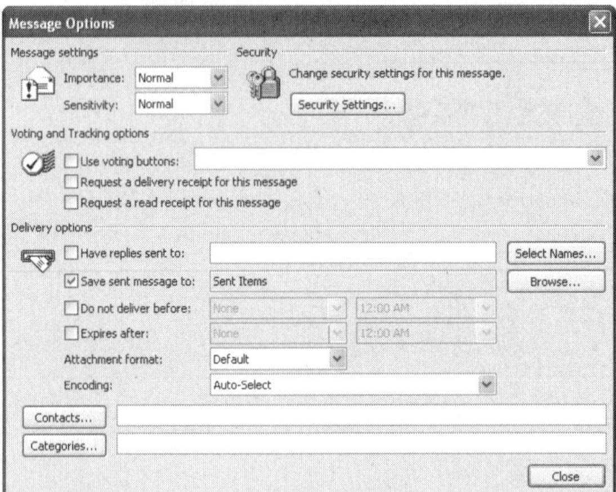

Figure 24-24. Click the Options button in the e-mail pane to access the Message Options dialog box.

The Message Options dialog box enables you to set the following options:

- **Importance** Lets you mark a message as Low, Normal, or High importance. For more information about indicating an e-mail message's importance, see "Setting E-Mail Priority" on page 659.
- **Sensitivity** Lets you specify whether the contents of a message are Normal, Personal, Private, or Confidential. This option serves as an indicator only; it doesn't protect your document in any way.
- **Security Settings** Displays the Security Properties dialog box, which enables you to encrypt e-mail messages and add digital signatures. For more information about security, see Chapter 28, "Addressing Document Protection and Security Issues."
- **Use Voting Buttons** Includes voting buttons in e-mail messages so that recipients can reply to a message by clicking buttons such as Approve or Reject.
- **Request A Delivery Receipt For This Message** Sends a message to you when your e-mail message arrives at the recipient's address.
- **Request A Read Receipt For This Message** Sends a message to you verifying the date and time your message was opened by the recipient. (Of course, this doesn't guarantee that the recipient actually read your message.)
- **Have Replies Sent To** Sends replies to the current message to another e-mail address you specify, such as an assistant's address. You can click Select Names to display the Have Replies Sent To dialog box, similar to the Select Names dialog box that appears when you click To in the e-mail pane.
- **Save Sent Message To** Saves the sent message in the specified folder. By default, sent messages are saved in the Sent Items folder in Outlook. You can click Browse to specify a different folder.
- **Do Not Deliver Before** Stores the message in your Outbox until the specified date and time.

- **Expires After** Allows you to specify a date after which the message becomes unavailable.
- **Attachment Format** Specifies the format to use when sending an attachment. You can choose the Default, MIME, UUEncode, or BINHEX format.
- **Encoding** Lets you specify the character set used in the message.
- **Contacts** Displays a list of contact names and addresses to which you can link the message in Outlook.
- **Categories** Helps you assign words you can use to find and group related items in Outlook.

After you configure the settings in the Message Options dialog box, click Close to accept the settings, and then continue creating your e-mail message.

Configuring HTML Options for E-Mail Messages

In addition to configuring settings in the Message Options dialog box, you can control a couple of options specific to HTML for e-mail messages you send that use HTML formatting. To access these options, follow these steps:

1. Choose Tools, Options, click the General tab, and then click E-Mail Options.
2. In the E-Mail Options dialog box, click the General tab, shown in Figure 24-25.

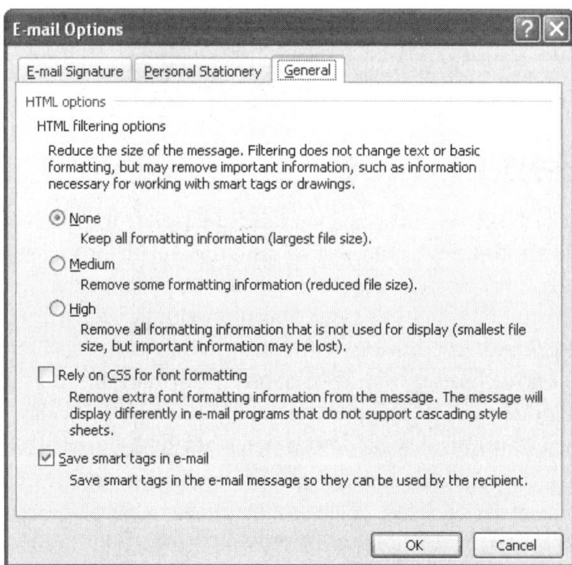

Figure 24-25. The General tab in the E-Mail Options dialog box presents three options for HTML that you can control when you send HTML e-mail messages.

The General tab provides the following options for HTML:

- **HTML Filtering Options** In Word 2002, HTML filtering for e-mail messages was an all-or-nothing deal—you either filtered your messages or you didn't. In Word 2003, you have a little more control over HTML filtering. When you select a filtering option,

Word reduces the size of your HTML e-mail message by removing "behind-the-scenes" formatting information (such as smart tags and some formatting functionality specific to Word) without altering the message's appearance. In Word 2003, you can remove some "behind-the-scenes" formatting by choosing the Medium setting or you can remove all formatting not related to display by choosing the High setting. When you use filtering, the file size is reduced because formatting information specific to Word is stripped from the message's HTML source code. If you plan to edit the document in Word later, you should keep the default None option selected, or maintain two copies of the file—one for editing in Word and one for online use.

- **Rely On CSS For Font Formatting** When you select this check box, you instruct Word to create a cascading style sheet (CSS) and attach it to an e-mail message formatted with HTML. The result of this action is usually to reduce the size of the message. The drawback is that if the recipient uses an e-mail application that doesn't support CSS, your document will not be displayed properly.
- **Save Smart Tags In E-Mail** If you know that recipients will view your message in Outlook or Word, you can instruct Word to use smart tags in the e-mail message. Selecting this check box and sending a message to a recipient who uses an e-mail application that doesn't support smart tags will have no effect. Note that if you choose the High HTML filtering option, the Save Smart Tags In E-Mail check box will not be available. If you choose the Medium filtering setting, you can specify whether you want to include smart tags in your e-mail message.

After you configure the settings in the E-Mail Options dialog box, click OK to save your settings, and then click OK again to close the Options dialog box.

Using Word to Send Faxes

Faxing is yet another fast, convenient way to get information from your office or home computer to other people around the country or around the world. Using Word, you can send faxes using your system's fax modem (if one is installed) or a fax service, which is the recommended process in Word 2003. In both cases, Word provides a Fax Wizard that walks you through most of the process. In addition, with the Office 2003 optical character recognition feature, you can edit online faxes to remove personal information. This part of the chapter addresses creating, sending, and working with faxes in Word 2003. To kick off the discussion, the standard approach of using a fax modem is described first.

> **Note** If you use Internet fax services, you'll probably have to pay a fee to a third-party vendor for the service. If you use a fax modem's software, you can send faxes using the Fax Wizard in Word. If you use the Microsoft Fax program with your fax modem, the Fax Wizard in Word 2003 automatically opens the Send Fax Wizard, as described later in this chapter.

Sending a Fax Using a Fax Modem

Word has long offered the ability to fax a document using a computer's fax modem. Word 2003 continues to offer this capability. To use a fax modem, you must have your fax modem set up on your system in the Printers And Faxes folder. To verify this, display the Control Panel, and then double-click the Printers And Faxes icon.

If a fax modem is installed on your computer, you can send a document as a fax directly to a recipient. To send a document as a fax, follow these steps:

1 Open your document, and choose File, Send To, Recipient Using A Fax Modem. The Fax Wizard appears, as shown in Figure 24-26.

Figure 24-26. The Fax Wizard walks you step-by-step through the process of creating and sending your fax.

Tip **Start a fax from scratch**

If you want to send a fax without first creating a new document—for those times when you simply want to send a file as an attachment or send only a cover page with a note—you start by opening the New Document task pane, as follows:

- Choose File, New. The New Document task pane appears.
- Click the On My Computer link in the Templates section. The Templates dialog box appears.
- Click the Letters & Faxes tab, click Fax Wizard, and then click OK. The Fax Wizard welcome page appears, as shown in Figure 24-26.

2 After the Fax Wizard opens, click Next to begin the process. The Document To Fax page allows you to specify which document you want to fax. By default, the current document is selected. If you have more than one document open and you want to choose a document other than the one shown, click the arrow for the list and select the document you want to send. You can also choose whether you want to include a cover sheet.

3 After you specify the fax document and your cover sheet preference, click Next to proceed to the Fax Software page of the wizard. The Fax Software page of the Fax Wizard enables you to select the fax program you want to use. You can choose

Microsoft Fax or another fax program using the list. If you don't see the program you want to use, click the Other button, and then navigate to the folder containing the fax program you need.

Tip **Print a document for faxing**
If you will be walking down the hall and using the office fax machine to send a fax, you can click the I Want To Print My Document So I Can Send It From A Separate Fax Machine option in the Fax Wizard to tell Word to print the selected document in fax format.

4 Click Next. If you chose to use Microsoft Fax, the Fax Wizard completes, and the Send Fax Wizard opens, which walks you through the process of completing the fax transmission. Otherwise, the Word Fax Wizard continues to the Recipients page. The Recipients page of the Fax Wizard lets you specify who you want to receive your fax. Here you can select individuals from your Address Book or you can type names and fax numbers in the boxes provided.

5 After you specify fax recipients, click Next to access the Cover Sheet page. Word provides three styles for the fax cover sheet—professional, contemporary, and elegant. Each is displayed on the Cover Sheet page of the Fax Wizard (which appears only if you selected a fax program that has cover sheet capability). Make your selection, and then click Next.

6 The Sender page of the Fax Wizard is about you—or your company. Fill in whatever information you want the recipient to know about you in the following boxes: Name, Company, Mailing Address, Phone, and Fax. Click Next to continue.

Tip **Save time by using the Address Book**
If you have created an entry for yourself with your company's information in an address book, you can have Word plug in the information automatically by clicking Address Book, choosing the address book you want to use (such as your Contacts folder in Outlook), and then selecting your name from the list. Word inserts the information you've entered on the Sender page so that you don't have to retype it.

7 The final page of the Fax Wizard simply tells you to click Finish to send the fax. Click Finish. Word starts your fax software, which dials the first number in your recipient list and begins to transmit the fax.

Tip **Help the fax program dial correctly**
If your fax program is having a hard time dialing a number correctly—for instance, it dials 1 before an area code when you'd rather it didn't—you can work around this without reconfiguring your area code rules. To do so, opt to bypass area code rules, and simply type the complete phone number (including area code) for the fax recipient in the fax phone number text box when you complete a fax wizard.

Troubleshooting

I can't find the Fax Wizard

If the Fax Wizard option is missing from the Letters & Faxes tab, you might need to install the Fax templates and wizard in Word. To do so, follow these steps:

1. Choose Start, Control Panel (or Start, Settings, Control Panel if you're using Classic View or a version of the Windows operating system earlier than Windows XP).
2. In the Control Panel, double-click Add Or Remove Programs, click Microsoft Office in the Currently Installed Programs list, and then click Change. The Microsoft Office 2003 Setup dialog box appears.
3. Select the Add Or Remove Features option, and then click Next.
4. Select the Choose Advanced Customization Of Applications check box, and then click Next.
5. Expand Microsoft Office Word, expand Wizards And Templates, click Faxes, and then choose Run From My Computer from the menu.
6. Click the Update button to install the Fax templates and wizard.

If you are using Office on a network, be sure to check with your network administrator before installing any new features.

Troubleshooting

The Microsoft Fax option is unavailable

If the Microsoft Fax option appears dimmed in the Fax Wizard, you might need to install it. To do so, follow these steps:

1. Choose Start, Control Panel (or Start, Settings, Control Panel if you're using Classic View or a version of Windows earlier than Windows XP).
2. In the Control Panel, double-click Add Or Remove Programs, and then click Add/Remove Windows Components. The Microsoft Setup Wizard appears.
3. Select Fax Services, and then click Next.
4. After the installation is complete, click Finish.

In addition, ensure that a fax modem is configured in the Printers And Faxes folder in the Control Panel.

Sending Faxes Using an Internet Fax Service

If you don't have a fax modem installed on your computer or you'd like to take advantage of features provided with online faxing, you can sign up to use an Internet fax service. Word 2003 works seamlessly with Internet fax services, and you'll find that you have quite a bit of control over faxes you send using this method.

To sign up with a fax service, choose File, Send To, Recipient Using Internet Fax Service. When you choose this option for the first time, you'll see a message box, as shown in Figure 24-27, that states that you must sign up with a fax service provider before you can use a fax service to send faxes. Click OK to access the Office Marketplace Web site, which offers a selection of available fax services.

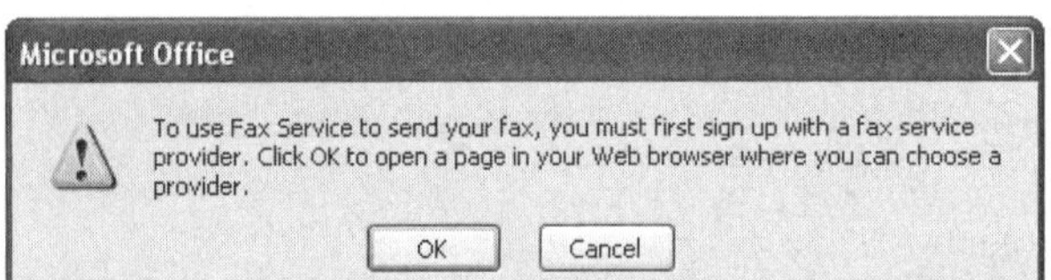

Figure 24-27. You must sign up with an Internet fax service before you can use Internet fax services in Word.

After you select and sign up with an Internet fax service provider, you can fax a Word document by performing the following steps:

1. Ensure that Outlook is installed, open the document you want to send in Word, and then choose File, Send To, Recipient Using Internet Fax Service. The Sent With Microsoft Office 2003 Fax Service message window opens with the current document name inserted in the Attach text box, as shown in Figure 24-28. Notice that the attached document carries the .tif extension. This is because Internet fax services convert documents into Tagged Image File Format (TIFF) graphic files.

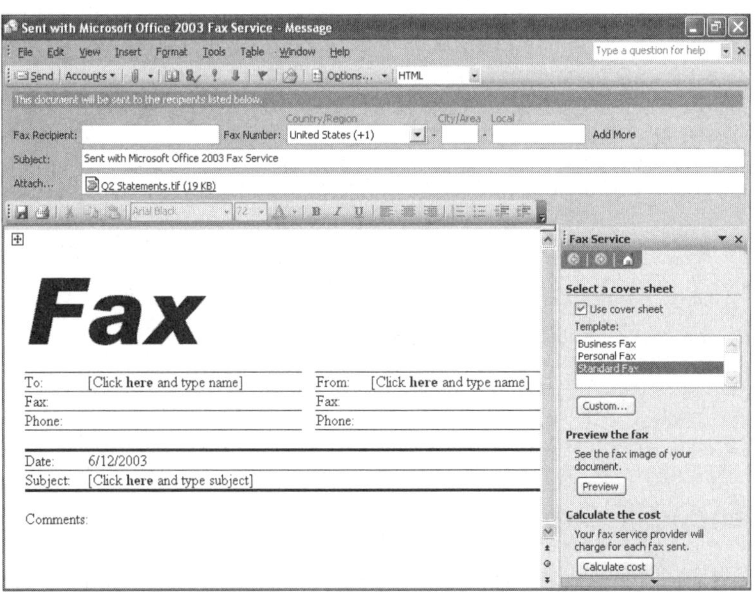

Figure 24-28. The Sent With Microsoft 2003 Fax Service message window opens automatically when you fax a document using an Internet fax service, and it includes the new Fax Service task pane.

> **Note** If Outlook is installed but not open when you send a fax, the fax will be placed in Outlook's Outbox, and your fax will be sent the next time mail is sent from Outlook. If you want to send your fax immediately, ensure that Outlook is open before you send the fax.

2. Enter the information in the Fax Recipient area. If you'd like to send the fax to more than one recipient, click Add More, and then enter additional recipient information.
3. In the Subject line, replace the *Sent With Microsoft Office 2003 Fax Service* text with your own text.
4. In the Fax Service task pane, specify whether you want to use a cover sheet (using a cover sheet is highly recommended). If you opt to use a cover sheet, you can choose from Business Fax, Personal Fax, Standard Fax, or Custom. If you click Custom, the existing fax cover letter is removed, and you can either create or insert a custom cover page. Keep in mind that headers and footers are not supported in blank cover pages.

> **Note** In addition to cover page options, the Fax Service task pane provides options that enable you to calculate the cost of sending the current fax and provides a link to your fax service's Web site.

5. Complete the cover page information. If you have Person Name smart tags enabled, you can use the smart tags to insert the To and From address information.
6. After you complete the cover page information, click Preview in the Fax Service task pane if you want to see how your fax transmission will appear to the recipient. You fax document will appear in the Microsoft Office Document Imaging window, as shown in Figure 24-29.

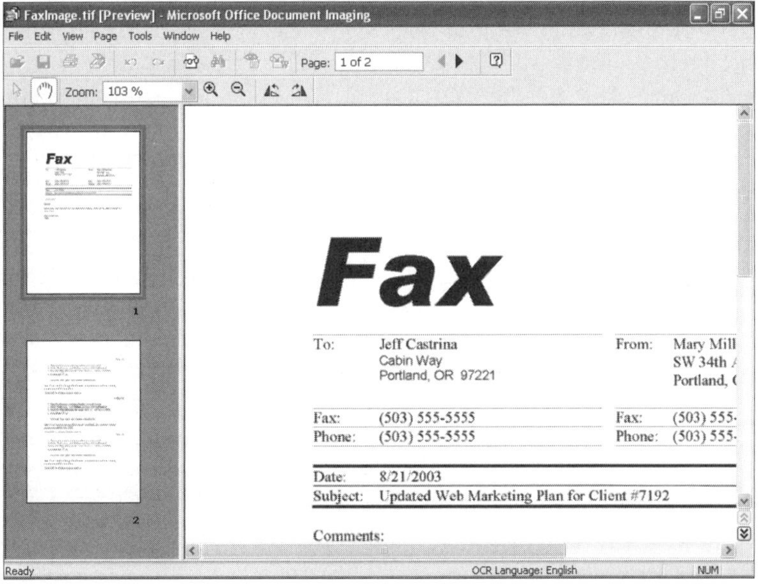

Figure 24-29. After Word creates a TIFF format version of your fax document and cover page, you can preview the information in the Microsoft Office Document Imaging window.

7. To view each page in the Microsoft Office Document Imaging window, click each thumbnail image in the Thumbnail pane. If everything looks good, close the Microsoft Office Document Imaging window to return to the fax message window.
8. Click Send in the fax message window's toolbar.

After you send a fax, most Internet fax services send a "success" or "failure" e-mail message to let you know if your fax transmission was successful.

Troubleshooting

I can't align the information on the default cover pages properly

If you experience alignment problems on your cover page, you might be placing your insertion point too close to the label on the default Business Fax, Personal Fax, or Standard Fax cover pages. If this occurs, click farther away from the label before typing. For instance, click below your address in the Fax field instead of clicking immediately after the *Fax* label. If you want to be sure about cursor placement, display hidden characters by showing the Standard toolbar (choose View, Toolbars, Standard), and then clicking Show/Hide to display hidden table cells and tab settings.

Troubleshooting

I can't send a fax using the Internet fax service

When you send a fax using an Internet fax service, you basically convert your document into a TIFF file and attach it to an e-mail message, which is then sent to the recipient's fax machine or fax modem. The body of the e-mail message contains the cover sheet, and the attached TIFF file is the fax document. By default, you must have both Outlook 2003 and Word 2003 installed and configured on your system to use an Internet fax service. If your fax isn't being sent or if you're not sure whether your fax was sent, you can perform the following checks:

- Verify whether Outlook 2003 sent your fax. To do so, open Outlook 2003, and then look in the Sent Items folder. Your fax will appear as an e-mail message with an attachment. If your fax message is sitting in the Outbox folder, click Send/Receive in the Outlook toolbar to send the fax.
- Check the Outlook 2003 Inbox to see if you received a message from your Internet fax service provider that states whether your fax transmission succeeded or failed. Generally, Internet fax services send confirmation messages to your Outlook inbox whenever you attempt to send a fax.

- Ensure that the Microsoft Office Document Image Writer print driver is installed in your Printers And Faxes folder. If it is missing, you can install it using the Microsoft Office 2003 Setup. To do so, click Start, Control Panel, Add Or Remove Programs, Microsoft Office, and then click the Change button. Then select Add Or Remove Features, click Next, select the Choose Advanced Customization Of Applications check box, click Next, expand Office Tools, expand Microsoft Office Document Imaging, click Microsoft Office Document Image Writer, click Run From My Computer, click Update, and then click OK after the update completes.
- Ensure that your Internet fax service is properly activated. If you're unsure, visit your Internet fax service provider's online help pages or contact their support group. Usually, after you sign up with an Internet fax service provider, you'll receive a welcome e-mail message verifying your status, user information, and login parameters.

Tip **Send merged faxes**
You can send multiple faxes that you create by using the Mail Merge Wizard. Start by opening the document you want to fax, and then choose Tools, Letters And Mailings, Mail Merge. The Mail Merge task pane opens. When the Mail Merge Wizard asks you to specify a print option, choose your fax application in the Name list in the Print dialog box. For more information about creating and working with mail-merged documents, see Chapter 30, "Performing Mail Merges."

Converting and Faxing Unsupported File Types

You can use Office 2003 capabilities to convert unsupported file types. To take advantage of this capability, you have to be able to open the unsupported file type in an application—such as opening a Portable Document Format (PDF) file in Adobe Acrobat Reader—and you must have the Microsoft Office Document Image Writer installed as a printer in the Print And Faxes folder in the Control Panel. If your system meets both those requirements, you can convert a file into a TIFF file. To do so, follow these steps:

1. Open the file, and then choose File, Print. The Print dialog box appears.
2. In the Name list in the Printer section, choose Microsoft Office Document Image Writer.
3. Click the Properties button, and then click the Advanced tab in the Microsoft Office Document Image Writer Properties dialog box.
4. In the Advanced tab, choose the TIFF – Monochrome Fax option, and then click OK.
5. In the Print dialog box, click OK. The Save As dialog box appears.
6. Specify a name and location for the TIFF file.

After you create a TIFF file, you can fax the TIFF file from Word. To do so, open Word, choose File, Send To, Recipient Using Internet Fax Service to start the fax service. In the message window, clear the Attach text box (by right-clicking in the text box, and then choosing Clear from the menu), click Attach to open the Insert File dialog box, and then navigate to the TIFF file. When you attach a TIFF file, it will be sent as a fax document. To view how the attachment will appear when it is sent, click Preview in the Fax Service task pane.

Tip **Send a TIFF File using Microsoft Office Document Imaging**
To send a TIFF file without opening Word, double-click the TIFF file to open it in the Microsoft Office Document Imaging window, and then choose File, Send To, Recipient Using Internet Fax Service.

Sending a PDF File

If your Internet fax service provider supports PDF documents, you can fax PDF documents using Word 2003 without first manually converting the PDF file into a TIFF file. To do this, open Word or Outlook, and then choose File, Send To, Recipient Using Internet Fax Service. In the fax message window, delete the file name in the Attach text box, click the Attach label to open the Insert File dialog box, and then use the Insert File dialog box to locate and insert the PDF file. After you attach a PDF file, complete the cover letter, and then click Send. You'll receive a message box stating that the information will be converted into a graphic. Click OK. Then you'll receive a message box stating that Office can't convert the attached file type, but possibly the Internet fax service provider can. Click Yes to indicate that you want to proceed, and then the document will be sent to your Internet fax service provider for further file conversion.

Note Because Office 2003 doesn't support the PDF file format, you can't preview a fax created with a PDF file. If you want to use the fax preview feature, you'll have to convert the PDF file into a TIFF file before you create your fax.

Forwarding an Online Fax Using Microsoft Office Document Imaging (MODI)

You can forward an online fax in a couple of ways. First, you can forward a fax as an e-mail with a TIFF attachment by forwarding the Outlook message stored in your Inbox or Sent Items folder in the same way you forward e-mails (select the message, and then choose Forward on the Outlook toolbar). Alternatively, if you'd like to create a new cover page, you can open the fax message's attachment by double-clicking the attachment icon or right-clicking the attachment file, and then choosing Open. By default, the attachment will open in MODI. After you open the fax document, you can create a new fax by choosing File, Send To, Recipient Using Internet Fax Service in the Microsoft Office Document Imaging window.

NEW FEATURE! Removing Personal Information from an Online Fax Using Microsoft Office Document Imaging

At times, you might want to share parts of a fax document, but remove sensitive or personal information. Using Microsoft Office Document Imaging (MODI), you can black out content in TIFF files or remove pages, such as a fax transmission's cover page. If you want to save changes you make to a TIFF file in MODI, ensure that the Make Annotations Permanent When Document Is Saved option is on. To access this option, in the MODI window choose Tools, Options, and then click the Annotations tab if necessary. In the Annotations tab, you can select the Make Annotations Permanent When Document Is Saved check box, and then click OK.

After you've determined whether you want to save document changes, you can edit a fax document or other TIFF file by performing the following steps:

1. Right-click the TIFF file attached to a fax you received in Outlook, choose Open, and then click Open in the message box. The file opens in MODI by default.
2. To remove a page, click on the page in the Thumbnail pane, and then choose Page, Cut Page (or press Ctrl+Shift+X).
3. To black out information, click the arrow on the Pen button on the Annotations toolbar, choose Pen Settings, select Chisel Marker (10.5 mm) in the Pen Settings tab in the Pen & Highlighter Settings dialog box, and then click OK.
4. With the Pen button selected, drag your cursor over the information you want to hide.
5. After you finish modifying the TIFF file, save the file (if desired), and then click File, Send To, Recipient Using Internet Fax Service to fax the file.

Conducting Online Meetings with NetMeeting

Word, like other Office applications, works with Internet Explorer to provide online collaboration. This pairing of technologies enables you to conduct online interactive meetings by using NetMeeting. NetMeeting is a conferencing application that includes the following components:

- Application sharing
- Audio capabilities
- File distribution and sharing
- Internet calling capabilities
- Text-based chat
- Video capabilities
- Virtual whiteboard

As you might imagine, using the audio and video capabilities requires that participants have speakers, microphones, and Web cameras installed on their systems. To use NetMeeting in Word, you must first configure NetMeeting in Internet Explorer, as described next.

Installing and Getting Familiar with NetMeeting

NetMeeting can be installed when you install Internet Explorer, so your system might already have NetMeeting installed. To find out whether NetMeeting is installed on your computer, open Internet Explorer, and then choose File, New, Internet Call. If NetMeeting is installed but you've never configured the application, the NetMeeting Wizard will appear. Simply complete the information in the NetMeeting Wizard, shown in Figure 24-30, to set up your NetMeeting application.

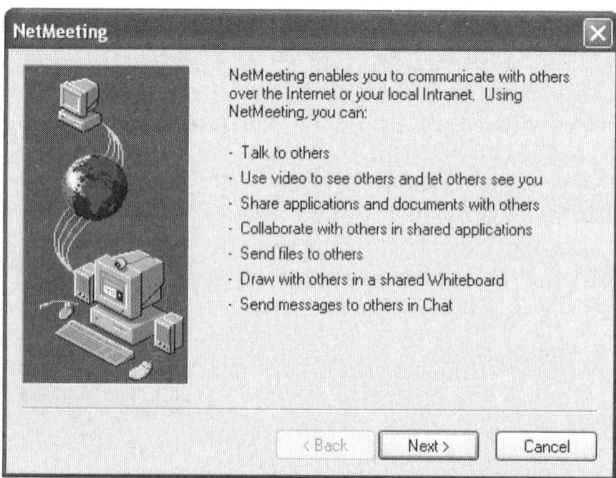

Figure 24-30. The NetMeeting Wizard walks you through setting up NetMeeting. The system's microphone and video camera should be installed before you run the NetMeeting Wizard.

If NetMeeting isn't installed on your computer, you can download the latest version of NetMeeting from Microsoft, at *www.microsoft.com/windows/netmeeting*. After you download NetMeeting, you'll need to work through the NetMeeting Wizard to configure your settings.

After you work through the NetMeeting Wizard, the NetMeeting window appears. To display the NetMeeting window from within Word in the future, you can choose Tools, Online Collaboration, Meet Now, or you can open NetMeeting from within Internet Explorer by choosing File, New, Internet Call. After you open Messenger, you can use the messenger window to send meeting information (including video) or you can use the Online Meeting toolbar.

After NetMeeting is running, you can check your video camera's operation and angle by clicking the Start Video button in the NetMeeting window. Figure 24-31 shows the NetMeeting interface with video turned on.

Figure 24-31. The NetMeeting interface provides features you need to collaborate online with others who have NetMeeting installed on their systems.

To get you up and running quickly, Table 24-2 describes the buttons available in the NetMeeting window.

Table 24-2. NetMeeting Tools

Button	Name	Description
	Place Call	Opens the Place A Call dialog box, from which you can place a call to another NetMeeting user.
	End Call	Disconnects your computer from a conference.
	Find Someone In A Directory	Opens the Find Someone dialog box, which contains a link to Windows Messenger. Windows Messenger capabilities replace the features provided by the Microsoft Internet Directory in earlier versions of NetMeeting.
	Start Video/ Stop Video	Starts and pauses video transmission.
	Picture-In-Picture	Displays your video as a small picture in the lower-right corner of the video screen so that you can see your video and the video of the other conference participant at the same time. (Note that only two people at a time can use video during a meeting, even if more than two people have video cameras.)

Table 24-2. NetMeeting Tools

Button	Name	Description
	Adjust Audio Volume View Participant List	Toggles between showing the microphone and speaker audio controls, and showing a list of the user names of meeting participants. When speaker controls are displayed, the button changes to View Participant List; you can click View Participant List to display the list of meeting participants' user names again.
	Share Program	Opens the Sharing dialog box, which enables you to share your computer's resources with other meeting participants.
	Chat	Opens the Chat window, which lets meeting participants communicate by entering text.
	Whiteboard	Opens the Whiteboard, which offers typical paint program capabilities.
	Transfer Files	Opens the File Transfer window, which enables you to transfer files to meeting participants.

For a full review of NetMeeting and its features, refer to the NetMeeting Help files (access by choosing Help, Help Topics in the NetMeeting window).

Joining Web Discussions

Another way to communicate online is to take part in Web Discussions. The Web Discussions features in Office enable you to attach comments to and insert comments in a Web page or any file you can open in an Office application and view in a Web browser (including .htm, .xls, .doc, and .ppt files). The comments you attach to the document appear within the document when it is displayed online but are stored on a discussion server, not in the document, and not necessarily on the same server that stores the document. Figure 24-32 shows a document containing discussion comments that is stored on a SharePoint Team Services Web site. Notice that some comments have been inserted directly in the document and others appear below the document. You can insert and view discussion comments in either location. Keep in mind that a server administrator must set up Web Discussions before you can use this feature.

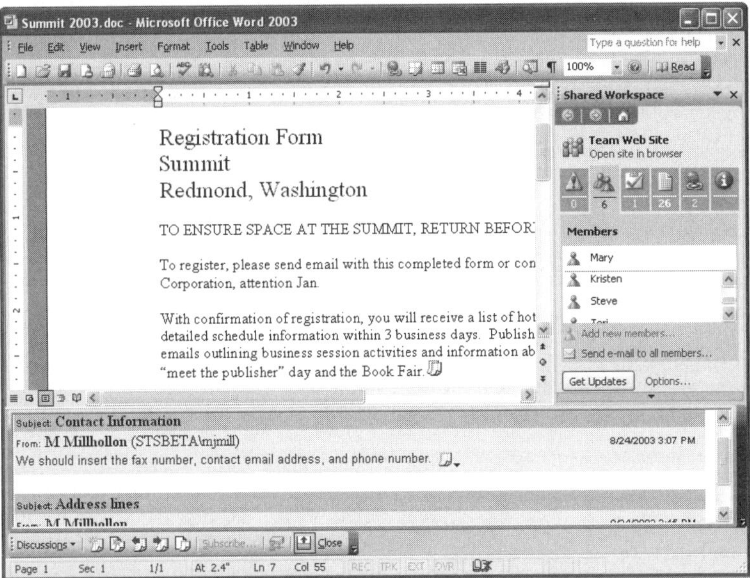

Figure 24-32. The Web Discussions feature in Office enables you to add comments to online documents for others to read and respond to.

For more information about team Web sites and SharePoint, see Chapter 25, "Working with Shared Documents."

Connecting to a Discussion Server

After your server administrator sets up the Web Discussions feature, you can connect to the discussion server and participate in Web Discussions. To connect to a discussion server, follow these steps:

1. Choose Tools, Online Collaboration, Web Discussions. The Web Discussions toolbar appears, as shown in Figure 24-33.

Figure 24-33. The Web Discussions toolbar provides buttons you can use to connect to discussion servers and participate in Web Discussions.

2. On the Web Discussions toolbar, click Discussions to display the Discussions menu, shown in Figure 24-34, and then choose Discussion Options. The Discussion Options dialog box appears.

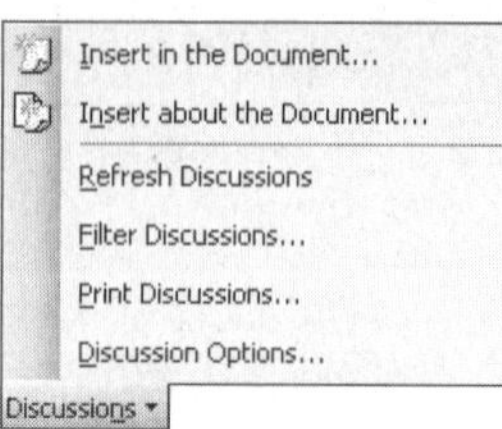

Figure 24-34. The Discussions button provides a menu of options for discussions.

3. To create a link to a new discussion server, click Add. The Add Or Edit Discussion Servers dialog box appears.
4. In the Type The Name Of The Discussion Server Your Administrator Has Provided box, type the name of a discussion server. If security is set up on your discussion server using the Secure Sockets Layer (SSL), select the Secure Connection Required (SSL) check box.
5. In the You Can Type Any Name You Want To Use As A Friendly Name For The Discussion Server box, type the name you want to use for the server. Click OK to close the dialog box.
6. In the Discussion Options dialog box, click OK to connect to the discussion server listed in the Select A Discussion Server list.

After you connect to a discussion server, you can navigate to the online document you want to discuss, and then add discussion comments, as described next.

Participating in a Discussion

After you've accessed an online document or a Web page, you can participate in Web Discussions by using the Web Discussions toolbar buttons. Table 24-3 describes the buttons on the Web Discussions toolbar.

Table 24-3. Web Discussions Toolbar Buttons

Button	Name	Description
Discussions ▾	Discussions	Provides a menu containing discussion-related actions you can perform, such as filtering, refreshing, and printing discussions.
	Insert Discussion In The Document	Inserts a discussion comment (and comment icon) at the insertion point location in a paragraph in the document.
	Insert Discussion About The Document	Inserts a discussion comment in the Discussion pane, which is a separate pane that appears below the active document.

Table 24-3. Web Discussions Toolbar Buttons

Button	Name	Description
	Previous	When discussions appear in the Discussion pane, click this button to move to the preceding comment.
	Next	When discussions appear in the Discussion pane, click this button to move to the next comment.
	Show General Discussions	Displays discussions below the document instead of as inline discussion comments.
Subscribe...	Get Notified When Changes Occur	Opens the Document Subscription window, which enables you to have the discussion server notify you when a file or folder changes by periodically sending you an e-mail message.
	Stop Communication With Discussion Server	Disconnects your computer from the Web Discussions server.
	Show/Hide Discussion Pane	Displays or hides the Discussion pane. You can drag the pane's border to adjust its viewing area.
Close	Close Web Discussions	Closes the Web Discussions feature and toolbar.

To add a discussion comment about an online document using the Web Discussion toolbar buttons, follow these steps:

1. To insert an inline discussion comment, position the insertion point in the paragraph you want to discuss, and then click Insert Discussion In The Document. To insert a general discussion below the document, click Insert Discussion About The Document. The Enter Discussion Text dialog box appears.
2. In the Enter Discussion Text dialog box, click in the Discussion Subject box, and type a subject for your comment.
3. Click in the Discussion Text area, enter your comment, and then click OK. Your comment appears in the Discussion pane.

If you want to respond to an existing comment, you can click the Show A Menu Of Actions icon located at the end of a discussion comment, and then choose an action from the shortcut menu, as shown in Figure 24-35.

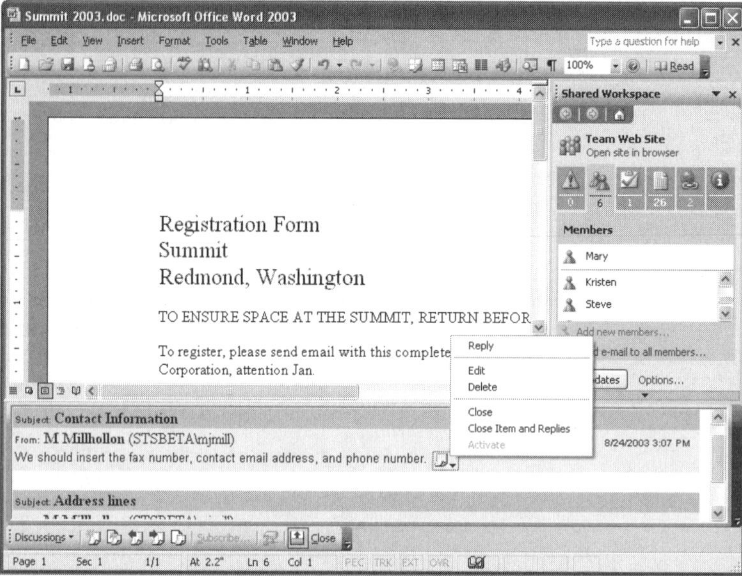

Figure 24-35. You can access a variety of actions by clicking the Show A Menu Of Actions icon that appears at the end of a discussion comment.

Most discussion features work with Office Server Extensions running on the network server. If you want to close and reactivate discussions or automatically store discussion comments on the same server as the document, the discussion server must be running Microsoft SharePoint Team Services. For more information about Microsoft SharePoint Team Services, see Chapter 25, "Working with Shared Documents."

Chapter 25

Working with Shared Documents

We live in an age of teamwork. If you haven't yet been assigned to a team—for creating next year's annual report, for analyzing and reporting on health care options, for designing and writing the new employee handbook—you probably will be before too long. Until now, you may have managed your team projects by keeping a folder full of revised files, gathering all the charts and images and notes and sending them as e-mail attachments to teammates as needed. The risk of managing large projects this way is twofold: an older version of a file might inadvertently be used instead of the most current file; and files (and people) could easily be left out of the process.

Word 2003 takes a huge step forward in helping you work collaboratively by enabling you to create an online Document Workspace where you can create a common area for storing, organizing, and managing the flow of information related to your team's project. This chapter shows you how to create and use a Document Workspace and use the Shared Workspace task pane to review, update, and exchange information about your shared documents.

Introducing SharePoint Team Services

The Shared Workspace feature in Word 2003 uses SharePoint Team Services, a group of Web products and services that enable you to organize, manage, share, and distribute information related to your team. A SharePoint Team Services site requires a Web server running Microsoft Windows 2000 Server or later, with Internet Information Services (IIS) 5, along with the Microsoft Data Engine (MSDE) or SQL Server 7 or later. However, to contribute to, access, or upload and download documents from a team site, you need only a Web browser. This makes it possible for team members all over the world—using different types of computers—to work effectively as one team.

You can get more information about SharePoint Products and Services by visiting *http://www.microsoft.com/sharepoint*.

How Will You Share Documents?

How will you first begin working with shared documents? Here are a few possible scenarios:

- You are at a team meeting when the leader selects you to write the first draft of the document you're all working on. This means you'll create the document in Word and then turn it into a shared document so others can review and comment on the draft. (The next section of the chapter will show you how to do that.)
- You are a member of a team and receive an e-mail message telling you that a copy of the first draft of the team document has been posted in the Document Workspace. How will you get to it? Read on.
- You are a member of the team and you receive an e-mail message with a shared file as an attachment. You can open the file as normal, make your changes, and then click Reply to send the revised file back to the teammate who sent it to you. In addition to sending the document back, the action also saves a copy of the document on the team site and ensures that each person works on the most recent version of the file.

The next sections of this chapter take a closer look at each of these aspects of working on a team and sharing documents. In addition to basic how-to's for viewing, sharing, and managing shared documents, you'll also learn how to customize and use the team Web site to keep your entire team moving in the right direction.

Sharing a Document

After writing, revising, and editing your draft of the new hiring policy, you think you're ready to distribute it to others on your team. You've reviewed it as well as you can—used the spelling checker, the grammar checker, and so on—and now you're ready to send your draft out for feedback. This is where you begin using Word's Shared Documents feature.

You have two choices when you're ready to share a document. You can create a shared Web site for the document or you can e-mail the document as a shared attachment to another person (or people). Either approach ends at the same place: a new team Web site on a shared server at a location you specify.

> **Tip** **Reserve your server space**
> To host a team Web site using the Document Workspace feature, you need Microsoft Windows 2000 Server or later, so check with your system administrator (or your Internet service provider [ISP]) to find out whether this option is available. Remember, however, that you can participate in using a team site if you use any Web browser running on any operating system.

Creating the Document Workspace

If you've just finished a draft of a document and you want to create a shared workspace so others can view the file, display the Tools menu and then choose Shared Workspace. The Shared Workspace task pane appears, as shown in Figure 25-1.

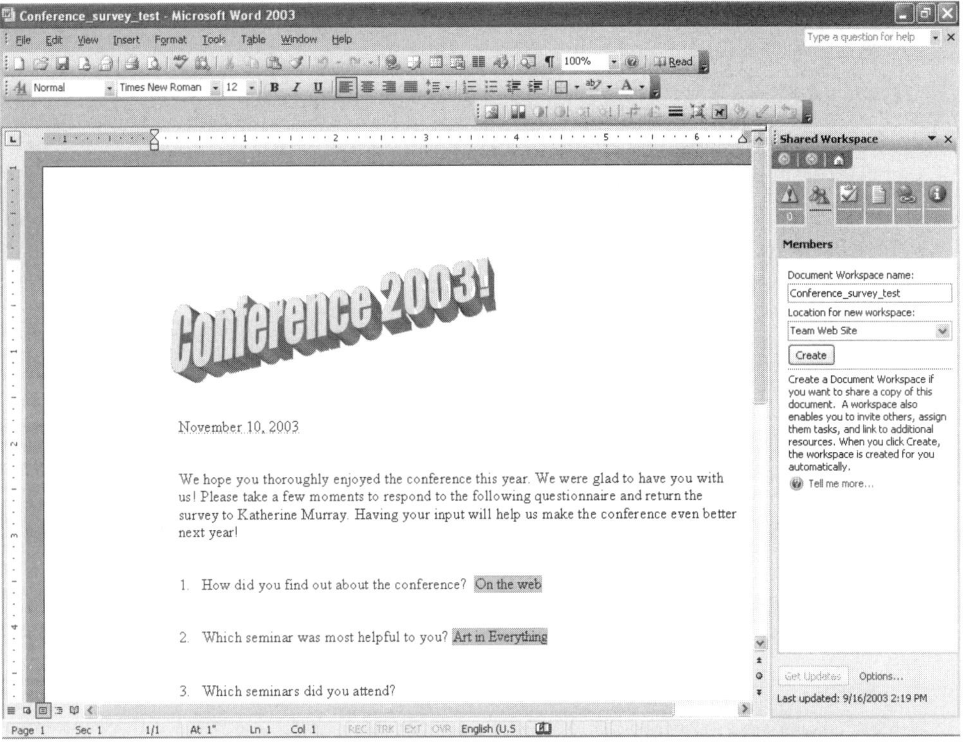

Figure 25-1. The Shared Workspace task pane contains everything you need to create and work with shared documents.

Click Create to begin the process. If you previously entered a Web address for your shared space, Word will find that address automatically and display the Connect box so that you can enter your user name and password. If you haven't already entered an address, you will be prompted to provide it. (Check with your system administrator or ISP for the address of the server space you can use.)

> **Note** Providing the address for the server space is necessary only if you are the one creating the shared workspace. If you are simply working with documents on a shared site (see the following two sections, "E-Mailing Shared Attachments" and "An Overview of the Shared Workspace Task Pane," for more information), the space already will have been created and you won't need to enter this information.

When the site is created, your name will appear in the Members tab (as shown in Figure 25-2) and the name of the document will appear at the top of the task pane.

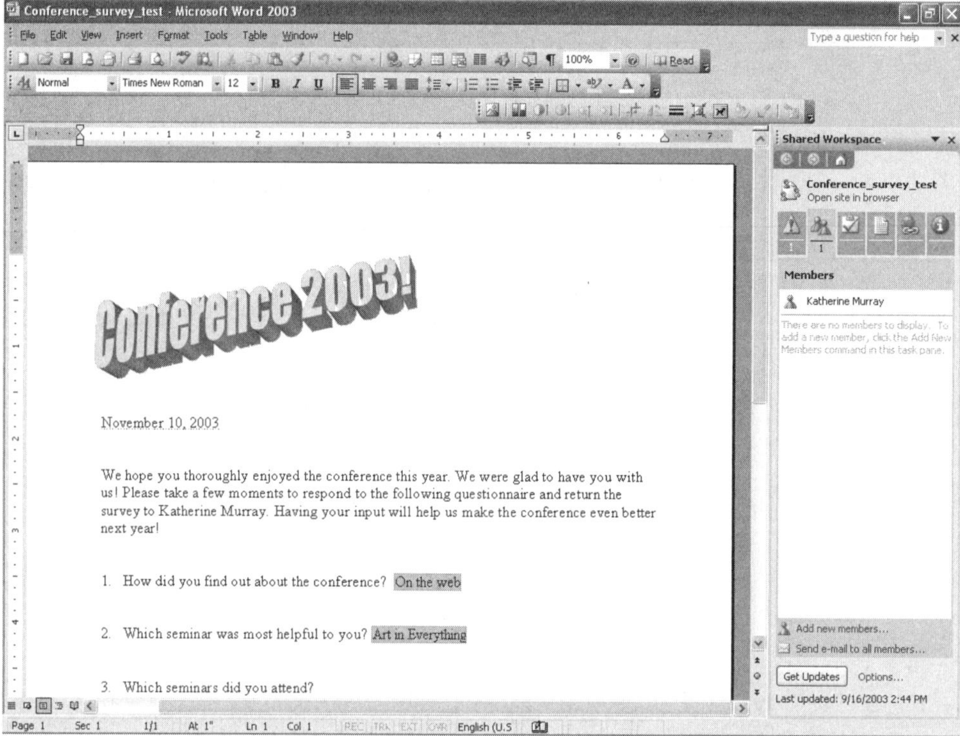

Figure 25-2. The Shared Workspace task pane shows you that the site has been created.

E-Mailing Shared Attachments

Perhaps the easiest way to create a shared workspace is simply to e-mail a shared attachment to someone else. Sound too simple to be true? Here's how it works:

1. Create and save your document as usual.
2. Display the File menu, and then choose Send To, Mail Recipient (For Review). An e-mail message appears, with the document in the Attachment line.
3. Click Attachment Options to the right of the message window. A task pane appears along the right edge of the message area.
4. Click Shared Attachments. A note is added to the body of the message, and the Document Workspace option becomes available, as shown in Figure 25-3.

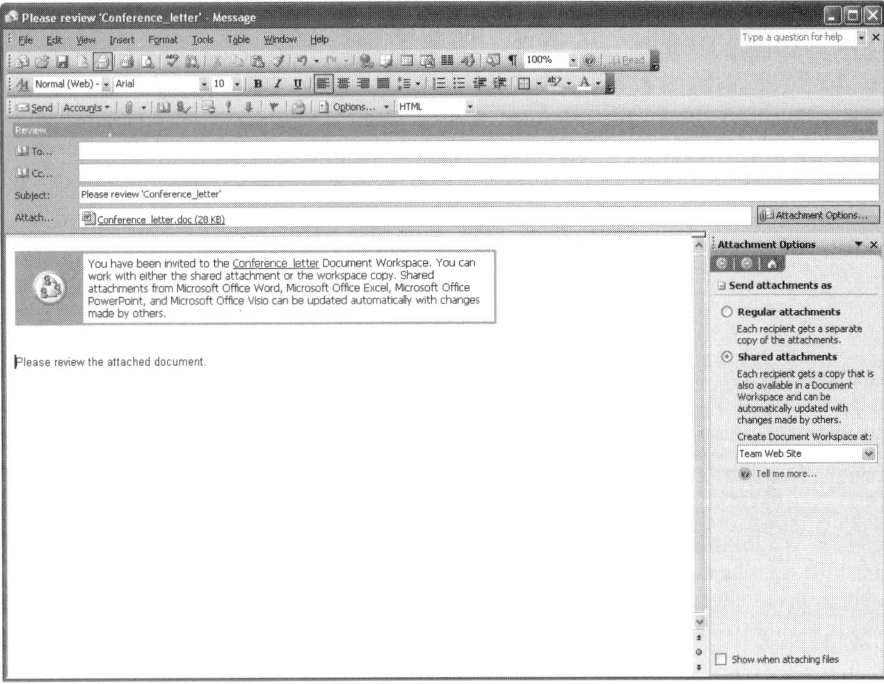

Figure 25-3. You can create a shared workspace by sending a shared attachment.

5 Click the Create Document Workspace At down arrow to choose where you want to create the team Web site, where the shared document will actually be stored.

6 Enter the names of the recipients in the To line, and then click Send.

With this simple procedure, a new shared workspace is created and the shared document is sent to all team members. When the recipients review and return the document to you, the most current version of the file will be kept on the team site so that the latest changes are automatically reflected in the final copy.

An Overview of the Shared Workspace Task Pane

Once you've created a shared workspace, the Shared Workspace task pane changes to provide information about the document and the site where it is stored. Figure 25-4 provides an overview of the elements in the task pane. Table 25-1 lists the tabs in the Shared Workspace task pane that can provide you with more information.

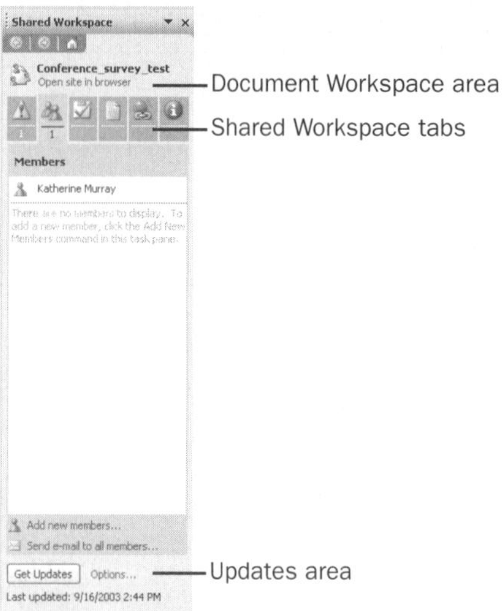

Figure 25-4. Elements in the Shared Workspace task pane give you information about your collaborative project.

You'll find the following tabs on the Shared Workspace task pane:

- The Document Workspace area enables you to access the site and perform other site functions, such as disconnecting from the site and deleting the site.
- The Shared Workspace tabs display additional information about different aspects of your site (see Table 25-1).
- The Updates area enables you to get instant updates on the information displayed in the task pane.

Table 25-1. Shared Workspace Tabs

	Status	Alerts you if the document needs to be updated, files have been checked in or out, or other changes have been made
	Members	Lists current members on the team site and displays options for adding members and sending e-mail to them
	Tasks	Lists all tasks assigned to each team member in the workspace
	Documents	Shows all documents currently stored in the shared workspace
	Links	Lists links that team members have provided as resources for the team
	Document Information	Gives pertinent information about the document that currently appears

Working with the Document Workspace

At the top of the Shared Workspace task pane, you see that you have the option of going to the team site that was just created. Position the pointer over the link and an arrow appears; click it to display a menu of choices as shown here:

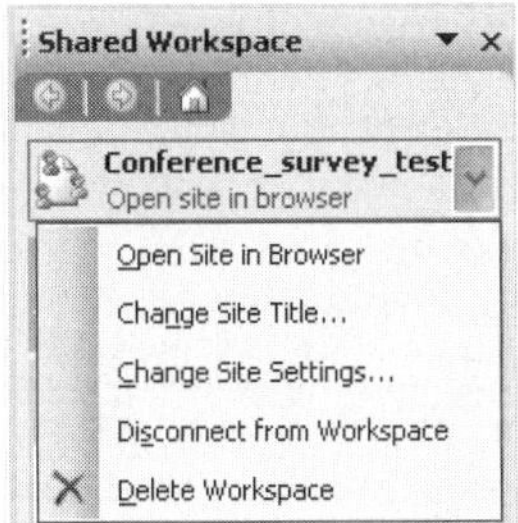

You can perform a number of site management tasks by using this menu; for now, however, click Open Site In Browser to go to the Web site. Figure 25-5 shows the team site in its default state.

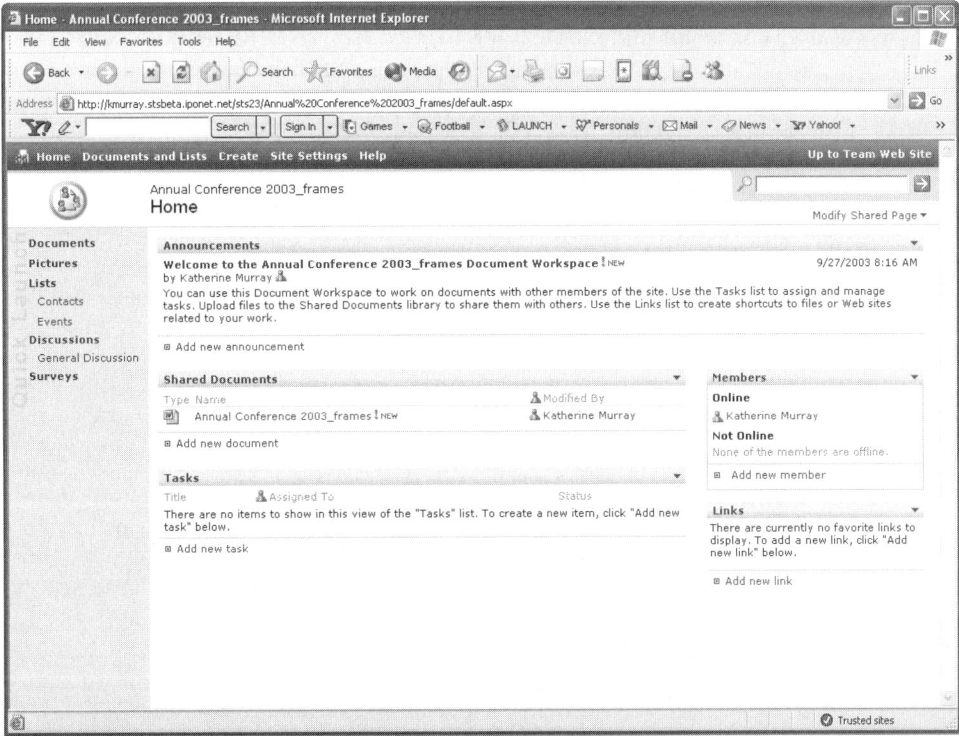

Figure 25-5. The new shared workspace team site includes areas for adding tasks, links, announcements, and more.

The following list describes the elements on the page:

- **Quick Launch** Serves as the navigation bar for your team Web site.
- **Announcements** You might want to post information about upcoming meetings, new resources, or after-work gatherings here. Click the Add New Announcement link to add your information.
- **Shared Documents** This is where your shared documents are listed. You can view, edit, check out, and discuss documents by clicking the items displayed here.
- **Tasks** When you assign tasks to various team members—one person is gathering the images for the report, another is getting the financial information from the accounting department—click Add New Task, and then add the information here.
- **Members** Shows all the members of your team and gives you the Add New Member link to expand your roster.
- **Links** Provides a common place for you to list helpful Web sites that can be used as resources for those working on your team.

Navigating the Site

The Quick Launch area, shown below, helps you navigate to various pages on the new team site. The Documents link takes you to a page that lists all shared documents stored on the site. Clicking Pictures enables you to create a library of images, movie clips, and diagrams you will be using in your team project. The Lists link takes you to a page where you can make changes to the lists SharePoint Team Services enable you to collect information for.

> **Note** All the data items you enter in the Document Workspace—announcements, contacts, events, links, and tasks—are stored in list form. You can modify the information that is shown, add information, and export list data to other Microsoft Office applications using the Lists view.

The General Discussion link enables you to create a message thread similar to those in newsgroups so that you can review and comment on the developing team project. Finally, the Surveys link takes you to a page that enables you to create online surveys to gather team opinions and reactions to topics related to the project.

Adding Information on the Site

As you can see, you can add information items on the shared workspace site, or you can add tasks, members, and other items by working with the Shared Workspace task pane in Word. Because the focus of this chapter is really sharing documents from within Word, we're going to return to the Shared Workspace task pane for most of the examples in this chapter. However, it's worth noting that there are a few actions that you'll want to perform on the site itself. On the team Web site, you will probably want to do the following:

- **Add announcements about upcoming team meetings** Click Add New Announcement to enter the information you want the team to know (as shown in Figure 25-6). Click the Choose Date From Calendar button to set the expiration date for the announcement.

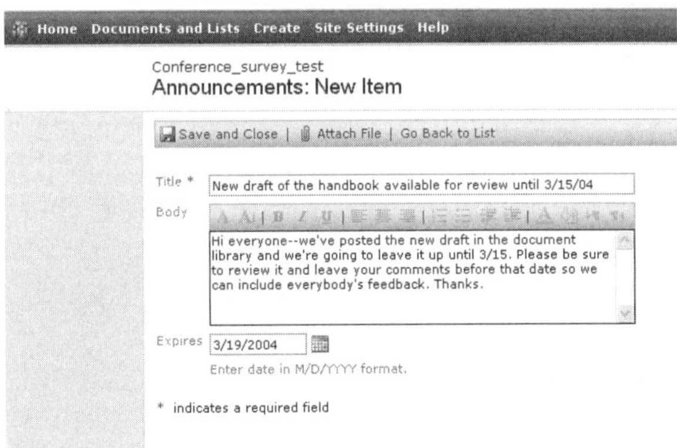

Figure 25-6. Use announcements to let team members know about changes to the site or upcoming events.

- **Create events to post upcoming deadlines or important meetings** Click Events in the Quick Launch area to create an event. Here you can enter the beginning and ending time, the location, and a description of the event. Additionally, you can create recurring appointments that continue indefinitely or are scheduled to end on a specific date (as shown in Figure 25-7).

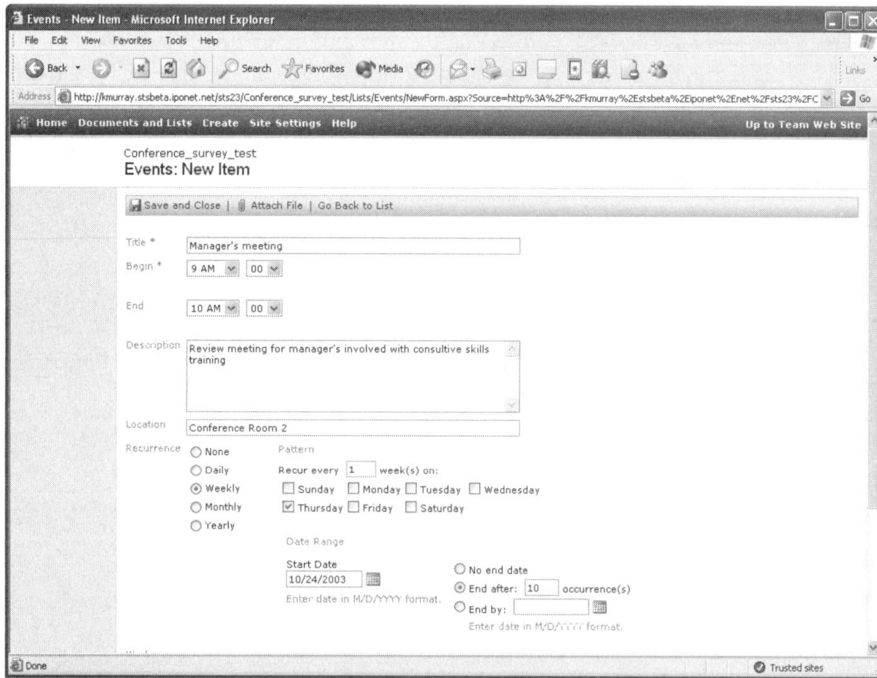

Figure 25-7. You can create events for the team and schedule face-to-face or virtual meetings online.

- **Have discussions about the project** On the team site, you can create a newsgroup-style discussion about issues related to your project. Click General Discussion in the Quick Launch area to go to the General Discussion page, where you can enter new postings and reply to other postings (as shown in Figure 25-8).

> **Tip** **Synchronize your schedule with Outlook**
> When you create events on the team site, you also have the option of synchronizing the schedule with your Outlook Calendar. On the Events page, Click Link To Outlook and a prompt will ask whether you want to add a new Events folder to Outlook. Click Yes. Now as you create, add, and remove events on the team site, the changes will be downloaded to your Outlook Events folder.

This is only a quick overview of some of the features on the shared workspace site you may want to try. The site is easy to use and modify—you'll want to spend some time exploring and experimenting to create just the right setup for your team.

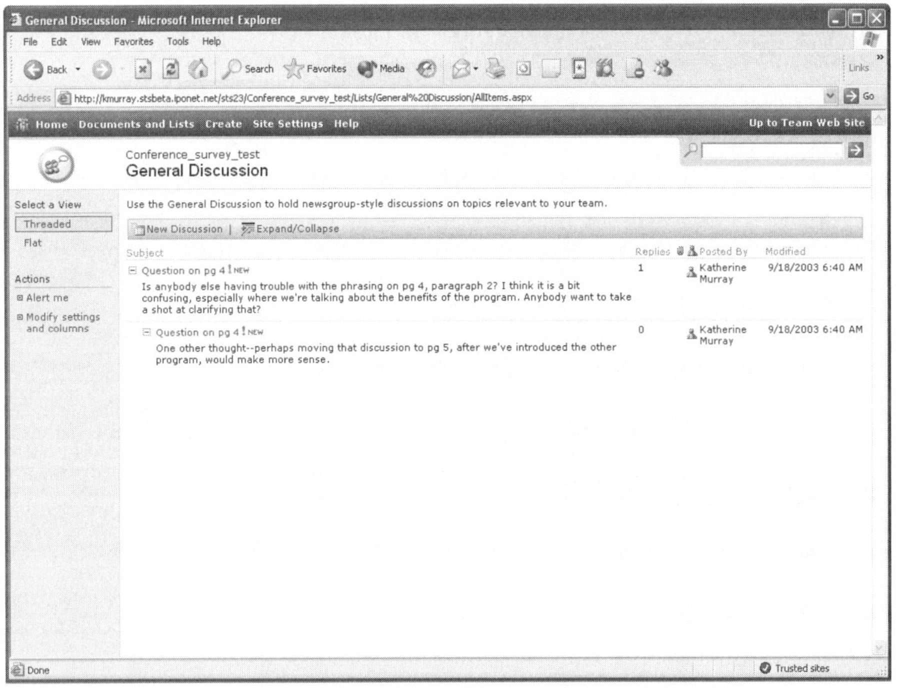

Figure 25-8. You can hold online discussions of issues related to your team project by using the General Discussion feature.

Working in the Shared Workspace Task Pane

Now that you know how to create a shared workspace and understand the site you've created online, you're ready to return to Word and use the features in the Shared Workspace task pane. This is where the benefits of these collaboration features really shine—you can manage, review, access, edit, and update your team documents, all right from within Word! This process is really no more difficult than working with any other document. This section of the chapter takes you through the major tasks you'll want to perform on shared documents.

Adding Team Members

One of the first things you'll want to do is add team members for your shared project. Open the Shared Workspace task pane (press Ctrl+F1 when your shared document is open on the screen), and then click the Members tab. This tab of the Shared Workspace task pane lists all active members, shows you whether they are online or not, gives you a link to add new members, and offers the option of sending e-mail to all members at once, as shown in Figure 25-9.

Figure 25-9. The Members tab enables you to add, organize, and contact members.

To add a new member, click the Add New Member link at the bottom of the task pane. In the Add New Members dialog box, type the names or e-mail addresses of others on your team, as shown in Figure 25-10.

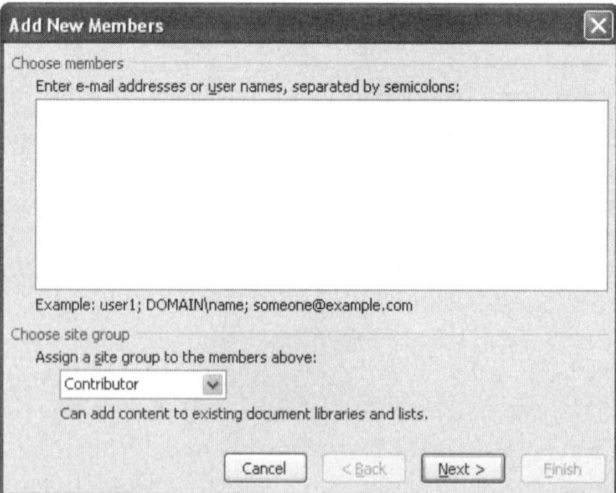

Figure 25-10. Enter the e-mail addresses of team members and assign them to a site group to control site access.

In the Choose Site Group section, you make selections that determine what kind of permissions you grant to the users you are adding. The four site groups and their permission levels are as follows:

- **Reader** Gives members read-only privileges
- **Contributor** Enables members to read and add postings on the site
- **Web Designer** Lets members read, post, and modify items on the site
- **Administrator** Includes full access; members of this group can read, post, modify, and add or delete users and pages

> **Note** The site group you select will be applied to all users you list in the Choose Members box in the Add New Members dialog box. This means that if you want to assign different users to different site groups, you'll need to add the members in batches.

Click Next. The member names and e-mail addresses appear in the next display. Enter a display name for each member, if you like, verify the addresses, and then click Finish. A message tells you that the members have been added and asks whether you'd like to send an e-mail message to the new participants, as shown here:

When you click OK, Word displays the e-mail message that will be sent to new team members. You can add your own message as needed and then click Send to deliver the message.

Adding Tasks

Delegation is a major part of getting any collaborative project done. Who does what is important, because everyone's work depends on everyone else. You can assign and review task assignments in the Shared Workspace task pane. Here's how:

1. With your document open, display the Shared Workspace task pane.
2. Click the Tasks tab, and then click Add New Task at the bottom of the task pane.
3. In the Task dialog box, shown in Figure 25-11, enter a title for the task. Then complete the Status, Priority, and Assigned To fields.

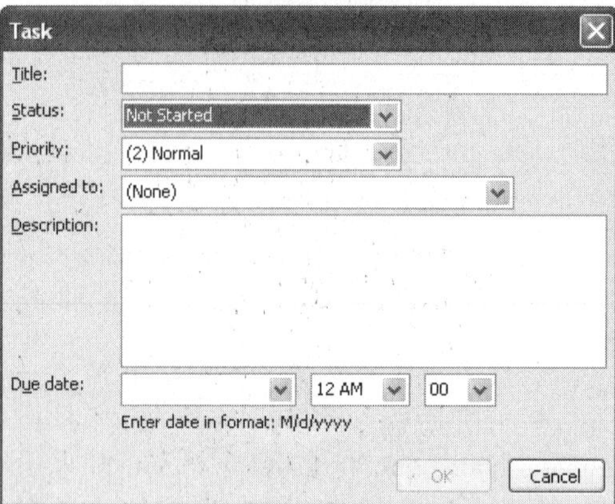

Figure 25-11. The Task dialog box collects information about the who, what, and when of any task that needs to be done.

4 If necessary, add a description to provide instructions about the task, and then enter a due date by selecting it from the calendar (click the arrow) or by typing it in the form *m/d/yyyy*.

5 Click OK to add the task.

After the task is added, you can view it at any time by clicking the Task tab. When you click the arrow to the left of the task, a list of task options appears. You'll use these options to update the status of your tasks or to remove tasks from the list.

Inside Out

Setting alerts

One of the great features of SharePoint Team Services and the Shared Workspace task pane is that they can automatically keep you in touch with any changes made on the team site or in your shared documents. Click Alert Me About Tasks in the bottom of the Tasks tab in the Shared Workspace task pane to go to the New Alert page of the team Web site. Here you can set up a notification system so that you receive e-mail messages whenever tasks are completed or items are added, updated, or removed. This keeps you up to date with the most recent happenings on the site and in your project, which helps everybody stay on the same page.

In addition, you can display information about a task (including any text that was entered in the Description field) by simply hovering the mouse pointer over it, as shown in Figure 25-12.

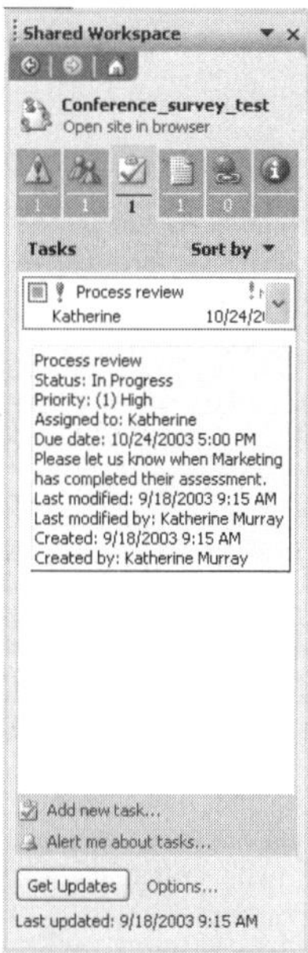

Figure 25-12. Get full information about a task by positioning the mouse pointer over it.

Working with Documents

Once you have enrolled the members and assigned the tasks, you can get down to the real business of working with your collaborative document. The Documents tab in the Shared Workspace task pane gives you everything you need to view, update, and work with the shared document. To see your options for working with a document, click the Documents tab and then click the arrow to the left of the document. A menu of document choices appears, as shown in Figure 25-13.

Note Some of the options shown in Figure 25-13 are disabled because the shared document is currently open on the screen. For example, you don't need the Open In Microsoft Office Word option when you're already working on the document. Similarly, after you make changes to the current document, the option Publish Back To Source Location becomes available.

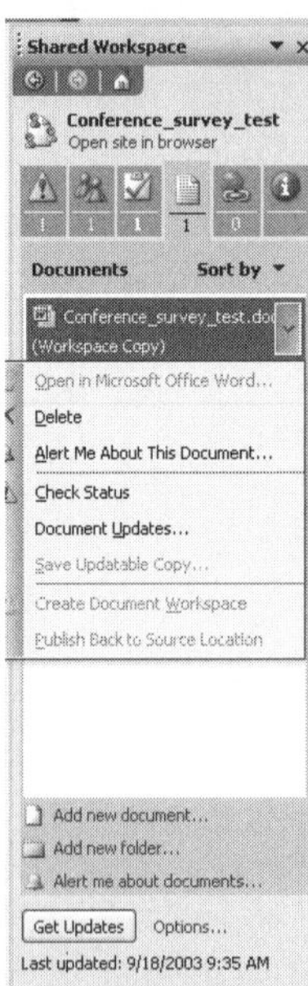

Figure 25-13. You can get information about the current document and update changes using the Documents tab.

Each time you open a shared document, a prompt will ask you whether you want to check for updates on the shared workspace site. If you click Get Updates, Word will compare the open document with the most recent version on the site. If the uploaded document is more current than the one you're opening, Word will display the Document Updates task pane so that you can compare and merge any necessary changes, as shown in Figure 25-14.

When you select Merge Copies, Word adds the changes to the current document but turns on tracking so that you can easily see the changes. You can then accept or delete changes as usual.

When you select Open Workspace Copy, Word displays both the copy of the document in the shared workspace and a task pane that gives you the option of keeping the workspace copy.

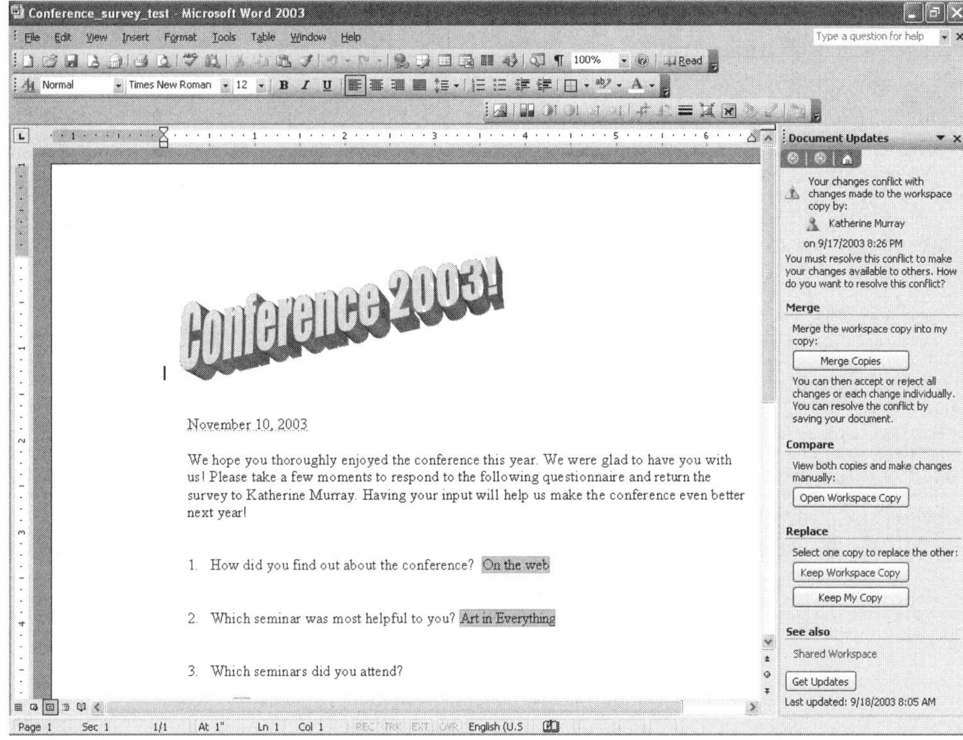

Figure 25-14. When you open a shared document, Word checks to see whether it is the most current version and gives you the option of comparing and merging changes.

Chapter 26

Creating Professional Web Sites

Many people are finding their way onto the World Wide Web, and they're following a variety of paths to get there. One approach you can take to building an online presence is to create your Web pages and Web sites using Word 2003. As you'll see in this chapter, Word provides enough Web page creation features that you can create professional-looking Web pages and Web sites in the same way you create Word documents—by entering and formatting information in a document. This chapter covers the Word features that you can use to create Web pages.

Understanding Web Page Creation Basics

In many ways, creating a Web page in Word is similar to creating any other document in Word. In fact, you can initiate Web page and Web site creation in Word by opening the New Document task pane (choose File, New) and then using any of the following methods:

- **Create a new, blank Web page.** Click the Web Page link to get started.
- **Base a Web page on an existing document.** Click the From Existing Document link, navigate to and select a copy of the file you want to use to create a Web page, and then click Create New.
- **Use the Save As dialog box.** You can save any open document as a Web page by choosing File, Save As Web Page or by choosing File, Save As, and then specifying a file type of Single File Web Page, Web Page, or Web Page, Filtered. For more information about the various types of Web page file formats, see "Saving Your Web Pages" on page 713.
- **Use Web page templates.** Click the On My Computer link in the Templates section to open the Templates dialog box, and then select theWeb Page template in the General tab. Or ensure that you're connected to the Internet, click Templates On Office Online in the Templates section, and then search the Microsoft Office Online Templates page using the phrase *Web site* as your search term.

Regardless of the method you use to create a Web page, you should know a bit about Web pages and how they differ from standard word processing documents before you start to create Web pages in Word. These two main differences stand out between standard Word documents and Web pages:

- **Most Web pages are created using multiple files.** A basic Web page generally consists of a text file that includes the Hypertext Markup Language (HTML) source code and a file for each graphic displayed on the Web page. The purpose of the source code in an HTML text file is to tell a browser how to display information. For example, the source code includes the page's text along with commands regarding how the text should be formatted. In addition, for each graphic on a Web page, the source code points to the location of the graphic file that should be displayed in a specified picture area within the Web page. When you view a Web page, you are actually viewing a number of files working together to create the appearance of a single page, as shown in Figure 26-1.

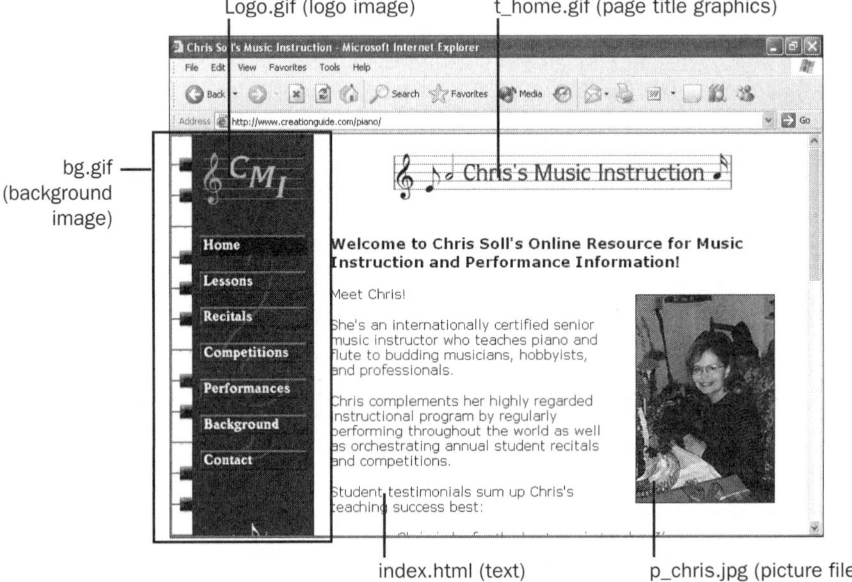

Figure 26-1. On this Web page, in addition to the HTML text file's content, a number of graphics files—including Graphics Interchange Format (GIF) and Joint Photographic Experts Group (JPEG) files—are displayed to create a single Web page.

- **Most Web page layouts are fluid.** As you know, people around the world view Web pages using a variety of browsers, operating systems, computers, and display settings. Therefore, Web pages need to be flexible enough to be displayed under a wide array of circumstances. To gain flexibility, Web designers have had to give up complete control over their Web page layouts—instead of strategically placing each element on a page as in traditional print design, Web page designers merely suggest where information should appear and how the page should flow. Figure 26-2 demonstrates how a Web page (in this case, the Web page example from Figure 26-1) can be displayed differently by viewing the same page at different resolutions.

Creating Professional Web Sites

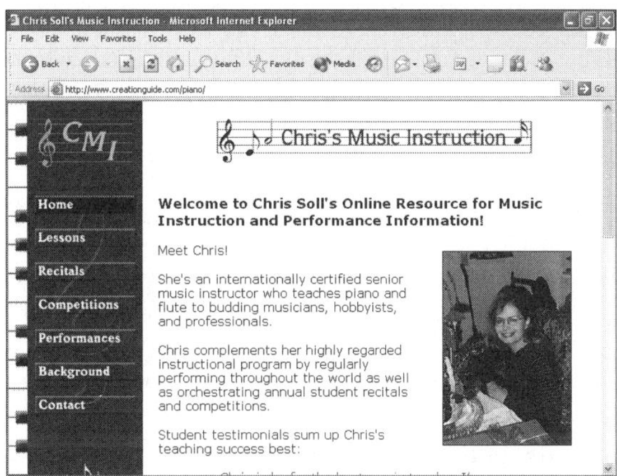

800 by 600

1024 by 768

Figure 26-2. As a designer, you usually need to consider how your Web page will appear in a variety of circumstances. This figure shows the Web page example from Figure 26-1 with the monitor set to 800 by 600 pixels and 1024 by 768 pixels.

Chapter 26

Of course, Web pages differ from printed documents in many other ways (for instance, hyperlinks don't link to anything on printed pages), and Web design philosophies and opinions abound. If you're interested in Web page design theory, you can find lots of information in bookstores, at online reference sites, and in magazines. In this chapter, you'll learn how to use some of Word's features to help you gain the technical expertise to express your creative side in your Web site design endeavors.

Configuring Web-Related Options

Before you start creating Web pages in Word, you should review Word's Web page–related options. Setting options might sound a little tedious compared to the prospect of creating Web pages, but controlling your working environment up front can save you headaches later. By paying attention to the Web options, you'll also give yourself a chance to think about your Web pages before you get started, and you'll be alerted to the types of details you might have to take into consideration. The options discussed in this part of the chapter can be found in the Web Options dialog box, which you can access by choosing Tools, Options, clicking the General tab, and then clicking Web Options. The first tab in theWeb Options dialog box is the Browser tab, so we'll start there.

Specifying Target Browser Options

When you create Web pages, you have to consider how people will be viewing your pages. One detail to consider is the range of browsers your audience will be using. If you're publishing Web pages on an intranet for your company, chances are that most users will be using the same browser and similar computer configurations—in that case, design considerations are easy because you can design for the company standard. On the other hand, if you're planning to post your pages on the Internet for people around the world, you'll have to take a broader approach to design because you won't know how users will be viewing your pages. (Will they use Macs, PCs, Microsoft Internet Explorer, Netscape Navigator, or something else?) In those cases, you need to define which browsers and which versions of those browsers you're going to cater to as you design your Web pages.

Word helps you design a particular browser standard, which means that working within browser and version limitations is easier than it sounds. In Word, you can turn on or off features not supported by selected Web browsers. To configure this setting, follow these steps:

1. Choose Tools, Options, click the General tab, and then click the Web Options button. The Web Options dialog box appears, as shown in Figure 26-3.
2. Click the Browsers tab, if necessary.
3. Ensure that the Disable Features Not Supported By These Browsers check box is selected.

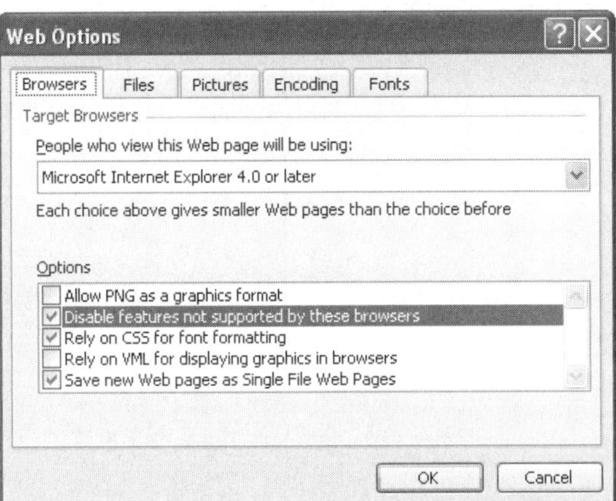

Figure 26-3. The Web Options dialog box provides options for specifying how Word handles some Web page creation tasks.

Caution If you clear the Disable Features Not Supported By These Browsers check box, you will be able to use every Web page feature built into Word regardless of whether any browser version can support it. In this case, "more" isn't better because you could very easily design a page that few people can view.

4 Click the People Who View This Web Page Will Be Using arrow, and then choose a browser type in the list. The check boxes in the Options list will be adjusted automatically based on the browser you select.

By default, Word is configured to use Internet Explorer 4 or later, which generally encompasses features of Netscape Navigator 4 or later as well. You can select the Microsoft Internet Explorer 4.0, Netscape Navigator 4.0, Or Later option to ensure that Netscape Navigator 4 features are supported. Either setting is a fair standard, because Internet Explorer 4 and Navigator 4 represent the most popular browser applications—and versions of the applications—in use today.

Reviewing File Options

After you specify a target browser for your intended Web audience, you should next consider how you want Word to handle your Web files. As mentioned, Web pages are made up of multiple files. When you create Web pages, you must keep your files organized—otherwise, you'll end up with pages containing broken links and missing components. Word offers a few ways you can organize your files, as well as a couple of default editor options, in the Files tab in the Web Options dialog box, shown in Figure 26-4.

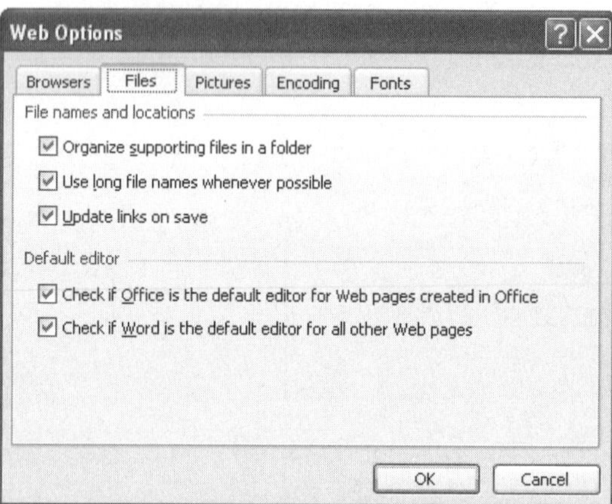

Figure 26-4. The Files tab helps control how Word organizes a Web page's files, and lets you specify whether you want Word to check automatically which program is registered as the default editor.

The Files tab enables you to specify the following preferences regarding files and folders:

- **Organize Supporting Files In A Folder** By default, Word saves supporting Web page files (such as graphics) in a separate folder within the folder that contains the HTML document. Generally, this setup works best, because you'll be able to find your HTML document easily as well as group the supporting files together in a logical subfolder. You should clear this check box only if you're working on a Web page that already has an existing hierarchy of folders or if you prefer to have your HTML documents and supporting files stored in the same folder. Regardless of how you store your Web page's files, you should note the page's file organization. Later, when you upload your Web page to a server, you'll need to re-create the organizational structure on the Web server to ensure that your links work properly.
- **Use Long File Names Whenever Possible** By default, this check box is selected. Nowadays, the only operating system that doesn't support long file names is Windows 3.*x* running on MS-DOS. If you know that some people who will be working with your files will be using Windows 3.*x* on MS-DOS, you'll want to clear this check box; otherwise, leave it selected.
- **Update Links On Save** By default, this option is selected, which means that Word checks the Web page's links each time you save a Web page document. If Word finds a broken link, you'll receive an error message that provides an option for fixing the link before saving.

In addition to folder options, the Files tab provides two check boxes related to the default editing applications associated with Web pages. You can specify that you want Word to check automatically whether Word or any other Microsoft Office System program is registered as the default editor for a Web page. By default, both options are selected. This means that pages built in Word will be displayed in Word, whereas pages built in Excel or FrontPage will be opened in those programs. Further, Web pages created in programs other than the ones in Office will be opened in Word.

Keep in mind that you can open a Web page in any Web editor application, regardless of which application is set as the default editor. To do so, simply open the application you want to use as a Web page editor, and then open the document from within the application.

Targeting Monitor Specifications

The Pictures tab in the Web Options dialog box, shown in Figure 26-5, is the same as in Word 2002 but has been pared down since Word 2000. In this tab, you simply define a couple of target monitor settings for typical viewers. Basically, when you configure these settings you're instructing Word to optimize a Web page for the selected monitor resolution. For most Web surfers, a typical monitor size is 800 by 600 pixels, with 96 pixels per inch. If you know that your audience uses other settings, you can optimize for those monitor settings. Regardless of your settings here, you should check all your Web pages using various screen settings before you post your pages live. As a Web designer, you want your Web pages to look their best for the largest possible number of people.

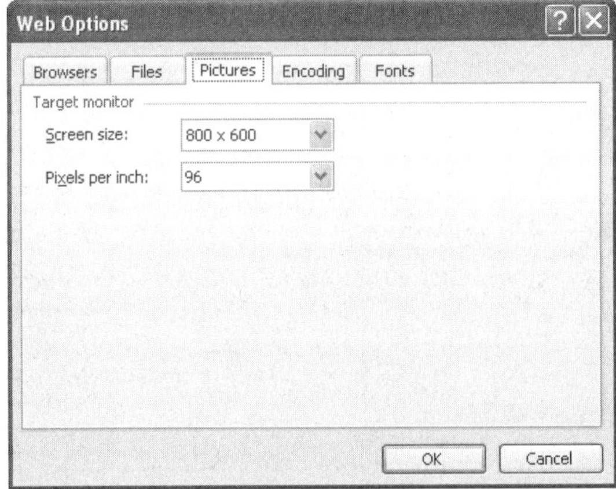

Figure 26-5. You can instruct Word to optimize a Web page for specific screen sizes and pixels-per-inch settings.

Selecting Encoding Options

The Encoding tab in the Web Options dialog box, shown in Figure 26-6, enables you to choose a language code from among those installed on your computer. *Encoding* refers to the byte or byte sequence that represents each character in your HTML or plain text files. You can choose a language code for the current page if the page is not already displayed with the correct language encoding (by selecting a language code in the Reload The Current Document As list). You can also save the current document with a particular language code by clicking the Save This Document As arrow, selecting a language code in the list, and then clicking OK. If you know that you always want to save Web pages using the encoding language selected in the Save This Document As list, you can select the Always Save Web Pages In The Default Encoding check box. This setting comes in handy if you reuse pages from other sources and want to store every page using one encoding language.

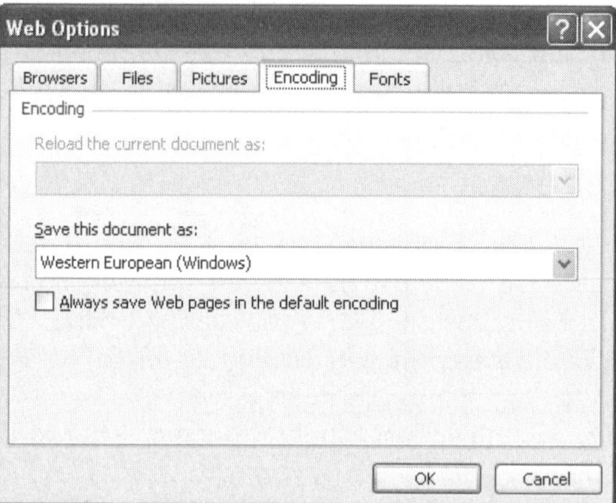

Figure 26-6. You can specify language encoding for documents that are currently displayed, for documents that are about to be saved, or for current and future Web pages you open in Word.

Choosing Default Fonts

The last tab in theWeb Options dialog box is the Fonts tab, shown in Figure 26-7.

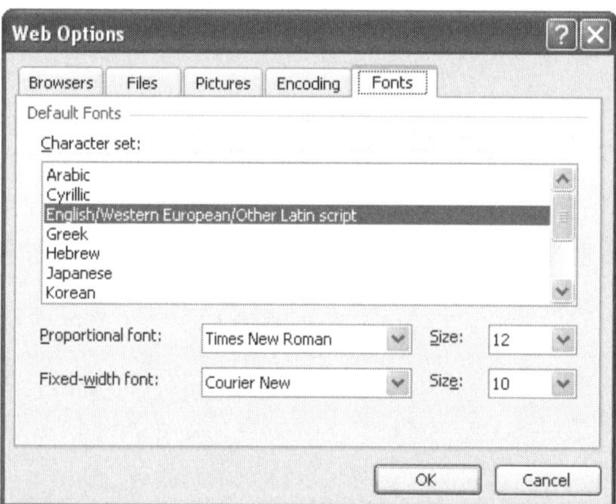

Figure 26-7. The Fonts tab enables you to set default font styles that will come into play when a Web page doesn't specifically assign a font style or size to text.

In the Fonts tab, you can configure the following default settings:

- **Character Set** Enables you to choose the character set that's used to encode the file. A character set is basically a mapping between the selected language's characters and a combination of numbers, letters, and symbols. For example, in ASCII (one of the most widely used character sets), the decimal code 65 maps to the letter *A*, whereas the HTML code A maps to the letter *A*. Most likely, the default setting is the character set you'll want to use for your Web pages.

- **Proportional Font** Specifies the font used for normal text if the Web page doesn't assign a font style. You can set a default font size in pixels in the Size box.
- **Fixed-Width Font** Specifies the font used for fixed-width elements if a Web page doesn't assign a font style. You can set a default font size in pixels in the Size box.

Universal Web Page Fonts

When you use fonts in your Web pages, keep in mind that only the following fonts are universally recognized as cross-platform fonts (which means they'll be displayed properly on both Macs and PCs):

Arial
Arial Narrow
Comic Sans MS
Courier New
Georgia
Times New Roman
Trebuchet MS
Verdana

If your Web pages will be viewed by a large, diverse audience (as would be the case on the Internet), you should consider sticking with these fonts when you design Web pages.

Building Web Pages and Web Sites

Now that you've mastered the details of configuring Word to serve as a Web page editor that meets your needs, you're ready to look at some of the Web page creation features in Word. As mentioned, you can use the Save As dialog box to save an existing document as a Web page, or you can open a new blank or existing Web page.

The process of saving existing documents as Web pages is discussed in "Saving Your Web Pages" on page 713.

New Web Page

To start by opening a blank Web page, display the New Document task pane (by choosing File, New), and then click the Web Page link. When you open a blank Web page, Word automatically disables features that aren't supported on the Web by the target browser(s) specified in the Browsers tab in the Web Options dialog box (as described in "Specifying Target Browser Options" on page 706). For example, underline colors aren't supported when you create Web pages. In addition, the New Blank Document icon on the Standard toolbar changes to a New Web Page icon, so that when you're working on a Web page you can quickly create a new, blank Web page by clicking the New Web Page button on the Standard toolbar.

To customize your Web pages, you can integrate a number of Word features, just as you do when you create other Word documents. The following features will come in especially handy when you're creating Web pages:

- **Cascading Style Sheets** A cascading style sheet (CSS) presents a Web page's formatting information in a specific place—either at the beginning of an HTML document or in a separate document—in a format that browsers can easily interpret and apply to the associated Web page or pages. When you use cascading style sheets, you can more easily control and modify text formatting on a Web site. For more information about cascading style sheets, see "Working with Cascading Style Sheets" on page 741.
- **Frames** You can display multiple Web pages at one time by using frames, as described in Chapter 17, "Formatting Layouts Using Text Boxes, Frames, Backgrounds, and Themes." The most common way to use frames in Web pages is to present a menu bar in a side or top frame that contains hyperlinks to the site's Web pages. As users click the hyperlinks in the menu frame, the associated Web page's contents appear in the main frame.
- **Graphics** As you know, Web designers include graphics on Web pages to help present information in a variety of ways, including showing logos, images, design elements (such as horizontal rules and bullets), and animated graphics. For more information about Web graphics, see "Working with Web Graphics" on page 727.
- **Hyperlinks** The Web makes heavy use of hyperlinks. You can work with text, graphical, and e-mail hyperlinks in Word. For more information about creating, editing, and removing hyperlinks in Word, see "Including Hyperlinks" on page 719.
- **Microsoft Script Editor** The Microsoft Script Editor enables you to view and edit HTML source code for all Office documents. Using the Script Editor, you can work with HTML, XML, Web scripts (such as VBScript and JScript), and cascading style sheets (CSS). For a quick introduction to the Script Editor, see "Editing Source Code Using the Microsoft Script Editor" on page 744.
- **Tables** When you create Web pages, you can use tables to control your page's layout. Using tables in Web pages is an extremely popular technique for page setup, and some Web site templates take advantage of tables. For more information about working with tables, see "Using Tables to Align Web Page Elements" on page 719, as well as Chapter 13, "Organizing Concepts in Tables."
- **Themes** You can quickly add a background, text formatting, bullets, horizontal rules, and link bars (if you're working on a Web page stored on a server that has FrontPage extensions installed) to Web pages by applying themes. For more information about themes, see Chapter 17, "Formatting Layouts Using Text Boxes, Frames, Backgrounds, and Themes."
- **Web Components** Using the Web Tools toolbar, you can add a number of Web page components to your Web pages, including movies, background sounds, and interactive forms. For more information about adding Web page components, see "Inserting Web Page Components" on page 734.

Remember, creating a Web page from a blank Web page document is the same as creating a document from a new, blank document.

Saving Your Web Pages

After you create a Web page document but before you get too far into Web page development, you need to save your Web pages. As with most document creation tasks, you should always (always, always, always) save your work frequently to avoid losing data due to unexpected system failures or power losses.

Saving Web pages involves a couple of key tasks that don't come into play when you save standard word processing documents. Specifically, you need to verify or add Web title bar text, and you need to determine whether you want to save your Web page so that you can continue to edit it in Word or save it in as streamlined a form as possible for publication on the Internet.

Inside Out

Creating backup files for Web pages

When you save a Web page, Word doesn't create a backup copy, even if you select the Always Create Backup Copy check box in the Save tab in the Options dialog box (which you access by choosing Tools, Options, and then clicking the Save tab). If you want to store a backup copy of a Web page, you'll need to use the Save As dialog box to save the document manually twice, using two different names or storing the files in two different locations.

Adding Title Bar Text

As you've probably noticed while surfing the Web, Web pages display text in your browser's title bar. The browser knows what text to display in the title bar by reading the HTML code in a Web page's header section. Using Word, you can add a title to a Web page without directly editing the document's source code. One of the most convenient ways to add title bar text to a Web page is to do so while saving the document, as described here:

1. With your Web page document open, choose File, Save As. The Save As dialog box appears.
2. In the Save As Type list, select Single File Web Page, Web Page, or Web Page, Filtered. (The differences among these three file types are described next, in "Choosing a Web Page Format: Web Page vs. Web Page, Filtered" and "Creating Single File Web Pages.") As soon as you choose a Web page file type, the Save As dialog box changes to include the Change Title button, as shown in Figure 26-8.

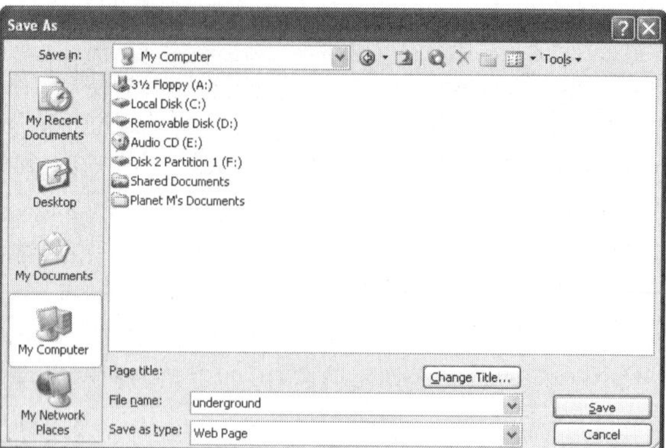

Figure 26-8. When you specify a Web page file type, the Save As dialog box changes to include the Change Title button.

3. Click Change Title. The Set Page Title dialog box opens, as shown in Figure 26-9.

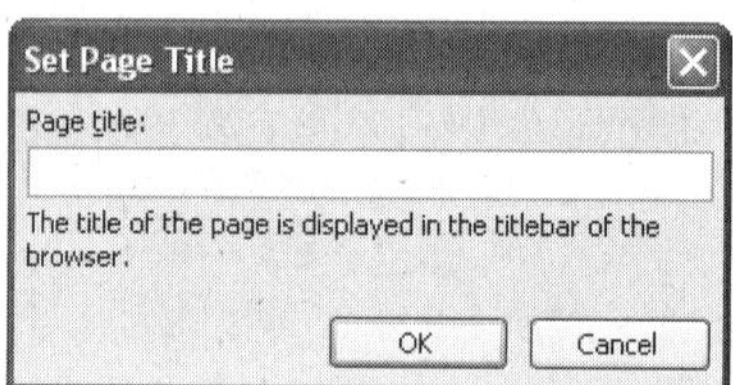

Figure 26-9. The Set Page Title dialog box enables you to add or modify a Web page's title bar text.

4. Type the title bar text for the Web page, and then click OK. The title text appears in the Save As dialog box next to the Page Title label.
5. Click Save to save your document.

When you display your Web page in a browser, the text you entered in the Set Page Title dialog box will appear in the browser's title bar. When you add title bar text, you should make the text as clear and descriptive as possible. The title text also appears on the Windows taskbar, so making the text concise and clear can help users find and return to your page if they're working with multiple windows open.

Tip **Change Web page title text using the Properties dialog box**
You can also change a document's title bar text by modifying the file's properties. To do so, open the file, choose File, Properties, click the Summary tab, and then type text in the Title box. Click OK to save your changes.

Choosing a Web Page Format: Web Page vs. Web Page, Filtered

As mentioned, you can save Web pages in three main formats: Single File Web Page, Web Page, and Web Page, Filtered. This section of the chapter looks at the Web Page and Web Page, Filtered file formats. The next section reviews the Single File Web Page format. Each file type serves a particular purpose.

When you save a document using the Web Page file type, the document can be viewed online. In addition, you can continue to edit the document in Word without a hitch because Word editing capabilities are also retained. In contrast, when you save a document using the Web Page, Filtered format, tags specific to Office are removed from the file's source code. This removal reduces the file size (and smaller file sizes mean faster download and display times when you're viewing files on the Web), but you lose some Office editing functionality, such as list formatting features and smart tags. If you save a document using Web Page, Filtered, and then reopen the file in an Office program, the text and general appearance of the page will be preserved, but some features might work differently or incorrectly.

You should follow these basic rules when saving Web pages in Word:

- If your Web page is a work in progress, save the document using the Web Page file type. That way, you'll retain full editing capabilities.
- If you've completed editing the Web page and you're ready to post it, save the document using the Web Page, Filtered file type to create the smallest possible document file with the cleanest HTML source code.
- If you've completed editing the Web page but you think you will work on it in the future, save two versions of the document. Use the Web Page file type to save a working copy on your local computer, and use the Web Page, Filtered file type to save a file that you can upload to a Web server.

After you decide how you'd like to save your Web page document, you can do so as follows:

1. While your Web page document is open, choose File, Save As.
2. Type a name for the file in the File Name box, click the Save As Type arrow, and then choose Web Page or Web Page, Filtered from the list.
3. Enter title text if necessary.
4. Using the Save In box, or the My Places Bar, navigate to the desired location, and then click Save.

When you save a Word document as a Web page that contains pictures, drawing objects, and other graphics not saved as Joint Photographic Experts Group (JPEG, or JPG), Graphics Interchange Format (GIF), or Portable Network Graphics (PNG) files, Word saves copies of the graphics with the HTML document using the JPG, GIF, or PNG format, as appropriate. (Pictures are saved as JPG graphics, and drawings are usually saved as GIF graphics.) When Word automatically converts images, it names and numbers the images image001.gif, image002.jpg, image003.png, and so forth.

Creating Single File Web Pages

Single File Web Page

In addition to saving Web page documents, you can create a single file Web page. A single file Web page contains all the elements of a Web page, including the text (HTML source code) and graphics files (pictures, background graphics, bullet images, and so forth), in a single file. Single file Web pages can be likened to HTML-formatted messages and complete Web pages that can be sent in many e-mail applications. The single file Web page encapsulation allows you to publish your entire Web site as a single MHTML (MIME [Multipurpose Internet Mail Extensions] encapsulation of aggregate HTML documents) file or send an entire Web site as an e-mail message or attachment. This format is supported by Internet Explorer 4 and later.

To save a Web page as a single file Web page, you simply specify the Single File Web Page file type in the Save As dialog box, as follows:

1. Open the Web page, and then choose File, Save As.
2. In the Save As dialog box, choose Single File Web Page in the Save As Type list.
3. Name the file, provide title text, specify the location where you want to store the file, and then click Save.

After you create a single file Web page, you can move the MHTML file anywhere without losing the graphics. In addition, a single file Web page tends to be smaller overall than the original Web page and associated graphics stored as separate files. The major drawback to single file Web pages is that not all browsers support MHTML yet, so if you use this format to post Web pages, you risk losing viewers who use browsers that don't support the MHTML format.

Configuring Web View Options

After you create your core Web page documents and save your documents (including adding title bar text), you're well into the process of Web page creation. As you design your Web pages, you're going to need to keep track of whether your content will be displayed according to your design plans when the page is displayed in Web browsers. To help you keep an eye on your pages, Word provides a number of Web-centric views you can use while you create and modify Web pages, as follows:

- **Web Layout view** Web Layout view is the working view in Word when you're creating Web pages and documents that will be viewed on the screen. When you're in this view, you can see backgrounds, text wrapping, and graphics appearing similarly to how the page will be displayed in a browser. To switch to Web Layout view, choose View, Web Layout, or click Web Layout View to the left of the horizontal scroll bar.
- **Web Page Preview** You can view your Web page documents in your browser at any time. You should do this frequently to ensure that your page will be displayed as planned. To view an open Web page document in your browser, choose File, Web Page Preview. If your browser isn't running, it starts automatically, and the current Web page document is displayed in your browser. To return to Word, close or minimize your browser and display the Word window again.

- **HTML source code** You can view and directly edit a Web page's HTML source code at any time. To do so, choose View, HTML Source. If you haven't used the Script Editor, you might have to insert your installation CD and install the editor. Similarly, if you don't see the HTML Source menu option, you need to install the Script Editor. To install the editor, ensure that your installation CD is handy (or that you know the network location of your installation files), and then choose View, HTML Source (if this option is available) or choose Tools, Macro, Microsoft Script Editor. For more information about editing source code, see "Editing Source Code Using the Microsoft Script Editor" on page 744.

In addition to using these views, you should always check your Web pages in a variety of browsers (including past and present versions of Internet Explorer and Netscape Navigator) and on various platforms (at least on the Mac and PC) before you publish your Web pages online. If you're designing for the Internet, you'll want your Web pages to look the best possible to the widest audience. Of course, if you're designing for a company intranet, you'll probably have to test your Web pages only on the browser types and versions used by employees.

Tip **View your pages on various platforms**
Although checking your Web pages on various platforms is highly recommended, it's not always easily accomplished. If you don't have a test network set up for this purpose, you can use some creative ingenuity to check your Web pages. For example, consider posting your pages online in a temporary directory. Then you can ask friends, relatives, and associates to view the temporary pages on their systems. You can also copy your files to a disk and take the disk to a nearby copy store to view your Web pages on their computers (for which you will probably be charged a fee). Or you can check out your Web pages on your local library's computers if it provides Internet access for members or allows you to bring your own disks. Finally, if you don't want to buy another computer or two for testing purposes, you can purchase software that enables you to install and run multiple operating systems on a single computer. Currently, VMware is a popular software package that enables you to run multiple operating systems. You can find out about the software by visiting the company's Web site at *http://www.vmware.com.*

Working with Web Page Text and Tables

When you create Web pages, you enter information the same way you enter information in other Word documents. The main concerns to address when creating Web text are to keep formatting simple, to ensure that text is concise, and to provide guidance for aligning components.

Adding Text and Headings

When you add text and headings to your Web pages, you should try to use Word's default styles, available in the Normal template. That way, if you later apply a theme to your Web page, the formatting will be applied directly to your document without extra formatting efforts on your part. Keep in mind that Web text is different from hard copy text. Generally, people read online text 25 percent more slowly than they read printed text. You can improve your Web pages' readability by keeping information concise and easy to scan. The following general rules of thumb might prove helpful when you create a Web page:

- Introduce a single idea per paragraph.
- Use simple sentence structure, and keep sentences short without oversimplifying your content.
- Limit paragraphs to 75 words or fewer.
- Use bulleted lists whenever possible.
- Use numbered lists when you're presenting a series of steps.
- Insert headings and subheadings to break up text and highlight key points.
- Keep headings simple and direct. (When in doubt, choose meaningful headings over clever ones.)
- Make sure that your information is presented in a logical hierarchy.
- Separate paragraphs with empty space (commonly referred to as *white space*).
- Avoid adding too many hyperlinks to your page's body text.
- Carefully check your spelling and grammar.
- Avoid tiny print, busy backgrounds, hard-to-see colors, and the like.

You want to make your main ideas jump out at readers. If your main ideas strike a chord with a reader, the reader will then move on to read the more detailed information. In addition to these text rules, remember that although theoretically Web pages are infinitely wide and infinitely long, you don't have to create ultra-long and ultra-wide documents. In most cases, a long Web page is usually easier to digest if it's divided into a number of shorter pages that are linked by means of hyperlinks on a menu bar.

Tip **Avoid underlining text that is not a link**
When you create Web text, avoid using underlining. Many people have become accustomed to associating underlined text in online documents with hyperlinks. If you underline text that isn't hyperlinked, viewers might become annoyed by clicking text and finding that it doesn't link to anything.

Inside Out

Using an animated GIF to create animated text for the Web

When you create Web text in Word, be aware that the animate text formatting feature found in the Text Effects tab in the Font dialog box doesn't work online (even though it seems like a natural fit). If you want to include animated text, consider creating an animated GIF. A number of free animated GIF builders and prebuilt animated GIFs are available for download on the Internet.

Using Tables to Align Web Page Elements

Many browsers (old and new) support tables without a hitch. Therefore, hordes of Web designers have gravitated toward using tables to help align information on Web pages. When you design Web pages, you'll frequently find that using a table simplifies your task. Fortunately, creating tables in Web pages is the same as creating tables in standard Word documents. You can format cells, borders, backgrounds, and so forth in the same manner. The main "trick" to using tables effectively in Web pages is to ensure that at least one cell is formatted to be a relative size (meaning that after the other table cells are displayed in a user's browser according to the table size settings, the relative table cell resizes to fit the remainder of the user's browser window). When you use tables in this manner, your Web page will resize to fit a browser's window.

For more information about creating and using tables, see Chapter 13, "Organizing Concepts in Tables."

Including Hyperlinks

If you create Web pages, you're going to want to include hyperlinks. After all, the ability to jump from document to document (or from file location to file location) using hyperlinks is a major drawing point of the Web. Imagine entering a Uniform Resource Locator (URL) in the Address box every time you wanted to visit a Web page! Because hyperlinks play such a large role in text navigation these days, Word provides convenient ways to create and modify hyperlinks in your documents.

Controlling Automatic Hyperlinks

By default, Web and e-mail addresses are automatically formatted as hyperlinks when you type them in a Word document if Word can easily recognize the text as a Web address or an e-mail address. For example, if you type **www.creationguide.com**, Word will format the text as a Web address, but if you type **creationguide.com**, Word won't format the text as a hyperlink. To work around this, you could type **www.creationguide.com**, and then after Word formats the hyperlink, you could delete the *www.* portion of the Web address. Similarly, you could add *http://* in front of a Web address that doesn't start with *www.* to indicate that the text is a Web address, as in *http://creationguide.com*.

This automatic formatting feature is usually welcome, but at times you might prefer to turn off the feature. To change this setting, you must configure the AutoCorrect options as follows:

1. Choose Tools, AutoCorrect Options, and then click the AutoFormat As You Type tab.
2. Clear the Internet And Network Paths With Hyperlinks check box under the Replace As You Type section, and then click OK.

After you turn off this AutoCorrect option, Word will no longer automatically format Web and e-mail addresses as hyperlinks in your documents. As you might expect, existing hyperlinks will not be affected.

As you probably know, hyperlinks are text or graphics that have been formatted to serve as links to other files, file locations, or e-mail addresses when users click them. Every hyperlink consists of two main components: an *anchor* and a *target*. The part of the hyperlink you click is the anchor, and the information you see in response to clicking an anchor is the target. When you create hyperlinks, you must specify the anchor information and enter the address or location of the target information. In addition, you can add a third component to hyperlinks, called *ScreenTips*. A ScreenTip is the text that appears when you hover your pointer over a hyperlink or that appears when the option to display graphics is turned off in an application (such as a browser). Using Word, you can easily create text, graphic, and e-mail hyperlinks, as described next.

Tip **Change the Ctrl+click hyperlink setting in Word**

By default, you must use Ctrl+click to follow a hyperlink while you're working in Word. This setup is convenient because it enables you to click within a hyperlink to edit its text. At times, though, you might find the combination is unnecessary or cumbersome. If that's the case, you can turn off this setting (so that you can simply click hyperlinks to follow them when you're working in Word). To remove the Ctrl+click setting, choose Tools, Options, click the Edit tab, and then clear the Use Ctrl+Click To Follow Hyperlink check box.

Creating Text Hyperlinks

Any text, including characters, words, phrases, headings, paragraphs, and so forth can be formatted to serve as a hyperlink. To create a text hyperlink, follow these steps:

1. Click in the word or select the text you want to format as a hyperlink, or position your insertion point where you want to insert a text hyperlink. Generally, it's easier to work with existing text, but you can also position the insertion point and then add the text as you build a hyperlink.

Insert Hyperlink

2. Click Insert Hyperlink on the Standard toolbar, or right-click the selected text or at the insertion point, and then choose Hyperlink from the shortcut menu. The Insert Hyperlink dialog box appears, as shown in Figure 26-10.

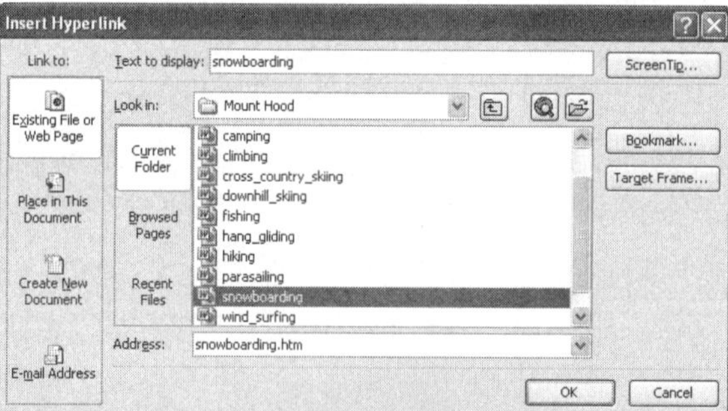

Figure 26-10. The Insert Hyperlink dialog box helps you specify the target for a hyperlink; you can choose an existing or new file, location within the current file, or e-mail address to serve as a hyperlink target.

> **Tip** In addition to using the Standard toolbar and right-click methods to access the Insert Hyperlink dialog box, you can also choose Insert, Hyperlink on the menu bar or press Ctrl+K.

3. Verify that the Text To Display box shows the text you want to use to create the hyperlink. If not, you can change the text to suit your needs. Keep in mind that the text you insert in this text box will appear on your page; it will be inserted at the insertion point or replace the text you selected in step 1.
4. Next, you need to specify the hyperlink's target file, file location, or e-mail address. To do so, click a button in the Link To to specify the type of hyperlink you'll be creating. You can select from among the following types of hyperlink targets:
   - *Existing File Or Web Page*—You can use this option if your hyperlink will link to an existing file or Web page. If the page you're linking to contains headings or bookmarks, you can format the hyperlink to jump directly to a particular heading or bookmark location. To do so, specify the file you want to link to, click Bookmark, and then click the bookmark or heading you want users to see when they click the hyperlink.
   - *Place In This Document*—You can create hyperlinks that jump to headings or bookmarks in the current document. When you click the Place In This Document button, the Insert Hyperlink dialog box changes to display a list of the headings and bookmarks in the current document, as shown in Figure 26-11. To create the hyperlink, verify the Text To Display text, click Place In This Document, click a listed heading or bookmark, and then click OK. This type of hyperlink comes in handy when you want to include a Return To Top link at the bottom of a page or if you have a long page with a list of links at the top of the page that enables viewers to jump to lower areas in the document.
   - *Create New Document*—You can use this option to create a hyperlink to a page that hasn't been created yet. When you click Create New Document, the Insert Hyperlink dialog box changes to display a text box you can use to name a new document. You can then specify whether you want to edit the new document now or later. When you name a new document, make sure you include the .htm or .html extension so that Word will create a Web page document instead of a Word document.
   - *E-Mail Address*—You can use this option to create hyperlinks that users can click to open a preaddressed e-mail message window. For more information about creating e-mail hyperlinks, see "Inserting E-Mail Hyperlinks" on page 724.

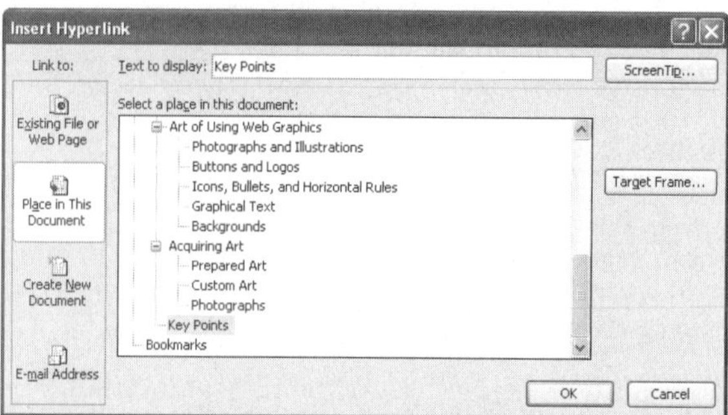

Figure 26-11. Using the Place In This Document option in the Link To area, you can configure a hyperlink to target a specific heading or bookmark in the current document.

> **Tip** **Create bookmarks to serve as hyperlink locations**
> To create a bookmark in your document, position your insertion point where you want to insert a bookmark, and choose Insert, Bookmark. Then, in the Bookmark dialog box, type a bookmark name without spaces and click Add. For more information about creating bookmarks, see Chapter 23, "Configuring Footnotes, Endnotes, and Cross-References."

5. After you choose a Link To option, select the file or file location you want the hyperlink to link to or type a Web address in the Address box. Figure 26-10 shows the Insert Hyperlink dialog box with information in the Address box, which links the hyperlink to another document stored in the current folder.
6. After you configure the hyperlink's target and text display information, click the ScreenTip button. The Set Hyperlink ScreenTip dialog box appears, as shown in Figure 26-12.

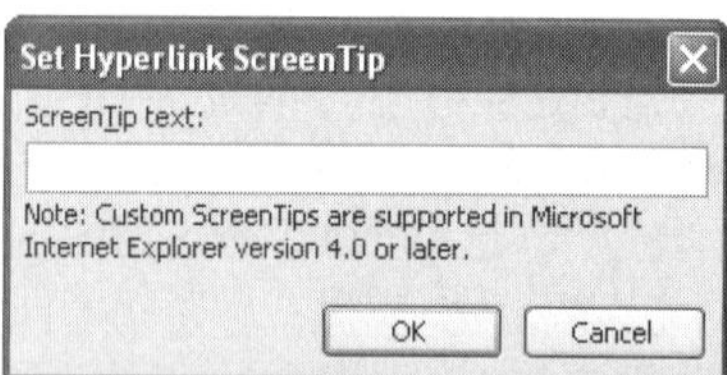

Figure 26-12. The Set Hyperlink ScreenTip dialog box enables you to specify the text that appears when users hover their pointers over a hyperlink.

7. Type text in the ScreenTip Text box, and then click OK.
8. Click OK in the Insert Hyperlink dialog box to complete the hyperlink creation process.

Using Drag-and-Drop to Create Hyperlinks

If you want to create a hyperlink in one document to access information in another document, you can use the right-click and drag method, as follows:

1. Open both documents, and arrange them so that you can see both documents at once.
2. In the target file (the file containing the information you want to link to), select text you want to use as the hyperlink's display text. Right-click the selected text, and then drag it into the other document. When the insertion point is positioned where you want to insert the hyperlink, release the right mouse button.
3. From the shortcut menu that appears, choose Create Hyperlink Here.

Keep in mind that you can't right-click and drag drawing objects to create hyperlinks; for those types of objects, you have to use the standard hyperlink procedures, as described in the next section, "Linking Graphics." If you use the right-click and drag method to create hyperlinks and you plan to post the Web pages online, you might find it easiest to store the files in the same folder. That way, you won't lose or confuse the hyperlink information when you upload the pages to the server.

Tip **Set the hyperlink base**
You can set the base address for a document if you want all hyperlinks to automatically include the base address information in their paths. To specify a base address, choose File, Properties, click the Summary tab, enter the base address in the Hyperlink Base box, and then click OK.

Linking Graphics

You can create graphics hyperlinks in the same way you create text hyperlinks. When you design Web pages, you'll find that some graphics make particularly intuitive hyperlinks, including the following:

- Graphic buttons that link to subpages in a Web site
- Logos that consistently link to a company's home page
- Small (thumbnail) pictures that link to larger versions of the pictures
- E-mail graphics that link to preaddressed e-mail message windows
- Pictures that link to Web pages elaborating on the pictures, such as a picture of the company's president that's linked to a Letter From The President page or Bio page

To access the Insert Hyperlink dialog box when you're formatting a graphic as a hyperlink, click the image or drawing object, and then click the Hyperlink button on the Standard toolbar, or right-click the picture or drawing object, and then choose Hyperlink from the shortcut menu. After you open the Insert Hyperlink dialog box, you configure the hyperlink information in the same way you configure text hyperlinks, as described in "Creating Text Hyperlinks" on page 720.

Creating Linked Banners and Navigation Buttons

You can combine Word features to create linked banners and buttons. For example, you can create banners using WordArt and you can create buttons by using Word's drawing tools, AutoShapes, and text boxes (see Chapter 12, "Enlivening Documents with Drawings and AutoShapes," for more information about this). After you create a banner or button in Word, you can format the object as a hyperlink by right-clicking the object and then choosing Hyperlink from the shortcut menu, or by clicking the object and then clicking the Hyperlink button on the Standard toolbar.

If you want to reuse a drawing object on several Web pages, you might want to save the object as a standard image file so that the button or banner appears consistently throughout your site. You'll need a drawing program such as Microsoft Paint to complete this procedure. To turn a drawing object into an image, follow these steps:

1. Display the WordArt, button, or other drawing object on the screen.
2. Press Print Scrn.
3. Open a drawing program and paste the contents of your system Clipboard into the program. For example, in Paint, choose Edit, Paste or press Ctrl+V.
4. Crop the WordArt or drawing object.
5. Resize the object to its approximate display size if necessary.
6. Save the image as a GIF file for use in your Web page.

After you create the GIF image, you can insert it in your Web page and format the image as a hyperlink, just as you insert and format other image files. For more information about inserting images in Web pages, see "Working with Web Graphics" on page 727.

Inserting E-Mail Hyperlinks

The last type of hyperlink we'll look at here is an e-mail hyperlink. E-mail hyperlinks are frequently used on Web pages to present an E-Mail The Webmaster link or other similar "contact us" types of link. When a user clicks an e-mail hyperlink, an e-mail message window opens, containing an e-mail address in the To box that you specified for the hyperlink. When you create an e-mail hyperlink, you can also automatically configure the Subject line's text.

To create an e-mail hyperlink, follow these steps:

1. Click in a word or select the text or graphic you want to display as a hyperlink, or position your insertion point where you want to insert the hyperlink.
2. Click Hyperlink on the Standard toolbar, or right-click and then choose Hyperlink from the shortcut menu, or press Ctrl+K.
3. In the Link To area in the Insert Hyperlink dialog box, click E-Mail Address. The Insert Hyperlink dialog box changes to accommodate creating e-mail hyperlinks.

Creating Professional Web Sites

4 In the E-Mail Address box, enter the e-mail address you want to associate with the hyperlink, or, if available, click the e-mail address in the Recently Used E-Mail Addresses list, as shown in Figure 26-13. Notice that when you enter an e-mail address, Word automatically adds the *mailto:* prefix.

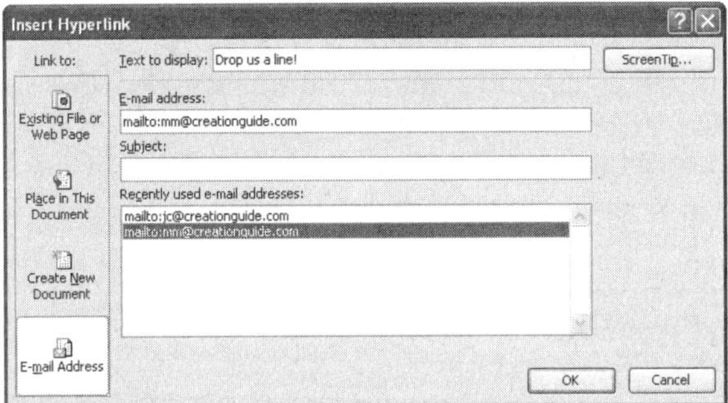

Figure 26-13. When you create an e-mail hyperlink, you can specify the To line e-mail address, ScreenTip information, and a Subject line for the e-mail message.

5 Verify or change the Text To Display text, and then type text in the Subject box, if desired.

6 Click the ScreenTip button, enter ScreenTip information in the Set Hyperlink ScreenTip dialog box, and then click OK.

7 Click OK in the Insert Hyperlink dialog box to complete the e-mail hyperlink.

> **Tip** **Use AutoCorrect to create e-mail hyperlinks**
> As mentioned, you can also create e-mail hyperlinks in your documents automatically by simply typing an e-mail address directly in the body of your document. By default, AutoCorrect formats e-mail addresses typed in a document as e-mail hyperlinks.

Editing Hyperlinks

After you create text hyperlinks, you can customize their appearance just as you customize other text by using standard formatting techniques such as applying font colors and font styles.

> **Tip** To easily select a hyperlink before applying formatting, right-click the hyperlink, and then choose Select Hyperlink from the shortcut menu.

In addition, you can edit text, graphics, and e-mail hyperlinks by modifying the hyperlinks' properties. For example, you can make the following changes:

- **Change a hyperlink's target.** To change a hyperlink's target, right-click the hyperlink, and then choose Edit Hyperlink from the shortcut menu. Then, in the Edit Hyperlink dialog box (which looks very much like the Insert Hyperlink dialog box), change the hyperlink's target information.

- **Change a text or an e-mail hyperlink's display text.** You can edit a hyperlink's text directly in the body of your document by typing over existing hyperlink text, or you can right-click a hyperlink, choose Edit Hyperlink from the shortcut menu, and then change the Text To Display text in the Edit Hyperlink dialog box.
- **Remove hyperlink formatting.** You can also remove hyperlink formatting from text, e-mail, and graphics hyperlinks. To do so, right-click the hyperlink, and then choose Remove Hyperlink from the shortcut menu. When you remove hyperlink formatting, the hyperlink is converted to regular, unlinked text or graphics. Keep in mind that formatted text retains its formatting, so if you manually applied boldface formatting or a font color to a hyperlink, the formatting remains intact even though the hyperlink is removed.

Troubleshooting

I want to remove hyperlink properties throughout a document without deleting the text or graphic anchors

Word doesn't provide a way to remove all hyperlink properties in a document in one fell swoop. But if you're a little flexible and your document doesn't contain extensive advanced formatting or a large number of components, you can remove hyperlink properties from a document without finding, selecting, and clearing each hyperlink. The trick is to temporarily turn off hyperlink formatting; once the hyperlink settings are removed, you can select all instances of the text formatted to look like hyperlinks, and then clear the text formatting. Here's how to accomplish this:

1. Open the document from which you want to remove all hyperlinks.
2. Choose Tools, Option, and then click the Save tab.
3. In the Save tab, click the Disable Features Introduced After check box, select Microsoft Word 6.0/95 in the list, and then click OK. You'll see a message box listing the changes that will be made to the document if you proceed with the format change. (If you don't see the message box, click Save on the Standard toolbar.) The message box should show how many instances of hyperlinks will be reformatted, similar to the following screenshot:

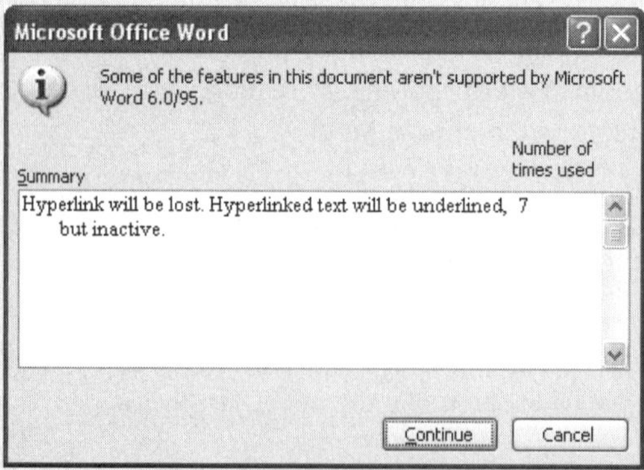

4 If the changes in the message box look acceptable, click Continue. (If some of the changes aren't acceptable, you won't be able to continue with this procedure; in that case, click Cancel, and then remove hyperlinks manually.)

5 At this point, your document won't contain any underlying hyperlink information, but text that served as hyperlink text anchors will continue to appear with hyperlink formatting (such as blue and underlined); therefore, you will probably want to clear the formatting. To clear all instances of hyperlink formatting at once, first right-click text that was a hyperlink, and then choose Select Text With Similar Formatting from the shortcut menu.

6 After selecting all instances of formatted text, press Ctrl+Spacebar to clear formatting from all selected text.

7 Finally, to reset the default Word format setting, choose Tools, Options, click the Save tab if necessary, clear the Disable Features Introduced After check box, and then click OK.

Tip **Modify hyperlink styles**

If you want to change the style of all hyperlinks used in your Web page, your best bet is to alter the Hyperlink and Followed Hyperlink styles in the Styles And Formatting task pane. For more information about modifying styles, see Chapter 9, "Using Styles to Increase Your Formatting Power."

Deleting Hyperlinks

In addition to changing hyperlinks and removing hyperlink properties, you might want to delete hyperlinks—anchors and all. You delete hyperlinks the same way you delete standard text and graphics. Select the information you want to delete, and then press Delete or Backspace.

Working with Web Graphics

As you've seen up to now in the chapter, creating Web pages is much like creating standard Word documents, with a few twists here and there. So you won't be surprised to learn that adding graphics to your Web pages is similar to adding graphics in standard Word documents. The main difference is that Web page graphics have to be stored as one of the following graphic file types so that browsers can display them:

- **GIF** GIFs are the most widely supported graphics type on the Web (which means that almost all browsers—old, new, and in-between—can display GIF images). GIF images can support up to 256 colors, and they are generally used for simple logos, line art, icons, cartoonlike illustrations, buttons, horizontal rules, bullets, backgrounds, and other graphics elements that require few colors. In addition, GIFs can include transparency and can be used to create simple animations, referred to as *animated GIFs.* (In a nutshell, an animated GIF can be likened a stack of GIF graphics that the browser flips through, like old movie flip cards, to create the appearance of movement.)

- **JPEG (or JPG)** The JPEG image file format was created by and named after the Joint Photographic Experts Group. This image format supports millions of colors (24-bit color), and JPEGs are almost universally supported by browsers. Because JPEGs can contain millions of colors, this file format is usually used to display photographic images online.
- **PNG** PNG (pronounced "ping") images are similar to GIF images. They're small files that load quickly and are limited to 256 colors. PNG images transmit slightly faster than GIF files, but PNGs are supported only on newer browsers. At this point, if your Web pages are going to be viewed by a diverse audience using a variety of browsers, you should use GIF files instead of PNG files.

For more information about transparency, see Chapter 12, "Enlivening Documents with Drawings and AutoShapes."

If you're creating a Web page in Word and you insert a graphic in your document that's stored as a file type other than these three file types, Word will create copies of the graphic and convert it to a JPG, GIF, or PNG file when you save the Web page document. Word will store copies of all graphics files in the HTML document's supporting files folder by default. This default action is desirable because when you use graphics files in your Web pages, you must store your files in an orderly manner to ensure that your HTML code works properly. And when you upload your Web pages to a server, you must retain your Web page's HTML and graphics file organization so that the server can properly find all graphics files referred to in your HTML document.

Now that we have some of the Web graphics particulars taken care of, let's look at how you can use graphics in your Web pages. Generally, graphics are used in Web pages to create the following components:

- Photographs and illustrations
- Buttons and logos
- Icons, bullets, and horizontal rules
- Graphical text
- Simple animations
- Backgrounds

As mentioned, inserting and adjusting graphics in Web pages is fundamentally the same as inserting and adjusting graphics in standard Word documents. But among Web graphics tasks, a few Web-specific topics stand out. In particular, when you create Web graphics, you'll want to specify alternative text for each graphic. Further, you'll probably want to insert horizontal rules, picture bullets, and animated clip art items. The next section of the chapter briefly addresses these topics.

For more information about working with graphics, objects, and WordArt, see Part 2, "Reinforcing Your Message with Tables, Charts, Diagrams, and Pictures," and for more information about inserting backgrounds, see Chapter 17, "Formatting Layouts Using Text Boxes, Frames, Backgrounds, and Themes."

Creating Professional Web Sites

Adding Alternative Text

When you use graphics on your Web pages, you should take a moment to think about the people who *won't* see your graphics, especially if your Web pages will be posted on the Internet. Because the Internet is worldwide, you can't accommodate all the types of Internet connections and browsers that people will be using to view your pages. It's highly likely that at least some of the people viewing your pages might be using text-only browsers or they might turn off the display of graphics in their browsers when they surf the Web so that they can display Web pages more quickly. As a Web page developer, you can specify alternative text (generally referred to as *ALT text* by Web designers) that will automatically appear while a graphic is loading or in a graphics area when a browser doesn't display graphics. Figure 26-14 shows how ALT text appears in a Web page with the graphics display turned off.

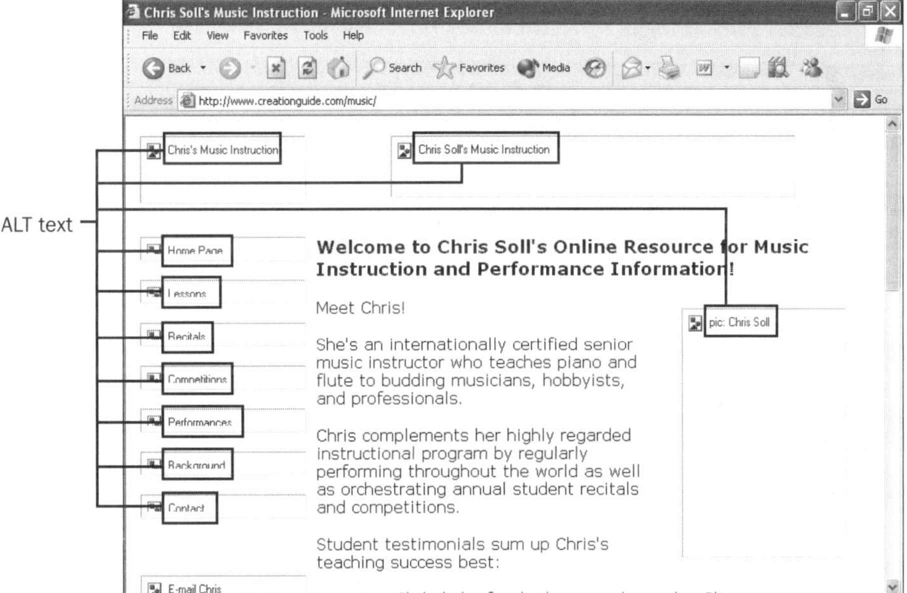

Figure 26-14. ALT text can be used to describe content areas to users who view your Web pages without graphics.

ALT text is displayed in place of images under the following conditions:

- When a browser doesn't support graphics
- When a browser's settings are configured to not show graphics
- When a user experiences slow downloads
- When viewers have special needs due to visual impairment

To specify ALT text for Web page graphics in Word, follow these steps:

1. With your Web page document open in Word, double-click the picture or drawing object in your Web page that you want to configure, and then click the Web tab in the Format Picture dialog box.

> **Tip** You can also display the Format Picture dialog box by right-clicking a picture or drawing object and then choosing Format Picture, or clicking the picture or drawing object and then choosing Format, Picture (or Format, AutoShape).

2. In the Alternative Text box, type the text you want to display in place of the graphic or when the viewer's pointer hovers over the graphic, and then click OK.

When you supply ALT text, you can insert as much text as you want, but keep in mind that some browsers might display only a limited number of characters. When you create ALT text, try to keep it concise and descriptive. Remember, the main purpose of ALT text is to provide information to viewers who won't be viewing your graphics or to explain graphics for Web page viewers.

Adding Horizontal Rules

A typical kind of graphic on Web pages is a horizontal rule. Horizontal rules can be created in two main ways: by typing HTML code directly into a Web page's source code or by inserting a graphical divider. To enter HTML code for a horizontal rule (you use the <HR> tag), you need to open the Microsoft Script Editor, and then add the source code. The Microsoft Script Editor is introduced in "Editing Source Code Using the Microsoft Script Editor" on page 744. This section of the chapter looks at the other typical way to insert horizontal rules, by inserting a graphic divider.

Word makes inserting horizontal rules in Web pages easy. You can access Word's default horizontal line graphics in two main ways:

- Position the insertion point where you want to insert a divider, display the Clip Art task pane, type **Web Dividers** in the Search For box, and then press Enter.
- Position the insertion point where you want to insert a divider, choose Format, Borders And Shading, click the Borders tab, and then click Horizontal Line.

As you can see in Figure 26-15, both approaches result in a similar display of available horizontal rules. To select a rule from either the Horizontal Line dialog box or the Clip Art task pane, double-click the line you want to include in your Web page.

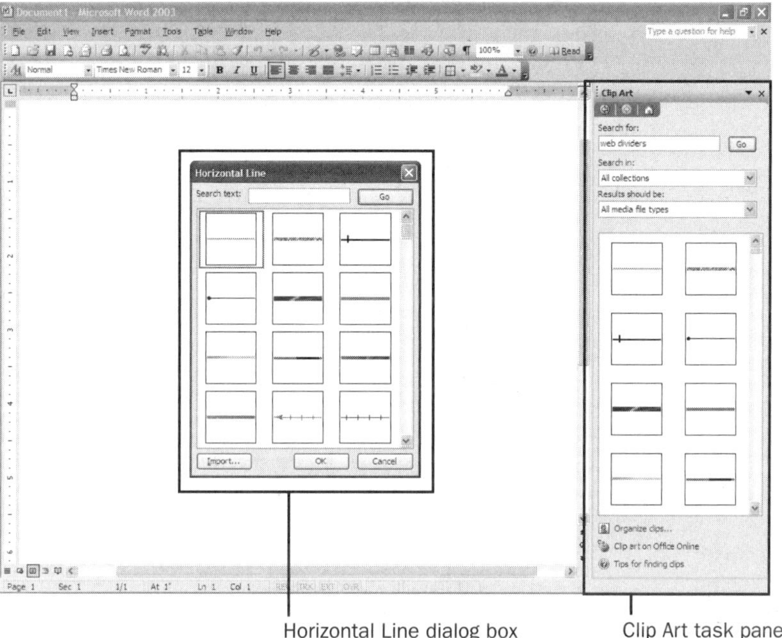

Figure 26-15. You can insert horizontal rules by displaying Word's default graphic lines and double-clicking the line you want to insert in your Web page.

After you insert a horizontal rule, you can modify its properties. If you inserted a rule using the Horizontal Line dialog box, you can right-click the line and then choose Format Horizontal Line from the shortcut menu (or click the line and then choose Format, Horizontal Line) to display the Format Horizontal Line dialog box, shown in Figure 26-16. Notice that you can control a line's width, height, color, and alignment using the Format Horizontal Line dialog box.

If you inserted the rule using the Clip Art task pane, you can right-click the line, and then choose Format Horizontal Line or Format Picture from the shortcut menu (or click the line, and then choose Format, Horizontal Line or Format, Picture depending on the available option) to display the Format Horizontal Line or Format Picture dialog box. In most cases, you'll use the Format Picture dialog box when you work with horizontal lines that you inserted using the Clip Art task pane. (The Format Picture dialog box is discussed in Chapter 11, "Adding Visual Impact with Pictures and Objects.")

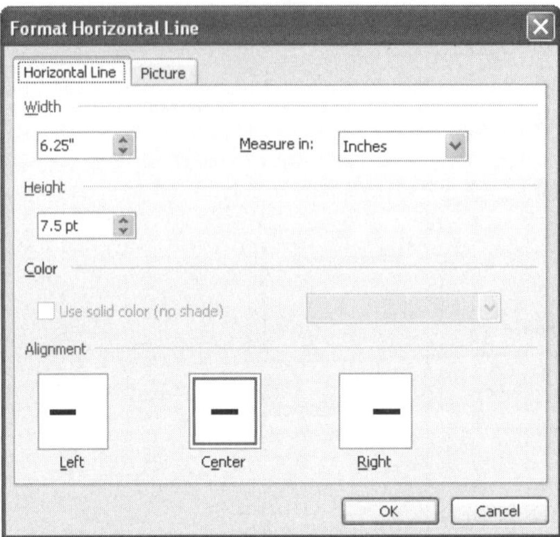

Figure 26-16. The Format Horizontal Line dialog box enables you to control the appearance of horizontal lines used in your Web pages.

Tip **Use AutoFormat to create horizontal lines**

By default, the AutoFormat As You Type tab in the AutoCorrect dialog box (which you can access by choosing Tools, AutoCorrect Options) is configured to replace some instances of repeated characters with formatted horizontal lines. For example, if you type --- (hyphens), ==== (equal signs), ____ (underscores), or **** (asterisks) and then press Enter, Word will replace the characters with a straight line, double line, thick line, or thick dotted line, respectively. For more in formation about AutoFormat features, see Chapter 7, "Putting Text Tools to Work."

Adding Picture Bullets

You can (and often should) use bulleted lists in your Web pages to help present information clearly and concisely. But being clear and concise doesn't have to be synonymous with boring. Instead of showing standard black dots every time you want to display a list, you might want to liven up your Web pages with graphics bullets. Word makes displaying a bulleted list with graphics a simple task, as described here:

1. Select the bulleted list you want to reformat with graphics bullets.
2. Choose Format, Bullets And Numbering, and then click the Bulleted tab.

3 Choose a bulleted list display box, and then click the Customize button. The Customize Bulleted List dialog box appears, as shown in Figure 26-17.

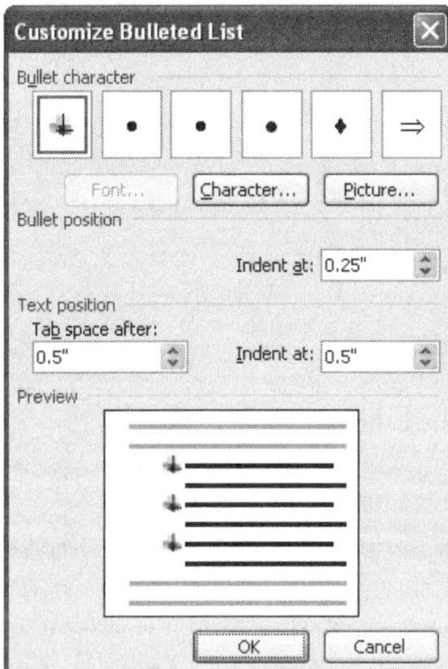

Figure 26-17. You can modify the layout of a bulleted list by configuring the Customize Bulleted List dialog box.

4 In the Customize Bulleted List dialog box, click the Picture button to open the Picture Bullet dialog box.

5 Double-click the bullet you want to use. Notice that some bullet options have a star in the lower-right corner. This star indicates that the bullet is displayed as an animated bullet when it is viewed in a browser.

6 Click OK in the Customize Bulleted List dialog box to reformat the bulleted list.

For more information about creating and modifying bulleted lists, see Chapter 8, "Aligning Information and Formatting Paragraphs and Lists."

Adding Animated Clip Art

Animated Clip Art

The Clip Art task pane includes some animated graphics that you can include in your Web pages. Animated clip art items in the Clip Art task pane can be identified by the small yellow star in the lower-right corner of the item's preview picture. You can insert animated clip art the same way you insert other clip art items—simply click the item in the Clip Art task pane. To view the animation, you must preview your document in a Web browser. To do so while working in Word, choose File, Web Page Preview.

Tip **Test animated clip art**
To see an animated clip art item in action, display the Clip Art task pane; type an action word, such as **walking**, in the Search For box; click Go; click an animated clip art item to insert it in your document; and then click File, Web Page Preview to view the animation.

Inserting Web Page Components

In addition to adding text and graphics to your Web pages, you can present multimedia information, including movies, background sounds, and scrolling text. Word makes inserting these types of components easy by providing toolbar buttons on the Web Tools toolbar. To display the Web Tools toolbar, choose View, Toolbars, Web Tools, or right-click a toolbar, and then choose Web Tools from the shortcut menu. In this part of the chapter, you'll learn how to insert multimedia components. The Web Tools toolbar also provides buttons that help you create interactive Web forms. Creating interactive Web forms is discussed in "Creating Interactive Forms" on page 739.

Inside Out

Keeping track of multimedia files

Multimedia files are not automatically stored in the HTML folder when you save a Web page in Word. Therefore, the best way to approach inserting a movie or sound file into your document is to copy the multimedia elements into your HTML folder before you add the components to your page. That way, the multimedia components will be easy to find when you insert them in your page, and the multimedia links will work properly after you upload your Web page files.

Inserting a Movie Component

When you create a Web page in Word, you can insert a movie directly in your Web page. Keep in mind that this option shows the movie directly on your page, similar to displaying a graphic. You can configure the movie to play when the Web page is opened, when the user moves the pointer over the movie, or in both instances. To insert a movie in your Web page, follow these steps:

Movie

1 Position your insertion point where you want to insert a link to a movie, and then click the Movie button on the Web Tools toolbar.

   The Movie Clip dialog box appears, as shown in Figure 26-18, and a default Movie icon appears in your document.

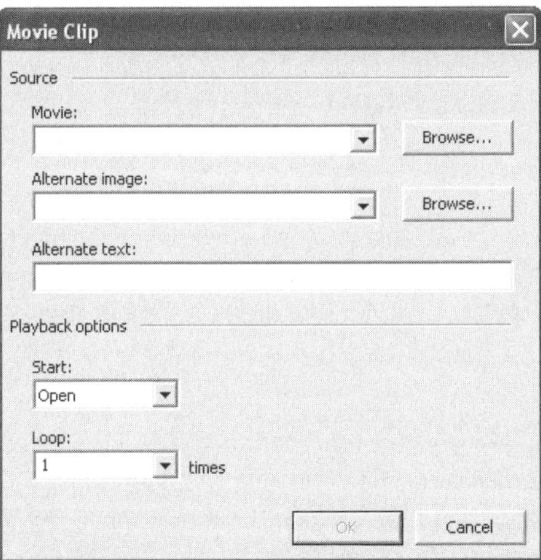

Figure 26-18. You use the Movie Clip dialog box to insert a movie in a Web page as well as to specify an alternative image, ALT text, and play options for the movie.

2 In the Movie box, type the path or address of the movie file you want to link to, or click Browse to locate the file.

> **Note** You can use AVI, MOV, Movie, MP2, MPG, MPEG, or QT movie formats in Web pages.

3 In the Alternate Image box, type the path or address of the graphics file you want to designate as a substitute when the user's browser doesn't support movies or when the user turns off the display of movies.

4 In the Alternate Text box, type the text you want to appear in place of the movie or alternative image and that will appear when a pointer is positioned over the alternative image.

5 Click the Start arrow, and then select one of the following options in the list:

- *Open*—Plays the movie when the user downloads the Web page.
- *Mouse-Over*—Plays the movie when the user moves the mouse pointer over it.
- *Both*—Plays the movie when the user downloads the Web page and whenever the user moves the mouse pointer over the movie image.

6 In the Loop box, enter the number of times you want the movie to repeat automatically, or click the arrow, and then select a number from 1 through 5 or Infinite, and then click OK.

Design Mode

Tip Control the movie's display and views of properties while you work

You can control your working environment by clicking the Design Mode toggle button on the Web Tools toolbar. When you're working with Web page components, you'll want to keep an eye on whether you're working in Design Mode or standard Web Page Layout view.

For instance, if you want to review a movie while you're working on your Web page document in Word, you'll need to ensure that Design Mode is off. When Design Mode is off, you can right-click the image representing the movie, and then choose Play from the shortcut menu. To stop the movie, right-click the movie, and then click Stop. To disable the movie altogether while you work, click the Design Mode button on the Web Tools toolbar to work in Design Mode.

If you're working in Design Mode and you want to return to the standard Web Layout view or display the Movie Clip dialog box, click the Design Mode button to turn off Design Mode. If you right-click a movie placeholder, and then choose Properties while working in Design Mode, the ActiveX control properties dialog box appears, which looks similar to a Visual Basic Application (VBA) dialog box used to configure macros or other VBA controls. To display the Movie Clip dialog box, you must turn off Design Mode, right-click the movie, and then choose Properties.

Generally, inserting a movie directly in a Web page isn't the best approach to take to Web page design. For the same reasons people turn off graphics or can't view graphics, some users also disable movies or can't view movies. In addition, people with slow Internet connections might not want to wait while movies download. Better design practice dictates that you copy the movie file into your Web page folder, and then create a hyperlink (text or graphic) that links to the movie file. That way, users can choose whether they want to view your movie instead of being forced to download it.

Movie Placeholder

To delete a movie from your Web page, click the Design Mode button on the Web Tools toolbar to enter Design Mode. Then right-click the Movie Placeholder icon, and then choose Cut from the shortcut menu.

Including Background Sounds and Sound Clips

Another multimedia element you can add to Web pages is background sound. Background sound refers to a sound file that plays when users display your Web page. You should use background sound sparingly. Many people find background sound annoying and a waste of bandwidth. If you find an instance in which a background sound adds to your page (maybe you're displaying a page about cricket chirps), you should feel comfortable adding the feature. Otherwise, your best bet is to provide a link to a sound file so that users can choose whether to play the sound file instead of being forced to run it. Here's how to add a background sound to a Web page when a background sound adds significantly to your Web page:

Sound

1 On the Web Tools toolbar, click Sound. The Background Sound dialog box appears, as shown in Figure 26-19.

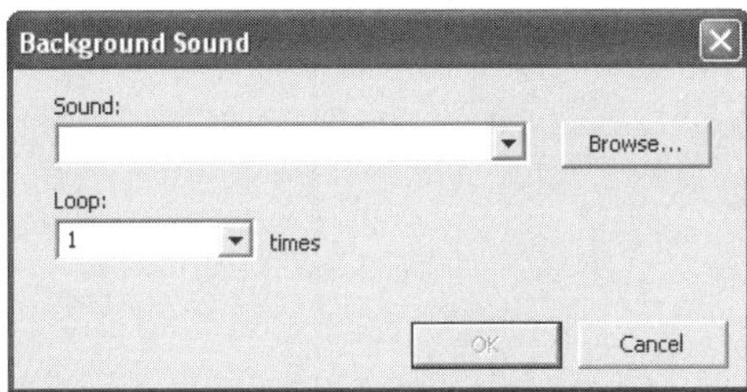

Figure 26-19. You can use the Background Sound dialog box to include background sound in your Web page.

2 In the Sound box, type the path or Web address of the sound file you want, or click Browse to locate the file.

Tip You can insert sound files in WAV, MID, MIDI, RMI, AU, AIF, AIFF, and SND formats.

3 In the Loop box, type the number of times you want the background sound to repeat, or click the arrow and then select from 1 through 5 or Infinite.

To stop the background sound from playing while you work on the Web page, click the Design Mode button on the Web Tools toolbar. (This button stops both movies and background sounds from playing.) To hear your background sound, click the Design Mode button to return to Web Page Layout view.

Tip To stop a background sound when you're viewing a Web page online, press Esc.

Sound Placeholder

To delete a sound from your Web page, click the Design Mode button, right-click the Sound Placeholder icon, and then choose Cut from the shortcut menu.

Adding Scrolling Text

Another type of multimedia component you can easily include on Web pages you build in Word is *scrolling text*, which is more commonly called *marquee text* by Web designers. Scrolling text is displayed like stock-ticker text—it enters on one side of your document and slides across to the other.

Note You should use scrolling text sparingly. Many browsers still don't support scrolling text and either will not display it at all or will display only part of it.

To insert scrolling text in your Web page document in Word, follow these steps:

Scrolling Text

1 On the Web Tools toolbar, click the Scrolling Text button. The Scrolling Text dialog box appears, as shown in Figure 26-20.

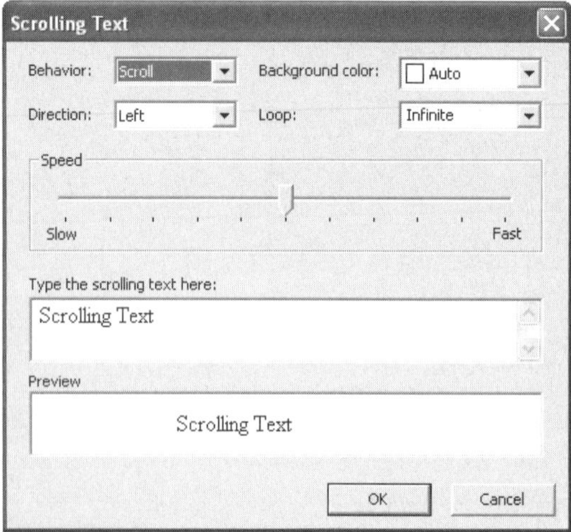

Figure 26-20. You use the Scrolling Text dialog box to include scrolling text in your Web page.

2 In the Behavior list, select from the following options. (To preview an option, select it, and then watch the sample text in the Preview box.)

- *Scroll*—Scrolls text across the screen. This is the default setting.
- *Slide*—Scrolls text once, stops at the other edge of the page, and then continues to display the scrolling text as static text.
- *Alternate*—Bounces the text back and forth between the left and right margins of the page.

3 In the Direction list, specify whether you want the text to scroll in from the left or right edge of the page.

4 If desired, click the Background Color list, and then select a color to be displayed behind the scrolling text. If you want to apply a background color, you must select one from the list; you can't apply custom colors to scrolling text items.

5 In the Loop box, type the number of times you want the text to scroll, or click the arrow, and then select 1 through 5 or Infinite. By default, scrolling text is configured to scroll infinitely (or so long as the page is displayed). If you select the Slide option in the Behavior list, the Loop option is unavailable because a slide implies only one scrolling action.

6 Drag the Speed slider to modify how fast or slow your text scrolls (or bounces) across the page.

7 Type the text you want to display in the Type The Scrolling Text Here box.

8 Click OK when you're satisfied with your scrolling text settings.

After you insert scrolling text, you can further modify the component by working with it in Design Mode (click the Design Mode button on the Web Tools toolbar). In Design Mode, you can enhance your scrolling text in the following ways:

- **Resize the scrolling text area.** Click the item and drag the component box's selection handles.
- **Format the scrolling text.** Use Word's text formatting tools, such as the Font dialog box and the Formatting toolbar buttons. Select the scrolling text component (you can't select the text), and then apply the font formatting settings.To view the settings, click the Design Mode button to run the scrolling text. To return to formatting mode, click the Design Mode button again.
- **Format the scrolling text component as a hyperlink.** Right-click the scrolling text component in Design Mode, and then choose Hyperlink from the shortcut menu. The Insert Hyperlink dialog box appears.

In general, you should use scrolling text to draw attention to a particular piece of information, and you shouldn't include critical information in this component (unless the information also appears elsewhere on the page). Users whose browsers don't support scrolling text might not see the message, so you want to make sure the information is "expendable" to some extent.

Creating Interactive Forms

If you've ever ordered an item online or used a Web search engine, you've used an interactive form. In Word, you can create online interactive forms in your Web page documents the same way you create standard forms. The main difference between creating standard Word forms and online forms is that you need to configure the properties of your online form's controls to work with your Web server. Because online forms created in Word require additional support files and server support, you should work with your network or Web administrator when planning and creating interactive Web forms.

Tip **Receive form responses as e-mail messages**

In addition to creating a *server-side online form* (a form that needs to work with a Web server that's configured to handle interactive forms), you can also create a Web form that sends an e-mail message to you each time the form is completed by a user. Whenever a user completes this type of form (often referred to as a *client-side form*) and then clicks a submit button, you receive an e-mail message containing the user's entries. To create this type of form, your best bet is to turn to a full-fledged HTML editor, such as FrontPage 2003.

When you create Web forms in Word, you can include 11 basic form controls, listed in Table 26-1. Word organizes the Web form controls for you on the Web Tools toolbar (right-click a toolbar, and then choose Web Tools from the shortcut menu, or choose View, Toolbars, Web Tools). Using the Web Tools toolbar, you can create a form by using any combination of these controls.

For an in-depth look at creating forms in Word, see Chapter 31, "Working with Field Codes and Custom Forms."

Table 26-1. Interactive Web Form Components

Web Tools Button	Control Name	Description
	Checkbox	Provides an option that's not mutually exclusive in a group of options or that appears as an independent option.
	Option Button	Provides options that are mutually exclusive in a group of options. Users can select only one item in a group of items.
	Drop-Down Box	Creates a list of options from which users can choose in list format.
	List Box	Inserts a box containing a list of items users can choose from. If the list is longer than the size of the box, users can scroll through the list to access additional options.
	Textbox	Creates a control in which users can enter one line of text.
	Text Area	Creates a control in which users can enter multiple lines of text.
	Submit	Sends the data that a user enters in the Web form. Every online form needs to include a Submit button or a Submit With Image button.
	Submit With Image	Displays a graphic that users can click to submit information.
	Reset	Resets the form to its default settings and removes any information entered by the user.
	Hidden	Inserts a hidden control that's used to pass information to a Web server (such as information about a user's computer operating environment) when the user submits the form.
	Password	Creates a text box that displays an asterisk to mask each character the user types in the text box.

Properties

To set a Web form control's properties, select the form control, and then click the Properties button on the Web Tools toolbar. To get information about the properties associated with each Web form control, consult the Word Help files. The Help topic titled "Form Controls You Can Use on a Web Page" provides property information for each of the 11 Web form controls.

Working with Cascading Style Sheets

Cascading style sheets (CSS) are used to format Web pages much in the same way traditional style sheets are used to format standard Word documents. The role of cascading style sheets is to present Web page formatting information in a specific place—either at the beginning of an HTML document or in a separate document—in a format that browsers can easily interpret and apply to the associated Web page or pages. Using cascading style sheets provides a convenient way to format several Web pages or a whole Web site. When cascading style sheets are in use, you can change the format of Web pages by making changes to the style sheet information instead of editing individual Web pages.

Because Word automatically creates your source code, you don't actually see that Word creates cascading style sheets. By default, Word uses cascading style sheets if your target browser option is set to Internet Explorer 4 or Netscape Navigator 4. (For more information about configuring your target browser, see "Specifying Target Browser Options" on page 706.) When Word creates a cascading style sheet, Word embeds the style sheet at the top of each Web page.

In addition to generating cascading style sheet information, you can use Word to attach, remove, and manage cascading style sheets for Web pages. You can also use Word to attach more than one style sheet to a Web page if necessary. For example, you might have one style sheet that's part of a large Web site, such as a style sheet for an international corporation, and another style sheet that defines a smaller group of related pages, such as a style sheet for a regional office. You can then specify which style sheet takes precedence over the other, in case conflicting styles are defined for the same element. When you attach a style sheet to your Web page in Word, the styles in the cascading style sheet will appear in the Styles And Formatting task pane.

For more information about the Styles And Formatting task pane, see Chapter 9, "Using Styles to Increase Your Formatting Power."

Working with Embedded Cascading Style Sheets

If you're familiar with coding HTML source code and cascading style sheets by hand, you might want to make changes directly to a style sheet that's embedded in a Web page. To do so, open the Web page, display the Web page's HTML Source code in the Script Editor (choose View, HTML Source), and then make changes directly to the code. Editing CSS code can come in handy if you want to tweak the code or make a quick change, such as changing the font family used for a style, as shown in Figure 26-21. After you make changes to source code in the Script Editor, you can save the changes, close or minimize the Script Editor, and then view the effects of your changes in the Web page document.

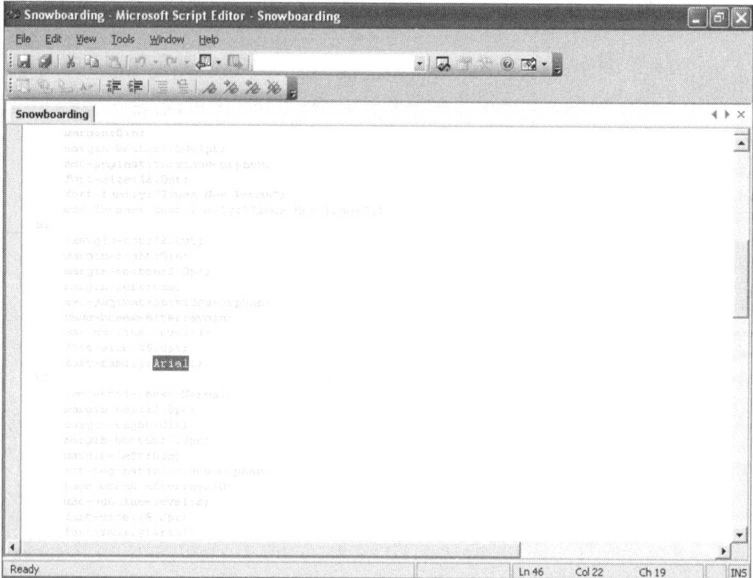

Figure 26-21. If you're comfortable editing HTML source code and working with CSS code, you can make changes directly to a Web page's embedded cascading style sheet.

> **Tip** For the latest information about CSS standards and sample code, visit the Cascading Style Sheets home page on the World Wide Web Consortium (W3C) Web site at *http://www.w3.org/Style/CSS*.

Attaching Cascading Style Sheets

If you have a cascading style sheet file, you can attach it to a Web page. Cascading style sheets carry the .css extension. You attach a cascading style sheet to a document the same way you attach a global template or an add-in. Specifically, you must complete the following steps:

1. Choose Tools, Templates And Add-Ins. The Templates And Add-Ins dialog box appears.
2. Click the Linked CSS tab, as shown in Figure 26-22.
3. Click the Add button. The Add CSS Link dialog box (which looks very similar to the Open dialog box) appears and displays any cascading style sheet files stored in your Templates folder.
4. If necessary, navigate to the cascading style sheet you want to add, select it, and then click OK.

Creating Professional Web Sites

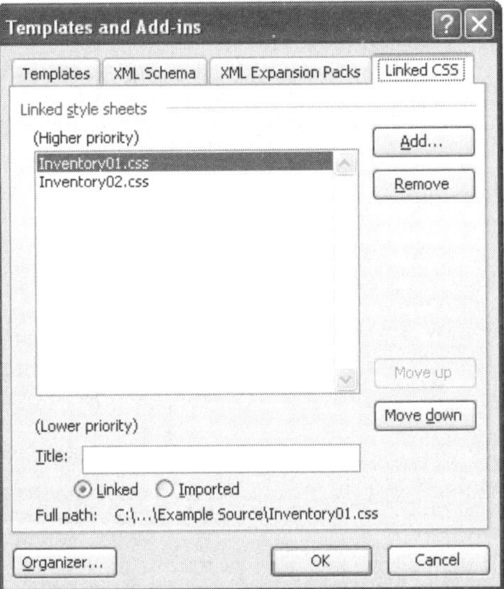

Figure 26-22. You can use the Linked CSS Style Sheets dialog box to attach, detach, and prioritize cascading style sheets.

5 To attach multiple style sheets to a document, repeat steps 3 and 4. After you've finished attaching cascading style sheets, click OK. A message box will appear, stating that the style sheet has changed and that you must save and reload the document. To have Word do this for you, click Yes.

After you attach a cascading style sheet to a document, the styles from the cascading style sheet will appear in the Styles And Formatting task pane.

Changing the Order of Cascading Style Sheets

The order of cascading style sheets provides a precedence that determines which styles are applied if two or more style sheets have conflicting settings for the same element. When you move a style sheet up in the list, you assign a higher priority to the style sheet. Likewise, when you move a style sheet down in the list, you assign a lower priority to the style sheet. To configure precedence among style sheets, follow these steps:

1 Choose Tools, Templates And Add-Ins. The Templates And Add-Ins dialog box appears.

2 Click the Linked CSS tab.

3 Select a style sheet in the list, and then click Move Up or Move Down to change the style sheet's precedence.

4 Click OK to close the Templates And Add-Ins dialog box.

Detaching Cascading Style Sheets

You can detach a cascading style sheet if you want to stop using the cascading style sheet to format a document. To do so, follow these steps:

1. Choose Tools, Templates And Add-Ins. The Templates And Add-Ins dialog box appears.
2. Click the Linked CSS tab.
3. Select the style sheet you want to remove, and then click Remove.
4. Remove any other style sheets you want to detach, and then click OK when you've finished. A message box will appear, stating that the style sheet has changed and that you must save and reload the document. To have Word do this for you, click Yes.

Keep in mind that when you remove a style sheet from the list, you don't delete the style sheet's file; you simply instruct the current document to stop referring to the style sheet.

Editing Source Code Using the Microsoft Script Editor

If you're comfortable working with HTML code, Web scripts, and cascading style sheet information, you might want to tweak your Web pages' source code directly from time to time. The Microsoft Script Editor allows you to view and edit your Web page documents' HTML source code. In addition, you can use the Microsoft Script Editor to add VBScript and JScript to your files.

To display a Web page's source code, open the document inWord, and then choose View, HTML Source. The first time you access the Microsoft Script Editor, you might see a message box stating that you have to install it. To do so, simply insert your installation CD, and then click Install. If you don't see the HTML Source menu option, choose Tools, Macro, Microsoft Script Editor to install the Script Editor. After the installation is complete, your Web page's source code will be displayed in the Microsoft Script Editor window, as shown in Figure 26-23.

You can edit and change the source code in the Microsoft Script Editor the same way you edit source code in other applications. In addition to displaying the code for the current page, the Project Explorer pane displays all other open documents so that you can easily display the source code for those documents as well. Notice too that the Standard toolbar contains two save buttons: Save and Save All. Use the Save All button if you've been working on the source code in a number of open documents and you're ready to save all your changes to the documents. After you save changes you've made in a document's source code, the document is updated to incorporate the changes.

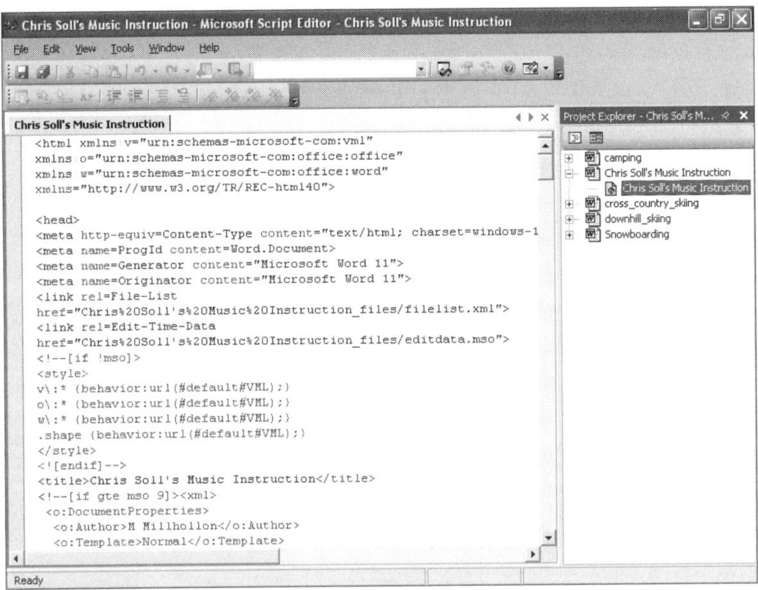

Figure 26-23. The Microsoft Script Editor provides a convenient way for Web page developers to edit Web page documents' source code.

Publishing Your Web Pages

The last stage of Web page creation entails publishing your Web pages. After you create and save your Web page documents, you're ready to publish your pages for the world (or at least your fellow employees, associates, or family members) to see. Publishing your Web pages simply means copying your Web page files and folders from your computer onto a Web server. Keep in mind that when you publish your Web pages, you must retain the hierarchical structure of your Web page files, including naming and organizational schemes. If your Web page stores all its graphics files in a subfolder, for example, you must publish the subfolder in addition to the contents of the folder without changing the name of the folder or files. (Remember, changing uppercase to lowercase constitutes changing the name of a file or folder name.)

The most common way to publish Web pages is to copy the files and folders on your system to a server by using a File Transfer Protocol (FTP) application. When you create Web pages in Word, you have another option. You can also save your Web page documents to a server by clicking the My Network Places button in the Save As dialog box and saving your Web page documents in a folder on your network location.

Whenever you publish Web pages, you should always view your live pages immediately after you upload them—that way, you'll be the first to see whether your pages are displayed properly. If your pages need to be fixed, change the local copy of your Web page document, and then save the updated file over the existing file on your Web server. After your Web pages are uploaded and live, you're ready for the next stage of Webmastering—maintaining and updating your Web site. (But that's a topic for another book!)

Chapter 27

Revising Documents Using Markup Tools

As you probably know, many finished documents (e.g., this book) reflect the efforts of a group of people who worked together to create a polished product. For example, you might be involved with a single document that was written by an author, modified by an editor, commented on by a technical reviewer, and inspected and approved by a project manager. Such team collaboration can be simplified tremendously by using Word.

In Word, numerous people can review the same document and incorporate their changes and comments with other people's changes and comments. After participants add their two cents' worth to a document, others in the group can insert responses directly into the document. Throughout the process,Word can dutifully track and color-code everyone's comments and changes, so long as you configure Word's markup features properly. Word 2003 incorporates modifications to the Track Changes feature that give you greater control over how changes and comments appear online. In addition, Word 2003 offers new ink options that you can use to add comments and annotations when you're using Word on a Tablet PC. In this chapter, you'll learn to use Word's markup features and reviewing options so that you can maximize your collaboration efforts when you work with others on documents.

Familiarizing Yourself with Markup Tools

When you collaborate on a document, you can use Word to track and merge people's changes and comments, highlight information to draw attention to selected text and graphics, store versions of documents throughout the development process, and add ink and voice comments. Specifically, Word provides the following reviewing and markup tools:

- **Comments** Enable you to annotate a document with suggestions and queries without actually changing the document. In Word 2003, you can add text, ink, and voice comments to documents. Comments are identified by comment markers in the text, which can be either insertion lines or parentheses, as described in "Adding and Managing Comments Effectively" on page 753.

- **The Highlight tool** Enables you to draw attention to particular information (including a letter, word, phrase, sentence, paragraph, graphic, and so forth) by adding a color background behind the information, as described in "Using the Highlight Tool" on page 750.

- **Ink support for tablet PCs** Enables you to draw and write on documents directly by using a stylus or other drawing device. Using ink on a Tablet PC is discussed in "Inserting Ink Comments and Annotations" on page 762.
- **The Track Changes feature** Records editing changes, including deletions, added content, and formatting changes made to a document. Word can track and color-code changes from multiple reviewers, and the changes can later be evaluated and accepted or rejected on a case-by-case or global basis. For more information about the Track Changes feature, see "Tracking Changes" on page 774.
- **The Versions feature** Maintains multiple versions of a document in a single file so that you can easily return to past versions of the changed document. "Working with Multiple Versions of a Document" on page 787, describes the Versions feature in more detail.

This chapter shows you how to make the most of these collaboration features. You'll find that many key collaboration features can be accessed from the Reviewing toolbar, shown in Figure 27-1. To open the Reviewing toolbar, right-click a toolbar and choose Reviewing on the shortcut menu, or choose View, Toolbars, Reviewing.

Figure 27-1. The Reviewing toolbar provides buttons you can use to add, modify, accept, and reject comments and tracked changes in documents.

As you can see in Figure 27-1, the Reviewing toolbar in Word 2003 is a slightly modified version of the Reviewing toolbar found in Word 2002. The most notable difference is the inclusion of the Insert Voice and Highlight buttons on the toolbar. The voice and highlight features were available in Word 2002, but they weren't easily accessible using toolbar buttons. Table 27-1 describes the buttons found on the Reviewing toolbar.

Table 27-1. Reviewing Toolbar Buttons

Button	Name	Description
Final Showing Markup	Display For Review	Controls how Word displays changes and comments in the current document. Available options are Final Showing Markup, Final, Original Showing Markup, and Original.
Show	Show	Accesses a menu that enables you to configure the display (Final or Original) and settings for Comments, Ink Annotations, Insertions And Deletions, Formatting, Reviewers, Balloons, Reviewing Pane, and Options.

Revising Documents Using Markup Tools

Table 27-1. Reviewing Toolbar Buttons

Button	Name	Description
	Previous	Jumps to the previous tracked change or comment in the current document relative to the insertion point.
	Next	Jumps to the next tracked change or comment in the current document relative to the insertion point.
	Accept Change	Accepts a selected tracked change in the current document, or enables you to accept all changes at once.
	Reject Change/ Delete Comment	Rejects a selected change or deletes a selected comment and returns the text to its original state, or enables you to reject all changes or delete all comments at once.
	Insert Ink Annotations (Tablet PCs Only)	Opens the Ink Annotations toolbar and enables you to add ink marks directly to the document as if you were writing on a paper version of the document.
	Ink Comment (Tablet PCs Only)	Inserts a new comment bubble that you can write in using a tablet pen, stylus, or other drawing device.
	Insert Comment	Inserts a new comment bubble that you can use to enter a text comment.
	Insert Voice	Opens the Sound Object dialog box and enables you to record a voice comment if the system has a microphone.
	Highlight	Controls whether the highlight tool is turned on or off; you use the highlight tool to draw attention to key information in documents.
	Track Changes	Controls whether the Track Changes feature is turned off or on.
Reply with Changes...	Reply With Changes	Appears when you're working on a document sent to you from another person using the Track Changes feature who mailed the document to you for review.
	Reviewing Pane	Shows or hides the Reviewing Pane, which displays the complete text of tracked changes and comments.

Now that you've had a quick introduction to the main document collaboration features, let's look at the finer details. This chapter starts with the simplest feature associated with marking up documents—the Highlight tool.

Using the Highlight Tool

As in earlier versions of Word, the Highlight tool is available for use in Word 2003, and its functionality remains the same. One minor difference regarding the Highlight tool in Word 2003 compared to Word 2002 is that you can access the tool from the Reviewing toolbar. Highlighting calls attention to important or questionable text in documents, as illustrated in Figure 27-2. Highlighting parts of a document works best when the document is viewed online, although you can use highlighting in printed documents if necessary. When you use the Highlight tool, the main tasks you'll perform are adding, removing, finding, and replacing highlighting. The next few sections briefly describe these procedures.

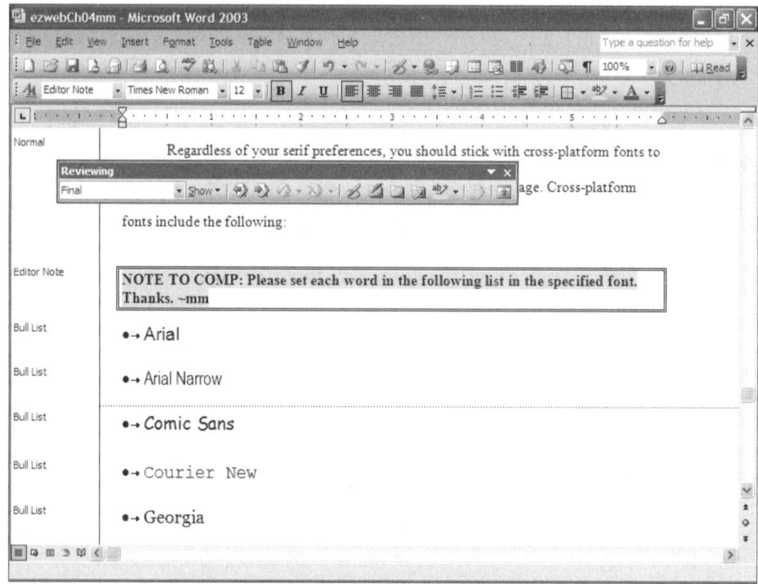

Figure 27-2. You can use the Highlight tool to draw attention to particular information in your Word document when you're collaborating with others.

Highlighting Information

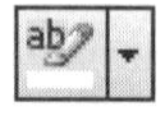

Highlight

You can apply highlighting to a single block of selected text or graphics, or you can apply highlighting to a series of text areas or graphics. To apply a single instance of highlighting to information, select the information and then click the Highlight button on the Reviewing toolbar or the Formatting toolbar. To apply highlighting to multiple blocks of information, click the Highlight button, select the text or graphic you want to highlight, and then select the next item in the document you want to highlight. The Highlight tool continues to highlight information as you select it. To turn off highlighting, click the Highlight button again, or press Esc.

You can change the highlight color by clicking the Highlight button arrow and choosing a color on the menu. The color you choose becomes the default highlight color until you select another color on the menu.

Tip **Choose highlight colors wisely**
Be sure to choose a light highlight color if you're going to print your document with highlighted text, especially if the document will be printed in monochrome (including grayscale) or on a dot-matrix printer. If more than one person is going to be adding highlighting to a document, consider assigning highlight colors to each person or standardize highlight colors to indicate a particular issue (for example, reviewers could use turquoise highlighting to specify that a page reference needs to be completed, bright green highlighting to draw attention to repeated information, and so forth).

Inside Out

Considering browsers when highlighting

If you save highlighted text as part of a Web page, Word stores the highlighting information as part of the Web page's cascading style sheet (CSS). This information will be understood and displayed properly in Internet Explorer 3 and Netscape Navigator 4 browsers and later versions, but earlier versions of those browsers (and other less widely used browsers) might not display the highlighting properly. If you're not sure which browsers viewers will be using to display your Web page, you should consider using another method to draw attention to the text in place of highlighting. For example, you could color the text itself, create a graphic of the highlighted text, or build a table and color the text's table cell to simulate a highlighted paragraph.

Removing Highlighting from Documents

You can remove the highlighting in a document when you no longer need to draw attention to the highlighted text or graphics. To remove highlighting, follow these steps:

1. Select the information you want to remove highlighting from, or press Ctrl+A to select the entire document.
2. Click the Highlight button arrow, and then choose None on the menu.

After you choose None, all instances of highlighting are removed from the selected text.

Tip **Display and hide highlighting**
You can display or hide highlighting (but not the text itself) on screen and in the printed document without permanently removing the highlighting. To do so, choose Tools, Options, click the View tab, clear or select the Highlight check box in the Show section, and click OK.

Finding Highlighted Items

If you want to jump from highlighted item to highlighted item, you can do so by using the Find And Replace dialog box. To find instances of highlighted text, follow these steps:

1. Choose Edit, Find, or press Ctrl+F.
2. Click More to expand the Find tab.
3. Click Format, and choose Highlight.
4. Click Find Next to jump to the next occurrence of highlighted text, and click Cancel when you've finished reviewing all other instances of highlighted text.

You can also select all instances of highlighted text at one time by following steps 1 through 3 above and then selecting the Highlight All Items Found In check box in the Find And Replace dialog box. Verify that Main Document is selected in the list below the check box and click Find All.

Tip **Clear the highlight format from the Find tab**
To stop the Highlight specification from being associated with the Find What text box on the Find tab, click No Formatting in the Find And Replace dialog box. For more information about the Find And Replace dialog box, see Chapter 4, "Honing Document Navigation Skills."

Reformatting Highlighted Items with Another Highlight Color

You can change a highlight color in a document, as well as change all instances of highlighting in a document to the same color. To change a single instance of a highlight color, choose another highlight color on the Highlight button menu, and then select the highlighted text. The existing highlight color changes to the newly selected color.

To change the color of multiple instances of highlighting, you can use the Find And Replace dialog box. Using this technique, you replace all existing highlighting (regardless of original highlight color) with a newly selected color, as follows:

1. Click the Highlight arrow, and select the color you want to assign to all highlighting.
2. Choose Edit, Replace, or press Ctrl+H. The Find And Replace dialog box appears.
3. If necessary, click More to expand the Replace tab.
4. Make sure that no text appears in the Find What and Replace With boxes, position your insertion point in the Find What box, and then click Format and choose Highlight.
5. Click in the Replace With box, and choose Format, Highlight.
6. Click Replace All, and then click OK in the message box that tells you how many replacements were made.
7. Click Close to close the Find And Replace dialog box.

In addition to replacing all highlighted text with a newly selected color, you can use the above procedure to replace selected instances of highlighting with a new color. To do so, click Find Next instead of Replace All in step 6. You can then specify which instances of highlighting are replaced with a new color on a case-by-case basis.

> **Note** You can also change all instances of highlighting to the same color by selecting all instances of highlighting using the Find tab, as described in "Finding Highlighted Items" on page 752, and then choosing a new color on the Highlight button menu.

Adding and Managing Comments Effectively

Comments allow people who collaborate on documents to ask questions, provide suggestions, insert notes, and generally annotate a document's contents without directly inserting any information into the body of the document. When you work with a document that contains comments, you can display the comments in the Reviewing Pane while viewing the document in any view or in a margin balloon if you're working in Web Layout, Print Layout, or Reading Layout view. When the Reviewing Pane is open, it is displayed below the document's editing window, along the bottom of the Word window. When you use balloons to display information, the balloons appear next to your document's contents in either the left or right margin. Figure 27-3 shows a sample document in Print Layout view, with a comment balloon and the Reviewing Pane visible.

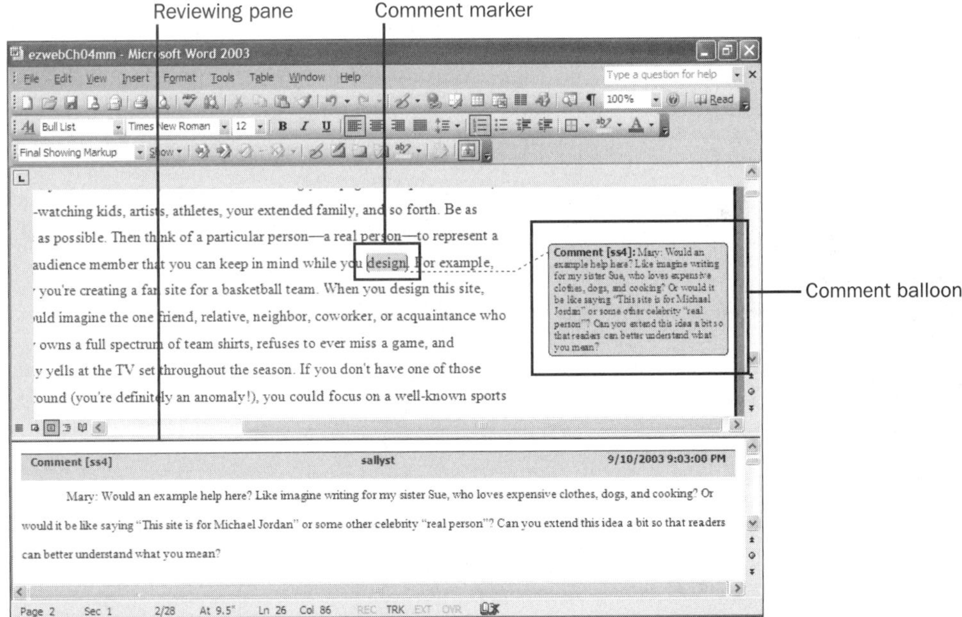

Figure 27-3. You can display color-coded comments in comment balloons or in the Reviewing Pane; in both views, each comment includes the initials of the person who created the comment and a numeric identifier.

In addition to comment balloons, Word 2003 implements a number of visual cues when displaying comments. For example, notice in Figure 27-3 that in both the balloon and the Reviewing Pane (in the shaded comment bar) the word "Comment" identifies the information as a comment. (You can also show insertions, deletions, and formatting changes in balloons and the Reviewing Pane, as described in "Tracking Changes" on page 774.) The balloons and comment bars in the Reviewing Pane can be color-coded to associate them with particular users, and each comment bar in the Reviewing Pane displays the user name of the person who inserted the comment.

As part of the new functionality in Word 2003, comments appear with the initials of the person who created the comment, and comments are automatically numbered sequentially throughout the document. In addition, the content associated with comments now appears shaded in the document to help visually link commented areas to corresponding comments. The shading of each instance of commented content matches the corresponding comment's balloon color, which simplifies identifying who created which comments. The new combination of user initials, comment numbering, and color-coded content shading makes identifying and referring to comments much easier than in past versions of Word, as you can see in Figure 27-3. All these small modifications are part of a new streamlined approach to using comments in Word.

Configuring Reviewers' User Names

Before you start inserting comments, you need to tell Word how to identify the comments you create. In other words, you need to configure your user name in Word. In fact, each person collaborating on the document must properly configure his or her user name to maximize Word's reviewing features. To set your user name information, you simply configure the settings on the User Information tab in the Options dialog box, as follows:

1. Choose Tools, Options, and click the User Information tab.
2. In the Name box, type the name you want to use to identify your comments, and enter your initials in the Initials box, as shown in Figure 27-4.

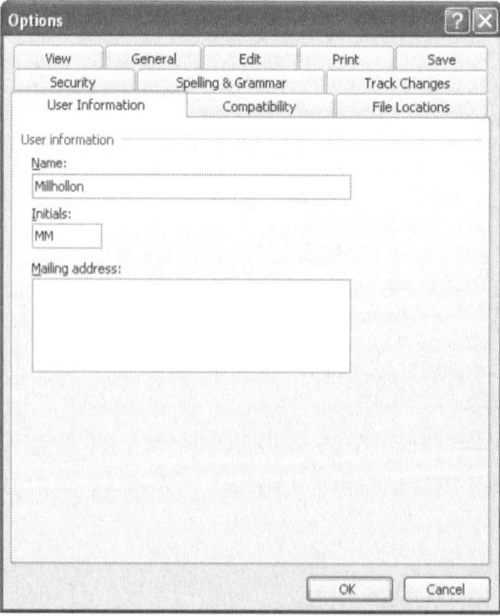

Figure 27-4. Word uses the User Information name to identify comments in documents.

3 Click OK to close the Options dialog box.

Keep in mind that the information you enter in the User Information tab is used by all Microsoft Office System programs. Any changes you make to these settings will affect future documents in other Office programs as well. Fortunately, this is not as dire as it sounds. For example, if you're temporarily using someone else's machine to review a document, you can change the name on the User Information tab before you work without affecting existing documents. Then, when you've finished working with the document on that machine, return to the User Information tab to replace the original information.

Configuring Colors Associated with Reviewers

By default, Word automatically uses a different color for each reviewer's comments and tracked changes in a document. If you prefer all comments and tracked changes to be displayed in a single color, you can change the default setting by accessing the Track Changes options using one of the following techniques:

- On the Reviewing toolbar, click Show and choose Options on the menu. The Track Changes dialog box opens, as shown in Figure 27-5.

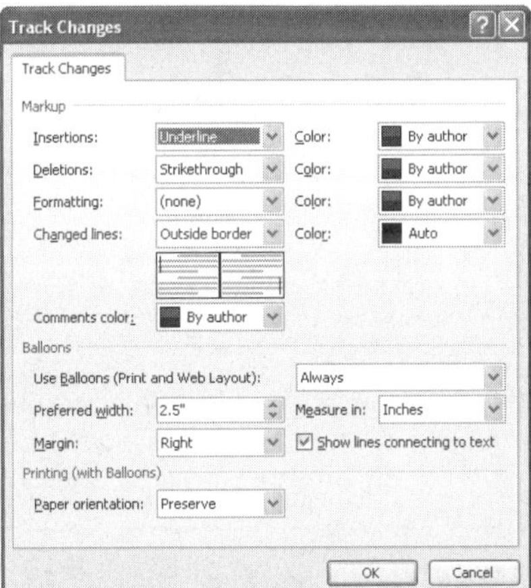

Figure 27-5. By default, comments, insertions, deletions, and formatting changes are displayed in a different color for each reviewer.

- Choose Tools, Options, and click the Track Changes tab. The options on the Track Changes tab in the Options dialog box are the same options available in the Track Changes dialog box.

On the Track Changes tab, you can specify a color for all comments, insertions, deletions, and formatting changes by selecting a color in the Color lists. By default, By Author is selected in the Color lists, which means that Word automatically assigns a different color to every person who inserts comments or tracked changes. Keep in mind that this setting doesn't always color-code each person's changes with the same color every time. Instead, the By Author option simply guarantees that every person's marks will appear in a distinct color—each person's color will most likely change each time someone reopens the document. For more information about configuring other Track Changes options, see "Adjusting the Appearance of Tracked Changes" on page 777.

If you're viewing a document that's color-coded for a number of reviewers, you can quickly see which colors are currently assigned to which reviewers. To do so, click Show on the Reviewing toolbar, and choose the Reviewers menu. You'll see a list of reviewer names accompanied by color-coded check boxes, as shown in Figure 27-6. (Of course, you can't see the color-coding here, but you can get an idea of how the color-coding system works.) In addition to seeing the reviewer color assignments, you can use the Reviewers menu to specify whose comments and tracked changes are displayed in the current document by selecting and clearing the check boxes next to reviewers' names. When you clear a check box while in Print Layout, Web Layout, or Reading Layout view, that reviewer's comment and tracked change balloons are hidden, and text inserted by the reviewer appears as regular body text. To redisplay a reviewer's comments and changes, reselect the reviewer's check box on the Reviewers menu.

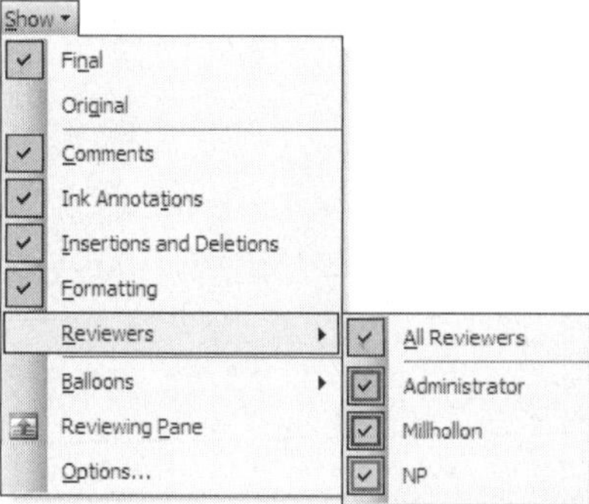

Figure 27-6. You can use the Reviewers menu to quickly see the colors currently assigned to reviewers and to control whose comments and changes are displayed in the current document.

Marking Text You Insert in E-Mail Responses

If Microsoft Outlook is your e-mail client and Word is set as your e-mail message editor, you can add comments to e-mail messages in the same way you add comments to standard documents. You can also configure Word to display your name or initials next to text you insert in e-mail responses, as follows:

1. Choose Tools, Options, and click the General tab.
2. Click E-mail Options, and then click the Personal Stationery tab in the E-mail Options dialog box.
3. Select the Mark My Comments With check box, and type the text (such as your name or initials) that you want to display in association with your comments, as shown on the next page:

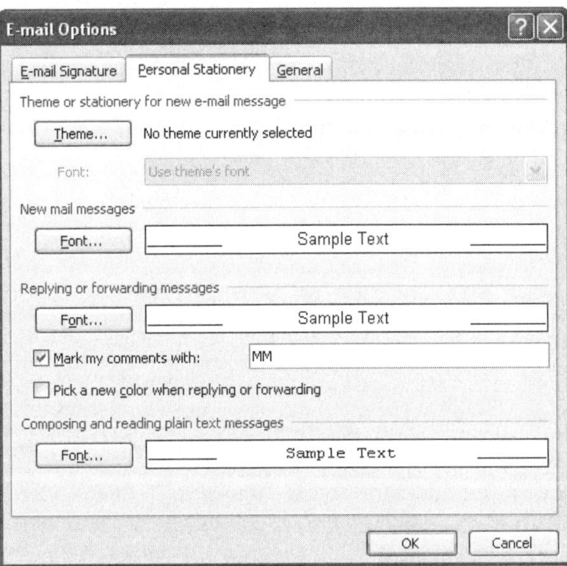

4 Click OK to close the E-mail Options dialog box, and then click OK to close the Options dialog box.

When you select the Mark My Comments With check box, only text you type next to previously written text in a message will display your name or initials next to it. To turn off this formatting in e-mail messages, clear the Mark My Comments With check box.

Inside Out

Optimizing a document's readability when some reviewer marks are hidden

If you're working in Normal view and you turn off the display of a reviewer's tracked changes, the text deleted by the reviewer appears restored and text inserted by the reviewer appears as regular text. As you can imagine, this can result in some strange mixtures of restored and added text. To avoid confusion, if you choose to hide a particular reviewer's comments and changes, be sure you're working in Print Layout, Web Layout, or Reading Layout view.

Allowing Reviewers to Use Only the Comments Feature

In addition to color-coding reviewers' comments, you can use Word to help control who can add comments to a document during the review phases. To do this, you use the Editing Restrictions setting in the Protect Document task pane, shown in Figure 27-7. Using the Editing Restrictions feature, you can ensure that the only modifications reviewers can make to your document are to add comments.

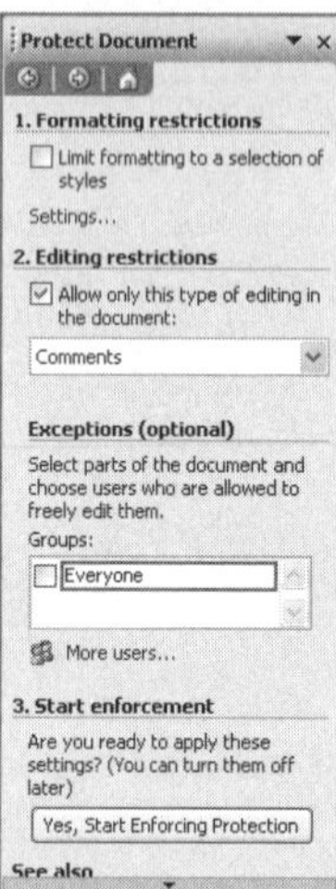

Figure 27-7. The Protect Document task pane enables you to limit reviewers' actions to only certain types of changes, such as comments.

To arrange this setup, follow these steps:

1. Choose Tools, Protect Document; or open the task pane (press Ctrl+F1), click the task pane title bar, and choose Protect Document.
2. In the Protect Document task pane, click the Allow Only This Type Of Editing In The Document check box, and choose Comments in the list below the check box option.
3. Specify any groups or users (click More Users) who are exceptions to the editing restriction.
4. Click Yes, Start Enforcing Protection. The Start Enforcing Protection dialog box opens.
5. If desired, type a password in the Password boxes, and click OK. If you specify a password, reviewers will have to enter the password before they can enter comments.

If you choose not to assign a password in step 5, reviewers will be restricted to inserting only comments by default. But if reviewers choose Tools, Unprotect Document, they'll be able to unlock the document and edit your document freely. In other words, this document protection plan is really more of a deterrent than a fail-safe protection, but many times a deterrent is all you really need. For more information about protecting documents and allowing particular groups or individuals to edit parts of a document, see Chapter 28, "Addressing Document Protection and Security Issues."

Troubleshooting

I forgot the document protection password

If you forget the password for a protected document, you can recover the document by circumventing the password protection. To do so, select the entire document (by pressing Ctrl+A), copy the document (by pressing Ctrl+C), and paste the document (by pressing Ctrl+V) into a new, blank document. This process creates a new document based on the existing document.

Fortunately, when you copy and paste a document that contains tracked changes and comments, the newly created document retains all the reviewers' marks and color-coded settings. However, in Word 2000 and earlier versions, when you copy and paste text that contains tracked changes, the changes are accepted in the newly copied version of the text regardless of whether you're ready to accept the changes.

Inserting Standard Comments

After you configure your user name information, specify how to color comments, and set any reviewer limitations, you're ready to insert comments into documents. Inserting a comment is a straightforward process. You can insert your comment at the insertion point, or you can select content that you want to associate with your comment. If you insert a comment at the insertion point, Word indicates the existence of your comment in the text by shading the nearest word and enclosing it in parentheses (see Figure 27-3 for an example). If you select content to be associated with a comment, Word marks the selected content in the same way, by shading the content and enclosing it in parentheses.

To insert a comment, follow these steps:

1. Position the insertion point where you want to insert a comment, or select the content you want to associate with your comment.
2. Perform any of the following three actions:
   - Choose Insert, Comment.
   - Click the Insert Comment button on the Reviewing toolbar.
   - Press Ctrl+Alt+M.

   If you're working in Web Layout, Print Layout, or Reading Layout view, an empty balloon opens by default when you insert a comment. If you're working in Normal or Outline view, the Reviewing Pane opens.

Note By default, comment balloons are turned on in Print Layout, Web Layout, and Reading Layout views. If your balloons are hidden, you can type comments in the Reviewing Pane when you're working in any view.

3 Type the comment text in the comment balloon or the Reviewing Pane, and then click outside of the balloon or Reviewing Pane to complete the comment.

Note After you enter a comment in a balloon, you can press Esc when you've finished typing to return the insertion point to the body text.

If you want to change a comment after you create it, you can do so by clicking inside the comment balloon or Reviewing Pane and then editing the text just as you edit standard text. If a comment is long and its contents aren't entirely displayed in a balloon, click the ellipsis in the balloon to open the Reviewing Pane. You can then modify the comment in the Reviewing Pane. If the Reviewing Pane isn't open or the ellipsis isn't visible, click the Reviewing Pane button on the Reviewing toolbar to open it. To close the Reviewing Pane, click the Reviewing Pane button on the Reviewing toolbar or press Alt+Shift+C.

Inside Out

Editing text in the Reviewing Pane

In both Word 2002 and Word 2003, you can't select and press Backspace to delete text in the Reviewing Pane. Therefore, to delete text while working in the Reviewing Pane, you need to either select text and use the Delete key, or position your cursor near the text you want to delete and then use the Backspace or Delete key to delete the information. Note that you can press Ctrl+Backspace or Ctrl+Delete to delete entire words at a time. If you want to replace existing text in the Reviewing Pane, you need to select the text you want to replace or position the cursor before the text you want to type over, double-click OVR in the status bar to turn on the Overtype feature, and then type the new comment text.

Inserting Voice Comments

Audio

In addition to inserting standard comments, you can include *voice comments* with documents. Basically, voice comments are WAV recordings you make and attach to a document. To create voice comments, your computer must have a sound card and a microphone. Likewise, others who review the document and listen to your voice comments must be using computers equipped with a sound card and speakers. Similar to text comments, voice comments appear as icons in balloons and in the Reviewing Pane. To create a voice comment, display the Reviewing toolbar and then follow these steps:

1 Open the Reviewing toolbar and click the Insert Voice button.

2 The Sound Object dialog box opens, as shown in Figure 27-8.

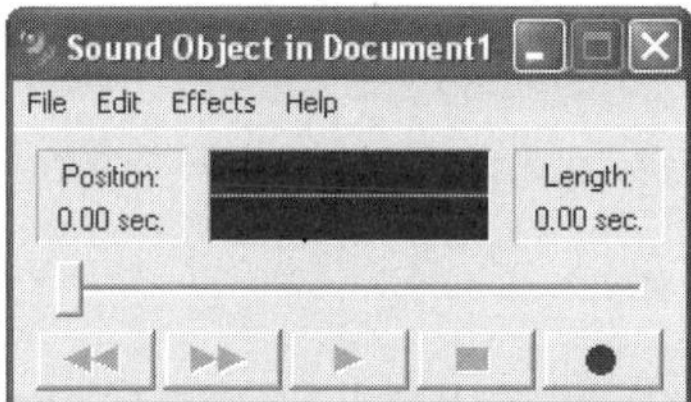

Figure 27-8. The Sound Object dialog box is a simple application you can use to include voice comments in documents.

Record

Stop

3 Click the Record button in the Sound Object dialog box and then speak into your microphone to record your comment.

4 Click Stop when you've finished recording your comment, and close the Sound Object dialog box to complete the voice comment. Voice comments appear in balloons and the Reviewing Pane, as shown in Figure 27-9.

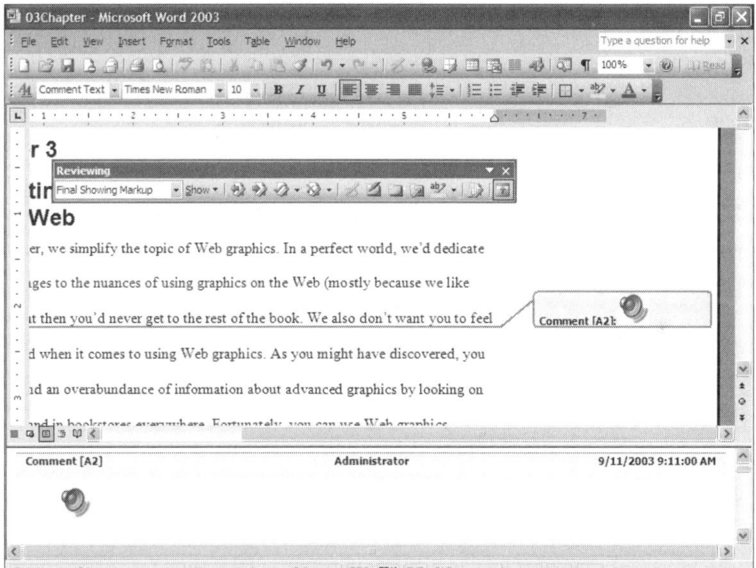

Figure 27-9. To listen to a voice comment, double-click the speaker icon in a comment balloon or Reviewing Pane.

After you create a voice comment, you can manipulate it in the following ways:

- **Listen to the voice comment.** Double-click the audio icon in the comment balloon. The comment plays without opening Sound Object.
- **Open Sound Recorder before listening to the voice comment.** Right-click the audio icon, and choose Sound Recorder Document Object, Edit on the shortcut menu.
- **Modify the voice comment.** Right-click the comment, and choose Sound Recorder Document Object, Edit on the shortcut menu.

- **Convert the voice comment from WAV format to another format.** Right-click the comment, and choose Sound Recorder Document Object, Convert on the shortcut menu.
- **Delete the voice comment.** Select the audio icon and press Delete; right-click the audio icon and choose Cut on the shortcut menu; or click the comment and click Reject Change/Delete Comment on the Reviewing toolbar.

If you decide to use voice comments, you should keep your messages short. By default, voice comments are WAV audio files attached to the document, and as you know, audio files can grow in size fairly rapidly.

Inserting Ink Comments and Annotations

If you're using a Tablet PC, you can use your tablet pen in Word 2003 to enter ink comments and add ink annotations directly in the body of documents. Ink comments are similar to standard comments except that you enter the comment information using your tablet pen instead of a keyboard. Figure 27-10 shows an ink comment. Notice that the written information can be displayed in a balloon or in the Reviewing Pane.

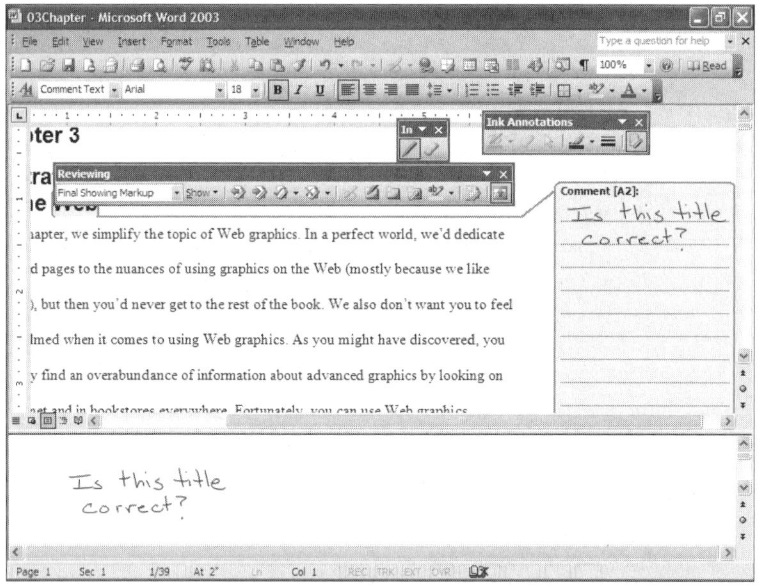

Figure 27-10. If you're using Word 2003 on a Tablet PC, you can use your tablet pen to add ink comments. After you add ink comments, others can view your comments on other types of systems.

In addition to creating ink comments, you can add ink annotations. Ink annotations are a little different from ink comments. When you use the ink annotation feature, you write directly on a document, as shown in Figure 27-11. Using ink annotations, you can write on an online document in the same way you write on paper documents. The next sections describe how to insert ink comments and annotations.

Revising Documents Using Markup Tools

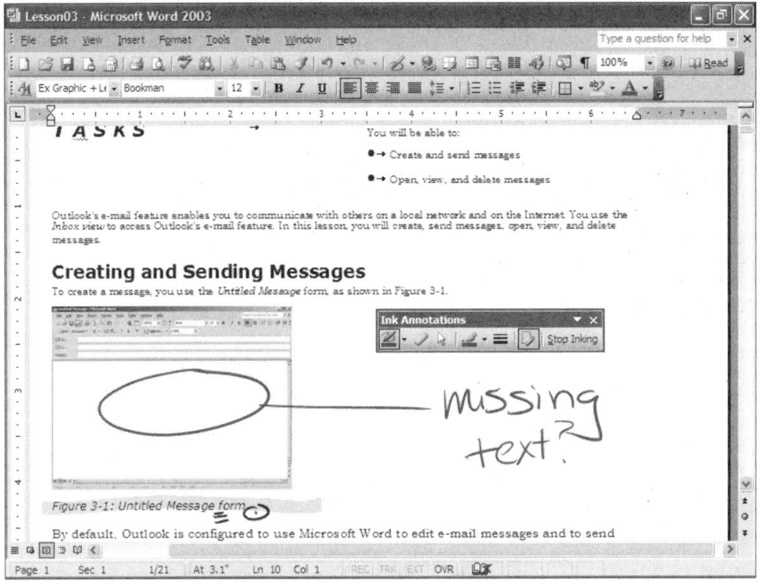

Figure 27-11. Ink annotations enable you to mark up documents onscreen in the same way you mark up printed pages with pens and highlighters.

NEW FEATURE!

Inserting Ink Comments

The procedure for inserting an ink comment is very similar to inserting standard comments. You must be working in Print Layout, Web Layout, or Reading Layout view to use ink comments. If you are working in Normal or Outline view and you attempt to add an ink comment, Word automatically switches to Print Layout view. To add an ink comment, perform the following steps:

1. Insert the cursor where you want to anchor the comment or select the content about which you want to add a comment.

Ink Comment

2. Tap the Ink Comment button on the Reviewing toolbar or choose Insert, Ink Comment from the menu bar. An empty balloon appears in the margin, and the Ink Comment toolbar appears, containing the Pen and Eraser buttons, as shown in Figure 27-12. By default, the pen is selected.

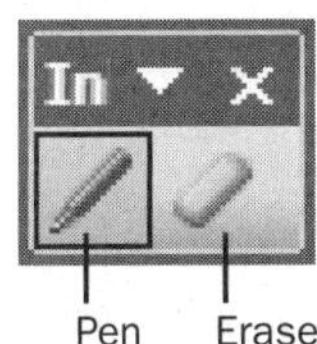

Figure 27-12. The Ink Comments toolbar contains the Pen and Eraser buttons. You can use the Eraser tool to remove some or all ink from a comment.

3. Tap in the comment balloon, and use the tablet pen to write or draw comment information.

When others view ink comments, the comments appear along with standard comments in the margin or in the Reviewing Pane. Figure 27-13 shows an ink comment being viewed on a desktop computer alongside a standard comment and tracked changes.

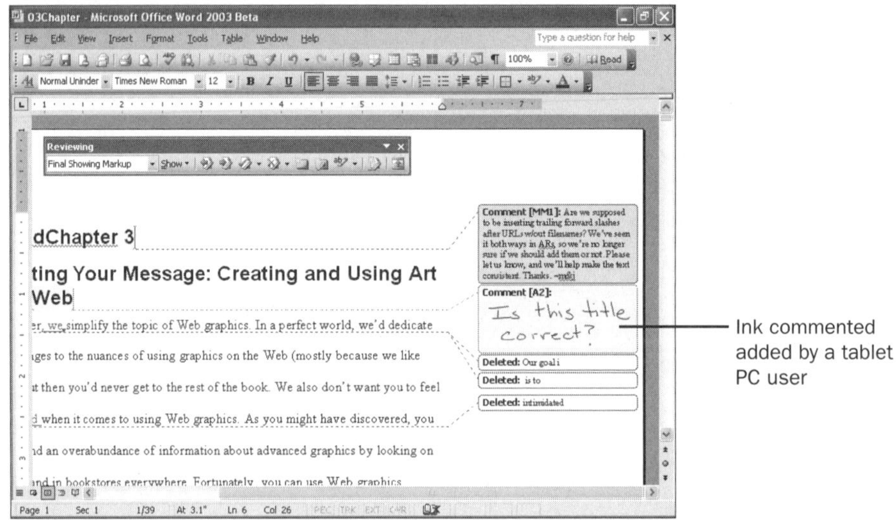

Figure 27-13. Ink comments appear alongside standard comments and tracked changes in a document's margin or Reviewing Pane. You can copy and delete ink comments, but you can't add text.

Adding Ink Annotations

Insert Ink

If you're using a Tablet PC, you can add ink annotations directly on top of content in documents. For instance, you can circle text, draw arrows on graphics, highlight key topics, or cross out chart elements. You must be running Word 2003 on a Tablet PC to use ink annotations, and it is recommended that you work in Print Layout view for optimal results. Furthermore, to ensure that ink annotations remain relevant and useful, you should lock the document's layout before you add ink annotations. This ensures that the content won't shift and render your ink annotations meaningless. Ink annotations are anchored to paragraphs, so if you add or remove paragraphs, your annotations will remain accurate and intact. But if any changes are made within a paragraph containing ink annotations—such as content is added or removed, font or margin sizes are changed, or other content is resized—the ink annotations will probably no longer line up correctly in your document. When you work with ink annotations, keep in mind that the ink marks are stored on a layer above the document's contents.

For more information about locking layouts and protecting documents, see Chapter 28, "Addressing Document Protection and Security Issues."

Tip If you add ink annotations while in Reading Layout view, make sure you click the Actual Page button on the Reading Layout toolbar before you add ink. Otherwise, your annotations might not align properly with content in the Print Layout and Web Layout views.

To add ink annotations, open the document, and click Insert, Ink Annotations on the menu bar or tap Insert Ink button on the Reviewing toolbar. When you add ink annotations, the Ink Annotations toolbar appears by default and contains tools you can use to customize your annotations. Table 27-2 describes the Ink Annotations toolbar buttons.

Table 27-2. Ink Annotations Toolbar Buttons

Button	Name	Description
	Ball Point Pens/ Felt Tip Pens/ Highlighters	Enables you to select a pen style and color. You can choose a black, red, or blue ballpoint or felt tip pen, or you can choose a yellow, turquoise, or pink highlighter. You can select additional colors by using the Line Color menu.
	Eraser	Turns on the eraser, which enables you to delete some or all of an ink annotation.
	Select Objects	Enables you to select objects, including ink annotation marks (this can come in handy if you want to move ink marks to another location on the page).
	Line Color	Enables you to select and apply line colors and patterns.
	Line Style	Enables you to specify line thickness and style.
	Show/Hide Markup	Displays and hides ink annotations in the current document.
Stop Inking Stop Erasing	Stop Inking/ Stop Erasing	Turns off the pen or eraser tool. This button changes its appearance depending on which tool is currently in use.

Configuring Comment Balloon and Reviewing Pane Options

When you work with comment balloons (and track change balloons, as discussed in "Tracking Changes" on page 774), you can control a variety of balloon options. Specifically, you can format balloon and Reviewing Pane label text (which is the text that is displayed on Reviewing Pane bars above each comment or tracked change), specify when balloons will be displayed, adjust balloon width and placement, and specify whether lines should connect balloons to text.

Changing the Style of Balloon and Reviewing Pane Labels

You can modify the style of balloon and Reviewing Pane labels (including the word "Comment" and user names) in the same manner you modify other styles in Word documents—by using the Styles And Formatting task pane. To modify the Balloon Text style, follow these steps:

1. Click the Styles And Formatting button on the Formatting toolbar to open the Styles And Formatting task pane.
2. In the Styles And Formatting task pane, click the Show arrow, and choose Custom to open the Format Settings dialog box.
3. In the Styles To Be Visible list, select the Balloon Text check box, and then click OK.
4. In the Styles And Formatting task pane, right-click the Balloon Text entry (this style also controls the Reviewing Pane label text) in the Pick Formatting To Apply box, and choose Modify on the shortcut menu. The Modify Style dialog box appears.
5. Select any options you want, and click Format to access additional style attributes.
6. After you configure the options you want, select the Automatically Update check box if you want to update all instances of balloon and Reviewing Pane labels, and then click OK.

For more information about working with styles, see Chapter 9, "Using Styles to Increase Your Formatting Power."

Inside Out

Opening the Format Settings dialog box

If the Format Settings dialog box doesn't open when you choose Custom in the Show list in the Styles And Formatting task pane, your insertion point might be positioned in the Reviewing Pane. The Format Settings dialog box won't open when you're working in the Reviewing Pane. To work around this little peculiarity, simply click in the document's body text, and then choose Custom in the Show list again.

Most style changes you make to the Balloon Text style affect only the balloons and the Reviewing Pane labels. To gain greater control over comment text formatting within balloons and the Reviewing Pane, you should also configure the Comment Text style, as discussed next.

Changing the Default Style for Text Inserted in Balloons and the Reviewing Pane

You can modify how comment text appears in balloons and in the Reviewing Pane by modifying the Comment Text style. When you modify this style, you change the appearance of text only (not the labels) in the comment balloons and comment entries in the Reviewing Pane (you do not modify the text displayed in tracked-change balloons or tracked-change Reviewing Pane entries, as discussed in "Tracking Changes" on page 774). To control how comment text appears follow the steps in the preceding section, but in steps 3 and 4 choose Comment Text instead of Balloon Text.

Showing and Hiding Balloons

If you prefer to work with the Reviewing Pane and not balloons, you can turn off balloons. Or if you prefer, you can use balloons only to show comments and formatting changes. To control balloon display in Web Layout, Print Layout, and Reading Layout views, you configure the Use Balloons option, as follows:

1. On the Reviewing toolbar, click Show and choose Balloons on the menu.
2. On the Balloon menu, specify a balloon setting by choosing Always, Never, or Only For Comments/Formatting.

If you hide balloons, comments will be displayed as ScreenTips when you position your mouse pointer over a comment marker, as shown in Figure 27-14.

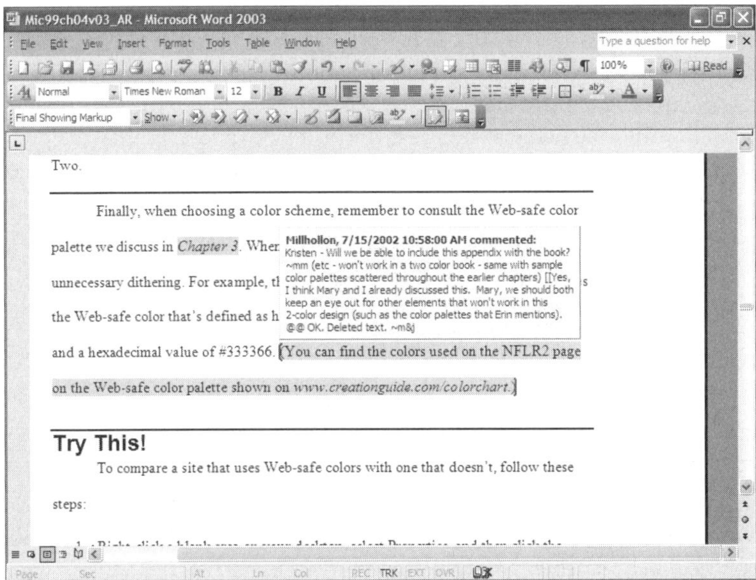

Figure 27-14. When balloons are hidden, comments are displayed as ScreenTips.

> **Note** You can also adjust balloon settings on the Track Changes tab. To access the tab, click Show, Options on the Reviewing toolbar or choose Tools, Options and click the Track Changes tab in the Options dialog box.

Note When you hide balloons, insertions and deletions will be shown in the body of the document, and formatting changes will be visible when you view your document in Final or Final Showing Markup mode. Final and Final Showing Markup modes are discussed in "Tracking Changes" on page 774.

Tip **Hide or display lines connecting text and balloons**
You can also specify whether the lines used to connect balloons to text are displayed or hidden by selecting or clearing the Show Lines Connecting To Text check box on the Track Changes tab. When you clear the Show Lines Connect To Text check box, balloons are displayed in the margin without a connector line when they aren't selected. When you select a comment, the comment is displayed with a solid line that connects the balloon to the comment marker in the text.

Adjusting Balloon Size and Location for Online Viewing

Balloons are a relatively new feature, first appearing in Word 2002; therefore, you might find that they take some getting used to, especially if you've frequently used comments and tracking tools in earlier versions of Word. To help you customize this new feature to suit your working style, Microsoft provides a couple of options you can use to control the size and position of balloons when you choose to view them. In fact, you can control balloon width and location for online viewing as well as for printing purposes. In this section, we'll look at configuring the online presentation of balloons. For more information about configuring balloons for printing, see "Printing Comments" on page 772.

To set balloon width and specify whether balloons are displayed in the right or left margin, you must configure the Track Changes dialog box (or the Track Changes tab in the Options dialog box), as follows:

1 Open the Track Changes dialog box by clicking Show on the Reviewing toolbar and choosing Options on the menu, or choose Tools, Options, and click the Track Changes tab.
2 Make sure that the Use Balloons (Print AndWeb Layout) list box is set to Always or Only For Comments/Formatting.
3 Click the Measure In arrow, and select whether you want to measure balloons by using inches or percent of the page. For more information about the Inches and Percent options, see the sidebar "Sizing Balloons—Inches vs. Percent."
4 In the Preferred Width box, enter a percentage or measurement (in inches) for the width of the balloons.
5 In the Margin box, choose the Left or Right option to specify on which side of the document text you want balloons to appear.
6 Click OK to apply the balloon settings.

Unfortunately, you can't preview how your balloon settings will be displayed from within the Track Changes tab. Your best bet when configuring balloons is to try a few settings and see which setting works best for you on your monitor.

Inside Out

Sizing balloons—inches vs. percent

When you size balloons, Word configures them without compromising the document's content area. This is accomplished by expanding the view of your document (not by reducing the document's content area). To clarify, let's look at the two sizing options: Inches and Percent.

When you use the Inches setting, you provide a set size in which your balloons will appear in your document's margin. For example, if you specify 2 inches, your page's view will expand so that balloons will be displayed within a 2-inch-wide area, starting from the document's margin.

Similarly, if you size balloons using the Percent option, the balloons will be displayed as a percentage of the page's size without compromising the document's content area. For example, if you specify balloons to be 100 percent, the balloons will be sized equal to 100 percent of the page, and the width of your page's view will be expanded accordingly (doubled, in this case).

You can easily see how balloons will be displayed relative to the current document by saving a setting (using Inches or Percent) and then viewing your document in Print Preview mode by clicking the Print Preview button on the Standard toolbar.

Reviewing Comments

Let's say your document has made its rounds, and now it's up to you to review the comments reviewers have inserted into the document. You can review comments only, or you can review comments while you review tracked changes. In this section, we'll look at the process of reviewing comments only. (For more information about reviewing tracked changes, see "Tracking Changes" on page 774.) To review only comments, you must first hide tracked changes. To show comments without displaying tracked changes, display your document in Web Layout, Print Layout, or Reading Layout view, and then follow these steps:

1. If necessary, choose View, Markup to show tracked changes and comments in your document. The Markup command on the View menu is a toggle command that you can use to show and hide markup in documents.
2. On the Reviewing toolbar, make sure that either Final Showing Markup or Original Showing Markup is selected in the Display For Review list.
3. Click Show on the Reviewing toolbar, and make sure that only the Comments option is selected on the menu. To accomplish this, you'll probably have to choose Ink Annotations, Insertions And Deletions, and Formatting to clear the check marks next to them.

After you complete these steps, comments and comment markers should be the only markup features visible in the current document. At this point, you can review the comments manually by scrolling through your document or the Reviewing Pane, or you can jump from comment to comment by clicking the Next and Previous buttons on the Reviewing toolbar.

Depending on the current view, clicking the Next or Previous button displays the next or previous comment as follows:

- In Normal view, the comment is displayed in the Reviewing Pane. If the Reviewing Pane isn't open, Word opens it automatically.
- In Print Layout, Web Layout, or Reading Layout view with balloons turned on, the comment balloon is displayed on screen and appears as the active comment, indicated by a dark outline, darker shading, and solid connector line.
- In Print Layout or Web Layout view with balloons turned off, the comment is displayed in the Reviewing Pane. If the Reviewing Pane isn't open, Word opens it automatically.
- In Reading Layout view with balloons turned off, the next comment is selected but the Reviewing Pane doesn't open. You can view the comment by positioning your cursor over the comment marker and reading the ScreenTip text.

> **Tip** **Browse from comment to comment**
> You can also browse from comment to comment by using the Select Browse Object feature (press Ctrl+Alt+Home) or the Go To tab in the Find And Replace dialog box (press Ctrl+G). On the Go To tab, you can select Comment in the Go To What list and then choose to view all reviewers' comments or a selected reviewer's comments by selecting Any Reviewer or a specific name in the Enter Reviewer's Name list. For more information about using the Browse Object feature and the Go To tab, see Chapter 4, "Honing Document Navigation Skills."

When you view comments in balloons, you might notice that some comments have an ellipsis in the lower-right corner. This symbol indicates that the entire comment text doesn't fit in the balloon. To view the remainder of the comment, click the ellipsis to open the Reviewing Pane, which will contain the entire contents of the comment.

Naturally, as you read through comments, you might want to respond to them while you work through the document. You can do so in the following ways:

- Type directly in a comment, in which case your response won't be color-coded according to your user name.
- Click in the comment you want to respond to, and then click New Comment on the Reviewing toolbar, press Ctrl+Alt+M,, or choose Insert, Comment. A new balloon opens directly below the balloon you're responding to, or a blank entry opens in the Reviewing Pane. Simply enter your response.

In addition to responding to comments, you might want to delete comments as you address them to help prepare the document for final publication, as described in the next section.

> **Tip** **Identify who created a comment and when**
> To quickly see when a comment was inserted and who created it, you can hover the mouse pointer over the comment balloon. When you do this, a ScreenTip appears that displays the comment's creation date and time as well as the user name of the person who created the comment. If you're working in the Reviewing Pane, each Reviewing Pane bar displays the user name and insertion date and time automatically.

Note If you notice that a name associated with tracked changes or comments changes to "Author" every time you save your document, you might have to reconfigure your Security tab settings in the Options dialog box. This automatic change from user names to Author occurs if you've selected the Remove Personal Information From This File On Save check box on the Security tab. When you select this option, names associated with tracked changes and comments are replaced with the word "Author." For more information about configuring your security settings, see Chapter 28, "Addressing Document Protection and Security Issues."

Deleting Comments

Generally, comments serve a temporary purpose—reviewers insert comments, someone addresses the comments, and then the comments are removed before the document's final publication (either online or in print). If you work with comments, you need to know how to delete them so that you won't unintentionally include them in your final publication. As you might expect, you can delete comments in several ways. Namely, you can delete a single comment, delete comments from a specific reviewer (or reviewers), or delete all comments, using the following techniques:

- **Delete a single comment.** Right-click a comment balloon and then click Delete Comment on the shortcut menu, or select a comment balloon and then click the Reject Change/Delete Comment button on the Reviewing toolbar.
- **Delete comments from a specific reviewer.** First clear the check boxes for all reviewers by clicking Show on the Reviewing toolbar and choosing Reviewers, All Reviewers. Next display only the comments you want to delete by clicking Show, choosing Reviewers, and then selecting the check box next to the reviewer's name whose comments you want to delete. (You can repeat this process to select additional reviewers as well.) To delete the displayed comments, click the Reject/Delete Comment arrow, and choose Delete All Comments Shown on the menu.
- **Delete all comments in the document.** Make sure that all reviewers' comments are displayed. (This is the default setting, but if all reviewers' comments aren't displayed, click Show on the Reviewing toolbar, and choose Reviewers, All Reviewers.) Click the Reject Change/Delete Comment arrow, and then choose Delete All Comments In Document on the menu.

Keep in mind that when you delete all comments at once by choosing the Delete All Comments In Document option on the Reject Change/Delete Comment menu, you delete all comments in the document, regardless of whether they are displayed on screen.

Tip **Delete a comment in the Reviewing Pane**
You can also delete comments one at a time from within the Reviewing Pane. To do so, click in the comment in the Reviewing Pane and click the Reject Change/Delete Comment button on the Reviewing toolbar, or right-click a comment in the Reviewing Pane and choose Delete Comment on the shortcut menu.

Tip The Reject Change/Delete Comment button includes the Delete All Ink Annotations In Document option, which enables you to delete all ink annotations in a document at once.

Printing Comments

As previously mentioned, you can control how comments are displayed on screen as well as in print. "Configuring Comment Balloon and Reviewing Pane Options" on page 765 addresses how to control the display of comments in balloons and in the Reviewing Pane. In this section, we look at the ways you can print comments. When you print a document containing comments (and tracked changes, for that matter), you can configure print settings in two areas: the Track Changes dialog box and the Print dialog box. Let's look first at the Track Changes dialog box.

In the Track Changes dialog box (accessed by clicking Show on the Reviewing toolbar and choosing Options), you can specify in the Printing (With Balloons) section how Word should adjust paper orientation to accommodate balloons. You can select any of the following settings in the Paper Orientation list:

- **Auto** Specifies that Word can determine the best orientation layout for your document automatically, based on your margin settings and balloon width settings.
- **Preserve** Prints the document with the orientation specified in the Page Setup dialog box.
- **Force Landscape** Prints balloons and the document in landscape format to allow the most room for the display of balloons.

After you choose how you want Word to handle page orientation issues when you print documents with comment balloons, you're ready to configure the Print dialog box.

In the Print dialog box (choose File, Print), you can specify whether to print the document showing markup (the default setting when comments and tracked changes are displayed), or you can opt to print just a list of the markup changes made in a document. Most likely, if you want to print a document's changes you'll want to print the document showing changes instead of printing a list of changes. When you print a list of changes, the list can become long and confusing.

The easiest way to print a document with its comments is to print the document with comment balloons in the margin and hide the other types of margin balloons (including balloons that show insertions, deletions, and formatting changes). To print comments in a document efficiently, follow these steps:

1. Display your document in Print Layout view.
2. On the Reviewing toolbar, click Show, and verify that only the Comments option is selected (and the Insertions And Deletions and Formatting options are cleared). By choosing just the Comments option, you'll be able to print the document and its comments, without cluttering your view with balloons denoting inserted, deleted, and reformatted information.
3. Choose File, Print to open the Print dialog box.

Revising Documents Using Markup Tools

4 In the Print dialog box, make sure that the Print What box shows Document Showing Markup and click OK.

The document will be printed with comment balloons in the margin. Word will reduce the view of the page to accommodate printing balloons in the margins. This doesn't affect your document's layout parameters—it's just a temporary modification for printing purposes when you're printing balloons along with a document.

Saving a Document with Comments as a Web Page

You can save a document that contains comments and other marked-up text as a Web page. When you do this, Word retains the comments and tracked changes in the text, although all reviewers' comments and changes are displayed in the same color. To save a reviewed document as a Web page, choose File, Save As, make sure that the Save As Type box shows Web Page in the Save As dialog box, and then click Save.

Keep in mind that the online display of comments and tracked changes in your document depends on your browser. In Microsoft Internet Explorer 4 and later, comments appear as dynamic ScreenTips, as shown in Figure 27-15. Also, revised text appears in a color other than black with underlining and strikethrough formatting (but remember, color-coding based on reviewers' user names is lost), similar to how you see markup changes in Word when a single color is selected to show markup. In browsers earlier than Internet Explorer 4 and in Netscape Navigator 4 and later, comments appear as footnotes beneath the main Web page instead of as dynamic ScreenTips.

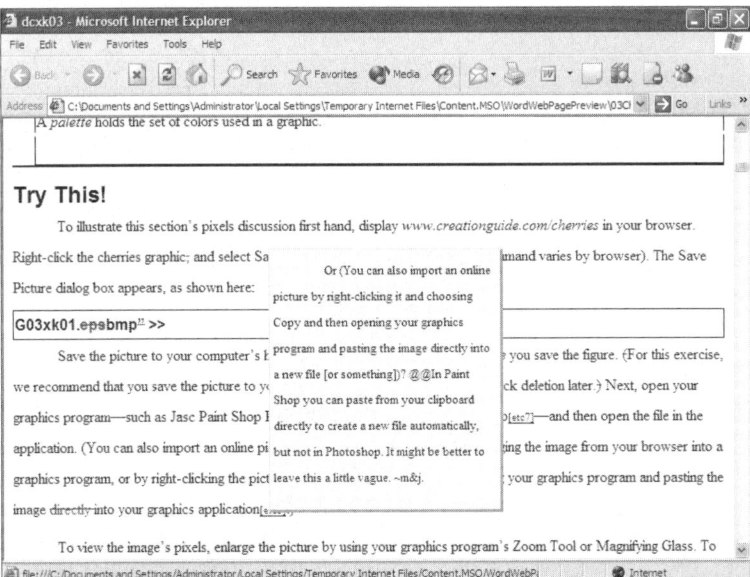

Figure 27-15. When you save a marked-up document as a Web page, Internet Explorer users can view comments in the form of dynamic ScreenTips by positioning the mouse pointer over a comment link.

Tracking Changes

Adding comments to documents is invaluable when reviewers need to annotate and query text, but you need another set of features when you want reviewers to conduct line-by-line edits to help smooth a document's text and layout. When your document is ready for detailed editing in a team setting, you'll want to turn to Word's Track Changes feature.

> **Note** If you've been using Word for a few versions now, you might still think of the Track Changes feature as the Revision Marks feature, which was the name of this feature in Word 95 and earlier.

When you turn on the Track Changes feature, Word records the deletions, insertions, and formatting changes made by each reviewer who modifies the document. By default, Word displays each reviewer's changes in a different color so that you can easily identify the sources of changes within your document. When you work with a document that has been modified by reviewers, you can use the Display For Review list on the Reviewing toolbar to display the changed document in four views, as described here:

- **Final Showing Markup** Shows deleted text in balloons and displays inserted text and formatting changes in line.
- **Final** Shows how the document would appear if you accepted all changes.
- **Original Showing Markup** Shows the inserted text and formatting changes in balloons and shows deleted text in line with strikethrough lines.
- **Original** Shows the original, unchanged document so that you can see how the document would look if you rejected all changes.

Being able to display your document in these ways can help you as you add, accept, and reject tracked changes. In addition, many configuration settings you use to control how comments are displayed (as discussed earlier in this chapter) also apply to tracked changes. In the sections discussing tracked changes that follow, you'll find references to topics covered in the comments sections in this chapter if the topic applies to both comments and tracked changes.

Before we get to the details of working with tracked changes, you should note that Word doesn't track some changes when you modify a document, including changes you make involving the following:

- AutoCaptions
- Background colors
- Embedded fonts
- Routing information
- Some custom options, such as custom toolbar buttons
- Some types of mail merge information, such as whether a file is a main document or a data file

For the most part you probably won't find that these limitations interfere with tasks involving tracked changes, but you should be aware of the exceptions, just in case.

> **Note** Word tracks changes when you resize or move graphics and other objects by showing the originally placed graphic or object as a deleted and reinserted item. Therefore, when you display a document with tracked changes, you might see a graphic or object in two locations—a deleted version and a newly placed version.

Tracking Changes While You Edit

When you track changes in a document, you can opt to display or hide the tracking marks while you work. Generally, it's easier to hide tracked changes if you're editing and writing text and better to view tracking marks when you're reviewing a document's changes. When Word tracks changes, it automatically records insertions or deletions in balloons (depending on your view, as described in the preceding section), which you can view in Print Layout, Web Layout, or Reading Layout view. Word marks tracked changes in a document as follows:

- **Added text** Appears in the reviewer's color with underlining.
- **Deleted text** Remains visible but is displayed in the reviewer's color with a strikethrough line indicating the deletion.
- **Text added and then deleted by the reviewer** Is displayed as if the text was never added. (In other words, no marks appears in a document in places where a reviewer adds information and then deletes the added information.)

In addition to these actions, Word automatically inserts a vertical line, called a *changed line*, along the left margin to indicate that an editing change has been made. This line appears wherever text or formatting changes are made while the Track Changes feature is turned on.

Figure 27-16 shows a document in Final Showing Markup view, which displays inserted text in line, deleted text in balloons, and both deleted and inserted text in the Reviewing Pane. Notice the changed line in the left margin, which specifies that the text next to the line has been modified in some way. For more information about configuring changed lines, see "Customizing the Appearance of Changed Lines" on page 778.

Notice in Figure 27-16 that the TRK button on the status bar is turned on (not dimmed); this indicates that the Track Changes feature is currently turned on. You can control whether the Track Changes feature is turned on or off simply by double-clicking TRK on the status bar.

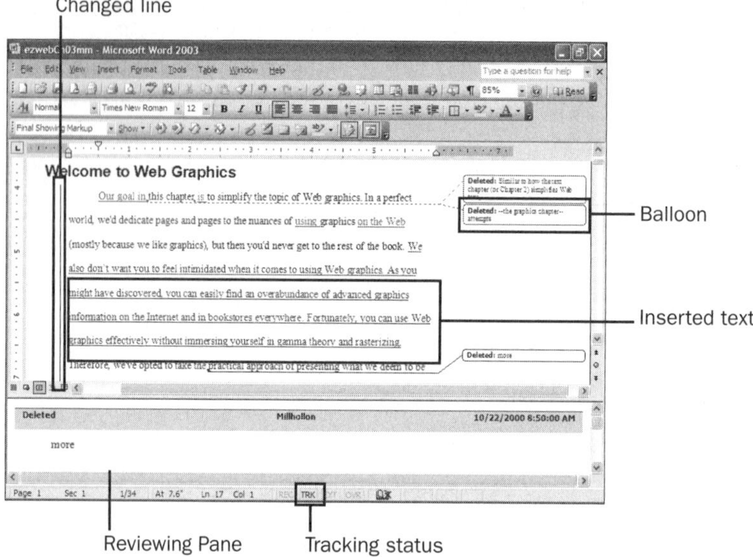

Figure 27-16. The Final Showing Markup view displays inserted text within the document and describes deletions in balloons in the margins. Of course, all changes are displayed in the Reviewing Pane regardless of the setting in the Display For Review box on the Reviewing toolbar.

You can track changes in a document by following these steps:

1. Open the document you want to edit, and choose whether you want to edit the document in Normal, Web Layout, Print Layout, or Reading Layout view.
2. Turn tracking on using one of the following techniques (all of which are toggle commands, which means that you can use the commands to turn Track Changes on or off):
   - Choose Tools, Track Changes.
   - Press Ctrl+Shift+E.
   - On the Reviewing toolbar, click the Track Changes button.
   - Double-click TRK on the status bar.
3. After Track Changes is turned on, make editorial changes, including inserting, deleting, moving, and reformatting. Word tracks your changes, regardless of whether your view reflects the tracked changes as marked-up text.

As mentioned, you can record changes while displaying tracked changes on screen or you can hide the tracking marks while you work. In addition, you can always tell whether changes are being tracked by looking at the TRK button on the status bar. If TRK appears black, you're tracking your changes, whether or not you can see the tracking marks on-screen. If TRK appears dimmed, the Track Changes feature is turned off, and any changes you make will not be tracked.

> **Tip** **Limit reviewers to making tracked changes only**
> You can control who can add tracked changes to your document by using the Protect Document task pane, as described in "Allowing Reviewers to Use Only the Comments Feature" on page 757. To limit reviewers to making only tracked changes, choose Tools, Protect Document to open the Protect Document task pane. In the Protect Document task pane, click the Allow Only This Type Of Editing In The Document check box, select Tracked Changes in the list, and click Yes, Start Enforcing Protection. Enter a password if desired, reenter the password, and click OK. When tracked changes are protected, all changes are marked and reviewers can't accept and reject changes made by other reviewers.

Adjusting the Appearance of Tracked Changes

Just as you can control the appearance of comments, you can control the appearance of tracked changes in your documents. A number of Track Changes options correspond to options available for comments, including the following:

- **Configuring user names** See "Configuring Reviewers' User Names" on page 754.
- **Configuring colors associated with reviewers** See "Configuring Colors Associated with Reviewers" on page 755.
- **Controlling balloon and Reviewing Pane options** See "Configuring Comment Balloon and Reviewing Pane Options" on page 765.

In addition to these options, you can specify how inserted text and objects should be marked, how formatting changes should be identified, and how changed lines should appear in your document. These options are discussed in the next several sections.

> **Note** The settings you configure for displaying tracked changes are global and will apply to all documents you open in Word that have Track Changes marks in them.

Specifying How Insertions and Formatting Changes Are Displayed

You can change how Word identifies inserted and reformatted information when the Track Changes feature is turned on. To configure these settings, you must access the Track Changes dialog box (or the Track Changes tab in the Options dialog box), as follows:

1. Click Show on the Reviewing toolbar and choose Options from the menu, or choose Tools, Options, and click the Track Changes tab.
2. Click the Insertions list, and select how you'd like inserted text to be identified. You can choose to show insertions without any special formatting (in which case inserted text looks like regular, non-color-coded text and is indistinguishable from the original text).

Or you can display inserted text in the reviewer's color only or in the reviewer's color and formatted as boldface, italic, underlined, double-underlined, or strikethrough. By default, inserted text appears in the reviewer's color with an underline.

3. Click the Deletions list, and select how you'd like deleted text to be identified. You can choose to show deletions without any special formatting (in which case deleted text looks like regular, non-color-coded text and is indistinguishable from the original text). Or you can display deleted text in the reviewer's color only or in the reviewer's color and formatted as boldface, italic, underlined, double-underlined, strikethrough, hidden, with a caret (^), or with a octothorpe (#). By default, deleted text appears in the reviewer's color as strikethrough text.
4. Click the Formatting list, and select how formatting changes should be marked. By default, formatting changes aren't marked in the body of the text (most likely because adding formatting to identify information that's been reformatted can sometimes create a confusing mix of formatting). The Formatting options are the same as the Insertions options.
5. Use the Color boxes to specify whether you want Word to assign author colors automatically. If you'd like, you can manually select a color to mark your changes, but you risk having your comments share a color with another reviewer if they also choose the same color. For clarity's sake, the By Author default setting is frequently used in team projects.
6. Click OK to save the settings.

Regardless of your selections for formatting inserted and reformatted information, you can still use changed lines to indicate in a general way where changes have occurred in a document. To learn how to configure changed lines, refer to the next section.

Customizing the Appearance of Changed Lines

As shown in Figure 27-16, Word automatically inserts a black vertical line, called a changed line, in the margin next to text that contains tracked changes. You can specify where changed lines are displayed on the page (along the right, left, or outside margins) and the color in which they are displayed. By default, changed lines are set to Auto and display as black lines. To configure how changed lines are displayed, follow these steps:

1. Click Show on the Reviewing toolbar and choose Options from the menu, or choose Tools, Options, and click the Track Changes tab.
2. In the Markup section, click the Changed Lines arrow and specify whether you want changed lines to be displayed along the left, right, or outside border. You can select the (None) setting if you'd rather not display changed lines when you use the Track Changes feature. To see how a particular setting works, select the option and refer to the preview box in the Track Changes tab. By default, changed lines are set to Outside Border.
3. To specify a color for changed lines, click the Color arrow next to the Changed Lines list, and then select a color. (You can't create a custom color for changed lines.)
4. Click OK to save your settings.

After you configure the changed lines settings, all documents you open that contain tracked changes will use the newly configured settings. In addition, any currently opened documents that contain tracked changes will be reformatted automatically to reflect the new settings.

Note In Normal view, all changed lines appear on the left, regardless of the setting you configure in the Markup section in the Track Changes dialog box (or on the Track Changes tab of the Options dialog box). The changed lines color setting applies in all views.

Accepting and Rejecting Proposed Edits

After a document has made the rounds and you receive a file containing a number of tracked changes, you can easily incorporate the edits by accepting or rejecting the changes. When you incorporate edits, you can address each edit on a case-by-case basis or you can accept multiple changes at once. In either case, you can reject and accept proposed changes by using the appropriate buttons on the Reviewing toolbar or by right-clicking changes and choosing options on the shortcut menu. Figure 27-17 shows the shortcut menu you see when you right-click deleted text. (If you right-click inserted text, the Accept Deletion and Reject Deletion options change to Accept Insertion and Reject Insertion.) In the next few sections, we'll look at the ways you can incorporate edits.

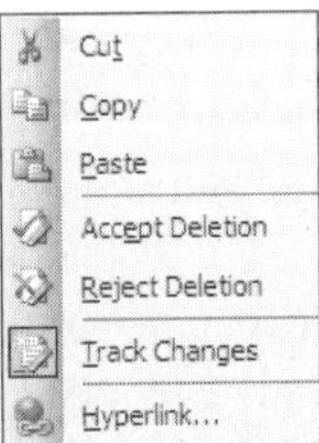

Figure 27-17. You can right-click tracked changes to access options that enable you to resolve the proposed changes.

Tip **Save your document with its markup before incorporating edits**
Before you start accepting and rejecting tracked changes and comments, consider saving a version of the document with all the tracked changes and comments intact. That way, if you want to return to the original marked-up version of the document, you'll have a copy on hand.

Addressing Tracked Changes One at a Time

The key to accessing the changes you want to review is to configure your view properly before you start navigating among changes and making editorial decisions. When you're ready to resolve tracked changes, you should configure the following settings:

- **Show document markup.** Show your document in either Final Showing Markup or Original Showing Markup view. You can do so by choosing either view name in the Display For Review list on the Reviewing toolbar. In addition, you can toggle document markup on and off by choosing View, Markup.

- **Specify the type(s) of changes to display.** Use the Show menu on the Reviewing toolbar to specify which types of changes you want to review. Available options are Comments, Ink Annotations, Insertions And Deletions, and Formatting. You can review any combination of the four types of document changes.
- **Display selected user comments.** Click Show on the Reviewing toolbar, click Reviewers to open the list of reviewers, and then pick and choose which reviewers' markup changes you want to resolve. You can resolve all changes at one time (by selecting the All Reviewers option), or you can select any combination of listed reviewers.
- **Specify how balloons should display.** Click Balloons on the Show menu, and then choose to always show balloons, never show balloons, or show only comments and formatting changes in balloons.
- **Show or hide the Reviewing Pane.** Decide whether you want the Reviewing Pane to be open while you work. To toggle the Reviewing Pane, click Reviewing Pane on the Show menu or click the Reviewing Pane button on the Reviewing toolbar.

After you display the changes you want to work with, you can move from tracked change to tracked change using the Next and Previous buttons on the Reviewing toolbar (in the same manner you jump from comment to comment), you can view and click edits in the Reviewing Pane, or you can scroll through the document and address edits in a less linear manner. Regardless of how you arrive at a tracked change, you can handle it in any of the following ways:

- Right-click a change (in the document body, in the Reviewing Pane, or in a balloon), and choose to accept or reject the addition or insertion by using the shortcut menu.
- Click in a change, and click the Accept Change or Reject Change button on the Reviewing toolbar.
- Select a range of text and click the Accept Change or Reject Change button on the Reviewing toolbar. All tracked changes in the selected text will be handled simultaneously.

After you accept or reject a change, Word displays the revised text as standard text. If you change your mind about a change, you can undo it by clicking Undo on the Standard toolbar or pressing Ctrl+Z.

Tip **Reject changes made to bullets**

If you're working with a formatted list, Word allows you only to accept formatting changes made to the bullets or numbers; you cannot reject these changes. However, you can accept or reject changes made in the list's text. If you want to reject formatting changes made to your list, you'll need to accept the change and then reformat the list so that it is displayed in its original formatting.

Accepting or Rejecting All Tracked Changes at Once

At times, you might want to accept or reject all changes in a document. For example, maybe you've gone through the document with a fine-tooth comb, reading and changing the document in Final view. When you're satisfied with the document, you want to simply accept all changes instead of resolving each change one by one. You can do so by executing a single command.

To accept or reject all changes in a document, you use the Accept All Changes In Document or Reject All Changes In Document commands. To access these commands, click the Accept Change or Reject Change/Delete Comment arrow on the Reviewing toolbar, and choose the appropriate command from the menu, as shown in Figure 27-18.

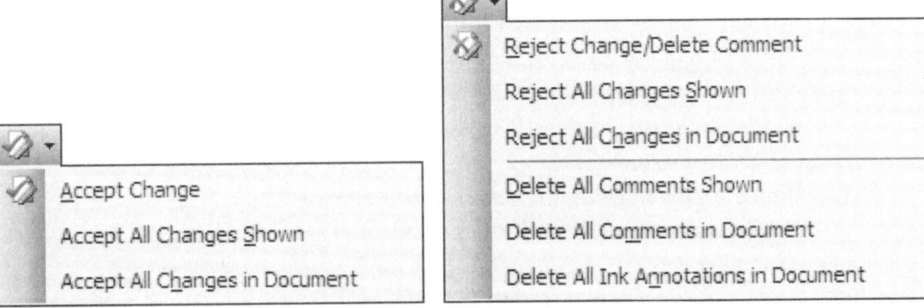

Figure 27-18. You can accept or reject all changes or changes by a particular user by using the Accept Change and Reject Change/Delete Comment menus, which are accessible from the Reviewing toolbar.

In addition to accepting or rejecting all changes in a document, you can show a subset of reviewers' changes and accept or reject just those changes.To control which changes are displayed in your document, click Show on the Reviewing toolbar, choose Reviewers, and then select which reviewers' changes you want to display and resolve. After you configure your display, click the Accept Change or Reject Change/Delete Comment arrow, and choose the Accept All Changes Shown or Reject All Changes Shown option.

Tip **Accept or reject changes in selected text**

Between resolving tracked changes one by one and accepting or rejecting all changes in one fell swoop lies the realm of accepting and rejecting edits contained in selected text. In other words, you can resolve editing issues on a piecemeal basis. To do so, select text—for example, you might want to select a paragraph or two that you've reviewed—and then click Accept Change or Reject Change/Delete Comment on the reviewing toolbar to accept or reject the tracked changes contained in the selected text.

Printing Documents That Contain Revisions

You can create printed versions of marked-up documents that include any revision marks and balloons. When you print a document with markup showing, by default Word chooses the zoom level and page orientation to best display your document's markup. In addition, you can print just a list of all markup in a document by selecting List Of Markup in the Print What box in the Print dialog box.

For more information about printing documents containing tracked changes, comments, and balloons, see "Printing Comments" on page 772.

To print a document showing markup, follow these steps:

1. Open your document and switch to Print Layout view.
2. Display the tracked changes in the manner you want them to be printed by using the Display For Review list on the Reviewing toolbar. In addition, select which reviewers' comments you want to display and print by clicking Show on the Reviewing toolbar, clicking Reviewers, and specifying which reviewers' comments should be displayed (and subsequently printed).
3. Choose File, Print to open the Print dialog box, make sure that Document Showing Markup is selected in the Print What list, and then click OK to print the document.

Tip **Create a Web page that shows tracked changes**
You can save a document containing tracked changes as a Web page and post the page online. For more information about saving a marked-up document as a Web page, see "Saving a Document with Comments as a Web Page" on page 773.

Comparing and Merging Documents

At times, you might want to expedite a reviewing process by sending reviewers separate copies of an original document. Then, when reviewers return the documents, you can merge their changes into the original version of the document or compare their changes side by side. In this section of the chapter, we look at merging and comparing documents after changes have been recorded.

Merging Documents

When you merge document revisions, you can merge any number of changed documents into a single document that will show each reviewer's changes.

Note Although it's best if reviewers work with Track Changes enabled when you're planning to merge documents, Word can detect and show changes even if a reviewer didn't turn on the Track Changes feature.

To merge comments and changes from several reviewers into one document, follow these steps:

1. Open the document into which you want to merge changes. Most likely, this will be the original version of the document you sent to reviewers.
2. Choose Tools, Compare And Merge Documents. The Compare And Merge Documents dialog box opens, as shown in Figure 27-19.

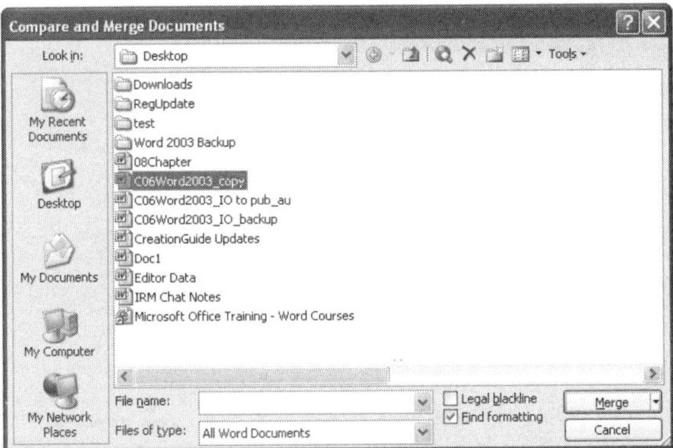

Figure 27-19. The Compare And Merge Documents dialog box looks similar to the Open dialog box, but it provides a couple of special merge-specific commands in the lower-right corner.

3. Navigate to and select the document that has changes to be merged.
4. Click the Merge button arrow and choose Merge Into Current Document on the menu, as shown in Figure 27-20.

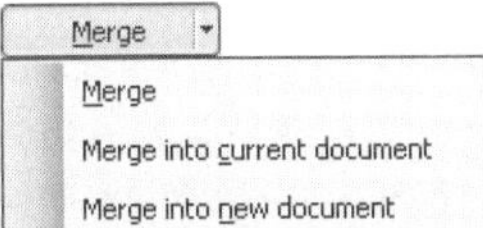

Figure 27-20. The Merge button enables you to control how Word merges the current and selected documents.

5. Repeat steps 2 through 4 to merge other reviewers' edits into the current document.

When you merge documents, you might see a message box stating that the documents being merged have one or more conflicting formatting changes, as shown in Figure 27-21. Word can store only one set of formatting changes at a time. When you merge multiple documents, you might have to choose whether you'd like to keep formatting from the current document (Your Document) or use the formatting in the document being merged (The Other Document). Select the document you want to use for formatting changes, and then click Continue With Merge. If you click Cancel, the merge procedure is aborted. If you don't want to incorporate formatting changes from the merged documents, you can clear the Find Formatting check box in the Compare And Merge Documents dialog box (shown previously in Figure 27-19) before you conduct a merge procedure.

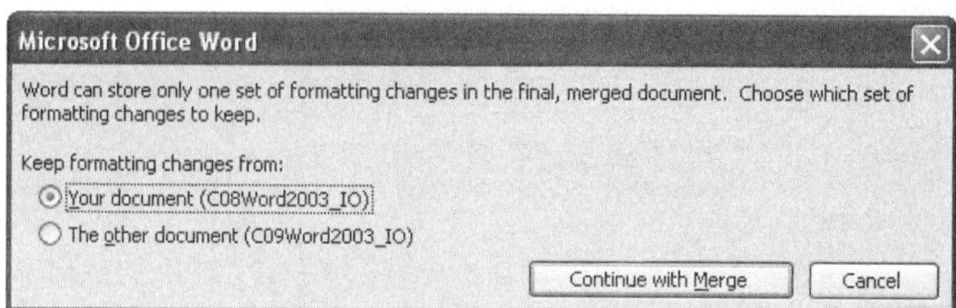

Figure 27-21. If you attempt to merge two documents with differing formatting, Word requires you to specify which document's formatting should take precedence.

> **Tip** For best results when merging changes from multiple reviewers, choose Tools, Options, click the Security tab, and verify that the Store Random Number To Improve Merge Accuracy check box in the Privacy Options section is selected.

Displaying Changes Between Two Documents in a Separate File

You can use the Legal Blackline option in the Compare And Merge Documents dialog box to compare two documents and display the changes in a separate file. When you do this, both documents remain unaltered and a new third document is created automatically. In the third document, the changes in the baseline document are accepted, and the changes in the compared document appear as tracked changes. You should use this option only when you're comparing two documents. If you need to compare more than two documents, you should use a different merge option, such as the Merge Into New Document option on the Merge menu in the Compare And Merge Documents dialog box.

To use the Legal Blackline option, follow these steps:

1. Open the baseline document, and choose Tools, Compare And Merge Documents.
2. In the Compare And Merge Documents dialog box, select the document you want to compare with the open document, select the Legal Blackline check box, and then click Compare.
3. If either or both of the documents has tracked changes, you'll see a message box stating that Word will treat the tracked changes as if they've been accepted. Click Yes to continue the comparing procedure.

The new document displays the changed text in an unnamed document file. You'll need to save and name the file if you want to store the file for future use.

> **Note** If you've used the Versions command on the File menu to save versions of a document in one file and you want to compare the current version with an earlier saved version, you can do so. First you need to save the earlier version as a separate file using a different name. Then you can compare the current document with the newly created file. For more information about working with versions of documents, see "Working with Multple Versions of a Document" on page 787.

Comparing Documents Side by Side

At times, you might want to compare documents without merging them. In Word 2003, you can easily compare two documents side by side. Using this feature, you can view and scroll through two documents at the same time to review differences between the two documents.

To use the Compare Side By Side feature, you must have at least two documents open. If you have more than two documents open, you can choose which two documents you want to compare by using the Window menu.

When you compare two documents side by side, Word displays the two documents vertically side by side along with the Compare Side By Side toolbar. The Compare Side By Side toolbar contains the following three buttons:

Synchronous Scrolling

Reset Window Position

- **Synchronous Scrolling** Enables you to control whether both documents should scroll simultaneously when you navigate through the documents.
- **Reset Window Position** Returns the view to showing the two documents vertically side by side on-screen.
- **Close Side By Side** Closes the side-by-side display and closes the Compare Side By Side toolbar.

When the Synchronous Scrolling option is turned on, you can use scrollbars, navigation keys (such as Page Up and Page Down), the Go To dialog box, mouse scroll wheels, and other document navigation tools to move through both documents simultaneously. In addition, you can change the view in both windows by changing the view in one window. For example, if both windows display the documents in Print Layout View, you can click the Normal View button in the horizontal scrollbar in one window, and both windows will change to Normal view. When the Synchronous Scrolling option is turned off, you can navigate through either document without changing the other document's view. Figure 27-22 shows two documents being compared side by side in Normal view along with the Compare Side By Side toolbar.

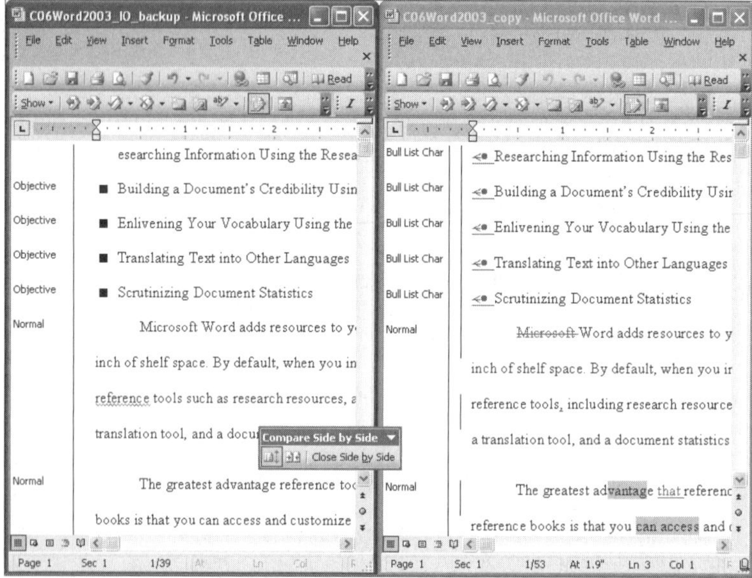

Figure 27-22. The Compare Side By Side feature in Word 2003 simplifies the task of viewing and navigating through two documents at once.

To compare two documents side by side, follow these steps:

1. Open both documents.
2. If you have more than two documents open, make one of the documents you want to compare the active document.
3. Choose Window, Compare Side By Side With.... Note that if you only have two documents open, the name of the other document will appear in the Window menu, in the following format: Compare Side By Side With *document name.*

When you finish comparing the two documents, click Close Side By Side on the Compare Side By Side toolbar. The windows will return to their previous sizes without closing. The document that is active when you close the side-by-side view displays as the active document. You can continue to access open documents by using the Window menu in Word.

> **Tip** **Reopen the Compare Side By Side toolbar**
>
> If you close the Compare Side By Side toolbar, you can reopen it later by using the Customize dialog box. To do so, choose Tools, Customize, click the Toolbars tab if necessary, select the Compare Side By Side check box, and then click Close.

Working with Multiple Versions of a Document

Another way you can record changes made to a document is to store versions of the document. Using Word, you can save multiple versions of a document within the same document. This method saves you from having to manage multiple files (with potentially similar file names) and saves disk space, because when you use the Versions feature, Word saves only the differences between versions, not an entire copy of the document for each version. After you've saved a version (or several versions) of a document, you can review, open, and delete earlier versions of a document.

You can create versions in two ways:

- **Manually** You can save a "snapshot" of a document at any time. To do this, you manually instruct Word to save a version of the current document in its current state.
- **Automatically** You can configure Word to save a version of your document automatically each time you close the document.

In the next few sections, you'll learn how to create and manage versions of documents manually as well as automatically.

Inside Out

Saving a document that contains versions as a Web page

Watch out when you're saving a document that contains versions as a Web page. Although Word maintains most aspects of your document when you save it as a Web page, it does not maintain versioning information. To preserve version information, save a copy of your file (as a Word document) before saving it as a Web page.

Saving a Version of a Document Manually

To take a snapshot of a document in its current state manually and save the snapshot as a version, follow these steps:

1. With the document open, choose File, Versions. The Versions dialog box appears, as shown in Figure 27-23. (The Versions dialog box in this example contains one saved version for illustrative purposes; when you create a version for the first time, the dialog box will be empty.)

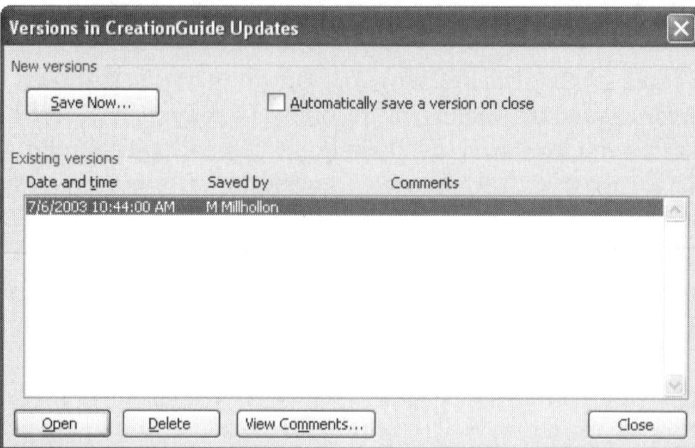

Figure 27-23. The Versions dialog box enables you to manually save a version of a document as well as access stored versions.

2 Click Save Now. The Save Version dialog box appears, as shown in Figure 27-24. You can use this dialog box to add comments regarding the version of the document you're saving.

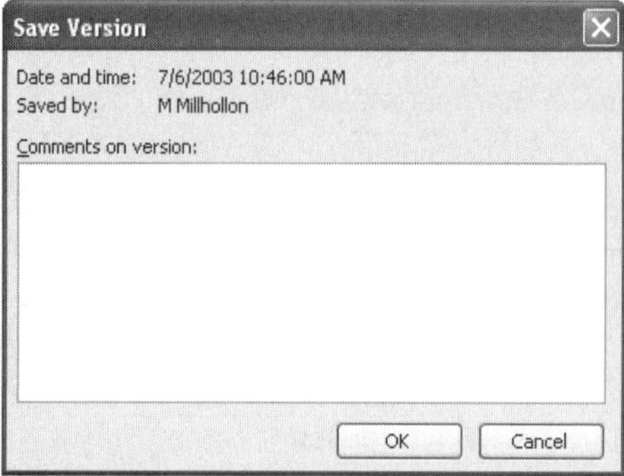

Figure 27-24. You can help differentiate between versions by entering comments about a version in the Save Version dialog box.

3 Enter descriptive information about the version you're saving, if desired, and then click OK.

The version of the document is saved, and an entry is inserted in the Versions dialog box. (You'll have to reopen the Versions dialog box to view the newly created entry.)

Tip **View comments associated with a version**

By default, comments associated with versions are displayed only partially in the Versions dialog box. If you want to view the comments in their entirety, open the Versions dialog box (by choosing File, Versions), select a version, and then click View Comments. The View Comments dialog box opens, containing comments added when the version was created. Click Close to close the View Comments dialog box, and click Close to close the Versions dialog box.

Saving Versions When You Close Documents

In addition to creating versions manually, you can configure Word to save a version whenever you close the document. Setting this feature is helpful if you need to frequently record versions of a document but you don't want to manually execute extra steps to save multiple versions. To save a version of a document each time you close the document, follow these steps:

1. With the document open, choose File, Versions.
2. In the Versions dialog box, select the Automatically Save A Version On Close check box.
3. Click Close.

When you open the Versions dialog box later, you'll see a list of versions saved each time the document was closed. Each listed entry includes the date and time the version was created, the user name of the person who saved the document and version, and any comments associated with the version.

Opening an Earlier Version of a Document

The main point of saving versions is to be able to access earlier versions of the document from before changes were implemented. You can open any version of a document from within the Versions dialog box (and as you might guess, when you open a version, it contains all versions created prior to the opened version). To open a specific version of a document, follow these steps:

1. With the document open, choose File, Versions.
2. Select the version you want to open and then click Open, or double-click the version you want to open. The current document and the older version of the document appear tiled horizontally in your Word window.

Because you're accessing archived information about a document, you can't modify an earlier version of a document after you open it. Instead, after you open an earlier version, you must use the Save As command to save the version as a new separate file. After you create a new file based on the earlier version, you can modify the new file just as you modify any other Word document.

Deleting Version Information

The final action associated with using versions is deleting version information. You can delete version information from within the Versions dialog box. To do so, open the Versions dialog box (by choosing File, Versions), select the version you want to delete, and click Delete. Word will display a message box asking whether you're sure you want to delete the version. Click Yes to complete the task.

> **Note** If you're planning to share a document with others (for review or other purposes), you might want to trim the document's size and avoid distributing unnecessary or possibly confidential information by deleting past versions from the current document.

Chapter 28

Addressing Document Protection and Security Issues

With the proliferation of personal computing and the recent surge of networking at all levels, sharing Word documents is more commonplace than ever. With this added increase in document swapping, you need to take an active role in making your information secure. Document security in Word comes in a number of forms. Most people know the importance of employing security measures at the network level, but you can also provide data integrity by securing your information at the document level. For example, you can perform the following document security tasks in Word:

- Control who can open, modify, distribute, and print your documents
- Specify the types of changes others can make to your documents
- Remove personal and hidden information
- Identify yourself as the author of a document (by using digital signatures)
- Protect yourself and others from macro viruses
- Control security settings when you send e-mail messages

In this chapter, you'll learn about the various document protection schemes available in Word. Keep in mind that the security features offered by Word can work independently as well as in combination with each other. Not surprisingly, you'll often find that the best security setup for your situation involves taking advantage of a combination of Word's security features.

Maximizing Document Protection with Information Rights Management (IRM)

Permission

Information Rights Management (IRM) is a document-focused information protection service that is available to users of Microsoft Office Professional Edition 2003 or the standalone versions of Word 2003, Excel 2003, PowerPoint 2003, or Outlook 2003. Further, these programs must work in conjunction with Microsoft Windows Server 2003 or the .NET Passport Service to provide IRM protection. Users who are not using the IRM-enabled applications can open IRM-protected documents by installing the Rights Management Add-on for Internet Explorer. For more information, visit *http://www.microsoft.com/windows/ie/downloads/addon/faq.asp*.

IRM was designed to help protect sensitive information from being leaked accidentally or by casual abusers. Fundamentally, IRM-protected documents are currently Word, Excel, and PowerPoint files with encrypted content. Note that IRM protects the *content* of the document itself, not just access to the document by means of a file system. By using IRM to protect a document, you can control who can access the document, as well as how the document can be handled by the people you share with or send the document to on your network or on the Internet. In other words, you determine which users you will trust with your document's contents, and you define the trust level for each person who is allowed to access the document, which directly affects what they can do with the information after they receive it.

Setting IRM Access Levels

With the IRM feature, Word 2003 enables you to restrict permission to documents and document content like never before. Basically, in addition to applying password protection and read-only settings—features available in earlier versions of Word—you can now take advantage of IRM settings to control whether documents can be forwarded, printed, or accessed after a specified number of days. You can use the IRM feature with Word 2003 to specify the following three access levels for Word documents:

- **Read** Enables specified users to read a document but not edit, print, or copy the content.
- **Change** Enables specified users to read, edit, and save changes to a document but not print the document.
- **Full Control** Gives specified users full authoring permissions and the freedom to do anything with a document. (Document authors always have Full Control access.)

To set access levels for specified users, you use the Permission dialog box, as shown in Figure 28-1. To open the Permission dialog box, click the Permission button on the Standard toolbar or choose File, Permission, Do Not Distribute. After the Permission dialog box appears, select the Restrict Permission To This Document check box to make the Read and Change boxes available.

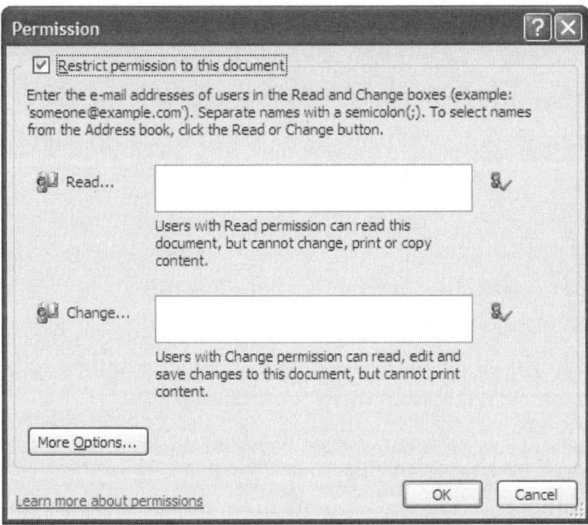

Figure 28-1. You use the Permission dialog box to grant Read or Change access to users by entering their e-mail addresses in the Read or Change boxes.

Customizing IRM Permissions

In conjunction with access levels, you can set additional permissions and settings using the Permission dialog box. To access the additional permissions and settings options, click More Options in the Permission dialog box. You can also change a user's access level in the More Options dialog box by clicking the Access Level setting next to the user's e-mail address and selecting a new access level, as shown in Figure 28-2.

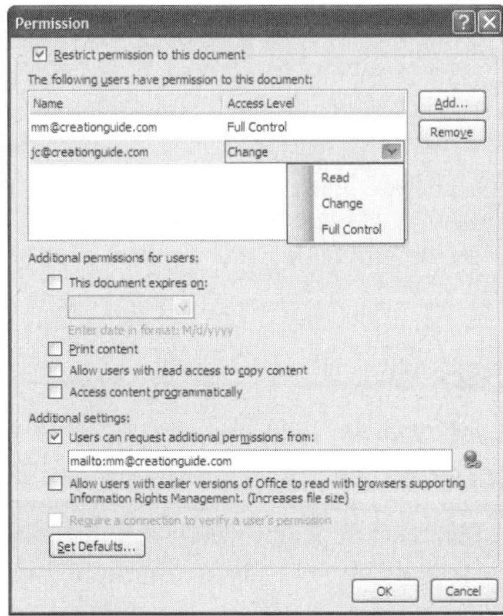

Figure 28-2. You can customize document permissions for each user who has access to the document.

Additional permissions and settings that you can set for each user include the following:

- **This Document Expires On** Enables you to set an expiration date for the document, after which the document will be unavailable to selected users.
- **Print Content** Enables you to grant printing capabilities to users with Read or Change access levels.
- **Allow Users With Read Access To Copy Content** Enables you to allow users with Read access to copy the document.
- **Access Content Programmatically** Enables you to allow users certain Word program features in the document, such as Smart Tags.
- **Users Can Request Additional Permissions From** Enables you to specify an address that users can use to request changes to their permission status.
- **Allow Users With Earlier Versions Of Office To Read With Browsers Supporting Information Rights Management (Increases File Size)** Enables you to allow users to open the IRM-protected document in their browser after they download and install the Rights Management Add-on for Internet Explorer from the Microsoft Web site. For more information on this, visit *http://www.microsoft.com/windows/ie/downloads/addon/faq.asp*.
- **Require A Connection To Verify A User's Permission** Enables you to require that users connect to the Internet to verify their credentials each time they access the document.
- **Set Defaults** Enables you to set the current settings as the default for documents with restricted permissions.

Sending IRM-Protected Documents to People Not Using Word 2003

If you send an IRM-protected document to someone who isn't using Word 2003, she or he can download the Rights Management Add-on For Internet Explorer or another browser that supports content with restricted permission. By default, the Rights Management Add-On For Internet Explorer Web page (*http://www.microsoft.com/windows/ie/downloads/addon/rmupdate.asp*) appears when a user tries to access an IRM-protected document or e-mail but she or he isn't running an Office application that supports IRM features. The user can download the add-on from that page to open the protected document in a Web browser.

Applying IRM Protection to Documents

To apply IRM protection to a document, follow these steps:

1. Open the document you want to protect.
2. Click the Permission button on the Standard toolbar. If you use multiple accounts and you want to specify which account will have Full Control as the author of the document,

choose File, Permission, Restrict Permission As to open the Select User dialog box. In the Select User dialog box, choose the account you want to use to create permissions, and then click OK.

3. In the Permission dialog box, select the Restrict Permission To This Document check box.
4. In the Permission dialog box, click the Change or Read label (hovering the mouse pointer over the label will change the label to a button) to access your address book or enter e-mail addresses of the users who can access the document in the Read or Change boxes. If you're entering more than one e-mail address, separate the addresses with a semicolon. If desired, click More Options to further configure user permissions.
5. Click OK to complete the setup.

After IRM permissions are set for a document, you can review the permission settings on the Status tab in the Shared Workspace task pane, as shown in Figure 28-3. Also, the Permission icon appears in the status bar. You can double-click the Permission icon to open the Permission dialog box.

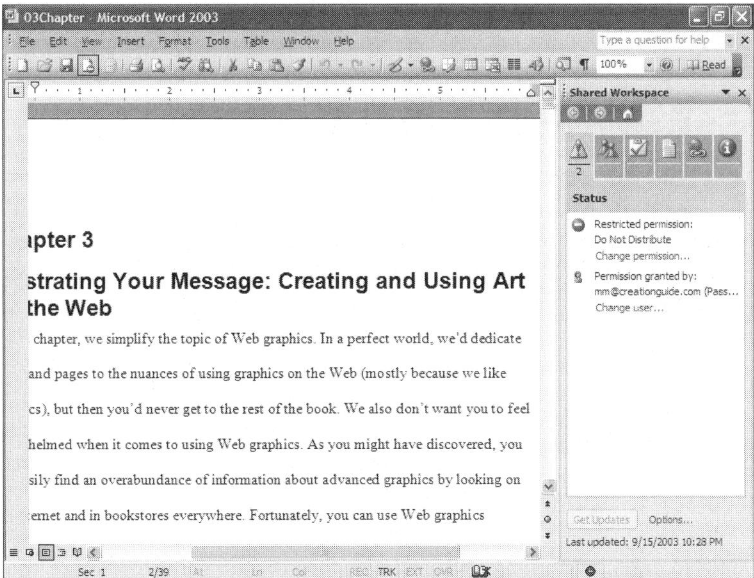

Figure 28-3. The Shared Document task pane provides information about a document's permission settings and links you can use to modify the permission settings.

Tip Keep an eye on IRM. Microsoft plans to increase the functionality of IRM in future versions of Office.

Understanding IRM Protection and E-Mail Messages

You can send an IRM-protected document as an attachment in an IRM-protected e-mail message. If you do this, the IRM permissions associated with the document will not be modified.

If you send a document that does not have IRM permissions associated with it as an attachment in an IRM-protected e-mail message, the document will inherit the IRM permissions associated with the e-mail message. Further, only documents supported by IRM will be restricted. Documents that don't support IRM and are attached to an IRM e-mail message will be fully accessible to users after they open the e-mail message.

At this time, only Word 2003, Excel 2003, and PowerPoint 2003 documents support IRM protection.

Adding Password Protection to Documents

Another way to restrict which users can open or modify a document is to use password protection. When you use password protection, users must enter a password before they can open or change the password-protected document. Standard passwords in Word are case sensitive; they can be up to 15 characters long, and they can contain any combination of letters, numerals, spaces, and symbols.

Tip **Create passwords longer than 15 characters**
If you want to create passwords that are longer than 15 characters (to a maximum of 255 characters), you can do so by choosing another encryption type for your document. To do this, choose Tools, Options, click the Security tab, click Advanced, and then choose an RC4 encryption type in the Encryption Type dialog box.

To protect a document by assigning a password, open the documenFt, choose Tools, Options, and click the Security tab in the Options dialog box, as shown in Figure 28-4. Many of Word's security features are accessible from the Security tab.

Addressing Document Protection and Security Issues

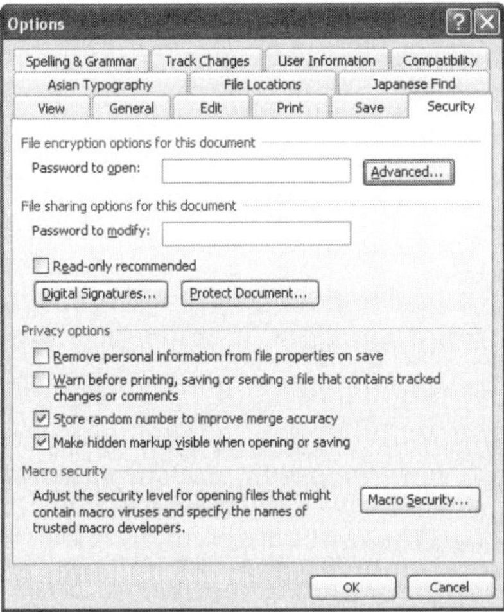

Figure 28-4. The Security tab in the Options dialog box provides a number of security-related settings.

After you display the Security tab, you can create a password that restricts who can open or modify the current document by performing one of the following actions:

- **Assign a password to open.** On the Security tab, enter a password in the Password To Open box and click OK. The Confirm Password dialog box appears. In the Reenter Password To Open box, type the password again and click OK. Save the document to complete the process.
- **Assign a password to modify.** On the Security tab, enter a password in the Password To Modify box and click OK. The Confirm Password dialog box appears. In the Reenter Password To Open box, type the password again and click OK. Save the document to complete the process.

After you assign a password to open a document, the Password dialog box will appear whenever a user attempts to open the document, as shown in Figure 28-5. To open the document, a user will have to enter the correct password and click OK. If a user doesn't know the password, he or she can click Cancel to abort the process.

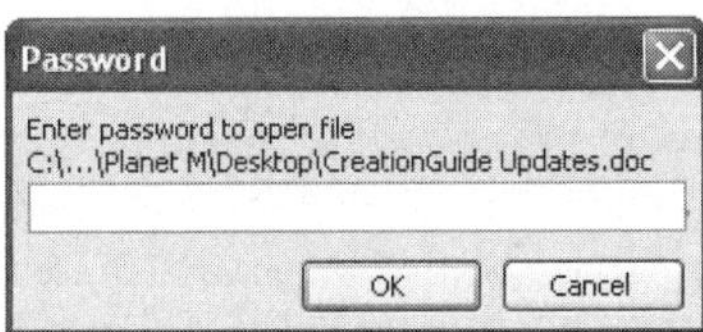

Figure 28-5. Before users can open a password-protected document, they must enter the correct password in the Password dialog box.

Chapter 28

Similarly, after you assign a password to grant users modification privileges, they'll see a Password dialog box like the one shown in Figure 28-6 when they open the document.

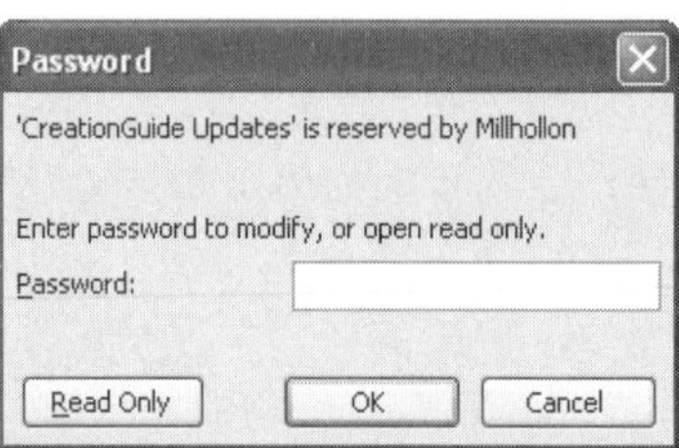

Figure 28-6. When a document is password-protected for modification, users can open the document in read-only format, even if they don't know the password required to make changes.

In this Password dialog box, users can perform any of the following actions:

- **Enter a password in the Password box and click OK** Enables users to open and modify the document.
- **Click Read Only** Enables users to view the document without allowing them to modify the original version of the document. If they make changes and try to save the document, the Save As dialog box appears.
- **Click Cancel** Aborts the entire process.

If users open the document by clicking Read Only, they'll be able to make changes to the document, but they'll only be able to save the modified document as a new file—they won't be able to replace the existing version of the file with their modified version.

Tip You can assign passwords to both the open and modify options on the Security tab, thereby providing two layers of protection and accessibility for your document.

To remove password protection, you must know the passwords to gain access to the document. After you open a password-protected document, you can delete the passwords on the Security tab; deleting password information on the Security tab removes the password protection. To do this, choose Tools, Options, click the Security tab, and delete the passwords (the letters of the password are masked) in the Password To Open and Password To Modify boxes. Then click OK and save the document to complete the procedure.

Note In most cases, you'll lose your password protection if you save your document in a format other than Word's document format. For example, if you save a Word document as a Web page, you'll lose your password protection. In addition, you cannot use Word's standard password protection options to add password protection to Web page documents.

Suggesting That a File Be Opened as Read-Only

As mentioned, you can attach a password to a document and thereby allow only certain people (the people who know the password) to modify the document. When a password is required to modify the document, those who don't know the password can open the document in read-only mode only. In addition to configuring a password, you can also configure a document to display a dialog box suggesting that users open the document as read-only. When you configure this setting, users can choose whether they want to open the document in normal or read-only mode, without entering a password.

You might want to configure a document with the Read-Only Recommended option if the document is a template, for example, and you want to encourage users to use the template in read-only mode to ensure that they don't inadvertently change the template. On the other hand, some users might have to modify the template at times, so you don't want to make the template read-only in all cases.

To configure a document so that it suggests to viewers that they open the document in read-only mode, follow these steps:

1. Choose Tools, Options, and click the Security tab.
2. Select the Read-Only Recommended check box, click OK, and save your document.

When users open a file with the Read-Only Recommended option turned on, they'll see a dialog box similar to the one shown in Figure 28-7. The dialog box asks whether the user wants to open the document in read-only format, and the user can click Yes, No, or Cancel. If users open the document as read-only, they can make changes to the document, but they must save the changed version with a new name (thereby not overwriting the original document).

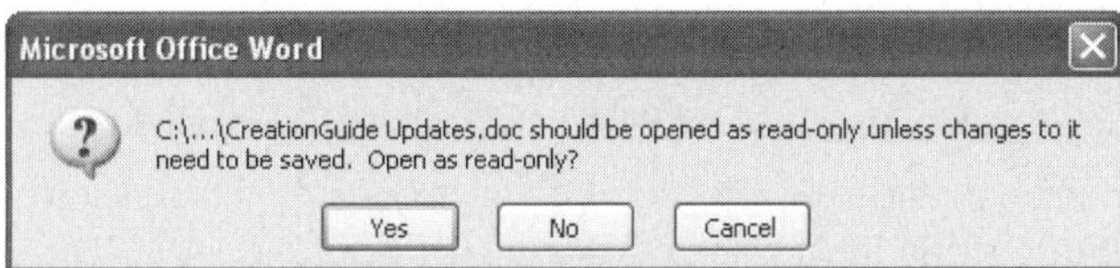

Figure 28-7. When the Read-Only Recommended check box is selected, users can click Yes to open a read-only version, click No to open the document normally, or click Cancel to bypass opening the document altogether.

Applying Formatting Restrictions

In Word 2003, you can restrict the available styles and formatting capabilities in a document. When you restrict formatting, users are able to open the document, but they can't format text other than applying approved styles. Most of the character formatting tools on the Formatting toolbar, along with other text formatting tools (such as formatting keyboard commands and menu items), are inaccessible when a document has formatting restrictions applied. Furthermore, the Styles And Formatting task pane shows only the allowable styles. To restrict formatting, you use the Protect Document task pane and the Formatting Restrictions dialog box, as shown in Figure 28-8.

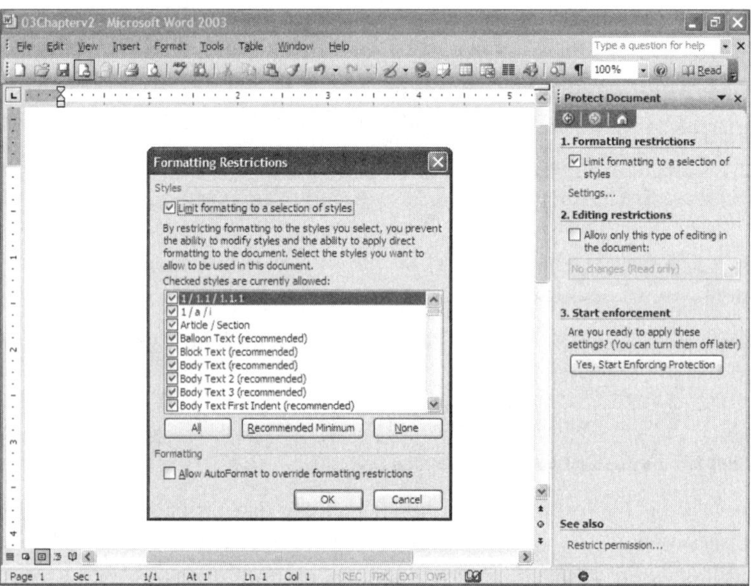

Figure 28-8. You can turn on formatting restrictions in the Protect Document task pane to stop users from applying character formatting or unapproved styles to document text.

To set up formatting restrictions, follow these steps:

1. Choose Tools, Protect Document. The Protect Document task pane appears.
2. Click the Limit Formatting To A Selection Of Styles check box, and then click the Settings link. The Formatting Restrictions dialog box appears.
3. In the Formatting Restrictions dialog box, specify which styles users are allowed to access by ensuring that the styles you want to make available are the only styles checked. You can take the following actions:
   - Manually select and unselect style check boxes to specify a group of styles that you want to allow users to access.
   - Click Recommended Minimum to limit styles to a recommended group of styles.
   - Click None if you don't want users to have access to any styles.
4. Click OK. If the document contains styles that you didn't select in step 3, a message box appears, stating that the document contains formatting or styles that aren't allowed and asking if you would like to remove them. Click No to apply the formatting settings without changing the document's current formatting, or click Yes to remove

the styles from the document. Keep in mind that if you clicked None in step 3 and then click Yes in the message box in this step, your document will be formatted in Normal style throughout. In most cases, you'll probably want to retain the current formatting in the document, so you should click No in the message box.

5 In the Protect Document task pane, click Yes, Start Enforcing Protection. The Start Enforcing Protection dialog box opens.

6 In the Start Enforcing Protection dialog box, enter a password in the Enter New Password (Optional) box, and then reenter the password in the Reenter Password To Confirm box. If you don't want to use password protection, leave the password boxes empty. Click OK to complete the procedure.

After formatting restrictions are enforced, users won't be able to apply character formats or use styles that aren't included on the approved list of styles.

To turn off formatting restrictions, display the Protect Document task pane, click Stop Protection in the Protect Document task pane, enter a password if required, and click OK.

Tip **Retain AutoFormatting functionality when restricting formatting**
If you want users to be able to use AutoFormatting features—such as replacing double hyphens (--) with dashes (—), ordinals (1st) with superscripts (1st), fractions (1/4) with fraction characters (¼), and so forth—select the Allow AutoFormat To Override Formatting Restrictions in the Formatting Restrictions dialog box. For more information about AutoFormatting, see Chapter 7, "Putting Text Tools to Work."

Restricting Tracked Changes, Comments, and Forms

In addition to granting users access and modification rights to a document, and formatting control, you can control how users can manipulate information within a document. Specifically, you can choose any of the following options:

- **Force changes made to the document to be tracked.** This option lets users change a document but highlights all changes made so that you can review them. When a document is protected for tracked changes, users can't turn off tracking, nor can they accept or reject changes.
- **Limit user changes to comments.** When this option is turned on, users can insert comments, but they can't make any other changes to the contents of the document.
- **Restrict data entry to forms.** This option protects a document from any changes other than entries in form fields or unprotected areas.
- **Prevent users from making any changes.** You can prevent users from making any changes to a document by making the document read-only.

To configure any of these editing limitations, follow these steps:

1. Open the document you want to protect, and then choose Tools, Protect Document (or press Ctrl+F1 to open the task pane, and then choose Protect Document in the task pane title bar list). The Protect Document task pane opens, as shown previously in Figure 28-8.
2. Click the Allow Only This Type Of Editing In The Document check box in the Editing Restrictions section.
3. Click the arrow, and then choose Tracked Changes, Comments, Filling In Forms, or No Changes (Read Only), depending on how you want to protect the document.
4. Click Yes, Start Enforcing Protection in the Protect Document task pane.
5. If you want to apply a password, type a password in the Enter New Password (Optional) box, type the password again in the Reenter Password To Confirm box, and click OK. If you don't include a password, users will be able to unprotect your document by choosing Tools, Unprotect Document or by clicking Stop Protection in the Protect Document task pane. If you do assign a password, users will have to enter the password before they can unprotect the document.

After you protect a document, users will be limited by the settings you've configured. You can turn off document protection by choosing Tools, Unprotect Document or clicking Stop Protection. If you assigned a password, you'll need to enter the password to unprotect the document. After you unprotect a document, it will remain unprotected until you reconfigure the settings in the Protect Document task pane.

Controlling Restrictions for Parts of Documents

Protecting a document from changes doesn't have to be an all-or-nothing affair. With a little planning, you can allow selected groups and users to freely edit certain sections of your document after you restrict the entire document by using the Comments or No Changes (Read Only) editing restriction.

When you choose either the Comments or No Changes (Read Only) option, the Protect Document task pane changes to show the Exceptions section, which lists access level groups (Everyone, Full Control, and Change) and a list of individual users who are permitted Full Access or Change permissions for the document, as shown in Figure 28-9. At this point, you can select portions of the document and use the Groups check boxes, in the Exceptions section, to specify which users can edit the selected portions of the document.You can make multiple selections for various user combinations throughout the document. For instance, you could select one area (or a number of areas by pressing Ctrl and selecting blocks of text), and specify that a particular set of individual(s) and/or group(s) can change that area or areas. Then, you can select other sections in the document text and assign another set of individual(s) and/or group(s) the ability to change this newly selected text. When you use multiple exceptions, the excepted text is offset in color-coded highlighting by default.

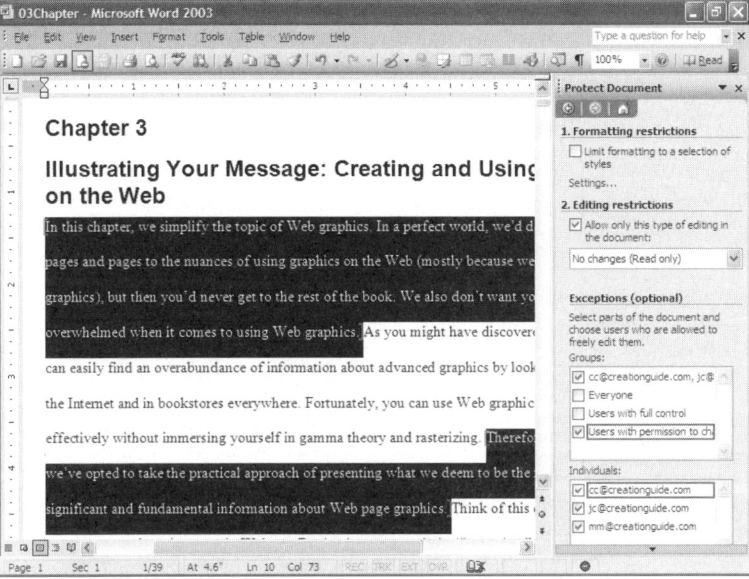

Figure 28-9. You can control the amount of editing allowed in a document by selecting areas in the document that can be edited and then assigning which users can edit which content areas.

The steps for creating editing exceptions are as follows:

1. After you assign the Comments or No Changes (Read Only) setting in the Editing Restrictions section in the Protect Document task pane, select text in the document that you want to enable for additional editing.
2. In the Protect Document task pane, choose all individuals and groups who will have full editing privileges for the selected text. If you choose more than one individual, a group is created that consists of the selected individuals. This simplifies the process of selecting the same group of individuals for subsequent procedures.
3. Continue to select and assign content until you have completed creating exceptions.
4. Click in a blank area of the document to clear the final excepted text. Each instance of excepted text will be highlighted in the color representing the individual or group allowed to edit the text.
5. Click the scroll arrow at the bottom of the Protect Document task pane (if necessary), and then click Yes, Start Enforcing Protection in the Start Enforcement section in the Protect Document taskbar. The Protect Document task pane adjusts to indicate that the document has special restrictions in effect, as shown in Figure 28-10. You can control whether excepted text appears highlighted by clearing or checking the Highlight The Regions I Can Edit check box in the Protect Document task pane.

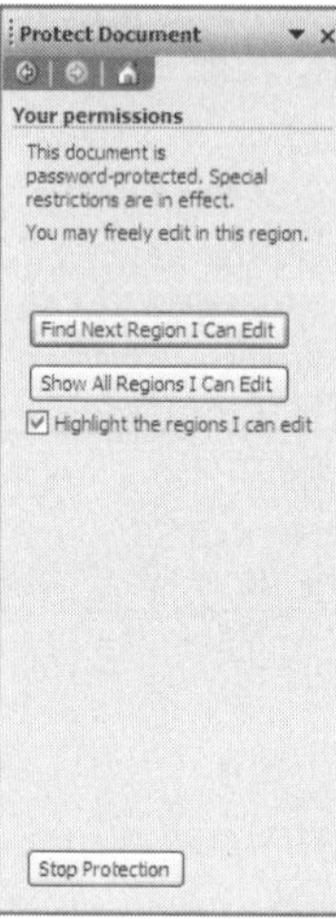

Figure 28-10. After you allow editing for sections of a document, the Protect Document task pane provides tools users can use to find and identify areas where they can change the document's contents.

You can clear excepted text by clicking Stop Protection in the Protect Document task pane (or choosing Tools, Unprotect Document), selecting an instance of excepted text, and changing the check boxes associated with the selected text.

To clear all exceptions from a document, click Stop Protection in the Protect Document task pane (or choose Tools, Unprotect Document), and then clear the Allow Only This Type Of Editing In The Document check box. A message box appears, stating that Word will ignore all the exceptions in the document. Click Yes to remove all exceptions.

Removing Personal Information and Hidden Data

One easy security measure you can take when sharing documents with others is to remove information you don't intend others to see. For example, you can remove personal information so that people who view your document won't be able to see the names of reviewers, the author of the document, and so forth. If your document contains other hidden information, such as version information or changes recorded by Word's fast save option, you'll want to eliminate that information as well. If you don't delete hidden information, other people who view your document might see information you'd rather they didn't, especially if they save your Word document in another file format (because information hidden in a Word document doesn't remain hidden when a Word document is saved in another format and viewed in another application). In the next few sections, we'll take a more detailed look at ways in which you can clear unnecessary personal information from documents before you share the documents with others.

In addition to removing personal information, removing version information, and removing fast save data, you might want to remove hidden text and accept or reject any tracked changes before you pass your document on to others. For more information about working with hidden text, see Chapter 2, "Mastering Document Fundamentals." For more information about accepting and rejecting tracked changes, see Chapter 27, "Revising Documents Using Markup Tools."

Removing Personal Information

Before you pass a document to others, you might want to remove hidden and personal information from the document. In Word, you can easily remove the following types of personal information:

- File properties, such as author name, manager name, company name, and last saved by information
- Names associated with comments (Word can change reviewers' names to *Author* automatically)
- Routing slips
- E-mail message header generated when you click the E-Mail button
- Names associated with versions (Word can change names associated with versions to *Author* automatically)

To hide these informational tidbits, you must configure the Security tab in the Options dialog box as follows:

1. With your file open, choose Tools, Options, and click the Security tab.
2. Select the Remove Personal Information From File Properties On Save check box, and then click OK.
3. Save the document.

Keep in mind that when you use this option, the names associated with information are deleted, but the actual information remains. For example, setting this option changes all names associated with comments to "Author" but the comments remain intact. The same holds true for versions—the name of the person who saved a version is changed to "Author" but the version of the document remains available for display.

Sending Documents Without Version Information

If you use the Versions feature in Word when you work with documents, the versions are saved as hidden information in the document. This enables you to retrieve the information later. When you send a document that contains versions to others, they can open past versions just as you open versions. In addition, versions of a document do not remain hidden if you or someone else saves the document in another format. To avoid sending extraneous information to others, you might want to remove the version information in documents before you pass them along. You can do so in two ways:

- **Distribute a separate document.** If you want to keep the previous versions of a document but you also need to pass the document on to others, you can save the current version as a separate document and then distribute the separate document instead of the document containing the versions. In this way, you create a "clean" document that doesn't include any version information. To do this, create a version to incorporate the latest changes (if necessary), and then choose File, Versions to open the Versions dialog box. Select the version of the document you want to save, and click Open. Then choose File, Save As to save this version as a new document.
- **Delete all version information.** If you don't need to retain information from prior versions, you can delete the version information stored in your document before you send the document to others. To do so, choose File, Versions to open the Versions dialog box, select the version(s) you want to remove (press Ctrl to select multiple versions), and click Delete.

After you remove versions from documents or create a clean copy of a document, you won't have to worry about others seeing version information if they open the document in an application other than Word. For more information about working with versions of documents, see Chapter 27, "Revising Documents Using Markup Tools."

Removing Fast Save Information

Another type of hidden information your Word documents might contain is information stored from fast saves. If you save a document with the Allow Fast Saves check box selected and then open the document as a text file, the document might contain information that you've deleted. This happens because fast saves save changes to a document instead of saving the entire document. To avoid this problem, you should fully save your document before you share it with someone else. To do so, follow these steps:

1. Open your document, choose Tools, Options, and click the Save tab in the Options dialog box.
2. Clear the Allow Fast Saves check box in the Save Options section, and click OK.
3. Click the Save button on the Standard toolbar to save your document.

An added bonus of this procedure is that when you turn off the fast save option and perform a full save, you usually reduce your document's file size because you're no longer saving all the changes made to your document along with the document's contents.

Using Digital Certificates to Digitally Sign Files and Macros

Office applications use Microsoft Authenticode technology to enable you to digitally sign a file or macro by using a digital certificate. Digital certificates can be likened to online identification cards that are attached to macros and documents. These IDs help confirm to others that a macro or document originated from the signer and hasn't been altered along the way. Digital certificates contain information about the person who obtained the certificate as well as information about the certification authority that issued the certificate.

Obtaining Digital Certificates

To obtain a digital certificate, you can purchase one from a certification authority (such as VeriSign, at *http://www.verisign.com*, or E-Lock, at *http://www.elock.com*), you can obtain one from your organization's security administrator or IT professional, or you can create a digital signature for limited local use. Since a certification authority doesn't sign the digital certificates you create, your "homemade" certificates will be considered unauthenticated, which means they'll generate a security warning if you send the certificate to a user whose security level is set to Medium or be completely disabled if the user's security level is set to High. (For more information about security levels, see "Setting Word Security Levels" on page 812.)

Working with Certificate Authorities and Security Administrators

When you obtain a digital certificate from a certification authority, you must submit an application to the authority and pay a fee (which is usually an annual rate based on the type of security you want to obtain). When you receive your digital certificate, the certification authority provides instructions for installation. Similarly, if you work with an in-house security administrator, you'll need to follow your organization's policies regarding how digital certificates are distributed and how digital signatures are added to your macros and files.

Creating Your Own Digital Certificates

If you want to create your own digital certificate to practice working with digital signatures or for your personal use, you can do so by using the Selfcert.exe application included with Office. Remember, this type of certification is unauthenticated, so it doesn't provide much security assurance to others outside of your local area network.

Installing the Selfcert.exe Application By default, Selfcert.exe is not installed with Office, so your first step in creating a digital certificate is to install the application from the Office installation CD, as follows:

1. Choose Start, Control Panel, and then double-click the Add Or Remove Programs icon.
2. Select Microsoft Office, and then click Change.
3. Choose Add Or Remove features, and then click Next.
4. Select Choose Advanced Customization Of Applications, and then click Next.
5. Expand Office Shared Features, click Digital Signature For VBA Projects, and choose Run From My Computer.
6. Click Update. When the updating is complete, a message box appears, stating that Office has been updated successfully. Click OK.

After you click Update, the Selfcert.exe feature is installed on your system. Usually, the application is installed in the C:\Program Files\Microsoft Office\Office11 folder.

Creating a Certificate After you install the Selfcert.exe application, you're ready to create a digital certificate. To do so, follow these steps:

1. Double-click the Selfcert.exe application. If the file isn't stored in the C:\Program Files\Microsoft Office\Office11 folder, choose Start, Search, For Files Or Folders, and run a search for **selfcert.exe.** When the search is completed, double-click the Selfcert.exe application. You'll see the Create Digital Certificate dialog box, as shown in Figure 28-11.

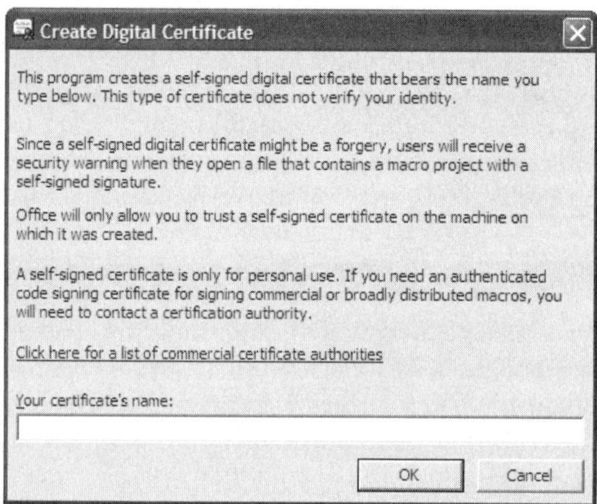

Figure 28-11. The Selfcert.exe application enables you to create an unauthenticated digital certificate that you can use for your own macros and files.

2. Type your name in the Your Certificate's Name box, and click OK. A message box appears, stating that you've successfully created a certificate, as shown in Figure 28-12. Click OK.

Figure 28-12. A message box appears after your certificate has been created.

At this point, you've successfully created an unauthorized digital certificate that you can use to sign and run macros on your local machine. You can also use your unofficial certificate to practice working with digital certificates. You can view your newly created certificate and attach it to your files and macros, as described in the next section.

Attaching a Digital Certificate to a File

After you obtain a digital certificate, you can authenticate your files and macros by digitally signing them. Basically, digitally signing a file or macro means that you've attached your digital certificate to the document. In this section, you'll learn how to digitally sign a file.

For information about digitally signing a macro, see Chapter 32, "Creating and Working with VBA Macros."

To attach a digital certificate to a file, follow these steps:

1 Open the document you want to digitally sign, and then choose Tools, Options, and click the Security tab.

2 Click Digital Signatures. The Digital Signature dialog box appears, as shown in Figure 28-13.

Figure 28-13. The Digital Signature dialog box lists the digital certificates attached to the current document and enables you to view, add, and remove certificates.

3 In the Digital Signature dialog box, click Add. The Select Certificate dialog box appears, as shown in Figure 28-14.

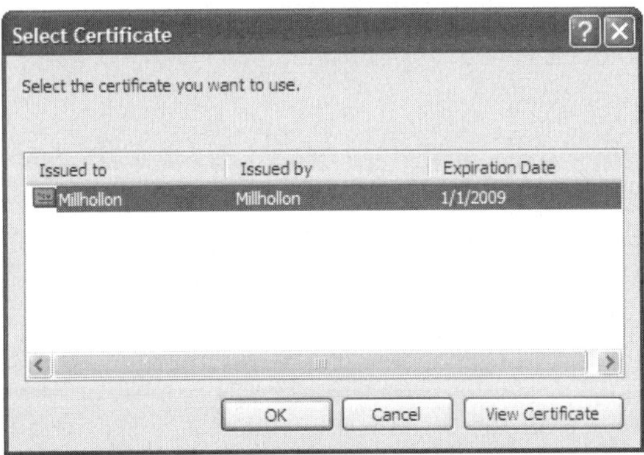

Figure 28-14. The Select Certificate dialog box lists the certificates you can use to digitally sign a file.

Note If you're working in Normal view when you click Add in step 3, or if ink annotations are included in the document, you might receive a message box that states that all text and pictures might not be visible in the current view. If you haven't saved the current document, you'll receive a message box stating that you must first save the document as a Word document before you can add a digital certificate. If you haven't accepted tracked changes, you might receive a message box that recommends that you accept or reject tracked changes before signing your document. In any message box, click Cancel if you want to proceed with the recommended actions or click Yes to continue.

4. Select the digital certificate you want to use. Click View Certificate to see more information about the selected certificate. The Certificate dialog box opens, displaying the General tab, as shown in Figure 28-15. Notice that the certificate icon has a red X mark in the lower right corner, indicating that the certificate is unauthorized. This certificate was created using the Selfcert.exe application, which, as mentioned, creates unauthorized certificates for your personal use.

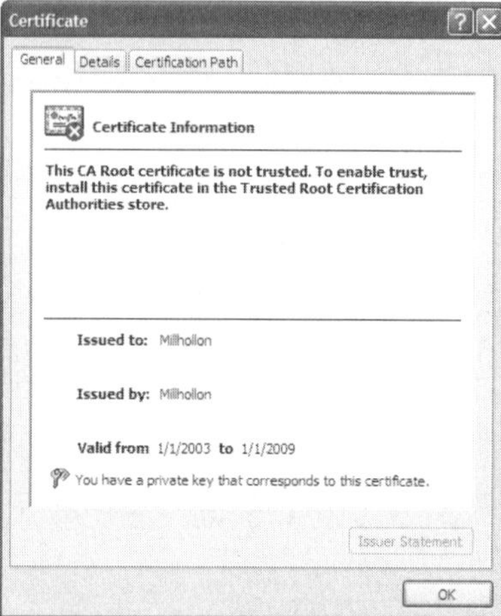

Figure 28-15. The Certificate dialog box shows you detailed information about a selected digital certificate.

5. Click OK to close the Certificate dialog box and return to the Select Certificate dialog box.
6. Click OK to add the certificate to the current document. The certificate will now be listed in the Digital Signature dialog box.
7. Click OK to close the Digital Signature dialog box, and then click OK to close the Options dialog box.

After you add a certificate to a document, you can remove it at any time. To do so, choose Tools, Options, and click the Security tab. Click Digital Signatures, select the digital certificate you want to remove, click Remove, and then click OK twice. This action removes the certificate's association with the current document—it doesn't delete the certificate.

Checking for the Red X

As mentioned, a digital certificate you create using the Selfcert.exe application will be displayed with a red X mark because the certificate is unauthenticated. A red X can also indicate the following security issues associated with a certificate:

- The signed file or macro has been tampered with.
- The certificate was not issued by a trusted certification authority.
- The certificate was issued without verification (such as a free certificate authority trial download).
- The certificate was invalid when it was used to sign the file or macros.

When you see a certificate with a red X, proceed with caution. This is a clear sign that something about the certificate is amiss.

Viewing Digital Certificates Attached to Files

If you're working with a file that's been digitally signed, you can easily view the digital certificates. The procedure for viewing digital signatures is similar to digitally signing a file. To view a digital signature, follow these steps:

1. Choose Tools, Options, click the Security tab, and click Digital Signatures.
2. Select the digital signature you want to learn about, and click View Certificate. The Certificate dialog box opens, showing details about the certificate.
3. Click OK three times to close all open dialog boxes.

If you want to export a certificate to a file (for instance, you might want to copy your certificate to disk and then install it on another machine), you can do so by using the Certificate Export Wizard. To access this wizard, click the Details tab in the Certificate dialog box and then click Copy To File. The wizard walks you through the process of exporting your digital certificate. Be careful when exporting your digital certificates. The security aspect of certificates relies entirely on the secrecy of the certificates' codes. If your codes become available to others, you've jeopardized your digital certificates' effectiveness.

Safeguarding Against Macro Viruses

Although the overriding purpose of macros is to streamline common tasks and procedures performed in Word and other applications, the unfortunate fact is that macros can also serve as a breeding ground for computer viruses. A macro virus is a type of computer virus that originates within a file, a template, or an add-in. As a Word user contemplating security issues, you need to be aware of macro viruses and how you can configure Word to assist you in recognizing when a macro might present a risk.

Note Microsoft devotes a number of areas on its Web site to security issues. For example, if you want to find out more about security, visit *http://www.microsoft.com/technet/security* and *http://ww.microsoft.com/security*. You can also visit the Office site, at *http://www.microsoft.com/office*, and search for **security** using the Search This Site text box.

Preventing Viruses in Word Documents

One strategy you can use to combat macro viruses when working in Word is to attach digital signatures to macros to identify their origin. Then, if you trust the origin of the digital signature, you're safe to enable the macro. Keep in mind that digital signatures enable you to identify and run macros from trusted sources; they do not locate and eliminate viruses.

In addition to using digital certificates, which can provide assurance regarding the person from whom a file or macro originated (as discussed in "Using Digital Certificates to Digitally Sign Files and Macros" on page 806), you can specify how you want Word to react when it encounters documents that contain macros. To do this, you set Word security levels, as described next.

Tip For the best protection against viruses, you should purchase and install third-party antivirus software to work in conjunction with Word's security settings.

Setting Word Security Levels

When Word encounters a document, it determines whether the document contains macros. If the document doesn't contain any macros, Word opens it without any warnings. If the document contains macros, Word opens it based on the current security settings. In Word, you can choose one of the following three levels of security:

- **High** This setting allows only signed and trusted macros to run. When you use this setting, you can run only macros that have been digitally signed and are listed as from a trusted source. Unsigned macros are disabled automatically before the file is opened.
- **Medium** This setting generates prompts asking whether you want to enable or disable macros on a file-by-file basis. Whenever a file containing macros is encountered that's signed by a source not listed as a trusted source, Word allows you to choose whether you want to enable or disable the macros when you open the file.
- **Low** This setting turns off all macro security warnings and trusts all macros. In other words, all files, including files that contain macros, will always open without a warning when you configure Word with the Low security level. You should consider using this setting only if you have installed the latest version of a virus scanner, if the most current virus signature files for your virus program are installed, and if you're absolutely sure that the documents you're opening can be trusted.

By default, Word's security is set to High, the recommended setting. To display Word's security options, choose Tools, Options, click the Security tab, and then click Macro Security. In the Security dialog box, click the Security Level tab, as shown in Figure 28-16. You can specify any security level, but you should consider retaining Word's High security level setting unless a particular need arises that requires you to lower your security settings.

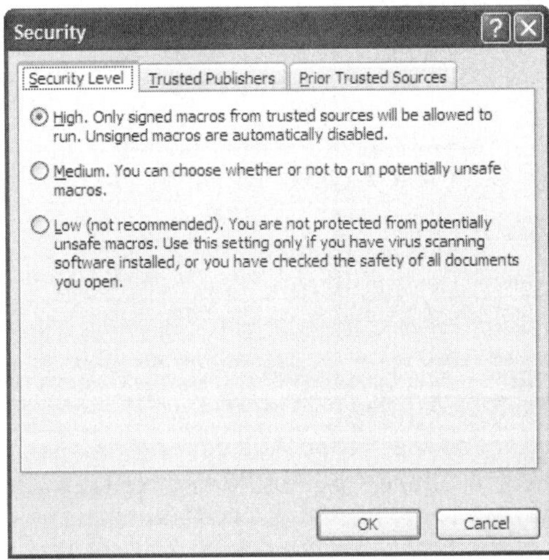

Figure 28-16. The Security Level tab in the Security dialog box enables you to specify how Word should react when you open a document that contains macros.

Viewing and Removing Trusted Sources

When you open a file that includes signed macros (and the signer isn't included on your trusted publishers list, as described in this section), you'll be asked whether you want to trust all macros from the signer. If you click Yes, the signer will be added to your list of trusted publishers. Before you add a signer, you should carefully review the publisher's certificate. You should especially review the certificate's Issued To, Issued By, and Valid From fields. After you add a signer to your trusted publishers list, Word will automatically enable macros signed by the publisher in the future. If you've upgraded to Word 2003 from an earlier version of Word, the Security dialog box includes the Prior Trusted Sources tab, which lists sources you've trusted in earlier versions of Word. As you add new trusted sources, they'll be added to the Trusted Publishers list.

If you later decide that you'd like to remove a signer from your trusted publishers list, you can do so at any time, as follows:

1. Choose Tools, Options, and click the Security tab.
2. Click Macro Security to open the Security dialog box.
3. Click the Trusted Publishers tab or the Prior Trusted Sources tab, as shown in Figure 28-17.

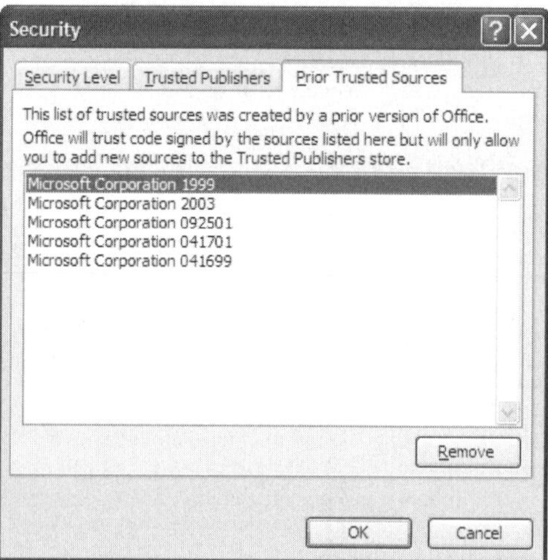

Figure 28-17. If you've added any sources to your trusted publishers list, they'll appear on the Trusted Publishers tab or the Prior Trusted Sources tab in the Security dialog box.

4 Select the publisher you want to remove, click Remove, and then click OK.

Microsoft digitally signs all templates, add-ins, and macros shipped with Office. After you add Microsoft to your list of trusted publishers for one of these installed files, all subsequent interactions with these files will not generate messages.

> **Tip** **Add your Selfcert.exe certificate to your trusted publishers list**
> Office applications will allow you to add the owner of an unauthenticated certificate (such as a Selfcert.exe certificate) to the list of trusted publishers only when the certificate is used on the same computer on which it was initially created. This means that you can create a certificate using Selfcert.exe and sign your own personal macros, and you can trust that certificate on your computer. But if you attempt to share your file with other users, they won't be able to run your macros if their security is set to High.

Accessing E-Mail Encryption Settings

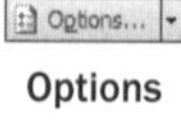

Options

One last type of security you might be concerned with when you're working in Word is e-mail security. If you're using Word to create e-mail messages, you should pay particular attention to the security settings associated with this feature. To access e-mail security settings, follow these steps:

1 If necessary, click the E-Mail button on the Standard toolbar to open the e-mail pane.
2 In the e-mail pane, click the Options button. The Message Options dialog box opens.
3 In the Message Options dialog box, click Security Settings. The Security Properties dialog box opens, as shown in Figure 28-18. You can use this dialog box to encrypt your message and attach a digital signature to it.

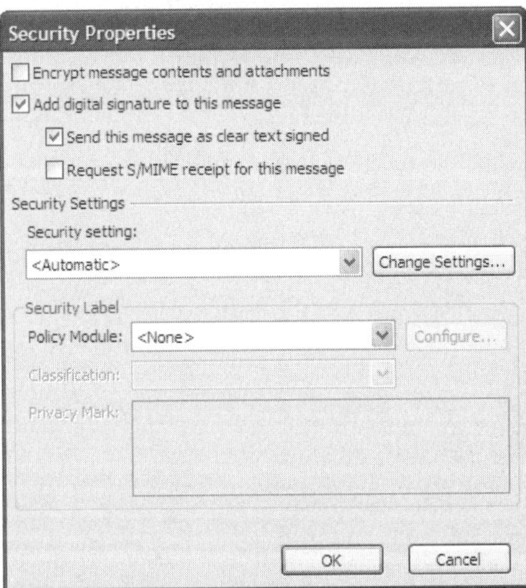

Figure 28-18. The Security Properties dialog box enables you to control security settings when you send e-mail messages from within Word.

4 After you configure your security settings, click OK, and then click Close to close the Message Options dialog box.

For additional information about providing security in e-mail messages, see the Microsoft Outlook Help files, visit the Outlook Web site (*http://www.microsoft.com/office/outlook*), or refer to an in-depth Outlook 2003 resource, such as *Microsoft Office Outlook 2003 Inside Out* (Microsoft Press, 2004).

Part 6

Advanced Word: XML, Forms, and VBA

Chapter 29

Working with XML

If you're not sure why people are so excited about XML, you're not alone. XML (which stands for Extensible Markup Language) has been around since 1998, but for the most part, it has been used only by people who are comfortable with technologies and programming languages for the World Wide Web. Now Word 2003 and the other core Office applications make XML an option for the rest of us.

The beauty of XML is its flexibility—you can create a document, save it as XML, and store it in such a way that it can be used across platforms, across countries, and across just about any data barrier you can imagine. Do you have gigabytes of data locked away in your old system that are inaccessible by today's software? Are there reports, legal briefings, analyses, and other documents spread over desktop PCs all over your organization that might offer valuable data if you could pull all the information together and actually put it in a usable form? Are you tired of writing the same type of information—marketing reports, statistical analyses, brochures, Web pages, and more—over and over again, when you could be using information already available in other files?

XML can change all that. In this chapter, you'll learn about the XML features in Word 2003 and find out how to create and save your own XML documents.

Note XML support is available only in the stand-alone version of Word 2003 and in Microsoft Office Professional Edition 2003.

Introduction to XML

The XML features in Word 2003 are so simple to use that you really don't need to know XML to enjoy its benefits. But knowing the basics of XML makes it easier to understand how it can be helpful in your own work. Toward that end, this section of the chapter gives you some XML fundamentals and definitions of some common terms you'll find used in connection with XML.

XML Glossary

Here are the XML terms you're sure to see in this chapter and other writings on XML:

- **DTD (Document Type Definition)** A definition of the data elements allowed in the XML document.
- **Element** A piece of data defined in an XML document, enclosed with start and end tags; for example, <TITLE>Microsoft Office Word 2003 Inside Out</TITLE>.
- **Cascading Style Sheets (CSS)** A collection of formatting instructions that control the display of the document. Stylesheets can be in a separate file and linked to the document or can be embedded in the document itself.
- **XML data** Also called an *XML document*, the .xml file is the raw XML data stored independently of the format for presenting it.
- **XML schema** A definition of the data elements allowed in the XML document. The XML schema is a superset of the DTD. You may also see the acronym XSD used to refer to an XML schema definition.
- **XSLT (XSL Transformations)** XSLT is used to convert XML documents into various document formats, most commonly HTML.
- **XSL (Extensible Stylesheet Language)** A language used to create stylesheets that can be used to transform XML into various document formats, using XSLT.
- **Well-formed** A well-formed XML document is one that adheres to the constraints defined by either the DTD or the XML schema.

XML Defined

Although it's hard to give XML a concise definition, the easiest and broadest approach says that XML is a highly flexible format for exchanging data and using it in applications. XML is an open standard for describing data in a format that is readable to humans, while also defining data elements within a document. Some people refer to XML as a markup language because, after all, that's what its name (Extensible Markup Language) says. But XML is more than a language of tags; XML actually lets you create a type of markup language that is specific to your data needs. With XML, you use specific rules to create your own tags and stylesheets; the individual tags describe the content and meaning of the data rather than its display format, which HTML controls.

In the big picture, the process goes like this:

1. You create or open a document in Word 2003.
2. You attach or create an XML schema or DTD.
3. You save the document as XML data only or in full XML format.
4. If you choose to transform the XML document, you can apply an XSLT to display the saved XML document in a specific view.

What Does XML Look Like?

XML is generally reader-friendly, meaning that people, not just machines, can easily read and follow the basic logic in the code. For example, the following simple example of an XML document contains information about a series of workshops offered by a sporting goods company:

```
<TRAINING>
  <CLASS>
    <TITLE>Mountain Biking</TITLE>
    <INTRUCTOR>Lee</INSTRUCTOR>
    <DATE>August 8, 2003</DATE>
    <DURATION>6 weeks</DURATION>
    <COST>$240</COST>
  </CLASS>
  <CLASS>
    <TITLE>Rappelling</TITLE>
    <INTRUCTOR>Jack</INSTRUCTOR>
    <DATE>June 24, 2003</DATE>
    <DURATION>4 weeks</DURATION>
    <COST>$160</COST>
  </CLASS>
  <CLASS>
    <TITLE>Kayaking</TITLE>
    <INTRUCTOR>Jason</INSTRUCTOR>
    <DATE>July 10, 2003</DATE>
    <DURATION>6 weeks</DURATION>
    <COST>$240</COST>
  </CLASS>
</TRAINING>
```

As you can see, each element has an opening tag and a closing tag (for example, the cost of a class is enclosed by a beginning tag, <COST>, and an ending tag, </COST>). The tagged elements are nested inside other tags; for example, each class record begins and ends with a <CLASS> tag; inside those tags are nested tags for each individual data item stored for that class.

> **Note** XML tags are case-sensitive by default. If you're creating an XML document that contains data to be used by various business systems, be sure to verify how the systems expect to operate with your tags before creating your document.

Chapter 29

Because XML allows you to name the content of the data, you can use that same class information as easily in a database as you can in a spreadsheet, a word processing document, a report, or an e-mail. Using an XML schema, which defines the rules for naming the XML data, and an XSLT, which is the template that will provide the format for the final document, you can make XML data usable in many different forms in all sorts of contexts, from one end of your organization to another.

By comparison, HTML (Hypertext Markup Language), the primary markup language used on the Web, is a tagging system that controls the way information is formatted, not the content of the data itself. A heading, for example, might have an <H1> or <H2> tag to designate the size of the heading; the <FONT> tag is used to specify the type family, size, color, and style of the text. But the HTML tags can't describe the content of the heading, and it's the content—the actual data itself—that can be used in other documents, such as databases, spreadsheets, reports, and so forth. The XML tags name the content of the data—not the formatting.

XML: A Public, International Standard

XML was developed by the World Wide Web Consortium (W3C) to create an easy-to use, easy-to-read standard that would allow information exchange across platforms all over the world. The W3C is a public organization with the sole purpose of creating standards and new technologies for the Internet. You can find out more about the W3C and its various activities (including in-depth information on the development and application of XML for businesses and individuals) by going to *http://www.w3.org.*

Note What is an "open standard"? A technology based on an open standard is open for use and development by the public; there are no licensing fees or proprietary standards owned by a specific company or organization.

The Benefit of Reusable Data

One aspect of XML's flexibility is the way it separates form from function. Because you are creating names that reflect the *content* and not the *format* of your data, you can pull that content into other forms by applying what's known as a *transform* (or template).

Suppose you're writing a marketing flyer about a new product. When you apply XML tags to the product name, specifications, and cost, you are coding that content so that it can be pulled easily into other documents—perhaps a catalog, a Web page, or an advertising brochure. This enables you not only to save keystrokes but also to reduce the margin for error—instead of having five different people write five different types of marketing copy about one product, you can have someone do it once, and then allow everyone to use the finalized document. This creates a consistent message (everybody says the same thing about the product, which is a great help toward consistent communication) and frees time others would spend rewriting the same text.

Make Your Own Rules

The XML support in Word 2003 gives you the option of attaching customized XSDs (XML Schema Definitions). This means that you can create your own rules for naming and storing your data—and you can also share schemas with others in your office, company, or industry.

You can choose to save your documents in Word's default schema (WordML) and attach your own customized (also called *arbitrary*) schema, which describes the language and functionality you need in your business.

> **Note** Creating a schema is a fairly complicated task—certain rules govern the development of "well-formed" code—but it's not as daunting as you might think. If you'd like to know more about XML and learn to develop your own schemas for your customized XML use, see *XML Step by Step, Second Edition* (Microsoft Press, 2002), by Michael J. Young.

XML in Word 2003

Now that you understand the basics of XML, let's take a look at the XML features you'll be using in Word 2003. The concept behind the addition of XML is simplicity—the developers wanted to make sure that anyone would be able to use the XML features to easily create, tag, save, and export XML data in their Word documents.

Here's a quick overview of the XML features you'll work with in Word 2003:

- **XML Structure task pane** XML now has its own task pane in Word, which leads you through the process of working with XML. The task pane, shown in Figure 29-1, first gives you the means to attach the XML schema you want to use, and then it shows the tree structure of your XML document so that you can easily tag items and navigate through the document.

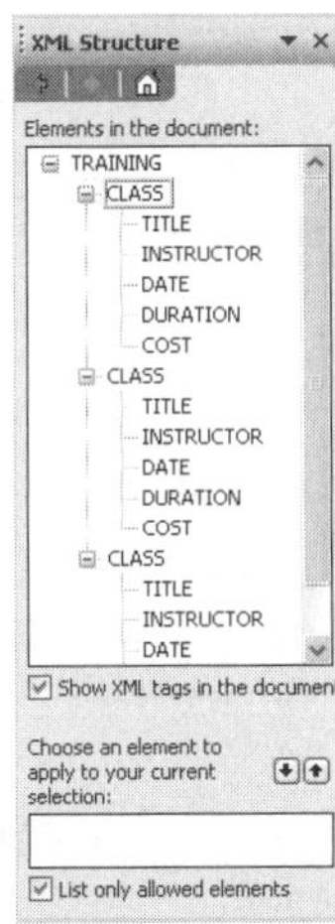

Figure 29-1. The task pane displays the tree structure of the current XML document and enables you to click and add tags while you work.

- **XML error checking** As you add XML tags to your document, Word checks the tags against the applied schema to make sure that the code is well formed.

- **View tags while you work** When you work on an XML document, all tags (existing tags and those you add) appear as graphical brackets around the word, phrase, paragraph, or entire document, as shown in Figure 29-2.

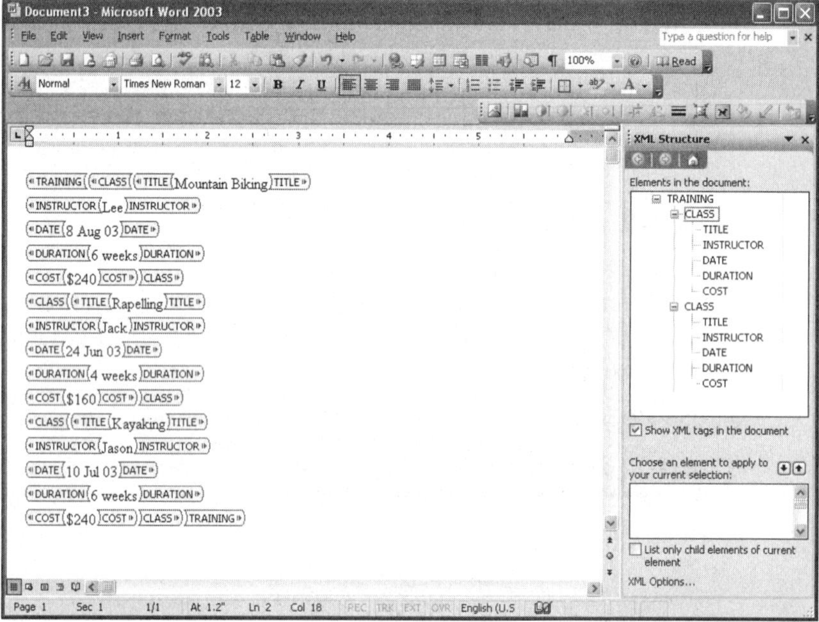

Figure 29-2. Tag view enables you to see at a glance where the XML tags are in your document and how they are nested.

> **Tip** You can turn Tag view off and on by clicking the Show XML Tags In The Document check box in the task pane.

- **Attach schemas easily** You can attach a schema two different ways—through the XML Structure task pane or by choosing Tools, Templates And Add-Ins.
- **Create a schema library** Because you might use more than one schema in a specific document (or create different schemas for different types of content), Word includes a Schema Library feature that makes it easy for you to organize and attach the schemas you need.

> **Tip** You can add more than one schema to a single document if you like. Word will apply both sets of definitions and rules and alert you if there is a conflict.

- **Opening an XML file** When you open an XML file in Word and choose XML Files in the Files Of Type list in the Open dialog box, you also have the option of applying an XSL transform as you open the file. To do this, click the arrow to the right of the Open button, and then select Open With Transform from the menu.

Note An XSL transform allows you to display an XML document in different views, or formats. For example, if you are opening a report file that you want to display on the Web, applying a transform lets you see the file in a Web-based format without making modifications to the file itself.

- **Saving an XML file** When you choose XML Document in the Save As Type list in the Save As dialog box (as shown in Figure 29-3), two options specific to XML appear to the left of the Save button. You can select the ApplyTransform check box, and then click the Transform button to choose the transform you want to apply, or, if you prefer, you can save data only.

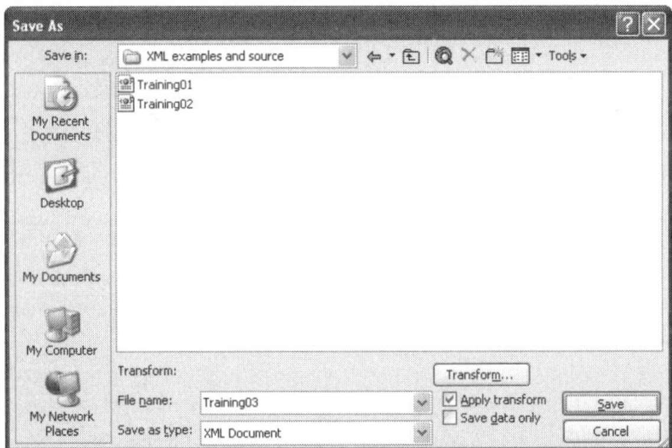

Figure 29-3. Word makes it easy to save an XML file in different formats.

Note You can manually attach an XML Schema Definition (XSD) file or apply an Extensible Stylesheet Language Transformation (XSLT) to an existing XML file, but Word adds another convenience to simplify this process. Word remembers associated files and gives the user the option of attaching the appropriate XSD or XSLT when a file that matches a recognized category is opened.

Creating an XML Document

Now that you know what to expect from Word's XML features, you're ready to work through the process. Start your XML document by following these steps:

1 Display the File menu, and then choose New.

2 In the New Document task pane, click XML Document, as shown in Figure 29-4.

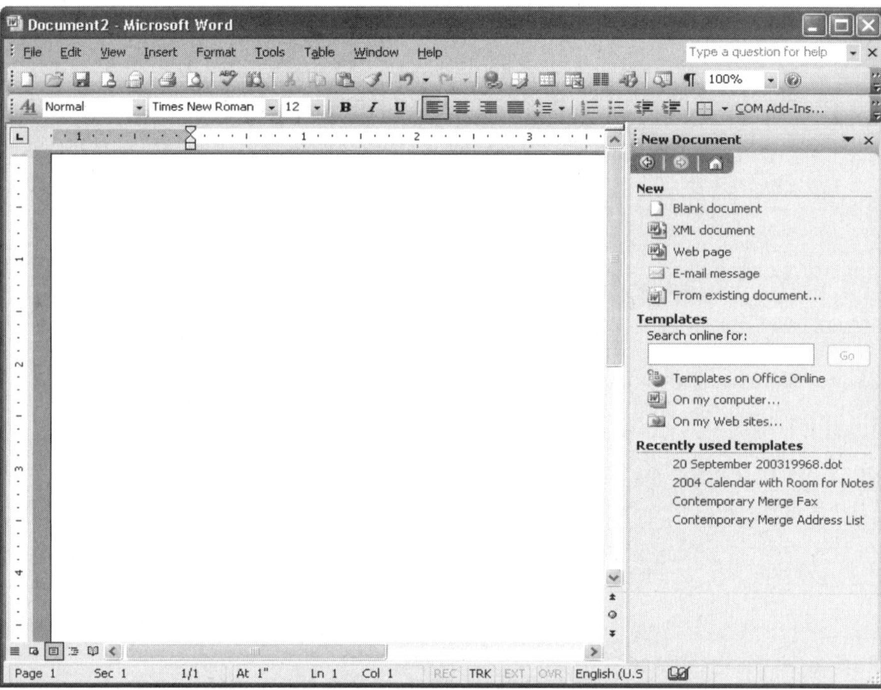

Figure 29-4. When you create a new document, Word 2003 gives you the option of creating an XML document.

Attaching a Schema

When the XML Structure task pane appears, click the Templates And Add-Ins link. The Templates And Add-Ins dialog box (shown in Figure 29-5) appears, where you can select the schema you want to use. The first time you attach a schema, however, the list will be blank.

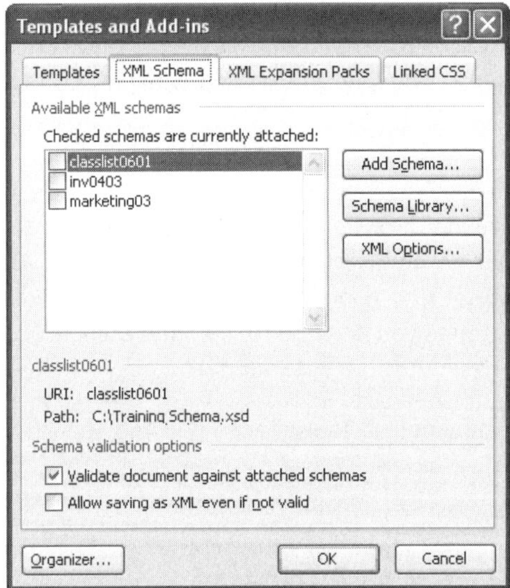

Figure 29-5. The XML Schema task pane includes tools for attaching, working with, and validating XML files.

To add a schema for the first time, follow these steps:

1. Click Add Schema. The Add Schema dialog box (shown in Figure 29-6) appears, where you can select the schema you want to use.

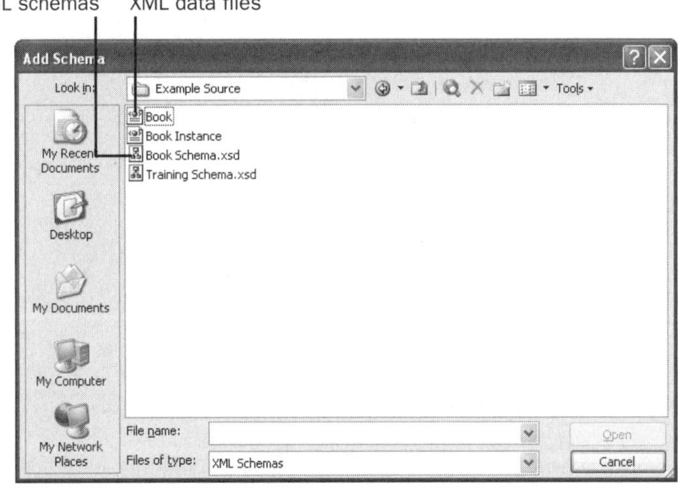

Figure 29-6. Select the schema you want to attach to your XML document in the Add Schema dialog box.

2 Click the schema, and then click Open. In the Schema Settings dialog box, enter a name under which the schema will be listed in the XML Schema tab (known as the *namespace alias*), and then click OK. The schema is added to the list and you can select it and then click OK to complete the process.

Note This section assumes that you have a schema to work with. If you have not been supplied an XML schema by your administrator or workgroup leader, you can search online for sample schemas to use or follow along with the XML examples in the book *XML Step by Step, Second Edition*, as mentioned earlier. The book includes a CD with numerous XML sample data files, schemas, and transforms you can use to learn more about XML.

Note You also can attach a schema by choosing Tools, Templates And Add-Ins, and then clicking the XML Schema tab.

An Overview of the Schema Library

The Schema Library, shown below, contains any XML schemas and XSLT (Extensible Stylesheet Language Transformation) files you will use to control the structure and format of your XML documents. To display the Schema Library, choose Tools, Templates And Add-Ins, and then click the XML Schemas tab. Select Schema Library.

The top portion of the Schema Library lists the XML schemas you've attached to the current document. The bottom portion of the dialog box enables you to add XSLT transforms, also called *solutions,* to the document. To add a solution, click Add Solution, navigate to the folder in which the transform is found, and then choose the XSLT transform from the list that appears. Click OK to add the transform and return to the Schema Library.

Chapter 29

Working with Tags

Most of your work with XML will rely on working with tags—the small code identifiers you attach to data to name the content. The tags available for use in a particular document depend on the schema attached to it—the schema contains the definitions for the tags, much as a style sheet defines the styles that are allowed in a document formatted for the Web.

Displaying Tags

You can easily show and hide XML tags while you work by pressing Ctrl+Shift+X. If you prefer, when the XML Structure task pane is visible, you can click Show XML Tags In The Document to remove the check mark and hide the tags.

In addition, to make finding the tag you want easier, you can choose which tags appear in the selection box in the bottom of the task pane by clicking the List Only Child Elements Of Current Element check box.

Adding Tags

Once you've attached the schema to the document, the next major step is to tag the content you want to use. To add XML tags to data in your current document, follow these steps:

1. Highlight the data you want to tag.
2. Click an XML element in the XML Structure task pane. The opening and closing tags for the item are added to your document, as shown in Figure 29-7.

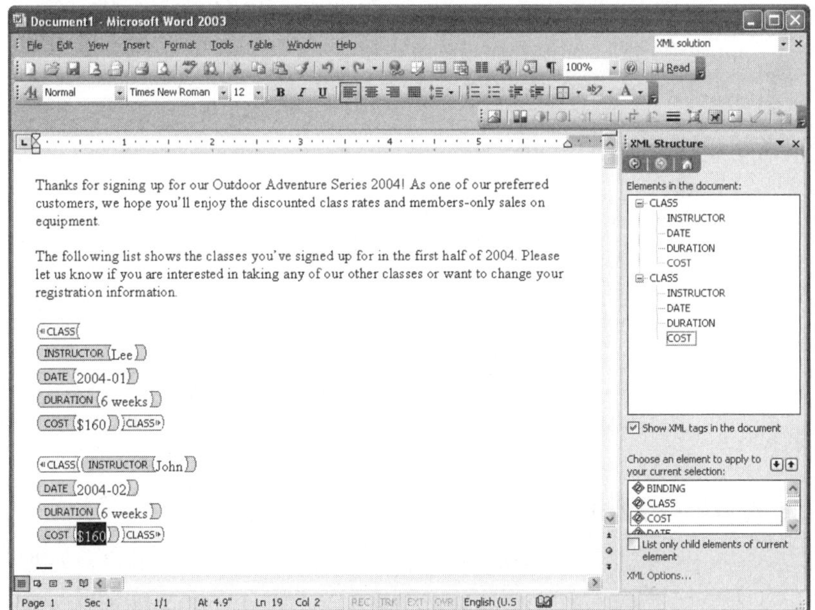

Figure 29-7. You can add XML tags easily by highlighting information in your document and clicking the tag you want to apply.

Adding Tag Attributes

XML attributes are special characteristics of an element that allow you to further categorize your data. For example, suppose that the training classes in the previous figure are offered to both groups and individuals. To help track the data on each type of training class independently, the CLASS tag could be assigned GROUP and INDIVIDUAL attributes.

To add an attribute, perform the following steps:

1 Right-click the XML element in the XML Structure task pane, and then click Attributes in the list, as shown below.

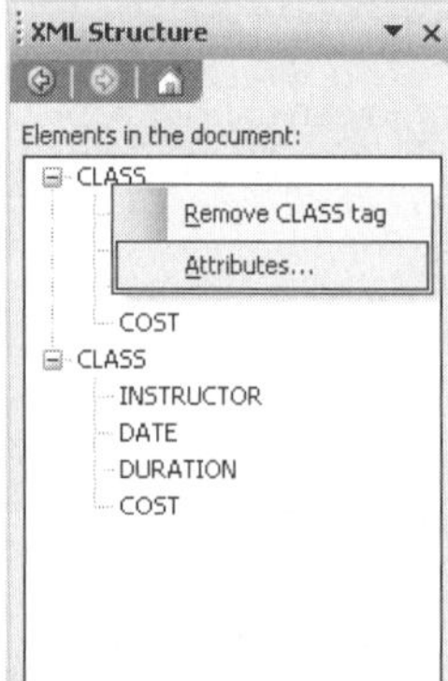

2 The Attributes dialog box appears. Click the attribute you want to use, enter an attribute value in the Value text box, click Add, and then click OK.

3 The new attribute is added to the list of available attributes. Now select the one you want and then click OK to add it to the XML element you selected.

Removing XML Tags

If you make a mistake entering a tag in your document and you want to remove it, simply right-click the tag you want to remove, and then choose Remove Tag. The data is still in your document but both the opening and closing tags are deleted.

Tip If you want to print your document complete with its XML tags, choose Tools, Options, and click the Print tab. Click the XML Tags check box in the Include With Document section, and then click OK to close the dialog box. Now print as usual (choose File, Print) or click the Print button on the Standard toolbar) and the XML tags will be printed in your document.

Setting XML Options

As you get more comfortable working with XML, you may want to modify some of the options to further control the way your XML files are saved, validated, and displayed. To display the XML Options dialog box, click the XML Options link at the bottom of the XML Structure task pane. The XML Options dialog box appears, as shown in Figure 29-8.

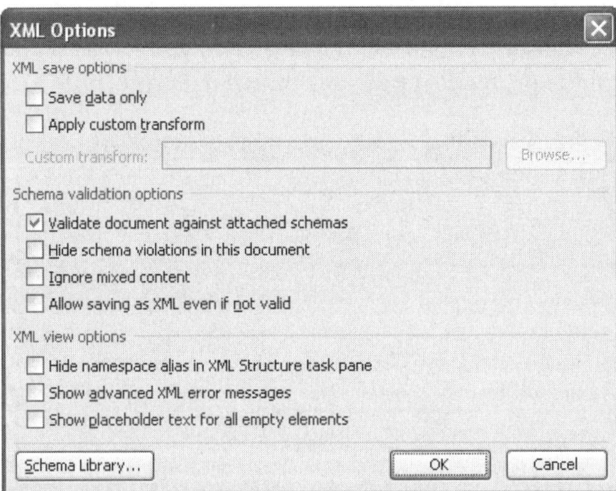

Figure 29-8. XML options enable you to control the way XML files are saved and to make choices about validation and display.

Saving XML

When you save your XML document (as you'll see more fully in "Saving XML Files"), you have the option of saving only XML data or saving the data and the format together. In the XML Options dialog box, you can make one of these settings the default choice for saving the current document. If you click the Save Data Only check box, the current XML document will be saved as data only. (You'll have the option to override this choice in the Save As dialog box, however.)

When you click the Apply Custom Transform check box, the Custom Transform field becomes available so that you can click Browse, and then choose the transform file you want to attach to the document.

Dealing with Schema Violations

If the tags you've added to your document—or the content they describe—create something that doesn't fit the schema you've attached, Word will let you know that you have a validation error. *Validation* is the process of checking the tags against the schema to make sure the code is properly formed. If Word finds a problem, it lets you know by displaying a purple wavy line along the left margin of the text, as shown here:

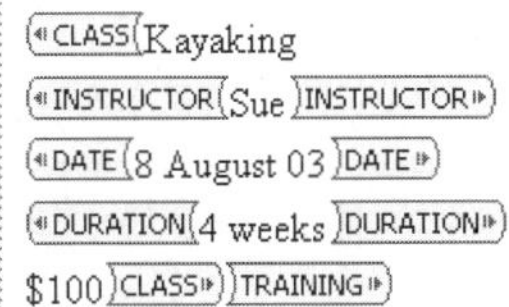

Chapter 29

In addition to the purple indicator, a small error icon appears in the XML Structure task pane next to the tag that is in error. To see a description of the problem, position the mouse pointer over the tag. A description of the problem appears, as shown in Figure 29-9.

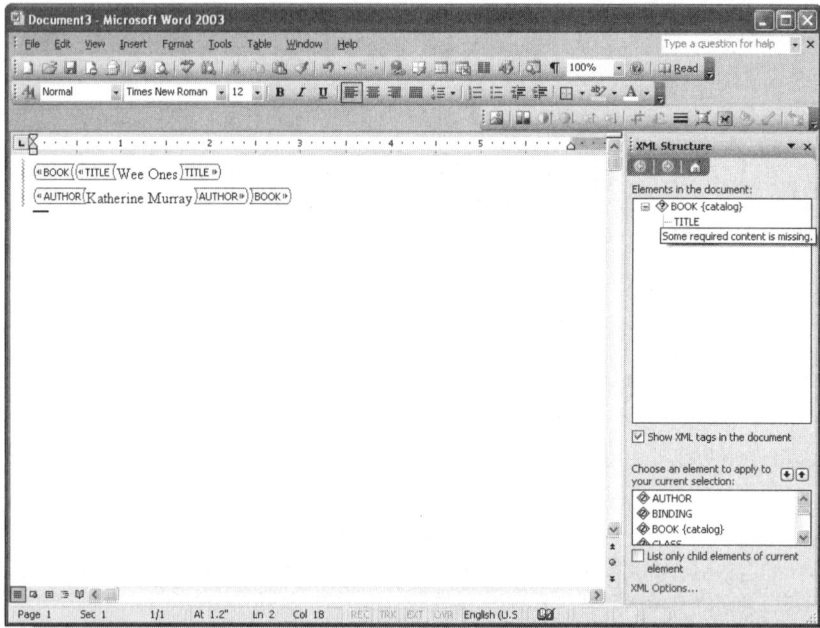

Figure 29-9. Word lets you know when an error occurs in your XML document.

The Schema Validation Options in the XML Options dialog box enable you to control how—and whether—Word checks your code for validation (this option is also available in the Templates And Add-Ins dialog box, where you first attach the schema). By default, the document will be validated against attached schemas. You can choose to hide errors in the current document, ignore mixed content, or even save the file as XML, errors and all. (You might want to do this, for example, if you have an error you can't figure out and you want to give the file to an XML guru for further investigation.)

View Options for XML

The XML View Options in the XML Options dialog box enable you to provide additional information about the XML elements you're working with. By default, the *namespace alias* (the name you assign to the schema or solution when you attach it) appears in the XML Structure task pane; you can hide it by selecting the Hide Namespace Alias In XML Structure

Task Pane check box. If you want to get additional information on the XML validation error messages you receive, select the Show Advanced XML Error Messages check box. Finally, if you want to see where empty elements occur in your document, select the last option, Show Placeholder Text for All Empty Elements.

If you are just learning how to use XML, you'll find that selecting the Show Advanced XML Error Messages feature will help you learn more quickly from your mistakes. The error messages that appear provide much more information about what's going on. For example, compare Figure 29-10 with the earlier, more limited error message shown in Figure 29-9.

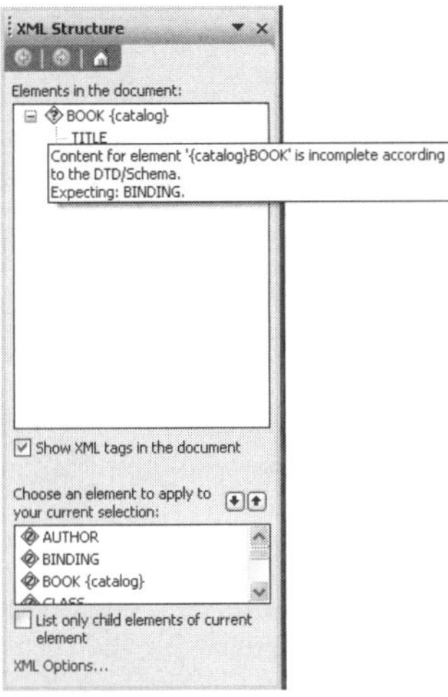

Figure 29-10. When the Show Advanced XML Error Messages option is checked, Word provides more explanation of validation problems.

Saving XML Files

Once you've created and tagged your XML document, you're ready to save it just the way you want it. Some documents are fine the way they are—in Word format, or saved using a particular XSLT transform. Other documents you'll want to preserve as data only so that they can be imported into other XML applications.

When you choose File, Save, the Save As dialog box appears as usual. As Figure 29-11 shows, the only difference is a small one: the addition of Apply Transform and Save Data Only check boxes. These are the choices for your XML document. If you want to save only the XML data, click the Save Data Only check box. If you want to apply a transform, select the Apply Transform check box, and then click Transform to choose the transform file you want to apply. Finally, click Save to complete the operation.

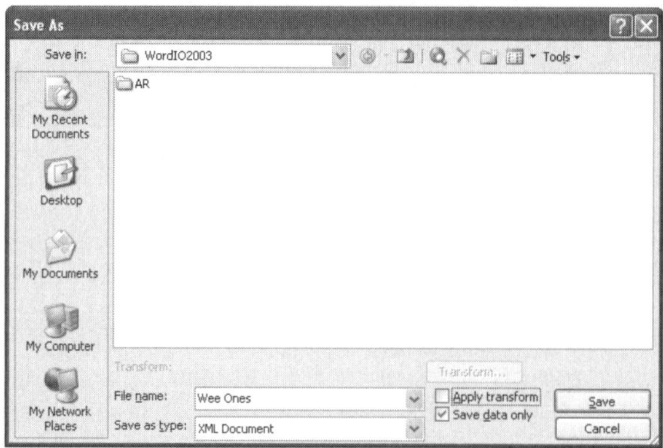

Figure 29-11. Choices in the Save As dialog box enable you to save your XML document as data only or to apply a transform.

Chapter 30

Performing Mail Merges

What did we ever do without mail merge? If it's part of your job to create marketing mailings, surveys, broadcast e-mail messages, or distributed faxes, you know how impossible (or at least time-consuming) it would be to try to complete a project like that by hand. Word's mail merge feature enables you to create a document once and use it many times, which cuts down on the time you spend creating and sending. Mail merge also enables you to use data you've saved elsewhere—in a mailing list database, an address list, or your Outlook Contacts list.

You might use mail merge to create and send projects like these:

- A direct mail campaign to your top 1,000 customers announcing a new service
- An e-mail press release announcing a new product release
- Mailing labels to affix to catalogs you send to new customers
- A form letter announcing a new rate increase
- An address listing of all the clients in your various databases

This chapter introduces you to the mail merge features in Word 2003 and shows you how to master the techniques for individual merge projects. You can capitalize on the work you've done by applying the "create it once, use it many times" techniques mail merge offers.

Getting an Overview of Mail Merge

Using Word's Mail Merge feature, you can create letters, faxes, e-mail messages, envelopes, labels, and directories once and use them many times. The merge process is basically the same for all document types. The Mail Merge Wizard will walk you through the following basic steps, regardless of the document type you're creating:

1. Select the document type you want to create. In this step, you tell Word whether you want to create a letter, e-mail message, envelope, labels, or directory.

2. Choose the document you want to start with. Here you select or create the file you want to use as the merge document.
3. Select the recipients. In this step, you choose your data list from an existing file, type data in the data source file, or select your Outlook Contacts list.
4. Write your letter (or e-mail message) and add the necessary merge fields.
5. Preview the merge operation and make any last minute changes.
6. Merge the document and the data source and print or send the results.

The next several sections explain more about each of these steps.

Know Your Merge Terms

The following terms might be new to you if you are learning about mail merge for the first time:

- **Main document** The letter, e-mail, envelope, or label into which the data will be merged.
- **Source file** Also known as the source list, the file from which the merge data is taken.
- **Merge fields** Identifiers inserted in the text that indicate to Word the position and type of data you want inserted at that point in the document.
- **Address block** Includes name and address information.
- **Greeting line** Adds the opening salutation, along with the name(s) of the recipient(s) you select.

Starting the Mail Merge Wizard

To start the mail merge process, you can begin with the document you want to use open on your screen, or you can create or open a document while you are using the wizard. To start the Mail Merge Wizard, chooseTools, Letters And Mailings, Mail Merge. The Mail Merge Wizard opens in the task pane on the right side of your Word window (shown in Figure 30-1).

Tip **Choose commands quickly from the Mail Merge toolbar**
It's a good idea to display the Mail Merge toolbar so that you have the option of using merge tools instead of following the Mail Merge Wizard. To display the toolbar, choose Tools, Letters And Mailings, Show Mail Merge Toolbar.

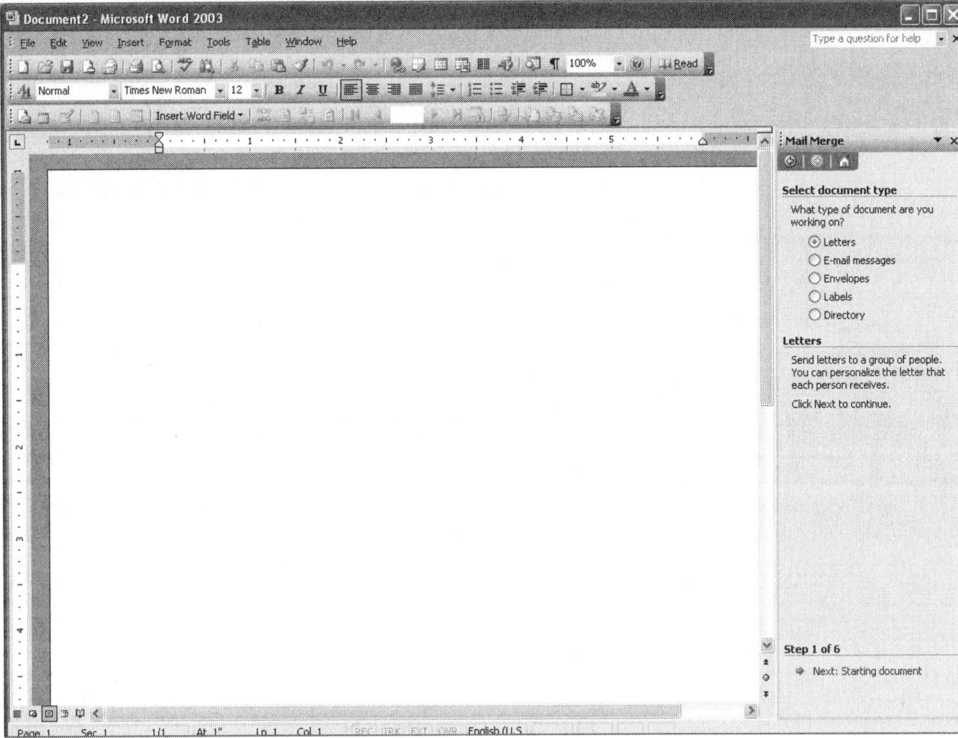

Figure 30-1. The Mail Merge Wizard leads you though a series of options to complete the merge operation.

Selecting the Document Type

Your first choice in the mail merge process involves selecting the type of document you want to create. Will you be sending a direct mail letter, an e-mail message, or a fax? Perhaps you want to start with envelopes and labels, or create a directory to store listings of data such as customer names and addresses, product info, and personnel contact data. Follow these steps to make your selection:

1. Choose Tools, Letters And Mailings, Mail Merge. The Mail Merge task pane appears along the right side of the work area.
2. In the Select Document Type section, choose the document you want to create for the merge operation.

Tip If the Mail Merge toolbar is displayed in your work area, you can click Main Document Setup to display the Main Document Type dialog box. You can then click the document type you want to use and click OK.

3 Once you've selected the type of document you want to create, click the Next link at the bottom of the task pane. The next step involves choosing the main document or form letter you want to use as the base document for the merge operation.

Note If you selected E-mail Messages as the document type for your merge, Word automatically changes the display to Web Layout view.

Starting Out with the Main Document

The main document is the document that holds the text that doesn't change—in other words, the boilerplate text that will appear on all the sales letters you send out or all your past due notices (or, for a happier example, all the birth announcements you send via e-mail). Word gives you a number of choices for the way in which you select your main document. You can do any of the following:

- Use the current document
- Start from a template
- Start from an existing document

Using the Current Document

If you elect to use the current document as the main document for your merge operation, you can simply type the text for the document as you want it to appear. You can omit the address information and the greeting at this point, becauseWord provides the means to do that automatically when you add the merge fields to your document. Figure 30-2 shows an example of a form letter used in a merge print.

One consideration, however: If you're creating an e-mail message you want to broadcast in a merge operation, remember that many graphic images or special text formats can create larger files and possibly require more time for downloading. For the convenience of your readers, consider going light on the graphical enhancements if you're creating an e-mail message.

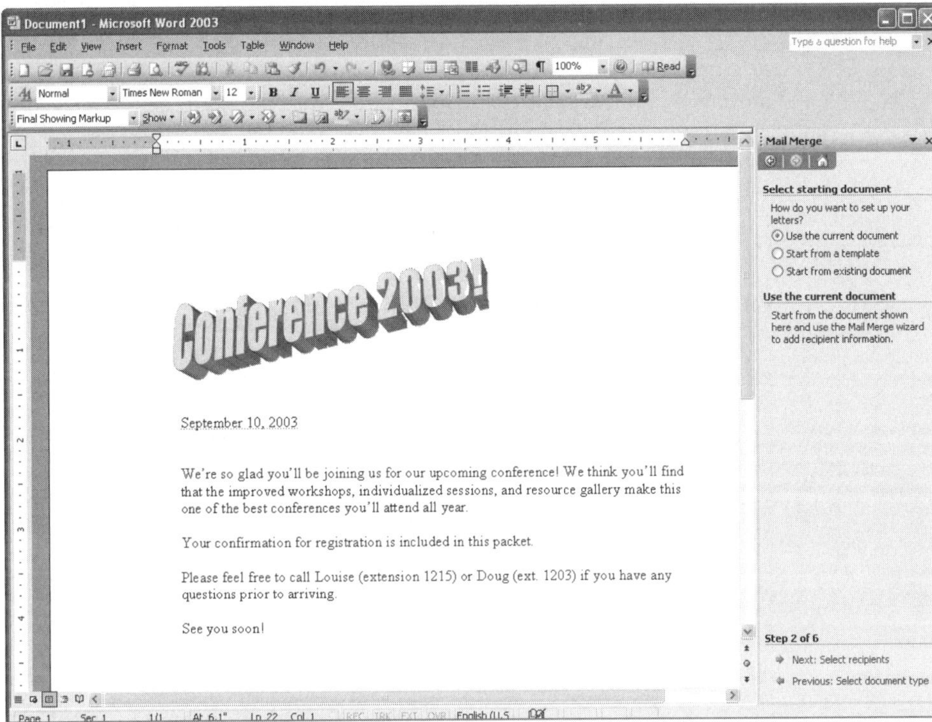

Figure 30-2. The main document stores the boilerplate text you'll use for the body of the message.

Working with the Letter Wizard

Creating a letter is a straightforward process in Word, but there might be those times when you'd like to have a little help. For this purpose, Word 2003 includes a Letter Wizard that enables you to choose the page design and letter style you want, in addition to choosing sender information and other details.

To start the Letter Wizard, choose Tools, Letters And Mailings, Letter Wizard. The Letter Wizard dialog box appears, where you can make choices about the design, style, and information you want to add. When you click OK, the letter is created, with the format and style you selected, in the current document window.

If you're using the letter with a merge operation, you can now begin the Mail Merge Wizard by choosing Tools, Letters And Mailings, Mail Merge.

Starting from a Template

If you don't want to work with the current document, you can choose a template instead. Word includes 10 mail merge templates you can start with and then modify to fit the document you want to send. To do this, perform the following steps:

1. Start by clicking Start From A Template in step 2 of the Mail Merge Wizard.
2. Click the Select Template link in the Start From A Template section to display the Mail Merge tab of the Select Template dialog box (shown in Figure 30-3).

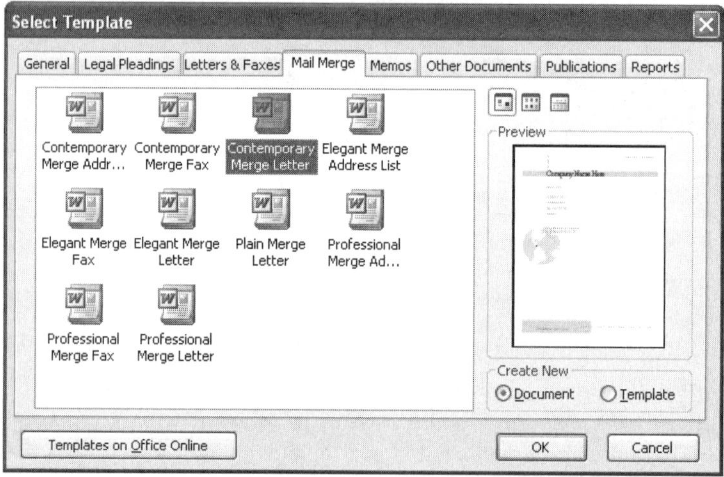

Figure 30-3. Word includes ten different templates you can use for mail merge operations.

3. You'll find a variety of templates for each of three document types—address list, fax, and letter.
4. Click the template you want, and then click OK. The template is displayed in the Word work area. You can then enter your text to personalize the list, fax, or letter for your purposes.

> **Tip** **Protect an open document**
> If you have a document open in the Word window, the program will prompt you that it will be replaced and any unsaved changes will be lost. If you want to leave that document open but also create a new merge document from a template, click New Document before starting the Mail Merge Wizard.

> **Tip** **Get more templates on Office Online**
> Word 2003 offers you a nearly instant way to get more templates for your mail merge work. When the Select Template dialog box is open, if you don't see a template you want to use, click Templates On Office Online. If you are currently connected to the Internet, you will be taken to the templates gallery of Microsoft Office Online, where you can view and download dozens of templates in more than 15 different categories.

Starting from an Existing Document

If you've used a letter in the past that was particularly effective, or if you want to save time by converting some of your marketing copy to an e-mail mailing, you can simply open that document and use it as the main document for your mailing. A main document can include text, images, borders, colors, shades, tables, and more—anything a traditional Word document can contain.

When you click Start From Existing Document in the Select Starting Document section in step 2 of the Mail Merge Wizard, a list appears in the Start From Existing section so that you can choose the merge file you want to use. To choose an existing merge file, click the file you want and click Open. Word loads the file into the work area.

> **Tip** **Use existing form letters**
> If you used a form letter in a past mail merge operation, you can always use it again, even if it was created in an earlier version of Word. Simply open the existing document before you start the Mail Merge Wizard and attach the data source as prompted. If you need to update any of the merge fields, you can delete, insert, or modify fields as needed as you go through the wizard steps.

> **Tip** **Save time by modifying existing text**
> If you want to send a simple merge document but don't want to invest the time in creating a document from scratch, you can open an existing merge document and simply modify it with your own text.

Choosing Your Recipients

When you get to the task pane view in which you choose the recipients for your merge operations, it's time to select your data list, which was referred to as the data source in previous Word versions. You can use an existing list, choose Outlook Contacts, or type a new list.

Using an Existing Data Source

Open Data Source

To select a list you've already created, click the Browse link in the Use An Existing List section of the Mail Merge Wizard. If you're using the Mail Merge toolbar, click the Open Data Source button. The Select Data Source dialog box appears so that you can choose a data list you've already created. Navigate to the folder containing the file you want, and then click Open. (If the file includes more than one data table, the Select Table dialog box will appear so that you can choose the one you want.) The Mail Merge Recipients dialog box appears, as shown in Figure 30-4.

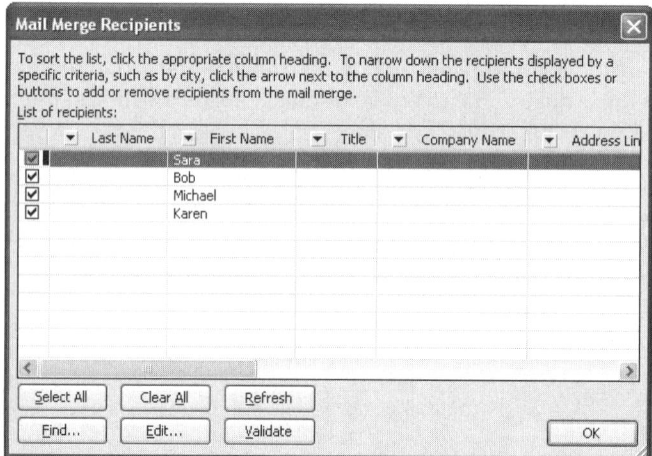

Figure 30-4. You can work with and modify the data in your data source in the Mail Merge Wizard.

If you don't want to change the recipient information in any way—in other words, you want to use the entire list just as it is—simply click OK to close the Mail Merge Recipients dialog box and continue using the Mail Merge Wizard.

Tip **Check data again later**

If you decide to pass up your opportunity to change the data in your recipient list now, don't worry—before you complete the merge operation you'll have a chance to preview and modify the recipients you've selected.

Choosing and Sorting Recipient Information

You use the Mail Merge Recipients dialog box to choose, sort, and edit the information in your data source file. If you plan to make changes, such as updating the address of a particular client, changing a company name, or deleting a customer you no longer work with, you can use the commands in this dialog box to carry out those tasks. Table 30-1 lists the various ways you can work with merge data.

Table 30-1. **Working with Merge Data**

Action	Result
Clear the check mark in the first column to deselect the recipient row.	Removes a recipient from the merge operation.
Select the check box in the first column.	Adds a recipient to the merge operation.
Click the arrow in the heading of the column by which you want to sort (for example, Last Name or City).	Reorders recipient records based on a particular field (if the listing was A to Z, clicking the heading will arrange the list Z to A).
Click an existing entry and click Edit. When the address list dialog box appears, click New Entry and enter the new recipient data. Click Close to close the dialog box.	Adds a new recipient to the list.
Click the Find button and type in the Find What box the data you want to locate. Click Find First to search for the recipient.	Finds a specific recipient (the first recipient record with the found data is highlighted in the Mail Merge Recipients dialog box).
Click the Select All button.	Selects all recipients (check marks appear in the left column in the dialog box).
Click the Clear All button.	Deselects all recipients (removes the check marks in the left column in the dialog box).
Click the Refresh button.	Updates the data displayed in the Mail Merge Recipient dialog box.
Click the Validate button.	Checks the data validity for your address data if you have a validation program installed.

Editing Your Data List

Mail Merge Recipients

Once you've added the data list to the merge document, you can edit it at any time during the merge procedure by clicking the Edit Recipient List link in the Mail Merge Wizard or by clicking the Mail Merge Recipients button on the Mail Merge toolbar. You might want to edit your list, for example, by selecting or deselecting fields to include, sorting data records, changing data entries, or modifying the order of fields.

When you click the Edit Recipient List link, the Mail Merge Recipients dialog box appears. Make any needed changes here and click OK to return to the wizard. Your changes are automatically saved.

Choosing Outlook Contacts

Perhaps the most seamless way of integrating up-to-date contact information with your main document for mailings and e-mail broadcasts is to use your contact manager, Outlook.

Since Outlook's contacts are kept up-to-date as you work, with smart tags that enable you to insert and update contact data on the fly, your Outlook contact information might be more current and complete than static data lists. E-mail addresses are added automatically from messages you receive and send, which means data is gathered for you while you go through your daily routine. Of course, the most complete data records—for example, client information that includes name, address, home and office phones, e-mail address, Web pages, and spouse names and birth dates—are available only because you entered them. This means that the degree to which Outlook can actually help you will depend on how consistently you've entered contact information.

To select your Outlook Contacts list, simply click Select From Outlook Contacts in the Select Recipients section of the Mail Merge task pane. Click the Choose Contacts Folder link, choose a profile name if prompted and click OK. The Select Contact List Folder dialog box appears, as shown in Figure 30-5. Select your Contacts list and click OK. The entries in your Contacts list appear in the Mail Merge Recipient dialog box.

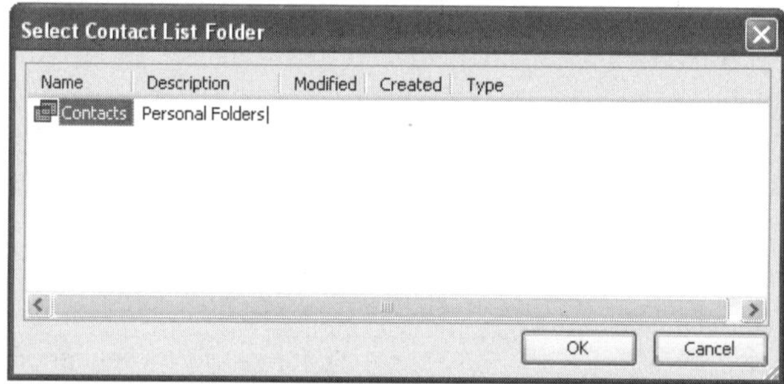

Figure 30-5. You can easily import your Outlook Contacts for use in your Word mail merge operations.

> **Tip** **Get more data by importing personal address books**
> Even if your Address Book in Outlook is incomplete, there is hope: Since you can create and load new address books in Outlook, you can work from others' data and use that information in your merge operations. If you have address book files saved in Microsoft Exchange Server, Outlook Express, Microsoft Internet Mail and News, Eudora Light and Pro, Netscape Mail and Messenger, or any other Messaging Application Programming Interface (MAPI)–compatible program, you can import them directly into Outlook and then use them in your Word merge operations.

Using an E-mail Distribution List as a Data Source

If you want to use a subset of your Outlook Contacts as the basis for your mail merge operation, you first need to export the selected data from Outlook in a way Word can recognize. This is a simple process. Here it is in a nutshell:

1. In Outlook, click Contacts.
2. Create a new folder for your distribution list (you can also do this with a selected subset of contacts that aren't part of a specific list) by choosing File, New, Folder. Name the folder (be sure the Contacts folder is selected) and click OK.
3. Copy the distribution list (or selected contacts) to the new folder by pressing and holding Ctrl while dragging the list (or contacts) to the new folder.
4. Select the new folder, choose File, Import And Export, and choose Outlook if more than one choice is available.
5. When the Import And Export Wizard dialog box appears, choose Export To A File and then click Next.
6. Choose the type of file you want to create and then click Next (typically, Access and Excel files are convenient for data lists and are saved in a form that can easily be used with other Office applications). If you are prompted to install the Translator, click Yes.
7. Choose the folder to export from, and then click Next.
8. Click Browse to choose the name and location for the destination file. You might want to store the exported file in your My Data Sources folder so the files will appear by default when you are ready to select the source file for your merge procedure. Click OK, Next, and then click Finish.
9. Back in Word, click the Select A Different List link and choose your new file from the list in the Select Data Sources dialog box.
10. Click Open to bring the contacts into Word for your mail merge project.

Creating Your Own New Data Source

Word gives you the option of entering your own data as part of the Mail Merge Wizard, if you're so inclined. When you're choosing the recipients for your document in the Mail Merge Wizard, click Type A New List in the Select Recipients section.

Note Any data you create in the New Address List will be saved in its own .mdb (mailing database) file, which means that you can use it with other mailings as well.

Click the Create link to display the New Address List dialog box (shown in Figure 30-6). You can now enter the information for the person or company you are adding.

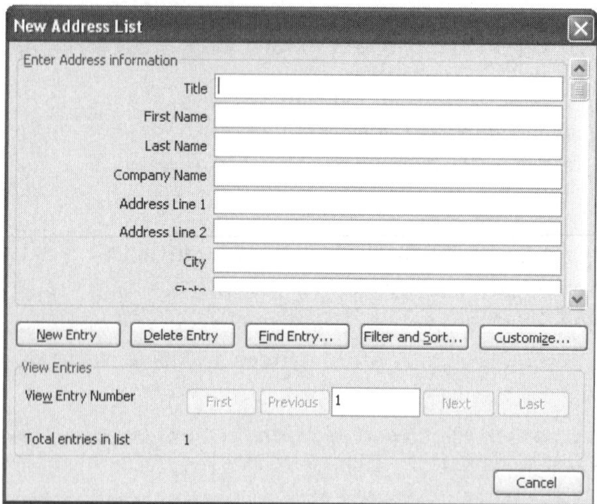

Figure 30-6. You can easily add your own data as you prepare your files for merging.

To add recipient information to the data source file, simply click in the field you want and type the information. Press Tab to move to the next item or scroll down through the list as needed. When you've finished entering information for that entry, click New Entry to display another blank form or, if you're completely finished, click Close to close the dialog box.

Customizing Address List Items

If you want to change the items listed in the New Address List dialog box, click Customize. The Customize Address List dialog box appears. You can make the following changes to the Field Names list:

- To add a field name, click Add. The Add Field dialog box appears. Type the name for the field you want to create and click OK.
- To delete a field and all the field information, select the field, click Delete, and then click Yes in the confirmation message box.
- To rename a field, select it and click Rename. Then enter a new name for the field and click OK.
- To move a field, select it and click either Move Up or Move Down to change its position in the list.

When you're finished making modifications to the field list, click OK to return to the New Address List dialog box. Add or edit your data as needed, then click Close to return to the wizard.

When you click Close, the Save Address List dialog box appears, with My Data Sources selected as the current folder, as shown in Figure 30-7. Enter a name for the file, and then click Save. The information is now displayed in the Mail Merge Recipients list, where you can sort, rearrange, and select or deselect recipients. Make any necessary selections, and click OK to close the dialog box and return to the wizard.

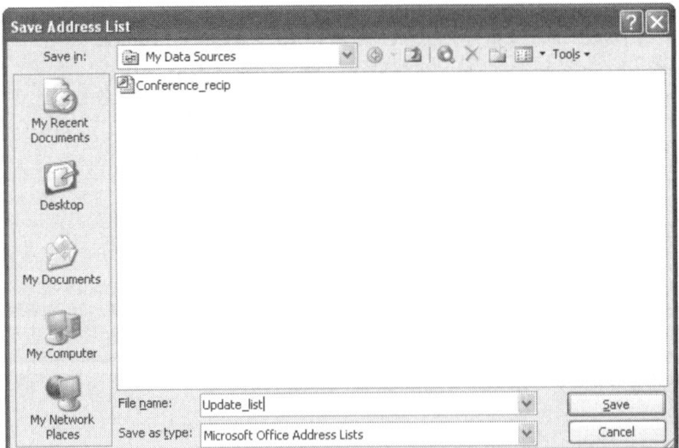

Figure 30-7. Microsoft Office Address List files are stored by default in the My Data Sources folder, where they can be accessed by all Office applications.

Adding Merge Fields

So now you've selected the document you want to use and you've identified the people to whom you want to send it. The next step involves adding the placeholders in the document where the data will be inserted for the individual recipients. When you click Next and the Mail Merge Wizard displays the page on which you create the letter for your merge operation, you see the following merge fields that can be inserted in your document:

- **Address Block** Displays the Insert Address Block dialog box so that you can add the name, street address, city, state, and postal code at the insertion point.
- **Greeting Line** Displays the Greeting Line dialog box, allowing you to select the salutation you want to use as well as the format for the recipient name.
- **Electronic Postage** Enables you to work with electronic postage if you've installed that feature.
- **Postal Bar Code** Displays the Insert Postal Bar Code dialog box so that you can choose the field after which you'd like to display the postal bar code.
- **More Items** Displays the Insert Merge Field dialog box, giving you the option of adding more fields to your main document.

Inserting an Address Block

The Address Block includes the collection of data you're likely to use most often. The block includes the recipient name, street address, city, state, and postal code. You can also include the company name and the country and region in the address if you choose. To add the Address Block to your main document, follow these steps:

1 Place the insertion point where you want to insert the Address Block.

Insert Address Block

2 In step 4 of the Mail Merge Wizard, click the Address Block link, or click the Insert Address Block button on the Mail Merge toolbar. The Insert Address Block dialog box appears, as shown in Figure 30-8.

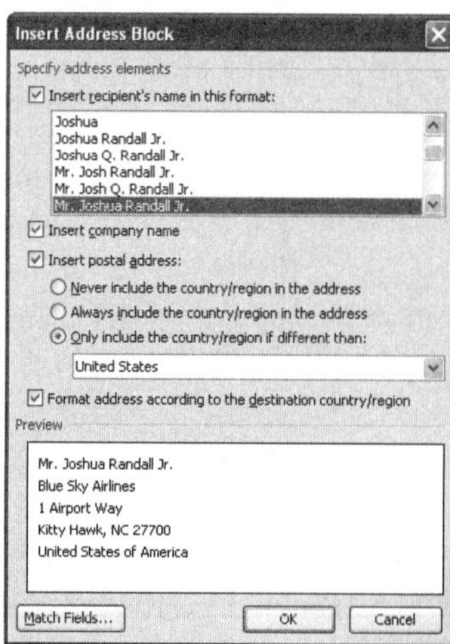

Figure 30-8. Specify the address format you want to use in the Insert Address Block dialog box.

3 Scroll through the Insert Recipient's Name In This Format list to choose the format you want to use for the recipient name; select the style you want to use.

4 If you want to omit the company name from the Address Block, clear the Insert Company Name check box.

5 To hide the postal information in the Address Block, clear the Insert Postal Address check box. The Preview section shows your current selections.

6 Click OK to close the dialog box. Word inserts the following code at the insertion point:

```
«AddressBlock»
```

Check for Errors

Tip Check for errors in your merge

You'll get a chance to preview your document with the data included before you do the actual merge. You can also use the Check for Errors button on the Mail Merge toolbar to do a test run before you execute the merge operation.

Tip Let Word format the address for you

A new address-formatting feature in Word 2003 takes some of the uncertainty out of sending international mail. How do they format postal codes in Denmark? On which line should you put the primary and secondary addresses? When you use the Insert Address Block feature in Word's mail merge process, be sure to click the check box Format Address According To The Destination Country/Region to let Word take care of those and other details for you.

Choosing a Greeting Line

The Greeting Line merge field enables you to say hello in the language and format you want. To add a Greeting Line, follow these steps:

1 Place the insertion point in the document where you want to add a Greeting Line.

2 Click the Greeting Line link in the Write Your Letter section of step 4 in the Mail Merge Wizard, or click the Insert Greeting Line button on the Mail Merge toolbar. The Greeting Line dialog box appears, as shown in Figure 30-9.

Insert Greeting Line

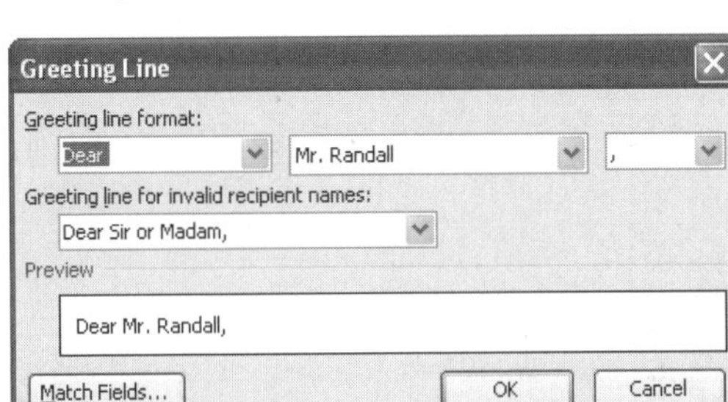

Figure 30-9. Choose the salutation and name format for your greeting in the Greeting Line dialog box.

3 For those recipients that show an empty or invalid name entry, you have the option of adding a generic phrase. Choose either Dear Sir Or Madam or To Whom It May Concern.

4 Click OK to close the dialog box and insert the Greeting Line. Word inserts the following code at the insertion point:

```
«GreetingLine»
```

Tip **Add a postal bar code**

If you're printing envelopes or labels on which you want a postal bar code to appear, click the Postal Bar Code link in step 4 of the Mail Merge Wizard. When the Insert Postal Bar Code dialog box appears, click the Merge Field With ZIP Code arrow and choose the field to which the postal code should refer.

Next, click the Merge Field With Street Address arrow to display the list of choices for the delivery address you want the postal code to reflect. Click your choice and click OK.

Inserting Merge Fields

Word offers a number of preset merge fields you can insert by pointing and clicking. You can further personalize your main document by adding address or database fields. To display the additional merge fields you can use in your document, click the More Items link in step 4 of the Mail Merge Wizard. The Insert Merge Field dialog box appears, as shown in Figure 30-10.

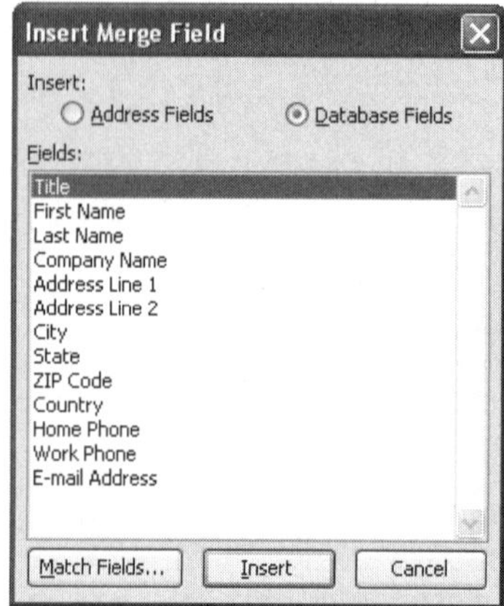

Figure 30-10. The Insert Merge Field dialog box enables you to choose either Address Fields or Database Fields.

If you want to use fields available in your Address Book, click the Address Fields option. You'll see quite a list of offerings, from basic contact info to spouse's name to nickname. When you click the Database Fields option, you'll see traditional database fields, including Title, First Name, Last Name, Company Name, Address Line 1, Address Line 2, City, State, ZIP Code, Country, Home Phone, Work Phone, and E-mail Address.

To insert one of Word's additional merge fields, follow these steps:

1. Place the insertion point where you want to add the field.
2. Click the More Items link in step 4 of the Mail Merge Wizard to display the Insert Merge Field dialog box, or click Insert Merge Fields on the Mail Merge toolbar.

3. Click Address Fields or Database Fields.
4. Click the field you want to add and click Insert.
5. When you're finished, click Close to return to your main document.

Figure 30-11 shows a form letter after two database fields, <<First_Name>> and <<Email_Address>>, have been added. When you're ready to preview your document with the merge data intact, click Next to proceed to the next wizard step.

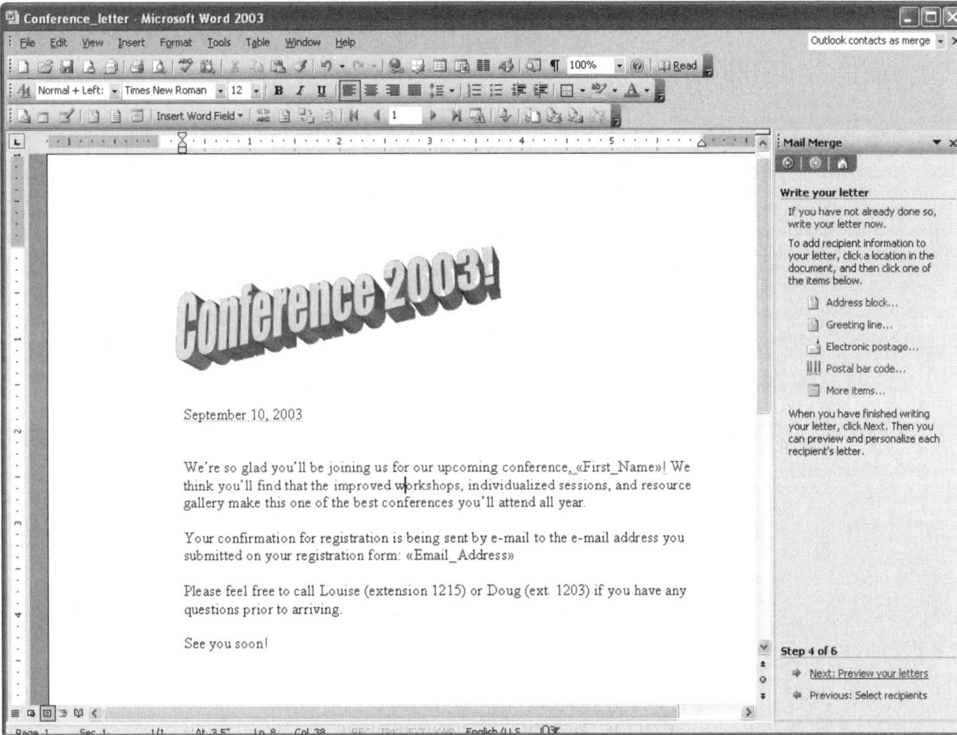

Figure 30-11. You can add database and address fields in the body of your document as needed.

> **Tip** **Display paragraph marks for accurate spacing**
>
> When you're adding merge fields to your document, turn on paragraph marks by clicking Show/Hide on the Standard toolbar. Displaying paragraph marks shows all paragraph marks, spaces, and tab characters so that you can better control the placement of merge fields in your document.

Matching Fields with Your Database

Word enables you to use data you've entered and organized in other programs—such as Access, Excel, other database programs, or compatible e-mail utilities—to serve as the source for your mail merge. If the fields you've created in your database don't match the fields in the address list, don't worry—you can use Word's Match Fields tool to equate the fields so data flows into the right place automatically.

You can display the Match Fields dialog box in several different ways:

Match Fields

- Click the Match Fields button on the Mail Merge toolbar.
- Click the Match Fields button in the Insert Address Block dialog box.
- Click the Match Fields button in the Greeting Line dialog box.

Tell Word how to match fields by clicking the arrow of the field you want to match. For example, if in your database file you have all addresses listed as Address Line 2, but in your Address List in the merge procedure you want it to be shown as Address Line 1, you can click the Address Line 1 arrow (shown in Figure 30-12) and select Address Line 2. When you select Address Line 2, Word places in Address Line 1 any data it finds tagged for Address Line 2. After you make your matches, click OK to close the dialog box and return to the document.

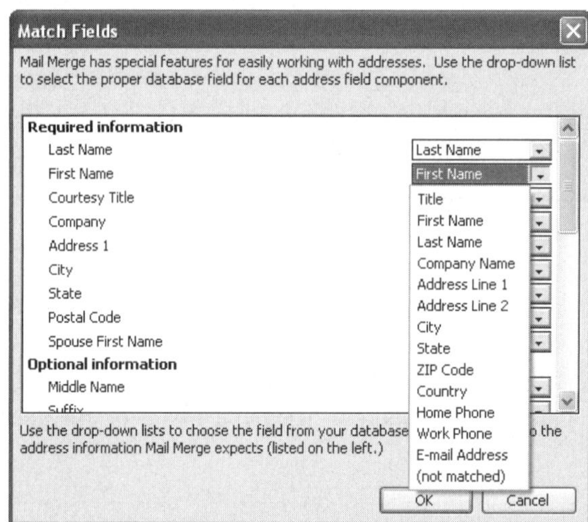

Figure 30-12. Use the Match Fields dialog box to tell Word how to correctly import the data you've created in other programs.

Adding Word Fields

Along with the merge fields you are given in the Mail Merge Wizard, you have another set of fields at your disposal. Word fields enable you to personalize your document, message, or form even further. You might want to add a Word field, for example, that skips a record based on the data in a particular field.

To add a Word field to your main document, follow these steps:

1. Place the insertion point in your document where you want to add the field.

Insert Word Field ▾

Insert Word Field

2. Click the Insert Word Field button on the Mail Merge toolbar. A menu appears, listing the Word field choices. Click your choice, and Word prompts you to add additional information. Table 30-2 gives you an overview of the Word fields available in mail merge operations.

Table 30-2. Word Fields for Mail Merge

Field	Description	Options
Ask	Adds a customized dialog box that asks for more information during a merge	You can use a predefined bookmark or add a new one to mark the placement of the Ask field.
Fill-In	Prompts user for additional information	You can choose to have Word ask for information with each merged record or only once, at the beginning of the process.
If...Then...Else	Creates conditional text segments that insert one phrase in one situation and another phrase in another	You can control the fields you want to compare as well as the qualifier (Equal To, Not Equal To, Less Than, Greater Than, Less Than Or Equal, Greater Than Or Equal, Is Blank, Is Not Blank).
Merge Record #	Adds the number of the current record to the merged document	Place the insertion point where you want the number to appear; no dialog box is displayed.
Merge Sequence #	Inserts numbering for all documents in the merge	Place the insertion point where you want the number to appear; no dialog box is displayed.
Next Record	Includes data from the next record in the current record	You can include several records at once; however, to list many records, create a directory.
Next Record If	Includes data from the next record if a certain condition is met	You can include record data if a field contains a value you seek.
Set Bookmark	Adds a bookmark and attached text in every merged document	You can use existing bookmarks or add new ones to accommodate the merge.
Skip Record If	Omits records depending on a specific condition	You can choose the fields to compare and the qualifier (Equal To, Not Equal To, Less Than, Greater Than, Less Than Or Equal, Greater Than Or Equal, Is Blank, Is Not Blank).

Previewing the Merge

The next step in the merge process involves reviewing the data merged into your document. The first document is displayed by default with your first recipient's data in the Word window (shown in Figure 30-13). You can page through the recipients by clicking the previous (<<) or next (>>) button in the wizard task pane.

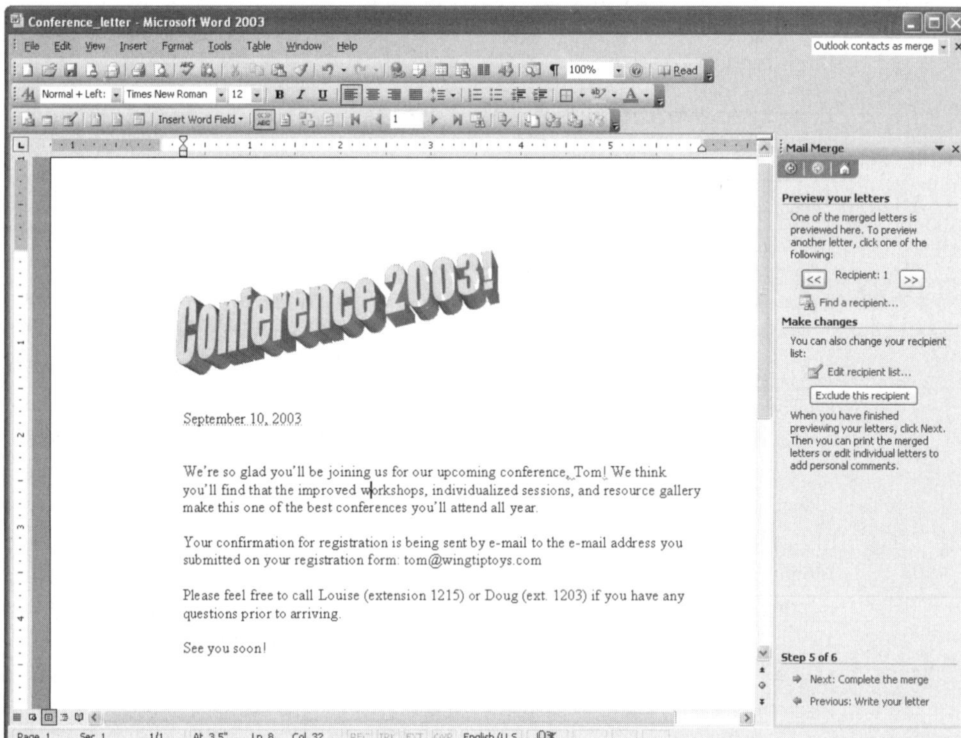

Figure 30-13. The merge data is shown automatically in your main document during Preview.

Finding a Specific Entry

Find Entry

If you want to locate a particular recipient in your list, click the Find A Recipient link in step 5 of the Mail Merge Wizard or click Find Entry on the Mail Merge toolbar. The Find Entry dialog box appears so that you can type in the Find box the data you'd like to locate. Specify the field you want to search, if necessary, and then click Find Next. Word locates the text you indicated in the merge document.

Excluding a Recipient

If you want to remove a recipient from the current merge operation, you can click Exclude This Recipient in the Make Changes section of the task pane. The entry is removed and the next recipient in the list is displayed.

If you change your mind and want to include the recipient after all, click the Edit Recipient List link to display the Mail Merge Recipients dialog box. Scroll to the recipient record you want to display, and select the check box in the left column. Click OK to close the dialog box. The recipient will be included in the merge.

> **Tip** Test before you print
> Before you go too far in designing your letter, print a sample to make sure it fits on your company stationery, particularly if you have a specialty logo or an unusual address line at the bottom of the page. Test your printout to make sure everything fits before you start the merge operation.

Checking for Errors

If you're preparing a merge operation with hundreds or thousands of records, it's an especially good idea to run a test before you perform the actual merge. Word gives you an easy way to run a quick check for errors. Simply click the Check For Errors button on the Mail Merge toolbar to display the Checking And Reporting Errors dialog box (shown in Figure 30-14). You have three choices for the way in which you test your merge: you can simulate the merge and save the errors in a new document; you can go ahead and run the merge operations, but have Word stop and alert you when an error is found; or you can complete the merge without pausing for errors and have Word report the errors in a new document.

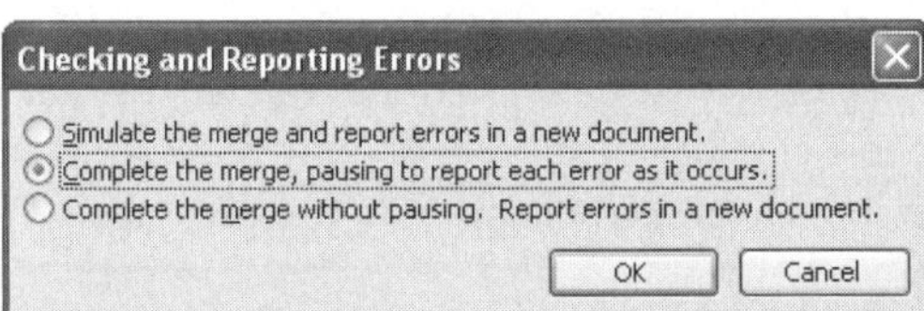

Figure 30-14. Select an error-checking method in the Checking And Reporting Errors dialog box.

The difference between these options is that one runs a "practice test" that reports on errors it finds but does not make changes in the document. The second option, the default, performs the merge but alerts you immediately whenever an error is found. If this is the first time you've used Word's mail merge utility, it's a good idea to test it out using the simulation until you feel comfortable proceeding with the real thing. The third option enables you to go ahead and print, but collects any errors in a separate document so that you can review them after the merge is complete.

Merging the Documents

The final step in the mail merge process involves printing, sending, or saving your document with the data intact. The actual merge is a bit anticlimactic. To finalize the merge, you simply click the Next button in the wizard or click the appropriate button on the Mail Merge toolbar, depending on whether you're merging to a new document, the printer, e-mail, or fax.

Choosing Merge Print Options

Merge To Printer

To prepare your merge documents for printing, click Print in step 6 of the Mail Merge Wizard or click Merge To Printer on the Mail Merge toolbar. The Merge To Printer dialog box appears, and you can choose from the following options:

- **All** Prints all records in the current document.
- **Current Record** Prints only the displayed record.
- **From And To** Enables you to set a page range—from record 2 to 5, for example—so that you can select only those records you want to print.

Troubleshooting

Fields are printed in my mail merge document instead of values

You went through all the steps in the Mail Merge Wizard, checked the merge for errors, and selected the merge process you wanted. Everything looked fine. But when you printed the merged documents, you see the merge field names instead of the values in the document. What's going on?

It might be that the Field Codes check box has been selected in your Word options, which causes fields to be displayed by default rather than the values they store. To check this option and change it if necessary, choose Tools, Options. When the Options dialog box appears, click the Print tab. Clear the Field Codes check box in the Include With Document section, and then click OK to close the dialog box and return to the document.

Merge to a New Document

If you're working with a letter document type, Word gives you the option of merging to a new document after the Mail Merge Wizard finishes so that you can further personalize the documents you've created.

Merge To New Document

To merge the information to a document, click the Edit Individual Letters link in step 6 of the wizard or click the Merge To Document button on the Mail Merge toolbar. The Merge To New Document dialog box opens, and you can choose whether you want to merge all records, the current record only, or a range of records you specify. Make your choices, and click OK to complete the merge.

Merge to E-mail

If you select the E-mail Message document type when you began the Mail Merge Wizard, the merge process involves putting the source data together with the main document in e-mail messages. After you preview the records and click Next, step 6 of the Mail Merge Wizard appears. Your only choice is Electronic Mail. When you click the link, the Merge To E-mail dialog box appears, as shown in Figure 30-15.

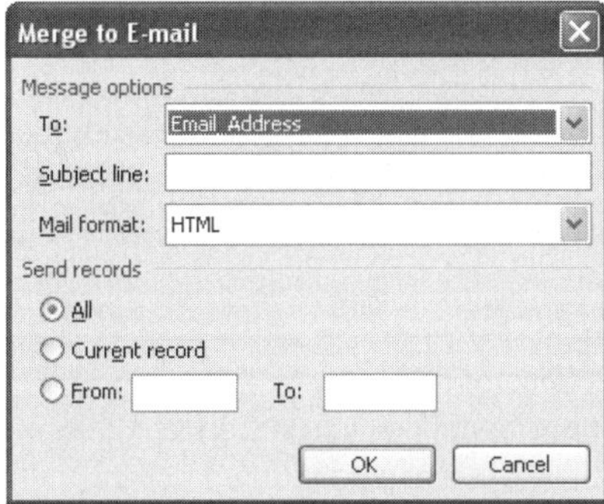

Figure 30-15. With Merge To E-mail, you combine source data with your main document and send the results to Outlook for delivery.

If you're creating your merge document by using the Mail Merge toolbar, you can click Merge To E-mail to begin the e-mail merge.

Your choices include the following:

- Click the To arrow to display the list of choices for the field containing the e-mail addresses to which you want to send the messages.
- Enter a Subject in the Subject Line box to tell recipients something about the incoming message.
- In the Mail Format list, select Attachment, Plain Text, or HTML to control the method by which you want to send the e-mail messages.
- In the Send Records section, choose the records you want to send. Your choices are All, Current Record, or From And To, which enables you to choose the range of recipients for your message.

Merge to Fax

You have one final option for where and how to merge your documents. If you have fax support set up on your system, you can use the Merge To Fax button on the Mail Merge toolbar to send faxes to groups of people. The Merge To Fax dialog box appears so that you can select the records to send (your choices are All, Current, and From And To). Click OK to send the faxes.

Reviewing the Merge

After Word merges your document, take the time to page through and make sure the results are what you expected. Two tools will help you see where your inserted fields appear in the main document: View Merged Data and Highlight Merge Fields.

Click the View Merged Data button on the Mail Merge toolbar to toggle the display between the field and values display. When you click View Merged Data the first time, Word displays the names in place of the merged data. When you click View Merged Data the second time, Word displays the data values inserted in the document.

Using the Highlight Merge Fields button, also on the Mail Merge toolbar, enables you to see at a glance where all the inserted fields are in your main document. When you click Highlight Merge Fields, all fields in the document appear highlighted. To suppress the highlight, click Highlight Merge Fields again.

Tip **Turn a merge document into a normal document**
If you want to change a form letter or merge document back into a standard Word document, simply display the document and then click the Main Document Setup button on the Mail Merge toolbar. When the submenu appears, click Normal Word Document, and then click OK. The document is then displayed as a normal document without the marked fields in place.

Creating a Directory

All the merge operations in this chapter thus far have covered ways you can take multiple data items and plug them into documents you can replicate easily. There will be times, however, when you will want a complete listing of the records in your source file. You might, for example, want to keep a listing of all the people you sent a catalog mailing to in fall 2003. To create a directory of records from your data source, you can use the Mail Merge Wizard. Here are the steps:

1. Start the wizard by choosing Tools, Letters And Mailings, Mail Merge. The wizard opens in the task pane.
2. In the Select Document Type section, click Directory. Click the Next link.
3. In the Select Starting Document section in step 2, choose whether you want to use the current document, select a template, or open an existing document for your directory. Click the Next link.
4. In the Select Recipients section in step 3, choose your data source by opening an existing file, using your Outlook Contacts list, or typing new source data. Again, click the Next link.
5. In the Arrange Your Directory section of step 4, click the fields you want to insert (most likely you'll want only Address Block). If you want to add additional fields, click the More Items link to display the Insert Merge Field dialog box and make your choices. Click the Next link.

6 In step 5, preview your document. Don't worry that only one record is shown in the document window to preview; you'll see an entire list when the merge is completed. Click the Next link.

7 In step 6, click the To New Document link in the Merge section. Click All and then OK in the Merge To New Document dialog box. The merge is completed and the directory is displayed in your document window. You can now save the directory file and use it for future merge operations.

Tip **Save time formatting by using templates**
Word includes several address list templates you can use as the basis for your directories. Unless you have a certain format you need to follow, you might as well benefit from the existing files already created. If you choose this option, click the Select Template link and choose one of the Address List templates in the Templates dialog box (or click Templates on Office Online to find more directory templates on the Office Online Web site).

Printing Envelopes and Labels

In some cases, you might want to print only a single envelope or an individual sheet of labels. In such a situation, working with the data source and inserting fields in a document isn't necessary—no merge is needed. When you want to print a simple envelope or set of labels, choose Tools, Letters And Mailings, Envelopes And Labels. The Envelopes And Labels dialog box appears, as shown in Figure 30-16.

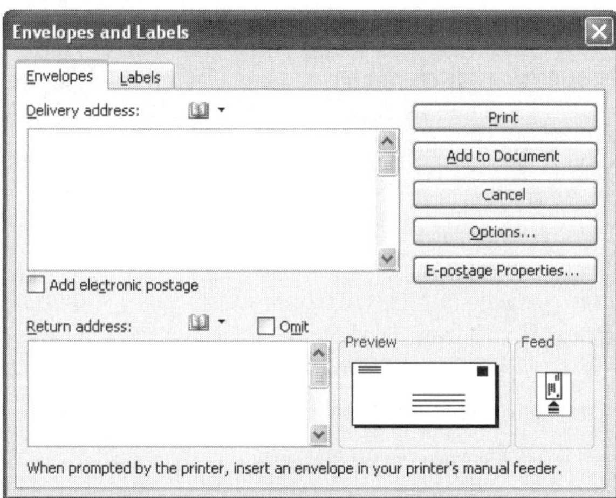

Figure 30-16. The Envelopes And Labels dialog box enables you to create and print individual envelopes and labels.

Note If you're working with an open document that has an Address Block inserted (or a default address you've entered yourself), the address will be shown automatically in the Envelopes And Labels dialog box.

The Envelopes tab includes a number of quick options you can set before printing an envelope. Here's an overview:

- **Print** Starts the print process, so make sure to set your other options and load the printer before clicking this button.
- **Add To Document** Adds the envelope to the current document so that the envelope and document can be printed together.
- **Cancel** Closes the Envelopes And Labels dialog box without saving settings.
- **Options** Displays the Envelope Options dialog box so that you can choose the envelope size and font specifications.
- **E-Postage Properties** Enables you to work with an e-postage account if you've previously set up an account on the Web.

To print an envelope, simply open the Envelopes And Labels dialog box and follow these steps:

1. If necessary, enter the recipient address in the Delivery Address box by typing it or by clicking the Insert Address button and selecting the recipient in the Select Name dialog box.
2. Enter the return address in the Return Address box by typing it or, again, you can click the Insert Address button and select the return address you want.
3. If you want to choose a non-standard size envelope or change the font used in the address blocks, click Options. The Envelope Options dialog box appears. Choose the envelope size and font you want to use and click OK.
4. If you've subscribed to an e-postage service and want to add electronic postage to the envelope, click E-Postage Properties to set postage options and select the Add Electronic Postage check box to enable the feature for the current envelope.
5. Make sure your printer is ready and the envelope is inserted as shown in the Feed section of the dialog box. If you want Word to save the created envelope with the document to be merged, click Add To Document.
6. Click Print. Word sends the information to the printer, and your envelope is printed as you specified.

Creating Labels

Instead of printing directly on envelopes, you might want to print mailing labels. Word makes it easy for you to print labels in a wide range of shapes and sizes. If you want to print single (or a few) labels and don't want to use mail merge to do it, you can use the Envelopes And Labels dialog box to print labels quickly. Here's how:

1. Choose Tools, Letters And Mailings, Envelopes And Labels. The Envelopes And Labels dialog box appears.
2. Click the Labels tab. The options here enable you to enter the label information, choose the way you want the label printed (a single label or a whole page of labels), and make selections about the label size and e-postage.
3. By default, Word prints a full page of labels. If you want to print only one, click the Single Label option in the Print section.
4. The selected label is shown in the Label section. If you want to select a different label, click Options to make a new choice.
5. When you have finished entering your choices, make sure your printer is loaded correctly and click Print. Word prints the labels as you selected.

Tip **Print many labels fast**

If you have a number of labels that you want to print quickly, it's best to use the Mail Merge Wizard to lead you through the steps for printing labels.

Troubleshooting

I can't feed envelopes from a loaded tray

If you've loaded envelopes in a paper tray and Word keeps prompting you to feed your envelopes to the printer manually, make sure that you've selected the correct paper feed choices. To check the settings, choose Tools, Letters And Mailings, Envelopes And Labels. Click the Envelopes tab, and click Options. In the Envelope Options dialog box, click the Printing Options tab and click the Feed From arrow. Choose the name of the tray in which you loaded the envelopes from the displayed list. Click OK to return to the Envelopes And Labels dialog box, and then click Print to print the envelope displayed.

Chapter 31

Working with Field Codes and Custom Forms

If you haven't used Word's data fields feature before now, Word 2003 gives you great reasons to give it a try. First, Microsoft Office Professional Edition 2003 and the stand-alone version of Word 2003 include full support for Extensible Markup Language (XML), which means that you can easily incorporate data from other documents and programs into your Word reports, letters, directories, and more. Second, Word developers now can create what are known as *smart documents*, which give users prompts, links, and resources as they work on common documents. By knowing how to insert, work with, and update field codes in your Word documents, you can take advantage of the new high-end features of Word 2003 that make your data management and processing tasks more efficient than ever.

The flexibility of Word 2003 gives you the means to create documents of all sorts—from simple letters to complex reports to documents that include indexes, footnotes and endnotes, diagrams, and more. But you aren't limited to creating documents that you simply print and distribute or post on the Web; you can use Word's field capabilities to insert variable information on the fly, or to give users the choice of entering certain data items automatically. You also can create forms that prompt users for information they enter, either by making field selections or typing the requested data.

In this chapter, you'll learn to use Word's tools to work with fields and create forms. Along the way, you'll discover what makes a fast, effective form, as well as find out how to make the most of Word's interactive data capabilities.

Why Use Fields and Forms in Word Documents?

A *field* is a kind of placeholder—a code inserted in your document that enables you to add variable data, launch another application, or ask for input from a user.

In its most basic sense, a field allows you to incorporate changeable data in your Word documents. For example, you might want to add information such as a product name, the number of pages in a document, or the current date. To do this, you insert field codes that tell Word to add text, graphics, page numbers, and other material to the document automatically. You can also use fields in your Word documents to do the following things:

- Calculate and display values in a document
- Add document information to headers and footers
- Prompt users to add more information during a mail merge operation
- Mark special items, such as table of content entries, index entries, and more

A *form* is a Word document that helps you capture the data you need for your applications. The only difference between a traditional document and a form is the addition of data fields that allow you to gather information. You'll learn how to create and work with forms later in this chapter.

Understanding Fields

A *field* lets Word know that there's additional information you want to include, or an action you want to perform, in a document. You add a field by choosing Insert, Field. The Field dialog box, shown in Figure 31-1, opens so that you can indicate the particular field and options you want to use.

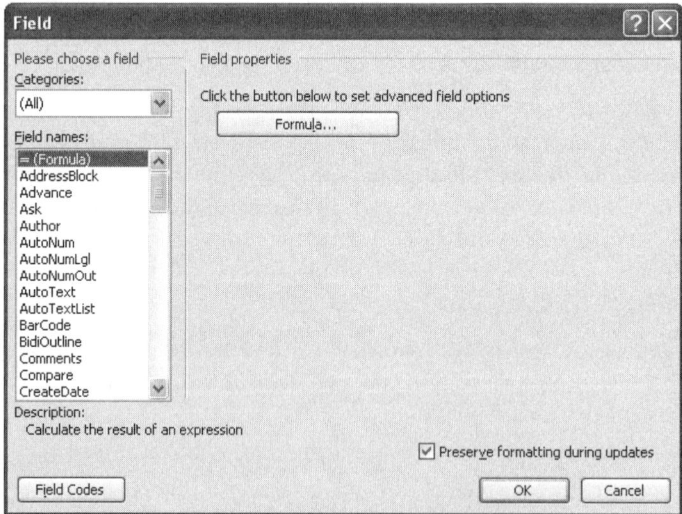

Figure 31-1. You insert a field by using the Field dialog box.

Field Anatomy

When you make the selections for a field, Word inserts a field code in the document at the insertion point. This is the code that tells Word what to insert or what action to call for when the user is working with the document. A field code like the following one includes four basic elements:

{ DATE \@ "dddd, MMMM dd, yyyy" * MERGEFORMAT }

- **Field identifiers** The curly braces { } are inserted when you create a field using the Field dialog box or press Ctrl+F9 to insert a field.
- **Field name** The name of the field—in this case, DATE—is the field you select or type between the braces.
- **Field instructions** The instructions—here shown as "dddd, MMMM dd, yyyy"—include any text you want to display as a prompt, a value or phrase, or a bookmark to be inserted.
- **Switches** A switch—shown in this example as MERGEFORMAT—is an option you set to specify the way in which you want the field to be displayed or formatted.

Field Functions

Fields have three basic functions in Word. You might use a field to perform a certain kind of action, to mark a specific item, or to display the results of a calculation.

- **Action fields** An action field asks for action from the user. Examples of action fields include the ASK field and the FILL-IN field, both of which prompt the user to enter more information.
- **Marker fields** A marker field marks an item for a specific purpose. For example, when you identify a word or phrase to be included in an index, Word inserts a field code to mark the index entry.
- **Result fields** A result field displays the results of a calculation or a file retrieval operation. One of the most common result fields you'll use is the FORMULA field; you'll also use DATE and TIME, as well as AUTOTEXT to display results in a field.

Fields You're Already Using

For some procedures, Word adds fields behind the scenes. When you create a table of contents, for example, Word adds {TOC} codes to your document. When you create an index, Word adds the index entry {XE} codes as field codes. Other examples of field codes that might already be in your documents include the following:

- If you've inserted a bookmark, a {BOOKMARK} field code is in your document.
- If you've used Insert, Date And Time to add the current date, a {DATE} code is in your document.
- If you've added a page number, {PAGE} is in your document.
- If you've added a hyperlink to a URL or another document, {HYPERLINK} is in your document.
- If you've added a footnote, {NOTEREF} is in your document.

Inserting Fields

When you want to insert a field into your document, start by choosing your location. You can add a field to the body of your document or you can insert a field in a header or footer. The process for adding a field is as follows:

1. Place the insertion point where you want to add the field.
2. Choose Insert, Field. The Field dialog box appears.
3. Click the Categories arrow and choose the category of field you want to add. Table 31-1 lists the various categories and provides a description of each.
4. Select any options you want to apply to the selected field, and click OK to add the field (see "Choosing Field Options" on page 869 for more information).

Note When you first add a field, Word displays the result of the field, not the actual field code, in the document. If you want to view the code itself, press Alt+F9.

Table 31-1. Field Categories

Field Category	Description	Field Codes
Date And Time	Fields for entering, editing, printing, and saving the current date and time. These fields cannot be modified by an end user.	CreateDate Date EditTime PrintDate SaveDate Time
Document Automation	Fields for comparing documents, moving to another section, starting a macro, or printing.	Compare DocVariable GoToButton If MacroButton Print
Document Information	Fields for inserting information automatically, including author name, document properties, file name, keywords, template, and the number of characters, pages, or words.	Author Comments DocProperty FileName FileSize Info Keywords LastSavedBy NumChars NumPages NumWords Subject Template Title
Equations And Formulas	Fields for adding formulas or entering an offset amount, scientific equation, or symbols.	=(Formula) Advance Eq Symbol
Index And Tables	Fields for entering index and table of contents entries. You can enter the codes from within the Field dialog box or allow Word to insert them automatically as you create the index or TOC.	Index RD TA TC TOA TOC XE

Table 31-1. Field Categories

Field Category	Description	Field Codes
Links And References	Fields for inserting text phrases and pictures and including links to various reference items, such as footnote references, literal quotes, pictures, bookmark text, and paragraphs.	AutoText AutoTextList Hyperlink IncludePicture IncludeText Link NoteRef PageRef Quote Ref StyleRef
Mail Merge	Fields for inserting merge fields, including address book data, greeting lines, database records, and more. You can also use ASK and FILL-IN fields to prompt users to enter information.	AddressBook Ask Compare Database Fill-In GreetingLine If MergeField MergeRec MergeSeq Next NextIf Set SkipIf
Numbering	Fields that insert automatic numbering of document pages and sections, as well as bar codes and list items.	AutoNum AutoNumLgl AutoNumOut BarCode ListNum Page RevNum Section SectionPages Seq
User Information	Fields that insert user information, including addresses, initials, and names.	UserAddress UserInitials UserName

Choosing Field Options

When you're working in the Field dialog box to enter field codes, you have a number of different options available to you, depending on what type of field you're adding. For example, when you insert an ASK field in your document, as shown in Figure 31-2, you need to provide the following additional information:

- The text prompt you want to use to prompt the user
- The bookmark name you want to use to mark the prompt

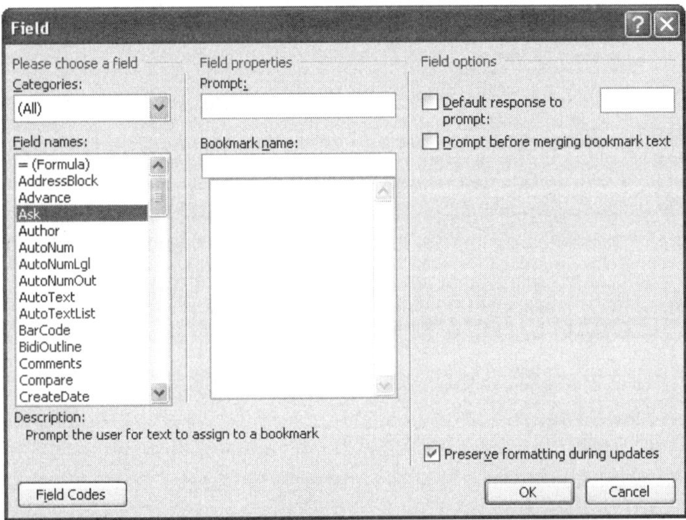

Figure 31-2. The Field dialog box provides field code options tailored to the field you select.

You can also add a default response to the prompt, if you want to provide one; in addition, you can have Word provide a prompt before the information is merged in a mail merge operation. Finally, the last choice in the Field dialog box asks whether you want to preserve the formatting of the field code when you update the field.

If you select another type of field, such as the FILESIZE field, another set of options is displayed, as shown in Figure 31-3. With the FILESIZE field, you can choose the following:

- The format of the number to be displayed
- The numeric format used
- Whether you want the file size to be displayed in kilobytes or megabytes

After you've made your field choices, click OK to close the Field dialog box. The field is placed in your document and the result will be displayed automatically.

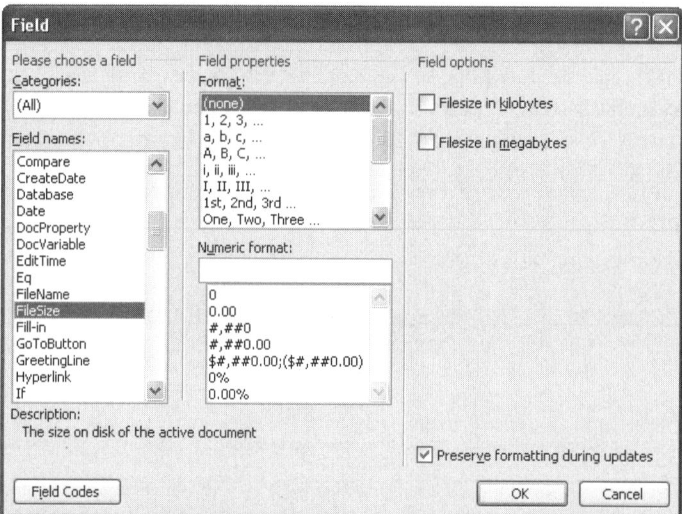

Figure 31-3. The Field dialog box gives different choices for a numeric field.

Typing Field Codes Directly

If you know the name of the field you want to insert, you can enter it directly into your document by placing the insertion point where you want to insert the field, pressing Ctrl+F9, and typing the field name. Word inserts the field code directly at the insertion point.

Tip **Use Ctrl+F9 to insert braces**

Although the curly braces surrounding the field code look like the regular braces you type from the keyboard, they're actually special characters Word inserts when you press the keyboard shortcut for entering a field. Instead of typing the braces, press Ctrl+F9 to add the braces.

In order to insert the complete field, you need to be able to type the field code name, any arguments you want to include, and the necessary switches.

Using Arguments in Field Codes

An *argument* is an additional piece of information that the field needs in order to complete the operation and display a result.You enter arguments in quotation marks. For example, if you're entering a code specifying the author of a document, you might enter

{ AUTHOR "Patricia Doyle" }

The argument in this case is "Patricia Doyle," and the field code is AUTHOR. If you're entering a one-word argument, you can type it without quotation marks, if you choose.

Entering Arguments in the Field Dialog Box

If you want to add arguments for the field code you're inserting by using the Field dialog box, follow these steps:

1. Place the insertion point where you want to add the field.
2. Choose Insert, Field. The Field dialog box appears.
3. Choose the field you want to add.
4. Specify any necessary field options in the Field dialog box.
5. Click the Field Codes button in the lower left corner of the dialog box. The Advanced Field Properties section of the Field dialog box appears, as shown in Figure 31-4.

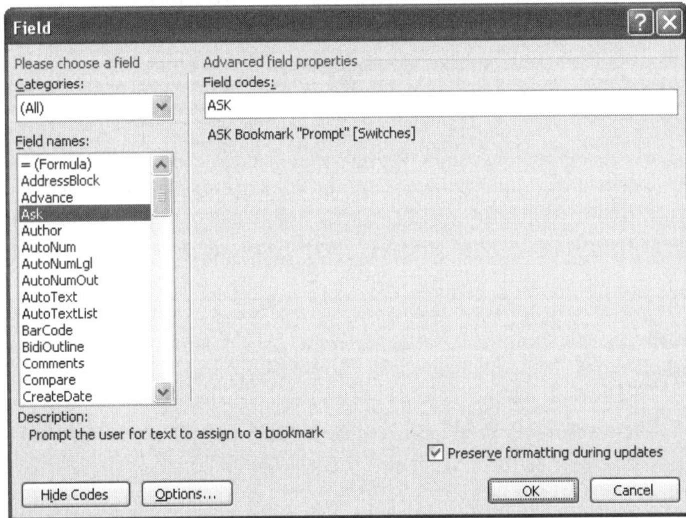

Figure 31-4. You can type field arguments in the Advanced Field Properties section of the Field dialog box.

6. If you want to add arguments to the field code you've selected, you can enter the text in the Advanced Field Properties area. (See the next section for additional information on how to specify switches for your field codes.)

Using Switches with Field Codes

Switches are special codes that change the way the field codes in your document act. There are two types of switches: general switches, which control the way the results of your field are formatted or displayed, and specific switches, which relate directly to the type of field you're using. Table 31-2 gives you an overview of the general switches you'll use with Word's field codes.

Table 31-2. Field Code Switches

Category	Identifier	Description	Example
Format	*	Changes the way field results are displayed	{AUTHOR * Lower}
Numeric Picture	\#	Specifies format settings for displaying a numeric result	{NUMPAGES \# "0"}
Date-Time Picture	\@	Specifies the formatting for the display of a date, time, or picture	{PRINTDATE \@ "MMMM d, yyyy"}
Lock Result	\!	Locks a BOOKMARK, INCLUDETEXT, or REF field, keeping it from being updated	{BOOKMARK C:\\Text\Myreport.doc \!}

Note The general switches shown in the preceding table will not work with the following fields: AUTONUM, AUTONUMGL, AUTONUMOUT, EMBED, FORMTEXT, TA, TC, XE, EQ, GOTOBUTTON, MACROBUTTON, RD, FORMCHECKBOX, FORMDROPDOWN, and LISTNUM. You'll be able to use field-specific switches with some of these fields, however.

Adding Switches

A field switch causes a specified action to be performed on a field result. For example, the * switch specifies a formatting action, and the \@ switch controls the display of a date, time, or picture entry.

If you're entering the switches by hand, you'll need to type the switches following the argument in the field code. If you're inserting the field using the Field dialog box, you can add the switches by following these steps:

1. Place the insertion point where you want to add the field.
2. Choose Insert, Field to display the Field dialog box.
3. Choose the field you want to add.
4. Make any necessary field choices in the Field dialog box.
5. Click the Field Codes button, and then click Options. The Field Options dialog box appears, as shown in Figure 31-5.

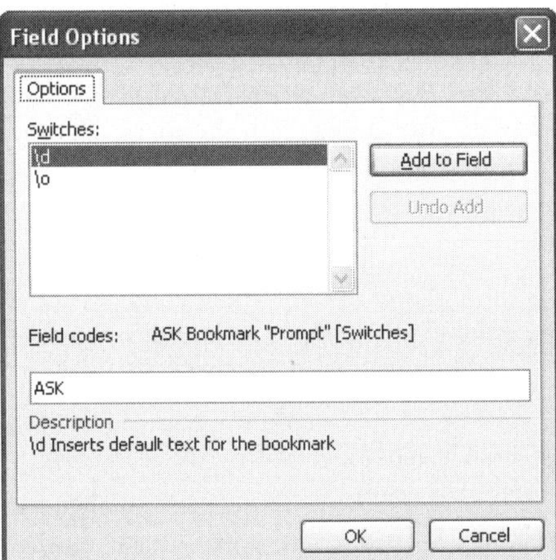

Figure 31-5. Add switches to your field in the Field Options dialog box.

6 Select the switch you want to use, and then click Add To Field.

7 Click OK to close the dialog box, and then click OK again to insert the field and return to the document.

> **Tip** Display specific switch functions
> The switches shown in the Field Options dialog box are field-specific switches; that is, they perform a unique action on the selected field. If you want to review the function of an individual switch, click the switch in the Field Options dialog box. The description of the switch's function appears in the Description section of the Field Options dialog box.

Viewing Codes and Fields

After you click OK in the Field dialog box to add a field, Word displays the field results in place of the field. This means that if you've inserted an AUTHOR field in your document, the name of the author will appear instead of the AUTHOR field code. If you've used the DATE field code to enter today's date, the date itself will appear instead of the code.

To switch between displaying field codes and field values, use one of these methods:

- To change the display of a single field, click in the field and press Shift+F9.
- To change the display of all fields in the document, press Alt+F9.

> **Tip** Change field code display
> If your field codes are displayed instead of the field values, choose Tools, Options to display the Options dialog box. If the Field Codes check box in the Show section, on the View tab is selected, the values will not be displayed. Clear the Field Codes check box to display values instead of codes, and click OK to close the dialog box.

Editing Fields

Once you've added a field to your document, you might want to make changes. To do this, simply right-click the field and click Edit Field on the shortcut menu, as shown in Figure 31-6. The Field dialog box appears, and you can make field changes as needed.

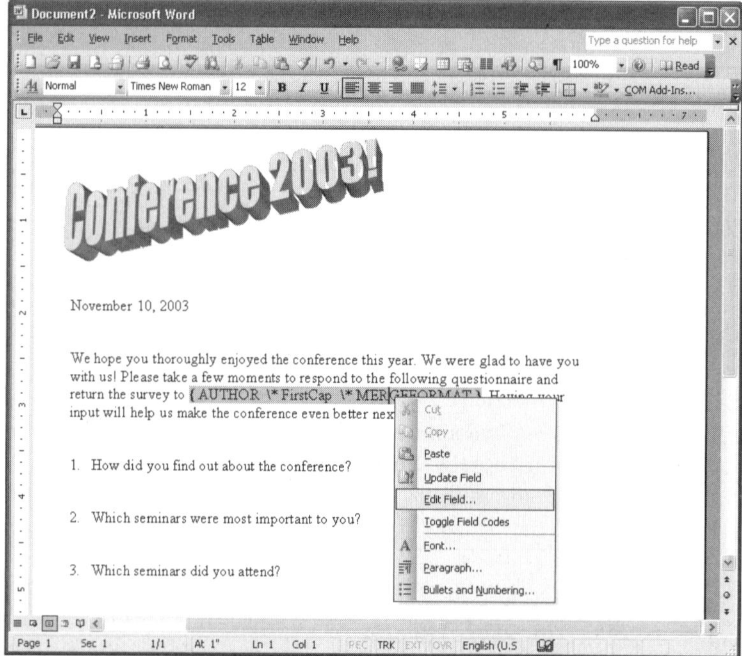

Figure 31-6. Right-click a field to display editing options.

> **Note** You can't make changes to a field in a form if the form is protected. If you need to make changes to a protected form, click the Protect Form button on the Forms toolbar to remove protection. For more information on creating and working with forms, see "Creating a Basic Form" on page 876.

Adding Field Shading

Field shading can help you show users where to enter their responses in a form you've created. If you want to make field entries stand out, you can add a background shade that calls a reader's eye to a field on your form. To add a shade to a field, follow these steps:

1 Open the document in which you've created your form and unprotect it, if necessary, by clicking Protect Form on the Forms toolbar.

2 Click Tools, Options. The Options dialog box appears.

3 Click the View tab. In the Show section, click the Field Shading arrow to display your choices, as shown in Figure 31-7. Choose Always, or When Selected.

Figure 31-7. You can have Word add shading to field entries to highlight data-entry fields for users.

4 Click OK to return to the document and have Word add the shading.

Note Field shading will appear only in those documents you use online or in electronic form. When you print the form, the shading will not appear.

Nesting Fields

You can create a *nested* field, which is a field within a field, to provide multiple levels of variable information. You can create a nested field by following these steps:

1 Create the first field by choosing Insert, Field, and then selecting the field options you want in the Field dialog box.

2 Click OK to close the Field dialog box and add the field to your document.

3 Press Alt+F9 to display field codes if necessary, and then place the insertion point inside the newly created field at the location you want to insert the second field code.

4 Choose Insert, Field to display the Field dialog box. Choose the second field and enter your field choices.

5 Click OK to create the nested field.

Updating Fields

If you make changes to fields as you work, either by changing the arguments or by modifying the data on which the fields are based, you need to have a way to update the fields to reflect these changes. To update the fields in your document, choose one of these methods:

- To update a single field, click in the field and press F9.
- To update multiple fields, select them by pressing Ctrl and clicking the fields, then press F9.
- To update all fields in the document, press Ctrl+A to select the entire document, then press F9.

Locking Fields

After all this work on the fields you've created, you don't want a coworker or user to be able to change the fields on the fly. You can lock a field to protect it. To do this, select the field and then press Ctrl+F11. This will keep the field from being modified. If you want to unlock a field, select it and then press Ctrl+Shift+F11. This returns the field to its normal, modifiable state.

If you want to protect an entire form, and not simply lock a field or two, you can use the Forms toolbar's Protect Form button to guard a form against further modification. For more information on protecting a form, see "Protecting Forms" on page 882.

Printing Field Codes

Before you print a document that includes field codes, make sure that you've performed an update to reflect all the latest changes. Here's how:

1. Choose Tools, Options and select the Print tab.
2. In the Printing Options section, select the Update Fields check box. When you click Print later, field codes will be updated automatically before the document is printed.

Note If you begin to print the document and find that one of the borders isn't printing, try changing your page margins to move the boundary inward.

Creating a Basic Form

Forms enable you to create interactive documents that call for more information from readers. You can create a fill-in-the-blanks form, with text boxes, check boxes, and drop-down lists. You can create tables for your forms and use all standard Word elements, such as borders, shading, columns, background designs, graphics, and more.

Word Forms vs. InfoPath—Which Is for You?

People use Word forms for all kinds of data collection needs. Whether you create an invoice, a data list, a travel log, or an expense listing, you can either save the form as a Word document and update it as needed or print the form and fill it in by hand. Either way, the Word form gives you a uniform way to collect the information you need.

Along with the introduction of the Microsoft Office System came a new program called Microsoft InfoPath. InfoPath is a sophisticated form-generation program that enables users to create custom forms that save data in XML format so that it can easily be added to a database, used in other applications, or shared with others without regard to the specific software they are using. InfoPath is intended for those users and businesses who rely heavily on form technologies to carry out their day-to-day work. If you use forms only occasionally (or generally print your forms, as opposed to saving them electronically), Word's form features are probably enough for your needs.

Planning the Form

A good form requires some thought. What types of information do you want to capture? How long or short should the form be? What types of questions will you ask? Your answers to these and other questions will give you what you need to build a form that does what you intend it to do. Consider these issues as you plan:

- **The shorter a form is, the better.** No one likes to be held captive by a long form with seemingly endless questions. Forms that ask too many questions—or that won't let you exit until you complete all the fields—can be a real turnoff for readers. Try to keep your form short, and limit the questions to those that ask about what you most need to know, in the order you need to know it.
- **Make it simple.** If you make your form easy for readers to understand and follow, with questions that are clear and to the point, you'll get better responses to your questions than if your form is complex and congested. Be concise and careful in your wording, and provide prompts and Help text where necessary, to explain to readers what you want them to do.
- **Order counts.** Readers will expect some kind of logical structure to your form. You might move from general questions to more specific questions, or you might follow a process. For example, if you're creating a customer response form that asks visitors to your Web site to evaluate their online shopping experience with your company, you might ask questions about their computer equipment and access, their ability to access your site, their experience using your site, how effective they feel your ordering system

is, how they feel about your sales security, and how they would like to be notified when their order is shipped.

- **Invite feedback.** Before you deploy your form for wide use, perform a few tests to see how effective it is. Ask coworkers or a few customers to use the form and evaluate it. You can then incorporate suggestions and make any necessary changes to improve the form.

Starting a Form with an Existing Document

If you have a document you've used for other things—perhaps a questionnaire or interview sheet you've previously printed and handed out—you can easily turn the document into an interactive form. To use an existing document, follow these basic steps:

1. Open the document you'd like to use as a form.
2. Delete any unnecessary information, and add text if needed.
3. Apply the styles and formats you want to use, complete with borders and shading as needed.
4. In the spots where you want users to add information, add spaces or placeholder characters (such as * or &).
5. Choose File, Save As, and save the form as a template (a .dot file).

> **Note** If you want to edit the form later, be sure to open the template and not the document. To make sure you're opening a template, choose File, Open, and in the Files Of Type field, select Document Templates.

Creating Your Own Form

You can create a form from a new Word document. You might want to use a table (as shown in Figure 31-8) to help provide the basic structure of the form—it'll make it easier for users to move from field to field by pressing Tab, and it helps provide an organized look for the document.

When you're creating your own form, you can add, modify, and enhance text and graphics just as you would a regular text document. For example, you might want to try the following things:

- Include your company logo in the form heading.
- Use styles to format headings and body text.
- Select a Table AutoFormat to apply a predesigned look to your form.
- Use the Draw Table button in the Tables And Borders toolbar to customize the way you draw lines for rows and columns.
- Add shading to highlight certain sections of your form.

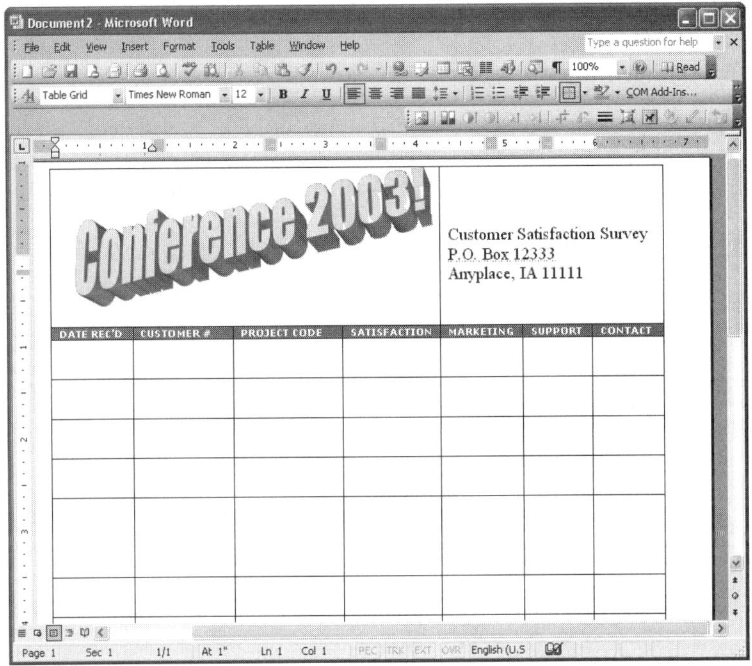

Figure 31-8. You can create a simple form quickly by using a Word table.

Tip **Save your form as a template**

After you design your form the way you want it, remember to save it as a template so you can use it to build the interactive features that will capture the data for you. To save the file as a template, choose File, Save As, and navigate to the folder in which you want to store the file. Click the Save As Type arrow, and choose Document Template (*.dot). Enter a name for the template in the File Name box and click Save.

Choosing a Form Template on the Web

Word also makes form templates available on the Web so that you can download existing forms and modify them to suit your needs. To find form templates online, follow these steps:

1. Establish your Internet connection.
2. Choose File, New. The New Document task pane appears.
3. Click the Templates On Office Online link. Your Web browser opens and displays the Microsoft Office Templates page, where you can find and download the templates you want to use.
4. In the Browse Templates section, click the links of the types of templates you'd like to see.
5. Scroll through the list of available templates and select a specific template to view it online.
6. When you find a template you like, click Download Now to download it to your computer. The template is displayed in Word 2003 and you are asked to express your opinion of it by clicking the number of stars in the task pane you want to assign to the template, as shown in Figure 31-9. (Your feedback helps to rate the template for other users.)

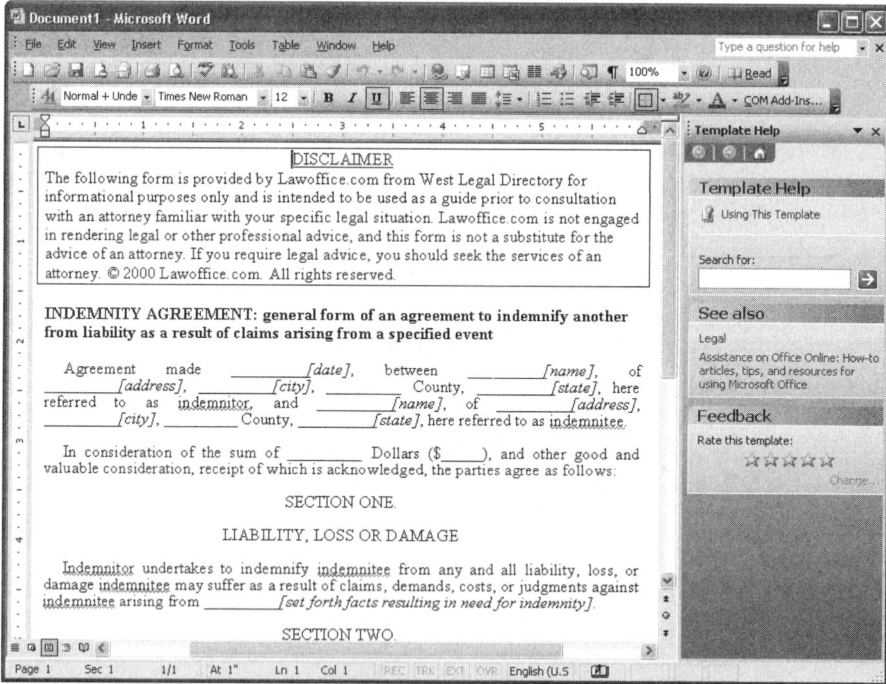

Figure 31-9. After you download a new template from Office Online, you can customize it to gather the data you want to capture.

7. Close your Web browser after you've finished downloading new form templates.

Working with the Forms Toolbar

You'll use the Forms toolbar to create and add form fields to your form. To display the toolbar, choose View, Toolbars, Forms. Table 31-3 describes the different functions of the Forms toolbar buttons.

Table 31-3. The Forms Toolbar

Button	Name	Description
	Text Form Field	Adds a text field at the insertion point so users can enter information
	Check Box Form Field	Inserts a check box field at the insertion point
	Drop-Down Form Field	Enables users to display a drop-down list of choices
	Form Field Options	Displays form field settings after a field has been added to the form
	Draw Table	Opens the Tables And Borders toolbar so that you can add tables and table elements to the form
	Insert Table	Lets you create a table with a selected number of rows and columns
	Insert Frame	Adds a floating frame on the form
	Form Field Shading	Works as a toggle to display and hide shading for text, check boxes, and drop-down fields
	Reset Form Fields	Resets form fields to their default settings
	Protect Form	Works as a toggle to protect and unprotect parts of the form or the entire form

Note Here's a quirk you might discover as you begin to create forms with Word: on the Forms toolbar, the name of a button may not seem to match the actual name of the tool you're using. For example, a combo box, which is the type of field that allows you to create a field that offers a combination of choices, is created with the Drop-Down Form Field button.

Form Terminology

If you're creating a form for the first time, you might see some terms that are new to you. Here's a quick introduction to form terms and phrases:

- *Control* is an item you use on the form, such as a text box, check box, scroll bar, or command button. The item is called a control because it enables you to control the form by making selections or adding information.
- *Form fields* store the data you enter. One form field, for example, might be CUSTOMER NAME, which enables you to enter each customer's name on the form.
- *Property* is a characteristic of an object, such as the color, size, location, or display of an item.

Protecting Forms

The Protect Form button is an important option on the Forms toolbar. Before you can see the form in the way the user will see it, you must protect the form.

Protect Forms

When you protect a form, you lock the fields in place so that no further changes can be made to field formats or specifications. Of course, you'll still be able to use the lists as intended, select check boxes, and enter text in text fields. To protect a form, click the Protect Form button; to unprotect a form, click the Protect Form button again. When a form is protected, the fields appear as the user will see them. When the form is unprotected, you see only the field name or the sample data you've entered for the field.

Password-Protecting the Form

You might want to assign a password to a form so that you can control when—and if—a form is unprotected. To protect a form in this way, follow these steps:

1. If necessary, unprotect the form by clicking the Protect Form button on the Forms toolbar.
2. Choose Tools, Options, and then click the Security tab, as shown in Figure 31-10. The top of the tab enables you to set two different kinds of passwords—one to open the document, and another to modify it.

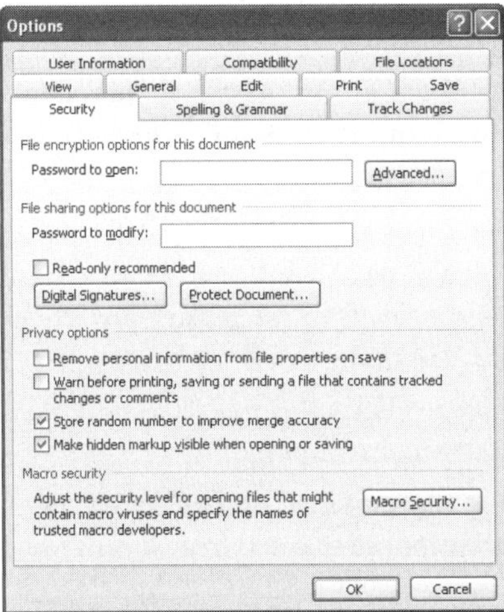

Figure 31-10. You can use the Security tab of the Options dialog box to assign a password to the form.

3. In the password box of your choice, type a password of up to 15 characters.
4. Click OK. Word displays a Confirm Password dialog box so that you can reenter the password you've chosen to verify that you've entered it correctly.
5. Type the password, and then click OK. The Word password protects the form.

Modifying a Password-Protected Form

If you want to modify a password-protected form at a later time, you can use your password to enable editing. When you open the file, a dialog box appears asking for your password. Type the password and click OK, and the form will appear as shown below.

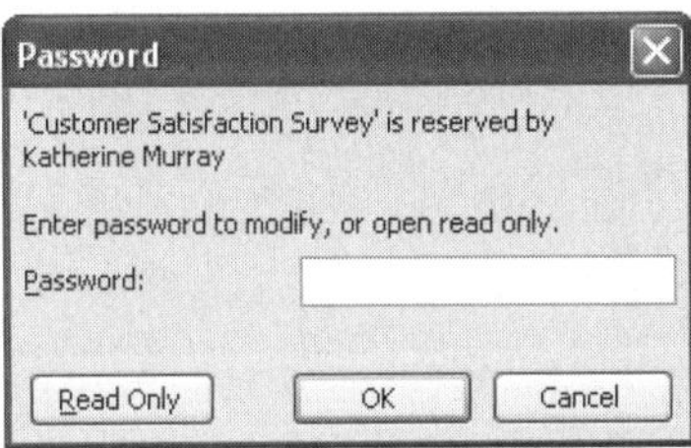

When you've finished making changes, save and close the file. Your changes will be saved and the form will be protected once again.

Entering Form Fields

Once you have the basic text and design for your form in place, you can add the features that make it truly interactive: the form fields. Word enables you to enter three different types of fields to your forms:

- **Text fields** Enable the user to type text, numbers, symbols, or perform calculations in text-entry boxes. Use this type of field when you're asking an open-ended question, when users are asked to provide comments or suggestions, or when you want to provide the flexibility for user-controlled input.
- **Check box fields** Enable the user to click a box to add a check mark. Use this type of field when users can select more than one response.
- **Drop-down fields** Provide a list of options for the user to review. This type of field is used when there can be only one response selected from a range of options.

The following sections go step by step through the process of adding each of these field types and choosing the options related to the type(s) you selected.

> **Note** The options for adding macros to the various form fields and customizing help to assist users in filling out forms are available in each of the Form Field Options dialog boxes for the various field types. For more information on working with macros and customized help in Word forms, see "Adding Help Messages to Forms" on page 890, and "Incorporating Form Macros" on page 892.

Viewing Fields

In the next section, you'll learn how to add fields to your form. Before you'll be able to see a field the way your users will see it, however, you need to protect the field. Simply click the field and then click the Protect Form button on the Forms toolbar. You'll then be able to see a field the way it will appear to users, as shown in Figure 31-11.

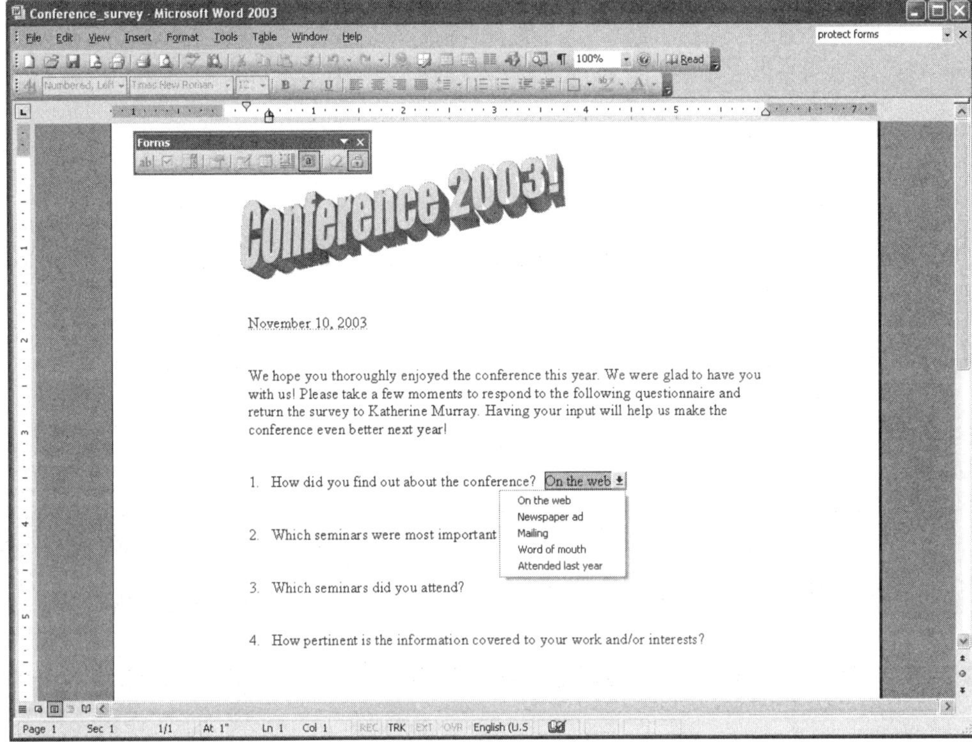

Figure 31-11. You can view a field you create by clicking the field and clicking the Protect Form button.

Inserting a Text Field

It is possible that the text field will be the type of field you use most often. A text field is a basic input tool—it records information you need that only the user can enter. For example, on a service request form, text fields would include the customer name, address, phone number, and e-mail address. Another text field would record any comments on the service to be performed.

To add a text field to your form, follow these steps:

ab|

Text Form Field

1. Place the insertion point where you want to add the text field.
2. Click the Text Form Field button on the Forms toolbar. Word inserts the field {FORMTEXT} in your document at the insertion point.

> **Note** The field codes that Word inserts automatically can't be modified; to change the settings for the inserted field type, use the Form Field Options button on the Forms toolbar.

Selecting Text Field Options

Form Field Options

Once the {FORMTEXT} field is placed in your form, you can select the Form Field Options you want to apply to the field. Click the Form Field Options button on the Forms toolbar, and the Text Form Field Options dialog box appears, as shown in Figure 31-12.

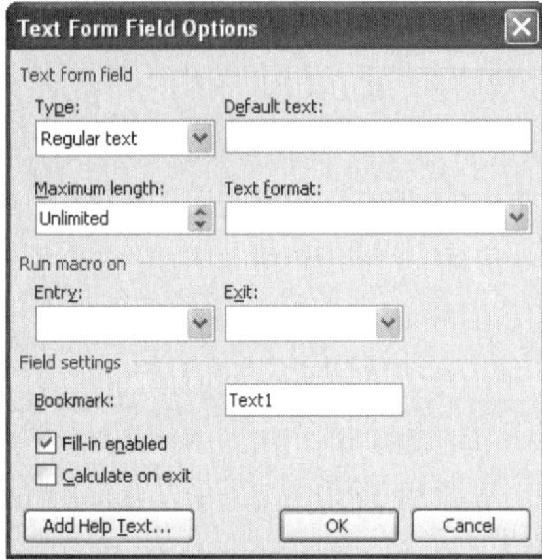

Figure 31-12. You make choices about the text field in the Text Form Field Options dialog box.

Choosing the Text Form Field Type

In the Text Form Field Options dialog box, you choose the type of text field you want to create and Word changes the code accordingly. In the Type list, select one of the following field types:

- **Regular Text** Includes text, numbers, symbols, and spaces
- **Number** Accepts numbers
- **Date** Requires dates
- **Current Date** Displays the current date and cannot be modified by users
- **Current Time** Displays the current time and cannot be modified by users
- **Calculation** Calculates numbers and cannot be modified by users

Tip **Add default entries for users**

You can include a default entry in a text form field so that your user doesn't have to enter it. Simply add the text you want to appear in the field after creating the text form field. In the Text Form Field Options dialog box, type the text in the Default Text box and select the Fill-In Enabled check box. The text you entered in the Default Text box will be displayed in the form until the user clicks in the field and types another entry.

Specifying Field Length

You can control the length of the text form field entry you will allow. If you've asked an open-ended question, perhaps requesting user comments about a new site feature you've added, you can leave a virtually unlimited space for user response. If, on the other hand, you want to limit the response to a few words, you can set the limit of the field length in the Text Form Field Options dialog box by following these steps:

1. Click the text form field code to select it.
2. Click the Form Field Options button on the Forms toolbar. The Text Form Field Options dialog box appears.
3. In the Maximum Length box, click the up arrow to display the number of characters you want to allow. Or, as an alternative, you can click in the field and type the number. A character can be a text character, a number, or a symbol.
4. Click OK to close the dialog box and return to the form.

Note If you want to link the text field to a bookmark you've previously created in your document, you can enter the name of the bookmark in the Bookmark box in the Text Form Field Options dialog box. Simply click in the box and type the bookmark name. For more information about creating and using bookmarks, see "Creating Bookmarks for Document Navigation" on page 133.

Controlling Text Display

If it matters to you or to your data management personnel how data is entered in the forms you create, you can control the capitalization of the text users enter in form fields. You can choose to display entries in all uppercase, lowercase, or in a variety of other displays. To choose the way text appears, follow these steps:

1. Click the text form field code to select it.
2. Click the Form Field Options button on the Forms toolbar. The Text Form Field Options dialog box appears.
3. Click the Text Format arrow. Choose from one of the following options:
   - *Uppercase* formats entries in uppercase letters.
   - *Lowercase* formats entries in lowercase letters.
   - *First capital* displays the entry with an initial first letter.
   - *Title case* treats the entry as though it is a title entry, with an initial capital letter in each word, with the exception of articles and short prepositions.
4. Click OK to close the dialog box and return to the form. Word adds the necessary field code so that the information entered is displayed as you selected.

> **Tip** **Calculate changes automatically**
> If you want Word to calculate the fields in your form each time you exit the form, select the Calculate On Exit check box in the Text Form Field Options dialog box and click OK. Each time you exit the form, Word updates the numeric fields and recalculates any equations in the form.

Adding a Check Box Field

If you want to include choices on your form in which users can select more than one option, you can create a list consisting of multiple check boxes. For example, suppose that your IT department is conducting a survey to find out how happy the employees are with the technical support services. You might include a question such as the following:

1. **Which of these services are important to you?**
   A. Same-day response times
   B. Talking to a tech support person as opposed to an automated system
   C. Being able to get a loaner machine while yours is in the shop

You can turn the list items into check boxes so that users can select all the choices that apply to them. To create a check box field, follow these steps:

Check Box Form Field

1. Place the insertion point where you want to add the check box field.
2. Click the Check Box Form Field button on the Forms toolbar. Word inserts a check box symbol at the insertion point and places the code {FORMCHECKBOX} on the form.
3. Add the check box label by pressing the Spacebar and typing the label of your choice.
4. Repeat as needed to insert additional check boxes.

> **Tip** **Display the form field codes**
> If you want to see which code Word is inserting in your document when you add fields using the Forms toolbar, simply press Alt+F9. The display changes to show the field codes. When you're ready to return to the original display, press Alt+F9 again.

Resizing the Check Box

By default, the check box field is created to match the size of surrounding text. If you want the box to stand out, you might want to modify the size of the check box character. To do this, you need to change the Check Box Size option in the Check Box Form Field Options dialog box by following these steps:

1. Double-click the check box or select it and click the Form Field Options button on the Forms toolbar. The Check Box Form Field Options dialog box appears, as shown in Figure 31-13.

Figure 31-13. The Check Box Form Field Options dialog box enables you to make choices about the way your check box field will look and act.

2. In the Check Box Size section of the dialog box, click Exactly, and increase or decrease the size value in the text box to match the size you want.
3. Click OK to save your changes and return to the form.

Note If you want to lock a check box field so that users can't alter it, select the Check Box Enabled check box in the Check Box Form Field Options dialog box.

Creating a Drop-Down Field

You use a drop-down field when you want to provide a list of choices for the user. In the example described above, you might want to give users the choice of rating the kind of experience they most recently had with tech support. To create a drop-down field, follow these steps:

1. Place the insertion point where you want to add the field.

Drop-Down Form Field

2. Select the Drop-Down Form Field button. Word adds a drop-down field to your form at the insertion point.
3. Double-click the form field or select it and click Form Field Options on the Forms toolbar to display the Drop-Down Form Field Options dialog box, shown in Figure 31-14.

Figure 31-14. The Drop-Down Form Field Options dialog box is where you'll enter the items for a drop-down list.

4. Add entries to the list by typing items in the Drop-Down Item box and clicking Add. Each item is added to the list.
5. Continue adding items as needed. Click OK to close the dialog box.

Adding Help Messages to Forms

If you think the users of your form will need help knowing how to enter the information you seek, you can create customized help messages to guide them along the way. To add help messages to your form, follow these steps:

1. Open the form template you want to use.
2. If necessary, click Protect Form on the Forms toolbar to unlock protection.
3. Double-click the form field you want to use. The Form Field Options dialog box for that field type appears (the text, check box, and drop-down form fields all have different Form Field Options dialog boxes).
4. In the displayed dialog box, click Add Help Text. The Form Field Help Text dialog box appears, as shown in Figure 31-15.
5. Choose your option as follows:
   - To display Help text in the status bar, click the Status Bar tab. Click in the text box, and type the text you want to appear in the status bar at the bottom of the Word window. Click OK to return to the form.
   - To show Help in a message box when the user presses F1, click the Help Key (F1) tab. Type the text you want to display in a help window when the user presses F1. Click OK to return to the form.

Figure 31-15. You can easily add your own help information to a form to show users how to enter information.

6 Click Protect Form on the Forms toolbar to enable form protection.

When you click in the form field that has help messages added to it, the messages will appear in the status bar if you chose Status Bar Help. If you created help messages to be displayed in a Help window, click in the field and press F1 to display the help message you entered in its own window, as shown in Figure 31-16.

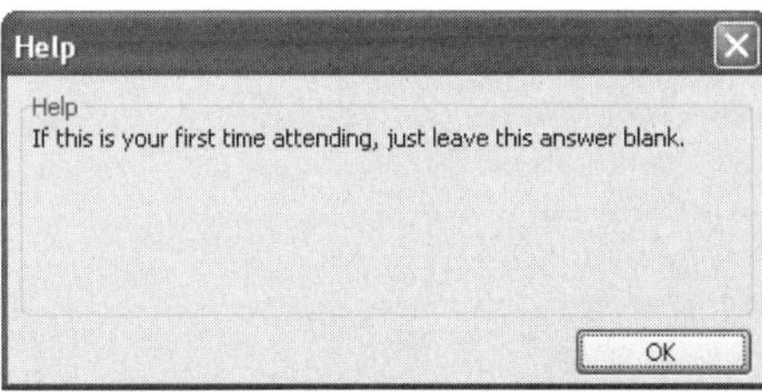

Figure 31-16. To display help messages you've created for a Help window, click in the protected field and press F1.

Note The message you enter for a Help window can contain up to 255 characters. If you create a message for the status bar, make sure the text is under 138 characters.

Incorporating Form Macros

In some cases, you might want an action the user selects to execute a macro you've added to the form. You can add a macro to your form template just as you would add a macro to any other document. Here are the steps:

1. Open the template to which you want to add the macro.
2. Click the field you want to use, and click Protect Form on the Forms toolbar to unprotect the field.
3. Double-click the field to display its Form Field Options dialog box.
4. Select the macro you want to use by making a choice in the Run Macro On section of the dialog box as follows:
   - If you want the macro to execute when the user enters, or selects, the field, click the Entry arrow and choose the macro you want to use from the list. The macros displayed in the list are those that are available in the document you are currently using. (For more information on adding macros to your form, see Chapter 32, "Creating and Working with VBA Macros.")
   - If you want the macro to execute after the user exits, or deselects, the field, click the Exit arrow and choose the macro from the list, as shown in Figure 31-17.

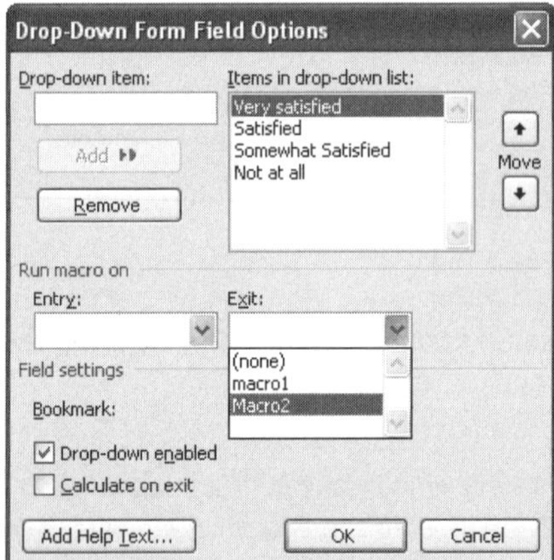

Figure 31-17. Choose whether you want Word to execute a macro when the user accesses or exits the field.

5. Click OK to close the Form Fields Options dialog box and save the settings.
6. Click the Protect Form button to protect the form once again. The macro is now enabled and will execute according to your selections when the user accesses the field.

Troubleshooting

I don't have any macros in the Entry or Exit lists

If you can't locate the macros you want to add, the trouble could be that you haven't added those macros to the current form. To add a macro to the current document, follow these steps:

1. Choose Tools, Templates And Add-Ins. The Templates And Add-Ins dialog box appears.
2. Click Organizer.
3. Click the Styles tab.
4. Click Close File on the left side of the dialog box; then click Open File, select the name of the file containing the macro you want to use, and then click Open.
5. Select the macro you want to use in the list on the left and click Copy. The item is placed in the list on the right side of the dialog box.
6. Click Close to save the change and return to the document.

Adding ActiveX Controls

For special situations, you might want to use an ActiveX control to carry out actions when your user selects an item on your form. You might use an ActiveX control, for example, to run a macro that automates a task. In order to use ActiveX controls, you should be comfortable with Microsoft Visual Basic for Applications (VBA) or Microsoft Script Editor. To add an ActiveX control to your form, follow these steps:

1. Open the template to which you want to add the control.
2. Click the Protect Form button on the Forms toolbar to unprotect the form.
3. Place the insertion point where you want to add the control.
4. Display the Control Toolbox toolbar by choosing View, Toolbars, Control Toolbox.
5. Click the ActiveX control button on the Control Toolbox toolbar that you want in the document. Word creates the control and displays the Exit Design Mode toolbar, as shown in Figure 31-18.

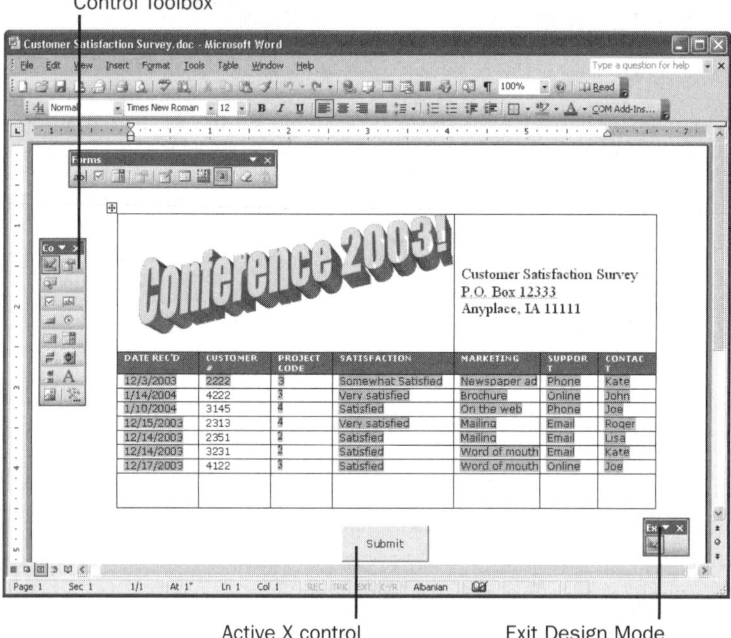

Figure 31-18. When you add an ActiveX control to your form, Word changes to Design Mode.

Note Use the controls you create with the Control Toolbox for forms you want to make available in Word, not for Web-based forms. Many browsers don't recognize the controls you create with the Control Toolbox toolbar.

Changing Control Properties

You can change the way an ActiveX control appears by modifying the control's properties. Right-click the control to display the shortcut menu, and then choose Properties. The Properties dialog box appears, as shown in Figure 31-19.

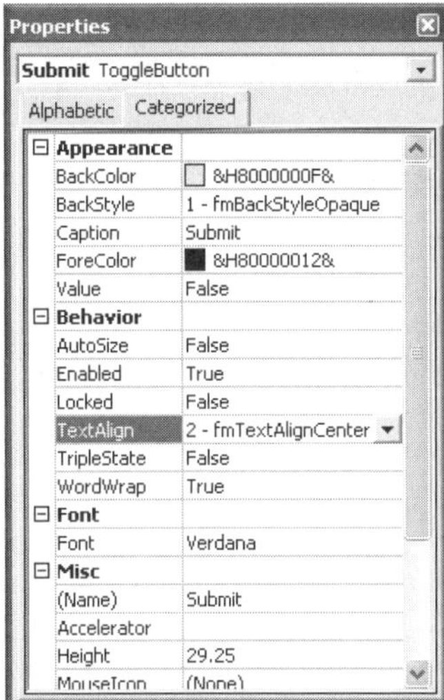

Figure 31-19. Change the way a control looks by making changes in the Properties dialog box.

Click the Categorized tab to see the various properties organized by category. If you want to make a change—for example, you might change the font—double-click the setting in the right column. When you double-click the font selection, the Font dialog box appears so that you can make the necessary changes and then click OK.

Programming a Control

Although an in-depth discussion of using VBA to program an ActiveX control is beyond the scope of this chapter, you can easily access the code window for scripting from your form. To access the code window, follow these steps:

1. Click the control to select it. Unprotect the field if necessary by clicking Protect Form on the Forms toolbar.
2. Click the View Code button on the Control Toolbox toolbar. Word displays the Visual Basic Editor, as shown in Figure 31-20.

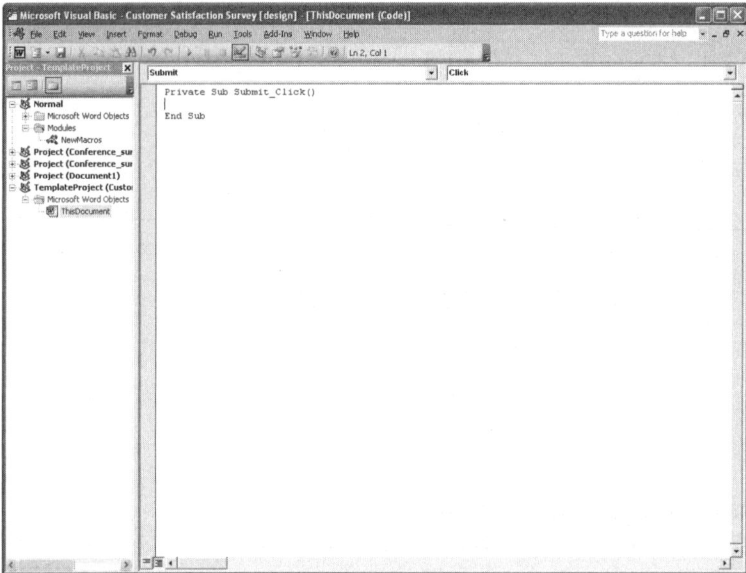

Figure 31-20. When you click View Code, the Visual Basic Editor opens so that you can enter the script for the control.

3 Enter the script for your Visual Basic program.
4 Click File, Close And Return To Microsoft Word to exit the editor and return to your form. Alternatively, you can simply press Alt+Q.

Using a Form

Designing a form is the first part of the story; using a form is the second part. To use a form, follow these steps:

1 Click File, New. The New Document task pane opens.
2 Click On My Computer. The Templates dialog box opens.
3 Click the General tab and select the form template you created; click OK. The form is displayed in the Word window.
4 Enter your responses on the form as requested.
5 When you're finished, press Ctrl+S to save the form. The Save As dialog box appears.
6 Select the folder in which you want to save the form and then click Save. This action saves the document as is, complete with text, data, and any graphics you've included in the form.

Note If you are using Microsoft Office Professional Edition 2003, or the stand-alone version of Word 2003, you also have the option of saving your form data as XML. To find out more about working with XML data, see Chapter 29, "Working with XML."

Saving Form Data

You save a form as you would save any document, by pressing Ctrl+S and choosing the location and file name you want for the file. If you want to save only the data in the form instead of the entire form, you can do this using a selection in the Options dialog box. Follow these steps:

1. Create a new form using the form template you created.
2. Choose Tools, Options.
3. Click the Save tab and select the Save Data Only For Forms check box in the Save Options section.
4. Click OK to save the setting and return to the form.

The first time you elect to save form data as a text file, Word displays the File Conversion dialog box to enable you to select how you want to save the data. You can choose the way you want Word to handle individual data items; the Preview section, in the File Conversion dialog box, shows you how the data will appear in the text file, as shown in Figure 31-21. Make any necessary changes, and then click OK to save the data.

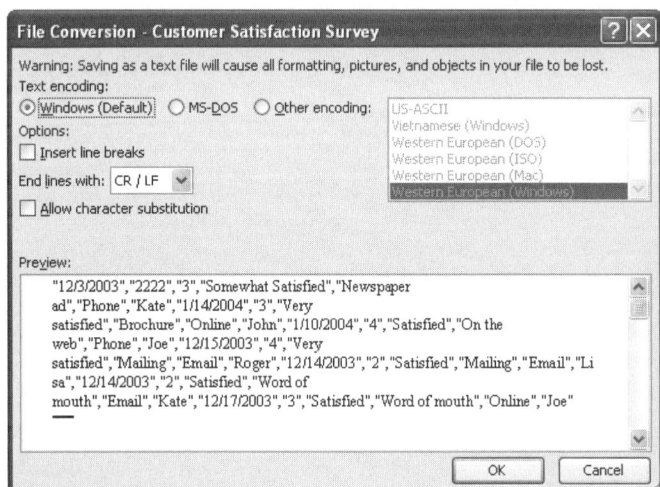

Figure 31-21. When you first save form data as a text file, Word displays your conversion options.

> **Note** Each time users open a copy of your form, they'll have to enable the Save Data Only For Forms option if you want only the data to be saved. You might want to add Help text or a form prompt to instruct users to select the option in the Options dialog box. You can also create a macro to handle the setting automatically for your users. For more about creating Word macros, see Chapter 32, "Creating and Working with VBA Macros."

Chapter 32

Creating and Working with VBA Macros

If you find that you perform certain tasks repeatedly, you might be able to simplify your life by creating Microsoft Visual Basic for Applications (VBA) macros. Properly used, VBA macros can perform some of your work for you. Many people find themselves cringing at the mere mention of the word macros, but there's really no reason to be intimidated. Simply put, a *macro* is a series of commands and instructions that are grouped together as a single command. For example, you can record a macro that creates a particularly formatted table and assign the macro to a toolbar button. Then, the next time you want to create a table with the same formatting, you simply click the toolbar button—nothing magical about it, but certainly a welcome convenience!

People typically create macros to perform the following kinds of tasks:

- Automating a complex series of steps or creating custom procedures
- Combining multiple commands, such as inserting and formatting tables with a single command
- Making menu commands and dialog boxes more accessible
- Speeding up editing and formatting procedures, such as applying custom borders, shading, backgrounds, or watermarks
- Accessing commonly opened documents, such as company procedure and policy manuals, in-house style sheets, or templates
- Inserting standard text from another document, such as a frequently used legal disclaimer or company slogan
- Inserting graphics or objects that are used repeatedly, such as an official logo, a "new item" identifier in a Web page or catalog, or other graphic or object

As you start to use macros, you'll find that they come in handy in a number of situations and let you customize your working environment to suit your needs.

In Word, you can create and run macros in a few main ways: you can view and run existing Word commands, record macros using the Macro Recorder, and hand-code macros using the Microsoft Visual Basic Editor (VBE). In this chapter, you'll be introduced to the built-in Word commands and you'll learn how to create a macro using the Macro Recorder. We'll also look briefly at the VBE (see the sidebar "Initiating a Macro in the VBE" on page 906), but learning all the ins and outs of using this tool is beyond the scope of this book.

Using Built-In Word Commands

Before you start to create your own macros, you should familiarize yourself with Word's built-in commands. As you might imagine, Word provides a number of built-in commands (over 1000), and many of them are already associated with toolbar buttons, menu commands, and keyboard shortcuts. For example, the FileClose command is attached to the File menu's Close command. You can view, run, and associate Word commands with toolbar buttons, menus, and keyboard shortcuts in the same ways you perform these actions with macros you create.

Viewing Existing Word Commands

You use some of the built-in Word commands regularly without realizing it (such as when you click the Print button on the Standard toolbar), but others aren't assigned to toolbar buttons or menu commands by default.

To view a list of Word's built-in commands, follow these steps:

1. Choose Tools, Macro, Macros, or press Alt+F8. The Macros dialog box appears.
2. Click the Macros In arrow, and select Word Commands in the list. The list of built-in Word commands appears, as shown in Figure 32-1.

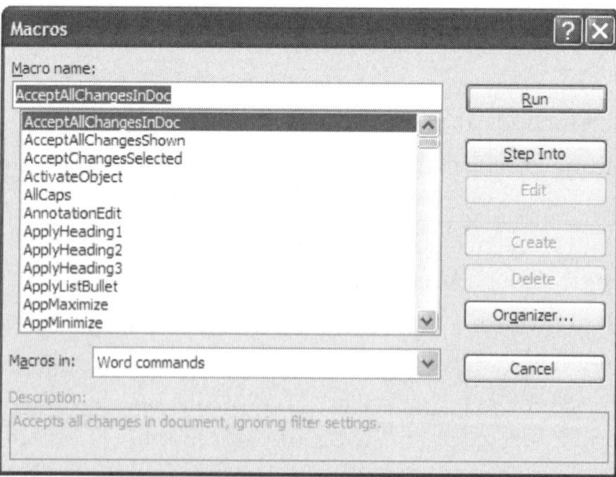

Figure 32-1. Using the Macros dialog box, you can display and run Word's built-in commands.

3 Scroll through the list of Word commands. When you select a Word command's name, the Description box shows a brief description of the command's action. To perform the described action, click the Run button. If you'd rather not perform any actions at this point, click Cancel to close the Macros dialog box.

To see a complete list of built-in Word commands along with short descriptions in table format, refer to this book's companion CD. If you see any commands you think you might be able to use, you can create toolbar buttons, menu commands, or keyboard shortcuts based on the Word commands, as described in the next section. The new Word commands available in Word 2003 are shown in Table 32-1 (as well as incorporated into the complete table on the companion CD).

Table 32-1. New Built-In Word Commands

Word command	Description
CloseReadingMode	Toggles Reading mode
CopyInkAsText	Copies the ink selection and puts its text equivalent on the Clipboard
DeleteAllInkAnnotations	Deletes all ink annotations
DisplaySharedWorkspacePane	Displays the Document Status pane
DocumentActionsPane	Displays the Smart Document pane
DoNotDistribute	Displays the Permission toggle button on toolbar
EditFindReadingMode	Finds the specified text or the specified formatting (opens the Find And Replace dialog box)
EmailAttachmentOptions	Toggles the display of the Attachment Options task pane
EmailChooseAccount	Activates the e-mail account chooser
FaxService	Sends a document to fax via the Internet
FilePermission	Restricts permission for a document
FileVersionsServer	Manages the server versions of a document
FormattingRestrictions	Applies the style lockdown settings
GettingStartedPane	Displays the Getting Started task pane
HelpCheckForUpdates	Opens the Internet browser and displays the Microsoft product updates page
HelpContactUs	Opens the Internet browser and displays the Microsoft Contact Us page
InsertInkAnnotations	Inserts ink annotations
InsertInkComment	Inserts an ink comment
InsertInkSplitMenu	Shows or hides ink annotations and Ink Annotations toolbar
InsertSoundComment	Inserts a sound object into a document

Table 32-1. New Built-In Word Commands

Word command	Description
NeverUseBalloons	Specifies to never use balloons
NoInsertionDeletionBalloons	Specifies to not include insertion and/or deletion balloons
ReadingMode	Toggles reading mode
ReadingModeGrowFont	Increases the font size in reading mode
ReadingModeInkOff	Unlocks a document for ink
ReadingModeLayout	Toggles reading mode
ReadingModeLookup	Opens reading mode lookup tools
ReadingModeMini	Toggles reading mode
ReadingModePageView	Uses actual layout in reading mode
ReadingModeShrinkFont	Decreases the font size in reading mode
Research	Initiates the Research task pane
ResearchLookup	Looks up a word in the research tool
ResetSideBySide	Resets the window position for side by side
ShowInkAnnotations	Shows or hides ink annotations
ShowSmPane	Displays the Document Updates task pane
SqmDialog	Opens the Service Options dialog box
SyncScrollSideBySide	Initiates synchronous scrolling of two windows side by side
ToggleReadingMode2Pages	Shows or hides two pages view in reading mode
ToggleReadingModeHelp	Provides help for ink annotations in reading mode
ToggleReadingModeInk	Enables ink annotations in reading mode
ToggleThumbnail	Shows or hides thumbnail view
ToggleXMLTagView	Toggles XML Tag view on or off
ToolsProtect	Sets protection for the active document or selection
ToolsThesaurusRR	Displays synonyms for the selected word in the Research task pane
UseBalloons	Specifies to always use balloons
ViewDocumentMapReadingMode	Toggles the state of the Heading Explorer
ViewXMLStructure	Shows the XML Structure task pane
WindowArrangeSideBySide	Arranges two windows side by side
XMLDocument	Applies XML transforms to a document
XMLOptions	Changes XML settings for a document

Assigning Shortcuts to Word Commands

After you're familiar with the built-in Word commands, you'll probably find that you would like quicker access to them. The process of displaying and running commands from the Macros dialog box isn't the most streamlined approach. To make selected Word commands more accessible, you can assign them to toolbar buttons, menu commands, or keyboard shortcuts, as follows:

1. Choose Tools, Customize. The Customize dialog box appears.
2. Click the Commands tab, and then select All Commands in the Categories list. The complete list of available Word commands that you can use for customization is displayed in the Commands list, as shown in Figure 32-2. As you scroll through this list, notice that a number of the Word commands have a custom toolbar button already associated with them, appearing in the shaded column to the left of the command names.

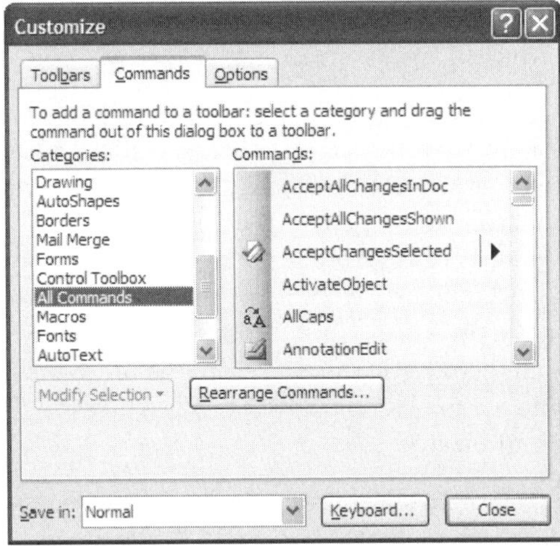

Figure 32-2. The Commands tab shows all available commands when you click All Commands in the Categories list.

> **Tip** If you want to remove a toolbar button or menu command—regardless of when it was added—you can drag the toolbar button or menu command off its toolbar or menu while the Customize dialog box is open.

3. To add a command to a toolbar or menu, select the command in the Commands list, and drag the command to the toolbar or menu. To create a keyboard shortcut, click Keyboard and configure the options in the Customize Keyboard dialog box. (For more information about creating toolbar buttons, menu commands, and keyboard shortcuts, see "Assigning a Macro to a Toolbar, a Menu, or a Keyboard Shortcut" on page 908.)

4 When you are finished with customizing your Word window, click Close in the Customize dialog box.

After you display a Word command as a menu command or toolbar button, you can right-click your newly created element to configure its display parameters, as described in "Assigning a Macro to a Toolbar or Menu," on page 908. Likewise, if you click Keyboard in the Customize dialog box to create a keyboard shortcut, you can configure your custom keyboard shortcut by completing the Customize Keyboard dialog box, as discussed in "Assigning a Macro to a Toolbar, a Menu, or a Keyboard Shortcut," on page 908.

Creating Macros Using the Macro Recorder

As mentioned, you can create macros by using the Macro Recorder, by entering VBA code in the VBE, or by using both tools in combination (for example, you could record the bulk of your macro's code using the Macro Recorder and then tweak the code in the VBE). In this section, we'll look at creating macros with the Macro Recorder.

Planning a Macro

Regardless of how you create a macro, you need to gather your thoughts before you start. This is especially true when you're creating macros using the Macro Recorder. When you run the Macro Recorder, it tracks all your movements—including any corrections you make along the way. As you can imagine, because Word records every action, the more movements and commands you perform (including any commands you undo), the larger your macro becomes. Therefore, you'll want to make sure that you've outlined the most streamlined approach to creating your macro before you start to record the procedure. If necessary, you might even jot down some notes before you start the recorder.You should consider the following items before creating your macro:

- Carefully plan the steps and commands you want the macro to perform.
- Make sure that you know the keyboard shortcuts you need to use, especially for moving within the document text. (You can't use the mouse in the body of the document when you use the Macro Recorder.) Also keep in mind that using keyboard shortcuts to move around your document is generally more accurate than using the arrow keys. (For example, pressing Ctrl+End to move to the end of your document is more efficient than pressing the Down Arrow key 10 times.)

> **Tip** For more information about using keyboard shortcuts, see Chapter 2, "Mastering Document Fundamentals."

- Conduct at least one practice run through the procedure and take notes, if necessary.
- Anticipate any messages that Word might display that might halt your macro or seem confusing when the macro is run. (For example, if your macro includes using the Find or Replace command on the Edit menu, click More on the Find or Replace tab, and

then click All in the Search box. Otherwise, if the macro searches only up or down in the document, it will stop when it reaches the beginning or end of the document and display a message box.)

- Make sure that your macro doesn't depend on the current document's content.

Tip **Create a macro that formats text**
If you want to create a macro that formats text, select the text before you start the Macro Recorder. Then run the Macro Recorder and format the selected text as desired, preferably by using keyboard shortcuts or clicking toolbar buttons instead of opening the Font dialog box.

After you've carefully planned the purpose and process of your macro, you're ready to run the recorder. Remember, running the recorder creates Visual Basic code, so you'll be able to view your macro and edit its code after you record it.

Initiating a Recording Procedure

To begin recording a macro, you must first open the Record Macro dialog box, shown in Figure 32-3, by choosing Tools, Macro, Record New Macro. The Record Macro dialog box enables you to set a number of macro parameters before you actually record your macro.

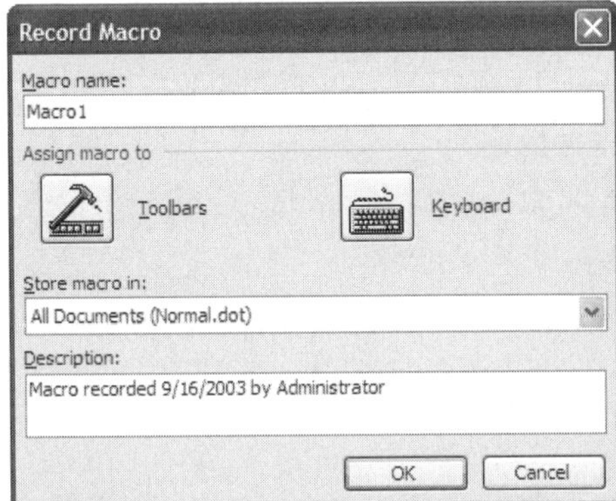

Figure 32-3. The Record Macro dialog box is a one-stop shop for configuring many macro settings.

Using the Record Macro dialog box, you can name your macro, specify how you'll access the macro after it's created, indicate where to store your macro, and add a description, if desired. Although you can configure and change these settings after you create the macro, your best bet is to address these issues up front, while the Record Macro dialog box is open and waiting for your input. If you postpone these tasks, you might forget to do them later.

Initiating a Macro in the VBE

This chapter focuses on using the Macro Recorder to create macros, but you can hand-code your macros from the start if you want. To begin creating a macro in the VBE, follow these steps:

1. Choose Tools, Macro, Macros.
2. In the Macros dialog box, type a name for your macro in the Macro Name box. (For information about naming macros, see the next section, "Naming a Macro.")
3. If necessary, ensure that the Macros In list displays the template or document in which you want to create the macro.
4. Click Create.

The VBE opens (as shown in Figure 32-9, later in this chapter); this is the editor in which you can enter VBA code to create your macro.

Naming a Macro

As Figure 32-3 shows, the Record Macro dialog box contains a Macro Name box. By default, Word provides a name for your macro, such as Macro1, Macro2, and so forth. This default naming scheme is very vague. Most likely, you'll want to associate a more descriptive name with your macro (and this practice is highly recommended). Fortunately, you can supply any name for your macro so long as you abide by the following guidelines:

- The macro name must begin with a letter.
- The macro name can contain up to 80 letters and numbers.
- The macro name can't contain spaces or symbols.

If you type a macro name that's invalid, an error message will appear after you click OK, as shown in Figure 32-4. If you see this error message, click OK, and then choose Tools, Macro, Record New Macro to restart the macro creation process.

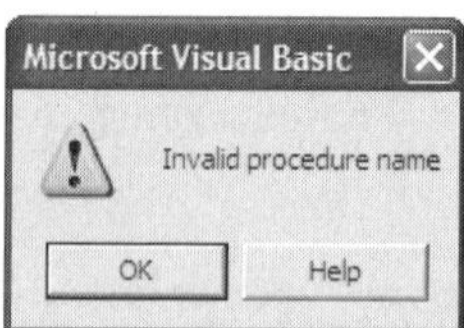

Figure 32-4. Word displays an error message if you type an invalid name in the Macro Name box in the Record Macro dialog box.

Caution If you give a new macro the same name as an existing macro or Word command, the new macro's actions will replace the existing macro's actions. You should be especially careful not to replace existing Word commands inadvertently. If you attempt to create a macro with the same name as an existing macro, Word will display a warning message box, asking whether you would like to replace the existing macro. At that point, you can click Yes to replace the existing macro or click No to return to the Record Macro dialog box (at which point you can enter a new name for your macro or click Cancel to halt the creation process).

Storing a Macro

In the Record Macro dialog box, you can also specify the location in which you'll store the macro. You can store macros in templates or in individual documents. Your macro is available only when the document or template in which it is stored is open. Most commonly, macros are stored in the Normal template, which means that the macros can be run at any time (because the Normal template is a global template, as described in Chapter 16, "Formatting Documents Using Templates, Wizards, Add-Ins, and XML Schemas"). You can store macros in the following locations:

- **Active document** If you plan to use a macro in a single document, you can store the macro directly in the document. When you choose this option, the macro will run only when that document is the active document.
- **All documents (Normal.dot)** You can store a macro in the Normal template, thereby making the macro available to all open files. By default, Word stores macros you create in the Normal template.
- **Template** You can store a macro in a template other than the Normal template if a template is attached to the current document or open when you create the macro. When you do this, the macro is available only when the template is opened or attached to the active document.

To specify where you want to store a macro, open the Record Macro dialog box (by choosing Tools, Macro, Record New Macro), click the Store Macro In list box, and then select the location where you'd like to store the macro.

Associating a Description with a Macro

The Record Macro dialog box also enables you to provide a brief description of macros you create. This description is helpful for future use, especially if you're planning to share the macro with others or if you modify or update an existing macro. By default, Word provides the date and author of a macro in the Description box. You can edit or delete this information and add custom information by typing in the Description box. Keep in mind that you can't edit text in the Description box for Word commands and other read-only macros.

Assigning a Macro to a Toolbar, a Menu, or a Keyboard Shortcut

When you create a macro, you can assign the macro to a keyboard shortcut, a toolbar button, a menu command, or a combination of these options (or you can choose not to create an association). If you choose to create a toolbar, menu, or keyboard shortcut association, the recording process will begin directly after you make the assignment. If you opt not to associate the macro with a toolbar, menu, or keyboard shortcut, you're ready to begin recording, as described in "Recording a Macro" on page 911. In this section, you'll learn how to create associations for your macros.

> **Note** If you don't assign some sort of shortcut to your macro, you'll need to open the Macros dialog box, select the macro name, and then click Run each time you want to run your macro.

Assigning a Macro to a Toolbar or Menu

As mentioned, you can associate a macro with a toolbar button or menu command to make the macro easily accessible. As you'll see, customizing your toolbars or menus with macro commands is similar to customizing toolbars and menus in general. To create a toolbar button or menu command association for your macro, follow these steps:

Toolbars

1. In the Record Macro dialog box (choose Tools, Macro, Record New Macro), enter the macro name in the Macro Name box, and then click the Toolbars button.
2. In the Customize dialog box, click the Commands tab, shown in Figure 32-5.

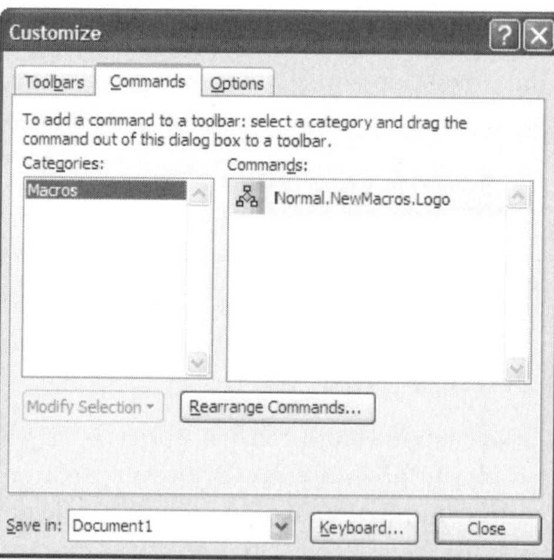

Figure 32-5. You can add a macro toolbar button or menu command by dragging the macro from the Customize dialog box onto a toolbar or menu.

3. In the Commands list, click the name of the macro you're recording, and drag the macro to the appropriate toolbar or menu.

> **Tip** **Create new toolbars for macro buttons**
>
> If you want to create a new toolbar to contain your macro button, click the Toolbars tab in the Customize dialog box, click New, and create a new toolbar. After you create a new toolbar, ensure that it appears on screen, click the Commands tab in the Customize dialog box, and then drag the macro icon from the Commands tab onto the newly created toolbar. For more information about creating custom toolbars, see Chapter 5, "Customizing Word and Enhancing Accessibility."

4 After you add a macro to a toolbar or menu and before you close the Customize dialog box, you can customize the appearance of the macro by right-clicking it and choosing options on the shortcut menu. Figure 32-6 shows the shortcut menu you can use to customize a toolbar button. Notice that you can assign a button image to your newly created macro toolbar button.

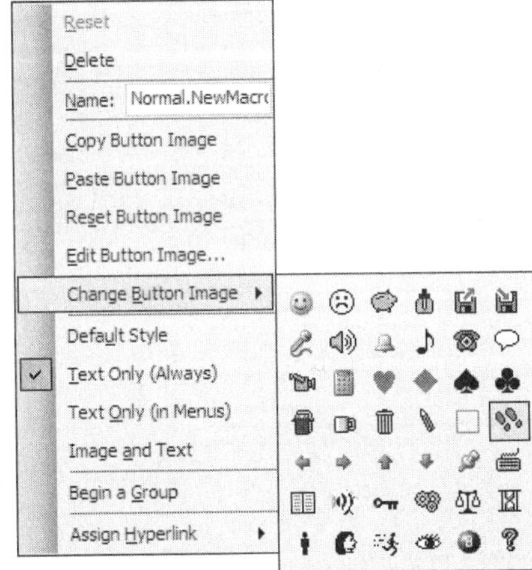

Figure 32-6. After you drag your macro to a toolbar or menu, you can customize its appearance by right-clicking it and choosing options on the shortcut menu.

The Customize dialog box also contains a Keyboard button (as shown in Figure 32-5). You can use this button to assign a keyboard shortcut to your macro in addition to creating a toolbar button or menu command, as described in the next section.

For more information about customizing menus and adding toolbar buttons, see Chapter 5, "Customizing Word and Enhancing Accessibility."

Assigning a Macro to a Keyboard Shortcut

In addition to creating toolbar buttons and menu commands, you can associate your macros with keyboard shortcuts. You might want to do this if a menu command already exists but you prefer to use a keyboard command instead of continually opening the menu. Perhaps you'd like to create a macro that turns the markup feature on and off and assign a keyboard shortcut to the macro. That way, instead of choosing View, Markup each time you want to view the markup in the current document, you could simply press a keyboard shortcut that toggles the changes on and off.

To assign a macro to a keyboard shortcut, follow these steps:

Keyboard

1 In the Record Macro dialog box (choose Tools, Macro, Record New Macro) or in the Customize dialog box (discussed in the preceding section), click the Keyboard button. The Customize Keyboard dialog box opens.

2 By default, the insertion point is in the Press New Shortcut Key box. Press the key combination you want to assign to your macro, as shown in Figure 32-7, click Assign, and then click Close.

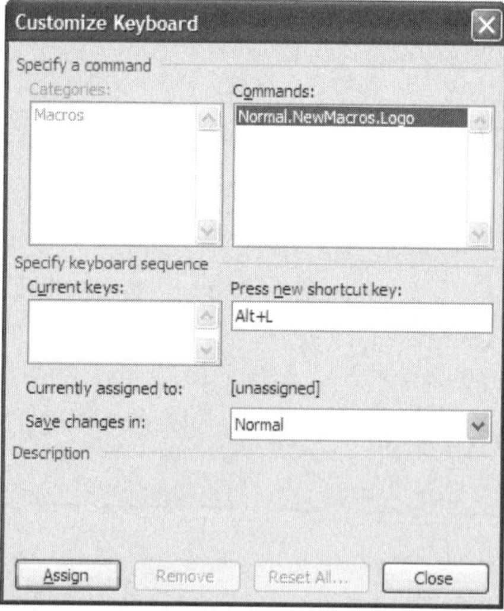

Figure 32-7. You can use the Customize Keyboard dialog box to assign keyboard shortcuts to your macros.

When you create keyboard shortcuts, make sure you don't overwrite an existing keyboard shortcut. In the example in Figure 32-7, the keyboard shortcut Alt+L is being assigned. The Currently Assigned To field indicates that the combination isn't assigned to another command in Word. If the command were already being used by another command, the dialog box would indicate that the combination is already in use and display the command that's using it. For example, if you attempt to assign Ctrl+P to a macro, Word would indicate that the FilePrint command already uses that keyboard shortcut. To assign another keyboard shortcut, delete the entry in the Press New Shortcut Key box and try another combination.

> **Note** When you create keyboard shortcuts, consider using Alt+*letter* instead of Ctrl+*letter*. Many Ctrl+*letter* keyboard combinations already exist in Word, so you might find it a bit tricky to find an available combination.

Recording a Macro

After you configure the settings in the Record Macro dialog box, you're ready to record your macro. To begin recording, click OK in the Record Macro dialog box. (If you assigned your macro to a toolbar button, menu command, or keyboard shortcut, the Macro Recorder will begin automatically after you complete the assignment procedure.) When the Macro Recorder begins, the Record Macro dialog box closes, and the Stop Recording toolbar, shown in Figure 32-8, is displayed. You're officially in record mode. The actions you take from this point on will be recorded in your macro.

Figure 32-8. The Stop Recording toolbar is small, but it contains the buttons you need to stop and pause your recording session.

> **Tip** **Avoid mixing macros and mouse movements**
> As mentioned in "Planning a Macro" on page 904, when you use the Macro Recorder, you can use your mouse to click commands, toolbar buttons, and menu commands, but the recorder won't record mouse movements in your document window. You'll need to use keyboard commands to record those movements. For example, if you're adding column headings in a table, you'll need to press Tab to indicate a movement from one cell to another instead of clicking in each cell.

If you need to, you can pause the recorder while recording a macro. You might want to do this to avoid adding extra (unnecessary) steps to your macro's VBA code. To pause the recorder while recording a macro, you use the Pause Recording button on the Stop Recording toolbar, as follows:

Pause Recording/ Resume Recording

1. On the Stop Recording toolbar, click the Pause Recording button.
2. Perform any actions you don't want to record.
3. To resume recording, click the Resume Recording button on the Stop Recording toolbar.

After you finish recording your macro, click the Stop Recording button on the Stop Recording toolbar, or choose Tools, Macro, Stop Recording. Your macro is now ready to run.

> **Tip** You should avoid adding extra steps to your macros whenever possible, since extra steps mean extra VBA coding, which in turn results in bigger macros and larger file sizes.

Saving Macros

When you create macros, they aren't automatically saved. In fact, macros aren't saved until you save the documents in which the macros are stored. Therefore, after you create a macro, you should immediately save your open documents by clicking Save on the Standard toolbar, pressing Ctrl+S, or choosing File, Save. After you save the documents containing your macros, you should run your macros to verify that they work as planned.

Tip If you have multiple files open, you can easily save all open documents and templates by using Word's Save All command. To do so, press Shift, and then choose File, Save All.

Editing and Viewing the VBA Code

If you encounter any undesirable traits or errors when you test a macro, you can edit the macro. To do so, you open the macro in the VBE, where you can make corrections, remove unnecessary steps, rename or copy the macro, or add instructions that you can't record in Word. To open a macro for editing in the VBE, follow these steps:

1. Choose Tools, Macro, Macros. The Macros dialog box opens.
2. In the Macro Name list, select the name of the macro you want to edit. If the macro you're looking for isn't displayed, click the Macros In arrow, and select a different document or template in the list.
3. Click Edit. The VBE appears, as shown in Figure 32-9.

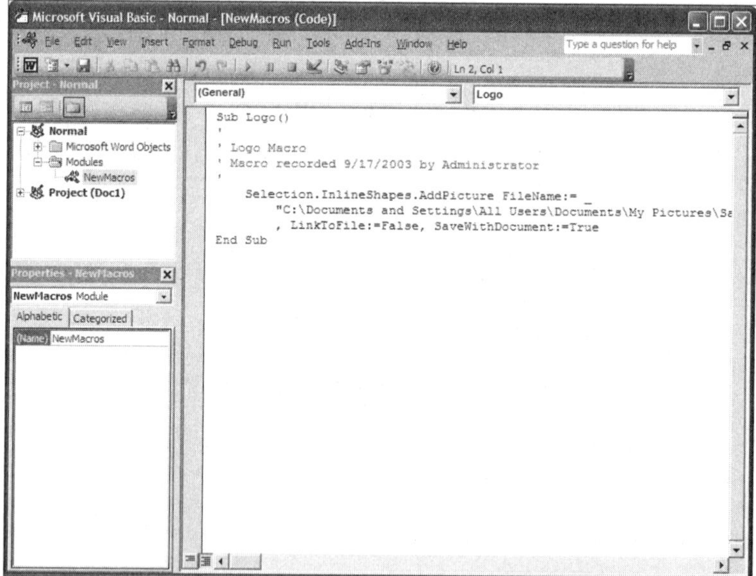

Figure 32-9. The VBE shows you the VBA code used to run your macros. This macro shows code used to insert a logo graphic.

Note If you select a macro that's read-only, the Edit button will be disabled and appear dimmed. Similarly, you can't edit macros in read-only documents.

Keeping Your Macro Code Trim

When you record a macro and add a command that displays a dialog box (such as choosing Format, Paragraph to open the Paragraph dialog box), Word records everything in the dialog box. In contrast, clicking toolbar buttons creates much more concise code. For example, let's say that part of your macro calls for right-aligning a paragraph. If you choose Format, Paragraph and set right-alignment by configuring the Paragraph dialog box settings while recording a macro, the following information will be inserted into your macro's code. (Notice that the alignment information is contained on a single line.)

```
With Selection.ParagraphFormat
        .LeftIndent = InchesToPoints(0)
        .RightIndent = InchesToPoints(0)
        .SpaceBefore = 0
        .SpaceBeforeAuto = False
        .SpaceAfter = 0
        .SpaceAfterAuto = False
        .LineSpacingRule = wdLineSpaceSingle
        .Alignment = wdAlignParagraphRight
        .WidowControl = True
        .KeepWithNext = False
        .KeepTogether = False
        .PageBreakBefore = False
        .NoLineNumber = False
        .Hyphenation = True
        .FirstLineIndent = InchesToPoints(0)
        .OutlineLevel = wdOutlineLevelBodyText
        .CharacterUnitLeftIndent = 0
        .CharacterUnitRightIndent = 0
        .CharacterUnitFirstLineIndent = 0
        .LineUnitBefore = 0
        .LineUnitAfter = 0
    End With
```

In contrast, if you click the Align Right button on the Formatting toolbar instead of opening the Paragraph dialog box, Word creates the following code for your macro:

```
Selection.ParagraphFormat.Alignment = wdAlignParagraphRight
```

In either case, your paragraph will be right-aligned, but the amount of VBA code used to create the effect differs dramatically. As you'd expect, using the single line of code approach is preferable because it's the more processor-efficient way of accomplishing a task.

You can compare how various procedures appear in VBA by repeatedly creating your macro, noting the different commands you use, and viewing your macro's code in the VBE. You can rework your macro and view the VBA code each time until you find the combination that's the most efficient.

Tip **Avoid editing VBA code**

If you prefer not to edit the VBA code to correct a macro, you can correct problems in many cases by deleting the macro and running the macro recorder again. Deleting macros is described in "Deleting Macros and Macro Projects" on page 918.

Running Macros

After you create a macro, you can run it using any of the following techniques:

- Click the macro's toolbar button or menu command.
- Press the macro's keyboard shortcut.
- Open the Macros dialog box (by pressing Alt+F8), select the macro in the Macro Name list, and click Run.

Users typically access macros by clicking toolbar buttons, choosing menu commands, or pressing keyboard shortcuts. But in some cases, you might want to store an infrequently used macro in your document or template without making the macro instantly accessible—in other words, you might want a macro to be available when you need it, but you don't need to use it every time you work in Word. In those cases, you should simply create and store your macro in your document or template and then run the macro from within the Macros dialog box whenever you need to complete the desired procedure.

Copying Macros to Other Templates or Documents

When you create macros in a document or template, Word stores the macros as a single *macro project*. Simply stated, a macro project is a collection of macros grouped under one name and stored as a single entity in a document or template. Each document or template has one macro project that contains all the macros you've created for that document or template. By default, when you record macros, Word stores the VBA code in a macro project named NewMacros. You can manipulate a macro project in a number of ways by using the Organizer. For instance, you can copy a macro project from one document or template to another document or template, you can delete a macro project, or you can rename it.

In this section, we'll look at copying macro projects to other documents or templates by using the Organizer. To do so, follow these steps:

1. Choose Tools, Macro, Macros (or press Alt+F8) to open the Macros dialog box.
2. Click Organizer, and then click the Macro Project Items tab. Figure 32-10 shows the Organizer dialog box with a macro project called NewMacros stored in the Normal template.

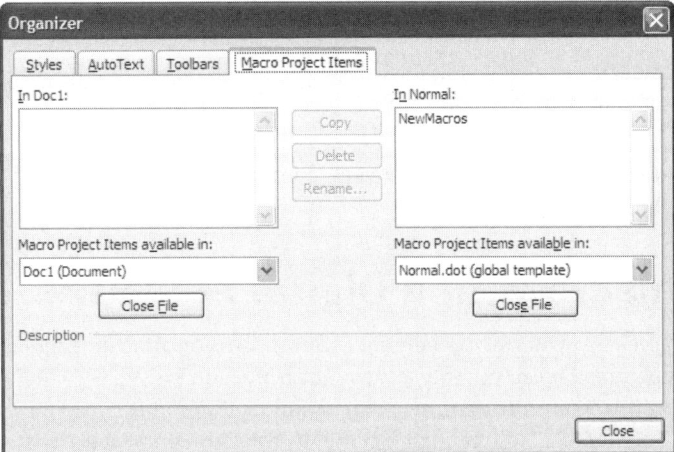

Figure 32-10. You can use the Organizer dialog box to copy, delete, and rename macro projects.

3. To copy the macro project from a template or document, click Close File and then click Open File to find and open the desired documents or templates.
4. Click the macro project you want to copy (in whichever list the item appears), and then click Copy to copy the macro project to the other currently displayed document or template (which should appear in the other list).
5. Click Close to close the Organizer dialog box.

Note If you have assigned macros to toolbars, you should also copy the toolbars by using the Toolbars tab in the Organizer dialog box. When you copy toolbars, you must also copy the macro project; otherwise, the toolbar buttons won't work.

When you copy a macro project to another document or template, you copy all the macros you've created to the other file. After you copy a macro project to another file, you can open the Macros dialog box in that file to edit, delete, or add individual macros.

Renaming Macro Projects

Renaming macro projects is similar to copying them. To rename a macro project, display the macro project in either list on the Macro Project Items tab in the Organizer dialog box, select the macro project name, and then click Rename. The Rename dialog box appears, as shown in Figure 32-11. This dialog box is extremely straightforward—you simply type a new name for your macro project and then click OK.

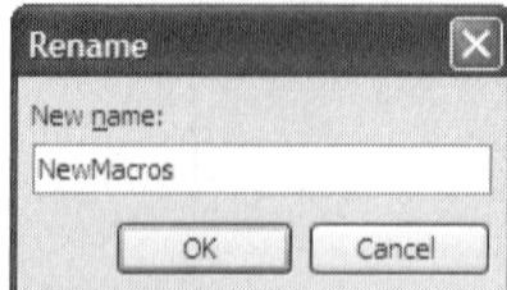

Figure 32-11. To rename a macro project, simply enter a new name in the Rename dialog box.

Signing a Macro with a Digital Signature

For added security, you can digitally sign your macros by attaching digital certificates to them. But before you can use this security measure, you must have a digital certificate installed on your computer. For more information about obtaining and using digital certificates, see Chapter 28, "Addressing Document Protection and Security Issues."

After you've installed a digital certificate, you can digitally sign a macro as follows:

1. Open the file that contains the macro project you want to sign.
2. Choose Tools, Macro, Visual Basic Editor, or press Alt+F11.
3. In the Project Explorer window of the VBE, select the macro project you want to sign.

Note When you open a macro project in VBE, all the macros are shown by default. If you prefer, you can display a selected macro only in the VBE by choosing Tools, Macro, Macros to open the Macros dialog box, selecting the macro you want to sign in the Macro Name list, and then clicking Edit. The VBE window opens and displays the code for the selected macro. Alternatively, you can double-click the macro project to open the macro window and then select a macro name in the Procedure list in the macro window.

4. Choose Tools, Digital Signature. The Digital Signature dialog box opens, as shown in Figure 32-12.

Figure 32-12. To help provide security, the Digital Signature dialog box enables you to sign your macros with a digital certificate.

5 In the Digital Signature dialog box, perform either of the following actions:

- If you haven't previously selected a digital certificate or want to assign a different certificate, click Choose. The Select Certificate dialog box appears, as shown in Figure 32-13. Select the certificate you want to use and then click OK. The digital certificate name displays in the Digital Signature dialog box. Click OK to close the Digital Signature dialog box.

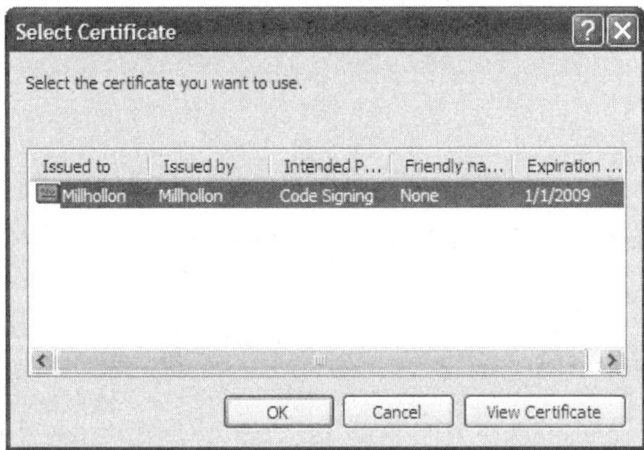

Figure 32-13. The Select Certificate dialog box displays a list of certificates that you can use to sign your macros.

- To use the current certificate, if one is specified, click OK.

6 After you sign your macro, close the VBE and save your document.

Changing the Security Level for Macro Virus Protection

Another security-related macro issue involves setting the security level in Word. You can specify whether you want Word to treat documents that contain macros with a high, medium, or low security level. To configure your security level, follow these steps:

1. Choose Tools, Macro, Security.
2. In the Security dialog box, click the Security Level tab, and then specify whether you want High, Medium, or Low security.
3. Click OK to apply the security level.

For more information about Word's security levels and how Word handles each security level, see Chapter 28, "Addressing Document Protection and Security Issues."

As a rule, you should digitally sign a macro only after you've completed the creation process, including testing the macro. Whenever signed code is modified, the digital signature is removed. If you have the proper digital certificate on your computer, the macro will then be signed again automatically when it is saved. As you can see, editing a signed macro causes your computer to perform extra processing. In addition, if you're working on a computer that doesn't contain your digital certificate information, modifying your macro will remove the digital certificate, and the certificate won't be reattached when you save your changes.

Deleting Macros and Macro Projects

The last technique you should master when creating macros is how to delete them. You'll find that deleting macros sometimes comes into play during the creation process. For example, you might want to test-drive a few versions of a particular macro before you settle on a final version. Or you might want to delete a macro simply because you don't need it anymore or you're trying to reduce your document's file size. Regardless of your reason for deleting macros, you can delete them in two ways: You can delete an individual macro, or you can delete an entire macro project (which contains all the macros in a selected document or template).

Deleting a Single Macro

You can easily delete any macro you create by opening the Macros dialog box and deleting the macro. To do so, follow these steps:

1. Choose Tools, Macro, Macros (or press Alt+F8) to open the Macros dialog box.
2. In the Macros dialog box, select the name of the macro you want to delete in the Macro Name list. If the macro isn't displayed, choose a different document, template, or list in the Macros In list.
3. Click Delete. Word displays a message box, verifying your decision to delete the macro.
4. Click Yes to proceed with the deletion; otherwise, click No.
5. Click Close to close the Macros dialog box.

Caution Once you delete a macro, it's gone. If you decide that you'd like to use the macro after you've deleted it, you'll have to re-create the macro from scratch.

Deleting a Macro Project

In addition to deleting individual macros from within the Macros dialog box, you can delete an entire macro project by using the Organizer. When you delete a macro project, you delete all the macros you've created and added to a document or template.

Caution After you delete a macro project and save the document or template, there's no way to recover the macro project.

To delete a macro project, follow these steps:

1. Choose Tools, Macro, Macros (or press Alt+F8) to open the Macros dialog box.
2. Click Organizer to open the Organizer dialog box.
3. Select the macro project you want to delete from the appropriate list and click Delete.
4. Word displays a message box asking whether you're sure you want to delete the macro project. Click Yes to proceed with the deletion; otherwise, click No.
5. Click Close to close the Organizer dialog box.

By default, Word displays the macro projects contained in the current document in the left list and the macro projects stored in the Normal template in the right list. You can use either list to navigate to the document or template of your choice.

Part 7

Appendixes

Appendix A

Installing and Repairing Word 2003

If you purchase Word 2003 as part of the Microsoft Office System, as most people do, Word is installed by default when you install Office. In most cases, the program will begin installing automatically when you put the first installation CD in the drive; however, if you want to add or remove programs or features later, you'll use Add Or Remove Programs in the Control Panel to make those changes. This appendix walks you through the process of installing and getting updates for your version of Word. You'll also learn how to detect and repair errors that may occur while you're working.

Note The Microsoft Office System does not work with systems that are running operating systems other than Microsoft Windows 2000 with Service Pack 3 (SP3) or later or Microsoft Windows XP. For system hardware and software requirements, see the sidebar "Hardware and Software Requirements for Word 2003."

Preparing to Install

The installation process is as simple as inserting the CD in the drive, starting the Setup utility, and then following the prompts on the screen. As you prepare to install Office on your computer, however, here are a few things to keep in mind:

- If you're working on a corporate network, contact your system administrator before installing anything on your individual system.
- If you're working on a home network or a stand-alone system, make sure that you have the hardware and software required before beginning the installation (see the sidebar "Hardware and Software Requirements for Word 2003," for a listing of requirements).
- If you have trouble with your version of Word, you can run Detect And Repair (available from Word's Help menu) any time after the first installation.
- You can update your version of Word from within the program by choosing Check For Updates from the Word Help menu.

Hardware and Software Requirements for Word 2003

Basic System Requirements

- Microsoft Windows 2000 Service Pack 3 or later or Microsoft Windows XP
- A computer capable of running Windows 2000 or Windows XP
- A Pentium 233 MHz processor (Pentium III recommended)
- 128 MB RAM or more
- Between 260 and 700 MB of available disk space (depending on the version and the features you install)
- CD-ROM drive

Special Considerations

- Microsoft Office Professional Edition 2003 requires the largest amount of hard disk space—190 MB for Outlook 2003 with Business Contact Manager and an additional 290 MB if you choose to keep the installation files cache.

Installing Office 2003

Be sure that you've backed up all important files before you begin your installation. Then follow these steps to install Office:

1. Insert the first Office 2003 CD in the drive and follow the instructions on your screen until the Choose The Type Of Installation page appears. (If setup doesn't start automatically when you insert the CD, display the contents of your CD, and then double-click Setup.exe to start setup.)
2. After you enter your product key, your user information, and agree to the license agreement, you are asked to select the type of installation you want. Select Typical Install, Complete Install, Minimal Install, or Custom Install. Typical Install installs the most commonly used Office components. Complete Install installs all the components in your version of Office. Minimal Install installs the minimum number of components, probably the best option if you're low on disk space. Custom Install enables you to choose only the Office components you want to install.
3. Click Next, and then follow the prompts on the screen to complete the installation.
4. When the Installation Wizard is finished copying files, a message box appears, telling you that the setup completed successfully. Click OK to close the message box.

Adding and Removing Items

At any time during your use of Word, you can add or remove features or change the way the various items work. To make changes to the features installed in Word, use Add Or Remove Programs in the Control Panel to start the Microsoft Office Professional Edition 2003 Configuration Wizard. Here are the steps:

1. Choose Start, Control Panel.
2. Double-click Add Or Remove Programs.
3. In the Currently Installed Programs list, select Microsoft Office Professional Edition 2003, and then click Change.
4. The wizard presents you with choices for modifying, repairing, or removing Office 2003, as shown in Figure A-1.

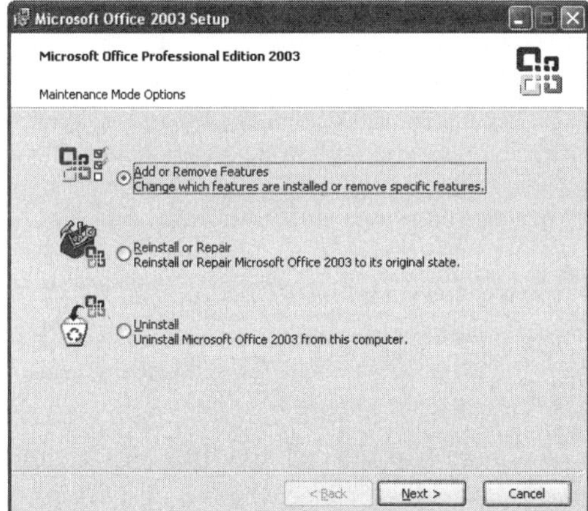

Figure A-1. You can use Add Or Remove Programs in the Control Panel to change, repair, or uninstall Office.

5. Follow the prompts to make changes as needed.

Repairing Word

From time to time, you might notice problems with Word. It happens to the best of us—after a series of lock-ups or badly timed power outages, we have bits and pieces of files on our computer that seem to hinder Word's performance or cause unexpected results.

Although Word's Crash Recovery and AutoRecover features help restore the data files you're using when a crash occurs, over time, repeated lock-ups can leave behind file fragments that slow down program performance. You can use Word's Detect And Repair command (available from the Help menu) to have Word look for and correct any of those barely noticed problems that might eventually get in your way.

Detect And Repair searches your Office installation for corrupted files, and then reinstalls any damaged files it finds. To use Detect And Repair, follow these steps:

1. Start Word, and then choose Help, Detect And Repair. The Detect And Repair dialog box appears, as shown in Figure A-2.

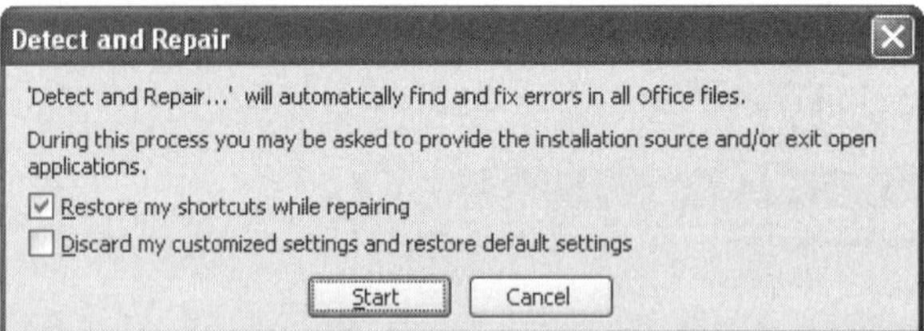

Figure A-2. Detect And Repair enables you to fix problems within Word.

2. If you want Word to restore any damaged shortcuts automatically, select the Restore My Shortcuts While Repairing check box, and then click Start. Word searches your installation and makes the necessary changes.

Getting Word Updates

Periodically, Microsoft publishes updates for the various Office applications and makes them available to all registered users. You can check to see whether updates are available for your version by connecting to the Internet, and then choosing Help, Check For Updates. Word connects you to the Updates page, shown in Figure A-3.

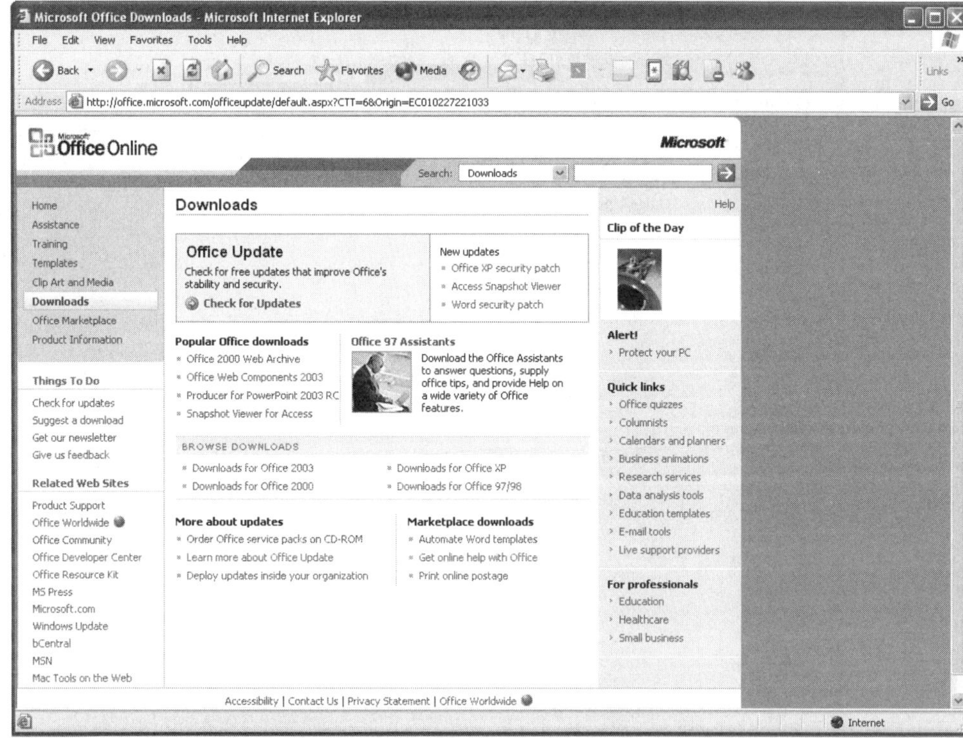

Figure A-3. Selecting the Check For Updates command from the Help menu takes you directly to Microsoft Office Online, where you can see whether any updates are available.

Click the Check For Updates link in the Office Update section and Office Update will check your system to see whether any updates are available, as shown in Figure A-4. If your system does need updating, the update links appear; you can then click the updates you want and they will be installed automatically without any further action from you.

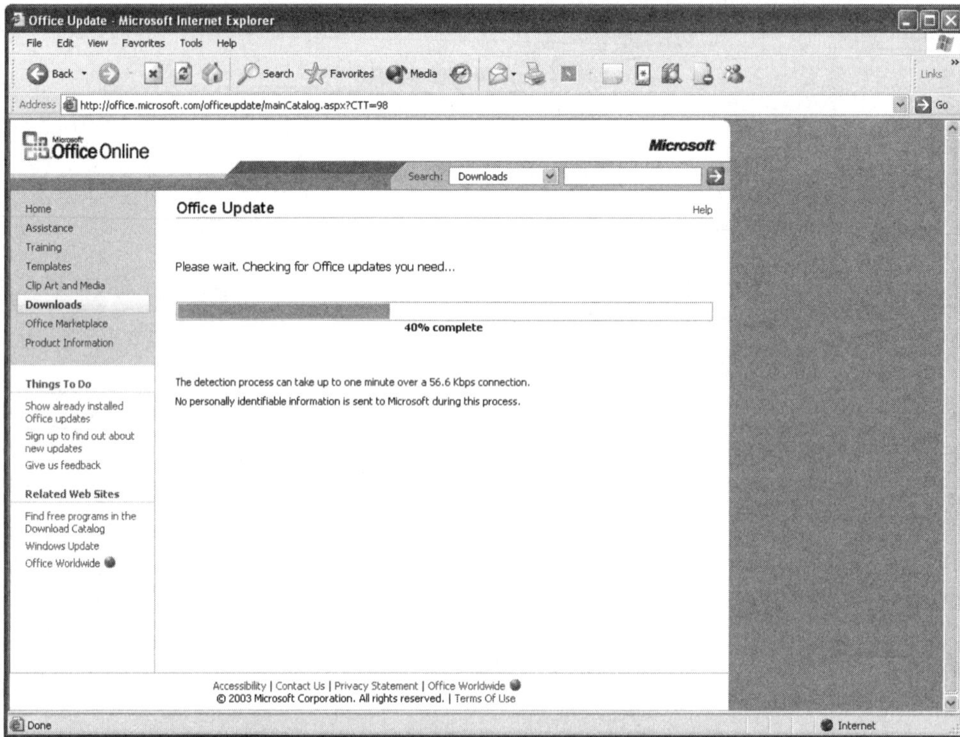

Figure A-4. Microsoft Office Online checks your system for available updates.

> **Note** It's a good idea to check for updates monthly to keep your version of Word 2003 up to date.

Appendix B

Implementing Multilanguage Features

If you work in a virtual office that spans the globe, or if you often trade documents with clients or co-workers on other continents, you'll find that the multilanguage features in Word 2003 are intuitive and easy to use. You might use multilanguage features, for example, to do any of the following:

- Find out automatically in which language a document was written, and use the necessary styles, punctuation, and editing techniques to edit that document accurately
- Create documents that include text in other languages, using special characters and symbols
- Edit languages that are written right to left
- Switch among documents in different languages to compare content and format
- Proofread documents created in other languages without having to use a third-party proofing program

This appendix introduces you to these multilanguage features and explains the enhancements now available with Word 2003. You'll find out how to enable the multilanguage capability and work with the options for multilanguage editing.

Understanding Multilanguage Support

The multilanguage support in Word comes to you courtesy of the Microsoft Office 2003 Multilingual User Interface (MUI) Pack. You'll find the MUI Pack on its own CD in your Microsoft Office System package; the Pack has its own installation utility that you can use to set up the languages for use with Word. (If you're working in a corporate setting, see your system administrator to obtain the Office 2003 MUI Pack.) After you install the MUI Pack, you'll be able to use the following features:

- **Automatic language detection** Word automatically detects up to 80 languages and uses the correct dictionaries, punctuation rules, and sorting conventions for each language.

- **Font support** All Office programs link to a second font if the primary font is missing characters that are specific to the language.
- **Date, time, and number formats** Word creates the date, time, and number formats applicable to each language.
- **Right-to-left editing** If you're working in a language that is written right to left, you can edit Word documents in that way.

Note Word uses Unicode text for multilanguage documents. Unicode is a standard way of storing text characters that provides for more than one byte for each character, enabling you to use a single character set to represent all languages.

Installing the MUI Pack

To install the MUI Pack features for the Microsoft Office System, insert the Language Pack CD from your Office CD set. Setup starts automatically, and then the Microsoft software agreement appears. After you accept the agreement, click Next, and then follow these steps:

1. The Setup Wizard asks you to choose the language you want to install. Select the languages you wish to install, and then click Next.
2. Choose the way you want menus and Help to appear. The three choices are set by default to match the system settings and the language you've selected for your system. To make changes, click the option down arrow, and then click your choice. Click Next to continue.
3. Select the type of installation you want: click Install Now to use the same components selected during your Office installation; click Complete, Proofing Tools Only, or Custom to install different configurations of the multilanguage features.
4. Click Install. Office installs the MUI Pack, and then prompts you to click OK when the installation is complete.

Tip **Change multilanguage options with Add Or Remove Programs**
After you install the MUI Pack, you can make further changes and enhancements to the feature. To do this, choose Start, Control Panel, and then double-click Add Or Remove Programs.

Entering Regional Options in Microsoft Windows

You can set up Microsoft Windows to recognize dates, times, and numbers entered in different languages automatically. After you've set up multilanguage support, you can configure

Windows to handle regional issues the way you want. To enter regional settings for multilanguage support, follow these steps:

1. Choose Start, Control Panel.
2. In Control Panel, double-click Regional And Language Options.
3. Click the Regional Options tab, as shown in Figure B-1.

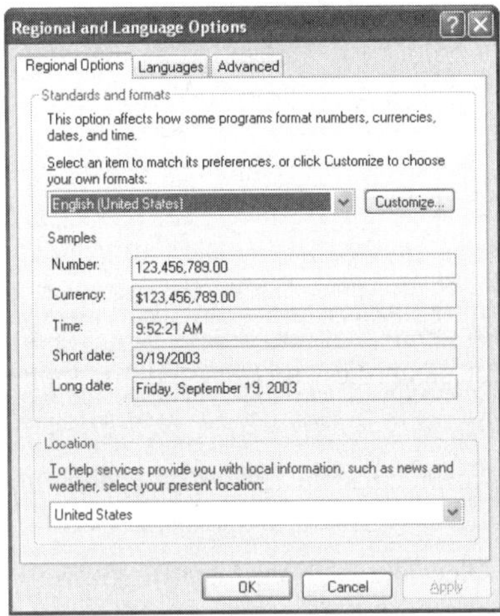

Figure B-1. Enter regional options for dates, times, and number formats in the Regional And Language Options dialog box.

4. In the Location section, click the arrow, and then select your location. Click OK to close the Regional And Language Options dialog box.

Choosing Keyboard Layouts

Some languages rely on different character sets, and if you've selected one of those languages, you'll need to modify your keyboard so that you'll be able to enter the necessary characters. You can change your keyboard layout to reflect the language change. To do this, follow these steps:

1. Choose Start, Control Panel.
2. In Control Panel, double-click Regional And Language Options.
3. Click the Languages tab, and then click Details. The Text Services And Input Languages dialog box appears, as shown in Figure B-2.

Figure B-2. Add a keyboard layout using the Text Services And Input Languages dialog box.

4 In the Default Input Language section, click the arrow, and then choose the language you want to use.

5 In the Installed Services section, select the keyboard layout you want to use.

6 Click OK twice to return to the desktop.

Setting Keyboard Shortcuts for Switching Languages

If you want to create a keyboard shortcut so you can switch between keyboard layouts easily, you can do so in the Text Services And Input Languages dialog box described in the previous steps. Follow these steps to select keyboard shortcuts for switching keyboard layouts:

1 In the Text Services And Input Languages dialog box, click Key Settings. The Advanced Key Settings dialog box appears.

2 Select the action to which you want to assign a keyboard shortcut.

3 Click Change Key Sequence. The Change Key Sequence dialog box appears, as shown in Figure B-3.

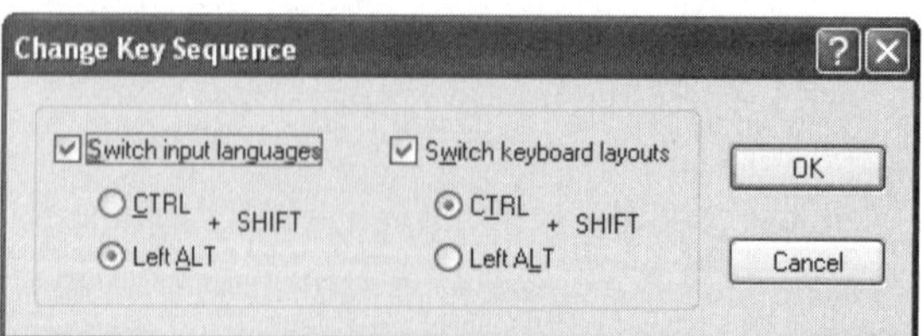

Figure B-3. You can assign a keyboard shortcut to make a quick keyboard change.

4 If you want to change the default selection (Left Alt+Shift) for the input languages, click the Ctrl option. The other option, Switch Keyboard Layouts, changes automatically.

5 Click OK to close the dialog box. The keyboard shortcut is recorded in the Advanced Key Settings dialog box.

> **Note** If your keyboard doesn't work when you enter text using the new language, make sure to use the keyboard shortcut sequence you selected to choose the new keyboard layout.

Enabling Languages

Before you can edit a document created in another language, you must make the language available in Word. When Word adds the new language, the Format menu shows additional commands that allow you to work with punctuation and characters unique to that language. To enable a language, follow these steps:

1 Choose Start, All Programs, Microsoft Office, Microsoft Office Tools, Microsoft Office 2003 Language Settings.

2 The Microsoft Office 2003 Language Settings dialog box appears, with the Enabled Languages tab selected, as shown in Figure B-4.

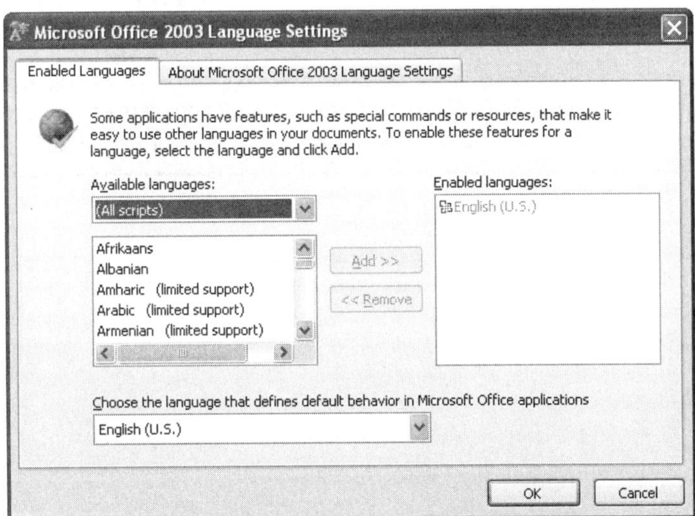

Figure B-4. Choose the languages you want to work with using Microsoft Office 2003 Language Settings.

3 In the Available Languages drop-down list, click the language you want to use.

4 Click Add. Office adds the language to the Enabled Languages list. Repeat for any additional languages you want to add.

5 If you want to change the default language for Office, click the Choose The Language That Defines Default Behavior In Microsoft Office Applications arrow, and then select the language you want to use.

6 Click OK. Office displays a message alerting you to restart your system to make the new language available.

7 Click Yes if you are ready to restart your system. Office updates your settings and makes the new language available for your use.

Using Input Method Editors

Another utility that helps you work with different languages in Word documents is an Input Method Editor (IME). An IME allows you to enter Asian characters in your documents by using your traditional, 101-key keyboard. The IME functions as an add-in utility for the multilanguage features. When you type, Word converts the text to the appropriate characters in the language you've selected.

If the version of Office 2003 you use is in Simplified Chinese, Traditional Chinese, Japanese, or Korean, the necessary IMEs are already available with your software. If you use another version of Office and want to be able to use IMEs, you can go to the Microsoft Office Download Center (*http://office.microsoft.com/OfficeUpdate/default.aspx*) and download the IMEs you need.

After you download and install the IMEs, they'll be available in your Language Bar. To select the IME you want to use, simply click the keyboard selection on the Language Bar to display the menu. Click your choice, and Office updates your keyboard settings.

Appendix C

Microsoft Office Specialist (MOS) Word 2003 Standards

In today's competitive computer market, many people are earning certification status to bolster their marketability and showcase their computer knowledge. One popular certification program designed for end users is the Microsoft Office Specialist (MOS) program. The MOS certification program enables you to demonstrate your proficiency in Office applications. As an experienced Word user, you can achieve two levels of MOS certification to become a Microsoft Office Specialist in Word by passing the Core Level and Expert Level exams. This appendix lists the objectives that you must master before you can become certified and points you to the sections of this book that describe the skills in detail. After you're proficient in these skills, you'll easily be able to pass the MOS exams and achieve Microsoft Office Specialist status.

To find out more about the MOS program and where you can take the exams, visit the Microsoft Training and Certification Web site at *http://www.microsoft.com/traincert*. On the main page, click the Microsoft Certifications link on the navigation bar, and then choose Microsoft Office Specialist.

MOS Word 2003 Core Level Standards

The MOS Word 2003 Core exam measures your ability to perform the following tasks:

- Create, organize, and format content
- Collaborate on documents
- Format and manage documents

This section presents the official list of specific skills you need to master before you can earn an MOS Word 2003 Core Level certification.

Creating Content

Insert and Edit Text, Symbols, and Special Characters

Inserting text, symbols, hidden text, and special characters

- See "Creating and Working with Content in Word," in Chapter 2.
- See "Inserting Symbols and Special Characters," in Chapter 2.
- See "Adding Text Effects and Animation," in Chapter 2.

Microsoft Office Word 2003 Inside Out

Deleting, cutting, copying, and pasting text and using the Clipboard

- See "Performing Basic Editing Tasks," in Chapter 2.

Checking spelling and grammar

- See "Building a Document's Credibility Using Spelling and Grammar Tools," in Chapter 6.

Checking language usage (e.g., Thesaurus)

- See "Enlivening Your Vocabulary Using the Thesaurus," in Chapter 6.

Insert Frequently Used and Predefined Text

Creating text for repeated use (e.g., AutoText)

- See "Making AutoText Work for You," in Chapter 7.

Inserting predefined text (e.g., AutoText and AutoCorrect)

- See "Using AutoCorrect to Fix Typos Effortlessly," in Chapter 7.
- See "Making AutoText Work for You," in Chapter 7.

Inserting date and time fields

- See "Inserting Date and Time Elements—The Quick Way," in Chapter 2.
- See "Inserting Fields," in Chapter 31.

Navigate to Specific Content

Finding and replacing text

- See "Finding Text and Elements Within the Current Document," in Chapter 4.
- See "Replacing Text," in Chapter 4.

Moving to selected content (e.g., Select Browse Object, Document Map)

- See "Accessing Document Areas Using the Document Map," in Chapter 4.
- See "Jumping to Document Areas Using the Go To and Select Browse Object Options," in Chapter 4.

Insert, Position, and Size Graphics

Inserting, positioning, and sizing graphics, text boxes, and shapes

- See "Enhancing Your Documents with Clip Art," in Chapter 11.
- See "Inserting Pictures," in Chapter 11.
- See "Resizing Pictures," in Chapter 11.
- See "Drawing Basic Lines and Shapes," in Chapter 12.
- See "Working with AutoShapes," in Chapter 12.
- See "Modifying Objects," in Chapter 12.

- See "Repositioning and Aligning Drawing Objects with Precision," in Chapter 12.
- See "Creating Text Boxes," in Chapter 17.
- See "Formatting Text Boxes and AutoShapes," in Chapter 17.

Create and Modify Diagrams and Charts

Creating and modifying charts and diagrams

- See "Creating a Basic Chart," in Chapter 14.
- See "Creating an Organization Chart," in Chapter 14.
- See "Designing Conceptual Diagrams," in Chapter 14.

Locate, Select, and Insert Supporting Information

Locating supporting information in local reference materials or on the Internet using the Research tool

- See "Researching Information Using the Research Task Pane," in Chapter 6.

Using the Research tool to select and insert supporting text-based information

- See "Researching Information Using the Research Task Pane," in Chapter 6.

Organizing Content

Insert and Modify Tables

Inserting new tables

- See "Creating a Simple Table," in Chapter 13.

Converting text to tables

- See "Changing Text to a Table," in Chapter 13.

Applying predefined formats to tables (e.g., AutoFormats)

- See "Enhancing Your Tables with Formatting," in Chapter 13.

Modifying table borders and shading

- See "Adding Borders and Shading," in Chapter 13.

Revising tables (insert and delete rows and columns, modify cell formats)

- See "Editing Tables," in Chapter 13.

Create Bulleted Lists, Numbered Lists, and Outlines

Customizing and applying bullets and numbering

- See "Creating a Quick List," in Chapter 8.
- See "Enhancing Bulleted Lists," in Chapter 8.
- See "Improving Numbered Lists," in Chapter 8.

Creating outlines

- See "Creating a New Outline," in Chapter 10.

Insert and Modify Hyperlinks

Inserting and modifying hyperlinks to other documents and Web pages

- See "Creating WordArt Hyperlinks," in Chapter 12.
- See "Including Hyperlinks," in Chapter 26.

Formatting Content

Format Text

Finding and modifying font typeface, style, color, and size

- See "Formatting Text Efficiently," in Chapter 2.

Applying styles to and clearing styles from text, tables, and lists

- See "Making Styles Work for You," in Chapter 9.

Applying highlights to text

- See "Using the Highlight Tool," in Chapter 27.

Applying text effects

- See "Formatting Text Efficiently," in Chapter 2.

Modifying character spacing

- See "Formatting Text Efficiently," in Chapter 2.

Format Paragraphs

Applying borders and shading to paragraphs

- See "Adding Borders to Sections and Paragraphs," in Chapter 18.
- See "Applying Shading Behind Content," in Chapter 18.

Indenting, spacing, and aligning paragraphs

- See "Formatting Paragraphs by Aligning and Indenting Text," in Chapter 8.

Setting, removing and modifying tab stops

- See "Controlling Alignment Using Tabs," in Chapter 8.

Apply and Format Columns

Applying and formatting columns

- See "Creating a Multi-Column Document," in Chapter 19.

Insert and Modify Content in Headers and Footers

Inserting and modifying content in document headers and footers

- See "Including Headers and Footers," in Chapter 15.

Inserting and formatting page numbers

- See "Adding Page Numbers," in Chapter 15.
- See "Including Headers and Footers," in Chapter 15.

Modify Document Layout and Page Setup

Inserting and deleting breaks

- See "Controlling Line and Page Breaks," in Chapter 8.
- See "Controlling Table Breaks," in Chapter 13.
- See "Controlling Page Breaks," in Chapter 15.
- See "Inserting Column Breaks," in Chapter 19.
- See "Removing Column Breaks," in Chapter 19.

Modifying page margins, page orientation

- See "Changing Margins and Orientation," in Chapter 15.

Collaborating

Circulate Documents for Review

Sending documents for review via e-mail

- See "Including an Introduction in an E-Mail Message," in Chapter 24.
- See "Sending a Document, E-Mail-Style," in Chapter 24.

Sending documents in an e-mail or as an e-mail attachment

- See "Sending a Document, E-Mail-Style," in Chapter 24.
- See "Sending an Attachment," in Chapter 24.

Compare and Merge Document Versions

Comparing and merging documents

- See "Comparing and Merging Documents," in Chapter 27.

Insert, View, and Edit Comments

Inserting, viewing and editing comments

- See "Adding and Managing Comments Effectively," in Chapter 27.

Track, Accept, and Reject Proposed Changes

Locating successive changes in a document

- See "Accepting and Rejecting Proposed Edits," in Chapter 27.

Tracking, accepting, and rejecting changes

- See "Tracking Changes While You Edit," in Chapter 27.
- See "Accepting and Rejecting Proposed Edits," in Chapter 27.

Formatting and Managing Documents

Create New Documents Using Templates

Creating new document types using templates

- See "Working with Templates and Wizards," in Chapter 2.
- See "Creating New Documents Based on Existing Templates," in Chapter 16.

Review and Modify Document Properties

Reviewing and modifying the document summary

- See "Getting to the Point with AutoSummarize," in Chapter 6.

Reviewing word, paragraph, and character counts (e.g., Word Count)

- See "Scrutinizing Document Statistics," in Chapter 6.

Organize Documents Using File Folders

Creating and using folders for document storage

- See "Saving Documents," in Chapter 2.
- See "Sharing Files and Folders," in Chapter 24.

Renaming folders

- See "Saving Files by Using the Save As Dialog Box," in Chapter 2.

Save Documents in Appropriate Formats for Different Uses

Converting documents to different formats for transportability (e.g., .rtf, .txt)

- See "Saving Documents," in Chapter 2.
- See "Sharing Files and Folders," in Chapter 24.

Saving documents as Web pages

- See "Saving Documents," in Chapter 2.
- See "Saving Your Web Pages," in Chapter 26.

Microsoft Office Specialist (MOS) Word 2003 Standards

Print Documents, Envelopes, and Labels

Printing documents, envelopes, and labels

- See "Printing Quickly and Efficiently," in Chapter 3.
- See "Controlling Print Jobs," in Chapter 3.
- See "Printing Envelopes and Labels," in Chapter 30.

Preview Documents and Web Pages

Previewing a document for printing

- See "Previewing Before Printing," in Chapter 3.

Previewing a Web page for publication

- See "Configuring Web View Options," in Chapter 26.

Change and Organize Document Views and Windows

Revealing formatting and hidden text

- See "Adding Text Effects and Animation," in Chapter 2.
- See "Seeing What's Going On Using Reveal Formatting," in Chapter 7.
- See "Modifying Paragraph Attributes Using Reveal Formatting," in Chapter 8.

Viewing reading layout, normal, outline, full screen, zoom views

- See "Viewing Documents in Various Lights," in Chapter 1.

Showing/hiding white space in a document

- See "Viewing Documents in Various Lights," in Chapter 1.

Splitting windows and arranging panes

- See "Viewing Documents in Various Lights," in Chapter 1.

MOS Word 2003 Expert Level Standards

The MOS Word 2003 Expert exam measures your ability to perform the following tasks:

- Format and organize content and documents at an advanced level
- Use Word's collaboration features
- Customize Word

This section presents the official list of skills you need to master before you can earn an MOS Word 2003 Expert Level certification.

Formatting Content

Create Custom Styles for Text, Tables, and Lists

Creating and applying custom styles for text, tables, and lists

- See "Creating New Styles," in Chapter 9.

Control Pagination

Controlling orphans and widows

- See "Controlling Line and Page Breaks," in Chapter 8.

Setting line and page breaks

- See "Controlling Line and Page Breaks," in Chapter 8.
- See "Controlling Page Breaks," in Chapter 15.

Format, Position, and Resize Graphics Using Advanced Layout Features

Wrapping text with graphics

- See "Controlling Text Wrapping," in Chapter 11.

Cropping and rotating graphics

- See "Cropping Pictures," in Chapter 11.
- See "Rotating Pictures," in Chapter 11.

Controlling image contrast and brightness

- See "Changing Picture Contrast and Brightness," in Chapter 11.

Scaling and resizing graphics

- See "Resizing Pictures," in Chapter 11.
- See "Modifying Objects," in Chapter 12.

Insert and Modify Objects

Inserting and modifying new objects and objects from files

- See "Inserting a Linked Object," in Chapter 11.
- See "Creating a New Embedded Object," in Chapter 11.

Create and Modify Diagrams and Charts Using Data from Other Sources

Creating and revising charts using data from other sources (e.g., Excel)

- See "Importing Data from Other Programs," in Chapter 14.

Organizing Content

Sort Content in Lists and Tables

Sorting content in lists and tables by specific categories

- See "Sorting Your Table Data," in Chapter 13.

Perform Calculations in Tables

Using formulas in tables

- See "Working with Functions in Tables," in Chapter 13.

Modify Table Formats

Modifying table formats by merging and/or splitting table cells

- See "Merging Cells," in Chapter 13.
- See "Splitting Cells," in Chapter 13.

Modifying text position and direction in a cell

- See "Changing Text Direction," in Chapter 13.

Modifying table properties

- See "Working with Table Properties," in Chapter 13.

Inserting and modifying fields

- See "Using Floating Frames for Comments, Footnotes, Tables, and Fields," in Chapter 17.
- See "Inserting Fields," in Chapter 31.
- See "Editing Fields," in Chapter 31.

Summarize Document Content Using Automated Tools

Summarizing relevant content using automated tools (e.g., AutoSummarize)

- See "Getting to the Point with AutoSummarize," in Chapter 6.

Analyzing content readability using automated tools (e.g., Readability Statistics)

- See "Judging a Document's Readability Level," in Chapter 6.
- See "Displaying Word Count Statistics," in Chapter 6.

Use Automated Tools for Document Navigation

Inserting bookmarks

- See "Creating Bookmarks for Document Navigation," in Chapter 4.

Using automation features for document navigation (e.g., Document Map, Thumbnails)

- See "Viewing Documents in Various Lights," in Chapter 1.
- See "Controlling How Print Preview Displays Documents," in Chapter 3.
- See "Accessing Document Areas Using the Document Map," in Chapter 4.

Merge Letters with Other Data Sources

Completing an entire mail merge process for form letters

- See Chapter 30, "Performing Mail Merges."

Merge Labels with Other Data Sources

Completing an entire mail merge process for mailing labels

- See "Creating Labels," in Chapter 30.

Structure Documents Using XML

Adding, deleting, updating, and modifying schemas, solutions, and settings in the Schema Library

- See "Attaching XML Schemas," in Chapter 16.
- See "Creating an XML Document," in Chapter 29.

Adding, deleting, and modifying schemas and transforms to documents

- See "Attaching XML Schemas," in Chapter 16.
- See "Creating an XML Document," in Chapter 29.

Managing elements and attributes in XML documents (e.g., adding, changing, deleting, cutting, copying)

- See "Creating an XML Document," in Chapter 29.

Defining XML options (e.g., applying schema validation options, applying XML view options)

- See "View Options for XML," in Chapter 29.

Formatting Documents

Create and Modify Forms

Creating and modifying forms

- See "Creating a Basic Form," in Chapter 31.
- See "Entering Form Fields," in Chapter 31.

Setting and changing options on form fields and check boxes

- See "Entering Form Fields," in Chapter 31.

Microsoft Office Specialist (MOS) Word 2003 Standards

Create and Modify Document Background

Creating watermarks

- See "Creating Backgrounds and Watermarks," in Chapter 17.

Creating and modifying themes

- See "Stylizing Documents with Themes," in Chapter 17.
- See "Formatting Messages with Stationery and Themes," in Chapter 24.

Creating and modifying document background colors and fill effects

- See "Creating Backgrounds and Watermarks," in Chapter 17.

Create and Modify Document Indexes and Tables

Creating and modifying document indexes, tables of contents, tables of figures, and tables of authorities

- See "Creating a TOC," in Chapter 21.
- See "Building a Table of Figures," in Chapter 21.
- See "Building a Table of Authorities," in Chapter 21.
- See Chapter 22, "Creating Effective Indexes."

Insert and Modify Endnotes, Footnotes, Captions, and Cross-References

Inserting, formatting, and modifying endnotes, footnotes, captions, and cross-references

- See "Adding Captions," in Chapter 21.
- See "Adding Footnotes and Endnotes," in Chapter 23.
- See "Using Cross-References," in Chapter 23.

Formatting numbering and marks for footnotes and endnotes

- See "Adding Symbols to Footnotes," in Chapter 23.
- See "Editing Footnotes and Endnotes," in Chapter 23.

Create and Manage Master Documents and Subdocuments

Creating master documents with three or more subdocuments

- See "Creating a Master Document," in Chapter 20.
- See "Creating Subdocuments," in Chapter 20.

Collaborating

Modify Track Changes Options

Setting reviewers' ink colors, setting balloon options, and showing and hiding reviewers

- See "Configuring Colors Associated with Reviewers," in Chapter 27.
- See "Configuring Comment Balloon and Reviewing Pane Options," in Chapter 27.
- See "Tracking Changes," in Chapter 27.

Publish and Edit Web Documents in Word

Opening and publishing Web pages in Word

- See "Displaying Existing Documents," in Chapter 2.
- See "Saving a File as a Web Page," in Chapter 2.
- See "Looking at Your Documents from the Web's Perspective," in Chapter 24.
- See "Saving Your Web Pages," in Chapter 26.
- See "Publishing Your Web Pages," in Chapter 26.

Inserting and modifying frames

- See "Adding Frames when Designing Online Documents," in Chapter 17.

Manage Document Versions

Creating, viewing, and deleting versions of documents

- See "Working with Multiple Versions of a Document," in Chapter 27.

Protect and Restrict Forms and Documents

Setting formatting restrictions

- See "Applying Formatting Restrictions," in Chapter 28.

Setting editing restrictions

- See "Restricting Tracked Changes, Comments, and Forms," in Chapter 28.

Adding users excepted from restrictions (groups and individuals)

- See "Controlling Restrictions for Parts of Documents," in Chapter 28.

Applying passwords to documents and forms

- See "Adding Password Protection to Documents," in Chapter 28.
- See "Restricting Tracked Changes, Comments, and Forms," in Chapter 28.

Attach Digital Signatures to Documents

Using digital signatures to authenticate documents

- See "Using Digital Certificates to Digitally Sign Files and Macros," in Chapter 28.

Microsoft Office Specialist (MOS) Word 2003 Standards

Customize Document Properties

Inserting and editing summary and custom information in document properties

- See "Printing Document Elements," in Chapter 3.
- See "Conducting Advanced File Searches Based on Document Properties," in Chapter 4.

Customizing Word

Create, Edit, and Run Macros

Creating and running macros

- See "Creating Macros Using the Macro Recorder," in Chapter 32.
- See "Running Macros," in Chapter 32.

Editing a macro using the Visual Basic Editor

- See "Editing and Viewing the VBA Code," in Chapter 32.

Customize Menus and Toolbars

Creating a custom menu

- See "Customizing Menus for Added Functionality," in Chapter 5.
- See "Assigning Shortcuts to Word Commands," in Chapter 32.
- See "Assigning a Macro to a Toolbar, a Menu, or a Keyboard Shortcut," in Chapter 32.

Adding and removing buttons from a toolbar

- See "Customizing Word Toolbars," in Chapter 5.
- See "Assigning Shortcuts to Word Commands," in Chapter 32.
- See "Assigning a Macro to a Toolbar, a Menu, or a Keyboard Shortcut," in Chapter 32.

Modify Word Default Settings

Changing the default file location for templates

- See "Specifying the Default Document's Location," in Chapter 5.

Setting a default dictionary

- See "Choosing a Default Dictionary," in Chapter 6.

Modifying default font settings

- See "Formatting Text Efficiently," in Chapter 2.
- See "Choosing Default Fonts," in Chapter 26.

Index to Troubleshooting Topics

Index to Troubleshooting Topics

Index

Symbols and Numbers

A

E

F

N

X

Z

About the Authors

Mary Millhollon is a certified Expert-level Microsoft Office Specialist in Word; a recognized Internet and Word expert, writer, and consultant; the co-owner of CreationGuide.com; and the instructional writer at Learning.com in Portland, Oregon. She has more than a dozen years of professional publishing, design, and computer experience, including hands-on experience in the book, magazine, newspaper, courseware, multimedia, and Web publishing industries. Mary is a freelance writer, Web designer, editor, sometime instructor, Internet expert, and instructional writer. She works daily (and nightly) with desktop applications and online technologies. Mary's educational background is a blend of art, English, journalism, and computer science, which lends itself well to today's constantly morphing computer technology. Her most recent book and courseware publications include *Microsoft Word Version 2002 Inside Out* (Microsoft Press), *Faster Smarter Web Page Creation* (Microsoft Press), and a collection of other computer-related books about Microsoft Office applications, Internet browsers, HTML (beginner and advanced), online communities, Web graphics, online auctions, and other desktop, Internet, network, application, and design topics. You can contact Mary via e-mail at *mm@creationguide.com* or visit *www.creationguide.com.*

Katherine Murray has been using technology to write about technology since the early 1980s. With more than 40 computer books (and a number of parenting books) to her credit, Katherine enjoys working on projects that teach new skills, uncover hidden talents, or develop mastery and efficiency in a chosen area. From books on general computer use to more specialized books on presentation graphics, Internet use, and Web animation, Katherine gets most excited about the programs that help people communicate, through print, sound, electronic, or visual expression—on or off the Web. For the last 15 years, Katherine has owned and operated reVisions Plus, Inc., a writing and publishing services company that relies on Word as the program of choice. Katherine also publishes a weblog for Microsoft Office 2003 and Office XP users (*www.revisionsplus.com/blogofficexp.html*) and is an occasional columnist for Microsoft Office Online. You can contact Katherine via e-mail at *kmurray@revisionsplus.com* or visit her company on the Web at *www.revisionsplus.com.*